THE SCOUTING REPORT: 1992

Produced by STATS, Inc.
(Sports Team Analysis and Tracking Systems, Inc.)

John Dewan, Editor
Don Zminda, Associate Editor

Statistics by STATS, Inc.

HarperPerennial
A Division of HarperCollins*Publishers*

The player photographs which appear in THE SCOUTING REPORT: 1992 were furnished individually by the 26 teams that comprise Major League Baseball. Their cooperation is gratefully acknowledged: Baltimore Orioles, Boston Red Sox, California Angels, Chicago White Sox, Cleveland Indians, Detroit Tigers, Kansas City Royals, Milwaukee Brewers, Minnesota Twins, New York Yankees, Oakland A's, Seattle Mariners, Texas Rangers, Toronto Blue Jays, Atlanta Braves, Chicago Cubs, Cincinnati Reds, Houston Astros, Los Angeles Dodgers, Montreal Expos, New York Mets, Philadelphia Phillies, Pittsburgh Pirates, St. Louis Cardinals, San Diego Padres and San Francisco Giants/Martha Jane Stanton.

FIRST EDITION

Designed by STATS, Inc.

ISSN 0743-1309

ISBN 0-06-273126-2

92 93 RRD 10 9 8 7 6 5 4 3 2 1

Table of Contents

Acknowledgments

Since this book is the result of many people working together as a team, I'd like to take this opportunity to acknowledge their contributions toward making this book a reality.

Don Zminda, who has been my associate editor for the last three years, has continued to do a tremendous job of coordinating the scouts. He is responsible for editing each and every report to create consistency in a book to which 26 different writers contributed. In addition, he is the author of all the minor league prospect reports for this book. This year again, the book is a credit to his baseball knowledge and writing skills.

Dr. Richard Cramer, founder and Chairman of the Board of STATS, Inc., is the one person primarily responsible for STATS' baseball systems which produced the charts appearing in this book. This information comes out of the same STATS system used by TV broadcasters, newspapers and Major League teams for inside information. Thanks to Dick for making this all possible.

Ross Schaufelberger is the production assistant for this year's book. He was copy editor, as well as assistant statistical editor. He also coordinated with the 26 Major League Teams to obtain all the player photos. This is his second year working on the book and the quality of his work shows through once again this year. This book would not be here without all his effort and talent.

Bob Mecca, statistical editor, has once again been old eagle eye for the third year in a row, as he reviewed the statistics within this book. He has verified all the statistics quoted in the reports for both relevance and accuracy. Thanks to Bob, STATS can be especially proud of accuracy of the numbers. Believe me, 26 scouts can toss around numbers in a lot of different ways. He makes sure that they are accurate and consistent.

Steve Moyer is our new assistant copy editor this year and he brings his own baseball knowledge into play. Thanks to Steve for his baseball insight that he brings to this book and the long hours that it took to apply it here.

In the last two months since the season ended, Jonathan Forman has worked practically non-stop, verifying and re-verifying the most detailed level of play-by-play within each game in the 1991 season. Once again this assures that all the statistics with in this book are the most accurate. At this point I believe he may be able recreate from memory all the games of the 1991 season (well at least the Cleveland games).

Thanks to Darren Grayson, Michael Canter and Tom Horowitz who assisted Ross in the photo collection and to Bud Podrazik who preformed the layout of the photos and charts. We also gratefully acknowledge all the teams who have provided these photos. Thanks to the rest of the STATS Inc. staff who kept the office rolling: Arthur Ashley, Assistant-VP, Bob Meyerhoff, Assistant-VP, Sue Dewan, VP, Chuck Miller, Statistician, Jim Musso, Statistician, and David Pinto, Analyst. On the Business Administration side, thanks go to Nadine Jenkins, Marge Morra and Suzette Neily.

Bill James' formula for player performance has once again helped us formulate the stars, bums and sleepers of 1992. Thanks for the insight, Bill.

The terrific statistics you find within this book would not be possible without the STATS, Inc. reporters who covered every game throughout the 1991 season. Thanks.

Finally, thanks to our editor at HarperCollins, Mary Kay Linge.

— John Dewan

The Scouting Staff

We know that you, the readers of this book, depend on STATS to give you interesting and insightful reports on more than 700 players. By the same turn, STATS depends on its writers -- both newspaper beat reporters and STATS reporters who cover major league games on a regular basis -- to produce those reports. We feel justifiably proud of their work, and we'd like to recognize them for their outstanding efforts.

The scouting reports in this book were written by the following people, in conjunction with our editors:

Baltimore Orioles — Kent Baker
Baltimore Morning Sun

Boston Red Sox — Peter Gammons
Boston Globe

California Angels — Dave King
STATS, Inc.

Chicago White Sox — Bob Mecca
STATS, Inc.

Cleveland Indians — Paul Hoynes
Cleveland Plain Dealer

Detroit Tigers — Doug Byron and
Dave Srinivasan
STATS, Inc.

Kansas City Royals — Marc Bowman
STATS, Inc.

Milwaukee Brewers — Matt Greenberger
STATS, Inc.

Minnesota Twins — Dennis Brackin
Minneapolis Star-Tribune

New York Yankees — John Benson
Diamond Analytics

Oakland Athletics — Chuck Hildebrand
Peninsula Times-Tribune

Seattle Mariners — Don Zminda
STATS, Inc.

Texas Rangers — Don Zminda
STATS, Inc.

Toronto Blue Jays — Howard Sinker
Minneapolis Star-Tribune

Atlanta Braves — Corey Seeman
STATS, Inc.

Chicago Cubs — Ross Schaufelberger
STATS, Inc.

Cincinnati Reds — Peter Pascarelli

Houston Astros — Joe Heiling
Beaumont Enterprise & Journal

Los Angeles Dodgers — Don Hartack
STATS, Inc.

Montreal Expos — Marco Bresba
STATS, Inc.

New York Mets — John Benson
Diamond Analytics

Philadelphia Phillies — Pete DeCoursey
Reading Eagle-Times

Pittsburgh Pirates — John Perrotto
Beaver County Times

St. Louis Cardinals — Matt Greenberger and
Rollie Loewen
STATS, Inc.

San Diego Padres — Peter Pascarelli

San Francisco Giants — Chuck Hildebrand
Peninsula Times-Tribune

The minor league prospect reports were written by Don Zminda.

This is STATS' third edition of **The Scouting Report**, and we feel it appropriate to recognize the writers who have worked on all three editions of the book: Kent Baker, John Benson, Marc Bowman, Dennis Brackin, Pete DeCoursey, Chuck Hildebrand, Joe Heiling, Paul Hoynes, Bob Mecca, Howard Sinker, and John Perrotto. Thanks to everyone who helped put together these books, but particularly to you guys.

On a personal level, I'd like to thank Peter Gammons and Peter Pascarelli, for their special efforts on helping this project to fruition; Ross Schaufelberger, who was responsible for so many details in finishing off this task; the STATS office people, including (among others) Art Ashley, Nadine Sanchez, Marge Morra, Suzette Neily, Steve Moyer and Jim Musso; and most especially, Dick Cramer and John and Sue Dewan, whose commitment to excellence helps make every STATS product a pleasure to be a part of.

— Don Zminda

Introduction

Today's baseball fan is more and more demanding -- player statistics are more commonly known, publications proliferate, and television contracts keep almost any game of interest available to viewers. Media and baseball experts know that it takes more and more effort to keep today's baseball fan happy with something new and cutting-edge. That's why when the editors of *The Scouting Report:1992* hear that TV announcers read annually from our book, or sportswriters carry it around in their briefcases, we know that we are accomplishing something very worthwhile. But when we heard that the players themselves read (and have verified!) its contents -- well, we think we've got a book that fans can learn from and enjoy.

This edition promises to be the best, most complete version of *The Scouting Report* yet produced. With our top-notch scouts and veteran writers like Peter Gammons and Peter Pascarelli, if you are looking for the most in-depth coverage of the real strengths and weaknesses of today's major leaguers, you've come to the right place. Welcome to both all our new readers and those of you who have scouted out the major leagues in our two previous editions. In this year's edition, we have again refused to sit on our hands: our newest feature is a special section on each team's top five prospects!

While adding new features, we didn't skimp on the meat and bones of the book: scouting reports on over 790 major and minor league baseball players are included. They are the most complete and detailed reports the general public has ever had the opportunity to see. We have also brought back our special hitting and pitcher charts based on the 1991 season. The hitting charts are well-known for displaying hitter's tendencies, while the pitcher charts measure the effectiveness of every pitcher (in four different situations) in performing his most basic task -- throwing a strike. Take a look at some of the players we have labelled as having "pinpoint control", like Zane Smith and Kevin Tapani, and you'll immediately realize the secret to their success through these charts!

Also returning for a second year is our popular section entitled "Stars, Bums and Sleepers." In this section, a fantasy/rotisserie smorgasbord, you'll get a feel for what to expect from each player in 1992: whether they will improve, decline, remain consistent, or even come out of nowhere to surprise! By looking through this section last season, players like Travis Fryman, Juan Gonzalez, and Marquis Grissom (tabbed sleepers in last year's Scouting Report) wouldn't have caught you asleep.

The Prospect Pages

We try to make every edition of *The Scouting Report* a little better than the previous one, and this year we're presenting something completely new: the "prospects page." We're sure you're well aware that a crucial part of every major league operation is its player development system, and the prospects page intends to address that.

For each team, we've chosen five outstanding minor league players -- many of them ready to make a major league impact in 1992, almost all of them expected to make an impact within two or three years. Much as we admire their work, we try to shy away from the Baseball America system of rating a club's "top ten prospects." That system relies heavily on front-office personnel for its ratings, and winds up trying to make the club look good. If a teams loses its third baseman to free agency, for example, you can bet the house that there will be two or three third sackers among its top ten. We prefer to avoid that, and make you (as a predictor), rather than the club, look good.

To help guide you with the prospects, we include "major league equivalencies" for the position players who played at the AA or AAA level in 1991. The MLE is a tool, adjusted for league and ball park, devised by Bill James to indicate how a minor league hitter would do at the major league level based on his minor league stats. Is this system necessary? Of course it's necessary; some minor leaguers compile their stats in a hitters' paradise like Colorado Springs (team batting average .298), while others struggle in a pitchers' yard like Tidewater (team batting average .256). Does the system work? Of course it works; the

James system was pointing out how Dodger and Brewer hitting prospects were overrated -- while Red Sox and Blue Jay prospects were underrated -- several years ago. All we can say to the doubtful is, keep track of these MLEs over the next several years. You'll see.

For each team, we've also included an organization overview. Some clubs are better developers of talent than others; the Red Sox of the 1980s, for example, nurtured and showed patience with their young talent, while the Yankees of the same period seemed to think a minor leaguer (a Willie McGee, for example, or a Fred McGriff) was only good as possible trade bait for someone else's fading veteran. If you want to project your club's future, you simply have to examine its recent past, and that's what we try to do here.

The Players

For each major league team there are 25 to 27 major league players scouted here. Most of the players are covered in depth, with a full page of scouting information. They are listed alphabetically with the team they last played for in 1991. The lesser players, four per team, follow the primary players on each team.

The Scouting Report Page

The Scouting Report page for primary players has two parts. The left side of the page provides an in-depth report by an expert scout/analyst who covers the teams on a daily basis. These reports are drawn from their day-to-day observation of the players.

The right-hand side of the page is chock full of information from the STATS computer. Starting at the top of the column it lists:

Position: The first position shown is the player's most common position in 1991. If a position player played at any other positions in 10 or more games, those positions are shown also. For pitchers, SP stands for starting pitcher and RP stands for relief pitcher. A second pitching position is shown if a starting pitcher relieved at least four times or a relief pitcher started at least twice.

Bats and Throws: L=left-handed, R=right-handed, B=both (switch-hitter).

Opening Day Age: This is the player's age on April 6, 1992.

Born: Birth date and place.

ML Seasons: This number indicates the number of different major league seasons in which this player has actually appeared. For example, if a player was called up to play in September in each of the last three seasons, the number shown would be three (3). Note that this is different from the term Major League Service, which only counts the actual number of days a player appears on a major league roster.

Overall Statistics: These are traditional statistics for the player's 1991 season and his career through 1991.

Pitcher Strike Charts

The pitcher strike charts answer the question "How Often Does He Throw Strikes?" The charts are constructed based on the most extreme pitchers at throwing strikes in baseball. Dennis Eckersley throws 70% of his pitches for strikes overall, and 81% for strikes when he's behind in the count (which, of course, is very rare). At the other extreme, Jim Deshaies threw only 46% of his pitches for strikes when he was ahead on the count in 1991. Therefore we've constructed the chart to represent the 40-80% range of throwing strikes.

Here are some ground rules: When you read your USA Today box score or hear an announcer state that a pitcher has thrown 97 pitches, 62 of them for strikes, the strike count includes swinging strikes, taken strikes, foul balls **and** balls hit in play. Even though not all balls hit into play are strikes, the theory is that most of them are, and the ones that aren't would be difficult to judge. Our charts reflect this. The charts are then broken into four categories. **All Pitches** is straight forward, as is **First Pitch.** We define **Ahead** as being any time there are more strikes than balls in the count (0-1, 0-2, 1-2). **Behind** includes counts with more balls than strikes (1-0, 2-0, 3-0, 2-1, 3-1, 3-2).

League averages are shown in each chart. If the pitcher is listed with an American League team, the AL average is shown. The NL average is shown for players whose report is with a National League team. Here are the 1991 league averages:

Strike Percentage by League — 1991		
	American	National
All Pitches	61.4%	62.5%
First Pitch	55.3%	56.8%
Ahead in the Count	56.4%	58.3%
Behind in the Count	68.5%	68.8%

You'll notice the National League throws a slightly higher percentage of strikes in all cases for the second straight year.

Hitting Diagrams

The hitting diagrams shown in these reports are the most advanced of their kind in baseball. For every game and every ball hit into play last year (both hits and outs), STATS' trained reporters entered data into the STATS computer. They kept track of the kind of batted ball -- ground ball, fly ball, pop-up, line drive or bunt, as well as the distance of each ball. Direction is kept by dividing the field into 26 "wedges" angling out from home plate. Distance is measured in 10-foot increments from home plate.

Below are switch-hitting Seattle second baseman Harold Reynolds' hitting diagrams. One chart shows where Reynolds hit the ball against left-handed pitchers (i.e. when he was batting right-handed); the other shows him against righties (batting lefty).

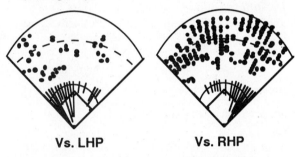

Vs. LHP   **Vs. RHP**

In the diagrams, ground balls and short line drives are shown by the various length lines in the infield: the longer the line, the more ground balls and liners were hit in that direction. Let's assume Seattle is playing the World Champion Minnesota Twins. It can be seen that Reynolds is a pull hitter on most balls hit to the infield, especially as a left-handed batter. When Reynolds is batting from the right side, against Allan Anderson, the third baseman Mike Pagliarulo and shortstop Greg Gagne should hold their positions, while second baseman Chuck Knoblauch moves closer to up-the-middle; big first baseman Kent Hrbek should play off the line to compensate, as Reynolds hits virtually nothing down the opposite field line. When Steve Bedrosian comes in and Reynolds is batting left-handed, Hrbek needs to hug the line and Knoblauch should move a few steps to his left, while Gagne closes toward the second base bag.

In the outfield, batted balls are shown by dots. The dotted line in the outfield is 300 feet away from home plate, indicating how deep an outfield normally plays. By examining the diagram, it is clear that Reynolds has very little power to the opposite field. Again, assume Seattle is playing the Twins. When Reynolds is hitting versus southpaw Mark Guthrie, he has almost no power to right field, so right fielder Shane Mack should play shallow and close to center. Similarly, center fielder Kirby Puckett can afford to play extremely shallow and towards left a shade, while left fielder Dan Gladden should be prepared to both cover the line and get back on the ball. If the Twins bring in Rick Aguilera to face Reynolds, he'll switch to batting lefty, and Mack and Puckett had better be ready: They'll need to play significantly deeper and be ready for balls in the right-center gap. Gladden needs to play Reynolds fairly honestly because Reynolds will occasionally hit one down the opposite field line, but in general Gladden should play very shallow.

Technical Information on the Diagrams

A lot of experimentation went into producing these charts. When we first started, we tried to show every single batted ball that was hit into play by each player. We found that the charts became very cluttered for everyday players. We began experimenting with trying to show only the most meaningful information. When all was said and done, here's what we ended up with:

a. Pop-ups and bunts are excluded. We excluded pop-ups because 95% of these are caught regardless of how fielders are positioned. We excluded bunts because defensing a bunt is a whole different strategy that is primarily used on a select number of players and situations.

b. Ground balls under 50 feet are excluded. These are swinging bunts and are somewhat rare. We exclude them because they don't provide a true indication of the direction of a batted ball reaching an infielder or going through the infield.

c. For everyday players, we excluded what we call isolated points in the outfield. If a player hit only one ball in a given area of the field with no other batted balls in the vicinity all season, we exclude it from the chart. We felt that one ball does not give a true indication of a tendency. This rule did not apply to balls hit farther than 380 feet; all batted balls over 380 feet are shown. See Cecil Fielder for many examples.

d. Similarly, for players who play infrequently, we expanded the data sample to create a larger pattern of dots in the outfield when he tended to hit in a given area more frequently.

e. For ground balls over 50 feet, we excluded only the rare isolated ground ball. For most players, almost all of their ground balls are shown.

Other notes of interest:

The field itself is drawn to precise scale, with the outfield fence reaching 400 feet in centerfield and 330 feet down the lines. Keep in mind that parks are configured differently so that a dot that is shown inside of the diagram might actually have been a home run. Similarly, a dot outside the fence in the diagram might actually have been in play.

Liners under 170 feet are part of the infield. We give responsibility for short line drives to the infielders.

No distinction is made between hits and outs.

1991 Situational Stats

There are eight situational breakdowns for every primary player. **Home** and **Road** show performance between playing in his home park versus on the road. **Day** and **Night** show performance in day games versus night games. For hitters, **LHP** and **RHP** show the player's performance versus left-handed pitchers and right-handed pitchers, respectively. For pitchers, **LHB** and **RHB** show how the opposition batters hit against that pitcher based on the side of the plate from which they hit. **Sc Pos** stands for Scoring Position. It shows batting performance when hitting with runners in scoring position. For pitchers, **Sc Pos** shows the opposition's batting statistics when there are men in scoring position against that pitcher.

The definition we use for **Clutch** here can be simply restated as the late innings of a close game. For those of you interested in the exact definition, clutch is when it is the seventh inning or later and the batting team is up by one run, tied, or has the tying run on base, at bat, or on deck. You'll notice a similarity to the save definition. This is intentional; it allows our definition of Clutch to be consistent with a very well-known statistic, the save.

1991 Rankings

This section shows how the player ranked against the league, against his teammates, and by position

in significant categories. Thanks to the power of the STATS computer, we not only include traditional categories, but also the less traditional categories as shown in the Major League Leaders section of this book. The Definitions and Qualifications section below provides some details on these lesser known categories. Due to space considerations, when a player ranked high in numerous categories, we omitted some of the less interesting rankings.

Major League Leaders

The chapter immediately following this introduction is a complete listing of Major League Leaders. The top three players in each category are shown for each league separately. You'll notice a STATS flavor to these leaders. Not only do we show the leaders for the common categories like batting average, home runs and ERA, but you'll also find less traditional categories like steals of third, percentage of extra bases taken as a runner and pitches thrown.

Definitions and Qualifications

The following are definitions and qualifications for the Major League Leaders and Rankings.

Definitions:

Times on Base -- Hits plus walks plus hit by pitch.

Groundball/Flyball Ratio -- The ratio of all ground balls hit to fly balls and pop-ups hit. Bunts and line drives are excluded completely.

Percentage of extra bases taken as a runner -- This figure measures how often a player takes an extra base on a single or double.

Runs scored per time reached base -- This is calculated by dividing Runs Scored by Times on Base.

Clutch -- This category shows a player's batting average in the late innings of close games: the seventh inning or later with the batting team ahead by one, tied, or has the tying run on base, at bat, or on deck.

Bases Loaded -- This category shows a player's batting average in bases loaded situations.

GDP per GDP situation -- A GDP situation exists any time there is a man on first with less than two outs. This statistic measures how often a player grounds into a double play in that situation.

Percentage of Pitches Taken -- This tells you how often a player lets a pitch go by without swinging.

Percentage of Swings Put into Play -- This tells you how often a player hits the ball into fair territory when he swings.

Run Support per Nine Innings -- This indicates how many runs are scored for a pitcher by his team while he was pitching translated into a per nine inning figure.

Baserunners per Nine Innings -- These are the hits, walks and hit batsmen allowed per nine innings.

Strikeout/Walk Ratio -- This is simply a pitcher's strikeouts divided by his walks allowed.

Stolen Base Percentage Allowed -- This figure indicates how successful opposing baserunners are when attempting a stolen base. It's stolen bases divided by stolen base attempts.

Save Percentage -- This is saves divided by save opportunities. Save opportunities include saves plus blown saves.

Blown Saves -- A blown save is given any time a pitcher comes into a game where a save situation is in place and he loses the lead.

Holds -- A hold is given to a pitcher when he comes into the game in a save situation, but is removed before the end of the game while maintaining his team's lead. The pitcher must retire at least one batter to get a hold.

Percentage of Inherited Runners Scored -- When a pitcher comes into a game with men already on base, these runners are called inherited runners. This statistic measures the percentage of these inherited runners that the relief pitcher allows to score.

First Batter Efficiency -- This statistic tells you the batting average allowed by a relief pitcher to the first batter he faces.

Qualifications:

In order to be ranked, a player had to qualify with a minimum number of opportunities. The qualifications are as follows:

Batters

Batting average, slugging percentage, on-base average, home run frequency, ground ball/fly ball ratio, runs scored per time reached base and pitches seen per plate appearance -- 502 plate appearances

Percentage of pitches taken, lowest percentage of swings that missed and percentage of swings put into play -- 1500 pitches seen

Percentage of extra bases taken as a runner -- 15 opportunities to advance

Stolen base percentage -- 20 stolen base attempts

Runners in scoring position -- 100 plate appearances with runners in scoring position

Clutch -- 50 plate appearances in the clutch

Bases loaded -- 10 plate appearances with the bases loaded

GDP per GDP situation -- 50 plate appearances with a man on first and less than two outs

Vs LHP -- 125 plate appearances against left-handed pitchers

Vs RHP -- 377 plate appearances against right-handed pitchers

BA at home -- 251 plate appearances at home

BA on the road -- 251 plate appearances on the road

Leadoff on-base average -- 150 plate appearances in the number-one spot in the batting order

Cleanup slugging percentage - 150 plate appearances in the number-four spot in the batting order

BA on 3-1 count -- 10 plate appearances putting the ball into play or walking on a 3-1 count

BA with 2 strikes -- 100 plate appearances with 2 strikes

BA on 0-2 count -- 20 plate appearances putting the ball into play or striking out on a 0-2 count

BA on 3-2 count -- 20 plate appearances with a 3-2 count

Pitchers

Earned run average, run support per nine innings, baserunners per nine innings, batting average allowed, on-base average allowed, slugging percentage allowed, home runs per nine innings, strikeouts per nine innings, strikeout/walk ratio, stolen base percentage allowed, GDPs per nine innings, pitches thrown per batter and groundball/flyball ratio off -- 162 innings pitched

Winning percentage -- 15 decisions

GDPs induced per GDP situation -- pitchers facing 30 batters in GDP situations

Save Percentage -- 20 save opportunities

Percentage of inherited runners scoring -- 30 inherited runners

First batter efficiency -- 40 games in relief

BA allowed, runners in scoring position -- pitchers facing 150 batters with men in scoring position

ERA at home -- 81 innings pitched at home

ERA on the road -- 81 innings pitched on the road

Vs LHB -- 125 left-handed batters faced

Vs RHB -- 377 right-handed batters faced

Relief Pitchers

ERA, batting average allowed, baserunners per 9 innings, strikeouts per 9 innings -- 54 innings in relief

Fielders

Percentage caught stealing by catchers -- catchers with 75 stolen base attempts against them

Fielding percentage -- 100 games at a position; 30 chances for pitchers

Major League Leaders

1991 American League Leaders

Batters

Batting Average
Julio Franco	.341
Wade Boggs	.331
Willie Randolph	.327
Ken Griffey Jr.	.327
Paul Molitor	.325
Cal Ripken	.323
Rafael Palmeiro	.322
Kirby Puckett	.319
Frank Thomas	.318
Danny Tartabull	.316

Home Runs
Jose Canseco	44
Cecil Fielder	44
Cal Ripken	34

Runs Batted In
Cecil Fielder	133
Jose Canseco	122
Ruben Sierra	116

Games Played
Joe Carter	162
Cecil Fielder	162
Cal Ripken	162

At Bats
Paul Molitor	665
Ruben Sierra	661
Steve Sax	652

Runs Scored
Paul Molitor	133
Rafael Palmeiro	115
Jose Canseco	115

Hits
Paul Molitor	216
Cal Ripken	210
Ruben Sierra	203
Rafael Palmeiro	203

Singles
Julio Franco	156
Paul Molitor	154
Steve Sax	148

Doubles
Rafael Palmeiro	49
Cal Ripken	46
Ruben Sierra	44

Triples
Paul Molitor	13
Lance Johnson	13
Roberto Alomar	11

Stolen Bases
Rickey Henderson	58
Roberto Alomar	53
Tim Raines	51

Caught Stealing
Luis Polonia	23
Rickey Henderson	18
Alex Cole	17

Walks
Frank Thomas	138
Mickey Tettleton	101
Rickey Henderson	98

Intentional Walks
Wade Boggs	25
Harold Baines	22
Ken Griffey Jr.	21

Hit by Pitch
Joe Carter	10
Jose Canseco	9
Dave Valle	9

Strikeouts
Rob Deer	175
Jose Canseco	152
Cecil Fielder	151

Ground into Double Play
Kirby Puckett	27
Albert Belle	24
Tony Pena	23
Randy Milligan	23

Sacrifice Bunts
Luis Sojo	19
Roberto Alomar	16
Harold Reynolds	14

Sacrifice Flies
John Olerud	10
Alvin Davis	10
9 Players with	9

Batter Plate Appearances
Paul Molitor	752
Harold Reynolds	728
Ruben Sierra	726

Times on Base
Frank Thomas	317
Paul Molitor	299
Rafael Palmeiro	277

Total Bases
Cal Ripken	368
Rafael Palmeiro	336
Ruben Sierra	332

Slugging Percentage
Danny Tartabull	.593
Cal Ripken	.566
Jose Canseco	.556

Slugging Pct off LHP
Shane Mack	.701
Cal Ripken	.677
Kirby Puckett	.658

Slugging Pct off RHP
Danny Tartabull	.614
Jose Canseco	.576
Rafael Palmeiro	.557

Cleanup Slugging Pct
Danny Tartabull	.610
Joe Carter	.527
Albert Belle	.526

On-Base Average
Frank Thomas	.453
Willie Randolph	.424
Wade Boggs	.421

On-Base Avg off LHP
Frank Thomas	.500
Dwight Evans	.468
Tony Phillips	.466

On-Base Avg off RHP
Wade Boggs	.456
Frank Thomas	.432
Rafael Palmeiro	.411

Leadoff On-Base Avg	
Wade Boggs	**.440**
Edgar Martinez	.405
Rickey Henderson	.401

HR Frequency - AB/HR	
Jose Canseco	**13.0**
Cecil Fielder	14.2
Danny Tartabull	15.6

Groundball/Flyball Ratio	
Carlos Quintana	**2.8**
Lance Johnson	2.6
Milt Cuyler	2.6

% Extra Bases Taken as Runner	
Terry Shumpert	**88.9%**
Luis Polonia	80.4
Ken Griffey Jr.	75.0

Runs/Time Reached Base	
Jose Canseco	**48.1%**
Rickey Henderson	45.5
Devon White	45.3

SB Success %	
Chuck Knoblauch	**83.3%**
Roberto Alomar	82.8
Kirk Gibson	81.8

Steals of Third	
Rickey Henderson	**21**
Roberto Alomar	**21**
Luis Polonia	17

BA Scoring Position	
Danny Tartabull	**.374**
Willie Randolph	.373
Darryl Hamilton	.368

BA Late & Close	
Carlos Quintana	**.394**
Darryl Hamilton	.389
Kent Hrbek	.389

BA Bases Loaded	
Greg Vaughn	**.636**
Willie Randolph	.545
Frank Thomas	.500

GDP/GDP Situation	
Lou Whitaker	**2.6%**
Rob Deer	**2.6%**
Kevin Maas	3.4

BA vs LH Pitchers	
Kirby Puckett	**.406**
Frank Thomas	.377
Julio Franco	.368

BA vs RH Pitchers	
Wade Boggs	**.361**
Rafael Palmeiro	.342
Julio Franco	.332

BA at Home	
Wade Boggs	**.389**
Frank Thomas	.371
Ken Griffey Jr.	.365

BA on the Road	
Cal Ripken	**.358**
Paul Molitor	.354
Julio Franco	.339

BA on 3-1 Count	
Luis Polonia	**1.000**
Warren Newson	1.000
Jerry Browne	.800

BA With 2 Strikes	
Willie Randolph	**.322**
Cal Ripken	.297
Luis Polonia	.291

BA on 0-2 Count	
Luis Rivera	**.379**
Ivan Rodriguez	.364
Joe Orsulak	.348
Kent Hrbek	.348

BA on 3-2 Count	
Rick Dempsey	**.467**
Lance Blankenship	.400
Steve Sax	.382

Pitches Seen	
Frank Thomas	**3015**
Devon White	2763
Robin Ventura	2712

Pitches Seen per PA	
Rickey Henderson	**4.34**
Frank Thomas	4.30
Rob Deer	4.25

% Pitches Taken	
Rickey Henderson	**68.2%**
Frank Thomas	65.4
Alvin Davis	64.2

% of Swings that Missed	
Wade Boggs	**5.3%**
Chuck Knoblauch	7.7
Jody Reed	8.3

% Swings Put Into Play	
B.J. Surhoff	**63.9%**
Don Mattingly	60.7
Chuck Knoblauch	59.7

Bunts in Play	
Milt Cuyler	**44**
Luis Sojo	43
Harold Reynolds	33

Pitchers

Earned Run Average	
Roger Clemens	**2.62**
Tom Candiotti	2.65
Bill Wegman	2.84
Jim Abbott	2.89
Nolan Ryan	2.91
Mike Moore	2.96
Kevin Tapani	2.99
Mark Langston	3.00
Jimmy Key	3.05
Bret Saberhagen	3.07

Wins	
Bill Gullickson	**20**
Scott Erickson	**20**
Mark Langston	19

Losses	
Kirk McCaskill	**19**
Greg Swindell	16
Charles Nagy	15

Win-Loss Percentage	
Joe Hesketh	**.750**
Scott Erickson	.714
Mark Langston	.704

Games Pitched	
Duane Ward	**81**
Gregg Olson	72
Mike Jackson	72

Games Started	
Bill Gullickson	**35**
Bob Welch	**35**
Roger Clemens	**35**
Dave Stewart	**35**
Jack Morris	**35**
Jack McDowell	**35**

Complete Games

Jack McDowell	15
Roger Clemens	13
Jack Morris	10
Jaime Navarro	10

Shutouts

Roger Clemens	4
Jack McDowell	3
Kevin Appier	3
Brian Holman	3
Scott Erickson	3

Games Finished

Bryan Harvey	63
Gregg Olson	62
Rick Aguilera	60

Innings Pitched

Roger Clemens	271.1
Jack McDowell	253.2
Jack Morris	246.2

Hits Allowed

Walt Terrell	257
Bill Gullickson	256
Dave Stewart	245

Batters Faced

Roger Clemens	1077
Jack Morris	1032
Jack McDowell	1028

Runs Allowed

Dave Stewart	135
Bob Welch	124
Jaime Navarro	117

Earned Runs Allowed

Dave Stewart	130
Bob Welch	112
Walt Terrell	103
Kevin Brown	103
Rich DeLucia	103

Home Runs Allowed

Rich DeLucia	31
Mark Langston	30
Frank Tanana	26

Walks Allowed

Randy Johnson	152
Mike Moore	105
Dave Stewart	105

Hit Batsmen

Kevin Brown	13
Mike Boddicker	13
Todd Stottlemyre	12
Randy Johnson	12

Strikeouts

Roger Clemens	241
Randy Johnson	228
Nolan Ryan	203

Wild Pitches

Jack Morris	15
Mike Moore	14
Erik Hanson	14

Balks

Denis Boucher	4
Jim Abbott	4
Kevin Tapani	3
David Wells	3
Kevin Brown	3
Wade Taylor	3
Chuck Finley	3
Chuck Crim	3

Run Support per 9 IP

Dave Stewart	6.1
Bill Gullickson	5.8
Scott Erickson	5.7

Baserunners per 9 IP

Nolan Ryan	9.3
Roger Clemens	9.6
Kevin Tapani	9.8

Batting Average Allowed

Nolan Ryan	.172
Randy Johnson	.213
Mark Langston	.215

Slugging Pct Allowed

Nolan Ryan	.285
Mike Moore	.318
Randy Johnson	.325

On-Base Average Allowed

Nolan Ryan	.263
Roger Clemens	.270
Kevin Tapani	.277

Home Runs per 9 IP

Tom Candiotti	.45
Mike Moore	.47
Roger Clemens	.50

Strikeouts per 9 IP

Nolan Ryan	10.6
Randy Johnson	10.2
Roger Clemens	8.0

Strikeout/Walk Ratio

Greg Swindell	5.5
Scott Sanderson	4.5
Roger Clemens	3.7

Stolen Bases Allowed

Jack Morris	32
Eric Plunk	28
Tom Candiotti	26

Caught Stealing Off

Bob Welch	16
Roger Clemens	16
Mark Langston	15

SB% Allowed

Greg Harris	14.3%
Scott Erickson	28.6
Rich DeLucia	30.8

GDPs induced

Walt Terrell	35
Kevin Brown	30
Greg Hibbard	27

GDPs Induced per 9 IP

Walt Terrell	1.4
Kevin Brown	1.3
Greg Hibbard	1.3

GDPs Induced/GDP Situation

Dave Eiland	31.0%
Wilson Alvarez	22.5
Russ Swan	21.7

Ground/Fly Ratio Off

Kevin Brown	2.8
Scott Erickson	2.4
Jim Abbott	2.1

BA Allowed Scoring Position

Joe Hesketh	.141
Jose Guzman	.162
Tom Candiotti	.189

Pitches Thrown

Roger Clemens	4025
Dave Stewart	3939
Tom Candiotti	3894

Pitches Thrown per Batter

Bill Gullickson	**3.27**
Greg Swindell	3.34
Walt Terrell	3.42

Pickoff Throws

Charlie Hough	**313**
Frank Tanana	214
Mike Boddicker	200

ERA at Home

Mike Moore	**2.14**
Greg Swindell	2.52
Jim Abbott	2.57

ERA on the Road

Tom Candiotti	**2.25**
Jimmy Key	2.64
Mark Langston	2.64

BA Off by LH Batters

Mike Flanagan	**.181**
Nolan Ryan	.183
Bryan Harvey	.183

BA Off by RH Batters

Scott Erickson	**.191**
Jack Morris	.210
Tom Candiotti	.212

Relievers

Relief ERA

Bryan Harvey	**1.60**
Todd Frohwirth	1.87
Mark Eichhorn	1.98

Relief Wins

Joe Klink	**10**
Mike Timlin	**10**
Mike Henneman	**10**

Relief Losses

Tom Gordon	**7**
Doug Jones	**7**
Mike Jackson	**7**
Paul Gibson	**7**

Saves

Bryan Harvey	**46**
Dennis Eckersley	43
Rick Aguilera	42

Blown Saves

Jeff Russell	**10**
Bobby Thigpen	9
Rick Aguilera	9
Jeff Reardon	9

Save Opportunities

Bryan Harvey	**52**
Dennis Eckersley	51
Rick Aguilera	51

Save Percentage

Tom Henke	**91.4%**
Bryan Harvey	88.5
Mike Henneman	87.5

Holds

Mark Eichhorn	**25**
John Habyan	20
Jeff Gray	19

Relief Innings

Duane Ward	**107.1**
Todd Frohwirth	96.1
Paul Gibson	96.0

Relief BA Allowed

Bryan Harvey	**.178**
Jeff Gray	.181
Rick Aguilera	.183

Runners/9 IP

Jeff Gray	**7.3**
Bryan Harvey	7.9
Dennis Eckersley	8.3

Relief Strikeouts/9 IP

Bryan Harvey	**11.6**
Duane Ward	11.1
Dennis Eckersley	10.3

% Inherited Runners Scored

Joe Klink	**15.2%**
Steve Bedrosian	16.3
Kenny Rogers	18.0

First Batter Efficiency

Todd Frohwirth	**.109**
Carl Willis	.114
Rick Aguilera	.127

Fielding

Errors by Pitcher

Randy Johnson	**5**
Bill Wegman	4
17 Pitchers with	3

Errors by Catcher

Terry Steinbach	**13**
Greg Myers	11
Ivan Rodriguez	10

Errors by First Base

Rafael Palmeiro	**12**
Randy Milligan	10
7 Players with	8

Errors by Second Base

Willie Randolph	**20**
Harold Reynolds	18
Chuck Knoblauch	18

Errors by Third Base

Robin Ventura	**18**
Gary Gaetti	17
Pat Kelly	16

Errors by Shortstop

Luis Rivera	**24**
Alvaro Espinoza	21
Ozzie Guillen	21

Errors by Left Field

Albert Belle	**9**
Rickey Henderson	8
Lloyd Moseby	6

Errors by Center Field

Alex Cole	**7**
Gary Pettis	6
Milt Cuyler	6

Errors by Right Field

Jose Canseco	**9**
Mark Whiten	7
Ruben Sierra	7
Rob Deer	7
Danny Tartabull	7

% CS by Catchers

Lance Parrish	**42.4%**
Carlton Fisk	40.7
Dave Valle	40.3

1991 National League Leaders

Batters

Batting Average
Terry Pendleton	.319
Hal Morris	.318
Tony Gwynn	.317
Willie McGee	.312
Felix Jose	.305
Barry Larkin	.302
Bobby Bonilla	.302
Will Clark	.301
Chris Sabo	.301
Ivan Calderon	.300

Home Runs
Howard Johnson	38
Matt D. Williams	34
Ron Gant	32

Runs Batted In
Howard Johnson	117
Barry Bonds	116
Will Clark	116

Games Played
Brett Butler	161
Mark Grace	160
Steve Finley	159

At Bats
Mark Grace	619
Brett Butler	615
Jay Bell	608

Runs Scored
Brett Butler	112
Howard Johnson	108
Ryne Sandberg	104

Hits
Terry Pendleton	187
Brett Butler	182
Chris Sabo	175

Singles
Brett Butler	162
Craig Biggio	130
Mark Grace	128

Doubles
Bobby Bonilla	44
Felix Jose	40
Todd Zeile	36
Paul O'Neill	36

Triples
Ray Lankford	15
Tony Gwynn	11
Steve Finley	10

Stolen Bases
Marquis Grissom	76
Otis Nixon	72
Delino DeShields	56

Caught Stealing
Brett Butler	28
Delino DeShields	23
Otis Nixon	21

Walks
Brett Butler	108
Barry Bonds	107
Fred McGriff	105

Intentional Walks
Fred McGriff	26
Barry Bonds	25
Eddie Murray	17

Hit by Pitch
Jeff Bagwell	13
Lonnie Smith	9
Luis Gonzalez	8

Strikeouts
Delino DeShields	151
Fred McGriff	135
Juan Samuel	133

Ground into Double Play
Benito Santiago	21
Dale Murphy	20
Jose Lind	19

Sacrifice Bunts
Jay Bell	30
Tom Glavine	15
Randy Tomlin	13
Zane Smith	13

Sacrifice Flies
Howard Johnson	15
Barry Bonds	13
Bobby Bonilla	11
Andy Van Slyke	11
Shawon Dunston	11

Batter Plate Appearances
Brett Butler	730
Mark Grace	703
Jay Bell	697

Times on Base
Brett Butler	291
Bobby Bonilla	266
Barry Bonds	260

Total Bases
Will Clark	303
Terry Pendleton	303
Howard Johnson	302

Slugging Percentage
Will Clark	.536
Howard Johnson	.535
Terry Pendleton	.517

Slugging Pct off LHP
Ivan Calderon	.627
Chris Sabo	.596
Barry Larkin	.585

Slugging Pct off RHP
Will Clark	.581
Paul O'Neill	.562
Howard Johnson	.559

Cleanup Slugging Pct
Howard Johnson	.592
Ron Gant	.589
Kevin Mitchell	.524

On-Base Average
Barry Bonds	.410
Brett Butler	.401
Fred McGriff	.396

On-Base Average off LHP
Ryne Sandberg	.456
Barry Larkin	.436
Lonnie Smith	.435

On-Base Average off RHP

Barry Bonds	**.425**
Bobby Bonilla	.418
Fred McGriff	.406

Leadoff On-Base Average

Brett Butler	**.401**
Lonnie Smith	.393
Lenny Dykstra	.387

HR Frequency - AB/HR

Howard Johnson	**14.8**
Fred McGriff	17.0
Matt D. Williams	17.3

Groundball/Flyball Ratio

Willie McGee	**4.0**
Brett Butler	3.7
Tony Gwynn	3.1

% Extra Bases Taken as Runner

Shawon Dunston	**94.7%**
Gerald Perry	81.3
Alfredo Griffin	75.0

Runs/Time Reached Base

Howard Johnson	**48.0%**
Ron Gant	46.5
Ray Lankford	45.1

SB Success %

Lenny Dykstra	**85.7%**
Gary Redus	85.0
Ced Landrum	84.4

Steals of Third

Marquis Grissom	**18**
Otis Nixon	13
Barry Larkin	10

BA Scoring Position

Tony Gwynn	**.377**
Pedro Guerrero	.350
Dave Justice	.347

BA Late & Close

Jeff Bagwell	**.361**
Mark Lemke	.359
Shawon Dunston	.357

BA Bases Loaded

Todd Zeile	**.600**
Ron Gant	.556
Felix Jose	.500

GDP/GDP Situation

Craig Biggio	**1.8%**
Howard Johnson	3.0
Gerald Perry	3.6

BA vs LH Pitchers

Ryne Sandberg	**.359**
Chris Sabo	.357
Ivan Calderon	.354

BA vs RH Pitchers

Hal Morris	**.336**
Will Clark	.334
Terry Pendleton	.328

BA at Home

Craig Biggio	**.343**
Terry Pendleton	.340
Chris Sabo	.339

BA on the Road

Willie McGee	**.345**
Tony Gwynn	.325
Will Clark	.319

BA on 3-1 Count

Glenn Braggs	**1.000**
Gary Carter	.667
Bip Roberts	.625

BA With 2 Strikes

Randy Ready	**.286**
Jeff Treadway	.283
Tony Gwynn	.282

BA on 0-2 Count

Dave Martinez	**.423**
Gregg Jefferies	.333
Jeff Treadway	.333

BA on 3-2 Count

Billy Hatcher	**.471**
Craig Biggio	.382
Terry Pendleton	.378

Pitches Seen

Brett Butler	**3064**
Delino DeShields	2853
Ryne Sandberg	2716

Pitches Seen per PA

Delino DeShields	**4.23**
Brett Butler	4.20
Darryl Strawberry	4.04

% Pitches Taken

Dave Magadan	**63.6%**
Delino DeShields	63.4
Orlando Merced	63.1

% of Swings that Missed

Tony Gwynn	**6.9%**
Ozzie Smith	8.8
Dave Magadan	9.0

% Swings Put Into Play

Tony Gwynn	**61.0%**
Ozzie Smith	55.5
Otis Nixon	54.2

Bunts in Play

Otis Nixon	**59**
Brett Butler	51
Steve Finley	40

Pitchers

Earned Run Average

Dennis Martinez	**2.39**
Jose Rijo	2.51
Tom Glavine	2.55
Tim Belcher	2.62
Pete Harnisch	2.70
Jose DeLeon	2.71
Mike Morgan	2.78
Randy Tomlin	2.98
Andy Benes	3.03
Doug Drabek	3.07

Wins

Tom Glavine	**20**
John Smiley	**20**
Steve Avery	18

Losses

Bud Black	**16**
Frank Viola	15
Doug Drabek	14
Tom Browning	14
David Cone	14

Win-Loss Percentage

John Smiley	**.714**
Jose Rijo	.714
Mitch Williams	.706

Games Pitched

Barry Jones	77
Paul Assenmacher	75
Mike Stanton	74

Games Started

Greg Maddux	37
John Smoltz	36
Charlie Leibrandt	36
Tom Browning	36

Complete Games

Tom Glavine	9
Dennis Martinez	9
Terry Mulholland	8

Shutouts

Dennis Martinez	5
Ramon Martinez	4
Bud Black	3
Zane Smith	3
Terry Mulholland	3

Games Finished

Lee Smith	61
Mitch Williams	60
Rob Dibble	57

Innings Pitched

Greg Maddux	263.0
Tom Glavine	246.2
Mike Morgan	236.1

Hits Allowed

Frank Viola	259
Doug Drabek	245
Tom Browning	241

Batters Faced

Greg Maddux	1070
Tom Glavine	989
Tom Browning	983

Runs Allowed

Tom Browning	124
Greg Maddux	113
Frank Viola	112

Earned Runs Allowed

Tom Browning	107
Frank Viola	102
Greg Maddux	98

Home Runs Allowed

Tom Browning	32
Frank Viola	25
Bud Black	25
Jack Armstrong	25

Walks Allowed

Jose DeJesus	128
Brian Barnes	84
Darryl Kile	84

Hit Batsmen

John Burkett	10
Juan Agosto	8
Mitch Williams	8

Strikeouts

David Cone	241
Greg Maddux	198
Tom Glavine	192

Wild Pitches

John Smoltz	20
David Cone	17
Jason Grimsley	14

Balks

Bud Black	6
Jim Deshaies	5
7 Pitchers	4

Run Support per 9 IP

Jose Rijo	5.6
Bryn Smith	5.5
Steve Avery	5.4

Baserunners per 9 IP

Jose Rijo	9.8
Tom Glavine	9.9
Mike Morgan	9.9

Batting Average Allowed

Pete Harnisch	.212
Jose Rijo	.219
Tom Glavine	.222

Slugging Pct Allowed

Jose Rijo	.305
Mike Morgan	.306
Dennis Martinez	.311

On-Base Average Allowed

Jose Rijo	.272
Tom Glavine	.277
Mike Morgan	.278

Home Runs per 9 IP

Jose DeJesus	.35
Jose Rijo	.35
Dennis Martinez	.37

Strikeouts per 9 IP

David Cone	9.3
Jose Rijo	7.6
Pete Harnisch	7.1

Strikeout/Walk Ratio

Zane Smith	4.1
David Cone	3.3
Jose Rijo	3.1

Stolen Bases Allowed

Charlie Leibrandt	35
Dwight Gooden	33
Doug Drabek	29

Caught Stealing Off

Mark Gardner	17
John Burkett	16
Dwight Gooden	16
Frank Viola	16

SB% Allowed

Frank Viola	27.3%
Trevor Wilson	40.0
Mark Gardner	43.3

GDPs induced

Zane Smith	27
Mike Morgan	23
Bud Black	20

GDPs Induced per 9 IP

Zane Smith	1.066
Bob Tewksbury	.895
Mike Morgan	.876

GDPs Induced/GDP Situation

Barry Jones	20.0%
Mike Remlinger	20.0
Rick Sutcliffe	19.4

Ground/Fly Ratio Off

Zane Smith	2.7
Mike Morgan	2.6
Greg Maddux	2.4

BA Allowed Scoring Position

Jeff Brantley	.161
Pete Harnisch	.188
Andy Benes	.196

Pitches Thrown

David Cone	3743
Greg Maddux	3658
Tom Glavine	3595

Pitches Thrown per Batter

Bob Tewksbury	3.10
Bryn Smith	3.26
Bruce Hurst	3.36

Pickoff Throws

David Cone	406
John Burkett	344
Jim Deshaies	295

ERA at Home

Dennis Martinez	2.16
Doug Drabek	2.40
Pete Harnisch	2.41

ERA on the Road

Jose Rijo	2.06
Mike Morgan	2.23
Andy Benes	2.33

BA Off by LH Batters

Trevor Wilson	.169
Randy Tomlin	.172
Chuck McElroy	.172

BA Off by RH Batters

John Smoltz	.182
Tim Belcher	.195
Tom Glavine	.205

Relievers

Relief ERA

Chuck McElroy	1.95
Juan Berenguer	2.24
Lee Smith	2.34

Relief Wins

Mitch Williams	12
Cris Carpenter	10
Roger McDowell	9

Relief Losses

John Franco	9
Barry Jones	9
Roger McDowell	9

Saves

Lee Smith	47
Rob Dibble	31
Mitch Williams	30
John Franco	30

Blown Saves

Tim Burke	10
Al Osuna	9
Paul Assenmacher	9
Mitch Williams	9

Save Opportunities

Lee Smith	53
Mitch Williams	39
Rob Dibble	36

Save Percentage

Lee Smith	88.7 %
Rob Dibble	86.1
John Franco	85.7

Holds

John Candelaria	19
Scott Terry	15
Mike Stanton	15

Relief Innings

Paul Assenmacher	102.3
Tim Burke	101.2
Chuck McElroy	101.1
Roger McDowell	101.1

Relief BA Allowed

Mitch Williams	.182
Stan Belinda	.184
Juan Berenguer	.189

Runners/9 IP

Juan Berenguer	9.2
Jeff Fassero	9.3
Jeff Innis	9.5

Relief Strikeouts/9 IP

Rob Dibble	13.6
Paul Assenmacher	10.3
Jim Gott	8.6

% Inherited Runners Scored

Dave Righetti	15.6 %
Scott Ruskin	16.7
John Candelaria	18.3

First Batter Efficiency

Dave Righetti	.071
Stan Belinda	.120
Mitch Williams	.145

Fielding

Errors by Pitcher

Ron Darling	6
Doug Drabek	5
Terry Mulholland	5
Tom Browning	5

Errors by Catcher

Benito Santiago	14
Gil Reyes	11
Joe Oliver	11

Errors by First Base

Pedro Guerrero	16
Fred McGriff	14
Orlando Merced	12
Jeff Bagwell	12

Errors by Second Base

Delino DeShields	27
Juan Samuel	17
Jeff Treadway	15

Errors by Third Base

Todd Zeile	25
Terry Pendleton	24
Ken Caminiti	23

Errors by Shortstop

Jay Bell	24
Alfredo Griffin	22
Shawon Dunston	21
Dickie Thon	21

Errors by Left Field

George Bell	10
Ivan Calderon	7
Kevin Mitchell	6

Errors by Center Field

Ron Gant	6
Ray Lankford	6
Marquis Grissom	5
Herm Winningham	5

Errors by Right Field

Dave Justice	7
Mike Simms	6
Darryl Strawberry	5
Dale Murphy	5
Hubie Brooks	5

% CS by Catchers

Gil Reyes	53.1 %
Tom Pagnozzi	44.9
Terry Kennedy	44.3

Stars, Bums and Sleepers — Who's Who in 1992

Stars, Bums and Sleepers —
Who's Who in 1992

The science of predicting the rise and fall of baseball players may be a lot of things, but one thing it isn't is EXACT. Our skepticism always leads us to the following question: "Why predict at all?" And our curiosity (and chutzpah) invariably leads us to answer: "Because it's fun, and we might learn something along the way."

What STATS has done in this section and in parts of its other publications is to try and stoke the fires of baseball debate and conversation, things that baseball fans enjoy most. That is not to say these predictions are light-hearted. Research by Bill James and John Dewan has created a system that puts an objective stamp on a player's ability. This system was used, along with the subjective advice of our scouts and staff experts, to create the following easy-to-use summarized prognostications, called "Stars, Bums, and Sleepers," and last year it proved to work quite well in delivering some useful hints.

For fantasy players who want a reliable gauge of a player abilities, we have created this section. For those fans who want to look at some reasoned evaluations that will stir up some good baseball talk, we have created this section. And for those fans who want someone to tell them to bet their salary that Terry Pendleton will bat .319 with 22 home runs . . . well, there's always Las Vegas. Have fun!

How To Use This Section

Every position is broken into four groups: Expect A Better Year in '92, Look for Consistency, Production Will Drop and 1992 Sleepers. Here's the key point to remember when looking at the first three of these categories. **A player is put into one of these three groups based on his 1991 performance.** For example, Cal Ripken is shown in the category Production Will Drop. That means that you probably shouldn't expect Cal to hit .323 again, especially in conjunction with 34 homers and 114 RBI. However, we still believe that Ripken could easily have the best year among all

shortstops in baseball, as he did in 1991. A year in which he knocks out 25 homers, drives in 96 runs and hits .275 would be hard for any shortstop to beat, but heck, it still is a drop from his mammoth MVP numbers.

We do things a little differently in the section entitled 1992 Sleepers, but we do them right (usually). Last year, our sleepers included Hector Villanueva, Hal Morris, Travis Fryman, Steve Buechele, Leo Gomez, Wes Chamberlain, Ray Lankford, Juan Gonzalez, Jay Buhner, Marquis Grissom, Bill Wegman, Scott Erickson, and Jeff Russell! You can bet (not literally, of course) that many of this year's crop of sleepers will hit the big time. The numbers we show in this section are each player's combined minor and major league performance for 1991. The idea here is to show what this player is **capable** of doing. We've tried to factor playing time into the equation as this book went to press in late 1991, but you'll get a better idea as the season starts as to who's playing and who's not.

Finally, within each grouping (for example, first basemen listed under Expect A Better Year) we've ranked the players based on our own expectations of performance from best performance to worst. Taking this example, we rank Mark McGwire ahead of John Olerud and Mark Grace. But we leave it up to you to decide (or you can ask us for more info) as to how much more Mark McGwire's offense will improve compared to Wally Joyner's anticipated decline.

How We Developed This Section

We broke down all 660+ regular major league players in this book into their most common position played in 1991. We then looked at every player in two basic ways: statistical analysis and subjective rating.

For our statistical model, we looked at historical patterns of performance to help us project performance for each player. Here are some of the factors that we plugged into our computer:

Career trends -- A player should not be judged simply based on his most recent year of performance, although the tendency for most fans (and many "experts") is to do just that. While it is possible that a player who had a good year in relation to the rest of his career has suddenly become a better ballplayer, it's much more likely that it was simply a good year. Meaning, of course, that it's likely he'll come down to a more normal performance the following year. While it is possible for a .246 career hitter like Otis Nixon to hit .297 again, it's much more likely he'll come back down to the .250 range that he's established for his career. The same is true about a bad season for most players. If his playing time does not get severely cut, a player with a bad season will usually rebound.

Player Age -- The best age for a player in baseball is 26 or 27. Based on historical studies, this is the age when players have their best years. So, the rule of thumb is that if a player is less than 26, you can expect some improvement over the level of play he's established so far in his career. If a player is over 27, you can expect some decrease in his playing performance from **the level of play he has established in recent years and over his career.**

Minor League Performance -- In his book *The Bill James Abstract*, Bill has found that minor league performance, when properly adjusted, is just as reliable in predicting major league performance as is prior major league performance. Therefore, we've looked at minor league performance here to help us project 1992, especially for the players we called "Sleepers."

We then added our own subjective considerations:

Playing Time -- When considering how good a player will be in a given year, you first have to determine how often he'll get a chance to play. This we've done by evaluating players compared to their teammates. Do your own research this spring to find out more about a team's plans for a player if you're not sure -- and don't forget to take into account a player's injury-prone nature.

Pitchers' Inconsistency -- For every five hitters you can name as being reasonably consistent from year to year, there is probably only one pitcher who can compare in consistency. Some of the most consistently tough pitchers in baseball over the past several years (Frank Viola, Doug Jones, Dave Stewart) can suddenly have a stinker. We used many subjective considerations in devising our pitcher evaluations.

Catcher

Expect A Better Year in '92

	1991 Statistics			
	Avg.	HR	RBI	SB
Mike Macfarlane	.277	13	41	1
Brent Mayne	.251	3	31	2
Chris Hoiles	.243	11	31	0
Darren Daulton	.196	12	42	5
Pat Borders	.244	5	36	0
Joe Oliver	.216	11	41	0
Ron Karkovice	.246	5	22	0

Look for Consistency

	1991 Statistics			
	Avg.	HR	RBI	SB
Craig Biggio	.295	4	46	19
Benito Santiago	.267	17	87	8
B.J. Surhoff	.289	5	68	5
Tom Pagnozzi	.264	2	57	9
Terry Steinbach	.274	6	67	2
Lance Parrish	.216	19	51	0
Tony Pena	.231	5	48	8
Mike Scioscia	.264	8	40	4
Greg Myers	.262	8	36	0
Don Slaught	.295	1	29	1
Dave Valle	.194	8	32	0
Mackey Sasser	.272	5	35	0
Mike Stanley	.249	3	25	0

Production Will Drop

	1991 Statistics			
	Avg.	HR	RBI	SB
Mickey Tettleton	.263	31	89	3
Brian Harper	.311	10	69	1
Matt Nokes	.268	24	77	3
Carlton Fisk	.241	18	74	1
Mike LaValliere	.289	3	41	2
Greg Olson	.241	6	44	1
Hector Villanueva	.276	13	32	0

1992 Sleepers

	1991 Statistics (includes minor leagues)			
	Avg.	HR	RBI	SB
Sandy Alomar Jr	.247	1	17	0
Todd Hundley	.257	15	73	1
Ivan Rodriguez	.268	6	55	1
Steve Decker	.221	11	38	0

First Base

Expect A Better Year in '92

	1991 Statistics			
	Avg.	HR	RBI	SB
Mark McGwire	.201	22	75	2
John Olerud	.256	17	68	0
Mark Grace	.273	8	58	3
Don Mattingly	.288	9	68	2
Dave Magadan	.258	4	51	1
Sid Bream	.253	11	45	0
Ricky Jordan	.272	9	49	0
Andres Galarraga	.219	9	33	5

Look for Consistency

	1991 Statistics			
	Avg.	HR	RBI	SB
Cecil Fielder	.261	44	133	0
Will Clark	.301	29	116	4
Fred McGriff	.278	31	106	4
Jeff Bagwell	.294	15	82	7
Kent Hrbek	.284	20	89	4
Eddie Murray	.260	19	96	10
Randy Milligan	.263	16	70	0
Pedro Guerrero	.272	8	70	4
Todd Benzinger	.262	3	51	4
Orlando Merced	.275	10	50	8
Brian Hunter	.251	12	50	0

Production Will Drop

	1991 Statistics			
	Avg.	HR	RBI	SB
Rafael Palmeiro	.322	26	88	4
John Kruk	.294	21	92	7
Wally Joyner	.301	21	96	2
Hal Morris	.318	14	59	10
Carlos Quintana	.295	11	71	1
Dan Pasqua	.259	18	66	0
Pete O'Brien	.248	17	88	0

1992 Sleepers

	1991 Statistics (includes minor leagues)			
	Avg.	HR	RBI	SB
Lee Stevens	.312	19	105	5
Glenn Davis	.230	11	31	4
Reggie Jefferson	.277	9	58	3
Mo Vaughn	.267	18	82	4

Second Base

Expect A Better Year in '92

| | 1991 Statistics | | | |
	Avg.	HR	RBI	SB
Gregg Jefferies	.272	9	62	26
Bip Roberts	.281	3	32	26
Billy Doran	.280	6	35	5
Craig Grebeck	.281	6	31	1
Jose Oquendo	.240	1	26	1
Terry Shumpert	.217	5	34	17
Geronimo Pena	.243	5	17	15
Mark Lemke	.234	2	23	1
Randy Ready	.249	1	20	2
Jerry Browne	.228	1	29	2
Tommy Herr	.209	1	21	9

Look for Consistency

| | 1991 Statistics | | | |
	Avg.	HR	RBI	SB
Roberto Alomar	.295	9	69	53
Jody Reed	.283	5	60	6
Harold Reynolds	.254	3	57	28
Delino DeShields	.238	10	51	56
Robby Thompson	.262	19	48	14
Juan Samuel	.271	12	58	23
Chuck Knoblauch	.281	1	50	25
Jeff Treadway	.320	3	32	2
Mariano Duncan	.258	12	40	5
Jose Lind	.265	3	54	7
Luis Sojo	.258	3	20	4
Keith Miller	.280	4	23	14
Lance Blankenship	.249	3	21	12

Production Will Drop

| | 1991 Statistics | | | |
	Avg.	HR	RBI	SB
Ryne Sandberg	.291	26	100	22
Julio Franco	.341	15	78	36
Steve Sax	.304	10	56	31
Lou Whitaker	.279	23	78	4
Willie Randolph	.327	0	54	4
Mike Gallego	.247	12	49	6
Casey Candaele	.262	4	50	9
Tim Teufel	.217	12	44	9

1992 Sleepers

| | 1991 Statistics (includes minor leagues) | | | |
	Avg.	HR	RBI	SB
Mickey Morandini	.251	2	29	15
Billy Ripken	.223	0	15	1

Third Base

Expect A Better Year in '92

| | 1991 Statistics | | | |
	Avg.	HR	RBI	SB
Kelly Gruber	.252	20	65	12
Gary Sheffield	.194	2	22	5
Kevin Seitzer	.265	1	25	4
Brook Jacoby	.224	4	44	2
Charlie Hayes	.230	12	53	3
Mike Sharperson	.278	2	20	1
Pat Kelly	.242	3	23	12

Look for Consistency

| | 1991 Statistics | | | |
	Avg.	HR	RBI	SB
Wade Boggs	.332	8	51	1
Matt D. Williams	.268	34	98	5
Edgar Martinez	.307	14	52	0
Todd Zeile	.280	11	81	17
Travis Fryman	.259	21	91	12
Carlos Baerga	.288	11	69	3
Tim Wallach	.225	13	73	2
Lenny Harris	.287	3	38	12
Mike Pagliarulo	.279	6	36	1
Scott Leius	.286	5	20	5
Craig Worthington	.225	4	12	0

Production Will Drop

| | 1991 Statistics | | | |
	Avg.	HR	RBI	SB
Howard Johnson	.259	38	117	30
Chris Sabo	.301	26	88	19
Robin Ventura	.284	23	100	2
Tony Phillips	.284	17	72	10
Terry Pendleton	.319	22	86	10
Ken Caminiti	.253	13	80	4
Gary Gaetti	.246	18	66	5
Steve Buechele	.262	22	85	0
Bill Pecota	.286	6	45	16
Jim Gantner	.283	2	47	4

1992 Sleepers

| | 1991 Statistics (includes minor leagues) | | | |
	Avg.	HR	RBI	SB
Leo Gomez	.238	22	64	1
Dean Palmer	.239	37	96	4
Jim Thome	.308	8	82	9

Shortstop

Expect A Better Year in '92

	1991 Statistics			
	Avg.	HR	RBI	SB
Tony Fernandez	.272	4	38	23
Alan Trammell	.248	9	55	11
Kurt Stillwell	.265	6	51	3
Walt Weiss	.226	0	13	6
Kevin Elster	.241	6	36	2
Manuel Lee	.234	0	29	7
Jeff Huson	.213	2	26	8

Look for Consistency

	1991 Statistics			
	Avg.	HR	RBI	SB
Barry Larkin	.302	20	69	24
Shawon Dunston	.260	12	50	21
Greg Gagne	.265	8	42	11
Jeff Blauser	.259	11	54	5
Luis Rivera	.258	8	40	4
Ozzie Guillen	.273	3	49	21
Spike Owen	.255	3	26	2
Dickie Thon	.252	9	44	11
Dick Schofield	.225	0	31	8
Dale Sveum	.241	4	43	2

Production Will Drop

	1991 Statistics			
	Avg.	HR	RBI	SB
Cal Ripken	.323	34	114	6
Jay Bell	.270	16	67	10
Ozzie Smith	.285	3	50	35
Bill Spiers	.283	8	54	14
Alvaro Espinoza	.256	5	33	4
Omar Vizquel	.230	1	41	7
Felix Fermin	.262	0	31	5

1992 Sleepers

	1991 Statistics (includes minor leagues)			
	Avg.	HR	RBI	SB
Bret Barberie	.328	12	66	10
Jose Offerman	.269	0	32	35
Andujar Cedeno	.278	16	91	9
Mark Lewis	.270	2	61	4

Left Field

Expect A Better Year in '92

	1991 Statistics			
	Avg.	HR	RBI	SB
Mike Greenwell	.300	9	83	15
Kevin Mitchell	.256	27	69	2
Kal Daniels	.249	17	73	6
Lloyd Moseby	.262	6	35	8
Pete Incaviglia	.214	11	38	1
Glenn Braggs	.260	11	39	11
Greg Briley	.260	2	26	23
Hensley Meulens	.222	6	29	3

Look for Consistency

	1991 Statistics			
	Avg.	HR	RBI	SB
Barry Bonds	.292	25	116	43
Rickey Henderson	.268	18	57	58
Greg Vaughn	.244	27	98	2
Tim Raines	.268	5	50	51
Ivan Calderon	.300	19	75	31
Albert Belle	.282	28	95	3
Luis Polonia	.296	2	50	48
George Bell	.285	25	86	2
Kevin McReynolds	.259	16	74	6
Kirk Gibson	.236	16	55	18
Luis Gonzalez	.254	13	69	10
Candy Maldonado	.250	12	48	4
Milt Thompson	.307	6	34	16
Dan Gladden	.247	6	52	15
Henry Cotto	.305	6	23	16
Bernard Gilkey	.216	5	20	14

Production Will Drop

	1991 Statistics			
	Avg.	HR	RBI	SB
Kevin Reimer	.269	20	69	0
Joe Orsulak	.278	5	43	6
Jim Eisenreich	.301	2	47	5
Lonnie Smith	.275	7	44	9
Billy Hatcher	.262	4	41	11
Otis Nixon	.297	0	26	72
Mike Felder	.264	0	18	21
Jerald Clark	.228	10	47	2

1992 Sleepers

	1991 Statistics (includes minor leagues)			
	Avg.	HR	RBI	SB
Wes Chamberlain	.245	15	70	16

Center Field

Expect A Better Year in '92

	1991 Statistics			
	Avg.	HR	RBI	SB
Lenny Dykstra	.297	3	12	24
Ellis Burks	.251	14	56	6
Ray Lankford	.251	9	69	44
Eric Davis	.235	11	33	14
Milt Cuyler	.257	3	33	41
Vince Coleman	.255	1	17	37
Jerome Walton	.219	5	17	7
Glenallen Hill	.258	8	25	6

Look for Consistency

	1991 Statistics			
	Avg.	HR	RBI	SB
Ken Griffey Jr	.327	22	100	18
Ron Gant	.251	32	105	34
Kirby Puckett	.319	15	89	11
Juan Gonzalez	.264	27	102	4
Roberto Kelly	.267	20	69	32
Brett Butler	.296	2	38	38
Mike Devereaux	.260	19	59	16
Robin Yount	.260	10	77	6
Brian McRae	.261	8	64	20
Marquis Grissom	.267	6	39	76
Lance Johnson	.274	0	49	26
Alex Cole	.295	0	21	27
Mike Huff	.251	3	25	14

Production Will Drop

	1991 Statistics			
	Avg.	HR	RBI	SB
Devon White	.282	17	60	33
Andy Van Slyke	.265	17	83	10
Steve Finley	.285	8	54	34
Dave Henderson	.276	25	85	6
Willie McGee	.312	4	43	17
Darryl Hamilton	.311	1	57	16
Darrin Jackson	.262	21	49	5
Daryl Boston	.275	4	21	15

1992 Sleepers

	1991 Statistics (includes minor leagues)			
	Avg.	HR	RBI	SB
Junior Felix	.299	4	36	15
Bernie Williams	.265	11	71	19
Reggie Sanders	.301	9	52	16
Von Hayes	.226	0	21	9
Darren Lewis	.302	3	67	45

Right Field

Expect A Better Year in '92

	1991 Statistics			
	Avg.	HR	RBI	SB
Dave Justice	.273	23	92	8
Jesse Barfield	.225	17	48	1
Dwight Smith	.228	3	21	2

Look for Consistency

	1991 Statistics			
	Avg.	HR	RBI	SB
Jose Canseco	.266	44	122	26
Ruben Sierra	.307	25	116	16
Darryl Strawberry	.265	28	99	10
Bobby Bonilla	.302	18	100	2
Tony Gwynn	.317	4	62	8
Shane Mack	.310	18	74	13
Jay Buhner	.244	27	77	0
Larry Walker	.290	16	64	14
Tom Brunansky	.229	16	70	1
Rob Deer	.179	25	64	1
Mark Whiten	.243	9	45	4
Dave Martinez	.295	7	42	16
Dwight Evans	.270	6	38	2
Randy Bush	.303	6	23	0
Gene Larkin	.286	2	19	2

Production Will Drop

	1991 Statistics			
	Avg.	HR	RBI	SB
Joe Carter	.273	33	108	20
Paul O'Neill	.256	28	91	12
Danny Tartabull	.316	31	100	6
Andre Dawson	.272	31	104	4
Felix Jose	.305	8	77	20
Dave Winfield	.262	28	86	7
Dale Murphy	.252	18	81	1
Mel Hall	.285	19	80	0
Dante Bichette	.238	15	59	14
Hubie Brooks	.238	16	50	3

1992 Sleepers

	1991 Statistics (includes minor leagues)			
	Avg.	HR	RBI	SB
Phil Plantier	.314	27	96	7
Pedro Munoz	.303	12	54	12
Chito Martinez	.295	33	83	3
Warren Newson	.329	6	44	7
Sammy Sosa	.220	13	52	22

Designated Hitter

Expect A Better Year in '92

	1991 Statistics			
	Avg.	HR	RBI	SB
Alvin Davis	.221	12	69	0

Look for Consistency

	1991 Statistics			
	Avg.	HR	RBI	SB
Frank Thomas	.318	32	109	1
Jack Clark	.249	28	87	0
George Brett	.255	10	61	2
Kevin Maas	.220	23	63	5
Sam Horn	.233	23	61	0
Chris James	.238	5	41	3

Production Will Drop

	1991 Statistics			
	Avg.	HR	RBI	SB
Paul Molitor	.325	17	75	19
Chili Davis	.277	29	93	5
Harold Baines	.295	20	90	0
Brian Downing	.278	17	49	1
Dave Parker	.239	11	59	3

1992 Sleepers

	1991 Statistics (includes minor leagues)			
	Avg.	HR	RBI	SB
Bo Jackson	.244	3	16	1
Carlos Martinez	.308	16	103	14

Starting Pitchers

Expect A Better Year in '92

	1991 Statistics				
	W	L	ERA	Sv	BR/9
David Wells	15	10	3.72	1	10.85
Jose DeLeon	5	9	2.71	0	11.67
Dave Stieb	4	3	3.17	0	11.61
Orel Hershiser	7	2	3.46	0	11.97
Frank Viola	13	15	3.97	0	12.22
Ron Darling	8	15	4.26	0	12.27
Frank Castillo	6	7	4.35	0	11.28
Bob Welch	12	13	4.58	0	13.17
Greg Swindell	9	16	3.48	0	10.40
Erik Hanson	8	8	3.81	0	12.37
Ben McDonald	6	8	4.84	0	12.11
Brian Barnes	5	8	4.22	0	12.66
Alex Fernandez	9	13	4.51	0	12.96
Rick Sutcliffe	6	5	4.10	0	13.13
Pete Schourek	5	4	4.27	2	13.24
Don Robinson	5	9	4.38	1	12.91
Eric King	6	11	4.60	0	12.72
Jim Deshaies	5	12	4.98	0	12.80
Dave Stewart	11	11	5.18	0	14.30
Danny Darwin	3	6	5.16	0	11.91
Ed Whitson	4	6	5.03	0	12.58
Ryan Bowen	6	4	5.15	0	14.07
Curt Young	4	2	5.00	0	14.49
Storm Davis	3	9	4.96	2	14.72
Jason Grimsley	1	7	4.87	0	14.46
Denny Neagle	0	1	4.05	0	15.75
Mark Gubicza	9	12	5.68	0	14.62
Jeff Johnson	6	11	5.88	0	13.82
Matt Young	3	7	5.18	0	14.92
Wade Taylor	7	12	6.27	0	15.78
Tim Leary	4	10	6.49	0	15.74
Arthur Rhodes	0	3	8.00	0	17.50
Kevin Ritz	0	3	11.74	0	24.07

Look for Consistency

	1991 Statistics				
	W	L	ERA	Sv	BR/9
Roger Clemens	18	10	2.62	0	9.59
Jose Rijo	15	6	2.51	0	9.82
Dennis Martinez	14	11	2.39	0	10.26

Nolan Ryan	12	6	2.91	0	9.31
Tom Candiotti	13	13	2.65	0	10.63
Bret Saberhagen	13	8	3.07	0	10.04
Andy Benes	15	11	3.03	0	10.37
Jimmy Key	16	12	3.05	0	10.92
Ramon Martinez	17	13	3.27	0	10.87
Greg Maddux	15	11	3.35	0	10.40
Bruce Hurst	15	8	3.29	0	10.68
Mike Moore	17	8	2.96	0	12.26
Juan Guzman	10	3	2.99	0	10.90
Chris Bosio	14	10	3.25	0	11.13
David Cone	14	14	3.29	0	10.91
Tim Belcher	10	9	2.62	0	11.44
Doug Drabek	15	14	3.07	0	11.89
Greg W. Harris	9	5	2.23	0	9.74
Kevin Appier	13	10	3.42	0	11.61
Bobby Ojeda	12	9	3.18	0	12.07
Randy Tomlin	8	7	2.98	0	11.83
John Smoltz	14	13	3.80	0	11.21
Bryn Smith	12	9	3.85	0	10.87
Jose Guzman	13	7	3.08	0	12.73
Dwight Gooden	13	7	3.60	0	11.56
Chuck Finley	18	9	3.80	0	12.43
Jaime Navarro	15	12	3.92	0	12.15
Luis Aquino	8	4	3.44	3	11.64
Frank Tanana	13	12	3.69	0	12.30
Chris Nabholz	8	7	3.63	0	11.30
Bud Black	12	16	3.99	0	11.59
Tom Browning	14	14	4.18	0	11.76
Bob Milacki	10	9	4.01	0	11.20
Mark Gardner	9	11	3.85	0	11.66
Brian Holman	13	14	3.69	0	13.18
Charlie Hough	9	10	4.02	0	12.28
Mike Boddicker	12	12	4.08	0	12.95
Mike Bielecki	13	11	4.46	0	11.87
Greg Hibbard	11	11	4.31	0	11.83
John Burkett	12	11	4.18	0	12.76
Kelly Downs	10	4	4.19	0	12.49
Mark Portugal	10	12	4.49	1	11.98
Randy Johnson	13	10	3.98	0	14.08
Bruce Ruffin	4	7	3.78	0	12.40
Darryl Kile	7	11	3.69	0	13.70
Bob Scanlan	7	8	3.89	1	12.73
Kirk McCaskill	10	19	4.26	0	13.27

	W	L	ERA	Sv	BR/9
Walt Terrell	12	14	4.24	0	13.91
Dennis Rasmussen	6	13	3.74	0	12.64
Kevin Gross	10	11	3.58	3	13.62
Neal Heaton	3	3	4.33	0	12.71
Tom Gordon	9	14	3.87	1	12.53
Wilson Alvarez	3	2	3.51	0	12.14
Charles Nagy	10	15	4.13	0	12.78
Chris Hammond	7	7	4.06	0	12.82
Mike Gardiner	9	10	4.85	0	12.95
John Cerutti	3	6	4.57	2	13.50
Oil Can Boyd	8	15	4.59	0	12.49
Jimmy Jones	6	8	4.39	0	13.10
David West	4	4	4.54	0	11.99
Allan Anderson	9	12	4.59	0	12.80
Rich Delucia	12	13	5.09	0	12.76
Danny Cox	4	6	4.57	0	12.14
Kevin Brown	9	12	4.40	0	14.35
Doug Simons	2	3	5.19	1	11.27
Dave Otto	2	8	4.23	0	12.51
Jack Armstrong	7	13	5.48	0	13.79
Joe Grahe	3	7	4.81	0	14.79
Shawn Boskie	4	9	5.23	0	14.44
Scott Aldred	2	4	5.18	0	13.81
Don August	9	8	5.47	0	14.05
Tom Bolton	8	9	5.24	0	15.38
Dave Eiland	2	5	5.33	0	14.00
Jose Mesa	6	11	5.97	0	15.72
Steve Searcy	3	3	6.59	0	15.85
Jack Morris	18	12	3.43	0	11.79
Terry Mulholland	16	13	3.61	0	10.98
Melido Perez	8	7	3.12	1	10.88
Todd Stottlemyre	15	8	3.78	0	11.55
Joe Hesketh	12	4	3.29	0	11.45
Bob Walk	9	2	3.60	0	11.27
Ken Hill	11	10	3.57	0	10.92
Trevor Wilson	13	11	3.56	0	11.36
Bob Tewksbury	11	12	3.25	0	11.73
Omar Olivares	11	7	3.71	1	11.51
Greg Harris	11	12	3.85	2	12.02
Russ Swan	6	2	3.43	2	12.47
Bill Krueger	11	8	3.60	0	13.27
Wally Whitehurst	7	12	4.18	1	11.54
Mark Leiter	9	7	4.21	1	12.10
Rod Nichols	2	11	3.54	1	11.86
Jose DeJesus	10	9	3.42	1	13.82
Jeff Shaw	0	5	3.36	1	12.82
Chris Beasley	0	1	3.38	0	12.49
Mark Guthrie	7	5	4.32	2	14.51
Paul McClellan	3	6	4.56	0	11.92
Adam Peterson	3	4	4.45	0	12.84
Brian Bohanon	4	3	4.84	0	13.35

1992 Sleepers

1991 Statistics
(includes minor leagues)

	W	L	ERA	Sv	BR/9
Sid Fernandez	2	3	2.10	0	8.65
Mike Mussina	14	9	2.87	0	10.29
Pascual Perez	2	4	3.08	0	11.16
Terry Mathews	9	6	3.54	2	12.20
Rheal Cormier	11	14	4.19	0	12.03
Rod Beck	5	4	2.77	7	10.04
Scott Kamieniecki	10	7	3.01	0	11.14
Teddy Higuera	4	2	4.00	0	12.00
Anthony Young	9	14	3.59	0	12.70
Ricky Bones	12	12	4.40	0	13.10
Kevin Morton	13	8	4.00	0	12.55
Chris Haney	9	11	3.18	0	13.02
Joe Slusarski	9	9	4.51	0	13.24
Pat Combs	4	8	5.42	0	16.16
Dan Gakeler	3	7	4.91	6	13.12
Kyle Abbott	15	12	4.05	0	11.52
Bobby Witt	4	8	5.68	0	15.83
Roberto Hernandez	7	2	3.46	0	11.21
Danny Jackson	1	5	6.42	0	16.89
Dana Kiecker	4	6	5.63	0	16.66

Production Will Drop

1991 Statistics

	W	L	ERA	Sv	BR/9
Eric Bell	4	0	0.50	0	5.50
Tom Glavine	20	11	2.55	0	9.92
Mike Morgan	14	10	2.78	1	9.94
John Smiley	20	8	3.08	0	10.44
Scott Erickson	20	8	3.18	0	11.74
Kevin Tapani	16	9	2.99	0	9.85
Mark Langston	19	8	3.00	0	10.52
Bill Wegman	15	7	2.84	0	10.38
Jim Abbott	18	11	2.89	0	11.11
Pete Harnisch	12	9	2.70	0	10.68
Zane Smith	16	10	3.20	0	10.46
Jack McDowell	17	10	3.41	0	10.57
Steve Avery	18	8	3.38	0	11.00
Scott Sanderson	16	10	3.81	0	10.04
Charlie Leibrandt	15	13	3.49	0	10.66
Tommy Greene	13	7	3.38	0	10.66
Bill Gullickson	20	9	3.90	0	12.09

Relief Pitchers

Expect A Better Year in '92

1991 Statistics

	W	L	ERA	Sv	BR/9
Rob Dibble	3	5	3.17	31	10.06
John Franco	5	9	2.93	30	13.01
Craig Lefferts	1	6	3.91	23	11.61
Norm Charlton	3	5	2.91	1	10.97
Jim Gott	4	3	2.96	2	11.37
Lee Guetterman	3	4	3.68	6	12.17
Randy Myers	6	13	3.55	6	13.43
John Candelaria	1	1	3.74	2	11.23
Bob Patterson	4	3	4.11	2	11.24
Dan Plesac	2	7	4.29	8	13.06
Scott Bailes	1	2	4.18	0	11.67
Rick Honeycutt	2	4	3.58	0	14.10
Jerry Don Gleaton	3	2	4.06	2	13.50
Mark Williamson	5	5	4.48	4	13.67
Chuck Crim	8	5	4.63	3	13.99
Bob Kipper	2	2	4.65	4	13.20
Kenny Rogers	10	10	5.42	5	15.43
Jeff Ballard	6	12	5.60	0	13.32
Jeff Robinson	0	3	5.37	3	13.74
Bob McClure	1	1	4.96	0	14.33
Dave Smith	0	6	6.00	17	16.09
Eric Plunk	2	5	4.76	0	15.39
Gene Nelson	1	5	6.84	0	15.90

Look for Consistency

	W	L	ERA	Sv	BR/9
Bryan Harvey	2	4	1.60	46	7.89
Dennis Eckersley	5	4	2.96	43	8.29
Jeff Reardon	1	4	3.03	40	10.77
Tom Henke	0	2	2.32	32	7.87
Steve Farr	5	5	2.19	23	10.54
Jeff Montgomery	4	4	2.90	33	11.30
Jay Howell	6	5	3.18	16	9.00
Larry Andersen	3	4	2.30	13	9.96
Gregg Olson	4	6	3.18	31	12.71
Jeff Russell	6	4	3.29	30	11.12
Bobby Thigpen	7	5	3.49	30	13.56
Dave Righetti	2	7	3.39	24	11.93
Alejandro Pena	8	1	2.40	15	10.49
Stan Belinda	7	5	3.45	16	10.23
Jeff Gray	2	3	2.34	1	7.30
Mark Eichhorn	3	3	1.98	1	8.60
Bill Landrum	4	4	3.18	17	11.20
Bill Swift	1	2	1.99	17	10.06
Paul Assenmacher	7	8	3.24	15	10.43
Jeff Brantley	5	2	2.45	15	12.74
Roger McDowell	9	9	2.93	10	13.32
Tim Burke	6	7	3.36	6	11.15
Mike Stanton	5	5	2.88	7	9.69
Barry Jones	4	9	3.35	13	11.17
Jeff Innis	0	2	2.66	0	9.46
Mike Timlin	11	6	3.16	3	12.05
Kent Mercker	5	3	2.58	6	11.29
Tim Crews	2	3	3.43	6	11.13
Mike Flanagan	2	7	2.38	3	10.25
Julio Machado	3	3	3.45	3	12.48
Les Lancaster	9	7	3.52	3	11.71
Scott Terry	4	4	2.80	1	12.10
Steve Bedrosian	5	3	4.42	6	12.57
Jim Clancy	3	5	3.91	8	10.84
Doug Piatt	0	0	2.60	0	11.94
Rob Murphy	0	1	3.00	4	12.56
Goose Gossage	4	2	4.25	1	11.91
Mike Magnante	0	1	2.45	0	12.76
Bob MacDonald	3	3	2.85	0	12.75
Rich Rodriguez	3	1	3.26	0	12.38
Scott Ruskin	4	4	4.24	6	12.72
Shawn Hillegas	3	4	4.34	7	12.47
Terry Leach	1	2	3.61	0	12.83
Jesse Orosco	2	0	3.74	0	13.40
Jim Corsi	0	5	3.71	0	11.47
Bill Sampen	9	5	4.00	0	14.13
Willie Fraser	3	6	5.08	1	13.25
Joe Boever	3	5	3.84	0	13.18
Mike Hartley	4	1	4.21	2	13.72
Steve Chitren	1	4	4.33	4	14.17
Jim Acker	3	5	5.20	1	11.72
Juan Agosto	5	3	4.81	2	14.55
Mike Jeffcoat	5	3	4.63	1	15.03
Edwin Nunez	2	1	6.04	8	14.57
Kevin D. Brown	2	4	5.51	0	14.28
Mike Fetters	2	5	4.84	0	16.93

1991 Statistics

Production Will Drop

	W	L	ERA	Sv	BR/9
Lee Smith	6	3	2.34	47	10.23
Rick Aguilera	4	5	2.35	42	9.78
Mitch Williams	12	5	2.34	30	12.84
Duane Ward	7	6	2.77	23	9.64
Juan Berenguer	0	3	2.24	17	9.23
Todd Frohwirth	7	3	1.87	3	8.78
Scott Radinsky	5	5	2.02	8	9.71
Mike Maddux	7	2	2.46	5	9.67
Mike Jackson	7	7	3.25	14	10.56
John Habyan	4	2	2.30	2	9.50
Jim Poole	3	2	2.36	1	8.79
Carl Willis	8	3	2.63	2	9.71
Roger Mason	3	2	3.03	3	8.49
Donn Pall	7	2	2.41	0	10.39
Chuck McElroy	6	2	1.95	3	11.55
Jose Melendez	8	5	3.27	3	9.80
Al Osuna	7	6	3.42	12	11.90
Marvin Freeman	1	0	3.00	1	9.75
Wally Ritchie	1	2	2.50	0	11.26
Steve Olin	3	6	3.36	17	13.58
Mel Rojas	3	3	3.75	6	10.50
Francisco Oliveras	6	6	3.86	3	10.44
Cris Carpenter	10	4	4.23	0	9.95
Ken Patterson	3	0	2.83	1	11.87
Dwayne Henry	3	2	3.19	2	12.24
Greg Cadaret	8	6	3.62	3	12.65
Vince Palacios	6	3	3.75	3	11.90
Ted Power	5	3	3.62	3	12.41
Joe Klink	10	3	4.35	2	12.48
Tony Fossas	3	2	3.47	1	12.63
Curt Schilling	3	5	3.81	8	14.04
Kip Gross	6	4	3.47	0	13.97
Scott Scudder	6	9	4.35	1	13.59
Mark Lee	2	5	3.86	1	13.83
John Barfield	4	4	4.54	1	12.74
Paul Gibson	5	7	4.59	8	15.28
Xavier Hernandez	2	7	4.71	3	14.00

1991 Statistics

1992 Sleepers

	W	L	ERA	Sv	BR/9
Doug Henry	5	3	1.73	29	9.61
Jeff Fassero	5	5	2.20	12	9.29
Mike Schooler	4	4	4.14	7	10.05
Steve Howe	5	2	1.22	8	9.36
Calvin Jones	3	3	2.99	9	13.37
Heathcliff Slocumb	3	1	3.55	2	12.20
Mark Wohlers	4	1	1.40	34	10.47
John Costello	2	2	2.66	3	13.15
Mark Davis	10	4	3.57	1	12.08
Doug Jones	6	10	4.73	14	12.73
Rob Mallicoat	8	7	4.59	3	13.50
Steve Frey	3	2	3.35	4	12.90
Ken Dayley	0	1	6.66	1	19.60

1991 Statistics (includes minor leagues)

American League Players

PITCHING:

Jeff Ballard started for the Orioles on Opening Day last year, but was buried deep in the Oriole bullpen by the end of the season. His effectiveness waned so much that he was optioned to Triple-A July 30 and did not return until rosters expanded in September. A late-season start against the Yankees showed nothing had changed. Ballard allowed six runs in less than three innings in what might have been his Oriole farewell.

Watching the Ballard of 1990 and '91, it's hard to believe that in 1989 he won more games (18) than any lefthander in the American League. People keep expecting Ballard to "regain his form," but it's very possible that his '89 numbers were a fluke. Ballard is 8-23 since then and 18-43 in his career except for that one big season.

A control pitcher, Ballard had a good spring training last year but never completely regained the command of the strike zone that he possessed in 1989. He appears to have lost movement on his sinker. His strikeout and walk totals remained typically low last year, and he was eminently hittable (.302 opposing average). Ballard must be around the plate to be effective, but the numbers suggest his location has been **too** good.

HOLDING RUNNERS AND FIELDING:

Intelligent and left-handed, Ballard keeps runners close and they take few liberties with him. Of course, runners haven't needed to steal with Ballard's tendency to give up a lot of hits. Ballard's defensive instincts are good and he moves well off the mound, but his best asset is his awareness of the game situation.

OVERALL:

After deciding to opt for free agency rather than accept an assignment to Rochester, Ballard appears to have no future with the Orioles. He says he is recovered from the two elbow operations of two years ago. The need for pitching around baseball being what it is, someone is bound to give him a chance.

JEFF BALLARD

Position: SP
Bats: L **Throws:** L
Ht: 6' 2" **Wt:** 203

Opening Day Age: 28
Born: 8/13/63 in Billings, MT
ML Seasons: 5

Overall Statistics

	W	L	ERA	G	GS	Sv	IP	H	R	BB	SO	HR
1991	6	12	5.60	26	22	0	123.2	153	91	28	37	16
Career	36	51	4.63	144	113	0	695.1	812	408	204	217	84

How Often He Throws Strikes

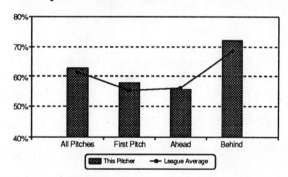

1991 Situational Stats

	W	L	ERA	Sv	IP		AB	H	HR	RBI	AVG
Home	0	8	5.93	0	44.0	LHB	88	16	1	9	.182
Road	6	4	5.42	0	79.2	RHB	418	137	15	72	.328
Day	2	3	5.06	0	37.1	Sc Pos	113	43	5	65	.381
Night	4	9	5.84	0	86.1	Clutch	16	5	0	3	.313

1991 Rankings (American League)

→ 1st worst batting average allowed vs. right-handed batters (.328)

→ 2nd worst winning percentage (.333)

→ Led the Orioles in losses (12)

HITTING:

Visions of 40 homers and 100 RBI danced in the heads of Orioles' fans when the Baltimore acquired Glenn Davis from the Houston Astros in January of 1991. After all, Davis was escaping the cavernous Astrodome and moving to the far chummier Memorial Stadium. Now Memorial Stadium is gone; the Orioles can only hope that Davis' prodigious bat, after an injury-riddled 1991 season, won't be gone also. Davis got only 176 at-bats (and ten homers) in '91, his free agent year.

Davis injured a nerve in his neck and wound up missing 105 games last year. As a result, the Orioles never found out what his bat could mean in their lineup. One of the top power hitters in the game, Davis is often fed a steady diet of breaking pitches away to avoid his strength. With a big, long swing, he has the perfect stroke for a slugger and the ball jumps off his bat. He is basically a pull hitter but was more inclined to go the opposite way last season. Davis will take a walk on occasion and will try for a single rather than a homer if the situation demands.

BASERUNNING:

As big men go, Davis is not a bad baserunner. He was successful in all four of his steal attempts last year and runs well for his size. The approach he takes is the same as his hitting: aggressive. He will go for the extra base and usually makes it.

FIELDING:

Davis is not a Gold Glover, but he has worked hard to improve his fielding, particularly after one nightmarish afternoon when he made four errors in a single game. He can scoop poor throws and has progressed at making his own accurately.

OVERALL:

The Orioles re-signed Davis for the 1992 season. He showed late in 1991 that he could come back from the injury, once thought career-threatening. Only 31, Davis is still capable of hitting 40 home runs over a full season.

GLENN DAVIS

Position: 1B/DH
Bats: R **Throws:** R
Ht: 6' 3" **Wt:** 200

Opening Day Age: 31
Born: 3/28/61 in Jacksonville, FL
ML Seasons: 8

Overall Statistics

	G	AB	R	H	D	T	HR	RBI	SB	BB	SO	AVG
1991	49	176	29	40	9	1	10	28	4	16	29	.227
Career	879	3208	456	835	159	11	176	546	27	326	519	.260

Where He Hits the Ball

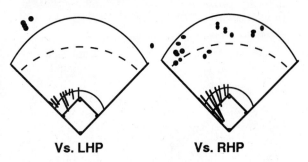

Vs. LHP   Vs. RHP

1991 Situational Stats

	AB	H	HR	RBI	AVG		AB	H	HR	RBI	AVG
Home	73	18	3	7	.247	LHP	47	12	5	7	.255
Road	103	22	7	21	.214	RHP	129	28	5	21	.217
Day	47	8	1	2	.170	Sc Pos	42	8	1	15	.190
Night	129	32	9	26	.248	Clutch	32	7	0	4	.219

1991 Rankings (American League)

➡ Led the Orioles in hit by pitch (5)

HITTING:

Mike Devereaux is not the classic leadoff hitter, but he adapted to the role as best he could last year. Making great strides as a power hitter, he hit a career-high 19 homers, providing a major threat at the top of the batting order. Devereaux's 56 extra base hits more than made up for his mediocre .260 average -- at least in terms of his overall value. But he struck out too much (115 times) and walked too seldom (47) to be a truly good number-one hitter.

Devereaux's legs help him beat out some hits, which is a plus in the top spot, but he still has a tendency to pull too many pitches. He is also very vulnerable to outside breaking pitches. Devereaux's personal preference is to bat lower in the order; with his power, he has the ability to drive in 85 runs or more. For now, though, the Orioles need Devereaux at leadoff, and he's doing the best he can with what he has.

BASERUNNING:

Devereaux led the team with 16 stolen bases, but was caught nine times. He has trackman's speed, yet he still doesn't read pitchers' moves well. Once he gets going, it only requires a few steps before he is flying, and no one on the team gets from first to third quicker.

FIELDING:

Devereaux gets an outstanding jump on fly balls and covers a lot of territory. His speed makes him the club's natural choice to play center. His arm is only average, however, and sometimes scatter-shot.

OVERALL:

Wherever he bats in the lineup, Devereaux is an asset to the Orioles. He has proven he can handle everyday play and is highly regarded in the clubhouse. For now, he will have to try to curb his strikeouts and raise his on-base percentage because the Orioles don't have anyone else to lead-off.

MIKE DEVEREAUX

Position: CF
Bats: R **Throws:** R
Ht: 6' 0" **Wt:** 193

Opening Day Age: 29
Born: 4/10/63 in Casper, WY
ML Seasons: 5

Overall Statistics

	G	AB	R	H	D	T	HR	RBI	SB	BB	SO	AVG
1991	149	608	82	158	27	10	19	59	16	47	115	.260
Career	428	1463	196	367	63	14	39	160	54	116	243	.251

Where He Hits the Ball

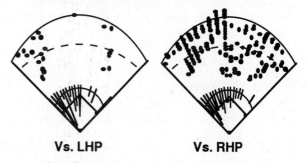

Vs. LHP   Vs. RHP

1991 Situational Stats

	AB	H	HR	RBI	AVG		AB	H	HR	RBI	AVG
Home	305	77	10	35	.252	LHP	167	49	6	16	.293
Road	303	81	9	24	.267	RHP	441	109	13	43	.247
Day	142	36	4	13	.254	Sc Pos	102	26	3	39	.255
Night	466	122	15	46	.262	Clutch	104	27	3	9	.260

1991 Rankings (American League)

➜ 4th in triples (10)

➜ 7th lowest on-base percentage vs. right-handed pitchers (.299)

➜ 9th lowest stolen base percentage (64.0%)

➜ Led the Orioles in triples, stolen bases (16), caught stealing (9), strikeouts (115), pitches seen (2,621), runs scored per time reached base (39.6%) and steals of third (3)

➜ Led AL center fielders in pitches seen per plate appearance (3.92)

HITTING:

Dwight Evans had something to prove last year, and he did it with a fine comeback season. In Evans' view, the Red Sox treated him like he was ready for the rocking chair, first confining him to DH duties, then letting him go via free agency. The Orioles took a chance and received both consistency and clutch hitting, though his power figures were a far cry from the ones he once posted.

Evans played 67 games in right field and, although slowed by an injured Achilles heel, he acquitted himself well. He was the team's top pinch hitter (10 for 25) and its leading stick both with men in scoring position and the bases loaded. Evans knows exactly what he wants to do at the plate and is an extremely patient hitter who will accept a walk. Evans' oft-troubled back held up last year, enabling him to drive pitches the other way more often.

BASERUNNING:

Now 40 years old, Evans will occasionally attempt a steal, but even the element of surprise doesn't help much: he was only two for five in steal attempts last year. He uses his intelligence and knowledge of the game on the base paths, but his aging legs won't permit him to take many chances.

FIELDING:

Once the consummate right fielder, a Hall of Fame caliber defender, Evans showed the Orioles that his years of experience haven't gone to waste. His cannon arm has diminished, but is still respected by opponents who remember it well. He can't play every day in right, but he can still play.

OVERALL:

Evans, only 15 homers away from 400 in his career, still has an outside chance to make the Hall of Fame. He probably won't be a regular this year, but he can still hit. He's a valuable man for pinch hitting and part-time duty, and it's a comfortable feeling to have him on the bench.

DWIGHT EVANS

Position: RF/DH
Bats: R **Throws:** R
Ht: 6' 3" **Wt:** 180

Opening Day Age: 40
Born: 11/3/51 in Santa Monica, CA
ML Seasons: 20

Overall Statistics

	G	AB	R	H	D	T	HR	RBI	SB	BB	SO	AVG
1991	101	270	35	73	9	1	6	38	2	54	54	.270
Career	2606	8996	1470	2446	483	73	385	1384	78	1391	1697	.272

Where He Hits the Ball

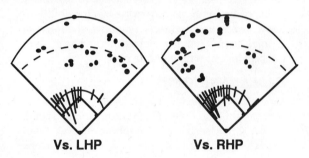

Vs. LHP   Vs. RHP

1991 Situational Stats

	AB	H	HR	RBI	AVG		AB	H	HR	RBI	AVG
Home	135	35	4	20	.259	LHP	107	33	1	10	.308
Road	135	38	2	18	.281	RHP	163	40	5	28	.245
Day	52	12	0	5	.231	Sc Pos	65	23	3	32	.354
Night	218	61	6	33	.280	Clutch	68	15	2	8	.221

1991 Rankings (American League)

→ 2nd highest on-base percentage vs. left-handed pitchers (.468)

→ Led the Orioles in on-base percentage vs. left-handed pitchers

→ Led AL right fielders in on-base percentage vs. left-handed pitchers

TOUGH ON LEFTIES

MIKE FLANAGAN

Position: RP
Bats: L **Throws:** L
Ht: 6' 0" **Wt:** 195

Opening Day Age: 40
Born: 12/16/51 in Manchester, NH
ML Seasons: 17

PITCHING:

One of the more inspirational stories of 1991, Mike Flanagan resurrected his career with his long-time team, the Orioles -- this time as a relief pitcher. Released by Toronto early in the '90 season, Flanagan couldn't hook on with anyone and sat out the rest of that year, his career seemingly over.

The Orioles invited him to their spring training camp last spring, but Flanagan's quiet comeback was lost in the hubbub surrounding ex-teammate Jim Palmer, who was making a much more publicized attempt at reviving his career. Flanagan prospered out of the limelight, not only making the team but becoming one of the club's best relievers. He finished the year by striking out the final two batters to ever face an Oriole pitcher at Memorial Stadium -- a fitting climax to an unlikely season.

Flanagan is wise, tough and a gutty competitor who always takes the ball. His sweeping curve and still-respectable fastball enable him to be effective against both lefties and righties; he can also drop down from the side when he needs to. He held left-handed batters to a .181 average while adapting quickly to the bullpen. One drawback: He takes a little longer than most relievers to get ready. But that was not a major problem.

HOLDING RUNNERS AND FIELDING:

Even by lefthanders' standards, Flanagan has an excellent move, one fine-tuned over his long career. It is so good that it sometimes fools the umpires and he is charged with a balk . . . one of which was costly in a loss last year. Difficult to steal against, Flanagan also has a lot of dexterity and is a heads-up fielder with sure hands.

OVERALL:

A "sentimental" invitee to the Orioles' camp last year, Flanagan recovered strongly from an arm injury to become a major part of their bullpen. His contract renewal was announced on the final day of the season. At age 40, he is still a viable and valuable commodity.

Overall Statistics

	W	L	ERA	G	GS	Sv	IP	H	R	BB	SO	HR
1991	2	7	2.38	64	1	3	98.1	84	27	25	55	6
Career	167	143	3.84	484	404	4	2735.1	2756	1267	867	1474	248

How Often He Throws Strikes

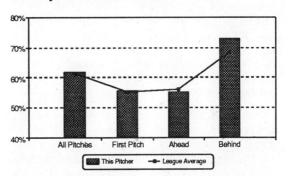

This Pitcher —•— League Average

1991 Situational Stats

	W	L	ERA	Sv	IP		AB	H	HR	RBI	AVG
Home	0	5	3.18	0	45.1	LHB	127	23	2	10	.181
Road	2	2	1.70	3	53.0	RHB	229	61	4	20	.266
Day	0	2	2.12	0	29.2	Sc Pos	85	16	2	25	.188
Night	2	5	2.49	3	68.2	Clutch	134	34	2	17	.254

1991 Rankings (American League)

→ 1st in lowest batting average allowed vs. left-handed batters (.181)

→ 4th in relief innings (94.1)

→ 5th in relief ERA (2.00) and relief losses (6)

→ 9th in holds (14)

→ Led the Orioles in holds, lowest batting average allowed vs. left-handed batters, relief losses and lowest percentage of inherited runners scored (25.5%)

PITCHING:

Spurned by Philadelphia, Todd Frohwirth may have found a home in Baltimore. After a checkered career with the Phillies -- he was up and down four times -- Frohwirth developed into a hitters' scourge in the American League. His sidewinding delivery baffled the opposition and his control and command overpowered them. Frohwirth finished the year with a 1.87 ERA and allowed only 94 baserunners in 96.1 innings.

Frohwirth has a slightly better-than-average fastball and a slurve (half slider, half curve). Both pitches are very effective coming from down under, an angle hitters rarely see. When he keeps the ball down in the strike zone, he is almost untouchable. Frohwirth is a also a pitcher who can work often without losing efficiency. While pitching the most innings of his career, he had the best winning percentage and lowest earned run average on the Oriole staff. He yielded only two homers, a .190 opposing batting average and was particularly hard on righties (.169 average).

Frohwirth received little work in spring training, but couldn't be ignored after leading the International League in saves during his stint at Rochester. Primarily a set-up man, he could be used to close games as well because his unorthodox delivery makes the ball difficult to pick up.

HOLDING RUNNERS AND FIELDING:

Because Frohwirth has a fairly slow delivery, baserunners will challenge him. But the Orioles do not want to fiddle with a delivery that confuses hitters, so his motion is not likely to change. A good fielder, he takes a little longer than most on ground balls because he also throws to first with an underarm motion.

OVERALL:

There is no question that Frohwirth is an integral part of the Orioles' 1992 plans. With Mark Williamson tailing off, Frohwirth could become the club's set-up man. He walks few, gives up few hits, pitches often and is a good influence in the clubhouse.

TODD FROHWIRTH

Position: RP
Bats: R **Throws:** R
Ht: 6' 4" **Wt:** 195

Opening Day Age: 29
Born: 9/28/62 in Milwaukee, WI
ML Seasons: 5

Overall Statistics

	W	L	ERA	G	GS	Sv	IP	H	R	BB	SO	HR
1991	7	3	1.87	51	0	3	96.1	64	24	29	77	2
Career	10	6	2.85	123	0	3	183.0	151	63	66	137	8

How Often He Throws Strikes

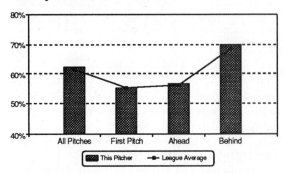

This Pitcher — League Average

1991 Situational Stats

	W	L	ERA	Sv	IP		AB	H	HR	RBI	AVG
Home	4	1	2.48	1	54.1	LHB	130	29	0	16	.223
Road	3	2	1.07	2	42.0	RHB	207	35	2	20	.169
Day	3	2	3.38	2	24.0	Sc Pos	100	19	1	35	.190
Night	4	1	1.37	1	72.1	Clutch	144	26	1	8	.181

1991 Rankings (American League)

→ 1st in first batter efficiency (.109)

→ 2nd in relief innings (96.1) and relief ERA (1.87)

→ 4th lowest batting average allowed by a relief pitcher (.190)

→ 5th in fewest baserunners allowed per 9 innings, relief pitcher (8.8)

→ Led the Orioles in first batter efficiency, relief ERA, relief innings, relief wins (7), lowest batting average allowed by a relief pitcher and fewest baserunners allowed per 9 innings, relief pitcher

HITTING:

Highly touted rookie Leo Gomez struggled early last season with the big club, went to Rochester to regain his timing and confidence, then returned to supplant Craig Worthington as the O's starting third baseman. Given the job on an everyday basis, Gomez wound up leading all major league rookies in homers with 16 and finished strongly, batting .280 from September 1.

Gomez hasn't yet been confused with Brooks Robinson, but it will be tough to dislodge him because he has a strong work ethic and tries hard to improve. Several parts of his offensive game still need work. Gomez probably won't ever hit for a high average and he still strikes out a lot, the result of a tentative approach to hitting. He sometimes hits like he doesn't want to hurt the ball.

Gomez was also weak in obvious RBI situations last year, but that's the sort of thing that can improve with experience. Some changes in his thinking helped when he returned from the minors, and his impressive gap power should keep him in the lineup.

BASERUNNING:

Caution is the operative word with Gomez, who was 1-for-2 in steal attempts. He requires the ball to be put in play -- hit and run or bunt -- to get going and won't blind anybody with his speed. He won't win any games with his footspeed.

FIELDING:

This is an area in which Gomez has made giant strides. He doesn't want to be known as simply a hitter and has worked hard with the glove. Despite the fact that he committed only one error in the last 82 games, Gomez went to the instructional league after the season to help his lateral movement. He is blessed with a strong, accurate arm.

OVERALL:

Until further notice, Gomez is the O's regular third-sacker. He is capable of 20 homers and 75 RBI, and his glove work has progressed dramatically. A dedicated player, Gomez has relaxed now that the job is totally his and Worthington is no longer a challenger.

LEO GOMEZ

Position: 3B
Bats: R **Throws:** R
Ht: 6' 0" **Wt:** 202

Opening Day Age: 25
Born: 3/2/67 in Carnovanas, Puerto Rico
ML Seasons: 2

Overall Statistics

	G	AB	R	H	D	T	HR	RBI	SB	BB	SO	AVG
1991	118	391	40	91	17	2	16	45	1	40	82	.233
Career	130	430	43	100	17	2	16	46	1	48	89	.233

Where He Hits the Ball

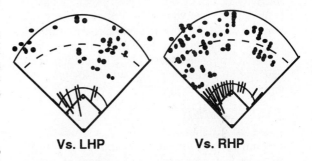

Vs. LHP   **Vs. RHP**

1991 Situational Stats

	AB	H	HR	RBI	AVG		AB	H	HR	RBI	AVG
Home	203	47	7	23	.232	LHP	114	25	6	16	.219
Road	188	44	9	22	.234	RHP	277	66	10	29	.238
Day	95	22	3	9	.232	Sc Pos	80	15	2	25	.188
Night	296	69	13	36	.233	Clutch	72	14	3	7	.194

1991 Rankings (American League)

➡ 3rd lowest batting average after the 6th inning (.170)

➡ 8th lowest batting average with runners in scoring position (.188)

➡ Led AL third basemen in sacrifice flies (7)

HITTING:

The Orioles badly want Chris Hoiles to mature into their No. 1 catcher, and there are signs that he is taking steps in that direction. After struggling (.190) in spot duty in 1990, Hoiles handled big league pitching better last season with 11 homers in 341 at-bats while lifting his average to .243. The O's think Hoiles can do a lot better, that he has the potential to hit 15 to 20 homers and knock in 75 runs.

At the major league level, Hoiles has had a tendency to become laid-back as a hitter instead of attacking the ball the way he did at AAA Rochester in 1990, when he hit a mighty .348 with 18 homers in only 247 at-bats. He showed more intensity down the stretch last year, a hopeful sign. A pull hitter who doesn't often go the other way, he could improve in situations with runners on base. Hoiles is not yet regarded as a tough out, and a lack of speed doesn't help his batting average. But he is showing slow and steady progress and could blossom in 1992.

BASERUNNING:

Like most catchers, Hoiles is heavy-footed and will infrequently attempt to steal. He was 0-for-2 stealing last year and is a one-base-at-a-time baserunner. Fortunately, he doesn't take many chances and avoids major blunders.

FIELDING:

The most surprising aspect of Hoiles' game last year was his glove. Hoiles did things his minor league career never suggested. He was effective throwing out runners (26 of 75 caught), he learned how to move behind the plate and he blocked balls well. Hoiles has made only one error in 136 major league games.

OVERALL:

If Hoiles can upgrade his hitting like he did his defense -- especially in run-producing situations -- he could be a major commodity. He appears to have a solid future now that he has overcome some bad habits behind the plate. The main focus is to get him to be more intense at the plate.

CHRIS HOILES

Position: C/DH
Bats: R **Throws:** R
Ht: 6' 0" **Wt:** 213

Opening Day Age: 27
Born: 3/20/65 in Bowling Green, OH
ML Seasons: 3

Overall Statistics

	G	AB	R	H	D	T	HR	RBI	SB	BB	SO	AVG
1991	107	341	36	83	15	0	11	31	0	29	61	.243
Career	136	413	43	96	19	0	12	38	0	35	76	.232

Where He Hits the Ball

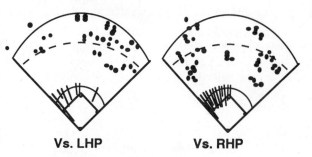

Vs. LHP   **Vs. RHP**

1991 Situational Stats

	AB	H	HR	RBI	AVG		AB	H	HR	RBI	AVG
Home	153	35	5	12	.229	LHP	113	29	6	8	.257
Road	188	48	6	19	.255	RHP	228	54	5	23	.237
Day	69	14	2	11	.203	Sc Pos	66	15	1	19	.227
Night	272	69	9	20	.254	Clutch	62	12	5	11	.194

1991 Rankings (American League)

→ Did not rank near the top or bottom in any category

HITTING:

Sam Horn is a free-swinging, feast-or-famine hitter who has always hit with tremendous power whenever he's been given a chance to play. Last year he was more dangerous than ever. Belting a career-high 23 homers in only 317 at-bats, more frequently than Cecil Fielder, over half of Horn's hits went for extra bases. He also hit .344 as a pinch-hitter with three home runs, a league high. On a team short of left-handed power, he became a prime force despite a lowly .233 average overall.

Horn reported to spring training trim last year, stayed fit throughout the season and applied himself while playing almost solely against righthanders. He has learned to hit the ball where it is pitched and is hitting more home runs to the opposite field. Earlier in his career, he tried to pull pitches on the outside corner, but that mistake has been abandoned. As a result, he has increased his market value with the Orioles and around the league. Understanding himself as a hitter has aided Horn immensely.

BASERUNNING:

Horn, who's hoping the American League adopts the "designated runner" sometime soon, lumbers on the bases, is easily doubled up on ground balls, and is absolutely no threat to steal. Horn's approach is to try and hit the ball into the seats; then he can run as slowly as he likes.

FIELDING:

Despite constant attempts, Horn has never developed with the glove. He has little range, trouble with low throws and as a fielder, makes a good DH. Fortunately for the Orioles, they won't have to use him except in an emergency because they are overloaded with first basemen.

OVERALL:

With the Orioles moving into a park that should favor left-handed power hitters, Horn should get lots of playing time in 1992, and that's all he's ever really needed to be productive. He may be a one-dimensional hitter, but that dimension is extremely important.

SAM HORN

Position: DH
Bats: L **Throws:** L
Ht: 6' 5" **Wt:** 250

Opening Day Age: 28
Born: 11/2/63 in Dallas, TX
ML Seasons: 5

Overall Statistics

	G	AB	R	H	D	T	HR	RBI	SB	BB	SO	AVG
1991	121	317	45	74	16	0	23	61	0	41	99	.233
Career	303	836	111	196	38	0	53	152	0	109	252	.234

Where He Hits the Ball

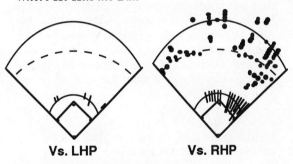

Vs. LHP   Vs. RHP

1991 Situational Stats

	AB	H	HR	RBI	AVG		AB	H	HR	RBI	AVG
Home	149	37	12	28	.248	LHP	18	2	1	1	.111
Road	168	37	11	33	.220	RHP	299	72	22	60	.241
Day	85	18	6	20	.212	Sc Pos	80	22	7	36	.275
Night	232	56	17	41	.241	Clutch	47	11	3	12	.234

1991 Rankings (American League)

➡ Did not rank near the top or bottom in any category

BALTIMORE ORIOLES

HITTING:

Drafted as a six-year minor league free agent following the 1990 season, Chito Martinez arrived in Baltimore last summer with a big splash. In two and a half months, he clouted 13 homers and had a .514 slugging percentage, figures that belie his small stature. Martinez had always hit with power as a Kansas City Royal farmhand, but seldom for average. His .269 mark with the O's was his highest since 1986, when he was in AA ball.

The secret to Martinez is his lightning bat speed. He gets the bat through the zone so quickly he can afford to wait a tad longer on pitches and still react to them. Often the result is a 400-foot drive that astounds opposing pitchers, because Martinez looks like he can't hit the ball that far. He did it often enough in 1991 to suggest he is for real, but the jury is still out. While Martinez eclipsed 20 homers at his last three minor league stops, he also averaged more than 130 strikeouts a season.

BASERUNNING:

Martinez once stole 20 bases in Class AA ball, but he seems to underrate his speed, which is pretty good. He approaches baserunning with caution and only unwinds when he has to, making him almost invisible on the base paths. He has more baserunning ability than he gives himself credit for.

FIELDING:

Martinez is adequate in right field. He has a powerful arm for a small player, but is sometimes fooled on fly balls and doesn't take the right angles in his approach to them. He needs some work on the basics, but his throwing ability is a good starting point.

OVERALL:

Martinez still must prove he can stand the grind of a full season in the majors, but at least now he is getting the chance. He should bunt once in a while to take more advantage of his legs, and cutting down on his strikeouts would help. But don't underestimate his power.

CHITO MARTINEZ

Position: RF
Bats: L **Throws:** L
Ht: 5'10" **Wt:** 180

Opening Day Age: 26
Born: 12/19/65 in Belize, Central America
ML Seasons: 1

Overall Statistics

	G	AB	R	H	D	T	HR	RBI	SB	BB	SO	AVG
1991	67	216	32	58	12	1	13	33	1	11	51	.269
Career	67	216	32	58	12	1	13	33	1	11	51	.269

Where He Hits the Ball

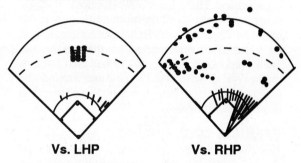

Vs. LHP   **Vs. RHP**

1991 Situational Stats

	AB	H	HR	RBI	AVG		AB	H	HR	RBI	AVG
Home	105	29	8	19	.276	LHP	29	6	1	1	.207
Road	111	29	5	14	.261	RHP	187	52	12	32	.278
Day	58	13	2	9	.224	Sc Pos	52	15	4	22	.288
Night	158	45	11	24	.285	Clutch	36	5	2	4	.139

1991 Rankings (American League)

→ Did not rank near the top or bottom in any category

PITCHING:

Some experts were prepared to stamp Ben McDonald's ticket to Cooperstown when he was the first player picked in the 1989 June draft. But thus far his career has been marked by too many injuries and too little promise fulfilled. In two-plus seasons, McDonald has been limited to 36 starts and a modest 15-13 record. Flashes of greatness are followed by breakdowns of fitness. McDonald was supposed to start last Opening Day, but had to be scratched because elbow problems put him on the disabled list. Then, shoulder stiffness ended his season almost a month early.

McDonald can still throw his fastball in the mid-90's when healthy, and he's working on spotting his change-up more diligently. That way, when he doesn't have his big, breaking curve working, he doesn't have to throw one fastball after another. At times McDonald still believes he has to strike everyone out and gets into a dangerous pitching pattern. Establishing the curve early is the key for McDonald, who had more trouble with right-handed batters (.313) than lefties. He is a hard worker and responds well to instruction, so no reason exists to give up on him yet.

HOLDING RUNNERS AND FIELDING:

A big man who takes a while to uncoil from his high leg kick, McDonald has improved his delivery time to the plate (1.6 seconds to 1.4). This keeps runners more honest, and a slide step also has helped. A former basketball player, McDonald has quick steps in both directions to reach proper fielding position, but his follow-through sometimes carries him too far to handle balls hit to his right.

OVERALL:

Perhaps the Orioles have expected too much, too early from McDonald. The club wanted him to step into the number-one spot in the rotation, but injuries and inconsistency prevented that from happening last season. If he can stay healthy, develop a more varied repertoire, and continue to mature, this may be the year.

BEN McDONALD

Position: SP
Bats: R **Throws:** R
Ht: 6' 7" **Wt:** 212

Opening Day Age: 24
Born: 11/24/67 in Baton Rouge, LA
ML Seasons: 3

Overall Statistics

	W	L	ERA	G	GS	Sv	IP	H	R	BB	SO	HR
1991	6	8	4.84	21	21	0	126.1	126	71	43	85	16
Career	15	13	3.82	48	36	0	252.1	222	114	82	153	27

How Often He Throws Strikes

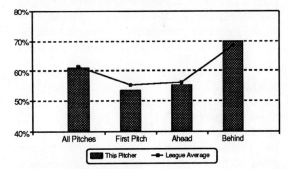

1991 Situational Stats

	W	L	ERA	Sv	IP		AB	H	HR	RBI	AVG
Home	2	4	3.70	0	73.0	LHB	256	55	8	30	.215
Road	4	4	6.41	0	53.1	RHB	227	71	8	32	.313
Day	0	1	5.59	0	29.0	Sc Pos	88	28	3	43	.318
Night	6	7	4.62	0	97.1	Clutch	27	7	2	6	.259

1991 Rankings (American League)

→ Led the Orioles in most stolen bases allowed (14)

HITTING:

Bob Melvin once fashioned himself as a slugger, but he has finally accepted the fact that he isn't one. Melvin hit only one homer last year and is now content to take the base hit or pass on pitches he can't handle. In short, he has become more disciplined and discovered what he can and can't do. As a result, Melvin's batting average has made a slow but steady rise; since 1987, he has batted .199, .234, .241, .243 and finally, last year's career-high .250.

While improving his average, Melvin's run-producing ability hasn't suffered. He is annually among the team leaders in hitting with men on base and in scoring position. Although he has played almost exclusively against lefthanders, he saw more righties last year and fared reasonably well. Basically a high-ball hitter, he now has the acumen to stay away from low pitches he can't hit.

BASERUNNING:

Melvin has been nabbed 11 out of the last 12 times he has tried to steal, so he wisely didn't attempt even once in 1991. A conservative baserunner, Melvin has little speed and the good sense to realize it. He won't take unnecessary risks.

FIELDING:

Defense is how Melvin makes his living. He is an ideal number-two catcher, one who works pitchers well, calls a splendid game and blocks balls in the dirt exceptionally well. His mind is always on top of the situation and he is an encouraging force for a pitching staff.

OVERALL:

With his skills -- excellent defense, enough hitting ability to make himself useful -- Melvin could last a long time as a backup catcher. The Orioles signed him to a two-year contract, realizing his value in working with their young pitchers. Melvin's bat will never pound people, but it has progressed. And his knack for clutch hitting can't be underrated.

BOB MELVIN

Position: C
Bats: R **Throws:** R
Ht: 6' 4" **Wt:** 206

Opening Day Age: 30
Born: 10/28/61 in Palo Alto, CA
ML Seasons: 7

Overall Statistics

	G	AB	R	H	D	T	HR	RBI	SB	BB	SO	AVG
1991	79	228	11	57	10	0	1	23	0	11	46	.250
Career	563	1676	151	388	73	6	31	179	4	85	332	.232

Where He Hits the Ball

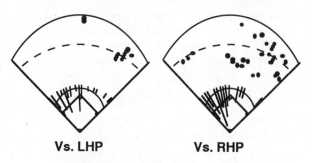

Vs. LHP   **Vs. RHP**

1991 Situational Stats

	AB	H	HR	RBI	AVG		AB	H	HR	RBI	AVG
Home	122	29	0	12	.238	LHP	78	21	0	5	.269
Road	106	28	1	11	.264	RHP	150	36	1	18	.240
Day	71	16	1	7	.225	Sc Pos	59	18	0	21	.305
Night	157	41	0	16	.261	Clutch	34	10	0	2	.294

1991 Rankings (American League)

➡ Did not rank near the top or bottom in any category

PITCHING:

What might have been a wasted 1991 season turned into a fine comeback for Bob Milacki. The big righthander led the Oriole staff in starts, innings, wins, complete games and strikeouts despite spending the first month of the season in Double-A ball. Milacki took the demotion well, applying himself and becoming the Orioles' most consistent starter during the second half.

Milacki has the most varied arsenal in the Baltimore rotation: two fastballs with different action, a curve, a slider and a change-up. When he's right, he can throw them for strikes on any count. But when Milacki is falling behind hitters, the danger signs arise. A pitcher's pitcher, Milacki sometimes sacrifices some velocity for control and command, which is usually effective for him. He was on a roll the final two months of 1991 and probably will enter 1992 as the O's top starter because of his experience.

Milacki has pitched better than his 31-29 career record would indicate, but the Oriole offense hasn't supported him very well. Sixteen times during his career he's pitched at least six innings while allowing two earned runs or less and still not won. Milacki tends to get in a groove late in the year. The Orioles are 14-5 in his career starts after September 1.

HOLDING RUNNERS AND FIELDING:

Milacki's ability to keep runners close is related to his control. If he is getting ahead, his concentration is generally better and his effectiveness improves. He is agile for a big man and will not hurt himself defensively.

OVERALL:

By working himself back into the rotation, Milacki again endeared himself to the Oriole management, which had begun to doubt him a bit after some mechanical problems early in the season. He is a complete pitcher with a lot of weapons when he's right. Milacki will take an important spot in the rotation again in 1992.

BOB MILACKI

Position: SP/RP
Bats: R **Throws:** R
Ht: 6' 4" **Wt:** 234

Opening Day Age: 27
Born: 7/28/64 in Trenton, NJ
ML Seasons: 4

Overall Statistics

	W	L	ERA	G	GS	Sv	IP	H	R	BB	SO	HR
1991	10	9	4.01	31	26	0	184.0	175	86	53	108	17
Career	31	29	3.86	98	89	0	587.1	560	266	211	299	57

How Often He Throws Strikes

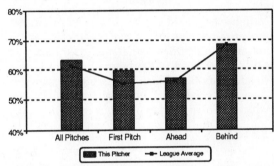

1991 Situational Stats

	W	L	ERA	Sv	IP		AB	H	HR	RBI	AVG
Home	4	4	5.16	0	83.2	LHB	360	92	5	41	.256
Road	6	5	3.05	0	100.1	RHB	332	83	12	41	.250
Day	2	2	3.03	0	32.2	Sc Pos	136	45	4	64	.331
Night	8	7	4.22	0	151.1	Clutch	46	9	2	3	.196

1991 Rankings (American League)

→ 1st in worst ERA at home (5.16)

→ 3rd in worst batting average allowed with runners in scoring position (.331)

→ 8th in lowest run support per 9 innings (4.1)

→ Led the Orioles in ERA (4.01), wins (10), games started (26), complete games (3), innings pitched (184), hits allowed (175), batters faced (758), strikeouts (108), pitches thrown (2,692), runners caught stealing (6), GDPs induced (18) and winning percentage (.526)

HITTING:

When Randy Milligan started the 1991 season in unfamiliar territory, left field, his offense understandably suffered. Once Glenn Davis was hurt and Milligan was able to return to his normal position, first base, he went on a batting tear and finished at about his normal level of production. Milligan finished the year with a respectable total of 16 homers and 70 RBI, the latter figure a career high.

Milligan battled through some nagging injuries to knock in those 70 runs. He walked 84 times, evidence of his continuing patience at the plate. He did strike out 108 times last year, but that's not an unusually high total for a power hitter who goes deep in so many counts.

Milligan has good power to all fields. He has proven to pitchers that he can pull the ball and is not jammed as often as he once was. Last year Milligan returned to the unusual trait of hitting righthanders better than lefties after a one-year change. A good clutch hitter, he batted over .300 with runners in scoring position.

BASERUNNING:

Milligan takes a while to get underway. Once he does, he has better-than- average speed and uses it to advantage. But he is not a base-stealer as shown by his 0-for-5 record in attempts last year. He can't be taken for granted, however.

FIELDING:

The left field experiment has ended, much to Milligan's satisfaction. Manager John Oates won't play him there in 1992; he will play only first base, where he is a little better than average defensively. Milligan works at defense, but he is unrefined and susceptible to occasional lapses.

OVERALL:

If Glenn Davis is available for the full 1992 season, it's likely that Milligan will alternate with Davis at first base with Milligan playing DH against lefthanders. Whether that works remains to be seen. But Milligan is not a complainer. He is a harmonious figure among teammates.

RANDY MILLIGAN

Position: 1B/DH
Bats: R **Throws:** R
Ht: 6' 1" **Wt:** 235

Opening Day Age: 30
Born: 11/27/61 in San Diego, CA
ML Seasons: 5

Overall Statistics

	G	AB	R	H	D	T	HR	RBI	SB	BB	SO	AVG
1991	141	483	57	127	17	2	16	70	0	84	108	.263
Career	417	1293	187	339	65	8	51	183	16	267	276	.262

Where He Hits the Ball

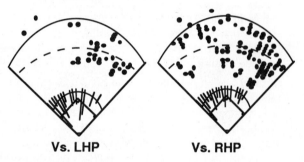

Vs. LHP   **Vs. RHP**

1991 Situational Stats

	AB	H	HR	RBI	AVG		AB	H	HR	RBI	AVG
Home	237	59	8	33	.249	LHP	140	32	5	19	.229
Road	246	68	8	37	.276	RHP	343	95	11	51	.277
Day	107	28	4	11	.262	Sc Pos	128	39	3	53	.305
Night	376	99	12	59	.263	Clutch	86	21	2	12	.244

1991 Rankings (American League)

→ 2nd in least runs scored per time reached base (26.8%)

→ 3rd in GDPs (23) and most GDPs per GDP situation (22.3%)

→ 5th in most pitches seen per plate appearance (4.17)

→ 6th lowest percentage of extra bases taken as a runner (26.5%)

→ Led the Orioles in walks, GDPs, most pitches seen per plate appearance, on-base average vs. right-handed pitchers (.384) and highest percentage of pitches taken (61.0%)

→ Led AL first basemen in GDPs, most pitches seen per plate appearance and highest percentage of pitches taken

FUTURE ALL-STAR

MIKE MUSSINA

Position: SP
Bats: R **Throws:** R
Ht: 6' 2" **Wt:** 185

Opening Day Age: 23
Born: 12/8/68 in
Williamsport, PA
ML Seasons: 1

PITCHING:

Mark down this name. Mike Mussina has already made a big impression on the American League in a little more than two months and just 12 starts. Mussina's debut, a 1-0, four-hit loss to Chicago's Charlie Hough, set the tone for his season; almost every start thereafter was top drawer. What made his performance even more remarkable was that Mussina had been pitching in professional ball for barely a year before reaching the majors.

Mussina has a major league arm, savvy beyond his years and solid confidence in his own abilities. With a fastball in the low 90s, a knuckle-curve that batters don't see well, a straight change-up and better than average control, he has the potential and assets to develop into the Orioles' number-one starter. His main problem at this early stage seems to be that he places very high expectations on himself. If Mussina can learn to relax a bit and let his defense help him, his efficiency may increase even more. Unfortunately, he often drew the opponents' top pitcher (114-79 record in his first 11 starts) and was plagued by weak offensive support.

HOLDING RUNNERS AND FIELDING:

Mussina, who does everything well, has a decent move to first for a righthander and is technically very sound. He lands well and knows how to get into fielding position. An intelligent and intense player, he is keenly aware of the game situation.

OVERALL:

A big future is in store for this former first round draft choice who earned an economics degree from Stanford in three and a half years. He tends to try to do too much himself, but that's certainly preferable to someone who tries to do too little. Going into spring training, he must be considered one of only two sure starters in the Baltimore rotation along with Bob Milacki.

Overall Statistics

	W	L	ERA	G	GS	Sv	IP	H	R	BB	SO	HR
1991	4	5	2.87	12	12	0	87.2	77	31	21	52	7
Career	4	5	2.87	12	12	0	87.2	77	31	21	52	7

How Often He Throws Strikes

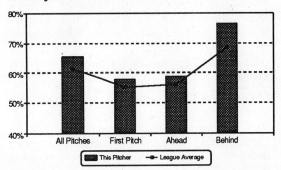

This Pitcher — League Average

1991 Situational Stats

	W	L	ERA	Sv	IP		AB	H	HR	RBI	AVG
Home	3	1	2.74	0	42.2	LHB	182	39	3	17	.214
Road	1	4	3.00	0	45.0	RHB	140	38	4	12	.271
Day	1	2	1.69	0	32.0	Sc Pos	55	15	1	21	.273
Night	3	3	3.56	0	55.2	Clutch	42	11	1	4	.262

1991 Rankings (American League)

➡ Led the Orioles in most GDPs induced per GDP situation (17.0%)

STOPPER

GREGG OLSON

Position: RP
Bats: R **Throws:** R
Ht: 6' 4" **Wt:** 209

Opening Day Age: 25
Born: 10/11/66 in
Omaha, NE
ML Seasons: 4

PITCHING:

Gregg Olson was so mad after blowing a game on "Turn Back The Clock" day last year that he trashed his 1966 Orioles' uniform and vowed he would never wear one again. That is a reflection of Olson's desire for perfection. He thinks he should never fail, a good quality for a closer. But Olson sometimes carries it too far, making it very tough on himself.

Olson had another good season in 1991, with 62 games finished and 31 saves. He has converted 83 percent of his save opportunities over the last three seasons. Nevertheless, there were signs that Olson was not up to his past level of excellence in 1991: He lost his first game ever at home, allowed a .294 batting average to righthanders and lost effectiveness down the stretch. Still, Olson's blazing fastball and pair of curves, including the devastating "Uncle Charlie," are top-quality pitches. His role as the Orioles' closer is not likely to change.

Olson, who allowed more than a hit an inning for the first time in his career, has a tendency to create jams for himself by throwing too much and pitching too little. But he is a valuable man whose rookie-year success would be almost impossible to match. Nobody remains unhittable forever, nor saves every game. Olson thinks he should.

HOLDING RUNNERS AND FIELDING:

Olson went to the Florida Instructional League after the season to work on holding runners. He remained so ineffective in this area last year that Oriole catchers often didn't bother to throw to second. He is not a slick fielder, either, tending to wasted motion and haste in his throws.

OVERALL:

Though his raw ability has not diminished, Olson must curb his appetite for blowing away hitters and let strike-zone location do the job more frequently. His self-critical demeanor can become a minus when he lets it go too far. Olson sometimes thinks the weight of the entire club is on him. A lot of pitchers in the big leagues would take his 1991 accomplishments.

Overall Statistics

	W	L	ERA	G	GS	Sv	IP	H	R	BB	SO	HR
1991	4	6	3.18	72	0	31	73.2	74	28	29	72	1
Career	16	14	2.43	210	0	95	244.0	198	69	116	245	6

How Often He Throws Strikes

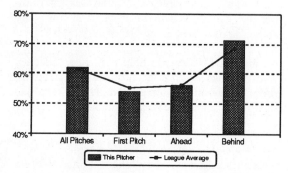

1991 Situational Stats

	W	L	ERA	Sv	IP		AB	H	HR	RBI	AVG
Home	3	1	3.15	13	34.1	LHB	139	32	1	15	.230
Road	1	5	3.20	18	39.1	RHB	143	42	0	21	.294
Day	0	5	7.08	7	20.1	Sc Pos	94	25	0	34	.266
Night	4	1	1.69	24	53.1	Clutch	194	52	1	29	.268

1991 Rankings (American League)

→ 2nd in games (72) and games finished (62)

→ 5th most blown saves (8) and most relief losses (6)

→ 6th in save opportunities (39)

→ 7th in saves (31) and most strikeouts per 9 innings, relief pitcher (8.8)

→ 8th in first batter efficiency (.182)

→ Led the Orioles in games, saves, games finished, wild pitches (8), blown saves and relief losses (6)

HITTING:

When Joe Orsulak's average hovered in the .230 range for the first four months of last season, there were concerns that he might be fading. Not to worry. Orsulak went on a 21-game hitting streak in August, finished with a flourish and landed at .278, one point above his career average. Orsulak did not go hitless in consecutive starts after July 28 and batted .384 in August.

Orsulak seemingly comes out of spring training every year as the Orioles' fourth outfielder and winds up with as much playing time as the regulars. He was in the lineup more often last season, taking days off only against certain tough left-handed pitchers. A blue-chip contact hitter, Orsulak uses the whole field and concentrates intently at the plate. He seems to guide the ball in with his eyes, then snaps at it quickly.

BASERUNNING:

Orsulak is not a bona fide base-stealer, but he can surprise on occasion, going 6-for-8 in thefts last year. An intelligent player who runs the bases with good sense, Orsulak takes fewer chances than he used to because he is not quite as fast. But when he goes, he almost always makes his goal.

FIELDING:

Somewhere, Orsulak "discovered" a cannon arm last season. Orsulak astonished one and all with a league-leading 22 outfield assists, as runners kept testing him and he kept throwing them out. The total was an Oriole record. He has a flair for sliding catches and banging into walls and is not afraid to expose his body to harm.

OVERALL:

This man is a professional hitter and that fact alone will keep him very active. Orsulak is a working man's hero, doing his job without undue commotion. He will probably stay in the game a long time because of his value as a DH and pinch hitter.

JOE ORSULAK

Position: LF/RF
Bats: L **Throws:** L
Ht: 6' 1" **Wt:** 203

Opening Day Age: 29
Born: 5/31/62 in Glen Ridge, NJ
ML Seasons: 8

Overall Statistics

	G	AB	R	H	D	T	HR	RBI	SB	BB	SO	AVG
1991	143	486	57	135	22	1	5	43	6	28	45	.278
Career	813	2544	339	704	113	26	33	226	77	193	232	.277

Where He Hits the Ball

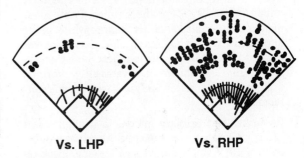

Vs. LHP	Vs. RHP

1991 Situational Stats

	AB	H	HR	RBI	AVG		AB	H	HR	RBI	AVG
Home	235	65	3	21	.277	LHP	64	15	0	6	.234
Road	251	70	2	22	.279	RHP	422	120	5	37	.284
Day	125	30	1	11	.240	Sc Pos	108	26	1	36	.241
Night	361	105	4	32	.291	Clutch	81	18	1	8	.222

1991 Rankings (American League)

→ 3rd highest batting average on an 0-2 count (.348)

→ Led the Orioles in least GDPs per GDP situation (9.7%), batting average with the bases loaded (.375) and batting average on an 0-2 count

→ Led AL left fielders in batting average on an 0-2 count

PITCHING:

A pleasant surprise, Jim Poole was a waiver pickup who filled a notable void in the Oriole bullpen when several other pitchers failed. Poole had put together a very impressive record as a reliever in the Dodger system, and his accomplishments for the Orioles proved that he may have simply been overlooked. For the final two-plus months, he was a highly productive Oriole reliever, allowing a ratio of about one batter in five faced to reach base. Poole wound up with a sparkling 2.36 ERA for his 29 games. Overall, he allowed only 29 hits and 12 walks in his 42 innings pitched.

Both the Dodgers and the Rangers had passed on Poole -- he'd compiled a 4.22 ERA in 16 games with L.A. in 1990. For the Orioles, Poole averaged nearly a strikeout an inning while being almost as effective against righthanders as he was against lefties. He was the toughest pitcher on the staff to hit and showed his versatility, working both in middle relief and as a situational left-hander.

Poole has two primary pitches, a fastball and a nasty slider that particularly fools right-handed batters. He is fairly durable, can bounce back on short rest, maintains a low profile, rarely walks people and sneaks up on the opposition. Poole was particularly strong at home, going 3-0 with an 0.75 earned run average at Memorial Stadium.

HOLDING RUNNERS AND FIELDING:

Being left-handed, Poole has a natural advantage in checking runners. Since he rarely falls behind in the count, would-be base stealers rarely get good base-stealing opportunities. He is a decent defensive player with good instincts and a feel for his position.

OVERALL:

The Orioles weren't quite sure what they had with Poole, but soon discovered he was a quality left-hander that they sorely needed. Manager John Oates likes the options two lefties in the bullpen give him. Poole figures to be one of them, coming off his startling Oriole debut.

JIM POOLE

Position: RP
Bats: L **Throws:** L
Ht: 6' 2" **Wt:** 190

Opening Day Age: 25
Born: 4/28/66 in
Rochester, NY
ML Seasons: 2

Overall Statistics

	W	L	ERA	G	GS	Sv	IP	H	R	BB	SO	HR
1991	3	2	2.36	29	0	1	42.0	29	14	12	38	3
Career	3	2	2.73	45	0	1	52.2	36	19	20	44	4

How Often He Throws Strikes

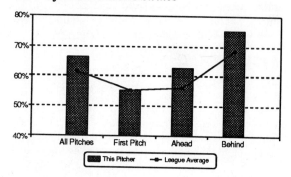

1991 Situational Stats

	W	L	ERA	Sv	IP		AB	H	HR	RBI	AVG
Home	3	1	1.55	1	29.0	LHB	69	13	2	10	.188
Road	0	1	4.15	0	13.0	RHB	79	16	1	6	.203
Day	1	0	1.04	0	8.2	Sc Pos	46	10	1	13	.217
Night	2	2	2.70	1	33.1	Clutch	41	6	1	3	.146

1991 Rankings (American League)

➡ Did not rank near the top or bottom in any category

HITTING:

It is impossible to figure out what to expect offensively from Billy Ripken, who has batted as high as .308 and as low as .207 in his five major league seasons. Last season's downer (.216) came only one year after he'd led the team in hitting with a .291 mark. The Orioles would probably take Ripken's .247 lifetime average, considering his outstanding defense. The trouble is, Ripken never has an "average" season.

Whether he's going well or not, Ripken makes consistent contact, especially on low fastballs, and he can execute the hit-and-run better than most. High pitches and breaking stuff have always bothered him. When he's in a slump, he'll chase a lot of bad pitches, and he'll seldom draw a walk.

Part of Ripken's problem last year was a painful rib injury which restricted his swing during the second half of the year. His poor finish has the O's thinking that the injury was more at fault than bad mechanics . . . though, of course, he's had bad years even when he's been healthy. Ripken usually hits ninth and is the team's most adept bunter; he annually tops the club list in sacrifices.

BASERUNNING:

For a middle infielder, Ripken is not especially fast and is not a strong base-stealing threat. However, he is well schooled in the fundamentals and doesn't embarrass himself on the bases. He can beat out a ground ball occasionally, but his injuries have slowed him.

FIELDING:

A master defensively, Ripken and brother Cal form one of the most effective double play combinations in the majors. He plays all out, catches the pop-up in shallow right as well as anyone, has good range and an ability to throw across his body quickly.

OVERALL:

Teammates consider Ripken to be funny, the practical joker of the club. But there's nothing funny about his up-and-down offensive performances. Unless he can find more consistency, he'll be in danger of losing his job -- despite his strong glove work.

BILLY RIPKEN

Position: 2B
Bats: R **Throws:** R
Ht: 6' 1" **Wt:** 182

Opening Day Age: 27
Born: 12/16/64 in Havre de Grace, MD
ML Seasons: 5

Overall Statistics

	G	AB	R	H	D	T	HR	RBI	SB	BB	SO	AVG
1991	104	287	24	62	11	1	0	14	0	15	31	.216
Career	556	1757	182	434	77	5	9	132	18	119	213	.247

Where He Hits the Ball

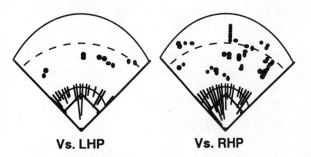

Vs. LHP   **Vs. RHP**

1991 Situational Stats

	AB	H	HR	RBI	AVG		AB	H	HR	RBI	AVG
Home	126	27	0	8	.214	LHP	100	27	0	7	.270
Road	161	35	0	6	.217	RHP	187	35	0	7	.187
Day	74	17	0	0	.230	Sc Pos	58	12	0	13	.207
Night	213	45	0	14	.211	Clutch	31	5	0	0	.161

1991 Rankings (American League)

➡ Led the Orioles in sacrifice bunts (11)

HITTING:

Without the self-imposed burden of having to carry the club on his own, Cal Ripken relaxed last year, made adjustments and had an epic MVP season. Ripken reached personal highs with a .323 batting average, 34 homers and 114 RBI, better numbers than in 1983, his other MVP season. His 85 extra-base hits led the majors and tied a club record. He also set a club record with 368 total bases and never went into a pronounced slump the entire season.

All this happened, of course, while Ripken was playing every day at arguably the most demanding defensive position. By finishing strongly he put to rest the idea that his consecutive game streak was giving him a tired bat. What was the difference? Ripken felt it was mechanical; he went back to his old stance, one with more of a crouch, and suddenly his 1983 thunder was back. Ripken also helped himself by remembering to let the ball come to him and by sticking with the old stance instead of changing it every two games or so, as he's done in the past.

BASERUNNING:

Establishing yet another career high, Ripken stole six bases last season and was caught only once. He is not fast, but uses his average speed beyond its limits because of his deep understanding of how to run.

FIELDING:

There was no way Ripken could surpass his 1990 season, when he committed only three errors. But his anticipation and sure-handedness led to the league lead in fielding percentage, putouts, assists, total chances and double plays. Ripken sacrifices a little range because of his size, but his rifle arm and instincts more than compensate.

OVERALL:

Ripken, the cornerstone of the Oriole franchise, is in his option year. He will be re-signed at almost any cost. Ripken's durability is peerless. He is on a string of 1,573 consecutive games and taking dead aim on Lou Gehrig's once-invincible record. He is a model player for all to emulate.

CAL RIPKEN

Position: SS
Bats: R **Throws:** R
Ht: 6' 4" **Wt:** 225

Opening Day Age: 31
Born: 8/24/60 in Havre de Grace, MD
ML Seasons: 11

Overall Statistics

	G	AB	R	H	D	T	HR	RBI	SB	BB	SO	AVG
1991	162	650	99	210	46	5	34	114	6	53	46	.323
Career	1638	6305	970	1762	340	33	259	942	28	688	747	.279

Where He Hits the Ball

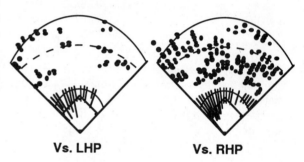

Vs. LHP   **Vs. RHP**

1991 Situational Stats

	AB	H	HR	RBI	AVG		AB	H	HR	RBI	AVG
Home	315	90	16	52	.286	LHP	164	57	12	31	.348
Road	335	120	18	62	.358	RHP	486	153	22	83	.315
Day	162	49	10	34	.302	Sc Pos	149	47	5	70	.315
Night	488	161	24	80	.330	Clutch	101	35	4	13	.347

1991 Rankings (American League)

→ 1st in total bases (368), games (162) and highest batting average on the road (.358)

→ 2nd in hits (210), doubles (46) and slugging percentage (.566)

→ 3rd in home runs (34) and sacrifice flies (9)

→ Led the Orioles in batting average (.323), home runs, at bats (650), runs (99), hits, doubles, total bases, RBI (114), games, slugging percentage, on-base percentage (.374), HR frequency (19.1 ABs per HR), lowest percentage of swings that missed (10.6%) and highest percentage of swings put into play (49.7%)

→ Led AL shortstops in fielding percentage (.986)

HITTING:

Intelligent and extremely coachable, David Segui increased his value last season by going to left field more and remaining poised and confident, things he didn't always do in his 1990 debut. A .244 hitter as a rookie, Segui raised his average by 34 points in 1991 to .278.

Segui will never be a prime power hitter, with 10 homers probably a maximum target. Instead, he hits line drives all over the field, makes contact and pinch hits very well for a young player. Switch-hitting is another plus for the son of former major league pitcher Diego Segui, although he hit more than 100 points higher from the right side in approximately the same number of at-bats. A hard-working player, Segui acquitted himself well in clutch situations, and his ability to hit from both sides makes opposing managers think twice before bringing in a specified relief pitcher.

BASERUNNING:

With average speed, Segui is not a daring sort and will probably never steal more than a few times per season. He is adequate on the base paths because he doesn't over react and doesn't make reckless mistakes. Overall, his baserunning is nothing special.

FIELDING:

Though he is only 25, Segui is already an accomplished first baseman who is often used for late-inning defense. He has good reactions, moves well to either side and handles throws nicely. In left field, a position he was forced to play on occasion, he had a few problems adjusting. By the end of the season, he had conquered most of them.

OVERALL:

With his ability to do a lot of things, Segui will probably be able to carve out a major league career. Switch-hitting is a major advantage, and he has shown he can come off the bench cold and perform with the bat or glove. He probably lacks the sock to play a power position regularly, but his versatility should keep him around.

DAVID SEGUI

Position: LF/1B
Bats: B **Throws:** L
Ht: 6' 1" **Wt:** 195

Opening Day Age: 25
Born: 7/19/66 in Kansas City, KS
ML Seasons: 2

Overall Statistics

	G	AB	R	H	D	T	HR	RBI	SB	BB	SO	AVG
1991	86	212	15	59	7	0	2	22	1	12	19	.278
Career	126	335	29	89	14	0	4	37	1	23	34	.266

Where He Hits the Ball

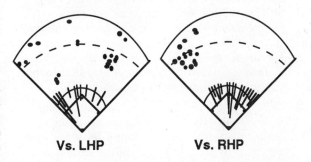

Vs. LHP	Vs. RHP

1991 Situational Stats

	AB	H	HR	RBI	AVG		AB	H	HR	RBI	AVG
Home	116	29	1	11	.250	LHP	98	33	1	12	.337
Road	96	30	1	11	.313	RHP	114	26	1	10	.228
Day	63	17	0	5	.270	Sc Pos	57	16	1	21	.281
Night	149	42	2	17	.282	Clutch	48	14	1	7	.292

1991 Rankings (American League)

➡ Did not rank near the top or bottom in any category

PITCHING:

Mark Williamson, once considered the most underrated Oriole, has backslid. Williamson was 18-7 with a 2.62 ERA and 10 saves in 1989-90 as the perfect complement to Gregg Olson. His figures last year (5-5, 4.48) were a far cry from that. Williamson has always had problems away from Baltimore, and last year he was hammered mercilessly on the road (53 hits in 36 innings, 6.69 ERA).

When a pitcher suddenly starts to lose effectiveness, all kinds of criticisms begin to surface. In Williamson's case, people began to talk about him as being injury prone; last year he lost time with a strained rib muscle, which paved the way for the emergence of Todd Frohwirth. They're also saying that Williamson has lost speed on his fastball. That would be a crucial loss for Williamson, because it reduces his ability to change speeds, always a hallmark of his strength. When Williamson's fastball gets closer in velocity to his palmball and slider, he's in trouble.

Once a part-time starter and occasional closer, Williamson will have to regain some strength during the winter or risk losing the set-up job permanently to Frohwirth. He has always been determined to pitch through injuries and has some vital experience which can help the young Oriole staff. But staying healthy is becoming a bigger problem for him every season.

HOLDING RUNNERS AND FIELDING:

With his arm speed waning, baserunners became more daring against Williamson, who had to throw over to first more often to hold them. He bounds from the mound deftly and doesn't hurt himself on defense. Rarely will Williamson make a mistake in judgement afield.

OVERALL:

Heretofore, Williamson was almost indispensable to the Orioles because no one else could fill his role. Now there is Frohwirth. Some talk has arisen about converting Williamson to a starter, but so far nothing serious has developed. For the first time in four years, Williamson will have to scramble to remain secure on the Oriole staff.

MARK WILLIAMSON

Position: RP
Bats: R **Throws:** R
Ht: 6' 0" **Wt:** 171

Opening Day Age: 32
Born: 7/21/59 in Corpus Christi, TX
ML Seasons: 5

Overall Statistics

	W	L	ERA	G	GS	Sv	IP	H	R	BB	SO	HR
1991	5	5	4.48	65	0	4	80.1	87	42	35	53	9
Career	36	29	3.77	277	12	19	515.2	504	231	174	310	47

How Often He Throws Strikes

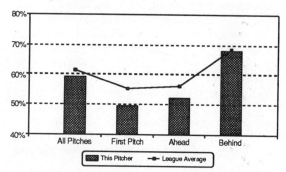

1991 Situational Stats

	W	L	ERA	Sv	IP		AB	H	HR	RBI	AVG
Home	3	4	2.66	1	44.0	LHB	121	30	2	16	.248
Road	2	1	6.69	3	36.1	RHB	195	57	7	35	.292
Day	2	0	5.25	4	24.0	Sc Pos	91	27	3	42	.297
Night	3	5	4.15	0	56.1	Clutch	150	36	4	17	.240

1991 Rankings (American League)

→ 10th highest batting average allowed by a relief pitcher (.275)

JUAN BELL

Position: 2B
Bats: B **Throws:** R
Ht: 5'11" **Wt:** 170

Opening Day Age: 24
Born: 3/29/68 in San Pedro de Macoris, Dominican Republic
ML Seasons: 3

Overall Statistics

	G	AB	R	H	D	T	HR	RBI	SB	BB	SO	AVG
1991	100	209	26	36	9	2	1	15	0	8	51	.172
Career	113	215	29	36	9	2	1	15	1	8	53	.167

HITTING, FIELDING, BASERUNNING:

Long considered an intriguing prospect, Juan "Tito" Bell received his first major league chance when Bill Ripken was injured last season. The results were mixed. Bell batted an anemic .172, but displayed some useful skills.

Bell's natural position is shortstop, but he won't play there with Cal Ripken firmly ensconced. He still has problems with mental mistakes at second base, where he has played only two years. Despite his weak average, Bell has some pop in his bat but he's still primarily a slashing hitter who strikes out too much (once every four at-bats) and does not make enough contact. One of the fastest Orioles, he can steal a base or move easily from first to third on a hit and is often used as a pinch runner. But he sometimes takes unnecessary chances and pays the price.

OVERALL:

The younger brother of George Bell has potential, but is still unpolished. At the plate, he is streaky and still needs to find consistency; cutting down on his strikeouts and making more contact to take advantage of his speed would be a start. A move to a team where he could play shortstop regularly would probably be good for him.

JOSE MESA

Position: SP
Bats: R **Throws:** R
Ht: 6' 3" **Wt:** 219

Opening Day Age: 25
Born: 5/22/66 in Azua, Dominican Republic
ML Seasons: 3

Overall Statistics

	W	L	ERA	G	GS	Sv	IP	H	R	BB	SO	HR
1991	6	11	5.97	23	23	0	123.2	151	86	62	64	11
Career	10	16	5.49	36	35	0	201.2	226	129	104	105	20

PITCHING, FIELDING & HOLDING RUNNERS:

Jose Mesa is the mystery man of the Baltimore staff. The Oriole management likes Mesa's ability, but wonders when, or if, he will ever become consistent. Mesa was leading the staff in everything for a month last year, then went winless in nine starts with an 8.29 ERA before being dispatched to Rochester.

Mesa had some problems last year with his right elbow, the same elbow which previously underwent major surgery. Supposedly the new injury was unrelated. Concentration lapses appear to be a bigger concern. Mesa can be pitching well, then suddenly lose his rhythm and get totally out of synch. He has four good pitches (fastball, curve, slider and change-up), all of which can be effective when he's healthy and focused. His wavering demeanor sometimes extends to holding baserunners, especially when he is struggling.

OVERALL:

The Orioles consider Mesa extremely talented, but wonder when he will put it all together with regularity. It's a tough situation, since he is alternately overpowering and perplexing. With his ability, he will undoubtedly get another chance.

ARTHUR RHODES

Position: SP
Bats: L **Throws:** L
Ht: 6' 2" **Wt:** 190

Opening Day Age: 22
Born: 10/24/69 in Waco, TX
ML Seasons: 1

Overall Statistics

	W	L	ERA	G	GS	Sv	IP	H	R	BB	SO	HR
1991	0	3	8.00	8	8	0	36.0	47	35	23	23	4
Career	0	3	8.00	8	8	0	36.0	47	35	23	23	4

PITCHING, FIELDING & HOLDING RUNNERS:

Refinement is the operative word for Arthur Rhodes, touted as the second coming of Vida Blue. A former second-round draft choice, Rhodes has excited Oriole followers for several years as he moved through their system while consistently striking out more than one batter per inning. Despite his strikeout totals, Rhodes simply wasn't ready for major league hitters in an eight-start trial at the end of last season, going 0-3 with an 8.00 ERA after spending most of the year at Double-A Hagerstown. He had only two quality starts and was hit hard (47 hits, 36 innings).

To complicate matters, Rhodes often had trouble finding the plate, averaging almost six walks per nine innings for the O's. He has a live fastball, but his curve and change-up need work. So far Rhodes has been overwhelmed by his major league surroundings. He simply has given opposing hitters too much credit. A good athlete who fields well, he rarely threw to first to hold runners.

OVERALL:

Never having pitched at Triple-A, Rhodes is likely to start the 1992 season at Rochester to get his feet planted more firmly. He needs more time to develop both his pitches and confidence. But the Orioles will wait for a pitcher with his caliber of arm.

CRAIG WORTHINGTON

Position: 3B
Bats: R **Throws:** R
Ht: 6' 0" **Wt:** 200

Opening Day Age: 26
Born: 4/17/65 in Los Angeles, CA
ML Seasons: 4

Overall Statistics

	G	AB	R	H	D	T	HR	RBI	SB	BB	SO	AVG
1991	31	102	11	23	3	0	4	12	0	12	14	.225
Career	335	1105	119	257	45	0	29	130	3	145	248	.233

HITTING, FIELDING, BASERUNNING:

After winning the Orioles' third base job last spring in a battle with Leo Gomez, Craig Worthington went downhill very quickly. He batted .225 in 31 games, injured a hamstring, went to Rochester, re-injured the hamstring and never was seen by the big club again. It was quite a comedown for Worthington, who was the International League MVP in 1988 and the Sporting News American League Rookie Player of the Year in 1989.

With Gomez firmly planted at third, Worthington's chances of returning to the Orioles have diminished. The two share some similarities, but Gomez has the added dimension of home run power, something Worthington can't match. Worthington has never regained the form at the plate that made him one of the team's top clutch hitters. He is slow on the base paths and no threat to steal. Just as damaging is the fact that his once-solid defense has suffered over the last two years. Besides the injury problems, Worthington did not adapt well to the demotion back to Rochester.

OVERALL:

With no alternative position, Worthington appears to have run out of time in Baltimore. A new start with a new team is probably the proper prescription for him. He needs to re-motivate himself, get healthy and begin anew.

ORGANIZATION OVERVIEW:

The once-great Oriole farm system hit the skids in the mid-to-late 1980s, when the O's neglected player development while seeking fading free agents like Freddie Lynn. Since Roland Hemond took over as general manager in late 1987, the O's have revived their system again, quickly developing players like Gregg Olson, Pete Harnisch, Mike Mussina and Leo Gomez, among others. Baltimore has also had a keen eye for talented players who were buried in other systems (Randy Milligan, Sam Horn and Chito Martinez are the best examples). The O's know how to nurture talent, though the cupboard is a little bare when it comes to help for 1992. Luis Mercedes is the best bet.

MANNY ALEXANDER

Position: SS   **Opening Day Age:** 21
Bats: R **Throws:** R   **Born:** 3/20/71 in San
Ht: 5' 10" **Wt:** 160   Pedro De Macoris, DR

Recent Statistics

	G	AB	R	H	D	THR	RBI	SB	BB	SO	AVG
90 A Wausau	44	152	16	27	3	1	0	11	8	12	41	.178
91 A Frederick	134	548	81	143	17	3	3	42	47	44	68	.261
91 AA Hagerstown	3	9	3	3	1	0	0	2	0	1	3	.333

Cal Ripken will probably be moved to a less demanding position in the next few years. Alexander and Ricky Gutierrez are the likely combatants to succeed Ripken as the Oriole shortstop. Yet another product of the shortstop factory at San Pedro de Macoris, D.R., Alexander has outstanding defensive skills, but hasn't shown a lot of consistency afield. He also needs to improve a lot at the plate, and is realistically two or three years away from making a major league impact.

RICKY GUTIERREZ

Position: SS   **Opening Day Age:** 21
Bats: R **Throws:** R   **Born:** 5/23/70 in Miami,
Ht: 6' 1" **Wt:** 175   FL

Recent Statistics

	G	AB	R	H	D	THR	RBI	SB	BB	SO	AVG
90 AA Hagerstown	20	64	4	15	0	1	0	6	2	3	8	.234
90 A Frederick	112	425	54	117	16	4	1	46	12	38	59	.275
91 AA Hagerstown	84	292	47	69	6	4	0	30	11	57	52	.236
91 AAA Rochester	49	157	23	48	5	3	0	15	4	24	27	.306
91 MLE	133	436	58	104	9	3	0	37	9	60	83	.239

The O's other "shortstop of the future," Gutierrez was once considered a shaky glove man, but he has improved over the last couple of years. His bat, much more dangerous than Alexander's (.306 in 157 at-bats at Rochester last year) keeps getting better, though he has never hit with much power.

LUIS MERCEDES

Position: OF   **Opening Day Age:** 24
Bats: R **Throws:** R   **Born:** 2/20/68 in San
Ht: 6' 0" **Wt:** 180   Pedro De Macoris, DR

Recent Statistics

	G	AB	R	H	D	THR	RBI	SB	BB	SO	AVG
91 AAA Rochester	102	374	68	125	14	5	2	36	23	65	63	.334
91 AL Baltimore	19	54	10	11	2	0	0	2	0	4	9	.204
91 MLE	102	357	53	108	12	3	1	28	16	50	66	.303

The Orioles are desperate for a bona-fide leadoff man, and Mercedes may well be the guy. He has hit .334 each of the last two years while displaying a good eye and a flair for stealing bases. There's little doubt about Mercedes' offensive skills. However, his glove is a big question. Mercedes couldn't handle second base, his original position, and he needs a lot of work in the outfield.

ANTHONY TELFORD

Position: P   **Opening Day Age:** 26
Bats: R **Throws:** R   **Born:** 3/6/66 in San
Ht: 6' 0" **Wt:** 184   Jose, CA

Recent Statistics

	W	L	ERA	GGS	Sv	IP	H	R	BB	SO	HR
91 AAA Rochester	12	9	3.95	27	25	0	157.1	166	82	48	115	18
91 AL Baltimore	0	0	4.05	9	1	0	26.2	27	12	6	24	3

An All-American at San Jose State, Telford was the Orioles' fourth-round pick in 1987, then suffered a serious shoulder injury. Telford has lost a lot off his fastball, but has a good curve and change, and he knows how to pitch. Telford had good outings with the Orioles in 1990 before spending most of last year at Rochester. He has an excellent chance to make the pitching-poor Oriole staff this season, though he has not been considered a potential star since his injury.

JEFF WILLIAMS

Position: P   **Opening Day Age:** 22
Bats: R **Throws:** R   **Born:** 4/16/69 in Salina,
Ht: 6' 4" **Wt:** 225   KS

Recent Statistics

	W	L	ERA	GGS	Sv	IP	H	R	BB	SO	HR
90 R Bluefield	2	0	1.59	9	0	0	11.1	7	3	5	14	0
90 A Frederick	2	1	4.68	16	0	1	25.0	23	17	17	31	2
91 A Frederick	1	2	2.70	12	0	6	16.2	17	6	6	20	1
91 AA Hagerstown	3	5	2.60	39	0	17	55.1	52	23	32	42	1

The Orioles' third pick in 1990, Williams is a big guy who was a high school football teammate of Detroit Lions' star Barry Sanders. He throws hard, striking out more than a man an inning at most of his minor league stops, and he recorded 23 saves last year. It would be no great shock to see him in the Baltimore pen this year.

HITTING:

One thing went back to normal: Wade Boggs was back in a batting race. After falling all the way -- for him -- to .302 in 1990, Boggs bounced back to bat .332. Unfortunately for him, a succession of injuries, the worst one being to his shoulder, battered him the last month and he ended up having to sit out the last week and bow out of the race against Julio Franco.

Most of Boggs' problems the previous season had stemmed from getting lost at the plate. He developed habits like getting too close to the plate, not flexing his right front knee to get an explosion in his swing and even losing his strike zone, details that Walter Hriniak had kept him aware of daily. Just how lost Boggs was at the plate was indicated by his 68 strikeouts in 1990. In 1991, he was pretty much back to normal: 89 walks, 32 strikeouts.

Boggs' Fenway and right-handed pitcher eccentricities are becoming more pronounced. In Fenway, he can take both the fastball on his fists and the fastball away and clank it off the Green Monster, balls that in Oakland, Anaheim and Minneapolis are routine fly ball outs. Against righthanders, he is a good breaking ball hitter. Against lefties, he tries to fight off breaking balls until he gets a mistake.

BASERUNNING:

Though he bats leadoff, Boggs, a 38 percent career base stealer, is no threat to take off. Understandably, his baserunning is on the conservative side.

FIELDING:

Even Boggs' detractors must give him his due as an underrated defensive third baseman. He has sure hands, a strong, accurate arm, charges topped balls well and makes the throw to the second baseman on the 5-4-3 double play as accurately as anyone in the league.

OVERALL:

The problem is, when you've batted .366 then hit .330, .302 and .332, people say you're on the decline. In Wade Boggs' case, the back and shoulder injuries that have become increasingly common are all that will put him in decline. He's still a tremendous player.

WADE BOGGS

Position: 3B
Bats: L **Throws:** R
Ht: 6' 2" **Wt:** 197

Opening Day Age: 33
Born: 6/15/58 in Omaha, NE
ML Seasons: 10

Overall Statistics

	G	AB	R	H	D	T	HR	RBI	SB	BB	SO	AVG
1991	144	546	93	181	42	2	8	51	1	89	32	.332
Career	1482	5699	1005	1965	400	43	78	637	15	930	439	.345

Where He Hits the Ball

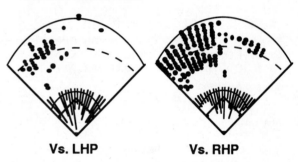

Vs. LHP   **Vs. RHP**

1991 Situational Stats

	AB	H	HR	RBI	AVG		AB	H	HR	RBI	AVG
Home	252	98	6	32	.389	LHP	166	44	2	13	.265
Road	294	83	2	19	.282	RHP	380	137	6	38	.361
Day	167	51	2	17	.305	Sc Pos	87	27	1	38	.310
Night	379	130	6	34	.343	Clutch	69	20	1	6	.290

1991 Rankings (American League)

→ 1st in intentional walks (25), batting average vs. right-handed pitchers (.361), leadoff on-base average (.440), on-base average vs. right-handed pitchers (.456), batting average at home (.389) and lowest percentage of swings that missed (5.2%)

→ 2nd in batting average (.331)

→ 3rd in on-base average (.421)

→ Led the Red Sox in batting average, runs (93), hits (181), singles (129), doubles (42), total bases (251), intentional walks, times on base (270), on-base average and batting average with runners in scoring position (.310)

BOSTON RED SOX

PITCHING:

This seemed to be a wonderful story. After 10 years in pro baseball, Tom Bolton was 10-5 in 1990 for the Red Sox and led them to the playoffs. Then, in 1991, Bolton started off 5-0, but by the end of the season he was out of the rotation and wondering again about his future.

Bolton is basically a fastball/change-up/curveball pitcher. When he was so successful in 1990, most observers felt that he simply had discovered the confidence to throw his fastball over the plate and challenge hitters. But last season, especially after he hurt his shoulder, he seemed unwilling to challenge anyone.

Batters began laying off Bolton pitches out of the strike zone -- fastballs away from righthanders and his curveball -- and forced him to come over the middle of the plate. It especially hurt him against righthanders, who batted .322 against him. Lefties batted .247 against Bolton, and overall opponents batted .308 and slugged .485 against him.

Forced to work out of the pen last year, Bolton turned in a 1.65 ERA over six games. Those were l-o-n-g appearances, averaging nearly three innings. There seems to be little doubt that Bolton is not a reliever because he doesn't have the slider for left-handed batters and is not effective pitching several days a week. He needs to work in a rotation and master his control so that he can paint the outside corner against right-handed batters.

HOLDING RUNNERS AND FIELDING:

Bolton is unexceptional in both categories. He lacks the slick pickoff move of many lefties, and is slow to the plate. Bolton permitted five steals in seven attempts last year.

OVERALL:

Ending the '91 season 8-9 with a 5.24 ERA puts Bolton in the familiar position of having to fight for his life. Like a lot of lefthanders who have to be very fine to succeed, what he needs are opportunity and innings.

TOM BOLTON

Position: SP/RP
Bats: L **Throws:** L
Ht: 6' 3" **Wt:** 175

Opening Day Age: 29
Born: 5/6/62 in Nashville, TN
ML Seasons: 5

Overall Statistics

	W	L	ERA	G	GS	Sv	IP	H	R	BB	SO	HR
1991	8	9	5.24	25	19	0	110.0	136	72	51	64	16
Career	20	21	4.54	107	39	1	339.0	386	186	149	208	29

How Often He Throws Strikes

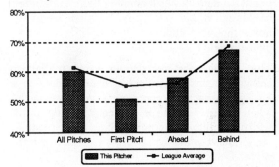

1991 Situational Stats

	W	L	ERA	Sv	IP		AB	H	HR	RBI	AVG
Home	5	5	4.68	0	65.1	LHB	81	20	2	10	.247
Road	3	4	6.04	0	44.2	RHB	360	116	14	50	.322
Day	4	5	5.40	0	50.0	Sc Pos	97	26	5	42	.268
Night	4	4	5.10	0	60.0	Clutch	21	10	1	1	.476

1991 Rankings (American League)

➡ 2nd highest batting average allowed vs. right-handed batters (.322)

HITTING:

As the 1991 season wore down, a Tom Brunansky watch developed. If Brunansky played in 145 games, his 1993 contract option was automatically picked up. It put Joe Morgan in a difficult situation, and general manager Lou Gorman -- who signed Brunansky to the two-year, $5.5 million guarantee although Brunansky was willing to take one year -- responded to criticism by saying, "If Brunansky were hitting .280, as I hoped, I'd be hearing it was a great contract."

Sorry, Lou, but Brunansky has never batted even .260 over a full season. Last year, as he struggled at .229 (which was only 19 points below his career average) the question arose about whether or not Brunansky was losing his skills. As a hitter, he has holes and is streaky. He's apt to hit six home runs and knock in 20 runs in six games, then struggle for a month.

That streakiness has driven some managers crazy; Brunansky would hit three homers in a 13-5 game, as one pointed out, but where was he when it was 3-2? He is a decent mistake hitter who can pull the hanging breaking ball or fastball out over the plate and can hit fastballs to right center with considerable power.

BASERUNNING:

Once a double-figures base stealer, Brunansky is a dismal 11-for-32 over the last three years. He is understandably sent less often than in the past, though he remains a smart baserunner.

FIELDING:

A solid right fielder with a decent arm throughout his career, Brunansky does not have the range that he had four years ago. He may have lost a couple of steps. He still has outstanding instincts, throws to the right base and hits cutoff men.

OVERALL:

Brunansky feels his erratic performance last year came about because he was in and out of the lineup so often. Some wonder. Brunansky may wish the Red Sox would have given him a one year deal, for he'd rather play than sit and collect his check. His desire has never changed.

TOM BRUNANSKY

Position: RF
Bats: R **Throws:** R
Ht: 6' 4" **Wt:** 216

Opening Day Age: 31
Born: 8/20/60 in Covina, CA
ML Seasons: 11

Overall Statistics

	G	AB	R	H	D	T	HR	RBI	SB	BB	SO	AVG
1991	142	459	54	105	24	1	16	70	1	49	72	.229
Career	1518	5402	713	1332	256	26	240	782	64	655	975	.247

Where He Hits the Ball

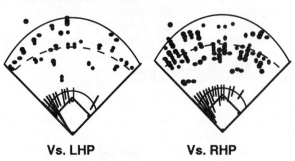

Vs. LHP   Vs. RHP

1991 Situational Stats

	AB	H	HR	RBI	AVG		AB	H	HR	RBI	AVG
Home	234	60	10	39	.256	LHP	142	36	5	22	.254
Road	225	45	6	31	.200	RHP	317	69	11	48	.218
Day	147	27	3	14	.184	Sc Pos	142	33	7	56	.232
Night	312	78	13	56	.250	Clutch	68	17	0	7	.250

1991 Rankings (American League)

➡ 2nd lowest batting average on the road (.200)
➡ 4th lowest batting average on an 0-2 count (.038)
➡ 5th lowest batting average (.229)
➡ 6th lowest groundball/flyball ratio (.74)
➡ 9th lowest on-base average (.303)
➡ Led the Red Sox in sacrifice flies (8)

ELLIS BURKS

Position: CF
Bats: R **Throws:** R
Ht: 6' 2" **Wt:** 202

Opening Day Age: 27
Born: 9/11/64 in
Vicksburg, MS
ML Seasons: 5

HITTING:

Last year was supposed to be the one Ellis Burks became a superstar. Burks turned out to have the worst year of his career. He batted .251, he hit only 14 homers, drove in 56 runs and was among the five worst players in the league for percentage of baserunners knocked in. Burks had bad knees and a bad back and, when the season was over, basically asked the Red Sox to trade him or expect him to eventually become a free agent.

Last year Burks was bothered by tendinitis in both knees and subsequently developed a bulging disc in his back which sidelined him in September. He became frustrated and over-anxious in clutch situations, regressed in terms of selectivity, and when he began to be booed, started chasing breaking balls and waving at bad pitches.

A quiet, laid-back Texan, Burks has never been comfortable in Boston, partially because he was the only black on the team until Mo Vaughn arrived, but also because Boston's frenetic pace is extreme for him. Some people feel that if Burks were to go to Texas or California he would rid himself of what Ken Brett called the worst curse in life, unlimited potential.

BASERUNNING:

Burks has terrific speed, but for the second year in a row was thrown out stealing more than he was successful. Now 27, he may never be a base stealer.

FIELDING:

Burks' gliding stride makes it look as if he isn't running as hard as he might, although he does go full out, but he has evolved from playing shallow to playing deep. Protecting his shoulder and back problems, he has balls fall in front of him that should be caught. The shoulder problems have also hampered his throwing.

OVERALL:

At 27, this is a pivotal year in Burks' career. If his back and knees are recovered, he should be one of the premier players in the league, as long as the third IF -- Boston -- is overcome.

Overall Statistics

	G	AB	R	H	D	T	HR	RBI	SB	BB	SO	AVG
1991	130	474	56	119	33	3	14	56	6	39	81	.251
Career	656	2559	405	725	152	24	85	357	88	226	402	.283

Where He Hits the Ball

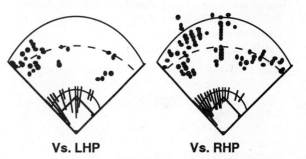

Vs. LHP   **Vs. RHP**

1991 Situational Stats

	AB	H	HR	RBI	AVG		AB	H	HR	RBI	AVG
Home	232	62	8	25	.267	LHP	135	35	5	23	.259
Road	242	57	6	31	.236	RHP	339	84	9	33	.248
Day	146	37	3	19	.253	Sc Pos	132	30	4	45	.227
Night	328	82	11	37	.250	Clutch	69	15	1	2	.217

1991 Rankings (American League)

➡ 7th in most caught stealing (11)

➡ Led the Red Sox in caught stealing, hit by pitch (6) and least GDPs per GDP situation (6.5%)

HITTING:

After signing him to a free agent contact, the Red Sox expected Jack Clark to give them a legitimate power force in the middle of a bunch of pure hitters. They wanted Clark to hit 25 homers, knock in around 90 runs to take the pressure off the Greenwells and Burks -- who are not pure cleanup hitters -- and murder left-handed pitching.

Which is almost precisely what Clark did. Only he ended up a villain in Boston, booed by the fans, ripped by the media. Clark can be his own worst enemy. He gets depressed -- usually when his team is losing -- and then says something outrageous. Last year he ripped being played at DH, was quoted as saying that he wanted to leave Boston, criticized Joe Morgan and yelled at a writer. But Jack's Jack, and admits, "I'm good for a half-dozen stupid statements a year."

Clark still stands way off the plate and tries to pull everything. He ends up taking strikes on the outer half and leaves breaking balls to take their course. He has said that he'd like to try pick out pitches in situations and try to drive them the other way, which might add 20 points to his average and another half-dozen homers to his resume.

BASERUNNING:

Clark did not steal a base in 1991, and is no threat to do so. He is an aggressive, but not always very alert, baserunner.

FIELDING:

Clark was strictly a DH last year, though he could play first base or the outfield in below-average fashion if required.

OVERALL:

Clark's strikeouts aren't a big deal if the Red Sox don't add too many other free-swinging sluggers. As long as his bat speed is there, he is a force. At the end of the year a poll of advance scouts listed Clark and Phil Plantier as being in the top three in bat speed in the American League. So don't start playing "Old Folks Boogie" yet.

JACK CLARK

Position: DH
Bats: R **Throws:** R
Ht: 6' 3" **Wt:** 205

Opening Day Age: 36
Born: 11/10/55 in New Brighton, PA
ML Seasons: 17

Overall Statistics

	G	AB	R	H	D	T	HR	RBI	SB	BB	SO	AVG
1991	140	481	75	120	18	1	28	87	0	96	133	.249
Career	1913	6590	1086	1772	321	39	335	1147	76	1206	1354	.269

Where He Hits the Ball

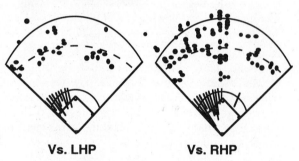

Vs. LHP   **Vs. RHP**

1991 Situational Stats

	AB	H	HR	RBI	AVG		AB	H	HR	RBI	AVG
Home	253	71	18	47	.281	LHP	117	38	6	20	.325
Road	228	49	10	40	.215	RHP	364	82	22	67	.225
Day	155	45	11	33	.290	Sc Pos	132	32	8	58	.242
Night	326	75	17	54	.230	Clutch	88	18	5	8	.205

1991 Rankings (American League)

→ 4th in walks (96), most pitches seen per plate appearance (4.25), on-base average vs. left-handed pitchers (.465) and lowest percentage of swings put into play (34.8%)

→ 5th in HR frequency (17.2 HRs per AB), lowest batting average vs. right-handed pitchers (.225) and lowest batting average on the road (.215)

→ Led the Red Sox in home runs (28), RBI (87), walks, strikeouts (133), slugging percentage (.466), HR frequency, pitches seen per plate appearance and batting average on a 3-1 count (.500)

→ Led designated hitters in strikeouts and HR frequency

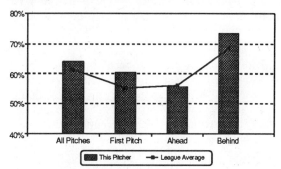

PITCHING:

Roger Clemens remains baseball's most consistent power pitcher. Last year Clemens started 6-0 and seemed to be on the verge of something akin to his 24-4 record in 1986, but was -- for him -- inconsistent from mid-May through July. Clemens finished 18-10 and led the league in ERA at 2.62. He is the game's winningest pitcher over the last six years at 118-52, and in that time only once has had an earned run average over 3.00.

In 1991 Clemens led the league in innings and strikeouts and was second in complete games, which is pure Roger Clemens. He has averaged 259 innings a year over these six years, including, of course, 1990 when he hurt his arm on Sept. 4 and started only twice the rest of the season.

Clemens is a horse. He throws in the low 90s -- on the Red Sox gun last year, he hit 96 and 97 MPH, figures reached by no Sox opponent. His concentration, approach and delivery keep that fastball remarkably consistent. Where some pitchers will throw one pitch at 93, the next at 86, Clemens last year had several games where he threw more than 75 pitches clocked at 90 or better.

HOLDING RUNNERS AND FIELDING:

When he was a rookie, Clemens had more than 40 consecutive baserunners steal successfully against him. After learning a slide step in his delivery to home plate with runners on base -- which he varies -- and developing a number of moves to first, along with constantly throwing there, Clemens has become difficult to run against. He's an average fielder.

OVERALL:

The one thing that bugs Clemens is that he's never had the Jack Morris finish to a season. He got sick in the playoffs in 1986 and wasn't himself in the World Series. He had a 2-0 lead in the seventh inning of his one start in '88 before giving up a game-tying homer to Jose Canseco. In 1990 he was hurt, leaving Game One with a 1-0 lead (the Athletics rallied and won) and leaving Game Four courtesy of Terry Cooney. Maybe in 1992?

ROGER CLEMENS

Position: SP
Bats: R **Throws:** R
Ht: 6' 4" **Wt:** 220

Opening Day Age: 29
Born: 8/4/62 in Dayton, OH
ML Seasons: 8

Overall Statistics

	W	L	ERA	G	GS	Sv	IP	H	R	BB	SO	HR
1991	18	10	2.62	35	35	0	271.1	219	93	65	241	15
Career	134	61	2.85	241	240	0	1784.1	1500	628	490	1665	117

How Often He Throws Strikes

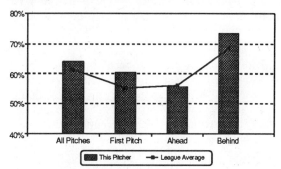

1991 Situational Stats

	W	L	ERA	Sv	IP			AB	H	HR	RBI	AVG
Home	8	5	2.59	0	142.2	LHB		563	123	3	45	.218
Road	10	5	2.66	0	128.2	RHB		430	96	12	37	.223
Day	6	2	2.22	0	73.0	Sc Pos		199	46	3	60	.231
Night	12	8	2.77	0	198.1	Clutch		125	28	0	8	.224

1991 Rankings (American League)

→ 1st in ERA (2.62), games started (35), shutouts (4), innings (271.1), batters faced (1,077), strikeouts (241), pitches thrown (4,025) and runners caught stealing (16)

→ 2nd in complete games (13) and lowest on-base average allowed (.270)

→ 3rd in strikeout/walk ratio (3.7), least home runs per 9 innings (.50) and most strikeouts per 9 innings (8.0)

→ Led the Red Sox in ERA, wins (18), games started, complete games, shutouts, innings, batters faced, hit batsmen (5), strikeouts, pitches thrown and strikeout/walk ratio

TONY FOSSAS

Position: RP
Bats: L **Throws:** L
Ht: 6' 0" **Wt:** 190

Opening Day Age: 34
Born: 9/23/57 in Havana, Cuba
ML Seasons: 4

PITCHING:

On dozens of summer mornings one could stop at Daisy Field on the Boston- Brookline line and see hundreds of inner-city kids playing baseball. Helping his brother coach was an unassuming man in his early thirties, proud that this was the field where he learned to play. The Red Sox sponsor a program for kids in the area -- most of whom are of Latin descent -- and Tony Fossas and Ellis Burks often volunteer to help the kids.

The 1991 season was a dream-come-true for Fossas. At the age of ten his family moved from Cuba to the Boston section of Jamaica Plain, less than two miles from Fenway Park. He grew up playing on Daisy Field, used to go into Fenway and root for the Red Sox. At the age of 33 and after 12 professional seasons, Fossas returned home to have one of the best unnoticed seasons in the American League.

There is nothing fancy about Fossas. He has no special pitch; he just slings his fastball and slider to hitters. He was especially effective stopping first hitters; they were 7-for-54 (.130) against him, the fourth best such prevention average in the American League.

Right-handed batters are more effective against Fossas, and too much exposure is often a problem. But, while Fossas isn't a long reliever, he can get up and pitch six days a week. And lefthanders will not hit him (.190 average last year).

HOLDING RUNNERS AND FIELDING:

For a lefty, Fossas does not do an exceptional job of holding baserunners. His release leaves him in an awkward position, and he is not a good fielder.

OVERALL:

"How many kids get to pitch out their dreams?" asks Fossas. "Not many. I'm one of the few." One of the best left-handed middle men in the American League last year, he hopes the dream will continue in 1992.

Overall Statistics

	W	L	ERA	G	GS	Sv	IP	H	R	BB	SO	HR
1991	3	2	3.47	64	0	1	57.0	49	27	28	29	3
Career	7	7	4.12	152	0	2	153.0	161	80	62	95	11

How Often He Throws Strikes

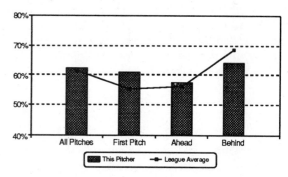

1991 Situational Stats

	W	L	ERA	Sv	IP		AB	H	HR	RBI	AVG
Home	1	0	2.45	1	22.0	LHB	84	16	2	13	.190
Road	2	2	4.11	0	35.0	RHB	124	33	1	18	.266
Day	0	0	2.18	0	20.2	Sc Pos	87	21	0	27	.241
Night	3	2	4.21	1	36.1	Clutch	63	11	1	9	.175

1991 Rankings (American League)

- 4th in holds (18) and first batter efficiency (.130)
- Led the Red Sox in games pitched (64), first batter efficiency and lowest percentage of inherited runners scored (28.2%)

PITCHING:

Acquired by the Red Sox at the end of spring training from the Seattle Mariners for reliever Rob Murphy, Mike Gardiner was in many ways Boston's biggest starting surprise. His record (9-10, 4.85) was hardly dominant, and he had problems the third time around batting orders. But the tough kid from Sarnia, Ontario showed some very positive signs.

Gardiner has an average -- and sometimes a shade above -- fastball and a decent slider. He is tough; he got hit in the leg by a line drive in Cleveland and wouldn't even rub it, even after manager Joe Morgan and trainer Charlie Moss came out to see him. He showed an ability to pitch inside, and a willingness to take the ball.

But new Red Sox pitching coach Rich Gale, who recommended Boston acquire Gardiner and coached him the first six weeks at Pawtucket, feels Gardiner got away from his basics last year. With the Red Sox, Gardiner was a fastball-slider pitcher with a big, slow curveball that often burned him; he gave up several of his 18 homers (in 130 innings) on that pitch. In the minors, Gardiner's most effective pitch had been his change-up, which he throws with the exact same arm action as his fastball. For some inexplicable reason, he got away from throwing it with the Red Sox.

HOLDING RUNNERS AND FIELDING:

Gardiner is only average in both holding runners and fielding. Last year runners were 11-for-16 stealing against him. He committed only one error.

OVERALL:

Gale believes that once Gardiner goes back to using the straight change, he can be a 200-plus innings horse who wins 12-15 games a year. That success would not be lost on the Blue Jays. Coming out of high school, Gardiner won an award as the top amateur player in Ontario, and the Blue Jays gave him a scholarship that paid part of his first two years' tuition at Indiana State.

MIKE GARDINER

Position: SP
Bats: B **Throws:** R
Ht: 6' 0" **Wt:** 185

Opening Day Age: 26
Born: 10/19/65 in Sarnia, Ontario
ML Seasons: 2

Overall Statistics

	W	L	ERA	G	GS	Sv	IP	H	R	BB	SO	HR
1991	9	10	4.85	22	22	0	130.0	140	79	47	91	18
Career	9	12	5.36	27	25	0	142.2	162	96	52	97	19

How Often He Throws Strikes

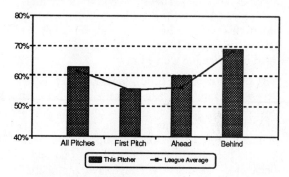

1991 Situational Stats

	W	L	ERA	Sv	IP		AB	H	HR	RBI	AVG
Home	4	5	4.30	0	75.1	LHB	247	64	4	23	.259
Road	5	5	5.60	0	54.2	RHB	264	76	14	41	.288
Day	3	2	4.28	0	40.0	Sc Pos	114	32	4	46	.281
Night	6	8	5.10	0	90.0	Clutch	15	6	1	3	.400

1991 Rankings (American League)

→ Did not rank near the top or bottom in any category

PITCHING:

On July 28, Jeff Gray was sitting in front of his locker, preparing to go out onto the field for his daily routine. He never made it. His right side went numb, and Gray suffered what was diagnosed as a kind of stroke, ending what had been a brilliant season. There were several players who later felt that the team's comeback from an 11½ game deficit to Toronto on August 11 was partly due to renewed dedication after Gray's unfortunate collapse.

How good was Jeff Gray before he was stricken? Probably the best middle reliever in the league. He allowed an astounding 39 hits in 61.2 innings. His ERA was 2.34. Lefties hit .200 against him, and they were lucky, because righties could manage only .165, and the .181 combined average against him was the best of any reliever but Bryan Harvey. He went down in July and still finished third in the league with 19 holds.

Part of the problem hitting against Gray is his deception. First, he takes a long time between pitches. Larry Bird told the Boston Globe's Bob Ryan that he "switches channels" when Gray is pitching. Gray has a slow windup, and when he lets the ball go it seems to jump in on hitters. Because of his delivery, Gray's average fastball seems a lot quicker. His big pitch is his forkball, which he throws perfectly with his fastball delivery. It breaks late. With the deliberate pace and the masking arm speed, the forkball is a devastating pitch.

HOLDING RUNNERS AND FIELDING:

The dawdling Gray would seem easy to steal on, but he's no pushover, allowing only five steals in eight attempts last year. He has good defensive reactions.

OVERALL:

You don't have to be a Red Sox fan to hope that Gray comes back from his illness. If toughness and character are truly important qualities, Gray has the makeup of a big-time middle man. The question this spring is whether or not health will allow him to do what he does so well.

JEFF GRAY

Position: RP
Bats: R **Throws:** R
Ht: 6' 1" **Wt:** 190

Opening Day Age: 29
Born: 4/10/63 in Alexandria, VA
ML Seasons: 3

Overall Statistics

	W	L	ERA	G	GS	Sv	IP	H	R	BB	SO	HR
1991	2	3	2.34	50	0	1	61.2	39	17	10	41	7
Career	4	7	3.33	96	0	10	121.2	104	48	29	96	10

How Often He Throws Strikes

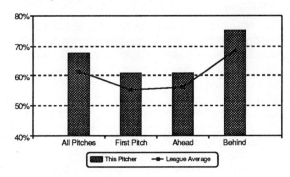

1991 Situational Stats

	W	L	ERA	Sv	IP		AB	H	HR	RBI	AVG
Home	1	1	2.12	1	29.2	LHB	95	19	2	12	.200
Road	1	2	2.53	0	32.0	RHB	121	20	5	14	.165
Day	0	0	2.08	1	13.0	Sc Pos	68	13	3	21	.191
Night	2	3	2.40	0	48.2	Clutch	134	27	4	17	.201

1991 Rankings (American League)

- ➡ 1st in least baserunners allowed per 9 innings, relief pitcher (7.3)
- ➡ 2nd lowest batting average allowed, relief pitcher (.181)
- ➡ 3rd in holds (19)
- ➡ 10th in relief ERA (2.34)
- ➡ Led the Red Sox in holds, relief ERA, lowest batting average allowed, relief pitcher and least baserunners allowed per 9 innings, relief pitcher

MIKE GREENWELL

Position: LF
Bats: L **Throws:** R
Ht: 6' 0" **Wt:** 200

Opening Day Age: 28
Born: 7/18/63 in
Louisville, KY
ML Seasons: 7

HITTING:

What has happened to this guy's power? Mike Greenwell hit one more home run than Luis Rivera last season. Luis Rivera? Back in 1988, Mike Greenwell hit 22 homers and knocked in 119 runs; in '91 he managed nine homers.

The concern about Greenwell's lack of power shouldn't take away from the fact that the man is a good hitter, period: at .311 lifetime, he is no slouch. And it doesn't matter if the pitcher's right-handed or left-handed. Greenwell was always pretty good hanging in against lefties, .288 lifetime going into 1991. But last season he actually hit better against lefties than he did righties.

The feeling with Greenwell is that he can and should hit for more power. Two things have happened. First, in 1990, he hurt his left foot; he stopped using this back foot for a trigger, and stopped driving off it as well. The result is that he has increasingly become a front-foot, lunge hitter who carves out a lot of hits because of his terrific hand-eye coordination and natural bat speed. The second reason for his reduced power is that he has misplaced his sense of working the count. Instead of using his ability to get ahead in counts and drive pitches, Greenwell is hitting like Matty Alou.

BASERUNNING:

An aggressive but not always wise baserunner, Greenwell has learned to pick his spots and channel that aggressiveness. He led the club with 15 steals; his 75% success rate was his career high.

FIELDING:

One of Greenwell's liabilities is that he is a below-average outfielder, although Fenway's left field is one of the easiest places to play once someone is used to it. He is aggressive, but sometimes too aggressive on the road, and tends to misplay balls into doubles and triples. His arm is below average.

OVERALL:

There are few better pure hitters alive than Greenwell. But over the last two years, he has increasingly become an opposite field hitter who'll occasionally pull a lefthander's soft stuff through the right side. When you hit one more homer than Luis Rivera, people in Boston notice.

Overall Statistics

	G	AB	R	H	D	T	HR	RBI	SB	BB	SO	AVG
1991	147	544	76	163	26	6	9	83	15	43	35	.300
Career	782	2800	402	870	165	26	82	471	58	294	211	.311

Where He Hits the Ball

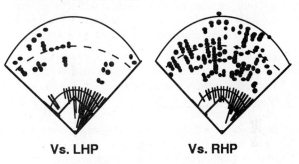

Vs. LHP   Vs. RHP

1991 Situational Stats

	AB	H	HR	RBI	AVG		AB	H	HR	RBI	AVG
Home	255	77	5	42	.302	LHP	168	55	4	34	.327
Road	289	86	4	41	.298	RHP	376	108	5	49	.287
Day	164	50	3	25	.305	Sc Pos	163	50	2	74	.307
Night	380	113	6	58	.297	Clutch	74	21	0	10	.284

1991 Rankings (American League)

→ 4th least pitches seen per plate appearance (3.00)

→ Led the Red Sox in triples (6), stolen bases (15), stolen base percentage (75.0%), batting average with the bases loaded (.458) and batting average on a 3-2 count (.318)

→ Led AL left fielders in batting average (.300), sacrifice flies (7), batting average vs. left-handed pitchers (.327), batting average at home (.302) and highest percentage of swings put into play (53.7%)

PITCHING:

What Red Sox fans will remember most about Greg Harris' 1991 season was that on September 26 in Baltimore he threw eight straight balls and walked in the winning run in the game that, for all intents and purposes, eliminated them. Harris hasn't exactly been Mr. September for the Red Sox; he was 1-4 in September and October the previous year and never even appeared in the playoffs.

But Harris has been an invaluable do-it-all utility pitcher in Boston, one who has started and relieved in virtually every role. Last year Harris was twice yanked out of the starting rotation and pitched the last two months of the season out of the bullpen. Harris' problem as a starter is that he basically is a fifth guy on a Red Sox staff that had a number-one starter and five number-fives.

Harris is predominantly a breaking ball pitcher. He has an outstanding curveball which he has learned to throw from a number of arm angles, making him very tough on right-handed hitters. But his curveball is tough on lefties as well, and he throws a tailing fastball that he spots well, and has a little split-finger for certain situations. He's almost like Mike Boddicker Jr., throwing every conceivable pitch in almost every conceivable situation.

HOLDING RUNNERS AND FIELDING:

Harris has proven to be a valuable pitcher in Fenway Park in part because he fields his position well and doesn't allow basestealing. He led the league with only one successful steal against him, and he's so tough to run on that only seven steals were attempted.

OVERALL:

A smart pitcher, Harris has been able to keep the ball away from both right-handed and left-handed batters, getting them to hit the ball to dead center where it dies with the new construction of the Boston ballpark. He's not a great pitcher, but he is a valuable one because of his versatility.

GREG HARRIS

Position: RP/SP
Bats: B **Throws:** R
Ht: 6' 0" **Wt:** 175

Opening Day Age: 36
Born: 11/2/55 in Lynwood, CA
ML Seasons: 11

Overall Statistics

	W	L	ERA	G	GS	Sv	IP	H	R	BB	SO	HR
1991	11	12	3.85	53	21	2	173.0	157	79	69	127	13
Career	59	66	3.64	470	96	40	1148.1	1043	529	490	870	101

How Often He Throws Strikes

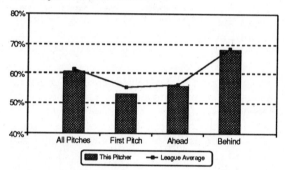

1991 Situational Stats

	W	L	ERA	Sv	IP		AB	H	HR	RBI	AVG
Home	4	6	3.80	2	71.0	LHB	303	74	5	35	.244
Road	7	6	3.88	0	102.0	RHB	342	83	8	40	.243
Day	4	4	4.45	0	54.2	Sc Pos	139	41	3	56	.295
Night	7	8	3.57	2	118.1	Clutch	121	23	1	9	.190

1991 Rankings (American League)

- → 1st lowest stolen base percentage allowed (14.3%)
- → 7th lowest run support per 9 innings (4.0)
- → 8th highest groundball/flyball ratio (1.6)
- → Led the Red Sox in losses (12), walks allowed (69), hit batsmen (5), groundball/flyball ratio, lowest stolen base percentage allowed, least pitches thrown per batter (3.73) and most GDPs induced per 9 innings (.88)

PITCHING:

Last year, Joe Hesketh came back from years of arm problems and two releases to pitch the way he had in 1985, when he was 10-5 with Montreal. Hesketh hopes his luck will be better this time around. The year after that 10-5 season, he was bothered by an impinged nerve in his left shoulder, then missed virtually all of 1987. While Hesketh did bounce back to some extent, he was still released by both the Expos and Braves in 1990 before signing with the Red Sox.

When Boston signed him, Hesketh expressed the opinion that if he could again be a starter, he could re-discover his career. He claimed that if he were on a regular program with four days rest and time to build the strength in his elbow -- rather than being on an irregular throwing program at the whim of managers who get pitchers up and down in the bullpen -- he could regain his rookie form. After all, Hesketh is built like a left-handed Oil Can Boyd.

It turned out he was right. Hesketh's fastball, which he runs away from righthanders and uses well against hitters from both sides of the plate, came back to the 88-89 MPH vicinity. Hesketh's best pitch, though, is a sharp slider he throws away from lefties and busts in on righthanders. It has such a late break that right-handed batters seemingly cannot lay off it, a la Steve Carlton.

HOLDING RUNNERS AND FIELDING:

Hesketh is difficult to run on, as he keeps runners at first base with his motion; basestealers were successful only seven times in 15 attempts. He fields his position fairly well.

OVERALL:

The biggest concern about Hesketh isn't his stuff, but his durability. At 170 pounds, he has never proven to be able to hold up over a full season. In 1985, he pitched a career high of 155 innings; last season, 153. But he is still a solid third or fourth starter, given regular four days rest.

JOE HESKETH

Position: RP/SP
Bats: L **Throws:** L
Ht: 6' 2" **Wt:** 170

Opening Day Age: 33
Born: 2/15/59 in Lackawanna, NY
ML Seasons: 8

Overall Statistics

	W	L	ERA	G	GS	Sv	IP	H	R	BB	SO	HR
1991	12	4	3.29	39	17	0	153.1	142	59	53	104	19
Career	41	29	3.46	256	64	19	645.2	606	280	245	505	57

How Often He Throws Strikes

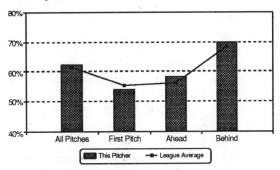

1991 Situational Stats

	W	L	ERA	Sv	IP		AB	H	HR	RBI	AVG
Home	7	1	2.04	0	70.2	LHB	87	21	2	9	.241
Road	5	3	4.35	0	82.2	RHB	481	121	17	44	.252
Day	3	3	3.96	0	61.1	Sc Pos	135	19	4	33	.141
Night	9	1	2.84	0	92.0	Clutch	40	7	0	1	.175

1991 Rankings (American League)

→ 1st in winning percentage (.750) and lowest batting average allowed with runners in scoring position (.141)

→ 8th in most GDPs induced per GDP situation (19.0%)

→ Led the Red Sox in home runs allowed (19), wild pitches (8), GDPs induced (19), winning percentage, most GDPs induced per GDP situation and lowest batting average allowed with runners in scoring position

PITCHING:

In the spring of 1990, Red Sox general manager Lou Gorman predicted that Kevin Morton might be in Boston by June. At the time, the kid was half a season out of Seton Hall. Then, Red Sox assistant farm director Ed Kenney, Jr. said "Morton is every bit as good as Steve Avery." Every week in a Boston newspaper there was a box titled, "The Phenom Watch," and the 1990 season turned into an emotional roller coaster for the youngster from Bridgeport, CT. He finished 8-14 at AA New Britain.

But in 1991, when the Red Sox became desperate for pitching help, they called him up and inserted him into the rotation. What they got was a 23 year old who seemed afraid to throw his fastball. Because Morton has a terrific change-up which seems to baffle right-handed hitters, Joe Morgan called for one change after another. While Morton had some moments, he also was tattooed, and his 6-5, 4.59 record summed up how inconsistent he was in his 15 starts.

One of new pitching coach Rich Gale's first priorities is to get Morton back to being a fastball/curveball/change-up pitcher. Morton had an average (86-87 MPH) fastball in Pawtucket and a sharp curveball. If he can establish them in the majors, he can be a successful pitcher because his change-up is unique. What makes it such a good pitch is Morton's neck movement; former Red Sox pitching coach Bill Fischer likens it to Stu Miller's.

HOLDING RUNNERS AND FIELDING:

An average fielder, (perhaps a little better), Morton played errorless ball last year. For a rookie, he also did a decent job of holding runners. Despite allowing a lot of men on base, Morton permitted only four stolen bases.

OVERALL:

The Red Sox haven't developed a 12 game winner since Roger Clemens came along in 1984. They hope that Morton is the next one to come out of their farm system. Another Steve Avery? Probably not. But what they saw last summer isn't all Kevin Morton's got.

KEVIN MORTON

Position: SP
Bats: R **Throws:** L
Ht: 6' 2" **Wt:** 185

Opening Day Age: 23
Born: 8/3/68 in Norwalk, CT
ML Seasons: 1

Overall Statistics

	W	L	ERA	G	GS	Sv	IP	H	R	BB	SO	HR
1991	6	5	4.59	16	15	0	86.1	93	49	40	45	9
Career	6	5	4.59	16	15	0	86.1	93	49	40	45	9

How Often He Throws Strikes

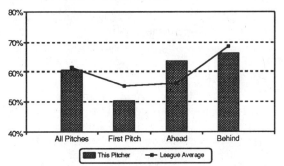

1991 Situational Stats

	W	L	ERA	Sv	IP		AB	H	HR	RBI	AVG
Home	4	2	4.91	0	44.0	LHB	41	11	2	5	.268
Road	2	3	4.25	0	42.1	RHB	287	82	7	36	.286
Day	2	0	6.30	0	20.0	Sc Pos	69	19	1	32	.275
Night	4	5	4.07	0	66.1	Clutch	4	1	1	1	.250

1991 Rankings (American League)

➡ Did not rank near the top or bottom in any category

HITTING:

Sit behind home plate at a Red Sox game and you will see Tony Pena run back and forth to his position, scramble after every foul ball and play a 12-5 game on a 90 degree July afternoon like a special teams football maniac. But as he turns 35 on June 4, there is concern that Pena's offensive days are behind him.

In Pena's defense, he plays every day, and last season played beaten up, with shoulder, rib, elbow and back ailments at different times of the season. But the fact remains that he's averaged only six homers a year the past five seasons, has knocked in 50 runs twice in that time, and last season saw his average slide to .231. Pena's on base percentage was .291, the fifth-worst of any American League qualifier.

As he has begun to age, Pena has increasingly become an inside-out, right field hitter. He is a free swinger who likes the fastball out over the plate so he can drive it the other way. He increasingly had difficulty laying off breaking balls from righthanders when behind in the count; his average against righties dropped to .215 last year.

BASERUNNING:

Pena swings so hard that it takes him a long time to get out of the batter's box. He is a big double play threat, grounding into 23 last season. He is a smart baserunner, however, and was 8-for-11 stealing last year despite his lack of speed.

FIELDING:

Red Sox pitchers swear by Pena, whose arm is still way above average (throwing out 40 of 121 attempted base stealers wasn't bad with this staff). He keeps on pitchers about being aggressive and allows them to maintain their own rhythm and pace.

OVERALL:

In good times and bad, Pena's enthusiasm never dies. Maybe the winter will allow him to recoup his strength, rest his body and come back in 1992 as strong as he was five years ago. He's at an important juncture in his career.

TONY PENA

Position: C
Bats: R **Throws:** R
Ht: 6' 0" **Wt:** 184

Opening Day Age: 34
Born: 6/4/57 in Monte Cristi, Dominican Republic
ML Seasons: 12

Overall Statistics

	G	AB	R	H	D	T	HR	RBI	SB	BB	SO	AVG
1991	141	464	45	107	23	2	5	48	8	37	53	.231
Career	1491	5140	545	1382	235	25	94	576	75	358	643	.269

Where He Hits the Ball

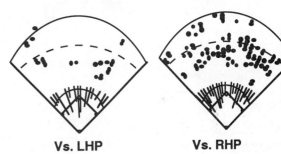

Vs. LHP   Vs. RHP

1991 Situational Stats

	AB	H	HR	RBI	AVG		AB	H	HR	RBI	AVG
Home	230	51	2	22	.222	LHP	106	30	4	17	.283
Road	234	56	3	26	.239	RHP	358	77	1	31	.215
Day	139	32	1	19	.230	Sc Pos	130	31	0	41	.238
Night	325	75	4	29	.231	Clutch	71	9	0	4	.127

1991 Rankings (American League)

→ 1st in lowest slugging percentage (.321), lowest slugging percentage vs. right-handed pitchers (.288) and lowest batting average after the 6th inning (.155)

→ 2nd in most GDPs per GDP situation (25.6%), lowest batting average vs. right-handed pitchers (.215) and lowest on-base average vs. right-handed pitchers (.278)

→ 3rd in GDPs (23)

→ 4th lowest batting average in the clutch (.127)

→ 5th lowest on-base average (.291)

→ Led the Red Sox in GDPs

→ Led AL catchers in stolen bases (8) and GDPs

FUTURE ALL-STAR

PHIL PLANTIER

Position: RF/LF
Bats: L **Throws:** R
Ht: 6' 0" **Wt:** 175

Opening Day Age: 23
Born: 1/27/69 in Manchester, NH
ML Seasons: 2

HITTING:

Is Phil Plantier the next big-time slugger? This 23-year-old outfielder came up for his third trial with the Red Sox on August 9 and by season's end was considered one of the most powerful young hitters in the game. In just 153 at-bats, Plantier hit 11 homers, knocked in 35 runs, batted .331 and slugged .615. The kid with what Joe Morgan called the "Toilet Seat Stance" demonstrated bat speed that puts him in the Jack Clark/Ronnie Gant/David Justice league.

What Plantier seems to be is a slightly different version of Fred Lynn, who hit .259 and .282 in the minors and found Fenway Park his nirvana (Lynn batted .350 in Fenway in a Boston uniform). Similarly, Fenway seems to make Plantier an even better, more dangerous hitter than he was in the minors. He has such tremendous power and elevation to the opposite field that he can wait on a pitch in Fenway, not hit the ball well and still loft it off The Wall or into the screen. Plantier's power isn't limited to Fenway (where he hit six of his 11 homers), but he believes that it can make him a better overall hitter.

BASERUNNING:

Plantier has only average speed, but he's learning to be a smarter baserunner. In 1990 he was 1-for-9 stealing at Pawtucket and Boston; in 1991 he was 7-for-8, though only 1-for-1 with the Sox.

FIELDING:

Plantier had developed a reputation as a DH type of outfielder. But then he found out that he was running on the heels of his feet, jolting his neck and head and making him lose track of the ball. When he learned to run on the balls of his feet, the improvement started, and he is now an above-average left fielder who may be asked to play the difficult Fenway Park left field. His arm is below average.

OVERALL:

He will have his weeks when he strikes out a lot, but Plantier looks like the legitimate home run hitter tailor-made for Fenway Park.

Overall Statistics

	G	AB	R	H	D	T	HR	RBI	SB	BB	SO	AVG
1991	53	148	27	49	7	1	11	35	1	23	38	.331
Career	67	163	28	51	8	1	11	38	1	27	44	.313

Where He Hits the Ball

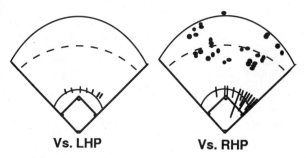

Vs. LHP   **Vs. RHP**

1991 Situational Stats

	AB	H	HR	RBI	AVG		AB	H	HR	RBI	AVG
Home	73	23	6	21	.315	LHP	25	8	3	13	.320
Road	75	26	5	14	.347	RHP	123	41	8	22	.333
Day	53	18	4	14	.340	Sc Pos	45	16	3	25	.356
Night	95	31	7	21	.326	Clutch	27	5	1	5	.185

1991 Rankings (American League)

➡ Did not rank near the top or bottom in any category

HITTING:

Carlos Quintana batted .287 as a rookie in 1990. Last year, he batted .295 and knocked in 71 runs in 478 at-bats. He hit .394 in late and close situations. He was second in the American League in average after the sixth inning (.340, a virtual tie with Julio Franco). Yet he can barely get a chance to play every day with the Red Sox. Part of the problem for "The Q" is that the Red Sox are loaded with first base/DH/outfield types.

As a rookie in 1990, Quintana was essentially a right field singles hitter. He never pulled fastballs, which gave him trouble when pitchers pounded him inside. But "The Q" is a highly intelligent, instinctive player who has demonstrated the ability to make adjustments. Last season, he went along with pitchers, looked for fastballs depending on counts and situations, and increasingly drove the ball to left field. Since his natural style is to hit the ball to right field, he is now beginning to use the whole field.

BASERUNNING:

Quintana has below-average speed, and like most of the Red Sox, runs conservatively, though his baserunning instincts are very good. He is no basestealer, though he was successful in his only attempt last year.

FIELDING:

Quintana was an outfielder throughout most of his minor league days, and really didn't convert to first base until a couple of years ago. But despite his bulky, seemingly gawky body, he has become an agile, accomplished first baseman. He has excellent hands, and stretches like someone who's played the position all his life.

OVERALL:

When the Red Sox acceded to media pressure and brought Mo Vaughn up, the players on the team rallied behind Quintana, criticizing the move and actually making life a little unpleasant for Vaughn. Eventually Vaughn found out that it was a reflection not on him, but on Quintana. If you start an all-star team of gamers, make sure "The Q" is on it.

CARLOS QUINTANA

Position: 1B/RF
Bats: R **Throws:** R
Ht: 6' 2" **Wt:** 195

Opening Day Age: 26
Born: 8/26/65 in Estado Miranda, Venezuela
ML Seasons: 4

Overall Statistics

	G	AB	R	H	D	T	HR	RBI	SB	BB	SO	AVG
1991	149	478	69	141	21	1	11	71	1	61	66	.295
Career	337	1073	132	306	54	1	18	146	2	122	155	.285

Where He Hits the Ball

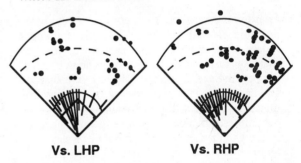

Vs. LHP   Vs. RHP

1991 Situational Stats

	AB	H	HR	RBI	AVG		AB	H	HR	RBI	AVG
Home	236	69	2	30	.292	LHP	153	52	5	26	.340
Road	242	72	9	41	.298	RHP	325	89	6	45	.274
Day	149	52	3	30	.349	Sc Pos	130	36	4	58	.277
Night	329	89	8	41	.271	Clutch	66	26	1	14	.394

1991 Rankings (American League)

→ 1st in groundball/flyball ratio (2.79) and batting average in the clutch (.394)

→ 2nd in batting average after the 6th inning (.340)

→ 7th in on-base average vs. left-handed pitchers (.436)

→ Led the Red Sox in groundball/flyball ratio, batting average in the clutch, batting average after the 6th inning and batting average vs. left-handed pitchers (.340)

→ Led AL first basemen in sacrifice bunts (6), groundball/flyball ratio, batting average in the clutch, batting average vs. left-handed pitchers, batting average after the 6th inning and bunts in play (7)

JEFF REARDON

STOPPER

Position: RP
Bats: R **Throws:** R
Ht: 6' 0" **Wt:** 200

Opening Day Age: 36
Born: 10/1/55 in Dalton, MA
ML Seasons: 13

PITCHING:

By the end of May 1992, Jeff Reardon will have more saves than any pitcher in baseball history. No one had hit the 40-save plateau before 1983; Reardon is one of two pitchers to have three 40-save seasons, including 1991. He has always been a willing, durable and tough workman. And can he pitch under pressure? He was on the mound when the Expos clinched the division in 1981, he was on the mound when the Twins clinched the division, pennant and World Series in 1987 and was on the mound when the Red Sox clinched the A.L. East in 1990. If being a we man means something to a team, Reardon and Jack Clark are the best teammates anyone could ask for.

Reardon is no longer the fireballer he was when he broke in with the Mets. He still challenges hitters with his fastball and tries to run it up on them, but he has actually now become a curveball pitcher first and foremost. The fact that Reardon still has the heart to go out to the mound anytime means he also is willing to challenge hitters, and sometimes will lose the challenge. He gave up four big ninth inning, two-out homers last season, including one to the Yankees' Roberto Kelly on September 22 that kept the Red Sox from moving into a first place tie and likely was the most memorable bad dream of the '91 season. Still, he had 40 saves in 49 chances.

HOLDING RUNNERS AND FIELDING:

Reardon does not do a good job of holding runners and has always been fairly easy to steal on. He is also a below-average fielder, with a delivery that leaves him out of position.

OVERALL:

It has been said many times that when it comes to the do-or-die world of short relievers, makeup is actually more important than stuff. In Jeff Reardon's case, the fastball may be only 85 MPH these days, but his heart is as big as the state of Vermont.

Overall Statistics

	W	L	ERA	G	GS	Sv	IP	H	R	BB	SO	HR
1991	1	4	3.03	57	0	40	59.1	54	21	16	44	9
Career	63	69	3.03	751	0	327	1003.0	850	361	336	799	96

How Often He Throws Strikes

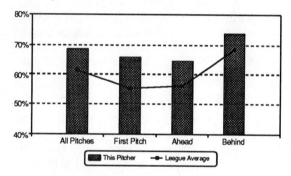

This Pitcher / League Average

1991 Situational Stats

	W	L	ERA	Sv	IP		AB	H	HR	RBI	AVG
Home	1	2	3.62	19	32.1	LHB	127	38	7	17	.299
Road	0	2	2.33	21	27.0	RHB	102	16	2	7	.157
Day	0	3	6.88	11	17.0	Sc Pos	61	13	2	17	.213
Night	1	1	1.49	29	42.1	Clutch	175	39	6	18	.223

1991 Rankings (American League)

→ 2nd in blown saves (9)

→ 4th in saves (40) and save opportunities (49)

→ 8th in games finished (51)

→ Led the Red Sox in saves, games finished (51), save opportunities, save percentage (81.6%) and blown saves

JODY REED

Position: 2B
Bats: R **Throws:** R
Ht: 5' 9" **Wt:** 165

Opening Day Age: 29
Born: 7/26/62 in Tampa, FL
ML Seasons: 5

HITTING:

What the Red Sox need to do is figure out some way to make Jody Reed believe that in April and May, he's actually back playing in Florida. Reed is a career .213 hitter in April, strange for a guy with a career .288 average. It happened to him in AA ball, it happened in AAA and last year . . .

Well, through April 27, Reed was 6-for-56, .107. But when the season was over, he had topped the 40-double mark for the third straight year and finished at .283 with career-highs of 87 runs, 175 hits, 60 RBI and five homers. "I've always had problems with cold weather," Reed admits. So if they played the first month in Winter Haven, Reed might win a batting title.

Reed's 5'-9" size belies his real skill: he is a little man with a big man's bat speed. Reed is outstanding at drilling fastballs on the inner half of the plate to left field. He wears out the left field corner in Fenway, where he had 27 of his 42 doubles, but that led to some bad habits as well. Reed actually batted only .263 at home and .304 on the road, basically because he became too much of a dead fastball, pull hitter at Fenway.

BASERUNNING:

Reed has only average speed, and usually steals at the Red Sox rate: four to six bases a year, with a success rate of about 50%. He is a smart, aggressive baserunner who will take the extra sack whenever he can.

FIELDING:

Reed has above-average range at second, plays hitters well, dives for balls and has a good second base arm for balls up the middle and double plays.

OVERALL:

Now that he's clearly settled as a second baseman and not bouncing back and forth between second and short, Reed -- like Chuck Knoblauch -- is just a step below the premier A.L. second basemen, Roberto Alomar and Julio Franco. But because his batting average and visibility aren't as high, he may never get the recognition.

Overall Statistics

	G	AB	R	H	D	T	HR	RBI	SB	BB	SO	AVG
1991	153	618	87	175	42	2	5	60	6	60	53	.283
Career	572	2108	297	607	153	6	14	187	16	257	183	.288

Where He Hits the Ball

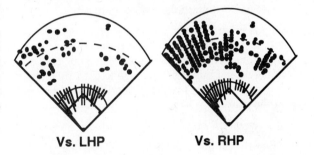

Vs. LHP   **Vs. RHP**

1991 Situational Stats

	AB	H	HR	RBI	AVG		AB	H	HR	RBI	AVG
Home	312	82	3	37	.263	LHP	165	44	0	6	.267
Road	306	93	2	23	.304	RHP	453	131	5	54	.289
Day	193	43	0	15	.223	Sc Pos	138	42	0	49	.304
Night	425	132	5	45	.311	Clutch	78	20	0	7	.256

1991 Rankings (American League)

→ 3rd lowest percentage of swings that missed (8.3%)

→ 4th in doubles (42)

→ 7th highest percentage of swings put into play (57.1%)

→ Led the Red Sox in at-bats (618), doubles, pitches seen (2,605), plate appearances (696), games (153), runs scored per time reached base (36.4%), batting average on the road (.304) and bunts in play (21)

→ Led AL second basemen in doubles

HITTING:

Listen to any talk show in Boston and you'll soon find out that Luis Rivera is one of the biggest reasons the Red Sox haven't won it all since 1918. Hey, even Matt Young ripped Rivera after Young lost what turned out to be his last start of the year. How bad was he?

He wasn't that bad at all. Rivera is one of those guys whom teammates respect more than anyone who sees him every couple of weeks. He's a tough gamer who played nearly the entire season with a very painful shoulder injury and never complained or begged out of the lineup. When Joe Morgan criticized Rivera in the press for a throw in Kansas City that the manager considered ill-advised, Rivera's teammates rallied to his defense and criticized the manager in turn.

Rivera is hardly a Cal Ripken, but he can bail and hit the inside fastball with pretty decent power, as his eight homers demonstrate. He also had 22 doubles, and raised his average to .258 by learning to go the other way with the ball on the outside of the plate.

BASERUNNING:

Rivera has slightly above-average speed, and he's a decent baserunner. But he's no basestealer. Last year's figures -- four for eight -- were typical numbers for him.

FIELDING:

Rivera led the league with 24 errors and had the worst fielding percentage of any regular shortstop. His range is above-average, however, and when his shoulder's healthy, so is his arm. A lot of the diminutive Rivera's errors come when he has played every day for a long period and gets physically and mentally tired. Tim Naehring's return should help in that regard.

OVERALL:

If he doesn't have to play too much, Rivera is a useful player. This season, Rivera will start as the regular with Naehring, his backup, coming off back surgery. The stats say the duo are as bad as the talk show callers' suggest. But they could fool a lot of people in '92.

LUIS RIVERA

Position: SS
Bats: R **Throws:** R
Ht: 5'10" **Wt:** 170

Opening Day Age: 28
Born: 1/3/64 in Cidra, Puerto Rico
ML Seasons: 6

Overall Statistics

	G	AB	R	H	D	T	HR	RBI	SB	BB	SO	AVG
1991	129	414	64	107	22	3	8	40	4	35	86	.258
Career	536	1652	192	390	89	8	24	158	14	122	314	.236

Where He Hits the Ball

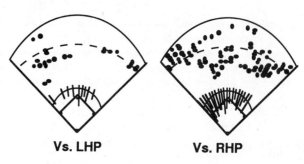

Vs. LHP   **Vs. RHP**

1991 Situational Stats

	AB	H	HR	RBI	AVG		AB	H	HR	RBI	AVG
Home	204	52	4	16	.255	LHP	108	34	4	16	.315
Road	210	55	4	24	.262	RHP	306	73	4	24	.239
Day	124	34	3	16	.274	Sc Pos	109	22	2	33	.202
Night	290	73	5	24	.252	Clutch	52	8	0	3	.154

1991 Rankings (American League)

→ 1st in highest batting average on an 0-2 count (.379)

→ 4th lowest batting average after the 6th inning (.186)

→ 6th lowest batting average in the clutch (.154)

→ 7th in sacrifice bunts (7)

→ Led the Red Sox in sacrifice bunts, batting average on an 0-2 count and batting average with 2 strikes (.241)

→ Led AL shortstops in errors (24) and batting average on an 0-2 count

HITTING:

The "Hit Dog" actually arrived at Fenway with higher acclaim than teammate Phil Plantier. And while Mo Vaughn struggled to make adjustments in this, his second full professional season, there seems little question that this beast of a man will hit and hit with impact.

First, Vaughn had to cope with being pounded inside with hard stuff. When he adjusted to that, he had to adjust to nothing but garbage, most of it out of the strike zone, especially down and in. He hadn't made all the adjustments by the end of the season, but he gave indications of what he can do.

Vaughn may be more of a pure hitter and less of a power hitter compared to Plantier. He likes to go with the ball away from him and drive it to left field, especially into the left field corner. He has awesome power -- as evidenced by the ball he almost hit out of Memorial Stadium -- but he saw little in the middle of the plate that he could get the bat head onto in his first month.

BASERUNNING:

Vaughn, who is 6-1 and weighs nearly 230 pounds, is obviously no speed burner. But he is fairly light on his feet and moves around the bases better than you might think. Don't expect him to steal, however.

FIELDING:

Vaughn looks like a Cecil Fielder or Hector Villanueva, but he actually is put together solidly and is a good athlete around first base. Also, he has such an intense work ethic that he has continually made himself a better defensive player.

OVERALL:

Vaughn is a warrior of a kid from a very strong family background; his father Leroy played for the Baltimore Colts and is now a high school principal. He also drives himself very hard, which added to his frustrations when he didn't hit as well as he had hoped. The "Hit Dog" really wants to be great, and that's a big part of the equation.

MO VAUGHN

Position: 1B/DH
Bats: L **Throws:** R
Ht: 6' 1" **Wt:** 225

Opening Day Age: 24
Born: 12/15/67 in Norwalk, CT
ML Seasons: 1

Overall Statistics

	G	AB	R	H	D	T	HR	RBI	SB	BB	SO	AVG
1991	74	219	21	57	12	0	4	32	2	26	43	.260
Career	74	219	21	57	12	0	4	32	2	26	43	.260

Where He Hits the Ball

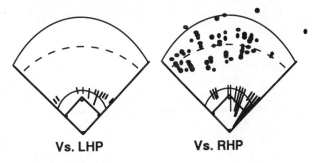

Vs. LHP   Vs. RHP

1991 Situational Stats

	AB	H	HR	RBI	AVG		AB	H	HR	RBI	AVG
Home	100	32	1	16	.320	LHP	33	7	0	7	.212
Road	119	25	3	16	.210	RHP	186	50	4	25	.269
Day	67	20	1	9	.299	Sc Pos	59	22	1	28	.373
Night	152	37	3	23	.243	Clutch	32	5	0	4	.156

1991 Rankings (American League)

→ 6th lowest batting average on a 3-2 count (.063)

PITCHING:

Oops. The Red Sox didn't know anything about Matt Young when they gave him $6.35 million for three years in '91. "We were reacting to losing Mike Boddicker, I admit it," said GM Lou Gorman at the end of the season. They found out in Boston what they'd already learned in Seattle, Oakland and Los Angeles. The man was 39-65 lifetime as a starter for a reason.

Young has a thing about throwing a baseball to another human being. Stuff? He has virtually unhittable stuff. But one night in Fenway, he threw five straight warmup pitches up onto the screen. He cannot even issue intentional walks. Maddeningly, he'll throw four great innings. Then comes the fifth, and there'll be a walk, a messed-up bunt, a bloop, another walk, and then the inevitable meatball.

Young averaged four wins a year in the three seasons prior to 1991. He did what should have been expected: three wins, seven losses, a 5.18 ERA for the Sox. And that seventh loss came in relief on Sept. 22 when Joe Morgan incredibly put him in against the Yankees in the tenth inning and, after getting an out, Young walked and hit the bases loaded to lose the game that cost them a first place tie.

HOLDING RUNNERS AND FIELDING:

Young is the worst fielding pitcher in modern baseball history. The man cannot pick up a ball and throw it to first; he will lob it underhand, run towards the bag, hold it, do anything, but he cannot field a ball in haste and throw it to a base. He does not hold baserunners very well, either, especially for a lefty.

OVERALL:

Had Young gone to Detroit or back to Seattle, perhaps, after three years of arm trouble, he might have put things together. But in Boston? "They've got an Ed Whitson situation," says former Sox pitching coach Bill Fischer. Whitson, as you may remember, could not pitch in New York but revived his career when he went back to San Diego.

MATT YOUNG

Position: SP
Bats: L **Throws:** L
Ht: 6' 3" **Wt:** 205

Opening Day Age: 33
Born: 8/9/58 in Pasadena, CA
ML Seasons: 8

Overall Statistics

	W	L	ERA	G	GS	Sv	IP	H	R	BB	SO	HR
1991	3	7	5.18	19	16	0	88.2	92	55	53	69	4
Career	54	85	4.33	283	147	25	1044.2	1063	574	466	735	84

How Often He Throws Strikes

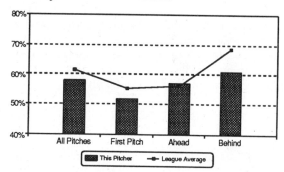

1991 Situational Stats

	W	L	ERA	Sv	IP		AB	H	HR	RBI	AVG
Home	2	3	4.53	0	45.2	LHB	51	13	1	4	.255
Road	1	4	5.86	0	43.0	RHB	295	79	3	33	.268
Day	1	2	4.91	0	18.1	Sc Pos	93	27	1	32	.290
Night	2	5	5.25	0	70.1	Clutch	22	7	0	0	.318

1991 Rankings (American League)

➡ Did not rank near the top or bottom in any category

DANNY DARWIN

Position: SP
Bats: R **Throws:** R
Ht: 6' 3" **Wt:** 190

Opening Day Age: 36
Born: 10/25/55 in
Bonham, TX
ML Seasons: 14

DANA KIECKER

Position: RP/SP
Bats: R **Throws:** R
Ht: 6' 3" **Wt:** 195

Opening Day Age: 31
Born: 2/25/61 in Sleepy
Eye, MN
ML Seasons: 2

Overall Statistics

	W	L	ERA	G	GS	Sv	IP	H	R	BB	SO	HR
1991	3	6	5.16	12	12	0	68.0	71	39	15	42	15
Career	114	115	3.46	500	220	29	1981.1	1847	859	596	1307	176

Overall Statistics

	W	L	ERA	G	GS	Sv	IP	H	R	BB	SO	HR
1991	2	3	7.36	18	5	0	40.1	56	34	23	21	6
Career	10	12	4.68	50	30	0	192.1	201	108	77	114	13

PITCHING, FIELDING & HOLDING RUNNERS:

The Red Sox lost Bruce Hurst and Mike Boddicker after the 1990 season, then had to find someone to fit into the number-two slot behind Roger Clemens. When they couldn't sign Bob Welch, they went for Danny Darwin and signed the veteran for an $11.8 million, four-year contract. Darwin was a disaster in Boston, going 3-6, 5.16 before going out for the year with a shoulder injury.

Darwin was suffering from the flu in his first start of the season, eventually contracted a severe case of walking pneumonia. His willingness to pitch hurt ultimately strained his shoulder. After a Fenway shelling, all he said to the media was, "I stunk." He never mentioned that he was sick.

Darwin hasn't been a big innings type of pitcher as a starter, and his fastball-slider style of challenging hitters makes him prone to the long ball in a park like Fenway. Darwin is a good fielder, but is no great shakes at holding runners.

OVERALL:

Darwin's best days in Houston were as a swing man. Butch Hobson may put Darwin back in the bullpen, or he may hope that Darwin can hold up as a starter, or perhaps try a little of both. His first concern, however, will be whether or not Darwin's arm can bounce back at the age of 36.

PITCHING, FIELDING & HOLDING RUNNERS:

Boston's biggest surprise of 1990 turned into one of their bigger disappointments in 1991. After surprising everyone by going 8-9 and allowing but one run in his only postseason start in '90, Dana Kiecker had a terrible sophomore year.

Kiecker started the season as the odd man out of the rotation, in long relief; then when did start, he developed some elbow problems. To compound this, he was afraid to tell the manager, which sent him, injured, to the doghouse and, eventually, Pawtucket. After the season it was decided that the 31-year-old veteran needed elbow surgery, making his winter even longer.

Kiecker is basically a sinker-slider pitcher who has to have his sinker working well to get ground balls and eat righthanders up. Last year he had no bite to either pitch. Hitters were patient, made him come at them and hit him hard (7.36 ERA, .344 opponents average). Kiecker is easy to run on, and not a good fielder.

OVERALL:

With Danny Darwin coming back, Greg Harris already established as a swing man and rookies Paul Quantrill and Peter Hoy favorite candidates of Butch Hobson and Rich Gale, it may be that Kiecker will have to move on to another organization and re-establish himself. Kiecker hasn't had a winning record on any level since his 1983 debut with Elmira.

STEVE LYONS

Position: CF/2B
Bats: L **Throws:** R
Ht: 6' 3" **Wt:** 192

Opening Day Age: 31
Born: 6/3/60 in Tacoma, WA
ML Seasons: 7

Overall Statistics

	G	AB	R	H	D	T	HR	RBI	SB	BB	SO	AVG
1991	87	212	15	51	10	1	4	17	10	11	35	.241
Career	776	2084	255	531	99	15	19	192	40	151	351	.255

HITTING, FIELDING, BASERUNNING:

When the Red Sox picked up utility man Steve Lyons, who'd been released by Chicago early in the 1991 season, they knew what they were getting. Lyons had come up through the Boston system, and it was there that he'd earned his beloved nickname, "Psycho." They weren't expecting Tony Phillips, in other words.

As it turned out, signing Lyons was a useful move. Lyons' strong suit is his versatility, and he wound up playing eight positions for the Sox (all except catcher); he even pitched a scoreless inning. Lyons played center most often, subbing for Ellis Burks, and did a competent job. Decent in an emergency, he's not really outstanding anywhere in the field. He lacks the range to be a good infielder, and the arm to be a good outfielder.

Lyons is no great shakes as a hitter, with little power or strike zone judgement. As a baserunner the usually-reckless Psycho did better than expected. His 10 steals were the second-best total of his career, and his 77 percent success rate was his best ever.

OVERALL:

Lyons was a free agent at season's end, and re-signing him was not exactly Boston's top priority. His versatility is a plus, but his performance as a pinch hitter last year (1-for-21) reduces his value considerably. He'll undoubtedly find a job somewhere.

TIM NAEHRING

Position: SS
Bats: R **Throws:** R
Ht: 6' 2" **Wt:** 190

Opening Day Age: 25
Born: 2/1/67 in Cincinnati, OH
ML Seasons: 2

Overall Statistics

	G	AB	R	H	D	T	HR	RBI	SB	BB	SO	AVG
1991	20	55	1	6	1	0	0	3	0	6	15	.109
Career	44	140	11	29	7	0	2	15	0	14	30	.207

HITTING, FIELDING, BASERUNNING:

When the 1991 season began, the Red Sox had major expectations for 24-year-old shortstop Tim Naehring. Naehring was Boston's shortstop on Opening Day, but that was probably the highlight of his season. The youngster batted only .109 in 55 at-bats before bowing out for the year with major back surgery.

Naehring played in the instructional league after the season, and expects to battle Luis Rivera for the shortstop job this spring. However, the operation involved transplanting part of Naehring's buttock muscle to his back, and his buttocks tightened up at times during instructional league play. Naehring doesn't think it'll be a problem this year, but he'll have to prove it.

If healthy, Naehring is still an exciting prospect. He has excellent power for a shortstop (15-plus homer potential) and good strike zone judgement. He doesn't have much running speed, however, and some question whether he has the range to play shortstop. The Sox think he does -- if he's healthy.

OVERALL:

Naehring has had back problems for a couple of years now, and the Red Sox don't really expect him to be 100 percent by the start of the season. They do feel he can be a semi-regular at short, however, filling in frequently for Rivera. If he can handle more than that, so much the better.

ORGANIZATION OVERVIEW:

Curiously underrated, the Red Sox farm system continues to produce top prospects -- Mo Vaughn and Phil Plantier, the 1991 recruits, were only the latest in a long line. One reason the Sox are sometimes forgotten as a top developer of talent is that they don't win a lot of minor league pennants; another is that their teams don't usually play in hitters' parks, where their prospects can rack up gaudy numbers. But this club knows how to develop players, patience being a key factor. Boston doesn't appear to have any impact players ready for '92, but Jeff McNeely and Frankie Rodriguez are starting to excite people.

SCOTT COOPER

Position: 3B
Bats: L **Throws:** R
Ht: 6' 3" **Wt:** 200

Opening Day Age: 24
Born: 10/13/67 in St. Louis, MO

Recent Statistics

	G	AB	R	H	D	THR	RBI	SB	BB	SO	AVG
91 AAA Pawtucket	137	483	55	134	21	2 15	72	3	50	58	.277
91 AL Boston	14	35	6	16	4	2 0	7	0	2	2	.457
91 MLE	137	472	41	123	21	1 11	54	1	38	62	.261

The possibilities for a young Red Sox third baseman -- and a left-handed hitter to boot -- are not exactly rosy as long as Wade Boggs is around. The Sox want to hold onto Boggs, so Cooper has become trade bait. He's outstanding defensively and has improved a lot with the bat, though he probably won't be a big home run hitter. Lots of clubs need a third baseman; Cooper will probably be playing for one of them in 1991.

PETE HOY

Position: P
Bats: L **Throws:** R
Ht: 6' 7" **Wt:** 220

Opening Day Age: 25
Born: 6/29/66 in Brockville, Ontario, Canada

Recent Statistics

	W	L	ERA	G	GS	Sv	IP	H	R	BB	SO	HR
90 A Winter Havn	2	10	3.56	52	3	7	108.2	110	54	30	48	3
91 AA New Britain	4	4	1.46	47	0	15	68.0	47	20	22	39	2
91 AAA Pawtucket	1	2	2.38	15	0	5	22.2	18	8	10	12	2

Tall and imposing, Hoy is one of three Canadian pitchers on the Red Sox 40-man roster, along with Paul Quantrill and Mike Gardiner. With Jeff Reardon now 36 years old, the Red Sox will be looking for a successor for their closer role, and Hoy is a candidate to fill it. Not very highly regarded before '91 (33rd round pick in '89), he had a big year with 20 saves at New Britain and Pawtucket. But the outstanding closers are usually able to blow away hitters; despite Hoy's size, he's yet to show that ability. Butch Hobson likes him, however, and Hoy has a chance to stick this year.

JEFF MCNEELY

Position: OF
Bats: R **Throws:** R
Ht: 6' 2" **Wt:** 190

Opening Day Age: 22
Born: 10/18/69 in Monroe, NC

Recent Statistics

	G	AB	R	H	D	THR	RBI	SB	BB	SO	AVG
90 A Winter Havn	16	62	4	10	0	0 0	3	7	3	19	.161
90 A Elmira	73	246	41	77	4	5 6	37	39	40	60	.313
91 A Lynchburg	106	382	58	123	16	5 4	38	38	74	74	.322

Boston's second-round pick in 1989, McNeely could give Boston something it hasn't had in years: both speed and on-base ability from the leadoff spot. The Red Sox also think McNeely has power potential, though he hasn't shown it so far. To top it off, he's an outstanding defensive outfielder. McNeely is probably a couple of years away from Boston, but if Ellis Burks is injured or traded, he could make it sooner than that.

PAUL QUANTRILL

Position: P
Bats: L **Throws:** R
Ht: 6' 1" **Wt:** 165

Opening Day Age: 23
Born: 11/3/68 in London, Ontario, Canada

Recent Statistics

	W	L	ERA	G	GS	Sv	IP	H	R	BB	SO	HR
90 A Winter Havn	2	5	4.14	7	7	0	45.2	46	24	6	14	3
90 AA New Britain	7	11	3.53	22	22	0	132.2	149	65	23	53	3
91 AA New Britain	2	1	2.06	5	5	0	35.0	32	14	8	18	2
91 AAA Pawtucket	10	7	4.45	25	23	0	155.2	169	81	30	75	14

Judging from his '91 stats -- a high ERA with not many strikeouts in AAA -- Quantrill doesn't appear to be much of a prospect. But new Sox manager Butch Hobson and pitching coach Rich Gale handled Quantrill at Pawtucket, and they just love him. He's another Canadian, a former hockey player, and a tough, aggressive kid. Though he's basically a finesse pitcher, Quantrill isn't afraid to challenge hitters. Give him a chance this year, on the recommendation of Hobson and Gale.

FRANK RODRIGUEZ

Position: P-SS
Bats: R **Throws:** R
Ht: 6' 1" **Wt:** 175

Opening Day Age: 19
Born: 12/11/72 in Brooklyn, NY

Recent Statistics

	G	AB	R	H	D	THR	RBI	SB	BB	SO	AVG
91 R Red Sox	3	14	3	7	0	1 0	3	0	0	1	.500
91 A Elmira	67	255	36	69	5	3 6	31	3	13	38	.271

One of baseball's most intriguing prospects, Rodriguez has glittering credentials both at shortstop and at pitcher (97-MPH fastball). "He'll be playing shortstop in the major leagues in one year," said one NY-Penn manager. The Red Sox, who drafted Rodriguez in '90 but couldn't sign him until last June, would prefer him to pitch, but so far have acceded to Rodriguez' wish to play short. At either spot he's drawn raves, and should move up quickly.

CY YOUNG STUFF

PITCHING:

It is not every Cy Young candidate who can say he was in danger of being sent to the minor leagues **during** the season. But that was precisely the case with Jim Abbott. The 24-year-old left-hander struggled early, but emerged as perhaps the outstanding starter in the American League after the All-Star break.

In early May, Abbott was 0-4 and had allowed 42 baserunners in 24 innings. His career was at a low point, and there was more than a whisper about a possible trip to Edmonton for the pitcher who had never worked in the minor leagues. Abbott's control was a little better than in seasons past, but he was consistently trying to work the ball inside and instead made frequent mistakes over the heart of the plate.

Two things helped turn Abbott's season around. First, he started moving his pitches around the strike zone more. He was particularly effective in keeping the ball away, which left batters unprepared for his inside stuff. The second reason was his rediscovery of the curve ball. Abbott's 90 MPH fastball is well known, but to study Abbott in the second half of the season was more like watching former teammate Bert Blyleven. Abbott learned to throw the curve effectively when behind in the count. After the 0-4 start, Abbott went 18-7.

HOLDING RUNNERS AND FIELDING:

In 1990, runners were successful 79% of the time against Abbott. In '91, that number dropped to a very impressive 46%. That difference was significant to Abbott's overall improvement. One noticeable change was the increase in the frequency with which he threw to first base. Abbott's fielding remains very solid.

OVERALL:

It remains to be seen if Abbott will be able to keep his place as one of the best starting pitchers in the AL. Nonetheless, 1991 will probably mark the turning point of Abbott's career. Barring injury, there is little doubt that he will be around for quite awhile.

JIM ABBOTT

Position: SP
Bats: L **Throws:** L
Ht: 6' 3" **Wt:** 210

Opening Day Age: 24
Born: 9/19/67 in Flint, MI
ML Seasons: 3

Overall Statistics

	W	L	ERA	G	GS	Sv	IP	H	R	BB	SO	HR
1991	18	11	2.89	34	34	0	243.0	222	85	73	158	14
Career	40	37	3.72	96	96	0	636.0	658	296	219	378	43

How Often He Throws Strikes

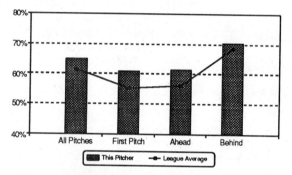

1991 Situational Stats

	W	L	ERA	Sv	IP		AB	H	HR	RBI	AVG
Home	8	7	2.57	0	129.1	LHB	142	43	3	18	.303
Road	10	4	3.25	0	113.2	RHB	767	179	11	57	.233
Day	9	2	3.21	0	73.0	Sc Pos	191	45	5	63	.236
Night	9	9	2.75	0	170.0	Clutch	91	24	2	10	.264

1991 Rankings (American League)

→ 1st in balks (4)

→ 3rd in highest groundball/flyall ratio (2.1) and lowest ERA at home (2.58)

→ 4th in ERA (2.89), wins (18) and runners caught stealing (14)

→ 5th in batters faced (1,002) and least home runs allowed per 9 innings (.52)

→ Led the Angels in ERA, games started (34), hits allowed (222), batters faced, balks, pick-off throws (178), strikeout/walk ratio (2.16), lowest slugging percentage allowed (.336) and groundball flyball ratio

PITCHING:

With the Angels' penchant for signing free agents, it's rare when there is any excitement over a first round pick (i.e., they seldom have any first round picks). Kyle Abbott is not only an exception to that statement, he is among the most eagerly anticipated arrivals in Anaheim in years. His first inning of major league work did nothing to dissuade his believers; Abbott struck out the side against the Texas Rangers (Julio Franco and Rafael Palmeiro included). Abbott, however, went on to lose the game.

It was that kind of experience in the majors for Abbott: flashes of brilliance together with some painfully bad innings. Opposing batters had a .414 on-base percentage against Abbott, as the 23 year old lefthander struggled with the strike zone (13 walks in just over 19 innings). Once Abbott gains some major league experience, his control should improve markedly. His strikeout-to-walk ratio in Edmonton last year was almost three-to-one.

Abbott has three good pitches: fastball, curve and change-up. At this point, only his curveball is at a major league level. He throws the fastball hard, but is not overpowering yet. He looked uncomfortable throwing the change from behind in the count, which allowed hitters to sit on the 2-1 or 3-1 fastball. If he can move both the fastball and the change to the next tier, look out!

HOLDING RUNNERS AND FIELDING:

Abbott shortened his stride a bit with a man on first, which worked; major leaguers stole just one base against him in three thries.

OVERALL:

Buck Rodgers said that he considered Abbott "a little bit ahead" of Scott Lewis and Joe Grahe in the race to become the Angels' fifth starter. However, with the three big-time lefties already on the Angels' staff, it could be that Abbott's baseball will be played somewhere other than Anaheim in 1992.

KYLE ABBOTT

Position: SP
Bats: L **Throws:** L
Ht: 6' 4" **Wt:** 195

Opening Day Age: 24
Born: 2/18/68 in Newbury Port, MA
ML Seasons: 1

Overall Statistics

	W	L	ERA	G	GS	Sv	IP	H	R	BB	SO	HR
1991	1	2	4.58	5	3	0	19.2	22	11	13	12	2
Career	1	2	4.58	5	3	0	19.2	22	11	13	12	2

How Often He Throws Strikes

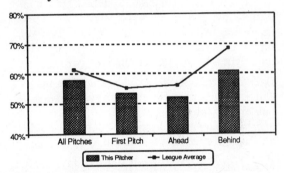

1991 Situational Stats

	W	L	ERA	Sv	IP		AB	H	HR	RBI	AVG
Home	0	2	5.06	0	10.2	LHB	13	4	0	2	.308
Road	1	0	4.00	0	9.0	RHB	60	18	2	7	.300
Day	0	1	7.71	0	4.2	Sc Pos	20	6	1	7	.300
Night	1	1	3.60	0	15.0	Clutch	4	1	0	0	.250

1991 Rankings (American League)

➡ Did not rank near the top or bottom in any category

PITCHING:

Scott Bailes is lucky to be in baseball. After a steady decline from his rookie year, when he won 10 games with the Cleveland Indians, Bailes discovered he suffered from a low blood-sugar condition which caused him to fatigue easily and also caused a 20-pound drop in weight. After altering his diet, Bailes pitched his way back onto the Angels staff in spring training last year, not allowing a run in 13 innings.

Bailes was not quite so dazzling during the regular season, but his work was better than his 4.18 ERA indicates. Bailes was actually second best on the squad in batting average allowed, and for the first time in his major league career, he allowed fewer hits than innings pitched. He ran into trouble by giving up walks and allowing too many long balls, a terrible combination. The word on Bailes is that opposing batters catch up to him quickly the second time around the batting order.

Bailes is a control pitcher who relies on a fastball and a sharp slider. He almost always keeps the ball around the plate, preferring to work outside, and has historically been a ground ball pitcher, although this was not the case in 1991.

HOLDING RUNNERS AND FIELDING:

Bailes has never helped himself a lot with his fielding. His follow-through is not conducive to good defense and he has had some problems with erratic throws to first -- many teams will try to bunt on him. Once considered poor at holding runners, Bailes is helped greatly by Lance Parrish's strong arm.

OVERALL:

Bailes' biggest obstacle is the pressure he puts on himself. A tremendous competitor, he landed himself on the disabled list last year when he jumped into the air after losing a Ping-Pong match, spraining his right ankle. With Whitey Herzog and Buck Rodgers now in charge, Bailes may need another strong spring in '92 to feel safe about his role with the Angels.

SCOTT BAILES

Position: RP
Bats: L **Throws:** L
Ht: 6' 2" **Wt:** 184

Opening Day Age: 29
Born: 12/18/62 in Chillicothe, OH
ML Seasons: 6

Overall Statistics

	W	L	ERA	G	GS	Sv	IP	H	R	BB	SO	HR
1991	1	2	4.18	42	0	0	51.2	41	26	22	41	5
Career	34	43	4.76	241	59	13	578.2	620	347	207	282	75

How Often He Throws Strikes

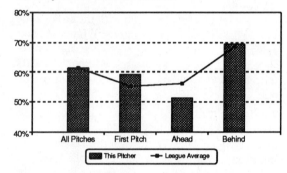

1991 Situational Stats

	W	L	ERA	Sv	IP		AB	H	HR	RBI	AVG
Home	0	2	3.80	0	21.1	LHB	77	19	3	16	.247
Road	1	0	4.45	0	30.1	RHB	111	22	2	9	.198
Day	0	0	3.00	0	9.0	Sc Pos	46	11	2	18	.239
Night	1	2	4.43	0	42.2	Clutch	36	10	1	6	.278

1991 Rankings (American League)

→ Did not rank near the top or bottom in any category

PITCHING:

The 1991 season was a very unlikely one for little-known Chris Beasley. A professional pitcher since 1984, Beasley had never even experienced AAA baseball until 1990. He was invited to the Angels' spring training camp as a non-roster invitee, but began the season in Edmonton. Pitching at the AAA level, he was 3-5 with a 5.26 ERA in July. But when the Angels decided to go with a four-man rotation and felt they needed more middle relief, Beasley got the call.

To add to the unlikelihood of the season, Beasley was slated to be sent back down on August 4th, but when Bryan Harvey had to leave the team to attend a funeral, Beasley stayed and posted 6.1 scoreless innings over his next three appearances. He continued to be very effective after his reprieve and ended up the season with a 3.38 ERA in 26 innings.

Beasley is a control pitcher who relies almost totally on location and the element of surprise for his fastball to be effective. Although his control wasn't all that good, Beasley held his own with runners on base, stranding 15 of the 20 runners he inherited. He is a ground ball pitcher who was successful at inducing critical double plays last year. As with most ground ball pitchers, the second Beasley gets the ball up, he is in trouble. On one of those occasions Kent Hrbek launched a 443-ft. home run off Beasley, one of the year's longest versus the Halos.

HOLDING RUNNERS AND FIELDING:

Beasley has a relatively quick delivery to the plate, and only one runner even attempted to run against him (he was caught). He has a good follow-through, and in limited time displayed good range coming off the mound.

OVERALL:

Beasley probably won't be in the long-term plans of the Angels unless he pitches even better than he did last year, which will be tough. However, the Angels are not strong in middle relief, and an effective spring training for Beasley might just earn him a spot on the roster.

CHRIS BEASLEY

Position: RP
Bats: R **Throws:** R
Ht: 6' 2" **Wt:** 190

Opening Day Age: 29
Born: 6/23/62 in Jackson, TN
ML Seasons: 1

Overall Statistics

	W	L	ERA	G	GS	Sv	IP	H	R	BB	SO	HR
1991	0	1	3.38	22	0	0	26.2	26	14	10	14	2
Career	0	1	3.38	22	0	0	26.2	26	14	10	14	2

How Often He Throws Strikes

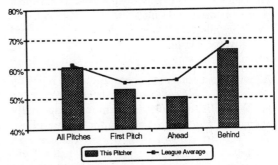

This Pitcher — League Average

1991 Situational Stats

	W	L	ERA	Sv	IP		AB	H	HR	RBI	AVG
Home	0	0	1.23	0	14.2	LHB	40	11	2	8	.275
Road	0	1	6.00	0	12.0	RHB	61	15	0	7	.246
Day	0	0	2.08	0	4.1	Sc Pos	32	9	0	12	.281
Night	0	1	3.63	0	22.1	Clutch	22	7	2	4	.318

1991 Rankings (American League)

→ Did not rank near the top or bottom in any category

PITCHING:

Mark Eichhorn moved comfortably into the role of set-up man for Bryan Harvey last year, enjoying his most successful season since his spectacular rookie campaign of 1986. Eichhorn's revival has been nothing short of amazing since his career appeared to bottom out with Atlanta in 1989.

To describe how Eichhorn gets batters out is a little like describing how a magician makes people disappear -- you see it happen, but you're never completely sure how. He is always near the plate, changing speeds and mixing the location of his pitches. He typically keeps the fastball away, preferring to challenge hitters with his enticing but effective change-up. When Eichhorn was in his long slump, his fastball appeared to have lost its movement and lefthanders were almost never fooled by him. Last year, Eichhorn rediscovered the movement in his pitches and allowed less than seven hits per nine innings.

As with most control pitchers, Eichhorn relies on keeping the ball down in the strike zone for his success. His double play support, especially against righthanders, is among the league's best. The two criticisms of Eichhorn are that he can't get lefties out consistently and that batters will eventually solve Eichhorn's riddle. Eichhorn was significantly worse in '91 against lefties (.262 against LHB versus an amazing .185 against RHB), but those numbers hardly rendered him useless. The second criticism might be more on the mark; Eichhorn tailed off significantly as the season wore down, with fatigue a contributing factor.

HOLDING RUNNERS AND FIELDING:

Holding runners is no longer one of Eichhorn's biggest problems. Only three of six runners who attempted to steal against him were successful. He is a solid fielder.

OVERALL:

The Angels are counting on Eichhorn to be Harvey's set-up man again in '92 and can hardly afford a major slip in his game. His re-emergence as a top flight reliever has been impressive and duly noted by Angel fans and baseball followers alike.

MARK EICHHORN

Position: RP
Bats: R **Throws:** R
Ht: 6' 3" **Wt:** 210

Opening Day Age: 31
Born: 11/21/60 in San Jose, CA
ML Seasons: 7

Overall Statistics

	W	L	ERA	G	GS	Sv	IP	H	R	BB	SO	HR
1991	3	3	1.98	70	0	1	81.2	63	21	13	49	2
Career	34	31	3.01	377	7	29	624.0	565	232	193	473	39

How Often He Throws Strikes

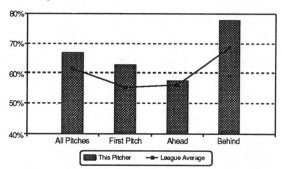

1991 Situational Stats

	W	L	ERA	Sv	IP		AB	H	HR	RBI	AVG
Home	2	2	1.30	1	41.2	LHB	126	33	2	13	.262
Road	1	1	2.70	0	40.0	RHB	162	30	0	14	.185
Day	1	1	1.82	1	24.2	Sc Pos	76	16	0	22	.211
Night	2	2	2.05	0	57.0	Clutch	145	30	0	13	.207

1991 Rankings (American League)

→ 1st in holds (25)

→ 3rd lowest relief ERA (1.98)

→ 4th least baserunners allowed per 9 innings, relief pitchers (8.6)

→ 5th in games (70)

→ 7th most GDPs induced per GDP situation (20.4%)

→ 9th in first batter efficiency (.185)

→ Led the Angels in games, holds, GDPS induced per GDP situation, first batter efficiency and relief innings (81.2)

HITTING:

Junior Felix was high on then Angel GM Mike Port's list of obtainable players at the end of the 1990 season. When he dealt Devon White and Willie Fraser for Felix and Luis Sojo, the Angels expected Felix to provide a combination of speed and power that White had not been providing for the past several years.

While White developed into the player for Toronto that the Angels had been waiting for, Felix suffered through a season of injury and inconsistency. As one of the Angels' few switch-hitters, Felix offers a decent bat from both sides of the plate. He stands in the batter's box better against left-handed pitchers but generates more power versus righties. Felix has good power to the alleys, but his home runs dropped from 15 with Toronto in 1990 to just two last season with the Angels.

Felix's development will depend greatly on how much he can improve his ability to hit the breaking ball. He has extremely poor judgment at the plate (11 walks in 230 at-bats for a strikeout-to-walk ratio of 5-1) and will show no discretion when he is behind in the count.

BASERUNNING:

Felix is one of the fastest players on the Angels, but his base-stealing technique is not very good yet. Buck Rodgers will likely put Felix at the top of the lineup to take advantage of his raw speed, but Felix is **not** a good leadoff man.

FIELDING:

It is questionable whether Felix will become a good major league center fielder. He might end up in left, where he'd have a much better chance to become an outstanding glove man. He has the tools, good speed and a decent throwing arm.

OVERALL:

Because of his injuries, the Angels will not write off Felix after one season. He did not make a good first impression, but the Angels are hopeful that Felix can play in 1992 as he did after returning from the disabled list last year (.325 in his last 83 at-bats).

JUNIOR FELIX

Position: CF
Bats: B **Throws:** R
Ht: 5'11" **Wt:** 165

Opening Day Age: 24
Born: 10/3/67 in Laguna Sabada, Dominican Republic
ML Seasons: 3

Overall Statistics

	G	AB	R	H	D	T	HR	RBI	SB	BB	SO	AVG
1991	66	230	32	65	10	2	2	26	7	11	55	.283
Career	303	1108	167	294	47	17	26	137	38	89	255	.265

Where He Hits the Ball

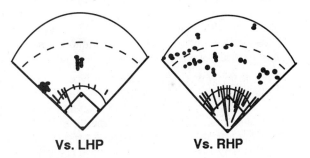

Vs. LHP   **Vs. RHP**

1991 Situational Stats

	AB	H	HR	RBI	AVG		AB	H	HR	RBI	AVG
Home	105	32	2	11	.305	LHP	55	16	0	9	.291
Road	125	33	0	15	.264	RHP	175	49	2	17	.280
Day	53	16	0	13	.302	Sc Pos	58	15	0	23	.259
Night	177	49	2	13	.277	Clutch	27	8	1	2	.296

1991 Rankings (American League)

➡ Did not rank near the top or bottom in any category

PITCHING:

Although Chuck Finley's record (18-9) last season duplicated that of 1990, Finley would probably be the first to admit that his 1991 performance was not nearly as satisfying. Finley's ERA rose almost a run and a half per game and he allowed a career high 23 home runs. While most pitchers would gladly take his numbers, it represented the first season in which Finley failed to progress.

One problem was his control. Finley, who had never walked more than 82 men in a season, allowed 101 free passes in '91. His strikeout total, which had risen every year of his career, also dropped slightly. Lefthanders had a lot more success against Finley than in the past few years. He allowed lefties to hit at a .257 clip against him with a .422 slugging percentage. Prior to last season, Finley had not allowed a home run to a lefty since 1988, but he gave up four last season. Finley also allowed 69 extra base hits, the seventh-highest total in the league.

Even so, Finley remains one of the best pitchers in the game. He is uncanny against right-handed batters (.242 batting average allowed) and a true clutch pitcher. While his strikeout total did dip a little, he was still among the league's top starters in K's per nine innings. He was a very consistent starter, as always, one who gives his team a chance to win in every game.

HOLDING RUNNERS AND FIELDING:

Finley is outstanding at keeping runners close to first base. In 227 innings, he allowed just 15 stolen bases in 29 attempts. His move is deceptive (he balked three times) and he does not have a particularly high leg kick. His fielding remains below average, however.

OVERALL:

Despite the slight regression last year, Finley is in the prime of his career and should continue to be an outstanding hurler. Along with Jim Abbott and Mark Langston, Finley helps comprise the best starting trio in the American League.

CHUCK FINLEY

Position: SP
Bats: L **Throws:** L
Ht: 6' 6" **Wt:** 214

Opening Day Age: 29
Born: 11/26/62 in
Monroe, LA
ML Seasons: 6

Overall Statistics

	W	L	ERA	G	GS	Sv	IP	H	R	BB	SO	HR
1991	18	9	3.80	34	34	0	227.1	205	102	101	171	23
Career	66	50	3.35	186	129	0	994.1	919	409	412	715	77

How Often He Throws Strikes

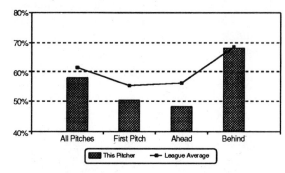

1991 Situational Stats

	W	L	ERA	Sv	IP		AB	H	HR	RBI	AVG
Home	9	3	3.03	0	124.2	LHB	109	28	4	8	.257
Road	9	6	4.73	0	102.2	RHB	730	177	19	80	.242
Day	4	3	4.36	0	43.1	Sc Pos	181	48	5	66	.265
Night	14	6	3.67	0	184.0	Clutch	95	20	3	8	.211

1991 Rankings (American League)

- ➡ 3rd in balks (3) and most pitches thrown per batter (3.99)
- ➡ 4th in wins (18), most walks allowed (101) and runners caught stealing (14)
- ➡ 5th in pitches thrown (3,810)
- ➡ Led the Angels in games started (34), shutouts (2), most walks allowed, hit batsmen (8), pitches thrown, stolen bases allowed (15), most run support per 9 innings (5.4) and strikeouts per 9 innings (6.8)

HITTING:

Gary Gaetti, like Mark Langston in 1990, was a high-priced free agent who was expected to take the Angels to a division title. But just as Langston struggled in '90, Gaetti disappointed people with his overall play in 1991. And of course, the Angels didn't win their division last year, either.

A unique hitter, Gaetti has consistently been worse against lefthanders than against righties over the past few years. While he has always been considered a pull hitter, he shows almost no discretion: whether the pitch is fast, slow, inside or outside, he'll try to pull it. His power is certainly not the threat it once was. Gaetti, who averaged 31 homers a year from 1986 to 1988, has averaged just 18 per season since then.

Gaetti is still an offensive threat, however. Even at his current level, he has more extra base power than most third basemen, and he's still a very effective hitter with men in scoring position.

BASERUNNING:

Though no speed burner, Gaetti is pretty adept on the bases. He is a very hard charger and takes the extra base with some regularity. The days of 10-15 stolen bases are long gone, however, as Gaetti's attempts to steal are now infrequent. He did steal five of ten last year.

FIELDING:

Gaetti's range, especially toward the hole, has slipped over the past few years, and he commits a good number of errors. Nonetheless, he led the league in assists, chances and double plays for third basemen last year. Gaetti might be the outstanding third baseman in the league at starting the 5-4-3 double play, and his reactions are still tremendous.

OVERALL:

Gaetti remains a better-than-average third baseman, but frankly the Angels were expecting a lot more from him than what he delivered in '91. California is now hoping that Gaetti's second season in an Angel uniform is as successful as Langston's was.

GARY GAETTI

Position: 3B
Bats: R **Throws:** R
Ht: 6' 0" **Wt:** 200

Opening Day Age: 33
Born: 8/19/58 in Centralia, IL
ML Seasons: 11

Overall Statistics

	G	AB	R	H	D	T	HR	RBI	SB	BB	SO	AVG
1991	152	586	58	144	22	1	18	66	5	33	104	.246
Career	1513	5575	704	1420	274	26	219	824	79	391	981	.255

Where He Hits the Ball

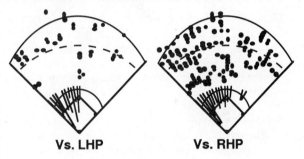

Vs. LHP   Vs. RHP

1991 Situational Stats

	AB	H	HR	RBI	AVG		AB	H	HR	RBI	AVG
Home	280	77	12	31	.275	LHP	159	38	6	26	.239
Road	306	67	6	35	.219	RHP	427	106	12	40	.248
Day	142	43	8	24	.303	Sc Pos	132	38	4	50	.288
Night	444	101	10	42	.227	Clutch	78	14	1	5	.179

1991 Rankings (American League)

- → 2nd in lowest percentage of pitches taken (42.5%)
- → 4th in hit by pitch (8) and lowest on-base percentage vs. right-handed pitchers (.289)
- → 6th lowest on-base percentage (.293)
- → 7th lowest batting average on the road (.219)
- → 10th lowest batting average (.246)
- → Led the Angels in hit by pitch and games (152)
- → Led AL third basemen in hit by pitch

HITTING:

In 1991, reserve outfielder Dave Gallagher enjoyed his best season since he burst onto the major league scene with the Chicago White Sox in 1988. Gallagher's career hit a low point when, over a four-month period in 1990, he was first released by the White Sox and then traded by the Baltimore Orioles. But last year Gallagher provided the Angels with solid backup play in the outfield and displayed an ability to come up with the clutch hit.

Not blessed with much power, Gallagher has learned how to hit to the opposite field effectively. He will also drive the ball up the middle if it is out over the plate. When he does manage an extra base hit, it is often down the opposite field line.

Gallagher will swing with abandon even when behind in the count, especially on high pitches. For a singles hitter, his command of the strike zone is not very good. He is always a threat to bunt and, despite his strikeout total, is competent on the hit-and-run.

BASERUNNING:

Gallagher is the definition of a quick player who is not very fast. He gets around the base paths pretty well and is aggressive taking the extra base. He is not a threat to steal a base, however, as his career stolen base percentage is below fifty percent.

FIELDING:

This remains the strongest aspect of Gallagher's game. He can play all three outfield positions and has great instincts. His arm, frequently challenged, is underrated (eight assists in '91). In just under 700 innings of defensive work, Gallagher did not make an error for the Angels last year.

OVERALL:

Because of his defensive prowess and his occasional offensive ability, Gallagher is an effective reserve outfielder. Injuries forced the Angels into playing him a little more than they would have hoped. But he showed them a lot and should make the trip from Arizona to Anaheim this spring.

DAVE GALLAGHER

Position: CF/RF
Bats: R **Throws:** R
Ht: 6' 0" **Wt:** 184

Opening Day Age: 31
Born: 9/20/60 in Trenton, NJ
ML Seasons: 5

Overall Statistics

	G	AB	R	H	D	T	HR	RBI	SB	BB	SO	AVG
1991	90	270	32	79	17	0	1	30	2	24	43	.293
Career	434	1380	179	380	59	7	7	115	15	108	179	.275

Where He Hits the Ball

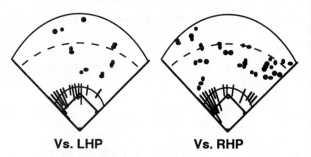

Vs. LHP   Vs. RHP

1991 Situational Stats

	AB	H	HR	RBI	AVG		AB	H	HR	RBI	AVG
Home	126	34	0	10	.270	LHP	110	33	0	9	.300
Road	144	45	1	20	.313	RHP	160	46	1	21	.287
Day	60	18	0	7	.300	Sc Pos	64	21	0	28	.328
Night	210	61	1	23	.290	Clutch	42	12	0	6	.286

1991 Rankings (American League)

→ Did not rank near the top or bottom in any category

PITCHING:

Despite having endured a season in the majors that he would just as soon forget, Joe Grahe may have the inside track on the Angels' number-five spot in the rotation for 1992. It was a long year indeed for Grahe, who lost the spring training battle for the final starting berth to Scott Lewis. Grahe was summoned to Anaheim in June, but failed to record a single out in his first start against Milwaukee (seven batters).

That outing was an indication of one of the troubles that haunted Grahe all year long: his inability to get out of the first inning or two. He was chided by ex-manager Doug Rader for not having enough command of his pitches. When the season ended, Grahe had struck out just seven more batters than he walked.

When Grahe was at the University of Miami, he finished third in the NCAA in strikeouts. Because of that, some Angel fans expected the second-round pick to become a power pitcher. But Grahe typically notches his strikeouts through location, not power. Since becoming a professional, Grahe's success has hinged on getting people out with men on base. At Edmonton he could do that, but in the bigs, his inability to get the key out has been perhaps his biggest problem.

HOLDING RUNNERS AND FIELDING:

Opposing managers run a lot on Grahe -- 14 times in 73 innings last year. Although a respectable five of the 14 were caught, look for this trend to continue. Grahe comes off the mound well and is a competent fielder.

OVERALL:

Grahe pitched better at the end of the season and will certainly get a long look in spring training. With Kirk McCaskill not expected to be back, Grahe and Mike Fetters could be the only right-handed starters returning next year. That fact works heavily in Grahe's favor as the 1992 season begins.

JOE GRAHE

Position: SP/RP
Bats: R **Throws:** R
Ht: 6' 0" **Wt:** 200

Opening Day Age: 24
Born: 8/14/67 in West Palm Beach, FL
ML Seasons: 2

Overall Statistics

	W	L	ERA	G	GS	Sv	IP	H	R	BB	SO	HR
1991	3	7	4.81	18	10	0	73.0	84	43	33	40	2
Career	6	11	4.87	26	18	0	116.1	135	73	56	65	5

How Often He Throws Strikes

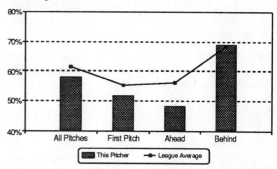

1991 Situational Stats

	W	L	ERA	Sv	IP		AB	H	HR	RBI	AVG
Home	1	3	3.53	0	43.1	LHB	143	43	1	20	.301
Road	2	4	6.67	0	29.2	RHB	149	41	1	21	.275
Day	1	1	3.38	0	18.2	Sc Pos	85	28	0	35	.329
Night	2	6	5.30	0	54.1	Clutch	25	6	1	2	.240

1991 Rankings (American League)

→ Did not rank near the top or bottom in any category

STOPPER

BRYAN HARVEY

Position: RP
Bats: R **Throws:** R
Ht: 6' 2" **Wt:** 219

Opening Day Age: 28
Born: 6/2/63 in
Chattanooga, TN
ML Seasons: 5

PITCHING:

Bryan Harvey gave the Angels their fourth Cy Young candidate last year (along with Jim Abbott, Mark Langston and Chuck Finley). There was simply no better reliever in the game than Harvey last year. Although he seemed to go unnoticed during much of the '91 season, Harvey's numbers deserve a closer look.

No American League pitcher struck out more batters per nine innings than Harvey (his 11.6 mark was bettered only by Cincinnati's Rob Dibble). His 46 saves were also the best in the AL (Lee Smith of St. Louis led the majors with 47). Harvey allowed ten less baserunners than innings pitched and just a .266 slugging percentage. He was particularly fearsome against righthanders, who hit him for just a .172 average and only three extra base hits in 122 at-bats.

Harvey's most effective pitch is a split-fingered fastball which explodes against right-handed batters. Against lefthanders Harvey will occasionally mix in a breaking pitch. In the past Harvey has had a problem with an occasional bout of wildness. But last season he walked just 17 batters, which resulted in an astounding strikeout-to-walk ratio of almost 6-1. Harvey did have intermittent problems surrendering the long ball (six in 78 innings), but rarely was anyone on base when the ball left the park.

HOLDING RUNNERS AND FIELDING:

Although it's doubtful that anyone will mess with Harvey's delivery at this point, allowing stolen bases is his greatest flaw. He permitted 12 (in 12 attempts) over 78 innings last year -- an amazing total considering how few runners even made it to first.

OVERALL:

Anyone who can notch 46 saves for a last place team has to be considered a force. If the Angels' offense ever improves and the team makes a run at the title, Harvey could launch his own assault on the American League record book for relievers.

Overall Statistics

	W	L	ERA	G	GS	Sv	IP	H	R	BB	SO	HR
1991	2	4	1.60	67	0	46	78.2	51	20	17	101	6
Career	16	16	2.45	225	0	113	279.0	197	87	115	331	20

How Often He Throws Strikes

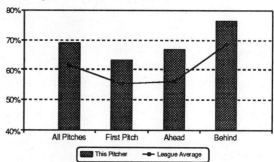

1991 Situational Stats

	W	L	ERA	Sv	IP		AB	H	HR	RBI	AVG
Home	2	2	2.06	22	39.1	LHB	164	30	4	14	.183
Road	0	2	1.14	24	39.1	RHB	122	21	2	11	.172
Day	0	0	0.79	11	22.2	Sc Pos	90	13	2	20	.144
Night	2	4	1.93	35	56.0	Clutch	214	40	4	23	.187

1991 Rankings (American League)

- ⟶ 1st in saves (46), games finished (63), save opportunities (52), relief ERA (1.60), lowest batting average allowed in relief (.178) and strikeouts per 9 innings in relief (11.6)
- ⟶ 2nd in save percentage (88.5%)
- ⟶ 3rd lowest batting average allowed vs. left-handed batters (.183)
- ⟶ 9th in blown saves (6)
- ⟶ 10th in games (67)
- ⟶ Led the Angels in saves, games finished, save opportunities, save percentage, blown saves and batting average allowed vs. left-handed batters

HITTING:

Wally Joyner reverted back to his old form in 1991, and then some, as he hit for a career-high .301 average and reached his highest home run total since 1987. After missing half the 1990 season with a stress fracture in his knee, Joyner also managed to elude significant injury last year, playing in 143 games.

Joyner remains one of the classiest hitters in the American League. On any given pitch he can do almost anything with the bat. He typically goes the other way against right-handed pitchers, and especially against lefthanders, but is very capable of pulling the ball hard. His power is to the alleys and his homers are almost always to right field. He is a contact hitter who can be put almost anywhere in the lineup except the number one spot. Joyner also managed to draw 52 walks last year.

Many felt that Joyner might not ever hit the 20 home run mark again after his 34 homer season of 1987, the homer season. But Joyner went on a power surge in mid-season and, although he tailed off at the end of the year, still ended up with 21 homers for the year.

BASERUNNING:

Thanks to several leg injuries, including one knee operation, Joyner no longer runs well. Once good for 5-8 steals a year, he now almost never attempts a steal. He is competent on the base paths, but pretty much station-to-station at this point.

FIELDING:

Joyner's fielding has taken a slight downturn in recent years. His range toward the line is not very good and he has an erratic arm. Overall he is no slouch, but his defense is no longer among the league's best.

OVERALL:

When Mike Port was general manager, the Angels and Joyner had several bitter salary negotiations and many people expect free agent Joyner to leave this winter. With Whitey Herzog now in charge, however, the Angels are expected to make a major effort to re-sign Joyner.

WALLY JOYNER

Position: 1B
Bats: L **Throws:** L
Ht: 6' 2" **Wt:** 203

Opening Day Age: 29
Born: 6/16/62 in Atlanta, GA
ML Seasons: 6

Overall Statistics

	G	AB	R	H	D	T	HR	RBI	SB	BB	SO	AVG
1991	143	551	79	166	34	3	21	96	2	52	66	.301
Career	846	3208	455	925	170	11	114	518	28	323	331	.288

Where He Hits the Ball

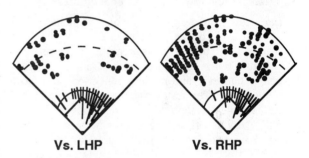

Vs. LHP   Vs. RHP

1991 Situational Stats

	AB	H	HR	RBI	AVG		AB	H	HR	RBI	AVG
Home	268	74	10	39	.276	LHP	189	52	5	28	.275
Road	283	92	11	57	.325	RHP	362	114	16	68	.315
Day	140	40	6	16	.286	Sc Pos	139	46	5	73	.331
Night	411	126	15	80	.307	Clutch	69	21	3	14	.304

1991 Rankings (American League)

➡ 5th in highest batting average with the bases loaded (.500) and highest batting average on the road (.325)

➡ 8th highest batting average with runners in scoring position (.331) and highest slugging percentage vs. right-handed pitchers (.511)

➡ Led the Angels in batting average (.301), doubles (34), total bases (269), RBIs (96), slugging percentage (.488), on-base average (.360), slugging percentage vs. right-handed pitchers, on-base percentage vs. right-handed pitchers (.384), batting average at home (.276) and highest percentage of swings put into play (48.0%)

PITCHING:

It has been widely perceived that Mark Langston's 1991 comeback was one of the league's best. A closer look suggests that, while Langston was certainly a better pitcher last season, his perceived "bad year" in 1990 wasn't all that bad. Langston won five of his last seven starts that season.

Whatever the case, Langston proved to his many critics (most notably ex-manager Dick Williams) that his "heart" should no longer be questioned. His disappointing first season with the Angels put enormous pressure on him as spring training began last March. He responded to the challenge and led the Angels in wins, winning percentage, strikeouts and fewest hits per nine innings.

Langston is the definition of a power pitcher. His fastball was noticeably more effective last year than in 1990; however, his breaking stuff was the real difference. Langston spotted his curveball better than ever and made a concerted effort to work inside. The result was that he dropped his walks per nine innings by almost one (4.20 to 3.51). A side effect was a huge increase in his home runs allowed. Langston gave up 30 home runs in 1991, the second highest total in his career (29 of the 30 were hit by righthanders!). But thanks to his improvement in the walk category, many of those homers did not hurt him.

HOLDING RUNNERS AND FIELDING:

Langston allowed only 10 steals in 25 attempts last year. This was the sixth-best rate in the American League. Langston's excellence in the field has earned him two Gold Gloves and he remains among the best fielding pitchers in the league.

OVERALL:

Mark Langston is just another one of the Angels' left-handed starters. On any other team that statement might not be much of a compliment, although it is high praise for Langston to be mentioned among Messrs. Finley and Abbott. Langston has the ability to make 1992 every bit as good as 1991.

MARK LANGSTON

Position: SP
Bats: R **Throws:** L
Ht: 6' 2" **Wt:** 184

Opening Day Age: 31
Born: 8/20/60 in San Diego, CA
ML Seasons: 8

Overall Statistics

	W	L	ERA	G	GS	Sv	IP	H	R	BB	SO	HR
1991	19	8	3.00	34	34	0	246.1	190	89	96	183	30
Career	115	101	3.76	267	264	0	1843.2	1611	862	868	1631	189

How Often He Throws Strikes

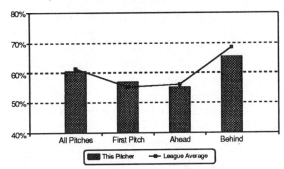

1991 Situational Stats

	W	L	ERA	Sv	IP		AB	H	HR	RBI	AVG
Home	9	3	3.33	0	127.0	LHB	129	28	1	7	.217
Road	10	5	2.64	0	119.1	RHB	755	162	29	75	.215
Day	3	3	3.51	0	66.2	Sc Pos	150	34	8	54	.227
Night	16	5	2.81	0	179.2	Clutch	98	22	3	5	.224

1991 Rankings (American League)

→ 2nd in most home runs allowed (30) and most home runs allowed per 9 innings (1.10)

→ 3rd in wins (19), most runners caught stealing (15), winning percentage (.704), lowest batting average allowed (.215), lowest ground-ball/flyball ratio allowed (.77) and ERA on the road (2.64)

→ 4th in innings pitched (246.1)

→ Led the Angels in wins, games started (34), complete games (7), innings pitched, home runs allowed, strikeouts, runners caught stealing, winning percentage, lowest batting average allowed, lowest on-base average allowed (.292) and lowest stolen base percentage allowed (40.0%)

PITCHING:

Kirk McCaskill was a much different pitcher in 1991 than he was in 1990, or for that matter his entire career. There was plenty of reason to believe that his steep decline was due to off-season bone chip surgery on his right elbow. There is no truth to the rumor that McCaskill has scheduled surgery to put the bone chips back in.

Whatever the reason for the decline, the Angels were concerned. McCaskill got pounded with regularity in '91, allowing too many hits and walks while striking out almost nobody (teammate Bryan Harvey struck out 30 more men in 100 less innings). Over the past few seasons, McCaskill's strikeout-to-walk ratio has deteriorated to the point that some observers believe his days in the majors are numbered.

McCaskill's fastball was dead all year long in '91. His outings depended on the success of his breaking pitches (he throws both a slider and a curve) and his change-up. Neither of the breaking pitches were consistently effective and the change-up was ineffective without a fastball to set it up. Lefthanders had a field day against McCaskill, nailing him for numbers that look like those of an offensive MVP (.313 BA, .355 OBP and .467 SLG).

HOLDING RUNNERS AND FIELDING:

A great athlete who was once an excellent National Hockey League prospect, McCaskill remains very effective in both holding runners and fielding. Although his stolen base percentage increased slightly, his move is one of the best in the league among righthanders. He is an exceptional fielder who makes good decisions on defense.

OVERALL:

The Angels turned down deal after deal for McCaskill, believing that they could never have enough pitching. Now he's a free agent who can leave on his own. It is believed that GM Whitey Herzog would like to re-sign McCaskill, but for less than the $2.1 million that he makes now. The marketplace will probably determine where McCaskill is pitching in 1992.

KIRK McCASKILL

Position: SP
Bats: R **Throws:** R
Ht: 6' 1" **Wt:** 205

Opening Day Age: 31
Born: 4/9/61 in Kapuskasing, Ontario
ML Seasons: 7

Overall Statistics

	W	L	ERA	G	GS	Sv	IP	H	R	BB	SO	HR
1991	10	19	4.26	30	30	0	177.2	193	93	66	71	19
Career	78	74	3.86	192	189	0	1221.0	1191	576	448	714	109

How Often He Throws Strikes

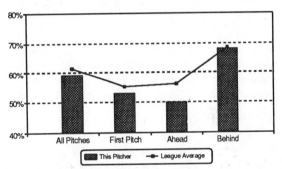

1991 Situational Stats

	W	L	ERA	Sv	IP		AB	H	HR	RBI	AVG
Home	4	10	4.08	0	92.2	LHB	351	110	11	50	.313
Road	6	9	4.45	0	85.0	RHB	330	83	8	33	.252
Day	2	2	2.28	0	27.2	Sc Pos	157	42	5	63	.268
Night	8	17	4.62	0	150.0	Clutch	35	7	2	4	.200

1991 Rankings (American League)

➡ 1st in losses (19) and least run support per 9 innings (3.1)

➡ 3rd in lowest winning percentage (.345), lowest strikeout/walk ratio (1.1), highest slugging percentage allowed (.435) and least strikeouts per 9 innings (3.6)

➡ 4th most GDPs induced per 9 innings (1.1)

➡ 5th in most GDPs induced (22), highest batting average allowed (.283) and highest on-base percentage allowed (.347)

➡ 7th in worst ERA (4.26) and most home runs allowed per 9 innings (.96)

➡ Led the Angels in losses, GDPs induced and most GDPs induced per 9 innings

HITTING:

The now-he's-finished now-he's-not history of Lance Parrish took a turn for the ugly in 1991. Parrish's average dropped 50 points from 1990 and was forty points lower than his career mark. Was this the end or just another dip in the road?

One encouraging sign was Parrish's power numbers, which per at-bat weren't down much from 1990. He has struggled against righthanders for several years, and may be nearing the part of his career where he will be platooned. He uncharacteristically struggled against lefties in '91 as well. Parrish belted just three of his 19 homers against southpaws and hit them at a mere .219 clip.

Parrish will go the other way, but his power is still to left field. Pitchers consistently keep the ball away and challenge him to dink a single to right instead of allowing him to hurt them with the long ball. Parrish comes to the plate to swing: his 35 walks were near a career low. His .285 on-base percentage was particularly glaring on a team which finished 13th in the league in that category.

BASERUNNING:

Parrish almost never takes the extra base and is not a threat to steal. It is doubtful that these conditions will change throughout the rest of his career.

FIELDING:

Parrish is very popular with the Angels' pitchers, and is very good at handling them. He will most likely keep a spot on someone's roster long after his effectiveness at the plate leaves him because of this skill. Parrish also retains his strong arm, finishing the year best in stolen base percentage allowed last year.

OVERALL:

The Angels have been high on prospect John Orton, but Orton hasn't hit, so Parrish's role looks to be very secure. Even in a frustrating season, Parrish drove in 51 runs and provided good defense. Still, he has just one year left on his contract and needs to have a good year in 1992 to continue his career with California.

LANCE PARRISH

Position: C
Bats: R **Throws:** R
Ht: 6' 3" **Wt:** 224

Opening Day Age: 35
Born: 6/15/56 in Clairton, PA
ML Seasons: 15

Overall Statistics

	G	AB	R	H	D	T	HR	RBI	SB	BB	SO	AVG
1991	119	402	38	87	12	0	19	51	0	35	117	.216
Career	1775	6468	803	1644	277	26	304	998	25	551	1372	.254

Where He Hits the Ball

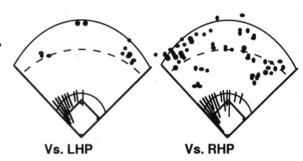

Vs. LHP   **Vs. RHP**

1991 Situational Stats

	AB	H	HR	RBI	AVG		AB	H	HR	RBI	AVG
Home	216	49	9	24	.227	LHP	105	23	3	10	.219
Road	186	38	10	27	.204	RHP	297	64	16	41	.215
Day	82	22	4	11	.268	Sc Pos	96	24	3	30	.250
Night	320	65	15	40	.203	Clutch	57	6	1	4	.105

1991 Rankings (American League)

- ➞ 1st in lowest batting average in the clutch (.105)
- ➞ 3rd lowest percentage of extra bases taken as a runner (20.0%)
- ➞ 5th highest percentage of swings that missed (29.8%)
- ➞ Led the Angels in strikeouts (117) and percentage of pitches taken (56.4%)
- ➞ Led AL catchers in highest percentage of runners caught stealing (42.4%) and fielding percentage (.997)

HITTING:

Luis Polonia picked up in 1991 right where he left off in '90. Polonia has provided the Angels with consistency in the leadoff spot and has turned into an offensive force.

Though he plays every day, Polonia has the stats of a platoon player. Last year he batted .238 against southpaws and .319 against righties. He doesn't possess much home run power, but did manage 38 extra base hits and is always a threat to put the ball in the gap.

An interesting development in Polonia's career was last season's dramatic increase in both walks and strikeouts. Polonia nearly doubled his previous career high in walks with 52 in what appeared to be a concerted effort to be more patient at the plate. However, he didn't seem to gain any better knowledge of the strike zone as he struck out 74 times, also a career high. Polonia led the league in batting on turf (.383), proof of what he can do when he puts the bat on the ball. If he cuts down on the K's, he could win a batting crown.

BASERUNNING:

One of the Angels' most exciting players, Polonia sometimes gets himself into trouble on the base paths. His judgement has historically been bad, but seemed to improve somewhat in '91. Not enough, however, as Polonia led the league in times caught stealing.

FIELDING:

Polonia appears on highlight films from time to time, but usually because of his gaffes rather than his successes. He has made some progress in the field, but his range is poor for someone with his speed and he often fails to cut off balls in the gap. Opposing teams often take advantage of Polonia's weak arm.

OVERALL:

Despite his faults, the Angels are happy with Polonia. His improved patience has made him a very solid leadoff man. He is also one of the few Angels with any speed. He may be asked to play DH in 1992 (something he hates), but he will be in the lineup.

LUIS POLONIA

Position: LF
Bats: L **Throws:** L
Ht: 5' 8" **Wt:** 150

Opening Day Age: 27
Born: 10/12/64 in Santiago City, Dominican Republic
ML Seasons: 5

Overall Statistics

	G	AB	R	H	D	T	HR	RBI	SB	BB	SO	AVG
1991	150	604	92	179	28	8	2	50	48	52	74	.296
Career	604	2163	343	653	79	37	13	207	144	155	265	.302

Where He Hits the Ball

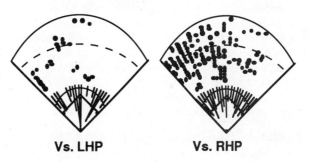

Vs. LHP   **Vs. RHP**

1991 Situational Stats

	AB	H	HR	RBI	AVG		AB	H	HR	RBI	AVG
Home	303	79	1	20	.261	LHP	168	40	0	17	.238
Road	301	100	1	30	.332	RHP	436	139	2	33	.319
Day	148	49	0	16	.331	Sc Pos	132	44	0	44	.333
Night	456	130	2	34	.285	Clutch	77	23	0	1	.299

1991 Rankings (American League)

→ 1st in most times caught stealing (23) and highest batting average on a 3-1 count (1.000)

→ 2nd highest percentage of extra bases taken as a runner (80.4%)

→ 3rd in highest batting average with 2 strikes (.291) and steals of third (17)

→ Led the Angels in at bats (604), runs (92), hits (179), singles, triples (8), stolen bases (48), caught stealing, times on base (232), pitches seen (2,462), plate appearances (662), runs scored per time reached base (39.6%) and batting average with runners in scoring position (.333)

PITCHING:

Now with his third team in four years, Jeff Robinson has seen his share of ups and downs. Optimistic after being signed in the off-season as a free agent, Robinson ran out of chances with the Angels after his frustrating 1991 campaign.

Robinson has good stuff: he throws a hard split-finger fastball and from time to time brings a big curveball to the mound in addition to a straight fastball. His inconsistency with the curveball gets him into a lot of trouble, however, and too often his pitches ended up hitting plastic seats rather than leather gloves. Opponents slugged .444 against Robinson, which included a frightening nine homers in 57 innings.

Robinson's split-finger is effective against righthanders, but lefties gave him a lot of trouble in '91. Despite his problems with the long ball, Robinson stranded 76% of the runners he inherited. Robinson has been used as a short man and as a starter from time to time in his career. Although his stuff is occasionally good enough to close games, his role will probably be to face several right-handed batters in middle relief.

HOLDING RUNNERS AND FIELDING:

Robinson's delivery to the plate is relatively slow, and he has been run on with moderate success in the past. The best chance runners have to advance against Robinson is via the wild pitch (he uncorked 10 in 57 innings last year). His move is below average and he has thrown a pickoff attempt into right field a time or two. Robinson's fielding is similarly hurt by erratic throwing, although he gets off the mound well.

OVERALL:

New General Manager Whitey Herzog stated his concern about the Angels' lack of depth in the bullpen, a comment that applied to Robinson, as the Angels decided not to pick up his option for 1992. Robinson's arm and recent history is good enough to warrant him a place on a roster somewhere, but it will not be in California after last year's disappointing season.

JEFF ROBINSON

Position: RP
Bats: R **Throws:** R
Ht: 6' 4" **Wt:** 200

Opening Day Age: 31
Born: 12/13/60 in Santa Ana, CA
ML Seasons: 8

Overall Statistics

	W	L	ERA	G	GS	Sv	IP	H	R	BB	SO	HR
1991	0	3	5.37	39	0	3	57.0	56	34	29	57	9
Career	42	54	3.87	405	57	38	823.1	804	404	309	583	70

How Often He Throws Strikes

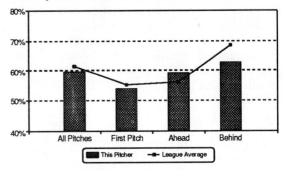

1991 Situational Stats

	W	L	ERA	Sv	IP		AB	H	HR	RBI	AVG
Home	0	1	2.30	1	31.1	LHB	98	27	4	16	.276
Road	0	2	9.12	2	25.2	RHB	118	29	5	17	.246
Day	0	0	7.63	1	15.1	Sc Pos	66	16	3	24	.242
Night	0	3	4.54	2	41.2	Clutch	68	15	1	8	.221

1991 Rankings (American League)

- 2nd worst relief ERA (5.37)
- 6th most strikeouts per 9 innings, relief pitchers (9.0)
- 8th lowest percentage of inherited runners scored (24.3%)
- 9th in wild pitches (10)
- Led the Angels in lowest percentage of inherited runners scored and wild pitches

HITTING:

Dick Schofield's career has undergone a meta-morphosis since his watershed year of 1986. Back then, Schofield was not only a defensive whiz but also a power hitting threat with good speed on the bases. The 1991 version of Schofield saw him suffer a decline in almost every aspect of his game.

Schofield's difficulties started with lefthanders last year. The righty-hitting Schofield batted just .183 (with one extra base hit) against southpaws last year, worst in the league in that category. While he increased his average to .240 against righties, his power numbers fell off the board against both sides. In 427 at-bats Schofield had just 12 extra base hits and, for the first time in his career, failed to hit a home run.

After returning from injury in '90, Schofield began developing more patience at the plate along with an ability to go the other way. He continued both of those traits in '91, but often lapsed into long bouts of trying to swing for the fences.

BASERUNNING:

Schofield stole eight of 12 bases last season, but is no longer a possibility to steal 20 as he used to be. One of the fastest righthanders out of the box in the league, Schofield remains a very difficult batter to double up, grounding into a double play only three times in 427 at-bats.

FIELDING:

One item of encouragement for the Angels was that Schofield's 1990 fielding slump ended in '91. While nobody was mentioning Gold Glove and Schofield in the same sentence, he is a solid shortstop without any particular weakness. He has twice led the AL in fielding percentage and might do so again before he's through.

OVERALL:

GM Whitey Herzog has let it be known that re-signing free agent Schofield is one of his top priorities. While it's true that good shortstops are hard to find (and Schofield is adequate), the underlying reason for the Angels' desperation is that they have nobody to replace Schofield. Still, nothing is certain for Schofield in 1992.

DICK SCHOFIELD

Position: SS
Bats: R **Throws:** R
Ht: 5'10" **Wt:** 179

Opening Day Age: 29
Born: 11/21/62 in Springfield, IL
ML Seasons: 9

Overall Statistics

	G	AB	R	H	D	T	HR	RBI	SB	BB	SO	AVG
1991	134	427	44	96	9	3	0	31	8	50	69	.225
Career	1060	3395	400	788	104	27	48	278	98	329	509	.232

Where He Hits the Ball

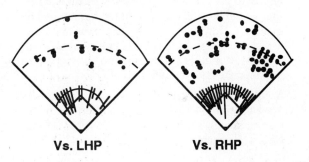

Vs. LHP   Vs. RHP

1991 Situational Stats

	AB	H	HR	RBI	AVG		AB	H	HR	RBI	AVG
Home	211	44	0	19	.209	LHP	115	21	0	8	.183
Road	216	52	0	12	.241	RHP	312	75	0	23	.240
Day	98	22	0	10	.224	Sc Pos	110	28	0	31	.255
Night	329	74	0	21	.225	Clutch	65	13	0	3	.200

1991 Rankings (American League)

→ 1st in lowest batting average vs. left-handed pitchers (.183) and lowest slugging percentage vs. left-handed pitchers (.191)
→ 4th in least GDPs per GDP situation (3.6%)
→ Led the Angels in least GDPs per GDP situation
→ Led AL shortstops in least GDPs per GDP situation and steals of third (2)

HITTING:

After two years in AAA in the Toronto organization, Luis Sojo knew he would eventually have to beat out Manuel Lee for the Blue Jays' starting second base position. Imagine Sojo's surprise when he was dealt to the Angels and was subsequently handed a starting job. After one year with California, the jury is still out on Sojo's offensive skills.

Sojo's minor league numbers seem to indicate that he would develop into a contact-style singles hitter. While there is a feeling that Sojo will eventually develop his doubles power and possibly have 8-12 home run potential in him, he did not display that potential in '91. He did show a great ability to put the ball in play with a strikeout rate that would have placed him in the top ten had he qualified. However, his slugging percentage was a disappointing .327, and he rarely hit the ball hard. Most of Sojo's success came when going to the opposite field and with infield hits.

Sojo's greatest offensive contribution comes via the bunt and the hit-and-run. Sojo led the AL in sacrifices with 19, and displays an aptitude in that area rarely seen anymore in baseball.

BASERUNNING:

Sojo is pretty fast once he gets going, but is not much of a base stealer. Once he feels comfortable in the league, he has the potential to steal 10-15 bases. All in all, speed is not a major factor in Sojo's game.

FIELDING:

A converted shortstop, Sojo's fielding was very solid in 1991. His instincts and reactions are very good at second base. He is very smooth afield and turns the double play nicely for having recently moved to second. His defense is good enough by itself to keep him in the majors awhile.

OVERALL:

Despite some glaring offensive problems, Sojo will almost certainly open the season at second for the Angels. His bunting and hit-and-run skills fit in perfectly with Buck Rodgers' scheme for the '92 Angels.

LUIS SOJO

Position: 2B
Bats: R **Throws:** R
Ht: 5'11" **Wt:** 175

Opening Day Age: 26
Born: 1/3/66 in Barquisimeto, Venezuela
ML Seasons: 2

Overall Statistics

	G	AB	R	H	D	T	HR	RBI	SB	BB	SO	AVG
1991	113	364	38	94	14	1	3	20	4	14	26	.258
Career	146	444	52	112	17	1	4	29	5	19	31	.252

Where He Hits the Ball

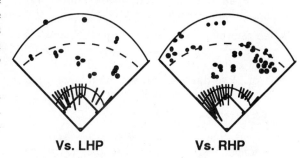

Vs. LHP   **Vs. RHP**

1991 Situational Stats

	AB	H	HR	RBI	AVG		AB	H	HR	RBI	AVG
Home	176	42	1	6	.239	LHP	114	34	0	5	.298
Road	188	52	2	14	.277	RHP	250	60	3	15	.240
Day	67	18	1	5	.269	Sc Pos	102	23	0	16	.225
Night	297	76	2	15	.256	Clutch	44	14	0	1	.318

1991 Rankings (American League)

→ 1st in sacrifice bunts (19)
→ 2nd in bunts in play (43)
→ 9th most GDPS per GDP situation (17.6%)
→ Led the Angels in sacrifice bunts, batting average in the clutch (.318) and bunts in play
→ Led AL second basemen in sacrifice bunts, hit by pitch (5) and bunts in play

HITTING:

Lee Stevens was a late Angel call-up in 1991 after spending almost all of his season at AAA Edmonton. This must have been a disappointment to the 24 year old who turned some heads with impressive minor league statistics and seven homers in 248 at-bats with the Angels in 1990.

Stevens had another solid year at Edmonton, batting .314 with 19 homers and 96 RBI. In very limited time with the Angels, Stevens hit the ball hard and for a good average, but continued to have problems making contact. When Stevens spent significant time with the Angels in 1990 he had some early success, but when pitchers started getting the book on him, Stevens had a terrible time laying the bat on the ball.

Stevens is a big man who will almost certainly hit with power in the majors. His swing is long and sweet, but susceptible to the inside pitch. He has also displayed a problem with the breaking ball (albeit with some noticeable improvement in '91).

BASERUNNING:

As a baserunner, Stevens has shown little proficiency in either stealing bases or taking the extra base. Although he has had very little time to display his ability in this area, Rickey Henderson won't be losing any sleep.

FIELDING:

Stevens has played both right field and first base. As a right fielder, he has limited range, but is pretty solid once he gets to the ball and possesses a decent arm. At first base, Stevens looks uncomfortable. He has made several errors in limited opportunities in the majors while playing first.

OVERALL:

As a heralded young prospect, Stevens is an insurance policy against the loss of Dave Winfield and the potential loss of Wally Joyner. He leaves California with a dilemma as a player who clearly has outgrown AAA, but hasn't shown a consistent ability to hit major league pitching. Is there a AAAA?

LEE STEVENS

Position: 1B
Bats: L **Throws:** L
Ht: 6' 4" **Wt:** 219

Opening Day Age: 24
Born: 7/10/67 in Kansas City, MO
ML Seasons: 2

Overall Statistics

	G	AB	R	H	D	T	HR	RBI	SB	BB	SO	AVG
1991	18	58	8	17	7	0	0	9	1	6	12	.293
Career	85	306	36	70	17	0	7	41	2	28	87	.229

Where He Hits the Ball

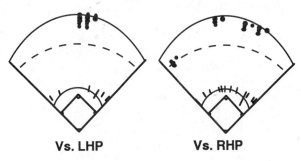

Vs. LHP   Vs. RHP

1991 Situational Stats

	AB	H	HR	RBI	AVG		AB	H	HR	RBI	AVG
Home	33	11	0	8	.333	LHP	17	5	0	5	.294
Road	25	6	0	1	.240	RHP	41	12	0	4	.293
Day	7	0	0	1	.000	Sc Pos	14	3	0	7	.214
Night	51	17	0	8	.333	Clutch	7	0	0	0	.000

1991 Rankings (American League)

→ Did not rank near the top or bottom in any category

HITTING:

Dave Winfield could have made things easier on the Angels if he would have made a modest contribution and then bowed out in a respectful way. Winfield messed up this simple plan by playing some of his best baseball in several seasons, and probably extended his career in the process.

Winfield had an excellent season in 1991, recording his first career three home run game and his first "cycle" performance. He led the team in homers with 28 and ended up with a respectable .262 average and 86 RBI. To state that those numbers represent a decrease from his pre-back surgery days is more of a testament to the man's career than a reflection of his play last season.

Winfield's bat seems to get slower every year and most pitchers work him consistently outside and then try to nail him with the fastball high and tight. Frequently he couldn't get around on it -- Winfield struck out a career-high 109 times last year. As has been his career-long pattern, Winfield provided clutch hitting, batting 10 points higher with runners in scoring position and two outs. Against lefthanders he is still as fearsome as ever, batting .300 against them last season.

BASERUNNING:

Winfield is such a big man that it takes him a while to get going, as evidenced by his 21 double plays. His overall speed is still good, and he even managed to steal seven of nine a year ago. He is still a fearsome sight breaking up the double play.

FIELDING:

Both Winfield's range and arm have begun to disappear, and his remaining days are probably as a designated hitter, a move he is fighting fiercely.

OVERALL:

The Angels had a $3 million option on Winfield for 1992, but chose instead to buy out his contract for less than half a million. They loved his leadership and clutch hitting ability, but were willing to let him test the open market. If Winfield doesn't come back, California will miss his presence -- and his offense.

DAVE WINFIELD

Position: RF/DH
Bats: R **Throws:** R
Ht: 6' 6" **Wt:** 246

Opening Day Age: 40
Born: 10/3/51 in St. Paul, MN
ML Seasons: 18

Overall Statistics

	G	AB	R	H	D	T	HR	RBI	SB	BB	SO	AVG
1991	150	568	75	149	27	4	28	86	7	56	109	.262
Career	2551	9464	1459	2697	460	80	406	1602	216	1044	1414	.285

Where He Hits the Ball

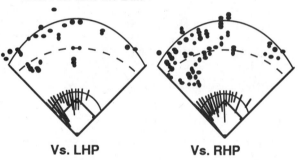

Vs. LHP   Vs. RHP

1991 Situational Stats

	AB	H	HR	RBI	AVG		AB	H	HR	RBI	AVG
Home	271	66	13	33	.244	LHP	160	48	11	27	.300
Road	297	83	15	53	.279	RHP	408	101	17	59	.248
Day	123	32	6	25	.260	Sc Pos	138	38	4	54	.275
Night	445	117	22	61	.263	Clutch	74	16	3	7	.216

1991 Rankings (American League)

➡ 6th in GDPs (21)

➡ 9th in home runs (28) and lowest on-base percentage vs. right-handed pitchers (.304)

➡ 10th in slugging percentage vs. left-handed pitchers (.575)

➡ Led the Angels in home runs, sacrifice flies (6), walks (56), GDPs, HR frequency (20.3 ABs per HR), most pitches seen per plate appearance (3.82), batting average vs. left-handed pitchers (.300) and batting average on an 0-2 count (.281)

➡ Led AL right fielders in GDPs (21), fielding percentage (.990) and groundball/flyball ratio (1.43)

SHAWN ABNER

Position: CF
Bats: R **Throws:** R
Ht: 6' 1" **Wt:** 194

Opening Day Age: 25
Born: 6/17/66 in
Hamilton, OH
ML Seasons: 5

Overall Statistics

	G	AB	R	H	D	T	HR	RBI	SB	BB	SO	AVG
1991	94	216	27	42	10	2	3	14	1	11	43	.194
Career	295	632	68	133	29	3	10	55	5	31	118	.210

HITTING, FIELDING, BASERUNNING:

Shawn Abner would certainly love to read a story without reference to his selection as the first pick in the 1984 draft by the Mets -- or his subsequent trades to the Padres and Angels. Over seven years, Abner's label has switched from "sure thing" to "role player," and as the latter Abner performed adequately for the Angels last year. He does not have a particular offensive strength; he doesn't hit for a high average, for power, or walk much. In the NL Abner saw a constant diet of breaking balls; in the AL he saw fewer but still had a lot of trouble with them. He figures to see more this year. Abner is an above-average defensive player with good range and a fair arm. His baserunning, which could be a strength with his speed, is less than remarkable.

OVERALL:

Abner commented at the end of the year that he might not be back with the Angels in '92 because of the team's overabundance of outfielders. However, Abner did not come cheaply (traded for Jack Howell) and it would not be surprising to see him make the 25-man squad at the end of spring training.

MIKE FETTERS

Position: RP/SP
Bats: R **Throws:** R
Ht: 6' 4" **Wt:** 212

Opening Day Age: 27
Born: 12/19/64 in Van Nuys, CA
ML Seasons: 3

Overall Statistics

	W	L	ERA	G	GS	Sv	IP	H	R	BB	SO	HR
1991	2	5	4.84	19	4	0	44.2	53	29	28	24	4
Career	3	6	4.51	46	6	1	115.2	135	66	49	63	14

PITCHING, FIELDING & HOLDING RUNNERS:

The career of Mike Fetters has not taken off like the Angels would have liked. A first round draft pick in 1986, Fetters has been in the majors for the better part of two years and has yet to show the potential that the club first envisioned.

Last year the Angels primarily used Fetters as a middle reliever, but he is capable of starting in a pinch. He has had periodic control problems which returned substantially in '91. His strikeout numbers have been steadily decreasing since leading the PCL in that category in 1989. Because he is very slow to the plate, holding runners on base remains a serious problem for Fetters, as does the wild pitch.

OVERALL:

Middle relief pitching is a very weak spot for the Angels, and Fetters has not done a lot to solidify it. In all fairness, he has not pitched a lot in the majors yet and may make a stronger impression given the opportunity. It is likely that his next chance will come with another team.

JOHN ORTON

Position: C
Bats: R **Throws:** R
Ht: 6' 1" **Wt:** 192

Opening Day Age: 26
Born: 12/8/65 in Santa Cruz, CA
ML Seasons: 3

Overall Statistics

	G	AB	R	H	D	T	HR	RBI	SB	BB	SO	AVG
1991	29	69	7	14	4	0	0	3	0	10	17	.203
Career	76	192	19	37	10	0	1	13	0	17	65	.193

HITTING, FIELDING, BASERUNNING:

The Angels are waiting patiently for John Orton to develop. Orton has made it to the majors on the force of a strong arm and an ability to call a good game behind the plate. Now, with the decline of Lance Parrish fairly imminent, the team wants Orton to hit.

After parts of three years in the majors, Orton has had just 192 at-bats and has a career average below .200. He has only moderate power with a fairly long swing that often fails to make contact. While he has struggled offensively, Orton had some success against lefties last year (.316, 6-for-19). He might be a candidate for a platoon spot except that Parrish, the man ahead of him, is also a right-handed hitter. On the bases Orton is pretty adept for a catcher (he once stole six bases in the minors).

OVERALL:

Under Mike Port the Angels were reluctant to keep Orton on the big league roster because they feared his development would be hindered if he did not play every day. That would offer some explanation for Orton's rough adjustment to the big leagues, and may indicate that Orton is ready for a breakthrough year in 1992.

BOBBY ROSE

Position: 2B
Bats: R **Throws:** R
Ht: 5'11" **Wt:** 185

Opening Day Age: 25
Born: 3/15/67 in W. Covina, CA
ML Seasons: 3

Overall Statistics

	G	AB	R	H	D	T	HR	RBI	SB	BB	SO	AVG
1991	22	65	5	18	5	1	1	8	0	3	13	.277
Career	43	116	14	31	6	3	3	13	0	7	24	.267

HITTING, FIELDING, BASERUNNING:

Bobby Rose is something of a late bloomer, although he will turn just 25 during spring training. Rose struggled in his first two years of minor league ball but turned the corner in 1988, showing a bit of power and hitting a career-high .284. After lighting up AA Midland in '89, Rose got the call to the bigs and has been up and down since. He has surprising power and has shown a propensity for hitting in the clutch (5-for-15 with runners in scoring position).

Rose is one of the Angels' most versatile players, able to play any infield position but shortstop and the outfield as well. Third base is his natural position. In '91 Rose impressed the Angels by slaughtering left-handed pitching for a .359 average (14-for-39). Like many of his teammates, Rose's speed is not much of a factor, though he did steal in double figures a couple of times in the minors.

OVERALL:

The play of Rose, both in the minors and the majors, has some people talking about trading Gary Gaetti. Rose's defensive versatility and good clutch hitting will work in his favor as the Angels' retool for 1992. So will the new Whitey Herzog-Buck Rodgers regime, which is expected to give young players more of a chance.

CALIFORNIA ANGELS MINOR LEAGUE PROSPECTS

ORGANIZATION OVERVIEW:

Never known for their great patience, the Angels have usually opted to work the free agent market -- a strategy which costs number one draft choices -- rather than develop their own players. When they do develop a player, like Dick Schofield and Jack Howell a few years ago, California has tended to develop unrealistic expectations of players with marginal skills. Whitey Herzog is expected to change all this . . . except one needs to remember that Herzog's Cardinal years were known more for making shrewd trades (Ozzie Smith, Jack Clark, Bruce Sutter) than for developing minor leaguers.

RUBEN AMARO

Position: OF   **Opening Day Age:** 27
Bats: B **Throws:** R   **Born:** 2/12/65 in
Ht: 5' 10" **Wt:** 170   Philadelphia, PA

Recent Statistics

	G	AB	R	H	D	THR	RBI	SB	BB	SO	AVG
91 AAA Edmonton	121	472	95	154	42	6	3	42	36	63	50	.326
91 AL California	10	23	0	5	1	0	0	2	0	3	3	.217
91 MLE	121	442	68	124	31	2	2	30	18	43	52	.281

The son of former Phillies shortstop Ruben Amaro is not like his dad -- Ruben Jr. is known more for his bat than his glove. Amaro's offensive skills are similar to Luis Polonia's, except that Amaro has a better batting eye. A former infielder, Amaro (just like Polonia) is nothing special on defense, but his bat gives him a chance to stick.

CHRIS CRON

Position: 1B   **Opening Day Age:** 28
Bats: R **Throws:** R   **Born:** 3/31/64 in
Ht: 6' 2" **Wt:** 200   Albuquerque, NM

Recent Statistics

	G	AB	R	H	D	THR	RBI	SB	BB	SO	AVG
91 AAA Edmonton	123	461	74	134	21	1	22	91	6	47	103	.291
91 AL California	6	15	0	2	0	0	0	0	0	2	5	.133
91 MLE	123	437	53	110	16	0	17	65	3	33	108	.252

If the Angels don't re-sign Wally Joyner, Cron has a chance to succeed him as the California first baseman. Originally an Atlanta signee, Cron didn't do much until the last couple of years, when he began to hit with some power and a good average. He's no superstar on defense, either. Don't expect another Joyner, in other words.

CHAD D. CURTIS

Position: 3B   **Opening Day Age:** 23
Bats: R **Throws:** R   **Born:** 11/6/68 in Marion,
Ht: 5' 10" **Wt:** 180   IN

Recent Statistics

	G	AB	R	H	D	THR	RBI	SB	BB	SO	AVG
90 A Quad City	135	492	87	151	28	1	14	65	63	57	76	.307
91 AAA Edmonton	115	431	81	136	28	7	9	61	46	51	58	.316
91 MLE	115	405	58	110	21	3	7	44	26	36	60	.272

A lowly 45th-round draft choice in 1989, Curtis came a long way in 1991, skipping AA ball and showing a good bat and excellent speed at Edmonton. He can play both second and third, though he's not considered a great glove man. Buck Rodgers loves base stealers, which gives Curtis a real chance this year.

GARY DISARCINA

Position: SS   **Opening Day Age:** 24
Bats: R **Throws:** R   **Born:** 11/19/67 in
Ht: 6' 1" **Wt:** 170   Malden, MA

Recent Statistics

	G	AB	R	H	D	THR	RBI	SB	BB	SO	AVG
91 AAA Edmonton	119	390	61	121	21	4	4	58	16	29	32	.310
91 AL California	18	57	5	12	2	0	0	3	0	3	4	.211
91 MLE	119	367	44	98	16	2	3	41	9	20	33	.267

As with Cron, DiSarcina's chances depend a lot on a potential free agent -- in his case, Angel shortstop Dick Schofield. DiSarcina improved a lot at the plate in his second year at Edmonton, and he's considered a competent glove man. He could probably replace Schofield if the Angels suddenly change their usual pattern and go with a rookie at a vital position. That's possible, but not likely. DiSarcina has a chance to stick as a utility man, however.

TIM SALMON

Position: OF   **Opening Day Age:** 23
Bats: R **Throws:** R   **Born:** 8/24/68 in Long
Ht: 6' 3" **Wt:** 210   Beach, CA

Recent Statistics

	G	AB	R	H	D	THR	RBI	SB	BB	SO	AVG
90 A Palm Sprngs	36	118	19	34	6	0	2	21	11	21	44	.288
90 AA Midland	27	97	17	26	3	1	3	16	1	18	38	.268
91 AA Midland	131	465	100	114	26	4	23	94	12	89	166	.245
91 MLE	131	439	63	88	19	1	16	59	5	47	177	.200

Rated the Angels' #1 prospect this spring by Baseball America, Salmon spent the year showing power (23 HR, 94 RBI) and patience (89 BB) at the AA level, but he hit only .245 and had 166 strikeouts. A good outfielder with an excellent arm, he's realistically a couple of years away.

PITCHING:

Two words describing the young White Sox starters are "poise" and "maturity," and 22-year-old lefthander Wilson Alvarez has plenty of both. Acquired from the Texas Rangers two years ago, Alvarez provided one of the biggest highlights in the White Sox season by tossing a no-hitter in his debut start for Chicago. It was quite a contrast from his first big league start for Texas in which Alvarez faced five batters and gave up two walks and two home runs without retiring a man.

Alvarez throws a slider and change-up, but he relies mainly on his fastball and curveball which he'll throw with hard sinking action. In his no-no against the Orioles, Alvarez got quite a few strikeouts when batters chased pitches that darted into the dirt. His high fastball is good enough to throw past major league hitters. Alvarez, at 6-1, is only 175 pounds, and he tended to wear down in the later stages of the game: opponents batted only .216 through his first 75 pitches, .286 after.

Alvarez had control problems in the minors, and it carried over to the big leagues. He walked 29 batters in 56 major league innings. The main culprit is his curveball, and he's going to need better control over it if he's going to use it effectively against righthanders.

HOLDING RUNNERS AND FIELDING:

Alvarez might not win any Gold Gloves, but he's more than adequate at fielding his position. He handled eight chances flawlessly last year. Alvarez has an outstanding move to first. Of the four runners who tried to steal off him, none were successful.

OVERALL:

Alvarez has been pitching professionally since he was 17, and the bumps along the way have made him a mature pitcher at a young age. His stuff impressed everybody last year, and he will definitely be given a shot at the White Sox rotation this spring. Fifteen wins are not out of the question if he's taking the ball every fifth day.

WILSON ALVAREZ

Position: SP
Bats: L **Throws:** L
Ht: 6' 1" **Wt:** 175

Opening Day Age: 22
Born: 3/24/70 in Maracaibo, Venezuela
ML Seasons: 2

Overall Statistics

	W	L	ERA	G	GS	Sv	IP	H	R	BB	SO	HR
1991	3	2	3.51	10	9	0	56.1	47	26	29	32	9
Career	3	3	3.99	11	10	0	56.1	50	29	31	32	11

How Often He Throws Strikes

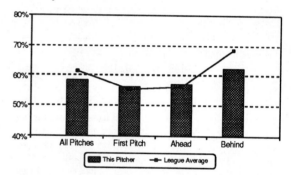

1991 Situational Stats

	W	L	ERA	Sv	IP		AB	H	HR	RBI	AVG
Home	1	1	2.79	0	19.1	LHB	18	4	0	0	.222
Road	2	1	3.89	0	37.0	RHB	186	43	9	18	.231
Day	3	0	1.98	0	27.1	Sc Pos	39	8	2	11	.205
Night	0	2	4.97	0	29.0	Clutch	2	1	0	0	.500

1991 Rankings (American League)

- → 2nd most GDPs induced per GDP situation (22.5%)
- → Led the White Sox in GDPs induced per GDP situation

HITTING:

Acquired in a trade from the San Diego Padres, Joey Cora took over the White Sox second base job from a slumping Scott Fletcher, hit well over .300 until the All-Star break, then went back to the bench when his bat and glove suddenly ran out of magic. Never given a chance in San Diego, Cora seemed at times a man possessed, or certainly like a man who wasn't going to let his job go without a fight. He tried to take command of the position when it was his, but while his intensity stayed high, his performance dropped steadily.

Cora is a slap hitter; he doesn't have much power and he doesn't draw walks. Because of his style, Cora is a good player to use on the hit and run. His speed usually prevents him from having his ground balls wind up as double plays.

BASERUNNING:

Cora's biggest offensive asset is his speed. He stole 11 bases in 17 attempts, a slightly higher percentage than the career 24-of-38 mark with which he began the season. A good baserunner, Cora was used frequently as a pinch runner.

FIELDING:

After an encouraging start, Cora had his problems in the field. He made more than twice as many errors (nine) as Fletcher and Craig Grebeck combined (four), and a couple of Cora mental lapses cost the Sox dearly. He'll need to improve on the double play, and he's got to use his agility and quickness to accomplish that, since his arm is not very strong.

OVERALL:

Cora's value lies in his speed and versatility, both at the plate (he's a switch-hitter) and in the field (he could play third or short in a pinch). He has the ability to become a quality second baseman, but last year he often seemed unsure of himself in crucial situations. Cora will have to have a very good spring to take the job away from Grebeck.

JOEY CORA

Position: 2B
Bats: B **Throws:** R
Ht: 5' 8" **Wt:** 152

Opening Day Age: 26
Born: 5/14/65 in Caguas, Puerto Rico
ML Seasons: 4

Overall Statistics

	G	AB	R	H	D	T	HR	RBI	SB	BB	SO	AVG
1991	100	228	37	55	2	3	0	18	11	20	21	.241
Career	240	588	77	145	13	5	0	34	35	55	56	.247

Where He Hits the Ball

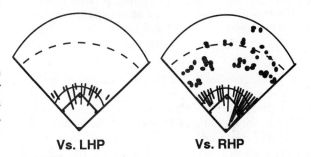

Vs. LHP   Vs. RHP

1991 Situational Stats

	AB	H	HR	RBI	AVG		AB	H	HR	RBI	AVG
Home	113	36	0	10	.319	LHP	57	17	0	1	.298
Road	115	19	0	8	.165	RHP	171	38	0	17	.222
Day	57	13	0	4	.228	Sc Pos	56	11	0	17	.196
Night	171	42	0	14	.246	Clutch	36	10	0	2	.278

1991 Rankings (American League)

→ Led AL second basemen in hit by pitch (5)

ALEX FERNANDEZ

Position: SP
Bats: R **Throws:** R
Ht: 6' 1" **Wt:** 205

Opening Day Age: 22
Born: 8/13/69 in Miami Beach, FL
ML Seasons: 2

PITCHING:

Despite some (very) rough outings last year, Alex Fernandez showed the stuff that continues to keep the White Sox very high on the young righthander. He had control problems (88 walks) throughout the season, but showed the ability to strike out hitters (6.8 strikeouts per nine innings), and keep them off base otherwise. Fernandez finished the season 9-13, but his record would have been better had he been given more than three and a half runs per game when he pitched.

Fernandez has four pitches, fastball, curve ball, slider, and change, and throws all of them hard. He works up in the strike zone, and uses his offspeed pitches to set up his high fastball, which is his strikeout pitch. Fernandez is often guilty of nibbling too much instead of trusting his fastball. The results are a lot of walks which hurt his ERA. He finally put it all together last September, going 3-1 with a 2.25 ERA.

The reason the White Sox are so high on Fernandez is his mental toughness. Only 22 years old, Fernandez showed the poise and confidence of a veteran. At 6-1 and 205 pounds, he looks like a workhorse, and despite being knocked out early in a lot of contests, he approached 200 innings pitched. He should be able to crack the 200-inning mark consistently.

HOLDING RUNNERS AND FIELDING:

Fernandez is a decent fielder, despite three miscues during the season. His move to first is not as quick or determined as teammate Jack McDowell's, but for a righthander, his 15/11 stolen base/caught stealing numbers are pretty good. Fernandez throws everything hard, which helps his catcher.

OVERALL:

Fernandez got knocked around quite a bit in 1991, but he's a tough pitcher with poise and confidence who figures in the White Sox long range plans. Able to pitch well over a lot of innings, Fernandez could easily explode to the 15-18 win mark in 1992 -- and stay there for quite a while.

Overall Statistics

	W	L	ERA	G	GS	Sv	IP	H	R	BB	SO	HR
1991	9	13	4.51	34	32	0	191.2	186	100	88	145	16
Career	14	18	4.29	47	45	0	279.1	275	140	122	206	22

How Often He Throws Strikes

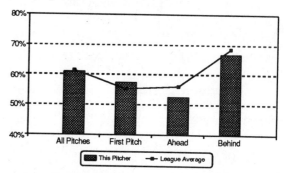

1991 Situational Stats

	W	L	ERA	Sv	IP		AB	H	HR	RBI	AVG
Home	5	7	4.48	0	96.1	LHB	330	83	4	32	.252
Road	4	6	4.53	0	95.1	RHB	389	103	12	54	.265
Day	2	4	7.32	0	39.1	Sc Pos	156	42	4	67	.269
Night	7	9	3.78	0	152.1	Clutch	53	12	1	4	.226

1991 Rankings (American League)

→ 2nd least run support per 9 innings (3.4)

→ 4th highest ERA (4.51)

→ 6th most strikeouts per 9 innings (6.8)

→ 7th in losses (13), most pitches thrown per batter (3.84) and highest ERA at home (4.48)

→ 9th lowest groundball/flyball ratio allowed (1.0) and most baserunners allowed per 9 innings (13.0)

→ Led the White Sox in losses, runners caught stealing (11) and strikeouts per 9 innings

CARLTON FISK

Position: C/1B/DH
Bats: R **Throws:** R
Ht: 6' 2" **Wt:** 223

Opening Day Age: 44
Born: 12/26/47 in
Bellows Falls, VT
ML Seasons: 22

HITTING:

Still catching regularly at age 44, Carlton Fisk has admitted that he's now entering "unexplored territory." The White Sox expressed an interest in funding the exploration, but not at Fisk's $2 million-plus price tag. After watching him endure a difficult September (9 for 70, .129), the Sox refused to pick up Fisk's option, making him a free agent.

If Fisk was washed up last year, there should be several dozen catchers ahead of him in the unemployment line this spring. Despite his sour finish, his 18 homers and 74 RBI ranked with the elite at his position. Fisk's RBI total was his best since 1985, when he was a kid of 37.

Even at his advanced age Fisk is primarily a pull hitter. Last year he batted .341 (95 for 279) when hitting the ball to left field, and only .168 (16 for 95) when going the other way. Because he tries to pull everything, a pitcher has to try to fool Fisk by mixing speed and location, and hope to catch him behind the fastball and ahead of the breaking ball.

BASERUNNING:

Although Fisk could probably beat some of baseball's older general managers in a foot race, his top speed would have to be marked down as "molasses slow." Fisk knows his limitations, and doesn't take too many risks on the bases.

FIELDING:

If his offense declined 25 percent, Fisk would still be valuable for his defensive skills. His ability to handle pitchers has had a lot to do with the success of the young White Sox staff. Fisk also has a lot left in his throwing arm: he threw out 41% of would-be base stealers.

OVERALL:

A sure Hall of Famer, Fisk would like to play in one more World Series. Despite his age, he still ranks as one of the major leagues' top receivers, and would be a valuable pickup even at a reduced offensive level. He may or may not be catching for the White Sox this year; he'll undoubtedly be catching for a contending team.

Overall Statistics

	G	AB	R	H	D	T	HR	RBI	SB	BB	SO	AVG
1991	134	460	42	111	25	0	18	74	1	32	86	.241
Career	2412	8515	1262	2303	417	46	372	1305	125	824	1337	.270

Where He Hits the Ball

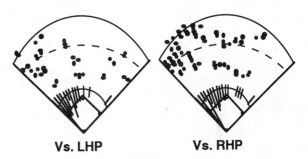

Vs. LHP   Vs. RHP

1991 Situational Stats

	AB	H	HR	RBI	AVG		AB	H	HR	RBI	AVG
Home	233	55	9	39	.236	LHP	157	36	5	28	.229
Road	227	56	9	35	.247	RHP	303	75	13	46	.248
Day	80	20	5	17	.250	Sc Pos	136	34	6	53	.250
Night	380	91	13	57	.239	Clutch	91	22	6	18	.242

1991 Rankings (American League)

➡ 2nd highest percentage runners caught stealing among catchers (40.7%)

➡ 5th most GDPs per GDP situation (19.8%)

➡ 6th lowest on-base average vs. left-handed pitchers (.274)

➡ 7th in hit by pitch (7)

➡ 9th lowest batting average at home (.236)

➡ Led the White Sox in hit by pitch and batting average on a 3-2 count (.316)

HITTING:

The 1991 season was a difficult pill for Scott Fletcher to swallow. He lost his starting job at second base in June and never really got a chance to win it back. While his glove work was up to standard, Fletcher found himself victimized by his shrinking bat.

Fletcher started the season on fire, and it appeared that his batting average, which had dropped between 11 and 20 points for four straight seasons, was headed back upwards. Fletcher batted .333 (18 for 54) with five doubles, a triple, a homer and 14 runs batted in April, not a bad month for a cleanup hitter let alone a number-eight hitter. But American League pitchers put out Fletcher's fire in May (.152) and June (.091), and Fletcher managed only five doubles and 14 runs batted in over the final five months of the season.

Never one to pile up walks, Fletcher became more impatient as the season dragged on. He was trying to use his scattered at-bats to hit his way back into the lineup. It didn't work, and Fletcher had zero walks in 72 at-bats after the All-Star break.

BASERUNNING:

Good for about a dozen stolen bases in his prime, Fletcher has stolen only three bases in three years while being called out six times. He still has average speed, though, and will take the extra base with two outs.

FIELDING:

Fletcher was the defensive star of the Cora/Fletcher/Grebeck trio that shared second base for the Sox last year, and the club's pitchers benefitted from his presence. Fletcher remains a solid keystone player on the double play. His arm, never great at shortstop, is more than adequate for second.

OVERALL:

The White Sox have a traffic jam at second base, and Fletcher went from the big wheel to the spare tire last season. A free agent, Fletcher could wind up on a team needing a solid defensive player and willing to gamble that he can hit .250 again. Given his ability and fiery attitude, that might be a chance worth taking.

SCOTT FLETCHER

Position: 2B
Bats: R **Throws:** R
Ht: 5'11" **Wt:** 173

Opening Day Age: 33
Born: 7/30/58 in Fort Walton Beach, FL
ML Seasons: 11

Overall Statistics

	G	AB	R	H	D	T	HR	RBI	SB	BB	SO	AVG
1991	90	248	14	51	10	1	1	28	0	17	26	.206
Career	1238	4025	504	1049	175	28	22	386	57	412	432	.261

Where He Hits the Ball

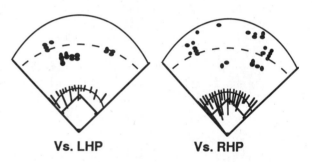

Vs. LHP   **Vs. RHP**

1991 Situational Stats

	AB	H	HR	RBI	AVG		AB	H	HR	RBI	AVG
Home	115	23	0	14	.200	LHP	101	19	0	5	.188
Road	133	28	1	14	.211	RHP	147	32	1	23	.218
Day	79	18	1	8	.228	Sc Pos	63	16	0	25	.254
Night	169	33	0	20	.195	Clutch	58	14	0	6	.241

1991 Rankings (American League)

➡ 7th lowest batting average with a 3-2 count (.067)

HITTING:

Craig Grebeck resembles the other White Sox middle infielders in size (he's only 5-7), and on first look most observers are tempted to pass him off as another good-field, no-hit player. Only the first half of that assumption would be true. Grebeck cracked the White Sox starting lineup after the All-Star break and provided some unexpected pop from the lower half of the order, batting .311 and slugging a hefty .492 after the break.

Though small in stature, Grebeck is probably one of the best fastball hitters on the White Sox team. While his .280 average is indicative of what he had done in the minor leagues, his .460 slugging percentage has surprised a lot of people. But Grebeck has shown he can hit a hard pitch a long way -- he's homered off the likes of Nolan Ryan. Patient at the plate, the diminutive Grebeck has also proven a tough target for pitchers, and he drew 38 bases on balls.

BASERUNNING:

Grebeck is an aggressive player, but that trait has not translated to the base paths. Slightly above-average in speed, he'll take an extra base in two-out situations or if the ball is hit to right, but he was only one for four in stolen bases.

FIELDING:

Grebeck rose through the ranks of the minor leagues as a shortstop, but is a better, more sure-handed second baseman. He made only one error in 159 chances at second, while making nine in 138 chances at third and short. He surprised a lot of people with his range, but needs some work around the bag on double plays.

OVERALL:

At 27, Grebeck may still need to fight first impressions concerning his size, but a second baseman who hits .280 with a dozen home runs and 75 walks is not something that many big league teams can pass on. They say that good things come in small packages, and Grebeck's strong showing in the second half gives him an edge come spring training.

CRAIG GREBECK

Position: 3B/2B/SS
Bats: R **Throws:** R
Ht: 5' 7" **Wt:** 160

Opening Day Age: 27
Born: 12/29/64 in Johnstown, PA
ML Seasons: 2

Overall Statistics

	G	AB	R	H	D	T	HR	RBI	SB	BB	SO	AVG
1991	107	224	37	63	16	3	6	31	1	38	40	.281
Career	166	343	44	83	19	4	7	40	1	46	64	.242

Where He Hits the Ball

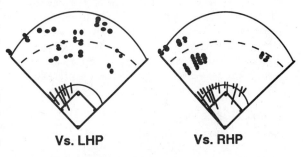

Vs. LHP   **Vs. RHP**

1991 Situational Stats

	AB	H	HR	RBI	AVG		AB	H	HR	RBI	AVG
Home	109	32	3	12	.294	LHP	115	35	5	21	.304
Road	115	31	3	19	.270	RHP	109	28	1	10	.257
Day	62	20	1	8	.323	Sc Pos	58	16	1	21	.276
Night	162	43	5	23	.265	Clutch	42	10	1	6	.238

1991 Rankings (American League)

→ Did not rank near the top or bottom in any category

HITTING:

Never atop the batting leaders in '91 like he had been in 1990, Ozzie Guillen was nonetheless a steadier hitter throughout the 1991 season. The results were a typical Guillen season: a decent average, very few walks, a lot of contact, and some surprises along the way.

Guillen is a nervous batsman who fidgets in the on-deck circle as well as the batter's box. Never still, he can usually be found fraternizing with fans in the box seats close to the field, and he carries this nervous energy into the batter's box. The bat and his body are constantly in motion, and the only time they move to the same end is when the pitch is released.

Guillen is a good fastball hitter, especially fastballs up in the strike zone. He usually pulls those pitches, slapping the ones down or away to left or up the middle. Lefthanders were especially tough on Guillen last year, retiring him consistently on low breaking pitches. Outfielders should play him shallow and around to left.

BASERUNNING:

Rarely a good percentage stealer, Guillen was only 21 for 36 in 1991 after going 13 for 30 in 1990. Playing nearly every day, he has had a tendency to get slow feet as the season wears on; he stole three bases and was caught nine times the final two months of the season. Ozzie is one of the faster White Sox players and will take his share of extra bases.

FIELDING:

The common impression is that Guillen, the Gold Glove winner at shortstop in 1990, was less than himself in the field in 1991. He did make more errors (21) than in 1990 (17), but fielded just as many chances per nine innings. He remains a flashy defender who makes outstanding plays routinely.

OVERALL:

Guillen's defensive brilliance would keep him in the lineup even if he hit .225. While you know what to expect from him offensively, it's on defense that Sox fans have learned to expect the unexpected.

OZZIE GUILLEN

Position: SS
Bats: L **Throws:** R
Ht: 5'11" **Wt:** 150

Opening Day Age: 28
Born: 1/20/64 in Oculare del Tuy, Venezuela
ML Seasons: 7

Overall Statistics

	G	AB	R	H	D	T	HR	RBI	SB	BB	SO	AVG
1991	154	524	52	143	20	3	3	49	21	11	38	.273
Career	1083	3801	427	1013	139	42	10	331	135	123	303	.267

Where He Hits the Ball

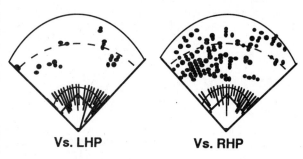

Vs. LHP   Vs. RHP

1991 Situational Stats

	AB	H	HR	RBI	AVG		AB	H	HR	RBI	AVG
Home	247	71	1	29	.287	LHP	161	34	1	9	.211
Road	277	72	2	20	.260	RHP	363	109	2	40	.300
Day	142	41	1	10	.289	Sc Pos	129	32	3	46	.248
Night	382	102	2	39	.267	Clutch	128	35	1	13	.273

1991 Rankings (American League)

→ 1st in least pitches seen per plate appearance (2.84), lowest on-base average vs. left-handed pitchers (.213), lowest batting average on a 3-2 count (.000) and lowest percentage of pitches taken (39.6%)

→ 2nd in lowest on-base average (.284) and lowest stolen base percentage (58.3%)

→ 3rd lowest slugging percentage vs. left-handed pitchers (.248)

→ Led the White Sox in sacrifice bunts (13), sacrifice flies (7), caught stealing (15), batting average vs. right-handed pitchers (.300), batting average on an 0-2 count (.298) and batting average with 2 strikes (.234)

PITCHING:

The 1991 season was full of ups and downs for Greg Hibbard, who rarely looked like the same pitcher who fooled American League hitters with his offspeed breaking stuff in 1990. Hibbard got off to a good start, suffered through a demotion to AAA Vancouver, then was recalled, first to the bullpen and finally back to his starting role. Though he won in double figures again, Hibbard's ERA was more than a run higher than in 1990.

Hibbard has four pitches: a sinking fastball, curve, slider, and a change-up, which is his bread-and-butter pitch. At Vancouver, the White Sox moved Hibbard from the first base side of the rubber to the third base side. That seemed to help his location, and he avoided the control problems which plagued him early in the year. When he is going well, Hibbard will get a lot of ground balls. He doesn't get many strikeouts, but when he does they usually come on his change-up, which he'll try to throw on the outside corner to righthanders.

While Hibbard's hits and walks per nine innings were nearly identical to his 1990 numbers, it's readily apparent why his ERA shot up: his home runs allowed jumped from 10 to 23, proof that his stuff wasn't sinking as dramatically as it had been.

HOLDING RUNNERS AND FIELDING:

Hibbard made two miscues in the field last year, but is a decent fielder; that is essential given all the ground balls hit at him. He has a good move to first, and runners stole only six bases in 14 attempts against him.

OVERALL:

Despite last year's troubles, the White Sox regard Hibbard as a solid major league starter. They may have been a little impatient in demoting him, though it was clear that Hibbard didn't pitch with the same confidence he displayed in 1990. Despite some steps backward in 1991 Hibbard should be in the rotation in '92.

GREG HIBBARD

Position: SP
Bats: L **Throws:** L
Ht: 6' 0" **Wt:** 190

Opening Day Age: 27
Born: 9/13/64 in New Orleans, LA
ML Seasons: 3

Overall Statistics

	W	L	ERA	G	GS	Sv	IP	H	R	BB	SO	HR
1991	11	11	4.31	32	29	0	194.0	196	107	57	71	23
Career	31	27	3.58	88	85	0	542.1	540	245	153	218	39

How Often He Throws Strikes

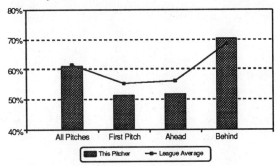

1991 Situational Stats

	W	L	ERA	Sv	IP		AB	H	HR	RBI	AVG
Home	4	5	3.44	0	91.2	LHB	120	30	5	19	.250
Road	7	6	5.10	0	102.1	RHB	617	166	18	71	.269
Day	2	3	5.43	0	56.1	Sc Pos	144	51	8	70	.354
Night	9	8	3.86	0	137.2	Clutch	64	15	1	4	.234

1991 Rankings (American League)

→ 1st highest batting average allowed with runners in scoring position (.354)

→ 2nd lowest strikeouts per 9 innings (3.3)

→ 3rd in most GDPs induced (27) and most GDPs induced per 9 innings (1.25)

→ 5th in most home runs allowed per 9 innings (1.1) and highest ERA on the road (5.10)

→ Led the White Sox in home runs allowed (23), GDPs induced, groundball/flyball ratio (1.56), lowest stolen base percentage allowed (42.9%), least pitches thrown per batter (3.49) and most GDPs induced per 9 innings

PITCHING:

Charlie Hough made his major league debut four months after teammate Wilson Alvarez was born, and to the White Sox, he's more than just a pitcher: he's a source of wisdom and experience for their young hurlers. The Sox were also looking for a starter to give some days off to their overworked bullpen last year, and Hough did that, making it into the seventh inning in 21 of his 29 starts. More often than not, they were quality innings. Only some tough luck and bad defense prevented Hough from winning 10 games for the tenth straight season.

With Hough, the hitters know what to expect, and his pitching pattern is no mystery: a knuckleball, followed by a knuckleball, usually followed by another knuckleball. Hough's "fastball," which he'll try to throw on the inside part of the plate when the hitter is (hopefully) not expecting it, is probably misnamed. Despite the knowledge of what's coming, the hitters still only managed 167 hits in Hough's 199.1 innings. (In his career, Hough has allowed more hits than innings pitched only once, in 1979). When the knuckler doesn't knuckle, the results become slowly, painfully obvious: walks (94) and home runs (21).

HOLDING RUNNERS AND FIELDING:

Despite his age, Hough has quick reflexes, and saved his only shutout by snaring a couple of line drives hit back through the box. Because of the knuckler, Hough spends a lot of time trying to prevent runners from stealing. He is the champ of the throw to first, leading the American League in pickoff tosses for the second straight year (313). Hough has been able to hold the running game in check: they stole only 10 bases in 19 tries in 1991.

OVERALL:

The White Sox exercised their option on Hough, more as an insurance policy on their young pitchers than anything else. If he remains in the rotation, expect more of the same from Hough. Bad games are part of the package, but the Sox are hoping there will be more good ones than bad.

CHARLIE HOUGH

Position: SP
Bats: R **Throws:** R
Ht: 6' 2" **Wt:** 190

Opening Day Age: 44
Born: 1/5/48 in Honolulu, HI
ML Seasons: 22

Overall Statistics

	W	L	ERA	G	GS	Sv	IP	H	R	BB	SO	HR
1991	9	10	4.02	31	29	0	199.1	167	98	94	107	21
Career	195	179	3.66	776	358	61	3306.0	2803	1536	1476	2095	327

How Often He Throws Strikes

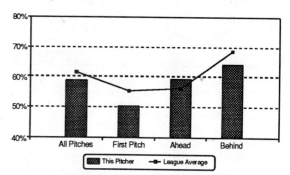

1991 Situational Stats

	W	L	ERA	Sv	IP		AB	H	HR	RBI	AVG
Home	5	5	3.38	0	106.2	LHB	355	84	8	45	.237
Road	4	5	4.76	0	92.2	RHB	374	83	13	45	.222
Day	4	3	2.45	0	69.2	Sc Pos	149	30	4	62	.201
Night	5	7	4.86	0	129.2	Clutch	72	19	3	9	.264

1991 Rankings (American League)

➡ 1st in pickoff throws (313)

➡ 5th in hit batsmen (11), lowest strikeout/walk ratio (1.1) and lowest batting average allowed with runners in scoring position (.201)

➡ 6th in walks allowed (94), highest ERA on the road (4.76) and lowest batting average allowed vs. right-handed batters (.222)

➡ Led the White Sox in walks allowed, hit batsmen, pickoff throws, ERA at home (3.38), lowest batting average allowed vs. right-handed batters and lowest batting average allowed with runners in scoring position

HITTING:

If there's a marketing consultant out there worth his salt, he'll have Bo Jackson appearing on "This Old House" soon, because Bo knows rehab. Following rehabilitation for what was first diagnosed to be a career-ending injury, Bo was back in baseball in September. Often criticized in his two-sport days for not paying enough attention to baseball, Jackson's offensive performance had, in fact, improved every year in the big leagues: his batting average, on-base and slugging percentage had risen steadily from 1986 to 1990.

Jackson now bats from an open stance, leaning back on his right leg, a slightly different posture than the straight-up style he employed as a Royal. The stance is a slight concession to the stiffness in his left hip, which inhibits his mobility. The injury definitely affects Bo's balance during his swing and there were times when he looked completely overmatched. He still gives his all on every cut, but he appeared to be a little more selective last year. Breaking pitches still give him trouble, but he can hit anything out over the plate a long way.

BASERUNNING:

Bo can still run the base paths, but the White Sox were careful about having him try to steal bases. Jackson hit into three double plays in September; the velocity at which he hits the ball, coupled with his slower running speed, were the main culprits.

FIELDING:

Jackson's defensive exploits -- great speed, cannon arm, strange lapses -- are well known, but it's doubtful that he'll get to show them off in '92. The Sox are very confident about his recovery, but whether or not he'll regain the mobility and durability to play effectively in the outfield remains a question.

OVERALL:

Jackson likes the silver and black -- of the White Sox, the only team willing to take a chance on the injured superstar. Despite the injury, Bo's 84 plate appearances were encouraging last year. If he is able to play every day in '92, look for him at DH. He could be the legitimate cleanup hitter the White Sox desperately need behind his former Auburn teammate, Frank Thomas.

BO JACKSON

Position: DH
Bats: R **Throws:** R
Ht: 6' 1" **Wt:** 235

Opening Day Age: 29
Born: 11/30/62 in Bessemer, AL
ML Seasons: 6

Overall Statistics

	G	AB	R	H	D	T	HR	RBI	SB	BB	SO	AVG
1991	23	71	8	16	4	0	3	14	0	12	25	.225
Career	534	1908	286	476	70	14	112	327	81	157	663	.249

Where He Hits the Ball

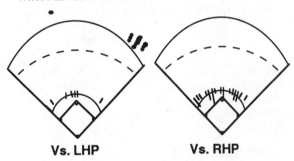

Vs. LHP   Vs. RHP

1991 Situational Stats

	AB	H	HR	RBI	AVG		AB	H	HR	RBI	AVG
Home	40	8	3	10	.200	LHP	26	6	2	6	.231
Road	31	8	0	4	.258	RHP	45	10	1	8	.222
Day	17	3	0	4	.176	Sc Pos	19	5	0	8	.263
Night	54	13	3	10	.241	Clutch	7	3	2	3	.429

1991 Rankings (American League)

→ Did not rank near the top or bottom in any category

GREAT RANGE

LANCE JOHNSON

Position: CF
Bats: L **Throws:** L
Ht: 5'11" **Wt:** 160

Opening Day Age: 28
Born: 7/6/63 in
Cincinnati, OH
ML Seasons: 5

HITTING:

Just call Lance Johnson "Mr. September." For the second straight year, Johnson hovered around the .260 mark, only to find his stroke late in the season. Johnson batted .343 in September-October, after batting .359 over the same period in 1990.

Johnson isn't good early in the season, and he isn't good batting early in the lineup. In 1990, he flopped as a leadoff man, and in '91 he was a weak link batting second. After being dropped to sixth or seventh, Johnson responded. He is a good bunter, and another in a long line of diminutive slap hitters populating the lower half of the White Sox order.

Extremely fast, Johnson is a ground ball hitter, using his speed to beat out infield hits and stay out of the double play. He can get around pretty quickly on the high fastball (the only pitches he'll try to pull), but had real trouble against lefthanders in '91. Johnson hit well against southpaws in 1990 (.321) but last year couldn't adjust to the steady diet of breaking balls being fed to him by lefties.

BASERUNNING:

More aggressive last year on the base paths, Johnson hit an astounding six triples in only 88 September at-bats. As a base stealer Johnson also improved: he was 26 for 37 (70%), better than his 1990 rate. Now, if he can only get on base more often . . .

FIELDING:

Johnson played at Gold Glove level all last year, saving White Sox pitchers numerous runs. A typical Johnson play was his great catch on a rapidly sinking fly ball to save Wilson Alvarez's no-hitter at Baltimore. Johnson's throwing arm is below average, however, and runners will take liberties on him.

OVERALL:

As a hitter, Johnson hits for a respectable average, but draws too few walks and has little power. It will be difficult to dislodge him from his starting role, however; on a club with a lot of shaky gloves, Johnson's defense is vital.

Overall Statistics

	G	AB	R	H	D	T	HR	RBI	SB	BB	SO	AVG
1991	160	588	72	161	14	13	0	49	26	26	58	.274
Career	427	1492	191	405	46	26	1	129	90	86	144	.271

Where He Hits the Ball

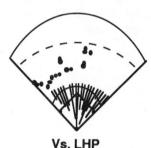 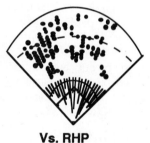

Vs. LHP   **Vs. RHP**

1991 Situational Stats

	AB	H	HR	RBI	AVG		AB	H	HR	RBI	AVG
Home	286	76	0	22	.266	LHP	164	40	0	8	.244
Road	302	85	0	27	.281	RHP	424	121	0	41	.285
Day	171	46	0	13	.269	Sc Pos	138	34	0	47	.246
Night	417	115	0	36	.276	Clutch	113	24	0	12	.212

1991 Rankings (American League)

- ➡ 1st in triples (13) and lowest HR frequency (no HRs in 588 at-bats)
- ➡ 2nd in groundball/flyball ratio (2.63)
- ➡ 5th in least pitches seen per plate appearance (3.07) and lowest slugging percentage vs. left-handed pitchers (.274)
- ➡ Led the White Sox in singles (134), triples, games (160), groundball/flyball ratio, batting average on the road (.282), bunts in play (25) and highest percentage of swings put into play (56.0%)
- ➡ Led AL center fielders in triples, games, groundball flyball ratio and highest percentage of swings put into play

RON KARKOVICE

STRONG ARM

Position: C
Bats: R **Throws:** R
Ht: 6' 1" **Wt:** 215

Opening Day Age: 28
Born: 8/8/63 in Union, NJ
ML Seasons: 6

HITTING:

In what promised to be a breakthrough season for him, patient White Sox catcher Ron Karkovice spent much of the 1991 campaign hampered by a torn ligament in his left thumb. Still, Karkovice's performance showed that the strides he made in 1989 and 1990 were not lost.

Under the tutelage of batting instructor Walt Hriniak, Karkovice has become a bona fide major league hitter. Over the last three seasons, Karkovice has amassed one season's worth of at-bats (532), and the numbers give an accurate reading of what he's capable of over a full season: .252 average, 32 doubles, 2 triples, 14 home runs, and 66 RBI. Not bad for any catcher who isn't Johnny Bench or Roy Campanella.

Karkovice is not a "come from behind" hitter (only .162 with two strikes), and practiced patience would put him at an advantage more often (he hit .313 after getting ahead in the count). Third basemen should be aware that Karkovice is a very good bunter.

BASERUNNING:

One benefit of being Carlton Fisk's backup is that Karkovice's knees have not yet taken the pounding that comes with catching 130 games a season (even though Karkovice would not have minded the trade-off). Thus, he still runs pretty well for a backstop. He's stolen 10 bases in 12 attempts in his career.

FIELDING:

Trying to steal bases when Karkovice is behind the plate is a losing proposition. In the last five years Karkovice has thrown out 86 of 175 baserunners, an astounding 49 percent. Further testament to his catching prowess are both the White Sox ERA while he was catching (3.66), and his passed ball total of two, despite catching knuckleballer Charlie Hough for 131 innings.

OVERALL:

It's often been said that Karkovice would be the starting catcher on most major league teams. In 1992, that team may finally be the White Sox. The Sox did not pick up Carlton Fisk's option at $2 million-plus; if they don't re-sign Fisk at a lower figure, Karkovice will be numero uno at last.

Overall Statistics

	G	AB	R	H	D	T	HR	RBI	SB	BB	SO	AVG
1991	75	167	25	41	13	0	5	22	0	15	42	.246
Career	336	829	106	184	43	2	23	95	10	64	257	.222

Where He Hits the Ball

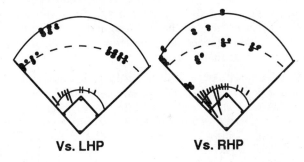

Vs. LHP   Vs. RHP

1991 Situational Stats

	AB	H	HR	RBI	AVG		AB	H	HR	RBI	AVG
Home	81	19	0	7	.235	LHP	61	18	3	8	.295
Road	86	22	5	15	.256	RHP	106	23	2	14	.217
Day	76	16	1	11	.211	Sc Pos	46	11	1	15	.239
Night	91	25	4	11	.275	Clutch	24	7	0	1	.292

1991 Rankings (American League)

→ Did not rank near the top or bottom in any category

JACK
McDOWELL

CY YOUNG STUFF

Position: SP
Bats: R **Throws:** R
Ht: 6' 5" **Wt:** 180

Opening Day Age: 26
Born: 1/16/66 in Van Nuys, CA
ML Seasons: 4

PITCHING:

While Jack McDowell's first album with his rock band V.I.E.W. didn't make the Billboard Top 10 last year, the guitar-playing righthander rarely struck a bad chord on the mound. McDowell was the workhorse of an otherwise shaky White Sox starting staff, tossing a '70s-style 15 complete games.

A fierce competitor, McDowell is a pitcher with an attitude and the stuff to back it up. Not afraid to throw inside, he relies primarily on two pitches: an 85 to 90-MPH fastball, and an excellent split-fingered fastball which he uses as his out pitch. McDowell's intensity will sometimes get the best of him, and he has a tendency to overthrow when he's pumped up. The result is less movement on his pitches, and without an adequate offspeed pitch, hitters can sit back and wait on the hard stuff.

McDowell can be wild high in the strike zone, and his periods of ineffectiveness usually come when his control is lacking. While many observers questioned the wiry McDowell's ability to withstand the string of complete games, he was a very economical pitcher: only five times in 35 starts did he throw more than 125 pitches.

HOLDING RUNNERS AND FIELDING:

Because of his loping delivery, McDowell invests a lot of effort at keeping baserunners close. He's got a quick move to first, and a whirling dervish move with runners on first and third which has caught a handful of napping baserunners. Despite his efforts, baserunners stole 22 bases in 32 attempts. McDowell is an excellent fielder, quick off the mound on bunts, and handled 52 chances without an error.

OVERALL:

Sporting a Fu Manchu to fit his "Black Jack" image, McDowell has become the ace of the White Sox staff. He almost singlehandedly pitched the club into the pennant race last June and July. With the development of an effective offspeed pitch to complement his hard stuff, McDowell could become a legitimate Cy Young contender year in and year out.

Overall Statistics

	W	L	ERA	G	GS	Sv	IP	H	R	BB	SO	HR
1991	17	10	3.41	35	35	0	253.2	212	97	82	191	19
Career	39	29	3.61	98	98	0	645.1	564	281	233	455	52

How Often He Throws Strikes

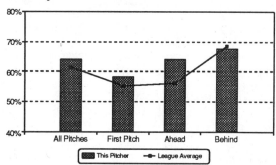

This Pitcher — League Average

1991 Situational Stats

	W	L	ERA	Sv	IP		AB	H	HR	RBI	AVG
Home	10	6	3.89	0	138.2	LHB	485	109	7	40	.225
Road	7	4	2.82	0	115.0	RHB	445	103	12	49	.231
Day	5	4	3.44	0	86.1	Sc Pos	193	52	4	59	.269
Night	12	6	3.39	0	167.1	Clutch	92	21	2	7	.228

1991 Rankings (American League)

→ 1st in games started (35), complete games (15) and fielding percentage by a pitcher (1.000)

→ 2nd in shutouts (3) and innings pitched (253.2)

→ 3rd in batters faced (1,028) and least GDPs induced per 9 innings (.43)

→ Led the White Sox in ERA (3.41), wins (17), games started, complete games, shutouts, innings pitched, batters faced, strikeouts (191), pitches thrown (3,828), stolen bases allowed (22), winning percentage (.630) and strikeout/walk ratio (2.3)

PITCHING:

Donn Pall's strong performance in 1990 enabled the White Sox to trade right-handed set-up man Barry Jones (along with Ivan Calderon) to Montreal for Tim Raines. Pall was even better in 1991, lowering his ERA by nearly a run. Only three bad outings by "The Pope," as he is nicknamed, kept Pall's season from being a truly religious experience; without them, his ERA would have been 1.43.

One reason for Pall's dramatic improvement was the addition of a slider to his repertoire. It was an excellent pitch for him, and gave hitters something else to think about. His main pitch is his exceptional split-finger fastball. Pall's curve is also designed to drop out of the strike zone and get hitters to chase it.

Those downward-moving pitches make Pall an exceptional reliever when a ground ball is required, and the White Sox took advantage (eight DPs in 51 double play situations with Pall on the mound). His hard-breaking pitches, including the splitter, can be difficult to control, but he issued only 17 unintentional walks in 71 innings last year.

The White Sox made a conscious effort not to use him against tough lefthanders last year, and Pall's performance against lefties improved significantly. He has a tendency to develop a tender arm, and the Sox limit his usage: he's never worked more than 56 games in a season, and his innings totals have been declining.

HOLDING RUNNERS AND FIELDING:

Pall is a decent fielder who lets his infielders handle the multitude of ground balls which shoot out of the batters box. He has a good move to first, and held runners to a 45% success rate in stolen base attempts.

OVERALL:

Working middle relief can be an anonymous job, but Pall's abilities hardly go unnoticed. He has never had a bad season, and 1991 was a step forward. Pall, a Chicago native who dreamed of playing for the White Sox as a kid, has quietly moved into an important role in the White Sox bullpen.

DONN PALL

Position: RP
Bats: R **Throws:** R
Ht: 6' 1" **Wt:** 183

Opening Day Age: 30
Born: 1/11/62 in Chicago, IL
ML Seasons: 4

Overall Statistics

	W	L	ERA	G	GS	Sv	IP	H	R	BB	SO	HR
1991	7	2	2.41	51	0	0	71.0	59	22	20	40	7
Career	14	14	3.08	177	0	8	262.2	251	101	71	153	24

How Often He Throws Strikes

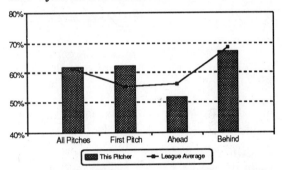

1991 Situational Stats

	W	L	ERA	Sv	IP		AB	H	HR	RBI	AVG
Home	5	0	2.19	0	37.0	LHB	106	20	1	4	.189
Road	2	2	2.65	0	34.0	RHB	149	39	6	21	.262
Day	0	0	2.19	0	24.2	Sc Pos	60	17	1	18	.283
Night	7	2	2.53	0	46.1	Clutch	101	25	2	5	.248

1991 Rankings (American League)

→ 6th in relief wins (7)
→ Led the White Sox in relief wins

HITTING:

The decision whether or not to sign Dan Pasqua should have been an easy one for the White Sox, who need a left-handed bat in the middle of their batting order. But given Pasqua's off season arrest on a misdemeanor drug charge, there was some concern. The White Sox are not likely to let this unduly affect their desire to retain Pasqua's services; prior to this incident, he had been considered a solid citizen.

Playing every day last year against righthanders, and occasionally against some lefties, Pasqua set career highs in many statistical categories, including runs scored (71), runs batted in (66) and walks (62). Save for a disastrous August, in which his bat fell silent (.169 with one home run and five RBI), Pasqua was a reasonably effective cleanup hitter.

Pasqua has good fly ball power to the gaps -- if he can get a pitcher's mistake out over the plate. Pitchers try to get him out by feeding him fastballs and curveballs inside. During the August drought, Pasqua was waving his uppercut swing at breaking pitches in on his fists.

BASERUNNING:

Pasqua's speed is below average, with only five steals in seven years. He did score 71 runs with no big guns hitting behind him, and will take an extra base on occasion.

FIELDING:

Pasqua played three defensive positions last year: left field, right field and first base. While he's generally sure-handed, Pasqua didn't have the range or arm for right field, the position he usually had to play. His soft hands helped him at first, and he was frequently shifted there for late-inning defense.

OVERALL:

Pasqua was a free agent at season's end. The Sox seemed interested in making a bid, even after Pasqua was arrested for having a small amount of marijuana delivered to his home. The Sox still like his left-handed bat, but with Tim Raines, Sammy Sosa, Frank Thomas and Bo Jackson available at the positions Pasqua normally plays, they can hardly offer Pasqua an everyday job.

DAN PASQUA

Position: 1B/RF
Bats: L **Throws:** L
Ht: 6' 0" **Wt:** 203

Opening Day Age: 30
Born: 10/17/61 in Yonkers, NY
ML Seasons: 7

Overall Statistics

	G	AB	R	H	D	T	HR	RBI	SB	BB	SO	AVG
1991	134	417	71	108	22	5	18	66	0	62	86	.259
Career	723	2156	291	541	101	13	104	333	5	273	525	.251

Where He Hits the Ball

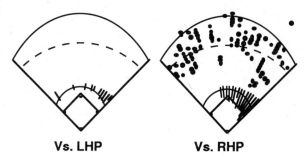

Vs. LHP   Vs. RHP

1991 Situational Stats

	AB	H	HR	RBI	AVG		AB	H	HR	RBI	AVG
Home	196	57	10	29	.291	LHP	49	13	3	8	.265
Road	221	51	8	37	.231	RHP	368	95	15	58	.258
Day	107	32	5	19	.299	Sc Pos	111	27	3	43	.243
Night	310	76	13	47	.245	Clutch	78	23	3	11	.295

1991 Rankings (American League)

→ Led the White Sox in least GDPs per GDP situation (7.9%) and batting average in the clutch (.295)

→ Led AL first basemen in triples (5)

PITCHING:

On the White Sox staff, Ken Patterson is Don Pall in reverse: a left-handed middle reliever who relies on a good fastball and breaking pitches high in the strike zone. As a result, Patterson permits nearly twice as many fly balls as he does ground balls. There aren't many instances when a manager will bring in a pitcher to get that long fly ball so Patterson has to be used carefully.

After turning in a 4.52 ERA as a rookie in 1988, Patterson has rapidly improved. He has lowered his ERA each season, while allowing fewer hits and home runs per nine innings. Control has always been a problem for him; despite his overall good numbers last year, he walked more batters than he struck out.

Patterson got off to a rocky start (6.75 April ERA), but settled down considerably after that. He pitched 11 scoreless innings in June, and crafted a 0.87 ERA over 20.2 innings in June and July. After being encouraged to bear down against righthanders if he wanted to stay in the big leagues, Patterson was very effective against them in 1991. His opponents average against righties last year dropped from .260 to .193.

HOLDING RUNNERS AND FIELDING:

Matt Young, the stone-fingered pitcher for the Red Sox, better not look back, because Ken Patterson might be gaining on him. Patterson made three errors in only 10 chances last year, a justifiable mark only for kids in T-ball. Patterson is fairly good at holding runners allowing only five steals in eight attempts.

OVERALL:

Though he generally pitches in the glamourless role of long relief, Patterson has done a fine job. He is a solid member of what is rapidly becoming (with Thigpen, Pall, Radinsky, Patterson, and Perez) one of the major leagues' deepest, most effective bullpens. Patterson's deteriorating strikeout-to-walk ratio bears watching, however -- it's often a sign of future trouble.

KEN PATTERSON

Position: RP
Bats: L **Throws:** L
Ht: 6' 4" **Wt:** 210

Opening Day Age: 27
Born: 7/8/64 in Costa Mesa, CA
ML Seasons: 4

Overall Statistics

	W	L	ERA	G	GS	Sv	IP	H	R	BB	SO	HR
1991	3	0	2.83	43	0	1	63.2	48	22	35	32	5
Career	11	4	3.70	145	3	4	216.1	195	97	104	123	24

How Often He Throws Strikes

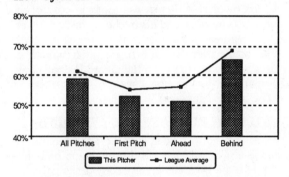

1991 Situational Stats

	W	L	ERA	Sv	IP		AB	H	HR	RBI	AVG
Home	3	0	2.53	1	32.0	LHB	63	17	1	12	.270
Road	0	0	3.13	0	31.2	RHB	161	31	4	20	.193
Day	2	0	3.00	0	15.0	Sc Pos	65	18	3	30	.277
Night	1	0	2.77	1	48.2	Clutch	21	2	0	1	.095

1991 Rankings (American League)

➡ 7th least strikeouts per 9 ininings in relief (4.5)

PITCHING:

A step back to the bullpen turned out to be a step forward for Melido Perez, the White Sox righthander who had been erratic last year as a starter. Perez had averaged 12 wins from 1988 to 1990, and was expected to be a mainstay of the White Sox rotation in 1991. He got off to a poor start, however, and stood at 1-4 with a 4.82 earned run average in late May.

Frustrated at his lack of progress, the White Sox sent Perez to the bullpen to work out the kinks. The difference was astonishing. Working first in long relief and later as a set-up man for Bobby Thigpen, Perez turned in a 7-3 bullpen record and a 2.22 ERA.

In his relief role, Perez was more in control of both his emotions and his pitches -- he had fewer walks in nearly twice as many innings in relief than as a starter. His split-finger pitch, which he uses as a counterpart to a high, hard fastball, was responsible for the lion's share of his strikeouts (128 in 135.2 innings).

HOLDING RUNNERS AND FIELDING:

Perez is a good fielder, quick off the mound to make a play, and has good reflexes on balls hit through the box. His energy sometimes gets the best of him, and he'll occasionally hurt himself by throwing a ball away. In the past, Perez has been effective at holding runners, but 15 of 20 base stealers were successful in '91.

OVERALL:

Perez took his "demotion" to the bullpen hard, but put aside his feelings with the idea of pitching himself back into the rotation. He has the stuff to be a starting pitcher: a good fastball, an excellent split-finger pitch, and a curve ball. In addition, he has the stamina and durability to be a starter. The Sox need Perez more as a starter than a reliever, and he should get a chance to crack the rotation once again this spring.

MELIDO PEREZ

Position: RP/SP
Bats: R **Throws:** R
Ht: 6' 4" **Wt:** 180

Opening Day Age: 26
Born: 2/15/66 in San Cristobal, Dominican Republic
ML Seasons: 5

Overall Statistics

	W	L	ERA	G	GS	Sv	IP	H	R	BB	SO	HR
1991	8	7	3.12	49	8	1	135.2	111	49	52	128	15
Career	45	46	4.26	150	109	1	723.1	679	383	305	573	80

How Often He Throws Strikes

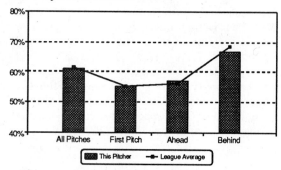

1991 Situational Stats

	W	L	ERA	Sv	IP		AB	H	HR	RBI	AVG
Home	2	3	3.61	0	62.1	LHB	223	45	6	25	.202
Road	6	4	2.70	1	73.1	RHB	272	66	9	25	.243
Day	1	0	2.21	0	20.1	Sc Pos	117	26	2	34	.222
Night	7	7	3.28	1	115.1	Clutch	152	32	5	13	.211

1991 Rankings (American League)

- ➡ 1st in lowest fielding percentage for a pitcher (.903)
- ➡ 4th worst first batter efficiency (.371)
- ➡ 6th in relief wins (7)
- ➡ 7th in wild pitches (11)
- ➡ 8th in relief ERA (2.23) and lowest batting average allowed vs. left-handed batters (.202)
- ➡ 9th in strikeouts per 9 innings in relief (8.6)
- ➡ Led the White Sox in wild pitches, lowest batting average allowed vs. left-handed batters, relief wins, relief innings (89) and strikeouts per 9 innings in relief

PITCHING:

Scott Radinsky displayed outstanding stuff in 1991, a definite jump from the often-erratic performance he turned in during his rookie year. Radinsky, who made the move from A ball to the big leagues two years ago, stayed in the groove all year long. He was an effective set-up man and sometime closer for the White Sox.

Blame it on rock and roll, but Radinsky, who played drums in his own rock band, "Scared Straight," has the same no-holds-barred approach to pitching as his guitar-playing teammate Jack McDowell: he comes right at hitters with heat, and never lets up. He possesses a great fastball and a slider which drops quickly out of the hitting zone. Radinsky showed much more control in his sophomore season. He stopped trying to throw every pitch at top speed; the result was a reduction in his strikeout rate, but much sharper control.

The game is often on the line when Radinsky enters the game, and he thrives on the pressure. Last year he retired 75% of the first batters he faced. Though he netted only eight saves on the season, he led the White Sox relievers in holds (15).

HOLDING RUNNERS AND FIELDING:

Radinsky has a decent move to first and a quick move towards home plate. Being left-handed also helps him keep runners close, and the way he rushes the ball to home plate at 90+ MPH makes baserunners think twice about going. Radinsky allowed only one stolen base last year. He's an average fielder, and executed 19 chances flawlessly.

OVERALL:

Radinsky is an intense pitcher who has a closer's presence stalking around the mound. He's got the pitches and the attitude to be a top-notch closer, and he proved last year that he can handle righthanders with his improved breaking pitch. Watch for Radinsky to get a few more save opportunities this year, and to continue excelling in the set-up role; like Rob Dibble in 1990.

SCOTT RADINSKY

Position: RP
Bats: L **Throws:** L
Ht: 6' 3" **Wt:** 190

Opening Day Age: 24
Born: 3/3/68 in Glendale, CA
ML Seasons: 2

Overall Statistics

	W	L	ERA	G	GS	Sv	IP	H	R	BB	SO	HR
1991	5	5	2.02	67	0	8	71.1	53	18	23	49	4
Career	11	6	3.20	129	0	12	123.2	100	47	59	95	5

How Often He Throws Strikes

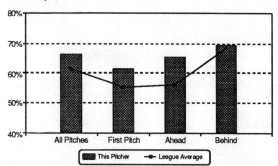

1991 Situational Stats

	W	L	ERA	Sv	IP		AB	H	HR	RBI	AVG
Home	1	2	1.51	6	41.2	LHB	78	16	3	11	.205
Road	4	3	2.73	2	29.2	RHB	179	37	1	13	.207
Day	1	2	1.64	2	22.0	Sc Pos	86	10	0	18	.116
Night	4	3	2.19	6	49.1	Clutch	157	33	2	15	.210

1991 Rankings (American League)

→ 6th in relief ERA (2.02) and lowest batting average allowed in relief (.206)

→ 7th in holds (15)

→ 8th in blown saves (7)

→ 9th in least runners per 9 innings in relief (9.7)

→ Led the White Sox in games pitches (67), holds, first batter efficiency (.186), lowest percentage of inherited runners scored (25.4%), relief ERA, lowest batting average allowed in relief and least runners per 9 innings in relief

HITTING:

Acquired in a big off season trade for Ivan Calderon and Barry Jones, Tim Raines suffered some dry spells adjusting to his new surroundings, but generally performed as expected. Though Raines finished at .268, the lowest average of his career, his performance from the leadoff spot was the best of any White Sox hitter in recent memory.

Raines hit .177 in April, got hot in May, batting .349 and stealing twelve bases, but suffered a frustrating July (.152), which sent his average tumbling back to the .260 range. Part of the problem was that Raines, who generates much of the force of his swing from his legs, was hampered by sore hamstrings in both legs. Unable to generate any real power, Raines could be seen frequently bouncing weak ground balls to the shortstop or second baseman.

Raines remains a good fastball hitter, but he dives into the ball and can be had by slow breaking pitches. His patience continues to be a big asset, and his 83 walks are a typical total for him.

BASERUNNING:

Despite being slowed for a while by sore legs, Raines stole 51 bases in 66 tries, an excellent 77% success rate. It was the eighth time in his career that he reached the 50 mark in steals. He is more than fast enough around the bases, and he scored 102 runs despite his low batting average.

FIELDING:

Raines had some problems in left field last year, misplaying some balls at inopportune times, but he was able to outrun most of his mistakes. The main problem with Raines' defense is his weak throwing arm. It is accurate, at least, as he threw out 12 baserunners last season.

OVERALL:

Though Raines had a few problems, the White Sox had to be pleased with their Canadian import. A personable man, Raines is one of the few veterans on the young White Sox team, and his clubhouse presence is a plus. With a year in the new league under his belt, Raines should have a steadier year in 1992.

TIM RAINES

Position: LF/DH
Bats: B **Throws:** R
Ht: 5' 8"   **Wt:** 185

Opening Day Age: 32
Born: 9/16/59 in Sanford, FL
ML Seasons: 13

Overall Statistics

	G	AB	R	H	D	T	HR	RBI	SB	BB	SO	AVG
1991	155	609	102	163	20	6	5	50	51	83	68	.268
Career	1560	5914	1036	1761	293	87	101	602	685	858	631	.298

Where He Hits the Ball

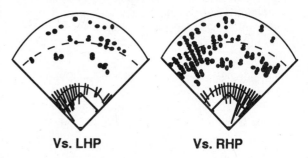

Vs. LHP   **Vs. RHP**

1991 Situational Stats

	AB	H	HR	RBI	AVG		AB	H	HR	RBI	AVG
Home	284	72	1	21	.254	LHP	208	58	2	17	.279
Road	325	91	4	29	.280	RHP	401	105	3	33	.262
Day	168	42	2	15	.250	Sc Pos	112	32	0	42	.286
Night	441	121	3	35	.274	Clutch	120	26	2	13	.217

1991 Rankings (American League)

→ 3rd in stolen bases (51)

→ 4th in caught stealing (15)

→ 6th lowest slugging percentage vs. right-handed pitchers (.344)

→ Led the White Sox in at-bats (609), stolen bases, caught stealing, plate appearances (709), stolen base percentage (77.3%), runs scored per time reached base (40.6%), lowest percentage of swings that missed (11.2%) and steals of third (2)

→ Led AL left fielders in at-bats, intentional walks (9), times on base (251), pitches seen (2,582), plate appearances, games (155) and lowest percentage of swings that missed

HITTING:

Sammy Sosa was expected to play a large part in the White Sox offense last year, and he looked like the real thing on Opening Day at Baltimore when he belted two home runs and drove in five runs. Unfortunately for Sosa and the White Sox, that was basically his season. Sosa's batting average and walks stayed down, while his strikeouts stayed up. The end result was a trip to the minor leagues in July, and not much more than pinch-hitting and running roles upon his recall.

Sosa's difficulties begin with his "swing hard at anything" style, which results in a lot of strikeouts (98) and almost no walks (14). Sosa loves to go after the first pitch, but far too often he swings and misses. Battling from behind too often to be effective, Sosa managed only a .132 average after he got down in the count.

Sosa is a dead fastball hitter who still has a lot of difficulty with breaking pitches. He definitely needs to acquire more patience if he's going to progress enough to warrant playing every day. His 17 walks in 117 at-bats during his minor league stint at AAA Vancouver last year was encouraging.

BASERUNNING:

Sosa runs the bases with abandon, and has the speed to back it up. He swiped 13 bases in 19 attempts, and scored five runs off the bench as a pinch-runner, including a couple of daring jaunts in close games late in the season.

FIELDING:

Sosa is an excellent outfielder who can play either center or right field effectively. He uses his speed to cover a lot of ground and make up for some youthful mistakes. Sosa has one of the strongest arms in the game, and runners are becoming reluctant to test it.

OVERALL:

Sosa is still young at 23, but with his lack of patience and problems making contact, he has a long way to go before becoming a solid everyday player. The Sox outfield is crowded entering the season, and Sosa will have to perform very well this spring to earn his starting role back.

SAMMY SOSA

Position: RF/CF
Bats: R **Throws:** R
Ht: 6' 0" **Wt:** 175

Opening Day Age: 23
Born: 11/12/68 in San Pedro de Macoris, Dominican Republic
ML Seasons: 3

Overall Statistics

	G	AB	R	H	D	T	HR	RBI	SB	BB	SO	AVG
1991	116	316	39	64	10	1	10	33	13	14	98	.203
Career	327	1031	138	235	44	11	29	116	52	58	295	.228

Where He Hits the Ball

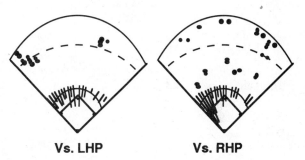

Vs. LHP   **Vs. RHP**

1991 Situational Stats

	AB	H	HR	RBI	AVG		AB	H	HR	RBI	AVG
Home	145	27	3	10	.186	LHP	128	29	5	11	.227
Road	171	37	7	23	.216	RHP	188	35	5	22	.186
Day	75	15	4	9	.200	Sc Pos	80	19	5	27	.237
Night	241	49	6	24	.203	Clutch	69	19	3	6	.275

1991 Rankings (American League)

→ 1st in lowest batting average on an 0-2 count (.000)

→ 7th in lowest batting average with 2 strikes (.122)

→ 9th lowest on-base average vs. left-handed pitchers (.277)

PITCHING:

Bobby Thigpen did not come close to repeating his 1990 record of 57 saves -- he didn't even get 40 save opportunities -- but a solid second half pushed him to the 30 save mark for the fourth season in a row. Thigpen's season was very reminiscent of his pre-1990 campaigns: not outstanding statistically, but effective in practice.

Thigpen has two main pitches, a fastball and a slider, which he'll mix with a curveball and occasional change-up. His fastball will start at the belt and wind up letter-high or higher (this is how he gets most of his strikeouts), and his slider moves down and away from righthanders. Thigpen needs to work frequently to keep sharp, and when he doesn't pitch regularly, his pitches flatten out and become more hittable. When he's high in the strike zone, Thigpen will give up more than his share of home runs. He was plagued by the home run ball again in 1991 (10).

Surprisingly for someone who throws so hard, Thigpen has never struck out a lot of batters. He has had problems with his control, and walked 38 batters in only 69.2 innings last year. Between the walks and the home runs, Thigpen blew nine saves, one more than he blew in all of 1990 when he had 65 opportunities.

HOLDING RUNNERS AND FIELDING:

Thigpen allowed eight stolen bases last year, a high figure considering the number of innings he pitched and the important situations he was usually pitching in. Thigpen does not have a good pickoff move, but fields his position well.

OVERALL:

Thigpen did not get many save chances in September, but he remains one of the game's top closers. It appears that he might need another pitch, perhaps a better offspeed breaking ball to offset the heat of his fastball and slider. Baseball is often a game of adjustment, and Thigpen would do well to stay one step ahead of the opposition.

BOBBY THIGPEN

Position: RP
Bats: R **Throws:** R
Ht: 6' 3" **Wt:** 195

Opening Day Age: 28
Born: 7/17/63 in Tallahassee, FL
ML Seasons: 6

Overall Statistics

	W	L	ERA	G	GS	Sv	IP	H	R	BB	SO	HR
1991	7	5	3.49	67	0	30	69.2	63	32	38	47	10
Career	27	30	2.89	344	0	178	452.0	393	161	179	298	42

How Often He Throws Strikes

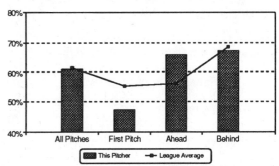

This Pitcher ■ League Average ●

1991 Situational Stats

	W	L	ERA	Sv	IP		AB	H	HR	RBI	AVG
Home	5	2	4.59	12	33.1	LHB	124	32	6	23	.258
Road	2	3	2.48	18	36.1	RHB	133	31	4	19	.233
Day	1	1	2.00	6	18.0	Sc Pos	88	19	2	30	.216
Night	6	4	4.01	24	51.2	Clutch	189	50	8	39	.265

1991 Rankings (American League)

→ 2nd in blown saves (9)

→ 3rd lowest save percentage (76.9%)

→ 5th in games finished (58)

→ 6th in save opportunities (39) and relief wins (7)

→ 8th in saves (30)

→ Led the White Sox in games pitches (67), saves, games finished, save opportunities, blown saves and relief wins

FRANK THOMAS

Position: DH/1B
Bats: R **Throws:** R
Ht: 6' 5" **Wt:** 240

Opening Day Age: 23
Born: 5/27/68 in
Columbus, GA
ML Seasons: 2

FUTURE MVP?

HITTING:

Only 23, Frank Thomas may be baseball's best all-around hitter. Only an August slide out of the pennant race by the White Sox prevented him from copping the American League's MVP Award in his first full major league season. The only players to reach Thomas' levels in batting average (.318), home runs (32), runs batted in (109), and walks (138) in one season are Babe Ruth and Ted Williams. Nice company.

Thomas' success is due in part to his ability to adjust to pitchers' strategies. The most common approach is to bust him with inside fastballs in hopes of either tying him up or getting a called strike from a generous umpire. Thomas simply will not swing unless he thinks the pitch is a strike, even with two strikes. If there are holes in his swing, American League pitchers have yet to find them.

Thomas has tremendous power to right field, and on occasion seems to hit the ball right out of the catcher's mitt. Late in the season, pitchers stopped trying to retire him in tight situations, preferring instead to pitch around him in hopes he'd chase some bad pitches and get himself out.

BASERUNNING:

Thomas' big strides help him get around the bases with good, but not exceptional, speed. He will not steal many bases, but he is aggressive and smart on the base paths.

FIELDING:

A sore shoulder kept Thomas at DH most of last year. When he played the injury hindered his throwing. In full health Thomas is an average or better fielder. He is expected to play regularly at first in 1992; watch for steady improvement.

OVERALL:

The White Sox are in dire need of a consistent bat behind Thomas in the batting order, or else they may find his walk total going up even more. But Thomas is a smart, fearsome hitter who's able to adjust to pitchers, and should continue to post great numbers no matter who's hitting behind him.

Overall Statistics

	G	AB	R	H	D	T	HR	RBI	SB	BB	SO	AVG
1991	158	559	104	178	31	2	32	109	1	138	112	.318
Career	218	750	143	241	42	5	39	140	1	182	166	.321

Where He Hits the Ball

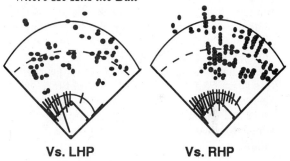

Vs. LHP   **Vs. RHP**

1991 Situational Stats

	AB	H	HR	RBI	AVG		AB	H	HR	RBI	AVG
Home	267	99	24	61	.371	LHP	170	64	11	35	.376
Road	292	79	8	48	.271	RHP	389	114	21	74	.293
Day	149	50	10	32	.336	Sc Pos	147	51	7	75	.347
Night	410	128	22	77	.312	Clutch	95	28	3	17	.295

1991 Rankings (American League)

→ 1st in walks (138), times on base (317), pitches seen (3,015), on-base average (.453) and on-base average vs. left-handed pitchers (.500)

→ 2nd in pitches seen per plate appearances (4.30), batting average vs. left-handed pitchers (.377), on-base average vs. right-handed pitchers (.432), batting average at home (.371) and highest percentage of pitches taken (65.4%)

→ Led the White Sox in batting average (.318), home runs (32), runs (104), hits (178), doubles (31), total bases (309), RBIs (109), walks, intentional walks (13), times on base, strikeouts (112), pitches seen, slugging percentage and on-base average

HITTING:

Robin Ventura is finally flashing the hitting form which made him Baseball America's College Player of the Decade for the 1980s. Moved from third to second in the batting order in late May, Ventura turned on the power and became one of the American League's top third basemen.

A patient hitter who draws walks (80), rarely strikes out (67), and hits the ball hard to all fields, Ventura turned out to be a perfect number-two hitter. He posted a .312 June average with seven extra base hits after being shifted up in the order, one more than he managed in April and May combined.

That was just the beginning, as Ventura started turning on the ball and pulling it. In one of the hottest months in Sox history, the lefty swinger clouted 12 home runs, drove in 33 runs, batted .357 and slugged .739 in July. He also provided one of the most dramatic moments in the White Sox season. Ventura capped Player of the Month Award honors by blasting a grand slam in the bottom of the ninth off Goose Gossage in front of a packed house to win the final game of the month.

BASERUNNING:

Ventura is no base stealer. He bounced into 22 double plays, and, given his foot speed (or lack thereof) and his ability to make contact, the White Sox might use him more on the hit-and-run to avoid the twin killing.

FIELDING:

While not yet of Gold Glove caliber, Ventura has the raw skills to be an excellent third baseman. He's got a strong arm that he puts on display with slow rollers, but sometimes makes an erratic throw, contributing to his 18 errors. He'll be a good one.

OVERALL:

Not many players hit 20 home runs and drive in 100 runs in their second season in the big leagues. The White Sox, who don't have a power-packed lineup, will be counting on the sweet swing of Ventura to keep up the pace he set for himself in '91.

ROBIN VENTURA

Position: 3B/1B
Bats: L **Throws:** R
Ht: 6' 1" **Wt:** 192

Opening Day Age: 24
Born: 7/14/67 in Santa Maria, CA
ML Seasons: 3

Overall Statistics

	G	AB	R	H	D	T	HR	RBI	SB	BB	SO	AVG
1991	157	606	92	172	25	1	23	100	2	80	67	.284
Career	323	1144	145	303	45	2	28	161	3	143	126	.265

Where He Hits the Ball

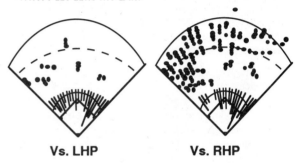

Vs. LHP   Vs. RHP

1991 Situational Stats

	AB	H	HR	RBI	AVG		AB	H	HR	RBI	AVG
Home	304	88	16	58	.289	LHP	192	50	5	20	.260
Road	302	84	7	42	.278	RHP	414	122	18	80	.295
Day	162	46	5	17	.284	Sc Pos	150	50	8	77	.333
Night	444	126	18	83	.284	Clutch	116	33	4	20	.284

1991 Rankings (American League)

→ 1st lowest fielding percentage at third base (.959)

→ 3rd in pitches seen (2,712)

→ 5th in GDPs (22)

→ Led the White Sox in sacrifice flies (7) and GDPs

→ Led AL third basemen in home runs (23), at-bats (606), total bases (268), RBIs (100), sacrifice flies, GDPs, pitches seen, plate appearances (705), HR frequency (26.4 ABs per HR), batting average with runners in scoring position (.333), batting average with the bases loaded (.461), errors (18) and bunts in play (18)

ROBERTO HERNANDEZ

Position: RP/SP
Bats: R **Throws:** R
Ht: 6' 4" **Wt:** 220

Opening Day Age: 27
Born: 11/11/64 in Santurce, PR
ML Seasons: 1

Overall Statistics

	W	L	ERA	G	GS	Sv	IP	H	R	BB	SO	HR
1991	1	0	7.80	9	3	0	15.0	18	15	7	6	1
Career	1	0	7.80	9	3	0	15.0	18	15	7	6	1

PITCHING, FIELDING & HOLDING RUNNERS:

A big, hard-throwing righty who resembles Lee Smith on the mound, Roberto Hernandez probably felt lucky to escape 1991 with his life, much less his major league prospects. Hernandez developed a serious blood clot while at Vancouver, and surgery was needed to replace a damaged vein in his arm with one from his leg.

Remarkably, Hernandez recovered quickly and was pitching in Chicago by September. His first start was everything the Sox had dreamed of: seven innings of one-hit ball against the Royals. Somewhat understandably, Hernandez couldn't sustain that excellent beginning, and in particular had trouble pitching from behind in the count. He made two more starts, not getting past the third inning, and finished the year in the bullpen.

Hernandez displayed his advertised 90-MPH fastball, and the pitch had nice downward movement. He also has a good slider, but needs to work on an offspeed pitch. He gets rid of the ball quickly, making him tough to steal on, and he showed good defensive reactions.

OVERALL:

If healthy this spring, Hernandez should make the club, and has a good chance to be a member of the starting rotation. After the surgery there are some concerns about his stamina, but he came a long way last year, and has the talent to be a star.

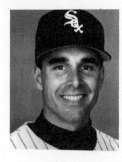

MIKE HUFF

Position: CF/RF
Bats: R **Throws:** R
Ht: 6' 1" **Wt:** 180

Opening Day Age: 28
Born: 8/11/63 in Honolulu, HI
ML Seasons: 2

Overall Statistics

	G	AB	R	H	D	T	HR	RBI	SB	BB	SO	AVG
1991	102	243	42	61	10	2	3	25	14	37	48	.251
Career	114	268	46	66	11	2	4	27	14	40	54	.246

HITTING, FIELDING, BASERUNNING:

Mike Huff is a speedy backup outfielder the White Sox picked up off the waiver wire from the Cleveland Indians. A Chicago-area product, Huff was a good acquisition for the White Sox. He was especially good in August, hitting .342.

Huff is a patient hitter (37 walks on the year) who has doubles power, but probably won't ever hit as many as 10 home runs in a full season. Huff is mainly an opposite-field hitter who will jump on a fastball and wait on a breaking pitch.

Huff's biggest asset is his speed. He stole 14 bases in 18 attempts, and was often used as a pinch runner by the Sox. His speed is also a plus on defense -- he can play all three outfield positions effectively. He has a good arm, suited mainly for center field rather than right.

OVERALL:

The White Sox' emphasis on speed and defense in the outfield is the main reason they got Huff. He'll be a bench player for the Sox, but he could be a good one, taking over for Lance Johnson in center field against tough lefthanders. Every team needs good bench players, and Huff's defensive and offensive abilities should be an asset to the Sox.

CHICAGO WHITE SOX

MATT MERULLO

Position: C/1B
Bats: L **Throws:** R
Ht: 6' 2" **Wt:** 200

Opening Day Age: 26
Born: 8/4/65 in Ridgefield, CT
ML Seasons: 2

Overall Statistics

	G	AB	R	H	D	T	HR	RBI	SB	BB	SO	AVG
1991	80	140	8	32	1	0	5	21	0	9	18	.229
Career	111	221	13	50	2	0	6	29	0	15	32	.226

HITTING, FIELDING, BASERUNNING:

Matt Merullo is the grandson of former Cubs shortstop Lennie Merullo (1941-47). Any resemblance, however, begins and ends with the last name. While Merullo the Elder was a quick, skinny right-handed hitting shortstop (5-11, 166 pounds), Merullo the Younger is a big, slow-footed (6-2, 200 pounds), left-handed hitting catcher.

The White Sox used Merullo primarily as a pinch hitter last season: he was only 7 for 41 (.171), but had a couple of home runs and seven RBI. He has solid minor league credentials, having hit .290. in his stints at AA Birmingham, though not with a lot of power. Like a lot of young hitters, Merullo hits the fastball well, but has trouble adjusting to the breaking pitch.

As a catcher, Merullo was not overly impressive in the minors, but could improve with more playing time at the major league level. He is very slow on the bases.

OVERALL:

The White Sox have tried to fill their bench with versatile players, and Merullo is an attractive addition in that regard. He can hit righthanders, and is useful as a third catcher. If Carlton Fisk should go elsewhere, Merullo could become an important part of the White Sox catching corps.

WARREN NEWSON

Position: RF/LF
Bats: L **Throws:** L
Ht: 5' 7" **Wt:** 190

Opening Day Age: 27
Born: 7/3/64 in Newnan, GA
ML Seasons: 1

Overall Statistics

	G	AB	R	H	D	T	HR	RBI	SB	BB	SO	AVG
1991	71	132	20	39	5	0	4	25	2	28	34	.295
Career	71	132	20	39	5	0	4	25	2	28	34	.295

HITTING, FIELDING, BASERUNNING:

If you're built like Warren Newson and can hit, you're inevitably compared to Tony Gwynn. If you're built like Warren and can't hit, you're compared to Tony's brother, Chris. Newson's not in Tony's class, but he definitely can hit. Acquired by the White Sox from San Diego along with Joey Cora, Newson quickly established himself as a "professional hitter," a guy who seems like he was born with a bat in his hands.

"The Deacon," as he's called by White Sox broadcasters, hit in whatever role he was used: he was 8-for-22 as the White Sox' premier pinch hitter, and hit .280 in regular duty. Newson can hit any type of pitch, and has good power to left and right center field. Among Newson's other pluses is an excellent eye at the plate, helping him draw 28 walks in only 132 at-bats.

Though he's built low to the ground, Newson is not slow, nor is he prone to baserunning blunders. He has average range in the outfield, but a weak arm.

OVERALL:

The long list of White Sox outfielders for 1992 should include Warren Newson. His abilities at the plate are numerous: he can hit for average, pop some home runs, and draw plenty of walks. Not a bad combination, especially for a White Sox team in need of some more solid offensive players.

ORGANIZATION OVERVIEW:

After a series of bad drafts in the early and mid-'80s eighties, the White Sox turned things around when Larry Himes became general manager in late 1986. In his four seasons as the Sox GM, Himes' number one picks were Jack McDowell, Robin Ventura, Frank Thomas and Alex Fernandez -- all key members of the club in 1991. Himes has since been deposed, and the new GM, Ron Schueler, hasn't been in charge long enough to show what he can do. But the Sox continue to do things the right way: they open up spots for their young players, and they don't panic if their players experience some growing pains. A lot of clubs could learn from their example.

ESTEBAN BELTRE

Position: SS
Bats: R **Throws:** R
Ht: 5' 10" **Wt:** 155

Opening Day Age: 24
Born: 12/26/67 in Ingenio Quisfuella, DR

Recent Statistics

	G	AB	R	H	D	THR	RBI	SB	BB	SO	AVG
91 AAA Denver	27	78	11	14	1	3	0	9	3	9	16	.179
91 AAA Vancouver	88	347	48	94	11	3	0	30	8	23	61	.271
91 AL Chicago	8	6	0	1	0	0	0	0	1	1	1	.167
91 MLE	115	410	44	93	9	3	0	29	7	24	79	.227

A diminutive shortstop with a major league glove, Beltre went from the Expo to Brewer to White Sox organization, finally making it to the bigs in September. When a guy gets traded that many times, there's usually an easy explanation, and in Beltre's case it's simple: he's not much of a hitter. Beltre raised his stock with a good year at Vancouver. He has a strong arm and could stick as a utility man.

RODNEY BOLTON

Position: P
Bats: R **Throws:** R
Ht: 6' 2" **Wt:** 190

Opening Day Age: 23
Born: 9/23/68 in Chattanooga, TN

Recent Statistics

	W	L	ERA	GGS	Sv	IP	H	R	BB	SO	HR
90 A Utica	5	1	0.41	6	6	0	44.0	27	4	11	45	0
90 A South Bend	5	1	1.94	7	7	0	51.0	34	14	12	50	4
91 A Sarasota	7	6	1.91	15	15	0	103.2	81	29	23	77	2
91 AA Birmingham	8	4	1.62	12	12	0	89.0	73	26	21	57	3

A 13th-round draft choice out of the University of Kentucky in 1990, Bolton was outstanding in his '90 debut and then was chosen White Sox minor league pitcher of the year for his '91 work. In 1990 he was 10-2, with a 1.23 ERA and a strikeout an inning at Utica and South Bend. Last year, moving up, he was 15-10, 1.78 at Sarasota and Birmingham, though his strikeout rate (while still impressive) went down. Some question Bolton's fastball, but his control is excellent, and you can't question his results thus far.

JEFF CARTER

Position: P
Bats: R **Throws:** R
Ht: 6' 3" **Wt:** 195

Opening Day Age: 27
Born: 12/3/64 in Tampa, FL

Recent Statistics

	W	L	ERA	GGS	Sv	IP	H	R	BB	SO	HR
91 AAA Vancouver	3	7	3.05	41	4	4	79.2	78	33	35	40	3
91 AL Chicago	0	1	5.25	5	2	0	12.0	15	8	5	2	1

Considered a minor player when traded in the Raines-Calderon deal by some, Carter was in fact an important part of the deal to the White Sox, who have an eye for pitching talent. Carter has had good numbers everywhere he's worked -- last year's 3.05 ERA was the highest of his minor league career. His fastball can reach 90 (though he doesn't get a lot of strikeouts), and he also relies a lot on a split-fingered pitch. Carter should get an extended look this spring.

JOHNNY RUFFIN

Position: P
Bats: R **Throws:** R
Ht: 6' 3" **Wt:** 174

Opening Day Age: 20
Born: 7/29/71 in Butler, AL

Recent Statistics

	W	L	ERA	GGS	Sv	IP	H	R	BB	SO	HR
90 A South Bend	7	6	4.17	24	24	0	123.0	117	86	82	92	7
91 A Sarasota	11	4	3.23	26	26	0	158.2	126	68	62	117	9

Signed at 16, Ruffin has been called a "young Dwight Gooden" -- a world-class exaggeration, considering that at Ruffin's current age, Gooden was winning 24 games with a 1.53 ERA, along with a Cy Young Award. Ruffin has a 97-MPH fastball, however, and an outstanding curve. Though he was only at Class A in 1991, Ruffin pitched extremely well. The Sox are not afraid to move young players up quickly, and Ruffin has the arm to reach the majors very soon.

ROBERT WICKMAN

Position: P
Bats: R **Throws:** R
Ht: 6' 1" **Wt:** 220

Opening Day Age: 23
Born: 2/6/69 in Green Bay, WI

Recent Statistics

	W	L	ERA	GGS	Sv	IP	H	R	BB	SO	HR
90 R White Sox	2	0	2.45	2	2	0	11.0	7	4	1	15	0
90 A Sarasota	0	1	1.98	2	2	0	13.2	17	7	4	8	0
90 A South Bend	7	2	1.38	9	9	0	65.1	50	16	16	50	1
91 A Sarasota	5	1	2.05	7	7	0	44.0	43	16	11	32	2
91 AA Birmingham	6	10	3.56	20	20	0	131.1	127	68	50	81	5

The next Three-Finger Brown? Another exaggeration: Wickman has all his digits, but lost the tip of his index finger in a farming accident (just like Brown, whose hand was gnarled in two separate farm mishaps). As with Brown, the injury seems to have given his offerings better movement. Wickman had a good year at AA Birmingham, despite his 6-10 record. He could be with the big club in 1992.

HITTING:

When Mike Aldrete stopped bouncing from one team to another last season, he landed in Cleveland. He went from Montreal to San Diego to Class AAA Colorado Springs before coming to rest in Cleveland on June 12. Aldrete went into the All-Star break hitting .410 for the Indians and didn't fall below the high .200s until September, when he seemed to tire.

Aldrete, 31, gave the Indians something they needed -- experience. While most of his teammates were still trying to figure out how to hit in the big leagues, Aldrete already knew. He's a smart, experienced left-handed hitter. He'll never be mistaken for a power hitter. Instead, he concentrates on hitting the ball to left field and up the middle.

A patient hitter, Aldrete drew 39 bases on balls in 198 at-bats last year. He only drove in 20 runs. He was one of the best hit-and-run men on the club.

BASERUNNING:

Aldrete isn't fast, but he runs the bases intelligently. In one game, he went from first to third on a sacrifice bunt -- the kind of heads up play that wasn't seen much in Cleveland last year. He knows how to go from first to third and slides well on close plays at the plate.

FIELDING:

First base is Aldrete's best position, although he did play some left field last year because of injuries and certain pitching match-ups. He has a good glove at first, but his arm is somewhat questionable -- especially on the 3-6-3 double play. He looked a little overmatched in left field, but caught most everything that was hit near him.

OVERALL:

After Aldrete was released by Montreal and San Diego, he said he thought about retiring. But he proved he could still be an effective role-player after the Indians signed him. If he's still with the Indians this season, that will be his job -- playing a little first base, pinch hitting and facing certain right-handed pitchers.

MIKE ALDRETE

Position: 1B/LF
Bats: L **Throws:** L
Ht: 5'11" **Wt:** 185

Opening Day Age: 31
Born: 1/29/61 in Carmel, CA
ML Seasons: 6

Overall Statistics

	G	AB	R	H	D	T	HR	RBI	SB	BB	SO	AVG
1991	97	198	24	48	6	1	1	20	1	39	41	.242
Career	618	1457	179	391	72	8	17	176	16	227	251	.268

Where He Hits the Ball

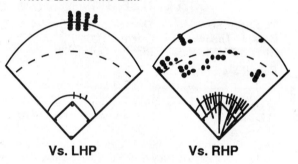

Vs. LHP   Vs. RHP

1991 Situational Stats

	AB	H	HR	RBI	AVG		AB	H	HR	RBI	AVG
Home	89	20	0	7	.225	LHP	12	2	0	1	.167
Road	109	28	1	13	.257	RHP	186	46	1	19	.247
Day	54	11	0	6	.204	Sc Pos	47	15	0	18	.319
Night	144	37	1	14	.257	Clutch	49	12	0	6	.245

1991 Rankings (American League)

➡ Did not rank near the top or bottom in any category

HITTING:

During the months leading to the 1991 season, Sandy Alomar scoffed at any mention of the sophomore jinx. He'd hit .290, drove in 66 runs and was named American League Rookie of the Year in 1990. Alomar said he wanted to do even better in 1991 and wouldn't listen to talk about a letdown.

Maybe he should have. Injuries to Alomar's right shoulder (inflamed rotator cuff) and right hip (strained hip flexor) limited him to 51 games. When Alomar is healthy, he's a line drive hitter who loves to hit through the middle or into right field. But last year, he looked lost at the plate.

Worried because he couldn't throw baserunners out due to his sore shoulder, Alomar let the injury affect his hitting. He didn't walk, struck out too much and stopped hitting in important situations. In 1990, he hit .307 with runners in scoring position. Last year he hit .096.

BASERUNNING:

When healthy, Alomar is an intelligent, but not overly fast, baserunner. Still, he gets down the line quickly for a big catcher (6-5, 215 pounds), and can go from first to third in the right situation.

FIELDING:

By the time Alomar said his right shoulder felt better, he strained the right hip flexor. As a result, he had trouble standing up behind the plate to throw out a potential base stealer. Despite the injuries, Alomar is still one of the most mobile catchers in the league. He has a habit of trying to throw runners out from his knees, but the Indians feel he puts too much strain on his arm that way.

OVERALL:

Alomar blamed himself for his injuries. He said he came to spring training overweight because of too many off season commitments following his Rookie-of-the-Year award. At the end of last year, Alomar went to the Indians' Florida Instructional League team to rebuild the strength in his shoulder and hip. If the Indians are to improve this season, they need a healthy and confident Alomar.

SANDY ALOMAR JR

Position: C
Bats: R **Throws:** R
Ht: 6' 5" **Wt:** 215

Opening Day Age: 25
Born: 6/18/66 in Salinas, Puerto Rico
ML Seasons: 4

Overall Statistics

	G	AB	R	H	D	T	HR	RBI	SB	BB	SO	AVG
1991	51	184	10	40	9	0	0	7	0	8	24	.217
Career	191	649	71	173	36	2	10	79	4	36	74	.267

Where He Hits the Ball

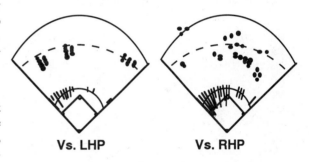

Vs. LHP **Vs. RHP**

1991 Situational Stats

	AB	H	HR	RBI	AVG		AB	H	HR	RBI	AVG
Home	69	17	0	0	.246	LHP	42	9	0	1	.214
Road	115	23	0	7	.200	RHP	142	31	0	6	.218
Day	61	16	0	2	.262	Sc Pos	52	5	0	6	.096
Night	123	24	0	5	.195	Clutch	40	6	0	4	.150

1991 Rankings (American League)

→ Did not rank near the top or bottom in any category

FUTURE ALL-STAR

CARLOS BAERGA

Position: 3B/2B
Bats: B **Throws:** R
Ht: 5'11" **Wt:** 165

Opening Day Age: 23
Born: 11/4/68 in San Juan, Puerto Rico
ML Seasons: 2

HITTING:

Some guys can hit, some guys can't. Carlos Baerga can hit. The tip-off came in Baerga's rookie season of 1990 when he hit .355 as a pinch hitter. Rookies aren't supposed to do that, but Baerga did. If there were any other doubts, Baerga erased them last year when he lifted his average 28 points to .288.

A switch-hitter, Baerga will chase a high fastball or breaking ball in the dirt now and then, but his discipline improved greatly last year. After hitting .255 through April, Baerga flirted with .300 for the rest of the season. He hit for a higher average right-handed, but showed more home run power left-handed -- nine homers and 49 RBI.

Overall, Baerga hit 11 homers last year, but his power was not consistent. After belting two homers on Aug. 22, he didn't hit another. But the Indians really weren't looking for power from Baerga. They wanted him to set the offense in motion as their number-three hitter, and that's exactly what Baerga did.

BASERUNNING:

Baerga is built along the lines of Kirby Puckett. He runs like a penguin. He's not a base stealer, but he can take an extra base if the opportunity presents itself.

FIELDING:

Baerga started the season at third base, but seemed uncomfortable. When he moved to second, he immediately looked like a natural. He's got good range and a strong throwing arm that allows him to play deep and steal hits. His strong arm helps him turn the double play quickly. He's fearless when it comes to making the pivot.

OVERALL:

Only 23, Baerga should continue to get better. He solidified the infield when he moved to second and gave the Indians a solid double play combination with shortstop Felix Fermin. He also helped give them some semblance of consistency with his production from the number-three spot. He's always smiling and loves to play. He's definitely a guy to watch.

Overall Statistics

	G	AB	R	H	D	T	HR	RBI	SB	BB	SO	AVG
1991	158	593	80	171	28	2	11	69	3	48	74	.288
Career	266	905	126	252	45	4	18	116	3	64	131	.278

Where He Hits the Ball

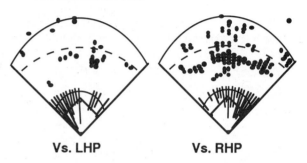

Vs. LHP   Vs. RHP

1991 Situational Stats

	AB	H	HR	RBI	AVG		AB	H	HR	RBI	AVG
Home	299	87	2	32	.291	LHP	161	53	2	20	.329
Road	294	84	9	37	.286	RHP	432	118	9	49	.273
Day	163	40	5	21	.245	Sc Pos	150	42	5	59	.280
Night	430	131	6	48	.305	Clutch	107	24	2	10	.224

1991 Rankings (American League)

→ 6th highest groundball/flyball ratio (2.3)

→ 8th in singles (130)

→ 10th in games (158)

→ Led the Indians in batting average (.288), at-bats (593), runs (80), hits (171), singles, intentional walks (5), hit by pitch (6), times on base (225), pitches seen (2,352), plate appearances (654), games (158), slugging percentage (.398), on-base average (.346), groundball/flyball ratio and runs scored per time reached base (35.6%)

→ Led AL third basemen in singles and games

HITTING:

Albert Belle has never found hitting a baseball to be difficult. He cannot say the same about other things connected to the game. Last year Belle was suspended by American League President Dr. Bobby Brown for hitting a taunting fan in the chest with a thrown baseball. He was also demoted to the minors for failing to run out a ground ball. Including a broken jaw that sidelined him for the last nine games of the season, Belle missed 32 games by his own actions, but still managed to hit .282 with 28 home runs and 95 RBI. Just think what this guy could do if he wore a white hat, signed autographs and said please and thank you.

Belle has a good idea of the strike zone. He's a dead fastball hitter, but can also handle breaking balls if he doesn't get overanxious. Like most power hitters, he gets into trouble when he tries to pull every pitch. He's much more effective when he concentrates on trying to hit the ball through the middle or to right field.

BASERUNNING:

Belle, who has ballooned close to 220 pounds, has average speed. He appeared to learn a lesson after being demoted on June 6 by the team for dogging it to first base. After his recall, he ran the bases hard. However, he showed poor judgement by colliding with Yankee catcher Matt Nokes late in the year. Belle suffered a broken jaw, costing him a chance for 30 homers and 100 RBI.

FIELDING:

Belle used to have a right fielder's arm, but weight lifting took the snap out of it and he's now better suited for left field. He worked hard on his defense, but still made nine errors. He has trouble when he has to go into the gap for balls and when he charges grounders.

OVERALL:

If Belle can control his temper and competitiveness, he can be a franchise player. He has excellent power and is intelligent enough to make adjustments to pitchers after they've adjusted to him.

FUTURE ALL-STAR

ALBERT BELLE

Position: LF/DH
Bats: R **Throws:** R
Ht: 6' 2" **Wt:** 200

Opening Day Age: 25
Born: 8/25/66 in Shreveport, LA
ML Seasons: 3

Overall Statistics

	G	AB	R	H	D	T	HR	RBI	SB	BB	SO	AVG
1991	123	461	60	130	31	2	28	95	3	25	99	.282
Career	194	702	83	183	39	6	36	135	5	38	160	.261

Where He Hits the Ball

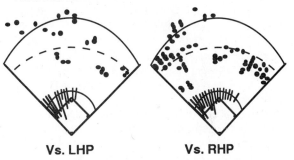

Vs. LHP　　　　**Vs. RHP**

1991 Situational Stats

	AB	H	HR	RBI	AVG		AB	H	HR	RBI	AVG
Home	236	60	8	35	.254	LHP	132	38	8	34	.288
Road	225	70	20	60	.311	RHP	329	92	20	61	.280
Day	132	40	11	36	.303	Sc Pos	126	39	6	61	.310
Night	329	90	17	59	.274	Clutch	66	13	2	10	.197

1991 Rankings (American League)

- → 2nd in GDPs (24)
- → 3rd in slugging percentage by a cleanup hitter (.526)
- → 4th most GDPs per GDP situation (20.9%)
- → 9th in home runs (28)
- → Led the Indians in home runs, doubles (31), total bases (249), RBIs (95), sacrifice flies (5), strikeouts (99), GDPs, batting average with runners in scoring position (.310) and slugging percentage vs. left-handed pitchers (.568)
- → Led AL left fielders in home runs, doubles, total bases, GDPs, errors (9) and slugging percentage vs. left-handed pitchers

HITTING:

Jerry Browne had a brutal year in 1991. He not only lost his starting job at second base, but he stopped hitting. In his first two years with the Indians Browne was a .285 hitter. Last year, he couldn't even hit .230.

As usual, Browne started the season slowly hitting .143 in April. He kept his second base job when rookie Mark Lewis was called up from the minors to fill in for injured shortstop Felix Fermin. But when Fermin came off the DL, Lewis moved to second and Browne was out of a job.

The switch-hitting Browne had a hard time adapting to his bench role. When he played, it was in unfamiliar spots, left field and third base. While Browne was learning two new positions, his hitting suffered. The one thing Browne did do well offensively was pinch hit. He led the Indians with a .324 average (11-for-34) as a pinch hitter.

BASERUNNING:

Browne is one of those players with decent speed but poor baserunning instincts. As a rookie with Texas in 1987, he stole 27 bases. He hasn't come close to those numbers since.

FIELDING:

Besides a slow start with the bat and the presence of Lewis and Carlos Baerga, Browne lost his job at second base for another reason -- he can't turn the double play. The problem first appeared toward the end of the 1990 season. Browne seemed to correct it in spring training, but it surfaced again early last year. He has good instincts at third base, but his arm is suspect. Later, Browne agreed to play left field, but this was purely a stopgap move at the time.

OVERALL:

The Indians think Browne can be a poor man's version of Detroit utility man Tony Phillips, and he went to the Instructional League to work on his outfield play. However, it's unlikely Browne will ever produce the kind of offense he did in 1989-1990 without getting consistent playing time.

JERRY BROWNE

Position: 2B/3B/LF
Bats: B Throws: R
Ht: 5'10" Wt: 170

Opening Day Age: 26
Born: 2/13/66 in St. Croix, Virgin Islands
ML Seasons: 6

Overall Statistics

	G	AB	R	H	D	T	HR	RBI	SB	BB	SO	AVG
1991	107	290	28	66	5	2	1	29	2	27	29	.228
Career	617	2093	298	564	89	19	14	182	62	254	225	.269

Where He Hits the Ball

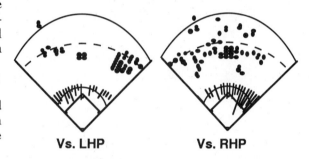

Vs. LHP   **Vs. RHP**

1991 Situational Stats

	AB	H	HR	RBI	AVG		AB	H	HR	RBI	AVG
Home	135	35	1	16	.259	LHP	78	18	0	6	.231
Road	155	31	0	13	.200	RHP	212	48	1	23	.226
Day	96	25	0	12	.260	Sc Pos	74	20	0	27	.270
Night	194	41	1	17	.211	Clutch	67	21	1	10	.313

1991 Rankings (American League)

→ 3rd in batting average on a 3-1 count (.800)

→ 7th in sacrifice bunts (12)

→ Led the Indians in least GDPs per GDP situation (10.0%), batting average in the clutch (.313) and batting average on a 3-1 count

→ Led AL second basemen in batting average on a 3-1 count

HITTING:

Last year Alex Cole did the one thing everyone wondered if he could do. He proved he could hit on a regular basis by leading Indians' regulars with a .295 average. Unfortunately, when it came to playing defense and running the bases -- things everyone thought Cole would do -- it was a different story.

Cole, a left-handed batter, is a good fastball hitter. He has a lot of patience at the plate, and it helped earn him an excellent .386 on-base percentage. He's a contact hitter who takes the ball up the middle or hits bloopers into short left field. If he hits the ball down the left field line, it's a sure double because of his speed.

After pressing too much in the first half, Cole put Rod Carew's spring training bunting lessons to use in the second half. It made him a better leadoff hitter.

BASERUNNING:

In 1990, Cole stole 40 bases in 63 games, while being caught only nine times. Last year the anticipation of what he could do over a full season bothered him. He stole 27 bases -- 18 coming after the All-Star break -- and was caught 17 times. Only Luis Polonia (23) and Rickey Henderson (18) were caught more often, and they stole 48 and 58 bases, respectively. A separated right shoulder in spring training made Cole hesitant to slide head-first.

FIELDING:

Cole, who played a promising center field in 1990, looked like he'd never played the game last season. His play was so shaky that he was moved to left field for a short time. When his replacement in center, Glenallen Hill, hurt his back, Cole got another chance. He took advantage and played decently in the second half.

OVERALL:

Cole is the Indians' only legitimate leadoff hitter, but his defense is so questionable he might have to DH. If Hill's back problem (bulging disk) is slow to heal, look for Cole to resume playing center. But can he cope with big-league pressure?

ALEX COLE

Position: CF
Bats: L **Throws:** L
Ht: 6' 2" **Wt:** 185

Opening Day Age: 26
Born: 8/17/65 in Fayetteville, NC
ML Seasons: 2

Overall Statistics

	G	AB	R	H	D	T	HR	RBI	SB	BB	SO	AVG
1991	122	387	58	114	17	3	0	21	27	58	47	.295
Career	185	614	101	182	22	7	0	34	67	86	85	.296

Where He Hits the Ball

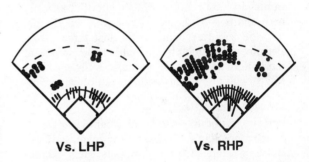

Vs. LHP   **Vs. RHP**

1991 Situational Stats

	AB	H	HR	RBI	AVG		AB	H	HR	RBI	AVG
Home	182	53	0	14	.291	LHP	62	24	0	8	.387
Road	205	61	0	7	.298	RHP	325	90	0	13	.277
Day	130	36	0	7	.277	Sc Pos	66	17	0	20	.258
Night	257	78	0	14	.304	Clutch	77	22	0	7	.286

1991 Rankings (American League)

→ 3rd in caught stealing (17)

→ 4th in highest percentage of pitches taken (64.1%)

→ 5th in leadoff on-base average (.382), steals of third (5) and worst stolen base percentage (61.4%)

→ 6th in batting average on a 3-1 count (.667) and lowest percentage of swings that missed (9.2%)

→ Led the Indians in stolen bases (27), caught stealing, walks (58), batting average on a 3-2 count (.333), bunts in play (21), highest percentage of pitches taken, lowest percentage of swings that missed, highest percentage of swings put into play (55.0%)

HITTING:

Felix Fermin is one of the best kept secrets in the American League. He's in the big leagues because he's an above-average defensive shortstop, but in the last two years he's also been an improved offensive player.

Fermin is strictly a singles hitter. He's hit one home run in 1,477 at-bats in the majors. Yet he's no longer strictly a right field hitter. Through weight lifting, he's become stronger and has been able to turn on the ball and get more hits to left field. Teams can no longer play their outfielders shallow and shift around to right against him.

Fermin loves any kind of fastball. He almost always makes contact, striking out just 76 times in his last 1,322 at-bats. He's a good hit-and-run man and one of the best bunters in the league, with 58 sacrifice bunts in the last three years. Fermin, who can hit in the number-two spot or at the bottom of the order, was also a decent hitter (.278) with runners in scoring position last year.

BASERUNNING:

Fermin is not a great baserunner. He's never stolen more than six bases in a big-league season. But he's smart and picks his spots. He's aggressive when it comes to stretching a single into a double.

FIELDING:

Rich Dauer, the Indians' former infield coach, called Fermin the best defensive shortstop in the league last year next to Chicago's Ozzie Guillen. He's got good range and enough arm to make the throw from the hole. Fermin made only 12 errors last season, his single-season low since he came to Cleveland. He runs the Tribe's infield.

OVERALL:

Fermin and youngster Mark Lewis will go into spring training competing for the same job. Fermin lacks Lewis' offensive potential, and it would be no reflection on his abilities if he loses out. If the Indians choose Lewis, some other clubs would undoubtedly be interested in Fermin.

FELIX FERMIN

Position: SS
Bats: R **Throws:** R
Ht: 5'11" **Wt:** 170

Opening Day Age: 28
Born: 10/9/63 in Mao, Valverde, Dominican Republic
ML Seasons: 5

Overall Statistics

	G	AB	R	H	D	T	HR	RBI	SB	BB	SO	AVG
1991	129	424	30	111	13	2	0	31	5	26	27	.262
Career	499	1477	142	373	35	7	1	98	17	105	95	.253

Where He Hits the Ball

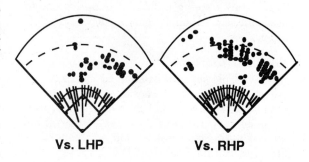

Vs. LHP   **Vs. RHP**

1991 Situational Stats

	AB	H	HR	RBI	AVG		AB	H	HR	RBI	AVG
Home	210	61	0	20	.290	LHP	121	34	0	8	.281
Road	214	50	0	11	.234	RHP	303	77	0	23	.254
Day	116	29	0	6	.250	Sc Pos	97	27	0	29	.278
Night	308	82	0	25	.266	Clutch	81	15	0	4	.185

1991 Rankings (American League)

→ 4th in sacrifice bunts (13)

→ 7th in batting average on a 3-1 count (.667)

→ 8th in most GDPs per GDP situation (19.1%) and lowest percentage of extra bases taken as a runner (30.3%)

→ Led the Indians in sacrifice bunts and batting average on an 0-2 count (.229)

→ Led AL shortstops in sacrifice bunts

HITTING:

The Indians wanted desperately to give Glenallen Hill the center field job after acquiring him from Toronto in the Tom Candiotti trade last year. There was one problem: Hill couldn't stay healthy. First, he pulled a groin muscle. Then he suffered a slight herniation of a disk in his back and was finished for the year.

The Indians envision Hill as a Rickey Henderson-type leadoff hitter, namely someone who can run and hit with power. Yet Hill has a history of not making contact, and it's questionable if he has the patience or the desire to be a successful leadoff hitter. Hill has indicated he'd like to hit lower in the order and have an opportunity to drive in runs.

The Indians say Hill gives the ball a better jolt than Albert Belle or Mark Whiten. Toronto GM Pat Gillick moaned and groaned about giving up Hill because of his long-range power potential.

BASERUNNING:

Hill once stole 42 bases in the minors (1985), but in two full big-league seasons he's never stolen more than eight. He is a big man with above-average speed, but it's questionable how much base stealing he's going to be doing after injuring his back last year.

FIELDING:

Hill looked comfortable in center field last year despite the fact that he hadn't played the position since 1989. He has good range and comes in on the ball well. His arm is decent. But again his bad back comes into play. He aggravated the injury making a diving catch; how many more will he be willing to attempt?

OVERALL:

Hill's bat has intriguing potential, but some scouts say he has a bad attitude and won't pay the price to get in shape. When he kept getting hurt after the trade, the Indians privately wondered if he was dogging it. But it turned out his injuries were legitimate. Hill should get a chance to silence the doubters in 1992.

GLENALLEN HILL

Position: CF/LF/DH
Bats: R **Throws:** R
Ht: 6' 2" **Wt:** 210

Opening Day Age: 27
Born: 3/22/65 in Santa Cruz, CA
ML Seasons: 3

Overall Statistics

	G	AB	R	H	D	T	HR	RBI	SB	BB	SO	AVG
1991	72	221	29	57	8	2	8	25	6	23	54	.258
Career	175	533	80	132	19	5	21	64	16	44	128	.248

Where He Hits the Ball

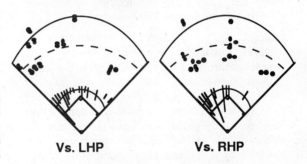

Vs. LHP   Vs. RHP

1991 Situational Stats

	AB	H	HR	RBI	AVG		AB	H	HR	RBI	AVG
Home	108	32	3	9	.296	LHP	96	27	4	12	.281
Road	113	25	5	16	.221	RHP	125	30	4	13	.240
Day	66	20	6	13	.303	Sc Pos	44	12	1	16	.273
Night	155	37	2	12	.239	Clutch	36	5	0	1	.139

1991 Rankings (American League)

→ Did not rank near the top or bottom in any category

PITCHING:

Shawn Hillegas lived through two seasons in 1991. He pitched very well in the first one and not so well in the second. Hillegas was the Indians' most effective reliever before the All-Star break. After starting the year in long relief, he moved into the closer role when Doug Jones and Steve Olin failed. At the break, he was 2-1 with five saves in five opportunities and a 2.11 earned run average.

After the break, Hillegas hit hard times. He had confidence, control and mechanical problems. The Indians were so befuddled by Hillegas' quick fall that they used him as a starter in his last three appearances to see if he could straighten his delivery out. They were also looking at him as a potential starter for the 1992 season.

Hillegas' best two pitches are a fastball and split-fingered fastball. In the first half, he showed no fear about throwing the fastball high in the strike zone and then coming back with the split-fingered pitch. The splitter would dive out of the strike zone, making batters look foolish. After the All-Star break, though, he recorded a blown save and a loss in two of his first four appearances and never really recovered. He started falling behind in the count and the batters would be waiting when he had to throw his fastball. His lack of control also led to gopher ball problems.

HOLDING RUNNERS AND FIELDING:

Hillegas is a decent fielder, but had some problems holding runners, especially late in a ball game. Like most closers -- at least when he held the job in the first half of the season -- he seemed more concerned about the batter than the baserunner.

OVERALL:

Even though Hillegas made his last three appearances as a starter, it's almost a sure thing he'll be back in the bullpen this year. The Indians like his arm strength and his versatility. They'd like to see him throw his slider more; he did so when he started and his control improved.

SHAWN HILLEGAS

Position: RP/SP
Bats: R **Throws:** R
Ht: 6' 2" **Wt:** 223

Opening Day Age: 27
Born: 8/21/64 in Dos Palos, CA
ML Seasons: 5

Overall Statistics

	W	L	ERA	G	GS	Sv	IP	H	R	BB	SO	HR
1991	3	4	4.34	51	3	7	83.0	67	42	46	66	7
Career	20	24	4.08	137	42	10	368.2	339	179	168	254	33

How Often He Throws Strikes

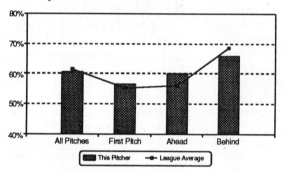

1991 Situational Stats

	W	L	ERA	Sv	IP		AB	H	HR	RBI	AVG
Home	3	2	3.07	5	55.2	LHB	142	32	1	14	.225
Road	0	2	6.91	2	27.1	RHB	158	35	6	29	.222
Day	0	1	6.83	1	29.0	Sc Pos	86	18	4	38	.209
Night	3	3	3.00	6	54.0	Clutch	125	27	4	19	.216

1991 Rankings (American League)

→ Led the Indians in games (51), holds (3), lowest batting average allowed vs. left-handed batters (.225), first batter efficiency (.189), relief innings (68.1), lowest batting average allowed in relief (.214) and most strikeouts per 9 innings in relief (7.8)

HITTING:

Chris James is a line drive hitter who can hit an occasional home run. When the Indians acquired him in the Joe Carter trade from San Diego before the 1990 season, they said he might hit 20 homers. James hasn't come close in two years, and was a hitting a lowly .238 when his 1991 season ended on September 5. James underwent arthroscopic surgery shortly thereafter to repair a torn rotator cuff in his right shoulder.

In 1990, James captured Cleveland's heart by hitting .299, driving in 70 runs and giving the Tribe a spark it sorely needed. The Indians seemed to feed off his competitiveness as they finished fourth in the AL East, their best finish since 1976. Last season, the always-streaky James had a nine-RBI game on May 4 against the A's and was hitting .303 on May 22. Unfortunately, he hit .207 (61-for-295) the rest of the year, and the May 4 game accounted for 22 percent of his season total of 41 RBI.

In 1990, James was used almost strictly as a DH. Last year, he saw some action in left and right field and at first base, and didn't seem as comfortable at the plate. He also lost playing time with the arrival of Glenallen Hill, Mark Whiten and Carlos Martinez. He never adjusted to the part-time role.

BASERUNNING:

James, whose brother Craig was an NFL running back, carries on the family tradition. He's not a base stealer, but he'll take an extra base on a fly ball and stretch a single into a double. He tries to lift a team through his aggressive baserunning.

FIELDING:

James never had a great throwing arm, and the shoulder injury won't help. But James will run into walls and throw his body onto the outfield grass to catch the ball.

OVERALL:

If James had stayed healthy, the Indians probably would have traded him last winter. He makes too much money to be a role player for a bottom-line team that's rebuilding. It's hard to see where he fits on this team for 1992.

CHRIS JAMES

Position: DH/1B/LF/RF
Bats: R **Throws:** R
Ht: 6' 1" **Wt:** 190

Opening Day Age: 29
Born: 10/4/62 in Rusk, TX
ML Seasons: 6

Overall Statistics

	G	AB	R	H	D	T	HR	RBI	SB	BB	SO	AVG
1991	115	437	31	104	16	2	5	41	3	18	61	.238
Career	668	2417	258	634	112	15	67	301	22	134	353	.262

Where He Hits the Ball

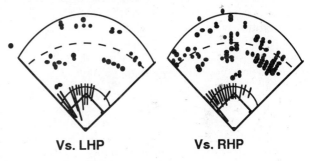

Vs. LHP   Vs. RHP

1991 Situational Stats

	AB	H	HR	RBI	AVG		AB	H	HR	RBI	AVG
Home	221	64	1	21	.290	LHP	131	26	2	12	.198
Road	216	40	4	20	.185	RHP	306	78	3	29	.255
Day	139	38	2	17	.273	Sc Pos	97	23	2	35	.237
Night	298	66	3	24	.221	Clutch	80	15	0	1	.188

1991 Rankings (American League)

➡ 2nd lowest on-base average vs. left-handed pitchers (.239)

➡ 5th lowest batting average vs. left-handed pitchers (.199)

➡ 10th lowest slugging percentage vs. left-handed pitchers (.298)

➡ Led the Indians in batting average with the bases loaded (.250)

➡ Led AL designated hitters in sacrifice bunts (2) and bunts in play (4)

PITCHING:

What happened to Doug Jones last season? The explanations were numerous, but one fact remained -- the closer with the third-most saves in the big leagues from 1988-1990 stopped saving ball games. Jones, relying on a decent fastball and a killer change-up, saved 112 games in his first three seasons as the Tribe's full-time closer, but last year late-inning disasters replaced late-inning heroics.

Jones hit bottom when the Indians outrighted him to Class AAA on July 25. When he left Cleveland, he was 1-7 with a 7.47 ERA and six saves in 11 chances. Some said Jones was tipping off his change-up. Others said he'd lost a couple of miles on his 88 MPH fastball, which took the surprise out of his slow-motion change. Jones had always been the master of disguise. Every pitch looked the same because every pitch was thrown with the same motion. Now it appeared hitters could see everything Jones threw before it left his hand.

Then there were those who said Jones, 34, had simply lost it, that he was finished. All along Jones said he just needed to pitch more. He got that chance in the minors, as the Indians made him a starter to give him more innings to increase his arm strength. When he returned to the Indians, he made four straight starts and went 3-1. He even struck out 13 batters in a game against Detroit.

HOLDING RUNNERS AND FIELDING:

Jones has improved his fielding since he broke into the big leagues. He starts the 1-6-3 double play very well. He's average at holding runners and hustles when he has to cover first.

OVERALL:

Jones added a cut fastball to his pitch selection when he returned as a starter. Yet, it's almost a certainty he'll be back in the bullpen this season if the Indians are able to solidify their rotation. Jones proved he could still pitch in the big leagues when he returned, but he'll need to re-certify his ability to save games on a consistent basis.

DOUG JONES

Position: RP/SP
Bats: R **Throws:** R
Ht: 6' 2" **Wt:** 195

Opening Day Age: 34
Born: 6/24/57 in Covina, CA
ML Seasons: 7

Overall Statistics

	W	L	ERA	G	GS	Sv	IP	H	R	BB	SO	HR
1991	4	8	5.54	36	4	7	63.1	87	42	17	48	7
Career	26	32	3.08	276	4	128	423.2	422	172	99	340	22

How Often He Throws Strikes

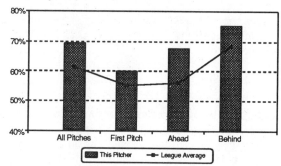

1991 Situational Stats

	W	L	ERA	Sv	IP		AB	H	HR	RBI	AVG
Home	1	4	6.41	1	26.2	LHB	132	45	4	25	.341
Road	3	4	4.91	6	36.2	RHB	140	42	3	20	.300
Day	1	0	4.00	4	9.0	Sc Pos	80	26	2	38	.325
Night	3	8	5.80	3	54.1	Clutch	91	37	4	26	.407

1991 Rankings (American League)

→ 1st in relief losses (7)

→ 5th highest batting average allowed vs. left-handed batters (.341)

→ Led the Indians in blown saves (5) and relief losses

PITCHING:

What kind of season did Eric King have in 1991? Well, he made bigger headlines for getting into a fight in an Arlington, Texas hotel, and later for coming down with chicken pox, than for anything he did on the mound. The one consistent attribute King showed was his visiting the disabled list with shoulder problems. He went on the DL on June 17 and missed more than a month of the season. It's the third straight season he's gone on the DL.

King has all the pitches to be an effective starter. He can beat you with curveballs and change-ups. Or he can beat you with his fastball. Yet his durability -- he's never pitched more than 159.1 innings in a season -- is questionable. King has also lost his ability to strike out hitters. In one stretch last year, he made four straight starts without striking out a single batter over 22 innings. Along with all that, some people question whether King can pitch in tight situations.

King seemed to have problems last year pitching with the Tribe's young and error-prone infield behind him. When an error occurred, he seemed to lose concentration. Manager Mike Hargrove also seemed to lose confidence in him toward the end of the season.

HOLDING RUNNERS AND FIELDING:

King is an average fielder. He handles bunts well and has a good throw to first. He does a decent job holding runners.

OVERALL:

The Indians gave King a vigorous off season conditioning program to follow. They want him to start this season with a sound right shoulder to avoid going on the disabled list yet again. When they acquired King from the White Sox, the Tribe said he was the kind of starter they could give the ball to every fifth day. Last year they found out he wasn't. Yet they are so short on starting pitching that King still figures in the team's plans for 1992.

ERIC KING

Position: SP
Bats: R **Throws:** R
Ht: 6' 2" **Wt:** 218

Opening Day Age: 28
Born: 4/10/64 in Oxnard, CA
ML Seasons: 6

Overall Statistics

	W	L	ERA	G	GS	Sv	IP	H	R	BB	SO	HR
1991	6	11	4.60	25	24	0	150.2	166	83	44	59	7
Career	48	39	3.85	186	99	15	784.0	724	360	305	414	61

How Often He Throws Strikes

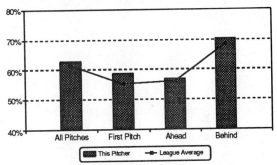

1991 Situational Stats

	W	L	ERA	Sv	IP		AB	H	HR	RBI	AVG
Home	2	7	5.95	0	65.0	LHB	326	93	5	44	.285
Road	4	4	3.57	0	85.2	RHB	268	73	2	28	.272
Day	4	3	4.16	0	75.2	Sc Pos	137	40	1	63	.292
Night	2	8	5.04	0	75.0	Clutch	25	12	0	5	.480

1991 Rankings (American League)

→ 4th lowest winning percentage (.353)
→ Led the Indians in shutouts (1) and ERA on the road (3.57)

MARK LEWIS

Position: 2B/SS
Bats: R **Throws:** R
Ht: 6' 1" **Wt:** 190

Opening Day Age: 22
Born: 11/30/69 in Hamilton, OH
ML Seasons: 1

HITTING:

Mark Lewis broke into the majors hard and fast last year. In his big-league debut on April 26, he singled against Nolan Ryan and hit a two-run double off Goose Gossage. It was the start of a sizzling month-and-a-half for the cocky 21 year old.

Lewis was hitting .415 (22-for-53) on May 12 when the Indians moved him from shortstop to second base to make room for Felix Fermin, who was coming off the disabled list. Lewis, a shortstop all his career, wasn't crazy about the move, but he kept hitting . . . for awhile. Then pitchers started jamming him with fastballs. Lewis, who has a very quick bat, began jumping at pitches in an effort to pull the ball. Instead he started hitting lazy fly balls to right.

By July 24, Lewis was down to .256 and was sent back to AAA Colorado Springs. There, manager Charlie Manuel worked at restoring the rookie's confidence and swing. When Lewis returned on Sept. 9, he hit .317 (19-for-60) in 15 games and looked much more comfortable at the plate.

BASERUNNING:

Lewis runs the bases hard and likes to get his uniform dirty with head-first slides. He'll steal a base if it's offered, but he's not going to give pitchers nightmares.

FIELDING:

Moved from short, Lewis didn't want to play second and didn't play it well. The experiment is over and Lewis stayed at short when he returned to Cleveland in September. Lewis is a very smooth fielder at his natural position. He does have problems catching high fly balls to short left field and slow bouncers while moving toward third. His throwing arm is outstanding.

OVERALL:

Lewis has outstanding offensive potential, but the Indians seem curiously reluctant to hand him their shortstop job. With a young infield, they feel they're going to need a steady hand at short. Still, Lewis has proven himself at the minor league level. He has earned a full shot at the starting shortstop job.

Overall Statistics

	G	AB	R	H	D	T	HR	RBI	SB	BB	SO	AVG
1991	84	314	29	83	15	1	0	30	2	15	45	.264
Career	84	314	29	83	15	1	0	30	2	15	45	.264

Where He Hits the Ball

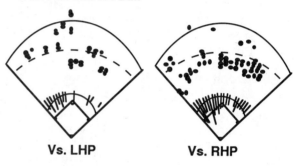

Vs. LHP   Vs. RHP

1991 Situational Stats

	AB	H	HR	RBI	AVG		AB	H	HR	RBI	AVG
Home	159	44	0	15	.277	LHP	87	24	0	7	.276
Road	155	39	0	15	.252	RHP	227	59	0	23	.260
Day	85	31	0	15	.365	Sc Pos	74	24	0	30	.324
Night	229	52	0	15	.227	Clutch	66	13	0	8	.197

1991 Rankings (American League)

➡ Led the Indians in sacrifice flies (5)

HITTING:

There were a lot of things Carlos Martinez did not prove last season. It's still debatable if he can play first base or if he'll ever be able to throw well enough again to play the outfield. But one thing is certain -- Martinez can hit.

After starting the season at Class AA Canton-Akron while recovering from a sore right elbow, Martinez was recalled to Cleveland. He was hitting .342 and in the midst of a career-high 16-game hitting streak on August 1. The streak ended loudly the next night when a Kevin Appier slider hit Martinez in the head. Martinez charged the mound, bumped an umpire and was ejected. He was also suspended and fined. Yeah, he's that kind of guy.

A line drive hitter, Martinez feasts on fastballs and can drive the ball into the gaps. Curveballs and sliders on the outside part of the plate can make him look silly. People have been waiting for Martinez to fill out his 6-5 frame for years. The wait is over. He now weighs 225 pounds (though media guides still list him at 175) and the extra muscle helped him hit five homers and 14 doubles in 257 at-bats.

BASERUNNING:

Martinez is a sight running the bases. He pumps his knees high and lifts his long arms up and down as if delivering countless karate chops on his way to first base. It's fun to watch, but he's no base stealing threat.

FIELDING:

The DH slot was made for this guy. The White Sox played Martinez all over the field and found him wanting. He played first base with the Tribe, but developed a problem. He kept dropping balls that hit him in the glove.

OVERALL:

For the most part, Martinez kept his temper under control in 1991. In fact, he did a stand-up comedy routine -- delivered in Spanish -- before almost every game that had the Latin players rolling in the aisles. He will be given a good chance to be the Indians' regular DH or a valuable bench player in '92.

CARLOS MARTINEZ

Position: DH/1B
Bats: R **Throws:** R
Ht: 6' 5" **Wt:** 175

Opening Day Age: 26
Born: 8/11/65 in La Guaira, Venezuela
ML Seasons: 4

Overall Statistics

	G	AB	R	H	D	T	HR	RBI	SB	BB	SO	AVG
1991	72	257	22	73	14	0	5	30	3	10	43	.284
Career	290	934	89	248	43	5	14	86	8	41	152	.266

Where He Hits the Ball

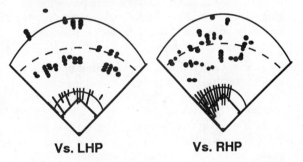

Vs. LHP   **Vs. RHP**

1991 Situational Stats

	AB	H	HR	RBI	AVG		AB	H	HR	RBI	AVG
Home	139	44	3	18	.317	LHP	80	27	4	13	.338
Road	118	29	2	12	.246	RHP	177	46	1	17	.260
Day	71	20	3	10	.282	Sc Pos	50	18	0	24	.360
Night	186	53	2	20	.285	Clutch	43	9	0	4	.209

1991 Rankings (American League)

→ 6th most GDPs per GDP situation (19.2%)
→ Led the Indians in sacrifice flies (5)

PITCHING:

Charles Nagy ended his rookie season as the Indians' most reliable starter. He showed the ability to pitch out of jams and keep his team in games even when he didn't have his best stuff. Nagy also showed durability -- 33 starts, 211.1 innings pitched and six complete games -- in his first full season. He went through a dead arm period in early August, but recovered to pitch some of his best ball of the season. Though Nagy lost his last three starts, his season was clearly a success.

Nagy's 15 losses were the third-most in the American League, but he pitched a lot better than his record indicates. The Indians' offense -- the lowest scoring team in baseball -- didn't do him justice. They averaged just 3.4 runs per game in Nagy's starts and scored three or fewer runs while he was in the game 25 times, including scoring no runs for him seven times.

Nagy's best pitch is a slider; he sets it up with a decent fastball and split-fingered pitch. He doesn't have any problem throwing strikes, recording 109 strikeouts and allowing 228 hits, the seventh most in the American League last year. What Nagy has to do is concentrate on throwing quality strikes. He also has to work on his performance in the early innings. Nagy allowed 44 runs and 84 hits in the first two innings of his 33 starts.

FIELDING AND HOLDING RUNNERS:

A good fielder, Nagy always hustles to first when he has to cover the bag. But he didn't hold runners very well and needs to make more throws to first.

OVERALL:

Nagy is not ready to be a number-one starter, but the role could be forced upon him now that the Indians have dealt Greg Swindell to Cincinnati. Nagy learned a lot last year: how to pitch with almost no offensive support and a shaky defense behind him, and how to pitch through slumps and dead-arm periods. The experience will help him.

CHARLES NAGY

Position: SP
Bats: L **Throws:** R
Ht: 6' 3" **Wt:** 200

Opening Day Age: 24
Born: 5/5/67 in Fairfield, CT
ML Seasons: 2

Overall Statistics

	W	L	ERA	G	GS	Sv	IP	H	R	BB	SO	HR
1991	10	15	4.13	33	33	0	211.1	228	103	66	109	15
Career	12	19	4.45	42	41	0	257.0	286	134	87	135	22

How Often He Throws Strikes

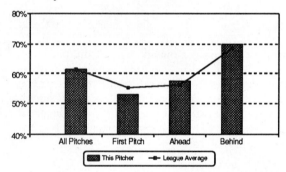

1991 Situational Stats

	W	L	ERA	Sv	IP		AB	H	HR	RBI	AVG
Home	6	5	3.56	0	93.2	LHB	460	133	7	47	.289
Road	4	10	4.59	0	117.2	RHB	368	95	8	42	.258
Day	3	6	4.45	0	64.2	Sc Pos	207	50	6	71	.242
Night	7	9	3.99	0	146.2	Clutch	72	17	0	3	.236

1991 Rankings (American League)

→ 3rd in losses (15) and lowest run support per 9 innings (3.4)

→ 4th highest groundball/flyball ratio (1.8)

→ 5th in GDPs induced (22) and highest stolen base percentage allowed (76.7%)

→ 7th in hits allowed (228)

→ Led the Indians in wins (10), games started (33), shutouts (1), walks allowed (66), hit batsmen (6), wild pitches (6), pitches thrown (3,262), stolen bases allowed (23), GDPs induced, winning percentage (.400), least home runs allowed per 9 innings (.64) and groundball/flyball ratio

PITCHING:

Versatile Rod Nichols filled many roles for the Indians in 1991 --starter, long reliever and set-up man. Nichols had a hard time winning (2-11 record), but that wasn't entirely his fault. He had a 3.98 ERA in 16 starts, but the Tribe scored only 25 runs (1.6 per game) while Nichols was on the mound. Nichols' only victories came in complete-game efforts against Oakland and Chicago.

Nichols, who bounced between Class AAA and Cleveland from 1988-1990, stuck in the majors last season after changing his pitching motion. He did away with the Louis Tiant back-to-the-hitter turn, and stopped relying on his slow curveball. Instead, he used a quicker, more efficient delivery. Suddenly, Nichols' fastball picked up a few miles an hour, and the bite to the curve and slider was much sharper. Nichols added a change-up to the mix around midseason. He calls the pitch a "forkle" -- a combination forkball/knuckleball. He holds it like a forkball, but it reacts like a knuckleball in flight.

Nichols, plagued by control problems in previous seasons, had better location with his reworked delivery. Yet he'd often say he was still experimenting to find out exactly what kind of pitcher he would become. Was he a finesse pitcher, who could get by on change-ups and breaking balls? Or was he more of a power pitcher, relying on a decent fastball and slider? Once the experimenting is over, Nichols will probably be a better pitcher.

FIELDING AND HOLDING RUNNERS:

Nichols is a good fielder, but tends to get frustrated when he makes a mistake defensively. Even though he's quickened his delivery, runners still get a good jump on him.

OVERALL:

The Indians must decide where Nichols can help them the most -- as a full-time starter or a spot starter/reliever. He seems better suited to be a starter, but didn't get upset when he bounced back and forth between the pen and the rotation. He's an aggressive pitcher, and isn't afraid to throw inside.

ROD NICHOLS

Position: SP/RP
Bats: R **Throws:** R
Ht: 6' 2" **Wt:** 190

Opening Day Age: 27
Born: 12/29/64 in Burlington, IA
ML Seasons: 4

Overall Statistics

	W	L	ERA	G	GS	Sv	IP	H	R	BB	SO	HR
1991	2	11	3.54	31	16	1	137.1	145	63	30	76	6
Career	7	27	4.34	61	39	1	294.1	323	160	83	152	25

How Often He Throws Strikes

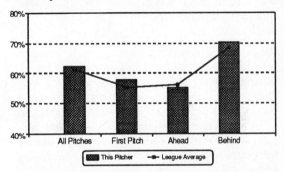

1991 Situational Stats

	W	L	ERA	Sv	IP		AB	H	HR	RBI	AVG
Home	1	7	4.08	0	75.0	LHB	272	81	2	35	.298
Road	1	4	2.89	1	62.1	RHB	260	64	4	25	.246
Day	1	3	4.26	0	38.0	Sc Pos	119	33	1	50	.277
Night	1	8	3.26	1	99.1	Clutch	87	13	1	4	.149

1991 Rankings (American League)

➡ Led the Indians in shutouts (1) and hit batsmen (6)

PITCHING:

Steve Olin has developed a pattern he would like to break. It goes like this - - he makes the Opening Day roster, struggles against left-handed batters, gets sent to the minors to correct the problem and finally returns to pitch well. The submarining righthander has done that for two straight seasons.

When Olin returned from Class AAA last July 15, he was given a major role -- he became the Indians' stopper because of the failures of Doug Jones and Shawn Hillegas. Olin handled it well. He converted 17 of his 22 save opportunities while showing the ability to work often. His delivery -- he's always thrown from down under -- doesn't put much strain on his arm and allows him to pitch frequently.

Olin's best pitch is a sinking fastball. He's been tough on right-handed hitters, but lefthanders give him fits. They hit .330 against him and opposing managers made sure he saw a steady stream of left-handed pinch hitters in save situations. Olin's problem is part confidence and part pitch location and selection. He has trouble jamming lefties with his slider and leaves it out over the plate. Lefthanders can see the pitch coming and wait for it.

HOLDING RUNNERS AND FIELDING:

A decent fielder, Olin sometimes has trouble with bouncers back to the mound. He gets off the mound quickly on bunts and rollers. Olin's submarine motion invites baserunners to steal, but not many do.

OVERALL:

Olin should be a vital member of the Indians' bullpen this season whether they decide to go with one stopper, or two, or three; after the way Jones struggled last year, Olin could well be the main guy. Olin saved 24 games at Class AAA in 1989, so he's no stranger to a closer's workload, but confidence is a key for him. Olin needs to develop the stopper's "live-for-today" attitude. His problems with lefthanders are also a concern.

STEVE OLIN

Position: RP
Bats: R **Throws:** R
Ht: 6' 2" **Wt:** 190

Opening Day Age: 26
Born: 10/4/65 in Portland, OR
ML Seasons: 3

Overall Statistics

	W	L	ERA	G	GS	Sv	IP	H	R	BB	SO	HR
1991	3	6	3.36	48	0	17	56.1	61	26	23	38	2
Career	8	14	3.46	123	1	19	184.2	192	83	63	126	6

How Often He Throws Strikes

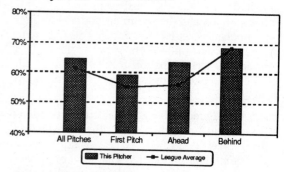

1991 Situational Stats

	W	L	ERA	Sv	IP		AB	H	HR	RBI	AVG
Home	0	1	3.80	7	21.1	LHB	103	34	1	11	.330
Road	3	5	3.09	10	35.0	RHB	120	27	1	18	.225
Day	1	2	2.76	4	16.1	Sc Pos	66	21	1	24	.318
Night	2	4	3.60	13	40.0	Clutch	132	31	1	15	.235

1991 Rankings (American League)

➡ 3rd worst first batter efficiency (.375)

➡ 4th worst save percentage (77.3%)

➡ 5th in relief losses (6)

➡ Led the Indians in saves (17), games finished (32), save opportunities (22), save percentage and blown saves

PITCHING:

Jesse Orosco's career continued its downward spiral in 1991. Orosco didn't make a single appearance for the worst team in the majors after September 13, which says something about the Indians' front office and even more about Orosco's ability to pitch.

Orosco needed 50 appearances last year to become the third pitcher in big-league history to work 50 or more games in 10 consecutive seasons. Working in 50 games would also have added $30,000 to Orosco's contract. But Orosco's season ended on Sept. 13 with appearance number 47, even though the Tribe didn't stop playing until Oct. 6. Orosco didn't complain much because he has a contract guaranteed through the 1992 season. Yet he did admit he wanted to be traded since the Indians were in a rebuilding mode and didn't seem to have much use for a 34-year-old left-handed reliever.

Orosco started last season in mop-up situations. When Mike Hargrove replaced John McNamara as manager, Orosco started pitching in tighter situations. The results were not good. Orosco was around mainly to pitch to lefties, but last year he had trouble getting them out. It got so bad that Hargrove wouldn't even use him in situations that clearly called for a lefthander. Orosco would throw in the bullpen, but it was only as a decoy. In three seasons with the Tribe, Orosco has only five saves -- none in 1991.

HOLDING RUNNERS AND FIELDING:

An excellent fielder, Orosco has made only three errors in his whole career. He has a decent move to first base, but runners will steal on him.

OVERALL:

Orosco's future with the Indians looks grim. The organization has lost confidence in him and he seems to have lost confidence in himself. Orosco's best pitch is a slider with which he's always been able to get lefthanders out. But last season, his slider deserted him and lefties hurt him. It would appear Orosco needs to change either ball clubs or careers.

JESSE OROSCO

Position: RP
Bats: R **Throws:** L
Ht: 6' 2" **Wt:** 185

Opening Day Age: 34
Born: 4/21/57 in Santa Barbara, CA
ML Seasons: 12

Overall Statistics

	W	L	ERA	G	GS	Sv	IP	H	R	BB	SO	HR
1991	2	0	3.74	47	0	0	45.2	52	20	15	36	4
Career	60	57	2.82	598	4	121	836.2	685	300	349	719	64

How Often He Throws Strikes

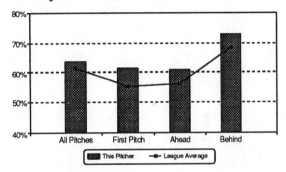

1991 Situational Stats

	W	L	ERA	Sv	IP		AB	H	HR	RBI	AVG
Home	1	0	1.90	0	23.2	LHB	63	18	1	8	.286
Road	1	0	5.73	0	22.0	RHB	119	34	3	22	.286
Day	0	0	3.29	0	13.2	Sc Pos	72	22	2	27	.306
Night	2	0	3.94	0	32.0	Clutch	40	13	0	9	.325

1991 Rankings (American League)

→ 7th fewest GDPs induced per GDP situation (3.6%)

→ 9th worst first batter efficiency (.326)

→ Led the Indians in holds (3) and lowest percentage of inherited runners scored (35.0%)

PITCHING:

Not many good things happened to the Indians last season. Just about everything that could go wrong did, but don't blame Dave Otto. The 6-7 rookie lefthander, who signed as a minor league free agent after spending six years in the Oakland organization, pitched well for the Tribe.

Of course, with the Indians, everything is relative. Just because someone pitched well doesn't mean they won many games. Otto, who didn't join the Tribe until June 28, went 2-8 in 18 appearances, the last 14 of them as a starter. While the record is poor, nine of Otto's outings were quality starts. Offensively, the Indians averaged just 2.5 runs in Otto's 14 starts while he was in the game.

When he pitched with Oakland Otto was considered a top prospect, but knee injuries and the overall talent of the A's pitching staff held him back. Last year he finally got a chance to pitch in the majors. More importantly, Otto's right knee, which had sidelined him for all but 4.1 innings in 1990, held up all season.

Otto throws a slider, fastball and forkball. He's sneaky fast (83-86 MPH), but is basically a finesse pitcher who must keep the ball down to be successful. He isn't afraid to throw inside, either. Otto showed good concentration and competitiveness on the mound.

HOLDING RUNNERS AND FIELDING:

The Indians were concerned about Otto's fielding because of his knee problems. In the minors, baserunners frequently ran on him because of his long delivery. However, Otto fielded his position well in Cleveland, hustling off the mound for bunts in front of the plate. He needs work holding runners, but a track meet didn't break out every time he pitched.

OVERALL:

Otto should be the Indians' number-three or four starter this season. He impressed the front office as a starter after a shaky start in the bullpen. But several times last season Otto made the wrong pitch at a crucial time, which always seemed to beat him. It's a problem he'll have to overcome.

DAVE OTTO

Position: SP
Bats: L **Throws:** L
Ht: 6' 7" **Wt:** 210

Opening Day Age: 27
Born: 11/12/64 in Chicago, IL
ML Seasons: 5

Overall Statistics

	W	L	ERA	G	GS	Sv	IP	H	R	BB	SO	HR
1991	2	8	4.23	18	14	0	100.0	108	52	27	47	7
Career	2	8	4.25	27	17	0	125.0	133	65	39	63	8

How Often He Throws Strikes

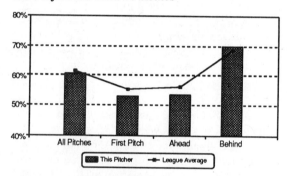

1991 Situational Stats

	W	L	ERA	Sv	IP		AB	H	HR	RBI	AVG
Home	1	6	4.12	0	59.0	LHB	69	21	0	11	.304
Road	1	2	4.39	0	41.0	RHB	313	87	7	31	.278
Day	0	1	2.20	0	16.1	Sc Pos	93	31	1	33	.333
Night	2	7	4.63	0	83.2	Clutch	50	16	2	7	.320

1991 Rankings (American League)

➡ Did not rank near the top or bottom in any category

HITTING:

Joel Skinner has always had trouble hitting breaking balls, and at 31, the problem isn't going away. Still, last season Skinner filled in for the injured Sandy Alomar and didn't do a bad job offensively. Skinner's .243 average was nothing to brag about, but he hit a lot better than that for most of the season.

Over the last couple of years hitting coach Jose Morales convinced Skinner to be patient and think fastball. When Alomar went on the DL in mid-May, Skinner came on strong. He ended May hitting .323 and was still batting .264 at the All-Star break. Skinner slumped thereafter, but easily bettered his .225 career average entering the season.

Skinner isn't a patient hitter. He walked 14 times last year, and that matched his second-highest total in nine big-league seasons. He has a little power and will hit an occasional home run when a pitcher makes a mistake with a fastball. He's a good bunter and will willingly hit behind a runner to move him up. When he gets two strikes on him, Skinner is usually easy pickings for big-breaking curveballs.

BASERUNNING:

Skinner might be the slowest catcher in the big leagues, which is saying something. He has trouble beating out even the surest of infield hits.

FIELDING:

This is where Skinner makes his money. He calls a good game and blocks balls in the dirt well. His best asset is his strong and accurate right arm. In one stretch last year, he threw out seven straight would-be base stealers. In fact, Skinner may have overdone it, as he missed the last two weeks of the season with a strained right shoulder.

OVERALL:

While the penny-wise Indians refused to offer long-term contracts to Tom Candiotti and Brook Jacoby, they signed Skinner to a three-year deal before the 1991 season. It turned out to be a smart move. Skinner gives the Indians consistent catching and veteran leadership for a young pitching staff.

JOEL SKINNER

Position: C
Bats: R **Throws:** R
Ht: 6' 4" **Wt:** 200

Opening Day Age: 31
Born: 2/21/61 in La Jolla, CA
ML Seasons: 9

Overall Statistics

	G	AB	R	H	D	T	HR	RBI	SB	BB	SO	AVG
1991	99	284	23	69	14	0	1	24	0	14	67	.243
Career	564	1441	119	329	62	3	17	136	3	80	387	.228

Where He Hits the Ball

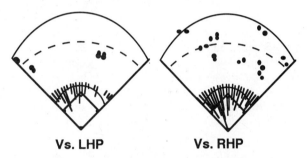

Vs. LHP   Vs. RHP

1991 Situational Stats

	AB	H	HR	RBI	AVG		AB	H	HR	RBI	AVG
Home	142	37	0	15	.261	LHP	88	27	0	7	.307
Road	142	32	1	9	.225	RHP	196	42	1	17	.214
Day	80	16	1	8	.200	Sc Pos	70	12	0	19	.171
Night	204	53	0	16	.260	Clutch	51	13	0	3	.255

1991 Rankings (American League)

➡ Did not rank near the top or bottom in any category

PITCHING:

Blame part of Greg Swindell's 1991 problems on the Indians' offense and defense -- the worst in the American League. Blame part of it on Swindell's attitude in the second half, which was something less than win-at-all-costs. Swindell clearly wanted out of Cleveland, and he got his wish, moving to Cincinnati in a big off season deal.

Swindell may have had his best season when it came to control and throwing all four of his pitches -- fastball, slider, change-up and curveball -- for strikes. His strikeout to walk ratio was outstanding (169-to-31). He led the league by averaging just 1.2 walks per nine innings.

But Swindell's control may have been a mixed blessing. Constantly keeping the ball around the plate, he allowed 241 hits, the fourth most in the league. As the season wore on and the Indians worked their way toward 105 losses, Swindell became obsessed with not walking people. He got to a point where he said if he was behind a hitter 2-0 or 3-0, he was going to groove a pitch no matter what the situation. This did not make a good impression on manager Mike Hargrove.

The Tribe's lack of offense and defense seemed to discourage Swindell in the second half. If an error was made in a critical part of the game, Swindell's concentration seemed to drift and, very often, so would his chance for victory.

HOLDING RUNNERS AND FIELDING:

Swindell is heavy and doesn't get off the mound quickly, but he fields his position decently. He has an excellent move to first base. Not many runners get a good jump on him.

OVERALL:

When the Indians traded Tom Candiotti to Toronto in late June, Swindell became the number-one starter on the Cleveland staff. But he didn't pitch like it. Swindell shouldn't have that pressure in Cincinnati, where Jose Rijo is the main guy. But he'll be expected to win 15 games or more -- something he hasn't done since 1988.

GREG SWINDELL

Position: SP
Bats: B **Throws:** L
Ht: 6' 3" **Wt:** 225

Opening Day Age: 27
Born: 1/2/65 in Fort Worth, TX
ML Seasons: 6

Overall Statistics

	W	L	ERA	G	GS	Sv	IP	H	R	BB	SO	HR
1991	9	16	3.48	33	33	0	238.0	241	112	31	169	21
Career	60	55	3.79	153	152	0	1043.0	1059	487	226	756	109

How Often He Throws Strikes

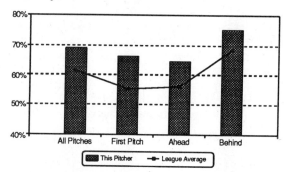

1991 Situational Stats

	W	L	ERA	Sv	IP		AB	H	HR	RBI	AVG
Home	7	9	2.52	0	153.1	LHB	153	42	1	14	.275
Road	2	7	5.21	0	84.2	RHB	763	199	20	88	.261
Day	3	5	2.75	0	68.2	Sc Pos	190	47	4	69	.247
Night	6	11	3.77	0	169.1	Clutch	139	35	1	7	.252

1991 Rankings (American League)

→ 1st in strikeout/walk ratio (5.5)

→ 2nd in losses (16), least pitches thrown per batter (3.34) and ERA at home (2.52)

→ 4th in hits allowed (241) and highest ERA on the road (5.21)

→ 5th least run support per 9 innings (3.6)

→ 6th in complete games (7)

→ Led the Indians in ERA (3.48), losses, games started (33), complete games, innings (241), strikeouts (169), batters faced (971), pickoff throws (146), runners caught stealing (11), strikeout/walk ratio and most run support per 9 innings

MARK WHITEN

STRONG ARM

Position: RF
Bats: B **Throws:** R
Ht: 6' 3" **Wt:** 215

Opening Day Age: 25
Born: 11/25/66 in
Pensacola, FL
ML Seasons: 2

HITTING:

Indians' players went through a series of physical exams at the end of last season to measure strength, quickness, conditioning, body fat and to determine areas for improvement during the winter. When Mark Whiten's results came back, they said he didn't need to do a thing. He was almost perfect.

Hitting a baseball, though, is another matter. Whiten, viewed as the key player in the Tom Candiotti deal with Toronto, was still classified as a rookie last year. The switch-hitter had problems making solid contact -- especially from the left side of the plate.

Whiten's one redeeming quality from the left side was his extra-base power. He hit for a higher average batting righty. Whiten looks like he can eventually be a home run threat, but he was more of a line drive hitter last year with 18 doubles and seven triples.

BASERUNNING:

Whiten can run, as his seven triples attest. He's also stolen as many as 49 bases in a minor league season (1987). Yet that kind of speed wasn't evident last year in Cleveland. He'll go hard into second to break up a double play, though.

FIELDING:

Manager Mike Hargrove needed to watch Whiten play right field for about a week after the June 27 trade before saying, "He's our best outfielder." Whiten went back well on the ball both to his left and right and made several nice catches against the fence. He has a strong throwing arm that makes runners fearful of taking the extra base.

OVERALL:

Whiten is a key part of the Indians' foundation. They dealt Candiotti to Toronto in an effort to add power, speed and athletic ability to the outfield. They think they did that with Whiten and Glenallen Hill. What Whiten needs now is playing time. There were too many talented bodies in front of him in Toronto. That's not the case in Cleveland.

Overall Statistics

	G	AB	R	H	D	T	HR	RBI	SB	BB	SO	AVG
1991	116	407	46	99	18	7	9	45	4	30	85	.243
Career	149	495	58	123	19	8	11	52	6	37	99	.248

Where He Hits the Ball

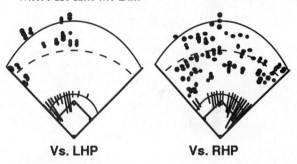

Vs. LHP   Vs. RHP

1991 Situational Stats

	AB	H	HR	RBI	AVG		AB	H	HR	RBI	AVG
Home	197	49	4	16	.249	LHP	109	28	2	10	.257
Road	210	50	5	29	.238	RHP	298	71	7	35	.238
Day	105	23	1	12	.219	Sc Pos	95	22	0	31	.232
Night	302	76	8	33	.252	Clutch	79	16	2	9	.203

1991 Rankings (American League)

→ 7th highest percentage of extra bases taken as a runner (72.4%)
→ 9th lowest batting average on an 0-2 count (.057)
→ 10th in triples (7)
→ Led the Indians in triples (4 with Cleveland)

ERIC BELL

Position: RP
Bats: L **Throws:** L
Ht: 6' 0" **Wt:** 165

Opening Day Age: 28
Born: 10/27/63 in Modesto, CA
ML Seasons: 4

REGGIE JEFFERSON

Position: 1B
Bats: B **Throws:** L
Ht: 6' 4" **Wt:** 210

Opening Day Age: 23
Born: 9/25/68 in Tallahassee, FL
ML Seasons: 1

Overall Statistics

	W	L	ERA	G	GS	Sv	IP	H	R	BB	SO	HR
1991	4	0	0.50	10	0	0	18.0	5	2	5	7	0
Career	15	15	4.97	51	33	0	212.0	206	132	101	140	37

Overall Statistics

	G	AB	R	H	D	T	HR	RBI	SB	BB	SO	AVG
1991	31	108	11	21	3	0	3	13	0	4	24	.194
Career	31	108	11	21	3	0	3	13	0	4	24	.194

PITCHING, FIELDING & HOLDING RUNNERS:

Eric Bell, a finesse pitcher who hadn't worn a big-league uniform since 1987, resurfaced last September in the Indians' bullpen. He looked unhittable, going 4-0 in 10 appearances and allowing only one earned run and five hits in 18 innings. That was the most wins any Indians' reliever had all season, which explains both how well Bell pitched and how bad the Tribe's bullpen performed.

Bell, a change-up, breaking ball pitcher, won 10 games for the Orioles in 1987, but then injuries set him back. He underwent Tommy John surgery on his left elbow in 1988 and has been trying to come back ever since. He started last season at Class AA Canton, going 9-5, 2.89, then made four effective starts for Class AAA Colorado Springs before getting called up. The Indians like him because he had success against both righties and lefties. He's a decent fielder and does a good job keeping runners close.

OVERALL:

Bell has starting rotation possibilities, but the Indians see him now as the left-handed reliever they need to strengthen their bullpen. Jesse Orosco has been unproductive for two years and, if Bell continues to pitch well, the Indians might finally have another option.

HITTING, FIELDING, BASERUNNING:

For several years, first sacker Reggie Jefferson was considered one of the top prospects in the Cincinnati organization, the budding superstar who would succeed Eric Davis. But when Cincinnati made a silly clerical error last summer in an attempt to save a few bucks, they were forced to deal Jefferson or lose him on waivers. The Indians were the lucky beneficiaries, and now Jefferson is considered a top prospect in the Cleveland organization, and indeed in all of baseball.

A switch-hitter, Jefferson showed some of his promised power after joining the Tribe -- especially from the left side of the plate. Jefferson has a long swing, particularly batting righty, and looked overmatched against breaking balls. But he'll hit a fastball a long way. He's not going to awe anyone with his speed and he's only average defensively, especially when it comes to turning the 3-6-3 double play.

OVERALL:

Since 1988, the Indians have tried veterans Willie Upshaw, Pete O'Brien and Keith Hernandez at first, with no luck. Jefferson, expected to turn that unimpressive string around, looked lost after he came to Cleveland. He'd dropped about 10 pounds because of pneumonia and was nursing a pulled chest muscle. That might explain his poor numbers. Jefferson should be the Opening Day first baseman unless he gets hit by a bus.

JEFF
SHAW

Position: RP
Bats: R **Throws:** R
Ht: 6' 2" **Wt:** 185

Opening Day Age: 25
Born: 7/7/66 in
Washington Courthouse,
OH
ML Seasons: 2

JIM
THOME

Position: 3B
Bats: L **Throws:** R
Ht: 6' 3" **Wt:** 200

Opening Day Age: 21
Born: 8/27/70 in Peoria,
IL
ML Seasons: 1

Overall Statistics

	W	L	ERA	G	GS	Sv	IP	H	R	BB	SO	HR
1991	0	5	3.36	29	1	1	72.1	72	34	27	31	6
Career	3	9	4.69	41	10	1	121.0	145	72	47	56	17

Overall Statistics

	G	AB	R	H	D	T	HR	RBI	SB	BB	SO	AVG
1991	27	98	7	25	4	2	1	9	1	5	16	.255
Career	27	98	7	25	4	2	1	9	1	5	16	.255

PITCHING, FIELDING & HOLDING RUNNERS:

Not many pitchers like the job, but Jeff Shaw found happiness in long relief last year. Shaw made nine starts with the Indians in 1990, most of them bad. He always seemed to get into trouble the second time through the batting order, which made for a quick exit.

Last year, Shaw joined the Indians on June 13 after being in the starting rotation at Class AAA. He made one start, a disaster, then moved to the pen. He went 0-5, but his ERA was a respectable 3.36 and, for the most part, he did what a long reliever is supposed to do -- give his team a chance to come back and win a game.

Shaw throws a fastball, slider and forkball. He still had trouble throwing strikes, but at least he stopped nibbling at the corners of the plate and went right after the hitters. He's a good fielder, but needs work when it comes to holding runners.

OVERALL:

Shaw didn't guarantee himself a spot in the Indians' bullpen for 1992, but he didn't eliminate himself either. He's still only 25, and if he could find the kind of control he had in 1987 when he struck out 117 and walked 56 in 184.1 innings at Class A Waterloo, he might develop into a competent reliever/spot starter. He took a step toward that goal last year.

HITTING, FIELDING, BASERUNNING:

Jim Thome made it to the big leagues and started 27 games at third base in 1991 -- not bad for a 21 year old who was in extended spring training in 1990. Considered an outstanding prospect, Thome made a good impression in those 27 games and figures to stick around this year.

The lefty-swinging Thome has a pretty inside-out swing that allows him to hit to the opposite field. In his major league debut on Sept. 4, he had two hits, both singles to left. He showed he could turn on the ball, too, hitting it with authority to right field on occasion. But last year, he seemed more intent to try and just make contact and take the ball the other way.

Thome is not a polished third baseman. His arm is average and he has some trouble going to the line. He made errors on routine plays and had trouble starting the 5-4-3 double play. Yet he didn't let it bother him. He was smart enough to know it was part of the learning process and didn't let it affect his next at-bat or play in the field. On the bases, he's no threat to steal.

OVERALL:

Unless Thome has a miserable spring training, he'll be the Indians' starting third baseman. The Tribe will probably spell him against tough left-handers until he gets more experience.

ORGANIZATION OVERVIEW:

When a club a) finishes at the bottom of the standings nearly every year and b) trades a lot of its veterans for younger (and cheaper) players, you'd expect it to have some good prospects. The Indians do, but that doesn't necessarily mean they know how to develop them. Last year's handling of shortstop Mark Lewis, considered their best youngster, creates doubts. The Tribe brought up Lewis, watched him go crazy with the bat, then attempted to shift him to second when the less-than-immortal Felix Fermin returned from the DL. They're probably still wondering why Lewis stopped hitting. The Indians do have some outstanding prospects, including Lewis, Jim Thome and Reggie Jefferson, but most of them are already in the majors, and who knows if Cleveland will be able to nurture and develop them? The players listed below are much farther away.

BRUCE EGLOFF

Position: P   **Opening Day Age:** 26
Bats: R **Throws:** R   **Born:** 4/10/65 in
Ht: 6' 2" **Wt:** 215   Denver, CO

Recent Statistics

	W	L	ERA	G	GS	Sv	IP	H	R	BB	SO	HR
91 AAA Colo Sprngs	1	2	3.38	15	0	2	29.1	31	14	13	17	2
91 AL Cleveland	0	0	4.76	6	0	0	5.2	8	3	4	8	0

Considered the heir-apparent to Doug Jones as Cleveland's closer, Egloff has spent most of his career battling injuries. He missed the entire 1988 season because of two rotator cuff operations, and lost most of 1991 after breaking his non-throwing hand in an apartment accident. Egloff still throws hard despite the operations, and has potential as a reliever, but he's a long shot to make the Indian staff this spring.

JEFF MUTIS

Position: P   **Opening Day Age:** 25
Bats: L **Throws:** L   **Born:** 12/20/66 in
Ht: 6' 2" **Wt:** 185   Allentown, PA

Recent Statistics

	W	L	ERA	G	GS	Sv	IP	H	R	BB	SO	HR
91 AA Canton-akrn	11	5	1.80	25	24	0	169.2	138	42	51	89	0
91 AL Cleveland	0	3	11.68	3	3	0	12.1	23	16	7	6	1

A first-round pick in 1988 (27th overall), Mutis has posted good numbers everywhere he's pitched, especially last year at AA Canton. Yet some people doubt his potential because he doesn't have a major league fastball (about 83 MPH). Mutis depends on control and changing speeds, and last year his stuff looked extremely hittable in three major league starts. He may need a year in AAA to fine-tune his pitches.

MANUEL RAMIREZ

Position: CF   **Opening Day Age:** 19
Bats: R **Throws:** R   **Born:** 6/20/72 in
Ht: 6'0" **Wt:** 190   Santiago, Dominican Republic

Recent Statistics

	G	AB	R	H	D	T	HR	RBI	SB	BB	SO	AVG
91 R Burlington	59	215	44	70	11	4	19	63	7	34	41	.326

The Indians' first draft choice last June, the 19-year-old Ramirez has had only 215 professional at-bats, but he's already made a big impression. He nearly won the Appalachian League triple crown with 19 homers and 63 RBI in those 215 at-bats, both league-leading totals, and a .326 average that ranked third. In addition, he has good speed. Ramirez is obviously a couple years away from the majors, but keep an eye on him.

RUDY SEANEZ

Position: P   **Opening Day Age:** 23
Bats: R **Throws:** R   **Born:** 10/20/68 in
Ht: 5' 11" **Wt:** 170   Brawley, CA

Recent Statistics

	W	L	ERA	G	GS	Sv	IP	H	R	BB	SO	HR
91 AA Canton-akrn	4	2	2.58	25	0	7	38.1	17	12	30	73	2
91 AAA Colo Sprngs	0	0	7.27	16	0	0	17.1	17	14	22	19	2
91 AL Cleveland	0	0	16.20	5	0	0	5.0	10	12	7	7	2

The hard-throwing Seanez is one of those guys who can throw a ball through a brick wall -- if he can find the wall. In 37.1 major league innings, Seanez has struck out 38, but walked 36, and his minor league numbers are basically the same. Seanez is still pretty young, but consider him a long, long shot at this point. Hmm . . . maybe, like Charlie Sheen in "Major League," he just needs glasses. Wild Thing, you make my heart sing.

EDDIE TAUBENSEE

Position: C   **Opening Day Age:** 23
Bats: L **Throws:** R   **Born:** 10/31/68 in
Ht: 6' 3" **Wt:** 205   Beeville, TX

Recent Statistics

	G	AB	R	H	D	T	HR	RBI	SB	BB	SO	AVG
91 AAA Colo Sprngs	91	287	53	89	23	3	13	39	0	31	61	.310
91 AL Cleveland	26	66	5	16	2	1	0	8	0	5	16	.242
91 MLE	91	268	35	70	17	2	6	26	0	20	62	.261

A tall, imposing catcher, Taubensee has done some traveling -- since the end of the 1990 season, he went from the Cincinnati to Oakland to Cleveland organizations. That would indicate he's not much of a prospect, but in fact he is; the A's picked him in the Rule 5 draft, then lost him to Cleveland when they tried to sneak him through waivers. Taubensee has always been considered a good defensive catcher, and over the last two years his hitting has improved greatly. There's a lot of demand for lefty-swinging catchers, so Taubensee figures to make it as a major leaguer.

HITTING:

Skeeter Barnes was signed as a minor league free agent by the Tigers before the 1991 season. Barnes had toiled for many years in the Cincinnati system, never getting a full shot in the majors until Detroit called him up on June 14.

At 34, Barnes probably knew this was his final major league chance, and he took full advantage of it. In July he really caught fire, hitting .313 and slugging .500 in full-time duty. He cooled down in August, but hit well enough in September to finish the season at .289.

Speed has always been the major part of Barnes' game, but the little man has some power as well. In '91 he showed pop in his bat by belting 13 doubles and five homers in 159 at-bats. Given a full season, he could be a threat to hit 25 doubles and 15 homers.

BASERUNNING:

Barnes stole 61 bases in his last two minor league seasons. However in Detroit, he was successful in only 10 of 17 attempts. He needs to learn to read the league's pitchers better before his basestealing success ratio will improve.

FIELDING:

Sparky Anderson once said of Barnes, "He reminds me of Tony Phillips. He busts his butt every day." In '91 Anderson used Barnes much like Phillips, playing him at every position except shortstop, catcher, and pitcher. In the outfield Barnes' speed affords him good range and his arm is above average. He doesn't embarrass himself in the infield either, though it wouldn't be surprising if Sparky limited him strictly to outfield duty in '92.

OVERALL:

Barnes is a little old to improve much as a hitter. But if he can turn in the kind of numbers he did in 1991, he doesn't need to improve. Anderson loves his work ethic, and he looks like he's got a lock on a job next year. Either Moseby or Incaviglia will wave goodbye in '92, so look for Barnes to be the recipient of much more playing time.

SKEETER BARNES

Position: 3B/LF/RF
Bats: R **Throws:** R
Ht: 5'11" **Wt:** 175

Opening Day Age: 35
Born: 3/7/57 in Cincinnati, OH
ML Seasons: 6

Overall Statistics

	G	AB	R	H	D	T	HR	RBI	SB	BB	SO	AVG
1991	75	159	28	46	13	2	5	17	10	9	24	.289
Career	150	268	40	63	14	2	8	27	12	20	35	.235

Where He Hits the Ball

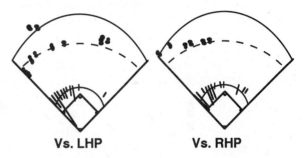

Vs. LHP   Vs. RHP

1991 Situational Stats

	AB	H	HR	RBI	AVG		AB	H	HR	RBI	AVG
Home	58	16	1	5	.276	LHP	85	24	3	11	.282
Road	101	30	4	12	.297	RHP	74	22	2	6	.297
Day	38	15	3	8	.395	Sc Pos	32	9	1	13	.281
Night	121	31	2	9	.256	Clutch	24	5	0	0	.208

1991 Rankings (American League)

➡ 9th in steals of third (4)

HITTING:

Dave Bergman is Sparky Anderson's favorite bench player, but Bergman saw limited duty in his traditional role as a pinch hitter and spot starter in 1991. Even though Bergman's batting average was his lowest since 1986, his '91 campaign was still solid.

Bergman has always been a very selective hitter, one who gets behind in the count a lot. He likes the fastball and will prolong the at-bat to get one. He has enough bat control to stand in the box with two strikes and foul off marginal pitches, settling for the free pass if he doesn't get an offering he likes.

Against right-handed hurlers Bergman hit .257 last year with surprising power. He has always been easy pickings for lefties, though, and Anderson used him only 19 times against them. Last year, Bergman struck out more times than he walked for the first time since 1985, but 11 of his 40 K's came against lefties.

Last year, Bergman hit only .120 as a pinch hitter, not good for a player who is often called off the bench. But he redeemed himself by batting .333 with runners in scoring position.

BASERUNNING:

At 38, Bergman has little speed. He is a smart veteran, though, and this helps compensate for the deficiency. He knows opposing fielders pretty well and knows when taking the extra base is warranted.

FIELDING:

Bergman is one of the better first basemen in the league. He scoops the throw in the dirt well, and was responsible for only one error. He is often used as a late-inning replacement for Cecil Fielder.

OVERALL:

Bergman was eligible for free agency over the winter. But considering Anderson's loyalty to players who have been good to him, and the fact that Rico Brogna, the Tiger's AA first base prospect, is still a year away, Bergman should be back in Detroit in 1992.

DAVE BERGMAN

Position: 1B
Bats: L **Throws:** L
Ht: 6' 2" **Wt:** 195

Opening Day Age: 38
Born: 6/6/53 in Evanston, IL
ML Seasons: 16

Overall Statistics

	G	AB	R	H	D	T	HR	RBI	SB	BB	SO	AVG
1991	86	194	23	46	10	1	7	29	1	35	40	.237
Career	1262	2498	295	648	97	16	53	279	18	360	328	.259

Where He Hits the Ball

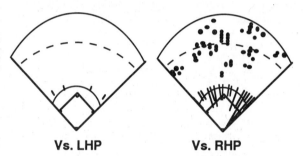

Vs. LHP   Vs. RHP

1991 Situational Stats

	AB	H	HR	RBI	AVG		AB	H	HR	RBI	AVG
Home	87	19	2	11	.218	LHP	19	1	0	1	.053
Road	107	27	5	18	.252	RHP	175	45	7	28	.257
Day	69	18	2	8	.261	Sc Pos	39	13	0	20	.333
Night	125	28	5	21	.224	Clutch	37	9	1	5	.243

1991 Rankings (American League)

→ Did not rank near the top or bottom in any category

PITCHING:

John Cerutti joined the Tigers in 1991 after spending six seasons trying to nail down a starting job in Toronto. He came to Detroit unsure of his role, and at the end of the season, he was just as confused.

Throughout his career, Cerutti has been given plenty of chances to prove he can be an effective starter. Except for a consistent 1989, he has never done what it takes. Sparky Anderson gave him only eight starts in 1991, and no one can blame him.

Cerutti began the season in good fashion, posting a 3.00 ERA in the bullpen. Anderson then gave him the chance to start, and in four games he posted an 0-2 mark with an ERA of 6.27. He finished the year with a 3-6 record and an ERA of 4.57.

Cerutti's arsenal features a curveball, a slider, a below-average fastball, and a sinker that he learned in 1989. He is notorious for serving up the long ball, so he uses the breaking pitches to keep hitters on their heels and the sinker to induce ground balls.

HOLDING RUNNERS AND FIELDING:

Cerutti has always been good with the leather, and in 1991 he got plenty of opportunities to prove it as hitters knocked numerous balls in his direction. He has a good move to first that keeps runners pretty close, and he is not afraid to throw over to the bag. Of the 133 runners Cerutti allowed last season, only seven attempted to steal.

OVERALL:

Cerutti's career is once again at a crossroads. It's obvious that without drastic improvement in his control, among other things, he cannot continue to pitch in the major leagues. At 31 he's not old enough to be washed up, but he's running out of chances. He'll scout the free-agent market during the off season, and despite the Tigers' desperate need for pitching, Cerutti probably will not be back in Motown in 1992.

JOHN CERUTTI

Position: RP/SP
Bats: L **Throws:** L
Ht: 6' 2" **Wt:** 200

Opening Day Age: 31
Born: 4/28/60 in Albany, NY
ML Seasons: 7

Overall Statistics

	W	L	ERA	G	GS	Sv	IP	H	R	BB	SO	HR
1991	3	6	4.57	38	8	2	88.2	94	49	37	29	9
Career	49	43	3.94	229	116	4	861.0	894	427	291	398	119

How Often He Throws Strikes

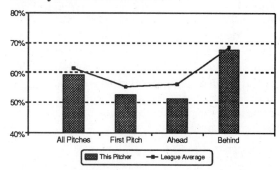

1991 Situational Stats

	W	L	ERA	Sv	IP		AB	H	HR	RBI	AVG
Home	3	1	4.24	0	40.1	LHB	69	13	2	16	.188
Road	0	5	4.84	2	48.1	RHB	271	81	7	44	.299
Day	0	2	10.13	1	13.1	Sc Pos	87	29	3	48	.333
Night	3	4	3.58	1	75.1	Clutch	59	10	1	7	.169

1991 Rankings (American League)

→ 3rd highest percentage of inherited runners scored (46.1%)

GREAT SPEED

MILT CUYLER

Position: CF
Bats: B **Throws:** R
Ht: 5'10" **Wt:** 185

Opening Day Age: 23
Born: 10/7/68 in Macon, GA
ML Seasons: 2

HITTING:

The 1991 season was supposed to be a "free year" for Milt Cuyler. Sparky Anderson gave him the center field job in spring training and vowed not to put any pressure on him. For the most part, Sparky lived up to his word, batting Cuyler in the bottom of the order and not talking him up to the press.

After the All-Star break, however, Anderson gave Cuyler a trial in the leadoff spot. The youngster struggled with a .235 batting average and an equally sub-par .320 on-base percentage in the number one spot. He did develop some useful skills, however. Cuyler, an admitted fly ball hitter, worked hard at slapping the ball on the ground. It paid off as he hit well over twice as many ground balls as fly balls and notched a .307 average on turf. Also, if the infield played him back, he would drop a bunt down and leg it out for a single.

In the minors, Cuyler's hitting would dropped off slightly with every promotion. The second year at each level, though, would bring improvement, so there is justification for the notion that Cuyler can learn to hit in the leadoff spot.

BASERUNNING:

Cuyler's blazing speed allowed him to swipe 41 bases last year with an 80 percent success rate. Even so, you can look for his stolen base totals to rise next year if he can get on base more.

FIELDING:

After only one full season in the majors, Cuyler is already considered by many to be the best center fielder in the American League. His speed allows him to flat out-run his mistakes and cut off potential gappers. Cuyler's arm is average at best, however.

OVERALL:

Anderson is very high on Cuyler, but if Cuyler cannot improve his discipline at the plate, his chances of becoming the Tigers' full-time leadoff hitter in 1992 will be diminished. He is still young, however, and has shown throughout his career that he is willing and able to learn.

Overall Statistics

	G	AB	R	H	D	T	HR	RBI	SB	BB	SO	AVG
1991	154	475	77	122	15	7	3	33	41	52	92	.257
Career	173	526	85	135	18	8	3	41	42	57	102	.257

Where He Hits the Ball

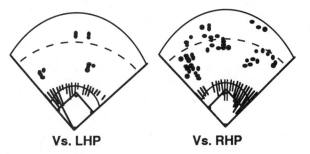

Vs. LHP   Vs. RHP

1991 Situational Stats

	AB	H	HR	RBI	AVG		AB	H	HR	RBI	AVG
Home	221	54	1	15	.244	LHP	122	33	0	8	.270
Road	254	68	2	18	.268	RHP	353	89	3	25	.252
Day	131	36	2	20	.275	Sc Pos	113	21	1	30	.186
Night	344	86	1	13	.250	Clutch	70	17	2	7	.243

1991 Rankings (American League)

→ 1st in bunts in play (44)

→ 3rd in lowest slugging percentage (.337) and highest groundball/flyball ratio (2.6)

→ 4th in steals of third (10)

→ 5th in stolen bases (41), stolen base percentage (80.4%) and lowest slugging percentage vs. right-handed pitchers (.337)

→ Led the Tigers in triples (7), sacrifice bunts (12), stolen bases, caught stealing (10), groundball/flyball ratio, stolen base percentage, runs scored per time reached base (43.0%), batting average in the clutch (.243), bunts in play and steals of third

HITTING:

Contrary to popular belief, Rob Deer's 1991 season was not a complete disaster. By hitting only .179, Deer set an all-time single-season record for the lowest average by a player with at least 400 at-bats. But Deer's on-base percentage was only a little below average at .314, and his 25 homers were nothing to sneer at.

Deer has the same problem Mickey Tettleton had in 1990: he sees too many pitches in each plate appearance. Deer usually gets behind in the count, takes two or three balls, then fans on eye-high fastballs. When Deer went for the first pitch, he slugged over .600 and hit .304. He needs to go after a few more first pitches to keep the pitchers honest.

Deer does not adjust to situations. If he commits to a pitch, he swings from the heels without fail. If he makes contact, it's almost always a fly ball.

BASERUNNING:

Since Deer hits fly balls almost exclusively, he grounds into only three or four double plays a year. He is no speed demon and was 1-for-4 in steal attempts (mainly broken hit-and-run tries). Deer should have his foot nailed to first in steal situations, but he is adequate in other facets of baserunning.

FIELDING:

Rob Deer may not be the best defensive right fielder in the American League, but he is awfully close. He is not fast, but he plays hitters well and gets an excellent jump on the ball. Deer's arm is decent and he can keep runners from going from first to third. Deer's weakness is that he is slightly error-prone.

OVERALL:

Despite his lowly 1991 average, Deer is quite capable of hitting .230 with 25-30 taters, a level he reached several times while with the Brewers. If he does so, he will return to his status as an acceptable regular in right field. If not, he'll be out of a job in two years.

ROB DEER

Position: RF
Bats: R **Throws:** R
Ht: 6' 3" **Wt:** 225

Opening Day Age: 31
Born: 9/29/60 in Orange, CA
ML Seasons: 8

Overall Statistics

	G	AB	R	H	D	T	HR	RBI	SB	BB	SO	AVG
1991	134	448	64	80	14	2	25	64	1	89	175	.179
Career	892	2972	437	649	108	11	173	472	34	452	1079	.218

Where He Hits the Ball

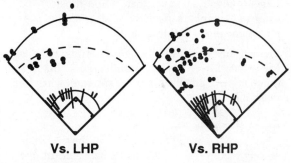

Vs. LHP   **Vs. RHP**

1991 Situational Stats

	AB	H	HR	RBI	AVG		AB	H	HR	RBI	AVG
Home	218	42	12	31	.193	LHP	138	27	9	18	.196
Road	230	38	13	33	.165	RHP	310	53	16	46	.171
Day	141	24	8	21	.170	Sc Pos	101	17	6	35	.168
Night	307	56	17	43	.182	Clutch	73	12	3	9	.164

1991 Rankings (American League)

→ 1st in lowest batting average (.179), strikeouts (175), least GDPs per GDP situation (2.6%), lowest batting average on the road (.165), highest percentage of swings that missed (34.7%) and lowest percentage of swings put into play (27.1%)

→ 3rd in lowest groundball/flyball ratio (.62), most pitches seen per plate appearance (4.25), lowest batting average with runners in scoring position (.168), lowest batting average at home (.193) and lowest batting average with 2 strikes (.103)

→ Led the Tigers in strikeouts, most pitches seen per plate appearance and least GDPs per GDP situation

FUTURE MVP?

CECIL FIELDER

Position: 1B/DH
Bats: R **Throws:** R
Ht: 6' 3" **Wt:** 230

Opening Day Age: 28
Born: 9/21/63 in Los Angeles, CA
ML Seasons: 6

HITTING:

Cecil Fielder weighed heavily on the minds of fans when he reported to Lakeland in the spring of '91. Fielder, listed in the Tigers' press guide at a sprightly 230 pounds, was a more Refrigerator Perry-like 300 pounds and many predicted a big drop in his production. Big Cecil's weight didn't affect his incredible bat speed, however, and homers aplenty flew off his bat in '91.

Fielder drove in 133 runs last season, the most by a Tiger in 30 years. He can be an easy out in bases empty situations, but when he smells an RBI, he's ferocious. Fielder pulls most of his homers, but will take a single by going the other way with breaking balls. His affinity for opposite-field hitting improved so much that, while most of his offensive numbers declined last year, he produced one more RBI than in '90.

Fielder still makes his living off lefties. He hits for great power against righthanders, but it's much more of an all-or-nothing situation when he faces them.

BASERUNNING:

Cecil's extra weight KILLS him here. He is among the five slowest men in baseball. In one week he was gunned down three times at second base after hitting drives into the gap or off the wall. Fielder probably loses 10 doubles a year because of his weight. In six seasons, he has yet to steal a base.

FIELDING:

Cecil is not a bad fielder. His range is about average, although his arm is poor. When Cecil can stay close to the bag he is adequate, but again, his weight hurts him on plays which require lots of movement.

OVERALL:

Fielder is a premium drawing card for a team which sorely needs one. There is a danger that Cecil could eat himself out of the league (or onto the DL). But as long as he retains the ability to whip the head of the bat through the strike zone with such great force, he'll earn every penny of his soon-to-be-prodigious salary.

Overall Statistics

	G	AB	R	H	D	T	HR	RBI	SB	BB	SO	AVG
1991	162	624	102	163	25	0	44	133	0	78	151	.261
Career	541	1703	273	445	69	3	126	349	0	214	477	.261

Where He Hits the Ball

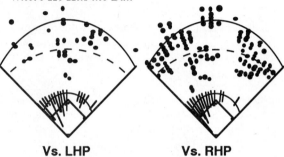

Vs. LHP   Vs. RHP

1991 Situational Stats

	AB	H	HR	RBI	AVG		AB	H	HR	RBI	AVG
Home	305	78	27	75	.256	LHP	159	47	13	31	.296
Road	319	85	17	58	.266	RHP	465	116	31	102	.249
Day	197	44	14	45	.223	Sc Pos	175	50	13	88	.286
Night	427	119	30	88	.279	Clutch	99	23	3	19	.232

1991 Rankings (American League)

- ➡ 1st in home runs (44), RBIs (133) and games (162)
- ➡ 2nd in HR frequency (14.2 ABs per HR) and highest percentage of swings that missed (32.1%)
- ➡ 3rd in strikeouts (151) and lowest percentage of swings put into play (34.5%)
- ➡ Led the Tigers in home runs, at bats (624), runs (102), hits (163), total bases (320), RBIs, hit by pitch (6), times on base (247), GDPs (17), pitches seen (2,667), plate appearances (712), games, slugging percentage (.513), HR frequency, batting average on an 0-2 count (.220)

FUTURE ALL-STAR

TRAVIS FRYMAN

Position: 3B/SS
Bats: R **Throws:** R
Ht: 6' 1" **Wt:** 194

Opening Day Age: 23
Born: 3/25/69 in Lexington, KY
ML Seasons: 2

HITTING:

Travis Fryman is one of those rare players with the potential to hit 350 career home runs while playing a key defensive position (shortstop/third base). In short, he looks like a Cal Ripken or Ernie Banks-type player who could be a major star at his position.

Fryman came up in 1990 without much flash. The pitchers thought he could be overpowered and challenged him, but Fryman handled the heat and walloped the ball with great consistency. In 1991, Fryman began seeing more off-speed stuff. Because of his inexperience and lack of selectivity, his average dipped.

His season was anything but a failure, however. Fryman's excellent power did not recede, and his ability to drive in runs improved. Fryman showed an ability to adjust to situations. He is definitely a better breaking-ball hitter than he was in '90. A career shortstop, he hit much better when playing his natural position.

BASERUNNING:

Fryman has slightly above-average speed and has mediocre judgement. He was 12-for-17 as a base thief and hit 13 double-play grounders. On the base paths Fryman is a little more aggressive than necessary, but this is the sort of thing he'll shake as he becomes a veteran.

FIELDING:

Fryman's arm is exceptional. Despite average range at short and a higher-than-normal tendency to make errors, Travis displayed an excellent ability to turn the double play. He has the potential to become a tremendous defensive player at the position. At third base, it was obvious that he was not comfortable and it affected his fielding and hitting tremendously. Fryman had terrible range at the hot corner and often booted balls hit hard right at him.

OVERALL:

Fryman exploded offensively when he replaced Trammell at short. He has excellent tools and with another year should become a defensive standout. With improved plate discipline expect his offensive totals to rise. As Trammell ages, Fryman needs to come to the forefront of the Tigers' plans at shortstop or his overall growth may be stunted.

Overall Statistics

	G	AB	R	H	D	T	HR	RBI	SB	BB	SO	AVG
1991	149	557	65	144	36	3	21	91	12	40	149	.259
Career	215	789	97	213	47	4	30	118	15	57	200	.270

Where He Hits the Ball

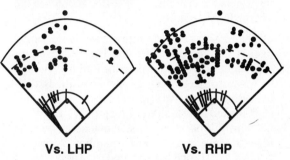

Vs. LHP   Vs. RHP

1991 Situational Stats

	AB	H	HR	RBI	AVG		AB	H	HR	RBI	AVG
Home	261	65	8	42	.249	LHP	152	45	5	23	.296
Road	296	79	13	49	.267	RHP	405	99	16	68	.244
Day	181	43	5	27	.238	Sc Pos	155	45	3	64	.290
Night	376	101	16	64	.269	Clutch	90	21	3	14	.233

1991 Rankings (American League)

→ 4th in strikeouts (149)
→ 5th lowest on-base average vs. right-handed pitchers (.293)
→ 6th lowest percentage of swings put into play (36.2%)
→ 7th lowest groundball/flyball ratio (.78)
→ 8th lowest batting average vs. right-handed pitchers (.244)
→ Led the Tigers in doubles (36)
→ Led AL third basemen in strikeouts

PITCHING:

Signed as a six-year minor league free agent in November of '90, Dan Gakeler jumped into the running to become the Tigers' fifth starter. He started the year at AAA Toledo, was called up June 9 when Mark Leiter went down, and immediately joined the starting rotation.

Gakeler got bombed in his first start against California, but responded by throwing 7.2 innings of two-hit ball in his next outing. Unfortunately, his next five starts were like his first, not his second, and he was exiled to the bullpen. Gakeler was sent back to Toledo after posting a terrible 1-3 record and allowing 44 hits and 22 walks in 39.1 innings. He was called up again in August and stayed with the Tigers for the remainder of the season. He did not distinguish himself.

Gakeler has no one but himself to blame for his dismal 1-4 record in 1991; the Tiger offense provided him with 4.8 runs per nine innings. Though he was considered a power pitcher and had excellent strikeout-to-walk ratios in the minors, his stuff looked a little short of major league quality. Obviously, Sparky Anderson saw something he liked in Gakeler, but considering how poorly he pitched in '91, one has to wonder what it was.

HOLDING RUNNERS AND FIELDING:

Gakeler is an average fielder. He charges the bunt pretty well for a big man and covers the bag at first, but don't expect a Gold Glove performance any time soon. His move to first is only average, and baserunners were 7-for-8 stealing while he was on the mound.

OVERALL:

After spending seven seasons in the minor leagues, Gakeler has learned about all he is going to learn down on the farm, so there isn't much point in keeping him there. Anderson has talked about using Gakeler in the set-up role next year, but he must first prove his effectiveness. More than likely, Gakeler will be invited to spring training in '92, but he will have to earn a spot on the Tigers' staff.

DAN GAKELER

Position: RP/SP
Bats: R **Throws:** R
Ht: 6' 6" **Wt:** 215

Opening Day Age: 27
Born: 5/1/64 in Mt Holly, NJ
ML Seasons: 1

Overall Statistics

	W	L	ERA	G	GS	Sv	IP	H	R	BB	SO	HR
1991	1	4	5.74	31	7	2	73.2	73	52	39	43	5
Career	1	4	5.74	31	7	2	73.2	73	52	39	43	5

How Often He Throws Strikes

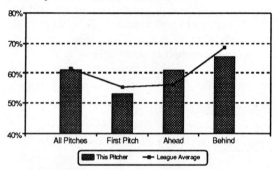

1991 Situational Stats

	W	L	ERA	Sv	IP		AB	H	HR	RBI	AVG
Home	0	1	6.00	1	36.0	LHB	116	35	2	14	.302
Road	1	3	5.50	1	37.2	RHB	169	38	3	27	.225
Day	0	2	7.31	0	28.1	Sc Pos	80	24	2	36	.300
Night	1	2	4.76	2	45.1	Clutch	39	9	1	7	.231

1991 Rankings (American League)

➡ 9th lowest GDPs induced per GDP situation (4.3%)

PITCHING:

From opening day until mid-May last year, Paul Gibson was among the best relievers in baseball, holding enemy batters under a .182 average in 26.1 innings. But as May ended, the roof caved in on Gibson and his season was lost. Gibson wound up with a 4.59 ERA, more than a run and a half higher than his 1990 mark.

Given his track record, Gibson couldn't be expected to maintain his early pace, but many people felt he simply came down with a tired arm. When Gibson was going well in May, Sparky Anderson, grateful to have an effective pitcher on his beleaguered staff, greatly increased the lefthander's workload. Gibson took the ball willingly, but the usage pattern took its toll. What really hurt him was a stretch from May 26 to June 5 in which he averaged three innings per stint.

Gibson is typical of a successful Tiger pitcher. When he's going well, he throws a sinker-slider combination that yields grounders or lazy fly balls. The grounders die in the grass and the fly balls are gobbled up by the outfielders. Gibson pitches well in Tiger Stadium but is in dire straits away from his home park.

HOLDING RUNNERS AND FIELDING:

Gibson has an above-average ability to hold runners. He has an average delivery to the plate and takes advantage of Mickey Tettleton's strong arm. Gibson gets out of the box quickly, has good range and is especially good at getting to bunts and soft grounders. He is not as sharp with hard-hit shots through the box.

OVERALL:

Like most of the Tiger relievers, Gibson needs to be worked carefully, not worn out in one month of overuse. Given more stable handling in '92, he should deliver a season more like his fine '90 (3.05 ERA) than his poor '91. The Tigers would gladly settle for that.

PAUL GIBSON

Position: RP
Bats: R **Throws:** L
Ht: 6' 1" **Wt:** 185

Opening Day Age: 32
Born: 1/4/60 in Center Moriches, NY
ML Seasons: 4

Overall Statistics

	W	L	ERA	G	GS	Sv	IP	H	R	BB	SO	HR
1991	5	7	4.59	68	0	8	96.0	112	51	48	52	10
Career	18	21	3.88	214	14	11	417.1	423	191	183	235	37

How Often He Throws Strikes

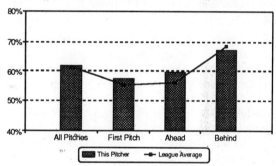

1991 Situational Stats

	W	L	ERA	Sv	IP		AB	H	HR	RBI	AVG
Home	4	3	4.08	4	53.0	LHB	113	39	6	30	.345
Road	1	4	5.23	4	43.0	RHB	264	73	4	29	.277
Day	2	2	4.45	1	28.1	Sc Pos	117	35	1	43	.299
Night	3	5	4.66	7	67.2	Clutch	174	48	7	26	.276

1991 Rankings (American League)

- ➡ 1st in relief losses (7)
- ➡ 3rd in relief innings (96) and most baserunners allowed per 9 innings in relief (15.3)
- ➡ 4th worst batting average allowed vs. left-handed batters (.345)
- ➡ 5th worst first batter efficiency (.350)
- ➡ 7th in games (68)
- ➡ Led the Tigers in games, holds (10), blown saves (5), relief losses and relief innings

PITCHING:

A well-traveled veteran, Jerry Don Gleaton turned in the best season of his career in 1990, recording 13 saves and a 2.94 ERA. The Tigers hoped that Gleaton could continue that sort of work in 1991, but instead he returned to earth with a 4.06 mark and only two saves. Since 1985, Gleaton's ERAs have ranged from that nifty 2.94 mark all the way up to 5.76, and he's never put good seasons back-to-back.

Gleaton had a typical roller coaster season during 1991. He couldn't get untracked during an especially cold April, but rallied when the temperatures rose, and his ERA shrank quickly. Despite solid work in May, Gleaton was hardly used in June and July. When he did pitch, he was excellent.

Then in August, Sparky Anderson rediscovered Gleaton . . . to say the least. Gleaton worked over 27 innings during the month, twice as many as he threw in June and July combined. Around mid-month his mechanics deteriorated and his pitches suffered. His fastball lost a couple of feet and his curveball no longer had its previous bite. Hitters treated Gleaton like they treated teammate Bill Gullickson: they devoured his strikes and disdained the base on balls. Gleaton entered August with a 3.46 ERA, but left it with a 4.05 mark.

HOLDING RUNNERS AND FIELDING:

Gleaton is solid in all aspects of fielding. His move is good, he is decent at fielding bunts and knocks down liners and grounders well.

OVERALL:

At 34, Gleaton is no star, but he can be a useful guy to have on a staff, especially against left-handed hitters. A free agent as the 1991 season ended, he figured to entertain several bids; Gleaton's the sort of "generic" lefty reliever who never seems to have trouble finding work. Chances are he'll turn up with a new major league team for the sixth time in his career.

JERRY DON GLEATON

Position: RP
Bats: L **Throws:** L
Ht: 6' 3" **Wt:** 210

Opening Day Age: 34
Born: 9/14/57 in Brownwood, TX
ML Seasons: 11

Overall Statistics

	W	L	ERA	G	GS	Sv	IP	H	R	BB	SO	HR
1991	3	2	4.06	47	0	2	75.1	74	37	39	47	7
Career	14	23	4.24	284	16	26	415.2	399	216	180	247	36

How Often He Throws Strikes

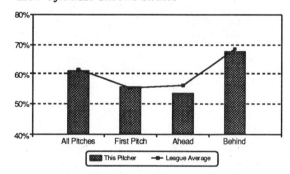

1991 Situational Stats

	W	L	ERA	Sv	IP		AB	H	HR	RBI	AVG
Home	2	1	4.46	0	34.1	LHB	76	20	1	12	.263
Road	1	1	3.73	2	41.0	RHB	199	54	6	27	.271
Day	0	0	5.30	2	18.2	Sc Pos	81	21	2	30	.259
Night	3	2	3.65	0	56.2	Clutch	85	25	3	15	.294

1991 Rankings (American League)

➡ 7th lowest percentage of inherited runners scored (23.9%)

➡ Led the Tigers in first batter efficiency (.205)

PITCHING:

When the Tigers signed righthander Bill Gullickson to a free agent contract before the 1991 season, they probably would have been pleased to have him match his 1990 figures: ten wins with a 3.82 earned run average. Gullickson's ERA actually rose last year to 3.90, but he pitched consistently enough -- and got enough offensive support -- to double his win total to a league-leading 20 (tied with Scott Erickson).

A lot of Gullickson's stats don't look like those of a 20-game winner. He allowed 256 hits, the second-highest total in the American League. He got cuffed around for a .288 opponent batting average, third worst among A.L. starters. He permitted 51 doubles, the highest total in the league. He allowed 22 homers, and he had a 4.95 ERA at Tiger Stadium, his home yard.

So how'd he do it? Mostly by throwing strikes, or at least by avoiding walks. Gullickson relies heavily on his breaking pitches, primarily a curve and slider, along with a sinking fastball. If he can get the hitter to chase a ball out of the strike zone, so much the better. When he had to throw strikes, he did, permitting only 31 unintentional walks in 226.1 innings. That, and run support to the tune of 5.8 runs per game (second best in the A.L.), was the secret to winning 20.

HOLDING RUNNERS AND FIELDING:

With the number of baserunners he allows, Gullickson gets plenty of chances to flash his above-average move to first. He has two pickoff moves (the first is slow and tentative, the second much quicker) and will nail his fair share of straying runners. Gullickson is sure-handed, but he is slow off the mound, and should be regarded as a sub-par fielder.

OVERALL:

Gullickson would probably be the first to admit that it took a good deal of luck for him to win 20 for the first time. He took a lot of lumps last year, but he hardly ever beat himself. A repeat performance seems unlikely, however.

BILL GULLICKSON

Position: SP
Bats: R **Throws:** R
Ht: 6' 3" **Wt:** 225

Opening Day Age: 33
Born: 2/20/59 in Marshall, MN
ML Seasons: 11

Overall Statistics

	W	L	ERA	G	GS	Sv	IP	H	R	BB	SO	HR
1991	20	9	3.90	35	35	0	226.1	256	109	44	91	22
Career	131	109	3.66	315	309	0	2063.1	2089	934	503	1080	195

How Often He Throws Strikes

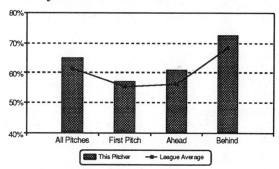

This Pitcher ▓ — League Average ●

1991 Situational Stats

	W	L	ERA	Sv	IP		AB	H	HR	RBI	AVG
Home	10	4	4.95	0	103.2	LHB	487	134	15	55	.275
Road	10	5	3.01	0	122.2	RHB	403	122	7	47	.303
Day	4	5	5.29	0	81.2	Sc Pos	184	57	5	73	.310
Night	16	4	3.11	0	144.2	Clutch	72	22	1	12	.306

1991 Rankings (American League)

→ 1st in wins (20), games started (35) and least pitches thrown per batter (3.27)

→ 2nd in hits allowed (256), highest slugging percentage allowed (.435) and highest run support per 9 innings (5.8)

→ 3rd in highest batting average allowed (.288)

→ 4th highest batting average allowed vs. right-handed batters (.303)

→ Led the Tigers in wins, games started, innings (226.1), batters faced (954), winning percentage, strikeout/walk ratio (2.1), lowest on-base percentage allowed (.321), least pitches thrown per batter, run support per 9 innings and ERA on the road (3.01)

PITCHING:

Despite a month on the disabled list, Mike Henneman had another solid season in 1991. Henneman's 2.88 ERA was his lowest since 1988, and he reached the 20-save mark for the third time in four years. Henneman's 87.5% save percentage was the third highest in the American League.

Henneman throws a sinking fastball that he mixes with an off speed forkball. Working the hitters down and away, he makes them chop the ball into Tiger Stadium's tundra of an infield. Henneman is not as effective on turf. Last year, his road ERA ballooned as choppers and hard grounders on artificial turf found holes in a defense conditioned to long grass. Though he sometimes lost his concentration with nobody on, he was tough with the bases occupied.

Sparky Anderson looks for the hot hand in his bullpen, and that tendency may have hampered Henneman. Used heavily early in the year, Henneman eventually fell victim to a sore shoulder that derailed him during the stretch drive. Henneman has spent time on the disabled list in three of the last four seasons, one reason why he's never had a 30-save year.

HOLDING RUNNERS AND FIELDING:

Henneman doesn't single-handedly stop the running game, but his pickoff move is adequate. He is an excellent fielder who can stab the shot up the middle with the best of them. The sacrifice bunt had better be a good one or he will gun down the lead runner.

OVERALL:

Sparky Anderson's relief pitchers must feel frustrated because they seldom get a chance to record the big save totals that relievers from other teams do. Anderson will often go to his ace as early as the seventh with the score tied or his team down by a run. While Henneman doesn't have the gaudy save totals, his lifetime won-lost record (49-21, with never a losing season) is a good indicator of how tough he is in close contests. When healthy, he's one of the best.

MIKE HENNEMAN

Position: RP
Bats: R **Throws:** R
Ht: 6' 4" **Wt:** 205

Opening Day Age: 30
Born: 12/11/61 in St. Charles, MO
ML Seasons: 5

Overall Statistics

	W	L	ERA	G	GS	Sv	IP	H	R	BB	SO	HR
1991	10	2	2.88	60	0	21	84.1	81	29	34	61	2
Career	49	21	2.90	309	0	80	456.2	413	170	172	313	25

How Often He Throws Strikes

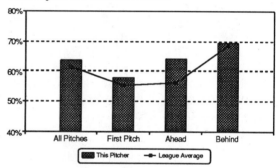

1991 Situational Stats

	W	L	ERA	Sv	IP		AB	H	HR	RBI	AVG
Home	7	0	1.95	15	50.2	LHB	127	34	0	11	.268
Road	3	2	4.28	6	33.2	RHB	187	47	2	24	.251
Day	5	0	2.84	5	25.1	Sc Pos	102	25	1	33	.245
Night	5	2	2.90	16	59.0	Clutch	224	52	1	25	.232

1991 Rankings (American League)

→ 1st in relief wins (10)

→ 3rd in save percentage (87.5%)

→ 6th lowest percentage of inherited runners scored (19.5%)

→ 9th in games finished (50)

→ Led the Tigers in saves (21), games finished, save opportunities (24), save percentage (87.5%), lowest percentage of inherited runners scored and relief wins

HITTING:

When Pete Incaviglia broke in with the Rangers in 1986, he did so with a bang, hitting 30 homers and driving in 88 runs. Unfortunately, that's been the high point of his career. The Tigers took a calculated risk by signing Inky before the beginning of the '91 season, and it blew up in their faces. After five straight 20-homer seasons, Incaviglia managed only 11 dingers last year, and his other numbers (.214 average, 38 RBI) were also career lows by a large margin.

Incaviglia started out the year slowly and was just starting to hit his groove when he was shelved in mid-June with a sore rib-cage muscle. Seventeen days after he got off the DL, he went back on with a sprained wrist, and after that he never really came back.

Incaviglia has a tendency to hit home runs to the opposite field because he likes the ball on the outside half of the plate. Pitchers know this by now, and they jammed him inside all year, making him more likely to ground out.

BASERUNNING:

Incaviglia is strictly a station-to-station baserunner. Going 1-for-4 as a base thief, he failed to reach the .500 mark for the third straight season. Pete is like a tank; when he goes into second hard to break up the double play, he raises a lot of dust.

FIELDING:

Incaviglia has gained a reputation as a gritty fielder who always hustles. He has good range for a big man and having Milt Cuyler in center field helps cut down on gappers as well. His arm is much better than Lloyd Moseby's, even though he doesn't cover as much territory.

OVERALL:

The Tigers knew Incaviglia was an all-or-nothing slugger who would strike out a ton, but they felt his run production justified his signing. Based on '91, they were wrong. Incaviglia is eligible for free agency, and with his bargaining power at a minimum, Detroit may be willing to give him another chance.

PETE INCAVIGLIA

Position: LF/DH
Bats: R **Throws:** R
Ht: 6' 1" **Wt:** 230

Opening Day Age: 28
Born: 4/2/64 in Pebble Beach, CA
ML Seasons: 6

Overall Statistics

	G	AB	R	H	D	T	HR	RBI	SB	BB	SO	AVG
1991	97	337	38	72	12	1	11	38	1	36	92	.214
Career	791	2786	371	679	132	14	135	426	27	255	880	.244

Where He Hits the Ball

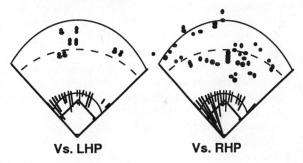

Vs. LHP   **Vs. RHP**

1991 Situational Stats

	AB	H	HR	RBI	AVG		AB	H	HR	RBI	AVG
Home	171	35	6	20	.205	LHP	97	20	0	5	.206
Road	166	37	5	18	.223	RHP	240	52	11	33	.217
Day	112	22	3	9	.196	Sc Pos	89	15	2	23	.169
Night	225	50	8	29	.222	Clutch	66	10	0	4	.152

1991 Rankings (American League)

→ 4th lowest batting average with runners in scoring position (.169)

→ 5th in lowest batting average in the clutch (.152) and lowest batting average on a 3-2 count (.063)

→ 7th lowest percentage of extra bases taken as a runner (26.7%)

PITCHING:

Mark Leiter made quite a comeback just by taking the mound for the Tigers in 1991. The fact that he was effective only makes his story that much more worthy of notice.

Leiter began his career as a wild, hard thrower in 1984 in the Oriole system. After missing three full years due to shoulder ailments, Leiter was released and picked up by the Yankees. Leiter didn't fit in with New York's plans and, after coming to Detroit before the '91 season, started the year with the Tigers in relief. He pitched adequately in the early going, showcasing an average fastball, a curve, slider and an occasional change-up.

Leiter was placed in the starting rotation in mid-July and responded to the increased exposure with a vengeance. He reeled off six straight wins from August 1 through September 1 and pitched well in eight of his first 11 starts (seven quality starts). After moving into the rotation, Leiter's strikeout rate dropped and his hits allowed rose, but his control improved dramatically. Tiger fans can take heart because the increased time on the mound helped loosen up Leiter's arm and the improved flexibility added velocity to his fastball, pushing it over the 90 MPH mark.

HOLDING RUNNERS AND FIELDING:

While he has a good move to first, Leiter is merely average in fielding his position. Some of this must be due to the time he has missed and problems with his shoulder, but some of it obviously is lack of concentration. This is definitely one area in which Leiter can improve his game.

OVERALL:

At 29, Leiter is not a candidate for superstardom, but he has a chance to be a good starter for several more years. Unless Scott Aldred takes a giant step forward with his control, expect the right-handed Leiter to battle Bill Gullickson for the staff ace role in 1992.

MARK LEITER

Position: RP/SP
Bats: R **Throws:** R
Ht: 6' 3" **Wt:** 210

Opening Day Age: 29
Born: 4/13/63 in Joliet, IL
ML Seasons: 2

Overall Statistics

	W	L	ERA	G	GS	Sv	IP	H	R	BB	SO	HR
1991	9	7	4.21	38	15	1	134.2	125	66	50	103	16
Career	10	8	4.64	46	18	1	161.0	158	86	59	124	21

How Often He Throws Strikes

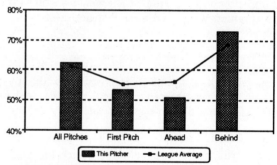

1991 Situational Stats

	W	L	ERA	Sv	IP		AB	H	HR	RBI	AVG
Home	4	3	4.11	1	72.1	LHB	230	55	9	26	.239
Road	5	4	4.33	0	62.1	RHB	281	70	7	41	.249
Day	4	3	3.60	1	45.0	Sc Pos	120	36	4	53	.300
Night	5	4	4.52	0	89.2	Clutch	41	13	0	6	.317

1991 Rankings (American League)

➡ Led the Tigers in hit batsmen (6)

HITTING:

When the Tigers acquired Lloyd Moseby as a free agent in 1990, they hoped he could again play like the legitimate power/speed threat he was in Toronto during the mid-80's. Instead, Moseby's play was mediocre in 1990, and injury-filled in 1991.

Moseby's '91 season was disjointed by the 50 days he spent on the disabled list. In late April, the Tigers lost him as a result of a bruised heel; in late May, a sore hamstring put him out of commission. And on August 29, he again went on the DL with fluid build-up in his right knee. Moseby suffered a drastic power outage in 1988, the first year he experienced back trouble, and he has yet to regain his health long enough to produce adequate numbers. Last year, Moseby produced only 22 extra-base hits in 260 at-bats.

Moseby feasts on high fastballs, but pitchers have been successful working him low and away with breaking stuff, resulting in more ground balls than fly balls. After suffering through a dismal first half, he fared slightly better after the All-Star break, giving Detroit some hope.

BASERUNNING:

Although Moseby's injuries have robbed him of the speed he once possessed, he is still adept at reading the pitcher. He managed eight stolen bases last year with his banged-up legs while being caught only once. Still, the third base coach has to be wary of sending him homeward on any play that looks close.

FIELDING:

Moseby lost his center field job to Milt Cuyler in 1991 and was switched to left, where he platooned with Pete Incaviglia. Although his range was slightly better than average, his arm continues to be the chief weakness in his game.

OVERALL:

Moseby blames ten years of playing on artificial turf for his physical ailments, and that may very well be true. At 32 he is old before his time, but Sparky Anderson is well known for squeezing useful performances from veteran players.

LLOYD MOSEBY

Position: LF
Bats: L **Throws:** R
Ht: 6' 2" **Wt:** 205

Opening Day Age: 32
Born: 11/5/59 in Portland, AK
ML Seasons: 12

Overall Statistics

	G	AB	R	H	D	T	HR	RBI	SB	BB	SO	AVG
1991	74	260	37	68	15	1	6	35	8	21	43	.262
Career	1588	5815	869	1494	273	66	169	737	280	616	1135	.257

Where He Hits the Ball

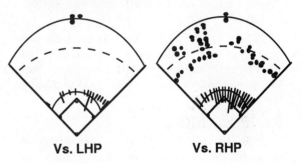

Vs. LHP   Vs. RHP

1991 Situational Stats

	AB	H	HR	RBI	AVG		AB	H	HR	RBI	AVG
Home	151	41	4	25	.272	LHP	46	11	1	9	.239
Road	109	27	2	10	.248	RHP	214	57	5	26	.266
Day	93	27	1	8	.290	Sc Pos	57	18	1	26	.316
Night	167	41	5	27	.246	Clutch	44	9	0	2	.205

1991 Rankings (American League)

➡ 8th in least GDPs per GDP situation (5.3%)

TONY PHILLIPS

OVERLOOKED

Position:
3B/2B/SS/LF/RF/DH
Bats: B **Throws:** R
Ht: 5'10" **Wt:** 175

Opening Day Age: 32
Born: 4/25/59 in Atlanta, GA
ML Seasons: 10

HITTING:

Sparky's jack-of-all-trades, Tony Phillips, turned in a stellar season at the age of 32. He played all over the diamond and his hitting remained excellent whether he was at third base, in left field, or anywhere else. Phillips posted career bests in average, hits, doubles, homers, RBI, on-base percentage and slugging percentage.

Phillips' did his best work when leading off. He had a solid .368 on-base percentage in that role and smacked 12 homers in the leadoff spot as well. What Phillips did best, however, was thump lefties. Phillips slugged .617 against them, a better mark than even Cecil Fielder. He also had a .466 OBP against southpaws. Like most of the Tigers, Phillips was more effective with runners on base.

Against righthanders Phillips reached base reasonably often, but his power was switched off. He's an excellent low ball hitter, especially batting lefty, and he's finally learned to stop chasing the high fastball.

BASERUNNING:

Phillips has been a poor baserunner throughout his career; his mediocre 10-for-15 performance in 1991 was his third best percentage ever. He is very aggressive when he reaches base and needs to be reigned in by his coaches. Phillips has decent speed and, despite his tendency to hit grounders, is tough to double up.

FIELDING:

Despite playing all over the place, Phillips displayed excellent skills wherever he roamed. He had phenomenal range at second and made a mere one error in 227 chances. At third, Phillips had excellent range and soft hands, but had trouble turning the 5-4-3 double play. Phillips was great in a short stint at shortstop. His double play skills when playing up the middle are incredible. In the outfield, Phillips displays surprising range and a solid arm.

OVERALL:

Last year was Phillips at his best, playing well everyday and everywhere. Though a hamstring problem hampered him in September and he finished the season weakly, you can expect him to play and hit well for several more years.

Overall Statistics

	G	AB	R	H	D	T	HR	RBI	SB	BB	SO	AVG
1991	146	564	87	160	28	4	17	72	10	79	95	.284
Career	1133	3725	538	953	158	34	58	386	85	520	670	.256

Where He Hits the Ball

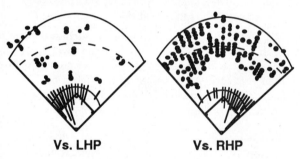

Vs. LHP   **Vs. RHP**

1991 Situational Stats

	AB	H	HR	RBI	AVG		AB	H	HR	RBI	AVG
Home	292	86	9	42	.295	LHP	154	55	11	25	.357
Road	272	74	8	30	.272	RHP	410	105	6	47	.256
Day	169	54	6	26	.320	Sc Pos	118	38	1	52	.322
Night	395	106	11	46	.268	Clutch	81	18	3	8	.222

1991 Rankings (American League)

- ➡ 3rd in on-base percentage vs. left-handed pitchers (.466)
- ➡ 6th in batting average vs. left-handed pitchers (.357)
- ➡ 7th in slugging percentage vs. left-handed pitchers (.617)
- ➡ Led the Tigers in batting average (.284), singles (111), batting average with runners in scoring position (.322), batting average with the bases loaded (.417), batting average, on-base percentage and slugging percentage vs. left-handed pitchers and batting average on the road (.272)

PITCHING:

Once one of baseball's great power pitchers, Frank Tanana has been strictly a junkballer for a number of years. Tanana relies on a curveball that he brings at a variety of speeds, a deceptive fastball, and a half-screwball change-up. Tanana gets the maximum from his repertoire, and at 38, with 220 career victories behind him, he shows no signs of decline.

The secret of Tanana's success is two-fold. First, his pitch selection is such that a hitter never sees the same sequence of pitches during the course of a game. Second, Tanana depends on pinpoint control to minimize the damage if the hitters successfully guess what is coming next. In 1991, Tanana allowed 12.3 baserunners per nine innings, so he wasn't effective keeping men off the bases. However, with runners on, Tanana became especially tough. Hitters managed a meager .235 average in such situations.

Tanana had the lowest strikeout-to-walk ratio of his career last season and allowed 26 home runs (third highest in the league). But for all this, Tanana still finished the year with more than 12 victories for the sixth time in eight seasons. While he pitched well, he also benefitted from splendid support. It's hard to lose often when given 5.2 runs per game.

HOLDING RUNNERS AND FIELDING:

Tanana has a variety of pickoff moves that he uses to keep runners honest. He allowed 17 stolen bases last year and runners were successful only 55 percent of the time. In the field, Tanana is quite sure-handed and will take out the lead runner on occasion. Last year, he committed his first error since 1988.

OVERALL:

At the end of the 1990 season many people were writing Tanana's epitaph. Tanana's been hearing that for years, but he always seems to find a way to keep surviving. Although he didn't set the world on fire last year, he did enough to silence his critics and prove, once again, his reliability.

FRANK TANANA

Position: SP
Bats: L **Throws:** L
Ht: 6' 3" **Wt:** 195

Opening Day Age: 38
Born: 7/3/53 in Detroit, MI
ML Seasons: 19

Overall Statistics

	W	L	ERA	G	GS	Sv	IP	H	R	BB	SO	HR
1991	13	12	3.69	33	33	0	217.1	217	98	78	107	26
Career	220	208	3.59	574	553	1	3797.1	3659	1698	1110	2566	398

How Often He Throws Strikes

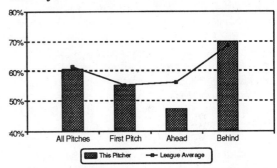

1991 Situational Stats

	W	L	ERA	Sv	IP		AB	H	HR	RBI	AVG
Home	7	5	4.10	0	120.2	LHB	159	37	5	17	.233
Road	6	7	3.35	0	96.2	RHB	659	180	21	70	.273
Day	4	5	3.16	0	77.0	Sc Pos	186	38	3	58	.204
Night	9	7	4.10	0	140.1	Clutch	38	15	0	9	.395

1991 Rankings (American League)

→ 2nd in pickoff throws (214)

→ 3rd in home runs allowed (26)

→ 4th in runners caught stealing (14) and most home runs allowed per 9 innings (1.08)

→ Led the Tigers in ERA (3.77), shutouts (2), home runs allowed, strikeouts (107), pitches thrown (3,423), pickoff throws, stolen bases allowed (17), runners caught stealing, lowest batting average allowed (.265) and lowest slugging percentage allowed (.412)

PITCHING:

When the Tigers signed Walt Terrell in July of 1990 they pretty much knew what they were getting: a pitcher who could eat up 150-200 innings per year and win 10 to 15 games. That was exactly what they got from Terrell in 1991.

Terrell began the '91 season with a dismal 4-9 record and a 4.69 ERA in 18 games, allowing 29 more hits than innings pitched. After the All-Star break he was relegated to the bullpen. Given a reprieve, Terrell responded by winning six of his next seven decisions, posting an ERA of 3.13 during the stretch. He wound up with a dozen wins, his most since 1987.

There's nothing flashy about Terrell. He walks to the mound, picks up the ball and goes right after the hitters. The only problem is that the hitters go right after him too. The opposition hit .301 against him while getting on base at a .358 clip in 1991. Terrell is a ground ball pitcher and he relies on keeping the ball low in the strike zone. His stuff seems perfect for the confines of Tiger Stadium, although his 1991 home ERA (4.84) indicates otherwise. Terrell was 9-7 at home last year and his high ERA is a result of a few bad outings. More often than not, his home starts were quality performances.

HOLDING RUNNERS AND FIELDING:

After Terrell starts his delivery, he gets the ball to the plate pretty quickly, so it's difficult to steal on him. He doesn't have a deceptive pickoff move, so he throws to first often to compensate. Terrell isn't a great fielder, either. He gets his glove down well, but lacks the mobility to make anything but routine plays.

OVERALL:

Almost every staff needs a guy who can take the ball every fifth day and get his fair share of wins given good support. Walt Terrell is exactly that sort of pitcher. The Tigers know what they can expect from him, so his immediate future seems safe.

WALT TERRELL

Position: SP
Bats: L **Throws:** R
Ht: 6' 2" **Wt:** 205

Opening Day Age: 33
Born: 5/11/58 in Jeffersonville, IN
ML Seasons: 10

Overall Statistics

	W	L	ERA	G	GS	Sv	IP	H	R	BB	SO	HR
1991	12	14	4.24	35	33	0	218.2	257	115	79	80	16
Career	104	114	4.14	285	280	0	1850.0	1927	945	700	868	173

How Often He Throws Strikes

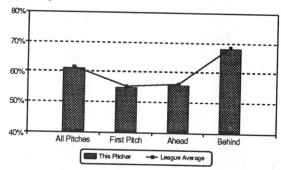

1991 Situational Stats

	W	L	ERA	Sv	IP		AB	H	HR	RBI	AVG
Home	9	7	4.84	0	111.2	LHB	461	141	9	55	.306
Road	3	7	3.62	0	107.0	RHB	392	116	7	44	.296
Day	5	3	3.72	0	65.1	Sc Pos	206	65	3	80	.316
Night	7	11	4.46	0	153.1	Clutch	77	23	1	8	.299

1991 Rankings (American League)

→ 1st in hits allowed (257), GDPs induced (35), lowest strikeout/walk ratio (1.0), highest batting average allowed (.301), most GDPs induced per 9 innings (1.44) and least strikeouts per 9 innings (3.3)

→ 2nd in highest on-base average allowed (.358)

→ Led the Tigers in losses (14), complete games (8), shutouts (2), hits allowed, batters faced (954), walks allowed (79), wild pitches (8), GDPs induced, groundball/flyball ratio (1.56), lowest stolen base percentage allowed (54.5%), least home runs allowed per 9 innings (.66) and most GDPs per GDP situation

HITTING:

After coming to Detroit in a mid-winter trade, Mickey Tettleton was greeted by many Tiger watchers with skepticism. The genial backstop brought his booming bat with him and silenced the skeptics with his finest season. Tettleton showed he could hit both righties and lefties (more power against lefties, better on-base percentage versus righties) and demonstrated a flair for delivering hits in the clutch.

Tettleton needs to work the pitcher in order to hit effectively. With the Orioles in 1990, he was too selective. He spent that year waiting for perfect pitches while striking out en masse and losing both average and power. Last year, Tettleton retained his trademark selectivity but became much more aggressive when the pitcher fell behind. The results included career highs in on-base percentage, homers, RBI and runs. As an added bonus, his aggressive attitude helped him lower his strikeout rate.

BASERUNNING:

Tettleton could probably beat Cecil Fielder in a foot race, but that's about it. He is an extremely slow runner and should take a station-to-station approach to running the bases.

FIELDING:

Sparky Anderson was suspicious of Tettleton's catching skills at the beginning of the year, but Tettleton rose to the challenge. In '91 Tettleton was among the league's best at preventing the stolen base and his pitch selection was outstanding. Simply put, once Tettleton learns his pitching staff, he gets the most out of their ability. He is not good at blocking the plate or handling wayward pitches, however.

OVERALL:

Anderson gave Tettleton a heavy workload, but carefully saw to it that the Mick wasn't overworked. Proving that his 1989 All-Star season wasn't a fluke, Tettleton re-established himself as one of the best catchers in baseball. He should be among the best for several more years.

MICKEY TETTLETON

Position: C/DH
Bats: B **Throws:** R
Ht: 6' 2" **Wt:** 212

Opening Day Age: 31
Born: 9/16/60 in Oklahoma City, OK
ML Seasons: 8

Overall Statistics

	G	AB	R	H	D	T	HR	RBI	SB	BB	SO	AVG
1991	154	501	85	132	17	2	31	89	3	101	131	.263
Career	775	2348	334	568	96	8	105	323	18	416	674	.242

Where He Hits the Ball

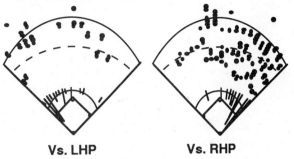

Vs. LHP   **Vs. RHP**

1991 Situational Stats

	AB	H	HR	RBI	AVG		AB	H	HR	RBI	AVG
Home	239	63	15	44	.264	LHP	109	27	9	25	.248
Road	262	69	16	45	.263	RHP	392	105	22	64	.268
Day	172	43	6	18	.250	Sc Pos	120	34	8	57	.283
Night	329	89	25	71	.271	Clutch	100	24	6	18	.240

1991 Rankings (American League)

- → 2nd in walks (101)
- → 4th in HR frequency (16.2 ABs per HR)
- → 6th in home runs (31) and most pitches seen per plate appearance (4.15)
- → 7th in strikeouts (131)
- → Led the Tigers in walks
- → Led AL catchers in home runs, runs (85), total bases (246), RBIs (89), walks, times on base (235), strikeouts, pitches seen (2,523), plate appearances (608), games (154), slugging percentage (.491), on-base percentage (.387), run scored per time reached base (36.2%) and pitches taken (61.5%)

HITTING:

At 34, Alan Trammell is beginning to show his age. Trammell played in pain almost the entire season and his power and average dropped precipitously. He missed most of July and August with knee, wrist and shoulder problems, and when he did play, he was a shadow of his former self. Trammell's average skidded 56 points to .248 last year, and his RBI total dropped from 89 to 55.

Trammell still makes good contact, but last year he couldn't turn on the ball because of his shoulder, and his bat speed dropped because of his wrist problem. His in-game stamina was also a problem. In the late innings, Trammell's hitting ability disappeared.

Trammell spent most of his time batting third or second in the order. He did move his game up a notch when he had a chance to drive in runs, but he still wasn't very impressive. More than anything, at the plate Trammell seemed to be showing the effects of 14 years of play at short.

BASERUNNING:

Trammell is still a quick, smart runner. He was 11-for-13 in steal attempts and has impeccable judgment for advancement. It's obvious that Trammell has lost some speed, but his skills in this area are seamless.

FIELDING:

Trammell still has good range, soft hands and is smooth when turning the double play. His arm is not strong, but he has a quick release and makes accurate pegs. This is no overestimation of his talent: his fielding remains Gold Glove caliber.

OVERALL:

Trammell had a difficult season last year, but it would be premature to write him off. He had a similar injury-riddled season in 1989 (.243), and bounced back with a .304 season in '90. At his age, however, a position switch may be a possibility, especially since it would ease pressure on his shoulder. Moving to third base and switching positions with Travis Fryman is one possibility. As long as Trammell hits, the Tigers will find a place for him.

ALAN TRAMMELL

Position: SS
Bats: R **Throws:** R
Ht: 6' 0" **Wt:** 180

Opening Day Age: 34
Born: 2/21/58 in Garden Grove, CA
ML Seasons: 15

Overall Statistics

	G	AB	R	H	D	T	HR	RBI	SB	BB	SO	AVG
1991	101	375	57	93	20	0	9	55	11	37	39	.248
Career	1936	7077	1066	2022	349	50	161	865	210	744	751	.286

Where He Hits the Ball

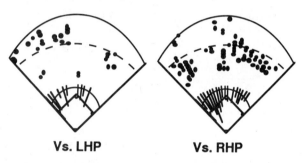

Vs. LHP   **Vs. RHP**

1991 Situational Stats

	AB	H	HR	RBI	AVG		AB	H	HR	RBI	AVG
Home	218	53	6	39	.243	LHP	113	24	4	17	.212
Road	157	40	3	16	.255	RHP	262	69	5	38	.263
Day	137	34	4	19	.248	Sc Pos	111	30	4	47	.270
Night	238	59	5	36	.248	Clutch	51	8	0	3	.157

1991 Rankings (American League)

→ 4th in lowest batting average with the bases loaded (.083) and lowest on-base percentage vs. left-handed pitchers (.268)

→ 7th lowest batting average in the clutch (.157)

→ 10th lowest batting average vs. left-handed pitchers

HITTING:

In 1991 Lou Whitaker did nothing to dispel the "Sweet" moniker he's earned while spending fifteen seasons in Detroit. In many ways, in fact, his '91 campaign was his sweetest. At the age of 34, when most players' abilities have begun to fade, Whitaker stepped forward and proved that he can still make adjustments as a hitter.

The most noticeable improvement Whitaker made last year was increased patience at the plate. Already the owner of a respectable .355 career on-base percentage, he increased his walk frequency, upping it from 75 per 500 at-bats (from 1987 to 1990) to 90 in thirty fewer at-bats. In addition to his career high in walks, his strikeout rate was his lowest ever.

When Detroit acquired Tony Phillips in '90, Whitaker faced a platoon situation for the first time in his career. However, being benched against some lefties was the best thing that could have happened to him. By slugging .489, Whitaker surpassed his career high of .462, a mark set in 1989 when he hit 28 dingers.

BASERUNNING:

Although his stolen base total doesn't show it, Whitaker is still an aggressive baserunner. While his speed has certainly diminished over the past few years, the mental part of his game hasn't. He is a smart baserunner who will take the extra base when warranted and will go into second hard to break up the double play.

FIELDING:

Whitaker is an exceptionally sure-handed fielder who can still turn the double play with the best in the league. His range has diminished a bit over the years, but it is still above average. This is due in part to the long infield grass of Tiger Stadium.

OVERALL:

Whitaker will return to Detroit in 1992 and fans will again fill the air with the traditional "Looouuu." Whitaker will bring his consistent style of play to Tiger Stadium for as long as he wants, and if 1991 is a sign of things to come, that should be for several more years.

LOU WHITAKER

Position: 2B
Bats: L **Throws:** R
Ht: 5'11" **Wt:** 180

Opening Day Age: 34
Born: 5/12/57 in New York, NY
ML Seasons: 15

Overall Statistics

	G	AB	R	H	D	T	HR	RBI	SB	BB	SO	AVG
1991	138	470	94	131	26	2	23	78	4	90	45	.279
Career	1965	7163	1134	1962	327	62	190	859	128	966	919	.274

Where He Hits the Ball

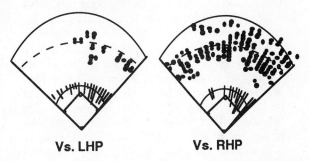

Vs. LHP   **Vs. RHP**

1991 Situational Stats

	AB	H	HR	RBI	AVG		AB	H	HR	RBI	AVG
Home	237	72	15	51	.304	LHP	97	24	2	14	.247
Road	233	59	8	27	.253	RHP	373	107	21	64	.287
Day	140	41	7	32	.293	Sc Pos	109	31	5	47	.284
Night	330	90	16	46	.273	Clutch	78	18	5	16	.231

1991 Rankings (American League)

→ 1st in least GDPs per GDP situation (2.6%)

→ Led the Tigers in sacrifice flies (8), on-base percentage (.391), least GDPs per GDP situation, batting average vs. right-handed pitchers (.287), slugging percentage vs. right-handed pitchers (.528) and on-base percentage vs. right-handed pitchers (.400)

→ Led AL second baseman in home runs (23), RBIs (78), sacrifice flies, walks (90), slugging percentage (.489), HR frequency (20.4 ABs per HR), pitches seen per plate appearance (3.88), runs scored per time reached base (42.1%), least GDPs per GDP situation and fielding percentage (.994)

SCOTT ALDRED

Position: SP
Bats: L **Throws:** L
Ht: 6' 4" **Wt:** 215

Opening Day Age: 23
Born: 6/12/68 in Flint, MI
ML Seasons: 2

Overall Statistics

	W	L	ERA	G	GS	Sv	IP	H	R	BB	SO	HR
1991	2	4	5.18	11	11	0	57.1	58	37	30	35	9
Career	3	6	4.90	15	14	0	71.2	71	43	40	42	9

PITCHING, FIELDING & HOLDING RUNNERS:

Considered one of the Tigers' top prospects, Scott Aldred has great stuff, but his control has always been suspect. Aldred began the '91 season at AAA Toledo knowing that barring a meltdown in his shoulder, he would see action in the majors. On July 17 he got the call. In Detroit, his control worries continued as he tried to nibble the corners and fell behind hitters too often. He was forced to take something off his 95-MPH fastball and the hitters had a field day. By the end of the season, Aldred's strikeout rate dropped and he allowed more hits than innings pitched for the first time in his career.

Aldred's season was not a complete wash as he finished very strongly. In his last five starts he averaged seven innings and logged an impressive 2.50 ERA. As a fielder he is a well-conditioned athlete who makes the routine plays with regularity. His pickoff move is only adequate, however.

OVERALL:

Sparky Anderson likes this young man quite a bit, so his chief concern going into spring training won't be earning a spot; it will be learning a new pitch. It's called the strike.

ANDY ALLANSON

Position: C
Bats: R **Throws:** R
Ht: 6' 5" **Wt:** 220

Opening Day Age: 30
Born: 12/22/61 in Richmond, VA
ML Seasons: 5

Overall Statistics

	G	AB	R	H	D	T	HR	RBI	SB	BB	SO	AVG
1991	60	151	10	35	10	0	1	16	0	7	31	.232
Career	455	1355	131	331	43	4	13	128	20	78	207	.244

HITTING, FIELDING, BASERUNNING:

In his role as Mickey Tettleton's caddy, Andy Allanson had good success in limited playing time against righties last year, but was impotent against lefties, the pitchers he was supposed to hit. Allanson batted mainly at the bottom of the order, where the main course on the menu is the fastball. Allanson was once a good fastball hitter, but his anemic production indicates that those days are gone. Allanson has little if any power, poor knowledge of the strike zone and no ability to hit for average. The result last year was a .266 on-base average and a .318 slugging percentage.

An adequate receiver, Allanson has soft hands and good plate-blocking skills. His game-calling skills are not on par with Tettleton, however, and he is not adept at throwing out runners. Allanson had decent speed as a youngster, but he has developed sluggish baserunning skills as he has aged. He primarily hits the ball in the air, but still grounds into a large number of double plays.

OVERALL:

Allanson is your typical backup catcher: he has decent defensive skills but can't hit a lick. That means he's always in danger of losing his spot on the roster.

SCOTT LIVINGSTONE

Position: 3B
Bats: L **Throws:** R
Ht: 6' 0" **Wt:** 190

Opening Day Age: 26
Born: 7/15/65 in Dallas, TX
ML Seasons: 1

Overall Statistics

	G	AB	R	H	D	T	HR	RBI	SB	BB	SO	AVG
1991	44	127	19	37	5	0	2	11	2	10	25	.291
Career	44	127	19	37	5	0	2	11	2	10	25	.291

HITTING, FIELDING, BASERUNNING:

Scott Livingstone faces playing-time prospects that are daunting to say the least. He is 26 and competing with Tony Phillips and Travis Fryman for time at third base. Nonetheless, Livingstone made a good impression as a rookie last year, batting .291 in 44 games.

Like many minor leaguers, Livingstone initially hit for an excellent average during his major league tenure. As the fastballs down the pipe were replaced by curves, changes and sliders, however, the average dipped and so did Livingstone's at-bats. He was able to handle the few lefties he faced, but overall Livingstone lacks power and consistent on-base ability.

Livingstone didn't steal bases in the minors and his two-for-three performance with the big club is probably his peak ability. He is an average fielder with a decent arm and is solid on the double play. He has been error-prone.

OVERALL:

Livingstone has been inconsistent in the minors and, given his advanced baseball age, he is unlikely to develop further offensive skills. He's a useful role-player who provides adequate defense. Livingstone is not a great prospect, but he does have a modicum of value to the Tigers.

KEVIN RITZ

Position: RP/SP
Bats: R **Throws:** R
Ht: 6' 4" **Wt:** 210

Opening Day Age: 26
Born: 6/8/65 in Eatonstown, NJ
ML Seasons: 3

Overall Statistics

	W	L	ERA	G	GS	Sv	IP	H	R	BB	SO	HR
1991	0	3	11.74	11	5	0	15.1	17	22	22	9	1
Career	4	13	6.05	27	21	0	96.2	106	75	80	68	3

PITCHING, FIELDING & HOLDING RUNNERS:

Going into the 1991 season, Kevin Ritz had yet to post a winning season at any level of professional baseball. The Tigers were still hopeful that he could salvage his career, and they were desperate enough for a fifth starter to call him up in June when they went with 12 pitchers.

In his five starts with the Tigers, Ritz was absolutely battered by opposing hitters. He survived past the second inning in only one of those five games. After a demotion in late June, Ritz was given another chance when Mike Henneman was sidelined. This time, he came out of the bullpen and looked like a different pitcher altogether. He notched a 2.84 ERA and his control improved greatly.

Ritz is a great fielder, showing excellent range and good instincts in '91. He has a good move to first and only three of the 39 baserunners he allowed attempted to steal.

OVERALL:

Ritz throws four pitches: a decent fastball, a sweeping curve, a slider, and a change-up. It seems a waste to use this varied repertoire in middle relief, but if Ritz is to ever pitch in the majors again, the bullpen is where he will probably end up.

ORGANIZATION OVERVIEW:

The Tigers, owned by a fast food king, have basically taken the "instant gratification" approach to building their ball club. They opt for veterans rather than youngsters. Detroit hasn't had a good farm system since the late seventies, when the Whitaker/Trammell/Morris group arrived. This summer the Tiger system was rated the worst in the majors by The Sporting News, and that seems like a fair assessment. Detroit does have a few good prospects in their system, and in the last two years they've come up with Milt Cuyler and Travis Fryman. For the most part, though, the pickings are pretty slim.

RICO BROGNA

Position: 1B
Bats: L **Throws:** L
Ht: 6' 2" **Wt:** 190

Opening Day Age: 21
Born: 4/18/70 in Turner Falls, MA

Recent Statistics

	G	AB	R	H	D	THR	RBI	SB	BB	SO	AVG
90 AA London	137	488	70	128	21	3	21	77	1	50	100	.262
91 AA London	77	293	40	80	13	1	13	51	0	25	59	.273
91 AAA Toledo	41	132	13	29	5	1	2	13	2	4	26	.220
91 MLE	118	413	45	97	15	0	14	55	1	22	93	.235

The Tigers' first pick in the 1988 draft, Brogna is generally considered their top prospect. His performance at AAA Toledo last year was disappointing, but he continued to show power potential with 13 homers in 293 at-bats at AA London. Considered a fine defensive first baseman, Brogna may be moved to right field due to Cecil Fielder's presence. Not yet 22, Brogna will almost certainly get a full year at AAA in 1992.

JOHN DESILVA

Position: P
Bats: R **Throws:** R
Ht: 6' 0" **Wt:** 193

Opening Day Age: 24
Born: 9/30/67 in Fort Bragg, CA

Recent Statistics

	W	L	ERA	GGS	Sv	IP	H	R	BB	SO	HR
90 A Lakeland	8	1	1.48	14	14	0	91.0	54	18	25	113	4
90 AA London	5	6	3.74	14	14	0	89.0	87	47	27	76	4
91 AA London	5	4	2.81	11	11	0	73.2	51	24	24	80	4
91 AAA Toledo	5	4	4.60	11	11	0	58.2	62	33	21	56	10

Though he doesn't throw as hard as Greg Gohr, DeSilva throws pitches that move, especially an excellent slider. He has routinely fanned around a man an inning throughout his minor league career, while also displaying excellent control. He comes from a fine college program at BYU and could well make the Tiger staff this year. He has some potential to be a major league winner.

GREG GOHR

Position: P
Bats: R **Throws:** R
Ht: 6' 3" **Wt:** 200

Opening Day Age: 24
Born: 10/29/67 in Santa Clara, CA

Recent Statistics

	W	L	ERA	GGS	Sv	IP	H	R	BB	SO	HR
90 A Lakeland	13	5	2.62	25	25	0	137.2	125	52	50	90	0
91 AA London	0	0	0.00	2	2	0	11.0	9	0	2	10	0
91 AAA Toledo	10	8	4.61	26	26	0	148.1	125	86	66	96	11

Detroit's first pick in '89, Gohr had a Tiger-sized ERA at Toledo last year (4.61). But he has a 90-MPH fastball, something the Tigers' staff sorely lacks. He moved to AAA all the way from Class A Lakeland. Gohr struck out 15 men in one game at Toledo toward the end of the year. If he can develop an off speed pitch, he should be pitching in Tiger Stadium this year. His skills are not as developed as DeSilva's at this point, but the Tigers like his potential more.

SHAWN HARE

Position: DH
Bats: L **Throws:** L
Ht: 6' 2" **Wt:** 190

Opening Day Age: 25
Born: 3/26/67 in St. Louis, MO

Recent Statistics

	G	AB	R	H	D	THR	RBI	SB	BB	SO	AVG
91 AA London	31	125	20	34	12	0	4	28	2	12	23	.272
91 AAA Toledo	80	252	44	78	18	2	9	42	1	30	53	.310
91 AL Detroit	9	19	0	1	1	0	0	0	0	2	1	.053
91 MLE	111	362	53	97	24	1	12	59	1	33	82	.268

An undrafted free agent signed in 1989, Hare finally got some attention this year by hitting .310 at Toledo. He doesn't have great power or great speed, but he has a good batting eye. A lefty swinger, he's a Dave Bergman type -- okay, but not very exciting.

RICH ROWLAND

Position: C
Bats: R **Throws:** R
Ht: 6' 1" **Wt:** 210

Opening Day Age: 25
Born: 2/25/67 in Cloverdale, CA

Recent Statistics

	G	AB	R	H	D	THR	RBI	SB	BB	SO	AVG
91 AAA Toledo	109	383	56	104	25	0	13	68	4	60	77	.272
91 AL Detroit	4	4	0	1	0	0	0	1	0	1	2	.250
91 MLE	109	368	45	89	20	0	11	55	2	49	83	.242

The Tigers could use a good backup to Mickey Tettleton, and Rowland may get that assignment this year. He's shown decent power and plate discipline at the minor league level, and his defensive skills, particularly his arm, are big league. He should make the ball club, but he doesn't figure to get a lot of work unless Tettleton gets hurt.

PITCHING:

In a repeat performance of 1990, Kevin Appier had a fine five month season in 1991. He started with a 4.34 ERA and was 1-5 through mid-May. As in 1990, though, a strong finish turned his season around. After a short bullpen stint helped him regain control of his good fastball, Appier returned to win his next two starts, both complete games. He went 9-3 with a 2.87 ERA over his final 20 starts, including a seven-game winning streak.

Appier throws hard enough to pitch up in the strike zone, but needs good control to be effective. He uses breaking pitches to set up his fastball, but early in the year he made costly mistakes with offspeed pitches by leaving them out over the plate. Appier had trouble getting out of tough jams and often let opponents fashion a big inning. Later in the year he was more effective in tight spots and had more confidence in his ability to bear down and blow away hitters; he was usually able to get strikeouts when he needed them. Appier used spacious Royals Stadium well, carrying a 2.79 ERA at home.

When Appier has good stuff the hitters have a hard time catching up with his fastball -- he throws harder as the game progresses. He's more effective against righthanders, who batted just .243 against him. However, lefties slugged .395 with eight homers.

HOLDING RUNNERS AND FIELDING:

A horrific fielder, Appier can turn any easy out into an adventure. His pickoff throws are unpredictable and randomly wild, but he still throws frequently to cut down runners' leads. Runners stole 10 bases in 18 attempts against Appier in 1991 after stealing 13 in 14 tries in 1990.

OVERALL:

At age 24 heading into 1992 "Ape" was the Royals best starting pitcher behind Bret Saberhagen in 1991, and is often sought by other teams in trade talks. If he can change his early-season luck in 1992, he'll become one of the league's top right-handed starters.

KEVIN APPIER

Position: SP
Bats: R **Throws:** R
Ht: 6' 2" **Wt:** 200

Opening Day Age: 24
Born: 12/6/67 in Lancaster, CA
ML Seasons: 3

Overall Statistics

	W	L	ERA	G	GS	Sv	IP	H	R	BB	SO	HR
1991	13	10	3.42	34	31	0	207.2	205	97	61	158	13
Career	26	22	3.43	72	60	0	415.0	418	186	127	295	29

How Often He Throws Strikes

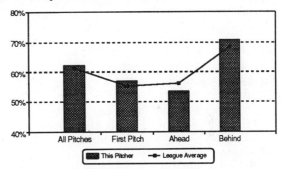

1991 Situational Stats

	W	L	ERA	Sv	IP		AB	H	HR	RBI	AVG
Home	5	5	2.79	0	96.2	LHB	403	108	8	41	.268
Road	8	5	3.97	0	111.0	RHB	400	97	5	38	.243
Day	4	3	1.93	0	70.0	Sc Pos	179	51	3	61	.285
Night	9	7	4.18	0	137.2	Clutch	84	19	0	4	.226

1991 Rankings (American League)

→ 2nd in shutouts (3)

→ 5th most strikeouts per 9 innings (6.8)

→ 7th least GDPs induced per 9 innings (.52)

→ 8th in strikeout/walk ratio (2.6), most pitches thrown per batter (3.83) and least home runs allowed per 9 innings (.56)

→ Led the Royals in wins (13), games started (31), shutouts, innings (207.2), hits allowed (205), batters faced (881), pitches thrown (3,376), most run support per 9 innings (4.7) and strikeouts per 9 innings

PITCHING:

In 1991, Luis Aquino changed from a marginally effective long reliever to a very effective starter, posting a 6-4 record as a member of the starting staff. While Aquino has been more effective out of the bullpen -- he has a career 2.85 ERA when pitching in relief compared to 3.80 as a starter -- he filled out the 1991 Royals' rotation admirably by going 5-2 in his last 13 starts after July 25th.

Aquino's strong finish proved he has fully recovered his arm strength after a muscle strain sidelined him for the last half of 1990. His 1991 numbers are quite similar to those of 1989, when he started 16 of his 34 games and posted a 3.50 ERA. Particularly encouraging was Aquino's strikeout-to-walk ratio, which was nearly two to one (as in 1989). In 1990, he walked nearly as many as he struck out.

The fastball is Aquino's out pitch, but he also throws a hard slider. Aquino doesn't overpower batters; he must change speeds and location to be effective. He is more successful against right-handed batters, limiting them to a .244 average, but they touched him for eight of his ten 1991 homers, often because he left a hittable fastball up in the strike zone. Stamina is a problem for Aquino -- he has trouble lasting past the sixth inning. A few of his victories came when he threw five or six innings and left with a substantial lead; the Royals scored early and often for him last year.

HOLDING RUNNERS AND FIELDING:

Aquino is a below-average fielder who doesn't help himself with the glove. He lacks a good pickoff move, but he partially makes up for it with a short, quick delivery to the plate. Opponents stole 10 bases in 16 tries.

OVERALL:

Aquino will probably battle Tom Gordon and Storm Davis for the fifth starter spot in 1992. Even if he doesn't win that job, he will get a long relief role and be available to step into the rotation again if injuries strike the starters.

LUIS AQUINO

Position: RP/SP
Bats: R **Throws:** R
Ht: 6' 1" **Wt:** 195

Opening Day Age: 26
Born: 5/19/65 in Santurce, Puerto Rico
ML Seasons: 5

Overall Statistics

	W	L	ERA	G	GS	Sv	IP	H	R	BB	SO	HR
1991	8	4	3.44	38	18	3	157.0	152	67	47	80	10
Career	20	14	3.45	106	42	3	407.0	406	177	129	192	25

How Often He Throws Strikes

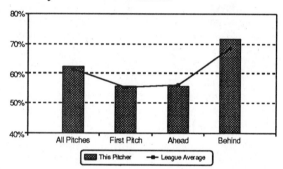

1991 Situational Stats

	W	L	ERA	Sv	IP		AB	H	HR	RBI	AVG
Home	3	1	3.13	1	77.2	LHB	289	76	2	32	.263
Road	5	3	3.74	2	79.1	RHB	312	76	8	35	.244
Day	2	0	2.47	2	43.2	Sc Pos	136	31	4	53	.228
Night	6	4	3.81	1	113.1	Clutch	79	16	1	6	.203

1991 Rankings (American League)

→ Did not rank near the top or bottom in any category

PITCHING:

After signing as a free agent with the Royals in 1991, Mike Boddicker was a bit of a disappointment. Expected to carry the load as a quality number-two starter, Boddicker was average at best. He started off well enough, posting a 2.03 ERA one month into the season. Then an elbow ligament strain put him on the disabled list for half of May, and Boddicker wasn't as effective the rest of the year. He was still a valuable starter, winning twelve games and throwing 180.2 innings -- both third-best on the Royals' staff.

Boddicker won't usually throw batters anything hittable, and they won't see the same pitch in the same location during a plate appearance against him. He moves the ball around and changes speeds often. Boddicker is more successful versus righthanders, who hit .240 and slugged .341 against him in 1991. Lefties hit .301 and slugged .470.

Boddicker has several different pitches and will throw each of them in a number of different ways. His most unorthodox pitch, the "fosh" -- a now-you-see-it, now-you-don't screwball change -- ties free swingers in knots. Boddicker occasionally loses control of his offspeed junk; he's hit 23 batters since 1990, including 13 in 1991. He strikes out few (less than four per game, among the league's lowest), but also walks few, and his sinkers induce lots of ground ball double plays, including a team leading 18 last season. It usually takes extended offensive sequences to beat Boddicker.

HOLDING RUNNERS AND FIELDING:

A fine fielder, Boddicker won a Gold Glove with the Red Sox in 1990. He positions himself well and throws to all bases accurately. Boddicker has a good pickoff move and is quick to the plate, making it difficult for runners to steal successfully.

OVERALL:

Signed for two more years, Boddicker remains KC property heading into 1992. The Royals hope he'll return to his 1990 form, but whether he does or not, his consistency and pitching savvy will still allow him to contribute to the team's success.

MIKE BODDICKER

Position: SP
Bats: R **Throws:** R
Ht: 5'11" **Wt:** 185

Opening Day Age: 34
Born: 8/23/57 in Cedar Rapids, IA
ML Seasons: 12

Overall Statistics

	W	L	ERA	G	GS	Sv	IP	H	R	BB	SO	HR
1991	12	12	4.08	30	29	0	180.2	188	89	59	79	13
Career	130	107	3.70	303	291	0	1983.0	1913	907	669	1259	177

How Often He Throws Strikes

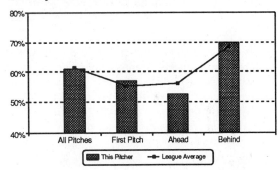

1991 Situational Stats

	W	L	ERA	Sv	IP		AB	H	HR	RBI	AVG
Home	7	8	4.07	0	110.2	LHB	355	107	7	43	.301
Road	5	4	4.11	0	70.0	RHB	337	81	6	37	.240
Day	4	3	5.40	0	40.0	Sc Pos	182	45	1	56	.247
Night	8	9	3.71	0	140.2	Clutch	63	17	1	6	.270

1991 Rankings (American League)

- ➡ 1st in hit batsmen (13)
- ➡ 3rd in pickoff throws (200)
- ➡ 5th least strikeouts per 9 innings (3.9)
- ➡ 8th lowest strikeout/walk ratio (1.3) and highest batting average allowed (.272)
- ➡ Led the Royals in hit batsmen, pickoff throws, runners caught stealing (10), GDPs induced (18), groundball/flyball ratio (1.3), most GDPs induced per 9 innings (.90) and lowest batting average allowed vs. right-handed batters (.240)

HITTING:

George Brett got off to his usual slow start last year, but failed to turn in a strong finish as he did in charging toward his third batting title in 1990. Brett finished 1991 with the worst batting average of his career, .255. Injuries plagued the veteran, who has missed fewer than 20 games only once since 1986. When Brett returned, it was strictly as a DH.

Brett had some good streaks in 1991, but never became the fearsome hitter of old. When he struggled, he became an out machine, striking out often and grounding into a team high 20 double plays. Brett was often fooled by hard sliders down and in, and had problems catching up to fastballs. Lefthanders gave him the most trouble. Brett hit lefties for a .234 average in 1991 -- down 82 points from 1990.

Brett remains a patient hitter who'll take a strike before swinging. He becomes more aggressive late in the game, but was unusually passive with runners in scoring position, drawing 30 walks in 140 plate appearances while hitting just .236. Leadoff hitter Brian McRae had more RBI than Brett's total of 61.

BASERUNNING:

Brett doesn't attempt to steal very often, but still picks his spots successfully. He was two for two in steal attempts in 1991 and is 39 for his 48 over the past four seasons. Brett no longer gambles on taking the extra base. His injury-riddled, 38-year-old legs don't get him around the bases well anymore.

FIELDING:

Brett was replaced at first base mainly to reduce his chance of further injury, but partly because his fielding skills have begun to erode. He still scoops low throws, but he now has very little range at first base. Brett's weak arm became less of a concern when he moved from third base to first in 1987.

OVERALL:

Bound for the Hall of Fame, Brett still has the capability for productive play. He'll DH full-time in 1992 with occasional duty at first base. Brett needs 164 hits to reach 3000; he'll need another big season to get there in 1992.

GEORGE BRETT

Position: DH
Bats: L **Throws:** R
Ht: 6' 0" **Wt:** 205

Opening Day Age: 38
Born: 5/15/53 in Glendale, WV
ML Seasons: 19

Overall Statistics

	G	AB	R	H	D	T	HR	RBI	SB	BB	SO	AVG
1991	131	505	77	129	40	2	10	61	2	58	75	.255
Career	2410	9197	1459	2836	599	129	291	1459	186	1022	772	.308

Where He Hits the Ball

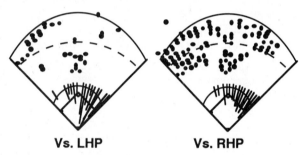

Vs. LHP   **Vs. RHP**

1991 Situational Stats

	AB	H	HR	RBI	AVG		AB	H	HR	RBI	AVG
Home	243	60	3	27	.247	LHP	167	39	2	18	.234
Road	262	69	7	34	.263	RHP	338	90	8	43	.266
Day	150	45	5	15	.300	Sc Pos	110	26	1	45	.236
Night	355	84	5	46	.237	Clutch	76	15	2	6	.197

1991 Rankings (American League)

→ 2nd lowest batting average on an 0-2 count (.000)

→ 9th in doubles (40) and GDPs (20)

→ Led the Royals in doubles, sacrifice flies (8), intentional walks (10), GDPs and batting average with the bases loaded (.444)

→ Led designated hitters in doubles and GDPs

PITCHING:

Year Two in the continuing saga of the Royals' Double Davis Disaster yielded an injury-plagued but passable season from Mark Davis. Twice he split a finger trying to snare sharply hit grounders bare-handed. But Davis spent his rehabilitation time well in Omaha and may have learned to pitch again.

The Royals hoped that Davis' former pitching coach, Pat Dobson, would help him regain control of his out pitch, a nasty breaking ball. But Dobson couldn't change Davis' fortunes. Davis walked nearly a batter an inning during the 17 games before his Omaha rehab stint. After pitching well as a starter in AAA, he earned five late-season starts with the Royals.

Although his major league starts weren't an overwhelming success, Davis lowered his ERA from 7.31 to 4.45 by season's end, including a 3.47 ERA after August 1st. However, he continued walking batters (more than 4.6 per game after his return), and was inconsistent from one outing to the next. Lefties hit Davis for average (.304); righthanders hit him for power (.387 slugging).

HOLDING RUNNERS AND FIELDING:

Baserunners distract Davis, and he occasionally has trouble concentrating on pitching while trying to hold them close. At these times he either forgets about the runner entirely or lets the batter hit a rope. In other facets, Davis is an average fielder.

OVERALL:

Davis showed better stuff at the end of 1991, but questions remain. Can he be consistent? Can he pitch well in games that mean something? Can he regain his confidence? Davis' future with the Royals depends on answers to these questions.

So, what can the Royals do with Davis? Even bad poker players know there's a time to cut losses. It won't be long before the Royals follow suit. At this point, they'll gladly accept any contribution Davis can make, as starter, closer, or set-up man. He'll try each role in 1992 until he succeeds somewhere. Barring any success, Davis might be released. He won't be traded because no other team will accept his huge contract.

MARK DAVIS

Position: RP/SP
Bats: L **Throws:** L
Ht: 6' 4" **Wt:** 210

Opening Day Age: 31
Born: 10/19/60 in Livermore, CA
ML Seasons: 11

Overall Statistics

	W	L	ERA	G	GS	Sv	IP	H	R	BB	SO	HR
1991	6	3	4.45	29	5	1	62.2	55	36	39	47	6
Career	48	75	3.90	498	79	92	989.2	884	473	431	874	102

How Often He Throws Strikes

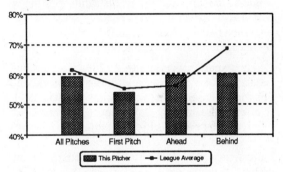

1991 Situational Stats

	W	L	ERA	Sv	IP		AB	H	HR	RBI	AVG
Home	4	1	4.66	0	29.0	LHB	56	17	0	6	.304
Road	2	2	4.28	1	33.2	RHB	173	38	6	30	.220
Day	0	2	7.11	0	19.0	Sc Pos	62	17	3	31	.274
Night	6	1	3.30	1	43.2	Clutch	22	9	1	8	.409

1991 Rankings (American League)

→ Did not rank near the top or bottom in any category

PITCHING:

In 1991, Storm Davis managed to go from bad to worse. One of the Royals' Dreadful Davis Duo, Storm first lost his starting spot, then bottomed out even further in the bullpen. He sputtered through nine starts until Mark Gubicza came off the disabled list, replacing Davis late in May. Davis was immediately awful in relief, allowing eight earned runs over 2.2 innings. But he eventually settled into his bullpen role, lowering his ERA to 3.57 by late July.

Unfortunately, Davis saved the worst for last. He finished the season by allowing 49 hits and 14 walks in his final 23.2 innings, with an ERA of 10.27. Overall, in 62.2 relief innings, Davis surrendered 83 hits and 28 walks while posting a 5.60 ERA. He struggled especially on the road, where he had a 5.73 ERA. Lefties mashed Davis by hitting .335 and slugging .498.

Davis primarily works hitters with a fastball, but he also throws an overhand curve and forkball. His forkball used to be more effective, but in 1991 it often came in flat. Davis doesn't throw hard enough to get fastballs by most hitters, so he must pick at corners and change speeds to succeed. Unfortunately, he didn't hit corners often enough, as his 3.6 walks per game indicate. Meanwhile, Davis' strikeout rate continued to drop, bottoming out at 4.2 per nine innings.

HOLDING RUNNERS AND FIELDING:

Runners have a hard time reading Davis' set position and don't often get a good jump; they stole just two bases in four attempts. He handles the glove well and sometimes comes through with defensive gems.

OVERALL:

Davis' 10-19 record and 4.85 ERA over two years in Kansas City (nearly a point higher than his two-plus Oakland years, when he was 36-15) are not what Royals' management expected when they signed him to a hefty three-year contract after the 1989 season. Davis must prove he still has major league stuff before the Royals give him an important role in 1992.

STORM DAVIS

Position: RP/SP
Bats: R **Throws:** R
Ht: 6' 4" **Wt:** 225

Opening Day Age: 30
Born: 12/26/61 in Dallas, TX
ML Seasons: 10

Overall Statistics

	W	L	ERA	G	GS	Sv	IP	H	R	BB	SO	HR
1991	3	9	4.96	51	9	2	114.1	140	69	46	53	11
Career	102	81	4.01	316	229	3	1545.1	1584	751	569	884	119

How Often He Throws Strikes

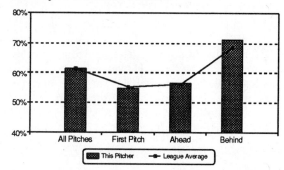

This Pitcher — League Average

1991 Situational Stats

	W	L	ERA	Sv	IP		AB	H	HR	RBI	AVG
Home	2	3	4.12	0	54.2	LHB	227	76	6	45	.335
Road	1	6	5.73	2	59.2	RHB	231	64	5	28	.277
Day	0	4	7.22	1	33.2	Sc Pos	131	39	2	58	.298
Night	3	5	4.02	1	80.2	Clutch	81	24	3	16	.296

1991 Rankings (American League)

→ 1st in worst relief ERA (5.60) and highest batting average allowed in relief (.326)

→ 2nd most baserunners allowed per 9 innings in relief (15.9)

→ 6th highest batting average allowed vs. left-handed batters (.335)

→ Led the Royals in holds (4), GDPs induced per GDP situation (14.0%) and first batter efficiency (.286)

HITTING:

Steady hitting is Jim Eisenreich's style. In his last three full seasons, he has hit .290 and slugged .414 while averaging 28 doubles and 39 extra-base hits. A line-drive hitter well suited to spacious Royals' Stadium, Eisenreich provides a good blend of batting average and power. He batted .311 at home in 1991.

One of baseball's most aggressive hitters, Eisenreich will swing at anything near the plate. He rarely walks (20 in 396 plate appearances) and also fans infrequently (35); he put the ball in play 86% of the time in 1991. Eisenreich has averaged fewer than one strikeout per ten at-bats over the last three years. He pulls the ball on the ground, but when he hits it in the air with power, it's usually to left or left-center. He's mainly a low ball hitter (all pitches) who has trouble with fastballs in on his fists. Eisenreich has often thrilled Royals fans with late-inning heroics. He also batted .324 with runners in scoring position in 1991.

BASERUNNING:

Eisenreich's baserunning continues to decline, as he stole just five bases (in eight attempts) in 1991, down from 12 steals in 1990 and 27 in 1989. He runs the bases with abandon, making some unnecessary outs. Eisenreich is fast out of the box and will occasionally gamble for extra bases.

FIELDING:

Despite a better fielding reputation, Eisenreich had worse range in left and made almost as many errors as Kirk Gibson in 1991 in half the innings. He has been a fine outfielder in the past, but was only average last season. Eisenreich has an average arm and usually reads fly balls well. He still has enough speed to succeed in center field, and he can fill in well in left and right.

OVERALL:

Eisenreich has been a steady and valuable performer as a fourth outfielder for the Royals over the last three years. He may get a chance to start, or at least platoon, if the Royals can't re-sign Danny Tartabull. Like Tartabull, Eisenreich's also a free agent, and he wants a starting job.

JIM EISENREICH

Position: LF/1B/CF/RF
Bats: L **Throws:** L
Ht: 5'11" **Wt:** 200

Opening Day Age: 32
Born: 4/18/59 in St. Cloud, MN
ML Seasons: 8

Overall Statistics

	G	AB	R	H	D	T	HR	RBI	SB	BB	SO	AVG
1991	135	375	47	113	22	3	2	47	5	20	35	.301
Career	585	1791	220	499	108	20	23	209	56	126	192	.279

Where He Hits the Ball

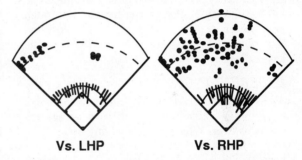

Vs. LHP   **Vs. RHP**

1991 Situational Stats

	AB	H	HR	RBI	AVG		AB	H	HR	RBI	AVG
Home	193	60	2	25	.311	LHP	87	28	1	16	.322
Road	182	53	0	22	.291	RHP	288	85	1	31	.295
Day	121	39	0	18	.322	Sc Pos	102	33	1	44	.324
Night	254	74	2	29	.291	Clutch	71	18	1	6	.254

1991 Rankings (American League)

→ 4th highest batting average with 2 strikes (.275)

→ Led the Royals in batting average with 2 strikes

→ Led AL left fielders in batting average after the 6th inning (.303)

KIRK GIBSON

Position: LF/DH
Bats: L **Throws:** L
Ht: 6' 3" **Wt:** 225

Opening Day Age: 34
Born: 5/28/57 in
Pontiac, MI
ML Seasons: 13

HITTING:

Kirk Gibson brought his gung-ho intensity to Kansas City in 1991 and gave the Royals much needed left-handed pop. Gibson's 16 homers, six triples and 81 runs scored were all second on the team. The Royals were disappointed in his .236 average and 55 RBI, but nagging injuries contributed to those low figures. Though Gibson missed 30 games, he always managed to contribute to the Royals' offense when he played.

Gibson is one of the few Royals' hitters who will take a pitch; his 69 walks led the team. Despite good power to all fields, Gibson's patience makes him a decent lead-off hitter, especially if his batting average gets closer to his career .269 average. He's primarily a low fastball hitter, but, in classic left-handed style, Gibson can hit any low pitch with power. A platoon role might suit Gibson at this point. He struggled with a .197 average against lefties.

BASERUNNING:

Age and injuries have failed to diminish Gibson's baserunning skills and he still runs as aggressively as ever. What's most amazing about Gibson is how successful he's been despite risky baserunning. He stole 18 bases in 22 attempts in 1991 and has succeeded in 87% of steal tries since 1988. Gibson always manages to take the seemingly impossible extra base.

FIELDING:

Gibson's fielding has been unfairly maligned of late. He is not the world's best outfielder, with below-average range and a weak arm. But that's less important now that he plays left field exclusively, and he doesn't remind the Royals of Lonnie Smith. Among his four 1991 errors was a deep fly ruled an error to protect Bret Saberhagen's no-hitter. Gibson gives top effort and makes most plays.

OVERALL:

Many in Kansas City were unimpressed with Gibson's results in '91. His low batting average and fielding were favorite targets. However, he gives the Royals sorely needed offense by getting on base and by having a powerful left-handed bat. Gibson will complete his two-year contract in '92 as the Royals' left fielder and leadoff man.

Overall Statistics

	G	AB	R	H	D	T	HR	RBI	SB	BB	SO	AVG
1991	132	462	81	109	17	6	16	55	18	69	103	.236
Career	1335	4782	809	1287	213	44	208	696	253	596	1056	.269

Where He Hits the Ball

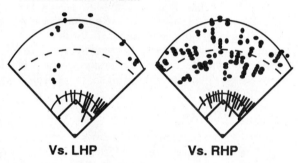

Vs. LHP   **Vs. RHP**

1991 Situational Stats

	AB	H	HR	RBI	AVG		AB	H	HR	RBI	AVG
Home	239	53	4	26	.222	LHP	132	26	2	11	.197
Road	223	56	12	29	.251	RHP	330	83	14	44	.252
Day	138	24	4	13	.174	Sc Pos	108	25	4	35	.231
Night	324	85	12	42	.262	Clutch	79	14	2	11	.177

1991 Rankings (American League)

→ 3rd highest stolen base percentage (81.8%)

→ 4th lowest batting average vs. left-handed pitchers (.197)

→ 5th lowest batting average at home (.222)

→ 6th most runs scored per time reached base (44.0%)

→ 7th lowest batting average (.236)

→ Led the Royals in walks (69), hit by pitch (6), stolen base percentage, most pitches seen per plate appearance (4.06) and steals of third (4)

→ Led AL left fielders in stolen base percentage

PITCHING:

Early in the 1991 season, Tom "Flash" Gordon appeared ready to make his big breakthrough. Gordon exuded confidence at the beginning of the campaign, throwing his out pitch, a sharp curve, on any count. However, due to minimal offensive support, Gordon wasn't winning despite fine performances. Posting only a 3-2 record in late May despite a 1.38 ERA, Gordon's confidence waned. He quickly became ineffective, eventually losing his rotation spot to Luis Aquino.

Unhappy with his demotion, Gordon showed annoyance when Hal McRae relieved him. He occasionally let his emotions affect his control, making bad situations worse. Gordon was unpredictable in relief. Sometimes he had good control and mowed down hitters. Other times Gordon would struggle with each delivery, running deep counts and filling the bases with runners. Gordon's 87 walks easily topped the Royals' staff.

Whether pitching well or poorly, Gordon always piles up strikeouts. He led the Royals with 167 whiffs and his average of 10.3 strikeouts per nine innings in relief ranked him fourth among all American League relievers. Gordon throws a fastball, but mainly for show to set up the curve. Later in the year as he lost confidence in his curve, he threw more fastballs, occasionally making costly mistakes by leaving it up and over the plate. Gordon's future success depends upon his ability to throw his curve for strikes. His curve is particularly difficult for righthanders, who hit only .191 against him.

HOLDING RUNNERS AND FIELDING:

Gordon's whirling motion and good pickoff move keep runners close. In 1991, opponents stole nine bases in 16 attempts after stealing eight bases in 18 tries in 1990, just a 50% success over the last two years. Gordon has improved his fielding since a marginal rookie performance.

OVERALL:

Gordon has lots of professional experience (532 innings) for his age (24). The Royals hope that once the experience starts showing, he will become a consistent starter. Gordon still has potential to be a great pitcher; 1992 could be his year.

TOM GORDON

Position: RP/SP
Bats: R **Throws:** R
Ht: 5' 9" **Wt:** 180

Opening Day Age: 24
Born: 11/18/67 in Sebring, FL
ML Seasons: 4

Overall Statistics

	W	L	ERA	G	GS	Sv	IP	H	R	BB	SO	HR
1991	9	14	3.87	45	14	1	158.0	129	76	87	167	16
Career	38	36	3.79	131	64	2	532.0	459	251	279	513	44

How Often He Throws Strikes

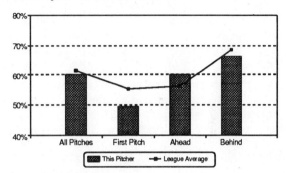

1991 Situational Stats

	W	L	ERA	Sv	IP		AB	H	HR	RBI	AVG
Home	2	8	4.00	1	92.1	LHB	302	75	4	31	.248
Road	7	6	3.70	0	65.2	RHB	283	54	12	32	.191
Day	5	3	2.01	0	53.2	Sc Pos	150	30	5	51	.200
Night	4	11	4.83	1	104.1	Clutch	142	37	1	5	.261

1991 Rankings (American League)

→ 1st in relief losses (7)

→ 4th in losses (14), lowest batting average allowed with runners in scoring position (.200) and most strikeouts per 9 innings in relief (10.3)

→ 7th lowest batting average allowed in relief (.207)

→ Led the Royals in losses, home runs allowed (16), walks allowed (87), strikeouts (167), holds (4), lowest batting average allowed with runners in scoring position, relief losses, lowest batting average allowed in relief, least baserunners allowed per 9 innings in relief (11.3) and most strikeouts per 9 innings in relief

PITCHING:

Off season shoulder surgery kept Mark Gubicza on the shelf until mid-May, and 1991 turned out to be his worst year in professional baseball. Gubicza's 5.68 ERA was more than a run higher than he'd ever carried at any professional level. Gubicza lacked sufficient strength to be effective; he couldn't get his best fastball past good hitters and his breaking pitches lacked bite. In particular, his usually tough slider often had little or nothing on it.

Opponents batted .308 against Gubicza, the highest opponent average against any regular Royals' pitcher. Lefties did the most damage, batting .326 and slugging .438; they racked Gubicza for twenty extra-base hits in 258 at-bats. His walk and strikeout rates remained consistent with recent seasons. Gubicza walked less than three per game while fanning more than twice as many as he walked.

For much of 1991, Gubicza worked under an 80-pitch limit, prescribed as an attempt to rebuild arm strength while preventing re-injury of his tender shoulder. He usually threw hard for a few innings, then tried to coast the rest of the way. Despite his ballooning ERA, Gubicza still managed a 9-12 record, a tribute to the fine run support given him by Royals hitters.

HOLDING RUNNERS AND FIELDING:

Gubicza lacks a good pickoff move. His delivery is slow to the plate, and his big leg kick gives runners a good jump. Runners stole against Gubicza with their usual success rate (75%) in 1991. Gubicza has been prone to making errors in pressure spots in the past but showed better composure in 1991. He remains a below-average fielder.

OVERALL:

The jury is still out on the success of Gubicza's return from the arm injury. Without full arm strength, his future is dim. He must throw his good fastball to succeed, but can't do that unless his shoulder is 100%. Gubicza enters 1992 as the team's fourth starter. Royals' fans hold their breath hoping that Gubicza can return to pre-injury form.

MARK GUBICZA

Position: SP
Bats: R **Throws:** R
Ht: 6' 5" **Wt:** 225

Opening Day Age: 29
Born: 8/14/62 in Philadelphia, PA
ML Seasons: 8

Overall Statistics

	W	L	ERA	G	GS	Sv	IP	H	R	BB	SO	HR
1991	9	12	5.68	26	26	0	133.0	168	90	42	89	10
Career	97	86	3.76	241	229	0	1540.1	1476	701	582	1010	89

How Often He Throws Strikes

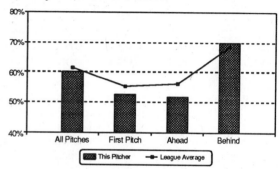

1991 Situational Stats

	W	L	ERA	Sv	IP		AB	H	HR	RBI	AVG
Home	4	6	5.21	0	65.2	LHB	258	84	3	36	.326
Road	5	6	6.15	0	67.1	RHB	287	84	7	45	.293
Day	3	3	6.19	0	36.1	Sc Pos	151	48	4	69	.318
Night	6	9	5.49	0	96.2	Clutch	11	1	0	0	.091

1991 Rankings (American League)

→ 6th in pickoff throws (189) and highest batting average allowed with runners in scoring position (.318)

→ 8th in highest batting average allowed vs. left-handed batters (.326)

→ Led the Royals in stolen bases allowed (18)

HITTING:

Kurt Stillwell's fielding difficulties gave rookie David Howard time to prove himself last year. Howard rode the bench until July 6th, going four-for-43 at the plate before the break. Though he finished the year with a lowly .216 average, Howard batted a more a little higher .239 when playing his natural position, shortstop.

A switch-hitter, Howard hits all pitching equally. He prefers high fastballs that he can drive and has more trouble with breaking pitches low or away. Howard hits the ball where it's pitched, but occasionally takes a big rip when he's ahead in the count.

Howard's steady minor league progress resulted in his best career offensive season at AA Memphis in 1990 with highs in batting average (.250), doubles (10), homers (5) and RBI (44). Solid spring performances in '91 helped him win an opening day roster spot. Howard handles the bat well; his nine sacrifice bunts were second on the team. By spraying the ball around the field Howard avoids double plays; he grounded into just one DP in 1991.

BASERUNNING:

Howard's lack of experience led to a few baserunning blunders in 1991. He doesn't possess great speed and won't steal many bases, but he usually has a good rate of success. Howard stole 15 bases in 19 attempts at Memphis in 1990 and reached double-digits in thefts in each of four minor league seasons.

FIELDING:

Steady glove work won Howard the starting shortstop job. He made some rookie mistakes immediately after taking over at short, but the errors lessened as Howard's experience grew. He has great range, but needs work on the DP pivot.

OVERALL:

The Royals liked what they saw of Howard in the second half of 1991. He should get a chance to win the shortstop job in spring training, but Howard needs to prove he can hit better over a full season. His glove is already of major league caliber.

DAVE HOWARD

Position: SS/2B
Bats: B **Throws:** R
Ht: 6' 0" **Wt:** 165

Opening Day Age: 25
Born: 2/26/67 in Sarasota, FL
ML Seasons: 1

Overall Statistics

	G	AB	R	H	D	T	HR	RBI	SB	BB	SO	AVG
1991	94	236	20	51	7	0	1	17	3	16	45	.216
Career	94	236	20	51	7	0	1	17	3	16	45	.216

Where He Hits the Ball

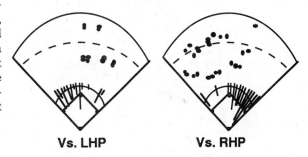

Vs. LHP　　　　Vs. RHP

1991 Situational Stats

	AB	H	HR	RBI	AVG		AB	H	HR	RBI	AVG
Home	116	24	0	7	.207	LHP	80	18	1	10	.225
Road	120	27	1	10	.225	RHP	156	33	0	7	.212
Day	79	15	0	4	.190	Sc Pos	66	16	1	17	.242
Night	157	36	1	13	.229	Clutch	29	5	0	1	.172

1991 Rankings (American League)

→ Did not rank near the top or bottom in any category

HITTING:

Mike Macfarlane was headed for his best season in 1991 when fate intervened, manifested in the person of Joe Carter. A day after hitting two home runs with five RBI, a career high, Macfarlane blocked the plate to prevent Carter from scoring, suffering torn knee ligaments. Nevertheless, Macfarlane's half-season provided the Royals with unexpected offense from the catcher's spot.

The biggest surprise was Macfarlane's power. He connected for 13 home runs after hitting a total of 12 career homers total prior to 1991. His .506 slugging average was 113 points better than his previous best. His .277 average was yet another career high.

Macfarlane is a dead pull hitter who likes fastballs. He fights off breaking pitches until getting a pitch to drive into the gap or down the line. Macfarlane struggles against finesse pitchers who needle the corners with offspeed pitches. He hit lefthanders particularly well in 1991, batting .321 and slugging .563 against them, but hadn't shown large platoon differences before last year.

BASERUNNING:

Lou Brock he'll never be: Macfarlane wisely tried just one steal (successfully) in 1991 after stealing the first base of his career in 1990. Macfarlane plays station-to-station baseball, rarely gambling for extra bases. His injury shouldn't have lasting impact on his baserunning -- he couldn't run before getting hurt anyway.

FIELDING:

Macfarlane initially made it to the majors with defensive prowess, and he continues to be a solid backstop. His throwing improved dramatically as he began shifting his feet better on throws to second. Last year Macfarlane thwarted 17 of 38 steal attempts (45%), up from just 17% in 1990. As demonstrated in the gruesome home-plate collision with Carter, he is hard-nosed and willing to make runners earn their way to the plate.

OVERALL:

As the Royals' incumbent catcher Macfarlane hopes to continue where he left off in 1991. He's in his prime and, if recovered, could be among the American League's best all-around catchers for the next few seasons.

MIKE MACFARLANE

Position: C
Bats: R **Throws:** R
Ht: 6' 1" **Wt:** 205

Opening Day Age: 28
Born: 4/12/64 in Stockton, CA
ML Seasons: 5

Overall Statistics

	G	AB	R	H	D	T	HR	RBI	SB	BB	SO	AVG
1991	84	267	34	74	18	2	13	41	1	17	52	.277
Career	355	1054	109	271	64	6	25	147	2	72	187	.257

Where He Hits the Ball

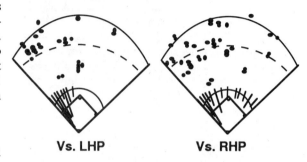

Vs. LHP   **Vs. RHP**

1991 Situational Stats

	AB	H	HR	RBI	AVG		AB	H	HR	RBI	AVG
Home	126	36	6	17	.286	LHP	112	36	5	14	.321
Road	141	38	7	24	.270	RHP	155	38	8	27	.245
Day	61	21	4	10	.344	Sc Pos	72	20	2	29	.278
Night	206	53	9	31	.257	Clutch	48	10	1	4	.208

1991 Rankings (American League)

→ 10th lowest batting average with the bases loaded (.111)
→ Led the Royals in hit by pitch (6) and least GDPs per GDP situation (6.9%)
→ Led AL catchers in least GDPs per GDP situation

HITTING:

In less than two full years as a professional, rookie Brent Mayne went from being the Royals' number-one pick in June, 1989 to their starting catcher in the majors. He got the job when Mike Macfarlane was lost to injury halfway through the season, and proved he can hit in the bigs. Mayne impressed the Royals with a .251 average, 31 RBI and fine clutch hitting (a .349 average with runners in scoring position) despite occasional lapses at the plate after initially replacing Macfarlane.

Mayne still has trouble against big league breaking pitches, especially from lefties with good control; he prefers to hit fastballs or sliders down. He'll take pitches away to left field, but mainly hits everything back up the middle. Mayne's a patient hitter who waits for a strike before swinging. He struck out a lot (42), but managed to walk some, too (23).

Left-handed Mayne is a fine complement to right-handed Macfarlane, particularly since Mayne can't hit lefties at all. Mayne had two hits in 22 at-bats against southpaws. Fortunately, he fares better against righthanders, hitting .268 and slugging .349 in 1991.

BASERUNNING:

Mayne has some speed but is only average on the base paths. He swiped two bases in six attempts in 1991 after stealing five in seven tries at AA Memphis in 1990. He needs more experience before he runs more often. Mayne wisely didn't take lots of chances on the bases in 1991.

FIELDING:

Mayne needs to work on throwing to second; opponents ran wild against him, stealing 53 bases in 76 attempts (70%). He is generally solid behind the plate defensively, but his lack of experience showed in his six errors, mostly on throws to second.

OVERALL:

The Royals must be pleased with Mayne's performance replacing Macfarlane. The offense didn't suffer with Mayne in the lineup, but he needs to work on throwing and overall defensive play. Mayne will very likely back up Macfarlane in 1992.

BRENT MAYNE

Position: C
Bats: L **Throws:** R
Ht: 6' 1" **Wt:** 190

Opening Day Age: 23
Born: 4/19/68 in Loma Linda, CA
ML Seasons: 2

Overall Statistics

	G	AB	R	H	D	T	HR	RBI	SB	BB	SO	AVG
1991	85	231	22	58	8	0	3	31	2	23	42	.251
Career	90	244	24	61	8	0	3	32	2	26	45	.250

Where He Hits the Ball

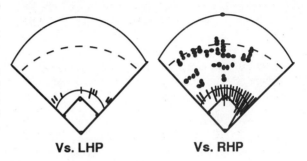

Vs. LHP   **Vs. RHP**

1991 Situational Stats

	AB	H	HR	RBI	AVG		AB	H	HR	RBI	AVG
Home	130	35	2	19	.269	LHP	22	2	0	3	.091
Road	101	23	1	12	.228	RHP	209	56	3	28	.268
Day	72	22	1	10	.306	Sc Pos	63	22	2	29	.349
Night	159	36	2	21	.226	Clutch	41	9	1	5	.220

1991 Rankings (American League)

➡ 9th highest batting average with a 3-1 count (.600)

➡ Led the Royals in batting average with a 3-1 count

➡ Led AL catchers in batting average with a 3-1 count

HITTING:

As the Royals' leadoff hitter during much of 1991, Brian McRae didn't get on base very consistently. But McRae provided some offensive spark by leading the Royals in runs scored (86) and connecting for 45 extra-base hits.

A line drive hitter with gap power, McRae walks too infrequently to be an effective leadoff hitter; in fact, he was eventually moved to the second spot in the order, to which he's better suited. McRae is a switch-hitter who hits lefties better (.294 vs. southpaws in '91, .361 in 1990). He strikes out too frequently, often falling behind in the count by flailing at first pitches out of the strike zone.

If McRae can learn to be more patient, he should see better pitches and draw more walks. He's still feeling his way around as a hitter. Halfway through the year, he shortened his swing to cut down on strikeouts, but instead lost most of his power. He hit just two homers in his last 298 at-bats.

BASERUNNING:

McRae, who's stolen 20 or more bases in each of his seven seasons of professional baseball, led the Royals in steals (20) and triples (9), but also tied for the team lead with 11 times caught stealing. McRae doesn't always use his great speed advantageously, sometimes becoming over-aggressive and running into outs.

FIELDING:

McRae's excellent speed also helps on defense. He has developed into a fine center fielder after beginning his career at second base. He has above average range and made several spectacular running grabs early in the year. He also committed only three errors. He has a weak arm, though, recording just two assists in '91.

OVERALL:

The Royals are impressed with McRae's steady outfield play, but want more consistent offensive production. At age 24, he's an important part of the team's youth movement; he's expected to steadily improve and eventually settle into the leadoff role. McRae should follow in the footsteps of Amos Otis and Willie Wilson as the next in a series of fine Royal center fielders.

BRIAN McRAE

Position: CF
Bats: B **Throws:** R
Ht: 6' 0" **Wt:** 185

Opening Day Age: 24
Born: 8/27/67 in Bradenton, FL
ML Seasons: 2

Overall Statistics

	G	AB	R	H	D	T	HR	RBI	SB	BB	SO	AVG
1991	152	629	86	164	28	9	8	64	20	24	99	.261
Career	198	797	107	212	36	12	10	87	24	33	128	.266

Where He Hits the Ball

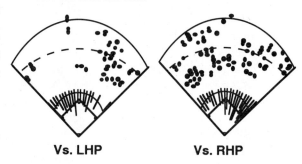

Vs. LHP   **Vs. RHP**

1991 Situational Stats

	AB	H	HR	RBI	AVG		AB	H	HR	RBI	AVG
Home	318	85	3	29	.267	LHP	204	60	2	19	.294
Road	311	79	5	35	.254	RHP	425	104	6	45	.245
Day	159	35	3	18	.220	Sc Pos	143	37	2	52	.259
Night	470	129	5	46	.274	Clutch	97	24	1	8	.247

1991 Rankings (American League)

- ➡ 1st in lowest leadoff on-base average (.284) and lowest on-base average vs. right-handed pitchers (.270)
- ➡ 3rd lowest on-base average (.288)
- ➡ 4th most runs scored per time reached base (45.3%)
- ➡ 5th most bunts in play (28)
- ➡ Led the Royals in at-bats (629), runs (86), hits (164), singles (119), triples (9), stolen bases (20), caught stealing (11), pitches seen (2,397), plate appearances (663), games (152), groundball/flyball ratio (1.62), runs score per time reached base and bunts in play

PITCHING:

Despite a few stumbles, Jeff Montgomery was reasonably successful as the Royals' stopper in 1991. His early season problems led manager Hal McRae to temporarily institute a bullpen by committee. Montgomery didn't like the set-up role, but it helped him regain focus and intensity. He persevered and eventually re-emerged as the Royals' best reliever. Montgomery finished strongly, blowing just two of his final 20 save chances after July 23rd. He also allowed only three earned runs in 33.2 innings over the final 27 games -- a 0.80 ERA. His 33 saves were a career best.

Montgomery still relies heavily on fastballs in the low 90s, but now mixes in more breaking balls. Using a slow curve as a change-up, he prevents hitters from sitting on his fastball. His high, tight heater is particularly tough on right-handed hitters, whom Montgomery has held to a .203 average since 1990.

Montgomery still lost control of his fastball on occasion last season, tossing six wild pitches in 90 innings. He maintained his usual three-to-one strikeout to walk ratio last year, although his strikeout rate declined slightly from his previous two full seasons. Montgomery often receives good offensive support which has helped him post a career 26-16 record.

HOLDING RUNNERS AND FIELDING:

Montgomery stays ahead of the hitters and throws hard, thereby keeping baserunners honest. His judgement of where to throw fielded balls has improved, but Montgomery remains an average fielder.

OVERALL:

Competitive teams need a good stopper and Montgomery has proven he can do the job. It took him four-and-a-half seasons to reach the big leagues, so he has relatively little major league experience for a 30 year old. Yet, he's still in his prime and will succeed as long as he has that hard fastball. Montgomery remains the incumbent Royals' closer entering 1992 and should fill the role well.

JEFF MONTGOMERY

Position: RP
Bats: R **Throws:** R
Ht: 5'11" **Wt:** 180

Opening Day Age: 30
Born: 1/7/62 in Wellston, OH
ML Seasons: 5

Overall Statistics

	W	L	ERA	G	GS	Sv	IP	H	R	BB	SO	HR
1991	4	4	2.90	67	0	33	90.0	83	32	28	77	6
Career	26	16	2.66	262	1	76	358.1	309	124	126	325	23

How Often He Throws Strikes

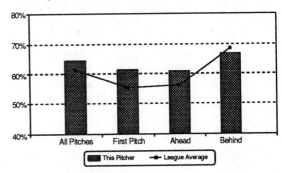

1991 Situational Stats

	W	L	ERA	Sv	IP		AB	H	HR	RBI	AVG
Home	3	3	3.44	15	49.2	LHB	168	44	4	31	.262
Road	1	1	2.23	18	40.1	RHB	170	39	2	12	.229
Day	0	1	4.50	9	24.0	Sc Pos	122	27	2	37	.221
Night	4	3	2.32	24	66.0	Clutch	255	62	5	39	.243

1991 Rankings (American League)

→ 5th in saves (33) and save percentage (84.6%)

→ 6th in save opportunities (39)

→ 7th in games finished (55)

→ 8th highest percentage of inherited runners scored (41.5%)

→ Led the Royals in games pitches (67), saves, games finished, save opportunities, save percentage, blown saves (6) and relief innings (90)

HITTING:

The Royals' most improved player in 1991, perennial super-sub Bill Pecota won the third base job with his glove and kept it with his bat. Pecota hit .289 with 20 extra-base hits after replacing Kevin Seitzer on July 7th. He managed career bests in homers (6), doubles (23) and on-base percentage (.356). For a second straight season, Pecota boosted his previous season's average 40 points, reaching a career-high .286 in 1991.

Pecota is a slap hitter who hits the ball where it's pitched, often taking inner-half breaking balls down the line for doubles. He likes pitches up and hits lefties better. His biggest weakness comes with sliders and fastballs low and away. Pecota shows early game patience but swings freely in late-inning situations. Pecota chokes up and punches at the ball with two strikes.

One of the Royals' better clutch hitters last year, Pecota batted .323 and slugged .440 with runners in scoring position, getting several big late-inning hits shortly after earning a full-time job. Pecota's also an accomplished bunter and had seven sacrifice hits in 1991.

BASERUNNING:

Past duties as a pinch runner make Pecota an experienced baserunner. He runs well enough to steal occasionally (41 thefts in 57 career attempts) and makes few judgement errors. Pecota gets a quick jump out of the box and stretches outfield hits for extra bases.

FIELDING:

Pecota's defensive prowess was particularly on display during a 68-game errorless streak at third base, but he's an accomplished fielder anywhere on the infield and can also play the outfield. Pecota has a strong and accurate arm and fields smoothly for his 6-2 frame.

OVERALL:

Will Pecota extend his impressive improvement into a third straight season? It's unlikely he'll get much better, but the Royals would happily accept a 1991 repeat. Formerly dubbed "I-29" for his frequent trips between Kansas City and Omaha, Pecota owns third base going into 1992. Versatility and defense make Pecota a valuable asset.

BILL PECOTA

Position: 3B/2B
Bats: R **Throws:** R
Ht: 6' 2" **Wt:** 190

Opening Day Age: 32
Born: 2/16/60 in Redwood City, CA
ML Seasons: 6

Overall Statistics

	G	AB	R	H	D	T	HR	RBI	SB	BB	SO	AVG
1991	125	398	53	114	23	2	6	45	16	41	45	.286
Career	445	1084	167	275	52	10	18	101	41	117	155	.254

Where He Hits the Ball

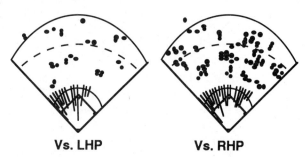

Vs. LHP   Vs. RHP

1991 Situational Stats

	AB	H	HR	RBI	AVG		AB	H	HR	RBI	AVG
Home	203	60	4	25	.296	LHP	128	43	2	17	.336
Road	195	54	2	20	.277	RHP	270	71	4	28	.263
Day	114	36	1	11	.316	Sc Pos	96	31	2	36	.323
Night	284	78	5	34	.275	Clutch	70	21	0	7	.300

1991 Rankings (American League)

➡ 4th highest batting average on a 3-2 count (.382)

➡ 5th highest batting average after the 6th inning (.328)

➡ Led the Royals in batting average vs. left-handed pitchers (.336), on-base average vs. left-handed pitchers (.414), batting average on a 3-2 count, batting average after the 6th inning, highest percentage of pitches taken (58.5%), lowest percentage of swings that missed (14.8%) and highest percentage of swings put into play (52.3%)

➡ Led AL third basemen in stolen bases (16), caught stealing (7) and stolen base percentage (69.6%)

STAFF ACE

BRET SABERHAGEN

Position: SP
Bats: R **Throws:** R
Ht: 6' 1" **Wt:** 200

Opening Day Age: 28
Born: 4/11/64 in
Chicago Heights, IL
ML Seasons: 8

PITCHING:

As expected, Bret Saberhagen regained his position among the American League's best pitchers last year. His 3.07 ERA placed him among the league leaders, and he topped Royals' hurlers in most pitching categories. Shoulder tendinitis caused Saberhagen to miss five starts, but a strong finish proved he had fully recovered.

When the weather was hot, Saberhagen was hotter. In five August starts, Sabes allowed just four earned runs on 20 hits over 41 innings (a 0.88 ERA) while tossing his first career no-hitter August 26th. During that span, he walked only seven. As usual, Saberhagen's control was good all year, as he fanned three times as many batters as he walked. He has averaged 1.76 walks per nine innings since 1989 and allowed opponents a minuscule .280 on-base percentage in 1991.

Saberhagen throws all of his pitches well, but his fastball, which he throws at several different speeds and with good movement, is one of the majors' best. Batters never see the same pitch in the same location during a game. Opponents need to get to Saberhagen early since he gets tougher as the game progresses; he has 48 complete games in 151 starts since 1987. Saberhagen used spacious Royals Stadium effectively last year, with a 2.76 ERA at home with just three homers allowed.

HOLDING RUNNERS AND FIELDING:

The recipient of a 1989 Gold Glove, Saberhagen remains among the best fielding pitchers in the majors. He throws well to all bases, and fields bunts and grounders flawlessly. Saberhagen will occasionally race into foul territory to snare popups unreachable by other fielders. He has an excellent move to first base and picks off many an unwary baserunner (four in '91).

OVERALL:

Perhaps due to his tremendous past workload, Saberhagen has traditionally slumped in even-numbered years in which he has a career mark of 36-48 (in odd-numbered years it's 74-30). If healthy this year, there's no reason he can't put an end to the pattern. The Royals' future success is closely linked to Saberhagen's.

Overall Statistics

	W	L	ERA	G	GS	Sv	IP	H	R	BB	SO	HR
1991	13	8	3.07	28	28	0	196.1	165	76	45	136	12
Career	110	78	3.21	252	226	1	1660.1	1551	650	331	1093	126

How Often He Throws Strikes

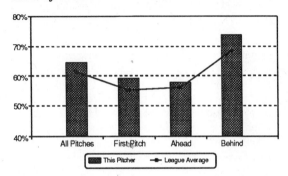

1991 Situational Stats

	W	L	ERA	Sv	IP		AB	H	HR	RBI	AVG
Home	7	3	2.76	0	94.2	LHB	354	76	9	36	.215
Road	6	5	3.36	0	101.2	RHB	370	89	3	27	.241
Day	4	4	3.09	0	64.0	Sc Pos	144	38	3	53	.264
Night	9	4	3.06	0	132.1	Clutch	102	23	2	9	.225

1991 Rankings (American League)

→ 4th lowest slugging percentage allowed (.327)

→ 5th highest strikeout/walk ratio (3.0) and lowest on-base average allowed (.280)

→ 6th in complete games (7) and shutouts (2)

→ 7th in lowest batting average allowed (.228), least home runs allowed per 9 innings (.55) and lowest ERA at home (2.76)

→ Led the Royals in ERA (3.07), wins (13), complete games, wild pitches (8), winning percentage (.619), strikeout/walk ratio, lowest stolen base percentage allowed (50.0%) and least pitches thrown per batter (3.67)

HITTING:

Like Lewis Carroll's Cheshire Cat, Kevin Seitzer's hitting has gradually faded from view, leaving behind a Royal frown of disappointment. Seitzer's batting average has dropped each year since 1987 to a career-low .265 in 1991. Most of his other offensive numbers have declined also. Formerly a contributor in many different facets, Seitzer is now more of a liability.

Seitzer is usually patient, hitting the ball to right for singles or lining doubles into gaps. He had tremendous pinch hitting success after his mid-season benching, going 11-for-20 off the bench. A platoon could help Seitzer, who hits lefthanders much better than righties: he batted .333 in 1991 and has slugged .447 against lefties since 1990.

Seitzer's RBI count fell for the fifth straight season to a career-low 25. He serves the Royals best by patiently setting the table for RBI men.

BASERUNNING:

Seitzer stole four bases in five attempts last year: the four steals were a career low. He still runs the bases aggressively, but made fewer baserunning mistakes in 1991. Knee problems contributed to Seitzer's lessened speed. His scheduled off season surgery should help.

FIELDING:

Seitzer's mobility was severely diminished by "medial plical shelves" in both knees -- a painful condition that limits movement. Unfortunately, there's no medical cure for his mishandling of the balls he does reach. Seitzer's .940 fielding percentage was among the league's worst. His fielding difficulties caused his mid-season benching. It's hard to see Seitzer, suddenly, at age 30, dramatically improving his fielding. The Royals do need more consistent glove work from him.

OVERALL:

Seitzer can still hit, but not enough to support his weak glove. If not traded, Seitzer will battle the suddenly solid Bill Pecota for the third base job. With consistent defensive play and renewed hitting, Seitzer can win the job and again give the Royals reason to smile.

KEVIN SEITZER

Position: 3B
Bats: R **Throws:** R
Ht: 5'11" **Wt:** 190

Opening Day Age: 30
Born: 3/26/62 in Springfield, IL
ML Seasons: 6

Overall Statistics

	G	AB	R	H	D	T	HR	RBI	SB	BB	SO	AVG
1991	85	234	28	62	11	3	1	25	4	29	21	.265
Career	741	2749	408	809	128	24	33	265	50	369	326	.294

Where He Hits the Ball

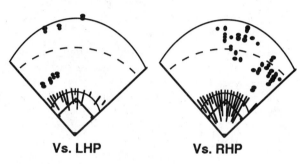

Vs. LHP   **Vs. RHP**

1991 Situational Stats

	AB	H	HR	RBI	AVG		AB	H	HR	RBI	AVG
Home	117	32	0	15	.274	LHP	66	22	1	7	.333
Road	117	30	1	10	.256	RHP	168	40	0	18	.238
Day	74	15	0	6	.203	Sc Pos	66	16	0	23	.242
Night	160	47	1	19	.294	Clutch	47	15	0	5	.319

1991 Rankings (American League)

➡ Led the Royals in batting average in the clutch (.319)

HITTING:

While the Royals didn't expect great hitting from Terry Shumpert in his first full season, 1991 was still disappointing. He hit a weak .217 and provided few offensive extras. A .339 streak in August provided some optimism, but Shumpert ended the season in a 7-for-54 slump.

Shumpert struck out too much (75) while walking too little (30). His .283 on-base percentage was among the league's worst for regulars. He tended to strike out in bunches, especially against hard throwers. Top right-handed power pitchers had overmatched Shumpert last year: he fanned 50 times in 234 at-bats against righthanders.

Early-season impatience left Shumpert seeing few first pitch strikes later in the year. He hit weak flies to right and grounders to shortstop by always trying to pull the ball. Shumpert has warning track power down the left field line and to the left-center gap. He's a decent bunter who led the Royals with ten sacrifice bunts, and he laid down several bunt singles early in the year.

BASERUNNING:

Shumpert swiped 17 bases last year, but tied for the team lead in being caught stealing with 11. He doesn't get a good jump off first base and has trouble reading a pitcher's move. Otherwise, Shumpert ran the bases well, using his raw speed to take extra bases on outfield hits.

FIELDING:

Excellent fielding got Shumpert to the big leagues early in 1990 and he often sparkled in 1991. However, he lacked the consistency that the Royals expected. Shumpert displayed good range, especially going to his left, and he turns the double play well for his lack of big league experience.

OVERALL:

Still only 25, Shumpert has lots of room for improvement. He enters 1992 under little pressure, as the Royals are committed to giving him the second base job. All they really expect is steady defensive play and gradual offensive improvement.

TERRY SHUMPERT

Position: 2B
Bats: R **Throws:** R
Ht: 5'11" **Wt:** 190

Opening Day Age: 25
Born: 8/16/66 in
Paducah, KY
ML Seasons: 2

Overall Statistics

	G	AB	R	H	D	T	HR	RBI	SB	BB	SO	AVG
1991	144	369	45	80	16	4	5	34	17	30	75	.217
Career	176	460	52	105	22	5	5	42	20	32	92	.228

Where He Hits the Ball

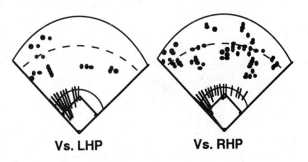

Vs. LHP   Vs. RHP

1991 Situational Stats

	AB	H	HR	RBI	AVG		AB	H	HR	RBI	AVG
Home	183	40	1	16	.219	LHP	135	28	2	12	.207
Road	186	40	4	18	.215	RHP	234	52	3	22	.222
Day	102	16	1	7	.157	Sc Pos	94	25	0	27	.266
Night	267	64	4	27	.240	Clutch	42	9	0	2	.214

1991 Rankings (American League)

➡ 1st highest percentage of extra bases taken as a runner (88.9%)

➡ 2nd worst fielding percentage at second base (.975)

➡ 4th lowest stolen base percentage (60.7%)

➡ 7th in caught stealing (11)

➡ Led the Royals in sacrifice bunts (10) and caught stealing (11)

➡ Led AL second basemen in caught stealing (11) and hit by pitch (5)

HITTING:

Kurt Stillwell's development took a definite downward turn in 1991. Only hot hitting in the spring kept him in the lineup as long as the All-Star break. Stillwell hit .317 in April and even temporarily led the American League in batting. But a May slide and a mediocre June prompted a change by Hal McRae, who decided that if his shortstop wasn't going to hit, he at least wanted some defense.

Stillwell was re-instated as the starting shortstop during the last three weeks and responded well, finishing with a career-best .265 average. He is mainly a singles hitter, but has doubles power to the gaps and down the lines. He likes to swing at first-pitch fastballs and won't take pitches unless they're entirely out of reach.

Stillwell's biggest problem is the slider away. He tries to pull them and ends up playing pepper with the middle infielders or hitting easy flies to the opposite field. A true switch-hitter, Stillwell hits right and lefthanded pitchers equally.

BASERUNNING:

Stillwell has succeeded in just three of six steal attempts since 1990 and managed just one triple in spacious Royals Stadium in '91 (half as many as slower-than-slow catcher Mike Macfarlane). He isn't fast, but he takes few risks.

FIELDING:

Poor fielding is at the heart of Stillwell's current problems. Although his glove and arm are usually dependable, Stillwell simply lacks sufficient range to make enough plays. He reached fewer balls than all other major league shortstops with his below-average lateral mobility. Even worse, most of his errors occurred at inopportune moments. He was finally benched in favor of .100 hitter David Howard.

OVERALL:

Unless Stillwell learns to hit like Cal Ripken Jr., his fielding must improve for him to retain an everyday job in the majors. The Royals have adequate defensive replacements, and free agent Stillwell may get a better offer elsewhere. It's make or break time; Stillwell must develop to remain a major league shortstop.

KURT STILLWELL

Position: SS
Bats: B **Throws:** R
Ht: 5'11" **Wt:** 185

Opening Day Age: 26
Born: 6/4/65 in Glendale, CA
ML Seasons: 6

Overall Statistics

	G	AB	R	H	D	T	HR	RBI	SB	BB	SO	AVG
1991	122	385	44	102	17	1	6	51	3	33	56	.265
Career	759	2487	304	630	126	25	30	268	28	223	353	.253

Where He Hits the Ball

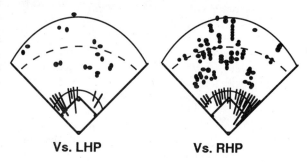

Vs. LHP   Vs. RHP

1991 Situational Stats

	AB	H	HR	RBI	AVG		AB	H	HR	RBI	AVG
Home	183	47	1	24	.257	LHP	109	29	1	15	.266
Road	202	55	5	27	.272	RHP	276	73	5	36	.264
Day	105	26	2	11	.248	Sc Pos	101	30	2	44	.297
Night	280	76	4	40	.271	Clutch	75	14	0	4	.187

1991 Rankings (American League)

➡ 2nd worst fielding percentage at shortstop (.959)

➡ 8th lowest batting average after the 6th inning (.208)

DANNY TARTABULL

Position: RF
Bats: R **Throws:** R
Ht: 6' 1" **Wt:** 210

Opening Day Age: 29
Born: 10/30/62 in Miami, FL
ML Seasons: 8

HITTING:

In 1991, Danny Tartabull turned in the big year that Royals' fans were long anticipating. He reached career bests and was among 1991's league leaders in most hitting categories. Tartabull had a powerful season in a poor power-hitting park. He smashed 13 of Kansas City's 47 Royals Stadium homers, slugging .571 at home.

Often during 1991, Tartabull *was* the Royals' offense. His teammates didn't set the table well for Tartabull, yet he made the most of limited opportunities, driving in 100 runs while hitting .374 and slugging .683 with runners in scoring position.

Tartabull patiently waits for his favorite pitch, a fastball up and away which he can drive deep to the outfield. If pitchers keep the ball down and in, Tartabull will hit grounders to the left side. Time and again in 1991, pitchers tried to overpower Tartabull (especially with runners on), only to watch him loft towering flies with his upper-cut swing. Pitchers who could change speeds gave him some difficulty, but Tartabull stopped hacking at bad pitches, drawing 65 walks for a .397 on-base percentage.

BASERUNNING:

Tartabull has been a below-average baserunner for years, but he runs the bases intelligently, rarely running into unnecessary outs. His six steals (in nine tries) in 1991 were his best since swiping eight in 1988.

FIELDING:

Tartabull led Royals' outfielders with seven errors and made fewer plays per nine innings (1.69) than all other major league right fielders except Darryl Strawberry. He's slow to pick up balls hit in his direction and lacks the necessary raw speed to close gaps in the spacious Royals Stadium outfield. Tartabull isn't in the lineup for his defense.

OVERALL:

The big question in Kansas City's hot stove league is: How much will free-agent Tartabull get? The answer: A bundle. The Royals can't afford to sign him, but they also can't afford not to. His absence from an already weak lineup could wreck Kansas City's offense. Tartabull is likely to go elsewhere and become very rich.

Overall Statistics

	G	AB	R	H	D	T	HR	RBI	SB	BB	SO	AVG
1991	132	484	78	153	35	3	31	100	6	65	121	.316
Career	823	2919	435	838	174	16	152	535	33	396	766	.287

Where He Hits the Ball

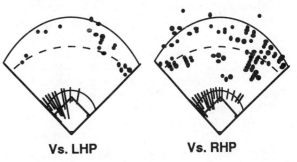

Vs. LHP   **Vs. RHP**

1991 Situational Stats

	AB	H	HR	RBI	AVG		AB	H	HR	RBI	AVG
Home	226	71	13	35	.314	LHP	142	42	8	22	.296
Road	258	82	18	65	.318	RHP	342	111	23	78	.325
Day	133	44	7	28	.331	Sc Pos	123	46	8	68	.374
Night	351	109	24	72	.311	Clutch	79	25	4	14	.316

1991 Rankings (American League)

→ 1st in slugging percentage (.593), batting average with runners in scoring position (.374), cleanup slugging percentage (.610), slugging percentage vs. right-handed pitchers (.614) and worst fielding percentage in right field (.965)

→ 3rd in HR frequency (15.6 ABs per HR) and highest percentage of swings that missed (32.0%)

→ Led the Royals in batting average (.316), home runs (31), total bases (287), RBIs (100), times on base (221), strikeouts (121), slugging percentage, on-base average (.397), HR frequency and batting average with runners in scoring position

The Scouting Report: 1992

TODD BENZINGER

Position: 1B/LF
Bats: B **Throws:** R
Ht: 6' 1" **Wt:** 190

Opening Day Age: 29
Born: 2/11/63 in Dayton, KY
ML Seasons: 5

Overall Statistics

	G	AB	R	H	D	T	HR	RBI	SB	BB	SO	AVG
1991	129	416	36	109	18	5	3	51	4	27	66	.262
Career	601	2048	233	523	99	12	46	286	17	134	376	.255

HITTING, FIELDING, BASERUNNING:

Todd Benzinger gained new life with a mid-season trade from Cincinnati to Kansas City last year. Benzinger had an immediate impact on the Royals' offense, hitting .346 with 19 RBI in his first three weeks. He batted .364 with runners in scoring position with the Royals and benefitted from Royal Stadium's wide-open spaces, hitting .326 and slugging .457 at home. After establishing himself as Kansas City's regular first baseman, Benzinger eventually cooled, but finished with a .294 average (.262, 51 RBI overall). He revived a stagnant career in the process.

Not a big home run hitter, the switch-hitting Benzinger sprays the ball around with gap power. He's a mediocre baserunner with a terrible basestealing percentage (38% over five years). An average first baseman, Benzinger can also play the outfield. He scoops low throws well enough at first base, but has a weak arm and little range in the outfield.

OVERALL:

Benzinger wants a full-time job and should get one from the Royals in 1992; they'll need him to drive in runs. Thus far in his career Benzinger has had flashes of brilliance, but he's been unable to consistently produce over the long haul. He should get another chance to prove himself in 1992.

MIKE MAGNANTE

Position: RP
Bats: L **Throws:** L
Ht: 6' 1" **Wt:** 180

Opening Day Age: 26
Born: 6/17/65 in Glendale, CA
ML Seasons: 1

Overall Statistics

	W	L	ERA	G	GS	Sv	IP	H	R	BB	SO	HR
1991	0	1	2.45	38	0	0	55.0	55	19	23	42	3
Career	0	1	2.45	38	0	0	55.0	55	19	23	42	3

PITCHING, FIELDING & HOLDING RUNNERS:

Mike Magnante surprised the Royals with a fine rookie campaign in 1991. He struggled in three early appearances and was sent to Omaha where he went 6-1 before being recalled when Bret Saberhagen went on the disabled list in mid-June. Magnante carried a 2.13 ERA in 35 games after his recall and by season's end was the Royals' most reliable set-up man.

Magnante sets up his fastball with offspeed breaking balls. He's what's known as "sneaky fast," utilizing an easy motion that hides his fastball's strength. With that repertoire, Magnante fanned 6.9 batters per nine innings, a fine ratio. Although Magnante succumbed to some rookie mistakes, he showed good composure as tough spots didn't rattle him. Magnante held runners at first well and fielded his position without incident.

OVERALL:

Magnante was exclusively a starter in the minors and could be called on to spot start. However, the Royals lack a reliable lefthander in the bullpen, so Magnante should enter 1992 in the lefty set-up role. His versatility is a plus.

TIM SPEHR

Position: C
Bats: R **Throws:** R
Ht: 6' 2" **Wt:** 205

Opening Day Age: 25
Born: 7/2/66 in Excelsior Springs, MO
ML Seasons: 1

Overall Statistics

	G	AB	R	H	D	T	HR	RBI	SB	BB	SO	AVG
1991	37	74	7	14	5	0	3	14	1	9	18	.189
Career	37	74	7	14	5	0	3	14	1	9	18	.189

HITTING, FIELDING, BASERUNNING:

Kansas City native Tim Spehr broke into the majors in 1991 when Mike Macfarlane was lost for much of the second half. Asked to back up Brent Mayne, Spehr showed some skills but couldn't handle major league pitching. He hit just .189.

Spehr was overmatched by most pitchers as long as they threw strikes. He displayed fine patience, drawing nine walks in 84 plate appearances, but he fanned 18 times. He's a spray hitter with some power to the alleys. He hit three homers.

Spehr's a below-average baserunner. He won't steal many bases and won't take many chances on the base paths. Fielding is his forte. He throws well, nailing 14 of 27 runners trying to steal last year. At Omaha, Spehr was rated the American Association's best defensive catcher in 1990.

OVERALL:

Despite spending half the season in the majors, Spehr is disappointed with his 1991 performance. He has major league defensive skills, but must hit better to have a shot at a big league catching job. Spehr will start 1992 in Omaha; he's currently the organization's third best catcher.

GARY THURMAN

Position: LF/RF
Bats: R **Throws:** R
Ht: 5'10" **Wt:** 175

Opening Day Age: 27
Born: 11/12/64 in Indianapolis, IN
ML Seasons: 5

Overall Statistics

	G	AB	R	H	D	T	HR	RBI	SB	BB	SO	AVG
1991	80	184	24	51	9	0	2	13	15	11	42	.277
Career	237	478	71	117	17	1	2	28	44	40	120	.245

HITTING, FIELDING, BASERUNNING:

A ligament injury sidelined Gary Thurman for a month last year, but despite that had what was easily the best year of his short big league career. Thurman reached career bests in most offensive categories while serving as a part-time outfielder in 1991. Considered a disappointment in the past, Thurman had never been give more than 87 at-bats to show what he could do. Given more of a chance, he produced.

A slap hitter who likes to beat balls into the turf, Thurman is aggressive, seldom walking while fanning often (13 walks and 54 whiffs since 1990). A fine baserunner with great speed, Thurman is 44 for 53 in steal attempts over five years. He runs aggressively, often taking extra bases on outfield hits. One of his two 1991 homers (the first two of his career) was an inside-the-park shot; he blazed around the bases, scoring without a throw. Thurman's speed helps on defense. He has a decent arm, but committed four errors in limited play.

OVERALL:

Thurman may be a platoon outfielder for the Royals in 1992 if Danny Tartabull isn't re-signed. Otherwise, he'll resume a reserve outfielder/pinch-hitter role. If healthy all year Thurman should again be a productive backup.

KANSAS CITY ROYALS MINOR LEAGUE PROSPECTS

ORGANIZATION OVERVIEW:

The Royals' farm system doesn't get much respect -- rated 19th in the majors last summer by The Sporting News -- but Kansas City has had a long tradition of producing solid major league players. That tradition shows no sign of dying out. The Royals still do one thing a lot of franchises never consider: when a position opens up at the major league level, KC usually looks to its farm system to fill the hole rather than bringing in a veteran from another team. A Terry Shumpert or a David Howard might not make it, but they'll still get a fair shot. The talent criticism is valid: the Royals have no one in the high minors who would be considered a potential superstar (if healthy, Jeff Conine might be the exception).

SEAN BERRY

Position: 3B
Bats: R **Throws:** R
Ht: 5' 11" **Wt:** 210

Opening Day Age: 26
Born: 3/22/66 in Santa Monica, CA

Recent Statistics

	G	AB	R	H	D	T	HR	RBI	SB	BB	SO	AVG
91 AAA Omaha	103	368	62	97	21	9	11	54	8	48	70	.264
91 AL Kansas City	31	60	5	8	3	0	0	1	0	5	23	.133
91 MLE	103	361	53	90	20	9	7	46	5	41	73	.249

The Royals have soured on third baseman Kevin Seitzer, and though Bill Pecota did a fine job last year, there should be some competition for the spot in '92. The husky Berry is one possibility: he has some power and surprising speed, though he hasn't hit much for average. He's also been error- prone throughout his career. It's his bat that will make or break him.

JEFF CONINE

Position: 1B
Bats: R **Throws:** R
Ht: 6' 1" **Wt:** 220

Opening Day Age: 25
Born: 6/27/66 in Tacoma, WA

Recent Statistics

	G	AB	R	H	D	T	HR	RBI	SB	BB	SO	AVG
90 AA Memphis	137	487	89	156	37	8	15	95	21	94	88	.320
90 MAJ Kansas City	9	20	3	5	2	0	0	2	0	2	5	.250
91 AAA Omaha	51	171	23	44	9	1	3	15	0	26	39	.257

Rated the Royals' top prospect a year ago after hitting .325 with 15 homers at Memphis, Conine missed much of 1991 with hand and wrist problems. Such injuries -- the latest the result of a bone broken while trying to check his swing -- often take a long time to heal, so his '91 figures can probably be discounted. If he's 100%, Conine will once again figure to be a top prospect. An outstanding athlete who's a world-class racquetball player, he can hit, hit with power, run and field, and has excellent plate discipline. Chances are he'll start 1992 at Omaha, but he could be in Kansas City by mid-summer.

BOB HAMELIN

Position: DH
Bats: L **Throws:** L
Ht: 6' 0" **Wt:** 230

Opening Day Age: 24
Born: 11/29/67 in Elizabeth, NJ

Recent Statistics

	G	AB	R	H	D	T	HR	RBI	SB	BB	SO	AVG
90 AAA Omaha	90	271	31	63	11	2	8	30	2	62	78	.232
91 AAA Omaha	37	127	13	24	3	1	4	19	0	16	32	.189

The Royals' top power-hitting prospect, Hamelin is a big, lumbering guy who will probably fit comfortably into Steve Balboni's old uniform. Weight is a problem for him, and so is a bad back -- he underwent surgery in midseason 1991, but is expected to be ready by the spring. Hamelin has great power and a good eye, but no speed, and he strikes out a lot. He's a longshot, but players of his ilk often fashion useful major league careers.

KEVIN KOSLOFSKI

Position: OF
Bats: L **Throws:** R
Ht: 5' 9" **Wt:** 160

Opening Day Age: 25
Born: 9/24/66 in Decatur, IL

Recent Statistics

	G	AB	R	H	D	T	HR	RBI	SB	BB	SO	AVG
90 AA Memphis	118	367	52	78	11	5	3	32	12	54	89	.213
91 AA Memphis	81	287	41	93	15	3	7	39	10	33	56	.324
91 AAA Omaha	25	94	13	28	3	2	2	19	4	15	19	.298
91 MLE	106	367	44	107	16	4	5	47	8	34	78	.292

A 20th-round draft choice back in 1984, Koslofski was stuck in A ball until the last two years, and 1991 was his best year at the plate by far. He has excellent speed and good discipline, and can definitely play in the majors if he hits like he did in 1991.

HARVEY PULLIAM

Position: OF
Bats: R **Throws:** R
Ht: 6' 0" **Wt:** 210

Opening Day Age: 24
Born: 10/20/67 in San Francisco, CA

Recent Statistics

	G	AB	R	H	D	T	HR	RBI	SB	BB	SO	AVG
91 AAA Omaha	104	346	35	89	18	2	6	39	2	31	62	.257
91 AL Kansas City	18	33	4	9	1	0	3	4	0	3	9	.273
91 MLE	104	338	30	81	17	2	4	33	1	26	65	.240

A marginal power-hitting prospect, Pulliam had a better year in 1990 than he did in '91. He has fair speed and can draw some walks, but lacks great defensive skills. He has a chance to make it as a spare outfielder in '92, but that's probably about it.

PITCHING:

After a year when his performance was limited to just 11 major league innings, most of it spent in the minors, Don August was released by the Brewers in October of 1990. He was invited to camp last spring, where he pitched pretty well, giving credit for the renewed pop in his pitches to an off season conditioning program with strength guru Mackie Shilstone.

Unfortunately, August still had a year much like 1990, except the Brewers let him have it in the majors this time. The good news is that he won eight games as a starter, posting an ERA of 2.48 in those winning outings. In his other 15 non-winning starts he had an ERA of 7.64 and lost eight games. August was among the bottom 10 in the league in strikeouts per nine innings, home runs allowed per nine innings, hits allowed per nine innings, and earned run average, both overall and in the first inning, when his ERA was 6.65.

As always, August depended on his sharp curveball breaking for strikes. He had a stretch of success in May, but his fastball proved hittable and his curveball inconsistent. His line against opposing hitters looks a great deal like he spent the year facing a collective Ivan Calderon: the opposition hit .301 with 18 homers.

HOLDING RUNNERS AND FIELDING:

August is easy to run on because he does not throw hard and the runners know it. Opposing runners stole 18 bases and were caught only four times. He has a sure glove, as his 32 total chances without an error attests, but his range is ordinary and he doesn't cover first all that well.

OVERALL:

The Brewers should have Bosio (if he isn't traded), Wegman, and Navarro, and with luck, Higuera and Ron Robinson as well as rookie Cal Eldred as starters this spring. It's somewhat surprising that August got as much work as he did in 1991. He relies on a curveball that hasn't been reliable in two years. It would be surprising if he found regular pitching work in 1992.

DON AUGUST

Position: SP/RP
Bats: R **Throws:** R
Ht: 6' 3" **Wt:** 190

Opening Day Age: 28
Born: 7/3/63 in Inglewood, CA
ML Seasons: 4

Overall Statistics

	W	L	ERA	G	GS	Sv	IP	H	R	BB	SO	HR
1991	9	8	5.47	28	23	0	138.1	166	87	47	62	18
Career	34	30	4.64	88	70	0	440.0	491	245	158	181	47

How Often He Throws Strikes

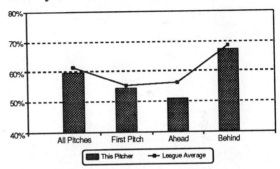

1991 Situational Stats

	W	L	ERA	Sv	IP		AB	H	HR	RBI	AVG
Home	8	5	4.13	0	80.2	LHB	302	96	10	50	.318
Road	1	3	7.34	0	57.2	RHB	249	70	8	29	.281
Day	1	2	10.26	0	16.2	Sc Pos	131	43	7	62	.328
Night	8	6	4.81	0	121.2	Clutch	38	13	3	8	.342

1991 Rankings (American League)

- ➡ 4th worst batting average allowed with runners in scoring position (.328)
- ➡ 10th worst batting average allowed vs. left-handed batters (.318)
- ➡ Led the Brewers in home runs allowed (18)

HITTING:

Dante Bichette came to the Brewers from the Angels in a trade for Dave Parker, and was a spring terror, hitting .295 with five homers and 15 RBI in 78 at-bats. But Bichette was his old self once the season started, and maybe a little worse.

It had looked like Bichette was learning during his 1990 season. Pitchers were denying him the good fastball on the first pitch, and he was learning to choke up when behind in the count and to slug when he was ahead of the pitcher. In 1991 he was hitting the first pitch successfully, and nothing else. He continued to strike out five times as much as he walked.

Bichette was a legitimate platoon player in 1990, with a pretty decent record against lefties, but in 1991 he declined against both lefties and righties. He had only one stretch, during midseason, when he hit for a decent average. He hit only three home runs after the break, when the rest of the team's offense was exploding.

BASERUNNING:

Never really a basestealing threat, Bichette ran more in 1991, with mixed results. His fourteen steals add a new dimension to his game, and being caught eight times seems to be more a lack of experience than speed. He is a good runner and could become a 20-steal man if he can get on base.

FIELDING:

Bichette took some of his troubles into the field with him, committing six errors in less than 1000 innings. He does have terrific range and an amazing arm, recording 14 kills on the bases and certainly quelling any nostalgia for the fine outfield play of the departed Rob Deer.

OVERALL:

What real hope is there for a hitter like Bichette? He relies on strength and speed, while still struggling, at age 29, to learn the strike zone and lay off the curve. It is hard to imagine Bichette as a starter for a team that expects to contend. His defense, speed, and power do make him a valuable bench player.

DANTE BICHETTE

Position: RF
Bats: R **Throws:** R
Ht: 6' 3" **Wt:** 225

Opening Day Age: 28
Born: 11/18/63 in West Palm Beach, FL
ML Seasons: 4

Overall Statistics

	G	AB	R	H	D	T	HR	RBI	SB	BB	SO	AVG
1991	134	445	53	106	18	3	15	59	14	22	107	.238
Career	312	978	107	236	42	4	33	135	22	44	217	.241

Where He Hits the Ball

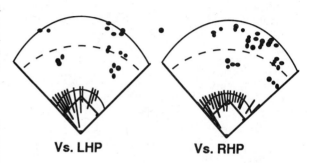

Vs. LHP   Vs. RHP

1991 Situational Stats

	AB	H	HR	RBI	AVG		AB	H	HR	RBI	AVG
Home	213	53	6	30	.249	LHP	154	39	6	18	.253
Road	232	53	9	29	.228	RHP	291	67	9	41	.230
Day	145	42	6	24	.290	Sc Pos	110	24	5	46	.218
Night	300	64	9	35	.213	Clutch	88	24	3	15	.273

1991 Rankings (American League)

→ 1st in lowest batting average with 2 strikes (.090)

→ 4th highest batting average with the bases loaded (.500)

→ 7th lowest stolen base percentage (63.6%)

→ 8th lowest percentage of pitches taken (45.2%), highest percentage of swings that missed (28.5%) and lowest percentage of swings put into play (36.9%)

→ Led the Brewers in caught stealing (8)

→ Led AL right fielders in batting average with the bases loaded

PITCHING:

It wasn't the breakthrough season that Brewer fans await annually from Chris Bosio. But after his 1990 season battling tendinitis in his knees, followed by off season knee surgery, 1991 has to be considered a triumph.

Bosio still threw his wide selection of hard stuff for strikes, and other than a mid season bout with a pulled hamstring, he took his turn in the rotation regularly, though he complained of leg problems down the stretch. His strikeout-to-walk ratio was down from his traditionally excellent 3-to-1 to a merely good 2-to-1. It isn't hard to look over his outings and project a record of 18-8 or even better, rather than 14-10.

Bosio had some by-now familiar tantrums last year over being yanked early in his first game back after his hamstring problem. He then went out and tossed a complete game six-hitter, beating the White Sox. The White Sox outing may be an indication that he has learned to harness his emotions and put them to work for himself and his team.

When Bosio did have trouble, there was a familiar pattern. He gets behind trying to hit the corners, and then has to come into the strike zone; his reluctance to issue the walk sometimes costs him.

HOLDING RUNNERS AND FIELDING:

Bosio has never been all that good in the field, mostly due to lack of range, but he doesn't hurt himself much either. He has improved his covering of first base, and was involved in four double plays. Runners will go on him, and in 1991 stole nine bases in 13 attempts.

OVERALL:

Trade rumors swirl around Bosio, but down the stretch the Brewers' rotation came together. There are questions, like whether he can get his strikeout rate back up, and whether his knee will hold up. Bosio is in a familiar position; he is a fine number-two or three starter, and with some luck and health, could still have a big season or two.

CHRIS BOSIO

Position: SP
Bats: R **Throws:** R
Ht: 6' 3" **Wt:** 225

Opening Day Age: 29
Born: 4/3/63 in Carmichael, CA
ML Seasons: 6

Overall Statistics

	W	L	ERA	G	GS	Sv	IP	H	R	BB	SO	HR
1991	14	10	3.25	32	32	0	204.2	187	80	58	117	15
Career	51	56	3.79	179	130	8	958.2	961	446	245	629	86

How Often He Throws Strikes

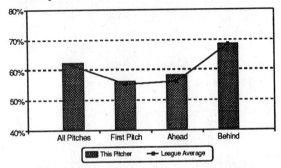

1991 Situational Stats

	W	L	ERA	Sv	IP		AB	H	HR	RBI	AVG
Home	5	6	3.83	0	96.1	LHB	418	105	6	39	.251
Road	9	4	2.74	0	108.1	RHB	348	82	9	33	.236
Day	4	3	3.50	0	69.1	Sc Pos	152	40	3	52	.263
Night	10	7	3.13	0	135.1	Clutch	64	19	2	6	.297

1991 Rankings (American League)

- → 4th least pitches thrown per batter (3.43)
- → 5th most GDPs induced (22)
- → 6th lowest ERA on the road (2.74)
- → 9th most GDPs induced per 9 innings (.97)
- → Led the Brewers in hit batsmen (8), strikeouts (117), GDPs induced (22), lowest slugging percentage allowed (.350), least pitches thrown per batter, least home runs allowed per 9 innings (.66), most GDPs induced per 9 innings, most strikeouts per 9 innings (5.1) and ERA on the road

PITCHING:

Chuck Crim and Dan Plesac both began to slide simultaneously two years ago, and in 1991 their ineffectiveness was at the core of Brewer bullpen troubles. Crim again pitched a large number of innings in middle relief. However, his ERA ballooned by more than a run over his 1990 figure, which was in turn over half a run higher than in 1989.

With his sinker ball even less effective than in 1990, and no curveball, Crim struggled. Nevertheless, Tom Trebelhorn kept trotting him out there until his ERA grew to 6.00 in July. In August, the Brewers' bullpen began to benefit from the yeoman pitching of Bosio, Navarro, and Wegman. Crim's workload began to lessen. The shorter outings seemed to gradually improve his pitching, and he was effective in September and October. In general, though, his second half pitching was worse than the first half.

Crim continues to suffer from an inability to induce the double play, and his reluctance to walk hitters shows, as he gave up more hits per inning than ever. There was almost no aspect of his game that didn't slip in 1991.

HOLDING RUNNERS AND FIELDING:

Base stealers were successful 12 times last year against Crim, and were only caught once. He doesn't have a good move to first, and though he will try to keep runners close, his sinking pitch makes it tough for the catcher to get off a good throw. His fielding is adequate, and he made just one error in 1991.

OVERALL:

Trebelhorn lived, and eventually died, with Crim and Plesac. New manager Phil Garner may not be so attached to Crim, and Plesac's days as closer appear to be over. There is some possibility that Crim can be successful in a lesser role, based on his late-season showing, but he was still giving up too many hits. If he's lost his workhorse capacity, his future as a set-up man is in doubt.

CHUCK CRIM

Position: RP
Bats: R **Throws:** R
Ht: 6' 0" **Wt:** 185

Opening Day Age: 30
Born: 7/23/61 in Van Nuys, CA
ML Seasons: 5

Overall Statistics

	W	L	ERA	G	GS	Sv	IP	H	R	BB	SO	HR
1991	8	5	4.63	66	0	3	91.1	115	52	25	39	9
Career	33	31	3.47	332	5	42	529.2	545	231	151	251	49

How Often He Throws Strikes

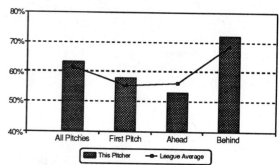

This Pitcher / League Average

1991 Situational Stats

	W	L	ERA	Sv	IP		AB	H	HR	RBI	AVG
Home	5	2	5.07	2	49.2	LHB	184	54	7	30	.293
Road	3	3	4.10	1	41.2	RHB	193	61	2	25	.316
Day	4	2	6.53	1	30.1	Sc Pos	110	40	3	47	.364
Night	4	3	3.69	2	61.0	Clutch	164	50	2	23	.305

1991 Rankings (American League)

→ 3rd in balks (3) and highest batting average allowed in relief (.305)

→ 4th in relief wins (8) and least strikeouts per 9 innings in relief (3.8)

→ 7th in worst first batter efficiency (.333) and most baserunners allowed 9 innings in relief (14.0)

→ 8th in relief innings (91.1)

→ 9th worst relief ERA (4.63)

→ Led the Brewers in games pitched (66), games finished (29), balks, relief wins and relief innings

HITTING:

Jim Gantner hit a steady .283 in 1991, producing, at age 37, a season that fits neatly into his long career. After a pronounced affection for left-handed pitching in 1990, he resumed his indifference in 1991, hitting both sides equally well, though he has more of his marginal power against righties. He cracked his first homer in four years in September (he hit two), ending a breathless watch among fans of punch-and-judy middle in-fielders.

The only noticeable change in Gantner's hitting was his drop in strikeouts per at bat, from an already low level to one that placed him just behind teammate B.J. Surhoff, fifth-lowest in the league. He is laying off the high pitch a little better than in the past. Consistent with his reputation of being a leader and a fiery player, Gantner was especially effective leading off an inning and in late and close situations.

BASERUNNING:

Gantner's knee surgery didn't seem to slow him in 1990, but in 1991 he was just 4-for-10, after a three year period in which he stole 58 bases in 75 attempts. However, he retained his hard edge on the bases.

FIELDING:

Gantner's versatility was never as valuable as in 1991, when he was forced to third base because of Gary Sheffield's injury and Dale Sveum's slow return to respectability. Gantner's .976 fielding percentage was the third best among fielders who had as many innings at third as he did. Age has diminished his defensive range.

OVERALL:

Gantner, who lost an arbitration bid before the 1991 season, became a free agent at the end of the year. Despite his steady play and versatility, he is a marginal producer, lacking power or the ability to draw a walk. He will be 38 in 1992, and has been on the DL in three of the last five years. But his skills should attract some interest now that his health is no longer a major question. The Brewers will have to choose between him and Willie Randolph, and his long career in Milwaukee could be over.

JIM GANTNER

Position: 3B/2B
Bats: L **Throws:** R
Ht: 5'11" **Wt:** 175

Opening Day Age: 38
Born: 1/5/54 in Eden, WI
ML Seasons: 16

Overall Statistics

	G	AB	R	H	D	T	HR	RBI	SB	BB	SO	AVG
1991	140	526	63	149	27	4	2	47	4	27	34	.283
Career	1700	5933	704	1633	250	37	46	550	131	371	484	.275

Where He Hits the Ball

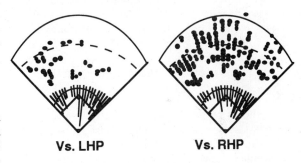

Vs. LHP   Vs. RHP

1991 Situational Stats

	AB	H	HR	RBI	AVG		AB	H	HR	RBI	AVG
Home	254	73	1	20	.287	LHP	139	37	0	13	.266
Road	272	76	1	27	.279	RHP	387	112	2	34	.289
Day	133	38	0	10	.286	Sc Pos	123	29	0	44	.236
Night	393	111	2	37	.282	Clutch	100	31	1	9	.310

1991 Rankings (American League)

➡ 3rd in least pitches seen per plate appearance (3.00)

➡ 5th lowest HR frequency (263 ABs per HR)

➡ 7th lowest slugging percentage vs. left-handed pitchers (.288)

➡ Led AL third basemen in triples (4) and highest batting average on an 0-2 count (.188)

HITTING:

In 1990 Darryl Hamilton faced lefties 11 times. Although he was one of the team's best hitters and a top clutch performer, any role beyond a platoon was questionable. But in 1991 Hamilton stepped into the vacuum that was the Brewers lineup and hit his way into a regular role. He recorded a .311 average that included a respectable .276 showing against lefties.

After a slow start Hamilton caught fire, hitting .327 after the break and operating as a perfect number-two hitter behind Paul Molitor. In the second slot he fashioned a .404 on-base average over 100 at-bats, which was better even than Molitor's pace. Though Hamilton takes a lot of pitches, he is a swinger like Molitor; he works the count to his favor for the hitting advantage it gives him. His 33 walks in 405 at-bats are not exceptional. Despite his lack of power, Hamilton drove in and scored 47 runs in the second half.

BASERUNNING:

Hamilton's reputation as a minor league speedster is justified, though he stole just 16 bases in 1991 and was caught six times. He may have been prevented from running more often by the presence of Molitor on base ahead of him. He could steal more if given the chance, and since the Brewers can use all the offense they can get, he should get that chance.

FIELDING:

Hamilton gained attention for his defensive skills, and they came in handy in '91 when Robin Yount had injury problems. Hamilton played three outfield positions, mostly in center and right. He committed only one error and showed his blazing speed and steady glove work.

OVERALL:

Given his first shot at regular duty last year, Hamilton made a very positive impression. He'll need to prove his performance against lefties was no fluke, and it would help if he could walk a little more. Batting near the top of a strong lineup, he has the potential to score 100 runs.

DARRYL HAMILTON

Position: CF/LF/RF
Bats: L **Throws:** R
Ht: 6' 1" **Wt:** 180

Opening Day Age: 27
Born: 12/3/64 in Baton Rouge, LA
ML Seasons: 3

Overall Statistics

	G	AB	R	H	D	T	HR	RBI	SB	BB	SO	AVG
1991	122	405	64	126	15	6	1	57	16	33	38	.311
Career	255	664	105	191	24	6	3	86	33	54	59	.288

Where He Hits the Ball

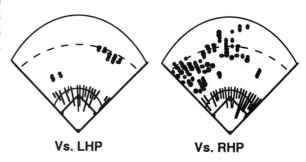

Vs. LHP   **Vs. RHP**

1991 Situational Stats

	AB	H	HR	RBI	AVG		AB	H	HR	RBI	AVG
Home	195	67	0	24	.344	LHP	87	24	0	11	.276
Road	210	59	1	33	.281	RHP	318	102	1	46	.321
Day	108	34	0	13	.315	Sc Pos	106	39	1	56	.368
Night	297	92	1	44	.310	Clutch	54	21	0	8	.389

1991 Rankings (American League)

- ➡ 2nd highest batting average in the clutch (.389)
- ➡ 3rd highest batting average with runners in scoring position (.368)
- ➡ 7th lowest percentage of swings that missed (9.6%)
- ➡ Led the Brewers in stolen base percentage (72.7%) and batting average in the clutch
- ➡ Led AL right fielders in sacrifice bunts (7), batting average in the clutch, batting average with 2 strikes (.246), bunts in play (19), lowest percentage of swings that missed and highest percentage of swings put into play (51.8%)

OVERLOOKED

DOUG HENRY

Position: RP
Bats: R **Throws:** R
Ht: 6' 4" **Wt:** 185

Opening Day Age: 28
Born: 12/10/63 in
Sacramento, CA
ML Seasons: 1

PITCHING:

It looked like Doug Henry's time had come back in 1988 when he rediscovered the heater that made him a dominating college pitcher at Arizona. Instead of reporting to the majors in 1989, though, he reported to elbow surgery. Henry looked pretty good in early 1990, and though he had a poor finish, he was showing signs of coming back, fanning better than a man per inning and earning 18 saves in the minors.

In 1991 Henry shined as the closer at Denver where he kept his ERA just above 2.00 in the thin mountain air, while striking out over twice as many as he walked. He was promoted in mid-July and gave up a run in his first outing. Three days later he gave up his only home run of the year, to Craig Grebeck of the White Sox. Those two were exactly half the total he would give up the rest of the season, as he allowed just 16 hits 14 walks in 36 innings. He blew his first save opportunity, but earned the win instead, and then converted 15 saves in a row.

Henry throws a fastball that approaches 90 MPH, along with a forkball and a hard slider. He held lefties and righties to identical .133 averages, in 60 at-bats from each side, and struck out 14 each way. That's what you call symmetry. He induces about an equal number of fly balls and grounders, and mixes his pitches well. Hitters can't count on a strike on the first pitch.

HOLDING RUNNERS AND FIELDING:

Henry is a good athlete, but his fielding skills are hard to assess since he has had very few opportunities. He handled five chances without a mishap. Only one of his rare baserunners attempted to steal, and he was caught.

OVERALL:

At 28, Henry is a mature pitcher with a closer's makeup and a variety of bewildering heat. He made almost no mistakes in 1991 and seems made for the role of one-inning stopper. You can depend on Henry to open the 1992 season as the ace of the Brewer pen.

Overall Statistics

	W	L	ERA	G	GS	Sv	IP	H	R	BB	SO	HR
1991	2	1	1.00	32	0	15	36.0	16	4	14	28	1
Career	2	1	1.00	32	0	15	36.0	16	4	14	28	1

How Often He Throws Strikes

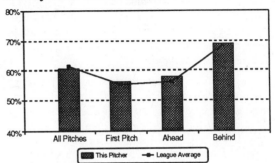

This Pitcher — League Average

1991 Situational Stats

	W	L	ERA	Sv	IP		AB	H	HR	RBI	AVG
Home	1	0	0.53	7	17.0	LHB	60	8	0	3	.133
Road	1	1	1.42	8	19.0	RHB	60	8	1	4	.133
Day	0	0	0.00	5	8.1	Sc Pos	29	4	0	6	.138
Night	2	1	1.30	10	27.2	Clutch	75	10	0	5	.133

1991 Rankings (American League)

➡ Led the Brewers in saves (15) and save opportunites (16)

PITCHING:

Teddy Higuera has been counted on as the ace of the Brewers' staff, and his continuing inability to answer the bell has contributed to the Brewers' annual pitching woes. In 1991 Higuera made only seven appearances and six starts. Though he resembled the Higuera of old, striking out almost three times as many hitters as he walked, he gave up a lot of hits and runs.

Higuera, despite knee, hamstring, ankle, and back problems, signed a four-year $13 million contract after the 1990 season, so the Brewers were obviously convinced of his health. But during the spring he reported pain even after soft-tossing, and blamed tendinitis. He started the season on the DL with what was diagnosed as a torn rotator cuff and inflammation. He had a couple of rehab assignments in the minors in May and pitched well. Catcher B.J. Surhoff reported that Higuera's fastball was really popping.

Unfortunately, everyone was positive except Higuera, who complained of stiffness, soreness, and not feeling at full strength. He had a couple of good outings but a load of pain, and for good reason. He needed major shoulder surgery in August and was through for the year. In the past Higuera has pitched with pain, but with the trouble in his shoulder, he had to shut down in '91.

HOLDING RUNNERS AND FIELDING:

Higuera has always been a good fielder who worked hard on his defense. He has great reflexes, but is getting older, as well as rusty. Higuera has one of the best pickoff moves in the game, but had few opportunities and little attention for base stealers in 1991.

OVERALL:

Naturally, the Brewers say that Higuera will be ready to throw in the spring; they have a big investment to protect. Despite his injuries, if he can pitch there is no reason to believe that he won't be effective; but there is no reason to believe that he will be able to pitch, either.

TEDDY HIGUERA

Position: SP
Bats: B **Throws:** L
Ht: 5'10" **Wt:** 178

Opening Day Age: 33
Born: 11/9/58 in Los Mochis, Sinaloa, Mexico
ML Seasons: 7

Overall Statistics

	W	L	ERA	G	GS	Sv	IP	H	R	BB	SO	HR
1991	3	2	4.46	7	6	0	36.1	37	18	10	33	2
Career	92	56	3.37	188	185	0	1291.1	1145	529	391	1019	114

How Often He Throws Strikes

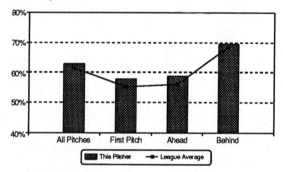

1991 Situational Stats

	W	L	ERA	Sv	IP		AB	H	HR	RBI	AVG
Home	2	0	4.50	0	20.0	LHB	32	7	0	3	.219
Road	1	2	4.41	0	16.1	RHB	109	30	2	15	.275
Day	2	1	3.24	0	16.2	Sc Pos	41	11	0	15	.268
Night	1	1	5.49	0	19.2	Clutch	3	0	0	0	.000

1991 Rankings (American League)

→ Did not rank near the top or bottom in any category

PITCHING:

The Brewers took a chance on Mark Lee, picking him up when the Royals released him in 1989 after he had undergone rotator cuff surgery. Lee came back to pitch that season, mostly as a starter, but not too effectively. In 1990, though, working out of the bullpen, he climbed two minor league levels to the majors, lowering his ERA at each stop and walking just 13 hitters with 56 strikeouts in 57 innings. With Milwaukee he posted a 2.11 ERA. Bill James, perhaps anticipating the imminent collapse of Dan Plesac, placed Lee, somewhat whimsically, tenth on his list of AL Rookie of the Year possibilities.

Lee was great in April, and looked like he would really help the Brewers, posting a 0.77 ERA for the month in nine games. But he showed signs of future trouble when he gave up a home run in his eighth appearance; homers were to be his nemesis. In one memorable game in May he was called upon to protect a 4-3 lead in Kansas City and gave up three homers while retiring only one batter. Obviously he wasn't fooling anyone, as his strikeouts dropped steadily and his hits and walks rose. Lee also had a big problem with the first hitter, though his .294 average looked pretty good compared to pen-mates Darren Holmes and Chuck Crim.

HOLDING RUNNERS AND FIELDING:

Lee is a decent, heads-up fielder who started three double plays in his limited mound time. He's more effective on ground balls than line drives. He made no errors. He kept base stealers under control, allowing six steals but nabbing four runners.

OVERALL:

In the Brewer pen a 3.86 ERA isn't too bad, and Lee led the team with 15 holds, though he blew six of seven save opportunities. And if you subtract the outings when he surrendered home runs, what a difference! A 1.69 ERA in 54 appearances and 49 hits in 58.2 innings. Regardless, unless he can find his strikeout pitch again, Lee will continue to be plagued by home runs.

MARK LEE

Position: RP
Bats: L **Throws:** L
Ht: 6' 3" **Wt:** 200

Opening Day Age: 27
Born: 7/20/64 in Williston, ND
ML Seasons: 3

Overall Statistics

	W	L	ERA	G	GS	Sv	IP	H	R	BB	SO	HR
1991	2	5	3.86	62	0	1	67.2	72	33	31	43	10
Career	3	5	3.45	77	0	1	94.0	98	40	36	57	11

How Often He Throws Strikes

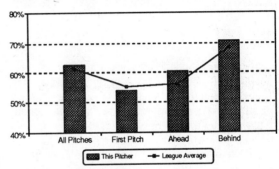

This Pitcher — League Average

1991 Situational Stats

	W	L	ERA	Sv	IP		AB	H	HR	RBI	AVG
Home	1	3	3.83	1	40.0	LHB	92	28	3	18	.304
Road	1	2	3.90	0	27.2	RHB	162	44	7	26	.272
Day	0	1	7.88	0	16.0	Sc Pos	74	24	3	35	.324
Night	2	4	2.61	1	51.2	Clutch	102	27	8	21	.265

1991 Rankings (American League)

- → 7th in holds (15)
- → 8th in highest batting average allowed in relief (.283)
- → 9th in blown saves (6)
- → Led the Brewers in holds and blown saves

PITCHING:

Julio Machado showed his stuff in late 1990 for the Brewers: inside rising heat and a good slider. In 1991 Machado made 54 appearances and struck out just a hair under 10 men per nine innings, which places him among the elite. He held hitters to a .211 batting average, tenth among A.L. relievers. He ate up lefties and righties alike.

Machado strikes out about twice as many batters as he walks, but since he fans so many, that means a lot of free passes. It isn't a big problem if he keeps his hits per inning down, as he did in 1991, but his tendency to put men on base makes him vulnerable to the home run. He has to challenge hitters more if he starts walking them, and homers tend to rattle him. Machado's increase in homers allowed is part of the reason his ERA went up almost a run from 1990, though the change in leagues has to take some of the blame.

If anything, Machado's overall pitching was better in 1991, and he learned to quit grooving the first pitch like he did in 1990. Given the disarray in the Brewers pen, especially early in the season, it's a wonder that he only got six save opportunities all year. Maybe it's because he blew three of them, two on homers. Perhaps he hasn't the makeup, even though he has the stuff, to be a closer.

HOLDING RUNNERS AND FIELDING:

Machado is an average fielder. His excessive motion does not lend itself to a good fielding stance, but his reflexes are good. He holds runners pretty well, and his heater gives his catcher a chance. Baserunners were only 5-for-10 against him.

OVERALL:

The departed Tom Trebelhorn was obviously not eager to make Machado the closer, though "Iguanaman" seems made for the role. Phil Garner might have a different opinion. Nevertheless, the excellent closing work of Doug Henry should keep Machado in middle relief where he is valuable.

JULIO MACHADO

Position: RP
Bats: R **Throws:** R
Ht: 5' 9" **Wt:** 165

Opening Day Age: 26
Born: 12/1/65 in Zulia, Venezuela
ML Seasons: 3

Overall Statistics

	W	L	ERA	G	GS	Sv	IP	H	R	BB	SO	HR
1991	3	3	3.45	54	0	3	88.2	65	36	55	98	12
Career	7	5	3.12	101	0	6	147.0	115	54	83	151	16

How Often He Throws Strikes

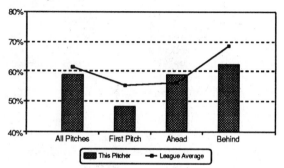

1991 Situational Stats

	W	L	ERA	Sv	IP		AB	H	HR	RBI	AVG
Home	1	1	2.76	1	45.2	LHB	151	33	8	25	.219
Road	2	2	4.19	2	43.0	RHB	157	32	4	19	.204
Day	2	1	3.13	1	31.2	Sc Pos	100	19	3	32	.190
Night	1	2	3.63	2	57.0	Clutch	91	20	3	10	.220

1991 Rankings (American League)

→ 5th most strikeouts per 9 innings in relief (9.9)

→ 7th in first batter efficiency (.156)

→ 10th lowest batting average allowed in relief (.211)

→ Led the Brewers in lowest batting average allowed vs. left-handed batters (.219), first batter efficiency, lowest percentage of inherited runners scored (25.9%), relief ERA (3.45), lowest batting average allowed in relief, least baserunners allowed per 9 innings in relief (12.5) and most strikeouts per 9 innings in relief

HITTING:

Paul Molitor bounced back from his 11th and 12th trips to the disabled list in 1990 to have a 1991 season that stands with the best he's ever produced. Molitor led the league in runs and hits, and his .325 average was solid across the board as he delivered in every situation. Line drives flew off his bat, and 325 total bases were the most of his splendid career.

Molitor even commanded 16 intentional walks, fourth in the AL, resulting in a career-best 77 walks for this notorious free-swinger. He said at the break that he saw little hope for the Brew Crew in the second half, yet he led their charge down the stretch. In August, when the Brewers stormed to a 19-10 record despite a team ERA of 4.30 for the month (383 baserunners and 34 homers allowed in 264 innings, if you can believe that), Molitor scored 31 runs in 29 games, drove in 20, and hit .357. When called upon to perform at first base, he slugged .524, like a proper first baseman. The only year that really could be considered a better year for Molly would be 1982, which is also the only year he played more games and had more at-bats.

BASERUNNING:

Molitor continues to be one of the very best baserunners in the American League. Though his 19 steals is one of his lowest full-season totals, his general baserunning is aggressive and successful. He led the Brewers in doubles, and tied for the league lead with 13 triples.

FIELDING:

Molitor is too valuable to play in the field where he keeps getting hurt. He did play 46 games at first base in 1991, and showed good range, but some inexperience.

OVERALL:

While injuries haunt Molitor, it is possible that the stints spent on the disabled list will allow him to extend his career. Happily, his uninjured seasons have been uniformly excellent. Should he avoid injury in 1992, look for a typical Molitor season, with a high batting average and runs scored totals among the league leaders.

PAUL MOLITOR

Position: DH/1B
Bats: R **Throws:** R
Ht: 6' 0" **Wt:** 185

Opening Day Age: 35
Born: 8/22/56 in St. Paul, MN
ML Seasons: 14

Overall Statistics

	G	AB	R	H	D	T	HR	RBI	SB	BB	SO	AVG
1991	158	665	133	216	32	13	17	75	19	77	62	.325
Career	1698	6911	1186	2086	369	79	148	701	381	682	816	.302

Where He Hits the Ball

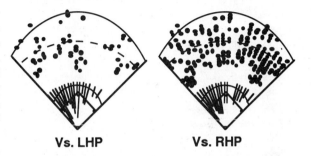

Vs. LHP   Vs. RHP

1991 Situational Stats

	AB	H	HR	RBI	AVG		AB	H	HR	RBI	AVG
Home	315	92	7	38	.292	LHP	174	56	5	17	.322
Road	350	124	10	37	.354	RHP	491	160	12	58	.326
Day	181	63	4	18	.348	Sc Pos	138	45	2	54	.326
Night	484	153	13	57	.316	Clutch	92	27	3	15	.293

1991 Rankings (American League)

→ 1st in at-bats (665), runs (133), hits (216), triples (13) and plate appearances (752)

→ 2nd in singles (154), times on base (299) and batting average on the road (.354)

→ 4th in total bases (325) and intentional walks (16)

→ Led the Brewers in at-bats, runs, hits, singles, doubles (32), triples, total bases, stolen bases (19), caught stealing (8), walks (77), intentional walks, hit by pitch (6), times on base, pitches seen (2,635), plate appearances, games (158), slugging percentage (.489) and runs scored per time reached base (44.5%)

PITCHING:

Jaime Navarro pitched up to his potential in 1991, exhibiting consistency and stamina and leading the Brewers in innings pitched while tying for first in victories with 15. Navarro's previous tendency to tire early in the game seems licked, as he tossed 10 complete games while throwing 90 or more pitches in 28 of 34 outings.

Navarro is a competent pitcher with a good fastball and a decent slider and change-up, but not much of a killer instinct. He prefers the ground out to the strikeout. One of his biggest problems occurred when he operated in the strike zone. Though his 18 homers allowed are not an extremely high total, they hurt Navarro. He was particularly vulnerable to lefties, who hit 13 dingers off him.

Navarro's starts divide easily into two groups: wins and everything else. When he won, his ERA was under 2.50; in all of his other starts it was close to 5.50. Coincidentally, but inconveniently, the Brewers scored 90 runs while he was pitching in games he won, but only 37 during his other time on the mound. The Brewers didn't win any of his no-decisions.

HOLDING RUNNERS AND FIELDING:

Navarro doesn't hold runners particularly well, and allowed 23 stolen bases against only seven caught. Much of the blame can be laid at the arm of B.J. Surhoff, who is among the league's worst catchers at nabbing base thieves. Navarro is not particularly graceful, but his fielding has improved a bit.

OVERALL:

Navarro's first and second half numbers are mirror images of each other, right down to the innings pitched and baserunners allowed. If he can keep pitching as well as he did in '91, he should continue to win around 15 games. With some luck, he could become the ace of the Brewers staff, but he needs a strikeout pitch to elevate his game and stand among the league's best pitchers.

JAIME NAVARRO

Position: SP
Bats: R **Throws:** R
Ht: 6' 4" **Wt:** 210

Opening Day Age: 25
Born: 3/27/67 in Bayamon, Puerto Rico
ML Seasons: 3

Overall Statistics

	W	L	ERA	G	GS	Sv	IP	H	R	BB	SO	HR
1991	15	12	3.92	34	34	0	234.0	237	117	73	114	18
Career	30	27	3.91	85	73	1	493.0	532	247	146	245	35

How Often He Throws Strikes

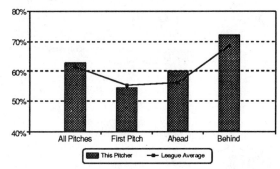

1991 Situational Stats

	W	L	ERA	Sv	IP		AB	H	HR	RBI	AVG
Home	9	3	3.58	0	113.0	LHB	480	130	13	59	.271
Road	6	9	4.24	0	121.0	RHB	428	107	5	45	.250
Day	5	2	3.00	0	60.0	Sc Pos	212	54	5	84	.255
Night	10	10	4.24	0	174.0	Clutch	94	22	3	10	.234

1991 Rankings (American League)

- → 3rd in complete games (10)
- → 4th highest stolen base percentage allowed (76.7%)
- → 5th in hits allowed (237) and batters faced (1,002)
- → Led the Brewers in wins (15), losses (12), games started (34), complete games (10), shutouts (2), innings (234), hits allowed, batters faced, home runs allowed (18), walks allowed (73), wild pitches (10), pitches thrown (3,602), stolen bases allowed (23) and runners caught stealing (7)

PITCHING:

The warning bells started ringing for Dan Plesac in 1990, when he allowed righty hitters to hit .286 with some power after holding them to a .207 mark in 1989. The hard slider that complemented Plesac's fastball seemed to desert him, and he complained of a lack of confidence. In 1991 even the lefties caught up with him.

Tom Trebelhorn had lost his confidence in Plesac in 1990, too, and didn't provide him with a save opportunity for the first month of the 1991 season. Plesac converted his first save in mid-May, and then went another month before he got another chance. He was pitching well and got a few more saves in June and July, but blew three in a row in late July. Then things got weird.

After a couple of outings where Plesac threw 47 and 65 pitches -- Trebelhorn was running some tests -- Plesac was moved into the rotation. In his first seven starts he went 2-3 with a 2.54 ERA, and kept the Brewers in his two no-decisions. His last three starts were disasters; he averaged three innings with an ERA of 14.00.

In all, the experiment provided more questions than answers. Plesac is still pretty effective for a few innings, but has obviously lost his ability to shut down a team as a closer. However, after 45 pitches, about three innings worth, opposing hitters hit .344 off him. The starter role, hailed by the Brewers, seems like a joke.

HOLDING RUNNERS AND FIELDING:

Plesac puts so much into his delivery that it affects his fielding, but he is far from terrible. He shows talent holding baserunners, and five of the nine who did run on him were caught.

OVERALL:

Plesac attracted a lot of attention from the Dodgers, both last spring and down the stretch. Now he is being projected as a Brewer starter in 1991, though the rotation could be crowded if Teddy Higuera and Ron Robinson come back from injury. Plesac still has the stuff to help a team --perhaps as a middle reliever, if not as a starter or finisher.

DAN PLESAC

Position: RP/SP
Bats: L **Throws:** L
Ht: 6' 5" **Wt:** 215

Opening Day Age: 30
Born: 2/4/62 in Gary, IN
ML Seasons: 6

Overall Statistics

	W	L	ERA	G	GS	Sv	IP	H	R	BB	SO	HR
1991	2	7	4.29	45	10	8	92.1	92	49	39	61	12
Career	24	33	3.25	321	10	132	445.1	396	179	151	394	38

How Often He Throws Strikes

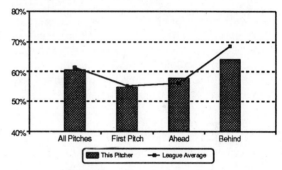

1991 Situational Stats

	W	L	ERA	Sv	IP		AB	H	HR	RBI	AVG
Home	0	4	5.63	5	48.0	LHB	64	19	4	14	.297
Road	2	3	2.84	3	44.1	RHB	286	73	8	38	.255
Day	0	1	4.12	2	19.2	Sc Pos	83	20	0	36	.241
Night	2	6	4.33	6	72.2	Clutch	61	18	4	15	.295

1991 Rankings (American League)

→ Did not rank near the top or bottom in any category

HITTING:

Change the date on the gold watch and don't rent out his bedroom yet. Willie Randolph had a fine spring as a Brewers non-roster invitee, and was projected to share time at second with Jim Gantner. But Gary Sheffield's injury forced Gantner to third, and Randolph became the regular at second. That turned out to be a big break for Milwaukee.

Randolph's .327 average, third in the AL, was by far the best of his 17-year career. His .424 on-base average was second in the league only to Frank Thomas. Randolph even drove home 54 runs, the third-highest total of his career.

Randolph didn't hit righties in 1990, posting just a .221 average against them, and at the same time his walk-to-strikeout ratio took a dangerous, there-goes-the-batting-eye drop. Voila! His batting eye came back in 1991. Since pitchers had to come in to Randolph or risk walking him, he improved to a .311 average against righties. He was also one of the league's best clutch hitters.

BASERUNNING:

If there is an area where Randolph is clearly not the player he once was, it's as a base thief. He attempted only six steals, and was caught twice. He is still a smart baserunner, and will break up the double play.

FIELDING:

Randolph is no longer a sure glove at second, leading the league with 20 errors. His range slid a little more as well, but he still gets the ball to first on time. His ability to turn the double play is legendary, and it's worthwhile to keep an eye on him to see his grace on the pivot.

OVERALL:

Randolph made noises at mid-season about playing one more year and then moving into management, where many observers believe he has a future. However, given his outstanding year, expect him to extend his playing career. Randolph was a free agent after the '91 season, and we may not have seen the last of him in postseason play.

WILLIE RANDOLPH

Position: 2B
Bats: R **Throws:** R
Ht: 5'11" **Wt:** 171

Opening Day Age: 37
Born: 7/6/54 in Holly Hill, SC
ML Seasons: 17

Overall Statistics

	G	AB	R	H	D	T	HR	RBI	SB	BB	SO	AVG
1991	124	431	60	141	14	3	0	54	4	75	38	.327
Career	2112	7732	1210	2138	305	64	52	672	270	1203	641	.277

Where He Hits the Ball

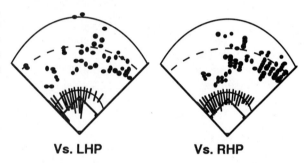

Vs. LHP   **Vs. RHP**

1991 Situational Stats

	AB	H	HR	RBI	AVG		AB	H	HR	RBI	AVG
Home	220	74	0	31	.336	LHP	148	53	0	21	.358
Road	211	67	0	23	.318	RHP	283	88	0	33	.311
Day	113	38	0	13	.336	Sc Pos	110	41	0	52	.373
Night	318	103	0	41	.324	Clutch	79	23	0	9	.291

1991 Rankings (American League)

→ 1st in batting average with 2 strikes (.322) and worst fielding percentage at second base (.969)

→ 2nd in on-base average (.424), lowest HR frequency (0 HRs in 431 at-bats), highest batting average with runners in scoring position (.373) and highest batting average with the bases loaded (.545)

→ 3rd in highest batting average (.327) and least runs scored per time reached base (27.8%)

→ Led the Brewers in batting average, on-base average and batting average with runners in scoring position

→ Led AL second basemen in errors (20)

HITTING:

Gary Sheffield's problems seem to be his shoulder, his wrist, his thumb, and his mouth. Sheffield's verbal attacks on management have cost him sympathy for his various injuries. Those injuries limited him to just 175 at-bats in '91, and his production reflected the physical problems that put him on the DL for good in July. He finally, and reluctantly, underwent shoulder surgery.

There is no reason to doubt Sheffield's talent. His unique toe-in stance generates power; though he had just 34 hits, 16 were for extra bases. He also managed to score 25 runs despite his limited appearances and pitiful on-base average, and maintained his traditional strikeout-to-walk ratio of about one-to-one.

In the spring, Sheffield followed up his 1989 complaint about not being allowed to play shortstop and his 1990 charges against Brewer management of racism with the comment that GM Harry Dalton was ruining the franchise. Dalton was fired after the season, so Gary wasn't alone in his thought. Sheffield does work hard, and spent the 1990 off season training with Sugar Ray Leonard, adding muscle and speed. His physical breakdown has to frustrate him terribly.

BASERUNNING:

Sheffield was five for ten on the base paths in 1991, showing his willingness to run, if not at the same level of competence as in 1990, when he was 25-for-35. A healthy Sheffield should be good for 20 to 30 steals per year.

FIELDING:

Sheffield's glove, an annual question mark, was no better in 1991. He committed eight errors, but his lackluster showing must partly be the result of his injuries and the rustiness that results from sporadic appearances.

OVERALL:

The Brewers have made some major management changes, but it's an open question whether that will help Sheffield succeed in Milwaukee. Can he put his past behind him, and moreover can his teammates? Sheffield is still only 23; there's plenty of time for him to mature. A lot of people still think he'll be a star, but fewer and fewer think he'll be a star for the Brewers.

GARY SHEFFIELD

Position: 3B
Bats: R **Throws:** R
Ht: 5'11" **Wt:** 190

Opening Day Age: 23
Born: 11/18/68 in Tampa, FL
ML Seasons: 4

Overall Statistics

	G	AB	R	H	D	T	HR	RBI	SB	BB	SO	AVG
1991	50	175	25	34	12	2	2	22	5	19	15	.194
Career	294	1110	138	287	61	3	21	133	43	97	96	.259

Where He Hits the Ball

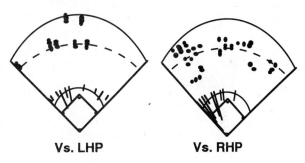

Vs. LHP   **Vs. RHP**

1991 Situational Stats

	AB	H	HR	RBI	AVG		AB	H	HR	RBI	AVG
Home	74	19	2	7	.257	LHP	43	6	0	4	.140
Road	101	15	0	15	.149	RHP	132	28	2	18	.212
Day	60	11	0	8	.183	Sc Pos	45	8	1	19	.178
Night	115	23	2	14	.200	Clutch	27	6	0	6	.222

1991 Rankings (American League)

→ 4th lowest batting average on a 3-1 count (.000)

HITTING:

Bill Spiers flashed unsuspected power in 1991, cracking eight home runs, but his big improvement came against right-handed pitching. He hit .306 and slugged .448 against righties, and due to this improvement raised his overall average 41 points over 1990.

Nagging injuries and recovery from surgery had hampered Spiers in 1990, and he started that season on the disabled list. It was a different story in 1991. On Opening Day of 1991 Spiers had two hits and a walk, stole two bases and scored twice. After five games he had hit three homers, one more than in all of 1990. Spiers is a streaky hitter, but he showed steady improvement during the season. His .386 average in August led the league. Spiers' primary weakness is his trouble with left-handed pitchers, but there is hope even there; though he hit a woeful .222, he managed to eke out a .305 on-base average. It could be worse.

BASERUNNING:

Spiers' baserunning didn't improve during his third season in the majors, but he wasn't much of a minor league thief either. His running game, both stealing and stretching hits, could use improvement, as he has the speed to do so.

FIELDING:

Spiers' shortstop play is solid rather than flashy. He has good range, but not enough to cover for his aging infield mates Randolph and Gantner. Although he committed 17 errors, he had only 10 through August. Spiers had a rash of bad throws down the stretch, a problem that plagued him all season. The problem does not appear chronic. He works well with Randolph on the double play.

OVERALL:

Spiers is among the most promising players on the Brewers. Still young, he had the kind of season that can establish a career. Instead of wondering where their next regular shortstop is coming from, the Brewers can wonder if Spiers, after Cal Ripken, is the most productive shortstop in the American League. When you look at the state of A.L. shortstop production, that may not be saying too much, but it's certainly one less problem for the troubled Brewers.

BILL SPIERS

Position: SS
Bats: L **Throws:** R
Ht: 6' 2" **Wt:** 190

Opening Day Age: 25
Born: 6/5/66 in Orangeburg, SC
ML Seasons: 3

Overall Statistics

	G	AB	R	H	D	T	HR	RBI	SB	BB	SO	AVG
1991	133	414	71	117	13	6	8	54	14	34	55	.283
Career	359	1122	159	293	37	12	14	123	35	71	163	.261

Where He Hits the Ball

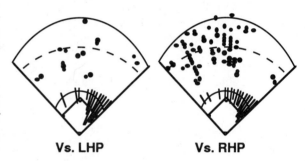

Vs. LHP   **Vs. RHP**

1991 Situational Stats

	AB	H	HR	RBI	AVG		AB	H	HR	RBI	AVG
Home	187	56	1	24	.299	LHP	117	26	2	12	.222
Road	227	61	7	30	.269	RHP	297	91	6	42	.306
Day	112	28	2	13	.250	Sc Pos	103	33	4	49	.320
Night	302	89	6	41	.295	Clutch	73	25	1	14	.342

1991 Rankings (American League)

➡ 6th lowest slugging percentage vs. left-handed pitchers (.282)

➡ 7th lowest stolen base percentage (63.6%)

➡ 9th in batting average in the clutch (.342)

➡ Led the Brewers in caught stealing (8) and bunts in play (23)

➡ Led AL shortstops in triples (6), stolen base percentage, batting average with runners in scoring position (.320), batting average with the bases loaded (.364) and highest percentage of pitches taken (57.5%)

HITTING:

Born to be a Brewer, one would think -- a low average hitter with really terrific power. Sure, Franklin Stubbs has weaknesses, like no real defensive position, and he strikes out more than twice as often as he walks. But the Brewers needed a first baseman and a lefty slugger; Stubbs has no platoon differential, could power 'em out of the Astrodome, and had just hit .291 and .261 the past two seasons.

Well, they were right about the platoon differential. He hit righties at .211 and lefties at .218. A glance at Stubbs' pre-1989 stats reveal what he might have been expected to deliver, but he couldn't even match those marginal numbers. Stubbs felt that the strike zone variation between the leagues was crossing him up, and that inside pitches that he was used to taking for a ball were being called strikes. He never got untracked. Unfortunately for the Brewers, they were short of bodies due to a revolving door to the DL, and Stubbs played regularly. Of course, his extended play may also be due to the fact that they're paying him millions of dollars.

BASERUNNING:

Stubbs runs well for a big guy, and picks his spots intelligently. He was 13-for-17 stealing in 1991, which is consistent with his history. He looks to take the extra base and stays out of double plays well. If he keeps his weight down, he can be an asset on the base paths.

FIELDING:

Stubbs is not particularly mobile at first base, but he is a heads-up player and he records more than his share of assists. He is not a good outfielder, with below-average range and throwing ability.

OVERALL:

Very few readers of this book, put in Harry Dalton's shoes, would have shelled out the money for a player with Stubbs' history. Now the Brewers are stuck with him, since his trade value is low and Milwaukee is not a rich franchise that can eat a contract. He could rebound to be a .240 hitter with 20 homers, but that won't win a pennant.

FRANKLIN STUBBS

Position: 1B
Bats: L **Throws:** L
Ht: 6' 2"   **Wt:** 208

Opening Day Age: 31
Born: 10/21/60 in Laurinburg, NC
ML Seasons: 8

Overall Statistics

	G	AB	R	H	D	T	HR	RBI	SB	BB	SO	AVG
1991	103	362	48	77	16	2	11	38	13	35	71	.213
Career	791	2187	273	507	87	11	93	287	63	214	531	.232

Where He Hits the Ball

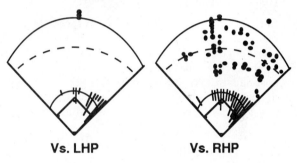

Vs. LHP   Vs. RHP

1991 Situational Stats

	AB	H	HR	RBI	AVG		AB	H	HR	RBI	AVG
Home	183	40	8	22	.219	LHP	87	19	2	10	.218
Road	179	37	3	16	.207	RHP	275	58	9	28	.211
Day	95	24	5	14	.253	Sc Pos	100	15	4	29	.150
Night	267	53	6	24	.199	Clutch	72	13	0	1	.181

1991 Rankings (American League)

- ➡ 1st in lowest batting average with runners in scoring position (.150)
- ➡ 7th fewest GDPs per GDP situation (5.1%)
- ➡ Led the Brewers in steals of third (2)
- ➡ Led AL first basemen in stolen bases (13), fewest GDPs per GDP situation and steals of third

HITTING:

Often considered a disappointment -- the curse of being the first player picked in the 1985 draft -- B.J. Surhoff continues to improve as a hitter. In 1990 Surhoff raised his average 28 points to .276; in 1991 he improved even more, to .289. But that's only part of the story.

What made Surhoff's 1991 season so intriguing was the dramatic improvement he made from month to month. He hit just .153 in April after an 0-for-17 start, and had only two extra-base hits through May. But he improved each month through August, when he hit .343. Surhoff slipped to a mere .339 in September/October. Toss out April and you have a .307 hitter; after the break he hit .323 with 46 RBI.

Surhoff is a contact hitter with good speed, especially for a catcher. He has learned to maximize his strengths by hitting almost everything on the ground. That style has raised his average, while costing him some power. Surhoff is good for five or six homers a year, with around 20 doubles. No one is complaining, now that Surhoff has raised his average to the .280 level.

BASERUNNING:

This area of Surhoff's game suffered in 1991, as his five steals with eight times caught is clearly the worst ratio in his career; his career average is 16 steals with nine times caught. Surhoff's doubles and triples remained about the same as always, so he may bounce back in 1992.

FIELDING:

Surhoff is one of the worst catchers in the game at tossing out runners, though he was better when the few Brewer pitchers who throw heat were on the mound. His agility behind the plate causes annual optimism that he will somehow learn how to get off a good throw, but it never happens.

OVERALL:

Surhoff has become a steady major league catcher and a useful offensive player. There has been talk of shifting him to another position, especially since the Brewers have some promising catching prospects. Wherever he plays, Surhoff should continue to be valuable; based on his play in 1991, he's a threat to hit .300.

B.J. SURHOFF

Position: C
Bats: L **Throws:** R
Ht: 6' 1" **Wt:** 200

Opening Day Age: 27
Born: 8/4/64 in Bronx, NY
ML Seasons: 5

Overall Statistics

	G	AB	R	H	D	T	HR	RBI	SB	BB	SO	AVG
1991	143	505	57	146	19	4	5	68	5	26	33	.289
Career	658	2303	251	624	100	15	28	288	69	159	178	.271

Where He Hits the Ball

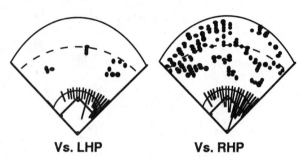

Vs. LHP   Vs. RHP

1991 Situational Stats

	AB	H	HR	RBI	AVG		AB	H	HR	RBI	AVG
Home	236	63	3	34	.267	LHP	102	26	0	11	.255
Road	269	83	2	34	.309	RHP	403	120	5	57	.298
Day	130	38	1	19	.292	Sc Pos	134	42	0	62	.313
Night	375	108	4	49	.288	Clutch	88	25	2	13	.284

1991 Rankings (American League)

→ 1st in highest percentage of swings put into play (63.9%)

→ 3rd in sacrifice flies (9)

→ 4th in sacrifice bunts (13) and groundball/flyball ratio (2.4)

→ 5th in lowest percentage of swings that missed (8.5%)

→ Led the Brewers in sacrifice bunts, sacrifice flies, caught stealing (8), GDPs (21), groundball/flyball ratio, lowest percentage of swings that missed and highest percentage of swings put into play

HITTING:

In 1991 Greg Vaughn made the prognosticators look like geniuses, as he did just about exactly what everyone thought he would do. He was expected to hit about .250 with 25 homers and 100 RBI, and he hit .244 with 27 homers and 98 RBI. Vaughn felt that he had earned the Brewer left field job in 1990, and expressed feelings of vindication when Candy Maldonado was traded to Toronto in August.

Vaughn hits everything in the air, and he also strikes out like Don Knotts at the Miss America pageant. His 125 K's ranked ninth in the league, but he took the sting out of the whiffs with 62 walks. That 2-to-1 strikeout/walk ratio was a vast improvement over his 3-to-1 rate in 1990.

When his stroke remains compact, Vaughn drives the fastball and can handle the curve; when he gets out of his groove he goes into terrible slumps. He had one in 1991 that lasted from mid-June to mid-August, during which he hit close to .180. When he came out of it, he hit over .280 the rest of the way. Vaughn is certainly explosive, and drove in five or more runs in a game five times in 1991.

BASERUNNING:

Vaughn was a wonderful minor league thief, good for 20-25 steals at an 80% success rate. He looked OK in 1991, but attempted only four steals in 1991, and was successful twice. It will be a big surprise if he doesn't take off more in 1992.

FIELDING:

Vaughn led AL left fielders in putouts by a wide margin. His defensive reputation is not great, and he may have had more opportunities, with the Brewer staff giving up a lot of shots to left. But he caught them, which is what counts. His arm is below average.

OVERALL:

Vaughn has established himself as one of the league's most productive left fielders, and there are untapped portions of his game that can make him even better. He is comfortable in the number-five spot, but Vaughn could become the Brewers' cleanup hitter in 1992.

GREG VAUGHN

Position: LF
Bats: R **Throws:** R
Ht: 6' 0" **Wt:** 193

Opening Day Age: 26
Born: 7/3/65 in Sacramento, CA
ML Seasons: 3

Overall Statistics

	G	AB	R	H	D	T	HR	RBI	SB	BB	SO	AVG
1991	145	542	81	132	24	5	27	98	2	62	125	.244
Career	303	1037	150	246	53	7	49	182	13	108	239	.237

Where He Hits the Ball

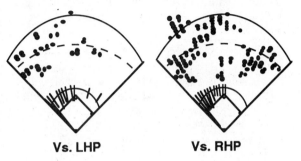

Vs. LHP   Vs. RHP

1991 Situational Stats

	AB	H	HR	RBI	AVG		AB	H	HR	RBI	AVG
Home	256	63	16	54	.246	LHP	154	35	5	22	.227
Road	286	69	11	44	.241	RHP	388	97	22	76	.250
Day	150	41	7	37	.273	Sc Pos	155	43	9	74	.277
Night	392	91	20	61	.232	Clutch	99	21	5	18	.212

1991 Rankings (American League)

→ 1st in highest batting average with the bases loaded (.636)

→ 3rd lowest batting average on an 0-2 count (.000)

→ 5th in lowest groundball/flyball ratio (.72) and least GDPs per GDP situation (4.2%)

→ Led the Brewers in home runs (27), RBIs (98), strikeouts (125), HR frequency (20.1 ABs per HR), most pitches seen per plate appearance (3.79) and least GDPs per GDP situation

→ Led AL left fielders in fielding percentage (.994), RBIs, sacrifice flies (7), strikeouts, slugging percentage (.456), HR frequency, least GDPs per GDP situation

PITCHING:

In posting 15 wins last season, Bill Wegman received considerable attention in Comeback Player of the Year discussions. And little wonder, because Wegman had missed most of 1989 and 1990 due to injuries. His list of ailments included tendinitis in his right shoulder, surgery to repair a torn right shoulder labrum, tendinitis in his right elbow, a bone spur and bone chips in the same elbow, and surgery to repair a partially torn medial collateral ligament. After all that, it's a wonder he could lift his arm.

Instead, Wegman returned to post a career best in wins. By racking up the third best ERA in the league at 2.84 (another career best), it appears as if he's "come back" to a place he's never been before. Prior to 1991, Wegman's career ERA was 4.63.

Wegman throws a good slider and fastball, complemented by a change-up. He keeps the ball down and gets a high number of ground ball outs, so if the Brewer infield defense improves, he will benefit. He seems fully recovered physically; after taking it easy during his first 10 starts, he went at least seven innings in 17 of his last 18, with seven complete games. He walked fewer than two men per nine innings, one of the best rates in the league.

HOLDING RUNNERS AND FIELDING:

Though he committed four errors last year, Wegman is one of the best fielding pitchers in baseball. A former high school shortstop, he comes off the mound like a fifth infielder. He led Brewer pitchers in putouts, assists, and total chances by a healthy margin. He holds runners well, and his rate of 41% caught stealing was far better than the team's 29%.

OVERALL:

Ever the optimists, the Brewers signed Wegman to a long-term contract after the season. It's a risk, and not only because of his history of arm problems. Finesse pitchers like Wegman (89 strikeouts, 40 walks in 193.1 innings) often have problems duplicating their success from one year to the next -- even when healthy.

BILL WEGMAN

Position: SP
Bats: R **Throws:** R
Ht: 6' 5" **Wt:** 220

Opening Day Age: 29
Born: 12/19/62 in Cincinnati, OH
ML Seasons: 7

Overall Statistics

	W	L	ERA	G	GS	Sv	IP	H	R	BB	SO	HR
1991	15	7	2.84	28	28	0	193.1	176	76	40	89	16
Career	51	51	4.25	151	140	0	914.0	952	486	216	410	118

How Often He Throws Strikes

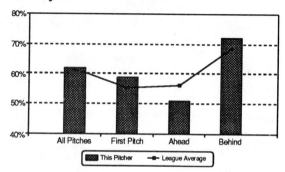

1991 Situational Stats

	W	L	ERA	Sv	IP		AB	H	HR	RBI	AVG
Home	7	4	2.62	0	103.0	LHB	384	85	6	34	.221
Road	8	3	3.09	0	90.1	RHB	344	91	10	28	.265
Day	5	1	1.87	0	62.2	Sc Pos	147	34	2	46	.231
Night	10	6	3.31	0	130.2	Clutch	73	16	4	8	.219

1991 Rankings (American League)

→ 3rd in ERA (2.84)

→ 5th lowest ERA at home (2.62)

→ 6th in complete games (7), shutouts (2), winning percentage (.682) and lowest on-base average allowed (.286)

→ 7th least pitches thrown per batter (3.48)

→ 8th most run support per 9 innings (5.2) and least strikeouts per 9 innings (4.1)

→ Led the Brewers in ERA, wins (15), shutouts, pickoff throws (157), runners caught stealing (7), winning percentage (.682) and strikeout/walk ratio (2.2)

HITTING:

After a miserable spring, Robin Yount burst out of the box last year, hitting with authority. Paul Molitor commented on the absence of the lazy fly balls that he'd seen during Robin Yount's disappointing 1990, and on the laser shots that led to a .342 average and five homers in April. On May 26th, Yount was still hitting .295. That night he slugged his ninth homer, and had 30 RBI and 24 runs in 42 games. Yount was back.

Well, maybe. Over the rest of the season, Yount hit .243 with one home run. In May there were rumors of headaches, and then reports of a bladder infection. His average plummeted in June, and he finally was forced out of the lineup in July by kidney stones, an extremely painful condition.

As has often been the case, Yount's return coincided with the improvement of the Brewers. He hit .327 in August with 11 walks, but little power. His illness may have drained his stamina, and he finished weakly. After getting his average up near .280 through August, he plunged to .260 by hitting .190 in September.

BASERUNNING:

The last time Yount failed to record double figures in steals was the strike year of 1981; his 6-for-10 in '91 was his worst rate since 1979. He still hits doubles and triples, and it is likely that if the rest of his game returns, so will his running game.

FIELDING:

Yount has established himself as an excellent center fielder, but did not seem quite as mobile in 1991. He may have been somewhat drained by his physical problems. He certainly didn't hurt the team out there, despite the fact that opposing baserunners took some liberties on his arm.

OVERALL:

The difference in Yount between 1990 and 1991 is that in '90, he only looked good in September; in '91, he looked like his old self whenever he was healthy. Age has taken its toll, and Yount will have trouble duplicating his MVP past. But he's still capable of having more fine years. Barring injury, he'll log his 3000th hit in 1992.

ROBIN YOUNT

Position: CF/DH
Bats: R **Throws:** R
Ht: 6' 0" **Wt:** 180

Opening Day Age: 36
Born: 9/16/55 in Danville, IL
ML Seasons: 18

Overall Statistics

	G	AB	R	H	D	T	HR	RBI	SB	BB	SO	AVG
1991	130	503	66	131	20	4	10	77	6	54	79	.260
Career	2579	9997	1499	2878	518	120	235	1278	247	869	1176	.288

Where He Hits the Ball

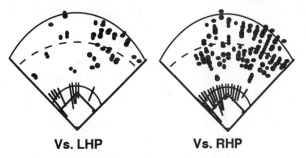

Vs. LHP   **Vs. RHP**

1991 Situational Stats

	AB	H	HR	RBI	AVG		AB	H	HR	RBI	AVG
Home	250	59	8	42	.236	LHP	129	33	2	18	.256
Road	253	72	2	35	.285	RHP	374	98	8	59	.262
Day	154	41	5	28	.266	Sc Pos	145	43	5	68	.297
Night	349	90	5	49	.258	Clutch	75	18	4	13	.240

1991 Rankings (American League)

→ 2nd lowest cleanup slugging percentage (.368)

→ 3rd in sacrifice flies (9)

→ 8th lowest batting average at home (.236)

→ 9th highest percentage of extra bases taken as a runner (71.8%)

→ Led the Brewers in sacrifice flies

→ Led AL center fielders in sacrifice flies

KEVIN D. BROWN

Position: SP/RP
Bats: L **Throws:** L
Ht: 6' 1" **Wt:** 185

Opening Day Age: 26
Born: 3/5/66 in Oroville, CA
ML Seasons: 2

Overall Statistics

	W	L	ERA	G	GS	Sv	IP	H	R	BB	SO	HR
1991	2	4	5.51	15	10	0	63.2	66	39	34	30	6
Career	3	5	4.67	22	13	0	86.2	82	46	42	42	7

PITCHING, FIELDING & HOLDING RUNNERS:

Acquired from the Mets, Kevin Brown pitched well in 23 innings with the Brewers in late 1990. Brown was in the Brewer rotation at the start of 1991, but didn't fool major league hitters.

Brown is a left-handed finesse pitcher with a so-so fastball and terrific control and craft. He walked very few hitters in the minors, though he gave up a fair number of hits, and was not a consistent strikeout pitcher. Last year with the Brewers he gave up a lot of hits, and when he tried painting the corners, his already-high walk total shot upward. After 10 starts he was demoted to the bullpen.

Brown was no better as a reliever, and the Brewers shipped him to Denver at the end of June. His ERA in Denver was good, but as usual, he gave up quite a few hits and had very few strikeouts. He is a decent fielder, and despite throwing slow stuff he keeps runners close and gives his catchers a chance.

OVERALL:

Brown is death on lefthanders, and it's surprising that he wasn't kept around by the Brewers to face them. If he can't learn to fool major league hitters as a starter, he may be back as a bullpen specialist against lefties.

RICK DEMPSEY

Position: C
Bats: R **Throws:** R
Ht: 6' 0" **Wt:** 184

Opening Day Age: 42
Born: 9/13/49 in Fayetteville, TN
ML Seasons: 23

Overall Statistics

	G	AB	R	H	D	T	HR	RBI	SB	BB	SO	AVG
1991	60	147	15	34	5	0	4	21	0	23	20	.231
Career	1757	4683	523	1092	223	12	96	471	20	590	735	.233

HITTING, FIELDING, BASERUNNING:

Rick Dempsey, after three undistinguished seasons backing up Mike Scioscia in Los Angeles, came to the Brewers as a spring invitee. He made the club when the Brewers elected to further develop prospects Dave Nilsson and Tim McIntosh in the minors. Dempsey had hit over .208 only once in the last five years, so the Brewers couldn't have expected much. The old pro had a pretty nice season, all things considered. He got hot in July and August, hitting .366 with nine walks and a couple of round-trippers. That made him so giddy he tried to steal two bases, but was caught both times.

Dempsey is like cholesterol on the base paths: he really clogs things up. He scored only 15 runs, even though he had Darryl Hamilton and Paul Molitor coming up behind him most of the time. Dempsey was no better than B.J. Surhoff at stopping opposition running, but, as always, he handled pitchers well. Dempsey has no mobility, but can still catch.

OVERALL:

The Brewers let Dempsey become a free agent after the season. His career should be over, but Dempsey hit pretty well in the second half, and was effective in the clutch. He could still be back with someone, even at age 42. As Earl Weaver said, Dempsey is a good man to have on your ball club.

EDWIN NUNEZ

Position: RP
Bats: R **Throws:** R
Ht: 6' 5" **Wt:** 240

Opening Day Age: 28
Born: 5/27/63 in
Humacao, Puerto Rico
ML Seasons: 10

DALE SVEUM

Position: SS/3B
Bats: B **Throws:** R
Ht: 6' 3" **Wt:** 185

Opening Day Age: 28
Born: 11/23/63 in
Richmond, CA
ML Seasons: 5

Overall Statistics

	W	L	ERA	G	GS	Sv	IP	H	R	BB	SO	HR
1991	2	1	6.04	23	0	8	25.1	28	20	13	24	6
Career	24	27	3.94	307	14	50	502.1	488	255	219	386	64

Overall Statistics

	G	AB	R	H	D	T	HR	RBI	SB	BB	SO	AVG
1991	90	266	33	64	19	1	4	43	2	32	78	.241
Career	511	1702	210	413	80	10	46	236	9	137	426	.243

PITCHING, FIELDING & HOLDING RUNNERS:

Edwin Nunez was a gamble that didn't pay off for the Brewers, though it's easy to see why they couldn't resist him. Nunez was a gamble because he's been on the disabled list eight times and been released once in the last eight years. He was hard to resist because he was healthy in 1990 and posted a 2.24 ERA in 80.1 innings for Detroit. Nunez is a big, hard thrower with a great splitter and fastball when he's sound.

In 1991 it was Nunez' back that betrayed him, and he underwent mid season surgery after throwing just 11 innings. He recovered quickly, and was able to participate in the Brewers' madcap August. He earned five saves and a win in August and September despite an ERA of 7.53 and 21 baserunners allowed in just 14.1 innings. Although his season ERA was 6.04, Nunez was a pro, converting eight of nine save opportunities and posting a 2-1 record. He allowed two stolen bases, and made an error in four chances, but after all, he had a bad back.

OVERALL:

Nunez will be starting his 11th major league season in 1992, but he won't be 29 till May. If he stays injury-free for a year, he could duplicate his good 1990 season with the Tigers. He was still throwing hard when he came off the DL.

HITTING, FIELDING, BASERUNNING:

Dale Sveum has had a long road back after suffering a serious leg fracture in September of 1988. Sveum missed the entire 1989 season while recovering from the break and resulting tendinitis. Then he logged just 117 major league at-bats in 1990, batting .197. At that point, many observers believed Sveum's career was over.

Given that prognosis, Sveum's return to semi-regular duty last year was quite remarkable. While his .241 average and four homers don't exactly spell superstar, Sveum batted .286 in the second half of 1991, with a .350 on-base average.

Sveum has always been a big run producer with a knack for getting the big hit. He drove in 43 runs in 266 at-bats, and though the figures seem fluky, he's done that sort of thing before (95 RBI in 1987). Sveum also gives runs back, committing 10 errors while filling in at second, third, and short, but he used to be worse. He's never been much of a basestealer, so his injury didn't hurt him in that area.

OVERALL:

Even at full health, it's doubtful that Sveum will hit 25 home runs again, as he did in homer-happy 1987. It's more likely that he's a .240-.250 hitter with a little pop in his bat. Assuming his talents remain in that range, he's a valuable bench player who plays the three middle infield positions, one who can help the Brewers.

MILWAUKEE BREWERS MINOR LEAGUE PROSPECTS

ORGANIZATION OVERVIEW:

The Brewer farm system of the mid-1980s was often described as the best in baseball, one that would guarantee future pennants. But the pennants never came, and a lot of the prospects (Glenn Braggs, Joey Meyer, etc) never panned out. What happened? One basic problem is the top Milwaukee farm clubs play in notorious hitters' parks in Denver and El Paso, where it's easy to post impressive numbers. The Brewers had some bad luck, too, like the injuries which derailed players like Juan Nieves. These days, no one rates the Brewer system at the top. If anything, it may be a little underrated now, as Milwaukee has several players who could make an impact in 1992. A couple of others (Angel Miranda, Jimmy Tatum) could easily have made this list.

CAL ELDRED

Position: P   **Opening Day Age:** 24
Bats: R **Throws:** R   **Born:** 11/24/67 in Cedar
Ht: 6' 4" **Wt:** 215   Rapids, IA

Recent Statistics

	W	L	ERA	GGS	Sv	IP	H	R	BB	SO	HR
91 AAA Denver	13	9	3.75	29 29	0	185.0	161	82	84	168	13
91 AL Milwaukee	2	0	4.50	3 3	0	16.0	20	9	6	10	2

Milwaukee's number-one choice in 1989, Eldred has yet to have a losing record at any level of professional ball. Eldred's fastball is only high-80s, but he has a good curve, and he's recorded a lot of strikeouts wherever he's played. Milwaukee needs starting pitching, and Eldred is almost certain to open the year in the Brewers' rotation. He has a good chance to succeed.

CHRIS GEORGE

Position: P   **Opening Day Age:** 25
Bats: R **Throws:** R   **Born:** 9/24/66 in
Ht: 6' 2" **Wt:** 200   Pittsburgh, PA

Recent Statistics

	W	L	ERA	GGS	Sv	IP	H	R	BB	SO	HR
91 AAA Denver	4	5	2.33	43 1	4	85.0	74	31	26	65	6
91 AL Milwaukee	0	0	3.00	2 1	0	6.0	8	2	0	2	0

The Brewers need help in their bullpen as well, and George is their main hope. A fastball/slider pitcher, he's put up good numbers wherever he's pitched, though he lacks the strikeout-an-inning credentials of a top closer. George's best chance this year appears to be in middle relief; it would be quite a surprise if he didn't make the Brewer staff this spring.

JOHN JAHA

Position: 1B   **Opening Day Age:** 25
Bats: R **Throws:** R   **Born:** 5/27/66 in
Ht: 6' 1" **Wt:** 195   Portland, OR

Recent Statistics

	G	AB	R	H	D	THR	RBI	SB	BB	SO	AVG
90 A Stockton	26	84	12	22	5	0 4	19	0	18	25	.262
91 AA El Paso	130	486	121	167	38	3 30	134	12	78	101	.344
91 MLE	130	452	82	133	31	1 20	91	7	45	108	.294

A 14th-round draft choice who's developed slowly, Jaha spent three years at Class A Stockton before breaking through in a big way at El Paso this year. Even adjusting for the "El Paso factor," his numbers are impressive, and the Brewers certainly need help at first base. If Phil Garner takes a liking to him, Jaha could well be the regular this year.

TIM McINTOSH

Position: C   **Opening Day Age:** 27
Bats: R **Throws:** R   **Born:** 3/21/65 in
Ht: 5' 11" **Wt:** 195   Minneapolis, MN

Recent Statistics

	G	AB	R	H	D	THR	RBI	SB	BB	SO	AVG
91 AAA Denver	122	462	69	135	19	9 18	91	2	37	59	.292
91 AL Milwaukee	7	11	2	4	1	0 1	1	0	0	4	.364
91 MLE	122	437	50	110	16	5 12	66	1	26	61	.252

The Brewers could use another catcher, either to spell B.J. Surhoff or to take over the job completely if Surhoff is shifted to another position. That gives McIntosh and Dave Nilsson a shot this year. McIntosh, who's older, is not the hitting prospect Nilsson is, and his defense (he's a converted outfielder) still needs some polish. But McIntosh can hit and field well enough to play in the majors.

DAVE NILSSON

Position: C   **Opening Day Age:** 22
Bats: L **Throws:** R   **Born:** 12/14/69 in
Ht: 6' 3" **Wt:** 185   Brisbane, Australia

Recent Statistics

	G	AB	R	H	D	THR	RBI	SB	BB	SO	AVG
90 A Stockton	107	359	70	104	22	3 7	47	6	43	36	.290
91 AA El Paso	65	249	52	104	24	3 5	57	4	27	14	.418
91 AAA Denver	28	95	10	22	8	0 1	14	1	17	16	.232
91 MLE	93	318	42	100	25	1 3	48	2	27	30	.314

Going into the '91 season, McIntosh was considered the Brewers' best catching prospect. But that was before the Australian-born Nilsson batted .418 in 249 at-bats at El Paso. Nilsson has always been considered a solid catcher with a strong arm, so the pecking order's now reversed. Two concerns about Nilsson: he hit only .232 in 95 at-bats at Denver, and he needed surgery on his non-throwing shoulder after the season. He's supposed to be 100 percent by spring, but it would be no shock if he started the season back at Denver.

RICK AGUILERA

Position: RP
Bats: R **Throws:** R
Ht: 6' 5" **Wt:** 205

Opening Day Age: 30
Born: 12/31/61 in San Gabriel, CA
ML Seasons: 7

PITCHING:

There is now no doubt that Rick Aguilera, the former Mets starter, is a legitimate closer. Aguilera proved convincingly last year that his outstanding 1990 season -- 5-3, 32 saves and 2.76 ERA -- was no fluke. He was even better in 1991, saving 42 games while posting a 2.35 ERA. Aguilera was superb after the All-Star break, earning saves in 20 of 23 opportunities and allowing just one earned run in 22.1 innings between July 19 and Sept. 25. He continued his brilliant work in the postseason with a win and five saves (and only one run allowed) in seven appearances.

There's no secret to Aguilera's success. He has excellent command of all his pitches, his best being a 90-MPH fastball that tends to rise and a split-fingered fastball that drops off the proverbial table. For good measure, Aguilera will mix in an occasional slider and curve. What makes Aguilera such an effective closer is that he's equally tough on left-handed and right-handed batters. Aguilera allowed only two homers against left-handed batters last year, the first he'd yielded to a lefty since August of 1989.

One more plus: Aguilera showed no symptoms of the shoulder stiffness that forced him to miss several games late in the 1990 season. This is one pitcher who appears to have found his niche in the bullpen.

HOLDING RUNNERS AND FIELDING:

Aguilera is a former college third baseman (Brigham Young University), and it shows. He's a sure-handed fielder (no errors in 63 games) with plenty of speed to cover first base on grounders to the right side. His move to first is unspectacular, and base stealers have had good success against him.

OVERALL:

The Twins, however briefly, toyed with the idea of moving Aguilera back into the starting rotation after the 1990 season. Forget about any such moves now. Aguilera is one of the game's best short men, and barring arm trouble (which he has had in several past seasons), he should be outstanding for years to come.

Overall Statistics

	W	L	ERA	G	GS	Sv	IP	H	R	BB	SO	HR
1991	4	5	2.35	63	0	42	69.0	44	20	30	61	3
Career	49	40	3.33	244	70	81	683.0	645	290	203	530	53

How Often He Throws Strikes

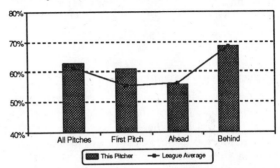

1991 Situational Stats

	W	L	ERA	Sv	IP		AB	H	HR	RBI	AVG
Home	2	0	1.00	23	36.0	LHB	136	25	2	14	.184
Road	2	5	3.82	19	33.0	RHB	104	19	1	13	.183
Day	3	1	1.16	7	23.1	Sc Pos	64	13	0	20	.203
Night	1	4	2.96	35	45.2	Clutch	184	34	1	24	.185

1991 Rankings (American League)

- → 2nd in save opportunities (51) and blown saves (9)
- → 3rd in saves (42), games finished (60), first batter efficiency (.127) and lowest batting average allowed in relief (.183)
- → 4th lowest batting average allowed vs. left-handed batters (.184)
- → Led the Twins in games pitched (63), saves, games finished, save opportunities, save percentage (82.3%), blown saves, lowest batting average allowed vs. left-handed batters, relief ERA (2.35), relief losses (5), lowest batting average allowed in relief and most strikeouts per 9 innings in relief (8.0)

ALLAN ANDERSON

Position: SP/RP
Bats: L **Throws:** L
Ht: 6' 0" **Wt:** 201

Opening Day Age: 28
Born: 1/7/64 in Lancaster, OH
ML Seasons: 6

PITCHING:

American League ERA leader in 1988 (2.45) and the league's winningest lefthander (33-19) in 1988-89. Anderson has hardly seemed like the same pitcher the last two years, as he's been raked unmercifully while compiling a terrible 12-29 record. The Twins' patience appeared to run out on Anderson last autumn when they left him off the 25-man postseason roster in favor of enigmatic David West and journeyman reliever Terry Leach.

What happened to Anderson remains a mystery. The prevailing opinion is that after four years in the big leagues, the hitters have him figured out. The lefthander has never been overpowering, relying on a curveball, better-than-average change-up and excellent location. The location hasn't been there consistently the past two years, and the Twins' coaches have, in turn, encouraged Anderson to be more aggressive, and to forget about trying to hit the corners.

It's time for Plan C, if there is one. Last year Anderson gave up more hits than innings pitched (148 hits, 134.1 innings) for the third straight season. More evidence of his lack of location was that he surrendered a team-high 24 home runs while pitching more than 100 fewer innings than Jack Morris and Kevin Tapani. Anderson was effective against left-handed batters, who hit .225 with just two homers. Righthanders, though, were a nightmare: .296 average with 22 home runs.

HOLDING RUNNERS AND FIELDING:

Anderson's problems throwing the baseball have not affected his fielding. He's smart and quick off the mound, and has an excellent move to first. Of course, he's gotten plenty of opportunity to perfect it.

OVERALL:

The consensus of all involved, Anderson included, is that the lefthander needs a change of scenery. Anderson indicated his desire for a trade when he was left off the postseason roster, and the Twins appear willing to comply. Anderson might be better-suited to the National League, simply because he needs to pitch in bigger parks.

Overall Statistics

	W	L	ERA	G	GS	Sv	IP	H	R	BB	SO	HR
1991	5	11	4.96	29	22	0	134.1	148	82	42	51	24
Career	49	54	4.11	148	128	0	818.2	901	424	211	339	87

How Often He Throws Strikes

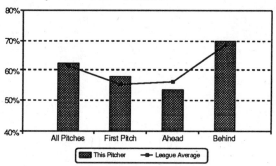

1991 Situational Stats

	W	L	ERA	Sv	IP		AB	H	HR	RBI	AVG
Home	2	4	4.52	0	67.2	LHB	111	25	2	9	.225
Road	3	7	5.40	0	66.2	RHB	416	123	22	65	.296
Day	0	4	5.24	0	22.1	Sc Pos	107	26	6	47	.243
Night	5	7	4.90	0	112.0	Clutch	43	14	2	3	.326

1991 Rankings (American League)

→ 1st in lowest winning percentage (.313)
→ 5th most home runs allowed (24)
→ 7th highest batting average allowed vs. right-handed batters (.296)
→ Led the Twins in home runs allowed and pickoff throws (94)

PITCHING:

The National League Cy Young Award winner in 1987, Steve Bedrosian made the transition from closer to set-up man in 1991. In his glory years, Bedrosian relied on power -- an excellent fastball and hard slider -- while striking out 156 batters in 179.1 innings in 1986 and 1987. Although he can still throw hard, Bedrosian is no longer an overpowering pitcher, as his 87 strikeouts in 156.2 innings the past two years will attest.

Bedrosian's biggest problem last year was location. As was true in his final season in San Francisco in 1990, Bedrosian struggled with his control, unable to hit the corners consistently and too often coming in high with his hard stuff. He allowed 11 homers last season, seven of them off the bats of right-handed hitters, whom Bedrosian historically has overpowered.

Bedrosian still has enough on the ball to make him difficult to hit, as witnessed by his .243 opponent batting average last season. Righthanders batted just .230, and over the preceding four seasons they compiled just a .205 average. Lefties hit him much better, so he has to be used carefully. In fairness, the Dome does Bedrosian no favors. He had a 5.52 ERA at home, compared to 2.97 on the road. In 1990, he had a 7.58 ERA on artificial turf; this year he was 4.99.

HOLDING RUNNERS AND FIELDING:

Bedrosian fits the mold of most other Twins' pitchers. First, he's a fine athlete who is helped by his own fielding skills. Second, he could do a better job of holding baserunners.

OVERALL:

Much about Bedrosian's decline the past two seasons remains a mystery. His three-year-old son, Cody, was diagnosed with leukemia in 1990, and that affected Bedrosian's concentration. Last year the veteran righthander suffered a mid-season circulatory problem that left his fingers cold and stiff. At age 34, time would seem to have run out on a return to his Cy Young form. But the personal and physical problems may leave the door open for improvement.

STEVE BEDROSIAN

Position: RP
Bats: R **Throws:** R
Ht: 6' 3" **Wt:** 205

Opening Day Age: 34
Born: 12/6/57 in Methuen, MA
ML Seasons: 11

Overall Statistics

	W	L	ERA	G	GS	Sv	IP	H	R	BB	SO	HR
1991	5	3	4.42	56	0	6	77.1	70	42	35	44	11
Career	70	73	3.39	608	46	184	1067.0	911	444	474	823	100

How Often He Throws Strikes

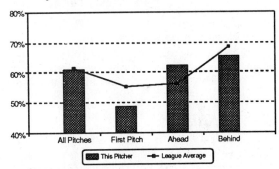

1991 Situational Stats

	W	L	ERA	Sv	IP		AB	H	HR	RBI	AVG
Home	2	3	5.52	2	44.0	LHB	123	32	4	17	.260
Road	3	0	2.97	4	33.1	RHB	165	38	7	23	.230
Day	1	1	10.42	2	19.0	Sc Pos	83	17	3	29	.205
Night	4	2	2.47	4	58.1	Clutch	127	31	3	19	.244

1991 Rankings (American League)

→ 2nd lowest percentage of inherited runners scored (16.3%)

→ 5th in first batter efficiency (.135)

→ Led the Twins in holds (10) and lowest percentage of inherited runners scored

HITTING:

Two characteristics mark Randy Bush's major league career. First, he is strictly a platoon player, batting solely against right-handed pitchers. Second, Bush is a very streaky hitter.

Taking these into consideration, 1991 was a very typical Bush year. On June 3, Bush was batting .173 (9-for-52) with no home runs and one RBI. At the time there was a general consensus that his days with the Twins might be nearing the end. But Manager Tom Kelly's patience was rewarded with dividends. From June 3 until the end of the regular season Bush batted .363 (41-for-113) with six homers and 22 RBI. Characteristically, Bush had 163 at-bats against righthanders last year, batting .307. He was 0-for-2 against lefthanders.

Bush is a true pull-hitter and a good fastball hitter, although he has some trouble with inside heat. When in a good streak, he has the ability to look inept on one offspeed pitch, then lace the next for a solid base hit. In a bad streak, he looks inept for days at a time.

BASERUNNING:

Bush hasn't stolen a base since 1989, going 0-for-5 the past two years. He suffered a severe hamstring injury in 1990, but appeared fit last year. Although he has never had great speed, he is an intelligent baserunner who knows when to take the extra base.

FIELDING:

Bush's lack of speed has always been his biggest drawback as an outfielder. He has a decent glove, thanks to hours of hard work early in his career. He is used almost exclusively in right field now, and was errorless in 33 games in right last season.

OVERALL:

Bush would be an asset to any contending team because of his ability to come off the bench and supply left-handed power. He led the AL with 13 pinch-hits in 1991, tying the league record with seven consecutive pinch hits between July 5 and Aug. 19. The extra plus with Bush is that he's a quality person, capable of accepting whatever role he's given.

RANDY BUSH

Position: RF
Bats: L **Throws:** L
Ht: 6' 1" **Wt:** 190

Opening Day Age: 33
Born: 10/5/58 in Dover, DE
ML Seasons: 10

Overall Statistics

	G	AB	R	H	D	T	HR	RBI	SB	BB	SO	AVG
1991	93	165	21	50	10	1	6	23	0	24	25	.303
Career	1084	2818	373	717	144	25	94	384	32	330	455	.254

Where He Hits the Ball

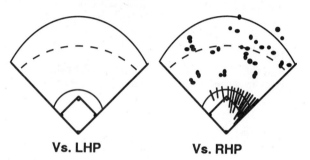

Vs. LHP   Vs. RHP

1991 Situational Stats

	AB	H	HR	RBI	AVG		AB	H	HR	RBI	AVG
Home	64	16	2	9	.250	LHP	2	0	0	0	.000
Road	101	34	4	14	.337	RHP	163	50	6	23	.307
Day	54	14	4	9	.259	Sc Pos	42	11	1	16	.262
Night	111	36	2	14	.324	Clutch	37	14	2	7	.378

1991 Rankings (American League)

→ Did not rank near the top or bottom in any category

HITTING:

The Angels grew disenchanted with Chili Davis when a lower-back problem limited him to 113 games and a career-low 58 RBI in 1990. The Twins signed Davis after losing free agent Gary Gaetti to the Angels, and Davis responded with a career-high 29 home runs while tying his career best with 93 RBI. Davis downplayed revenge as a factor, but he does admit working hard on an off season conditioning program put him in excellent condition. Chili homered 19 times in the season's first 75 games.

Davis was a critical acquisition to the Twins, as his switch-hitting ability was the perfect complement to a batting order dominated by right-handed batting Kirby Puckett and left-handed hitting Kent Hrbek. Though he hits well from both sides of the plate, Davis has traditionally been better from the left side, and that was true again in 1991.

Davis likes the ball low from both sides of the plate, and is sometimes vulnerable to pitches up in the strike zone. That vulnerability looked fatal at times in 1990, when Davis batted only .219 with runners in scoring position. Last year, however, he improved his performance to .283.

BASERUNNING:

Age and the back problems have taken a toll on Davis who was in double figures in stolen bases each his first six years in the majors. Last year he only managed five steals in 11 attempts. He showed poor judgement on the bases several times early in the season, but Twins manager Tom Kelly, a stickler for detail, quickly corrected those mental lapses.

FIELDING:

A poor defensive player in his years with the Angels, Davis became a full-time designated-hitter last year at the age of 31. The history of back problems makes it unlikely he will break from that role.

OVERALL:

Kelly credits Davis' fast start with helping the Twins forget about their last place finish of 1990. With Davis batting between Puckett and Hrbek, the Twins have a potent "heart of the order."

CHILI DAVIS

Position: DH
Bats: B **Throws:** R
Ht: 6' 3" **Wt:** 210

Opening Day Age: 32
Born: 1/17/60 in Kingston, Jamaica
ML Seasons: 11

Overall Statistics

	G	AB	R	H	D	T	HR	RBI	SB	BB	SO	AVG
1991	153	534	84	148	34	1	29	93	5	95	117	.277
Career	1452	5254	736	1410	248	26	185	752	113	634	1011	.268

Where He Hits the Ball

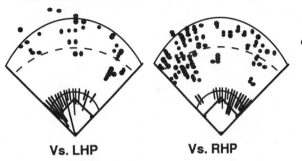

Vs. LHP   **Vs. RHP**

1991 Situational Stats

	AB	H	HR	RBI	AVG		AB	H	HR	RBI	AVG
Home	267	81	14	45	.303	LHP	174	47	11	32	.270
Road	267	67	15	48	.251	RHP	360	101	18	61	.281
Day	144	38	7	24	.264	Sc Pos	152	43	8	64	.283
Night	390	110	22	69	.282	Clutch	70	24	3	14	.343

1991 Rankings (American League)

- → 5th in walks (95)
- → 6th in intentional walks (13)
- → 7th lowest percentage of swings put into play (36.7%)
- → Led the Twins in home runs (29), doubles (34), RBIs (93), walks, intentional walks, times on base (244), strikeouts (117), pitches seen (2,469), games (153), slugging percentage (.507), on-base average (.385), HR frequency (18.4 ABs per HR) and most pitches seen per plate appearance (3.89)

PITCHING:

For the first half of 1991 Scott Erickson was the most dominating pitcher in the major leagues. The righthander was 12-2 with a 1.39 ERA on June 24, with a team-record 12 straight victories. Erickson was simply overpowering at that point, relying on a naturally sinking fastball that often was clocked in the low-90s.

But then Erickson underwent a transition that would be difficult for any pitcher, let alone a 23 year old just two years out of the University of Arizona. An elbow problem that first surfaced in early May landed Erickson on the disabled list just before the All-Star break. After his return Erickson relied more on his change-up and over-hand curveball, using his offspeed assortment to set-up a fastball that lacked its former velocity.

Erickson made progress after returning from the DL, although the final results are rather inconclusive. He was 8-6 after June 24, but his ERA was 5.54. As the season progressed, he appeared to regain some of the movement on his sinking fastball, making him tough with runners on base. He was spotty in the postseason, neither winning nor losing any of his three starts. In two of those starts he didn't make it past the fifth inning.

HOLDING RUNNERS AND FIELDING:

Erickson drew the ire of Twins' manager Tom Kelly for mental lapses fielding his position in 1990. He improved last year, and his natural athletic ability makes him a potentially outstanding fielder. He has a decent move to first, although it could stand improvement.

OVERALL:

An intriguing question for the Twins in 1992 is how Erickson will rebound from his elbow woes. Club officials feel that he must learn to rely more on his offspeed pitches if he is to have a successful career. But Erickson on several occasions in the postseason still proclaimed himself a power pitcher, saying the Twins had not had enough time yet to draw such conclusions. If he matures as the Twins hope, he should be a consistent 18-to-20 game winner.

SCOTT ERICKSON

Position: SP
Bats: R **Throws:** R
Ht: 6' 4" **Wt:** 225

Opening Day Age: 24
Born: 2/2/68 in Long Beach, CA
ML Seasons: 2

Overall Statistics

	W	L	ERA	G	GS	Sv	IP	H	R	BB	SO	HR
1991	20	8	3.18	32	32	0	204.0	189	80	71	108	13
Career	28	12	3.07	51	49	0	317.0	297	129	122	161	22

How Often He Throws Strikes

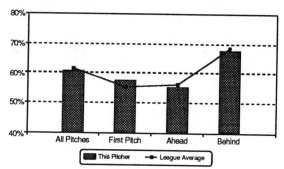

1991 Situational Stats

	W	L	ERA	Sv	IP		AB	H	HR	RBI	AVG
Home	10	3	3.53	0	97.0	LHB	417	123	8	38	.295
Road	10	5	2.86	0	107.0	RHB	345	66	5	34	.191
Day	7	4	3.52	0	84.1	Sc Pos	161	38	2	52	.236
Night	13	4	2.93	0	119.2	Clutch	63	16	1	7	.254

1991 Rankings (American League)

→ 1st in wins (20) and lowest batting average allowed vs. right-handed batters (.191)

→ 2nd in shutouts (3), winning percentage (.714), groundball/flyball ratio (2.4) and lowest stolen base percentage allowed (28.6%)

→ 3rd most run support per 9 innings (5.7)

→ 5th most GDPs induced (22)

→ Led the Twins in wins, shutouts, hit batsmen (6), runners caught stealing (10), winning percentage, groundball/flyball ratio, lowest stolen base percentage allowed, most run support per 9 innings, least home runs allowed per 9 innings (.57) and most GDPs induced per 9 innings (.97)

HITTING:

Twins' first-year hitting coach Terry Crowley made Greg Gagne one of his special projects last year, and found a prize pupil. Gagne batted only .235 in 1990, many of the outs coming when he would flail at two-strike sliders that broke into the dirt. After working with Crowley, Gagne hit .265 last year, matching the second-best mark of his career. He also struck out only 72 times, his lowest total for a full season.

There were noticeable improvements in two long-time Gagne problem spots: batting with runners in scoring position and against right-handed pitchers. Gagne batted .228 against righthanders from 1988 to 1990; he batted .259 against them last summer. The shortstop batted only .182 with runners in scoring position in 1990, seeing largely a diet of sliders low and away. Last year, a more selective Gagne lifted his scoring position mark to .252. Another evidence of improvement: between 1987 and 1990, Gagne's averages with two outs and runners in scoring position were .211, .194, .164, and .111. Last year: .286.

BASERUNNING:

Gagne has long been the Twins' fastest player, although young Jarvis Brown has probably wrestled away that title. The mystery is that Gagne has never stolen more than 15 bases. Last year he was successful on just 11 of 20 attempts. Gagne is excellent at going from first-to-third; he is an intelligent runner with excellent speed.

FIELDING:

The Twins wish the Gold Glove balloting had taken place after Gagne had demonstrated his defensive skills in postseason play. Gagne broke his own club record with 76 consecutive errorless games last year, the second-longest streak in American League history. More than sure-handed, Gagne has better range than most give him credit for, especially going into the hole.

OVERALL:

Gagne doesn't get the publicity of Puckett and Hrbek, but those who watch the Twins everyday contend his value is just as great. He's a superb shortstop on turf and last year was no longer a liability in clutch situations.

GREG GAGNE

Position: SS
Bats: R **Throws:** R
Ht: 5'11" **Wt:** 172

Opening Day Age: 30
Born: 11/12/61 in Fall River, MA
ML Seasons: 9

Overall Statistics

	G	AB	R	H	D	T	HR	RBI	SB	BB	SO	AVG
1991	139	408	52	108	23	3	8	42	11	26	72	.265
Career	994	2947	399	736	160	35	62	296	73	169	593	.250

Where He Hits the Ball

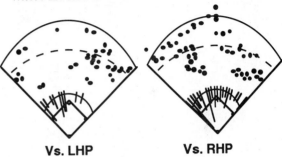

Vs. LHP   **Vs. RHP**

1991 Situational Stats

	AB	H	HR	RBI	AVG		AB	H	HR	RBI	AVG
Home	194	51	3	18	.263	LHP	118	33	2	12	.280
Road	214	57	5	24	.266	RHP	290	75	6	30	.259
Day	118	36	3	14	.305	Sc Pos	111	28	3	34	.252
Night	290	72	5	28	.248	Clutch	42	7	0	3	.167

1991 Rankings (American League)

- → 1st lowest stolen base percentage (55.0%)
- → 2nd best fielding percentage at shortstop (.984)
- → 8th highest percentage of extra bases taken as a runner (72.0%)
- → Led the Twins in caught stealing (9)

DAN GLADDEN

Position: LF
Bats: R **Throws:** R
Ht: 5'11" **Wt:** 181

Opening Day Age: 34
Born: 7/7/57 in San Jose, CA
ML Seasons: 9

HITTING:

Somehow, the numbers just don't add up. For the fifth straight season, Dan Gladden has been the primary leadoff man for the hard-hitting Twins, despite lowly on-base percentages of .312, .325, .331, .314 and .306. Gladden has struck out more than he's walked every year he's been in the majors, fanning 60 times last season while walking 36. Yet Gladden has now been the leadoff hitter for two world championship teams.

Gladden's main attributes as a leadoff man are a brashness that seems to rub off on teammates and better-than-average power for a number-one hitter. He had nine triples, six homers and 52 RBI last season in 461 at-bats. Gladden is a good fastball hitter, but can be fooled with off speed offerings. He's a streaky hitter, beginning last season by going 1-for-31 and ending the regular season batting .189 (27-for-143) in his last 40 games. He hits lefthanders (.254) and righthanders (.245) about the same, although he is more likely to pull the ball against lefties.

BASERUNNING:

Gladden will turn 35 this summer, and the first signs of the inevitable "lost step" may have come in 1991. He stole only 15 bases in 24 attempts, breaking a seven-season stretch in which he'd swiped at least 23 sacks each year. As he demonstrated in the World Series, Gladden runs the bases full-tilt.

FIELDING:

Gladden's major trait as a player -- aggressiveness -- is his main strength as a defensive player. He's unafraid of both walls and turf, going all-out for all flies and liners. Gladden has a very good glove (three errors in 246 chances), and an adequate arm.

OVERALL:

Fan favorite Gladden became a free agent after last season, and there's some question as to whether the Twins will be an active bidder considering that Pedro Munoz is apparently ready for regular duty. Gladden's fiery personality is an asset when he's playing regularly, but could he be happy being a fourth outfielder? The Giants didn't think so when they sent him to the Twins in 1987. Now it's the Twins' turn to decide.

Overall Statistics

	G	AB	R	H	D	T	HR	RBI	SB	BB	SO	AVG
1991	126	461	65	114	14	9	6	52	15	36	60	.247
Career	993	3728	554	1014	167	37	54	348	210	286	511	.272

Where He Hits the Ball

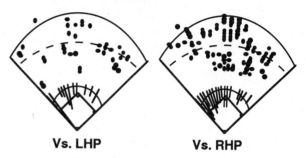

Vs. LHP   **Vs. RHP**

1991 Situational Stats

	AB	H	HR	RBI	AVG		AB	H	HR	RBI	AVG
Home	244	65	3	27	.266	LHP	118	30	1	19	.254
Road	217	49	3	25	.226	RHP	343	84	5	33	.245
Day	104	20	1	7	.192	Sc Pos	108	24	1	41	.222
Night	357	94	5	45	.263	Clutch	53	10	2	13	.189

1991 Rankings (American League)

➡ 3rd lowest leadoff on-base percentage (.313)

➡ 6th in highest percentage of extra bases taken as a runner (73.2%), triples (9) and lowest stolen base percentage (62.5%)

➡ Led the Twins in triples, caught stealing (9), runs scored per time reached base (41.9%) and batting average with the bases loaded (.444)

➡ Led AL left fielders in triples

HITTING:

Four years ago Brian Harper was loading trucks in the off season, wondering whether his dreams of a major league career might be over. Today, Harper is a key player on a world championship team, and is one of the league's finest offensive catchers. Harper has compiled a .307 batting average in four seasons with the Twins.

Harper batted .311 last season with career highs in home runs (10) and RBI (69). He's a line drive hitter who sprays the ball to all fields. He is also an excellent fastball hitter, and although some scouts believe he can be fooled by breaking balls, the numbers don't agree.

A great contact hitter, Harper has struck out only 77 times -- total -- in four seasons (1,471 at-bats) with the Twins. He was equally effective against left- and right-handed pitching last year, batting .316 against lefties, .309 against righties. Clutch hitting? He batted .313 with men in scoring position in 1991. And there's power in his line drives, as he's averaged 31 doubles in his three full seasons with Minnesota.

BASERUNNING:

The number of doubles Harper has amassed in recent seasons is all the more impressive because none of them were stretched singles due to speed. He's is an intelligent but slow baserunner, stealing one base in three attempts last year.

FIELDING:

If Minnesota lets Harper leave this winter via free agency, one reason will be that manager Tom Kelly has never been sold on his Harper's defense. Harper threw out only 28 of 126 (22 percent) would-be base stealers last year, but a lot of that could be attributed to his pitchers. Harper seems to handle pitchers well, and as Lonnie Smith can attest, he blocks home plate fearlessly.

OVERALL:

Harper has proven himself to be a superb major league hitter and an adequate catcher. Considering the current state of major league catching, he is certain to attract heavy bidding in the free agent market. The only question is whether the Twins will be willing to match the going rate.

BRIAN HARPER

Position: C
Bats: R **Throws:** R
Ht: 6' 2" **Wt:** 205

Opening Day Age: 32
Born: 10/16/59 in Los Angeles, CA
ML Seasons: 12

Overall Statistics

	G	AB	R	H	D	T	HR	RBI	SB	BB	SO	AVG
1991	123	441	54	137	28	1	10	69	1	14	22	.311
Career	648	1861	206	543	120	6	38	250	7	69	118	.292

Where He Hits the Ball

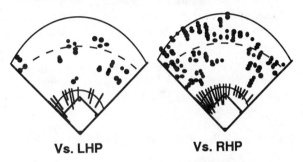

Vs. LHP   **Vs. RHP**

1991 Situational Stats

	AB	H	HR	RBI	AVG		AB	H	HR	RBI	AVG
Home	217	74	4	35	.341	LHP	114	36	2	14	.316
Road	224	63	6	34	.281	RHP	327	101	8	55	.309
Day	99	27	3	13	.273	Sc Pos	131	41	4	56	.313
Night	342	110	7	56	.322	Clutch	68	22	3	17	.324

1991 Rankings (American League)

→ 1st in lowest percentage of runners caught stealing as a catcher (22.2%)

→ 8th highest batting average on an 0-2 count (.320)

→ 9th lowest batting average on a 3-2 count (.074)

→ Led the Twins in hit by pitch (6); highest batting average with runners in scoring position (.313)

→ Led AL catchers in batting average in the clutch (.324) and batting average with 2 strikes (.245)

CLUTCH HITTER

HITTING:

There are scouts who still contend that Kent Hrbek should hit .300 with 30 homers and 100 RBI every year. Hrbek's a natural when it comes to hitting, and the biggest rap on him is that he hasn't worked to improve upon his natural skills. Even so, Hrbek is among the most feared left-handed hitters in the game. He's hit at least 20 home runs in eight straight seasons, and he has at least 75 RBI in every one of his 10 full major league campaigns.

Though he had a miserable postseason last year, Hrbek has proven he's tough in the clutch, batting .310 with runners in scoring position in '91. Some teams shift their defense toward right field against him, but that's more in hopes that he'll go the other way. Hrbek has always been able to hit to all fields, although his most prodigious homers are to right.

Hrbek loves a fastball down around his knees. The best hope pitchers have is to bust a fastball in on his fists, waist-high. For a power hitter, Hrbek has an excellent eye, drawing more walks than strikeouts in each of the last five seasons. And he hit lefties (.281) as well as righties (.284) in 1991.

BASERUNNING:

Hrbek once had decent speed, but that was in his younger, slimmer days. He stole just four bases in eight attempts last year, but he's a smart runner who knows when to take the extra base.

FIELDING:

Twins' officials insist that Hrbek is the best fielding first baseman in the major leagues, and the argument has merits. He has surprising range, and there is no one better at making diving stops to his right. He's superb at digging throws out of the dirt and running down pop fouls.

OVERALL:

Admittedly, Hrbek is never going to be Ted Williams or Stan Musial, though some thought he had that kind of potential. But he's a tremendous asset to the Twins, both in the field and at the plate.

KENT HRBEK

Position: 1B
Bats: L **Throws:** R
Ht: 6' 4" **Wt:** 253

Opening Day Age: 31
Born: 5/21/60 in Minneapolis, MN
ML Seasons: 11

Overall Statistics

	G	AB	R	H	D	T	HR	RBI	SB	BB	SO	AVG
1991	132	462	72	131	20	1	20	89	4	67	48	.284
Career	1431	5132	757	1484	270	17	243	892	28	659	657	.289

Where He Hits the Ball

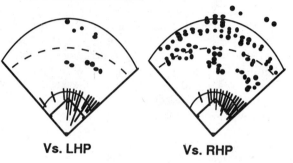

Vs. LHP   **Vs. RHP**

1991 Situational Stats

	AB	H	HR	RBI	AVG		AB	H	HR	RBI	AVG
Home	236	75	11	52	.318	LHP	128	36	6	25	.281
Road	226	56	9	37	.248	RHP	334	95	14	64	.284
Day	134	36	4	24	.269	Sc Pos	126	39	7	64	.310
Night	328	95	16	65	.290	Clutch	54	21	4	15	.389

1991 Rankings (American League)

→ 3rd in highest batting average in the clutch (.389) and highest batting average with an 0-2 count (.348)

→ Led the Twins in batting average in the clutch and batting average with an 0-2 count

→ Led AL first basemen in batting average with an 0-2 count

HITTING:

The haunting memories of Tommy Herr, Wally Backman, Fred Manrique and Nelson Liriano were finally laid to rest by Chuck Knoblauch in 1991. The Twins had been seeking a solid second baseman since Steve Lombardozzi, the regular during their championship season of 1987, was benched the next spring in favor of the newly acquired -- and quickly disappointing -- Herr. Last year the Twins gave the job to rookie Knoblauch . . . and not coincidentally, won another world championship.

Knoblauch, a 5-9, 175-pound spark plug, not only filled a gaping hole at second base, but solved another problem by emerging as a reliable number-two man in the batting order. Knoblauch is a solid contact hitter, capable of spraying line drives to all fields. The son of a highly-successful Texas high school coach struck out only 40 times in 565 at-bats. He also has a good eye at the plate, drawing 59 walks while batting .281.

A hard-nosed kid, Knoblauch showed his toughness in clutch situations, batting .308 with runners in scoring position. He also excelled in postseason play, hitting .326. Knoblauch hit just one home run, but showed promise for better power in the future with 24 doubles and six triples.

BASERUNNING:

Knoblauch plays the game like the coach's son he is. He quickly established himself as the Twins' best base stealing threat, swiping 25 in 30 attempts. He has better-than-average speed, plus plenty of smarts.

FIELDING:

Knoblauch made the transition from college shortstop to second baseman in his brief season and a half in the minor leagues. He committed 18 errors, but only three in the final 45 games. He has very good range and turns the double play adequately for someone so new to the position.

OVERALL:

Knoblauch is a fiery, intense player who was a perfect fit for the team's blue-collar image. The Twins found their second baseman of the future in 1991, and the one-time gaping hole should be a team strength for the next decade.

CHUCK KNOBLAUCH

Position: 2B
Bats: R **Throws:** R
Ht: 5' 9" **Wt:** 175

Opening Day Age: 23
Born: 7/7/68 in Houston, TX
ML Seasons: 1

Overall Statistics

	G	AB	R	H	D	T	HR	RBI	SB	BB	SO	AVG
1991	151	565	78	159	24	6	1	50	25	59	40	.281
Career	151	565	78	159	24	6	1	50	25	59	40	.281

Where He Hits the Ball

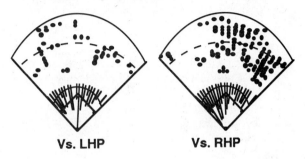

Vs. LHP   **Vs. RHP**

1991 Situational Stats

	AB	H	HR	RBI	AVG		AB	H	HR	RBI	AVG
Home	287	94	1	26	.328	LHP	148	38	0	6	.257
Road	278	65	0	24	.234	RHP	417	121	1	44	.290
Day	151	46	0	20	.305	Sc Pos	117	36	0	46	.308
Night	414	113	1	30	.273	Clutch	78	21	0	5	.269

1991 Rankings (American League)

→ 1st in highest stolen base percentage (83.3%)

→ 2nd in lowest percentage of swings that missed (7.7%)

→ 3rd in lowest HR frequency (565 ABs per HR) and highest percentage of swings put into play (59.7%)

→ Led the Twins in stolen bases (25), groundball/flyball ratio (1.9), stolen base percentage, least GDPs per GDP situation (6.7%), batting average vs. right-handed pitchers (.290), batting average at home (.327), batting average with 2 strikes (.265), highest percentage of pitches taken (59.7%), lowest percentage of swings that missed and highest percentage of swings put into play

HITTING:

The arrival of Chili Davis as the Twins' full-time designated hitter lessened Gene Larkin's playing time, but the former Columbia University star still knew how to make himself useful. How much more useful can you get than driving in the winning run in the seventh game of the World Series -- as Larkin did?

Larkin batted .286 in 255 at-bats last year, noteworthy because in his first four major league seasons, his averages were .266, .266, .267 and .269. He had batted at least 400 times the previous three seasons, but team officials decided more power was needed at the DH position. Larkin, although a powerfully-built at 6'-3", 205 pounds, is a line drive, contact hitter. A switch-hitter, he's effective from both sides of the plate, batting .293 against righties and .273 against lefties last season.

Larkin's Series-winning hit had an ironic twist to it. He's been adequate in the clutch in seasons past, but in 1991 he hit just .190 with runners in scoring position. He was also just 3-for-19 as a pinch hitter last year . . . but he was 2-for-4 in the Series, including the clinching hit.

BASERUNNING:

Larkin is not blessed with an abundance of speed (2-for-5 in stolen bases), but like most Twins his baserunning is a plus because he knows when to take the extra base. He's not afraid of contact if a catcher is blocking the plate.

FIELDING:

Larkin played both first base and right field last year, but has a way to go before becoming an accomplished outfielder. His lack of speed hurts his range. He played very well at first base, making just one error, though he lacks Hrbek's range.

OVERALL:

The Twins once thought Larkin had the potential to be a hitting star. It now appears he'll be a .270, line-drive hitter, which isn't bad. He lacks the power to be a full-time designated hitter, and has Hrbek in front of him at first base. But even if he never gets another hit for the Twins, they'll always remember his one big blow.

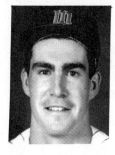

GENE LARKIN

Position: RF/1B
Bats: B **Throws:** R
Ht: 6' 3" **Wt:** 205

Opening Day Age: 29
Born: 10/24/62 in Astoria, NY
ML Seasons: 5

Overall Statistics

	G	AB	R	H	D	T	HR	RBI	SB	BB	SO	AVG
1991	98	255	34	73	14	1	2	19	2	30	21	.286
Career	587	1840	220	497	106	10	25	205	16	219	219	.270

Where He Hits the Ball

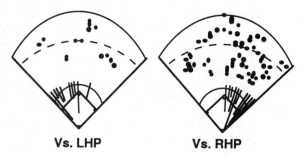

Vs. LHP   Vs. RHP

1991 Situational Stats

	AB	H	HR	RBI	AVG		AB	H	HR	RBI	AVG
Home	131	41	0	12	.313	LHP	88	24	1	6	.273
Road	124	32	2	7	.258	RHP	167	49	1	13	.293
Day	97	36	0	7	.371	Sc Pos	58	11	0	16	.190
Night	158	37	2	12	.234	Clutch	46	10	0	5	.217

1991 Rankings (American League)

→ Did not rank near the top or bottom in any category

PITCHING:

A grizzled veteran of 38, Terry Leach was strictly a fringe pitcher on the Twins' staff by season's end. Leach only got a spot on the playoff roster when Allan Anderson and Tom Edens faltered in late-August starts. He didn't appear at all in the championship series against Toronto, and, except for a one-batter appearance in Game Three, his World Series action consisted of two indifferent innings in Atlanta's 14-5 Game Five blowout. It was hardly the sort of action to make a fellow feel secure about his long-term future.

Leach has a classic submarine delivery, one carefully developed over his 16-year professional career. His best pitch is a sinking fastball that makes him effective in double play situations. He needs excellent location and movement to be pitch well, because his velocity is lacking.

Leach's skills have narrowed to the point where he is best only when pitching to one or two righthanders per game. He's usually in trouble if a lefty comes up. Last year opposing right-handed batters hit just .240 (35-for-146) against Leach, while lefthanders hit .367 (47-for-128). In this case, the numbers don't lie.

HOLDING RUNNERS AND FIELDING:

Leach's unorthodox delivery leaves him in an awkward position, making it difficult for him to snatch balls hit up the middle. He is steady on balls he does nab. His move to first is acceptable, but his assortment of offspeed deliveries makes him an inviting target to steal against.

OVERALL:

Leach's role with the Twins was sharply reduced last year, and if he is to continue in the majors it will likely be as a specialist. Leach needs a team that can afford to carry a pitcher with the specific role of going against a right-handed batter or two every couple of games. That team probably won't be the Minnesota Twins.

TERRY LEACH

Position: RP
Bats: R **Throws:** R
Ht: 6' 0" **Wt:** 190

Opening Day Age: 38
Born: 3/13/54 in Selma, AL
ML Seasons: 9

Overall Statistics

	W	L	ERA	G	GS	Sv	IP	H	R	BB	SO	HR
1991	1	2	3.61	50	0	0	67.1	82	28	14	32	3
Career	32	22	3.30	311	21	9	610.0	616	257	175	306	36

How Often He Throws Strikes

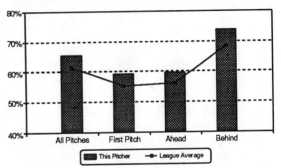

1991 Situational Stats

	W	L	ERA	Sv	IP		AB	H	HR	RBI	AVG
Home	0	0	2.54	0	39.0	LHB	128	47	1	20	.367
Road	1	2	5.08	0	28.1	RHB	146	35	2	20	.240
Day	0	1	2.03	0	26.2	Sc Pos	98	28	1	36	.286
Night	1	1	4.65	0	40.2	Clutch	54	16	0	11	.296

1991 Rankings (American League)

➤ 2nd highest batting average allowed vs. left-handed batters (.367)

➤ 4th highest batting average allowed in relief (.299)

➤ 6th in highest percentage of inherited runners scored (42.1%) and least strikeouts per 9 innings in relief (4.3)

SCOTT LEIUS

Position: 3B/SS
Bats: R **Throws:** R
Ht: 6' 3" **Wt:** 185

Opening Day Age: 26
Born: 9/24/65 in
Yonkers, NY
ML Seasons: 2

HITTING:

One of last summer's pleasant surprises for the Twins was the strong contribution of rookie Scott Leius, who platooned at third base with veteran Mike Pagliarulo. The Twins mulled over trading for a third sacker at times during the year -- Steve Buechele and Kevin Seitzer were two of the names mentioned -- but eventually realized that the Pagliarulo-Leius platoon was doing the job. The platoon continued to do the job in postseason play as well. Leius hit .357 in the World Series and belted an eighth-inning homer to win Game Two.

Leius, a right-handed hitter, proved ideal in his platoon role, batting .305 against lefthanders (.254 vs. righties). Still, Leius' ability as a hitter remains a question. After he led the Southern League with a .303 average in 1989, Leius batted only .229 at AAA Portland in 1990. Last year he showed a tendency to chase offspeed breaking balls out of the strike zone.

Leius struck out 35 times while walking 30 times last year, but hit .271 with runners in scoring position. Leius had some of the season's more curious numbers, batting .368 at the Metrodome, .212 on the road. He showed adequate power with five home runs.

BASERUNNING:

Leius is an adequate baserunner, not blazing fast but capable of taking an extra base when the opportunity presents itself. He stole five bases in 10 attempts.

FIELDING:

Leius went to spring training last year as a shortstop and switched to third base just before the start of the season. Considering that, he had a good first season at the hot corner, committing seven errors in 148 chances. He has very good hands and agility, with an average arm by third base standards.

OVERALL:

Leius could be the Twins' full-time third baseman of the future if he can prove that he can hit righthanders consistently. At worst he will be a valuable utility man, platooning at third base while backing up at shortstop and perhaps second base.

Overall Statistics

	G	AB	R	H	D	T	HR	RBI	SB	BB	SO	AVG
1991	109	199	35	57	7	2	5	20	5	30	35	.286
Career	123	224	39	63	8	2	6	24	5	32	37	.281

Where He Hits the Ball

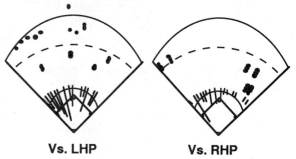

Vs. LHP   **Vs. RHP**

1991 Situational Stats

	AB	H	HR	RBI	AVG		AB	H	HR	RBI	AVG
Home	95	35	2	10	.368	LHP	128	39	3	13	.305
Road	104	22	3	10	.212	RHP	71	18	2	7	.254
Day	61	19	2	8	.311	Sc Pos	48	13	0	13	.271
Night	138	38	3	12	.275	Clutch	23	9	1	1	.391

1991 Rankings (American League)

➡ 9th highest on-base average vs. left-handed pitchers (.427)

HITTING:

Proof that organizations can still be guilty of colossal mistakes --even in the computer age -- is offered by Shane Mack's performance as a Twin. The Padres didn't even bother protecting the outfielder on their 40-man major league roster after the 1989 season. Two lackluster seasons in limited action (.239 and .244) had convinced San Diego that Mack was too nervous and tentative to make it as a major leaguer. Wrong. Very wrong. Mack has batted .317 the past two seasons, and showed the kind of power last summer that led the Padres to draft Mack in the first round of the amateur draft in 1984.

Mack was batting just .239 on July 12 last year, but from that point on he was the Twins' most productive offensive player. He hit .360 with 10 home runs and 45 RBI over the final three months. Mack, who finished with 18 homers, has excellent power to the opposite field. Because of that most teams try to pitch him inside. He still strikes out far more than he walks, fanning 79 times while walking 34 times in 1991. He was brutal versus lefties, leading the majors with a .701 slugging percentage against them.

BASERUNNING:

Mack is an excellent natural athlete, swiping 13 bases in 22 attempts. He's a hustler on the bases, unafraid to go hard into second and break up double plays.

FIELDING:

Mack was scheduled to become the Twins' center fielder last season, with the master plan moving Kirby Puckett to right. Mack's early slump ended that experiment, but it showed the confidence the Twins have in his range and athletic ability. Mack suffered a serious elbow injury with the Padres, but his recovery has reached the stage where his throwing arm is once again adequate.

OVERALL:

The Twins appear to have uncovered a budding star in Mack. The next step for Mack will be moving into a prominent spot in the batting order -- numbers three, four or five. To this point he has been more comfortable in the bottom third, but if he is as good as his last two seasons indicate, he will pass that test, too.

SHANE MACK

Position: RF/LF/CF
Bats: R **Throws:** R
Ht: 6' 0" **Wt:** 190

Opening Day Age: 28
Born: 12/7/63 in Los Angeles, CA
ML Seasons: 4

Overall Statistics

	G	AB	R	H	D	T	HR	RBI	SB	BB	SO	AVG
1991	143	442	79	137	27	8	18	74	13	34	79	.310
Career	429	1112	170	325	51	15	30	155	35	95	216	.292

Where He Hits the Ball

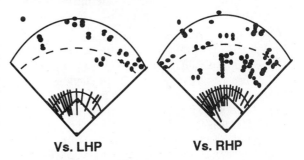

Vs. LHP   **Vs. RHP**

1991 Situational Stats

	AB	H	HR	RBI	AVG		AB	H	HR	RBI	AVG
Home	213	71	4	34	.333	LHP	137	48	9	29	.350
Road	229	66	14	40	.288	RHP	305	89	9	45	.292
Day	137	44	7	22	.321	Sc Pos	113	30	6	54	.265
Night	305	93	11	52	.305	Clutch	62	12	2	8	.194

1991 Rankings (American League)

→ 1st in highest slugging percentage vs. left-handed pitchers (.701)

→ 3rd lowest stolen base percentage (59.1%)

→ 8th in triples (8) and batting average vs. left-handed pitchers (.350)

→ Led the Twins in caught stealing (9), hit by pitch (6) and slugging percentage vs. left-handed pitchers

→ Led AL right fielders in triples, caught stealing, batting average vs. left-handed pitchers and slugging percentage vs. left-handed pitchers

WORKHORSE

JACK MORRIS

Position: SP
Bats: R **Throws:** R
Ht: 6' 3" **Wt:** 200

Opening Day Age: 36
Born: 5/16/55 in St. Paul, MN
ML Seasons: 15

PITCHING:

At the age of 36, Jack Morris is back on top of the baseball world. Returning to his native Twin Cities after signing a lucrative free agent contract, Morris capped an amazing season by winning four postseason games and the World Series MVP award. Even a young Jack Morris, the winningest pitcher of the 1980s, would have been hard-pressed to equal the aging Jack's ten-inning, 1-0 masterpiece in Game Seven.

Reversing a two-year downward slide in which his record (with the Tigers) was only 21-32, Morris pitched over 200 innings for the ninth time in 10 seasons. He led the Twins' staff with 10 complete games and strikeouts with 163. Morris' out pitch remains a nasty forkball, and his fastball is consistently in the upper 80s.

Morris has annually been among the league leaders in home runs allowed, and there were predictions that he would meet his doom pitching in the hitter-friendly Metrodome. The predictions were wrong. Morris, who was raised in St. Paul, was 13-3 with a 3.31 ERA at the Dome, 5-9 with a 3.57 ERA on the road. He allowed only seven home runs in 133.1 innings at home, 11 homers in 113.1 away. There were times when Jack displayed flashes of the temper that earned him the moniker "Mt. Morris" in Detroit, but he seldom let his frustration with questionable calls get the best of him.

HOLDING RUNNERS AND FIELDING:

Morris has long had problems holding runners. Standing 6-3, and his high leg kick makes him an inviting target to opposing base stealers. He is an excellent athlete and one of the better fielding pitchers on the Twins staff (zero errors in 49 chances).

OVERALL:

The Twins got more than they could possibly have hoped for when they signed Morris to an incentive-laden contract before the 1991 season. That contract allowed Morris to opt for free agency when the season ended, and Morris wants to test his resurgent market value. If the Twins want to keep their local hero, they'll have to ante up.

Overall Statistics

	W	L	ERA	G	GS	Sv	IP	H	R	BB	SO	HR
1991	18	12	3.43	35	35	0	246.2	226	107	92	163	18
Career	216	162	3.71	465	443	0	3290.0	2993	1489	1178	2143	339

How Often He Throws Strikes

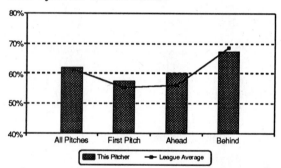

| | All Pitches | First Pitch | Ahead | Behind |

■■■ This Pitcher ━●━ League Average

1991 Situational Stats

	W	L	ERA	Sv	IP		AB	H	HR	RBI	AVG
Home	13	3	3.31	0	133.1	LHB	456	128	9	52	.281
Road	5	9	3.57	0	113.1	RHB	466	98	9	45	.210
Day	8	4	3.84	0	91.1	Sc Pos	212	57	9	83	.269
Night	10	8	3.19	0	155.1	Clutch	111	27	2	11	.243

1991 Rankings (American League)

→ 1st in games started (35), wild pitches (15) and stolen bases allowed (32)

→ 2nd in batters faced (1,032) and lowest batting average allowed vs. right-handed pitchers (.210)

→ 3rd in complete games (10), innings (246.2) and highest stolen base percentage allowed (80.0%)

→ Led the Twins in losses (12), games started, complete games, innings, hits allowed (226), batters faced, walks allowed (92), strikeouts (163), wild pitches, pitches thrown (3,735), stolen bases allowed, GDPs induced (23), lowest batting average allowed (.245) and lowest slugging percentage allowed (.347)

HITTING:

Since Detroit's Tony Phillips is actually an everyday player, a strong argument can be made that Al Newman has been baseball's most versatile utility man since joining the Twins in 1987. Newman is the first player in major league history to play at least 25 games at second base, shortstop and third base in four consecutive seasons.

The only hole in that argument revolves around the hole in Newman's bat. The infielder batted only .191 last year, down 51 points from his 1990 average. In his best season, 1989, Newman hit .253 with 18 doubles, 38 RBI, 59 walks and 25 stolen bases. His numbers last year dropped to five doubles, 19 RBI, 23 walks, 21 strikeouts and four stolen bases.

Newman at his best is a slap hitter. He has almost no power, having gone homerless in his last 1,725 at-bats, the longest active streak in the major leagues. His only homer came on July 6, 1986 at Atlanta while playing for Montreal. The switch-hitter batted a respectable .242 against lefties in 1991, but hit only .172 against righties.

BASERUNNING:

Newman is an exceptionally bright player who seldom makes mistakes on the base paths. At the age of 31, however, he appears to have slowed a step, stealing just four bases in nine attempts last season.

FIELDING:

There may have been dropoffs in Newman's offense and base stealing, but his defense was as steady as ever last year. He's a natural second baseman, but fills in capably at shortstop and third base. Last season he made only one error in 129 chances at second, two errors in 155 chances at shortstop and one error in 27 chances at third, all exceptional figures.

OVERALL:

Newman entered the off season a free agent and there was a question whether the Twins would pay for his return. His lack of production offensively concerns team officials, but they also fear they could miss his steady glove and steadying influence in the clubhouse.

AL NEWMAN

Position: SS/2B/3B
Bats: B **Throws:** R
Ht: 5' 9" **Wt:** 198

Opening Day Age: 31
Born: 6/30/60 in Kansas City, MO
ML Seasons: 7

Overall Statistics

	G	AB	R	H	D	T	HR	RBI	SB	BB	SO	AVG
1991	118	246	25	47	5	0	0	19	4	23	21	.191
Career	738	1861	239	422	63	7	1	144	82	202	186	.227

Where He Hits the Ball

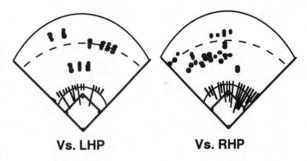

Vs. LHP   Vs. RHP

1991 Situational Stats

	AB	H	HR	RBI	AVG		AB	H	HR	RBI	AVG
Home	117	21	0	10	.179	LHP	66	16	0	8	.242
Road	129	26	0	9	.202	RHP	180	31	0	11	.172
Day	104	18	0	8	.173	Sc Pos	74	14	0	19	.189
Night	142	29	0	11	.204	Clutch	43	5	0	2	.116

1991 Rankings (American League)

→ 2nd lowest batting average in the clutch (.116)

→ 3rd lowest batting average on a 3-2 count (.045)

HITTING:

A number of scouts wrote off Mike Pagliarulo after his 1990 season, figuring he was no longer an effective player. The Twins disagreed, signing Pags to a free agent contract, and the third baseman responded with a solid, if unspectacular, season. Pagliarulo was platooned, and while it is true that he showed only a glimpse of the power that enabled him to hit 60 homers with the Yankees in 1986-87, Pags batted a career-high .279, and finished the year with two postseason homers. Pagliarulo's tenth-inning home run won Game Three of the playoffs in Toronto, a key contest in Minnesota's championship drive.

Although he had just six home runs during the regular season, Pagliarulo showed line drive power with 20 doubles. A pull hitter early in his career, he now sprays hits to all fields. Pagliarulo's power comes primarily when he's able to pull low pitches in the strike zone. Most teams pitch him up and away, and his vulnerability to such pitches was obvious in his .195 average (17-for-87) with runners in scoring position.

BASERUNNING:

Pagliarulo's best attribute on the bases is his aggressiveness. He lacks speed, stealing just one base in three attempts last season. But he's the kind of heady, no-nonsense player preferred by Twins' manager Tom Kelly.

FIELDING:

The question marks about Pagliarulo after 1990 extended to his defense. The word was that his range was poor and his arm too weak. Both reports were inaccurate. Pagliarulo's range won't put him in the Brooks Robinson category, but he made numerous diving stops. His arm, which required surgery in 1987 to remove elbow bone chips, was strong enough and extremely accurate.

OVERALL:

When the season started, Pagliarulo, signed to a one-year contract, was considered an interim third baseman. The Twins inquired about the availability of Steve Buechele, Tim Wallach and Kevin Seitzer during the year. However, Pags was a personal favorite of Kelly, and for that reason it's likely he'll get another contract for 1992.

MIKE PAGLIARULO

Position: 3B
Bats: L Throws: R
Ht: 6' 2" Wt: 195

Opening Day Age: 32
Born: 3/15/60 in Medford, MA
ML Seasons: 8

Overall Statistics

	G	AB	R	H	D	T	HR	RBI	SB	BB	SO	AVG
1991	121	365	38	102	20	0	6	36	1	21	55	.279
Career	1002	3185	370	753	161	14	121	425	11	301	670	.236

Where He Hits the Ball

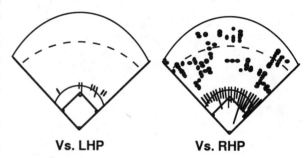

Vs. LHP   Vs. RHP

1991 Situational Stats

	AB	H	HR	RBI	AVG		AB	H	HR	RBI	AVG
Home	190	54	4	27	.284	LHP	16	3	0	1	.188
Road	175	48	2	9	.274	RHP	349	99	6	35	.284
Day	101	28	3	10	.277	Sc Pos	87	17	1	25	.195
Night	264	74	3	26	.280	Clutch	53	13	0	5	.245

1991 Rankings (American League)

- 9th lowest batting average with runners in scoring position (.195)
- Led the Twins in batting average on a 3-1 count (.444)

HITTING:

Twins' veteran Kent Hrbek says some of his favorite moments as a major leaguer have come when he's followed Kirby Puckett to the plate and listened to the catcher grumble about the pitch Puckett just slashed for a base hit. Puckett is truly a one-of-a-kind offensive player, a notorious free swinger who strikes out twice as many times as he walks and still manages to hit well above .300. He had a typical season in 1991, batting .319 with 15 homers, 89 RBI, 31 walks and 78 strikeouts -- all before helping lead the Twins to the World Championship.

Puckett tried to be more patient in 1990, when he walked a career-high 57 times while striking out 73. But for all his patience that season, he batted .298 -- breaking a string of four straight .325-plus seasons -- and failed to homer in his final 74 games. So, in 1991, it was back to slashing bad pitches to all corners of the park, especially right field, which remains his power alley. The Twins didn't complain at all.

BASERUNNING:

Puckett may look like a human bowling ball, but he still has decent speed, swiping 11 bases in 16 attempts. He stole more than 20 bases in each of his first two seasons in the majors, but isn't likely to steal 20 again.

FIELDING:

Puckett has his detractors defensively, his perceived negatives being that he plays too deep and doesn't cover the ground he once did. There is some basis in the criticisms. But the bottom line is that Puckett catches almost everything that comes his way (six errors in 363 chances) and has a strong, accurate arm (13 assists).

OVERALL:

Puckett is simply one of the best players in the major leagues. And his ample physical attributes are enhanced by a friendly, outgoing personality that has made him one of the most popular players ever to wear a Twins uniform. After eight splendid seasons and two world titles, he's starting to be talked about as a future Hall of Famer.

KIRBY PUCKETT

Position: CF/RF
Bats: R **Throws:** R
Ht: 5' 8" **Wt:** 216

Opening Day Age: 31
Born: 3/14/61 in Chicago, IL
ML Seasons: 8

Overall Statistics

	G	AB	R	H	D	T	HR	RBI	SB	BB	SO	AVG
1991	152	611	92	195	29	6	15	89	11	31	78	.319
Career	1222	5006	716	1602	266	47	123	675	100	275	639	.320

Where He Hits the Ball

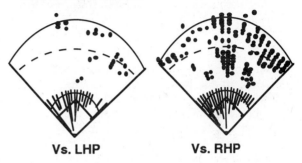

Vs. LHP   **Vs. RHP**

1991 Situational Stats

	AB	H	HR	RBI	AVG		AB	H	HR	RBI	AVG
Home	328	107	7	45	.326	LHP	155	63	7	24	.406
Road	283	88	8	44	.311	RHP	456	132	8	65	.289
Day	178	55	6	27	.309	Sc Pos	153	46	1	65	.301
Night	433	140	9	62	.323	Clutch	74	28	3	15	.378

1991 Rankings (American League)

→ 1st in GDPs (27) and batting average vs. left-handed pitchers (.406)

→ 3rd in slugging percentage vs. left-handed pitchers (.658) and batting average after the 6th inning (.337)

→ 4th in singles (145) and batting average in the clutch (.378)

→ Led the Twins in batting average (.319), at-bats (611), runs (92), hits (195), singles, total bases (281), sacrifice bunts (8), sacrifice flies (7), GDPs, plate appearances (661), batting average/on-base average (.436) vs. left-handed pitchers, batting average on the road (.311), batting average after the 6th inning and bunts in play (18)

KEVIN TAPANI

Position: SP
Bats: R **Throws:** R
Ht: 6' 0" **Wt:** 187

Opening Day Age: 28
Born: 2/18/64 in Des Moines, IA
ML Seasons: 3

PITCHING:

Everything about Kevin Tapani is low-key, from his personality to his seemingly effortless pitching style. But over the course of the 1991 season, the soft-spoken righthander was the Twins' most consistent pitcher. Tapani worked at least six innings in 29 of his 34 starts, and his 2.99 ERA was the lowest among Twins' starters. Tapani won only one of his four postseason starts -- the second game of the World Series -- but his season was obviously a big success.

Tapani's record last year would have been much better, save for a six-game losing streak in the first two months. The slump had more to do with his teammates than with Tapani. The Twins scored one run or less in four of the six games, and two runs in another. Once he began to get better support, Tapani went 9-0 with a 2.22 ERA in nine starts between July 21 and Sept. 6.

The secret to Tapani's success is excellent control of each of his four pitches -- fastball, slider, change-up and forkball. He didn't walk a batter in 13 of his 34 starts, and went four successive starts without a walk, spanning 29.2 innings, between July 21 and Aug. 5. Tapani's smooth delivery makes him appear less than overpowering, but his fastball is in the 90-MPH vicinity. It's worth nothing that lefthanders batted only .235 off him. Some people are concerned about the 23 home runs Tapani allowed, but that's not unusual for a hard thrower with great control.

HOLDING RUNNERS AND FIELDING:

Tapani's excellent mechanics make him a challenge for any would be base stealer. He's consistent defensively, making only one error in 52 chances last year.

OVERALL:

Tapani proved last season that his strong first-half rookie showing in 1990 (11-5 on Aug. 1 before a series of injuries) was no fluke. A legitimate Cy Young candidate last year, Tapani should be a consistent 15-to-18 game winner for several years to come.

Overall Statistics

	W	L	ERA	G	GS	Sv	IP	H	R	BB	SO	HR
1991	16	9	2.99	34	34	0	244.0	225	84	40	135	23
Career	30	19	3.45	70	67	0	443.1	428	177	81	259	38

How Often He Throws Strikes

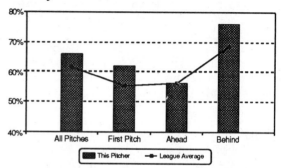

1991 Situational Stats

	W	L	ERA	Sv	IP		AB	H	HR	RBI	AVG
Home	10	5	2.79	0	132.1	LHB	520	122	8	42	.235
Road	6	4	3.22	0	111.2	RHB	397	103	15	34	.259
Day	3	2	2.72	0	53.0	Sc Pos	185	38	1	46	.205
Night	13	7	3.06	0	191.0	Clutch	74	19	2	6	.257

1991 Rankings (American League)

→ 2nd highest stolen base percentage allowed (85.7%)

→ 3rd in balks (3) and lowest on-base percentage allowed (.277)

→ 4th highest strikeout/walk ratio (3.4)

→ 5th in innings (244) and least pitches thrown per batter (3.47)

→ Led the Twins in ERA (2.99), balks, strikeout/walk ratio, lowest on-base percentage allowed, least pitches thrown per batter, ERA at home (2.79) and lowest batting average allowed with runners in scoring position (.205)

PITCHING:

David West continued his enigmatic tradition through the 1991 season, when his performance resulted in another season of shuttling between the starting rotation and the bullpen. Once considered the best prospect in the Mets' pitching-rich farm system, the lefthander posted a 4.54 ERA, still high, but his best figure since joining the Twins. West raised Minnesota hopes during the Championship Series against Toronto, shutting out the Jays (a team he's always handled) in two appearances over 5.2 innings. But in the World Series against Atlanta, West literally couldn't get anyone out. In two appearances versus the Braves, he allowed two hits and four walks without retiring a man, a typically West-like pattern of undependability.

The Twins spent two years trying to improve West's mechanics, the theory being that when his arm dropped -- and it generally did when he first came from the Mets -- his pitches would rise in the strike zone. Now they want West to change his mental approach by challenging hitters consistently rather than nibbling at corners. West still lacks the quality offspeed pitch to make him an effective nibbler.

West is 6-6, 231 pounds and has a fastball worthy of his frame. There were signs that West may be on the brink of finally living up to his advance billing. Opponents batted only .244 (righthanders were .229) and he walked only 28 in 71.1 innings. That was a big improvement over 1990 when he walked 78 in 146.1 innings.

HOLDING RUNNERS AND FIELDING:

West is no gazelle on the mound. While many of the Twins' pitchers are excellent natural athletes, West is rather awkward in his movements. He does, however, have a decent move to first.

OVERALL:

West entered last season with a 5.54 career ERA, the highest of any active pitcher who had managed to survive 200 innings. Though he pitched a little better last year, especially in the playoffs, the moment of truth for him will occur in 1992. The Twins still envision West as a major league star, but it's now or never time.

DAVID WEST

Position: SP
Bats: L **Throws:** L
Ht: 6' 6" **Wt:** 231

Opening Day Age: 27
Born: 9/1/64 in Memphis, TN
ML Seasons: 4

Overall Statistics

	W	L	ERA	G	GS	Sv	IP	H	R	BB	SO	HR
1991	4	4	4.54	15	12	0	71.1	66	37	28	52	13
Career	15	17	5.29	67	47	0	287.1	287	176	142	197	43

How Often He Throws Strikes

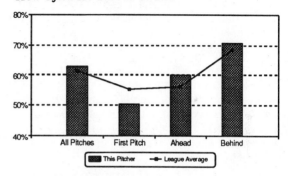

1991 Situational Stats

	W	L	ERA	Sv	IP		AB	H	HR	RBI	AVG
Home	1	3	7.46	0	25.1	LHB	35	12	2	4	.343
Road	3	1	2.93	0	46.0	RHB	236	54	11	32	.229
Day	1	2	5.03	0	19.2	Sc Pos	59	13	1	21	.220
Night	3	2	4.35	0	51.2	Clutch	13	1	0	0	.077

1991 Rankings (American League)

→ Did not rank near the top or bottom in any category

PITCHING:

How big a surprise was Carl Willis last year? When the 1990 season ended, Willis returned to college to complete work on his degree, figuring he might soon need it. He turned 30 over the winter and was coming off a season at Colorado Springs in which he posted a 6.39 ERA. With the exception of six appearances with the White Sox in 1988, Willis had spent the four seasons between 1987 and 1990 in the minors.

After all that, if someone had told Willis that he would finish 1991 as the steadiest middle reliever on a world championship ball club, even Carl wouldn't have believed it. Purchased from Portland on April 17, Willis turned in a 2.63 ERA in 40 appearances. By season's end Tom Kelly had developed such confidence in Willis that he chose the righty as his key set-up man in postseason play.

Willis has a decent fastball and a split-fingered pitch with excellent movement. (Some say Willis' splitter is actually a spitter, but consider him innocent until proven guilty.) Twins' scouts correctly gambled that the heavy air at Colorado Springs, coupled with a slight elbow problem, was to blame for Willis' 1990 stats.

Between July 6 and Aug. 11, Willis was 4-0 with one save and a perfect 0.00 ERA in nine relief appearances spanning 23.2 innings. Those figures underscore Willis' stamina; in the playoffs and Series, Kelly could confidently use him for two innings or more. The key to his success is that he consistently pitched ahead in the count. He walked only 19 batters in 89 innings.

HOLDING RUNNERS AND FIELDING:

Willis is an adequate fielder, though lacking somewhat in natural quickness. His move to first is similarly unspectacular, but adequate.

OVERALL:

The Twins would gladly settle for a repeat of Willis' 1991 performance next year. Team officials are confident that as long as his elbow is sound, as it was last year, his control and split-fingered fastball will make him a valuable long man out of the bullpen.

CARL WILLIS

Position: RP
Bats: L **Throws:** R
Ht: 6' 4" **Wt:** 212

Opening Day Age: 31
Born: 12/28/60 in Danville, VA
ML Seasons: 5

Overall Statistics

	W	L	ERA	G	GS	Sv	IP	H	R	BB	SO	HR
1991	8	3	2.63	40	0	2	89.0	76	31	19	53	4
Career	10	9	4.39	103	2	4	192.2	201	107	70	96	16

How Often He Throws Strikes

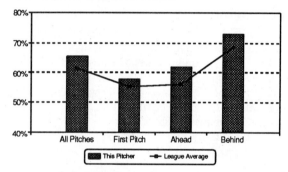

1991 Situational Stats

	W	L	ERA	Sv	IP		AB	H	HR	RBI	AVG
Home	7	2	2.84	0	50.2	LHB	130	37	0	10	.285
Road	1	1	2.35	2	38.1	RHB	198	39	4	19	.197
Day	1	0	2.61	1	20.2	Sc Pos	79	19	1	25	.241
Night	7	3	2.63	1	68.1	Clutch	69	16	2	4	.232

1991 Rankings (American League)

➡ 2nd in first batter efficiency (.114)
➡ 4th in relief wins (8)
➡ 8th least baserunners allowed per 9 innings in relief (9.7)
➡ Led the Twins in first batter efficiency, relief wins, relief innings (89) and least baserunners allowed per 9 innings in relief

MARK GUTHRIE

Position: RP/SP
Bats: B **Throws:** L
Ht: 6' 4" **Wt:** 196

Opening Day Age: 26
Born: 9/22/65 in Buffalo, NY
ML Seasons: 3

Overall Statistics

	W	L	ERA	G	GS	Sv	IP	H	R	BB	SO	HR
1991	7	5	4.32	41	12	2	98.0	116	52	41	72	11
Career	16	18	4.11	78	41	2	300.0	336	149	101	211	26

PITCHING, FIELDING & HOLDING RUNNERS:

Lefthander Mark Guthrie began last season in the Twins' starting rotation, but spent the final half of the season as a long reliever. It was a step backward, since Guthrie ended the 1990 season by pitching into the seventh inning in his last 11 starts and posting a 2.51 ERA over his final 61 innings. Guthrie handled the demotion, however, and did some nice relief work in the postseason. In six games covering 6.1 innings against the Blue Jays and Braves, Guthrie allowed only one run. Manager Tom Kelly was never afraid to go to him in important situations.

Guthrie doesn't have an overpowering fastball, and needs excellent control, especially of his forkball, to be effective. He has one of the best pickoff moves in the major leagues, and is a good fielder.

OVERALL:

Guthrie appeared to have a bright future when the 1990 season ended, but now is one of many question marks on the staff. Since the Twins have an abundance of prospects in the minor league system, he may only get one more shot at earning a rotation spot. Based on his fine work in the playoffs and Series, however, Guthrie could find a lot of work in the bullpen.

PEDRO MUNOZ

Position: RF
Bats: R **Throws:** R
Ht: 5'10" **Wt:** 200

Opening Day Age: 23
Born: 9/19/68 in Ponce, Puerto Rico
ML Seasons: 2

Overall Statistics

	G	AB	R	H	D	T	HR	RBI	SB	BB	SO	AVG
1991	51	138	15	39	7	1	7	26	3	9	31	.283
Career	73	223	28	62	11	2	7	31	6	11	47	.278

HITTING, FIELDING, BASERUNNING:

Still only 23 years old, Pedro Munoz is the best young hitting prospect in the Twins system. After batting .316 at AAA Portland -- his second straight solid season at that level -- Munoz hit .283 in 138 at-bats with Minnesota last year. The Toronto Blue Jays must be kicking themselves; they gave up Munoz (and Nelson Liriano) in late July 1991 in order to get two months of service from John Candelaria.

Munoz is a line drive hitter who, like many young players, hits fastballs better than breaking balls. He has shown excellent power potential, hitting seven homers during his limited playing time. One of the impressive things about Munoz is that he hits both righthanders (.277) and lefthanders (.295). He has better than average speed, swiping three bases in as many attempts. The biggest rap on Munoz when he arrived from Toronto was that he was a defensive liability. However, he has looked to be adequate during his time with Minnesota, displaying a decent glove and average arm.

OVERALL:

The Twins will give Munoz a shot at winning the left field job in spring training. He looks to be a solid .280-type hitter. If he can do the job defensively, he could become a Twins regular.

DENNY NEAGLE

Position: RP/SP
Bats: L **Throws:** L
Ht: 6' 4" **Wt:** 200

Opening Day Age: 23
Born: 9/13/68 in Prince Georges County, MD
ML Seasons: 1

Overall Statistics

	W	L	ERA	G	GS	Sv	IP	H	R	BB	SO	HR
1991	0	1	4.05	7	3	0	20.0	28	9	7	14	3
Career	0	1	4.05	7	3	0	20.0	28	9	7	14	3

PITCHING, FIELDING & HOLDING RUNNERS:

While Denny Neagle was piling up impressive victory totals in the minors the past two summers, there remained some skepticism in Minnesota because the lefthander lacks an overpowering fastball. The Twins had seen this type of lefty before (Allan Anderson, Mark Guthrie) and weren't going to get overly excited.

Neagle eased some of those doubts in his seven 1991 appearances. He might not possess a 90-MPH fastball, but he's an aggressive pitcher with a major league change-up. Neagle, who'd always racked up impressive strikeout totals during his minor league career, fanned a decent total, (14), in his 20 major league innings. One negative sign was that righthanders batted .359 compared to .238 for lefties.

Neagle had some flaws in his follow-through when he first arrived, and he was hit in the forearm by a line drive in his major league debut. The flaws appear to have been corrected, and Neagle showed signs of being a smooth fielder with a decent pickoff move.

OVERALL:

Neagle will be given a chance to move into the starting rotation in spring training. The Twins need a lefty, and his minor league numbers warrant a long look.

JUNIOR ORTIZ

Position: C
Bats: R **Throws:** R
Ht: 5'11" **Wt:** 181

Opening Day Age: 32
Born: 10/24/59 in Humacao, Puerto Rico
ML Seasons: 10

Overall Statistics

	G	AB	R	H	D	T	HR	RBI	SB	BB	SO	AVG
1991	61	134	9	28	5	1	0	11	0	15	12	.209
Career	539	1325	100	347	49	4	5	133	6	93	162	.262

HITTING, FIELDING, BASERUNNING:

After batting .335 in 1990, the colorful Junior Ortiz returned to earth -- as much as he ever does, anyway -- in 1991 with a .209 average. Ortiz is a decent contact hitter, striking out just 12 times in 134 at-bats last year, which allowed the Twins to use him in hit-and-run situations. Ortiz is primarily a line drive hitter, with five doubles and one triple his only extra-base hits. Surprisingly, he had more trouble with left-handed pitchers (.143 batting average, 6-for-42), than righties (.239, 22-for-92).

Ortiz is a smart baserunner but lacks speed (zero stolen bases). His strength is in his catching skills. He was the Twins' designated catcher for Scott Erickson's starts, and Erickson responded with 20 victories. Ortiz has an adequate arm and did a good job catching Erickson's hard slider.

OVERALL:

At 32, Ortiz is the prototype backup catcher, a good glove man who doesn't hit consistently enough to warrant regular duty. Ortiz has had some good years with the bat, but even when he doesn't hit, he provides value. There's no reason why his talents shouldn't keep him in the majors for several more years.

ORGANIZATION OVERVIEW:

The Twins' world championship last year was a result of contributions from seasoned veterans Hrbek, Puckett), free agent signings (Davis, Morris), players recently developed by the Twin system (Erickson, Knoblauch) and youngsters acquired from other teams (Aguilera, Tapani). The constants are that Minnesota has a good eye for talent and manager Tom Kelly has the patience to give young players a fair shot. Still, when you need to sign three free agents, as the Twins did last winter, your farm system isn't doing all it should. The Twins' best prospects are mostly pitchers, and there are some doubts.

WILLIE BANKS

Position: P **Opening Day Age:** 23
Bats: R **Throws:** R **Born:** 2/27/69 in Jersey
Ht: 6' 1" **Wt:** 185 City, NJ

Recent Statistics

	W	L	ERA	GGS Sv	IP	H	R	BB	SO	HR
91 AAA Portland	9	8	4.55	25 24 0	146.1	156	81	76	63	6
91 AL Minnesota	1	1	5.71	5 3 0	17.1	21	15	12	16	1

The first pitcher chosen (and third overall pick) in the 1987 draft, Banks has moved slowly through the Twin system, going 9-8 at Portland and making five lackluster appearances (1-1, 5.71) for the big club last year. Banks has a major league fastball and change, but his breaking stuff is iffy, and his control has always been a huge problem. His stats at Portland induce doubts; he's now a questionable prospect, though pitchers with his stuff can develop in a hurry.

RICH GARCES

Position: P **Opening Day Age:** 21
Bats: R **Throws:** R **Born:** 5/18/70 in
Ht: 6' 0" **Wt:** 200 Maracay, Venezuela

Recent Statistics

	W	L	ERA	GGS Sv	IP	H	R	BB	SO	HR
90 A Visalia	2	2	1.81	47 0 28	54.2	33	14	16	75	2
90 AA Orlando	2	1	2.08	15 0 8	17.1	17	4	14	22	0
90 MAJ Minnesota	0	0	1.59	5 0 2	5.2	4	2	4	1	0
91 AAA Portland	0	1	4.85	10 0 3	13.0	10	7	8	13	1
91 AA Orlando	2	1	3.31	10 0 0	16.1	12	6	14	17	0

A year ago, the Twins thought so highly of Garces that they were seriously considering moving Rick Aguilera to their starting rotation and giving Garces, then only 19, the closer role. That plan quickly died when Garces reported to camp overweight. He proceeded to have an absolutely miserable year, going AWOL a couple of times and suffered some strange injuries, including a skin rash. Garces still has a terrific arm. He'll have to get his act together dramatically, though, if he wants to make the Twins staff in 1992.

PAT MAHOMES

Position: P **Opening Day Age:** 21
Bats: R **Throws:** R **Born:** 8/9/70 in Bryan,
Ht: 6' 3" **Wt:** 198 TX

Recent Statistics

	W	L	ERA	GGS Sv	IP	H	R	BB	SO	HR
90 A Visalia	11	11	3.30	28 28 0	185.1	136	77	118	178	14
91 AA Orlando	8	5	1.78	18 17 0	116.0	77	30	57	136	5
f91 AAA Portland	3	5	3.44	9 9 0	55.0	50	26	36	41	2

A sixth-round pick in 1988, Mahomes developed quickly last year at age 21, blowing away hitters at AA Orlando (including a 16-strikeout performance) and then doing reasonably well in nine starts at Portland. Mahomes' fastball and especially his breaking ball are considered major league quality. He's clearly Minnesota's best pitching prospect now, and maybe their best overall. The Twins, with room on their staff, give Mahomes an excellent chance of making the big club this year.

PAUL SORRENTO

Position: 1B **Opening Day Age:** 26
Bats: L **Throws:** R **Born:** 11/17/65 in
Ht: 6' 2" **Wt:** 205 Somerville, MA

Recent Statistics

	G	AB	R	H	D	THR	RBI	SB	BB	SO	AVG
91 AAA Portland	113	409	59	126	30	2 13	79	1	62	65	.308
91 AL Minnesota	26	47	6	12	2	0 4	13	0	4	11	.255
91 MLE	113	398	46	115	29	1 10	62	0	50	62	.289

Now 26, Sorrento has seen some action with the Twins in each of the last three seasons, and made their postseason roster last year. He has a little power, good patience and an ability to hit for average. His defense at first is so-so. Playing behind Kent Hrbek, Sorrento probably won't get much action with the Twins. A trade would help, and there's always the expansion draft. He has the hitting skills to help a major league team; all he needs is a chance to play.

LENNY WEBSTER

Position: C **Opening Day Age:** 27
Bats: R **Throws:** R **Born:** 2/10/65 in New
Ht: 5' 9" **Wt:** 187 Orleans, LA

Recent Statistics

	G	AB	R	H	D	THR	RBI	SB	BB	SO	AVG
91 AAA Portland	87	325	43	82	18	0 7	34	1	24	32	.252
91 AL Minnesota	18	34	7	10	1	0 3	8	0	6	10	.294
91 MLE	87	317	34	74	17	0 5	27	0	19	30	.233

With Brian Harper a free agent, Webster has a chance to become the Twins' regular catcher this year; barring that, he still figures to make the club as a backup. Webster has major league defensive skills (good arm, great rapport with pitchers), but his bat won't excite anybody. He'll have to be a **very** strong defensive catcher to last as a regular.

STRONG ARM

HITTING:

Jesse Barfield is a classic pull hitter with power that is still outstanding. When his 1991 season ended July 28 with a fractured foot bone, Barfield was on a pace to hit 30-plus home runs. The negative side of 1991 included his lowest on-base percentage since 1988 (when he had a serious wrist injury) and his lowest batting average ever. Barfield was simply having trouble getting around on hard stuff from right-handed pitchers.

Barfield-watchers have been scrutinizing his walk/strikeout ratio as a key indicator during the past few years. The strikeouts are always plentiful, but when Barfield is selective and draws walks, he gets better pitches and produces more at the plate. The evidence from 1991 was unfavorable: his worst ratio since 1988. Barfield doesn't try to hit singles. As a hard swinger, he needs to pick his pitches more carefully than he did in 1991.

BASERUNNING:

Not since he stole 22 bases in 1985 has Barfield been a real threat to steal. He has gradually given up the stolen base as a weapon, but he remains a smart and alert runner who will move aggressively in the right situations.

FIELDING:

Second among active players with 159 career outfield assists, Barfield is widely recognized as having one of the strongest and most accurate arms in the American League. Despite the reputation, runners still become over-optimistic at times; usually they pay the price. Barfield has good range, gets to base hits quickly, and always knows what to do with the ball.

OVERALL:

Barfield's injury coincided with the arrival of Bernie Williams, who pushed Roberto Kelly to left field and the Hall/Meulens platoon into right. With Barfield back in the picture, the Yankees simply have too many outfielders. If they are seriously committed to a youth movement, Barfield must be considered a candidate either for a trade or increased bench time. Barfield will make a solid contribution wherever he plays. He is a quiet leader with a very positive attitude.

JESSE BARFIELD

Position: RF
Bats: R **Throws:** R
Ht: 6' 1" **Wt:** 206

Opening Day Age: 32
Born: 10/29/59 in Joliet, IL
ML Seasons: 11

Overall Statistics

	G	AB	R	H	D	T	HR	RBI	SB	BB	SO	AVG
1991	84	284	37	64	12	0	17	48	1	36	80	.225
Career	1398	4664	707	1206	214	30	239	709	65	542	1207	.259

Where He Hits the Ball

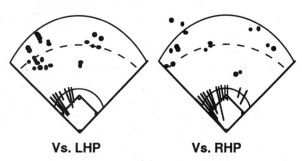

Vs. LHP **Vs. RHP**

1991 Situational Stats

	AB	H	HR	RBI	AVG		AB	H	HR	RBI	AVG
Home	130	30	11	30	.231	LHP	108	34	9	24	.315
Road	154	34	6	18	.221	RHP	176	30	8	24	.170
Day	69	15	3	10	.217	Sc Pos	75	19	4	31	.253
Night	215	49	14	38	.228	Clutch	44	12	2	5	.273

1991 Rankings (American League)

➡ 5th highest percentage of extra bases taken as a runner (73.7%)

➡ 8th highest slugging percentage vs. left-handed pitchers (.602)

➡ Led the Yankees in slugging percentage vs. left-handed pitchers and on-base percentage vs. left-handed pitchers (.408)

PITCHING:

For the third consecutive year, Greg Cadaret was Mr. Versatility on the Yankee staff, working as a starter, long reliever, set-up man, and occasional closer. And for the third consecutive year, Cadaret was clearly superior in relief appearances (2.85 ERA) and seriously deficient as a starter (6.00 ERA). People are beginning to wonder when the Yankees are going to catch on.

Cadaret is essentially a power pitcher. He loves to challenge hitters and work inside. He simply runs out of gas after 40 to 45 pitches (.224 opponents' batting average on first 45 pitches, .320 BA thereafter). Cadaret has a curve and a forkball that are great assets when working in relief, but these pitches are not sharp enough to round out a starter's repertoire.

Cadaret needs the good fastball to be effective. When his velocity drops a little after a few innings, hitters can look for the fastball and clobber it. He doesn't have sufficient command of the breaking pitches to rely on them when he's behind in the count.

HOLDING RUNNERS AND FIELDING:

Cadaret has a good pickoff move and gets the ball to the catcher quickly. In 1990-1991 opposing baserunners failed in 60% of their steal attempts against Cadaret, yet they keep trying. Cadaret is a superior fielder who often helps himself by pouncing on bunts or grabbing shots through the middle. He is one of the best defensive assets on the Yankee pitching staff.

OVERALL:

Cadaret is a solid, reliable relief pitcher. The Yankees' repeated attempts to use him as a starter since they acquired him in June 1989, are evidence of stubborn, wishful thinking by management. Year after year, Cadaret's full season numbers have been ruined by his appearances in a starting role; behind these stats, Cadaret is one of the top lefty relievers in the American League.

GREG CADARET

Position: RP/SP
Bats: L **Throws:** L
Ht: 6' 3" **Wt:** 214

Opening Day Age: 30
Born: 2/27/62 in Detroit, MI
ML Seasons: 5

Overall Statistics

	W	L	ERA	G	GS	Sv	IP	H	R	BB	SO	HR
1991	8	6	3.62	68	5	3	121.2	110	52	59	105	8
Career	29	19	3.83	255	24	9	474.1	457	224	240	359	31

How Often He Throws Strikes

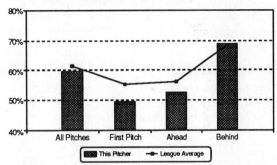

1991 Situational Stats

	W	L	ERA	Sv	IP		AB	H	HR	RBI	AVG
Home	4	3	4.72	0	61.0	LHB	118	29	0	11	.246
Road	4	3	2.52	3	60.2	RHB	329	81	8	43	.246
Day	4	4	4.39	2	55.1	Sc Pos	111	33	2	44	.297
Night	4	2	2.98	1	66.1	Clutch	122	28	2	14	.230

1991 Rankings (American League)

➡ 7th in games pitched (68) and relief innings (91.2)

➡ Led the Yankees in games pitched, runner caught stealing (8), first batter efficiency (.189) and relief innings

HITTING:

Alvaro Espinoza is a great bat-handler and contact hitter. He is a free swinger, but he tries only to put the ball in play, not to hit for power. Espinoza doesn't walk enough. He went through one streak in 1991 with only two walks in 210 plate appearances. He strikes out too much for a singles hitter, and swings at too many pitches that put the ball exactly where the defense wants it.

In early 1991, Espinoza showed progress after working with batting coach Frank Howard. He learned to swing harder on selected pitches, while still making contact. He didn't pull the ball, but he gave the opposition fielders more to think about. During April and early May, Espinoza hit over .300 against both righties and lefties. The pitchers and defenses soon caught up with him, however, and made him a .245 hitter for the remainder of the season.

BASERUNNING:

Espinoza has average speed, meaning he is slow for a shortstop. His main strength as a runner is that he knows how to handle all situations, and he concentrates intensely on every pitch. Combined with his superior knowledge of opposition pitchers, this intensity helps him take a good lead, get a good jump, and capitalize on every opportunity.

FIELDING:

Concentration and knowledge are Espinoza's main assets in the field. He isn't among the most gifted athletes playing shortstop, but he positions himself extremely well and gets to many balls that would elude some of the flashier shortstops. He is sure-handed and good at completing double plays.

OVERALL:

As a young prospect, Espinoza was let go by the Twins and Astros. After three decent seasons in New York, he is now age 30 and past his prime. The Yankees have their eye on 24-year-old Dave Silvestri, who had a big year at AA Albany in 1991. When Silvestri is ready, displacing Espinoza won't be a major obstacle.

ALVARO ESPINOZA

Position: SS
Bats: R **Throws:** R
Ht: 6' 0" **Wt:** 189

Opening Day Age: 30
Born: 2/19/62 in
Valencia, Venezuela
ML Seasons: 7

Overall Statistics

	G	AB	R	H	D	T	HR	RBI	SB	BB	SO	AVG
1991	148	480	51	123	23	2	5	33	4	16	57	.256
Career	517	1523	142	387	61	5	7	104	8	48	190	.254

Where He Hits the Ball

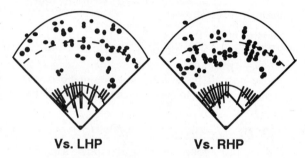

Vs. LHP   **Vs. RHP**

1991 Situational Stats

	AB	H	HR	RBI	AVG		AB	H	HR	RBI	AVG
Home	254	63	2	14	.248	LHP	161	42	1	15	.261
Road	226	60	3	19	.265	RHP	319	81	4	18	.254
Day	151	40	3	10	.265	Sc Pos	100	25	1	27	.250
Night	329	83	2	23	.252	Clutch	75	15	0	3	.200

1991 Rankings (American League)

→ 1st in lowest on-base average (.282)

→ 2nd least pitches seen per plate appearance (2.93)

→ 3rd lowest percentage of pitches taken (43.1%)

→ 5th highest batting average on a 3-2 count (.375)

→ 7th lowest slugging percentage (.344)

→ Led the Yankees in sacrifice bunts (9), highest batting average with the bases loaded (.167) and batting average on a 3-1 count (.500)

→ Led AL shortstops in batting average on a 3-2 count

PITCHING:

Steve Farr has never been regarded as having great "closer stuff" -- no overpowering fastball like the best ace relievers, and no devastating forkball or trick pitch. Before 1991, he had an inconsistent record as a closer, but it's clear that Farr can do the job.

Farr's bread and butter is a good major league fastball which he complements with a curve and slider. Having three good pitches makes his 90 MPH fastball more effective than it would be in a two-pitch repertoire. Working in short relief makes his pitches more effective than they would be if hitters got three or four looks at them in a game.

Farr's outstanding control is the key factor that helps him get strikeouts in critical situations. His three-to-one strikeout/walk ratio tells the story. The fastball is just good enough that a hitter can't adjust to it if he is looking for a breaking ball. Yet the hitter can't just look for a fastball because of Farr's excellent command of the other two pitches. Farr is a resilient worker who can appear three consecutive days when needed. However, he doesn't get stale with four or five days off.

HOLDING RUNNERS AND FIELDING:

Farr helps himself with alert play around the mound. He watches runners carefully and usually throws over at least once in every steal situation. The opposition got away with only two steals in 1991. As a fielder, Farr covers his position well. He has good range, sure hands, and an accurate throwing arm.

OVERALL:

The Yankees were oddly reluctant to nominate Farr as their top reliever before the start of the 1991 season. Instead they held open the possibility that other candidates might share that role or even take it away from him. Farr clearly won the job on the basis of merit, and his role for 1992 is definitely not in question.

STEVE FARR

Position: RP
Bats: R **Throws:** R
Ht: 5'11" **Wt:** 200

Opening Day Age: 35
Born: 12/12/56 in Cheverly, MD
ML Seasons: 8

Overall Statistics

	W	L	ERA	G	GS	Sv	IP	H	R	BB	SO	HR
1991	5	5	2.19	60	0	23	70.0	57	19	20	60	4
Career	42	40	3.22	380	28	73	697.0	632	273	269	572	55

How Often He Throws Strikes

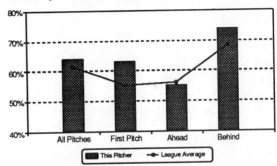

1991 Situational Stats

	W	L	ERA	Sv	IP		AB	H	HR	RBI	AVG
Home	3	3	2.56	12	38.2	LHB	116	28	2	10	.241
Road	2	2	1.72	11	31.1	RHB	144	29	2	15	.201
Day	2	1	0.87	6	20.2	Sc Pos	64	12	2	20	.188
Night	3	4	2.74	17	49.1	Clutch	171	37	3	19	.216

1991 Rankings (American League)

→ 5th lowest save percentage (79.3%)

→ 7th lowest ERA in relief (2.19)

→ 9th in blown saves (6)

→ 10th in saves (23), games finished (48) and save opporunties (29)

→ Led the Yankees in save, games finished, save opportunities, save percentage, blown saves, lowest batting average allowed vs. left-handed batters (.241), lowest percentage of inherited runners scored (25.8%), relief ERA and lowest batting average allowed in relief (.219)

PITCHING:

Overshadowed by Dave Righetti for three years, Lee Guetterman had a chance to emerge with more closer duty in 1991. Guetterman couldn't seize the opportunity, mainly because he couldn't do the job against right-handed hitters. By mid-season, it was obvious that the Yankees were looking to Steve Farr whenever the game was on the line. Guetterman returned to his familiar middle relief role and, as usual, handled it reasonably well.

A big man at 6-8, Guetterman has a big repertoire. He is basically a sinker ball pitcher, but he also throws a curve, slider and change-up. He can also straighten out his fastball when he wants to give a different look. With all those pitches, you might wonder why Guetterman isn't a starter. The answer is simple: he lacks stamina. Guetterman is rarely seen on the mound after about 40 pitches. Eight hitters got to face him after 45 pitches in 1991; Guetterman retired only two of them.

Guetterman understands that with his lack of overpowering stuff, he can't waste his energy by nibbling and falling behind in the count. So he simply comes in and throws strikes. Although Guetterman has been generally successful with this approach, he had obvious trouble with right-handed hitters in 1991 (.305 batting average). His stats probably would have been much better if the Yanks had saved him to work against lefties, but last year 71% of the hitters he faced were right-handed.

HOLDING RUNNERS AND FIELDING:

Over the years, Guetterman has improved his move to first and ability to hold runners. Few runners will attempt to steal on him. Last year, he gave up only four steals in seven attempts. Guetterman is a fine fielder, as you would expect from a former first baseman.

OVERALL:

Going into 1992, no one was talking about Guetterman as a co-closer any more, but he remains a useful reliever. The best use for Guetterman now is set-up work against lefty hitters.

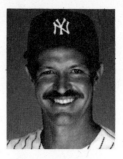

LEE GUETTERMAN

Position: RP
Bats: L **Throws:** L
Ht: 6' 8" **Wt:** 235

Opening Day Age: 33
Born: 11/22/58 in Chattanooga, TN
ML Seasons: 7

Overall Statistics

	W	L	ERA	G	GS	Sv	IP	H	R	BB	SO	HR
1991	3	4	3.68	64	0	6	88.0	91	42	25	35	6
Career	31	26	4.03	287	23	21	518.1	552	260	158	231	40

How Often He Throws Strikes

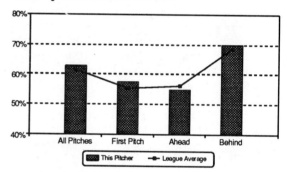

1991 Situational Stats

	W	L	ERA	Sv	IP		AB	H	HR	RBI	AVG
Home	2	1	4.18	4	51.2	LHB	97	17	2	8	.175
Road	1	3	2.97	2	36.1	RHB	243	74	4	31	.305
Day	2	1	3.71	2	26.2	Sc Pos	95	22	3	34	.232
Night	1	3	3.67	4	61.1	Clutch	120	35	4	16	.292

1991 Rankings (American League)

→ 1st in least strikeouts per 9 innings in relief (3.6)

PITCHING:

John Habyan was the Orioles' third-round draft pick back in 1982, but for many years he was considered a major disappointment. The Orioles gave up on Habyan as a starter after repeated trials, and finally swapped him to the Yankees in a 1989 minor league deal. While at AAA Columbus, Habyan was shifted to the bullpen, and that move has turned his career around. Working out of the Yankee bullpen last year, Habyan was one of the most consistent performers on the Yankee staff. He gave up more than three hits just twice in 66 appearances and he walked more than one hitter only once.

Habyan has a cool disposition, well suited to coming into games in pressure situations. He's not overpowering. His main pitch is the slider and he also throws a sinking fastball, pitching to spots and keeping the ball low. He's a very efficient worker, averaging the fewest pitches per inning (13.2) of anyone on a team of control pitchers.

Habyan was a starter as recently as 1990. Although the Yankees now prefer to keep his appearances short, he has the stamina to work four innings or more when required. Habyan likes working as a short reliever, believing that the frequent appearances help to keep him sharp.

HOLDING RUNNERS AND FIELDING:

Habyan watches baserunners carefully. Although he doesn't have a great move to first base, his compact, quick delivery and constant attention make him difficult to steal on. Habyan is also an above-average fielder. He moves off the mound quickly, fields with sure hands, and rarely makes a mistake in judgement.

OVERALL:

After finishing his first successful major league season in 1991, Habyan said, "There were no highlights. Just being healthy, being consistent. I enjoyed the whole year." Habyan isn't likely to become an ace reliever, because he isn't overpowering and isn't especially effective against lefty hitters, but at 28 he has a bright future as a middle-inning, situational reliever.

JOHN HABYAN

Position: RP
Bats: R **Throws:** R
Ht: 6' 2" **Wt:** 195

Opening Day Age: 28
Born: 1/29/64 in Bayshore, NY
ML Seasons: 6

Overall Statistics

	W	L	ERA	G	GS	Sv	IP	H	R	BB	SO	HR
1991	4	2	2.30	66	0	2	90.0	73	28	20	70	2
Career	13	12	3.72	114	18	3	258.2	242	125	84	158	27

How Often He Throws Strikes

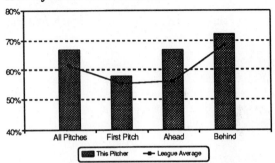

1991 Situational Stats

	W	L	ERA	Sv	IP		AB	H	HR	RBI	AVG
Home	3	0	1.33	2	47.1	LHB	114	31	0	16	.272
Road	1	2	3.38	0	42.2	RHB	210	42	2	19	.200
Day	2	1	3.26	1	19.1	Sc Pos	90	23	1	30	.256
Night	2	1	2.04	1	70.2	Clutch	148	37	1	15	.250

1991 Rankings (American League)

- ➡ 2nd in holds (20)
- ➡ 6th least baserunners allowed per 9 innings in relief (9.5)
- ➡ 9th in relief ERA (2.30)
- ➡ Led the Yankees in holds and least baserunners allower per 9 innings in relief

HITTING:

Mel Hall is an aggressive, pull hitter with good power to right field. He loves fastballs. Over the years, Hall hasn't paid much attention to the strike zone or the pitch count. Last year, however, he suddenly became a patient hitter. His strike-out/walk ratio made an astounding drop from 7.7 in 1990 to 1.5 in 1991, the kind of improvement rarely seen except in very young minor leaguers. Another dramatic change was Hall's great success against southpaws, who had previously held him to a career average of just .156.

Always the optimist, Hall found nothing surprising as he hit over .300 for most of the season; he talked about hitting .325. He attributes all his success to increased playing time and nothing more. Hall hates sitting on the bench and has often expressed his feelings.

BASERUNNING:

Hall is noted for his effort and enthusiasm on the base paths. He has good natural speed but is often too aggressive and has never shown much knowledge of situations. The Yankees rarely let him try to steal.

FIELDING:

Although he makes many spectacular plays and keeps his error count low, Hall is undependable in the field. Too often he gets a poor jump, and he doesn't pay enough attention to situations and cutoffs. His arm is well below average.

OVERALL:

Hall astounded his friends and critics alike by coming back strong from a weak 1990 season and producing his career year at age 30. But his new-found ability to hit lefties puts the Yankees in an awkward situation. With Bernie Williams and Roberto Kelly playing every day, and right-handed hitters Hensley Meulens and Jesse Barfield both highly credible candidates for the third outfield job, there is a natural platoon role for Hall in 1992, but no full-time job. Hall has long been unhappy and unproductive as a part-timer. Something will have to change: either Hall's attitude or the Yankee roster.

MEL HALL

Position: RF/LF/DH
Bats: L **Throws:** L
Ht: 6' 1" **Wt:** 218

Opening Day Age: 31
Born: 9/16/60 in Lyons, NY
ML Seasons: 11

Overall Statistics

	G	AB	R	H	D	T	HR	RBI	SB	BB	SO	AVG
1991	141	492	67	140	23	2	19	80	0	26	40	.285
Career	1099	3629	498	1005	193	22	119	534	27	237	518	.277

Where He Hits the Ball

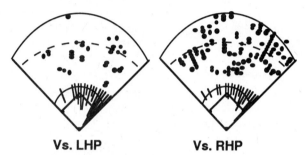

Vs. LHP   **Vs. RHP**

1991 Situational Stats

	AB	H	HR	RBI	AVG		AB	H	HR	RBI	AVG
Home	245	67	13	48	.273	LHP	162	50	5	27	.309
Road	247	73	6	32	.296	RHP	330	90	14	53	.273
Day	174	51	7	33	.293	Sc Pos	144	36	5	59	.250
Night	318	89	12	47	.280	Clutch	78	17	5	15	.218

1991 Rankings (American League)

- ➡ 7th least pitches seen per plate appearance (3.18)
- ➡ 9th least GDPs per GDP situation (5.4%)
- ➡ 10th lowest percentage of pitches taken (46.4%)
- ➡ Led the Yankees in RBIs (80), slugging percentage (.455) and runs scored per time reached base (39.6%)

PITCHING:

Steve Howe is back. After recording only four saves in seven years (1984-1990) and spending more time on the suspended list than on a major league roster, Howe emerged as a key pitcher in the Yankee bullpen in 1991. Through numerous failed comeback attempts at places like San Jose, Tabasco and Oklahoma City, he kept his 93-MPH fastball. At AAA Columbus in 1991, Howe worked 18 innings without yielding a single earned run and reappeared in the majors on May 11. Before he fell on a slippery infield and hyperextended his elbow on August 10, Howe put up numbers that compare to his best season (1983) in every category but saves.

Howe has a basic repertoire featuring the sharp fastball. On a good day he doesn't need another pitch, but he also possesses a hard-biting slider, and throws an occasional straight change. With that assortment, Howe is especially tough on left-handed hitters (.128 batting average). He handles the righties adequately too, using more sliders. The low, hard slider, breaking down and in to right-handed hitters, is remarkably reminiscent of Dave Righetti's toughest pitch.

HOLDING RUNNERS AND FIELDING:

Howe has a fine pickoff move and pays careful attention to baserunners. With a quick delivery and the good fastball, he doesn't give runners much time to do anything on the bases. There was only one attempted stolen base against him in 1991. He is above average in fielding range and situational knowledge.

OVERALL:

Howe arrived at 1991 spring training with a very good fastball and a very bad reputation. He had only a few supporters who believed that he could rise above the substance-abuse problems that had plagued him through the 1980s; he had even fewer who believed he could regain his past form at age 33. In this context, Howe's 1991 performance was one of the great surprises of the season. With his stuff as good as ever, he won't surprise anyone if he continues to pitch well this year.

STEVE HOWE

Position: RP
Bats: L **Throws:** L
Ht: 6' 1" **Wt:** 180

Opening Day Age: 34
Born: 3/10/58 in Pontiac, MI
ML Seasons: 7

Overall Statistics

	W	L	ERA	G	GS	Sv	IP	H	R	BB	SO	HR
1991	3	1	1.68	37	0	3	48.1	39	12	7	34	1
Career	32	32	2.59	305	0	63	427.2	406	152	96	246	14

How Often He Throws Strikes

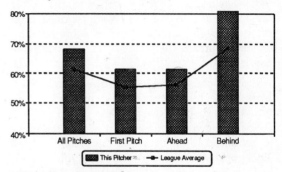

1991 Situational Stats

	W	L	ERA	Sv	IP		AB	H	HR	RBI	AVG
Home	2	1	2.28	0	23.2	LHB	47	6	0	2	.128
Road	1	0	1.09	3	24.2	RHB	129	33	1	9	.256
Day	1	0	1.65	0	16.1	Sc Pos	41	10	1	11	.244
Night	2	1	1.69	3	32.0	Clutch	70	20	0	3	.286

1991 Rankings (American League)

➡ 5th most GDPs induced per GDP situation (21.2%)

PITCHING:

Jeff Johnson was part of the Yankees "kiddie corps" last year, a group which included Dave Eiland, Scott Kamieniecki, Pat Kelly, Hensley Meulens, Wade Taylor and Bernie Williams. All the youngsters struggled in their on-the-job training, and no one struggled more than Johnson, who went 6-11 with a 5.88 ERA. Johnson looked excellent during a seven-game stretch from June 19 to July 24, when he went 4-1 with a 1.88 ERA. After that, the league's hitters made some adjustments, and Johnson wasn't able to overcome them.

Johnson is a very direct pitcher. His basic repertoire is a 90-MPH fastball and a slider, but he has variations on the two main pitches. Mark Connor taught him how to throw a sinker by taking a little off the fastball, and he also has a big-bending slider that breaks sharply down and in to a right-handed hitter.

Although Johnson is a hard thrower who likes to work inside, his success depends mainly on control. He isn't overpowering enough to get the fastball by anyone who is looking for it, so he has to get ahead in the count. In the second half of 1991, opposition hitters often beat Johnson by looking for a fastball on the first pitch and jumping on it.

HOLDING RUNNERS AND FIELDING:

For a left-handed pitcher, Johnson is much too easy to steal on. In 1991 he gave up 18 stolen bases in 22 attempts. Jeff needs both increased attention to runners and work on a sharper pickoff move. His defensive reactions are on the slow side and he is no better than average in the field at this point in his career.

OVERALL:

At 25, Johnson is going through that long and difficult period when young pitchers learn how to be consistent. The problem for him is learning to throw his breaking pitches for strikes. With more experience and increased confidence he can be a winner in the major leagues, but he isn't there yet.

JEFF JOHNSON

Position: SP
Bats: R **Throws:** L
Ht: 6' 3" **Wt:** 200

Opening Day Age: 25
Born: 8/4/66 in Durham, NC
ML Seasons: 1

Overall Statistics

	W	L	ERA	G	GS	Sv	IP	H	R	BB	SO	HR
1991	6	11	5.88	23	23	0	127.0	156	89	33	62	15
Career	6	11	5.88	23	23	0	127.0	156	89	33	62	15

How Often He Throws Strikes

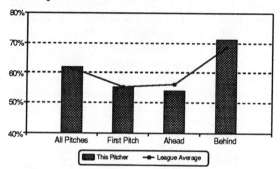

This Pitcher — League Average

1991 Situational Stats

	W	L	ERA	Sv	IP		AB	H	HR	RBI	AVG
Home	2	6	5.57	0	64.2	LHB	52	12	1	7	.231
Road	4	5	6.35	0	62.1	RHB	460	144	14	70	.313
Day	1	4	7.97	0	35.0	Sc Pos	128	42	3	58	.328
Night	5	7	5.18	0	92.0	Clutch	24	6	2	3	.250

1991 Rankings (American League)

➡ 2nd lowest fielding percentage for a pitcher (.906)

➡ 3rd highest batting average allowed vs. right-handed pitchers (.313)

➡ 4th lowest winning percentage (.353)

➡ 5th highest batting average allowed with runners in scoring position (.328)

PITCHING:

Righthander Scott Kamieniecki first appeared for the Yankees last June 18 and promptly reeled off seven consecutive quality starts, going 4-2 with an ERA of 2.68. In his next two starts, Kamieniecki gave up 10 earned runs in 8.1 innings and then went on the DL for the remainder of the season with a strained back.

Kamieniecki is basically a power pitcher. He throws in the 90s, but he also pitches to locations and changes speeds effectively. He has two breaking pitches, a curve and a slider, and also throws a straight change. The Yankees used Kamieniecki carefully in 1991. He pitched into the eighth inning only once and never threw more than 111 pitches in any game. Although he normally worked within limits of 100 pitches or seven innings, he never showed much fatigue. He loses some sharpness off his control after about 80 pitches, but of the 24 batters who faced him after the seventh inning, only four got hits last year.

Kamieniecki was a mature rookie at age 27 in 1991. He showed experience by using his entire repertoire and pitching to both sides of the plate. The Yankees were especially pleased with Kamieniecki's consistency in finishing at least six innings in every one of his first seven outings. Ex-manager Stump Merrill: "He's a good competitor. You know when he goes out there, he's going to carry you to the seventh inning and not beat up your bullpen."

HOLDING RUNNERS AND FIELDING:

A shortstop in high school, Kamieniecki is a sure-handed fielder who covers his position well and knows what to do with the ball. He is adequate at holding runners (four steals in six attempts in 1991) but could improve this part of his game.

OVERALL:

Kamieniecki was off to a promising start last year before injuries put him on the shelf. The Yankees would love to have this healthy young starter back again, and plan to have him in the 1992 rotation if he can recover physically.

SCOTT KAMIENIECKI

Position: SP
Bats: R **Throws:** R
Ht: 6' 0" **Wt:** 195

Opening Day Age: 27
Born: 4/19/64 in Mt. Clemens, MI
ML Seasons: 1

Overall Statistics

	W	L	ERA	G	GS	Sv	IP	H	R	BB	SO	HR
1991	4	4	3.90	9	9	0	55.1	54	24	22	34	8
Career	4	4	3.90	9	9	0	55.1	54	24	22	34	8

How Often He Throws Strikes

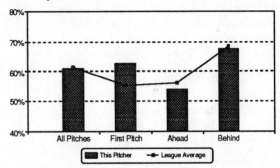

1991 Situational Stats

	W	L	ERA	Sv	IP		AB	H	HR	RBI	AVG
Home	2	2	3.76	0	26.1	LHB	116	31	5	13	.267
Road	2	2	4.03	0	29.0	RHB	95	23	3	10	.242
Day	1	1	4.97	0	12.2	Sc Pos	50	9	1	13	.180
Night	3	3	3.59	0	42.2	Clutch	10	2	1	1	.200

1991 Rankings (American League)

→ Did not rank near the top or bottom in any category

HITTING:

Pat Kelly was hitting .336 at AAA Columbus when the Yankees brought him up in May. He had been a .283 career hitter in the lower minors, but isn't yet ready to hit .280 in the majors. Kelly struggled in his 96-game debut last year, batting only .242 while showing an impatient bat.

Kelly has a little power and excellent speed, which helps him beat out some infield hits. He did not show a lot of bat speed last year, often going to the opposite field, and he needs to improve his knowledge of the strike zone. A line-drive spray hitter, he'll have to walk more to become a positive influence in the batting order.

When he first came up, Kelly was obviously overmatched by major league pitching. He made some progress at learning the pitchers and becoming more selective, but in clutch situations, pitchers handled Kelly with relative ease.

BASERUNNING:

Speed is Kelly's greatest offensive asset. He averaged 29 steals per year in three minor league seasons and appears capable of maintaining that pace in the majors. Kelly is good at reading pitchers and situations. He gets a good lead and a good jump, is alert to opportunities, and rarely makes a mistake. His 92% stolen base success rate (12/13) is rarely seen in a rookie.

FIELDING:

The Yankees brought up Kelly to play second base, but quickly moved him to third. He was obviously unfamiliar with the position and made numerous rookie mistakes. His athletic ability is obvious, but it's too early to rate him as a third baseman.

OVERALL:

Most organizations wouldn't have played Kelly in the major leagues in 1991 and certainly not at a new position. He's still young at 24 and should have a good career ahead of him. But the Yankees' high-priced extension of Steve Sax for four years and their stated desire for power from the third base position both indicate confusion about what to do with Kelly.

PAT KELLY

Position: 3B/2B
Bats: R **Throws:** R
Ht: 6' 0" **Wt:** 180

Opening Day Age: 24
Born: 10/14/67 in Philadelphia, PA
ML Seasons: 1

Overall Statistics

	G	AB	R	H	D	T	HR	RBI	SB	BB	SO	AVG
1991	96	298	35	72	12	4	3	23	12	15	52	.242
Career	96	298	35	72	12	4	3	23	12	15	52	.242

Where He Hits the Ball

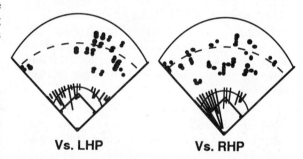

Vs. LHP   Vs. RHP

1991 Situational Stats

	AB	H	HR	RBI	AVG		AB	H	HR	RBI	AVG
Home	150	38	3	12	.253	LHP	99	26	1	7	.263
Road	148	34	0	11	.230	RHP	199	46	2	16	.231
Day	95	20	2	8	.211	Sc Pos	64	12	0	17	.188
Night	203	52	1	15	.256	Clutch	42	11	1	4	.262

1991 Rankings (American League)

→ 3rd most errors at third base (16)

→ Led the Yankees in triples (4), hit by pitch (5) and bunts in play (15)

→ Led AL third basemen in triples and steals of third (3)

HITTING:

At 27, Roberto Kelly is quietly putting together an excellent career. Despite missing more than five weeks with a wrist injury in 1991, Kelly joined Jose Canseco and Joe Carter as the only 20 homer/20 steal players in the American League. Kelly's batting averages have declined since he hit .302 in 1989, but the important numbers, his homer and RBI totals, have been getting better.

Kelly is a classic fastball hitter with a very quick bat. The only safe place to throw him a fastball is up and in or way off the plate. He will swing at pitches out of the strike zone whenever he feels he can drive the ball. Within his own definition of the strike zone, he is showing better patience and had his career high in walks last year (45).

With Don Mattingly past his prime, Kelly has been appearing more as the third or fourth hitter in the Yankee order. With more patience he could be a good leadoff hitter, but his increased power output makes him well suited to the heart of the order.

BASERUNNING:

Kelly's speed gave him an average of 36 stolen bases per year over the last three seasons. He is still learning pitchers and situations and can improve further. In clutch situations Kelly is always ready to be aggressive and take an extra base.

FIELDING:

The Yankees installed Bernie Williams in center field when Kelly was injured. A fine center fielder himself, with great range and a decent arm, Kelly bristled somewhat when he found himself in left field after coming off the DL. He adjusted quickly, however, and played some of the best left field seen in Yankee Stadium since Rickey Henderson lost his enthusiasm.

OVERALL:

The Scouting Report has been calling Kelly a top star since 1989. The New York fans, media and front office are finally beginning to catch on. Whenever another organization talks trade with the Yankees now, the one person they want from the Yanks is Roberto Kelly.

ROBERTO KELLY

Position: CF/LF
Bats: R **Throws:** R
Ht: 6' 2" **Wt:** 192

Opening Day Age: 27
Born: 10/1/64 in
Panama City, Panama
ML Seasons: 5

Overall Statistics

	G	AB	R	H	D	T	HR	RBI	SB	BB	SO	AVG
1991	126	486	68	130	22	2	20	69	32	45	77	.267
Career	486	1697	239	479	79	10	46	192	123	127	344	.282

Where He Hits the Ball

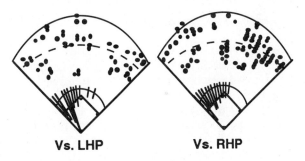

Vs. LHP   **Vs. RHP**

1991 Situational Stats

	AB	H	HR	RBI	AVG		AB	H	HR	RBI	AVG
Home	232	72	11	30	.310	LHP	159	47	9	26	.296
Road	254	58	9	39	.228	RHP	327	83	11	43	.254
Day	141	40	5	21	.284	Sc Pos	117	35	6	52	.299
Night	345	90	15	48	.261	Clutch	81	22	6	15	.272

1991 Rankings (American League)

→ 2nd lowest leadoff on-base average (.304)

→ 8th in stolen bases (32)

→ 9th in stolen base percentage (78.0%), lowest batting average on the road (.228) and steals of third (4)

→ Led the Yankees in stolen bases, hit by pitch (5), stolen base percentage and batting average at home (.310)

PITCHING:

Tim Leary developed a forkball in the Mexican winter league before the 1988 season and enjoyed his only winning season that year. Except for that one campaign he is a career 41-74 pitcher with a horrendous .357 winning percentage. Leary has had his share of bad luck, but he has also thrown more than his share of bad pitches.

It is extremely difficult to find anything positive in Leary's 1991 performance. Once regarded as the staff ace, he couldn't hold his spot in the starting rotation in 1991 and just barely stayed on the major league roster. The Yankees wanted him to work a few games at AAA Columbus to search for his past form, but Leary resisted that idea and instead became a seldom-used reliever.

Leary has a large repertoire, but at this point none of his pitches are outstanding. In addition to the forkball, he has a fastball, curve and slider. Leary has lost the ability to throw his fastball by anyone, and now depends on good control to be effective. In 1991 he obviously didn't have that control. After he posted a 6.30 ERA as a starter through July 5, most observers figured that Leary couldn't do any worse working out of the bullpen; they were wrong. Leary had a 7.78 ERA in relief and often looked like a batting practice pitcher.

HOLDING RUNNERS AND FIELDING:

Leary has never been good at holding runners. Because he wasn't getting batters out, fewer runners took chances against him in 1991; even so, 10 of 15 were successful. One of Leary's few remaining strengths is that he is a good fielder who covers plenty of ground.

OVERALL:

Leary at this point projects as a number ten or eleven pitcher, even on a weak staff like the Yankees'. By refusing to work out his problems in the minor leagues, he raised doubts about his attitude as well. He will have to turn things around in a hurry if he wants to stay in the majors.

TIM LEARY

Position: SP/RP
Bats: R **Throws:** R
Ht: 6' 3" **Wt:** 212

Opening Day Age: 33
Born: 12/23/58 in Santa Monica, CA
ML Seasons: 10

Overall Statistics

	W	L	ERA	G	GS	Sv	IP	H	R	BB	SO	HR
1991	4	10	6.49	28	18	0	120.2	150	89	57	83	20
Career	58	85	4.07	227	171	1	1160.0	1211	580	379	765	110

How Often He Throws Strikes

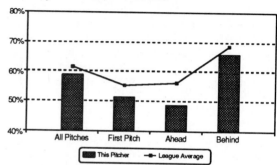

1991 Situational Stats

	W	L	ERA	Sv	IP		AB	H	HR	RBI	AVG
Home	1	4	5.75	0	56.1	LHB	267	81	9	38	.303
Road	3	6	7.13	0	64.1	RHB	214	69	11	37	.322
Day	1	2	11.45	0	30.2	Sc Pos	118	40	6	57	.339
Night	3	8	4.80	0	90.0	Clutch	29	7	1	4	.241

1991 Rankings (American League)

→ 2nd highest batting average allowed with runners in scoring position (.339)

→ 9th in wild pitches (10)

→ Led the Yankees in wild pitches

HITTING:

After bursting into the major leagues in 1990 by hitting 11 home runs faster than any rookie in history, Kevin Maas found that pitchers were making some adjustments. He hasn't been the same since. Maas belted 23 homers in his first full season last year, but after a strong start -- a .276 average through May 31 -- he hit only .176 over the next three months.

Maas can hit any fastball when he knows it's coming. Pitchers simply won't give in to him now, no matter what the count. Maas still hits for good power, and he walks enough to make up for his low batting average. Though his patience helps him get ahead on numerous counts, he presses too much and doesn't take advantage. That tendency to press also showed up with runners in scoring position, where Maas hit only .179. Maas needs to learn when to look for the breaking ball and how to hit it when he knows it's coming.

BASERUNNING:

Maas is still recovering from a knee injury that slowed him down considerably in 1989. In the minors he stole as many as 14 bases in one year. In 1991 he started to show that speed again; he was caught only once in six attempted steals. Maas has a mature knowledge of situations and rarely hurts his team on the base paths.

FIELDING:

Maas is a competent first baseman, but he got only 35 starts at first with Don Mattingly healthy during 1991. Possibly due to lack of practice, he made six errors in that limited time on the field. For defensive purposes, Maas must be regarded as just a backup.

OVERALL:

Maas is still only 27 and has a great deal of untapped potential. If he can make some adjustments and hit curveballs with authority, he could become a great power hitter. On the downside, Maas is in a crowded situation with good lefty hitters like Mel Hall looking for playing time and he might get pushed aside before he has time to develop.

KEVIN MAAS

Position: DH/1B
Bats: L **Throws:** L
Ht: 6' 3" **Wt:** 206

Opening Day Age: 27
Born: 1/20/65 in Castro Valley, CA
ML Seasons: 2

Overall Statistics

	G	AB	R	H	D	T	HR	RBI	SB	BB	SO	AVG
1991	148	500	69	110	14	1	23	63	5	83	128	.220
Career	227	754	111	174	23	1	44	104	6	126	204	.231

Where He Hits the Ball

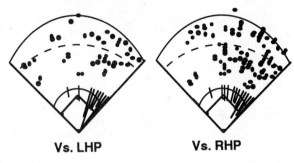

Vs. LHP   Vs. RHP

1991 Situational Stats

	AB	H	HR	RBI	AVG		AB	H	HR	RBI	AVG
Home	236	42	8	25	.178	LHP	181	40	9	31	.221
Road	264	68	15	38	.258	RHP	319	70	14	32	.219
Day	149	39	5	24	.262	Sc Pos	123	22	4	40	.179
Night	351	71	18	39	.202	Clutch	85	23	6	18	.271

1991 Rankings (American League)

→ 1st lowest batting average at home (.178)

→ 2nd lowest groundball/flyball ratio (.60)

→ 3rd lowest batting average (.220) and least GDPs per GDP situation (3.4%)

→ 6th lowest batting average with runners in scoring position (.179)

→ 7th most pitches seen per plate appearance (4.13)

→ Led the Yankees in walks (83), strikeouts (128), HR frequency (21.7 ABs per HR), most pitches seen per plate appearance, least GDPs per GDP situation and highest percentage of pitches taken (59.7%)

HITTING:

The big question for Don Mattingly in 1991 was whether he could overcome a sore back that ruined his 1990 campaign. Could Mattingly regain the power stroke that drove in 684 runs in six seasons? The answer was: probably not. At 30, a prime age when most hitters are blasting more long balls, Mattingly has become more of a singles hitter. In 1991, 26% of his hits went for extra bases, up from 21% in the disastrous 1990 season, but still far below the 41%, 36% and 38% that he showed in his best years, 1985-1987.

Mattingly was among the first to admit that he is no longer an ideal number-three hitter. He still has a great eye and fast hands. He is surely among the smartest hitters of all time. However, Mattingly can no longer be considered a slugger. Nonetheless, he is quickly adapting to get the most from his superb bat-handling abilities.

BASERUNNING:

Mattingly steals one or two bases every year, just to give the opposition one more problem to worry about. He is intensely aware of every situation, takes every possible advantage, and knows more about sliding than many recognized speedsters do. Even as a slow runner he is a baserunning asset.

FIELDING:

A perennial Gold Glove winner, Mattingly masters first base by knowing pitchers' intentions and opposition hitters' tendencies. He positions himself perfectly. Mattingly's soft hands often take away hits and save throwing errors. His smart play makes him appear to have range and quickness beyond his true abilities.

OVERALL:

While no longer the great slugger of a few years ago, Mattingly remains a dangerous hitter, a great fielder, and a powerful presence on the field. One of the toughest outs in baseball, he is a gritty competitor who can bear down in pressure situations, evidenced by his .292 average with runners in scoring position during 1991. Mattingly is a natural, quiet leader on a team that needs leadership.

DON MATTINGLY

Position: 1B/DH
Bats: L **Throws:** L
Ht: 6' 0" **Wt:** 193

Opening Day Age: 30
Born: 4/20/61 in Evansville, IN
ML Seasons: 10

Overall Statistics

	G	AB	R	H	D	T	HR	RBI	SB	BB	SO	AVG
1991	152	587	64	169	35	0	9	68	2	46	42	.288
Career	1269	5003	719	1570	323	15	178	827	11	388	300	.314

Where He Hits the Ball

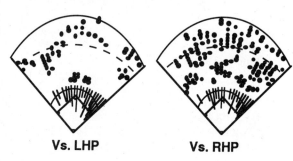

Vs. LHP   Vs. RHP

1991 Situational Stats

	AB	H	HR	RBI	AVG		AB	H	HR	RBI	AVG
Home	266	81	7	40	.305	LHP	227	60	5	29	.264
Road	321	88	2	28	.274	RHP	360	109	4	39	.303
Day	168	46	1	19	.274	Sc Pos	137	40	2	57	.292
Night	419	123	8	49	.294	Clutch	89	27	4	15	.303

1991 Rankings (American League)

➡ 2nd lowest batting average with the bases loaded (.000) and highest percentage of swings put into play (60.7%)

➡ 3rd in sacrifice flies (9)

➡ 4th least runs scored per time reached base (29.2%) and lowest percentage of swings that missed (8.4%)

➡ Led the Yankees in sacrifice flies, intentional walks (11), GDPs (21), batting average in the clutch (.303), batting average vs. right-handed pitchers (.303), slugging percentage vs. right-handed pitchers (.400), on-base average vs. right-handed pitchers (.350), lowest percentage of swings that missed and highest percentage of swings put into play

HITTING:

Hensley Meulens is a young and developing power hitter who has had considerable success at the minor league level. As a rookie last year, Meulens was in and out of the lineup all season, though in truth he didn't do a lot to merit regular duty. Meulens' .222 average and six homers were well below expectations.

Meulens can drive any pitcher's fastball, but he is over-eager. He strikes out too much and is easy prey for crafty pitchers who can change speeds and throw breaking balls for strikes. Not a true pull hitter, Meulens goes to left field only with inside pitches. When he connects on mistakes out over the plate, he is equally likely to hit a home run to right-center or left-center.

Meulens uses an open stance, off the plate, and hasn't yet learned to cover outside pitches. The needed improvement is easy to state but difficult to put into practice: crowd the plate and cover the whole strike zone.

BASERUNNING:

Meulens is a smart, aggressive runner with fair speed, and he once stole 14 bases in the minors. The Yankees haven't called on him to steal very often, but he can shift into high gear in critical situations. At worst he will not hurt his team on the bases, and often he will create a run.

FIELDING:

Meulens never played outfield before 1990, even as a youngster. He moved from third base to left field and adjusted quickly two years ago; he then moved to right field when Jesse Barfield was injured in 1991. He has all the basic tools, fair range and a good arm. But he can't be rated higher than adequate given his lack of experience.

OVERALL:

The Yankees are facing a crowded outfield again in 1992, but Meulens will surely get his share of playing time. At age 24 he has valuable major league experience while many of his contemporaries are just moving from Double-A to Triple-A.

HENSLEY MEULENS

Position: LF/RF/DH
Bats: R **Throws:** R
Ht: 6' 3" **Wt:** 212

Opening Day Age: 24
Born: 6/23/67 in Curacao, Netherlands Antilles
ML Seasons: 3

Overall Statistics

	G	AB	R	H	D	T	HR	RBI	SB	BB	SO	AVG
1991	96	288	37	64	8	1	6	29	3	18	97	.222
Career	127	399	51	89	15	1	9	40	4	29	130	.223

Where He Hits the Ball

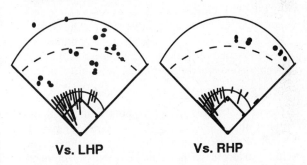

Vs. LHP   Vs. RHP

1991 Situational Stats

	AB	H	HR	RBI	AVG		AB	H	HR	RBI	AVG
Home	154	33	4	16	.214	LHP	178	42	5	19	.236
Road	134	31	2	13	.231	RHP	110	22	1	10	.200
Day	103	26	0	11	.252	Sc Pos	67	16	1	22	.239
Night	185	38	6	18	.205	Clutch	33	5	0	3	.152

1991 Rankings (American League)

→ 10th lowest batting average with 2 strikes (.132)

HITTING:

Matt Nokes has gradually developed a left-handed power stroke just right for Yankee Stadium. As a result, he's become a feared power hitter again, just as he was in 1987-88, when he totaled 48 homers for the Tigers. Nokes was one of the few Yankee players to hit more home runs at home than on the road in 1991.

Ever since he hit 32 home runs as a rookie in 1987, pitchers have feared Nokes and tried to keep the ball away from him. Last year he re-worked his swing and the result was the return of his old power. Combined with the growing confidence that comes with increased playing time, the sweet swing has made Nokes one of the team's most productive hitters.

In late 1991, Nokes showed a new capacity to stay hot when he finds his groove. He produced five two-homer games, all after July 6, equaling his previous total for four and a half years. Nokes has been a good clutch hitter throughout his career.

BASERUNNING:

Nokes makes his offensive contributions at the plate, not on the bases. He was three for five in steal attempts during 1991. You will never see him run any more than that. His main objective on the bases is avoiding mistakes.

FIELDING:

By going to instructional camp in autumn 1990, Nokes believes he improved his ability to throw out runners, to the point where the Yankees had to make him their number-one catcher. With a young pitching staff to handle in 1991 there were no complaints about Nokes as a game-caller and defensive player. He still has troubles with balls in the dirt, but he catches well enough to stay in the lineup.

OVERALL:

Still just age 28 with good health, Nokes is poised to produce some of the best seasons ever by a Yankee catcher. His 24 home runs in 1991 were the most by a Yankee backstop since Elston Howard in 1963, and the most by a left-handed hitting catcher since Yogi Berra in 1956.

MATT NOKES

Position: C
Bats: L **Throws:** R
Ht: 6' 1" **Wt:** 191

Opening Day Age: 28
Born: 10/31/63 in San Diego, CA
ML Seasons: 7

Overall Statistics

	G	AB	R	H	D	T	HR	RBI	SB	BB	SO	AVG
1991	135	456	52	122	20	0	24	77	3	25	49	.268
Career	641	1995	227	524	74	3	95	303	8	137	271	.263

Where He Hits the Ball

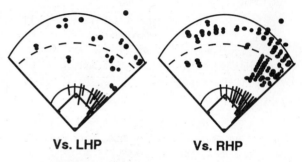

Vs. LHP   Vs. RHP

1991 Situational Stats

	AB	H	HR	RBI	AVG		AB	H	HR	RBI	AVG
Home	200	52	13	43	.260	LHP	111	29	7	23	.261
Road	256	70	11	34	.273	RHP	345	93	17	54	.270
Day	157	38	11	29	.242	Sc Pos	125	32	6	49	.256
Night	299	84	13	48	.281	Clutch	75	21	2	13	.280

1991 Rankings (American League)

→ 2nd lowest percentage of runners caught stealing as a catcher (26.7%)

→ 5th lowest percentage of pitches taken (44.6%)

→ 9th highest batting average on an 0-2 count (.320)

→ Led the Yankees in home runs (24), hit by pitch (5) and batting average on an 0-2 count

PITCHING:

Still recovering from 1990 shoulder surgery, Pascual Perez was on the disabled list for most of the 1991 season. He didn't pitch at all during spring training. Remaining in Florida to compete in the "extended spring" schedule for Tampa, he was highly effective: 35 strikeouts, just two walks, and a 2.73 ERA in 26.1 innings. The Yankees activated him on May 14, but Perez developed stiffness and went back on the DL for another 69 games from June 1 to August 16. He ultimately made 14 major league starts, working past the sixth inning just once. He was still on a limit of 100 pitches when the season ended.

Perez has outstanding control. His out pitch is a slider which he can pinpoint with devastating effectiveness. Perez also has a good major league fastball. He isn't a consistent 90-MPH thrower like he was a few years ago, but he can still reach back and bring it when the situation requires. The best aspect of Perez' fastball is that it can move in any direction; even his catcher doesn't know what to expect. To round out his repertoire, Perez throws a straight change, an occasional curve, and a crowd-pleasing lob change-up.

HOLDING RUNNERS AND FIELDING:

Perez is among the best-fielding pitchers in the American League. His animated behavior on the field is a self-caricature revealing his intense concentration. He is never fooling around in competitive situations. Pascual holds runners effectively and yielded only four steals (with four runners caught) in 1991.

OVERALL:

By year end, Perez and his catchers agreed that he had 99% of his pre-surgery velocity back and was sharp as ever with his control and movement on the fastball. Though it's risky to count on an oft-injured pitcher who will soon be 35, the Yankees need a healthy Perez to anchor their shaky rotation. The Yankees will handle him carefully this year and keep their fingers crossed.

PASCUAL PEREZ

Position: SP
Bats: R **Throws:** R
Ht: 6' 3" **Wt:** 183

Opening Day Age: 34
Born: 5/17/57 in San Cristobal, Dominican Republic
ML Seasons: 11

Overall Statistics

	W	L	ERA	G	GS	Sv	IP	H	R	BB	SO	HR
1991	2	4	3.18	14	14	0	73.2	68	26	24	41	7
Career	67	68	3.44	207	193	0	1244.0	1167	541	344	822	107

How Often He Throws Strikes

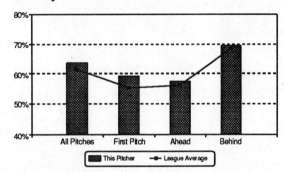

1991 Situational Stats

	W	L	ERA	Sv	IP		AB	H	HR	RBI	AVG
Home	1	3	3.53	0	43.1	LHB	140	39	5	15	.279
Road	1	1	2.67	0	30.1	RHB	132	29	2	10	.220
Day	0	0	2.65	0	17.0	Sc Pos	54	12	3	19	.222
Night	2	4	3.34	0	56.2	Clutch	6	2	0	0	.333

1991 Rankings (American League)

→ 6th most GDPs induced per GDP situation (21.2%)

SCOTT SANDERSON

Position: SP
Bats: R **Throws:** R
Ht: 6' 5" **Wt:** 200

Opening Day Age: 35
Born: 7/22/56 in
Dearborn, MI
ML Seasons: 14

PITCHING:

Scott Sanderson has three main pitches: a fastball, a slow curve, and a forkball. He also throws an occasional straight change. Ten years ago, Sanderson's fastball moved at 93 MPH, but today Sanderson himself admits that he can't throw the heater by anyone. Although not overpowering, Sanderson is a better pitcher in the 1990's than he was before. His strikeout/walk ratio of 4.5 in 1991 was the best of his career and among the highest of any major league starter.

Sanderson's success now depends on pinpoint control: "When I can hit my spots, I have a good game." Sanderson feels it is a big advantage pitching with a lead because it widens his margin of error. The Yankees now keep Sanderson on a modest pitch limit. Often he works only five or six innings. Twice in 1991 they let him throw a complete game (both were shutouts) but they never let him go over 118 pitches.

HOLDING RUNNERS AND FIELDING:

Although he doesn't have quite the high leg kick that he did in previous years, Sanderson is still one of the easier pitchers to steal a base on. He gives most of his concentration to the hitter, not to baserunners, and he takes a while to get the ball to the catcher. Sanderson is a smooth and steady fielder. He moves well and knows what to do with the ball when he gets it.

OVERALL:

Sanderson has a lot of mileage on him. He has survived back spasms, torn ligaments in the knee and thumb, and elbow and shoulder problems. Nonetheless he just put together the best back-to-back winning seasons in his 14-year major league career. Sanderson is a classic example of the experienced pitcher who has made the conversion from power to finesse. No one touted him as the Yankee ace going into 1991, but when he was selected for the All-Star team there was no doubt he was the best Yankee starter.

Overall Statistics

	W	L	ERA	G	GS	Sv	IP	H	R	BB	SO	HR
1991	16	10	3.81	34	34	0	208.0	200	95	29	130	22
Career	131	110	3.61	377	320	5	2034.1	1972	895	507	1339	211

How Often He Throws Strikes

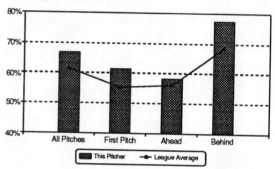

1991 Situational Stats

	W	L	ERA	Sv	IP		AB	H	HR	RBI	AVG
Home	7	6	4.66	0	92.2	LHB	437	114	15	54	.261
Road	9	4	3.12	0	115.1	RHB	358	86	7	35	.240
Day	3	5	4.00	0	72.0	Sc Pos	153	41	4	62	.268
Night	13	5	3.71	0	136.0	Clutch	32	6	0	1	.188

1991 Rankings (American League)

→ 2nd highest strikeout/walk ratio (4.5)

→ 4th lowest on-base average allowed (.279) and lowest groundball/flyball ratio (.85)

→ Led the Yankees in ERA (3.81), wins (16), games started (34), complete games (2), shutouts (2), innings (208), hits allowed (200), batter faced (837), home runs allowed (22), strikeouts (130), pitches thrown (3,171), GDPs induced (19), winning percentage (.615), strikeout/walk ratio, lowest batting average allowed (.252), lowest on-base average allowed, lowest slugging percentage allowed (.405) and lowest groundball/flyball ratio

HITTING:

Steve Sax returned to the top rank of American League hitters in 1991. To those who know him best he had never been away. Sax is simply one of the best professional hitters in the game today. He can handle just about any pitch in any location in any situation. He is a genuine terror in clutch situations as shown by his .318 average with runners in scoring position.

Sax produced a career high 10 homers in 1991. No, he isn't suddenly becoming a power hitter. He simply drives the ball well, and sometimes it goes over the fence. Sax is essentially a singles and doubles hitter who uses the whole ballpark. An outstanding contact hitter, he knows the strike zone as well as anyone.

BASERUNNING:

Sax does not have the raw speed of Rickey Henderson or Tim Raines, but he is their equal in every other aspect of the running game. He has exceeded 30 steals in each of the last six seasons, and nine times in all. Sax's success rate is consistently over 70%. He gets a good jump and knows how to slide.

FIELDING:

Because he had some well-publicized throwing problems for a couple of years, Sax got an undeserved rap as a shaky fielder. It's nonsense. In his first year in the American League, he led all second basemen in fielding and he hasn't made more than 10 errors in a season since 1988. He has both good range and excellent positioning and has been a perennial leader in double plays since he came to the Yankees.

OVERALL:

Even while Julio Franco had his career year and Roberto Alomar emerged as a budding superstar, Steve Sax remained arguably the best overall second baseman in the American League. Yankee management has shown a peculiar lack of appreciation with actions like placing Pat Kelly at second base and Sax at third for a short trial period last year, but he is undeniably All-Star material.

STEVE SAX

Position: 2B
Bats: R **Throws:** R
Ht: 6' 0" **Wt:** 183

Opening Day Age: 32
Born: 1/29/60 in Sacramento, CA
ML Seasons: 11

Overall Statistics

	G	AB	R	H	D	T	HR	RBI	SB	BB	SO	AVG
1991	158	652	85	198	38	2	10	56	31	41	38	.304
Career	1562	6230	817	1781	247	42	49	494	407	505	534	.286

Where He Hits the Ball

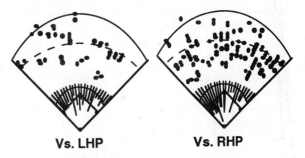

Vs. LHP   Vs. RHP

1991 Situational Stats

	AB	H	HR	RBI	AVG		AB	H	HR	RBI	AVG
Home	327	95	6	27	.291	LHP	215	74	5	20	.344
Road	325	103	4	29	.317	RHP	437	124	5	36	.284
Day	201	58	3	24	.289	Sc Pos	132	42	2	44	.318
Night	451	140	7	32	.310	Clutch	103	25	1	7	.243

1991 Rankings (American League)

→ 2nd highest fielding percentage at second base (.990)

→ 3rd in at-bats (652), singles (148) and highest batting average on a 3-2 count (.382)

→ 4th in highest percentage of swings put into play (58.2%)

→ 5th in steals of third (5)

→ Led the Yankees in batting average (.304), at-bats, runs (85), hits (198), singles, doubles (38), total bases (270), caught stealing (11), times on base (242), pitches seen (2,451), plate appearances (707), games (158), on-base average (.345), groundball/flyball ratio (2.1) and batting average with runners in scoring position (.318)

PITCHING:

Wade Taylor spent 1991 getting on-the-job training in the major leagues. Not many teams would let a rookie pitcher keep working with an ERA over 6.00 all year, but the Yankees had faith that Taylor would find eventual success. He got better at every level as he advanced through the Yankee farm system, finishing as a dominant starter at AAA Columbus.

Taylor is a basic fastball/curveball/change-up pitcher. His 89-90 MPH fastball isn't overpowering, but he can make it run down and in against a right-handed hitter or throw it straight to selected spots. Taylor must have good location on all his pitches to be successful. He needs to move the ball around in the strike zone, pitch inside to control the plate, and stay ahead in the count. It's not easy to do all those tasks simultaneously, and Taylor usually failed in one or more of them in each outing.

It is hard to find any statistical breakdowns that put Taylor in a favorable light in 1991. Home/away, grass/turf, day/night and month-by-month splits all tell a story of consistent failure. A month after arriving in the major leagues, Taylor summed up his situation simply: "I'm just feeling my way around in the dark. I pitch to my strengths and find out what the hitters can do with it." Generally, they did enough to beat him.

HOLDING RUNNERS AND FIELDING:

Taylor covers his position well as you would expect from a former collegiate shortstop. Taylor held runners fairly well during 1991, but he was giving up more stolen bases later in the season after opponents had time to study him.

OVERALL:

Taylor's adjustment to the major leagues obviously isn't complete. Judging from his fine minor league record, the Yankees figure to be patient with him. However, he will have to begin showing some consistency to stay in the rotation in 1992.

WADE TAYLOR

Position: SP
Bats: R **Throws:** R
Ht: 6' 1" **Wt:** 185

Opening Day Age: 26
Born: 10/19/65 in Mobile, AL
ML Seasons: 1

Overall Statistics

	W	L	ERA	G	GS	Sv	IP	H	R	BB	SO	HR
1991	7	12	6.27	23	22	0	116.1	144	85	53	72	13
Career	7	12	6.27	23	22	0	116.1	144	85	53	72	13

How Often He Throws Strikes

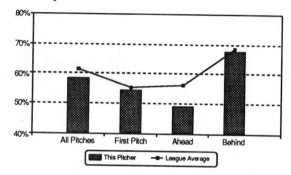

1991 Situational Stats

	W	L	ERA	Sv	IP		AB	H	HR	RBI	AVG
Home	5	6	5.34	0	62.1	LHB	206	67	6	30	.325
Road	2	6	7.33	0	54.0	RHB	253	77	7	43	.304
Day	2	4	7.97	0	35.0	Sc Pos	127	41	2	54	.323
Night	5	8	5.53	0	81.1	Clutch	2	2	1	2	.000

1991 Rankings (American League)

→ 3rd in balks (3)

→ 8th lowest winning percentage (.368)

→ 9th highest batting average allowed vs. left-handed batters (.325)

→ Led the Yankees in losses (12), hit batsmen (7), balks and pickoff throws (156)

TOP PROSPECT

BERNIE WILLIAMS

Position: CF
Bats: B **Throws:** R
Ht: 6' 2" **Wt:** 180

Opening Day Age: 23
Born: 9/13/68 in San Juan, Puerto Rico
ML Seasons: 1

HITTING:

While the Yankees were unloading minor league talent in pursuit of elusive championships in the late 1980s, the front office wisely kept Bernie Williams' name out of the negotiations. Williams finally arrived in New York last summer, and though he batted only .238, he did a lot to make the Yankees glad they held onto him.

Williams is a classic, all-around offensive threat. He can hit for average, hit for power, and can use his speed to get on base and make things happen. A switch-hitter, Williams uses the whole field and can go with any pitch. He generates more power batting left-handed, meaning he is well-suited to Yankee Stadium. In his peak years, Williams should be hitting 10 to 20 homers every season.

Williams is still getting accustomed to major league pitching. He can hit anybody's fastball, and has excellent strike zone judgement, but he has a little trouble with the sharp breaking stuff and offspeed pitches that are so common in the A.L. The league's pitchers showed Williams unusual respect in 1991, reflecting the glowing reports of minor league scouts.

BASERUNNING:

Williams showed just a little of his speed with 10 steals in half a season in 1991; he is capable of much more. As a rookie, he preferred to study pitchers and take advantage of obvious opportunities. In the future he will be a threat to steal 30 or 40 bases.

FIELDING:

The installation of Williams in center field when Roberto Kelly got injured showed the Yankees' high expectations. Leaving him in center for the rest of the season showed that he was living up to them. Williams gets a good jump and moves extremely well. His long, smooth strides give him great range, a vital attribute in the huge New York pasture.

OVERALL:

Williams has just scratched the surface of his talent in major league competition. At age 23, he has already become a fixture in the Yankee outfield.

Overall Statistics

	G	AB	R	H	D	T	HR	RBI	SB	BB	SO	AVG
1991	85	320	43	76	19	4	3	34	10	48	57	.238
Career	85	320	43	76	19	4	3	34	10	48	57	.238

Where He Hits the Ball

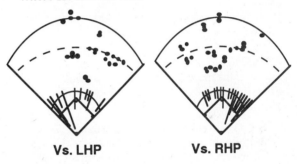

Vs. LHP **Vs. RHP**

1991 Situational Stats

	AB	H	HR	RBI	AVG		AB	H	HR	RBI	AVG
Home	159	42	1	19	.264	LHP	104	21	2	13	.202
Road	161	34	2	15	.211	RHP	216	55	1	21	.255
Day	112	31	1	19	.277	Sc Pos	67	23	0	29	.343
Night	208	45	2	15	.216	Clutch	55	12	0	8	.218

1991 Rankings (American League)

➡ 7th lowest batting average on an 0-2 count (.048)
➡ Led the Yankees in triples (4)

DAVE EILAND

Position: SP/RP
Bats: R **Throws:** R
Ht: 6' 3" **Wt:** 205

Opening Day Age: 25
Born: 7/5/66 in Dade City, FL
ML Seasons: 4

BOB GEREN

Position: C
Bats: R **Throws:** R
Ht: 6' 3" **Wt:** 228

Opening Day Age: 30
Born: 9/22/61 in San Diego, CA
ML Seasons: 4

Overall Statistics

	W	L	ERA	G	GS	Sv	IP	H	R	BB	SO	HR
1991	2	5	5.33	18	13	0	72.2	87	51	23	18	10
Career	5	9	5.16	32	27	0	150.0	177	99	45	52	23

Overall Statistics

	G	AB	R	H	D	T	HR	RBI	SB	BB	SO	AVG
1991	64	128	7	28	3	0	2	12	0	9	31	.219
Career	249	620	54	147	15	1	19	70	0	36	151	.237

PITCHING, FIELDING & HOLDING RUNNERS:

Righthander Dave Eiland has been a star at the minor league level, winning International League Pitcher of the Year honors after going 16-5 at AAA Columbus in 1990. That success has eluded Eiland at the major league level, especially in '91. Eiland was hit hard last year while going 2-5 in 18 appearances.

Eiland's main pitch is the sinker. He tries to keep the ball down and generate groundouts. He isn't overpowering and expects to give up a few hits every time he takes the mound. In 1991, too many pitches stayed up in the strike zone, and Eiland didn't have the control that is vital if he is going to be successful.

A former collegiate defensive end, Eiland fields his position well. His range and poise are commendable. Eiland watches the baserunners carefully and holds them adequately, but in 1991 he simply had too many baserunners to handle.

OVERALL:

In his fourth chance to stick on the major league roster, Eiland finally did so in 1991. He couldn't hold his spot in the starting rotation, however. To be successful, Eiland simply must show better control than he had in 1991. One positive factor is that he is still young enough (25) to improve.

HITTING, FIELDING, BASERUNNING:

Pitchers caught up with Bob Geren in 1990, and things got no better for the 30-year old receiver in 1991. After batting .288 as a rookie in 1989, Geren has produced averages of just .213 and .219 the last two seasons. One opposition catcher said that Geren never did learn how to hit a major league slider. Pitchers have had success throwing him high fastballs and low breaking balls.

Geren has decent power although he didn't show it in 1991. After totalling 17 home runs in 1989-90, he had only two a year ago. Never a very patient hitter, he struck out in nearly a quarter of his at-bats last year. As a baserunner, he is slow and simply tries to avoid mistakes.

Geren's greatest strength is defense, including pitcher-handling, game-calling, and throwing out runners. The emergence of Matt Nokes as a respected defensive presence was a major factor in Geren's loss of playing time.

OVERALL:

Geren still has one of the best throwing arms in baseball, but that isn't enough when your team has another catcher who can hit 20 home runs and handle the backstop chores as well. The gradual development of John Ramos, a good right-handed hitting catcher, could mean that Geren becomes even more obscure in 1992.

ERIC PLUNK

Position: RP/SP
Bats: R **Throws:** R
Ht: 6' 5" **Wt:** 217

Opening Day Age: 28
Born: 9/3/63 in
Wilmington, CA
ML Seasons: 6

RANDY VELARDE

Position: 3B/SS
Bats: R **Throws:** R
Ht: 6' 0" **Wt:** 190

Opening Day Age: 29
Born: 11/24/62 in
Midland, TX
ML Seasons: 5

Overall Statistics

	W	L	ERA	G	GS	Sv	IP	H	R	BB	SO	HR
1991	2	5	4.76	43	8	0	111.2	128	69	62	103	18
Career	31	29	4.11	247	41	8	582.0	512	294	372	522	62

Overall Statistics

	G	AB	R	H	D	T	HR	RBI	SB	BB	SO	AVG
1991	80	184	19	45	11	1	1	15	3	18	43	.245
Career	264	650	71	151	27	5	13	58	4	53	140	.232

PITCHING, FIELDING & HOLDING RUNNERS:

Eric Plunk developed a large repertoire in 1990 but couldn't do much with it in 1991. Plunk might have won a key relief role last year, possibly even sharing saves with Steve Farr. In his first 3.1 innings of 1991, however, he gave up nine hits seven walks, and four earned runs and never got on track.

Plunk has a 90-MPH fastball and a curve, slider, straight change and forkball. All these pitches simply deserted him early last year. He lost velocity off the fastball and couldn't control the breaking ball. As a result his ERA nearly doubled, from 2.72 in 1990 to 4.76 in 1991. Hitters simply teed off on Plunk, belting 18 homers in only 111.2 innings.

Plunk gave up an astounding 28 stolen bases in 31 attempts in 1991 after yielding only three steals in 1990. After Plunk gets his pitches back, he will need to go to work on watching baserunners again. He is not a good defensive player.

OVERALL:

With outstanding seasons from Farr and John Habyan, the Yankees moved Plunk into the starting rotation in mid August, where he was inconsistent at best. Plunk hasn't had success as a starter in past seasons and his role for 1992 is in question.

HITTING, FIELDING, BASERUNNING:

Over the last few years, Randy Velarde has proven himself to be a useful bench player, the kind that any club likes to have around. Though no star with the bat, Velarde is a good fastball hitter and not an easy out. He is basically a singles hitter who tries to make contact and use the entire field. Velarde is susceptible to breaking pitches and change-ups, and is not a dangerous hitter when the pitcher approaches him carefully.

Defensively, Velarde is a competent professional at second, short or third. He needs to be versatile because he isn't outstanding at any position and doesn't hit well enough to be a regular. Velarde has good range and positions himself well, but he is definitely error prone, both physically and mentally. On the bases, Velarde has above-average speed but only fair judgement.

OVERALL:

Velarde has been a utility player ever since he arrived in the majors. He offers a wide assortment of skills though he isn't outstanding in any aspect of the game. He's not a key player, but the Yankees will probably have a place for him in 1992.

NEW YORK YANKEES MINOR LEAGUE PROSPECTS

ORGANIZATION OVERVIEW:

The Yankees of the 1980s had to be a farm director's nightmare. In their mania for signing free agents, the Yanks sacrificed their number one draft choice every year of the decade except one, usually to get such blue-chippers as Dave Collins, Al Holland and Gary Ward. Sometimes they'd lose all three of their top picks. When the Yanks did develop a player, he'd usually be traded. Willie McGee went for Bob Sykes, Fred McGriff for Dale Murray, Doug Drabek for Rick Rhoden. No wonder their last pennant was in 1981. Now that the Yankees have hit the skids and George Steinbrenner is (they insist) out of the picture, New York is "building with youth." The Yanks, surprisingly, still have some quality prospects, but most of them were rushed to the majors in 1991. What's left on the farm are players who are mostly a few years away.

ED MARTEL

Position: P   **Opening Day Age:** 23
Bats: R **Throws:** R   **Born:** 3/2/69 in Mt.
Ht: 6' 1" **Wt:** 185   Clemens, MI

Recent Statistics

	W	L	ERA	GGS	Sv	IP	H	R	BB	SO	HR
90 A Pr William	8	13	4.08	25 25	0	143.1	134	77	65	95	8
91 AA Albany	13	6	2.81	25 24	0	163.1	129	67	55	141	8

An 11th-round pick in 1987, Martel didn't create much interest until this season when he turned in an outstanding season at Albany. Martel has an excellent fastball and the rest of his stuff is improving. With the Yankees hurting for pitching, he could be pitching for the big club this year.

ALAN MILLS

Position: P   **Opening Day Age:** 25
Bats: R **Throws:** R   **Born:** 10/18/66 in
Ht: 6' 1" **Wt:** 189   Lakeland, FL

Recent Statistics

	W	L	ERA	GGS	Sv	IP	H	R	BB	SO	HR
91 AAA Columbus	7	5	4.43	38 15	8	113.2	109	65	75	77	3
91 AL New York	1	1	4.41	6 2	0	16.1	16	9	8	11	1

Mills, a hard-throwing righty, was rushed to the majors from A ball in 1990 and pitched reasonably well for the Yanks in 36 games. His control was bad, however, and he spent 1991 at Columbus, starting, relieving, and walking people. The Yankees say they still like him as a reliever, but Mills still has a lot to prove.

JOHN RAMOS

Position: C   **Opening Day Age:** 26
Bats: R **Throws:** R   **Born:** 8/6/65 in Tampa,
Ht: 6' 0" **Wt:** 190   FL

Recent Statistics

	G	AB	R	H	D	THR	RBI	SB	BB	SO	AVG
91 AAA Columbus	104	377	52	116	18	3 10	63	1	56	54	.308
91 AL New York	10	26	4	8	1	0 0	3	0	1	3	.308
91 MLE	104	362	42	101	16	1 7	51	0	45	56	.279

Matt Nokes' big year in 1991 alleviated the Yankees' need for a regular catcher, but the backup position is open. Ramos definitely has the bat. He has good discipline, the ability to hit for average, and some power. His glove is the question mark. In 1988 Ramos committed 25 errors in 96 games -- that's 25 errors at catcher, a total which would be a lot for a shortstop in 96 games. They say Ramos' defense is "improving." It better be.

DAVE SILVESTRI

Position: SS   **Opening Day Age:** 24
Bats: R **Throws:** R   **Born:** 9/29/67 in St.
Ht: 6' 0" **Wt:** 180   Louis, MO

Recent Statistics

	G	AB	R	H	D	THR	RBI	SB	BB	SO	AVG
90 A Pr William	131	465	74	120	30	7 5	56	37	77	90	.258
90 AA Albany	2	7	0	2	0	0 0	2	0	0	1	.286
91 AA Albany	140	512	97	134	31	8 19	83	20	83	126	.262
91 MLE	140	495	80	117	28	4 15	68	14	58	134	.236

Silvestri, a member of the 1988 Olympic team, came to the Yankees from Houston in a 1990 minor league deal. The Yankees need a shortstop like Steinbrenner needs a pardon, so Silvestri's powerful year at Albany created a lot of interest. His glove apparently is adequate (decent range, too many errors thus far); now all he needs to do is hit for a better average, since the rest of his offensive game is very good.

WILLIE E. SMITH

Position: P   **Opening Day Age:** 24
Bats: R **Throws:** R   **Born:** 8/27/67 in
Ht: 6' 6" **Wt:** 240   Savannah, GA

Recent Statistics

	W	L	ERA	GGS	Sv	IP	H	R	BB	SO	HR
90 AA Albany	1	1	0.00	9 0	4	8.2	6	1	5	12	0
90 AAA Columbus	3	1	6.23	33 0	7	34.2	38	24	29	47	3
91 AA Albany	7	7	4.15	21 21	0	108.1	99	65	72	104	7

Call him Wil-LEE Smith, because in size and demeanor, Smith resembles the Cardinal reliever. He has the fastball, also, though he doesn't always know where it's going. Smith, who came to the Yanks in the Don Slaught deal (now **there's** a switch), has averaged around a strikeout per inning wherever he's pitched, whether starting or relieving. He has definite star potential, the most in this group . . . if he can get the ball over the plate.

HITTING:

Amid the turbulence that was a constant all year in the Oakland Athletics' clubhouse, Harold Baines was an oasis of tranquility. And he was one of the few A's who put together a solid start-to-finish season.

In his first full season in Oakland, Baines gave the A's the dependable left-handed bat they had lacked in the middle of their order. With dangerous hitters in front and behind him in the order, Baines saw an opportunity to return to his pull-hitting style of the early 1980s. He was able to enhance his power numbers without doing undue damage to his average.

Baines' Mel Ott-like kickout tends to tempt opposing pitchers to throw him a lot of offspeed stuff, but he showed last season that he can combat that tactic by moving his hands down and wristing the ball to left field. He is a good low-ball hitter who almost never offers at a pitch above his waist unless the A's need a fly ball.

BASERUNNING:

Baines' knee problems have made him a virtual non-entity in base-stealing situations. But he isn't completely helpless, and knows his limitations. The A's know he won't run them out of many innings.

FIELDING:

It had been thought that the A's would relegate Baines exclusively to designated hitter duties, but a shortage of outfielders early in the season prompted A's manager Tony La Russa to use Baines occasionally in the outfield. Although his range is obviously limited, he still has a good arm and seemed to react well to the ball.

OVERALL:

As usual, Harold Baines let his work on the field do his talking for him. He went about his business quietly and efficiently, and looked more spry than he had in recent seasons. The A's would appear set at the designated hitter post for the next few years, and it's possible they might even find more outfield openings for Baines in 1992.

HAROLD BAINES

Position: DH
Bats: L **Throws:** L
Ht: 6' 2" **Wt:** 195

Opening Day Age: 33
Born: 3/15/59 in Easton, MD
ML Seasons: 12

Overall Statistics

	G	AB	R	H	D	T	HR	RBI	SB	BB	SO	AVG
1991	141	488	76	144	25	1	20	90	0	72	67	.295
Career	1704	6266	807	1809	316	46	225	990	29	588	956	.289

Where He Hits the Ball

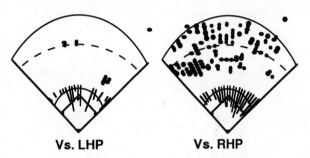

Vs. LHP   Vs. RHP

1991 Situational Stats

	AB	H	HR	RBI	AVG		AB	H	HR	RBI	AVG
Home	227	60	11	52	.264	LHP	83	25	4	18	.301
Road	261	84	9	38	.322	RHP	405	119	16	72	.294
Day	154	51	7	33	.331	Sc Pos	133	37	6	69	.278
Night	334	93	13	57	.278	Clutch	73	15	3	10	.205

1991 Rankings (American League)

→ 2nd in intentional walks (22)

→ 6th highest batting average on the road (.322)

→ 8th highest batting average on a 3-1 count (.625)

→ Led the A's in batting average (.295), intentional walks, groundball/flyball ratio (1.8), batting average vs. right-handed pitchers (.294), batting average on a 3-1 count, batting average on the road and highest percentage of swings put into play (50.0%)

→ Led designated hitters in intentional walks, groundball/flyball ratio and batting average on a 3-1 count

HITTING:

Mike Bordick originally was an undrafted free agent, and never had batted better than .270 in five minor league seasons. So the A's knew what they were getting when they made him their regular shortstop after Walt Weiss was injured last summer. Bordick didn't surprise, hitting a very weak .238.

Bordick is a back-foot hitter who will wait on the ball and then try to jab it where it is pitched, even if he has to come close to dislodging the ball from the catcher's mitt. He has almost no power, but doesn't overswing, and he seemed to react fairly well to breaking pitches. Fastballs up and in kept him pretty well handcuffed most of the time. He can and will bunt, and the A's will use him as the triggerman on the hit-and-run from time to time.

BASERUNNING:

Bordick isn't particularly fast and isn't a threat to steal, especially when Rickey Henderson is at bat -- as was the case much of the time when Bordick reached base last season. However, he is a heady, aggressive baserunner who won't hesitate to take a big turn.

FIELDING:

The A's were more than satisfied with Bordick's work at shortstop in Weiss' stead. He still has a lot to learn about playing the hitters, but he has a good first step in either direction, turns the double play without difficulty and is fearless. His arm is good but not great, and he had some problems making long throws from the hole.

OVERALL:

Bordick clearly was a stopgap player for the A's. They first tried Lance Blankenship at second and Mike Gallego at short before moving Gallego back to second and installing Bordick at short. Bordick is a smart, total-effort player who also can function at other infield positions. He's not likely to win a full-time job with the A's, but seems to be an ideal utility man.

MIKE BORDICK

Position: SS
Bats: R **Throws:** R
Ht: 5'11" **Wt:** 175

Opening Day Age: 26
Born: 7/21/65 in Marquette, MI
ML Seasons: 2

Overall Statistics

	G	AB	R	H	D	T	HR	RBI	SB	BB	SO	AVG
1991	90	235	21	56	5	1	0	21	3	14	37	.238
Career	115	249	21	57	5	1	0	21	3	15	41	.229

Where He Hits the Ball

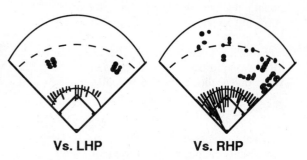

Vs. LHP   Vs. RHP

1991 Situational Stats

	AB	H	HR	RBI	AVG		AB	H	HR	RBI	AVG
Home	106	24	0	7	.226	LHP	58	13	0	6	.224
Road	129	32	0	14	.248	RHP	177	43	0	15	.243
Day	68	19	0	10	.279	Sc Pos	52	18	0	20	.346
Night	167	37	0	11	.222	Clutch	17	4	0	0	.235

1991 Rankings (American League)

→ 7th in sacrifice bunts (12)
→ Led the A's in sacrifice bunts and bunts in play (18)

JOSE CANSECO

IN HIS PRIME

Position: RF/DH
Bats: R **Throws:** R
Ht: 6' 4" **Wt:** 240

Opening Day Age: 27
Born: 7/2/64 in Havana, Cuba
ML Seasons: 7

HITTING:

Jose Canseco seemed to feel very alone in 1991. Some of his teammates ostracized him because of his proclivity for drawing attention to himself, intentionally or otherwise. Later, his remarks about the Oakland Athletics' fans earned him a lot of boos. But he was virtually alone among his big-name teammates for a more important reason: he kept putting up the big numbers.

Canseco's habit of tinkering with his stance accounted in large part for his poor start, which left him in the .220s in June. Finally, he settled on a slightly open stance with his hands moved back a bit. This stance enabled him to extend his arms on outside pitches without losing his ability to turn on the inside pitch. It also helped him become a better low-ball hitter. Canseco, however, had more trouble with offspeed pitches than in the past.

Pitchers had some success throwing Canseco hard stuff outside, then breaking balls and change-ups. Still, he is at the point where he will hit almost any mistake -- and a lot of non-mistakes -- hard.

BASERUNNING:

Canseco regained his former aggressiveness on the bases in 1991. His 26 steals were his best total since his 40/40 year of 1988, and his 81% success rate was the second best of his career. The only problem was that he ran into more than a few foolish outs.

FIELDING:

Canseco's right field arm remains one of the strongest in baseball, and his range to his left almost takes away the right-field line from opposing hitters. However, he was more erratic than usual last year, sometimes showing lapses in concentration.

OVERALL:

Canseco twice last season strongly indicated that he wanted out of Oakland because of what he considered verbal abuse by fans. Partially because of his hefty $23 million contract, very few teams would give the A's equal value in a trade. Despite all the furor, he's a once-in-a-generation talent.

Overall Statistics

	G	AB	R	H	D	T	HR	RBI	SB	BB	SO	AVG
1991	154	572	115	152	32	1	44	122	26	78	152	.266
Career	853	3216	540	867	156	8	209	647	122	370	870	.270

Where He Hits the Ball

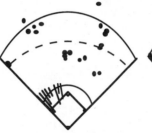

Vs. LHP **Vs. RHP**

1991 Situational Stats

	AB	H	HR	RBI	AVG		AB	H	HR	RBI	AVG
Home	267	72	16	46	.270	LHP	136	34	8	21	.250
Road	305	80	28	76	.262	RHP	436	118	36	101	.271
Day	188	56	11	42	.298	Sc Pos	154	41	14	85	.266
Night	384	96	33	80	.250	Clutch	97	23	9	28	.237

1991 Rankings (American League)

➡ 1st in home runs (44), HR frequency (13 ABs per HR), runs scored per time reached base (48.1%) and errors in right field (9)

➡ 2nd in runs (115), RBIs (122), hit by pitch (9), strikeouts (152) and slugging percentage vs. right-handed pitchers (.576)

➡ 3rd in slugging percentage (.556)

➡ Led the A's in home runs, at-bats (572), runs, total bases (318), RBIs, hit by pitch, times on base (239), strikeouts, GDPs (16), pitches seen (2,638), plate appearances (665), slugging percentage, HR frequency, stolen base percentage (81.3%) and runs scored per time reached base

PITCHING:

Like a lot of the younger pitchers in the Oakland Athletics' organization, Steve Chitren was rushed into a breach created by injuries to their veteran relief pitchers. Chitren, in only his third season of professional baseball, spent a lot of time as the A's set-up man for Dennis Eckersley, and led the staff in appearances for much of the season.

Considering his inexperience, Chitren's performance would have to be considered promising. But he had a tendency to be too confrontational for his own good. Chitren has an above-average major league fastball that he likes to ride in on right-handed hitters. The problem was that he left it over the plate too often, especially in situations where hitters were content to wait through the rest of his modest repertoire. Chitren has a sinker and a slider to go with his fastball, but they don't differ radically in speed or movement from his fastball.

To continue his improvement, Chitren needs to develop both an offspeed pitch and more riding-in movement on his fastball. He was particularly vulnerable against lefthanders because he had nothing to keep them off the plate. Some of the Walt Hriniak-influenced hitters around the league could dive into his offerings almost with impunity.

HOLDING RUNNERS, FIELDING:

Like most pitchers developed at Stanford, Chitren has a good feel for the non-pitching aspects of the game. He has a reasonably good move to first and is persistent about throwing over. He also fields his position well.

OVERALL:

Chitren pitched better than his numbers might indicate, largely because of a few games that over-inflated his ERA. If he is to function other than as a closer, he probably will have to develop a pitch that provides contrast to the stuff he already has. It's not likely the A's will tamper with him too much, though, because he's their most likely candidate to succeed Dennis Eckersley within a few years.

STEVE CHITREN

Position: RP
Bats: R **Throws:** R
Ht: 6' 0" **Wt:** 180

Opening Day Age: 24
Born: 6/8/67 in Tokyo, Japan
ML Seasons: 2

Overall Statistics

	W	L	ERA	G	GS	Sv	IP	H	R	BB	SO	HR
1991	1	4	4.33	56	0	4	60.1	59	31	32	47	8
Career	2	4	3.58	64	0	4	78.0	66	33	36	66	8

How Often He Throws Strikes

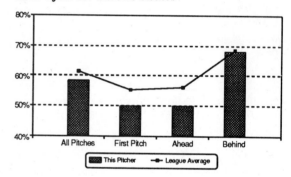

1991 Situational Stats

	W	L	ERA	Sv	IP		AB	H	HR	RBI	AVG
Home	0	0	5.28	1	29.0	LHB	96	28	4	18	.292
Road	1	4	3.45	3	31.1	RHB	133	31	4	25	.233
Day	0	1	7.45	0	19.1	Sc Pos	71	21	1	32	.296
Night	1	3	2.85	4	41.0	Clutch	86	21	3	19	.244

1991 Rankings (American League)

→ 6th most baserunners allowed per 9 innings in relief (14.2)

→ 9th in holds (14)

→ 10th highest percentage of inherited runners scored (40.0%)

PITCHING:

The Oakland Athletics got more than they had any right to expect when they acquired Ron Darling from the Montreal Expos in August. Darling clearly had outlasted his usefulness after eight good seasons with the New York Mets, and his elbow problems had made it apparent that he no longer was the superior power pitcher he once had been.

Once with the A's, though, Darling reacted positively to the change in clubhouses and ballparks. Although he doesn't rely exclusively on his fastball anymore, he still produces a lot of fly balls, and the Oakland Coliseum is the ideal park for such a pitcher.

Darling gave the A's immediate quality work after they picked him up, although his early-season lack of work became obvious in the later innings for the A's. He lost his last seven Oakland decisions after winning his first three, but poor support was largely responsible. Oakland averaged only 2.8 runs per game for Darling during his 12 starts.

With the A's, Darling expanded his previous experimentation with a forkball, and he figures to get better at it if he stays with Oakland because pitching coach Dave Duncan teaches that pitch so well. He also made more extensive use of a change-up.

HOLDING RUNNERS, FIELDING:

Darling had difficulty holding runners; 24 of 27 basestealers were successful with Darling on the mound (all three teams he pitched for combined). He sometimes had a tendency to give the catcher insufficient help with throws to first, though. His fielding was not a problem.

OVERALL:

Darling is one of the most learned pitchers in baseball. While with the A's he seemed ready, even eager, to begin the transformation he will have to make now that he is losing his great fastball. Darling, albeit belatedly, was to the A's what Scott Sanderson was to them in 1990. It wouldn't be a surprise to see Darling as a regular member of the rotation next season -- if the free agent re-signs with Oakland.

RON DARLING

Position: SP
Bats: R **Throws:** R
Ht: 6' 3" **Wt:** 195

Opening Day Age: 31
Born: 8/19/60 in Honolulu, HI
ML Seasons: 9

Overall Statistics

	W	L	ERA	G	GS	Sv	IP	H	R	BB	SO	HR
1991	8	15	4.26	32	32	0	194.1	185	100	71	129	22
Career	102	79	3.56	272	256	0	1712.0	1562	766	657	1219	168

How Often He Throws Strikes

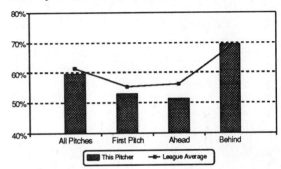

1991 Situational Stats

	W	L	ERA	Sv	IP		AB	H	HR	RBI	AVG
Home	3	9	5.40	0	90.0	LHB	391	93	8	42	.238
Road	5	6	3.28	0	104.1	RHB	336	92	14	47	.274
Day	1	5	5.60	0	54.2	Sc Pos	179	52	5	66	.291
Night	7	10	3.74	0	139.2	Clutch	45	12	2	6	.267

1991 Rankings (American League)

→ 9th lowest batting average allowed vs. left-handed batters (.207)

→ Led the A's in lowest batting average allowed vs. left-handed batters

DENNIS ECKERSLEY

Position: RP
Bats: R **Throws:** R
Ht: 6' 2" **Wt:** 195

Opening Day Age: 37
Born: 10/3/54 in
Oakland, CA
ML Seasons: 17

PITCHING:

The load that Dennis Eckersley had to carry in 1991 was in direct proportion to the A's desperation in competent set-up men. At times, it showed. Eckersley was brilliant most of the season, walking only nine men in 76 innings to give him a total of only 16 walks in 207 innings over the past three seasons.

But Eckersley complained of arm fatigue in August, and he was tagged for 11 home runs, some of which were catastrophic as the A's tumbled out of the American League West race. At other times, the A's staff was so ineffective that Eckersley's workload was reduced too much. This seemed to affect the sharpness on his pitches.

Even so, it hardly was a season that suggested that Eckersley has lost his position as a premier reliever. He still is almost uncanny in his ability to paint the corners and maintain uniform motion. He is starting to reduce speed on his breaking pitches in an effort to make his fastball appear more lively. In any case, the advice to hitters in 1991 was familiar: go up there hacking.

HOLDING RUNNERS AND FIELDING:

Eckersley never has been overly conscious of holding runners. His move is average, although the economy of his motion somewhat compensates for this once he releases the ball. He is becoming a trifle awkward getting off the mound, and teams are starting to bunt more when facing him.

OVERALL:

Any decrease in Eckersley's productivity tends to loom larger only because he has been so dominant since converting to the bullpen full-time in 1987. His complaints about shoulder fatigue sounded ominous at the time, but he finished reasonably well. The combination of Eckersley's mechanics and his conditioning should enable him to continue to madden hitters for some time to come.

Overall Statistics

	W	L	ERA	G	GS	Sv	IP	H	R	BB	SO	HR
1991	5	4	2.96	67	0	43	76.0	60	26	9	87	11
Career	174	144	3.47	671	361	188	2891.1	2685	1207	668	2025	302

How Often He Throws Strikes

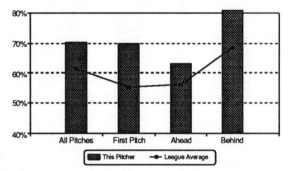

1991 Situational Stats

	W	L	ERA	Sv	IP		AB	H	HR	RBI	AVG
Home	5	1	1.83	18	39.1	LHB	150	34	5	18	.227
Road	0	3	4.17	25	36.2	RHB	138	26	6	15	.188
Day	2	1	1.59	17	34.0	Sc Pos	78	12	3	22	.154
Night	3	3	4.07	26	42.0	Clutch	220	45	7	29	.205

1991 Rankings (American League)

- 1st in least GDPs induced per GDP situation (0.0%)
- 2nd in saves (43) and save opportunities (51)
- 3rd in least baserunners allowed per 9 innings in relief (8.3) and most strikeouts per 9 innings in relief (10.3)
- 4th in games finished (59)
- 5th in blown saves (8)
- Led the A's in games pitched (67), saves, game finished, save opportunities, save percentage (84.3%), blown saves, relief ERA (2.96), relief innings (76), lowest batting average allowed in relief (.208), least baserunners per 9 innings in relief and most strikeouts per 9 innings in relief

HITTING:

One of the most hilarious episodes of the Oakland A's season involved Mike Gallego the night he was issued the first intentional pass of his career. Gallego stared out at the pitcher, transfixed. "I didn't know what he was doing," he said later. "When the first ball went wide, I thought the pitcher wanted a new ball."

Humor aside, though, Gallego earned more than that token measure of respect. He hit 12 home runs, one more than he had hit in his entire career prior to 1991. With the increase in power, his batting average also improved 41 points, indicating across-the-board plate improvement.

Even though Gallego is only 5-foot-8, he has a powerful frame. Firmly established as a regular and given more latitude by A's manager Tony La Russa, he is looking to attack pitches instead of trying to work counts. He has a short, compact stroke, but the stroke never lacked power, and most of Gallego's home runs were line drives. He didn't seem to be bothered when pitchers began throwing him more curveballs.

BASERUNNING:

Nobody on the team goes in harder on a takeout than Gallego, and nobody on the team has stretched more singles into doubles. He isn't turned loose in steal situations often, which is just as well; he was 6-for-15 in 1991, and has a lowly 45% success rate in his career.

FIELDING:

Even when he was hitting in the low .200s, Gallego's glove was good enough to get him lots of playing time. He has excellent range and balance at second, and he committed only seven errors last year. He is not quite as good at shortstop, where his lack of arm strength can be a handicap.

OVERALL:

Finally given the A's second base job from Day One last year, Gallego's confidence soared, and so did his numbers. He's an above-average major league second baseman -- as the free-agent contract he'll get will attest -- and 1992 could be the season he becomes an All-Star.

MIKE GALLEGO

Position: 2B/SS
Bats: R **Throws:** R
Ht: 5' 8" **Wt:** 160

Opening Day Age: 31
Born: 10/31/60 in Whittier, CA
ML Seasons: 7

Overall Statistics

	G	AB	R	H	D	T	HR	RBI	SB	BB	SO	AVG
1991	159	482	67	119	15	4	12	49	6	67	84	.247
Career	729	1743	219	404	63	9	23	160	21	196	271	.232

Where He Hits the Ball

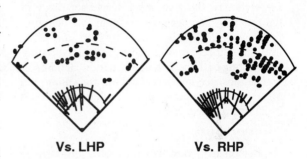

Vs. LHP   Vs. RHP

1991 Situational Stats

	AB	H	HR	RBI	AVG		AB	H	HR	RBI	AVG
Home	230	62	6	20	.270	LHP	122	38	5	13	.311
Road	252	57	6	29	.226	RHP	360	81	7	36	.225
Day	146	37	4	9	.253	Sc Pos	100	25	2	36	.250
Night	336	82	8	40	.244	Clutch	80	25	3	11	.313

1991 Rankings (American League)

→ 3rd highest fielding percentage at second base (.989)

→ 4th lowest batting average vs. right-handed pitchers (.225) and lowest slugging percentage vs. right-handed pitchers (.325)

→ 8th in games (159) and lowest batting average on the road (.226)

→ Led the A's in triples (4), games, batting average in the clutch (.313), batting average after the 6th inning (.313) and bunts in play (18)

→ Led AL second basemen in hit by pitch (5)

HITTING:

Dave Henderson was one of many reasons the Oakland A's fell out of the American League West hunt in August. He was also one of the few reasons they were in it that long.

Before the All-Star break, Henderson was on the way to the best season of his career; because of him, the A's were able to survive epochal slumps by many of their other big-name hitters. Batting in the number-two spot behind Rickey Henderson seemed to have the same effect on him as it had on Carney Lansford during the two previous seasons. He was consistently getting fastballs to hit because Rickey represented an automatic steal if a pitcher threw a curveball.

Later, though, the A's moved Henderson down in the order, and he became too intent on swinging for power. His average dropped from the .340s into the still-respectable .280s, but his yearning for the long ball boomeranged on him. Henderson went almost six weeks without hitting a home run after the All-Star break, although his season total of 25 was a career high.

BASERUNNING:

Henderson isn't much of a stealing threat anymore, but he attacks baserunning with unremitting zeal. Some of the most violent collisions of the past few years at the Coliseum have involved Henderson.

FIELDING:

Henderson is one of the best defensive center fielders in baseball. He sometimes is maligned because of his showboating in the outfield, but he's all business when a difficult chance comes his way. He has a good throwing arm.

OVERALL:

Henderson has emerged during the latter stages of his career as an All-Star caliber player. It's almost forgotten now that he was once considered a chronic underachiever. He's a mature, stabilizing influence on the Oakland team, and it would seem highly unlikely that the A's will be looking to replace him in the near future.

DAVE HENDERSON

Position: CF
Bats: R **Throws:** R
Ht: 6' 2" **Wt:** 220

Opening Day Age: 33
Born: 7/21/58 in Dos Palos, CA
ML Seasons: 11

Overall Statistics

	G	AB	R	H	D	T	HR	RBI	SB	BB	SO	AVG
1991	150	572	86	158	33	0	25	85	6	58	113	.276
Career	1355	4487	645	1182	252	16	172	622	48	415	948	.263

Where He Hits the Ball

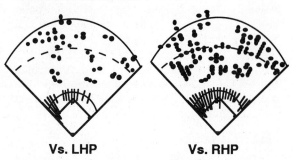

Vs. LHP   **Vs. RHP**

1991 Situational Stats

	AB	H	HR	RBI	AVG		AB	H	HR	RBI	AVG
Home	282	73	15	39	.259	LHP	144	51	8	24	.354
Road	290	85	10	46	.293	RHP	428	107	17	61	.250
Day	178	51	12	32	.287	Sc Pos	152	43	6	58	.283
Night	394	107	13	53	.272	Clutch	96	26	1	7	.271

1991 Rankings (American League)

→ 2nd highest fielding percentage in center field (.997)

→ 6th highest slugging percentage vs. left-handed pitchers (.618)

→ 7th highest batting average vs. left-handed pitchers (:354)

→ 8th highest batting average with the bases loaded (.461)

→ Led the A's in at-bats (572), hits (158), singles (100), doubles (33), least GDPs per GDP situation (6.1%), batting average vs. left-handed pitchers and slugging percentage vs. left-handed pitchers

→ Led AL center fielders in batting average with the bases loaded

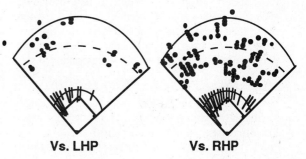

HALL OF FAMER

RICKEY HENDERSON

Position: LF
Bats: R **Throws:** L
Ht: 5'10" **Wt:** 190

Opening Day Age: 33
Born: 12/25/58 in Chicago, IL
ML Seasons: 13

HITTING:

The oft-whispered contention around the Oakland Athletics last year was that Rickey Henderson, in the aftermath of his contract dispute, spent much of 1991 hitting to suit Rickey Henderson rather than the A's. Henderson had been the prototypical leadoff hitter since his return to Oakland, spraying the ball throughout the park in addition to providing middle-of-the-order power.

In 1991, though, Henderson often tried to pull pitches he either would have taken or tried to wrist into play previously. Pitchers went after him with inside fastballs -- not previously a good idea because of Henderson's open stance and quick hands -- and got away with it because Henderson would try to loft the ball. Lefthanders backdoored him with breaking balls because he sometimes tried to pull those pitches, too.

Most of Henderson's hitting totals were down last year. Although his strikeout-to-walk ratio was about the same as in 1990, those stats are deceptive because they reflect his excellent work during the middle and very end of the season, and hide his very poor work while the A's were toppling out of the race.

BASERUNNING:

Henderson had a lot of trouble with his oft-damaged legs in 1991; his success rate (76%) was his lowest since 1982. He did break Lou Brock's career stolen-base record early in the season, and won his 11th American League basestealing title in 12 seasons.

FIELDING:

Henderson often was laconic last year in left field, and the accuracy and strength of his throws decreased appreciably. Teams have begun to take the extra base on him almost as they please. He remains very good at balls hit to either side or behind him.

OVERALL:

One year after winning the MVP award, Henderson sulked and played selfishly. A lot of the blame for the A's demise in 1991 can be laid at his feet. The A's need a motivated Rickey Henderson in 1992 if they are to return to the top of the American League West.

Overall Statistics

	G	AB	R	H	D	T	HR	RBI	SB	BB	SO	AVG
1991	134	470	105	126	17	1	18	57	58	98	73	.268
Career	1742	6483	1395	1888	311	51	184	679	994	1191	869	.291

Where He Hits the Ball

Vs. LHP   Vs. RHP

1991 Situational Stats

	AB	H	HR	RBI	AVG		AB	H	HR	RBI	AVG
Home	248	69	8	28	.278	LHP	114	33	8	17	.289
Road	222	57	10	29	.257	RHP	356	93	10	40	.261
Day	144	41	6	19	.285	Sc Pos	91	21	6	41	.231
Night	326	85	12	38	.261	Clutch	71	17	3	15	.239

1991 Rankings (American League)

→ 1st in stolen bases (58), most pitches seen per plate appearance (4.34), lowest fielding percentage in left field (.970), highest percentage of pitches taken (68.2%) and steals of third (21)

→ 2nd in caught stealing (18) and runs scored per time reached base (45.4%)

→ 3rd in walks (98)

→ Led the A's in stolen bases, caught stealing, walks, on-base average (.400), most pitches seen per plate appearance, on-base average vs. right-handed pitchers (.399), batting average with 2 strikes (.219), highest percentage of pitches taken, lowest percentage of swings that missed (11.6%) and steals of third

PITCHING:

The shoulder injury that cost the Oakland Athletics Rick Honeycutt for half the 1991 season easily was the most disastrous to hit their pitching staff. Honeycutt functioned in so many roles during the previous three seasons that the A's, whose staff is top-heavy with righthanders, never found a way to replace him. After his return Honeycutt himself wasn't as effective as in previous seasons, but he was still one of the better workmen on the Oakland staff.

Honeycutt, who will be entering his 16th season, is a craftsman on the mound. He doesn't throw particularly hard, but he sinks almost everything and is particularly effective with his slider against left-handed hitters. Honeycutt is not, however, strictly a lefty-vs.-lefty specialist. He'll use his curve and occasionally a slider on the outside corner against righties, and last year started experimenting with a change-up occasionally.

HOLDING RUNNERS AND FIELDING:

Honeycutt is so adept at keeping runners chained to first base that manager Tony La Russa has been known to use him against right-handed hitters solely because a man on first has speed that must be negated. Honeycutt has a number of effective devices that he uses to keep runners guessing on first. Afield, he isn't adroit, but knows what he's doing and is almost never guilty of a mental mistake. He had some trouble covering bunts last season -- as, seemingly, did almost all of the A's pitchers.

OVERALL:

Honeycutt is signed through this coming season, and he's one of the individuals the A's are counting upon most to provide a healthy, uninterrupted season. The single biggest void the A's pitching staff had last season was the lack of a lefty set-up man for Dennis Eckersley. Honeycutt's shoulder apparently is fine, and the A's will need a typical season from him to return to their accustomed status.

RICK HONEYCUTT

Position: RP
Bats: L **Throws:** L
Ht: 6' 1" **Wt:** 191

Opening Day Age: 37
Born: 6/29/54 in Chattanooga, TN
ML Seasons: 15

Overall Statistics

	W	L	ERA	G	GS	Sv	IP	H	R	BB	SO	HR
1991	2	4	3.58	43	0	0	37.2	37	16	20	26	3
Career	99	131	3.73	534	268	27	1959.0	1989	942	600	914	168

How Often He Throws Strikes

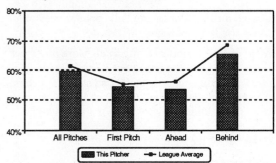

1991 Situational Stats

	W	L	ERA	Sv	IP		AB	H	HR	RBI	AVG
Home	0	2	2.14	0	21.0	LHB	54	11	1	4	.204
Road	2	2	5.40	0	16.2	RHB	88	26	2	10	.295
Day	1	1	3.07	0	14.2	Sc Pos	32	6	1	8	.188
Night	1	3	3.91	0	23.0	Clutch	103	26	1	8	.252

1991 Rankings (American League)

→ 9th in holds (14)
→ Led the A's in first batter efficiency (.191)

HITTING:

Brook Jacoby initially responded well to his escape from Cleveland, and the Oakland Athletics thought he would provide ballast to the lower half of their order. But Jacoby, who was batting .234 at the time he switched teams, hit only .213 in an Oakland uniform.

Jacoby was coming off a .293 season for the Indians, but with the A's, his previously-considerable bat speed simply didn't seem to be there. Jacoby didn't try to hit for power and didn't hesitate to try to poke the ball to right field, but he had trouble doing even that most of the time. Oddly -- because this never was his reputation -- he seemed more comfortable with breaking balls than with fastballs. He managed only 12 extra base hits, all doubles, with the A's for a measly .277 slugging percentage.

On the plus side, Jacoby is a count-worker and made pitchers get him out with quality offerings. He seemed to have more success with low pitches, and knows the strike zone fairly well. The main problem was that he was swinging through a lot of high strikes that, in the past, he almost certainly would have hit hard.

BASERUNNING:

Jacoby had two steals in 1991 after recording only a single theft in 1990. However, he is an intelligent baserunner who anticipates situations well, and he'll go in hard on a takeout situation.

FIELDING:

Jacoby's third base play tightened the A's left-side defense demonstrably. Although he's extremely sure-handed and has a better-than-average arm, his first step isn't inordinately quick. Jacoby also plays first base more than acceptably, and was used there in place of Mark McGwire frequently toward the end of the year.

OVERALL:

Jacoby's sudden absence of bat speed mystified both himself and his employers, but given his work habits, the A's did not think his problem was permanent. He was a positive addition to the clubhouse; he also gives the A's a valuable insurance policy in case Lansford can't regain his pre-injury form, or if the A's decide to move McGwire.

BROOK JACOBY

Position: 3B/1B
Bats: R **Throws:** R
Ht: 5'11" **Wt:** 195

Opening Day Age: 32
Born: 11/23/59 in
Philadelphia, PA
ML Seasons: 10

Overall Statistics

	G	AB	R	H	D	T	HR	RBI	SB	BB	SO	AVG
1991	122	419	28	94	21	1	4	44	2	27	54	.224
Career	1191	4229	505	1144	197	24	116	509	16	411	710	.271

Where He Hits the Ball

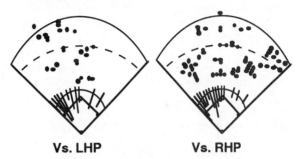

Vs. LHP   Vs. RHP

1991 Situational Stats

	AB	H	HR	RBI	AVG		AB	H	HR	RBI	AVG
Home	190	41	2	27	.216	LHP	116	29	1	13	.250
Road	229	53	2	17	.231	RHP	303	65	3	31	.215
Day	142	29	0	13	.204	Sc Pos	104	26	1	39	.250
Night	277	65	4	31	.235	Clutch	85	16	2	4	.188

1991 Rankings (American League)

➡ 6th lowest batting average after the 6th inning (.188)

➡ 8th lowest batting average with 2 strikes (.122)

PITCHING:

Joe Klink surprised many with his 10 win total in 1991, but it was a deceptive number. The typical Klink game would involve him entering in the seventh or eighth inning, giving up a run or two and then getting the win when the A's rallied.

Klink was adequate, no more, when thrust into the left-handed set-up role left vacant by Rick Honeycutt's shoulder injury. His previous role during two seasons with the A's was primarily as a one-batter pitcher against left-handed hitters. He had to expand that role out of necessity last year, and had a lot of trouble against righthanders.

Klink is predominantly a curveball pitcher who tends to get his breaking ball high in the strike zone. This tendency usually doesn't hurt him much in the spacious Coliseum, but he was battered on a regular basis when he hung curveballs on the road. His fastball strictly is for show, and he has a lot of trouble when he drops his arm angle from the regular straight over the top delivery. He was among the staff leaders in appearances all year and this workload brought on fatigue that at times caused the arm to drop.

HOLDING RUNNERS AND FIELDING:

Klink will throw over to first base a lot to try to help his catcher, but there's very little deception in anything he does on the mound, and he doesn't vary his techniques. In the field, he's not athletic and well below average in just about every respect.

OVERALL:

If the A's can return Klink to his 1989-90 role next season, they can continue to get decent mileage out of him. He could be called the Ken Dayley of the 1990s: a guy who can get lefty hitters out in a one-time-only situation. His big advantage on this staff is that he doesn't make much money, and the A's aren't likely to spend a ton of cash to find somebody to replace him.

JOE KLINK

Position: RP
Bats: L **Throws:** L
Ht: 5'11" **Wt:** 175

Opening Day Age: 30
Born: 2/3/62 in Johnstown, PA
ML Seasons: 3

Overall Statistics

	W	L	ERA	G	GS	Sv	IP	H	R	BB	SO	HR
1991	10	3	4.35	62	0	2	62.0	60	30	21	34	4
Career	10	4	4.04	114	0	3	124.2	131	57	50	70	9

How Often He Throws Strikes

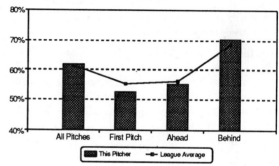

1991 Situational Stats

	W	L	ERA	Sv	IP		AB	H	HR	RBI	AVG
Home	4	1	3.34	1	32.1	LHB	98	22	2	9	.224
Road	6	2	5.46	1	29.2	RHB	133	38	2	20	.286
Day	1	1	2.84	1	19.0	Sc Pos	73	21	1	24	.288
Night	9	2	5.02	1	43.0	Clutch	103	24	2	10	.233

1991 Rankings (American League)

→ 1st in lowest percentage of inherited runners scored (15.2%) and relief wins (10)

→ 6th in holds (16)

→ Led the A's in holds, most GDPs induced per GDP situation (17.0%), lowest percentage of inherited runners scored and relief wins

HITTING:

Mark McGwire's season-long slump was one of the most over-analyzed aspects of the Oakland Athletics' disappointing 1991 season. No solution became evident, as McGwire's power output hit a career low and he struggled most of the season to keep his average above .200. Over-analysis by McGwire himself might have been one of the reasons.

McGwire is an inveterate videotape watcher, and it seemed as if every tape that he saw of himself led to another adjustment of his stance. He tried everything: moving back from the plate, opening his stance, holding his hands in various positions. Nothing worked, and it could have been that McGwire was so concerned with his mechanics that his concentration was affected.

In any case, he could or would not try to use the entire field, and he could or would not adjust the upward plane of his swing. The result was a succession of long fly balls, pop-ups and strikeouts. Getting McGwire out wasn't much of a mystery: tempt him to pull, and he would invariably try to do so.

BASERUNNING:

McGwire is no threat on the bases and generally is content with station-to-station baserunning. He usually is an intelligent baserunner who knows his limitations, but he seemed less willing upon occasion to break up double plays and slide hard.

FIELDING:

McGwire's work at first base last year was again of Gold Glove quality; he did not let his batting problems affect his defensive concentration. McGwire is outstanding at roaming the vast foul-ground area of the Coliseum, and he throws better than most first basemen.

OVERALL:

Nobody thought in 1987, when McGwire batted .289 with 49 homers as a rookie, that he would become the next Dave Kingman. But that's what happened in 1991. To be sure, McGwire is a far better all-around player, but he must learn to use the entire field and take the uppercut out of his swing. Otherwise, he will be doomed to more frustration as "Son of Kong."

MARK McGWIRE

Position: 1B
Bats: R **Throws:** R
Ht: 6' 5" **Wt:** 225

Opening Day Age: 28
Born: 10/1/63 in Pomona, CA
ML Seasons: 6

Overall Statistics

	G	AB	R	H	D	T	HR	RBI	SB	BB	SO	AVG
1991	154	483	62	97	22	0	22	75	2	93	116	.201
Career	777	2656	417	647	106	5	178	504	6	437	592	.244

Where He Hits the Ball

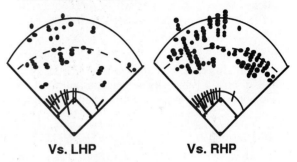

Vs. LHP   Vs. RHP

1991 Situational Stats

	AB	H	HR	RBI	AVG		AB	H	HR	RBI	AVG
Home	243	45	15	48	.185	LHP	130	26	5	19	.200
Road	240	52	7	27	.217	RHP	353	71	17	56	.201
Day	167	32	12	37	.192	Sc Pos	129	31	9	57	.240
Night	316	65	10	38	.206	Clutch	65	11	4	15	.169

1991 Rankings (American League)

→ 1st in lowest groundball/flyball ratio (.55) and lowest batting average vs. right-handed pitchers (.201)

→ 2nd in lowest batting average (.201), lowest batting average at home (.185), lowest batting average with 2 strikes (.093) and highest fielding percentage at first base (.997)

→ 6th in walks (93), lowest batting average vs. left-handed pitchers (.200) and lowest batting average on the road (.217)

→ 9th lowest batting average in the clutch (.169)

→ Led the AL first basemen in walks

PITCHING:

While the rest of the Oakland Athletics staff was noisily crumbling around him, Mike Moore pieced together one of his best seasons in 1991. Two factors seemed to be paramount in his turn-around after an even-worse-than-it-looks 13-15 campaign in 1990: increased aggressiveness and a lower arm angle.

Moore got in trouble in 1990 because he was trying to pinpoint the ball instead of attacking hitters. That got him behind on counts, and the result was that he gave up too many walks and fat-pitch hits. In 1991, Moore had a much better strike-to-ball ratio on his initial pitches, which enabled him to work with more confidence on pitches other than his fastball -- particularly the forkball, which all but deserted him in '90.

Late in the season, Moore also dropped down from straight over to three-quarters with his arm motion. This change enabled him to ride his fast-ball in on right-handed hitters, and gave him a weapon against hitters who had been crowding the plate.

HOLDING RUNNERS AND FIELDING:

Moore showed particular improvement last year at holding baserunners; if a runner stole success-fully, more often the steal was on the catcher, and that hasn't always been the case with Moore. He has a slide step that he mixes in with his normal motion from time to time. Moore is a good athlete who fields his position very well.

OVERALL:

The mystery of Mike Moore was solved to a large extent last season, and it couldn't have come at a better time for him -- 1991 was the final season of the contract he signed with the A's in 1989. There's no question that the A's will try hard to re-sign Moore, who at age 32 is on the verge of reaching the maturity level that could take him to the 20-game winner plateau.

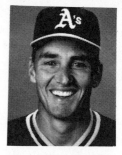

MIKE MOORE

Position: SP
Bats: R **Throws:** R
Ht: 6' 4" **Wt:** 205

Opening Day Age: 32
Born: 11/26/59 in Eakly, OK
ML Seasons: 10

Overall Statistics

	W	L	ERA	G	GS	Sv	IP	H	R	BB	SO	HR
1991	17	8	2.96	33	33	0	210.0	176	75	105	153	11
Career	115	130	4.06	328	318	2	2108.0	2071	1053	807	1335	185

How Often He Throws Strikes

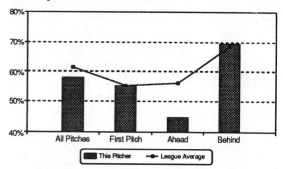

1991 Situational Stats

	W	L	ERA	Sv	IP		AB	H	HR	RBI	AVG
Home	11	3	2.14	0	117.2	LHB	394	90	4	32	.228
Road	6	5	4.00	0	92.1	RHB	374	86	7	33	.230
Day	8	1	3.79	0	71.1	Sc Pos	181	38	0	51	.210
Night	9	7	2.53	0	138.2	Clutch	54	16	0	4	.296

1991 Rankings (American League)

- 1st in ERA at home (2.14)
- 2nd in walks allowed (105), wild pitches (14), lowest slugging percentage allowed (.318) and least home runs allowed per 9 innings (.47)
- 4th in most pitches thrown per batter (4.00)
- 5th in winning percentage (.680) and ground-ball/flyball ratio (1.77)
- Led the A's in ERA (2.96), wins (17), shutouts (1), walks allowed, strikeouts (153), wild pitches, pickoff throws (122), GDPs induced, winning percentage, strikeout/walk ratio (1.5), lowest batting average allowed (.229), lowest slugging percentage allowed and low-est on-base average allowed (.324)

PITCHING:

Coming off the best year of his career, Gene Nelson didn't even have a year in 1991, for all intents and purposes. In any case, it will be one he would just as soon forget.

It started on Opening Night when a foul ball into the A's dugout caught Nelson on one of his pitching fingers. The fracture kept him out for two months, and when Nelson finally did return, he was completely without rhythm or comfort on the mound. His motion was out of sync, and often his arm was far ahead of his body when he released the ball. That meant that he was high with just about all his pitches, and if he wasn't walking people -- 13 against four strikeouts at one point -- he was being bludgeoned relentlessly. Nelson's entire season was a struggle to get his earned run average below a run an inning.

Nelson also lost command of his forkball, which made his good-but-not-great fastball a festive main dish. As his troubles worsened, he fell into the trap of overthrowing, and the result was that he never had command of any of his pitches. At the end of August, hitters had a .493 on-base percentage against him, and manager Tony La Russa was unable to use him in anything other than mop-up situations as the A's tumbled out of the race.

HOLDING RUNNERS AND FIELDING:

Nelson's problems with his pitching carried over to the other aspects of his work. His defense, improved in 1990, fell off, and he was so nonplussed by the merry-go-round of baserunners surrounding him that he seldom paid any attention to them.

OVERALL:

It's far too early for the A's to give up on Nelson, especially considering his age (31) and his excellent work over the previous three years. His arm apparently is healthy. Nelson has revived his career before under less favorable circumstances, and the chances are decent that he'll rebound strongly in 1992.

GENE NELSON

Position: RP
Bats: R **Throws:** R
Ht: 6' 0" **Wt:** 174

Opening Day Age: 31
Born: 12/3/60 in Tampa, FL
ML Seasons: 11

Overall Statistics

	W	L	ERA	G	GS	Sv	IP	H	R	BB	SO	HR
1991	1	5	6.84	44	0	0	48.2	60	38	23	23	12
Career	50	58	4.08	413	66	23	967.1	933	472	372	597	109

How Often He Throws Strikes

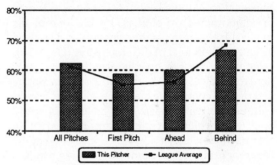

1991 Situational Stats

	W	L	ERA	Sv	IP		AB	H	HR	RBI	AVG
Home	0	1	5.27	0	27.1	LHB	76	27	3	18	.355
Road	1	4	8.86	0	21.1	RHB	120	33	9	34	.275
Day	0	2	4.96	0	16.1	Sc Pos	65	19	5	40	.292
Night	1	3	7.79	0	32.1	Clutch	83	27	6	25	.325

1991 Rankings (American League)

➡ Did not rank near the top or bottom in any category

PITCHING:

The airlines that service the Seattle-Tacoma airport certainly profited from the travels of Joe Slusarski last year. It is to be questioned whether the same can be said of Slusarski, the Oakland Athletics' second-round draft choice in 1988.

Slusarski made the trip between Class AAA Tacoma and the A's no less than five times in 1991. When the A's needed an emergency starter, which was often, they usually turned to Slusarski. And it usually was Slusarski who returned to Tacoma when the crisis subsided. He didn't get to pitch on a regular basis for any extended period, and his inconsistency during his first major league season therefore was quite understandable.

Slusarski took some beatings, but he also turned in some impressive outings. He has one of the liveliest fastballs in the organization, and showed he can use it in a lot of different ways. He cuts it, rides it and turns it over in a pattern that only rarely was discernible to opposing hitters. But he had trouble controlling his curve, slider and forkball, and he really doesn't yet have an offspeed pitch with which to complement his heater. He also had a tendency to let up on hitters when he found himself behind in the count. This resulted in a flurry of early-season home runs that made his overall work look less effective than it was in actuality.

HOLDING RUNNERS, FIELDING:

Slusarski did a surprisingly good job in the non-pitching phases. He has a quick move to first, although he tended to give it away. He's also a fine athlete who is very agile in the field.

OVERALL:

Slusarski remains one of the shining stars in the A's organization. The likelihood is that he'll probably be in the minor leagues most or all of next season unless the A's have another pitching meltdown. But he's only 25, and is still expected to be a successful major leaguer down the road.

JOE SLUSARSKI

Position: SP
Bats: R **Throws:** R
Ht: 6' 4" **Wt:** 195

Opening Day Age: 25
Born: 12/19/66 in Indianapolis, IN
ML Seasons: 1

Overall Statistics

	W	L	ERA	G	GS	Sv	IP	H	R	BB	SO	HR
1991	5	7	5.27	20	19	0	109.1	121	69	52	60	14
Career	5	7	5.27	20	19	0	109.1	121	69	52	60	14

How Often He Throws Strikes

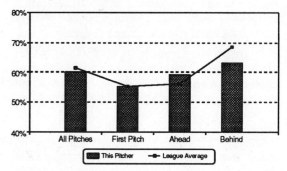

1991 Situational Stats

	W	L	ERA	Sv	IP		AB	H	HR	RBI	AVG
Home	2	3	5.36	0	43.2	LHB	253	75	7	25	.296
Road	3	4	5.21	0	65.2	RHB	174	46	7	28	.264
Day	2	3	5.72	0	50.1	Sc Pos	101	29	4	40	.287
Night	3	4	4.88	0	59.0	Clutch	13	5	1	3	.385

1991 Rankings (American League)

→ Did not rank near the top or bottom in any category

HITTING:

Perhaps some of the Oakland Athletics' pitchers missed former catcher Ron Hassey last year, but Terry Steinbach did not. Freed of his semi-platoon role by Hassey's departure, Steinbach put together the most productive season of his six-year major league career. He attained career highs in almost every category and proved he is an All-Star caliber catcher.

Before last season, Steinbach could never piece together two strong halves. In 1991, though, he lifted his average near .300 early in the season and kept it there for almost the entire six-month run. His power output remained similar to his career norm, but his clutch hitting was best on the club next to Dave Henderson.

During previous seasons, Steinbach usually was played in the gaps because he didn't hit the ball much down either line. But in 1991 he littered the entire field with base hits. A good breaking ball hitter who likes to extend his arms, he still could stand to make pitchers work him more.

BASERUNNING:

Steinbach is a good baserunner, even though he is not even a remote threat to steal. He almost never takes the A's out of innings with thoughtless baserunning, and will take the extra base if an outfielder isn't paying attention to him.

FIELDING:

Steinbach is an above-average defensive catcher who handles pitchers fairly well. He has a strong arm, but needs to work on releasing the ball more quickly and streamlining his footwork. Steinbach has become more of a take-charge guy in the infield, and even the A's older players respond to his direction.

OVERALL:

Steinbach was one of the few players who brought stability to the A's in 1991. He easily assumed the everyday catcher mantle, and finally put an end to his tendency to hit in peaks and valleys. There was some question after 1990 as to whether the A's wanted to commit to Steinbach as their number-one catcher. His work in 1991 probably answered most of those questions.

TERRY STEINBACH

Position: C
Bats: R **Throws:** R
Ht: 6' 1" **Wt:** 195

Opening Day Age: 30
Born: 3/2/62 in New Ulm, MN
ML Seasons: 6

Overall Statistics

	G	AB	R	H	D	T	HR	RBI	SB	BB	SO	AVG
1991	129	456	50	125	31	1	6	67	2	22	70	.274
Career	605	2046	230	553	94	8	49	277	7	137	315	.270

Where He Hits the Ball

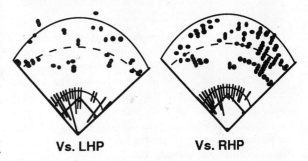

Vs. LHP   Vs. RHP

1991 Situational Stats

	AB	H	HR	RBI	AVG		AB	H	HR	RBI	AVG
Home	220	61	1	31	.277	LHP	139	37	3	15	.266
Road	236	64	5	36	.271	RHP	317	88	3	52	.278
Day	131	42	3	27	.321	Sc Pos	130	37	2	60	.285
Night	325	83	3	40	.255	Clutch	86	25	0	10	.291

1991 Rankings (American League)

→ 2nd lowest fielding percentage by a catcher (.980)

→ 3rd in sacrifice flies (9)

→ 5th highest batting average with the bases loaded (.500)

→ 7th in hit by pitch (7)

→ Led the A's in sacrifice flies, batting average with runners in scoring position (.285) and batting average with the bases loaded

→ Led AL catchers in doubles (31), sacrifice flies, batting average with the bases loaded, batting average vs. left-handed pitchers (.266), batting average after the 6th inning (.282) and errors (13)

PITCHING:

Even in the midst of a professional season of torment, the persona of Dave Stewart remained admirable. At one point, he told some Oakland Athletics beat writers that their criticism of his work was not severe enough. Stewart said he didn't want anybody judging him now on the basis of the four straight 20-win seasons he had compiled before 1991.

Stewart's class was about the only aspect of his game that didn't disappear during 1991. Even when he won, he seldom was the regal presence on the mound that he had been throughout the previous four seasons. Stewart constantly had to pitch from behind in the count. And in the big-game situations that used to stimulate him most, he couldn't come through.

Stewart's most obvious problem last year was the pitch that originally rescued him from oblivion: the forkball. He never seemed to have the same release point on it, and he left it high in the zone more often than not. Although he has other good pitches, he had come to depend almost exclusively on the forkball as his offspeed pitch. When it turned out he needed more than the forkball, he had no other pitch to turn to.

HOLDING RUNNERS AND FIELDING:

Stewart still is one of the best athletes among pitchers in baseball, but he tended to force some plays that he wouldn't have attempted during his 20-game seasons. He threw less to first base than he had in the past, but he still has a well-above-average move and gets rid of the ball quickly.

OVERALL:

Stewart's 1991 season was a reminder to many, and to himself, that without his forkball, as was the case prior to 1986, he is a fringe major lea-guer. He might be at the stage where he will have to develop another offspeed pitch -- like a change-up -- to regain his elite status. His problems do not seem uncorrectable, and the A's still think of him as the cornerstone of their pitching staff and, to a large degree, of their franchise.

DAVE STEWART

Position: SP
Bats: R **Throws:** R
Ht: 6' 2" **Wt:** 200

Opening Day Age: 35
Born: 2/19/57 in
Oakland, CA
ML Seasons: 12

Overall Statistics

	W	L	ERA	G	GS	Sv	IP	H	R	BB	SO	HR
1991	11	11	5.18	35	35	0	226.0	245	135	105	144	24
Career	134	96	3.70	428	253	19	2053.2	1926	923	782	1346	179

How Often He Throws Strikes

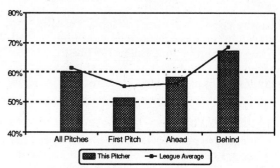

1991 Situational Stats

	W	L	ERA	Sv	IP		AB	H	HR	RBI	AVG
Home	8	3	4.21	0	115.1	LHB	444	134	8	71	.302
Road	3	8	6.18	0	110.2	RHB	436	111	16	55	.255
Day	6	3	4.58	0	70.2	Sc Pos	221	64	7	102	.290
Night	5	8	5.45	0	155.1	Clutch	45	14	1	7	.311

1991 Rankings (American League)

→ 1st in highest ERA (5.18), games started (35), highest run support per 9 innings (6.1) and highest ERA on the road (6.18)

→ 2nd in walks allowed (105), pitches thrown (3,939) and most baserunners allowed per 9 innings (14.3)

→ 3rd in hits allowed (245)

→ Led the A's in games started, shutouts (1), innings (226), hits allowed, batters faced (1,014), walks allowed, pitches thrown, stolen bases allowed (23), GDPs induced (19) and run support per 9 innings

HITTING:

Walt Weiss was batting only .226 when a freak ankle injury ended his 1991 season in mid-June. One reason for the low average was the fact he batted only .194 from the right side of the plate. The A's were seeing few left-handed pitchers at that stage of the season, and Weiss, who in 1990 had hit almost as well right-handed as left-handed, never got into any kind of groove against southpaws.

Still, Weiss is one of those hitters whose usefulness is understated by his numbers. Usually batting eighth or ninth, he seldom strikes out and almost always does something of value even when he doesn't end up on base. He has a very quick bat and likes low pitches onto which he can drop the bat. He is perhaps the best bunter on the team, and without him the A's lost a couple of games in which they needed a crucial bunt and didn't get it.

BASERUNNING:

The A's also missed Weiss' baserunning expertise. He was six for six in basestealing attempts at the time he was hurt, and on a team that sometimes runs the bases recklessly, Weiss was a paragon of intelligence and stability on the bases.

FIELDING:

More than anything, the A's simply couldn't replace Weiss defensively. His footwork is so efficient that he makes everything look easy, and he has the ability to throw from just about any position. Whether he can continue to do that after two knee operations -- and now a serious ankle injury -- will be an important element in the A's 1992 season.

OVERALL:

The A's were 32-20 and in first place in the American League West when Weiss was lost for the year. Without him, Oakland was a below-.500 ball club. Weiss' ankle is expected to be fine going into spring training, but his inability to stay healthy leaves him as a major question mark. If he isn't able to regain his old form, the A's are in serious trouble.

WALT WEISS

Position: SS
Bats: B **Throws:** R
Ht: 6' 0" **Wt:** 175

Opening Day Age: 28
Born: 11/28/63 in Tuxedo, NY
ML Seasons: 5

Overall Statistics

	G	AB	R	H	D	T	HR	RBI	SB	BB	SO	AVG
1991	40	133	15	30	6	1	0	13	6	12	14	.226
Career	425	1292	142	328	55	5	8	109	26	116	164	.254

Where He Hits the Ball

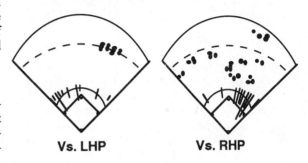

Vs. LHP   Vs. RHP

1991 Situational Stats

	AB	H	HR	RBI	AVG		AB	H	HR	RBI	AVG
Home	78	13	0	4	.167	LHP	31	6	0	1	.194
Road	55	17	0	9	.309	RHP	102	24	0	12	.235
Day	48	11	0	4	.229	Sc Pos	33	7	0	12	.212
Night	85	19	0	9	.224	Clutch	17	6	0	4	.353

1991 Rankings (American League)

➡ Did not rank near the top or bottom in any category

PITCHING:

Unlike teammate Dave Stewart, Bob Welch's fall from the numerical pantheon wasn't reflected by a startling decrease in overall effectiveness. Even though he went from 27-6 to 12-13, and his ERA rose from 2.95 to 4.58. Welch had stretches of effectiveness which recalled his Cy Young form. Unfortunately, they were matched by similar strings of ineffectiveness.

One problem was the fact Welch wasn't getting anywhere near the 5.9 runs per game that the A's scored for him in 1990. Another was the fact the A's didn't re-sign catcher Ron Hassey, who virtually had been his personal catcher. All parties downplayed that aspect of Welch's decline, but Welch seemed to have more problems pacing himself and funneling his emotions in 1991 than he had with Hassey behind the plate.

Welch remains a power pitcher who works primarily on the inside to set up the outside corner. In 1991 though, he often failed to get "on top" of the ball, and the results were often pitches that came across at the thigh instead of the knee. Welch has a solid curveball and forkball, but usually will stay outside the strike zone with them. Hitters seemed more cognizant of that in 1991, and he had trouble forcing them to chase those pitches early in the count.

HOLDING RUNNERS AND FIELDING:

Few pitchers are quicker and more combative in fielding situations, but Welch sometimes lets his aggression get the better of him -- especially in terms of decision-making. He has a decent move, releases quickly and isn't easy to run against, although he sometimes suffers from batter myopia with runners on base.

OVERALL:

A smattering of horrendous outings early in the season and general ineffectiveness in September inflated Welch's ERA last year, and reduced run support hurt his record. Still, he reverted on many occasions to the over-excitable, hyperactive Bob Welch who used to take himself out of games too often. Welch has to find a way to regain the sense of calm that he was able to project in 1990.

BOB WELCH

Position: SP
Bats: R **Throws:** R
Ht: 6' 3" **Wt:** 198

Opening Day Age: 35
Born: 11/3/56 in Detroit, MI
ML Seasons: 14

Overall Statistics

	W	L	ERA	G	GS	Sv	IP	H	R	BB	SO	HR
1991	12	13	4.58	35	35	0	220.0	220	124	91	101	25
Career	188	122	3.27	431	406	8	2732.1	2493	1105	892	1815	219

How Often He Throws Strikes

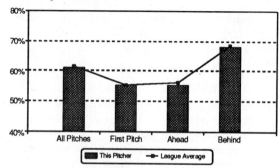

1991 Situational Stats

	W	L	ERA	Sv	IP		AB	H	HR	RBI	AVG
Home	8	7	3.60	0	125.0	LHB	430	117	8	57	.272
Road	4	6	5.87	0	95.0	RHB	405	103	17	55	.254
Day	5	4	3.28	0	79.2	Sc Pos	190	59	4	82	.311
Night	7	9	5.32	0	140.1	Clutch	86	21	3	9	.244

1991 Rankings (American League)

- ➡ 1st in games started (35) and runners caught stealing (16)
- ➡ 2nd highest ERA on the road (5.87)
- ➡ 3rd highest ERA (4.58)
- ➡ 4th most home runs allowed (25) and lowest strikeout/walk ratio (1.1)
- ➡ 5th in hit batsmen (11)
- ➡ Led the A's in losses (13), games started, complete games (7), shutouts (1), home runs allowed, hit batsmen, runners caught stealing, lowest stolen base percentage allowed (42.9%) and least pitches thrown per batter (3.71)

HITTING:

Willie Wilson knew when he came to Oakland that he would fill a backup role for the first time in his illustrious career. But he was not a backup for long, because the A's were hit by a steady succession of injuries to outfielders. Wilson was pressed into service on almost a regular basis, and he performed fairly well, although his numbers reflected the degree to which his skills have eroded.

Wilson played in almost as many games as he had the previous year with Kansas City. He gave the A's much-needed speed on the bases, and he had some impressive hitting streaks. But he did not compensate for his low batting average with a high on-base percentage, and did nothing to use his speed to complement his batting. Wilson doesn't bunt much, won't try to hit the ball on the ground and does not work for walks.

BASERUNNING:

Wilson still can run with the best of them. He doesn't steal as much as he used to, and often was caught up in the A's penchant for station-to-station baseball. But his baserunning alone will undoubtedly make him useful to somebody for another year or two.

FIELDING:

Wilson, a center fielder for almost his entire career in Kansas City, was asked to play left field most of the time in 1991, and responded admirably. He did have some trouble with center fielder Dave Henderson in terms of communication early in the season, but that was worked out. Playing left field eliminated some problems for Wilson since he does not throw well.

OVERALL:

Wilson probably isn't at the end of the line just yet, but his speed is the only aspect of his game that hasn't been affected by his age, so he must use it. The A's no longer have the surplus of outfielders that they once did, and A's manager Tony La Russa liked Wilson's attitude. He may be back.

WILLIE WILSON

Position: LF/CF/RF
Bats: B **Throws:** R
Ht: 6' 3" **Wt:** 200

Opening Day Age: 36
Born: 7/9/55 in Montgomery, AL
ML Seasons: 16

Overall Statistics

	G	AB	R	H	D	T	HR	RBI	SB	BB	SO	AVG
1991	113	294	38	70	14	4	0	28	20	18	43	.238
Career	1900	7093	1098	2038	255	137	40	537	632	378	1033	.287

Where He Hits the Ball

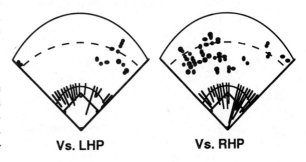

Vs. LHP   Vs. RHP

1991 Situational Stats

	AB	H	HR	RBI	AVG		AB	H	HR	RBI	AVG
Home	132	33	0	16	.250	LHP	99	25	0	6	.253
Road	162	37	0	12	.228	RHP	195	45	0	22	.231
Day	106	23	0	11	.217	Sc Pos	66	19	0	28	.288
Night	188	47	0	17	.250	Clutch	42	10	0	4	.238

1991 Rankings (American League)

→ 7th in stolen base percentage (80.0%)

→ Led the A's in triples (4)

LANCE BLANKENSHIP

Position: 2B/3B/LF
Bats: R **Throws:** R
Ht: 6' 0" **Wt:** 185

Opening Day Age: 28
Born: 12/6/63 in
Portland, OR
ML Seasons: 4

JAMIE QUIRK

Position: C
Bats: L **Throws:** R
Ht: 6' 4" **Wt:** 200

Opening Day Age: 37
Born: 10/22/54 in
Whittier, CA
ML Seasons: 17

Overall Statistics

	G	AB	R	H	D	T	HR	RBI	SB	BB	SO	AVG
1991	90	185	33	46	8	0	3	21	12	23	42	.249
Career	244	449	74	101	16	1	4	35	20	51	97	.225

Overall Statistics

	G	AB	R	H	D	T	HR	RBI	SB	BB	SO	AVG
1991	76	203	16	53	4	0	1	17	0	16	28	.261
Career	906	2089	180	505	93	6	41	236	5	161	407	.242

HITTING, FIELDING, BASERUNNING:

The ankle injury that ended Walt Weiss' season gave Lance Blankenship his first free-and-clear shot at a full-time job. The Oakland Athletics moved Mike Gallego to shortstop and inserted Blankenship at second base. Unfortunately, he couldn't hold the job.

Blankenship has a little power, but he couldn't integrate it into his overall hitting approach. He overswung far too often and thus easily was victimized by breaking balls. He also was pitched away with success because he had trouble going to the opposite field. He showed no patience and couldn't fight back from down in the count.

Blankenship also was overanxious on the bases, as if his brazen running would prove to his bosses that he was gutsy enough to be a regular. On defense, Blankenship barely was adequate. He's a fine athlete with the equipment -- arm, range, toughness on the double play -- to play regularly, but he seems fidgety with his hands.

OVERALL:

Blankenship couldn't hold the second base job when it was handed to him, and his eagerness and aggression seem to work to his disadvantage, making him too hyped up. If he has a future with the A's -- and that's now debatable -- it could be as an outfielder.

HITTING, FIELDING, BASERUNNING:

With the departure of Ron Hassey, Jamie Quirk settled into a snug role as the Oakland Athletics' backup catcher. It was a comfortable fit for both. Quirk gave the A's solid offensive production with occasional power, along with a valuable left-handed bat off the bench.

Quirk didn't match his 1990 numbers, which were among the best of his 16-year career, but he hit consistently in '91. He's a lowball hitter who will almost never offer at anything above the waist. Quirk isn't quick-wristed enough to fight off inside fastballs, but he seldom tries. He hits more often to the left side than to the right, and usually will try to flick the ball, although he'll lengthen his swing if he's expecting a fastball.

Quirk isn't any threat on the bases and in fact often is replaced by a pinch-runner late in games. Defensively, he knows how to handle pitchers. He isn't a polished receiver, but throws well and gets rid of the ball fairly quickly. He also can fill in at first, third and the outfield.

OVERALL:

Quirk is an ideal backup catcher for the A's, and the fact he is a left-handed hitter probably will keep him around in 1992. His versatility works prominently in his favor.

ERNEST RILES

Position: 3B/SS
Bats: L **Throws:** R
Ht: 6' 1" **Wt:** 180

Opening Day Age: 31
Born: 10/2/60 in Bainbridge, GA
ML Seasons: 7

CURT YOUNG

Position: RP
Bats: R **Throws:** L
Ht: 6' 1" **Wt:** 180

Opening Day Age: 31
Born: 4/16/60 in Saginaw, MI
ML Seasons: 9

Overall Statistics

	G	AB	R	H	D	T	HR	RBI	SB	BB	SO	AVG
1991	108	281	30	60	8	4	5	32	3	31	42	.214
Career	786	2300	289	594	83	20	42	260	18	222	358	.258

Overall Statistics

	W	L	ERA	G	GS	Sv	IP	H	R	BB	SO	HR
1991	4	2	5.00	41	1	0	68.1	74	38	34	27	8
Career	64	50	4.33	225	152	0	1024.2	1039	539	343	512	140

HITTING, FIELDING, BASERUNNING:

Because Carney Lansford missed almost the entire 1991 season, the Oakland Athletics made Ernest Riles their regular third basemen against righthanders for much of the year. Alas, Riles confirmed the contention that his former team, the Giants, had long held: Riles is more valuable off the bench.

As a regular, Riles seemed to think that he was expected to provide power to a team that already had plenty, and he went after many more high pitches than he usually does. He would work the count, then nullify any advantage he would get by swinging at ball three and ball four. He was especially vulnerable to pitches high and tight.

Riles is a good baserunner, although he almost never attempts to steal. He fielded acceptably at third base most of the time, but he had a tendency to force throws from awkward positions. Only Mark McGwire's dexterity at first base saved him from a number of errors.

OVERALL:

Though he flopped in a regular role, Riles can play any infield or outfield position adequately, and with the Giants in 1990 was an exceptional pinch hitter. The A's would much prefer to use him in those roles, and if he's with them next year, that's likely what he'll be doing.

PITCHING, FIELDING & HOLDING RUNNERS:

In previous seasons, Curt Young had one of the most difficult roles on the Oakland A's staff: that of swing starter. Because the bullpen was so depleted in 1991, Young found himself functioning as a set-up/middle relief pitcher, and the change did not seem to benefit him.

Young fared reasonably well against lefthanders last year, but righthanders punished him at a .312 clip. His tendency to snip at the plate instead of challenging hitters worked to his advantage as a starter, but as a reliever with little margin for error, he was unwilling to challenge hitters. Young walked 34 while striking out 27, and his numbers against righthanders were appalling: 25 walks, eight strikeouts.

In the past, Young has done a good job against baserunners, but last year he was working much more often with runners on base and they got a better look at him. He is an average fielder.

OVERALL:

Young's work as a relief pitcher indicated that while he can be effective in single-batter, lefty-against-lefty situations, his stuff and his temperament are far better suited to starting. Ideally, he should be the number-five starter as he was in 1990. If the A's don't plan to use him in that capacity, they're likely to shop him.

ORGANIZATION OVERVIEW:

It's hard to remember, but the A's of the early and mid-eighties were a struggling, low-budget franchise which had to produce its own players in order to survive. Survival was a great motivator, and the A's developed such stars as Jose Canseco and Mark McGwire, while keeping a keen eye out for undervalued players on other teams (Dave Stewart, Dennis Eckersley, Dave Henderson). The A's rode those horses to three straight pennants. Baseball, however, is a game of "What have you done for me lately?" . . . and last year, when Oakland reached down to its farm system for help, it didn't get much. The A's do have some fine prospects, but all of them are pitchers, and it'll be awhile before they pan out.

KEVIN CAMPBELL

Position: P
Bats: R **Throws:** R
Ht: 6' 4" **Wt:** 225
Opening Day Age: 27
Born: 12/6/64 in Marianna, AR

Recent Statistics

	W	L	ERA	GGS	Sv	IP	H	R	BB	SO	HR
91 AAA Tacoma	9	2	1.80	35	0	2	75.0	53	18	35	56	1
91 AL Oakland	1	0	2.74	14	0	0	23.0	13	7	14	16	4

Campbell, a righty acquired from the Dodger system before the 1991 season, is one of the few Oakland farm players who did a good job for the big club last year; he allowed only 13 hits in 23 innings while compiling a 2.74 ERA for the A's. Campbell's career has taken off since shifting to the bullpen and developing a slider. He's much farther along than most of the A's other pitching prospects, and could get a lot of work with the big club this year.

KIRK DRESSENDORFER

Position: P
Bats: R **Throws:** R
Ht: 5' 11" **Wt:** 180
Opening Day Age: 22
Born: 4/8/69 in Houston, TX

Recent Statistics

	W	L	ERA	GGS	Sv	IP	H	R	BB	SO	HR
91 AAA Tacoma	1	3	10.88	8	7	0	24.0	31	29	20	19	4
91 AL Oakland	3	3	5.45	7	7	0	34.2	33	28	21	17	5

A graduate of the pitching factory at the University of Texas, Dressendorfer began 1991 in the Oakland rotation with only four professional starts under his belt -- a tall order, even for a Texan. Not surprisingly, Dressendorfer had some problems, though he gave up less than a hit an inning. After being sent to Tacoma, he got belted around mercilessly, developed an ear infection and then needed shoulder surgery, putting him out for the year. He's supposed to be ready by spring of '92. If healthy, he's highly regarded enough to make the A's forget his 1991 troubles and give him another shot at their Oakland rotation.

DON PETERS

Position: P
Bats: R **Throws:** R
Ht: 6' 0" **Wt:** 190
Opening Day Age: 22
Born: 10/7/69 in Oak Lawn, IL

Recent Statistics

	W	L	ERA	GGS	Sv	IP	H	R	BB	SO	HR
90 A Sou Oregon	1	1	0.76	11	7	0	35.2	20	7	17	34	0
91 AA Huntsville	4	11	5.00	33	20	0	126.0	131	89	70	59	14

Don Peters was Oakland's first draft choice in 1990. After pitching 11 games in rookie ball in 1990, he jumped to AA in '91, appearing in 33 games. He may have been overmatched; certainly he didn't have the stats of a top prospect. But Oakland loves Peters' 92-MPH fastball and his makeup as well. They'll take their time with him, but realistically Peters is at least a couple of years away from Oakland.

TODD VAN POPPEL

Position: P
Bats: R **Throws:** R
Ht: 6' 5" **Wt:** 210
Opening Day Age: 20
Born: 12/9/71 in Hinsdale, IL

Recent Statistics

	W	L	ERA	GGS	Sv	IP	H	R	BB	SO	HR
91 AA Huntsville	6	13	3.47	24	24	0	132.1	118	69	90	115	2
91 AL Oakland	0	0	9.64	1	1	0	4.2	7	5	2	6	1

Considered a franchise pitcher before he even entered professional ball, Van Poppel had a poor won-lost record at AA Huntsville last year. His control was a problem, but he has a great curve and a 94-MPH fastball, which helped him blow away a lot of hitters. In his one major league start in September, he looked like he belonged. The A's want to be careful with him, so consider Van Poppel two years away. Considering his tender age, he's performed very well.

DAVE ZANCANARO

Position: P
Bats: B **Throws:** L
Ht: 6' 1" **Wt:** 170
Opening Day Age: 23
Born: 1/8/69 in Carmichael, CA

Recent Statistics

	W	L	ERA	GGS	Sv	IP	H	R	BB	SO	HR
90 A Sou Oregon	3	0	3.86	10	8	0	44.1	44	22	13	42	2
90 A Modesto	1	2	6.23	4	2	0	13.0	13	9	14	7	1
91 AA Huntsville	5	10	3.38	29	28	0	165.0	151	87	92	104	7

Another product of the 1990 draft, Zancanaro was a first round compensation pick that year (34th overall). Like Peters and Van Poppel, Zancanaro labored at Huntsville last year, and also like the other two, he had a terrible won-lost record. There were compensations. Zancanaro's ERA was the best of the three and he showed an ability to dominate hitters. He threw consistently in the 90s, and the A's liked his tenacity. Zancanaro's control is a problem, but he is not that far away from a major league opportunity.

HITTING:

Over the last three seasons Greg Briley has been a semi-regular in the Seattle outfield, logging 300-400 at-bats while hitting between .245 and .260. But after belting 13 homers in 1989, Briley has totaled only seven four-baggers over the last two seasons. Since Briley doesn't hit many doubles and triples or draw a lot of walks, his overall lack of production has the Mariners concerned.

Briley is compact at 5-8 and 165, and since he came up as a second baseman, he was sometimes compared to Hall-of-Famer Joe Morgan. To hit with Morgan's kind of power, he needs to hit the ball in the air, and over the last two years Briley has become a pronounced ground ball hitter . . . perhaps in an effort to utilize his good speed. The payoff, however, should be more singles, and he has yet to do that with any consistency. One hopeful sign is that he batted .308 after the All-Star break last year.

Briley remains a good lowball hitter, one with a tendency to chase pitches up and out of the strike zone. This tendency has increased in recent years, and last year Briley walked at a lower rate than in any of his three Seattle seasons.

BASERUNNING:

Briley stole a career-high 23 bases in 1991, while being thrown out 11 times, another career high. He has the speed and intelligence to do a better job.

FIELDING:

Originally an infielder, Briley has yet to completely master outfield play. He has enough speed to cover left field, but he does not have the natural instincts of someone who has played the outfield all his life. His throwing arm is weak and runners can take advantage of it.

OVERALL:

The Mariners have some good young outfield prospects, and might even switch Pete O'Brien to left field on a part-time basis. If Briley wants to get his 300 at-bats in 1992, he is going to have to show more pop with the bat.

GREG BRILEY

Position: LF/RF
Bats: L **Throws:** R
Ht: 5' 8" **Wt:** 165

Opening Day Age: 26
Born: 5/24/65 in Greenville, NC
ML Seasons: 4

Overall Statistics

	G	AB	R	H	D	T	HR	RBI	SB	BB	SO	AVG
1991	139	381	39	99	17	3	2	26	23	27	51	.260
Career	393	1148	137	296	59	9	21	111	50	108	187	.258

Where He Hits the Ball

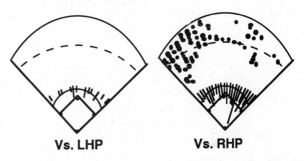

Vs. LHP   Vs. RHP

1991 Situational Stats

	AB	H	HR	RBI	AVG		AB	H	HR	RBI	AVG
Home	185	46	2	12	.249	LHP	39	9	0	9	.231
Road	196	53	0	14	.270	RHP	342	90	2	17	.263
Day	87	26	0	6	.299	Sc Pos	70	17	1	22	.243
Night	294	73	2	20	.248	Clutch	79	21	1	6	.266

1991 Rankings (American League)

→ 7th in caught stealing (11)
→ Led the Mariners in caught stealing

HITTING:

Keep Jay Buhner healthy for a season, people have always said, and then watch what he can do. Playing in 137 games and logging 406 at-bats -- both career highs by large margins -- Buhner came through in 1991 as predicted, belting 27 homers.

When he connects, Buhner can hit a ball as far as anyone. On an East Coast road trip in early August, Buhner hit a couple of tape measure shots -- particularly one in Yankee Stadium -- that had fans and writers gaping. That August surge put Buhner among the league leaders in home runs; then, as often happens with him, his bat went cold. The streaky Buhner belted his 24th homer on August 13, but didn't get his 25th until September 30. Typically, that started Buhner on another hot streak and he whacked three round-trippers during the last week of the season.

Buhner showed some signs of maturing as a hitter last year. He lowered his always prolific strikeout rate, while walking more than ever before. An excellent low-ball hitter, he can still be made to look foolish by pitchers who work him fastballs in and breaking balls away.

BASERUNNING:

With his history of sprains and broken bones, Buhner is no threat to steal. He's not horribly slow, however, and he's an aggressive, gung-ho baserunner who always looks to take the extra base.

FIELDING:

Buhner takes that same aggressiveness to the outfield, where he's never afraid to crash into a fence. He has good range and an excellent throwing arm. His 14 assists tied him for the league lead in right field.

OVERALL:

Predicting stardom for a brittle player like Buhner is always risky; just when you think he's turned the corner, he gets hurt again. But Buhner will be 27 this year, an age at which a lot of players have their best seasons. If healthy, he could easily be among the A.L. home run leaders.

JAY BUHNER

Position: RF
Bats: R **Throws:** R
Ht: 6' 3" **Wt:** 205

Opening Day Age: 27
Born: 8/13/64 in
Louisville, KY
ML Seasons: 5

Overall Statistics

	G	AB	R	H	D	T	HR	RBI	SB	BB	SO	AVG
1991	137	406	64	99	14	4	27	77	0	53	117	.244
Career	338	1056	143	261	56	6	56	182	4	118	321	.247

Where He Hits the Ball

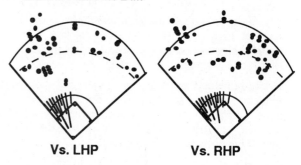

Vs. LHP   Vs. RHP

1991 Situational Stats

	AB	H	HR	RBI	AVG		AB	H	HR	RBI	AVG
Home	212	45	14	41	.212	LHP	146	35	9	26	.240
Road	194	54	13	36	.278	RHP	260	64	18	51	.246
Day	96	22	8	19	.229	Sc Pos	108	23	4	42	.213
Night	310	77	19	58	.248	Clutch	72	16	3	12	.222

1991 Rankings (American League)

- → 4th lowest batting average at home (.212)
- → 7th lowest batting average with the bases loaded (.111)
- → 9th lowest batting average with 2 strikes (.129)
- → Led the Mariners in home runs (27), strikeouts (117) and slugging percentage vs. left-handed pitchers (.486)
- → Led AL right fielders in highest percentage of pitches taken (58.9%)

HITTING:

Though few people noticed, Henry Cotto was having his best major league season last year when an injury abruptly ended it. Cotto, who suffered a tear in his right rotator cuff, didn't play after August 2 and underwent surgery in mid-August.

The Mariners are keeping their fingers crossed, because as he enters his thirties, Cotto seems to be becoming a smarter hitter. A .258 lifetime hitter entering the season, Cotto batted .305 last year, easily a career high. More than anything, his secret seemed to be that he's finally becoming a more selective hitter. Once very prone to jump on the first pitch, Cotto worked the count to great advantage last year; on plate appearances that started with ball one, he batted a hefty .361. Cotto still lacks the patience to work a walk, however, drawing a typically low total (10) last year. A good lowball hitter, he likes to jump on pitchers' mistakes.

If Cotto can hit .300 again he may force more playing time. The M's are content with him just as he is, as a fourth outfielder who fills in superbly for the regulars. Given regular duty in the past, Cotto has hit well for long stretches but then worn down.

BASERUNNING:

Cotto is Seattle's best baserunner and one of the very best in baseball. At 31 he shows no signs of slowing down. He was 16-for-19 stealing last year and has an outstanding 83 percent success rate for his career.

FIELDING:

The versatile Cotto handles all three outfield positions in style, showing excellent range at each post. The shoulder injury has to concern him and the Mariners, however, because his arm was never much more than average.

OVERALL:

Rotator cuff surgery is always a little scary, even for a position player. Cotto is the sort of solid bench player who can help any major league club -- but first he'll have to prove he's healthy.

HENRY COTTO

Position: LF/CF
Bats: R **Throws:** R
Ht: 6' 2" **Wt:** 180

Opening Day Age: 31
Born: 1/5/61 in Bronx, NY
ML Seasons: 8

Overall Statistics

	G	AB	R	H	D	T	HR	RBI	SB	BB	SO	AVG
1991	66	177	35	54	6	2	6	23	16	10	27	.305
Career	668	1644	229	433	68	8	34	162	91	88	263	.263

Where He Hits the Ball

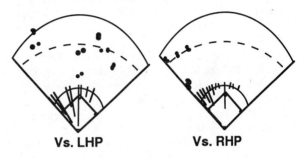

Vs. LHP   **Vs. RHP**

1991 Situational Stats

	AB	H	HR	RBI	AVG		AB	H	HR	RBI	AVG
Home	73	22	2	13	.301	LHP	96	31	4	13	.323
Road	104	32	4	10	.308	RHP	81	23	2	10	.284
Day	56	19	1	7	.339	Sc Pos	39	12	2	16	.308
Night	121	35	5	16	.289	Clutch	32	7	0	1	.219

1991 Rankings (American League)

➡ Did not rank near the top or bottom in any category

HITTING:

The Mariners' all-time leader in most offensive categories, Alvin Davis suffered through an unhappy -- and unsuccessful -- 1991 season. A .289 lifetime hitter entering the season, Davis batted an anemic .221, a career low by 50 points. His on-base percentage (.299) was almost 100 points below his career average of .391. And Davis, who'd never hit fewer than 17 homers in seven previous seasons, managed only a dozen round-trippers.

If this wasn't the same Alvin Davis, it was easy to understand why. Davis was in the last year of his Mariner contract and the club showed no interest in signing him to a new pact. The longtime hero suddenly found himself number three among Seattle first basemen at year-end, ranking behind both Pete O'Brien and AAA star Tino Martinez. Davis logged a lot of time in the DH slot, but as in 1990, he never seemed comfortable in the role. He also seemed to be losing his patience: long one of the majors' most selective hitters, Davis has seen his walk total drop from 101 to 85 to 56 over the last three seasons. Meanwhile his strikeout totals have gone up as pitchers have learned they can challenge him more often than they could in the past.

BASERUNNING:

Davis has always been very slow, and now that he's in his thirties, he would have trouble outrunning a tortoise. Over the last six seasons he's stolen exactly one base. As they say, he knows his limitations.

FIELDING:

Davis is not a big liability at first base, but he's not a big asset, either. His problem is lack of range, mostly in reaching balls down the line. He is good at handling low throws in the dirt, however.

OVERALL:

In his best years, Davis' power stats were always very dependent on the friendly Seattle ballpark. Of his 160 career homers, 101 came at the Kingdome. At 31 he is young enough to bounce back, but he'll probably need a small home yard to reach his former level of play.

ALVIN DAVIS

Position: DH/1B
Bats: L **Throws:** R
Ht: 6' 1" **Wt:** 190

Opening Day Age: 31
Born: 9/9/60 in Riverside, CA
ML Seasons: 8

Overall Statistics

	G	AB	R	H	D	T	HR	RBI	SB	BB	SO	AVG
1991	145	462	39	102	15	1	12	69	0	56	78	.221
Career	1166	4136	563	1163	212	10	160	667	7	672	549	.281

Where He Hits the Ball

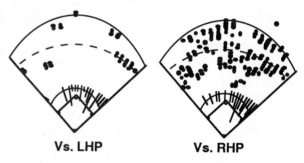

Vs. LHP   Vs. RHP

1991 Situational Stats

	AB	H	HR	RBI	AVG		AB	H	HR	RBI	AVG
Home	226	52	6	35	.230	LHP	101	24	4	14	.238
Road	236	50	6	34	.212	RHP	361	78	8	55	.216
Day	128	30	5	19	.234	Sc Pos	108	28	1	46	.259
Night	334	72	7	50	.216	Clutch	75	16	4	11	.213

1991 Rankings (American League)

→ 1st in sacrifice flies (10) and least runs scored per time reached base (24.7%)

→ 2nd lowest slugging percentage (.336)

→ 3rd in lowest batting average vs. right-handed pitchers (.216), lowest slugging percentage vs. right-handed pitchers (.324), lowest on-base average vs. right-handed pitchers (.388) and highest percentage of pitches taken (64.2%)

→ 4th in lowest batting average (.221), lowest groundball/flyball ratio (.67), lowest percentage of extra bases taken as a runner (20.8%) and lowest batting average on the road (.212)

→ Led the Mariners in sacrifice flies and highest percentage of pitches taken

PITCHING:

Rich DeLucia made the Mariner rotation last year based on a good minor league record and an impressive September stint with the M's in 1990 (2.00 ERA in five starts). DeLucia pitched reasonably well for most of the year before an horrendous September (1-5, 9.64 ERA) saddled him with a losing record and a 5.09 ERA, second-worst among American League starters for the year.

DeLucia is primarily a fastball pitcher who works upstairs in the strike zone; he had the highest fly ball-to-ground ball ratio in the American League last year. A pitcher can be successful doing that -- number two and three were Nolan Ryan and Mark Langston -- but he needs either an outstanding fastball, excellent control, or both. Unfortunately for DeLucia, his fastball registers only about 85 MPH, and his control, usually very good during his minor league career, deserted him last year. As a result, he allowed 31 homers, another category in which he led the league.

Though his struggles were obvious, DeLucia showed some positives last year. He held his own until his September disaster -- undoubtedly a sign of fatigue -- and he allowed less than a hit an inning, a sign that he has major league stuff. He might need to warm up a little more; through his first 15 pitches he was hammered by the opposition (.345 opponents' average).

HOLDING RUNNERS AND FIELDING:

DeLucia does an excellent job of holding baserunners. He allowed only four steals all year, and his opponents' stolen base percentage, a meager 30.8%, was third-best in the league. He fielded his position well, not committing an error all season.

OVERALL:

DeLucia had a full shot to prove himself as a major league starter last year and the jury is still out. The Mariners have some outstanding pitching prospects who are about ready to make a major league impact. If one or two of them make the grade next spring, DeLucia will be hard-pressed to keep his job.

RICH DELUCIA

Position: SP
Bats: R **Throws:** R
Ht: 6' 0" **Wt:** 180

Opening Day Age: 27
Born: 10/7/64 in Reading, PA
ML Seasons: 2

Overall Statistics

	W	L	ERA	G	GS	Sv	IP	H	R	BB	SO	HR
1991	12	13	5.09	32	31	0	182.0	176	107	78	98	31
Career	13	15	4.58	37	36	0	218.0	206	116	87	118	33

How Often He Throws Strikes

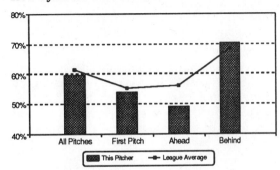

1991 Situational Stats

	W	L	ERA	Sv	IP		AB	H	HR	RBI	AVG
Home	7	4	4.72	0	89.2	LHB	320	92	11	42	.287
Road	5	9	5.46	0	92.1	RHB	358	84	20	54	.235
Day	3	5	6.23	0	47.2	Sc Pos	125	34	6	63	.272
Night	9	8	4.69	0	134.1	Clutch	25	10	4	5	.400

1991 Rankings (American League)

→ 1st in home runs allowed (31), lowest ground-ball/flyball ratio (.68), highest slugging percentage allowed (.457) and most home runs allowed per 9 innings (1.53)

→ 2nd highest ERA (5.09)

→ 3rd in lowest stolen base percentage allowed (30.8%) and highest ERA on the road (5.46)

→ Led the Mariners in home runs allowed, lowest stolen base percentage allowed and highest run support per 9 innings (5.5)

FUTURE MVP?

KEN GRIFFEY JR

Position: CF
Bats: L **Throws:** L
Ht: 6' 3" **Wt:** 200

Opening Day Age: 22
Born: 11/21/69 in Donora, PA
ML Seasons: 3

HITTING:

Even the best young ballplayers need a wake up call sometimes and Ken Griffey, Jr. got one at the All-Star break last year. Griffey's nine homers and .280 average weren't good enough for Seattle columnist Steve Kelly, who bluntly asked whether Griffey wanted to just get by, or whether he wanted to fulfill his destiny and be a superstar. "The article made me think," Griffey admitted, and from then on he was a terror, batting .372 with 64 RBI in 75 games after the break. By year's end Griffey's overall stats -- 22 homers, 100 RBI, a .327 average -- were exactly what you'd expect from a budding young superstar.

Still a baby at 22, Griffey seems to be a player who can do just about everything. He already has impressive bat speed, great power to the gaps, and improving discipline. He doesn't even strike out much, keeping his K total at around the 80 mark.

As is true with any great hitter, pitchers try to keep Griffey off balance, working him in and out and feeding him a lot of offspeed stuff. Griffey even has a cure for that. When he feels sure a curveball is coming, he'll sometimes step up in the box and blast away, as he did on a game-winning curveball against Melido Perez in Chicago.

BASERUNNING:

Griffey has outstanding speed, but he's still learning to use it on the bases. He stole 18 bases in 24 attempts last season, his best work yet. He's capable of doing a lot better.

FIELDING:

Already a Gold Glove winner at his young age, Griffey is improving in the field as well. His putout totals have increased as he's learned to play the hitters, and he's cut his error total each year. His throwing arm is not overwhelmingly powerful, but it's plenty good enough.

OVERALL:

What's next for Griffey -- 30 homers, 120 RBI, a batting title? Anything seems possible for this remarkable young player . . . just as long as he stays motivated.

Overall Statistics

	G	AB	R	H	D	T	HR	RBI	SB	BB	SO	AVG
1991	154	548	76	179	42	1	22	100	18	71	82	.327
Career	436	1600	228	478	93	8	60	241	50	178	246	.299

Where He Hits the Ball

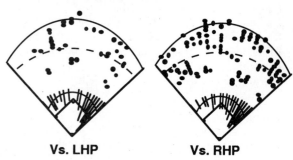

Vs. LHP   **Vs. RHP**

1991 Situational Stats

	AB	H	HR	RBI	AVG		AB	H	HR	RBI	AVG
Home	282	103	16	59	.365	LHP	159	50	5	26	.314
Road	266	76	6	41	.286	RHP	389	129	17	74	.332
Day	144	47	6	25	.326	Sc Pos	167	55	6	76	.329
Night	404	132	16	75	.327	Clutch	81	23	2	13	.284

1991 Rankings (American League)

➡ 3rd in highest percentage of extra bases taken (75.0%), sacrifice flies (9), intentional walks (21) and batting average at home (.365)

➡ 4th in batting average (.327), doubles (42), highest batting average vs. right-handed pitchers (.332), highest slugging percentage vs. right-handed pitchers (.550) and highest on-base average vs. right-handed pitchers (.405)

➡ Led the Mariners in batting average, hits (179), doubles, total bases (289), RBIs (100), intentional walks, slugging percentage (.527), HR frequency (24.9 ABs per HR), least GDPs per GDP situation (8.5%) and batting average with runners in scoring position (.329)

PITCHING:

Erik Hanson's 1991 experiences recall Graig Nettles' description of Sparky Lyle's Yankee career: from Cy Young to Sayonara. The big righthander hasn't yet copped a Cy Young award, but after his 18-win, 211-strikeout 1990 campaign, people were dusting off the mantlepiece. Fast-forward a year, however, and suddenly people are talking about Hanson in very different terms -- as possible trade bait.

Plagued by early-season shoulder problems, Hanson won only eight games in 1991. He went on the disabled list twice in May, and when he returned, he was nothing like the dominant hurler of 1990. Some people thought Hanson was babying his arm, worried about getting hurt again. That might be why he was throwing so many offspeed and breaking pitches instead of cutting loose with his 90-plus fastball. Others bluntly questioned Hanson's toughness, saying he couldn't handle the pressure of close games. Hanson missed only one turn after returning from the DL in June. His work was hardly disastrous (3.81 ERA, 7.4 strikeouts per nine innings), but he never managed to win more than two games in any month.

When he's on, Hanson has the stuff to be one of baseball's best pitchers. All his pitches (fastball, curve, change-up) are excellent, and he mixes them in a way that keeps hitters guessing. The problem in 1991 was that he wasn't on very often.

HOLDING RUNNERS AND FIELDING:

One very positive aspect of Hanson's work last year was his improvement at controlling the running game. Base stealers were only 11-for-21 with Hanson on the mound, an impressive performance for a power pitcher. A natural athlete, he fields his position well.

OVERALL:

If the Mariners are serious about peddling Hanson -- and new manager Bill Plummer might want to offer his input on that idea -- they'll probably find no shortage of bidders. Hanson is only 26, and lots of people will take a chance on a talent like his.

ERIK HANSON

Position: SP
Bats: R **Throws:** R
Ht: 6' 6" **Wt:** 210

Opening Day Age: 26
Born: 5/18/65 in Kinnelon, NJ
ML Seasons: 4

Overall Statistics

	W	L	ERA	G	GS	Sv	IP	H	R	BB	SO	HR
1991	8	8	3.81	27	27	0	174.2	182	82	56	143	16
Career	37	25	3.40	83	83	0	565.2	525	231	168	465	42

How Often He Throws Strikes

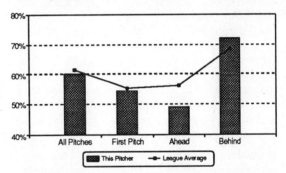

1991 Situational Stats

	W	L	ERA	Sv	IP		AB	H	HR	RBI	AVG
Home	4	5	4.25	0	89.0	LHB	355	85	10	47	.239
Road	4	3	3.36	0	85.2	RHB	321	97	6	22	.302
Day	1	3	4.47	0	44.1	Sc Pos	150	35	3	49	.233
Night	7	5	3.59	0	130.1	Clutch	63	15	0	6	.238

1991 Rankings (American League)

- → 2nd in wild pitches (14)
- → 4th most strikeouts per 9 innings (7.4)
- → 7th highest slugging percentage allowed (.414)
- → 8th highest ERA at home (4.25)
- → 9th in strikeout/walk ratio (2.6) and highest batting average allowed (.269)
- → Led the Mariners in wild pitches, caught stealing (10), strikeout/walk ratio, lowest on-base average allowed (.323) and ERA on the road (3.36)

PITCHING:

One of three young pitchers the Mariners received from Montreal in the 1989 Mark Langston deal, Brian Holman has pitched well for Seattle while fighting injury problems, the latest of which appears to be serious. Holman has yet to have a winning season, but his 13-14 mark last year was largely the result of poor run support. The Mariners averaged only 3.6 runs a game for him last year, making him the sixth-worst supported starter in the American League.

Though he stands 6-4, Holman is on the slender side at 185 pounds, and he's not a power pitcher like teammate Randy Johnson, who arrived from Montreal in the same deal. Holman has a good fastball and can strike hitters out, so it's not quite correct to label him a finesse pitcher. His best pitch is a good sinking fastball, one which he likes to work outside against lefthanders. Holman also throws a slurve -- a big-breaking slider -- which can be very effective against righties. Holman's best pitches arrive low in the strike zone, and as a result he gets a good number of ground ball outs and double plays. He's not afraid to work inside, plunking 10 batters last year.

Holman underwent elbow surgery for bone chips in September of 1990, so there was naturally some concern early last year about his arm strength. Holman's elbow proved okay, but later in the year he developed shoulder problems and had to undergo rotator cuff surgery at season's end.

HOLDING RUNNERS AND FIELDING:

Holman does not have an outstanding pickoff move, but he delivers the ball quickly, making him tough to steal on. Runners were only 4-for-9 against Holman in '91. He fields his position well.

OVERALL:

Tough and aggressive, Holman has proven himself to be a capable major league starter. Unfortunately, his rotator cuff problems have clouded his Mariner future. Holman may not be ready for the start of the 1992 season and no one knows exactly when he'll be able to return.

BRIAN HOLMAN

Position: SP
Bats: R **Throws:** R
Ht: 6' 4" **Wt:** 185

Opening Day Age: 27
Born: 1/25/65 in Denver, CO
ML Seasons: 4

Overall Statistics

	W	L	ERA	G	GS	Sv	IP	H	R	BB	SO	HR
1991	13	14	3.69	30	30	0	195.1	199	86	77	108	16
Career	37	45	3.71	109	99	0	676.2	682	303	254	392	47

How Often He Throws Strikes

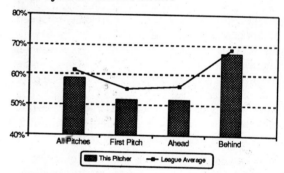

1991 Situational Stats

	W	L	ERA	Sv	IP		AB	H	HR	RBI	AVG
Home	9	7	2.65	0	118.2	LHB	391	111	6	42	.284
Road	4	7	5.28	0	76.2	RHB	352	88	10	35	.250
Day	3	8	3.50	0	79.2	Sc Pos	172	39	3	57	.227
Night	10	6	3.81	0	115.2	Clutch	53	10	1	2	.189

1991 Rankings (American League)

→ 2nd in shutouts (3)

→ 4th in losses (14)

→ 5th in GDPs induced (22) and most GDPs induced per 9 innings (1.0)

→ Led the Mariners in wins (13), losses, complete games (5), shutouts, hits allowed (199), GDPs induced, groundball/flyball ratio (1.63), most GDPs induced per 9 innings, ERA at home (2.66) and lowest batting average allowed with runners in scoring positon (.227)

PITCHING:

Still only 27, Mike Jackson has a 96-MPH fastball and the sort of stuff that makes people think "closer." Jackson had the perfect opportunity to nail down his reputation in 1991. Mike Schooler, the Mariner relief ace, missed the first half of the season with shoulder problems, and Jackson was one of the M's first choices to fill the breach. But Jackson didn't seize the opportunity, blowing eight save opportunities in 22 attempts during the course of a very enigmatic season.

Looking back on last season, one finds a lot to like. A workhorse, Jackson appeared in 72 games, second-most in the AL. He held the opposition to a .201 batting average and he struck out an impressive 7.5 batters per nine innings. Jackson's walk total -- 34 in 88.2 innings -- seems high, but 11 of those walks were intentional, so there's nothing wrong with his control. He allowed only five homers and his six hit batters are a sign that he's fearless about pitching inside.

Jackson's problem, pure and simple, is consistency. Look at his monthly ERAs: April 3.86, May 0.95, June 4.26, July 4.85, August 0.00 (in 15 games), September 9.26, October 0.00. There's a lot of good pitching in there, but the main word that comes to mind is "erratic."

HOLDING RUNNERS AND FIELDING:

Jackson has a better move to first than most power pitchers, but opponents were successful on all five of their stolen base opportunities last year. He's a former infielder who does a good job of fielding his position.

OVERALL:

Jackson has proven he's a good reliever, although he hasn't proven to be a good closer. He's the sort of pitcher who intrigues opposing general managers. Whatever his role, and wherever he works in 1992, there's no question that Mike Jackson can be a pitcher of considerable value.

MIKE JACKSON

Position: RP
Bats: R **Throws:** R
Ht: 6' 0" **Wt:** 200

Opening Day Age: 27
Born: 12/22/64 in Houston, TX
ML Seasons: 6

Overall Statistics

	W	L	ERA	G	GS	Sv	IP	H	R	BB	SO	HR
1991	7	7	3.25	72	0	14	88.2	64	35	34	74	5
Career	25	35	3.53	326	7	29	487.1	383	217	235	409	49

How Often He Throws Strikes

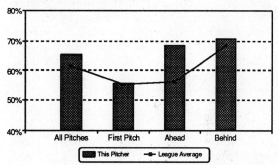

1991 Situational Stats

	W	L	ERA	Sv	IP		AB	H	HR	RBI	AVG
Home	3	2	2.64	6	47.2	LHB	119	30	2	12	.252
Road	4	5	3.95	8	41.0	RHB	200	34	3	21	.170
Day	2	1	4.24	1	17.0	Sc Pos	87	19	1	27	.218
Night	5	6	3.01	13	71.2	Clutch	208	46	4	26	.221

1991 Rankings (American League)

→ 1st in lowest save percentage (63.6%) and relief losses (7)

→ 2nd in games pitched (72)

→ 5th in blown saves (8), lowest percentage of inherited runners scored (19.2%) and lowest batting average allowed in relief (.201)

→ Led the Mariners in games pitched, games finished (35), save opportunities (22), blown saves, first batter efficiency (.147), relief wins (7), relief losses, lowest batting average allowed in relief and most strikeouts per 9 innings in relief (7.5)

PITCHING:

The biggest pitcher in major league history at 6-10, Randy Johnson is also one of the most overpowering. Johnson has a fastball that approaches 100 MPH, a sharp-breaking curve and a change-up that can keep hitters guessing. At his best he is simply unhittable. He tossed a no-hitter at the Tigers in June of 1990 and just missed another one against Oakland last August 14, losing it on a ninth-inning single by Mike Gallego.

Unfortunately, Johnson has a simple problem: when he winds up, no one -- not Johnson, nor his catcher, nor his manager, nor the hitter -- has much of an idea where the ball is going. When Johnson walked a league-leading 120 batters in 1990, many people chalked it up to inexperience and figured that his control would improve in '91. Figure again. In '91 Johnson walked the staggering total of 152, 47 more than Mike Moore and Dave Stewart, who were far back in second place. Johnson even performed the dubious feat of allowing more walks than hits (151).

With his long delivery, Johnson never finds it easy to find the sort of rhythm that will allow him to throw strikes consistently. He showed some improvement in his control for awhile after the All-Star game, but that was only temporary. In September-October he was the same old Randy, walking 32 men in 38 innings.

HOLDING RUNNERS AND FIELDING:

Johnson has enough trouble getting the ball in the strike zone to worry much about controlling basestealers. His delivery leaves him in a bad fielding position and when he gets the ball he often boots it. Johnson's fielding average last year was a hideous .821.

OVERALL:

Johnson is a major talent, but he'll have trouble becoming a big winner if he doesn't cut down on his walks. Consistent winning with his style is possible -- the young Bob Feller and Nolan Ryan come to mind -- but it's an uphill struggle.

RANDY JOHNSON

Position: SP
Bats: R **Throws:** L
Ht: 6'10" **Wt:** 225

Opening Day Age: 28
Born: 9/10/63 in Walnut Creek, CA
ML Seasons: 4

Overall Statistics

	W	L	ERA	G	GS	Sv	IP	H	R	BB	SO	HR
1991	13	10	3.98	33	33	0	201.1	151	96	152	228	15
Career	37	34	4.01	99	98	0	607.2	495	307	375	577	57

How Often He Throws Strikes

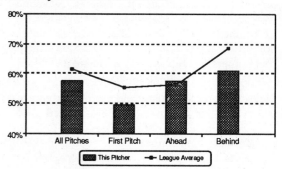

This Pitcher ■ League Average ●

1991 Situational Stats

	W	L	ERA	Sv	IP		AB	H	HR	RBI	AVG
Home	6	5	3.92	0	105.2	LHB	85	18	2	14	.212
Road	7	5	4.05	0	95.2	RHB	623	133	13	67	.213
Day	3	1	6.10	0	38.1	Sc Pos	190	45	4	65	.237
Night	10	9	3.48	0	163.0	Clutch	61	15	0	3	.246

1991 Rankings (American League)

➡ 1st in walks allowed (152), most pitches thrown per batter (4.18) and errors by a pitcher (5)

➡ 2nd in strikeouts (228), lowest batting average allowed (.213) and most strikeouts per 9 innings (10.2)

➡ 3rd in hit batsmen (12), lowest slugging percentage allowed (.325) and highest on-base average allowed (.358)

➡ Led the Mariners in wins (13), games started (33), innings (201.1), batters faced (889), walks allowed, hit batsmen, strikeouts, pitches throwns (3,714), most stolen bases allowed (18), GDPs induced (22) and least home runs allowed per 9 innings (.67)

PITCHING:

Calvin Jones was the Mariners' first-round choice in the January, 1984 draft. The righthander finally reached Seattle last June after a long minor league apprenticeship. At 27, Jones hadn't even pitched at the AAA level until this 1991, and he'd never been on Seattle's 40-man roster or gotten an invitation to their major league training camp. Mariner expectations were modest. But Jones made an immediate impression, turning in a 2.53 ERA and averaging nearly a strikeout an inning in 27 appearances. Allowing only 33 hits in 46.1 innings, he held lefties to a .164 average and did not yield a homer.

A big man at 6-3 and 185 pounds, Jones has a fastball which tops 90, but his best pitch is a forkball that he learned two years ago while still in the Class A California League. Jones has long fingers, ideal for a forkball pitcher, and he picked up the pitch quickly; his forker, which got him to the majors within two years, has been described as "unhittable" by more than one observer.

Jones worked most often as a long man/middle reliever last year, the lowest rung on the bullpen ladder, but his work has the Mariners thinking he can handle much bigger responsibilities. The one reservation about him concerns his control. Jones walked a lot of batters throughout his minor league career and the problem continued in Seattle last year.

HOLDING RUNNERS AND FIELDING:

Jones needs to work on controlling the running game. Although he pitched a low number of innings, runners were successful five times in six stolen base attempts against him. He fields his position well and did not allow an error last year.

OVERALL:

Though Jones seemingly came out of nowhere last year, he figures heavily in Seattle's 1992 plans. A set-up role, replacing Mike Jackson, is a strong possibility. If Mike Schooler isn't 100 percent, Jones might even get a chance as a finisher.

CALVIN JONES

Position: RP
Bats: R **Throws:** R
Ht: 6' 3" **Wt:** 185

Opening Day Age: 28
Born: 9/26/63 in Compton, CA
ML Seasons: 1

Overall Statistics

	W	L	ERA	G	GS	Sv	IP	H	R	BB	SO	HR
1991	2	2	2.53	27	0	2	46.1	33	14	29	42	0
Career	2	2	2.53	27	0	2	46.1	33	14	29	42	0

How Often He Throws Strikes

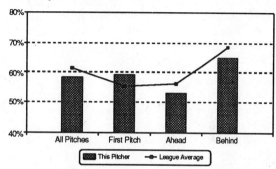

1991 Situational Stats

	W	L	ERA	Sv	IP		AB	H	HR	RBI	AVG
Home	2	1	1.44	0	25.0	LHB	67	11	0	4	.164
Road	0	1	3.80	2	21.1	RHB	91	22	0	11	.242
Day	1	1	2.45	0	11.0	Sc Pos	42	14	0	15	.333
Night	1	1	2.55	2	35.1	Clutch	48	10	0	3	.208

1991 Rankings (American League)

→ Did not rank near the top or bottom in any category

PITCHING:

Now 33, veteran lefthander Bill Krueger didn't exactly set pulses racing when he signed a free-agent contract with the Mariners in December 1990. However, what the M's got was a starting pitcher who stood tall at a time when Seattle desperately needed help. Krueger wound up with an 11-8 record and a 3.60 ERA, easily the best season of his nine-year major league career.

If Krueger has learned a thing or two about pitching over the years, it's easy to understand how. He broke in at Medford in 1980, and he's spent a lot of his baseball life pitching in minor league towns like West Haven, Tacoma, Madison and Albuquerque. He's also had major league stops in Oakland, Los Angeles and Milwaukee. Krueger's fastball isn't going to bust any radar guns and neither will his breaking pitch. In order to be successful, he needs to mix his pitches and demonstrate good control.

Krueger did exactly that through most of 1991. He kept his walk total down -- always a problem for him -- and was able to succeed even while allowing well over one hit an inning. Krueger stunned the baseball world, and probably himself as well, by going 4-0 with a 1.19 ERA during the month of July. He cooled off after that, but he put together a very solid season.

HOLDING RUNNERS AND FIELDING:

Krueger has a good move to first, but one that's compromised by a high leg kick when he delivers to the plate. Runners were successful in 11 of 16 attempts against him last year. He fields his position well and did not commit an error in 1991.

OVERALL:

A free agent at season's end, Krueger might not get much of an offer from the Mariners, a club with a good deal of young pitching talent. But he can rest assured that there are always a lot of teams which need pitching.

BILL KRUEGER

Position: SP/RP
Bats: L **Throws:** L
Ht: 6' 5" **Wt:** 205

Opening Day Age: 33
Born: 4/24/58 in Waukegan, IL
ML Seasons: 9

Overall Statistics

	W	L	ERA	G	GS	Sv	IP	H	R	BB	SO	HR
1991	11	8	3.60	35	25	0	175.0	194	82	60	91	15
Career	47	49	4.19	197	114	4	845.1	908	476	378	417	67

How Often He Throws Strikes

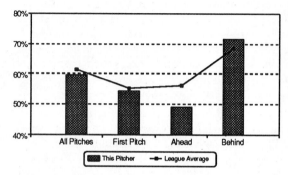

1991 Situational Stats

	W	L	ERA	Sv	IP		AB	H	HR	RBI	AVG
Home	7	3	3.73	0	94.0	LHB	140	43	2	16	.307
Road	4	5	3.44	0	81.0	RHB	532	151	13	56	.284
Day	2	2	3.15	0	34.1	Sc Pos	146	38	0	54	.260
Night	9	6	3.71	0	140.2	Clutch	50	17	1	4	.340

1991 Rankings (American League)

➡ 2nd highest batting average allowed (.289)

➡ 6th highest slugging percentage allowed (.418) and highest on-base average allowed (.346)

➡ 7th most GDPs induced per 9 innings (.98)

➡ Led the Mariners in ERA (3.60), pickoff throws (163), winning percentage (.579) and least pitches thrown per batter (3.54)

OVERLOOKED

EDGAR MARTINEZ

Position: 3B
Bats: R **Throws:** R
Ht: 5'11" **Wt:** 175

Opening Day Age: 29
Born: 1/2/63 in New York, NY
ML Seasons: 5

HITTING:

In his second full season as the Mariners' third baseman, Edgar Martinez did everything Seattle expected -- and then some. There was nothing shabby about Martinez' .302, 11-homer performance in 1990, but in '91 he exceeded it, improving his offensive numbers in virtually every category.

Though not exactly the Mike Schmidt type, Martinez belted 14 homers last year, and his 35 doubles indicate his power to the gaps. However, Martinez's real forte is getting on base. He's one of the most patient hitters in baseball, seldom swinging at a first pitch and drawing a good number of walks (84 last year). Because of his on-base ability -- and because the M's lacked a viable alternative -- Martinez spent much of last year in the leadoff spot. Though he's not exactly Rickey Henderson, Martinez scored a club-high 98 runs.

With his quick hands, Martinez can turn on a fastball and pull it with power. But for the most part he prefers to use the whole field. Because he lacks speed and hits a lot of hard grounders, Martinez is very prone to the double play ball (19 last year).

BASERUNNING:

As a leadoff man, Martinez is the West Coast Wade Boggs -- on the bases as well as at bat. Martinez had no successful steals last year and is 3-for-11 lifetime in five seasons. Call him a conservative, but fairly-smart, baserunner.

FIELDING:

After committing 27 errors in 1990, Martinez knew he had to improve in the field, and he did. He reduced his error total to 15 and showed improved range, ranking second in the league in assists and third in total chances. He's become a very solid glove man.

OVERALL:

Now a regular after years spent waiting for his chance, Martinez is young enough at 29 to hold his job for years to come. Very quietly, he's become one of the best third basemen in the American League.

Overall Statistics

	G	AB	R	H	D	T	HR	RBI	SB	BB	SO	AVG
1991	150	544	98	167	35	1	14	52	0	84	72	.307
Career	386	1277	195	380	76	5	27	131	3	181	172	.298

Where He Hits the Ball

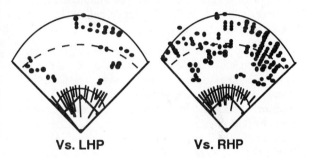

Vs. LHP   Vs. RHP

1991 Situational Stats

	AB	H	HR	RBI	AVG		AB	H	HR	RBI	AVG
Home	250	80	8	28	.320	LHP	156	56	2	12	.359
Road	294	87	6	24	.296	RHP	388	111	12	40	.286
Day	143	37	2	14	.259	Sc Pos	105	23	2	33	.219
Night	401	130	12	38	.324	Clutch	65	23	1	10	.354

1991 Rankings (American League)

- → 2nd in leadoff on-base average (.405)
- → 4th in hit by pitch (8), batting average vs. left-handed pitchers (.359) and batting average after the 6th inning (.336)
- → 5th in on-base average (.405)
- → Led the Mariners in runs (98), singles (117), walks (84), times on base (259), GDPs (19), on-base average (.405), groundball/flyball ratio (1.53), most pitches seen per plate appearance (4.08), batting average in the clutch (.354) and batting average vs. left-handed pitchers

HITTING:

Tino Martinez will finally get his chance to become the Mariners' full-time first baseman in 1992 -- at last. After batting .320 with 17 homers and 93 RBI for AAA Calgary in 1990, Martinez thought he'd done everything he needed to do to prove himself ready for the major leagues. But with Pete O'Brien and Alvin Davis still around last spring, Martinez found himself back in Canada, like it or not.

To his credit, Martinez didn't pout and have himself a bad season. Instead he posted numbers that were, if anything, even better: .326 average, 18 homers, 86 RBI, 82 walks. At the end of the year he was chosen the Pacific Coast League's Most Valuable Player and Portland manager Russ Nixon, a long-time major leaguer, called him "the best hitting prospect in the league."

That said, there are a number of people who question whether Martinez will become an impact player at the major league level. The Calgary stats are impressive, but they were logged in a hitter's park and a hitter's league. Martinez hasn't hit well in September trials for the Mariners in either 1990 (.221) or 1991 (.205), though admittedly those were based on only 180 combined at-bats. Martinez has proven himself to be a good off-speed hitter, but some baseball men doubt his ability to hit a major league fastball.

BASERUNNING:

A big man at 6-2 and 205, Martinez seems to be an intelligent baserunner but he doesn't have a lot of speed. He's never stolen in double figures in the minors and he's yet to swipe a major league base.

FIELDING:

A natural first baseman, Martinez handles himself very well around the bag. He has good footwork, excellent range and good hands. He's never been tried in the outfield and probably won't be, given his prowess at first.

OVERALL:

All Martinez has really wanted is a fair chance, and he seems certain to get it this year. Now it's up to him to prove himself and make the doubters eat their words.

TINO MARTINEZ

Position: 1B
Bats: L **Throws:** R
Ht: 6' 2" **Wt:** 205

Opening Day Age: 24
Born: 12/7/67 in Tampa, FL
ML Seasons: 2

Overall Statistics

	G	AB	R	H	D	T	HR	RBI	SB	BB	SO	AVG
1991	36	112	11	23	2	0	4	9	0	11	24	.205
Career	60	180	15	38	6	0	4	14	0	20	33	.211

Where He Hits the Ball

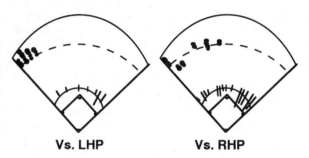

Vs. LHP   **Vs. RHP**

1991 Situational Stats

	AB	H	HR	RBI	AVG		AB	H	HR	RBI	AVG
Home	57	13	3	6	.228	LHP	35	9	1	1	.257
Road	55	10	1	3	.182	RHP	77	14	3	8	.182
Day	30	3	1	3	.100	Sc Pos	28	2	0	5	.071
Night	82	20	3	6	.244	Clutch	25	9	1	2	.360

1991 Rankings (American League)

→ Did not rank near the top or bottom in any category

PITCHING:

When the Mariners obtained lefthander Rob Murphy from Boston for pitcher Mike Gardiner right before the start of the 1991 season, they hoped they were obtaining at least a semblance of the Murphy who'd proven himself to be one of baseball's best and most durable relievers from 1986 to 1989. They definitely didn't want the Murphy of 1990, the one who'd been lit up for a 6.32 ERA and a .348 opponents' batting average in his last year with the Red Sox.

What they got, for the most part, was the old Murphy. At age 31 and after working in 305 games from 1987 to 1990, Murphy no longer had the fastball to strike out over a man an inning as he had done in the past. But used carefully -- Murphy only worked 48 innings despite appearing in 57 games -- he turned in a creditable effort, recording a 3.00 ERA and converting all four of his save opportunities. Murphy's season ended in early September when he suffered an ankle injury. His arm was showing signs of fatigue by then, so the early finish to his season probably protected his ERA.

The Mariners got Murphy primarily to pitch to left-handed hitters, and he did the job, holding lefty swingers to a .203 average. After Murphy was raked by righties at a .404 clip in '90, there was understandable concern that he couldn't handle them any more. Murphy eased those worries by holding righties to a .281 mark in '91, not great, but enough to keep him in the league.

HOLDING RUNNERS AND FIELDING:

Murphy has never been a good defensive player, and he wasn't in 1991, booting two of his 12 chances. Usually good at controlling the running game, he was victimized for five steals in five attempts in '91.

OVERALL:

Murphy didn't overwhelm anyone in 1991, but he proved he could still retire major league hitters. Even marginal lefty relievers always seem to find work, so if the Mariners don't want Murphy in 1992, someone probably will.

ROB MURPHY

Position: RP
Bats: L **Throws:** L
Ht: 6' 2" **Wt:** 215

Opening Day Age: 31
Born: 5/26/60 in Miami, FL
ML Seasons: 7

Overall Statistics

	W	L	ERA	G	GS	Sv	IP	H	R	BB	SO	HR
1991	0	1	3.00	57	0	4	48.0	47	17	19	34	4
Career	19	25	3.15	398	0	27	448.2	417	175	185	405	32

How Often He Throws Strikes

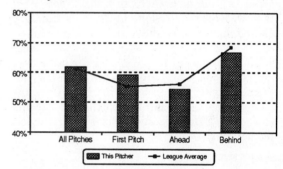

1991 Situational Stats

	W	L	ERA	Sv	IP		AB	H	HR	RBI	AVG
Home	0	0	1.40	3	25.2	LHB	74	15	2	11	.203
Road	0	1	4.84	1	22.1	RHB	114	32	2	17	.281
Day	0	0	3.45	2	15.2	Sc Pos	64	16	1	20	.250
Night	0	1	2.78	2	32.1	Clutch	56	15	0	7	.268

1991 Rankings (American League)

→ Did not rank near the top or bottom in any category

HITTING:

After flopping horrendously in 1990 -- the first season of his four-year, $7.6 million Mariner contract -- Pete O'Brien turned in a much more satisfying performance in 1991. The difference was stunning. O'Brien, who'd hit only five homers in 1990, belted 17 in 1991, his highest total since 1987. After driving in 27 runs in 1990, O'Brien drove home 88 in '91, matching the second-highest total of his career. After batting a dismal .156 with runners in scoring position in '90, O'Brien batted a very healthy .287 in those situations in 1991. O'Brien's .248 batting average was nothing to brag about, but even that was an increase of 24 points over 1990.

What was the difference? In truth, it was 1990 that was the aberration. O'Brien is not Lou Gehrig, but he's certainly no .224 singles hitter, either. O'Brien is now 34, and after his dismal 1990 performance, there was concern that he was no longer able to get around on a good fastball. O'Brien put those fears to rest in 1991. He retains his weakness on up-and-in fastballs, but it seems clear that O'Brien is still getting enough good pitches to hit.

BASERUNNING:

As a basestealer, O'Brien is looking forward to that old rocking chair; he hasn't had a successful steal since 1989. He's not an overly aggressive baserunner, but he is a fairly smart one.

FIELDING:

O'Brien has never won a Gold Glove for his first base work, but his defense has always been excellent. He committed only three errors in 1991 and his .997 fielding was a career high. O'Brien has good range and soft hands, and his defensive prowess aids the Mariner pitchers. O'Brien is not at all a good defensive player in left field, a position he is sometimes forced to play.

OVERALL:

O'Brien restored his reputation as a solid ballplayer in 1991. Unfortunately, the Mariners have Tino Martinez waiting in the wings. O'Brien faces a fight to hold his first base job, but his 1991 performance will help his case.

PETE O'BRIEN

Position: 1B/LF/DH
Bats: L **Throws:** L
Ht: 6' 2" **Wt:** 195

Opening Day Age: 34
Born: 2/9/58 in Santa Monica, CA
ML Seasons: 10

Overall Statistics

	G	AB	R	H	D	T	HR	RBI	SB	BB	SO	AVG
1991	152	560	58	139	29	3	17	88	0	44	61	.248
Career	1361	4831	584	1279	232	20	148	657	22	575	515	.265

Where He Hits the Ball

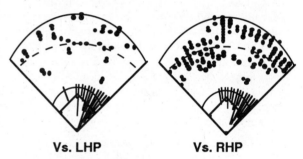

Vs. LHP   **Vs. RHP**

1991 Situational Stats

	AB	H	HR	RBI	AVG		AB	H	HR	RBI	AVG
Home	290	69	12	53	.238	LHP	179	42	4	27	.235
Road	270	70	5	35	.259	RHP	381	97	13	61	.255
Day	147	43	5	26	.293	Sc Pos	174	50	7	75	.287
Night	413	96	12	62	.232	Clutch	98	20	3	19	.204

1991 Rankings (American League)

➡ 3rd in sacrifice flies (9)

➡ 6th lowest batting average with the bases loaded (.111)

➡ 8th lowest on-base average (.300)

➡ 9th least runs scored per time reached base (31.5%)

➡ Led AL first basemen in fielding percentage (.997)

HITTING:

Honored by President George Bush in 1990, Harold Reynolds is a certifiable Point of Light (Number 167 on the White House list) and one of the great players in the short history of Seattle baseball. Reynolds' 1991 season, with its .254 average, was not one of his greatest, but it was nothing to apologize for, either. His 57 RBIs were a career high and his 95 runs scored were the second-highest total of his career. Reynolds also drew 72 walks, his second-best total ever.

Now 31, Reynolds has decent power to the gaps. His 34 doubles last year were the second-highest total of his career. He is a good bunter and an excellent contact hitter. Reynolds has never struck out more than 63 times in a season, his total in 1991.

A switch-hitter, Reynolds has usually been better from the right side, and he has been a better lowball than highball hitter. He is a tough out in clutch situations, hitting .301 with men in scoring position in 1990 and .322 in those situations in 1991.

BASERUNNING:

Reynolds stole 60 bases in 80 attempts in 1987, but during the next three years he stole about half that many while being thrown out at a high rate. In 1991 Reynolds swiped only 28, but his success rate was an excellent 78 percent . . . a sign that he's becoming a smarter runner.

FIELDING:

A three-time Gold Glove winner (1988-90), Reynolds led the American League in putouts, assists, chances and double plays in 1991, and has topped AL second basemen in assists each of the last five years. The downside is that he has also led the league in errors four times, though not in '91. As long as he continues to show his great range the Mariners will accept the errors.

OVERALL:

An excellent player and a pillar of the Seattle community, Reynolds would appear to be in no danger of losing his job anytime soon. The M's would love to have a few more players just like him.

GREAT RANGE

HAROLD REYNOLDS

Position: 2B
Bats: B **Throws:** R
Ht: 5'11" **Wt:** 165

Opening Day Age: 31
Born: 11/26/60 in Eugene, OR
ML Seasons: 9

Overall Statistics

	G	AB	R	H	D	T	HR	RBI	SB	BB	SO	AVG
1991	161	631	95	160	34	6	3	57	28	72	63	.254
Career	1015	3632	488	950	177	45	14	262	213	346	311	.262

Where He Hits the Ball

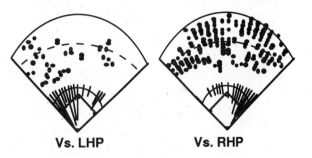

Vs. LHP   Vs. RHP

1991 Situational Stats

	AB	H	HR	RBI	AVG		AB	H	HR	RBI	AVG
Home	314	94	1	27	.299	LHP	174	46	1	16	.264
Road	317	66	2	30	.208	RHP	457	114	2	41	.249
Day	157	31	1	16	.197	Sc Pos	146	47	1	51	.322
Night	474	129	2	41	.272	Clutch	97	30	1	15	.309

1991 Rankings (American League)

→ 2nd in plate appearances (728) and errors at second base (18)

→ 3rd in sacrifice bunts (14), lowest batting average on the road (.208) and bunts in play (33)

→ 4th in pitches seen (2,705) and games (161)

→ 5th lowest slugging percentage (.341)

→ Led the Mariners in at-bats (631), singles (117), triples (6), sacrifice bunts, stolen bases (28), pitches seen, plate appearances, games, stolen base percentage (77.8%), most runs scored per time reached base (40.1%) and bunts in play

PITCHING:

Previously Mr. Big in the Mariner bullpen, Mike Schooler missed half the 1991 season with shoulder problems that first appeared toward the end of the '90 campaign. Schooler appeared in 34 games after the All-Star break, a sign that he was fully recovered, but the cautious Mariners went to a bullpen-by-committee and Schooler received only ten save opportunities for his half season of work. Perhaps they were right; Schooler converted only seven of those opportunities and his 3.67 ERA was a career high.

When he's healthy and in top form, Schooler is one of baseball's top closers. Now 29, he has a 90-plus fastball, an excellent slider, and a curve he can mix in to throw hitters off balance. He had 33 saves in 1989 and 30 in 1990, and he has the talent to reach that level (or even better) consistently as long as his arm is 100 percent.

Though the Mariners treated Schooler with kid gloves after his return last July, there's a lot of reason to believe he can be as good as ever in 1992. Schooler held the opposition to a .198 batting average; he struck out 31 men in 34.1 innings while walking only 10 and he gave up only two home runs. When you hold your opponents to a .255 on-base percentage and a .278 slugging percentage, you have to be doing **something** right. Those are not the statistics of a sore-armed pitcher.

HOLDING RUNNERS AND FIELDING:

Like most power pitchers, Schooler concentrates on delivering the ball to the plate with maximum effect, rather than diverting his attention to a baserunner. Despite that, he does a pretty good job of holding runners. He's also a fine fielder who did not commit an error in 1991.

OVERALL:

While treating Schooler cautiously, the Mariners discovered that Bill Swift could also be a reliable closer. They also have Mike Jackson but when Schooler's right, he's The Man.

MIKE SCHOOLER

Position: RP
Bats: R **Throws:** R
Ht: 6' 3" **Wt:** 220

Opening Day Age: 29
Born: 8/10/62 in Anaheim, CA
ML Seasons: 4

Overall Statistics

	W	L	ERA	G	GS	Sv	IP	H	R	BB	SO	HR
1991	3	3	3.67	34	0	7	34.1	25	14	10	31	2
Career	10	22	2.96	190	0	85	215.2	198	80	69	199	13

How Often He Throws Strikes

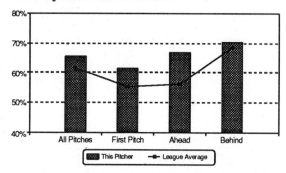

This Pitcher — League Average

1991 Situational Stats

	W	L	ERA	Sv	IP		AB	H	HR	RBI	AVG
Home	2	1	2.45	4	18.1	LHB	57	10	1	7	.175
Road	1	2	5.06	3	16.0	RHB	69	15	1	9	.217
Day	0	2	8.22	2	7.2	Sc Pos	37	11	1	15	.297
Night	3	1	2.36	5	26.2	Clutch	57	11	2	10	.193

1991 Rankings (American League)

→ Did not rank near the top or bottom in any category

PITCHING:

Lefthander Russ Swan was a starter throughout his minor league career, mostly in the Giant chain. But when the Mariners had an opportunity for a lefty middle reliever in 1991, Swan wasn't about to pass up the chance. Swan acquitted himself well enough last year, recording a decent 3.43 ERA in 63 appearances. It was a good performance, especially considering that it came in a new role, but it was not an overwhelming one.

Swan has had arm problems during his career. At his best, he can get his fastball up to 90 MPH. However, he is primarily a finesse pitcher, relying on a good sinker, a slider that drops down in the strike zone, and a split-fingered fastball. He is very much a ground ball pitcher, with a ratio of 3.3 grounders for every fly ball in 1991.

With that kind of stuff, Swan is likely to permit more than a hit an inning (81 in 78.2 IP last year) and unlikely to strike out a lot of hitters (only 33). Very clearly, he needs good control in order to succeed. Swan had that last year, allowing only 21 unintentional walks. But he also permitted eight homers, another indication of how marginal his repertoire is.

HOLDING RUNNERS AND FIELDING:

Swan is the sort of pitcher who needs to help himself with his defense. There are no big problems with his glove work, but Swan's ability to hold runners is suspect. Last year opponents stole seven bases in eight attempts with Swan on the mound -- a very unsatisfactory ratio.

OVERALL:

If he can produce a 3.43 ERA like he did in 1991, Swan will have no problems holding onto his role in 1992. Despite his good ERA, his peripheral stats make him a somewhat shaky bet to be quite as successful again.

RUSS SWAN

Position: RP
Bats: L **Throws:** L
Ht: 6' 4" **Wt:** 215

Opening Day Age: 28
Born: 1/3/64 in Fremont, CA
ML Seasons: 3

Overall Statistics

	W	L	ERA	G	GS	Sv	IP	H	R	BB	SO	HR
1991	6	2	3.43	63	0	2	78.2	81	35	28	33	8
Career	8	8	3.88	78	11	2	134.2	140	71	54	51	15

How Often He Throws Strikes

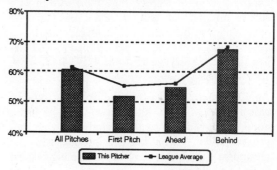

1991 Situational Stats

	W	L	ERA	Sv	IP		AB	H	HR	RBI	AVG
Home	1	2	5.28	0	30.2	LHB	119	23	1	9	.193
Road	5	0	2.25	2	48.0	RHB	182	58	7	24	.319
Day	1	0	1.61	0	22.1	Sc Pos	91	22	2	24	.242
Night	5	2	4.15	2	56.1	Clutch	119	30	3	11	.252

1991 Rankings (American League)

→ 3rd in most GDPs induced per GDP situation (21.7%) and least strikeouts per 9 innings in relief (3.8)

→ 4th lowest percentage of inherited runners scored (19.0%)

→ 7th lowest batting average allowed vs. left-handed batters (.193)

→ 8th worst first batter efficiency (.328)

→ Led the Mariners in most GDPs induced per GDP situation, lowest batting average allowed vs. left-handed batters and lowest percentage of inherited runners scored

PITCHING:

Mike Schooler's injury problems over the last year and a half may have hampered the Mariners, but they had one benefit -- the M's now know that Bill Swift can be an effective closer. How can anyone complain about a relief ace who's given 18 save opportunities and converts 17 of them? Swift logged six of those saves after September first last year, when Seattle was fighting to achieve its first winning season. From the All-Star break on, his ERA was an outstanding 1.36.

The second player chosen in the 1984 draft, Swift has always had impressive stuff. He made the majors a year later, but for a long time the Mariners seemed uncertain how to use him. Over the course of several seasons they worked him as a starter, middle man and late man, and the role-switching may have slowed his development. Develop he did, however -- since 1986, Swift's ERA has dropped every year: 5.46, 4.59, 4.43, 2.39, 1.99.

As a late man, Swift is not the Schooler-type of closer who can blow hitters away, but he has a good, hard, sinking fastball along with an improving slider. At his best, he produces lots of grounders and double play balls. The big benefit is that he seldom yields a homer, allowing only seven dingers in 218.1 innings over the last two years.

HOLDING RUNNERS AND FIELDING:

A fine athlete, Swift has always fielded his position very well. His move to first is not eye-catching, but he unloads the ball to the plate so quickly that he's very tough to steal on. Swift allowed only one steal in 1990-91 combined.

OVERALL:

The ground ball-type finisher was once common in baseball, but these days most clubs prefer a closer who has a big strikeout pitch. For the Mariners, that means Schooler, assuming he's healthy. But Swift has considerable value as a set-up man, and the M's now know for certain that he can handle the closer's role if needed.

BILL SWIFT

Position: RP
Bats: R **Throws:** R
Ht: 6' 0" **Wt:** 180

Opening Day Age: 30
Born: 10/27/61 in South Portland, ME
ML Seasons: 6

Overall Statistics

	W	L	ERA	G	GS	Sv	IP	H	R	BB	SO	HR
1991	1	2	1.99	71	0	17	90.1	74	22	26	48	3
Career	30	40	4.04	253	86	24	759.0	827	395	253	292	37

How Often He Throws Strikes

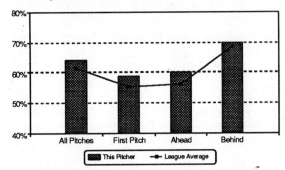

1991 Situational Stats

	W	L	ERA	Sv	IP		AB	H	HR	RBI	AVG
Home	1	2	1.65	7	43.2	LHB	123	29	1	9	.236
Road	0	0	2.31	10	46.2	RHB	207	45	2	22	.217
Day	0	0	1.47	3	18.1	Sc Pos	99	18	1	28	.182
Night	1	2	2.13	14	72.0	Clutch	169	43	1	14	.254

1991 Rankings (American League)

- → 4th in games pitched (71), most GDPs induced per GDP situation (21.3%) and relief ERA (1.99)
- → 9th in relief innings (90.1)
- → Led the Mariners in saves (17), holds (13), relief ERA, relief innings and least baserunners allowed per 9 innings in relief (10.1)

DAVE VALLE

Position: C
Bats: R **Throws:** R
Ht: 6' 2" **Wt:** 200

Opening Day Age: 31
Born: 10/30/60 in
Bayside, NY
ML Seasons: 8

HITTING:

Dave Valle spent the first half of 1991 heading toward a dubious batting record. Valle reached the All-Star break with a batting average of .135. A check of the record books revealed that back in 1909, a Dodger catcher named Bill Bergen had batted .139, the lowest mark ever for a player with 300 or more at-bats. Fortunately for Valle, his bat heated up considerably in the second half (.261). A late hot streak had him threatening the Mendoza line before he finally finished at .194, a career low.

Never much of a batsman, Valle hasn't hit over .240 since 1987, the year he became the regular Mariner catcher. He's always had a hitch in his swing, one which causes him to open up his front shoulder. That makes him easy prey for breaking pitches. Valle is aware of the problem and corrects it at times, but then lapses back into his old bad habits. Valle crowds the plate and can blast an occasional long one, but his slugging average has gone down every year since 1986.

Though he suffered through a terrible season, Valle was finally able to stay healthy in 1991 after spending time on the disabled list for four straight seasons. His 132 games played were a career high by a big margin.

BASERUNNING:

An all-around offensive liability, Valle runs the bases about as well as he hits. He's stolen only three bases in eight seasons and he's prone to making foolish baserunning mistakes.

FIELDING:

Defense is the reason Valle has been able to hold a regular position. He handles pitchers well and is one of the best throwing catchers in the game. He'd be a Gold Glove candidate, but they usually don't give that award to .194 hitters.

OVERALL:

Unless the Mariners make a deal or sign a free agent, Valle will have no serious challengers to his position this year. Valle may be comforted by the knowledge that the new Seattle manager, Bill Plummer, was a catcher with a .188 lifetime average.

Overall Statistics

	G	AB	R	H	D	T	HR	RBI	SB	BB	SO	AVG
1991	132	324	38	63	8	1	8	32	0	34	49	.194
Career	586	1712	192	391	69	9	50	225	3	150	242	.228

Where He Hits the Ball

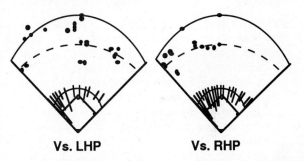

Vs. LHP   Vs. RHP

1991 Situational Stats

	AB	H	HR	RBI	AVG		AB	H	HR	RBI	AVG
Home	173	28	0	8	.162	LHP	112	26	6	17	.232
Road	151	35	8	24	.232	RHP	212	37	2	15	.175
Day	74	13	3	9	.176	Sc Pos	86	14	2	24	.163
Night	250	50	5	23	.200	Clutch	56	12	2	5	.214

1991 Rankings (American League)

→ 1st in most GDPs per GDP situation (31.2%) and lowest batting average on a 3-1 count (.000)

→ 2nd in hit by pitch (9) and lowest batting average with runners in scoring position (.163)

→ 5th lowest batting average on an 0-2 count (.040)

→ Led the Mariners in hit by pitch and GDPs (19)

→ Led AL catchers in hit by pitch

HITTING:

Omar Vizquel comes from a long line of Venezuelan shortstops -- a line which has produced the likes of Chico Carrasquel, Luis Aparicio, Dave Concepcion and Ozzie Guillen. Vizquel has the glove to rank in such distinguished company, but his bat is another matter.

After raising some hopes by batting .247 in 1990, his second season as the Mariners' shortstop, Vizquel skidded to .230 in 1991. However, he did improve in some areas. Vizquel had 21 extra-base hits, tripling his meager 1990 total of seven. He showed more patience than ever before, drawing a career-high 45 walks. He also hit the ball on the ground more, something the Mariners want him to do.

Vizquel's biggest improvement came with men on base. In 1990, he hit an anemic .171 with runners in scoring position. In '91 the figure was a very solid .312. As a result Vizquel drove in 41 runs, exceeding his total for 1989 and 1990 combined (38). That kind of production won't scare Cal Ripken, but it was a big step up from someone who used to be the All-American out in clutch situations.

BASERUNNING:

A smart baserunner, Vizquel is probably more conservative than he needs to be. Last year he stole seven bases in nine attempts, and over the last two years he's 11-for-14. With a success rate like that, he should be stealing more.

FIELDING:

There's never been anything wrong with Vizquel's glove work. He has fine range, soft hands and the ability to turn the double play. He has improved in the latter area particularly, more than doubling his DP total from 1990 to 1991. Vizquel doesn't make many errors either, fielding a solid .980 each of the last two years.

OVERALL:

A very solid defensive player, Vizquel would have little trouble holding his job if could hit .250-.260. That seems unlikely, so he'll probably have to fight to maintain his regular position in 1992.

OMAR VIZQUEL

Position: SS
Bats: B **Throws:** R
Ht: 5'9" **Wt:** 165

Opening Day Age: 24
Born: 4/24/67 in Caracas, Venezuela
ML Seasons: 3

Overall Statistics

	G	AB	R	H	D	T	HR	RBI	SB	BB	SO	AVG
1991	142	426	42	98	16	4	1	41	7	45	37	.230
Career	366	1068	106	246	26	9	4	79	12	91	99	.230

Where He Hits the Ball

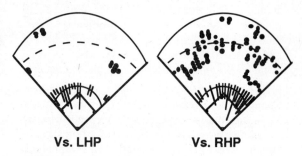

Vs. LHP   **Vs. RHP**

1991 Situational Stats

	AB	H	HR	RBI	AVG		AB	H	HR	RBI	AVG
Home	206	52	1	24	.252	LHP	87	20	0	11	.230
Road	220	46	0	17	.209	RHP	339	78	1	30	.230
Day	115	32	0	13	.278	Sc Pos	109	34	0	39	.312
Night	311	66	1	28	.212	Clutch	74	15	0	3	.203

1991 Rankings (American League)

- → 2nd lowest slugging percentage vs. right-handed pitchers (.298)
- → 6th in lowest batting average vs. right-handed pitchers (.230) and bunts in play (27)
- → 8th lowest percentage of swings that missed (9.7%)
- → Led the Mariners in lowest percentage of swings that missed
- → Led AL shortstops in bunts in play, lowest percentage of swings that missed and highest percentage of swings put into play (52.3%)

SCOTT BRADLEY

Position: C
Bats: L **Throws:** R
Ht: 5'11" **Wt:** 185

Opening Day Age: 32
Born: 3/22/60 in Montclair, NJ
ML Seasons: 8

Overall Statistics

	G	AB	R	H	D	T	HR	RBI	SB	BB	SO	AVG
1991	83	172	10	35	7	0	0	11	0	19	19	.203
Career	597	1642	148	422	75	6	18	183	3	102	109	.257

HITTING, FIELDING, BASERUNNING:

A smart player who's often considered coaching or managerial material in the future, Scott Bradley probably felt more like a coach than a player in 1991. After several years in which he shared the Mariners' catching job with Dave Valle, Bradley all but disappeared late last year, starting only one of the M's last 41 games. A .263 lifetime hitter entering the campaign, Bradley had an all-around depressing season, finishing with a .203 average.

Now 32, Bradley needs to hit for a decent average in order to earn his keep on offense. He has little power, with only seven extra-base hits and no homers in 1991. He also doesn't draw many walks, though he's fine contact hitter who won't strike out much. Bradley is not a good mechanical receiver, but he calls a good game and pitchers like working with him. He's an intelligent baserunner, but no threat to steal.

OVERALL:

It was obvious by season's end that Bradley didn't fit into the Mariners' future plans. The change in managers might alter that status, but there's a strong chance that Bradley will be modeling another uniform in 1992. He'll be an asset in the clubhouse and the dugout, but if he wants to help on the diamond, he'll have to hit a lot better.

DAVE COCHRANE

Position: LF/C/3B
Bats: B **Throws:** R
Ht: 6' 2" **Wt:** 180

Opening Day Age: 29
Born: 1/31/63 in Riverside, CA
ML Seasons: 4

Overall Statistics

	G	AB	R	H	D	T	HR	RBI	SB	BB	SO	AVG
1991	65	178	16	44	13	0	2	22	0	9	38	.247
Career	153	362	33	83	19	1	6	31	0	28	95	.229

HITTING, FIELDING, BASERUNNING:

At age 29, Dave Cochrane has turned himself into a useful major leaguer by doing a little of everything. A switch-hitter, Cochrane hits about as well from the right side (.245) as he does from the left (.248). He's got power potential, having hit 15 or more homers six times during his minor league career. He's versatile, and has played six positions in his three seasons with the Mariners (1B, 2B, 3B, SS, LF and RF). He can help as a pinch hitter, going 4-for-16 in that role last year. He could even pitch in an emergency; he worked eight games for the Hawaii club back in 1987.

Cochrane's problem is that, while he can do a lot of things, he can't do any of them very well. In the majors he's never displayed that potent home run bat, and he's never hit much for average. He doesn't have outstanding speed, and he's no great shakes at any of his many positions. Cochrane's best potential might be as a catcher. He has a strong arm and the willingness to learn the position.

OVERALL:

Cochrane might want to get serious about his future as a catcher, especially if the M's deal Scott Bradley. Whether that happens or not, his versatility makes him a good bet to hold onto a major league job.

TRACY JONES

Position: LF/DH
Bats: R **Throws:** R
Ht: 6' 3" **Wt:** 220

Opening Day Age: 31
Born: 3/31/61 in Inglewood, CA
ML Seasons: 6

JEFF SCHAEFER

Position: SS/3B
Bats: R **Throws:** R
Ht: 5'10" **Wt:** 170

Opening Day Age: 31
Born: 5/31/60 in Patchogue, NY
ML Seasons: 3

Overall Statistics

	G	AB	R	H	D	T	HR	RBI	SB	BB	SO	AVG
1991	79	175	30	44	8	1	3	24	2	18	22	.251
Career	493	1303	173	356	56	6	27	164	62	100	140	.273

Overall Statistics

	G	AB	R	H	D	T	HR	RBI	SB	BB	SO	AVG
1991	84	164	19	41	7	1	1	11	3	5	25	.250
Career	154	281	32	64	10	1	1	17	8	8	38	.228

HITTING, FIELDING, BASERUNNING:

Once considered one of the best prospects in an organization brimming with talent (Cincinnati), Tracy Jones has been reduced to part-time status by injuries and lack of production. Since arriving in the majors in 1986, Jones has only made it through one season (1987) without spending some time on the disabled list. Last year it was a quadriceps injury which caused him to miss a month starting in mid-June. Typically, it happened just when he was swinging a hot bat. Jones struggled after his return, batting just .214 in the second half.

Jones did make himself useful as a pinch hitter last year, batting .300 (6-for-20). If he wants to stay in the majors, he'll probably have to accept that sort of fill-in status. Jones stole 31 bases in 1987, but knee injuries have robbed him of most of his speed. That limits his outfield range, but Jones gets a good jump and possesses a strong arm.

OVERALL:

Jones was a free agent after the '91 season and the Mariners may want to make room for some of their young outfielders rather than offer him another contract. He figures to earn a bid from a club looking for a righty bat off the bench.

HITTING, FIELDING, BASERUNNING:

Like his teammate Dave Cochrane, Jeff Schaefer hung around the minor leagues for a long time before finally landing a major league job with the Mariners. Like Cochrane, Schaefer's long suit is his versatility. He can play second, short or third, and he's a fine glove man at each position.

Schaefer only has to hit a little bit to make himself useful, and in 1991 he did just that -- he hit a little bit. Schaefer's .250 average was acceptable, but he didn't draw walks or hit with power, so it was a fairly weak .250. He wasn't much in clutch situations, batting only .171 with men in scoring position. Schaefer has good speed, and he's a fine bunter. His primary value is defensive -- this fellow can throw some leather. He is comfortable at both short and second, and won fielding honors at both positions during his minor league career.

OVERALL:

Schaefer got some playing time filling in for Omar Vizquel as the Mariner shortstop last year and did a very nice job. At 31 he's not much of a threat to win a regular job, but if he can keep hitting at the .250 level, he has a good chance to make the club as a bench player again in 1992.

HITTING:

After two .300 seasons as a part-time player for the Rangers, Jack Daugherty suffered through a forgettable, injury-racked campaign in 1991. Daugherty figured to get lots of starts in the outfield and at DH when Texas released Pete Incaviglia before the start of the season. Instead, he missed half the year with two unrelated injuries and wound up batting a miserable .194. Prior to '91, Daugherty had never hit below .250 in his professional career.

Things didn't go well for Daugherty at any time last year. As the season began, the Rangers signed Brian Downing, and Downing immediately began swinging a red-hot bat. That cut into Daugherty's playing time, and so did an early slump: he was only 2-for-17 in April. Before he could regain his stroke, he strained some finger ligaments and had to go on the disabled list. Daugherty finally returned on June 22 -- for exactly one day. He had to go on the shelf again, this time with appendicitis. He returned in September, but by then it was a lost season.

The Rangers probably aren't too concerned because Daugherty looks like he could hit .280 falling out of bed -- as long as he's healthy. He needs to hit for a good average in order to earn his keep. Daugherty lacks home run power, and he's not the most patient hitter, either.

BASERUNNING:

Daugherty was a fine basestealer in the minors, but he's never shown that ability since coming to the Rangers. Last year's performance, one-for-one, was typical. He seldom runs himself into outs.

FIELDING:

Though not a superior glove man, Daugherty can play both first base and the outfield competently. He has neither great range nor a great arm, but he gets the job done.

OVERALL:

After everything that happened to him last year, Daugherty has to figure he's due for better luck. If he can regain his '89-'90 stroke, he shouldn't have much trouble winning a roster spot.

JACK DAUGHERTY

Position: LF
Bats: B **Throws:** L
Ht: 6' 0" **Wt:** 190

Opening Day Age: 31
Born: 7/3/60 in Hialeah, FL
ML Seasons: 4

Overall Statistics

	G	AB	R	H	D	T	HR	RBI	SB	BB	SO	AVG
1991	58	144	8	28	3	2	1	11	1	16	23	.194
Career	246	570	60	154	28	6	8	69	3	49	96	.270

Where He Hits the Ball

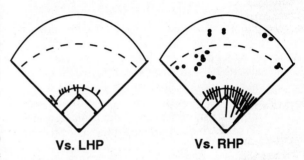

Vs. LHP   Vs. RHP

1991 Situational Stats

	AB	H	HR	RBI	AVG		AB	H	HR	RBI	AVG
Home	63	12	0	2	.190	LHP	30	7	0	2	.233
Road	81	16	1	9	.198	RHP	114	21	1	9	.184
Day	35	7	0	1	.200	Sc Pos	39	5	0	9	.128
Night	109	21	1	10	.193	Clutch	29	4	0	4	.138

1991 Rankings (American League)

→ Did not rank near the top or bottom in any category

HITTING:

At age 41, Brian Downing is nearing the end of an outstanding, though largely unnoticed, career. A proud man who was one of the best players in the short history of the California Angels, Downing probably would have retired a year ago if he'd felt the Angels were showing him proper appreciation. When that didn't happen, Downing signed with Texas and immediately said "In your face, California!" by batting .733 (11 for 15), with six walks, in his first five Ranger games. Downing settled down after that, but nonetheless put together a fine season, batting .278 with 17 homers. Even that record is deceptive. Except for horrendous slumps in June and October, months in which he batted a combined .106 (9 for 85), Downing had a hefty .337 average for the year.

Despite his advanced age, Downing remains an excellent fastball hitter, and he's particularly tough on high pitches. With his open stance, he has always been inclined to pull the ball, but as his bat has slowed a little bit, he has begun to use the whole field. Downing has always been a very patient hitter and he remained one in 1991, drawing 58 walks and recording a fine .377 on-base average. Because of that ability the Rangers used him mostly from the leadoff spot in 1991 despite the fact that he's painfully slow.

BASERUNNING:

Downing stole a base in 1991, pretty exciting stuff for a guy whose last successful steal had come in 1988. He didn't let it go to his head, remaining a smart and conservative baserunner.

FIELDING:

Downing may still keep a glove in his locker, but if he does it's strictly for old-time's sake. Once a sure-handed outfielder, Downing last played in the field in 1987.

OVERALL:

A free agent, Downing has longed to play in a World Series at least once in his career. His solid 1991 season guarantees that he'll get some offers. He may well retire, but an offer from a contending club might tempt him.

BRIAN DOWNING

Position: DH
Bats: R **Throws:** R
Ht: 5'10" **Wt:** 194

Opening Day Age: 41
Born: 10/9/50 in Los Angeles, CA
ML Seasons: 19

Overall Statistics

	G	AB	R	H	D	T	HR	RBI	SB	BB	SO	AVG
1991	123	407	76	113	17	2	17	49	1	58	70	.278
Career	2237	7533	1135	2010	342	28	265	1034	49	1135	1069	.267

Where He Hits the Ball

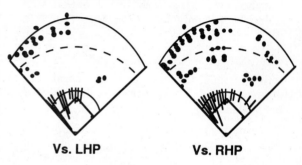

Vs. LHP   Vs. RHP

1991 Situational Stats

	AB	H	HR	RBI	AVG		AB	H	HR	RBI	AVG
Home	204	52	8	23	.255	LHP	139	39	9	17	.281
Road	203	61	9	26	.300	RHP	268	74	8	32	.276
Day	77	19	3	11	.247	Sc Pos	89	23	3	33	.258
Night	330	94	14	38	.285	Clutch	75	22	2	14	.293

1991 Rankings (American League)

→ 4th in hit by pitch (8)
→ 10th in highest percentage of pitches taken (61.6%)
→ Led the Rangers in hit by pitch and highest percentage of pitches taken
→ Led designated hitters in hit by pitch

HITTING:

The consummate professional hitter, Julio Franco didn't like it when his batting average slipped twenty points to .296 in 1990 after four straight .300 seasons. Franco came back with a vengeance in 1991, winning his first American League batting title with a career-high .341 average. Franco batted a mighty .366 after the All-Star break and held off a host of challengers that included five-time champion Wade Boggs.

With his unusual stance -- hands high, bat parallel to the ground with the barrel almost pointed at the pitcher -- Franco would seem unable to get around on a good fastball. But he uncoils quickly and is deadly against the high heater. That's particularly true against southpaws: Franco batted .368 against lefthanders last year, with an awesome .626 slugging percentage. The ability to handle the fastball has helped make Franco an outstanding clutch hitter. He batted .322 with runners in scoring position last year.

An intelligent hitter, Franco uses the whole field. In 1990, he went to right so much that teams began playing him as though he were a left-handed hitter. In 1991, he kept the opponents honest by driving the ball more often, and the result was a career-high 15 homers.

BASERUNNING:

Always an excellent base stealer, Franco seems to be improving with age. In 1991, he stole a career-high 36 bases while being thrown out only nine times. He's aggressive at trying to take extra bases, sometimes getting thrown doing so.

FIELDING:

Franco appeared to be improving at second base, but in 1991 he had a bad year in the field. He did succeed in reducing his errors from 19 to 14, but all too often messed up easy plays. His range seemed reduced as well. Franco has the tools for the position, but some question his desire.

OVERALL:

If Franco could field anywhere near as well as he hits, he'd be mentioned with Ryne Sandberg and Roberto Alomar as one of the great all-around second basemen. However, his bat is so potent that the Rangers will forgive his lapses in the field.

JULIO FRANCO

Position: 2B
Bats: R **Throws:** R
Ht: 6' 1" **Wt:** 188

Opening Day Age: 30
Born: 8/23/61 in San Pedro de Macoris, Dominican Republic
ML Seasons: 10

Overall Statistics

	G	AB	R	H	D	T	HR	RBI	SB	BB	SO	AVG
1991	146	589	108	201	27	3	15	78	36	65	78	.341
Career	1367	5309	788	1605	242	40	84	671	219	484	620	.302

Where He Hits the Ball

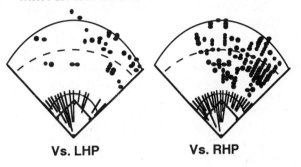

Vs. LHP   Vs. RHP

1991 Situational Stats

	AB	H	HR	RBI	AVG		AB	H	HR	RBI	AVG
Home	294	101	7	40	.344	LHP	155	57	8	29	.368
Road	295	100	8	38	.339	RHP	434	144	7	49	.332
Day	108	35	2	16	.324	Sc Pos	149	48	2	57	.322
Night	481	166	13	62	.345	Clutch	103	34	2	6	.330

1991 Rankings (American League)

→ 1st in batting average (.341), singles (156) and batting average after the 6th inning (.340)

→ 3rd in batting average vs. left-handed pitchers (.368), batting average vs. right-handed pitchers (.332) and batting average on the road (.339)

→ 4th in on-base average (.408), slugging percentage vs. left-handed pitchers (.626) and batting average at home (.343)

→ Led the Rangers in batting average, singles, stolen bases (36), on-base average, groundball/flyball ratio (1.89), stolen base percentage (80.0%) and most pitches seen plate appearance (3.84)

FUTURE ALL-STAR

JUAN GONZALEZ

Position: CF/LF
Bats: R **Throws:** R
Ht: 6' 3" **Wt:** 200

Opening Day Age: 22
Born: 10/16/69 in Vega
Baja, Puerto Rico
ML Seasons: 3

HITTING:

Juan Gonzalez' first full season in a Texas uniform was everything the Rangers had hoped for -- and then some. A 21-year-old picture of confidence, Gonzalez handled major league pitching in the same impressive fashion that he'd handled AAA hurlers at Oklahoma City in 1990. In 1990, the young slugger hit 29 homers with 101 RBI and a .258 average in the American Association; in 1991, he hit 27 homers with 102 RBI and a .264 average in the American League. If he hadn't logged 20 at-bats too many in September trials with the Rangers in 1989 and 1990, Gonzalez would have been a runaway choice for Rookie of the Year.

Of course, Gonzalez wasn't perfect. Like a lot of young sluggers, he chased bad breaking pitches far too often. An impatient hitter, took only 42 walks while striking out 118 times. He batted so-so .265 with runners in scoring position, and he found his power neutralized at Arlington Stadium, where he hit only seven homers. He was swinging a tired bat at the end of the season, batting only .155 with a homer and eight RBI in 110 at-bats after September 1. But those are quibbles; it was an awfully impressive performance, particularly for someone so young.

BASERUNNING:

Gonzalez was never a basestealer at the minor league level, so it was no great surprise that he stole only four bases in eight attempts last year. He's not slow by any means, but lacks good baserunning instincts.

FIELDING:

Gonzalez is a fine outfielder, but lacks the speed to be a superior center fielder. With his strong arm, he could be outstanding in right, but the Rangers already have Ruben Sierra there. Gonzalez will most likely wind up in left field eventually.

OVERALL:

Coming up through the Ranger system, Gonzalez continued to improve at each level. Not the type to let success go to his head, he'll be working hard to improve the few flaws in his game.

Overall Statistics

	G	AB	R	H	D	T	HR	RBI	SB	BB	SO	AVG
1991	142	545	78	144	34	1	27	102	4	42	118	.264
Career	191	695	95	179	44	2	32	121	4	50	153	.258

Where He Hits the Ball

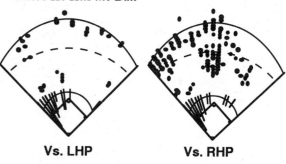

Vs. LHP   **Vs. RHP**

1991 Situational Stats

	AB	H	HR	RBI	AVG		AB	H	HR	RBI	AVG
Home	262	70	7	40	.267	LHP	147	44	9	27	.299
Road	283	74	20	62	.261	RHP	398	100	18	75	.251
Day	83	26	5	23	.313	Sc Pos	170	45	7	68	.265
Night	462	118	22	79	.255	Clutch	93	20	7	21	.215

1991 Rankings (American League)

→ 7th in RBIs (102)

→ 8th lowest on-base average vs. right-handed pitchers (.304)

→ Led the Rangers in home runs (27), strikeouts (118) and HR frequency (20.2 ABs per HR)

→ Led AL center fielders in home runs, strikeouts and HR frequency

PITCHING:

The unerasable image of Goose Gossage is that of the young fireballer who blew away hitters for the mighty Yankees of the late '70s. That image will linger long after people have forgotten a more recent one from last July 31: Gossage standing on the Comiskey Park mound, watching Robin Ventura's game-ending grand slam homer sail over the fence for a crushing 10-8 Ranger defeat.

Though he's now 40 years old, Gossage can still get his fastball up into the low 90's. The Rangers love power pitchers, and since the Goose is a good three and a half years younger than Nolan Ryan, Texas was the natural team to give him a chance after he'd spent the 1990 season in Japan. For a while it looked like a brilliant move. Gossage made the club with a strong spring and didn't permit his first run until his twelfth appearance on May 9.

Then reality set in. Gossage got cuffed around in June, then spent a month on the disabled list with a shoulder injury. He got his only save of the year -- the 308th of his career -- on July 23, but didn't get any more save opportunities after the Ventura grand slam. Gossage went back on the DL shortly after that. He finished the year with eight straight scoreless outings, but those stints totaled only 6.2 innings.

HOLDING RUNNERS AND FIELDING:

Gossage has never been known for his great move to first, but he allowed only two steals in four attempts in his 40.1 innings of work last year. The Goose's delivery leaves him in an awkward defensive position, so it's no surprise that he has a .923 career fielding average.

OVERALL:

Gossage burned his bridges from Texas late in the year when he ripped Bobby Valentine for the way he'd been used. What are the job prospects for bad-tempered, sore-shouldered, 40-year-old relievers who still think they should be closing games? Not very good.

GOOSE GOSSAGE

Position: RP
Bats: R **Throws:** R
Ht: 6' 3" **Wt:** 225

Opening Day Age: 40
Born: 7/5/51 in Colorado Springs, CO
ML Seasons: 19

Overall Statistics

	W	L	ERA	G	GS	Sv	IP	H	R	BB	SO	HR
1991	4	2	3.57	44	0	1	40.1	33	16	16	28	4
Career	117	100	2.94	897	37	308	1676.1	1372	610	672	1407	102

How Often He Throws Strikes

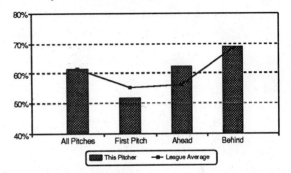

1991 Situational Stats

	W	L	ERA	Sv	IP		AB	H	HR	RBI	AVG
Home	2	0	2.01	1	22.1	LHB	48	9	1	8	.188
Road	2	2	5.50	0	18.0	RHB	97	24	3	23	.247
Day	0	1	4.00	0	9.0	Sc Pos	59	13	1	24	.220
Night	4	1	3.45	1	31.1	Clutch	68	17	2	21	.250

1991 Rankings (American League)

→ 5th least GDPs induced per GDP situation (3.0%)

→ 7th most inherited runners scored (41.5%)

→ 10th worst first batter efficiency (.325)

PITCHING:

In a 1991 season which featured some amazing comebacks, there was none more dramatic than that of Ranger righthander Jose Guzman. After missing two complete seasons with shoulder problems, Guzman came back in 1991 and went 13-7 with a 3.08 ERA, decidedly the best season of his five-year major league career. How remarkable was that? Since 1901 only eight pitchers have missed two full years and then come back to win at least ten games in a season. The vast majority of those missed time due to military service (the last of them being Vinegar Bend Mizell back in 1956; Guzman was the very first to do so after an injury.

Looking over Guzman's 1991 season, it's easy to forget that he was ever away. He didn't make his first appearance until May 23, and didn't record his first victory until June 14, although he'd already made several strong starts by then. He really hit his stride after the All-Star break, going 9-4 with a 3.22 earned run average. Guzman's arm showed no sign of fatigue late in the year; he was 4-2 after September 1.

Guzman has always possessed an above-average fastball, one which sinks naturally. Though he gets his share of strikeouts (6.6 per nine innings last year), he is primarily a ground ball pitcher. Guzman also throws a change-up and a slider. Controlling his pitches is sometimes a problem, but Guzman's pitches are hard to hit out of the park.

HOLDING RUNNERS AND FIELDING:

Guzman has always been regarded as a good fielder, and showed no effects of the long layoff last year. He was once easy to steal on, but last year allowed only 12 steals in 25 attempts.

OVERALL:

Despite his long layoff, Guzman won't turn 29 until the start of the 1992 season. A club always has to keep its fingers crossed about a player with a long history of injuries, but the popular Guzman enters 1992 as one of the Rangers' top starters.

JOSE GUZMAN

Position: SP
Bats: R **Throws:** R
Ht: 6' 3" **Wt:** 198

Opening Day Age: 29
Born: 4/9/63 in Santa Isabel, Puerto Rico
ML Seasons: 5

Overall Statistics

	W	L	ERA	G	GS	Sv	IP	H	R	BB	SO	HR
1991	13	7	3.08	25	25	0	169.2	152	67	84	125	10
Career	50	51	3.97	126	119	0	789.2	754	395	322	536	86

How Often He Throws Strikes

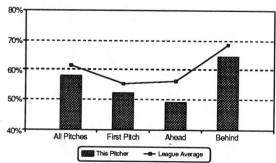

1991 Situational Stats

	W	L	ERA	Sv	IP		AB	H	HR	RBI	AVG
Home	5	3	3.86	0	60.2	LHB	283	69	6	30	.244
Road	8	4	2.64	0	109.0	RHB	353	83	4	21	.235
Day	2	0	2.23	0	32.1	Sc Pos	154	25	0	36	.162
Night	11	7	3.28	0	137.1	Clutch	67	14	1	3	.209

1991 Rankings (American League)

→ 2nd lowest batting average allowed with runners in scoring position (.162)

→ 4th lowest ERA on the road (2.64)

→ 6th least home runs allowed per 9 innings (.53)

→ 7th in runners caught stealing (13)

→ Led the Rangers in wins (13), complete games (5), runners caught stealing (13), most run support per 9 innings (5.2), least home runs allowed per 9 innings, lowest ERA on the road, lowest batting average allowed vs. right-handed batters (.235) and lowest batting average allowed with runners in scoring position

HITTING:

Jeff Huson's 1990 success may have caused the Rangers to have unrealistic expectations for him. Texas had Huson penciled in for a utility/backup role when the Rangers obtained him from Montreal prior to the '90 campaign. But Jeff Kunkel's failures and Huson's hot hitting soon landed him a role as a platoon shortstop against righties. Though Huson's average faded to .240 by season's end that year, his play impressed the Ranger brass.

Huson entered 1991 in a shortstop platoon again, this time alternating with Mario Diaz. He soon showed that he couldn't handle it. Huson reached the All-Star break batting only .200, and batted only slightly better over the second half. By then, he was in and out of the lineup, often appearing as a late-inning replacement.

Huson has a few virtues as a hitter. He's a good contact hitter, usually putting the ball on the ground to utilize his fine speed. He's also a fine bunter. He has an excellent batting eye, drawing 39 walks in a little over 300 plate appearances last year. He has hit reasonably well in the clutch, batting .261 with men in scoring position. He's a decent enough fastball hitter, but he doesn't appear capable of handling major league breaking stuff.

BASERUNNING:

Very speedy, Huson was a prolific base stealer in the minors, and has shown some potential at the major league level. He was eight-for-11 stealing last year, but he'd probably swipe a lot more given regular duty.

FIELDING:

Huson came to the Rangers with a reputation as a fine glove man, but he's yet to prove himself at the major league level. He does have good range, but his bad throws lead to numerous errors. He fielded only .964 at shortstop in 1991.

OVERALL:

Huson has proven pretty convincingly that he can't cut it as a regular major league shortstop. Still, he is versatile -- able to play second, short and third -- and if he hits a little better, he has a chance to stick with the club in a utility role.

JEFF HUSON

Position: SS
Bats: L **Throws:** R
Ht: 6' 3" **Wt:** 180

Opening Day Age: 27
Born: 8/15/64 in
Scottsdale, AZ
ML Seasons: 4

Overall Statistics

	G	AB	R	H	D	T	HR	RBI	SB	BB	SO	AVG
1991	119	268	36	57	8	3	2	26	8	39	32	.213
Career	316	780	101	177	27	5	2	59	25	95	95	.227

Where He Hits the Ball

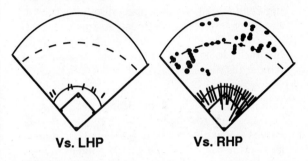

Vs. LHP   Vs. RHP

1991 Situational Stats

	AB	H	HR	RBI	AVG		AB	H	HR	RBI	AVG
Home	141	25	1	15	.177	LHP	27	2	0	0	.074
Road	127	32	1	11	.252	RHP	241	55	2	26	.228
Day	68	15	0	7	.221	Sc Pos	61	16	1	21	.262
Night	200	42	2	19	.210	Clutch	37	10	0	0	.270

1991 Rankings (American League)

→ 4th highest percentage of extra bases taken as a runner (75.0%)

MIKE JEFFCOAT

Position: RP
Bats: L **Throws:** L
Ht: 6' 2" **Wt:** 190

Opening Day Age: 32
Born: 8/3/59 in Pine
Bluff, AR
ML Seasons: 8

PITCHING:

Over the course of several seasons with the Rangers, Mike Jeffcoat has transformed himself from a marginal starter to the sort of journeyman lefty reliever who never seems to have trouble finding a job. Pitchers of this ilk often go on and on whether they're effective or not, and in 1991, Jeffcoat was anything but effective. His earned run average was a lofty 4.63, and opponents of all sorts padded their averages against him, batting .324 when Jeffcoat was on the mound. A tough year, for sure, but one that wouldn't look out of place in the long career logs of Dan Schatzeder or Paul Mirabella.

Jeffcoat might have a good excuse for his problems last year. He appeared in 70 games, a career high and a total which topped all other lefties in the American League. Jeffcoat took the ball without complaint all year, but the heavy workload obviously took its toll. From June through September his monthly ERAs were 3.14, 3.52, 5.06 and 7.59.

Jeffcoat's fastball won't break any speed guns, so he relies on throwing the hitter's timing off with curves and split-fingered pitches. His biggest asset is his control, which was as good as always in 1991 -- only 2.5 unintentional walks per nine innings. However, he's always going to give up a lot of hits, having allowed more hits than innings pitched in seven of his eight seasons.

HOLDING RUNNERS AND FIELDING:

A fine defensive player, Jeffcoat did not commit an error in 1991. He has a decent pickoff move, but last year runners were successful in five or their seven stolen base attempts with him on the mound.

OVERALL:

Though Jeffcoat suffered in 1991, he has a big asset -- a healthy left arm. Used more carefully than he was in 1991, he can be an effective reliever, with a proven ability to spot-start in his recent past. If the Rangers aren't interested in Jeffcoat for 1992, someone else probably will be.

Overall Statistics

	W	L	ERA	G	GS	Sv	IP	H	R	BB	SO	HR
1991	5	3	4.63	70	0	1	79.2	104	46	25	43	8
Career	25	25	4.22	245	42	7	477.2	544	250	144	235	45

How Often He Throws Strikes

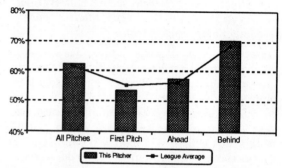

1991 Situational Stats

	W	L	ERA	Sv	IP		AB	H	HR	RBI	AVG
Home	4	0	4.82	1	37.1	LHB	121	35	2	15	.289
Road	1	3	4.46	0	42.1	RHB	203	69	6	31	.340
Day	0	0	3.50	0	18.0	Sc Pos	86	28	2	35	.326
Night	5	3	4.96	1	61.2	Clutch	105	29	2	10	.276

1991 Rankings (American League)

- ➡ 2nd highest batting average allowed in relief (.321)
- ➡ 4th most baserunners allowed per 9 innings in relief (15.0)
- ➡ 5th in games pitched (70)
- ➡ 6th worst first batter efficiency (.344)
- ➡ Led the Rangers in games pitched and relief innings (79.2)

PITCHING:

A fifth-round draft choice in 1987, Terry Mathews has posted unimpressive stats throughout most of his career. Promoted to Texas by a somewhat-desperate Ranger club during the 1991 season, Mathews suddenly looked like a different pitcher, especially during the second half. What was the difference? Mathews was finally moved to the bullpen, where it's likely he belonged all along.

Throughout his minor league career, Mathews was used primarily as a starter. He showed a good fastball, and, for the most part, above-average control. His repertoire is not sensational, however, and as a starter it always seemed a little short. Freed of the burden of pacing himself, Mathews was suddenly able to let loose. With the Rangers last year he fanned 51 batters in 57.1 innings, a strikeout ratio he'd never displayed as a minor leaguer. His control was outstanding, with only 15 unintentional walks (2.4 per game).

It took awhile for Mathews to discover himself, and maybe for the Rangers to discover him. He worked in long relief after being called up in June, and even started a couple of games. His work was so mediocre that he earned a quick ticket back to Oklahoma City. Recalled on August 10 when Goose Gossage had to go on the disabled list, Mathews looked like a different pitcher. In his last 26 appearances he posted a 2.40 ERA, fanning 37 while walking only 11 in 41.1 innings. He did not surrender a home run after his recall.

HOLDING RUNNERS AND FIELDING:

Possessing a fairly long motion, Mathews is pretty easy to steal on. He allowed eight steals in 11 attempts in his limited action. He sets himself well after his delivery, and played errorless ball last year.

OVERALL:

The Rangers can use some relief help, and Mathews' performance last year made a strong impression. But questions remain. He was easy pickings for left-handed hitters (.305 average), and he's yet to prove himself over a full season. Mathews should begin 1992 in a set-up role, and if Jeff Russell falters, he might get bigger responsibilities.

TERRY MATHEWS

Position: RP
Bats: L **Throws:** R
Ht: 6' 2" **Wt:** 200

Opening Day Age: 27
Born: 10/5/64 in Alexandria, LA
ML Seasons: 1

Overall Statistics

	W	L	ERA	G	GS	Sv	IP	H	R	BB	SO	HR
1991	4	0	3.61	34	2	1	57.1	54	24	18	51	5
Career	4	0	3.61	34	2	1	57.1	54	24	18	51	5

How Often He Throws Strikes

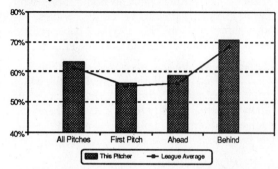

1991 Situational Stats

	W	L	ERA	Sv	IP		AB	H	HR	RBI	AVG
Home	2	0	3.42	1	26.1	LHB	82	25	2	8	.305
Road	2	0	3.77	0	31.0	RHB	133	29	3	14	.218
Day	4	0	2.45	0	14.2	Sc Pos	52	10	0	13	.192
Night	0	0	4.01	1	42.2	Clutch	83	16	0	5	.193

1991 Rankings (American League)

➡ Did not rank near the top or bottom in any category

IN HIS PRIME

HITTING:

In three seasons with the Texas Rangers, Rafael Palmeiro has increased his batting average from .275 to .319 to .322. He has raised his on-base percentage from .354 to .361 to .389. He has lifted his slugging average from .374 to .468 to .532. And, most significantly, he has increased his home run total from eight to 14 to 26. If the Rangers are a little bit excited about their young first baseman, it's easy to understand why.

When Palmeiro arrived in Texas in a big trade with the Cubs before the 1989 season, the knock on him was that he was a potential power hitter who insisted on trying to hit for average. That criticism has subsided after 1991, a year in which Palmeiro showed he could do both. Along with the 26 homers, Palmeiro belted 49 doubles, another career high, and his 336 total bases ranked second in the league only to Cal Ripken.

Palmeiro also showed increased discipline last year. He raised his walk total from 40 to 68, while striking out only 72 times. A decided fastball hitter who has usually hit the ball where it's pitched, he learned to pull for power in 1991 -- a key factor in his increased home run output.

BASERUNNING:

Palmeiro stole a dozen bases in 14 attempts for the 1988 Cubs, but that appears to be an aberration. His 1991 figures -- four out of seven --are more typical of his career. He's a reasonably intelligent baserunner, but definitely lacking in speed.

FIELDING:

Palmeiro was primarily an outfielder before coming to Texas, and he will probably never be a great first baseman. He is not a butcher around the bag, but he led all AL first sackers with 12 errors.

OVERALL:

When he first came up with the Cubs in 1986, Palmeiro was considered a future batting champion. He seemed nearly ready to achieve that potential in 1991, as he led the league for much of the season. Now he's added power to the combination as well; at age 27 he appears to have many big years ahead of him.

RAFAEL PALMEIRO

Position: 1B
Bats: L **Throws:** L
Ht: 6' 0" **Wt:** 188

Opening Day Age: 27
Born: 9/24/64 in Havana, Cuba
ML Seasons: 6

Overall Statistics

	G	AB	R	H	D	T	HR	RBI	SB	BB	SO	AVG
1991	159	631	115	203	49	3	26	88	4	68	72	.322
Career	727	2662	379	805	167	19	73	336	26	233	245	.302

Where He Hits the Ball

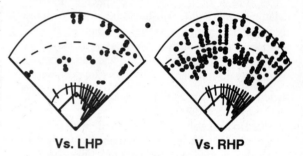

Vs. LHP   Vs. RHP

1991 Situational Stats

	AB	H	HR	RBI	AVG		AB	H	HR	RBI	AVG
Home	298	101	12	43	.339	LHP	186	51	9	26	.274
Road	333	102	14	45	.306	RHP	445	152	17	62	.342
Day	125	40	3	17	.320	Sc Pos	142	33	2	49	.232
Night	506	163	23	71	.322	Clutch	107	26	6	17	.243

1991 Rankings (American League)

→ 1st in doubles (49), lowest batting average with the bases loaded (.000) and errors at first base (12)

→ 2nd in runs (115), total bases (336) and highest batting average vs. right-handed pitchers (.342)

→ 3rd in hits (203), times on base (277), slugging percentage vs. right-handed pitchers (.557) and on-base average vs. right-handed pitchers (.411)

→ Led the Rangers in runs, hits, doubles, total bases, walks (68), intentional walks (10), times on base, GDPs (18) and slugging percentage (.533)

TOP PROSPECT

DEAN PALMER

Position: 3B/LF
Bats: R **Throws:** R
Ht: 6' 1" **Wt:** 190

Opening Day Age: 23
Born: 12/27/68 in
Tallahassee, FL
ML Seasons: 2

HITTING:

Dean Palmer arrived in Texas last June rated as the best power-hitting prospect in the minor leagues. He displayed that power with 15 homers in 268 at-bats, and the Rangers were impressed enough to trade their regular third sacker, free-agent-to-be Steve Buechele, and hand the job to Palmer. But Palmer's Ranger average last year was only .187, and now some people are wondering whether he'll make it.

There's no question about Palmer's ability to hit the long ball. Between Texas and Oklahoma City last year, he blasted 37 homers with 96 RBI. He has a short, quick stroke, and the ball simply jumps off his bat. But Palmer has always had a tendency to chase bad pitches, and last year he struck out in over one-third of his Ranger at-bats, and 159 times for the year including his AAA numbers. If a pitcher got two strikes on him, the at-bat was essentially over; Palmer hit only .117 as a two-strike hitter. Pitchers tended to work him down and in, hoping to neutralize his great strength.

BASERUNNING:

Palmer has some speed, recording 15 stolen bases at Tulsa in 1989. He didn't show it at the major league level last year, going 0-for-2. He'll probably swipe a few as he gets to know American League pitchers, but speed is not a big part of his game.

FIELDING:

The Rangers had been to accustomed the stellar glove work of Steve Buechele at third, and Palmer suffered by comparison. He showed a strong arm and made some fine plays, but he also committed a lot of careless errors. However, he definitely has the tools for the position, and should improve greatly with experience.

OVERALL:

Palmer's figures were disappointing last year, but it's important to note that he's still only 23. At that age, Mike Schmidt was just breaking in for the Phillies with stats very much like Palmer's: .196, 18 homers, 136 Ks in 367 at-bats.

Overall Statistics

	G	AB	R	H	D	T	HR	RBI	SB	BB	SO	AVG
1991	81	268	38	50	9	2	15	37	0	32	98	.187
Career	97	287	38	52	11	2	15	38	0	32	110	.181

Where He Hits the Ball

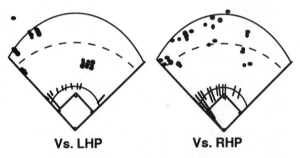

Vs. LHP   **Vs. RHP**

1991 Situational Stats

	AB	H	HR	RBI	AVG		AB	H	HR	RBI	AVG
Home	114	16	6	11	.140	LHP	81	20	9	16	.247
Road	154	34	9	26	.221	RHP	187	30	6	21	.160
Day	60	15	3	10	.250	Sc Pos	55	13	6	25	.236
Night	208	35	12	27	.168	Clutch	46	13	5	11	.283

1991 Rankings (American League)

→ 2nd lowest batting average on a 3-2 count (.038)

→ 6th lowest batting average with 2 strikes (.117)

HITTING:

As the Rangers prepared for the 1991 season, Kevin Reimer shaped up strictly as a spare part. With Pete Incaviglia, Juan Gonzalez and Ruben Sierra in the outfield and Jack Daugherty and Gary Pettis as able reserves, Reimer figured to log somewhere around the 100 at-bats he'd compiled in 1990, mostly as a pinch-hitter. Then funny things began to happen. Incaviglia got released, Daugherty got hurt and Pettis stopped hitting. Given his first chance at regular duty, Reimer came through in a big way, batting .269 with 20 homers in only 394 at-bats.

Reimer, who had seasons of 21 and 16 home runs in the minors, has always had power potential. But for a long time he didn't show it at the major league level, hitting only seven homers in his first 307 big league at-bats. Then, during the second half of 1991, Reimer changed his stance, adopting the high leg-kick employed by teammate Ruben Sierra. The result was fairly amazing. Reimer, who'd hit only four home runs in 177 at-bats during the first half, came through with 16 homers (and 45 RBI) after the All-Star break.

Reimer has always been an excellent fastball hitter. That helps explain why he's so devastating on first pitches, batting .458 (33-for-72 with seven homers) last year. Reimer is not nearly so effective with offspeed and breaking stuff, but he won't be intimidated by any pitcher.

BASERUNNING:

A big man at 6-2 and 215, Reimer has never stolen many bases, and last year he was 0-for-3. He's a good, aggressive baserunner, who stretches many singles into doubles.

FIELDING:

Reimer doesn't have a lot of range in left field but has worked hard and is improving. He gets a much better jump on the ball than he used to. His arm is below average.

OVERALL:

With the way he played in the second half of 1991, Reimer has insured that he'll get plenty of playing time in 1992. Tough as nails, he's still only 27, and could be in line for a big year.

KEVIN REIMER

Position: LF/DH
Bats: L **Throws:** R
Ht: 6' 2" **Wt:** 225

Opening Day Age: 27
Born: 6/28/64 in Macon, GA
ML Seasons: 4

Overall Statistics

	G	AB	R	H	D	T	HR	RBI	SB	BB	SO	AVG
1991	136	394	46	106	22	0	20	69	0	33	93	.269
Career	215	524	53	135	31	1	23	86	0	43	122	.258

Where He Hits the Ball

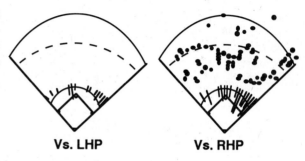

Vs. LHP   **Vs. RHP**

1991 Situational Stats

	AB	H	HR	RBI	AVG		AB	H	HR	RBI	AVG
Home	184	50	13	41	.272	LHP	36	8	1	4	.222
Road	210	56	7	28	.267	RHP	358	98	19	65	.274
Day	83	27	4	13	.325	Sc Pos	102	29	9	53	.284
Night	311	79	16	56	.254	Clutch	56	20	2	6	.357

1991 Rankings (American League)

→ 5th highest batting average in the clutch (.357)

→ 7th in hit by pitch (7)

→ Led the Rangers in batting average in the clutch

→ Led AL left fielders in hit by pitch, batting average in the clutch and slugging percentage vs. right-handed pitchers (.492)

STRONG ARM

IVAN RODRIGUEZ

Position: C
Bats: R **Throws:** R
Ht: 5' 9" **Wt:** 165

Opening Day Age: 20
Born: 11/30/71 in Vega Baja, Puerto Rico
ML Seasons: 1

HITTING:

Watching Ivan Rodriguez break in last year, it was almost impossible to believe that the young receiver was only 19 years old and playing the most games behind the plate as a teenager since Frankie "Blimp" Hayes back in the 1930s. Rodriguez made his strongest impression on defense, but he also did some fine work at bat, hitting a respectable .264.

Though very young, Rodriguez has more than 300 games of professional ball under his belt. A native of Puerto Rico, he signed with Texas at age 16 before breaking in at Class A Gastonia as a 17 year old in 1989. At every level he's shown a maturity beyond his years, and that was doubly true in his Ranger debut in 1991. Compact at 5-9 and 165, he has not shown much home run ability thus far, although he did belt 16 doubles in 280 at-bats. He loves the fastball and is primarily a ground ball hitter, one who usually makes contact.

Rodriguez' main drawback last year was his tendency to swing at everything. He drew only five walks in 88 games, and he'll need to show more discipline if he's going to be a successful major league hitter.

BASERUNNING:

Some young catchers have good speed, but Rodriguez is not one of them. He did not steal a base last year, but he did show good judgement on the bases.

FIELDING:

Throughout his professional career, Rodriguez has been talked about as a future Gold Glove winner. Ranger scout Luis Rosa, who signed him, rates Rodriguez' throwing arm with Benito Santiago's and Sandy Alomar's; some say it's better than either one. Rodriguez moves very well behind the plate and handles pitchers like a veteran.

OVERALL:

The Rangers were excited about Rodriguez long before he reached the majors, and it's easy to understand why. His defense is so good that he won't need to hit much to be a very valuable player. The bonus is that his bat has definite potential.

Overall Statistics

	G	AB	R	H	D	T	HR	RBI	SB	BB	SO	AVG
1991	88	280	24	74	16	0	3	27	0	5	42	.264
Career	88	280	24	74	16	0	3	27	0	5	42	.264

Where He Hits the Ball

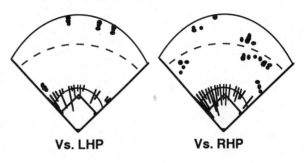

Vs. LHP   Vs. RHP

1991 Situational Stats

	AB	H	HR	RBI	AVG		AB	H	HR	RBI	AVG
Home	135	32	3	18	.237	LHP	71	17	1	9	.239
Road	145	42	0	9	.290	RHP	209	57	2	18	.273
Day	38	8	0	2	.211	Sc Pos	51	17	1	23	.333
Night	242	66	3	25	.273	Clutch	47	11	0	1	.234

1991 Rankings (American League)

- ➡ 2nd in batting average on an 0-2 count (.364)
- ➡ Led the Rangers in batting average on an 0-2 count
- ➡ Led AL catchers in batting average on an 0-2 count

PITCHING:

After watching Kenny Rogers turn in two fine seasons as a durable lefty reliever, the Rangers had a new plan for 1991 -- turn Rogers into a starter. The move seemed sensible, because Texas had a real need for a southpaw in their rotation, and Rogers appeared to have enough stuff to make the switch. What clinched it was that Rogers had looked good in a three-start trial late in the '90 season.

Unfortunately, what looked good in theory didn't work out on the field. Rogers made nine starts last season, and, thanks to some good offensive support, managed to turn in a 4-4 record. But his ERA as a starter was 7.53, and he allowed 65 hits and 31 walks in only 43 innings. Eventually, Rogers went back to the pen, where he should have been all along. It took him a while to get back in the groove, but after the All Star break his ERA was 3.18 in 40 appearances.

Rogers has a decent low-90s fastball, an above-average change and a curveball which can be an effective pitch. Working out of the pen, Rogers didn't have to worry about his stamina, and he threw hard enough to strike out 7.2 batters per nine innings. In his starting efforts he seemed to be taking something off his pitches, as he averaged only 4.2 strikeouts per nine. Whether as a starter or as a reliever, Rogers was very susceptible to the home run ball last year, permitting 14 in 109.2 innings. Poor location was the primary cause.

HOLDING RUNNERS AND FIELDING:

With a good move to first and a quick delivery to the plate, Rogers is very tough to steal against. He allowed only one steal last year in four attempts. He's a decent fielder.

OVERALL:

Texas' need for a starter might tempt them to experiment with Rogers again, but that's less likely after 1991. He has a strong arm and remains tough on lefties. With better control, he should return to his 1989-90 form.

KENNY ROGERS

Position: RP/SP
Bats: L **Throws:** L
Ht: 6' 1" **Wt:** 205

Opening Day Age: 27
Born: 11/10/64 in Savannah, GA
ML Seasons: 3

Overall Statistics

	W	L	ERA	G	GS	Sv	IP	H	R	BB	SO	HR
1991	10	10	5.42	63	9	5	109.2	121	80	61	73	14
Career	23	20	3.97	205	12	22	281.0	274	148	145	210	22

How Often He Throws Strikes

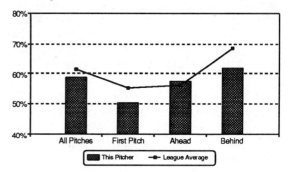

1991 Situational Stats

	W	L	ERA	Sv	IP		AB	H	HR	RBI	AVG
Home	6	5	5.59	3	46.2	LHB	98	22	3	16	.224
Road	4	5	5.29	2	63.0	RHB	332	99	11	50	.298
Day	1	2	6.35	0	17.0	Sc Pos	119	35	6	56	.294
Night	9	8	5.24	5	92.2	Clutch	124	26	4	9	.210

1991 Rankings (American League)

- → 3rd lowest percentage of inherited runners scored (18.0%)
- → 5th in highest batting average allowed vs. right-handed batters (.298) and relief losses (6)
- → Led the Rangers in holds (11), first batter efficiency (.196), lowest percentage of inherited runners scored, relief wins (6), relief losses and lowest batting average allowed in relief (.233)

PITCHING:

After missing half of the 1990 season while recovering from surgery on his right elbow, Jeff Russell made a fine comeback in 1991. Though Russell blew ten save opportunities and seemed to be fatigued late in the year, he recorded 30 saves, tying him for the eighth-highest total in the league. Russell held the opposition to a .198 average with runners in scoring position and a .208 mark in the late innings of close games. He did not completely erase the concerns about his elbow, however.

When he's healthy, Russell possesses a fastball that can reach the high 90s He also throws a change-up and a slider, but it's the heater which was primarily responsible for his 38-save season in 1989. Since his elbow surgery in 1990, Russell has not shown the ability to fan a batter an inning as he did in 1989. But he can still be plenty effective. Russell's control was sometimes a problem in the past, but last year it was excellent. He permitted less than one walk for every three innings pitched, an above average ratio.

The Rangers were fairly pleased with Russell's 1991 performance, but have to be concerned about the way he pitched in the second half. Before the All-Star break, his ERA was 2.93; after it, the figure was 3.78. After September 1, Russell allowed 18 hits in 12 innings with a 5.25 ERA. Russell also permitted 11 homers last season, his highest total since 1988, when he was a starter.

HOLDING RUNNERS AND FIELDING:

Russell has improved his ability to hold baserunners, and last year permitted only one steal (in one attempt) over 79.1 innings. He has always been a smooth fielder.

OVERALL:

Russell's elbow problems are chronic, the kind that can return at any time; because of that, his second-half slump in 1990 has to worry the Rangers. He'll begin 1992 as the Texas closer, but once again they'll have to keep their fingers crossed.

JEFF RUSSELL

Position: RP
Bats: R **Throws:** R
Ht: 6' 3" **Wt:** 205

Opening Day Age: 30
Born: 9/2/61 in Cincinnati, OH
ML Seasons: 9

Overall Statistics

	W	L	ERA	G	GS	Sv	IP	H	R	BB	SO	HR
1991	6	4	3.29	68	0	30	79.1	71	36	26	52	11
Career	46	57	3.96	345	79	83	857.1	834	436	329	528	83

How Often He Throws Strikes

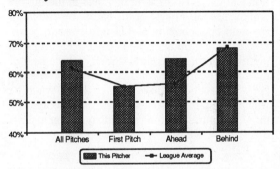

1991 Situational Stats

	W	L	ERA	Sv	IP		AB	H	HR	RBI	AVG
Home	2	1	3.00	18	39.0	LHB	145	35	2	28	.241
Road	4	3	3.57	12	40.1	RHB	156	36	9	24	.231
Day	2	3	3.72	6	19.1	Sc Pos	101	20	1	34	.198
Night	4	1	3.15	24	60.0	Clutch	226	47	8	37	.208

1991 Rankings (American League)

- → 1st in blown saves (10)
- → 2nd in lowest save percentage (75.0%) and worst first batter efficiency (.390)
- → 5th in save opportunities (40)
- → Led the Rangers in saves (30), games finished (56), save opportunities, blown saves, most GDPs induced per GDP situation (15.6%), relief ERA (3.29), relief wins (6) and least baserunners allowed per 9 innings in relief (11.1)

NOLAN RYAN

Position: SP
Bats: R **Throws:** R
Ht: 6' 2" **Wt:** 212

Opening Day Age: 45
Born: 1/31/47 in Refugio, TX
ML Seasons: 25

PITCHING:

Nolan Ryan will be 45 in 1992, and about the only question left is -- how long can he go on? Only a few pitchers have remained effective at such an advanced age, and all of them were very different pitchers than Ryan. Spitballer Jack Quinn went 18-7 with a 2.90 ERA in 1928, a year in which he turned 45 in midseason. Knuckleballers Hoyt Wilhelm (7-7, 2.20, 14 saves) and Phil Niekro (16-8, 3.09) were still excellent pitchers at 45. None of the above were power pitchers like Ryan; as he is in so many ways, Ryan is totally unique.

With a couple of reservations, the Ryan we saw in 1991 showed no signs of slowing down (and any number of hitters will agree). He held the opposition to a .172 batting average, best in the majors and the second-lowest of his career by one point (he held opponents to a .171 mark twenty years ago, in 1972). He permitted only 9.3 baserunners per nine innings, best in baseball and the best of his 25-year career. Ryan's 2.91 earned run average was his second-lowest since 1981, when he was pitching in the Astrodome. And of course he threw his unprecedented seventh no-hitter against the division-winning Blue Jays on May first.

The only negatives in Ryan's 1991 season concerned his health. He missed some time in June with back problems, and he had to go on the disabled list in late July with shoulder troubles. Such are the perils of being in your mid-forties.

HOLDING RUNNERS AND FIELDING:

A career .893 fielder entering the '91 season, Ryan went out and played errorless ball; maybe he's getting ready to win a Gold Glove sometime after he turns 50. Ryan has no tricks when it comes to holding baserunners -- he permitted 24 steals in 32 attempts.

OVERALL:

At Ryan's age, most careers are long since over -- and the ones that are still going can end overnight. But Ryan is no ordinary citizen. He epitomizes the virtues that Texans hold dear: strength and quiet endurance.

Overall Statistics

	W	L	ERA	G	GS	Sv	IP	H	R	BB	SO	HR
1991	12	6	2.91	27	27	0	173.0	102	58	72	203	12
Career	314	278	3.15	767	733	3	5163.1	3731	2056	2686	5511	307

How Often He Throws Strikes

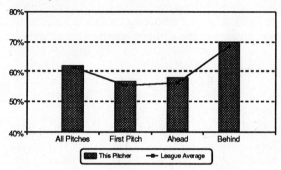

1991 Situational Stats

	W	L	ERA	Sv	IP		AB	H	HR	RBI	AVG
Home	10	4	3.08	0	131.2	LHB	345	63	5	27	.183
Road	2	2	2.40	0	41.1	RHB	249	39	7	27	.157
Day	3	0	1.90	0	42.2	Sc Pos	117	27	4	44	.231
Night	9	6	3.25	0	130.1	Clutch	49	7	1	2	.143

1991 Rankings (American League)

- ➡ 1st in lowest batting average allowed (.172), lowest slugging percentage allowed (.285), lowest on-base average allowed (.263), least GDPs induced per 9 innings (.31) and most strikeouts per 9 innings (10.6)
- ➡ 2nd in lowest groundball/flyball ratio (.70), most pitches thrown per batter (4.12) and lowest batting average allowed vs. left-handed batters (.183)
- ➡ 3rd in strikeouts (203)
- ➡ 4th in stolen bases allowed (24)
- ➡ 5th in ERA (2.91)
- ➡ Led the Rangers in ERA, shutouts (2), strikeouts, most stolen bases allowed and winning percentage (.667)

RUBEN SIERRA

FUTURE MVP?

Position: RF
Bats: B **Throws:** R
Ht: 6' 1" **Wt:** 200

Opening Day Age: 26
Born: 10/6/65 in Rio Piedras, Puerto Rico
ML Seasons: 6

HITTING:

One mark of a truly great performer is that the following is considered a "down" season: a .280 average with 16 homers and 96 RBI. Those were Ruben Sierra's figures for the 1990 campaign. In 1991, Sierra improved those numbers to .307, 25 and 116, and nobody was complaining.

It's important to remember that Sierra is still only 26, an age when most players are still establishing themselves as major leaguers. He's had his growing pains in prime time, not down in the bushes, so perhaps that's one reason why people have been overly critical of him. Throw in the fact that he's Latin, in some limited vocabularies a synonym for "moody" and "selfish," and you might develop a little more perspective on his Texas career.

Sierra silenced most of his critics in 1991. As usual, the switch-hitter was better batting righty, but he improved markedly from the left side, raising his average from .255 to .296. Often impatient in the past, Sierra drew a career-high 56 walks. He continued to use the whole field and remained a great clutch hitter, batting .342 with runners in scoring position. Pitchers usually try to change speeds and get him to go fishing for a bad offering, but Sierra is a very smart hitter.

BASERUNNING:

Sierra drew some heat in 1990 when he attempted only nine steals, all of them successful. In 1991 he was much more aggressive, going 16 for 20. His raw speed is excellent, and he'll take an extra base whenever he can.

FIELDING:

Sierra's defensive work also drew criticism in 1990, when he committed ten errors and threw out only seven runners despite a cannon arm. In '91 he reduced the errors to seven and had 14 assists, tying him for most in the league among right fielders.

OVERALL:

The Rangers have never even won a division title, and because of that, a lot of people don't consider Sierra a "winning" player. He sure looked like a winner in 1991, and there are about 25 other clubs who would be willing to take a chance on winning with him.

Overall Statistics

	G	AB	R	H	D	T	HR	RBI	SB	BB	SO	AVG
1991	161	661	110	203	44	5	25	116	16	56	91	.307
Career	909	3543	505	993	196	37	139	586	74	253	529	.280

Where He Hits the Ball

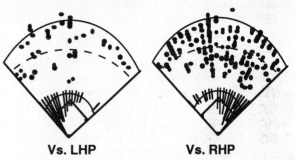

Vs. LHP   Vs. RHP

1991 Situational Stats

	AB	H	HR	RBI	AVG		AB	H	HR	RBI	AVG
Home	328	105	12	61	.320	LHP	188	63	7	32	.335
Road	333	98	13	55	.294	RHP	473	140	18	84	.296
Day	122	41	6	23	.336	Sc Pos	187	64	9	92	.342
Night	539	162	19	93	.301	Clutch	114	33	4	20	.289

1991 Rankings (American League)

→ 2nd in at-bats (661)

→ 3rd in hits (203), doubles (44), total bases (332), RBIs (116), sacrifice flies (9), and plate appearances (726)

→ 4th in runs (110) and games (161)

→ 5th highest batting average with runners in scoring position (.342)

→ Led the Rangers in at-bats, hits, triples (5), RBIs, sacrifice flies, pitches seen (2,642), plate appearances, games, runs scored per time reached base (42.5%), batting average with runners in scoring position and batting average with the bases loaded (.444)

HITTING:

Once considered to be the Texas Rangers' catcher of the future, Mike Stanley has settled comfortably into a part-time platoon role over the last couple of seasons. It's a role he handles pretty well. While Stanley's average was on the low side last year (.249), his on-base percentage was a fine .372, and over one-third of his hits were for extra bases.

A righty swinger, Stanley does almost all of his damage against southpaws. In 1990, he batted .277 vs. lefties, .173 vs. righties; in '91 his figures were .277 vs. LHP, .218 vs. RHP. All five of his homers over the last two years have come against lefthanders. He's decidedly a fastball hitter and a good lowball hitter. Righties who pitch away from these strengths can usually handle Stanley without much problem. Against lefties it's a different story, however.

BASERUNNING:

Stanley probably has a little more speed than most catchers, but only a little. He's a very intelligent baserunner and a perfect 6-for-6 as a basestealer in his career. Knowing his limitations, he was a perfect 0-for-0 in 1991.

FIELDING:

A versatile player, Stanley logged defensive time at first, third, and left field last year, along with his primary position, catcher. Stanley has never been a very good mechanical receiver, and his throwing arm is a liability. But pitchers like working with him and he's an adequate backup. With "Pudge" Rodriguez now established behind the plate, Stanley figures to use his fielder's glove more this year. He's below average wherever he plays.

OVERALL:

Any catcher playing behind Ivan Rodriguez figures to be spending most of his time on the bench. Fortunately for Stanley, he's proven that he can be an effective hitter in part-time roles. With his versatility, there's no reason he can't continue to get his usual 150-200 at-bats.

MIKE STANLEY

Position: C
Bats: R **Throws:** R
Ht: 6' 0" **Wt:** 190

Opening Day Age: 28
Born: 6/25/63 in Ft. Lauderdale, FL
ML Seasons: 6

Overall Statistics

	G	AB	R	H	D	T	HR	RBI	SB	BB	SO	AVG
1991	95	181	25	45	13	1	3	25	0	34	44	.249
Career	452	987	114	248	43	4	16	120	6	147	215	.251

Where He Hits the Ball

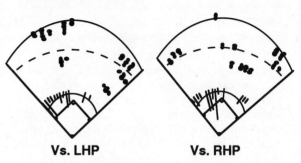

Vs. LHP   **Vs. RHP**

1991 Situational Stats

	AB	H	HR	RBI	AVG		AB	H	HR	RBI	AVG
Home	96	27	1	17	.281	LHP	94	26	3	15	.277
Road	85	18	2	8	.212	RHP	87	19	0	10	.218
Day	41	10	2	6	.244	Sc Pos	55	14	0	21	.255
Night	140	35	1	19	.250	Clutch	39	9	1	9	.231

1991 Rankings (American League)

➡ Did not rank near the top or bottom in any category

PITCHING:

Bobby Witt is a terrible tease; he always promises greatness, only to revert to his old struggling ways. Witt seemed to have arrived for good in 1990, when he won 17 games with a 3.36 earned run average and 221 strikeouts. However, last year it was back to square one again. Witt managed only three wins and a 6.09 ERA over the course of a maddening, injury-riddled campaign.

Witt never really got it going in '91. He was off to a 3-3 start last May when some shoulder soreness was diagnosed as a slight tear of the rotator cuff, forcing him to the disabled list. Rest was prescribed and Witt missed two months, including a rehab stint at AAA Oklahoma City, before returning to the Rangers on August 1. He was deemed healthy but hardly looked it, not making it past the fourth inning until his fifth start. Finally, in September, Witt revealed that he was experiencing elbow pain when he threw his slider. He ultimately underwent arthroscopic surgery to smooth a bone spur and is scheduled to be ready for spring training.

When he's healthy, Witt possesses an overpowering 95-MPH fastball, along with the slider and a curveball. Even with all his problems last year, he continued to strike out nearly a man an inning. Witt seemed to have his career-long control problems licked in 1990, but in '91 they returned, as he walked 74 men in only 88.2 innings.

HOLDING RUNNERS AND FIELDING:

With his high leg kick and poor control, Witt has always been easy to run on. Though he worked only 88.2 innings last year, he permitted 18 steals in 22 attempts. Witt has improved somewhat as a fielder, but is still below average.

OVERALL:

Even when completely healthy, Witt was never able to put together back-to-back winning seasons . . . and now his arm is questionable. For the moment, the Rangers are just hoping that Witt will return to full health.

BOBBY WITT

Position: SP
Bats: R **Throws:** R
Ht: 6' 2" **Wt:** 205

Opening Day Age: 27
Born: 5/11/64 in Arlington, VA
ML Seasons: 6

Overall Statistics

	W	L	ERA	G	GS	Sv	IP	H	R	BB	SO	HR
1991	3	7	6.09	17	16	0	88.2	84	66	74	82	4
Career	59	59	4.63	160	157	0	980.0	841	556	682	951	71

How Often He Throws Strikes

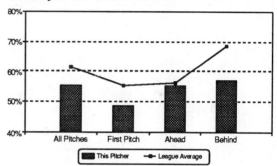

1991 Situational Stats

	W	L	ERA	Sv	IP		AB	H	HR	RBI	AVG
Home	0	5	6.30	0	40.0	LHB	151	35	2	21	.232
Road	3	2	5.92	0	48.2	RHB	180	49	2	33	.272
Day	0	1	4.50	0	14.0	Sc Pos	106	27	1	47	.255
Night	3	6	6.39	0	74.2	Clutch	11	2	0	2	.182

1991 Rankings (American League)

→ Did not rank near the top or bottom in any category

TEXAS RANGERS

OIL CAN BOYD

Position: SP
Bats: R **Throws:** R
Ht: 6' 1" **Wt:** 160

Opening Day Age: 32
Born: 10/6/59 in
Meridian, MS
ML Seasons: 10

Overall Statistics

	W	L	ERA	G	GS	Sv	IP	H	R	BB	SO	HR
1991	8	15	4.59	31	31	0	182.1	196	96	57	115	21
Career	78	77	4.04	214	207	0	1389.2	1427	680	368	799	166

PITCHING, FIELDING & HOLDING RUNNERS:

Is the Can empty? When the Rangers acquired Dennis Boyd from Montreal last July 21, it looked like a deal which might lead to a division title. Boyd had posted a 2.93 ERA for the Expos in 1990, and though his '91 work with Montreal before coming to Texas wasn't as good (6-8, 3.52), it was plenty good enough for the pitching-poor Rangers.

That was the plan, but Boyd turned out to be a disaster in Texas. In 12 Ranger starts he posted a 6.68 ERA, the highest of his career, and allowed 81 hits in only 62 innings. He pitched competently, but only for short stretches. For his first 45 pitches (about three innings worth), Boyd's opponents' batting average was .241; after that, it was .310. Runners took off frequently against Boyd, but with a tricky motion and good-throwing catchers, he permitted only 14 steals in 26 attempts. He played errorless ball during the season.

OVERALL:

Boyd was a free agent when the season ended, but his performance was so bad that the Rangers seemed unlikely to make a bid. At 32, he's hardly old enough to be over the hill. But Boyd weighs only 160 pounds, and his work last year suggests he's now wearing out too quickly to be an effective starter. Boyd might be better off working in relief, though he'd probably despise the idea.

MARIO DIAZ

Position: SS/2B
Bats: R **Throws:** R
Ht: 5'10" **Wt:** 160

Opening Day Age: 30
Born: 1/10/62 in
Humacao, Puerto Rico
ML Seasons: 5

Overall Statistics

	G	AB	R	H	D	T	HR	RBI	SB	BB	SO	AVG
1991	96	182	24	48	7	0	1	22	0	15	18	.264
Career	203	373	43	90	13	1	2	42	0	25	37	.241

HITTING, FIELDING, BASERUNNING:

The Rangers have been hurting for a shortstop for several years. When they signed Mario Diaz as a free agent last winter, it looked like a good opportunity for the veteran infielder who'd never really received a chance in the major leagues. At 29, Diaz finally got 182 major league at-bats last year. He didn't bowl anyone over, but he batted a respectable .264.

Diaz' bat shouldn't really have surprised anybody. Coming up through the Seattle organization, he'd hit .300 or thereabouts at numerous stops. He's not the most disciplined hitter, but he's a good contact man and a tough out. Last year he batted .313 with runners on base.

Diaz has played all four infield positions, but he's primarily a shortstop. His glove work is about average, with a decent arm and range. He won't dazzle anyone in the field, but he won't hurt much, either. His speed is definitely below average, and he's no threat to steal.

OVERALL:

Diaz has been in organized ball since 1979, and yet, despite good credentials, he's never been given a real shot at an everyday job. At this point his chances of becoming a regular are, as Bill James put it, "roughly the same as your chance of getting a date with Kelly McGillis." Diaz' best hope would be to make a major league roster as a utility man.

GENO PETRALLI

Position: C
Bats: L **Throws:** R
Ht: 6' 1" **Wt:** 190

Opening Day Age: 32
Born: 9/25/59 in Sacramento, CA
ML Seasons: 10

Overall Statistics

	G	AB	R	H	D	T	HR	RBI	SB	BB	SO	AVG
1991	87	199	21	54	8	1	2	20	2	21	25	.271
Career	656	1549	157	431	66	9	22	161	6	174	212	.278

HITTING, FIELDING, BASERUNNING:

Geno Petralli is 32 years old, has a bad back, can't run a lick, and has spent most of his adult life chasing passed balls back to the screen. Oh, and he can't throw very well, either. As this book went to press, Petralli didn't have a contract for 1992. But not to worry: Petralli's a lefty-swinging catcher, and he can hit. That means he'll find work.

Petralli missed a lot of the 1991 season while suffering from back problems. By the time he came back Ivan Rodriguez had established himself as the Ranger catcher. But when Petralli played, he hit: .308 in May, .327 in August, .344 in September. Petralli doesn't have much power, but with a lifetime average of .278 and a disciplined bat (.352 lifetime on-base average), he doesn't have to hit homers.

As a catcher, Petralli is better than a lot of people think. His arm is a little below average, but it's not horrible, and he handles pitchers pretty well. He's not the most mobile guy in the world, but those years chasing Charlie Hough knuckleballs created too negative an impression.

OVERALL:

Lefty-swinging catchers can always find a job, even the ones who can't hit as well as Petralli. The only question is whether he'll play for the Rangers, or someone else. His destination probably depends on his salary demands.

GARY PETTIS

Position: CF
Bats: B **Throws:** R
Ht: 6' 1" **Wt:** 160

Opening Day Age: 34
Born: 4/3/58 in Oakland, CA
ML Seasons: 10

Overall Statistics

	G	AB	R	H	D	T	HR	RBI	SB	BB	SO	AVG
1991	137	282	37	61	7	5	0	19	29	54	91	.216
Career	1105	3470	541	823	104	46	20	247	340	492	913	.237

HITTING, FIELDING, BASERUNNING:

Gary Pettis will be 34 when the 1992 season starts, and his days as a major league regular are probably over. Pettis batted only .216 in 1991, which is not to say he can't still be a useful player.

Even at a fairly advanced age, Pettis' game is all speed and defense. Though his basestealing skills have declined, he's swiped at least 20 bases every year since 1983, including 29 last year. He remains an outstanding center fielder with marvelous range. Last year the Rangers worked Pettis into 137 contests, putting his glove out there every chance they could.

As a youngster, Pettis was considered a hitting prospect by the over-optimistic Angels. They used to say that he was too undisciplined and he had to learn to hit the ball on the ground to take advantage of his speed. So Pettis learned to draw some walks and became primarily a ground ball hitter. He's still never hit .260 in a season in which he's had 100 at-bats. Some guys just can't hit.

OVERALL:

Pettis is signed through 1992, so unless the Rangers choose to eat his contract, he'll have the same role this year that he had in 1991. He'll start only occasionally, but will almost always be in the field when the Rangers have a lead in the late innings.

ORGANIZATION OVERVIEW:

Over the last couple of years, the Rangers have fearlessly moved veterans aside, or off their roster, while working players such as Juan Gonzalez, Ivan Rodriguez and Dean Palmer into their lineup. That's laudable, and something many clubs just don't have the guts to do. The main negative with the Rangers has been their record in developing pitchers -- namely the arm problems that hampered the development, or wrecked the careers of Edwin Correa, Bobby Witt and Jose Guzman, among others. Texas seems aware of the problem and appears to be showing more care with their young arms.

HECTOR FAJARDO

Position: P   **Opening Day Age:** 21
Bats: R **Throws:** R   **Born:** 11/16/70 in
Ht: 6' 2" **Wt:** 195   Michoacan, Mexico

Recent Statistics

	W	L	ERA	G	GS	Sv	IP	H	R	BB	SO	HR
91 A Augusta/Salem	4	3	2.65	12	12	0	68.0	48	29	25	86	2
91 AA Carolina	3	4	4.13	10	10	0	61.0	55	32	24	53	4
91 AAA Buffalo	1	0	0.96	8	0	1	9.1	6	1	3	12	0
91 AL Texas	0	2	6.75	6	5	0	25.1	35	20	11	23	2

One of two top pitching prospects Texas received in the Steve Buechele trade, Fajardo is older and farther along than Kurt Miller. He saw some major league action this year; though his ERA wasn't very good, Fajardo displayed an excellent fastball and split-fingered pitch and had a 2-to-1 strikeout/walk ratio. One concern about Fajardo -- especially for the Rangers -- is that he's from Mexico where pitchers are often given heavy usage at a young age. Fajardo has shown no ill-effects thus far, however.

MONTY FARISS

Position: 2B   **Opening Day Age:** 24
Bats: R **Throws:** R   **Born:** 10/13/67 in
Ht: 6' 4" **Wt:** 200   Leedey, OK

Recent Statistics

	G	AB	R	H	D	THR	RBI	SB	BB	SO	AVG
91 AAA Okla City	137	494	84	134	31	9 13	73	4	91	143	.271
91 AL Texas	19	31	6	8	1	0 1	6	0	7	11	.258
91 MLE	137	475	63	115	26	7 9	54	2	68	172	.242

The Rangers have had a frustrating wait for Fariss, the sixth player chosen in the 1988 draft, for several seasons Fariss has shown some hitting promise, but also some holes in his swing with 143 strikeouts this year at Oklahoma City. The main concern has been defensive, however. As both a shortstop and second baseman, Fariss has suffered from "Steve Sax disease" -- unexplainable throwing errors on routine plays. The latest plan involves switching him to left field.

BARRY MANUEL

Position: P   **Opening Day Age:** 26
Bats: R **Throws:** R   **Born:** 8/12/65 in
Ht: 5' 11" **Wt:** 180   Mamou, LA

Recent Statistics

	W	L	ERA	G	GS	Sv	IP	H	R	BB	SO	HR
91 AA Tulsa	2	7	3.29	56	0	25	68.1	63	29	34	45	5
91 AL Texas	1	0	1.13	8	0	0	16.0	7	2	6	5	0

People keep underestimating Barry Manuel. Though he saved 36 games at Charlotte in 1990 -- a Florida State League record -- he wasn't listed as one of the Rangers' top prospects this spring. In '91 he saved 25 more at AA Tulsa, but still wasn't listed as a Baseball America top ten prospect. Manuel is finally getting some notice after a strong late-season performance with the Rangers. One reason he's been underestimated is that he doesn't have an eye-popping fastball. But Manuel keeps getting hitters out, and has a very good chance to stick in the Rangers' pen this year.

ROB MAURER

Position: 1B   **Opening Day Age:** 25
Bats: L **Throws:** L   **Born:** 1/7/67 in
Ht: 6' 3" **Wt:** 200   Evansville, IN

Recent Statistics

	G	AB	R	H	D	THR	RBI	SB	BB	SO	AVG
91 AAA Okla City	132	459	76	138	41	3 20	77	2	96	134	.301
91 AL Texas	13	16	0	1	1	0 0	2	0	2	6	.063
91 MLE	132	438	57	117	34	2 15	57	1	72	161	.267

The Rangers don't really need a first baseman with Rafael Palmeiro around, but Maurer might force his way onto the Texas roster this year. Maurer has excellent power and great patience at the plate; the negative is that he's always struck out a lot. He's also very slow. One thing worth noting about Maurer is that he's consistently improved, always doing better over the second half of a season. He has an excellent chance to stick with the Rangers this year, possibly in a DH role.

KURT MILLER

Position: P   **Opening Day Age:** 19
Bats: R **Throws:** R   **Born:** 8/24/72 in
Ht: 6' 5" **Wt:** 200   Tucson, AZ

Recent Statistics

	W	L	ERA	G	GS	Sv	IP	H	R	BB	SO	HR
90 A Welland	3	2	3.29	14	12	0	65.2	59	39	37	61	3
91 A Augusta	6	7	2.50	21	21	0	115.1	89	49	57	103	6

Considered Pittsburgh's top prospect -- and one of the top pitching prospects in all of baseball -- Miller came to the Rangers with Fajardo in the Buechele trade. With a fastball clocked at 94 MPH and a developing curve, Miller has the stuff to justify the lofty ranking. Having lost some good pitchers to injury over the last few years, the Rangers will bring Miller along s-l-o-w-l-y. He's expected to start the year in Class A.

PITCHING:

When the Blue Jays were introduced for the first home game of the American League playoffs, Jim Acker got a noisier reception than most players. Trouble was, Acker was being booed by the home fans. It was a tough season for the middle reliever, who was knocked around consistently in '91. Acker has never been able to get over the hump of pitching consistently for an extended period, doing just well enough to keep his place on the staff without threatening its stronger members.

Acker's strength is that he can pitch for several days in a row when his team needs him to. He also has the potential to be tough on left-handed batters, but the fact that they knocked him around pretty handily last season is a measure of his overall problems. Acker also gave up a frightening number of home runs last season -- a career-high 16 in only 88.1 innings. That's more than in the previous two seasons combined.

When Acker is on his game he gets a lot of grounders. Otherwise, he gets into a lot of trouble with a fastball that doesn't stay down and an average slider. Acker also has a change as his third pitch. He's does a pretty good job mixing them up, probably because none of his pitches are good enough for him to fall in love with any one in particular.

HOLDING RUNNERS AND FIELDING:

Acker's defense has improved with time. He handles bunts well and is usually in good position to field ground balls. He has a good enough move to keep baserunners from running too often and too successfully.

OVERALL:

At this stage of his career, Acker is probably the ninth or tenth man on the pitching staff, and he needs to be effective to keep his job. He'll probably never be more than a middle-inning guy, keeping his team in high-scoring games or working the ugly innings of blowouts.

JIM ACKER

Position: RP/SP
Bats: R **Throws:** R
Ht: 6' 2" **Wt:** 215

Opening Day Age: 33
Born: 9/24/58 in Freer, TX
ML Seasons: 9

Overall Statistics

	W	L	ERA	G	GS	Sv	IP	H	R	BB	SO	HR
1991	3	5	5.20	54	4	1	88.1	77	53	36	44	16
Career	33	49	3.92	450	32	30	873.2	873	428	317	471	78

How Often He Throws Strikes

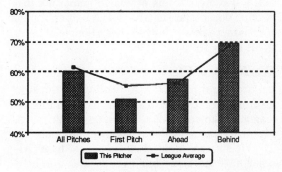

1991 Situational Stats

	W	L	ERA	Sv	IP		AB	H	HR	RBI	AVG
Home	2	2	4.92	0	53.0	LHB	126	37	5	18	.294
Road	1	3	5.60	1	35.1	RHB	197	40	11	39	.203
Day	2	1	5.46	0	29.2	Sc Pos	74	24	6	44	.324
Night	1	4	5.06	1	58.2	Clutch	93	17	2	11	.183

1991 Rankings (American League)

➡ 5th highest percentage of inherited runners scored (45.2%)

GREAT SPEE

ROBERTO ALOMAR

Position: 2B
Bats: B **Throws:** R
Ht: 6' 0" **Wt:** 175

Opening Day Age: 24
Born: 2/5/68 in Ponce, Puerto Rico
ML Seasons: 4

HITTING:

A bit of a second banana to Joe Carter in the big four-player trade with San Diego, Roberto Alomar quickly established himself as one of the most popular players ever to wear the Toronto colors. Alomar had a wonderful season at the plate, giving the Jays a number-two hitter with great speed and surprising power (61 extra base hits). Alomar is an opposite-field hitter who handles the bat so skillfully he's fun to watch.

Alomar had the best on-base percentage among the Toronto regulars, showing a good eye along with his ability to drive the ball either into the gaps or down the lines. A switch-hitter, he was especially dangerous from the left side. If there's still a weakness to his offensive game, it's that Alomar doesn't fare nearly as well batting righty. He has more power, but also has a couple of holes in his swing from that side.

BASERUNNING:

An exciting runner, Alomar is always a threat to go from first to third, and he was second in the league in stolen bases. He brought with him a National League tendency to steal third, nabbing 21 of his career-high 53 steals at that base. Alomar runs the bases intelligently and is a hard slider.

FIELDING:

Sometimes Alomar is a victim of his own prowess, making a great stop because of his extraordinary range -- only to commit an error on a throw he should have thought twice about making. He has very good hands and is a Gold Glove candidate even though he makes more errors than some of his peers.

OVERALL:

After four outstanding seasons, Alomar is still only 24 years old. He should keep improving, and has the potential to be a .300-plus hitter and big-time catalyst in the Toronto order. The team didn't have a surplus of power hitters last year, so the Jays need the kind of spark that he provides.

Overall Statistics

	G	AB	R	H	D	T	HR	RBI	SB	BB	SO	AVG
1991	161	637	88	188	41	11	9	69	53	57	86	.295
Career	609	2391	334	685	119	23	31	226	143	205	317	.286

Where He Hits the Ball

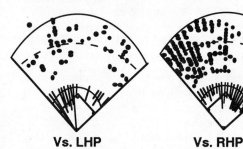

Vs. LHP   **Vs. RHP**

1991 Situational Stats

	AB	H	HR	RBI	AVG		AB	H	HR	RBI	AVG
Home	313	93	6	40	.297	LHP	191	47	5	27	.246
Road	324	95	3	29	.293	RHP	446	141	4	42	.316
Day	197	48	2	27	.244	Sc Pos	157	44	1	58	.280
Night	440	140	7	42	.318	Clutch	105	30	2	15	.286

1991 Rankings (American League)

➡ 1st in steals of third (21)
➡ 2nd in sacrifice bunts (16), stolen bases (53) and stolen base percentage (82.8%)
➡ 3rd in triples (11)
➡ 4th in plate appearances (719), games (161) and bunts in play (31)
➡ 5th in pitches seen (2,702)
➡ Led the Blue Jays in batting average (.295), hits (188), singles (127), triples, sacrifice bunts, stolen bases, caught stealing (11), times on base (249), plate appearances, on-base average (.354) and stolen base percentage

HITTING:

Just when the Jays thought they'd found a first-string catcher, Pat Borders had a 1991 season that cast some doubt about whether he can hold down that role in the future. Borders seemed to establish himself as someone who could hit for some power and a good average during 1990. He'd held his own against righthanders and had broken the habit of chasing bad pitches. But then in '91, he had some of the problems that had raised questions about him in the past.

What happened? Borders could still turn on a fastball that's put over the inside half of the plate. But he chased too many pitches that turned into weak ground balls and pop-ups. He still hasn't broken the habit of going after sliders in the dirt, and he doesn't draw many walks. Borders spends a lot of time behind the plate observing hitters; the Jays are still waiting for him to bring some of those lessons to the batter's box when he's the one with a bat in his hands.

BASERUNNING:

Borders doesn't steal bases and doesn't even think about taking an extra base. He's slow. He's also a big guy who could be a factor in take-outs at second base or home, if only he'd get there in time.

FIELDING:

A converted third baseman, Borders doesn't have the smoothest release on his throws to second, but he's had a very good record at throwing out base stealers. He gets rid of the ball quickly. He has a problem with blocking home plate, which hurt Toronto a couple of times during the playoffs.

OVERALL:

Last year, there was talk that Borders could be on his way to becoming one of the better catchers in the league. All bets are off now, however, and the question will be whether he can regain his starting role. The Jays would still like to believe that he can be a .270 hitter and belt 15 homers.

PAT BORDERS

Position: C
Bats: R **Throws:** R
Ht: 6' 2" **Wt:** 200

Opening Day Age: 28
Born: 5/14/63 in Columbus, OH
ML Seasons: 4

Overall Statistics

	G	AB	R	H	D	T	HR	RBI	SB	BB	SO	AVG
1991	105	291	22	71	17	0	5	36	0	11	45	.244
Career	380	1032	95	274	58	6	28	135	2	43	171	.266

Where He Hits the Ball

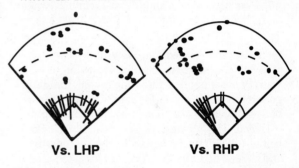

Vs. LHP   Vs. RHP

1991 Situational Stats

	AB	H	HR	RBI	AVG		AB	H	HR	RBI	AVG
Home	146	36	2	18	.247	LHP	147	35	1	14	.238
Road	145	35	3	18	.241	RHP	144	36	4	22	.250
Day	103	20	1	11	.194	Sc Pos	65	19	3	30	.292
Night	188	51	4	25	.271	Clutch	59	16	1	10	.271

1991 Rankings (American League)

- ➡ 5th lowest on-base percentage vs. left-handed pitchers (.271)
- ➡ Led the Blue Jays in batting average on an 0-2 count (.240)

WORKHORSE

TOM CANDIOTTI

Position: SP
Bats: R **Throws:** R
Ht: 6' 2" **Wt:** 200

Opening Day Age: 34
Born: 8/31/57 in Walnut Creek, CA
ML Seasons: 8

PITCHING:

The Jays picked up Tom Candiotti midway through last season and his steady work was one of the reasons they were able to outlast Boston for the Eastern Division title. Though Candiotti received such poor support that he posted only a .500 record despite ranking second in the league in ERA, he never appeared to get flustered. He pitched at least seven innings in 24 of his 34 starts.

Candiotti is a knuckleballer, one of only two major leaguers (along with Charlie Hough) who rely on the pitch. In earlier seasons, he fought the notion of being considered a knuckleball pitcher, but the fact was that his other pitches just weren't good enough. "The Candy Man" gets hurt when he feels the need to throw a 3-and-1 fastball.

The righthander throws the knuckler at three different speeds -- medium, slow and slower. He also has a slow curve that features a big downward break when he's throwing it well. Candiotti gets into trouble when the curve is flat because batters already are expecting his stuff to be offspeed. His slowest pitch is usually clocked below 60 MPH. Candiotti also throws a fastball and slider, but really shouldn't use them too often.

HOLDING RUNNERS AND FIELDING:

Candiotti is quick to cover first base and gets off the mound well to field bunts and slow grounders. He is not afraid to slow down the pace of the game by throwing to first. He needs to do that, because the knuckler doesn't give him much of a chance to thwart basestealers.

OVERALL:

Candiotti was a free agent at season's end, and the Jays were expected to make a major effort to sign him. He has a good approach to the game, knowing what he needs to do to be successful. He especially relishes pitching against teams whose lineups are filled with free-swinging sluggers. To wit: He was 5-0 against Oakland, Detroit and Texas, allowing only seven earned runs in 52 innings.

Overall Statistics

	W	L	ERA	G	GS	Sv	IP	H	R	BB	SO	HR
1991	13	13	2.65	34	34	0	238.0	202	82	73	167	12
Career	84	78	3.51	213	205	0	1404.2	1349	626	461	878	115

How Often He Throws Strikes

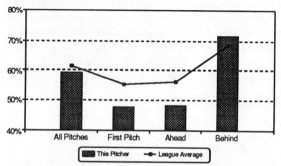

1991 Situational Stats

	W	L	ERA	Sv	IP		AB	H	HR	RBI	AVG
Home	6	6	3.11	0	110.0	LHB	449	109	6	40	.243
Road	7	7	2.25	0	128.0	RHB	438	93	6	27	.212
Day	6	4	2.10	0	77.0	Sc Pos	212	40	3	55	.189
Night	7	9	2.91	0	161.0	Clutch	95	19	0	4	.200

1991 Rankings (American League)

→ 1st in least home runs allowed per 9 innings (.45) and lowest ERA on the road (2.25)

→ 2nd in lowest ERA (2.65) and least GDPs induced per 9 innings (.34)

→ 3rd in pitches thrown (3,894), most stolen bases allowed (26), lowest batting average allowed vs. right-handed batters (.212) and lowest batting average allowed with runners in scoring position (.189)

→ 4th lowest run support per 9 innings (3.5)

→ 5th lowest batting average allowed (.228) and most pitches thrown per batter (3.97)

→ Led the Blue Jays in complete games (3)

HITTING:

Last year, Joe Carter became the first player to drive in more than 100 runs for three different teams in consecutive seasons. That is not necessarily a compliment. Carter has established himself as the kind of player that teams will take extensive measures to acquire . . . and then subsequently, to get rid of.

Carter has averaged 109 RBI per year over the last six years, and that sort of production has to be admired. His weakness, as Hall of Famer Joe Morgan has pointed out, is that he's only doing part of his job. In his desire to drive in runs, Carter forgets that it's important that he himself get on base for others to drive home. Swinging at bad pitches to drive runners in, he won't draw many walks, and he makes far more outs than necessary (a mediocre .308 lifetime on-base percentage). Carter's value last year was boosted by Sky-Dome, where he batted .290 and hit 23 of his 33 homers; on the road, his figures weren't as formidable.

BASERUNNING:

Carter can go from first to third needing only a small lapse by the defense, and he's taken out a few second basemen over the years with his hard slides. A consistent threat to steal, he's swiped 20 or more bases in six of the last seven years.

FIELDING:

Playing mostly in right and left field, Carter had 13 assists, but that's a deceptive statistic because teams tend to run on him. He has difficulty hitting cutoff men and doesn't have outstanding range. Yet Carter always gives an honest effort in the outfield. He led the Jays with eight outfield errors.

OVERALL:

Carter has played every game for more than three seasons, and any questions about his desire have long been answered. But despite his hefty RBI totals, there are still some remaining doubts about his overall value. Those doubts probably won't be erased until Carter has appeared in a World Series.

JOE CARTER

Position: RF/LF
Bats: R **Throws:** R
Ht: 6' 3" **Wt:** 215

Opening Day Age: 32
Born: 3/7/60 in Oklahoma City, OK
ML Seasons: 9

Overall Statistics

	G	AB	R	H	D	T	HR	RBI	SB	BB	SO	AVG
1991	162	638	89	174	42	3	33	108	20	49	112	.273
Career	1186	4579	630	1206	234	27	208	754	169	266	742	.263

Where He Hits the Ball

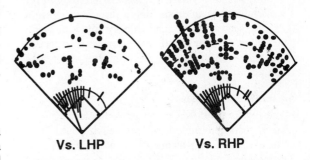

Vs. LHP   **Vs. RHP**

1991 Situational Stats

	AB	H	HR	RBI	AVG		AB	H	HR	RBI	AVG
Home	321	93	23	64	.290	LHP	188	63	10	32	.335
Road	317	81	10	44	.256	RHP	450	111	23	76	.247
Day	200	49	10	30	.245	Sc Pos	183	49	9	76	.268
Night	438	125	23	78	.285	Clutch	107	21	1	9	.196

1991 Rankings (American League)

→ 1st in hit by pitch (10) and games (162)

→ 2nd in cleanup slugging percentage (.527)

→ 3rd in sacrifice flies (9) and lowest batting average with the bases loaded (.077)

→ 4th in home runs (33), doubles (42) and lowest percentage of pitches taken (43.9%)

→ 5th in total bases (321)

→ Led the Blue Jays in home runs, doubles, total bases, RBIs (108), intentional walks (12), hit by pitch, games, slugging percentage (.503) and HR frequency (19.3 ABs per HR)

HITTING:

Last season wasn't the one by which Kelly Gruber should be judged. Gruber missed a portion of the year with an injured right hand, and ended up playing in a little over two-thirds of Toronto's games. He still showed a lot of power, finishing second on the team in homers to Joe Carter. But Gruber didn't hit for average and in clutch situations the way he had in 1990, the best season of his career.

Gruber has always been able to pull the ball, and at his best he knows when to swing for the fences and when to cut down on his stroke. Most of his homers are pulled, but he can hit for power to right-center and right field. He came to the majors as a high fastball hitter, but has learned to wait for a pitch that he can drive. His timing, as one might expect, seemed to be thrown off a bit from being sidelined. Gruber could be a bit more selective at the plate. He drew only 26 unintentional walks last year.

BASERUNNING:

The Jays don't need Gruber to steal a lot of bases, but he can be counted upon to reach double figures. Last season was one of his worst in terms of efficiency, however (63%). Gruber is a hard slider and a heady runner who will take the extra base when given a chance.

FIELDING:

Gruber has a strong but erratic arm, and his thumb problems apparently contributed to the number of errors that he committed in 1991. He has good range and makes plays that go for doubles into the corner against lesser third basemen.

OVERALL:

If he can stay healthy, Gruber should be a consistent threat to hit 25-30 homers and be in the 100 RBI range, especially if the top of the Jays order continues to be productive. You can still count him among the best in the game at third base.

KELLY GRUBER

Position: 3B
Bats: R **Throws:** R
Ht: 6' 0" **Wt:** 185

Opening Day Age: 30
Born: 2/26/62 in Bellaire, TX
ML Seasons: 8

Overall Statistics

	G	AB	R	H	D	T	HR	RBI	SB	BB	SO	AVG
1991	113	429	58	108	18	2	20	65	12	31	70	.252
Career	801	2648	379	698	129	21	103	391	73	169	421	.264

Where He Hits the Ball

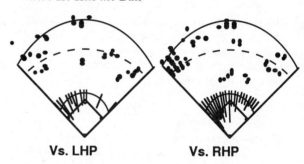

Vs. LHP   Vs. RHP

1991 Situational Stats

	AB	H	HR	RBI	AVG		AB	H	HR	RBI	AVG
Home	221	58	8	31	.262	LHP	112	31	8	18	.277
Road	208	50	12	34	.240	RHP	317	77	12	47	.243
Day	135	41	8	24	.304	Sc Pos	131	31	3	42	.237
Night	294	67	12	41	.228	Clutch	76	17	3	11	.224

1991 Rankings (American League)

→ 2nd lowest fielding percentage at third base (.962)

→ 4th highest batting average on a 3-1 count (.800) and 4th lowest batting average on a 3-2 count (.056)

→ 6th lowest percentage of pitches taken (44.8%)

→ Led the Blue Jays in batting average with the bases loaded (.400) and batting average on a 3-1 count

→ Led AL third basemen in caught stealing (7), least GDPs per GDP situation (8.1%) and batting average on a 3-1 count

PITCHING:

Juan Guzman had never shown much in the minors, and he wasn't seen as much more than a fifth starter when the Jays called him up to fill Dave Stieb's spot in the rotation. But Guzman turned out to be the team's most effective pitcher over the final two months of the season, and was the only one to win a game during the AL playoffs.

There is nothing fancy about Guzman's portfolio. He's a hard thrower, a guy who uses the fastball and slider and is just wild enough to keep his opponents off balance. Guzman won all 10 of his games consecutively, setting a team record that had been held by Stieb. He obviously did more than take a spot in the rotation.

Imagine what it must have felt like for a team to face Tom Candiotti, the knuckleballer one night, and then feel Guzman's smoke the next. Guzman gets his fastball into the mid-90s, and the pitch has good movement. He wasn't any easier to hit for teams that loaded their batting orders with left-handed hitters. Guzman got into trouble when he walked too many batters. His games were marked by deep counts, but he usually managed to recover from the holes that he dug.

HOLDING RUNNERS AND FIELDING:

As with many hard throwers, Guzman's motion leaves him in bad position to field balls hit up the middle. He committed three errors in only 17 chances, an .824 fielding average. He has an average move to first base, but helps his catcher by delivering the ball quickly.

OVERALL:

Calling Guzman a surprise is an understatement. He wasn't even on the major league roster after the 1990 season, and no other team took a chance on drafting him. He looks like he should be in the majors to stay, and it will be interesting to see if teams can figure out ways to make adjustments when facing him.

JUAN GUZMAN

Position: SP
Bats: R **Throws:** R
Ht: 6' 0" **Wt:** 190

Opening Day Age: 25
Born: 10/28/66 in Santo Domingo, DR
ML Seasons: 1

Overall Statistics

	W	L	ERA	G	GS	Sv	IP	H	R	BB	SO	HR
1991	10	3	2.99	23	23	0	138.2	98	53	66	123	6
Career	10	3	2.99	23	23	0	138.2	98	53	66	123	6

How Often He Throws Strikes

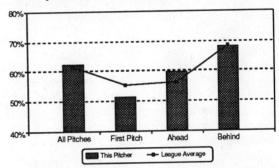

1991 Situational Stats

	W	L	ERA	Sv	IP		AB	H	HR	RBI	AVG
Home	5	1	3.82	0	63.2	LHB	238	46	1	15	.193
Road	5	2	2.28	0	75.0	RHB	259	52	5	30	.201
Day	3	1	2.09	0	43.0	Sc Pos	116	23	2	36	.198
Night	7	2	3.39	0	95.2	Clutch	35	6	1	3	.171

1991 Rankings (American League)

→ 6th lowest batting average allowed vs. left-handed batters (.193)

→ 9th in wild pitches (10)

→ Led the Blue Jays in wild pitches

STOPPER

TOM HENKE

Position: RP
Bats: R **Throws:** R
Ht: 6' 5" **Wt:** 225

Opening Day Age: 34
Born: 12/21/57 in
Kansas City, MO
ML Seasons: 10

PITCHING:

Tom Henke put together another standout year for the Jays in 1991, even though he was hindered at times by injuries. Henke missed a month of the campaign -- parts of April and May -- with a pulled groin muscle, and pitched only four times during the last three weeks of the regular season because of tendinitis in his right shoulder.

When healthy, though, few relievers were more consistent. Henke had 25 saves before blowing his first save opportunity of the year in August. He averaged more than one strikeout per inning for the sixth time in seven seasons -- the one season he didn't, he had 66 K's in 68 innings pitched. His ERA was under 3.00 for the fifth straight season. Despite his injuries and the depth of the Toronto bullpen, Henke recorded more than 30 saves for the third time in his career.

In other words, Henke is still "The Terminator," the affectionate nickname that has been bestowed upon him by Toronto fans. That's what you get for owning a blazing fastball, a pretty good slider and a close to flawless record. Henke also has a forkball that helps drive opponents crazy when thrown in concert with his high, hard fastball.

HOLDING RUNNERS AND FIELDING:

Because Henke tends to get strikeouts and fly balls, he doesn't get too many chances to field grounders. That's not a bad thing because he doesn't have a great glove. He sometimes has trouble covering first base and doesn't get to balls that other pitches would field. Because of his great fastball, it's hard to run against Henke even though he doesn't have a good pickoff move or a quick motion.

OVERALL:

At 34, Henke appears to have lots of juice left in his arm. He was effective during the A.L. playoffs, showing little sign of the discomfort that plagued him in the final weeks of the season. The combination of Henke and Duane Ward in the bullpen means the Jays always have a fresh closer.

Overall Statistics

	W	L	ERA	G	GS	Sv	IP	H	R	BB	SO	HR
1991	0	2	2.32	49	0	32	50.1	33	13	11	53	4
Career	29	28	2.68	430	0	186	567.1	437	181	176	649	44

How Often He Throws Strikes

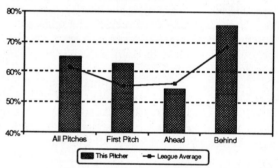

1991 Situational Stats

	W	L	ERA	Sv	IP		AB	H	HR	RBI	AVG
Home	0	1	2.31	14	23.1	LHB	95	17	3	10	.179
Road	0	1	2.33	18	27.0	RHB	84	16	1	6	.190
Day	0	0	1.29	8	14.0	Sc Pos	36	8	2	12	.222
Night	0	2	2.72	24	36.1	Clutch	118	18	2	11	.153

1991 Rankings (American League)

→ 1st in save percentage (91.4%)

→ 6th in saves (32)

→ 9th in save opportunities (35)

→ Led the Blue Jays in saves, save opportunities, save percentage and first batter efficiency (.188)

PITCHING:

Jimmy Key re-established himself as one of the workhorses of the Jays rotation last season, putting together solid numbers and staying healthy for the entire season. He allowed less than a hit per inning and had the pinpoint control that makes him one of the nastier finesse pitchers in the league.

A master of the pitching craft, Key will loop his curveball, trying to catch the outside corner of the plate and fool the hitter into a fruitless lunge. He'll continue working the outside corner, and then bust a fastball on the fists. He has a deep bag of tricks, and will rarely give a batter the same look twice during a game.

Key's fastball comes in about the mid-80s, and he has that uncanny knack for knowing when to keep it off the plate and when he can challenge an opposing hitter. He yielded only 12 homers, testimony to the lack of mistakes. Key shows a slider once in a while, but it isn't as important as his other three pitches. He isn't afraid to lollypop a very slow change from time to time, a pitch that looks more hittable than it is. The wise batters lay off it.

HOLDING RUNNERS AND FIELDING:

Watch pitchers who routinely fall off the mound, allowing grounders up the middle to end up in center field, and you appreciate Key even more. He makes all of the plays that good mechanics allow and is quick off the mound to field bunts and dribblers. He doesn't have a great pickoff move, but keeps runners close by paying attention to them, making a serious attempt from time to time.

OVERALL:

Key is still the main lefty in what has become a very deep group of Jays starters. There's no reason why he shouldn't be a threat to win 16 to 20 games every season, providing the Jays can score enough runs for him.

JIMMY KEY

Position: SP
Bats: R **Throws:** L
Ht: 6' 1" **Wt:** 190

Opening Day Age: 30
Born: 4/22/61 in Huntsville, AL
ML Seasons: 8

Overall Statistics

	W	L	ERA	G	GS	Sv	IP	H	R	BB	SO	HR
1991	16	12	3.05	33	33	0	209.1	207	84	44	125	12
Career	103	68	3.41	284	217	10	1479.0	1419	622	345	827	141

How Often He Throws Strikes

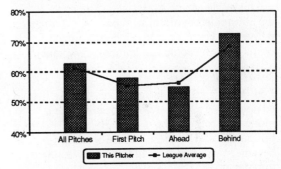

This Pitcher — League Average

1991 Situational Stats

	W	L	ERA	Sv	IP		AB	H	HR	RBI	AVG
Home	7	8	3.43	0	110.1	LHB	112	32	2	9	.286
Road	9	4	2.64	0	99.0	RHB	703	175	10	57	.249
Day	5	3	2.07	0	65.1	Sc Pos	176	36	3	49	.205
Night	11	9	3.50	0	144.0	Clutch	67	19	2	7	.284

1991 Rankings (American League)

→ 2nd in ERA on the road (2.64)

→ 4th least home runs allowed per 9 innings (.52)

→ 6th in strikeout/walk ratio (2.8)

→ Led the Blue Jays in ERA (3.05), wins (16), losses (12), shutouts (2), hits allowed (207), GDPs induced (14), strikeout/walk ratio, lowest slugging percentage allowed (.347), lowest on-base average allowed (.293), groundball/flyball ratio (1.2), most run support per 9 innings (4.6), least home runs allowed per 9 innings (.52) and lowest ERA at home (3.43)

HITTING:

Manuel Lee isn't in the lineup for his bat, but in part it's his lack of offense that causes the Jays to consider other candidates to play shortstop. It's hard to be happy with someone who can't get on base, one way or another, at least 30 percent of the time -- and Lee just hasn't been able to do that.

As has been his pattern, Lee continued to be stronger against left-handed pitchers last season. He strikes out too much, almost as frequently as slugging Joe Carter last season. When a player doesn't hit a single home run, he shouldn't be striking out close to once in every four at-bats, which is the case with Lee.

Lee is an opposite-field hitter from either side of the plate. He can be overpowered by some pitchers and fooled by those who have good offspeed deliveries. He has become a better bunter, a part of his game he could use to more advantage.

BASERUNNING:

Lee doesn't steal a lot of bases, but he'll take advantage of a pitcher who doesn't have a good motion or forgets about him. He isn't a daring baserunner and he doesn't cause opposing second basemen and shortstops to tremble when he tries to break up the double play.

FIELDING:

Lee finally got to play his natural position, shortstop, last season. He goes to his right better than most, but he can also take away potential hits up the middle. Perhaps it was because he'd been away from the position for so long, but Lee turned far fewer double plays than other shortstops who played a comparable number of innings.

OVERALL:

Lee doesn't have a lock on the shortstop position; he was rightfully considered a weak link in the Blue Jay lineup last year. He can expect a stiff challenge from number-one draft choice Eddie Zosky, who saw some action when Lee was out with a groin injury last summer.

MANUEL LEE

Position: SS
Bats: B **Throws:** R
Ht: 5' 9" **Wt:** 161

Opening Day Age: 26
Born: 6/17/65 in San Pedro de Macoris, Dominican Republic
ML Seasons: 7

Overall Statistics

	G	AB	R	H	D	T	HR	RBI	SB	BB	SO	AVG
1991	138	445	41	104	18	3	0	29	7	24	107	.234
Career	625	1756	182	443	57	16	13	160	20	108	353	.252

Where He Hits the Ball

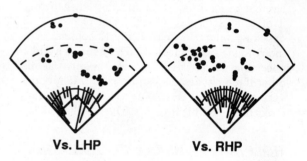

Vs. LHP   **Vs. RHP**

1991 Situational Stats

	AB	H	HR	RBI	AVG		AB	H	HR	RBI	AVG
Home	213	53	0	12	.249	LHP	144	41	0	11	.285
Road	232	51	0	17	.220	RHP	301	63	0	18	.209
Day	138	29	0	4	.210	Sc Pos	105	23	0	28	.219
Night	307	75	0	25	.244	Clutch	80	16	0	5	.200

1991 Rankings (American League)

→ 5th lowest batting average on a 3-1 count (.000)

→ Led AL shortstops in strikeouts (107)

BOB MacDONALD

Position: RP
Bats: L **Throws:** L
Ht: 6' 2" **Wt:** 180

Opening Day Age: 26
Born: 4/27/65 in East Orange, NJ
ML Seasons: 2

PITCHING:

Until David Wells returned to the bullpen late in the '91 season, Bob MacDonald was the main left-handed relief pitcher for the Jays. MacDonald shuttled between the majors and Class AAA Syracuse during the early part of 1991, but came back to stay on June 2.

MacDonald had good success early in the season, putting together a string of 19 scoreless innings over 13 appearances from mid-May until a week after the All Star break. In fact, his ERA was under 1.00 for the first half of the season. MacDonald was showing himself to be especially tough on right-handed batters, who batted only .208 against him for the year.

MacDonald doesn't throw overly hard, but at times he was hurt by a lack of control. Especially during the second half of the season. He walked 10 batters in 10 innings during July and got less work as the season neared its close. He had no saves, blew all four of his save opportunities, and generally finished games only when the outcome was pretty well decided. He didn't appear at all in Toronto's five postseason games.

HOLDING RUNNERS AND FIELDING:

MacDonald helps his catcher by paying attention to baserunners, and he has a pretty good move to first base.He didn't get enough action on the mound to draw conclusions about his fielding prowess. He handled all nine chances without an error, but wasn't involved in any double plays.

OVERALL:

By the end of last season, MacDonald was the ninth or 10th man on the staff, depending on how much respect you give Jim Acker. He could fill an important middle relief role if he stays with the Jays, especially if Wells remains in the bullpen and the team goes with a mainly right-handed starting rotation. He's always been a reliever, but at age 26, it's too soon to draw many conclusions about the direction of his career.

Overall Statistics

	W	L	ERA	G	GS	Sv	IP	H	R	BB	SO	HR
1991	3	3	2.85	45	0	0	53.2	51	19	25	24	5
Career	3	3	2.73	49	0	0	56.0	51	19	27	24	5

How Often He Throws Strikes

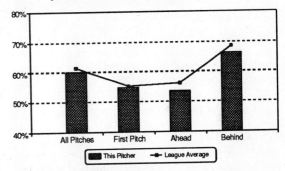

1991 Situational Stats

	W	L	ERA	Sv	IP		AB	H	HR	RBI	AVG
Home	1	1	2.84	0	31.2	LHB	77	25	2	18	.325
Road	2	2	2.86	0	22.0	RHB	125	26	3	17	.208
Day	1	1	1.89	0	19.0	Sc Pos	70	21	2	30	.300
Night	2	2	3.37	0	34.2	Clutch	65	16	2	14	.246

1991 Rankings (American League)

→ 9th highest percentage of inherited runners scored (40.8%)

HITTING:

Either Candy Maldonado is a good luck charm, or he's a better player than many people think. In the past nine seasons, Maldonado's played for five division champions, in each of the odd-numbered years: the '83 and '85 Dodgers, the '87 and '89 Giants, and now the '91 Blue Jays. Expect a huge bidding war for Candy's 1993 services.

After signing with Milwaukee (a team which could use some luck), Maldonado spent the first half of the 1991 season on the disabled list with a broken bone in his left foot. Acquired by Toronto in August, he became their regular left fielder and provided some needed offensive boost in the closing weeks of the season. He was especially hot during the last five weeks when some of the other Jays went south with their bats.

Maldonado has developed some patience over the years, although he strikes out more often than he should. He's primarily a lowball hitter and can poke a low slider a long way to center or right field. He can be blown away with high fastballs and fooled badly with breaking pitches.

BASERUNNING:

Maldonado's never been much of a threat to steal, and missing half of last season didn't do anything to help. He runs hard, unafraid to bowl over a catcher or take out a middle infielder if he can get there in time. If he had speed, he'd use it well.

FIELDING:

Maldonado has a strong arm, but it isn't always accurate. Well suited for left field, he seemed to welcome playing at the usually climate-controlled SkyDome, where the wind and sun couldn't play tricks on him the way they had during his San Francisco years.

OVERALL:

There wasn't a place for him in Milwaukee, nor in Cleveland, who didn't try to re-sign Maldonado after a good 1990 season. Instead he found a home with Toronto, the most consistent team in the A.L. East. It will be interesting to see what kind of numbers he can put up if given 400-450 at-bats.

CANDY MALDONADO

Position: LF/RF
Bats: R **Throws:** R
Ht: 6' 0" **Wt:** 195

Opening Day Age: 31
Born: 9/5/60 in Humacao, Puerto Rico
ML Seasons: 11

Overall Statistics

	G	AB	R	H	D	T	HR	RBI	SB	BB	SO	AVG
1991	86	288	37	72	15	0	12	48	4	36	76	.250
Career	1059	3114	373	795	174	12	104	475	30	257	613	.255

Where He Hits the Ball

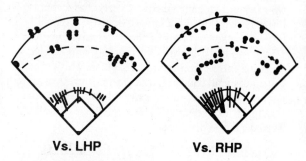

Vs. LHP   **Vs. RHP**

1991 Situational Stats

	AB	H	HR	RBI	AVG		AB	H	HR	RBI	AVG
Home	127	29	7	22	.228	LHP	76	21	3	12	.276
Road	161	43	5	26	.267	RHP	212	51	9	36	.241
Day	82	18	4	13	.220	Sc Pos	80	20	5	35	.250
Night	206	54	8	35	.262	Clutch	49	6	2	5	.122

1991 Rankings (American League)

→ 3rd lowest batting average in the clutch (.123)

HITTING:

The various personnel moves made by the Jays last season worked in Rance Mulliniks' favor, as he was the primary DH against right-handed pitching for much of the season. His role was diminished over the final few weeks when Toronto, looking for more power, acquired Dave Parker for that role. But Mulliniks was back in the DH spot for the playoffs.

Mulliniks has been a platoon player for most of his career because he's never been able to hit lefties with consistency. He is a low fastball hitter who'll drive the ball into the gaps; he is quite adept at going to the opposite field. He still doesn't usually get overpowered, and he has a very good eye at the plate. A pitcher has to put the ball in the strike zone to get Mulliniks to offer.

Mulliniks' value to the team will be based wholly on how well he can continue hitting. If the Jays go looking for more power in the DH role, he'll probably wind up as a pinch hitter, a role which he's handled very well for most of his career.

BASERUNNING:

Mulliniks never had much speed in his prime, and he's not much more than a base-to-base advancer at age 36. He's a heady enough player, however, that he won't get into trouble on the bases.

FIELDING:

At this stage, Mulliniks will carry a glove only as a backup or fill-in player. He's still a competent fielder, but the lack of action hasn't helped his game. At best, he strictly has an average glove and an average arm.

OVERALL:

Mulliniks is the 24th or 25th man on the team, a classy guy who isn't prone to complaining about his diminished role. There seems to be a sense of respect for what Mulliniks meant to the Jays when they first were becoming competitive in the mid-1980s. It's nice to see a team show some loyalty to a player.

RANCE MULLINIKS

Position: DH
Bats: L **Throws:** R
Ht: 6' 0" **Wt:** 175

Opening Day Age: 36
Born: 1/15/56 in Tulare, CA
ML Seasons: 15

Overall Statistics

	G	AB	R	H	D	T	HR	RBI	SB	BB	SO	AVG
1991	97	240	27	60	12	1	2	24	0	44	44	.250
Career	1322	3567	444	971	226	17	73	435	15	459	555	.272

Where He Hits the Ball

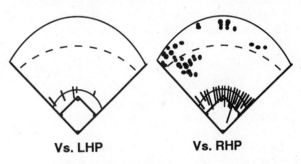

Vs. LHP   Vs. RHP

1991 Situational Stats

	AB	H	HR	RBI	AVG		AB	H	HR	RBI	AVG
Home	120	30	1	11	.250	LHP	12	1	0	0	.083
Road	120	30	1	13	.250	RHP	228	59	2	24	.259
Day	76	17	0	6	.224	Sc Pos	50	20	0	21	.400
Night	164	43	2	18	.262	Clutch	41	9	1	5	.220

1991 Rankings (American League)

→ Did not rank near the top or bottom in any category

HITTING:

For most of last season Greg Myers was the lefty-batting part of the Jays catching platoon. But he tailed off during the second half of the season and found himself on the bench even against right-handed starters. The fact that he's never started a game against a left-handed pitcher shows that the Jays have limited hopes for the 26-year-old catcher. Myers swings an average bat, has average power and has a pretty good eye at the plate. In other words, nothing outstanding, but nothing to worry the Jays too much, either.

As a part-time player, Myers led the Jays in grounding into double plays, which is a double whammy for a left-handed batter. Myers doesn't have very good bat control and is not a good bunter. Most of his power is to right field, although he can handle pitches that are up in the strike zone and take them to left-center. Offspeed pitches are a problem.

BASERUNNING:

Myers hasn't stolen a base in the majors and didn't even try in 1991. He's a plodder who doesn't often get to second base in time to be a factor in breaking up double plays. The Jays pinch run for Myers when they need an extra run in the late innings.

FIELDING:

Myers has good hands; which is the good news. The bad news is his erratic arm that leads to numerous errors. He's had elbow and shoulder problems during his career, and runners are likely to gamble with him behind the plate. Myers' defense, as much as anything, keeps him from getting more playing time.

OVERALL:

The Jays like to think that a Myers/Borders platoon will make them solid behind the plate for the next few years. But Myers still has to show some improvement, especially defensively, to live up to his end of the bargain. He's more likely to become an outright second-string catcher than an everyday player.

GREG MYERS

Position: C
Bats: L **Throws:** R
Ht: 6' 2" **Wt:** 206

Opening Day Age: 25
Born: 4/14/66 in Riverside, CA
ML Seasons: 4

Overall Statistics

	G	AB	R	H	D	T	HR	RBI	SB	BB	SO	AVG
1991	107	309	25	81	22	0	8	36	0	21	45	.262
Career	218	612	59	146	31	1	13	59	0	45	90	.239

Where He Hits the Ball

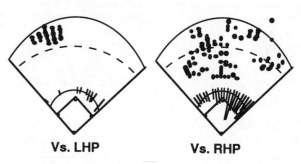

Vs. LHP   Vs. RHP

1991 Situational Stats

	AB	H	HR	RBI	AVG		AB	H	HR	RBI	AVG
Home	145	42	5	20	.290	LHP	35	6	1	3	.171
Road	164	39	3	16	.238	RHP	274	75	7	33	.274
Day	89	23	2	12	.258	Sc Pos	81	19	3	30	.235
Night	220	58	6	24	.264	Clutch	53	14	0	3	.264

1991 Rankings (American League)

→ 1st in lowest percentage of extra bases taken as a runner (19.0%) and lowest fielding percentage as a catcher (.979)

→ 3rd lowest percentage of runners caught stealing as a catcher (26.9%)

→ 7th most GDPs per GDP situation (19.1%)

→ Led the Blue Jays in GDPs (13), batting average on a 3-2 count (.333) and batting average with 2 strikes (.211)

HITTING:

The Jays had enough confidence in John Olerud's potential that they tradee Fred McGriff before last season. At first, it didn't look like such a good idea. Olerud got off to a slow start and was platooned for much of the year, sitting on the bench against lefties. But he came around as the season progressed, and showed some of the pure hitting form that Toronto is hoping to get from him for many years to come.

Olerud hits line drives and he can hit them far, going deep to left or right. He has a good eye at the plate, but sometimes lapses into stretches where he has trouble making contact, driving up his strikeout total. There are people who believe he'll become the kind of player who will put up Jack Clark-like numbers, 25 homers and 100 walks -- the kind of guy an opposing manager hates to see come up in the clutch. He'll need to do a better job against lefties to reach that status, though.

BASERUNNING:

The Jays are a team that's built for speed, and Olerud is a glaring exception. He doesn't steal bases and isn't a threat to take an extra base. On his behalf, Olerud knows that he isn't a speedster and doesn't get himself into trouble.

FIELDING:

In college, Olerud had a pretty good move to first base, but we won't see it because the Jays rejected the idea of having him take the mound. At first base, he makes all the plays that he should. He has good reach and average range.

OVERALL:

Olerud never played in the minor leagues, and he's learned a lot of things the hard way. He seems to be continuing to learn well, and could turn into quite a power threat. A more immediate goal for Olerud would be to get his name on the lineup card no matter who's pitching.

JOHN OLERUD

Position: 1B
Bats: L **Throws:** L
Ht: 6' 5" **Wt:** 218

Opening Day Age: 23
Born: 8/5/68 in Seattle, WA
ML Seasons: 3

Overall Statistics

	G	AB	R	H	D	T	HR	RBI	SB	BB	SO	AVG
1991	139	454	64	116	30	1	17	68	0	68	84	.256
Career	256	820	109	214	45	2	31	116	0	125	160	.261

Where He Hits the Ball

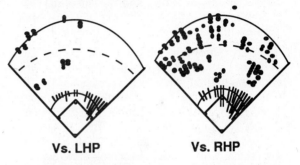

Vs. LHP   Vs. RHP

1991 Situational Stats

	AB	H	HR	RBI	AVG		AB	H	HR	RBI	AVG
Home	226	61	7	39	.270	LHP	83	18	3	16	.217
Road	228	55	10	29	.241	RHP	371	98	14	52	.264
Day	133	32	6	29	.241	Sc Pos	116	27	3	45	.233
Night	321	84	11	39	.262	Clutch	89	23	2	13	.258

1991 Rankings (American League)

→ 1st in sacrifice flies (10)

→ 3rd highest fielding percentage at first base (.996)

→ 8th lowest batting average with the bases loaded (.111)

→ Led the Blue Jays in sacrifice flies, walks (68), highest percentage of pitches taken (60.3%), lowest percentage of swings that missed (15.0%) and highest percentage of swings put into play (47.2%)

→ Led AL first basemen in sacrifice flies and hit by pitch (6)

PITCHING:

Dave Stieb pitched less than 60 innings last season because of a severe back problem that could threaten his career. Unfortunately, there's no guarantee that Stieb will be back in 1992. Watching Stieb work out in the outfield during the American League Championship Series last October, gingerly doing knee bends to pick up the baseball, was a sad sight.

The vintage Stieb, the one that Toronto hopes to see again, is a hard thrower with a fastball in the 90-MPH range and a wicked slider that has a stunning down-and-away drop to right-handed batters. He's come to terms with the slider, which dropped from his favor a few years ago because he thought it was taking a toll on his arm. Last season he threw it about one out of every three pitches and also relied on the good fastball.

Stieb also throws a curve and change-up, and once in a while drops down from his straight overhand motion when facing a righthander. He sometimes suffers from control problems, but Stieb has a knack for pitching himself out of trouble. At times, Stieb's competitive fires have worked against him when mistakes caused him to get rattled; with age has also come more control of that aspect of his game.

HOLDING RUNNERS AND FIELDING:

Stieb has a jerky move to first: he pivots, makes a little hop and then throws. It's good enough to keep runners close, as long as he doesn't get into a set pattern. Stieb was a college outfielder, and he still has those raw defensive skills. He handles his position well, fielding bunts and covering first better than most.

OVERALL:

The Jays won the division without Stieb in 1991, and he doesn't have to rush his return for the sake of the team. If he can come back, it'll be a bonus that will give the Jays enough flexibility with thir pitching staff to make them the envy of their peers.

DAVE STIEB

Position: SP
Bats: R **Throws:** R
Ht: 6' 1" **Wt:** 195

Opening Day Age: 34
Born: 7/22/57 in Santa Ana, CA
ML Seasons: 13

Overall Statistics

	W	L	ERA	G	GS	Sv	IP	H	R	BB	SO	HR
1991	4	3	3.17	9	9	0	59.2	52	22	23	29	4
Career	170	126	3.33	399	391	1	2726.2	2389	1119	960	1586	209

How Often He Throws Strikes

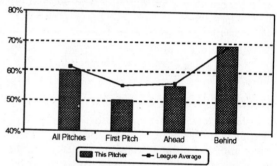

1991 Situational Stats

	W	L	ERA	Sv	IP		AB	H	HR	RBI	AVG
Home	1	2	5.50	0	18.0	LHB	117	28	2	11	.239
Road	3	1	2.16	0	41.2	RHB	97	24	2	10	.247
Day	2	3	3.62	0	32.1	Sc Pos	50	11	2	17	.220
Night	2	0	2.63	0	27.1	Clutch	15	2	0	1	.133

1991 Rankings (American League)

➡ Led the Blue Jays in most GDPs induced per GDP situation (15.2%)

TORONTO BLUE JAYS

PITCHING:

In 1991, Todd Stottlemyre finally established himself as a force on the Jays staff, working his way up from fifth starter status to a pitcher who had the respect of his opponents. Stottlemyre was the workhorse of the Jays staff last year and had a couple of stretches -- at the beginning of the year and again at midseason -- where opponents just couldn't do anything against him. It was the first time in his four-year career that he'd posted a winning record.

Stottlemyre can change speeds on all three of his pitches -- fastball, curve and slider -- although he sometimes gets into trouble by walking too many batters. He can throw his fastball in the low 90s, and it usually has pretty good movement. He can be overpowering at times, a real bat-breaker. He seemed to learn last season that even if his fastball was working well, he needed to use his other pitchers in order to be successful. One measure of change in that regard was that Stottlemyre had much better success against lefties than in previous years. He isn't afraid to come inside.

HOLDING RUNNERS AND FIELDING:

You need to divide Stottlemyre's defense into three parts. He's about as good as it gets when it comes to covering first base, but he doesn't field balls around the mound as well as many pitchers, and his move to first base still needs work. Opponents can run on him.

OVERALL:

Stottlemyre has worked hard to iron out some of the wrinkles in his game. He's had the sort of career that's somewhat common, a promising youngster who learns in the majors instead of in the bush leagues. Stottlemyre's improvement isn't exactly a shock, and it would not be a huge surprise to see him put together similar seasons to 1991 on a regular basis throughout the '90s.

TODD STOTTLEMYRE

Position: SP
Bats: L **Throws:** R
Ht: 6' 3" **Wt:** 195

Opening Day Age: 26
Born: 5/20/65 in Yakima, WA
ML Seasons: 4

Overall Statistics

	W	L	ERA	G	GS	Sv	IP	H	R	BB	SO	HR
1991	15	8	3.78	34	34	0	219.0	194	97	75	116	21
Career	39	40	4.27	122	101	0	647.2	654	324	234	361	65

How Often He Throws Strikes

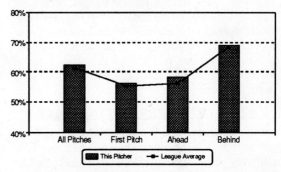

1991 Situational Stats

	W	L	ERA	Sv	IP		AB	H	HR	RBI	AVG
Home	9	3	3.96	0	116.0	LHB	422	102	11	33	.242
Road	6	5	3.58	0	103.0	RHB	404	92	10	51	.228
Day	3	3	4.48	0	66.1	Sc Pos	169	40	4	57	.237
Night	12	5	3.48	0	152.2	Clutch	58	17	1	3	.293

1991 Rankings (American League)

→ 1st in highest stolen base percentage allowed (88.9%)

→ 3rd in hit batsmen (12)

→ 4th in most stolen bases allowed (24) and least GDPs induced per 9 innings (.45)

→ Led the Blue Jays in games started (34), innings (219), batters faced (921), walks allowed (75), hit batsmen (12), pitches thrown (3,331), pickoff throws (184), most stolen bases allowed, winning percentage (.652), lowest batting average allowed (.235) and lowest batting average allowed vs. right-handed batters (.228)

PITCHING:

Another one of the hard-throwing righthanders in the Toronto bullpen, Mike Timlin demonstrated one very valuable trait: he was effective while working on short rest. It wasn't uncommon for Timlin to go a couple of innings in consecutive games or work three times in four days. Aside from a rough time during the second half of May, Timlin pitched well for most of the season. He kept the team in games in which Jays starters got into trouble early, often picking up the win after Toronto rallied. He tied for the league lead in wins by a reliever.

Timlin's best pitch is his fastball. It breaks on the fists to right-handed batters, who sometimes look like they don't have a chance against him. Last year he didn't have the same success against lefties. It would help Timlin if he could come up with a better offspeed pitch, and it isn't uncommon for a hard-throwing pitcher to develop a good change-up after he's already established himself in the majors.

HOLDING RUNNERS AND FIELDING:

Timlin is an average fielder. He doesn't always get to first base as quick as you'd like, but he's still very green, having pitched in Class A ball as recently as 1990. There's time for him to learn. He's usually in good position to field balls and is competent at handling bunts. He doesn't take chances when it comes to throwing to a base. He's unexceptional when it comes to holding runners.

OVERALL:

With Tom Henke and Duane Ward in the bullpen, Timlin is probably destined to stay in the role of middle reliever. But his presence means that the Jays don't have to stay with a starting pitcher who doesn't bring his good stuff to the mound. Timlin could take advantage of that role, coming into winnable games and racking up an impressive winning percentage while biding his time until he gets a chance at a more glamourous role.

MIKE TIMLIN

Position: RP/SP
Bats: R **Throws:** R
Ht: 6' 4" **Wt:** 205

Opening Day Age: 26
Born: 3/10/66 in Midland, TX
ML Seasons: 1

Overall Statistics

	W	L	ERA	G	GS	Sv	IP	H	R	BB	SO	HR
1991	11	6	3.16	63	3	3	108.1	94	43	50	85	6
Career	11	6	3.16	63	3	3	108.1	94	43	50	85	6

How Often He Throws Strikes

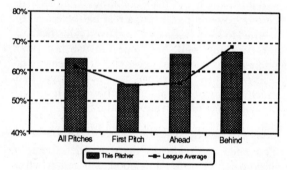

1991 Situational Stats

	W	L	ERA	Sv	IP		AB	H	HR	RBI	AVG
Home	7	2	2.35	1	61.1	LHB	169	50	3	22	.296
Road	4	4	4.21	2	47.0	RHB	235	44	3	30	.187
Day	4	2	2.45	0	40.1	Sc Pos	115	33	2	45	.287
Night	7	4	3.57	3	68.0	Clutch	158	37	3	20	.234

1991 Rankings (American League)

- ➡ 1st in relief wins (10)
- ➡ 4th highest percentage of inherited runners scored (45.4%)
- ➡ 5th most relief innings (93.2)
- ➡ Led the Blue Jays in blown saves (5) and relief wins

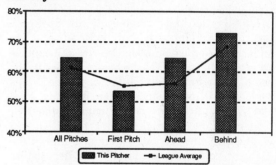

WORKHORSE

DUANE WARD

Position: RP
Bats: R **Throws:** R
Ht: 6' 4" **Wt:** 215

Opening Day Age: 27
Born: 5/28/64 in Parkview, NM
ML Seasons: 6

PITCHING:

Last season marked a turning point of sorts for Duane Ward. He finally got the chance to show that, in addition to being a workhorse who can pitch day after day, he was capable of closing games -- nailing down the tough saves that have typically gone to Tom Henke.

Because Henke was hurt for various parts of the season, Ward got the chance to show what he could do as a closer. He did very well, striking out well over one batter per inning and blowing only four of 27 save opportunities. Even Toronto fans, who'd taken out their hostilities on Ward in previous years, made him one of their favorites in 1991.

With his 95-MPH fastball, Ward has established himself as one of the hardest throwers in baseball. He also throws a nice hard slider, giving him two pitches that are overpowering. He's cut down on his wildness, reducing his walk total each season since 1988. Ward has also learned that pitching an inning or two means not having to worry about finesse. He comes out firing.

Ward has also developed a smoother motion, which decreases his chance of arm problems. The Jays obviously count on Ward to pitch more innings than most teams expect from their relievers.

HOLDING RUNNERS AND FIELDING:

Ward has a high leg kick, and therefore is pretty easy to steal against. His move to first isn't much better than average, and it's not a natural-looking move, either. Ward handles the balls he can reach, but his follow-through puts him in worse position than most other pitchers.

OVERALL:

With two pitchers who can finish off a team, the Jays have no shortage of options. In the playoffs, Manager Cito Gaston said he wouldn't be above flip-flopping Ward and Henke in the closer and set-up roles. Ward could probably rack up 40 saves in a different situation, but being with Toronto means he'll be with a contender more often than not.

Overall Statistics

	W	L	ERA	G	GS	Sv	IP	H	R	BB	SO	HR
1991	7	6	2.77	81	0	23	107.1	80	36	33	132	3
Career	23	29	3.59	308	2	64	491.0	415	214	217	476	23

How Often He Throws Strikes

[Bar chart showing percentages for All Pitches, First Pitch, Ahead, Behind, with y-axis from 40% to 80%. Legend: "This Pitcher" (bars), "League Average" (line)]

1991 Situational Stats

	W	L	ERA	Sv	IP		AB	H	HR	RBI	AVG
Home	5	4	3.14	14	63.0	LHB	187	36	3	18	.193
Road	2	2	2.23	9	44.1	RHB	199	44	0	20	.221
Day	3	2	2.04	10	39.2	Sc Pos	100	28	2	37	.280
Night	4	4	3.19	13	67.2	Clutch	237	50	2	25	.211

1991 Rankings (American League)

- → 1st in games (81) and relief innings (107.1)
- → 2nd most strikeouts per 9 innings in relief (11.1)
- → 4th in save percentage (85.2%)
- → 5th in holds (17), lowest batting average allowed vs. left-handed batters (.192) and relief losses (6)
- → Led the Blue Jays in games, games finished (46), strikeouts (132), holds, lowest batting average allowed vs. left-handed batters, lowest percentage of inherited runners scored (27.8%), relief ERA (2.77), relief losses, relief innings, lowest batting average allowed in relief (.207) and most strikeouts per 9 innings in relief

PITCHING:

What to do with David Wells? In 1990, Wells went from being the lefthander in the Jays bullpen to a spot in the starting rotation, with excellent results (11-6, 3.14). Wells worked in the rotation for most of 1991, and for more than half the year, he was brilliant. After beating the White Sox on July 24, Wells was 12-4 with a 2.73 ERA and had won 11 of his last 12 decisions.

But then fatigue seemed to set in. Wells got hammered in five straight starts, losing them all. The Jays needed a lefty in their bullpen, and in mid-September he went back to relief work. Again he did well, not allowing a run in nine of his last 11 outings.

Working as a starter led Wells to change his game a little. He added a change-up to his repertoire, which helped him pace himself. He became less of a strikeout pitcher, though he was still capable of getting the big strikeout when he needed it. His control also improved. On the downside, Wells gave up 10 more homers than in 1990, even though he pitched about the same number of innings. He needs to pick his spots for a challenge a little bit better. Patient batters take him to the opposite field, and sometimes Wells' fiery nature gets the best of him.

HOLDING RUNNERS AND FIELDING:

Wells is a good fielder, finishing off his delivery in good position to take grounders. He sometimes doesn't get to first base as quickly as he should. He holds baserunners very well, last year permitting only eight steals in 21 attempts.

OVERALL:

Toronto's needs will probably determine how Wells is used this year. Based on 1991, there have to be concerns about whether he can be effective over a full season in the starting rotation. Wells has shown he can be a very effective starter for long stretches, however, and his ability to handle both starting and relief roles is a big plus for the Blue Jays.

DAVID WELLS

Position: SP/RP
Bats: L **Throws:** L
Ht: 6' 4" **Wt:** 225

Opening Day Age: 28
Born: 5/20/63 in Torrance, CA
ML Seasons: 5

Overall Statistics

	W	L	ERA	G	GS	Sv	IP	H	R	BB	SO	HR
1991	15	10	3.72	40	28	1	198.1	188	88	49	106	24
Career	40	28	3.44	196	55	11	567.1	521	235	165	387	55

How Often He Throws Strikes

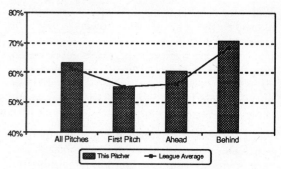

This Pitcher — League Average

1991 Situational Stats

	W	L	ERA	Sv	IP		AB	H	HR	RBI	AVG
Home	6	5	4.81	0	86.0	LHB	130	27	3	9	.208
Road	9	5	2.88	1	112.1	RHB	617	161	21	61	.261
Day	1	4	7.61	0	36.2	Sc Pos	133	33	5	41	.248
Night	14	6	2.84	1	161.2	Clutch	98	25	2	7	.255

1991 Rankings (American League)

➡ 3rd in balks (3) and most home runs allowed per 9 innings (1.1)

➡ 4th highest ERA at home (4.81)

➡ 5th in most home runs allowed (24), lowest stolen base percentage allowed (38.1%) and least GDPs induced per 9 innings (.50)

➡ 6th lowest groundball/flyball ratio (.91)

➡ 7th most runners caught stealing (13)

➡ Led the Blue Jays in home runs allowed, wild pitches (10), runners caught stealing, lowest stolen base percentage allowed, least pitches thrown per batter (3.53) and least baserunners allowed per 9 innings (10.8)

GREAT RANGE

DEVON WHITE

Position: CF
Bats: B **Throws:** R
Ht: 6' 2" **Wt:** 172

Opening Day Age: 29
Born: 12/29/62 in
Kingston, Jamaica
ML Seasons: 7

HITTING:

The main reason that California traded Devon White to Toronto was that the Angels' front office felt he had regressed as a hitter. The regression is over. White filled the leadoff spot for the Jays and quickly showed that he can make a big impact with the bat, along with maintaining his defensive skills that are outstanding.

White improved his hitting from the left side of the plate and was a terror whenever he got to bat from the right. He finished 27 points higher than his career average, and had career bests in several offensive categories. He was eighth in the A.L. in multi-hit games, and his production was enough to keep the Jays from fretting too much about his 135 strikeouts, an extraordinary number for a leadoff batter. White still swings at too many pitches out of the strike zone and is a mark for offspeed pitches, especially low ones, once the pitcher gets ahead in the count.

BASERUNNING:

One of the fastest men around, White has stolen as many as 44 bases in a season, and can improve on his 1991 total of 33. He's an intelligent baserunner and teams aren't likely to gun him down when he tries to go from first to third or second to home.

FIELDING:

Considered by many to be the best center fielder in the game, White gets an unnaturally fast jump on fly balls, sometimes seeming to be in motion before the ball is in the air. He routinely charges hits, which keeps runners from going more than base at a time, and teams don't run on his arm. His low error total (one) is not deceptive.

OVERALL:

In 1991, White established himself as a better player than the Angels thought he could be. There are still a couple of areas for improvement --contact and hitting from the left side -- but if can stay at his current level, White will be extremely valuable.

Overall Statistics

	G	AB	R	H	D	T	HR	RBI	SB	BB	SO	AVG
1991	156	642	110	181	40	10	17	60	33	55	135	.282
Career	768	2873	447	732	131	34	76	301	156	199	610	.255

Where He Hits the Ball

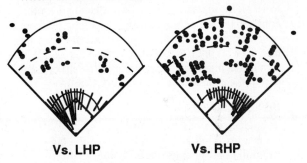

Vs. LHP   Vs. RHP

1991 Situational Stats

	AB	H	HR	RBI	AVG		AB	H	HR	RBI	AVG
Home	326	97	9	33	.298	LHP	199	60	8	20	.302
Road	316	84	8	27	.266	RHP	443	121	9	40	.273
Day	206	67	4	17	.325	Sc Pos	128	22	1	37	.172
Night	436	114	13	43	.261	Clutch	108	33	0	8	.306

1991 Rankings (American League)

→ 1st highest fielding percentage in center field (.998)

→ 2nd most pitches seen (2,763)

→ 3rd most runs scored per time reached base (45.3%)

→ 4th in runs (110) and triples (10)

→ 5th in at-bats (642), strikeouts (135), lowest batting average with runners in scoring position (.172) and steals of third (5)

→ Led the Blue Jays in at-bats, runs, strikeouts, pitches seen, groundball/flyball ratio (1.6), most pitches seen per plate appearance (3.86), runs scored per time reached base, batting average in the clutch (.306) and batting average at home (.298)

HITTING:

When he played for the New York Mets in the prime of his career, Mookie Wilson often found himself platooned with Len Dykstra, playing almost exclusively against lefties. Last year, the Jays rarely used the switch-hitter unless there was a righthander on the mound.

Wilson is a fastball hitter who doesn't have much patience at the plate; it can be very hard for an opposing pitcher to walk him. The Jays took to using him toward the bottom of the order, instead of the leadoff spot where he spent much of his career. Wilson's 1991 average was the lowest of his career, which began in 1980.

Wilson's playing time was cut in half from 1990 to 1991, hiding some of his flaws. He made better contact last season than in '90. Opposing pitchers can't drive Wilson off the plate, but they can tie him up with pitches that are low and inside. He'll also chase pitches that are wide of the strike zone and in the dirt. Wilson doesn't bunt well.

BASERUNNING:

Young players still can learn a lot from Wilson. He is a textbook slider who can avoid a tag even when the ball gets to the base ahead of him. He doesn't make many running mistakes. He's lost a step from his prime, but he doesn't try to steal unless he has a good chance of taking the base.

FIELDING:

Wilson doesn't throw well. Never has, never will. Other teams know that and are quick to take the extra base against him. Hey, Mookie would run on himself. He has pretty good range, and takes away some balls that might otherwise go into the gap.

OVERALL:

The Jays appear to have a settled outfield situation, so they might decide not to bid on Wilson, a free agent. His value is as a veteran who has seen many tough situations over the years. He'll undoubtedly catch on somewhere.

MOOKIE WILSON

Position: LF/DH
Bats: B **Throws:** R
Ht: 5'10" **Wt:** 174

Opening Day Age: 36
Born: 2/9/56 in Bamberg, SC
ML Seasons: 12

Overall Statistics

	G	AB	R	H	D	T	HR	RBI	SB	BB	SO	AVG
1991	86	241	26	58	12	4	2	28	11	8	35	.241
Career	1403	5094	731	1397	227	71	67	438	327	282	866	.274

Where He Hits the Ball

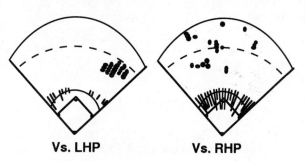

Vs. LHP   Vs. RHP

1991 Situational Stats

	AB	H	HR	RBI	AVG		AB	H	HR	RBI	AVG
Home	115	31	1	14	.270	LHP	43	9	0	1	.209
Road	126	27	1	14	.214	RHP	198	49	2	27	.247
Day	79	20	0	5	.253	Sc Pos	68	20	1	27	.294
Night	162	38	2	23	.235	Clutch	53	12	0	9	.226

1991 Rankings (American League)

➡ Did not rank near the top or bottom in any category

KEN DAYLEY

Position: RP
Bats: L **Throws:** L
Ht: 6' 0" **Wt:** 180

Opening Day Age: 33
Born: 2/25/59 in
Jerome, ID
ML Seasons: 10

Overall Statistics

	W	L	ERA	G	GS	Sv	IP	H	R	BB	SO	HR
1991	0	0	6.23	8	0	0	4.1	7	3	5	3	0
Career	33	45	3.64	383	33	39	573.0	563	271	221	404	42

PITCHING, FIELDING & HOLDING RUNNERS:

The Jays signed Ken Dayley as a free agent before last season, and then suffered along with the lefthander as injuries limited him to only 4.1 innings for the season. First Dayley had an inner-ear problem that caused dizziness. He returned in late May, pitched several times, and then suffered a strained muscle in his pitching arm. While being treated for that problem, he started suffering dizziness again -- and the Jays called it a season.

It will be interesting to see how much of his old form Dayley can regain. He's a power pitcher who has, more often than not, been very tough on lefty batters during his career. He throws a rising fastball, but his curve, which comes in to righty batters, has become his "out" pitch. Dayley has been able to remain effective while pitching for several days in succession. He is an excellent fielder, with only one error in 377 career chances. His move to first is unspectacular.

OVERALL:

Dayley has two strikes against him. Toronto has a lot of talented pitchers and, at age 33, there's no guarantee that he'll be able to come back from almost a full season of inactivity. If healthy, he'll give the Jays another left-handed option.

DAVE PARKER

Position: DH
Bats: L **Throws:** R
Ht: 6' 5" **Wt:** 250

Opening Day Age: 40
Born: 6/9/51 in Jackson, MS
ML Seasons: 19

Overall Statistics

	G	AB	R	H	D	T	HR	RBI	SB	BB	SO	AVG
1991	132	502	47	120	26	2	11	59	3	33	98	.239
Career	2466	9358	1272	2712	526	75	339	1493	154	683	1537	.290

HITTING, FIELDING, BASERUNNING:

Dave Parker's production slipped markedly last season, and the Angels released him in September. The Jays picked him up for the last few weeks when they were looking for a lefty pitch-hitter and designated hitter. Parker didn't seem to have the quick bat that marked his more productive years in the majors, and he could be had by fastballs up in the strike zone and offspeed stuff. There were times with the Angels, especially early in the season, when he looked very unimpressive at the plate. At age 40, you have to wonder if he can come back. Parker has gradually become more of an opposite-field hitter.

Parker is no longer an effective defensive player, as his range has been cut to the point of making his strong arm useless. He has always been an enthusiastic baserunner, but again, age has taken its toll. He knows better than to take risks on the bases.

OVERALL:

Whether or not he finds a team to play for in 1992, Parker's career is definitely in its twilight. He was a force during his younger years with the Pirates and contributed to several teams as he got older. If his career is over, it's been an outstanding one.

ED SPRAGUE

Position: 3B/1B
Bats: R **Throws:** R
Ht: 6' 2" **Wt:** 215

Opening Day Age: 24
Born: 7/25/67 in Castro Valley, CA
ML Seasons: 1

Overall Statistics

	G	AB	R	H	D	T	HR	RBI	SB	BB	SO	AVG
1991	61	160	17	44	7	0	4	20	0	19	43	.275
Career	61	160	17	44	7	0	4	20	0	19	43	.275

HITTING, FIELDING, BASERUNNING:

A first-round draft pick in 1988, Ed Sprague made it to the majors last season and filled in at third base when Kelly Gruber went on the disabled list. Sprague batted .391 in his first 17 games, but then tailed off. At times, he showed enough patience at the plate to coax walks. Other times, though, he could be fooled by the same pitch in consecutive at-bats.

The facet of his game which most reduced Sprague's playing time later in the season was his defense. It wasn't good. He had trouble with his glove, he had trouble with his throwing. He had enough trouble that he made 12 errors in 35 games (31 starts) at third base. His fielding percentage was only .870. Gruber, whose fielding suffered because of a thumb injury that hindered his throwing, made one more error all season -- in 250 more chances. Sprague has never been much of a threat on the bases. He was thrown out in all three of his steal attempts last season.

OVERALL:

Sprague is a player with offensive potential and, to this point in his career, defensive limitations. He can play several positions, none of them well. A lot of people think he'll have to make the team as a catcher, his former position. The Jays might be able to use some help there.

PAT TABLER

Position: DH/1B
Bats: R **Throws:** R
Ht: 6' 2" **Wt:** 200

Opening Day Age: 34
Born: 2/2/58 in Hamilton, OH
ML Seasons: 11

Overall Statistics

	G	AB	R	H	D	T	HR	RBI	SB	BB	SO	AVG
1991	82	185	20	40	5	1	1	21	0	29	21	.216
Career	1153	3776	443	1067	185	25	47	496	16	364	545	.283

HITTING, FIELDING, BASERUNNING:

Over his career, Pat Tabler has been a line drive hitter who could come to the plate in any situation, against any pitcher, and be dangerous. His teams usually found a defensive spot for him. Now, however, Tabler is more of a designated hitting and pinch hitting specialist. He started some games at first base last season for the Jays, but has limited range and does little to help his fielders when it comes to handling bad throws.

Tabler saw most of his action as a DH last year against left-handed pitchers. Also, he was used a pinch hitter more often than any other Toronto player, going 9 for 21 with six RBI. He is basically a singles hitter. Tabler has also gained quite a reputation over the years for his ability to hit with the bases loaded. After going 2 for 6 in those situations last year, an off year by his standards, his career mark is 42-for-86. Tabler is a slow runner, and hasn't stolen a base since 1988.

OVERALL:

After batting only .216 last season, Tabler will probably be reduced to pinch hitting and occasional fill-in duty this year. At 34, he's young enough to handle those roles. If Toronto doesn't want him back, he should be able to find a team that needs an extra bat.

ORGANIZATION OVERVIEW:

The Blue Jays built an outstanding organization in large part by tapping into markets other teams were neglecting. Toronto aggressively scouted Latin America, in particular the Dominican Republic, and brilliantly used the Rule 5 draft to pick up unprotected players, notably George Bell and Kelly Gruber, from other clubs. Other clubs eventually caught on to what they were doing, and the Jays no longer have the edge they once enjoyed. But Toronto still has an eye for young talent; anxious as they are to finally win a pennant, it will be interesting to see if the Jays show their traditional patience with their hottest prospects.

DEREK BELL

Position: OF **Opening Day Age:** 23
Bats: R **Throws:** R **Born:** 12/11/68 in
Ht: 6' 2" **Wt:** 200 Tampa, FL

Recent Statistics

	G	AB	R	H	D	THR	RBI	SB	BB	SO	AVG
91 AAA Syracuse	119	457	89	158	22	12	13	93	27	57	69	.346
91 AL Toronto	18	28	5	4	0	0	0	1	3	6	5	.143
91 MLE	119	441	72	142	20	8	11	75	19	46	72	.322

Only 22, Bell had a monster year in the International League (a pitcher's league) and was chosen Baseball America's Minor League Player of the Year. He has speed, power, patience, the ability to hit for average -- all the offensive skills. He needs to improve a lot defensively, but he has the tools. If Toronto is committed to him, they won't let Candy Maldonado stand in Bell's way. It's possible he'll have to go back to Syracuse, but based on 1991, Bell looks like a star.

CARLOS DELGADO

Position: C **Opening Day Age:** 19
Bats: L **Throws:** R **Born:** 6/25/72 in
Ht: 6' 3" **Wt:** 206 Aguadilla, PR

Recent Statistics

	G	AB	R	H	D	THR	RBI	SB	BB	SO	AVG
90 A St. Cath	67	226	29	64	13	0	6	39	2	35	65	.283
91 A Myrtle Bch	132	441	72	126	18	2	18	71	9	74	97	.286
91 AAA Syracuse	1	3	0	0	0	0	0	0	0	0	2	.000

Now **this** is a prospect -- a big, strong kid, great arm, good catcher, excellent hitting credentials, outstanding attitude. He's 19 years old, but one South Atlantic League manager called him "a man playing against boys." The only concern about Delgado has to do with some knee problems which were aggravated by crouching behind the plate. Not to worry; Delgado has the skills to make it at another position if he can't handle the strain of catching.

ROB DUCEY

Position: OF **Opening Day Age:** 26
Bats: L **Throws:** R **Born:** 5/24/65 in
Ht: 6' 2" **Wt:** 180 Toronto, Ontario, Canada

Recent Statistics

	G	AB	R	H	D	THR	RBI	SB	BB	SO	AVG
91 AAA Syracuse	72	266	53	78	10	3	8	40	5	51	58	.293
91 AL Toronto	39	68	8	16	2	2	1	4	2	6	26	.235
91 MLE	72	258	43	70	9	2	7	32	3	41	60	.271

The Blue Jays have yearned for Canadian players, yet they've never given much of a shot to Toronto-born Rob Ducey, who's spent five long years in AAA ball. Ducey's a fine outfielder and a hitter with patience and a little power; certainly he could have done at least as much for the Jays the last two years as Mookie Wilson did. A minor league free agent, Ducey may finally get a chance with another team this year. If not, there's always expansion.

TURNER WARD

Position: OF **Opening Day Age:** 26
Bats: B **Throws:** R **Born:** 4/11/65 in
Ht: 6' 2" **Wt:** 185 Orlando, FL

Recent Statistics

	G	AB	R	H	D	THR	RBI	SB	BB	SO	AVG
91 AAA Colo Sprngs	14	51	5	10	1	1	1	3	2	6	9	.196
91 AAA Syracuse	59	218	40	72	11	3	7	32	9	47	22	.330
91 AL Toronto	48	113	12	27	7	0	0	7	0	11	18	.239
91 MLE	73	260	35	73	10	2	7	28	7	42	32	.281

If Toronto doesn't re-sign Wilson, they have a ready-made replacement in Ward, a switch-hitter with speed and a lot more discipline than Mookie. He doesn't figure to be an impact player -- both the Yankees and the Indians have already dealt him away -- but Ward has a good chance of making the Jays' roster as a spare outfielder this year.

EDDIE ZOSKY

Position: SS **Opening Day Age:** 24
Bats: R **Throws:** R **Born:** 2/10/68 in
Ht: 6' 0" **Wt:** 170 Whittier, CA

Recent Statistics

	G	AB	R	H	D	THR	RBI	SB	BB	SO	AVG
91 AAA Syracuse	119	511	69	135	18	4	6	39	9	35	82	.264
91 AL Toronto	18	27	2	4	1	1	0	2	0	0	8	.148
91 MLE	119	497	56	121	16	2	5	31	6	28	86	.243

The Jay's weren't exactly overwhelmed by Manuel Lee's shortstop play last year, and seem about ready to hand the job to Zosky, their first pick in 1989. There seems little doubt that Zosky has a major league glove, but his hitting is another matter. Zosky's 1991 stats suggest a low-average, punch- and-judy hitter. That sounds a lot like Manuel Lee, so what does Toronto have to lose?

National League Players

CY YOUNG STUFF

PITCHING:

What a difference a year makes. In 1990, Steve Avery relied almost exclusively on his great fastball. While the 90+ MPH heater was awesome, it was basically his only pitch. Hitters soon caught up with it and Avery had trouble keeping opponents off base; great fastball or not, hitters tattooed him for a .302 average. He ended up 3-11 with a 5.64 ERA in 21 games. Everyone agreed that Avery needed a new pitch or two if he were to fulfill his potential.

Before the '91 season began, there was talk about starting Avery at AAA Richmond. However, before his fortunes could get any worse, Avery took charge of his career and turned it completely around. He came to spring training with a few more pounds of muscle and two surprises: a curveball and change-up. Avery's new pitches were so successful that his biggest problem became whether he should pitch the ninth inning or not. The new Avery won 18 games, showing a poise beyond his years in clutch situations.

With the addition of the curveball and change, Avery's outstanding fastball has become much tougher to hit. He can regularly throw the curve for strikes, freezing batters into striking out. Spurred on by the Braves' much improved defense, he is very aggressive on the mound and prefers simply to "grip and rip."

HOLDING RUNNERS, FIELDING, HITTING:

Young fastball pitchers usually are inclined to go at the hitters rather than keep runners close. Avery did an acceptable job in that area (21 SB in 32 attempts against) and with the glove. As a hitter, he is one of the best in the league, with a .215 batting average including one four-hit game.

OVERALL:

Avery's outstanding postseason performance, particularly his two crucial victories over the Pirates (no runs allowed in 16.1 innings) proved to just about everyone that he is the best young pitcher in baseball. Another season like 1991 and he might be able to remove the word "young" from that statement.

STEVE AVERY

Position: SP
Bats: L **Throws:** L
Ht: 6' 4" **Wt:** 190

Opening Day Age: 21
Born: 4/14/70 in Trenton, MI
ML Seasons: 2

Overall Statistics

	W	L	ERA	G	GS	Sv	IP	H	R	BB	SO	HR
1991	18	8	3.38	35	35	0	210.1	189	89	65	137	21
Career	21	19	4.10	56	55	0	309.1	310	168	110	212	28

How Often He Throws Strikes

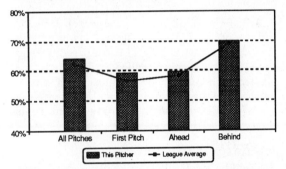

1991 Situational Stats

	W	L	ERA	Sv	IP		AB	H	HR	RBI	AVG
Home	9	5	3.75	0	105.2	LHB	164	30	3	10	.183
Road	9	3	3.01	0	104.2	RHB	624	159	18	70	.255
Day	6	3	4.24	0	63.2	Sc Pos	164	41	5	57	.250
Night	12	5	3.01	0	146.2	Clutch	35	5	0	3	.143

1991 Rankings (National League)

➡ 3rd in wins (18) and most run support per 9 innings (5.4)

➡ 4th in winning percentage (.692)

➡ 5th in games started (35)

➡ 6th in home runs allowed (21), highest ERA at home (3.75) and lowest batting average allowed vs. left-handed batters

➡ Led the Braves in shutouts (1), home runs allowed, winning percentage, most run support per 9 innings and lowest batting average allowed vs. left-handed batters

GREAT RANGE

RAFAEL BELLIARD

Position: SS
Bats: R **Throws:** R
Ht: 5' 6" **Wt:** 160

Opening Day Age: 30
Born: 10/24/61 in
Pueblo Nuevo,
Dominican Republic
ML Seasons: 10

HITTING:

The Braves' newcomers who attracted all the media attention were impact players like Terry Pendleton, Sid Bream and Otis Nixon. While shortstop Rafael Belliard did not get much notice, he had the best season of his career and was a valuable asset to the Braves' rise from worst to first.

When the Braves signed Belliard as a free agent, he was looked on mostly as a backup, someone who would give General Manager Schuerholz the flexibility to trade either Jeff Treadway or Jeff Blauser. Both players wound up staying in Atlanta, but manager Bobby Cox considered good defense at short to be imperative, and Belliard became his main shortstop.

A .218 lifetime hitter entering the season, Belliard batted a career-high .249 last year. It was a weak .249, however, with only 11 extra-base hits, and an on-base percentage rivalled by the Braves ace pitcher, Tom Glavine. Belliard has never shown much selectivity at the plate, and pitchers with good fastballs can usually overpower him. He is a very competent bunter.

BASERUNNING:

Though the 5-6 Belliard looks like a stolen base threat, he has had only one great year for thefts, nabbing 42 way back in 1981 with Alexandria of the Carolina League. He would probably steal a few more, but batting eighth, he rightfully never takes a chance with the pitcher at the plate.

FIELDING:

Belliard is the Braves' version of Ozzie Smith in the middle of their infield. He covers an acre of ground and has an adequate arm to throw runners out from the hole. Belliard can also play second and third competently, but he played only short last year.

OVERALL:

Along with Pendleton and Bream, Belliard provided the Braves' pitchers with the confidence to put the ball in play and let the defense take care of the rest. If the rest of the team continues to hit well, look for the Braves to retain their defensive specialist at short during the 1992 season.

Overall Statistics

	G	AB	R	H	D	T	HR	RBI	SB	BB	SO	AVG
1991	149	353	36	88	9	2	0	27	3	22	63	.249
Career	633	1404	151	317	25	11	1	99	38	107	231	.226

Where He Hits the Ball

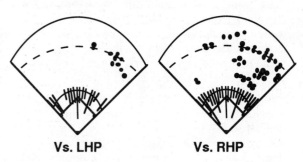

Vs. LHP   **Vs. RHP**

1991 Situational Stats

	AB	H	HR	RBI	AVG		AB	H	HR	RBI	AVG
Home	173	44	0	15	.254	LHP	95	23	0	4	.242
Road	180	44	0	12	.244	RHP	258	65	0	23	.252
Day	88	24	0	5	.273	Sc Pos	78	21	0	27	.269
Night	265	64	0	22	.242	Clutch	44	10	0	2	.227

1991 Rankings (National League)

→ 2nd lowest fielding percentage at shortstop (.967)

→ 5th lowest batting average on a 3-1 count (.000)

→ 6th highest percentage of extra bases taken as a runner (69.2%)

PITCHING:

When the Braves signed the veteran Juan Berenguer as a second-look free agent before the 1991 season, some people suspected it was Ted Turner's doing; the colorful, Fred Flintstone-sized "Senor Smoke" seemed a natural for the WTBS comedy lineup. As for Berenguer's pitching prospects, one Chicago columnist indicated that Atlanta's signing of Berenguer was one of the worst of the year: "He'll mope when he realizes he's not the closer," the scribe wrote.

Closer? It's doubtful that Berenguer had any illusions about being the close. He had been in the majors for 13 seasons, and had saved a total of 14 games. But in the Braves' storybook season, closer is exactly what Berenguer became. To the wonderment of many, Berenguer posted a 2.24 ERA and 17 saves in 18 opportunities. The save total would have been higher, except that Berenguer missed the last month, and the postseason, when he injured his forearm while playing with his kids. (The plot for a TNT made-for-TV movie, perhaps?)

Even at his advanced age, the hard-throwing Berenguer still has a great fastball. Strictly a power pitcher (he also throws a slider), Berenguer seemed to benefit from coming over to the "fastball league." He stranded all but one of 25 inherited runners and kept opposing hitters below a .200 batting average. He was especially tough on right-handed hitters.

HOLDING RUNNERS, FIELDING, HITTING:

Berenguer's hard-throwing style does not lend itself well to either fielding the ball or keeping runners close. But when you strike out almost one an inning and your opponents only bat .189, this is not a huge problem. He struck out three times in five at-bats as a hitter, par for the course.

OVERALL:

People keep waiting for Berenguer to start showing his age. On opening day he'll be 37 and might have some problems with his injury, which healed more slowly than initially thought. If he comes back, he will have to fend off Alejandro Pena, Mike Stanton and Mark Wohlers for the closer's job.

JUAN BERENGUER

Position: RP
Bats: R **Throws:** R
Ht: 5'11" **Wt:** 223

Opening Day Age: 37
Born: 11/30/54 in Aguadulce, Panama
ML Seasons: 14

Overall Statistics

	W	L	ERA	G	GS	Sv	IP	H	R	BB	SO	HR
1991	0	3	2.24	49	0	17	64.1	43	18	20	53	5
Career	63	57	3.79	443	93	31	1127.2	957	524	568	930	106

How Often He Throws Strikes

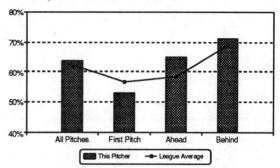

This Pitcher ■ League Average

1991 Situational Stats

	W	L	ERA	Sv	IP		AB	H	HR	RBI	AVG
Home	0	1	2.76	9	32.2	LHB	106	21	1	2	.198
Road	0	2	1.71	8	31.2	RHB	122	22	4	14	.180
Day	0	1	1.96	6	18.1	Sc Pos	56	8	0	7	.143
Night	0	2	2.35	11	46.0	Clutch	116	19	3	8	.164

1991 Rankings (National League)

- ➡ 1st in least baserunners allowed per 9 innings in relief (9.2)
- ➡ 2nd in relief ERA (2.24)
- ➡ 3rd lowest batting average allowed in relief (.189)
- ➡ 7th in saves (17)
- ➡ 9th in first batter efficiency (.170)
- ➡ Led the Braves in saves, games finished (35), save opportunities (18), first batter efficiency, relief ERA, lowest batting average allowed in relief and least baserunners allowed per 9 innings in relief

PITCHING:

While his former Cub teammate Greg Maddux was battling for the league lead in tough losses, Mike Bielecki was being showered with gifts of surplus runs galore. Firmly embracing the old adage that a pitcher's wins are a stand-alone measure of ability, many people talked as though Bielecki's 13 wins actually were a result of fine pitching. To complete the fantasy, Bielecki was traded along with Damon Berryhill from a sinking ship to a rising star, joining the Braves the last week of September, for Yorkis Perez and Turk Wendell.

The truth is that Bielecki has good control and not much else to cheer about. That is normally not enough to become a 13-game winner . . . unless you receive five runs of support per nine innings, which he did. Bielecki was effective early on, keeping his split-fingered pitch down continually and mixing in a curve and slider for strikes. But as the splitter started to rise, so did Bielecki's ERA, totalling 4.76 after the All-Star break.

Bielecki has developed one of the slowest curves in baseball, clocked at 51 MPH, which he slops up to nemesis lefties like Will Clark the second time around the order. The trick pitch helped, but he'll have trouble tricking an 82-MPH fastball by hitters enough to win 13 games again.

HOLDING RUNNERS, FIELDING, AND HITTING:

Bielecki worked hard to improve his hitting, which didn't improve above dismal, and his pick-off move, which moved up to good. He moves off the mound pretty well and helps himself with the glove. He played errorless ball last year and started three double plays.

OVERALL:

On a staff with so many talented righthanders, Bielecki faces a real struggle to make the staff as a swing-man/long reliever. Anticipating the good health of Juan Berenguer and development of Mark Wohlers and Marvin Freeman, he would do well to head over to the American League and try to become another nicer Scott Sanderson.

MIKE BIELECKI

Position: SP/RP
Bats: R **Throws:** R
Ht: 6' 3" **Wt:** 195

Opening Day Age: 32
Born: 7/31/59 in Baltimore, MD
ML Seasons: 8

Overall Statistics

	W	L	ERA	G	GS	Sv	IP	H	R	BB	SO	HR
1991	13	11	4.46	41	25	0	173.2	171	91	56	75	18
Career	51	48	4.19	184	134	1	846.2	842	434	349	489	72

How Often He Throws Strikes

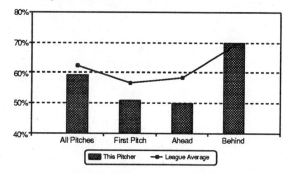

1991 Situational Stats

	W	L	ERA	Sv	IP		AB	H	HR	RBI	AVG
Home	8	7	4.74	0	95.0	LHB	345	95	10	42	.275
Road	5	4	4.12	0	78.2	RHB	308	76	8	41	.247
Day	6	7	4.89	0	84.2	Sc Pos	160	42	1	59	.262
Night	7	4	4.04	0	89.0	Clutch	72	21	2	14	.292

1991 Rankings (National League)

- → 1st in highest ERA at home (4.74)
- → 2nd in highest ERA (4.46), lowest strikeout/walk ratio (1.3) and least strikeouts per 9 innings (3.9)
- → 3rd highest slugging percentage allowed (.420)
- → 5th most home runs allowed per 9 innings (.93)
- → 6th in highest on-base average allowed (.319) and most run support per 9 innings (5.0)
- → 7th highest batting average allowed (.262)

HITTING:

The highlight of Jeff Blauser's career occurred last June, when he went nine-for-13 with three homers and 12 RBI in a weekend series at Philadelphia. However, the Braves media relations department forgot to enter Blauser's name for consideration as National League player of the week, and he was passed over for the honor. That's the kind of season Blauser had.

Blauser essentially shared the Braves' shortstop job with Rafael Belliard (though Blauser also played second and third). They had an almost identical number of at-bats, 353 for Belliard, 352 for Blauser. Yet Blauser had nearly three times as many extra base hits (28 to 11), twice as many RBI (54 to 27), and two-and-a-half times as many walks (54 to 22). Blauser had 11 homers, Belliard none. But while Belliard's good defense was rightfully considered an Atlanta asset, Blauser's good offense was, once again, forgotten.

Credited or not, Blauser is a fine offensive player, especially for a middle infielder, and can turn on a fastball; projected to 550 at-bats, his figures would have been 17 homers, 84 RBI. Blauser's strikeout/walk ratio has improved every year, and he has become a dangerous hitter with men on base.

BASERUNNING:

Blauser has never been able to regain the speed he had in his early years in the minors. He stole only five bases in 11 tries. He gets around the bases with decent speed but rarely has the ability to take extra bases.

FIELDING:

When healthy, Blauser has below average range, but his arm is good. He was suffering from an elbow injury last year, and that led to many of his 17 errors. At full strength, he's competent enough to play regularly.

OVERALL:

The Braves feel that their orientation toward defense was a big key to winning the pennant last year. That puts Blauser in a bench role. Lots of teams could use his hitting skills, however, and if their offense sags, the Braves might be one of them.

JEFF BLAUSER

Position: SS/2B/3B
Bats: R **Throws:** R
Ht: 6' 1" **Wt:** 180

Opening Day Age: 26
Born: 11/8/65 in Los Gatos, CA
ML Seasons: 5

Overall Statistics

	G	AB	R	H	D	T	HR	RBI	SB	BB	SO	AVG
1991	129	352	49	91	14	3	11	54	5	54	59	.259
Career	455	1426	176	374	71	12	35	161	20	147	275	.262

Where He Hits the Ball

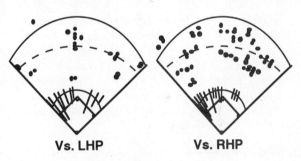

Vs. LHP   Vs. RHP

1991 Situational Stats

	AB	H	HR	RBI	AVG		AB	H	HR	RBI	AVG
Home	174	47	7	32	.270	LHP	128	39	4	26	.305
Road	178	44	4	22	.247	RHP	224	52	7	28	.232
Day	99	19	2	9	.192	Sc Pos	98	31	4	43	.316
Night	253	72	9	45	.285	Clutch	72	17	2	7	.236

1991 Rankings (National League)

→ 1st in lowest batting average on an 0-2 count (.040)

→ 5th highest batting average with the bases loaded (.444)

→ 7th lowest batting average with 2 strikes (.132)

→ Led the Braves in highest percentage of pitches taken (61.2%)

→ Led NL shortstops in least GDPs per GDP situation (5.4%), batting average with runners in scoring position (.316), batting average with the bases loaded (.444) and highest percentage of pitches taken

HITTING:

When John Schuerholz moved from Kansas City to Atlanta, one of his goals was to improve the shaky Braves' defense. Another was to add veterans who were a good influence on a ball club. With Sid Bream, he was able to fill both needs. Though the oft-injured Bream got into only 91 games, there's a pennant flying at Fulton County Stadium, and the Braves were very pleased with Bream's contributions.

Bream's signing paid early dividends as he batted near .290 with nine home runs before going down with yet another of his chronic knee injuries. Undoubtedly pressing, Bream couldn't get his bat going after his return and batted only .176 in the postseason. But Atlanta felt he had done his job.

Primarily a line drive hitter throughout most of his career, Bream has become more of a power hitter as a result of working with weights. He can turn on a high fastball, and given a full season of health, would be a threat for 20 to 25 homers in the Atlanta ballpark. Bream did not take advantage of the Launching Pad last year, hitting only three of his 11 homers there.

BASERUNNING:

Years of knee problems have cost Bream his speed. Once a threat to steal 10 bases or so, he was 0-for-3 last year. He is a very conservative runner who will rarely take second on a ball that does not get past the outfielder.

FIELDING:

Despite all his injuries, Bream is one of the finest defensive first baseman in the National League. He turns the 3-6-3 double play about as well as Keith Hernandez did in his prime. Bream's defense was a major reason Atlanta signed him, and he didn't disappoint.

OVERALL:

Bream's fitness is always a concern, but when healthy he will continue as Atlanta's primary first baseman, quite possibly in a platoon with Brian Hunter. A hard worker who's an excellent influence on the Braves' younger players, Bream showed Atlanta why Pittsburgh's Jim Leyland was so upset that Bream got away.

SID BREAM

Position: 1B
Bats: L **Throws:** L
Ht: 6' 4" **Wt:** 220

Opening Day Age: 31
Born: 8/3/60 in Carlisle, PA
ML Seasons: 9

Overall Statistics

	G	AB	R	H	D	T	HR	RBI	SB	BB	SO	AVG
1991	91	265	32	67	12	0	11	45	0	25	31	.253
Career	800	2398	281	629	147	10	71	352	40	267	347	.262

Where He Hits the Ball

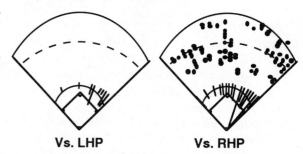

Vs. LHP   **Vs. RHP**

1991 Situational Stats

	AB	H	HR	RBI	AVG		AB	H	HR	RBI	AVG
Home	115	31	3	21	.270	LHP	40	6	1	7	.150
Road	150	36	8	24	.240	RHP	225	61	10	38	.271
Day	66	17	5	15	.258	Sc Pos	78	20	4	36	.256
Night	199	50	6	30	.251	Clutch	32	7	0	3	.219

1991 Rankings (National League)

→ 6th highest batting average on a 3-2 count (.353)

→ Led NL first basemen in batting average on a 3-2 count

PITCHING:

Veteran pitchers are supposed to have a resurgence when they are traded from a cellar-dweller to a contender. The move from last place Houston to contending Atlanta didn't exactly revive Jim Clancy's career, though he had some good moments in an Atlanta uniform. Overall, however, Clancy pitched a lot better out of the Houston bullpen (2.78 ERA, five saves) than he did out of Atlanta's (5.71 ERA, three saves).

Now 36, Clancy is a power pitcher who still relies heavily on a sinking fastball which can reach 90 MPH. He also throws a cut fastball and a slider that has a quick downward break. He throws an occasional change-up, but only for variety's sake. Clancy's pitches have good movement when they're working, but they're sometimes hard to control. He tossed 10 wild pitches in less than 90 innings last year.

Clancy got off to a fast start with the Braves. His ERA for Atlanta was under 3.00 early in August, but he slumped thereafter. Bobby Cox wasn't afraid to go to Clancy in the postseason, however, using him in four games, including three in the World Series. The long-time veteran will always be able to tell people that he was the winning pitcher in the memorable third game of the Series, though he worked only a third of an inning.

HOLDING RUNNERS, FIELDING, HITTING:

Clancy does not excel at the little things and seems miserable when he is on the mound. He is an adequate fielder but does not possess a great move to first. He was almost never called on to bat in his role with the Braves.

OVERALL:

The Braves have a crowded bullpen and probably won't have a lot of interest in free agent Clancy. Given that he was making a transition to the bullpen after 14 years as a starter, his work was probably good enough to earn a bid from someone, as long as his salary demands are reasonable.

JIM CLANCY

Position: RP
Bats: R **Throws:** R
Ht: 6' 4" **Wt:** 220

Opening Day Age: 36
Born: 12/18/55 in Chicago, IL
ML Seasons: 15

Overall Statistics

	W	L	ERA	G	GS	Sv	IP	H	R	BB	SO	HR
1991	3	5	3.91	54	0	8	89.2	73	42	34	50	8
Career	140	167	4.22	472	381	10	2518.2	2513	1304	947	1422	244

How Often He Throws Strikes

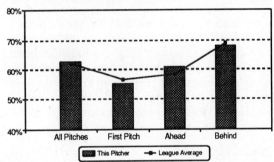

1991 Situational Stats

	W	L	ERA	Sv	IP		AB	H	HR	RBI	AVG
Home	2	3	4.28	3	40.0	LHB	147	33	2	21	.224
Road	1	2	3.62	5	49.2	RHB	180	40	6	18	.222
Day	2	1	4.66	2	29.0	Sc Pos	84	24	3	30	.286
Night	1	4	3.56	6	60.2	Clutch	99	20	2	10	.202

1991 Rankings (National League)

→ 7th in wild pitches (10)
→ 8th in relief innings (89.2)
→ 9th in highest relief ERA (3.91) and least strikeouts per 9 innings in relief (5.0)

IN HIS PRIME

RON GANT

Position: CF
Bats: R **Throws:** R
Ht: 6' 0" **Wt:** 172

Opening Day Age: 27
Born: 3/2/65 in Victoria, TX
ML Seasons: 5

HITTING:

In his first 37 at-bats last year, Ron Gant had only four hits (.108), one homer and three RBIs. Gant has had a very unpredictable career, and a lot of people flashed back to 1989, a year in which Gant batted .177 and was demoted to the low minors.

Fortunately, Gant soon caught fire and began to make his way up the National League leader boards. He culminated another great season by hitting his 30th homer, thus joining Willie Mays and Bobby Bonds as the only players to reach 30 home runs and 30 stolen bases in consecutive seasons. Gant's .251 average marked a 52-point drop from 1990, but there was no complaining about his career-high 105 RBI or his 101 runs scored.

Gant is a very similar batter to the Mets' Howard Johnson (and even puts up very similar numbers in almost every category): a dead fastball hitter who loves to pull the ball. He has very little power to right field, but his great speed keeps opposing managers from exercising an exaggerated shift to left field. Gant has become a more patient hitter, and last year drew a career-high 71 walks.

BASERUNNING:

With the exception of Otis Nixon, Gant is the fastest, and smartest, baserunner on the Atlanta team. Though his 69 percent regular season success rate was nothing to brag about, Gant was 8-for-8 in the postseason. If he can improve his batting average, stealing 40 or 50 bases is not out of the question.

FIELDING:

A converted infielder, Gant is still working on his center field play. He has the range for the position, but his arm is definitely below average. His limitations were never so clear as when compared head-to-head with Pittsburgh's Andy Van Slyke in the NLCS.

OVERALL:

Over the last three seasons, Gant has batted .177, .303 and .251, so predicting his batting average is fairly pointless. There are few doubts left, however, about his power or his speed. He is undoubtedly one of the most exciting -- and productive -- players in baseball.

Overall Statistics

	G	AB	R	H	D	T	HR	RBI	SB	BB	SO	AVG
1991	154	561	101	141	35	3	32	105	34	71	104	.251
Career	548	2042	328	529	109	17	94	283	99	188	382	.259

Where He Hits the Ball

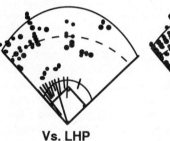

Vs. LHP   **Vs. RHP**

1991 Situational Stats

	AB	H	HR	RBI	AVG		AB	H	HR	RBI	AVG
Home	258	72	18	52	.279	LHP	164	47	10	37	.287
Road	303	69	14	53	.228	RHP	397	94	22	68	.237
Day	138	39	8	29	.283	Sc Pos	172	45	6	69	.262
Night	423	102	24	76	.241	Clutch	83	14	3	20	.169

1991 Rankings (National League)

→ 1st in errors in center field (6)
→ 2nd in runs scored per time reached base (46.5%), batting average with the bases loaded (.556) and cleanup slugging (.589)
→ 3rd in home runs (32) and lowest ground-ball/flyball ratio (.71)
→ Led the Braves in home runs, runs (101), doubles (35), RBIs (105), walks (71), strike-outs (104), pitches seen (2,410), games (154), HR frequency (17.5 ABs per HR), most pitches seen per plate appearance (3.75), runs scored per time reached base, least GDPs per GDP situation (4.6%) and batting average with the bases loaded

PITCHING:

The only trouble Tom Glavine encountered during the 1991 season was in the first couple of innings of almost every start. Once he settled down, Glavine switched on the cruise control. After three up and down seasons, the former second-round draft pick realized his great potential with a 20-win season and the National League Cy Young Award.

Glavine is a master at changing speeds. His fastball, which reaches 90 MPH, has fine movement and drops down in the strike zone, but his quick-breaking curveball is probably his best pitch. Glavine also has an excellent change-up; he turns it over a little bit, so that it breaks away from right-handed hitters. As a result, he was more effective against righties (.205) than lefties (.294) in '91. Glavine's most effective when he has great control, and Baseball America ranked him as the pitcher with the second best control in the National League (behind Dennis Martinez) last year.

The most noticeable change in Glavine in 1991 was the confidence he took to the mound. Catcher Greg Olson said the Atlanta pitchers didn't "go out there scared anymore." Glavine's renewed confidence put fear into the minds of opposing batters. Working a career-high 246.2 innings, he wore down toward the end of the season, but he still posted a 2.96 ERA in four postseason starts.

HOLDING RUNNERS, FIELDING, HITTING:

Glavine does a good job in keeping runners close. He allowed only 18 stolen bases in 28 attempts without the benefit of a great arm behind the plate. He's an able fielder who comes off the mound in good position to field the ball. One of the best hitting pitchers in baseball, he batted .230 with 15 sacrifice hits.

OVERALL:

Glavine was the subject of trade rumors before the 1991 season, including a proposed trade for Kal Daniels of the Dodgers. If that trade was made, the Dodgers would have clinched the West sometime in August. Glavine is an exceptional pitcher who may have not yet shown us his best.

TOM GLAVINE

Position: SP
Bats: L **Throws:** L
Ht: 6' 1" **Wt:** 190

Opening Day Age: 26
Born: 3/25/66 in Concord, MA
ML Seasons: 5

Overall Statistics

	W	L	ERA	G	GS	Sv	IP	H	R	BB	SO	HR
1991	20	11	2.55	34	34	0	246.2	201	83	69	192	17
Career	53	52	3.81	139	139	0	892.2	861	427	283	515	72

How Often He Throws Strikes

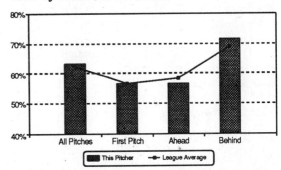

1991 Situational Stats

	W	L	ERA	Sv	IP		AB	H	HR	RBI	AVG
Home	10	4	2.71	0	106.1	LHB	170	50	4	18	.294
Road	10	7	2.44	0	140.1	RHB	735	151	13	56	.205
Day	6	4	2.79	0	71.0	Sc Pos	172	43	2	51	.250
Night	14	7	2.46	0	175.2	Clutch	91	21	0	7	.231

1991 Rankings (National League)

→ 1st in wins (20), complete games (9) and fielding percentage as a pitcher (1.000)

→ 2nd in innings (246.2), batters faced (989), lowest on-base average allowed (.277) and sacrifice bunts as a hitter (15)

→ 3rd in ERA (2.55), strikeouts (192), pitches thrown (3,595), lowest batting average allowed (.222) and lowest batting average allowed vs. right-handed batters (.205)

→ Led the Braves in ERA, wins, complete games, shutouts (1), innings, batters faced, strikeouts, pitches thrown, pickoff throws (238), GDPs induced (19), strikeout/walk ratio (2.8) and sacrifice bunts as a hitter

HITTING:

In the Braves 1991 Media Guide photo, Brian Hunter seems completely asleep. Other photographs of Hunter show the same glossed over-sleepy look. And yet, put a bat in his hand and he wakes up both himself and the Braves.

Hunter was having a good year at AAA Richmond (.260-10-30) when he moved from the Richmond outfield to the Fulton County infield on May 31. He made 63 starts at first base while Sid Bream was injured, and then continued in a platoon role when Bream returned. With the varsity, Hunter continued to show a good deal of power (one home run every 22.6 at-bats).

Strong, with a stocky frame, Hunter has a short but powerful stroke. Throughout his minor league career he hit with good power, including double-digit home runs for four consecutive years (1988-1991) at various levels while maintaining a respectable batting average. Last year Hunter excelled when the game was on the line by batting over one hundred points higher with runners on base than with no one on (.305 vs. .203).

BASERUNNING:

While not a basestealer, Hunter shows a real exuberance on the base paths, hustling and aggressively taking the extra base. He shows no fear in taking out both pivot-men at second and catchers at the plate. He showed some smarts on the bases, especially for a rookie.

FIELDING:

The career outfielder was given the unenviable task Dave Justice had in 1990: learning first base on the job at Fulton County Stadium. Unlike Justice, Hunter proved to be an able defensive first baseman. He also dabbled in left field where he might play more regularly if Lonnie Smith and/or Otis Nixon is not retained.

OVERALL:

Hunter should be very valuable to the Braves in 1992. Whether in left field, at first base or as the Braves' primary pinch hitter, he'll provide the Braves with a great deal of flexibility. If Sid Bream gets hurt again, Hunter could become the regular at first -- or in left, depending on what happens with Smith and Nixon.

BRIAN HUNTER

Position: 1B
Bats: R **Throws:** L
Ht: 6' 0" **Wt:** 195

Opening Day Age: 24
Born: 3/4/68 in Toro, CA
ML Seasons: 1

Overall Statistics

	G	AB	R	H	D	T	HR	RBI	SB	BB	SO	AVG
1991	97	271	32	68	16	1	12	50	0	17	48	.251
Career	97	271	32	68	16	1	12	50	0	17	48	.251

Where He Hits the Ball

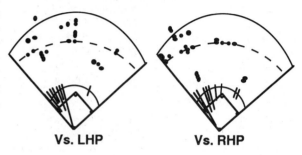

Vs. LHP   Vs. RHP

1991 Situational Stats

	AB	H	HR	RBI	AVG		AB	H	HR	RBI	AVG
Home	141	38	7	33	.270	LHP	121	33	6	22	.273
Road	130	30	5	17	.231	RHP	150	35	6	28	.233
Day	70	19	3	6	.271	Sc Pos	91	29	3	37	.319
Night	201	49	9	44	.244	Clutch	50	12	3	12	.240

1991 Rankings (National League)

➡ 3rd lowest batting average on a 3-2 count (.000)

➡ 6th highest batting average on a 3-1 count (.571)

➡ 8th lowest batting average with 2 strikes (.133)

➡ Led the Braves in batting average on a 3-1 count

DAVE JUSTICE

Position: RF
Bats: L **Throws:** L
Ht: 6' 3" **Wt:** 200

Opening Day Age: 25
Born: 4/14/66 in Cincinnati, OH
ML Seasons: 3

HITTING:

Blessed with one of the finest swings in baseball, Dave Justice had a second consecutive outstanding year in 1991. Justice put up big numbers despite missing almost two months with a bad back. He might have had a 30-homer, 120-RBI season if not for the injury.

Justice is a strong line drive hitter who continues to bat equally well against lefties and righties. While he insists he is not necessarily a power hitter, his figures belie that notion. In two-plus years Justice has averaged a home run every 18 at-bats, one of the top marks in baseball. He does not owe his home runs to the intimacy of Fulton County Stadium, where he hit 11 of his 21 homers. With his balanced swing and great bat speed, Justice should be a major home run threat for years to come.

Though he batted only .231 in the postseason, Justice led the Braves with eight RBI, and his three homers tied Lonnie Smith for the club lead. He was a key factor in Atlanta making it to the seventh game of the Series.

BASERUNNING:

Even though the Braves beat Pittsburgh in the NLCS, many talked about Justice's miss of third base in Game Five. That play was not indicative of Justice's baserunning skills, as he normally makes few mistakes. He was fast enough to steal eight bases in 109 games and will likely improve on that in 1991. He'll have to improve his 50% success rate, though.

FIELDING:

Justice led National League right fielders with seven errors despite manning his position well. He is fleet of foot, has a powerful arm and finished with nine outfield assists, fourth at the position. He is sure to continue to improve with experience.

OVERALL:

A surprise star as a rookie, Justice has convinced most people he's for real. In two full seasons he's recorded slugging averages of .535 and .503 -- figures which place him among baseball's elite. There's little doubt that he's one of the best young hitters in baseball.

Overall Statistics

	G	AB	R	H	D	T	HR	RBI	SB	BB	SO	AVG
1991	109	396	67	109	25	1	21	87	8	65	81	.275
Career	252	886	150	245	51	3	50	168	21	132	182	.277

Where He Hits the Ball

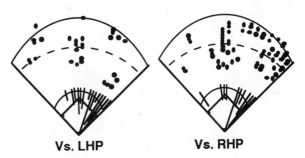

Vs. LHP   Vs. RHP

1991 Situational Stats

	AB	H	HR	RBI	AVG		AB	H	HR	RBI	AVG
Home	175	47	11	41	.269	LHP	155	43	7	39	.277
Road	221	62	10	46	.281	RHP	241	66	14	48	.274
Day	95	20	7	21	.211	Sc Pos	124	43	6	66	.347
Night	301	89	14	66	.296	Clutch	58	15	2	13	.259

1991 Rankings (National League)

→ 1st in lowest fielding percentage in right field (.968)

→ 3rd highest batting average with runners in scoring position (.347)

→ 4th in batting average with the bases loaded (.444) and lowest percentage of swings put into play (37.4%)

→ Led the Braves in intentional walks (9) and batting average with runners in scoring position

→ Led NL right fielders in least GDPs per GDP situation (4.8%) and errors (7)

PITCHING:

In many people's minds, the image of Charlie Leibrandt will always be that of a "loser" -- walking slowly off the field, head down, after yielding a game-ending home run to Kirby Puckett in Game Six of the World Series. Leibrandt's record in postseason play is now 1-6, which only underscores the negative image. But Leibrandt's earned run average in those games is a respectable 3.73, and this classy veteran is anything but a loser.

Leibrandt is the odd member of the power-pitching Braves staff. Unlike his teammates, he can't challenge batters with hard stuff in the strike zone; his fastest pitches rarely break the low 80s. He throws a fastball, curve and a very good change-up, keeping his pitches on the borders of the strike zone. His control is so good that he makes hitters go after pitches that are off the plate but too close to take. Leibrandt walked only 2.2 batters per nine innings.

A veteran who's won in double figures seven different times, Leibrandt provides matchless experience to the youthful Braves rotation. With his put-it-in-play style, he would figure to have benefitted from Atlanta's much improved defense in 1991, but in fact his ERA rose from 3.16 to 3.49. Still, Leibrandt had a very successful year, winning 15 games, the first time he's reached that mark since 1987 when he won 16 for Kansas City.

HOLDING RUNNERS, FIELDING, HITTING:

Leibrandt's excellent move to first helped erase 11 baserunners in 1991, though 35 were successful. He is a very strong fielder who comes off the mound ready and able to field his position. He's no hitter, but he can bunt. Leibrandt's 12 sacrifices were second on the Braves.

OVERALL:

After his crushing postseason defeats, a lot of people were saying Leibrandt might never recover. They said the same thing after his tough losses in the 1985 Series, but Leibrandt came back to do some of the best pitching of his career. At his age (35) arms can go quickly, but people should know better than to question Charlie Leibrandt's heart.

CHARLIE LEIBRANDT

Position: SP
Bats: R **Throws:** L
Ht: 6' 3" **Wt:** 200

Opening Day Age: 35
Born: 10/4/56 in Chicago, IL
ML Seasons: 12

Overall Statistics

	W	L	ERA	G	GS	Sv	IP	H	R	BB	SO	HR
1991	15	13	3.49	36	36	0	229.2	212	105	56	128	18
Career	116	102	3.68	336	289	2	1964.2	2030	906	569	928	148

How Often He Throws Strikes

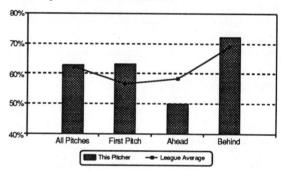

1991 Situational Stats

	W	L	ERA	Sv	IP		AB	H	HR	RBI	AVG
Home	6	8	4.35	0	101.1	LHB	190	52	2	20	.274
Road	9	5	2.81	0	128.1	RHB	674	160	16	71	.237
Day	2	6	4.23	0	66.0	Sc Pos	170	48	8	74	.282
Night	13	7	3.19	0	163.2	Clutch	77	20	1	4	.260

1991 Rankings (National League)

- ➡ 1st in stolen bases allowed (35) and least GDPs induced per 9 innings (.24)
- ➡ 2nd in games started (36) and highest ERA at home (4.35)
- ➡ 5th in sacrifice bunts as a hitter (12)
- ➡ 6th in losses (13)
- ➡ 7th in wins (15) and pickoff throws (230)
- ➡ Led the Braves in losses, games started, shutouts (1), hits allowed (212), hit batsmen (4), stolen bases allowed and least pitches thrown per batter (3.61)

MARK LEMKE

Position: 2B/3B
Bats: B **Throws:** R
Ht: 5' 9" **Wt:** 167

Opening Day Age: 26
Born: 8/13/65 in Utica, NY
ML Seasons: 4

HITTING:

Lloyd Waner's nickname, "Little Poison," is already taken, but the Minnesota Twins might have wanted to hang it on Mark Lemke. Lemke stands about 5-9 in his elevator shoes, but against the Twins he was a tower of strength, batting .417 and slugging .708 in the World Series.

It's ironic that the whole world now thinks of Lemke as a pint-sized slugger, because it's been Lemke's failure to become just that which has kept him from a regular job with the Braves. Lemke's Series performance wasn't a fluke by any means. In the minors he proved he can turn on a fastball, averaging 18 homers a year in 1986-88. In the majors Lemke has managed only four home runs, but he has belted 30 doubles in 621 lifetime at-bats.

With the Braves, Lemke has always been tough to strike out, and he draws an occasional walk. But even after batting a career-high .234 in 1991, his lifetime average is still a lowly .225. The Braves don't expect the Lemke of the World Series on an everyday basis; all they'd like is a semblance of the Lemke they saw coming up through their system (respectable average, occasional power).

BASERUNNING:

People rarely confuse Lemke with Otis Nixon on the bases. He's stolen only one major league base, having been caught six times. Again, the Braves would like to see the minor league Lemke who stole as many as 18 bases in a season.

FIELDING:

This is one area where the Braves have no complaint. One of the more gifted infielders in baseball, second sacker Lemke can turn the double play with the best in the league. His range is also very good. Lemke can also handle shortstop, though he lacks a great arm.

OVERALL:

Braves' Manager Bobby Cox, who appreciates defense, would love to use Lemke every day. All Lemke really needs to do is improve his batting average. His World Series performance should help his self-confidence; as the 1992 season begins, the second base job should be his to lose.

Overall Statistics

	G	AB	R	H	D	T	HR	RBI	SB	BB	SO	AVG
1991	136	269	36	63	11	2	2	23	1	29	27	.234
Career	268	621	70	140	30	3	4	56	1	59	61	.225

Where He Hits the Ball

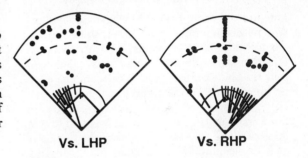

Vs. LHP   **Vs. RHP**

1991 Situational Stats

	AB	H	HR	RBI	AVG		AB	H	HR	RBI	AVG
Home	132	37	2	14	.280	LHP	114	29	0	11	.254
Road	137	26	0	9	.190	RHP	155	34	2	12	.219
Day	57	18	0	4	.316	Sc Pos	74	17	0	20	.230
Night	212	45	2	19	.212	Clutch	53	19	0	9	.358

1991 Rankings (National League)

→ 2nd highest batting average in the clutch (.359)

→ 5th lowest batting average with an 0-2 count (.053) and highest batting average with a 3-2 count (.368)

→ Led the Braves in batting average in the clutch

→ Led NL second basemen in batting average in the clutch and batting average on a 3-2 count

PITCHING:

With the arrival of Juan Berenguer, Mark Wohlers and Alejandro Pena, Kent Mercker surrendered the closer's role he had assumed for the Braves in late 1990. Mercker moved to a middle-man/spot-starter role, and he put up even better numbers than he posted in 1990. In his new role, Mercker was still able to pick up six saves. He walked a batter nearly every other inning, but he was usually able to pitch himself out of jams.

The hard-throwing Mercker's fastball consistently tops 90 MPH, and is often in the mid-90 range. The lefthander uses the heater about 80 percent of the time, mixing in an occasional curve. As a reliever he doesn't mess with his change-up much, using it more as a starter.

Late in the season, Braves Manager Bobby Cox, who needed a number-five starter, shifted Mercker to the rotation. Mercker, who had been an effective starter in the minors, responded with four fine outings that included a combined 1-0 no-hitter (with Wohlers and Pena) against San Diego on September 11. Mercker was only 1-0 in those four games, but the Braves went on to win three of them. As a starter, Mercker had an ERA of 2.79, walking 10 and striking out 17 in 19.1 innings.

HOLDING RUNNERS, FIELDING, HITTING:

Mercker needs to improve his move to first base. He did not foil a single attempted base theft in 10 attempts. He is a decent fielder who comes off the mound in good position to stop balls hit up the middle. If Mercker stays in the rotation, he will improve on his .100 average as a hitter.

OVERALL:

The Braves are in the happy position of being able to use Mercker as either a reliever or starter. With a deep bullpen, they probably have more use for him in the rotation; the problem is that they already have three other lefty starters. As long as Mercker's fastball is working, he is sure to have an important job.

KENT MERCKER

Position: RP/SP
Bats: L **Throws:** L
Ht: 6' 2" **Wt:** 195

Opening Day Age: 24
Born: 2/1/68 in Dublin, OH
ML Seasons: 3

Overall Statistics

	W	L	ERA	G	GS	Sv	IP	H	R	BB	SO	HR
1991	5	3	2.58	50	4	6	73.1	56	23	35	62	5
Career	9	10	3.14	88	5	13	126.0	107	51	65	105	11

How Often He Throws Strikes

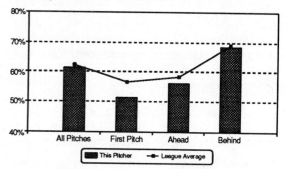

1991 Situational Stats

	W	L	ERA	Sv	IP		AB	H	HR	RBI	AVG
Home	4	1	2.48	5	36.1	LHB	72	14	1	6	.194
Road	1	2	2.68	1	37.0	RHB	194	42	4	18	.216
Day	2	1	1.69	1	16.0	Sc Pos	67	16	3	20	.239
Night	3	2	2.83	5	57.1	Clutch	105	24	3	13	.229

1991 Rankings (National League)

➝ 8th in relief ERA (2.50)
➝ Led the Braves in most strikeouts per 9 innings in relief (7.5)

GREAT SPEED

OTIS NIXON

Position: LF/CF/RF
Bats: B **Throws:** R
Ht: 6' 2" **Wt:** 180

Opening Day Age: 33
Born: 1/9/59 in
Evergreen, NC
ML Seasons: 9

HITTING:

In 1991, Otis Nixon was having the finest offensive season of his career, thriving as Atlanta's leadoff man. A career .228 hitter entering the season, the "new Nixon" was batting .297. He was well on his way to dethroning Vince Coleman as the stolen base champ, and was helping lead the Braves to a division title.

And then it all came crashing down. At a crucial point in the pennant race, Nixon was suspended for sixty days for violating baseball's drug policy. Nixon was vilified by some, given sympathy by others. Realistically, it represented a tragic ending to a Cinderella story.

Nixon was always considered a baserunner par excellence. However, his inability to get on base consistently doomed him to a life on the bench. Always a decent fastball hitter, Nixon has long been able to handle the bat, and he improved his patience and his ability against breaking stuff in his last year with the Expos. Given an opportunity to play every day by the Braves, he responded with his best offensive season ever. In truth, he was probably playing over his head; after a strong first half, Nixon had been slumping.

BASERUNNING:

Nixon would have easily won the stolen base crown had he not been suspended. He successfully stole over 75% of the time and took extra bases almost at will.

FIELDING:

Nixon proved to be a solid outfielder for the Braves, as he used his speed to make up for his weak arm. He would routinely come out of nowhere to snag line drives off opponents' bats.

OVERALL:

Nixon became a free agent after the 1991 season. Some teams won't go near him, but he'll almost certainly get some offers. The question is whether Atlanta will be one of the bidders. The Braves have other outfield options, and may simply choose not to retain Nixon.

Overall Statistics

	G	AB	R	H	D	T	HR	RBI	SB	BB	SO	AVG
1991	124	401	81	119	10	1	0	26	72	47	40	.297
Career	749	1540	302	379	39	8	4	101	264	169	210	.246

Where He Hits the Ball

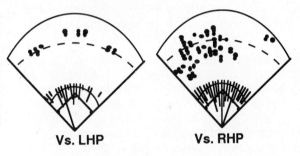

Vs. LHP   **Vs. RHP**

1991 Situational Stats

	AB	H	HR	RBI	AVG		AB	H	HR	RBI	AVG
Home	207	68	0	15	.329	LHP	95	29	0	7	.305
Road	194	51	0	11	.263	RHP	306	90	0	19	.294
Day	100	34	0	10	.340	Sc Pos	77	24	0	26	.312
Night	301	85	0	16	.282	Clutch	54	19	0	4	.352

1991 Rankings (National League)

→ 1st in bunts in play (59)

→ 2nd in stolen bases (72) and steals of third (13)

→ 3rd in caught stealing (21) and highest percentage of swings put into play (54.2%)

→ 4th in batting average in the clutch (.352)

→ Led the Braves in stolen bases, caught stealing, stolen base percentage (77.4%), bunts in play, highest percentage of swings put into play and steals of third

→ Led NL right fielders in sacrifice bunts (7), stolen bases, caught stealing, stolen base percentage, batting average in the clutch, bunts in play, highest percentage of pitches taken (61.2%) and steals of third

HITTING:

At the end of the 1990 season, Manager Bobby Cox played Ernie Whitt, with his sub-.200 average, at catcher over Atlanta's only All-Star game representative, Greg Olson. Cox's lack of confidence in Olson was somewhat understandable. Olson was 30, had played in the Met and Twin organizations without making much of an impression, and his numbers had faded in the second half of 1990.

Any trace of that lack of confidence was completely gone by the end of the 1991 season. In the midst of a pennant race, Cox used Olson behind the plate for 41 consecutive games, sitting him out only for the season finale, after Atlanta had clinched the N.L. West. Olson, who was given the position outright after Mike Heath's injury, also caught every inning of the postseason and batted a solid .275 in the NLCS and World Series.

Olson's handling of the staff was the main reason he won Cox's confidence, but his hitting was good enough to keep him in the lineup. Olson is basically a .250 hitter with some patience and a touch of power. He showed the wear of catching every day by hitting only .191 during September and October, lowering his batting average to .241. He has a nice line drive stroke and can hit the ball to all fields. He's not a huge RBI guy, but he hit significantly better with men on base (.281 vs. .215).

BASERUNNING:

Olson scored a lot of points with the TBS broadcasting crew when he was successful in stealing a base in 1991, thereby matching his 1990 total. He rarely takes a lead of more than two steps.

FIELDING:

Always a solid receiver, Olson made further improvements in his defensive game in 1991. While he will never be a Santiago or Alomar in throwing runners out, he calls a good game and has improved greatly in blocking the plate.

OVERALL:

Greg Olson represents the American Dream, personal and financial reward for hard work and determination. While he is by no means the best catcher in baseball, this blue-collar athlete has won a lot of fans.

GREG OLSON

Position: C
Bats: R **Throws:** R
Ht: 6' 0" **Wt:** 200

Opening Day Age: 31
Born: 9/6/60 in Marshall, MN
ML Seasons: 3

Overall Statistics

	G	AB	R	H	D	T	HR	RBI	SB	BB	SO	AVG
1991	133	411	46	99	25	0	6	44	1	44	48	.241
Career	236	711	82	178	37	1	13	80	2	74	99	.250

Where He Hits the Ball

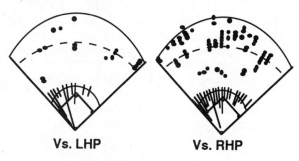

Vs. LHP   **Vs. RHP**

1991 Situational Stats

	AB	H	HR	RBI	AVG		AB	H	HR	RBI	AVG
Home	202	58	6	31	.287	LHP	100	29	2	17	.290
Road	209	41	0	13	.196	RHP	311	70	4	27	.225
Day	105	24	1	6	.229	Sc Pos	93	27	1	33	.290
Night	306	75	5	38	.245	Clutch	75	14	0	6	.187

1991 Rankings (National League)

- ➡ 2nd in lowest batting average after the 6th inning (.212) and highest fielding percentage at catcher (.995)
- ➡ 3rd lowest batting average with 2 strikes (.121)
- ➡ 4th most GDPs per GDP situation (18.3%)
- ➡ 5th highest percentage of swings put into play (54.1%)
- ➡ Led the Braves in lowest percentage of swings that missed (12.8%)
- ➡ Led NL catchers in doubles (25) and batting average with runners in scoring position (.290)

PITCHING:

Alejandro Pena wasn't exactly shocked when the Mets dealt him to the Braves last August. Pena had pitched well in nearly two seasons in New York, and his ERA was 2.71 at the time of the deal. But for some reason he had never been one of manager Bud Harrelson's favorites, and he was seldom used in important situations. In addition, he was to become a free agent at the end of the '91 season.

With Atlanta, Pena not only jumped feet-first into a pennant race; he jumped right into the Braves' closer role. After an injury to late man Juan Berenguer, Bobby Cox and GM John Schuerholz wanted a veteran for the job, and Pena became their man. In a word, he was brilliant. Down the stretch Pena went 2-0 with a perfect 11 saves in 11 opportunities while posting a 0.51 ERA. Pena continued his great work in the playoffs, saving three of the Braves' four wins against Pittsburgh. A lot of people could share credit for bringing Atlanta its first pennant, but Pena deserved as much as anyone.

As a closer, Pena relied mostly on his fine fastball and continually challenged opposing batters. He used his change and slider less often, but with great effect -- like the solitary change-up he used to strike out Andy Van Slyke with the tying run on third to end Game Six of the playoffs.

HOLDING RUNNERS, FIELDING, HITTING:

Pena does a good job of keeping runners close, even though he allowed eight stolen bases in 1991. He has a decent move to first and is an accomplished fielder. He's not much of a hitter.

OVERALL:

With each slap of Pena's mitt after getting an important out late in the season, Schuerholz got a slap on the back for bringing the reliever south. Now Schuerholz's job will be to re-sign the free agent, who figures to have some good years left. After his work late last year, Pena won't come cheap.

ALEJANDRO PENA

Position: RP
Bats: R **Throws:** R
Ht: 6' 1" **Wt:** 203

Opening Day Age: 32
Born: 6/25/59 in Cambiaso Puerto Plata, Dominican Republic
ML Seasons: 11

Overall Statistics

	W	L	ERA	G	GS	Sv	IP	H	R	BB	SO	HR
1991	8	1	2.40	59	0	15	82.1	74	23	22	62	6
Career	49	42	2.90	392	72	52	927.1	838	355	288	709	54

How Often He Throws Strikes

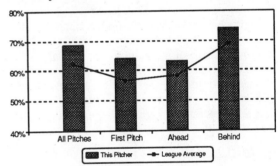

This Pitcher — League Average

1991 Situational Stats

	W	L	ERA	Sv	IP		AB	H	HR	RBI	AVG
Home	4	1	3.05	5	38.1	LHB	150	29	3	14	.193
Road	4	0	1.84	10	44.0	RHB	152	45	3	16	.296
Day	2	0	2.89	3	18.2	Sc Pos	69	19	3	27	.275
Night	6	1	2.26	12	63.2	Clutch	147	34	2	19	.231

1991 Rankings (National League)

- → 4th in relief wins (8)
- → 5th in lowest save percentage (75.0%) and lowest relief ERA (2.41)
- → 8th in lowest batting average allowed vs. left-handed batters (19.3%) and first batter efficiency (.170)
- → 9th in blown saves (5)

HITTING:

When Terry Pendleton became a free agent after batting .230 for the Cardinals in 1990, only two teams showed interest, the Braves and the Yankees. Atlanta, which had suffered from shaky defense at third for several seasons, was primarily interested in Pendleton's glove. All they asked was that he hit respectably.

Pendleton hit respectably, all right -- enough to wind up as the National League's Most Valuable Player. Pendleton defined what is meant by "career year": he recorded personal bests in hits (187), doubles (34), triples (8), homers (22), runs scored (94), on-base percentage (.363) and slugging average (.517). He followed up by batting .367 in the World Series.

What was the difference? A lot of it had to with changing ballparks, from the big St. Louis yard to the cozy Atlanta park. Pendleton hit .340 at Fulton County, with 13 of his 22 homers. While he still didn't draw many walks, he curbed his tendency to chase bad pitches. He has also improved as a lefty swinger; he is more of a lowball hitter batting lefty, preferring high pitches from the right side.

BASERUNNING:

Pendleton brought to the Braves the savvy of the Cardinals' running attack. While his pudgy frame does not get around the bases in record time, he was a smart enough baserunner to steal in double figures for the first time since 1987.

FIELDING:

Statistics will never adequately show what Pendleton means to the Braves. While always considered a great glove man, his presence was one of the main reasons the Braves' young pitchers oozed with confidence. Pendleton is great on turf and was the first Atlanta third baseman in a long time to bounce a throw over to first, and mean it.

OVERALL:

Pendleton will have trouble duplicating his 1991 numbers; when a veteran hitter's numbers jump one season, they usually return to earth the next. But with his intelligence and his ability to take advantage of the Atlanta park, Pendleton should be able to have another good year -- if not an MVP-type year -- in '92.

TERRY PENDLETON

Position: 3B
Bats: B **Throws:** R
Ht: 5' 9" **Wt:** 195

Opening Day Age: 31
Born: 7/16/60 in Los Angeles, CA
ML Seasons: 8

Overall Statistics

	G	AB	R	H	D	T	HR	RBI	SB	BB	SO	AVG
1991	153	586	94	187	34	8	22	86	10	43	70	.319
Career	1080	4019	498	1075	189	32	66	528	109	295	500	.267

Where He Hits the Ball

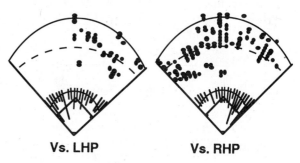

Vs. LHP   Vs. RHP

1991 Situational Stats

	AB	H	HR	RBI	AVG		AB	H	HR	RBI	AVG
Home	285	97	13	48	.340	LHP	177	53	4	23	.299
Road	301	90	9	38	.299	RHP	409	134	18	63	.328
Day	153	43	6	24	.281	Sc Pos	169	54	7	66	.320
Night	433	144	16	62	.333	Clutch	88	30	1	12	.341

1991 Rankings (National League)

→ 1st in batting average (.319), hits (187) and total bases (303)

→ 2nd in batting average at home (.340) and errors at third base (24)

→ 3rd in slugging percentage (.517), highest batting average vs. right-handed pitchers (.328) and batting average on a 3-2 count (.378)

→ Led the Braves in batting average, at-bats (586), hits, singles (123), triples (8), total bases, sacrifice flies (7), times on base (231), GDPs (16), plate appearances (644), slugging percentage (.517), on-base average (.363) and groundball/flyball ratio (1.3)

HITTING:

Still a useful veteran at age 36, Lonnie Smith has played in World Series for the Phillies, Cardinals, Royals and now the Braves. Smith didn't get his fourth world championship ring last year, but that was hardly his fault. He homered in Games Three, Four and Five of the Series -- the only games Atlanta won.

Smith began spring training last year as the Braves' starting left fielder. However, he suffered a knee injury that required arthroscopic surgery. While on the DL he lost his job twice: once to Deion Sanders and then to Otis Nixon. When he returned to the Braves' active list, Smith was used off the bench, though he saw frequent action. He only returned to the everyday lineup when Otis Nixon was suspended for drugs in September.

Many observers thought Nixon's suspension would kill the Braves, but Smith picked up the pace in left field and in the leadoff spot. He's not a major power threat, but as his Series homers showed, he can smack the longball. A very disciplined hitter, he has an excellent .371 lifetime on-base average.

BASERUNNING:

Smith seemed to have regained the spring in his step late in the season. While he certainly could not have replaced Nixon's stolen base skill at the top of the batting order, he showed much of the aggressive baserunning that Nixon, and a younger Lonnie Smith, always showed.

FIELDING:

"Skates" Smith has always been known for his defensive misadventures. His weakness seemed amplified after he took over for Nixon. By the playoffs, however, he seemed to have regained his confidence and played surprisingly well. His arm is very inaccurate.

OVERALL:

Smith's playing time triggered an automatic renewal of his contract for 1992. However, he doesn't figure strongly in Atlanta's plans. He still has the offensive skills to interest an American League team that needs a DH. If Smith stays in Atlanta, it will likely be in a bench role.

LONNIE SMITH

Position: LF
Bats: R **Throws:** R
Ht: 5' 9" **Wt:** 190

Opening Day Age: 36
Born: 12/22/55 in Chicago, IL
ML Seasons: 14

Overall Statistics

	G	AB	R	H	D	T	HR	RBI	SB	BB	SO	AVG
1991	122	353	58	97	19	1	7	44	9	50	64	.275
Career	1391	4730	830	1375	256	52	84	471	356	544	742	.291

Where He Hits the Ball

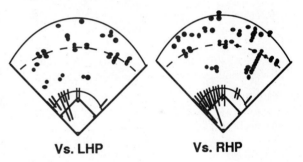

Vs. LHP   Vs. RHP

1991 Situational Stats

	AB	H	HR	RBI	AVG		AB	H	HR	RBI	AVG
Home	193	56	6	31	.290	LHP	115	39	0	11	.339
Road	160	41	1	13	.256	RHP	238	58	7	33	.244
Day	78	22	1	10	.282	Sc Pos	96	28	1	36	.292
Night	275	75	6	34	.273	Clutch	56	13	0	1	.232

1991 Rankings (National League)

- ➡ 2nd in hit by pitch (9) and leadoff on-base average (.393)
- ➡ 3rd highest on-base average vs. left-handed pitchers (.435)
- ➡ 5th highest batting average vs. left-handed pitchers (.339)
- ➡ 6th highest percentage of swings that missed (25.7%)
- ➡ 7th lowest percentage of swings put into play (39.0%)
- ➡ Led the Braves in hit by pitch, batting average vs. left-handed pitchers and on-base average vs. left-handed pitchers

PITCHING:

Whatever he does over the rest of his career -- and he's not yet 25 years old -- John Smoltz will long be remembered for the way he matched Jack Morris pitch for pitch in Game Seven of the memorable 1991 World Series. A Detroit native, Smoltz had idolized Morris while growing up, and even more as he was coming up through the Detroit system. Under intense pressure, the young righthander never blinked; if Bobby Cox hadn't removed him in the eighth inning of a scoreless tie, Smoltz and Morris might still be matching zeroes.

Over the second half of 1991, Atlanta got used to that kind of pitching from Smoltz. After starting the season 2-11, Smoltz was 12-2 with a 2.63 ERA after the All-Star break. From August 1 on, Smoltz went 8-1 with a 1.49 ERA, holding opponents to a .236 batting average. In postseason play Smoltz was just as impressive -- 2-0, 1.52, with 26 strikeouts and only four walks in 29.2 innings.

Smoltz gave a lot of credit for his second-half turnaround to Jack Llewellyn, a sports psychologist he began seeing around the All-Star break. The counseling did a lot to keep Smoltz focused, particularly in pressure situations. Of course, it helps when you have a 92 MPH fastball, a good curve, a fine change-up, and a slider that's been described as "unhittable."

HOLDING RUNNERS, FIELDING, HITTING:

Smoltz has an adequate move to first base and keeps runners close. Catchers threw out 13 of 27 attempted stolen bases with him on the mound. He is a very good defensive pitcher. At the plate, he managed three doubles and three RBIs with a .108 batting average.

OVERALL:

Smoltz has always had the arm to be a big winner, but up to now, he's never been able to put it together for a full season. He may finally be ready. Working with Llewellyn seemed to help him a lot; working over hitters in the postseason (including 16.1 scoreless innings in the two Game Sevens) probably helped his confidence even more. Smoltz seems ready to win 18 games or more.

JOHN SMOLTZ

Position: SP
Bats: R **Throws:** R
Ht: 6' 3" **Wt:** 185

Opening Day Age: 24
Born: 5/15/67 in Detroit, MI
ML Seasons: 4

Overall Statistics

	W	L	ERA	G	GS	Sv	IP	H	R	BB	SO	HR
1991	14	13	3.80	36	36	0	229.2	206	101	77	148	16
Career	42	42	3.72	111	111	0	733.0	646	329	272	523	61

How Often He Throws Strikes

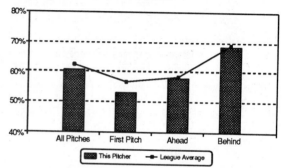

1991 Situational Stats

	W	L	ERA	Sv	IP		AB	H	HR	RBI	AVG
Home	9	7	4.10	0	136.0	LHB	486	140	10	56	.288
Road	5	6	3.36	0	93.2	RHB	363	66	6	33	.182
Day	1	2	3.31	0	35.1	Sc Pos	192	50	4	71	.260
Night	13	11	3.89	0	194.1	Clutch	42	9	0	3	.214

1991 Rankings (National League)

- 1st in wild pitches (20) and lowest batting average allowed vs. right-handed batters (.182)
- 2nd in games started (36)
- 4th highest ERA at home (4.10)
- 6th in losses (13), walks allowed (77) and GDPs induced (18)
- 7th in complete games (5)
- Led the Braves in losses, games started, walks allowed, wild pitches, runners caught stealing (13), lowest stolen base percentage allowed (51.8%), most GDPs induced per 9 innings (.71) and lowest batting average allowed vs. right-handed batters

PITCHING:

Any lad who grows up near Alvin, Texas, has hopes that there will be a touch of Nolan Ryan in his blood. Mike Stanton, who attended Alvin Community College, certainly can be counted in that group even though he's a lefty. Stanton doesn't have Ryan's fastball, but his heater can reach 90, and he also has a very fine slider along with a good curve and fine control.

A few years ago, Stanton seemed ready to become the closer that the Braves had been looking for. He was first called up in late 1989 and struck out 27 batters in 24 innings while recording seven saves. But in 1990, Stanton developed shoulder problems. Instead of accepting the rest he needed, he decided to pitch through the pain. After Stanton's ERA ballooned to 18.00 in '90 he went on the disabled list, and when the pain continued during a rehab stint at AA Greenville, he underwent surgery for a torn labrum in his left shoulder.

Recovering quickly, Stanton was ready by spring training and proved he was completely healthy by working in 74 games in '91, third-most in the National League. He was the left-handed set-up man to Juan Berenguer and then Alejandro Pena, and was tough against both lefties and righties. He held up brilliantly under postseason pressure, turning in a 0.82 ERA in eight games. He was unscored upon in five World Series appearances.

HOLDING RUNNERS, FIELDING, HITTING:

Stanton's high-kick delivery makes him an easy target for baserunners (nine stolen bases in 10 attempts against him). He fields his position well and led all Braves' hitters with a .500 batting average (3 for 6) with a double and a RBI.

OVERALL:

Stanton's outstanding postseason pitching clinched his role as the main lefthander in the Braves bullpen. If Berenguer can't come back and the Braves don't re-sign Pena, he might even get a second chance to become the Braves' closer. With his recent history of shoulder problems, he will most likely continue in a set-up role for now.

MIKE STANTON

Position: RP
Bats: L **Throws:** L
Ht: 6' 1" **Wt:** 190

Opening Day Age: 24
Born: 6/2/67 in Houston, TX
ML Seasons: 3

Overall Statistics

	W	L	ERA	G	GS	Sv	IP	H	R	BB	SO	HR
1991	5	5	2.88	74	0	7	78.0	62	27	21	54	6
Career	5	9	3.55	101	0	16	109.0	95	47	33	88	7

How Often He Throws Strikes

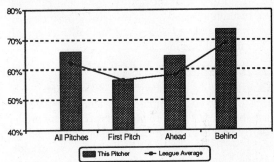

1991 Situational Stats

	W	L	ERA	Sv	IP		AB	H	HR	RBI	AVG
Home	1	1	2.21	4	40.2	LHB	103	20	1	4	.194
Road	4	4	3.62	3	37.1	RHB	183	42	5	31	.230
Day	1	1	3.63	1	17.1	Sc Pos	80	17	2	28	.213
Night	4	4	2.67	6	60.2	Clutch	162	32	1	19	.198

1991 Rankings (National League)

→ 2nd in holds (15)

→ 3rd in games pitched (74)

→ 4th least baserunners allowed per 9 innings in relief (9.7)

→ 7th lowest batting average allowed in relief (.217)

→ Led the Braves in games pitched, holds, blown saves (3), lowest percentage of inherited runners scored (27.6%) and relief innings (78)

HITTING:

Despite the media horde that followed Atlanta during the last few weeks of the season, Jeff Treadway had a great deal of solitude. Treadway does not have the home run stroke of Ron Gant or the defensive ability of Terry Pendleton, and he spent a lot of the stretch drive, and almost all of the postseason, on the bench. Still, Treadway was a very important part of the Braves' drive for the pennant.

Treadway is a solid major league hitter, one who has been able to increase his batting average each full year in the majors. He has a textbook line drive swing with doubles power to the gaps. A good contact man, Treadway is an excellent number-two hitter with the ability to hit-and-run and the discipline to take pitches with a base stealer on first. Treadway is a good fastball hitter, and likes the ball inside.

BASERUNNING:

Treadway is not gifted with great speed, and plays accordingly. He attempted only four stolen bases last season and runs conservatively on the bases (partly because he's in front of Pendleton, Justice and Gant). Don't look for him to break his major league high of three steals any time in the near future.

FIELDING:

Despite sharing time with both Jeff Blauser and Mark Lemke, Treadway improved his play at second base. Two areas that stand out are his increased range and more accurate arm. He's also better on the double play, but for the most part his defensive skills are still below average for a second baseman.

OVERALL:

With his good bat, there's little doubt that Treadway could be the regular second baseman for a lot of clubs. Unfortunately, the defense-oriented Braves don't seem to be one of them. A trade might be good for Treadway's career, though he helps the Braves considerably in a bench role.

JEFF TREADWAY

Position: 2B
Bats: L **Throws:** R
Ht: 5'11" **Wt:** 170

Opening Day Age: 29
Born: 1/22/63 in Columbus, GA
ML Seasons: 5

Overall Statistics

	G	AB	R	H	D	T	HR	RBI	SB	BB	SO	AVG
1991	106	306	41	98	17	2	3	32	2	23	19	.320
Career	494	1638	194	467	78	11	26	158	11	107	135	.285

Where He Hits the Ball

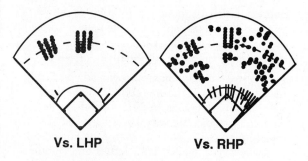

Vs. LHP   Vs. RHP

1991 Situational Stats

	AB	H	HR	RBI	AVG		AB	H	HR	RBI	AVG
Home	159	42	1	12	.264	LHP	20	5	0	0	.250
Road	147	56	2	20	.381	RHP	286	93	3	32	.325
Day	79	24	0	8	.304	Sc Pos	66	22	1	27	.333
Night	227	74	3	24	.326	Clutch	37	9	0	6	.243

1991 Rankings (National League)

→ 2nd highest batting average with 2 strikes (.283)

→ 3rd in highest batting average on an 0-2 count (.333) and errors at second base (15)

→ Led the Braves in batting average with 2 strikes and batting average on an 0-2 count

TOP PROSPECT

MARK WOHLERS

Position: RP
Bats: R **Throws:** R
Ht: 6' 4" **Wt:** 207

Opening Day Age: 22
Born: 1/23/70 in Holyoke, MA
ML Seasons: 1

PITCHING:

Mark Wohlers has one basic pitch: a devastating fastball clocked in the upper 90s. He has a very smooth motion and then, in the words of coach Leo Mazzone, "Pow"! Wohlers moved through the Braves system last year about as quickly as his fastball, pitching at AA Greenville, AAA Richmond and finally Atlanta. He worked in a total of 68 games, recording 34 saves and impressing observers at every stop.

Wohlers' ERA, while impressive, jumped with each step (0.57 at AA, 1.03 at AAA and 3.20 with Atlanta), and he had some control problems with the Braves, with ten unintentional walks in less than 20 innings. He's had a problem with walks throughout his career, but his control has been improving as he's matured.

Good as his heater is, Wohlers will need other pitches to complement his fastball. Last year he worked on adding a cut fastball and a slider, but those pitches still need some work. As a late reliever, he won't have a lot of need for offspeed pitches.

HOLDING RUNNERS, FIELDING, HITTING:

Like a lot of young power pitchers, Wohlers has had some problems holding baserunners. He was very easy to run on last year (five steals in five attempts at the major league level), and he'll have to improve. For a big man, Wohlers moves off the mound pretty well and has good defensive reactions. He won't be batting enough for his stick work to make any difference.

OVERALL:

June trade talks with the Expos for reliever Tim Burke broke down when the Expos insisted on Wohlers. He has a world of potential and should be a valuable part of the Atlanta bullpen for years to come. If the Braves retain either Alejandro Pena or Juan Berenguer, Wohlers may be the kind of reliever Bobby Cox would love to use to shut down rallies in the middle innings. If neither returns, however, he could well become the closer.

Overall Statistics

	W	L	ERA	G	GS	Sv	IP	H	R	BB	SO	HR
1991	3	1	3.20	17	0	2	19.2	17	7	13	13	1
Career	3	1	3.20	17	0	2	19.2	17	7	13	13	1

How Often He Throws Strikes

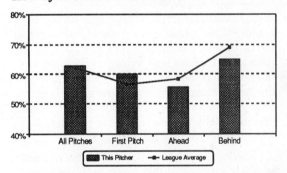

1991 Situational Stats

	W	L	ERA	Sv	IP		AB	H	HR	RBI	AVG
Home	1	0	1.64	1	11.0	LHB	28	9	1	4	.321
Road	2	1	5.19	1	8.2	RHB	43	8	0	7	.186
Day	0	1	8.44	0	5.1	Sc Pos	33	9	0	10	.273
Night	3	0	1.26	2	14.1	Clutch	33	9	1	5	.273

1991 Rankings (National League)

→ Did not rank near the top or bottom in any category

MARVIN FREEMAN

Position: RP
Bats: R **Throws:** R
Ht: 6' 7" **Wt:** 222

Opening Day Age: 29
Born: 4/10/63 in Chicago, IL
ML Seasons: 5

Overall Statistics

	W	L	ERA	G	GS	Sv	IP	H	R	BB	SO	HR
1991	1	0	3.00	34	0	1	48.0	37	19	13	34	2
Career	6	5	4.32	74	18	2	166.2	141	85	88	117	9

PITCHING, FIELDING, HITTING & HOLDING RUNNERS:

In his first full season in Atlanta, Marvin Freeman put up some impressive numbers while serving as the main set-up man for closer Juan Berenguer. He was well on his way to making 1991 his first full season at the major league level. However, Freeman's season ended prematurely in late August. After pitching with back troubles the entire year, he finally needed surgery to repair a herniated disc and was out for the season.

A towering 6-7, Freeman is a hard thrower with an excellent fastball that can overpower hitters; he also throws a slider and a split-fingered fastball, but the heater is his money pitch. Throughout most of his career, he's been plagued with control problems, but with the Braves he's finally been able to get the ball over the plate consistently. Freeman is an able athlete who does the little things to help his cause while on the mound. He is rarely called on to hit for the Braves.

OVERALL:

Should Freeman recover from his back injury, he most certainly has a role with the Braves in 1992 as one of the main set-up guys to the Braves' closer. Freeman probably would not be suited for any other role (starter or stopper) on the staff.

MIKE HEATH

Position: C
Bats: R **Throws:** R
Ht: 5'11" **Wt:** 180

Opening Day Age: 37
Born: 2/5/55 in Tampa, FL
ML Seasons: 14

Overall Statistics

	G	AB	R	H	D	T	HR	RBI	SB	BB	SO	AVG
1991	49	139	4	29	3	1	1	12	0	7	26	.209
Career	1325	4212	462	1061	173	27	86	469	54	278	616	.252

HITTING, FIELDING, BASERUNNING:

One of the first deals worked out by Braves' new General Manager John Schuerholz was to sign Mike Heath, a second-look free agent. As they say, it seemed like a good idea at the time. The Braves needed catching help since Ernie Whitt had flopped in 1990 and Greg Olson had looked like a half-season wonder. The sturdy Heath, who'd hit steadily while playing 122 games in each of 1989 and 1990, seemed like one of the safer bets around.

As it turned out, this was one of the few Schuerholz plans which didn't pan out. Heath began the year as the Braves' top catcher, but didn't hit and soon lost playing time to Olson. In July, Heath's depressing year ended when he went out for the season with a bone spur requiring surgery on his right elbow.

At full health, Heath has been a good-hitting catcher with a strong arm and a take-charge attitude. Some people like his fire; others, including some of his pitchers, find him abrasive and hard to work with. Heath didn't play long enough for Atlanta to reach a conclusion.

OVERALL:

Heath is now 37, and he's nearing the end of his career. He'll battle Olson and September acquisition Damon Berryhill for playing time this spring; he has a chance to stick, but only if he's healthy.

KEITH MITCHELL

Position: LF
Bats: R **Throws:** R
Ht: 5'10" **Wt:** 180

Opening Day Age: 22
Born: 8/6/69 in San Diego, CA
ML Seasons: 1

Overall Statistics

	G	AB	R	H	D	T	HR	RBI	SB	BB	SO	AVG
1991	48	66	11	21	0	0	2	5	3	8	12	.318
Career	48	66	11	21	0	0	2	5	3	8	12	.318

HITTING, FIELDING, BASERUNNING:

Still only 22 years old, outfielder Keith Mitchell came a long way last year. Mitchell began the year at AA Greenville, but was summoned to Atlanta after Dave Justice went on the disabled list. He went down to AAA Richmond after Justice came back, but got some more playing time in September after Otis Nixon's drug suspension. He made Atlanta's postseason roster.

Keith is the second cousin of the Giants' Kevin Mitchell, and though he lacks his cousin's power, he appears to have major league hitting skills. He's an above-average line drive hitter, has good discipline, and has the potential to hit ten or 15 homers -- maybe more in Atlanta's Launching Pad.

Mitchell also has good speed, stealing 15 bases between the majors and minors this year, but his judgement wasn't always the best. He's considered a good outfielder, though his arm is not outstanding. He has the speed, but needs to get a better jump on the ball.

OVERALL:

Atlanta's left field job will be up for grabs this spring, with Lonnie Smith aging and Nixon possibly leaving via free agency. Mitchell has a fine chance to nail down a job. He's young enough to straighten out some personal problems he's had and continue his promising career.

DEION SANDERS

Position: LF
Bats: L **Throws:** L
Ht: 6' 1" **Wt:** 195

Opening Day Age: 24
Born: 8/9/67 in Ft. Myers, FL
ML Seasons: 3

Overall Statistics

	G	AB	R	H	D	T	HR	RBI	SB	BB	SO	AVG
1991	54	110	16	21	1	2	4	13	11	12	23	.191
Career	125	290	47	53	5	4	9	29	20	28	58	.183

HITTING, FIELDING, BASERUNNING:

After starting his career with the Yankees, Deion Sanders made up his mind to play baseball in the same city where he plays football. He moved to Atlanta last year and received enormous attention by playing for both the Braves and the NFL Falcons in the same week. Sanders has proven he can play in the NFL; the question is, can he play in the major leagues?

After a terrific spring training that detoured plans to send him to AAA Richmond, Sanders found himself in the Braves starting lineup, subbing for the injured Lonnie Smith in left field. He soon played himself back to Richmond, then left in August to report to the Falcons' camp.

Sanders briefly returned to the Braves -- amid great fanfare -- in September. He was used strictly as a pinch runner, which suggests his offensive limitations. Sanders' main asset, and possibly his only baseball skill, is his blinding speed, both in the outfield and on base. Strikeouts continue to be a big problem for Sanders, with one whiff every five at-bats.

OVERALL:

After 290 major league at-bats, Sanders has a .183 lifetime average. He's shown enough power to raise hopes, but most people don't think he can cut it unless he makes baseball a bigger priority. That seems unlikely.

ORGANIZATION OVERVIEW:

Basking in the glow of their surprise pennant, the Braves deservedly took some bows for the way they developed young talent. Why not, with the way Steve Avery, Tom Glavine, Dave Justice and company were strutting their stuff? Several people deserve credit, but none more than Bobby Cox, who stuck by his plan to go with youth through some lean years during his tenure as both Atlanta's general manager and now manager. Get pitching and more pitching was Cox's credo, and it finally paid off. Atlanta still has some fine players down on the farm; we'll have to wait and see if the Braves show the same commitment to youth, now that they've made it to the top.

TYLER HOUSTON

Position: C
Bats: L **Throws:** R
Ht: 6' 2" **Wt:** 205

Opening Day Age: 21
Born: 1/17/71 in Long Beach, CA

Recent Statistics

	G	AB	R	H	D	THR	RBI	SB	BB	SO	AVG
90 A Sumter	117	442	58	93	14	3 13	56	6	49	101	.210
91 A Macon	107	351	41	81	16	3 8	47	10	39	70	.231

The Braves are in dire need of a young catcher, and Houston, the second player chosen in the 1989 draft (after Ben McDonald) has been their big hope. Thus far it's been a struggle; Houston has size and defensive skills, but he hasn't hit much, and his surly attitude (six ejections this year) isn't winning him any friends. Houston's been psychoanalyzed to death, but if he doesn't start hitting better than .231, it won't matter if he turns into Mr. Rogers.

CHIPPER JONES

Position: SS
Bats: B **Throws:** R
Ht: 6' 3" **Wt:** 185

Opening Day Age: 19
Born: 4/24/72 in Deland, FL

Recent Statistics

	G	AB	R	H	D	THR	RBI	SB	BB	SO	AVG
90 R Braves	44	140	20	32	1	1 1	18	5	14	25	.229
91 A Macon	136	473	104	153	24	11 15	98	39	69	70	.323

Chipper Jones was the Braves' consolation prize in 1990, when they had the first pick in the draft but didn't dare use it to draft Todd Van Poppel. Van Poppel insisted he wouldn't sign with the Braves at any price. The pick looked more like a booby prize in 1990, when Jones batted .229 in rookie ball, and early in '91, when he had hitting problems and committed 28 errors in his first two months at Macon. But Jones then went crazy with the bat, hitting for both average and power. There's little question that Jones is a major league hitting prospect; but he'll have to prove he can play shortstop. If he keeps hitting like he did in '91, they'll find a place for him.

MIKE KELLY

Position: OF
Bats: R **Throws:** R
Ht: 6' 4" **Wt:** 195

Opening Day Age: 21
Born: 6/2/70 in Los Angeles, CA

Recent Statistics

	G	AB	R	H	D	THR	RBI	SB	BB	SO	AVG
91 A Durham	35	124	29	31	6	1 6	17	6	19	47	.250

By finishing last so many times, Atlanta got lots of premium picks, and this year they wound up with Kelly, Arizona State's star outfielder. The Braves shrewdly sent Kelly to Durham, where Crash Davis and Annie Savoy helped him . . . sorry, wrong movie. Kelly looks good: he shows speed, power, defense and could move up to Atlanta quickly. Judging by what he showed in his first taste of professional ball, it could happen.

RYAN KLESKO

Position: 1B
Bats: L **Throws:** L
Ht: 6' 3" **Wt:** 220

Opening Day Age: 20
Born: 6/12/71 in Westminster, CA

Recent Statistics

	G	AB	R	H	D	THR	RBI	SB	BB	SO	AVG
90 A Sumter	63	231	41	85	15	1 10	38	13	31	30	.368
90 A Durham	77	292	40	80	16	1 7	47	10	32	53	.274
91 AA Greenville	126	419	64	122	22	3 14	67	14	75	60	.291
91 MLE	126	409	51	112	19	1 12	53	8	48	63	.274

Big and strong, Klesko had an outstanding year in AA ball, showing about everything you'd want in a young hitter -- he hit for average and power while displaying fine discipline and speed to boot. A former pitcher, he is fairly new to first base but has the athletic skills to master the position. Klesko is considered a potential superstar by some, though he'll have to hit more homers to move into that category. With Sid Bream and Brian Hunter still blocking his way, Klesko will probably hone his skills in AAA ball for at least a year.

JAVY LOPEZ

Position: C
Bats: R **Throws:** R
Ht: 6' 3" **Wt:** 210

Opening Day Age: 21
Born: 11/5/70 in Ponce, PR

Recent Statistics

	G	AB	R	H	D	THR	RBI	SB	BB	SO	AVG
90 A Burlington	116	422	48	112	17	3 11	55	0	14	84	.265
91 A Durham	113	384	43	94	14	2 11	51	10	25	87	.245

If Tyler Houston can't make it, Javier Lopez is Plan B as Atlanta's catcher of the future. Thus far he's displayed an outstanding arm, and his other defensive skills are considered major league caliber. As a hitter, he has a long way to go. Lopez showed good speed, with 10 steals, and some power, with 11 homers. His 25 walks were a lot for him -- he had only 14 in 1990. Latin players sometimes take a while to adjust to life in America, and Lopez has had more problems than most. Given that, he still has to be considered a good prospect, and ahead of Houston at this point.

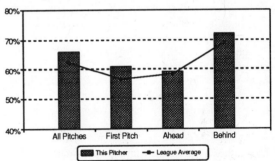

TOUGH ON LEFTIES

PITCHING:

In characteristically subdued style last year, Paul Assenmacher filled various roles in the muddled Chicago bullpen. After blowing seven of 10 saves at Wrigley in 1990, he rebounded in '91 to record a 2.07 home ERA and close out eight of 11 games successfully. He became the only Cub closer not met by the fans with instant trepidation.

The left-handed Assenmacher brings to the mound a basic complement of three average pitches (88 MPH tailing fastball, slider, change-up) that are made more effective by a quick-breaking, paralyzing curveball. A fast worker, Assenmacher loves to use this breaking ball to get ahead of hitters and his sweeping slider to punch them out. More often than not, the pitch combination works well: Assenmacher's rate of 117 strikeouts in 102.2 IP (10.3 per nine innings) trailed only Rob Dibble among all N.L. pitchers.

Forced into stopper duty last season, Assenmacher recorded a career-high 15 saves, but blew nine other chances -- in 1990, he blew 10 of 20 save opportunities. He is much better suited to the workhorse set-up role, in which he has logged 74+ games and 100+ IP each of the last two seasons. A tendency to allow the longball with his hittable fastball, especially after getting behind to righties, hurts his effectiveness in game-deciding situations. Assenmacher is simply devastating vs. lefties; he struck out 33% of all lefties he faced and allowed them a .179 batting average.

HOLDING RUNNERS, HITTING, FIELDING:

Assenmacher has an average move to first and prefers going after the hitters quickly to paying too much attention to baserunners. He is extremely sure-handed and accurate with his throws. He made his first career error in April after 323 mistake-free games.

OVERALL:

A big favorite of Don Zimmer and Jim Essian, Assenmacher was often seen warming up four or more straight games (he pitched in 14 of the team's first 26 games before getting hammered mercilessly in May). With more careful use, Assenmacher will continue to be valuable as a set-up man/spot closer.

PAUL ASSENMACHER

Position: RP
Bats: L **Throws:** L
Ht: 6' 3" **Wt:** 200

Opening Day Age: 31
Born: 12/10/60 in Detroit, MI
ML Seasons: 6

Overall Statistics

	W	L	ERA	G	GS	Sv	IP	H	R	BB	SO	HR
1991	7	8	3.24	75	0	15	102.2	85	41	31	117	10
Career	33	25	3.34	389	1	39	484.2	440	203	177	457	40

How Often He Throws Strikes

[Bar chart showing strike percentages by situation]

- All Pitches: ~66%
- First Pitch: ~61%
- Ahead: ~59%
- Behind: ~73%

Legend: This Pitcher | League Average

1991 Situational Stats

	W	L	ERA	Sv	IP		AB	H	HR	RBI	AVG
Home	4	2	2.07	8	61.0	LHB	134	24	1	14	.179
Road	3	6	4.97	7	41.2	RHB	247	61	9	33	.247
Day	4	1	2.85	9	53.2	Sc Pos	104	27	2	36	.260
Night	3	7	3.67	6	49.0	Clutch	279	61	7	35	.219

1991 Rankings (National League)

→ 1st in relief innings (102.2)

→ 2nd in games pitched (75), blown saves (9) and most strikeouts per 9 innings in relief (10.3)

→ 3rd lowest save percentage (62.5%)

→ 4th in holds (14), highest percentage of inherited runners scored (41.2%) and relief losses (8)

→ Led the Cubs in games pitched, games finished (31), save opportunities, holds, blown saves, relief wins (7), relief losses, relief innings, least baserunners allowed per 9 innings in relief (10.4) and most strikeouts per 9 innings in relief

HITTING:

When compared to the other two free agents the Cubs signed over the 1990 off season -- Danny Jackson and Dave Smith -- George Bell was a veritable godsend. Bell came from the American League with a reputation as a prolific power hitter, a true fastball devourer, and many had ideas that Bell would put up Dawson-like 40-homer numbers in his first year in the Friendly Confines.

While Bell's 25 homers and 86 RBI were certainly more than respectable (the HRs were his most since his MVP '87 season), a surprise was that Bell hit far better on the road (16 homers, .526 slugging percentage), than at Wrigley where he continually pressed.

With his upright stance, Bell looks for inside, belt-high heat, his specialty. He'll take high stuff the opposite way, but is still vulnerable to offspeed pitches that tail low and away. Pitchers adjusted to Bell in the second half, throwing him fewer fastballs, and his run production declined. The 32 year old must increase his anemic walk total (32) before his bat speed begins to decline.

BASERUNNING:

Bell is not a slow baserunner, but sometimes the Cubs wish he were. He was gunned down six of the eight times he attempted to steal in 1991 and his aggressive style of baserunning often did not befit the result.

FIELDING:

As Bell logged more innings in left field than anyone in the N.L. but Barry Bonds, the Cubs found out the hard way that his bad-glove reputation was based in fact. His 10 errors were most of any major league outfielder. Bell's forward/backward mobility is poor and his arm is below average.

OVERALL:

George Bell remains eager to win, and was one of many Cubs to question the team's desire and lack of fundamentals in a season-long slew of finger-pointing. One of the better power-hitting left fielders in baseball, he nevertheless shares many of the same weaknesses of the club as a whole. Nagging injuries may prevent him from going much beyond his 1991 numbers.

GEORGE BELL

Position: LF
Bats: R **Throws:** R
Ht: 6' 1" **Wt:** 202

Opening Day Age: 32
Born: 10/21/59 in San Pedro de Macoris, Dominican Republic
ML Seasons: 10

Overall Statistics

	G	AB	R	H	D	T	HR	RBI	SB	BB	SO	AVG
1991	149	558	63	159	27	0	25	86	2	32	62	.285
Career	1330	5086	704	1453	264	32	227	826	61	287	625	.286

Where He Hits the Ball

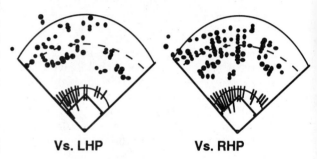

Vs. LHP   **Vs. RHP**

1991 Situational Stats

	AB	H	HR	RBI	AVG		AB	H	HR	RBI	AVG
Home	288	77	9	45	.267	LHP	208	60	15	34	.288
Road	270	82	16	41	.304	RHP	350	99	10	52	.283
Day	269	73	11	46	.271	Sc Pos	149	35	6	60	.235
Night	289	86	14	40	.298	Clutch	100	26	·5	18	.260

1991 Rankings (National League)

→ 1st in lowest fielding percentage in left field (.962)

→ 7th in sacrifice flies (9) and lowest on-base average vs. right-handed pitchers (.313)

→ Led the Cubs in GDPs (10), batting average vs. right-handed pitchers (.283), batting average on a 3-1 count (.357), batting average on the road (.304) and batting average with 2 strikes (.236)

→ Led NL left fielders in errors (10), at-bats (558), hits (159), singles (107) and batting average with the bases loaded (.333)

PITCHING:

As has been the case with Cub youngsters recently, 22-year-old Frank Castillo burst into the rotation with an exclmation point, yet ended the season as a question mark. The pitching-poor Cubs hope Castillo's string of excellent outings from June through August are more indicative of his future than those of September.

If Castillo is to become a successful major leaguer, he must continue to master his already credible control. The possessor of a below-average fastball that tops out around 86 MPH, the righthander is very dependent upon getting ahead of hitters and keeping the ball down in the zone. His fastball has downward movement, producing grounders, and he throws a slower-than-normal curve to keep his fastball honest. His best pitch is a tremendous straight change-up, from which he records most of his strikeouts. Working quickly, he often starts batters with a decent slider to try and get ahead.

When he threw strikes and used his change, Castillo showed the ability to go the distance, notching four complete games. He also was extremely tough on right-handed batters, holding them to a .226 on-base percentage with no homers. However, Castillo suffered a strained right shoulder in early August, and after returning from the DL two weeks later, he pitched very poorly. He left his last outing in October badly hurting with tightness in that same shoulder.

HOLDING RUNNERS, HITTING, FIELDING:

Very sound fundamentally, Castillo has a quick move to first which limited theft attempts to just 11 in his 18 starts. His movements off the mound are professional. He can lay down a good sacrifice, but needs work as a hitter.

OVERALL:

A youngster with a likeable attitude and poise, Castillo was the Cubs number-two starter and a favorite of then-manager Jim Essian before the arm injury. Keeping a careful eye on what may have been just a tired arm, Castillo has the make-up to develop a career as a solid third starter.

FRANK CASTILLO

Position: SP
Bats: R **Throws:** R
Ht: 6' 1" **Wt:** 180

Opening Day Age: 23
Born: 4/1/69 in El Paso, TX
ML Seasons: 1

Overall Statistics

	W	L	ERA	G	GS	Sv	IP	H	R	BB	SO	HR
1991	6	7	4.35	18	18	0	111.2	107	56	33	73	5
Career	6	7	4.35	18	18	0	111.2	107	56	33	73	5

How Often He Throws Strikes

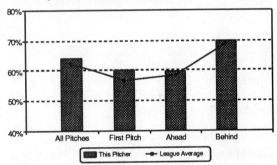

1991 Situational Stats

	W	L	ERA	Sv	IP		AB	H	HR	RBI	AVG
Home	3	3	3.73	0	50.2	LHB	273	77	5	28	.282
Road	3	4	4.87	0	61.0	RHB	152	30	0	16	.197
Day	4	4	3.88	0	53.1	Sc Pos	105	31	1	39	.295
Night	2	3	4.78	0	58.1	Clutch	37	10	0	2	.270

1991 Rankings (National League)

→ Did not rank near the top or bottom in any category

HITTING:

Doug Dascenzo had a memorable 1991 season, but not because of any real progress into full-time duty with the Cubs. Dascenzo became the first position player to pitch in three games in a season since 1988. His four scoreless innings made the laughter surrounding suggestions he join the struggling Cub bullpen sound a bit nervous.

As a hitter, the 5-8 Dascenzo is paid to work his way on base and create havoc. He is something less than perfect in this role, however, except when leading off or with the bases empty. In those situations, Dascenzo is patient enough to draw walks or fire a line drive up the middle and put his speed to use. When he is used as a pinch hitter or bats with runners on, however, Dascenzo becomes too aggressive, hacks early in the count and usually ends up grounding out.

A good handler of the bat, Dascenzo is the best bunter on the team and is dependable on the squeeze. Rob Dibble found this ability to his dismay and threw the ball at him in a noted incident.

BASERUNNING:

Dascenzo stole 14 bases in 21 attempts in 1991, consistent with his typical seasonal numbers. His speed is functional, not blinding, and he retains an aggressive style on the base paths.

FIELDING:

Dascenzo is as sure-handed an outfielder as there is in the N.L. From the start of his career until last August, he compiled the third-longest stretch of consecutive games without an error (242) by an outfielder in history. His range is average in both center and left, but his arm is very weak.

OVERALL:

With all the Cubs' center field turmoil in 1991, it's a safe bet that if Dascenzo couldn't win a regular job then, he never will. He is a useful role player for speed, defense, and contact hitting, but he needs to keep himself in perspective. After giving himself an A+ midseason review, Dascenzo went 0-for-28 and 1-for-40.

DOUG DASCENZO

Position: CF/LF
Bats: B **Throws:** L
Ht: 5' 8" **Wt:** 160

Opening Day Age: 27
Born: 6/30/64 in Cleveland, OH
ML Seasons: 4

Overall Statistics

	G	AB	R	H	D	T	HR	RBI	SB	BB	SO	AVG
1991	118	239	40	61	11	0	1	18	14	24	26	.255
Career	304	694	96	161	24	5	3	60	41	67	61	.232

Where He Hits the Ball

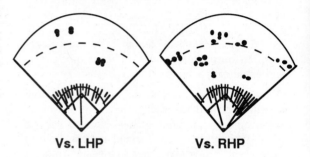

Vs. LHP   **Vs. RHP**

1991 Situational Stats

	AB	H	HR	RBI	AVG		AB	H	HR	RBI	AVG
Home	125	29	0	8	.232	LHP	87	26	0	8	.299
Road	114	32	1	10	.281	RHP	152	35	1	10	.230
Day	107	25	0	6	.234	Sc Pos	60	10	0	16	.167
Night	132	36	1	12	.273	Clutch	59	20	0	9	.339

1991 Rankings (National League)

→ 9th highest batting average in the clutch (.339)

→ Led NL center fielders in batting average in the clutch

HITTING:

"This is one of my worst years . . . it is mind-boggling . . . everything is in disarray." This is how Andre Dawson summed up a season in which he smashed 31 homers and drove in 104 runs, his second-highest such totals over the past eight years. Never content with personal success, Dawson felt the sting of the team turmoil and a one-game suspension when his temper flared out of control.

"The Hawk" has one key weakness as a hitter, and it continued last season: he just loves to swing the lumber. His walks dipped to a career low of 22, of which three were intentional. In addition, Dawson's batting average, slugging percentage, and on-base percentage all dropped considerably while his strikeouts rose.

Dawson can't be beaten with any kind of heat below waist level that allows him to extend his arms. He likes to drive more than pull, and he feasts on hard throwers who keep their heat moving down and away. Not much has changed with the plate-diver: he'll lunge after low-and-away sliders and try to take on high heat unsuccessfully.

BASERUNNING:

Dawson's steal totals went from 16 in 1990 to four in 1991, while his caught stealings went from two to five. This startling downturn shows Dawson is protecting his bothersome knees; his days of double-digit steals are probably over. He still runs the bases hard.

FIELDING:

To hear some tell it, Dawson is still Gold Glove caliber, but in reality, he has slipped to the middle of the pack defensively. His range to his right is prodigious, but he has loads of problems to his left and especially going back on the ball. His right arm, still fearsome, was hampered by a shoulder spur in 1991.

OVERALL:

Heading into his 16th full season in 1992, Dawson continues to swing away as one of baseball's great power hitters. Any doubts about his ability to hold up at age 36 with repaired knees seem useless. The Hawk should one day soar into Cooperstown.

ANDRE DAWSON

Position: RF
Bats: R **Throws:** R
Ht: 6' 3" **Wt:** 195

Opening Day Age: 37
Born: 7/10/54 in Miami, FL
ML Seasons: 16

Overall Statistics

	G	AB	R	H	D	T	HR	RBI	SB	BB	SO	AVG
1991	149	563	69	153	21	4	31	104	4	22	80	.272
Career	2167	8348	1199	2354	417	92	377	1335	304	522	1279	.282

Where He Hits the Ball

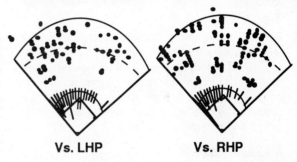

Vs. LHP   Vs. RHP

1991 Situational Stats

	AB	H	HR	RBI	AVG		AB	H	HR	RBI	AVG
Home	280	82	22	59	.293	LHP	223	66	16	47	.296
Road	283	71	9	45	.251	RHP	340	87	15	57	.256
Day	274	80	19	58	.292	Sc Pos	158	47	12	76	.297
Night	289	73	12	46	.253	Clutch	118	26	7	19	.220

1991 Rankings (National League)

➡ 4th in home runs (31) and lowest percentage of pitches taken (44.1%)

➡ 6th in RBIs (104), lowest on-base average (.302), HR frequency (18.2 ABs per HR) and slugging percentage vs. left-handed pitchers (.556)

➡ Led the Cubs in home runs, RBIs, GDPs (10), slugging percentage (.488), HR frequency, batting average with the bases loaded (.364) and batting average on a 3-2 count (.333)

➡ Led NL right fielders in home runs, RBIs, hit by pitch (5) and slugging percentage vs. left-handed pitchers

GREAT SPEED

HITTING:

When Don Zimmer was fired last May, his prize pupil Shawon Dunston struggled both at the plate and in the field. Dunston awoke from a semi-platoon stupor in August just in time to win himself a four-year contract, making him baseball's highest paid shortstop at $3 million per year.

Dunston does not have $3 million-per-year offensive capabilities. In his first full season in 1986, Dunston hit .250 with a .278 on-base percentage and a .411 slugging percentage. He also scored 66 runs and drove in 68. Last season, at age 28, Dunston hit .260 with a .292 OBP and .407 slugging, scoring 59 runs while driving in 50. It is maddening to see a skilled young player playing at the same level six years after his debut at age 22.

Dunston's continuing weaknesses include an inability to recognize the slider, which causes him to take full swings at balls low and away. When he got hot in the second half, it was no coincidence to see him taking outside pitches to the opposite field while jerking balls on the inner half with his good power.

BASERUNNING:

Dunston is a dynamo on the base paths, always taking the extra base and running full blast. He stole 21 of 27 in '91 and would easily be capable of 40 steals if he ever got on base regularly.

FIELDING:

The excitement Dunston generates isn't limited to his speed; he continues to be one of the game's most recognizable fielders on the strength of his famous arm. Less renowned is the hitch and wind-up he uses to show the arm off, which creates careless errors. His range is excellent, but he over-relies on the arm on slow grounders, and is not a Gold Glove candidate.

OVERALL:

Dunston is an emotional player who needs a supportive manager. He didn't respond well to sharing time with Jose Vizcaino, but he got hot at just the right time. Dunston will never stop his hustling play despite the new contract, but it's doubtful that he'll ever take that big step forward, either.

SHAWON DUNSTON

Position: SS
Bats: R **Throws:** R
Ht: 6' 1" **Wt:** 175

Opening Day Age: 29
Born: 3/21/63 in Brooklyn, NY
ML Seasons: 7

Overall Statistics

	G	AB	R	H	D	T	HR	RBI	SB	BB	SO	AVG
1991	142	492	59	128	22	7	12	50	21	23	64	.260
Career	900	3260	399	840	154	37	73	340	131	134	569	.258

Where He Hits the Ball

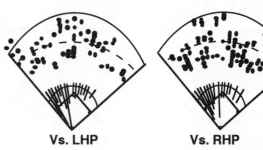

Vs. LHP   **Vs. RHP**

1991 Situational Stats

	AB	H	HR	RBI	AVG		AB	H	HR	RBI	AVG
Home	237	70	7	26	.295	LHP	194	45	5	19	.232
Road	255	58	5	24	.227	RHP	298	83	7	31	.279
Day	231	66	7	25	.286	Sc Pos	107	29	1	35	.271
Night	261	62	5	25	.238	Clutch	112	40	3	13	.357

1991 Rankings (National League)

→ 1st in highest percentage of extra bases taken as a runner (94.7%)

→ 2nd least pitches seen per plate appearance (3.23)

→ 3rd in sacrifice flies (11), lowest on-base average (.292), batting average in the clutch (.357) and batting average after the 6th inning (.333)

→ 4th lowest batting average on the road (.227)

→ Led the Cubs in triples (7), sacrifice flies, batting average in the clutch, batting average after the 6th inning and bunts in play (18)

→ Led NL shortstops in sacrifice flies, hit by pitch (4), batting average in the clutch and batting average after the 6th inning

HITTING:

The possessor of a career .297 batting average despite his '91 average of .273, Mark Grace mirrored his team last year: lackluster halves, disappointing overall. The most oft-quoted Cub in the local media, Grace unfortunately talked a lot better than he played. After trying to spur the team on with motivational newspaper quotes before one key series, Grace went 0-for-the-series and committed a game-losing error.

As their most prominent left-handed hitter, Grace was expected to pop versus tough righties and patience versus lefthanders. Grace was decent in the former role and a bust in the latter. He'll smoke a right-handed fastball when in a groove, primarily for gap singles and doubles, even showing rare aggressiveness; when slumping, he is passive, does not pull with authority and gets himself completely mixed up in the box. Against southpaws, Grace's .270 batting average was a mirage: he had but 12 extra-base hits and an on-base percentage of .333 in 280 plate appearances.

BASERUNNING:

Moved from his customary third spot, Grace saw much less need to run in front of the big boys, and attempted only seven steals, a third as many as his usual. His speed on the bases and out of the box has truly slipped, although because of his smarts, he is not daring needlessly.

FIELDING:

Grace is gathering steam for a run at a Gold Glove. He has good, not great, quickness and has impressive range, especially with outfield pops. He is top-notch at scoops in the dirt, but his arm is not accurate and created a few of his eight errors.

OVERALL:

The rumblings of a trade to the American League are a sign of Cub impatience with Grace's pop-gun power at first. Whether he goes or not, Grace is the one expendable marquee-value Cub that could land them a young starter.

MARK GRACE

Position: 1B
Bats: L **Throws:** L
Ht: 6' 2" **Wt:** 190

Opening Day Age: 27
Born: 6/28/64 in Winston-Salem, NC
ML Seasons: 4

Overall Statistics

	G	AB	R	H	D	T	HR	RBI	SB	BB	SO	AVG
1991	160	619	87	169	28	5	8	58	3	70	53	.273
Career	593	2204	298	655	111	13	37	276	35	269	192	.297

Where He Hits the Ball

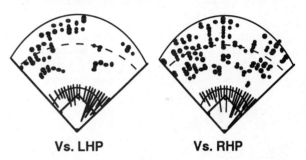

Vs. LHP **Vs. RHP**

1991 Situational Stats

	AB	H	HR	RBI	AVG		AB	H	HR	RBI	AVG
Home	322	93	5	32	.289	LHP	252	68	2	19	.270
Road	297	76	3	26	.256	RHP	367	101	6	39	.275
Day	313	88	7	38	.281	Sc Pos	131	30	1	46	.229
Night	306	81	1	20	.265	Clutch	118	28	1	10	.237

1991 Rankings (National League)

→ 1st in at-bats (619)

→ 2nd in plate appearances (703) and games (160)

→ 3rd in singles (128)

→ 4th highest batting average on an 0-2 count (.324)

→ Led the Cubs in at-bats, singles, intentional walks (7), plate appearances, games, ground-ball/flyball ratio (1.6), least GDPs per GDP situation (4.6%), batting average on an 0-2 count, on-base average vs. right-handed pitchers (.355), lowest percentage of swings that missed (11.9%) and highest percentage of swings put into play (53.6%)

PITCHING:

One Cub fan said to another regarding Danny Jackson's Cub debut in 1991, "There's some good news and some bad news. We've still got three more years left on his contract." To which the other Cub fan answered "So what's the good news?"

To the Cubs and Jackson, 1991 was no joke. In what seemed like a different century come October, Jackson was tabbed Opening Day starter for the Cubs last season by Don Zimmer; signed in November of '90 as one of the team's free agent triumvirate, no Cub was deemed more important to the team's success. Sadly, the opener was the only time he pitched into the eighth inning in any of his 14 starts in 1991 and he recorded just one lone victory for the season.

Two injuries (a scout partly attributed the first to his Opening Day weight) helped do Jackson in: a torn groin which shelved him from late April until June, and a related stomach muscle problem which disabled him from mid-June to August. When he returned, he showed the same lack of strike zone command he exhibited in early April. When healthy, Jackson is a fastball/slider pitcher whose velocity reaches into the low 90s; the slider is perennially one of the league's best, swooping in hard on righthanders. The problem is, he's seldom healthy.

HOLDING RUNNERS, HITTING, FIELDING:

Jackson's move to first is lackluster, and his movement off the mound was hampered by the groin injury and an overall slowdown. Opponents stole eight of 10 with Jackson pitching, and his hitting has degenerated over the last two years to a pitiful level.

OVERALL:

Jackson obviously felt the weight of expectation on his left shoulder last season, and because of injury, can't be put entirely to blame for failing. Jackson is a proud competitor and his velocity hasn't diminished. His chances of a comeback, with Billy Connors' fine-tuning, do exist . . . barring his now-customary two or three trips per season to the DL.

DANNY JACKSON

Position: SP
Bats: R **Throws:** L
Ht: 6' 0" **Wt:** 205

Opening Day Age: 30
Born: 1/5/62 in San Antonio, TX
ML Seasons: 9

Overall Statistics

	W	L	ERA	G	GS	Sv	IP	H	R	BB	SO	HR
1991	1	5	6.75	17	14	0	70.2	89	59	48	31	8
Career	73	79	3.83	213	197	1	1277.0	1251	622	521	768	78

How Often He Throws Strikes

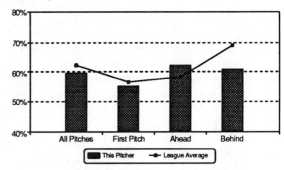

1991 Situational Stats

	W	L	ERA	Sv	IP		AB	H	HR	RBI	AVG
Home	0	2	7.20	0	40.0	LHB	60	18	0	12	.300
Road	1	3	6.16	0	30.2	RHB	228	71	8	37	.311
Day	0	3	8.27	0	32.2	Sc Pos	98	31	3	41	.316
Night	1	2	5.45	0	38.0	Clutch	19	10	2	6	.526

1991 Rankings (National League)

→ Did not rank near the top or bottom in any category

PITCHING:

Les Lancaster was expected to take on any and every role on the beleaguered Cub staff in 1991. He started as the middle relief man, moved into the decimated starting rotation in June, was shifted to the role of right-handed closer in August, and ended up somewhere between all three come October. When all was through, Lancaster was not amused.

The veteran righthander brings the standard bag of tricks to the mound, none of which are well beyond average. He throws a straight-boring fastball and a cutter which top out at 88 MPH, a fairly hard slider, and a normal curve and change-up. In general, when Lancaster gets himself into a good, quick-moving rhythm, he is successful. Like most of the non-hard throwers on the Cub staff, Lancaster gets pounded when he falls behind in the count.

In danger of being demoted in April, Lancaster gamely battled back and regained effectiveness, befitting his reputation as a competitor. Lancaster joined the rotation in June (where he and his agent firmly believed he belonged all along) and unfurled a new forkball for the occasion. It didn't help him much, as he compiled a 4.48 ERA as a starter.

HOLDING RUNNERS, HITTING, FIELDING:

Lancaster has a decent move, but runners often find him an inviting target for base thievery; his compact delivery gave his catchers a good chance in 1991 and they nabbed 50% of the 28 runners who tried to steal. He is a very quick fielder, one of the team's best, and packed a decent stick on his infrequent plate visits.

OVERALL:

Conventional wisdom, and a 2.69 ERA in 83.2 IP as a reliever, seem to indicate that Lancaster should return to his long-man role and get an occasional spot start or closing opportunity. However, Les spouted off when taken out of the rotation in August, saying he wanted to pitch someplace where "I could be a third or fourth starter." Chances are the Cubs will accommodate him.

LES LANCASTER

Position: RP/SP
Bats: R **Throws:** R
Ht: 6' 2" **Wt:** 200

Opening Day Age: 29
Born: 4/21/62 in Dallas, TX
ML Seasons: 5

Overall Statistics

	W	L	ERA	G	GS	Sv	IP	H	R	BB	SO	HR
1991	9	7	3.52	64	11	3	156.0	150	68	49	102	13
Career	34	23	3.82	232	38	22	555.2	558	255	189	337	44

How Often He Throws Strikes

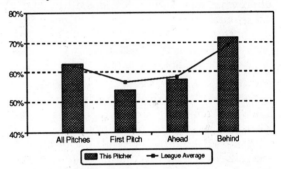

1991 Situational Stats

	W	L	ERA	Sv	IP		AB	H	HR	RBI	AVG
Home	7	2	3.46	1	83.1	LHB	310	81	6	36	.261
Road	2	5	3.59	2	72.2	RHB	277	69	7	36	.249
Day	6	1	3.62	1	74.2	Sc Pos	134	42	6	62	.313
Night	3	6	3.43	2	81.1	Clutch	135	39	1	15	.289

1991 Rankings (National League)

- ➡ 3rd highest batting average allowed with runners in scoring position (.313)
- ➡ 5th highest percentage of inherited runners scored (40.9%)
- ➡ 6th worst first batter efficiency (.313)
- ➡ 7th most runners caught stealing (14)
- ➡ Led the Cubs in runners caught stealing

STAFF ACE

GREG MADDUX

Position: SP
Bats: R **Throws:** R
Ht: 6' 0" **Wt:** 170

Opening Day Age: 25
Born: 4/14/66 in San Angelo, TX
ML Seasons: 6

PITCHING:

Greg Maddux is the most valuable member of the Cubs. Averaging 17 wins, 35 starts, and 247 innings over the last four years, Greg Maddux has been a beacon of strength in the sea of turmoil known as Cubs' pitching. The Cub staff ERA excluding Maddux over the last two seasons is 4.35; Maddux's ERA in the same period is 3.40.

The staff ace, who will turn 26 during the first week of the season, carries a varied repertoire that relies on intelligence over raw explosiveness. Maddux doesn't consider himself a power pitcher, yet the variable-speed fastball (reaching 90 MPH) is his most common offering. He also brings a slider that he tends to overthrow, an improving curveball, a tough splitter, and a deadly circle change-up that was his most effective pitch in 1991. Maddux surpassed his previous career-high in strikeouts by more than 50, in large part due to this outstanding change-up.

Not all was rosy for Maddux. Lapses in concentration seemed to befall him at all the wrong times and caused him to allow a disproportionate number of big innings due to the longball (18 HR allowed) and leadoff walk. While not always perfect game-to-game, Maddux literally saved the injured Cubs from disaster as the league leader in innings and starts, and was an anathema to righties, holding them to a .214 average.

HOLDING RUNNERS, HITTING, FIELDING:

Maddux continually works on all parts of his game, including his fielding, hitting, and pickoff move. His move improved to above-average, but he nevertheless allowed 25 of 32 runners to steal safely. A Gold Glover, he is probably the best fielding pitcher in the National League. Under Richie Zisk's tutelage, Maddux improved his already solid hitting and slugged a homer.

OVERALL:

Woe be the Cubs if for any reason Greg Maddux were to ever have an off year. Fortunately, key indices like his strikeouts per inning (and per walk) and hits per inning were all significant career bests; if anything, it looks as though the best from Greg Maddux is yet to come.

Overall Statistics

	W	L	ERA	G	GS	Sv	IP	H	R	BB	SO	HR
1991	15	11	3.35	37	37	0	263.0	232	113	66	198	18
Career	75	64	3.61	177	173	0	1174.0	1151	547	385	738	75

How Often He Throws Strikes

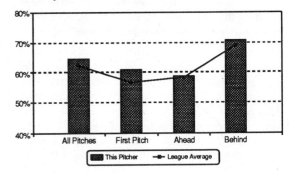

1991 Situational Stats

	W	L	ERA	Sv	IP		AB	H	HR	RBI	AVG
Home	7	5	3.45	0	127.2	LHB	587	148	14	65	.252
Road	8	6	3.26	0	135.1	RHB	392	84	4	29	.214
Day	7	8	3.72	0	138.0	Sc Pos	212	55	4	70	.259
Night	8	3	2.95	0	125.0	Clutch	111	37	2	17	.333

1991 Rankings (National League)

→ 1st in games started (37), innings (263) and batters faced (1,070)

→ 2nd in strikeouts (198) and pitches thrown (3,658)

→ 3rd in groundball/flyball ratio (2.4)

→ Led the Cubs in ERA (3.35), wins (15), losses (11), games started, complete games (7), shutouts (2), innings, hits allowed (232), batters faced, most home runs allowed (18), walks allowed (66), hit batsmen (6), strikeouts, pitches thrown, pickoff throws (168), most stolen bases allowed (25), winning percentage (.577) and sacrifice bunts as a batter (11)

PITCHING:

Chuck McElroy, who came to the Cubs on Opening Day along with Bob Scanlan in the Mitch Williams trade, was not met with great expectations by the Chicago organization or media. After the Dave Smith bomb went off, however, and McElroy kept pitching inning after scoreless inning of relief, the 23-year-old rookie's work began to draw more and more attention.

McElroy is a bespectacled lefthander with an exceptionally smooth, compact three-quarter arm delivery. His fastball crackles with authority up to 92 MPH and he complements it with a quick-breaking slider and above-average splitter. He occasionally throws some offspeed stuff with mixed results; he's better off spotting the slider and busting his good heat inside. McElroy is an extremely quick worker, sometimes too quick, causing him to lose strike-zone command. He walked 57 in 101.1 innings, a figure he needs to improve. He's already shown his dominance over left-handed hitters, holding them to a .172 batting average last year.

McElroy had a chance to wrest the left-handed closer role from Paul Assenmacher in mid-August, but blew a save and was sent back to set-up duty. He also blew two saves in October, when all semblance of control briefly left him. These situations indicated an inability to pitch effectively when he fell behind in the count.

HOLDING RUNNERS, HITTING, FIELDING:

McElroy has a very sneaky move that runners must be conscious of; baserunners were only 12-for-22 with him on the mound. He has good balance after his release and fields his position well. He is a good athlete, runs well, and is no slouch at the plate.

OVERALL:

McElroy has an excellent chance of nailing down a left-handed closer role with the Cubs next season. If he works on his control and stays composed, he has the arm to handle late-relief duties. His performance thus far has certainly helped take some of the sting off the re-emergence of Mitch Williams with Philadelphia.

CHUCK McELROY

Position: RP
Bats: L **Throws:** L
Ht: 6' 0" **Wt:** 160

Opening Day Age: 24
Born: 10/1/67 in Galveston, TX
ML Seasons: 3

Overall Statistics

	W	L	ERA	G	GS	Sv	IP	H	R	BB	SO	HR
1991	6	2	1.95	71	0	3	101.1	73	33	57	92	7
Career	6	3	2.58	98	0	3	125.2	109	48	71	116	8

How Often He Throws Strikes

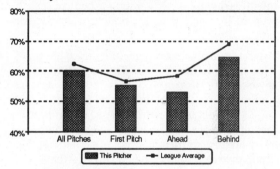

1991 Situational Stats

	W	L	ERA	Sv	IP		AB	H	HR	RBI	AVG
Home	3	1	1.53	3	58.2	LHB	122	21	3	15	.172
Road	3	1	2.53	0	42.2	RHB	225	52	4	23	.231
Day	4	0	1.32	2	54.2	Sc Pos	85	19	3	33	.224
Night	2	2	2.70	1	46.2	Clutch	147	36	3	13	.245

1991 Rankings (National League)

→ 1st in relief ERA (1.95)

→ 3rd in lowest batting average allowed vs. left-handed batters (.172) and relief innings (101.1)

→ 6th in games pitches (71) and lowest batting average allowed in relief (.210)

→ 7th in highest percentage of inherited runners scored (36.2%) and most strikeouts per 9 innings in relief (8.2)

→ Led the Cubs in lowest batting average allowed vs. left-handed batters, relief ERA and lowest batting average allowed in relief

HITTING:

The Rodney Dangerfield of his team, Luis Salazar has never been one to pop off about his irregular role as the sometime starting third baseman. Salazar might not get much respect, but when the Cubs are done with their yearly experiment at the hot corner, he always gets plenty of playing time.

While "rare" is not a word usually used in conjunction with Salazar, last season he attempted to join an elite group of players who have played in 100 or more games in a season and recorded more total home runs than walks (his teammate Shawon Dunston beat him into the group in 1990). With 14 HRs in 333 at-bats, Salazar's lone intentional walk of the season pushed his season total of free passes to 15, ruining a chance for immortality.

Salazar is an above-average utility third baseman who takes lefties downtown for a living; he smacked 10 HRs in 166 ABs in 1991 against southpaws. He is as undisciplined as a hitter can be. To paraphrase Deion Sanders, inside heat is the wife he loves, while breaking balls down and away are the girlfriends he could do without. He is effective at getting around on high fastballs and retains good bat speed.

BASERUNNING:

A below-average runner, Salazar doesn't try anything fancy on the bases except the occasional caught stealing. He grounded into the most double plays per opportunity on the club.

FIELDING:

Salazar does not have Matt Williams looking over his shoulder. His range is average, he makes big errors without ever making gems, and his relays when starting double plays are inconsistent. He can play first base with some ability if needed.

OVERALL:

Salazar is a useful player as a pinch-hitter and spot starter versus lefties, and could carry this role on a winning team. He will probably again lose playing time to the latest Cub third base prospect, whoever he may be -- at least for awhile.

LUIS SALAZAR

Position: 3B
Bats: R **Throws:** R
Ht: 5' 9" **Wt:** 180

Opening Day Age: 35
Born: 5/19/56 in
Barcelona, Venezuela
ML Seasons: 12

Overall Statistics

	G	AB	R	H	D	T	HR	RBI	SB	BB	SO	AVG
1991	103	333	34	86	14	1	14	38	0	15	45	.258
Career	1204	3846	418	1017	137	31	89	430	116	168	619	.264

Where He Hits the Ball

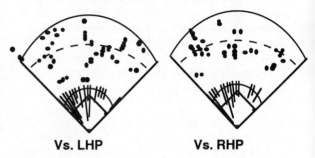

Vs. LHP   **Vs. RHP**

1991 Situational Stats

	AB	H	HR	RBI	AVG		AB	H	HR	RBI	AVG
Home	165	43	8	20	.261	LHP	166	45	10	25	.271
Road	168	43	6	18	.256	RHP	167	41	4	13	.246
Day	149	30	6	14	.201	Sc Pos	73	14	3	24	.192
Night	184	56	8	24	.304	Clutch	73	24	3	11	.329

1991 Rankings (National League)

➡ Did not rank near the top or bottom in any category

HITTING:

At first glance, his 1991 numbers look like expected fare from robotic Ryne Sandberg. The unlikelihood of another 40 home run season means Sandberg's power decline to 26 homers was to be expected, as was a slight drop in batting average to his career norm. Watching the star play game-in and game-out in '91, however, one could notice some significant changes in his approach.

In his career season of 1990, Sandberg tuned up righties to a .334 batting average, a .616 slugging percentage and 30 home runs; those figures dropped to .253, .441 and 18. The reason: Sandberg simply was not thrown anything on the inner half of the plate, his red zone. Doing what superstars do, Sandberg adjusted into the most patient phase of his career, resulting in a career-high 87 walks and .379 on-base percentage.

Sandberg's new attitude took its toll on lefties, as he hit a hundred points higher than in '90 for a league-leading .359 average against them. He handled lefty breaking balls better, smacking them to the right-center field gap, and was content to try and dump balls the opposite way when behind in the count.

BASERUNNING:

Sandberg remains one of the game's heady base thieves despite only above-average acceleration from first base. With his 22 steals, Sandberg surpassed 20 SBs for the ninth time in 10 seasons, a career 78% success rate. His baserunning is nearly flawless.

FIELDING:

The man of streaks, Sandberg's latest is 730+ straight assist streak without a throwing error. He is nonpareil in turning two, and while his range is not the league's best, he still makes the sublime routine, and vice versa.

OVERALL:

One has to look hard for flaws in Ryne Sandberg, given his new-found patience. After getting a badly-bruised hand close to the break and being diagnosed as out for over a week, Sandberg returned within two games and played well. Barring injury in the next two years, he will become baseball's all-time home run hitting second baseman.

RYNE SANDBERG

Position: 2B
Bats: R **Throws:** R
Ht: 6' 2" **Wt:** 180

Opening Day Age: 32
Born: 9/18/59 in Spokane, WA
ML Seasons: 11

Overall Statistics

	G	AB	R	H	D	T	HR	RBI	SB	BB	SO	AVG
1991	158	585	104	170	32	2	26	100	22	87	89	.291
Career	1547	6093	976	1753	288	59	205	749	297	551	875	.288

Where He Hits the Ball

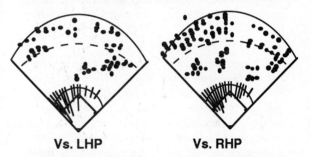

Vs. LHP   **Vs. RHP**

1991 Situational Stats

	AB	H	HR	RBI	AVG		AB	H	HR	RBI	AVG
Home	291	90	15	54	.309	LHP	209	75	8	27	.359
Road	294	80	11	46	.272	RHP	376	95	18	73	.253
Day	289	93	13	47	.322	Sc Pos	136	46	8	70	.338
Night	296	77	13	53	.260	Clutch	111	28	3	19	.252

1991 Rankings (National League)

→ 1st in batting average vs. left-handed pitchers (.359), on-base average vs. left-handed pitches (.456) and fielding percentage at second base (.995)

→ 3rd in runs (104) and pitches seen (2,716)

→ 4th in times on base (259), plate appearances (684) and games (158)

→ Led the Cubs in batting average (.291), runs, hits (170), doubles (32), total bases (284), caught stealing (8), walks (87), times on base, strikeouts (89), pitches seen, on-base average (.379), pitches seen per plate appearance (3.97), most runs scored per time reached base (40.1%) and batting average with runners in scoring position (.338)

PITCHING:

Traded to the Cubs in the Mitch Williams deal last spring, Bob Scanlan left Philadelphia convinced that he simply needed to be given an opportunity to pitch. As it turned out, he came to the right place, and may have salvaged a chance for a big league career in the Cubs bullpen.

Though Scanlan has a 94-MPH fastball, nothing in his minor league stats suggested he could be an effective major league pitcher. Put in the Cub rotation in early May, he showed off a wide array of mediocre pitches, including a curve, slider, straight change and splitter. One big problem hindered Scanlan in the minors: a growing loss of control that forced him to bring in his hard-but-straight heater. Nevertheless, he achieved instant success in his first four starts (a Cub specialty), and credited former pitching coach Jim Wright with improving his strike-zone command.

The improvement was illusory, as Scanlan's old control problems re-emerged; rather than allow walks, he forced too many fastballs in the hitting zone on favorable counts. Scanlan was switched to the bullpen, where he had some success in short, hard-throwing stints. He pitched inside, and exhibited an ability to consistently throw strikes, although strikeouts were infrequent. Scanlan fanned only 44 men in 111 innings, not exactly a closer-type ratio.

HOLDING RUNNERS, HITTING, FIELDING:

Scanlan needs a ton of work on his mound fundamentals. He is slow off the mound and has an erratic arm, coupled with unsure instincts. His move is good enough to hamper opposition runners. Scanlan ranks among the worst hitting pitchers in the N.L. (1 for 24 in '91).

OVERALL:

The Scanlan saga is not over, as he was sent to winter ball with whispers about having a shot at becoming the Cubs' right-handed closer. Given Scanlan's inability to blow hitters away despite his great fastball, the closer spot may be a bit of wishful thinking. But with better control this season, Scanlan can definitely help the Cub bullpen.

BOB SCANLAN

Position: RP/SP
Bats: R **Throws:** R
Ht: 6' 7" **Wt:** 215

Opening Day Age: 25
Born: 8/9/66 in Los Angeles, CA
ML Seasons: 1

Overall Statistics

	W	L	ERA	G	GS	Sv	IP	H	R	BB	SO	HR
1991	7	8	3.89	40	13	1	111.0	114	60	40	44	5
Career	7	8	3.89	40	13	1	111.0	114	60	40	44	5

How Often He Throws Strikes

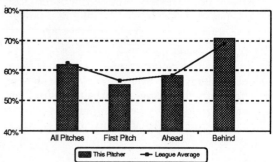

1991 Situational Stats

	W	L	ERA	Sv	IP		AB	H	HR	RBI	AVG
Home	5	5	5.49	1	59.0	LHB	225	58	2	25	.258
Road	2	3	2.08	0	52.0	RHB	199	56	3	30	.281
Day	3	4	5.33	0	54.0	Sc Pos	126	40	2	50	.317
Night	4	4	2.53	1	57.0	Clutch	72	15	1	7	.208

1991 Rankings (National League)

➡ Led the Cubs in errors by a pitcher (2)

PITCHING:

The man with the unusual name, Heathcliff Slocumb was the Cubs' only rookie pitcher to come north last spring. It would be nice to report that Slocumb also had an unusual amount of success, but in fact Slocumb was sent to AAA Iowa in August to work on throwing strikes. His work was hardly a disaster, however, with a 3.45 ERA in 52 games.

Slocumb is basically a power pitcher, with a 90-MPH fastball and a tough-breaking slider. Those pitches are effective enough when he gets ahead in the count and can mix in a mid-80s cut fastball. Slocumb continually works low in the zone, and is prone to throwing his slider in the dirt. He tossed a club-leading nine wild pitches in 62.2 innings. Keeping the ball down, Slocumb is very stingy in allowing the gopher ball; despite pitching in Wrigley Field, he allowed only three homers last year, all to lefties. His slider is very tough versus righties, who hit only .180 against him.

Developing confidence in his pitches is essential if Slocumb is going to improve. Given a brief shot at closing games last summer, he blew two of three saves with wildness and overthrown balls. He couldn't be used on a daily basis, either; when pitching on consecutive days, he allowed 15 earned runs in only 20.2 IP.

HOLDING RUNNERS, FIELDING, HITTING:

Along with control of his pitches, Slocumb needs to learn to control the running game. He is prone to absolute forgetfulness with baserunners, and his pickoff move is hardly deceptive. Runners stole 12 of 13 successfully with Slocumb pitching. His fielding prowess is average.

OVERALL:

With the anticipated departure of Les Lancaster and the uncertainty surrounding Dave Smith and Bob Scanlan, Slocumb has a chance to nail down a role in the Cub bullpen this year. Slocumb would love to be a closer or a set-up man, but he needs a lot of improvement before he can be effective in those roles.

HEATHCLIFF SLOCUMB

Position: RP
Bats: R **Throws:** R
Ht: 6' 3" **Wt:** 210

Opening Day Age: 25
Born: 6/7/66 in Jamaica, NY
ML Seasons: 1

Overall Statistics

	W	L	ERA	G	GS	Sv	IP	H	R	BB	SO	HR
1991	2	1	3.45	52	0	1	62.2	53	29	30	34	3
Career	2	1	3.45	52	0	1	62.2	53	29	30	34	3

How Often He Throws Strikes

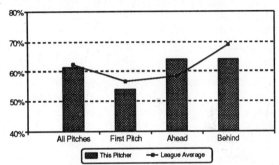

1991 Situational Stats

	W	L	ERA	Sv	IP		AB	H	HR	RBI	AVG
Home	2	0	3.00	1	33.0	LHB	107	31	3	14	.290
Road	0	1	3.94	0	29.2	RHB	122	22	0	16	.180
Day	2	0	4.99	1	30.2	Sc Pos	90	19	1	24	.211
Night	0	1	1.97	0	32.0	Clutch	55	10	1	8	.182

1991 Rankings (National League)

→ 3rd least GDPs induced per GDP situation (2.0%)

→ 4th in first batter efficiency (.146)

→ 6th least strikeouts per 9 innings in relief (4.9)

→ Led the Cubs in wild pitches (9), first batter efficiency and lowest percentage of inherited runners scored (32.5%)

PITCHING:

It would be impossible to imagine a much more disastrous campaign for a stopper than that of Dave Smith in 1991. While some skeptics predicted failure in his move from the Astrodome to Wrigley Field, no one could have foreseen the depths to which Smith would fall.

As with his free agent compadre Danny Jackson, injuries plagued Smith all season long. But unlike Jackson, the belief is that there was more behind his ineffectiveness than the back spasms and arm swelling Smith experienced. Smith has never had much velocity; he relies upon his good split-finger pitch frequently and mixes in an occasional mid-80s fastball, slow curve, and change-up. Able to get by with guile, knowledge of the hitters, and the occasional long fly ball while in the Astrodome, Smith's control of the splitter was not sharp enough to survive at Wrigley.

There was one brief bright spot in Smith's winless, six-blown-save season that gives the Cubs hope. In May he was flawless, racking up seven saves in seven tries and allowing no runs for the month. But the success was short-lived. Smith had no prayer against lefties, who slugged close to .700.

HOLDING RUNNERS, HITTING, FIELDING:

Smith is an accomplished fielder who knows the game situation at all times and never makes mistakes. His pickoff move is fair and his quick delivery helps keep runners from getting a big jump. But without velocity it was still impossible for the Cub catchers to stop any of the three stolen bases he permitted.

OVERALL:

After saving 16 of 21 games in the first half, Smith evaluated himself at a "C" level to the local media. He blew the first game after the break, and saved only one more the rest of the way, which surely dropped that grade to "F." Whether the "F" stands for "finished" will depend on the 37 year old's health and split-finger control.

DAVE SMITH

Position: RP
Bats: R **Throws:** R
Ht: 6' 1" **Wt:** 195

Opening Day Age: 37
Born: 1/21/55 in San Francisco, CA
ML Seasons: 12

Overall Statistics

	W	L	ERA	G	GS	Sv	IP	H	R	BB	SO	HR
1991	0	6	6.00	35	0	17	33.0	39	22	19	16	6
Career	53	53	2.67	598	1	216	795.1	685	276	279	545	34

How Often He Throws Strikes

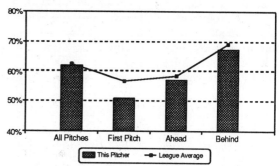

1991 Situational Stats

	W	L	ERA	Sv	IP		AB	H	HR	RBI	AVG
Home	0	3	5.60	10	17.2	LHB	74	28	4	21	.378
Road	0	3	6.46	7	15.1	RHB	55	11	2	7	.200
Day	0	3	6.38	10	18.1	Sc Pos	43	13	2	20	.302
Night	0	3	5.52	7	14.2	Clutch	99	33	5	24	.333

1991 Rankings (National League)

→ 4th lowest save percentage (73.9%)

→ 7th in saves (17) and blown saves (6)

→ 8th in save opportunites (23) and relief losses (6)

→ Led the Cubs in saves and save percentage

PITCHING:

In a season of personal dramatics, Rick Sutcliffe spurned injury, demotion, ineffectiveness and even retirement to finish the 1991 season very strongly. As the Cubs' lone free agent, no one would accuse the top-notch competitor of putting on a salary drive, but Sutcliffe's string of excellent August/September outings revived almost extinct marketability.

Coming off arm surgery in 1990, the 35-year-old righthander came out of the chute in mid-April throwing fairly effectively despite a lack of usual velocity and movement on his pitches. This caught up with him by the end of May and he was first sent to the bullpen, then the DL. While rehabbing in the minors, Sutcliffe was despondent enough to talk about retiring. To the rescue came an old friend, pitching coach Billy Connors, who fixed his delivery and stride, and the results proved to Sutcliffe his arm was fine. On August 11, Sutcliffe faced a no-out bases loaded jam already trailing 2-0. Connors came out to the mound, Sutcliffe wriggled free, and from that point on he had a superb win-loss record of 4-1.

Sutcliffe relies on mixing his basic four pitches in and out to the batter. His curve and slider started breaking much more sharply in August and his velocity returned to average levels. He remained very tough on righties with his characteristic tricky slider, inducing many ground ball double plays.

HOLDING RUNNERS, FIELDING, HITTING:

Sutcliffe has a good quick move to first, but his exaggeratedly slow delivery makes him one of the league's easiest pitchers to run on. Opponents stole 21 of 23 against Sutcliffe. He is very slow off the mound despite good instincts, and can be bunted on.

OVERALL:

Not all the Cub pitching stories were dismal, Sutcliffe proved. His 2.33 ERA after the break may go a long way in his bank account, but the money may not come from Chicago. Thanks to Connors' save, a team should find interest in the apparently healthy veteran gamer. He could fill a number-four spot on a winning team.

RICK SUTCLIFFE

Position: SP
Bats: L **Throws:** R
Ht: 6' 7" **Wt:** 215

Opening Day Age: 35
Born: 6/21/56 in Independence, MO
ML Seasons: 15

Overall Statistics

	W	L	ERA	G	GS	Sv	IP	H	R	BB	SO	HR
1991	6	5	4.10	19	18	0	96.2	96	52	45	52	4
Career	139	110	3.84	376	314	6	2227.0	2106	1036	901	1464	182

How Often He Throws Strikes

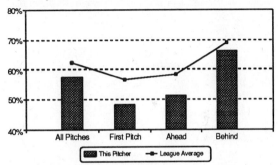

1991 Situational Stats

	W	L	ERA	Sv	IP		AB	H	HR	RBI	AVG
Home	3	1	3.18	0	56.2	LHB	218	63	4	30	.289
Road	3	4	5.40	0	40.0	RHB	146	33	0	14	.226
Day	3	2	3.97	0	45.1	Sc Pos	103	25	1	38	.243
Night	3	3	4.21	0	51.1	Clutch	7	2	0	0	.286

1991 Rankings (National League)

- ➡ 3rd most GDPs induced per GDP situation (19.4%)
- ➡ Led the Cubs in GDPs induced per GDP situation

HITTING:

"When I'm hitting, people say I'm strong. When I'm not hitting, they say I'm fat," complained Hector Villanueva during one of his common hitting tears during the '91 season. Such periods usually resulted in labored discussions by the Cubs on how to get Villanueva's potent bat into the everyday lineup.

This 6-1, 220 pound catcher can hit -- with 20 home runs, a .275 batting average, and a .529 slugging percentage in 306 at-bats since 1990, it's obvious. Villanueva gets into grooves during which he becomes as good as any hitter on the team: last September, he took his frustrations out on opposing pitchers by batting .333 in 22 games with five homers, 11 RBI, a .395 on-base percentage and a .638 slugging percentage.

A patient hitter, Villanueva dares pitchers to throw him fastballs that he can pull, and he has had success in hitting breaking ball mistakes. His short, powerful arms make him prey to outside nibbling, but so far his good eye has kept this from blossoming into a larger weakness.

BASERUNNING:

Villanueva is about as slow a runner as there is in the National League, which is certainly detrimental to him hitting higher than sixth or seventh in the order.

FIELDING:

Villanueva showed a little improvement as a catcher last year, but even after gunning down six Cardinals in his last two games, his caught stealing percentage was a lowly 28%. Villanueva does less harm at first base, but the Cubs already have Mark Grace there.

OVERALL:

Villanueva again went to play winter ball in Puerto Rico where he won the triple crown after the 1990 major league season. This year he wanted to work on his catching, but upon arrival found that his teammate Rick Wilkins had also been signed to his winter-league team. Shifted to first base as a result, Villanueva's career as a full-time catcher with the Cubs seems to be at a dead-end. If he shows an ability to field at first base, however, the Cubs may realize some interesting trade possibilities.

HECTOR VILLANUEVA

Position: C
Bats: R **Throws:** R
Ht: 6' 1" **Wt:** 220

Opening Day Age: 27
Born: 10/2/64 in San Juan, Puerto Rico
ML Seasons: 2

Overall Statistics

	G	AB	R	H	D	T	HR	RBI	SB	BB	SO	AVG
1991	71	192	23	53	10	1	13	32	0	21	30	.276
Career	123	306	37	84	14	2	20	50	1	25	57	.275

Where He Hits the Ball

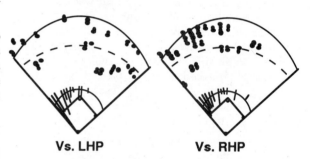

Vs. LHP   Vs. RHP

1991 Situational Stats

	AB	H	HR	RBI	AVG		AB	H	HR	RBI	AVG
Home	105	34	11	24	.324	LHP	100	28	6	16	.280
Road	87	19	2	8	.218	RHP	92	25	7	16	.272
Day	95	30	9	18	.316	Sc Pos	43	10	3	17	.233
Night	97	23	4	14	.237	Clutch	44	12	1	5	.273

1991 Rankings (National League)

➡ Did not rank near the top or bottom in any category

HITTING:

A journeyman of 15 pro seasons, most of which were spent in the minors, Chico Walker finally put in a full major league season in 1991. Walker's switch-hitting and multi-position abilities helped him land a job in the spring, and when the season had ended, Walker had compiled nearly as many big league at-bats (374) as he had in his first 15 years combined (377).

Though a semi-regular, Walker's greatest contribution came as a pinch hitter, batting .406 with 13 pinch hits and a .500 on-base percentage. A lack of ability to hit right-handed didn't deter Jim Essian from playing Walker full-time as a third baseman against righties and center fielder against lefties. Batting left-handed, Walker is a fairly patient hitter who can hit anyone's fastball, occasionally for power. He is content to go to the opposite field when behind in the count. Against southpaws, he is eaten up by breaking stuff and rarely has a good at-bat unless he gets a high heater to drive.

BASERUNNING:

Lacking dazzling speed, Walker nevertheless is an effective base stealer. He can read a pitcher's moves and usually gets a good jump, traits he learned after swiping 413 bases in his minor league career. A great bunter, Walker occasionally beat out bunt hits.

FIELDING:

Walker shuttled between center field and third all season and was not especially effective at either position. He is better in center, where he is tentative picking up the ball but generally sure-handed. At the hot corner, Walker is often cold; he is uncomfortable with hard-hit shots and lets the ball play him. He has stated his dislike for playing third.

OVERALL:

Walker is a pleasant, native South Side Chicagoan whom fans liked to pull for as the underdog. He should find a position on the bench as a utility player next season. If he winds up with any amount of playing time resembling that of 1991, though, the Cubs will surely be in the midst of another long season.

CHICO WALKER

Position: 3B/CF
Bats: B **Throws:** R
Ht: 5' 9" **Wt:** 170

Opening Day Age: 34
Born: 11/25/57 in Jackson, MS
ML Seasons: 9

Overall Statistics

	G	AB	R	H	D	T	HR	RBI	SB	BB	SO	AVG
1991	124	374	51	96	10	1	6	34	13	33	57	.257
Career	285	751	106	178	18	5	8	59	45	68	133	.237

Where He Hits the Ball

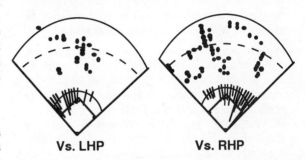

Vs. LHP   Vs. RHP

1991 Situational Stats

	AB	H	HR	RBI	AVG		AB	H	HR	RBI	AVG
Home	200	54	4	19	.270	LHP	119	25	3	12	.210
Road	174	42	2	15	.241	RHP	255	71	3	22	.278
Day	189	48	3	11	.254	Sc Pos	84	24	2	28	.286
Night	185	48	3	23	.259	Clutch	95	31	1	11	.326

1991 Rankings (National League)

→ 4th lowest leadoff on-base average (.306) and lowest on-base average vs. left-handed pitchers (.256)

→ 9th lowest batting average vs. left-handed pitchers (.210)

HITTING:

Only two seasons removed from winning the 1989 Rookie of the Year award, Jerome Walton has endured a steady and mysterious decline. After suffering an injury-filled sophomore season, expectations were that Walton would re-emerge in '91 as a productive leadoff hitter. Instead, Walton disappeared.

After showing some patience in 1990 (.350 on-base percentage), Walton began last season as the Cubs leadoff hitter, but drew just two walks in his first 35 games. After Walton compiled a .238 OBP in May, the Cubs started to explore other center field options. New manager Jim Essian gave Walton a chance in June, but Walton failed to improve. Essian then buried the '89 hero so deep on the bench he could only manage 79 at-bats for a .139 average in the second half.

Walton has exaggerated his hitting weaknesses with a confused batting stance that causes him to dive in to the plate in an effort to pull the ball. He is easy prey for inside fastballs and waves feebly at sliders. Despite coaches' efforts to change his stance to help versus lefties, Walton still can't get comfortable; he seems uninterested in just making contact or looking for a walk.

BASERUNNING:

Walton didn't get on base enough to display what is normally fine speed. He stole seven bases in 10 attempts, but ran the bases as if in a fog at times.

FIELDING:

Accompanying his hitting dropoff were small slides in Walton's fielding ability. In the past, Walton was a shallow-playing gambler who had the range to pick off balls in the gaps. Walton showed little intensity and committed notable mental errors in 1991. He had average range and, even though his arm is weak, was still used to replace Chico Walker late in games.

OVERALL:

Potential seems to be an albatross around the neck of Jerome Walton. He certainly might regroup at age 26, but in '91 he showed an odd lack of spark or desire to improve himself. A trade to a turf-playing team might help him.

JEROME WALTON

Position: CF
Bats: R **Throws:** R
Ht: 6' 1" **Wt:** 175

Opening Day Age: 26
Born: 7/8/65 in Newnan, GA
ML Seasons: 3

Overall Statistics

	G	AB	R	H	D	T	HR	RBI	SB	BB	SO	AVG
1991	123	270	42	59	13	1	5	17	7	19	55	.219
Career	340	1137	169	301	52	6	12	84	45	96	202	.265

Where He Hits the Ball

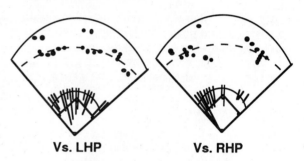

Vs. LHP   Vs. RHP

1991 Situational Stats

	AB	H	HR	RBI	AVG		AB	H	HR	RBI	AVG
Home	120	27	3	6	.225	LHP	128	25	0	6	.195
Road	150	32	2	11	.213	RHP	142	34	5	11	.239
Day	128	29	1	7	.227	Sc Pos	52	9	0	11	.173
Night	142	30	4	10	.211	Clutch	56	9	1	6	.161

1991 Rankings (National League)

→ 1st in lowest leadoff on-base average (.264), lowest slugging percentage vs. left-handed pitchers (.242) and lowest fielding percentage in center field (.983)

→ 5th lowest batting average in the clutch (.161)

→ 6th lowest on-base average vs. left-handed pitchers (.261)

→ 7th lowest batting average vs. left-handed pitchers (.195)

→ 9th lowest percentage of extra bases taken as a runner (30.0%)

HITTING:

Left-handed hitting Rick Wilkins is the latest in a line of promising young catchers to visit Wrigley Field for a summer. If Wilkins can make offensive adjustments to major league pitching, he might be able to last longer than Damon Berryhill and Joe Girardi.

Wilkins has exhibited good power at all his minor league stops, and impressed the Cubs with homers in three straight games in late June. However, there is not much more than the home run in Wilkins' offensive arsenal; he never hit above .251 in four minor league seasons before 1991, and batted only .186 after the All-Star break for the Cubs last year.

Opposing pitchers found out that Wilkins could handle major league heat after he slugged .537 in June. They soon discovered he was far less competent with breaking balls and hard sliders, which became his bland diet the rest of the season. Wilkins showed signs of adjusting after bottoming out in an 0-for-20 streak, but Hector Villanueva kept him watching from the bench in the fall. Wilkins has a fairly good eye, but his long swing makes him prone to the strikeout.

BASERUNNING:

Wilkins possesses fairly good speed, which allowed him to steal three bases in six attempts for the Cubs. He was often used as a runner and defensive replacement for Villanueva.

FIELDING:

Wilkins is an excellent receiver with a beautiful release and strong arm. While occasionally hurrying his throws, he gunned down a who's who of National League base stealers on the way to a 39% caught stealing rate. He was timed at 3.1 seconds (from catch, through throw, to reception at second base) in nabbing Otis Nixon.

OVERALL:

Catchers with Wilkins' defensive ability invariably win jobs in the major leagues. Although he was hyped by some media members as a future All-Star, that seems unlikely. A more accurate projection would be a career similar to that of his crosstown backstop Ron Karkovice: defensive specialist with some power but a limited batting average.

RICK
WILKINS

Position: C
Bats: L **Throws:** R
Ht: 6' 2" **Wt:** 210

Opening Day Age: 24
Born: 7/4/67 in
Jacksonville, FL
ML Seasons: 1

Overall Statistics

	G	AB	R	H	D	T	HR	RBI	SB	BB	SO	AVG
1991	86	203	21	45	9	0	6	22	3	19	56	.222
Career	86	203	21	45	9	0	6	22	3	19	56	.222

Where He Hits the Ball

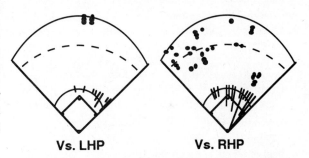

Vs. LHP   **Vs. RHP**

1991 Situational Stats

	AB	H	HR	RBI	AVG		AB	H	HR	RBI	AVG
Home	103	18	2	9	.175	LHP	38	9	1	5	.237
Road	100	27	4	13	.270	RHP	165	36	5	17	.218
Day	107	17	2	9	.159	Sc Pos	43	10	2	17	.233
Night	96	28	4	13	.292	Clutch	46	14	1	5	.304

1991 Rankings (National League)

- → 6th in hit by pitch (6)
- → 10th lowest batting average with 2 strikes (.135)
- → Led the Cubs in hit by pitch
- → Led NL catchers in sacrifice bunts (7)

SHAWN BOSKIE

Position: SP/RP
Bats: R **Throws:** R
Ht: 6' 3" **Wt:** 205

Opening Day Age: 25
Born: 3/28/67 in
Hawthorne, NV
ML Seasons: 2

Overall Statistics

	W	L	ERA	G	GS	Sv	IP	H	R	BB	SO	HR
1991	4	9	5.23	28	20	0	129.0	150	78	52	62	14
Career	9	15	4.57	43	35	0	226.2	249	120	83	111	22

PITCHING, FIELDING, HITTING & HOLDING RUNNERS:

Shawn Boskie entered the 1991 season in the Cubs' rotation after a respectable rookie campaign which ended early due to elbow surgery. After cruising through his first few starts, the 25 year old endured a winless slump that stretched from late April to mid-June (eight starts). The slump destroyed Boskie's confidence and put his Cub future in jeopardy.

Boskie throws four undistinguished pitches, the best of which is a sporadically effective curveball. Lacking the confidence to throw his breaking ball early in the count, Boskie starts off too many hitters with juicy mid-80s fastballs. In general, his fastball has little movement and he tends to get it up in the zone, a certain recipe for failure in The Friendly Confines. Boskie allowed 14 HRs in his 129 IP, including 10 to lefties, who wore him out all season.

Seemingly distracted by his mound woes, Boskie made two throwing errors which cost the Cubs wins. He is a nimble athlete and has some hitting ability.

OVERALL:

After the season, Boskie headed to the Dominican winter league to work on a split-fingered pitch and control of his breaking stuff. He needs both improvements to make the Cubs' opportunity-laden staff: he hasn't regained his old velocity since the surgery and thus needs to be ultra-fine.

CED LANDRUM

Position: CF/LF
Bats: L **Throws:** R
Ht: 5' 7" **Wt:** 167

Opening Day Age: 28
Born: 9/3/63 in Butler, AL
ML Seasons: 1

Overall Statistics

	G	AB	R	H	D	T	HR	RBI	SB	BB	SO	AVG
1991	56	86	28	20	2	1	0	6	27	10	18	.233
Career	56	86	28	20	2	1	0	6	27	10	18	.233

HITTING, FIELDING, BASERUNNING:

The Cubs single season stolen base record was set 88 years ago by Frank Chance with 67. Blinding-fast Ced Landrum has an outside shot at the record if he can hit consistently enough.

A rookie at age 27, Landrum forced his way to the big leagues after posting a league-leading .336 average for two months at AAA Iowa last year; that came on the heels of a .296 campaign with Iowa in 1990. Despite the good minor league numbers, there is still doubt about whether Landrum can hit well enough to stick. The 5-7, 167-pound Landrum looks like he can't get around on a good fastball. Landrum has absolutely no power and has been trained well to keep the ball on the ground when he does make contact. He often tries to work the count for a walk, intelligently.

Landrum's great speed allowed him to swipe 27 of 32 bases, mainly as a pinch runner. It's virtually impossible for a catcher to nab him when he gets even a slight jump. His good outfield range rivals that of the pre-1991 Jerome Walton.

OVERALL:

With as much speed as any player in baseball, Landrum may sprint his way into the plodding Cub lineup. Landrum headed to winter ball to practice the bunt-and-slap. The Cubs have visions of an Otis Nixon-clone jump-starting the top of their order.

DWIGHT SMITH

Position: RF/CF
Bats: L **Throws:** R
Ht: 5'11" **Wt:** 175

Opening Day Age: 28
Born: 11/8/63 in
Tallahassee, FL
ML Seasons: 3

Overall Statistics

	G	AB	R	H	D	T	HR	RBI	SB	BB	SO	AVG
1991	90	167	16	38	7	2	3	21	2	11	32	.228
Career	316	800	102	225	41	8	18	100	22	70	129	.281

HITTING, FIELDING, BASERUNNING:

Dwight Smith, the other half of the Cubs Rookie-of-the-Year disappearing duo along with Jerome Walton, had all the makings of a professional hitter until about halfway through the 1990 season. Since then, the highlight for Smith was singing the national anthem before a game at Wrigley in 1991. With the way he hit last season, it was prudent for him to be checking out an alternative profession.

Formerly an excellent hitter against righties, Smith batted just .235 against them in 1991. He has become easy prey for high heat and has started swinging from his heels on breaking stuff. Last year Smith alternated between slap-happy passivity and pull-hungry over-aggressiveness, and never received enough playing time to get into a groove.

Considered a poor left fielder with an average arm at best, Smith was used in center by Jim Essian last year. The experiment will not be repeated. His baserunning, once excellent, is now shoddy and he is clearly not as fast as he used to be.

OVERALL:

Despite a rocky last two years, Smith is only 28 and showed some real hitting ability in the not-too-distant past. With a more mature approach and flexible stance, he could return as an extremely valuable left-handed stick in a fresh environment.

JOSE VIZCAINO

Position: SS/3B
Bats: B **Throws:** R
Ht: 6' 1" **Wt:** 180

Opening Day Age: 24
Born: 3/26/68 in
Palenque de San
Cristobal, Dominican
Republic
ML Seasons: 3

Overall Statistics

	G	AB	R	H	D	T	HR	RBI	SB	BB	SO	AVG
1991	93	145	7	38	5	0	0	10	2	5	18	.262
Career	137	206	12	54	6	1	0	12	3	9	27	.262

HITTING, FIELDING, BASERUNNING:

Shortstop Jose Vizcaino joined the Cubs before the '91 season, mostly as a hedge in case Shawon Dunston left via free agency when the campaign ended. When Dunston struggled after Don Zimmer was removed, Vizcaino worked himself into an unacknowledged semi-platoon with Dunston under new manager Jim Essian. Unfortunately for Jose, the more the Cubs watched Vizcaino's fly-weight bat, the more they began to appreciate Dunston. If it's any comfort to Vizcaino, he may have helped Dunston became baseball's richest shortstop.

Lacking both extra-base power and plate discipline, Vizcaino has marginal effectiveness as a punch-type hitter against junkballing righties. A fly ball from Vizcaino occurs slightly more frequently than a major league minority hiring.

Vizcaino runs very well, and has some potential as a basestealer. His greatest strength is in the field, where he shows good range and a fine arm at shortstop as well as an ability to play second and third.

OVERALL:

Vizcaino picked up in '91 where Curtis Wilkerson left off for the Cubs. That being said, Vizcaino has a decent chance to improve into a useful backup infielder who can steal a base and play solid defense. The question is whether at age 24 (and after 200 major league at-bats) he's ready to accept that role for good.

ORGANIZATION OVERVIEW:

When Dallas Green took over the Cubs in the early 1980s, he candidly admitted that the club's player development program was a disaster. That became his top priority, and over the next few years the Cubs began producing players like Lee Smith, Rafael Palmeiro, Mark Grace and Shawon Dunston. Green was later deposed, and the Jim Frey regime wasn't able to produce the same kind of talent. Now Larry Himes, the man who built the current White Sox, has taken over on the North Side. Expect improvement, but expect it to take a few years.

LANCE DICKSON

Position: P
Bats: R **Throws:** L
Ht: 6' 1" **Wt:** 185
Opening Day Age: 22
Born: 10/19/69 in Fullerton, CA

Recent Statistics

	W	L	ERA	G	GS	Sv	IP	H	R	BB	SO	HR
90 A Geneva	2	1	0.53	3	3	0	17.0	5	1	4	29	1
90 A Peoria	3	1	1.51	5	5	0	35.2	22	9	11	54	1
90 AA Charlotte	2	1	0.38	3	3	0	23.2	13	1	3	28	0
90 MAJ Chicago	0	3	7.24	3	3	0	13.2	20	12	4	4	2
91 AAA Iowa	4	4	3.11	18	18	0	101.1	85	39	57	101	5

The Frey regime had some bad luck, especially in the case of Dickson. The Cubs' first draft choice in 1990, he was supposed to do for the Cubbies what Jack McDowell did for the White Sox. Dickson has a major league curveball, but his progress has been delayed by bizarre injuries -- a leg infection in 1990, a stress fracture in his foot in 1991. Between injuries he did some solid work at AAA Iowa, and unless a safe falls on his head (possible, considering his luck), he figures as a Cub starter this year.

ELVIN PAULINO

Position: 1B
Bats: L **Throws:** R
Ht: 6' 1" **Wt:** 190
Opening Day Age: 25
Born: 10/6/66 in Moca, DR

Recent Statistics

	G	AB	R	H	D	THR	RBI	SB	BB	SO	AVG
90 A Winston-sal	109	409	69	107	23	2	14	63	5	49	66	.262
91 AA Charlotte	132	460	67	118	27	1	24	81	9	55	110	.257
91 MLE	132	451	53	109	24	0	22	65	5	35	115	.242

If the Cubs grow weary of waiting for Mark Grace to develop some power, they might take a look at Paulino, a Dominican native who had a low-average, but high-power year in AA last year. Paulino has some speed, decent plate discipline, and intriguing home run power. He's increased his home run total every year since 1988. His play this year, presumably at AAA Iowa, will be closely watched.

YORKIS PEREZ

Position: P
Bats: L **Throws:** L
Ht: 6' 0" **Wt:** 160
Opening Day Age: 24
Born: 9/30/67 in Bajos De Haina, DR

Recent Statistics

	W	L	ERA	G	GS	Sv	IP	H	R	BB	SO	HR
91 AAA Richmond	12	3	3.79	36	10	1	107.0	99	47	53	102	7
91 NL Chicago	1	0	2.08	3	0	0	4.1	2	1	2	3	0

It's hard to believe Perez is only 24; he's been considered a prospect for a long time while moving from Minnesota to Montreal to Atlanta to Chicago. Perez was signed by the Twins at age 15, so he's done a lot of pitching for a 24 year old. He has an excellent fastball, but control problems have always held him back. His control improved at Richmond last year, and with Himes probably putting a premium on youthful new faces, Perez could see a lot of action out of the Cub bullpen this year.

REY SANCHEZ

Position: SS
Bats: R **Throws:** R
Ht: 5' 10" **Wt:** 180
Opening Day Age: 24
Born: 10/5/67 in Rio Piedras, PR

Recent Statistics

	G	AB	R	H	D	THR	RBI	SB	BB	SO	AVG
91 AAA Iowa	126	417	60	121	16	5	2	46	13	37	27	.290
91 NL Chicago	13	23	1	6	0	0	0	2	0	4	3	.261
91 MLE	126	400	43	104	13	2	1	33	7	25	27	.260

Rey Sanchez had this dream: he'd have a solid year at Iowa, the Cubs wouldn't re-sign free agent Shawon Dunston, and Sanchez would take over as the Chicago shortstop in 1992. Alas, the Cubs re-signed Dunston, so Sanchez might have to endure another year at AAA. It might not hurt, since he missed the entire 1990 season after elbow surgery. Sanchez has a decent glove and speed. He does not seem like the Gold Glove type, so his bat is the key. A utility role is possible.

TURK WENDELL

Position: P
Bats: L **Throws:** R
Ht: 6' 2" **Wt:** 175
Opening Day Age: 24
Born: 5/19/67 in Pittsfield, MA

Recent Statistics

	W	L	ERA	G	GS	Sv	IP	H	R	BB	SO	HR
91 AA Greenville	11	3	2.56	25	20	0	147.2	130	47	51	122	4
91 AAA Richmond	0	2	3.43	3	3	0	21.0	20	9	16	18	3

The Cubs are in both the baseball and TV businesses, and in Turk Wendell, who came to Chicago with Yorkis Perez for Mike Bielecki and Damon Berryhill, they might have someone who can pad both bottom lines. The Turk throws right but bats left, chews licorice on the mound, brushes his teeth between innings and won't catch a ball thrown by an umpire. Wendell's work last year indicates that he has major league stuff and every cable TV operator in America is praying that he's for real, not to mention the licorice and toothpaste manufacturers.

PITCHING:

Jack Armstrong's 1991 season began with a spring training walkout triggered by unhappiness with his contract. As things turned out, the Reds might have been happier if he had never come back. When the season ended they shipped the unhappy righthander upstate to Cleveland in the Greg Swindell deal.

All the wheels came off last year for the headstrong Armstrong. He was ineffective all season while being hampered by elbow problems and assorted other aches and pains -- physical woes which belie a ballyhooed fitness regimen that has not translated into pitching durability.

Armstrong's control had improved markedly in 1990, but last season he consistently pitched from behind in counts. He averaged three-and-a-half walks per nine innings with opposing hitters compiling a very high .354 on-base percentage against him.

Even more unsettling for the Reds was Armstrong's penchant for allowing home runs. Prior to the 1991 season, he had allowed 22 homers in 274 career innings of pitching. Last season, he was ripped for 25 homers in only 139.2 innings. The reason rested with his loss of control and loss of velocity on both his slider and high-80s fastball. Said one NL coach, "He hasn't overpowered anybody since those first dozen or so starts in 1990." One warning is the success enjoyed by right-handed batters against Armstrong. With his slider ineffective, righties batted over .300 against him.

HOLDING RUNNERS, FIELDING, HITTING:

Armstrong has a better than average pickoff move and a fairly quick delivery home which helps him combat base stealers. He also helps himself in the field because of his excellent athletic skills. Those skills don't extend to batting where he now has all of nine career hits in 102 at-bats.

OVERALL:

The All-American Boy now takes his act to Cleveland, where at least he'll begin with a clean slate. It's been a season and a half since he was a factor, and this is definitely a "put up or shut up" season for Armstrong.

JACK ARMSTRONG

Position: SP
Bats: R **Throws:** R
Ht: 6' 5" **Wt:** 215

Opening Day Age: 27
Born: 3/7/65 in Englewood, NJ
ML Seasons: 4

Overall Statistics

	W	L	ERA	G	GS	Sv	IP	H	R	BB	SO	HR
1991	7	13	5.48	27	24	0	139.2	158	90	54	93	25
Career	25	32	4.61	79	72	0	413.2	412	230	172	271	47

How Often He Throws Strikes

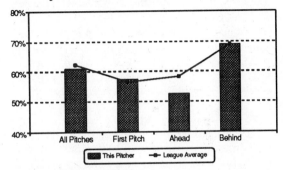

This Pitcher — League Average

1991 Situational Stats

	W	L	ERA	Sv	IP		AB	H	HR	RBI	AVG
Home	4	8	6.38	0	66.1	LHB	297	83	13	48	.279
Road	3	5	4.66	0	73.1	RHB	243	75	12	36	.309
Day	2	3	3.31	0	32.2	Sc Pos	113	41	7	59	.363
Night	5	10	6.14	0	107.0	Clutch	18	5	0	1	.278

1991 Rankings (National League)

→ 2nd most home runs allowed (25)

→ 4th lowest winning percentage (.350)

→ 6th most losses (13)

→ Led the Reds in pickoff throws (204) and runners caught stealing (8)

HITTING:

A valuable member of Cincinnati's 1990 championship team who saved the playoffs with a leaping, Game Six catch, Glenn Braggs had his 1991 season cut short by a midseason shoulder problem. The irony was that after doing nothing for the first two months, Braggs rebounded by late May and had his average up to .260 with 11 homers when his season finally ended after 85 games. Unfortunately for Braggs and the Reds, the injury could still have implications into this season.

Possessing one of the best builds in baseball, Braggs is a legitimate power threat when he can get his arms extended and turn on a fastball. Teams try to bust him inside with fastballs but must get in on his hands. If they don't get far enough inside, Braggs, a powerful pull hitter, will punish them. Lefthanders will waste breaking pitches away and he is also vulnerable to offspeed stuff. He hit 44 points better against lefties, but his power is comparable against righthanders.

BASERUNNING:

Braggs has above-average speed and has improved his selectivity in steal attempts. He was successful in 1991 on 11 of 14 attempts. He is also tough on the base paths. With his speed and huge frame, Braggs is not a very welcome sight for opposing middle infielders trying to turn double plays.

FIELDING:

Probably a better right fielder, Braggs nevertheless has to play left field for Cincinnati. His range is limited no matter where he plays and he also has poor hands, which results in a few drops every year. Before his shoulder was injured, Braggs had an above-average arm which now might be suspect.

OVERALL:

Until his injury, Braggs had overcome a slow start and seemed on his way to the 20 or 25-home run season long predicted for him. Assuming he returns to good health, this now could be a make-or-break year. He's young enough and talented enough to emerge as a quality front-line player.

GLENN BRAGGS

Position: LF/RF
Bats: R **Throws:** R
Ht: 6' 4" **Wt:** 220

Opening Day Age: 29
Born: 10/17/62 in San Bernardino, CA
ML Seasons: 6

Overall Statistics

	G	AB	R	H	D	T	HR	RBI	SB	BB	SO	AVG
1991	85	250	36	65	10	0	11	39	11	23	46	.260
Career	600	2070	268	538	86	13	62	283	55	175	424	.260

Where He Hits the Ball

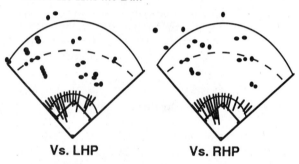

Vs. LHP   Vs. RHP

1991 Situational Stats

	AB	H	HR	RBI	AVG		AB	H	HR	RBI	AVG
Home	120	36	8	23	.300	LHP	124	35	5	23	.282
Road	130	29	3	16	.223	RHP	126	30	6	16	.238
Day	53	15	6	14	.283	Sc Pos	63	19	1	26	.302
Night	197	50	5	25	.254	Clutch	44	9	1	4	.205

1991 Rankings (National League)

➡ 1st in batting average on a 3-1 count (1.000)

WORKHORSE

TOM BROWNING

Position: SP
Bats: L **Throws:** L
Ht: 6' 1" **Wt:** 195

Opening Day Age: 31
Born: 4/28/60 in Casper, WY
ML Seasons: 8

PITCHING:

It wasn't the best of years for Tom Browning in 1991. He had the second-highest earned run average of his career, and though 32 games above .500 lifetime, he was only 14-14 last season. That said, it is a measure of his dependability that he was among league leaders in innings pitched and victories, as usual.

In an age when consistent 200-inning pitchers are becoming rare, Browning is a throwback. Since 1985, he has averaged 235 innings per season, more than any other National League pitcher. As one NL manager said, "Innings pitched is one of the most under-appreciated statistics in the game. When you have a guy who you know will pile up innings, it is a source of great security."

Browning's pitching style never changes much. He relies on his control, spotting a fastball which he turns over to right-handed hitters, and changing speeds which he does as well as anyone. However, his control can get him in trouble. Since he is always around the plate, he is annually among the league leaders in hits and home runs allowed. One NL scout says, "He doesn't overpower you, so if he's just off a little in his spots, he will get hit." Browning's hits-per-inning ratio has gone up each year since 1988, a source of at least minor concern to the Reds.

HOLDING RUNNERS, FIELDING, HITTING:

Browning has a good pickoff move to first and also quickens his delivery to the plate to aid his catchers in throwing out base stealers. He is also one of the best fielding pitchers in the NL. Browning is a better-than-average hitting pitcher, a dependable bunter and a deceptively good baserunner.

OVERALL:

Browning isn't necessarily the ace of the Cincinnati pitching staff with Jose Rijo around. But he's the glue that holds the rotation together. In an age when performance wildly fluctuates from year to year, no pitcher in baseball is more consistent than Browning.

Overall Statistics

	W	L	ERA	G	GS	Sv	IP	H	R	BB	SO	HR
1991	14	14	4.18	36	36	0	230.1	241	124	56	115	32
Career	107	75	3.80	256	255	0	1669.1	1617	774	445	889	205

How Often He Throws Strikes

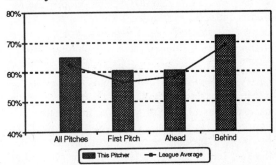

1991 Situational Stats

	W	L	ERA	Sv	IP		AB	H	HR	RBI	AVG
Home	10	4	3.50	0	121.0	LHB	212	43	4	22	.203
Road	4	10	4.94	0	109.1	RHB	694	198	28	92	.285
Day	6	6	3.66	0	91.0	Sc Pos	175	56	4	74	.320
Night	8	8	4.52	0	139.1	Clutch	71	23	3	9	.324

1991 Rankings (National League)

→ 1st in home runs allowed (32), highest slugging percentage allowed (.427), most home runs allowed per 9 innings (1.25) and highest batting average allowed with runners in scoring position (.320)

→ 2nd in games started (36), lowest ground-ball/flyball ratio (.85) and highest batting average allowed vs. right-handed pitchers (.285)

→ 3rd in highest ERA (4.18), losses (14), hits allowed (241) and batters faced (983)

→ Led the Reds in losses, games started, innings (230.1), hits allowed, batters faced, home runs allowed, pitches thrown (3,363) and most stolen bases allowed (21)

PITCHING:

Amid assorted physical woes, lefthander Norm Charlton bounced between the bullpen and the Reds rotation in 1991. He continued to pitch well when healthy last year (2.91 ERA), but after winning 12 games in 1990, he posted only three wins in 1991. All the shifting of both Charlton and Randy Myers was confusing, since one of the biggest factors in the Reds' 1990 success was the awesome bullpen combination of Charlton, Rob Dibble and Myers.

Many observers feel that Charlton still has not developed a varied enough pitching approach to make him an effective starter. When he's behind in counts, he relies too much on his fastball. And while he's maintained 90+ MPH velocity, he remains hittable. Opposing hitters have also become accustomed to his penchant for throwing inside to right-handed and left-handed batters alike.

Charlton also tends to over-use his forkball to the detriment of his fastball. He has an outstanding back-door breaking ball which he throws to right-handed hitters almost exclusively. However, he has no similar out pitch to lefties, as evidenced by the fact that lefthanders batted 22 points higher against him than righthanders. Like Dibble, Charlton needs to find more poise. His admission that he deliberately threw at the Dodgers' Mike Scioscia underscored his need for a more mature attitude.

HOLDING RUNNERS, FIELDING, HITTING:

Charlton has a decent pickoff move, though runners can still time his high leg kick. He is also an adequate fielder of his position. However, don't expect him to help himself with the bat. He had only one hit in 23 at-bats last year, perhaps another indication that he is a reliever at heart.

OVERALL:

One of the Reds' big decisions will be whether to use Charlton as a starter or in relief. It is a dilemma that will not likely sort itself out until spring training. He has the talent to be successful anywhere, but it would seem his future lies in the bullpen.

NORM CHARLTON

Position: RP/SP
Bats: B **Throws:** L
Ht: 6' 3" **Wt:** 200

Opening Day Age: 29
Born: 1/6/63 in Fort Polk, LA
ML Seasons: 4

Overall Statistics

	W	L	ERA	G	GS	Sv	IP	H	R	BB	SO	HR
1991	3	5	2.91	39	11	1	108.1	92	37	34	77	6
Career	27	22	3.00	174	37	3	419.1	350	155	164	331	27

How Often He Throws Strikes

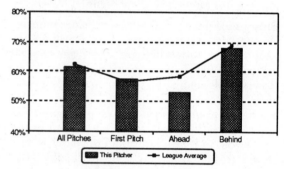

1991 Situational Stats

	W	L	ERA	Sv	IP		AB	H	HR	RBI	AVG
Home	0	4	4.01	1	42.2	LHB	87	22	0	16	.253
Road	3	1	2.19	0	65.2	RHB	303	70	6	30	.231
Day	0	3	6.04	0	28.1	Sc Pos	99	24	1	36	.242
Night	3	2	1.80	1	80.0	Clutch	94	22	1	14	.234

1991 Rankings (National League)

→ 5th in wild pitches (11)
→ 7th in hit batsmen (6)
→ Led the Reds in wild pitches and hit batsmen

HITTING:

There were few bigger disappointments in baseball last year than Eric Davis. He missed much of spring training while recovering from off season knee surgery. He remained weak all season, a by-product of the torn kidney he suffered in the 1990 World Series. And he harbored resentment all year at what he perceived to be mistreatment at the hands of Reds' owner Marge Schott.

All in all, it made for an ugly season. Well known for missing extended chunks of every campaign, Davis became invisible in 1991. When healthy, Davis hits with power to all fields and can be one of the most fearsome streak hitters in the game. However, he has never adjusted to what has become a well-established pitching pattern against him -- crowd him inside with hard stuff and then stay away from him with breaking balls out of the strike zone. With his bat slowed last year, many clubs didn't even worry about location but instead just threw him fastballs with which he could not catch up.

BASERUNNING:

Davis' injuries have slowed him, and he seems like he's lost his desire to run. As one NL manager said, "You used to prepare for him like he was Rickey Henderson. Now he's just another guy who might steal a base here and there." Davis is less of a threat to take an extra base, and he did not hit a triple last season.

FIELDING:

If he's not traded, Davis will likely move to left field to make room in center for rookie Reggie Sanders. When he is 100 percent, Davis is one of the best outfielders in the game. However, his range has decreased in recent years. He has a strong, accurate arm.

OVERALL:

There are bad feelings on both sides between Davis and the Reds and there's a strong possibility he will end up elsewhere, like San Diego. Wherever he winds up, he can still be one of the game's biggest stars, but he's become such a physical risk that it's a gamble to count on him.

ERIC DAVIS

Position: CF
Bats: R **Throws:** R
Ht: 6' 3" **Wt:** 185

Opening Day Age: 29
Born: 5/29/62 in Los Angeles, CA
ML Seasons: 8

Overall Statistics

	G	AB	R	H	D	T	HR	RBI	SB	BB	SO	AVG
1991	89	285	39	67	10	0	11	33	14	48	92	.235
Career	856	2857	554	767	119	18	177	532	247	424	753	.268

Where He Hits the Ball

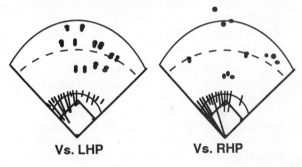

Vs. LHP   Vs. RHP

1991 Situational Stats

	AB	H	HR	RBI	AVG		AB	H	HR	RBI	AVG
Home	140	34	5	18	.243	LHP	105	24	3	11	.229
Road	145	33	6	15	.228	RHP	180	43	8	22	.239
Day	79	22	4	8	.278	Sc Pos	69	15	2	21	.217
Night	206	45	7	25	.218	Clutch	39	6	2	5	.154

1991 Rankings (National League)

→ 2nd lowest batting average with 2 strikes (.116)

→ 4th highest batting average on a 3-1 count (.611)

→ Led NL center fielders in hit by pitch (5) and batting average on a 3-1 count

STOPPER

ROB DIBBLE

Position: RP
Bats: L **Throws:** R
Ht: 6' 4" **Wt:** 230

Opening Day Age: 28
Born: 1/24/64 in
Bridgeport, CT
ML Seasons: 4

PITCHING:

In some ways, Rob Dibble is becoming the baseball equivalent of Mike Tyson. Dibble's constant brushes with the game's authority have begun to overshadow anything he does on the pitcher's mound. All the suspensions and controversies took their toll in 1991. It was a difficult year for Dibble, despite 31 saves in his first season as a full-time closer.

After a first half in which Dibble was virtually unhittable, he became very mortal over the season's final months. Dibble blew five saves, saw his earned run average inflate to 3.17 (a career high by over a run), and served up one of the year's most memorable home runs to Atlanta's Dave Justice in the season's final week. As a NL coach said, "For over a year he had that aura of a guy who no one could hit. But he lost some of that this season."

Scouts say that Dibble might have lost a little off his fastball down the stretch, dropping from routine radar clockings in the high 90s to late-season readings that would top out in the 92-93 range. Regardless, Dibble remains one of baseball's hardest throwers, and also incorporates an overpowering slider. He has tried mixing in an offspeed pitch that turns over like a forkball.

HOLDING RUNNERS, FIELDING, HITTING:

Don't look for Dibble to help himself with the so-called "little things." He is easy to run on because of his big leg-kick and slow delivery to the plate. He is rarely in position to field the ball on those rare occasions when batters hit it against him, and is vulnerable to the bunt. He remains hitless in his major league career.

OVERALL:

Maturity is often an over-used word. But in Dibble's case, it is very apt. He needs to become less of a cartoon character, avoid the suspensions and just go about the business of being this generation's Goose Gossage.

Overall Statistics

	W	L	ERA	G	GS	Sv	IP	H	R	BB	SO	HR
1991	3	5	3.17	67	0	31	82.1	67	32	25	124	5
Career	22	14	2.21	246	0	44	338.2	234	89	119	460	14

How Often He Throws Strikes

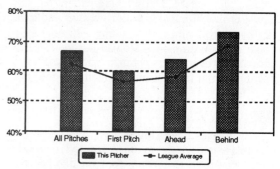

1991 Situational Stats

	W	L	ERA	Sv	IP		AB	H	HR	RBI	AVG
Home	1	4	5.26	18	39.1	LHB	173	34	2	14	.197
Road	2	1	1.26	13	43.0	RHB	128	33	3	20	.258
Day	1	0	1.35	8	20.0	Sc Pos	104	23	3	32	.221
Night	2	5	3.75	23	62.1	Clutch	215	53	4	30	.247

1991 Rankings (National League)

→ 1st in strikeouts per 9 innings in relief (13.6)
→ 2nd in saves (31), save percentage (86.1%) and least GDPs induced per GDP situation (1.7%)
→ 3rd in games finished (57) and save opportunities (36)
→ Led the Reds in saves, games finished, save opportunities, save percentage, blown saves (5), lowest batting average allowed vs. left-handed batters (.197), first batter efficiency (.259), lowest percentage of inherited runners scored (19.1%), relief ERA (3.17), batting average allowed in relief (.223), least baserunners per 9 innings in relief (10.1) and strikeouts per 9 innings in relief

BILLY DORAN

Position: 2B
Bats: B **Throws:** R
Ht: 6' 0" **Wt:** 175

Opening Day Age: 33
Born: 5/28/58 in
Cincinnati, OH
ML Seasons: 10

HITTING:

By midseason last year, Billy Doran had proven that he was most of the way back from the back problems that plagued him in 1990 and throughout spring training. Doran closed fast, batting .328 over the last four weeks. The fast finish brought his average to .280 and likely cemented his role as the Reds' regular second baseman.

His recovery was good news for the Reds, who gave the Cincinnati native a three-year contract after the 1990 season. He remains a solid switch-hitter, competent from both sides of the plate, though he hit 23 points better batting left-handed last year. Always a good fastball hitter who hits the ball to all fields, Doran can be retired from either side of the plate with breaking stuff and change of speeds low and away. He is also a fairly selective hitter who has maintained a solid walk-to-strikeout ratio throughout his career.

BASERUNNING:

Doran's days as a base stealer are likely behind him. He stole only five bases last year in nine attempts, and has been reduced to the kind of average runner who can only steal in certain situations against pitchers with below-average moves. He remains very aggressive in trying for the extra base and breaking up double plays.

FIELDING:

As long as he stays at second, Doran is a capable fielder. His range is limited but he helps make up for a lack of mobility with knowledgeable positioning. He can fill in at third but his arm is below average for that position, as are his reactions.

OVERALL:

With Mariano Duncan likely departing as a free agent, Doran will probably get a chance this year to return to everyday status. He's not too old to remain a solid performer, provided his physical problems are finally behind him.

Overall Statistics

	G	AB	R	H	D	T	HR	RBI	SB	BB	SO	AVG
1991	111	361	51	101	12	2	6	35	5	46	39	.280
Career	1293	4684	672	1262	200	37	76	444	201	639	557	.269

Where He Hits the Ball

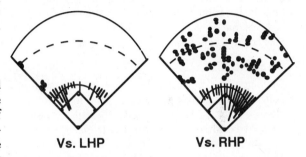

Vs. LHP   Vs. RHP

1991 Situational Stats

	AB	H	HR	RBI	AVG		AB	H	HR	RBI	AVG
Home	169	50	3	18	.296	LHP	80	21	2	8	.262
Road	192	51	3	17	.266	RHP	281	80	4	27	.285
Day	96	26	2	12	.271	Sc Pos	82	22	0	28	.268
Night	265	75	4	23	.283	Clutch	78	19	1	11	.244

1991 Rankings (National League)

→ Led the Reds in lowest percentage of swings that missed (13.5%) and highest percentage of swings put into play (51.7%)

HITTING:

One of several Reds who experienced dropoffs from their 1990 production, Mariano Duncan at least finished strongly enough to receive some serious interest as a free agent. He hit six of his career-high 12 home runs in the season's last month and got his average up to .258 after spending much of the season near the Mendoza Line.

Once a switch-hitter, the right-handed Duncan remains a far more dangerous hitter against southpaws. He hit nearly 100 points higher vs. left-handed pitching, the second straight year he had such a huge disparity. However, Duncan hit seven of his home runs against righties. Recent efforts to improve his strength, and a shortening of his swing have obviously paid some dividends because he is no longer the automatic out against righties that he once was. Duncan is very vulnerable to any breaking stuff low and away.

BASERUNNING:

Duncan was frequently bothered by hamstring pulls last year, and the physical problems cut into his base stealing. He attempted only nine steals all year, five of them successful. His triples dropped to only four after leading the league in 1990 with 11. If Duncan is healthy and bats in the top part of the lineup, he could again be a 20-30 stolen base threat.

FIELDING:

Duncan has always been an erratic fielder, whether at short, which is his more natural position, or second. He has decent range and a good arm, but his errors are most often caused by his arm, not his hands.

OVERALL:

Yes, he can still be a wild swinger. Yes, he can still scare you in the field. And yes, he is still a low .200s hitter against righthanders. But Duncan has produced some pretty good offensive numbers in his career, especially for a middle infielder. That's something a lot of clubs should find desirable when Duncan hits the open market.

MARIANO DUNCAN

Position: 2B/SS
Bats: R **Throws:** R
Ht: 6' 0" **Wt:** 185

Opening Day Age: 29
Born: 3/13/63 in San Pedro de Macoris, Dominican Republic
ML Seasons: 6

Overall Statistics

	G	AB	R	H	D	T	HR	RBI	SB	BB	SO	AVG
1991	100	333	46	86	7	4	12	40	5	12	57	.258
Career	646	2256	297	569	83	24	45	203	124	129	428	.252

Where He Hits the Ball

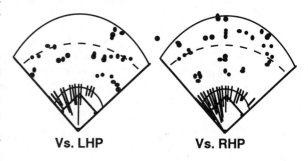

Vs. LHP   Vs. RHP

1991 Situational Stats

	AB	H	HR	RBI	AVG		AB	H	HR	RBI	AVG
Home	167	52	10	25	.311	LHP	140	44	5	19	.314
Road	166	34	2	15	.205	RHP	193	42	7	21	.218
Day	84	20	3	12	.238	Sc Pos	73	25	2	28	.342
Night	249	66	9	28	.265	Clutch	52	12	0	6	.231

1991 Rankings (National League)

→ 7th lowest batting average with an 0-2 count (.071)
→ Led the Reds in triples (4)

PITCHING:

Kip Gross came to Cincinnati from the Mets as an obscure part of the memorable John Franco-Randy Myers trade. With Myers' status in limbo, Gross could wind up being a more important part of the Reds' future. Gross actually posted a lower ERA (3.47) than Myers did (3.55) last season.

Used as a swing man in both the majors and minors, Gross made nine starts in 1991. Though he had mixed results, he will likely get an opportunity to win a job in the rotation during spring training. However, because he has also spent much of his minor league career as a reliever, he could end up in a middle-inning or set-up role, especially if the Reds juggle their personnel. Cincinnati used Gross mostly in relief over the final month, indicating that the bullpen might be the way they're leaning with him.

Gross will need to work on his control, which gave him trouble in a number of his starts. He also allows more than his share of home runs while giving up more hits than innings pitched. Not an overpowering pitcher, Gross relies on a big-breaking, overhand curve with which he spots an average fastball, which he will usually try to sink. He also has a better than average change of speed pitch. However, he needs to spot all his pitches well to have success.

HOLDING RUNNERS, FIELDING, HITTING:

Gross needs to develop a better pickoff move while learning how to better hold runners on. His fielding is adequate. He never batted in the majors until last year, and was 2-for-22.

OVERALL:

Cincinnati will need to decide what role Gross can fill best. The Reds' starting rotation appears to have at least one opening, but Gross might be a little short stuff-wise to fill it. Instead, it's likely he'll end up in some kind of relief job.

KIP GROSS

Position: RP/SP
Bats: R **Throws:** R
Ht: 6' 2" **Wt:** 190

Opening Day Age: 27
Born: 8/24/64 in Scottsbluff, NE
ML Seasons: 2

Overall Statistics

	W	L	ERA	G	GS	Sv	IP	H	R	BB	SO	HR
1991	6	4	3.47	29	9	0	85.2	93	43	40	40	8
Career	6	4	3.52	34	9	0	92.0	99	46	42	43	8

How Often He Throws Strikes

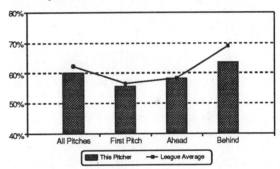

1991 Situational Stats

	W	L	ERA	Sv	IP		AB	H	HR	RBI	AVG
Home	1	3	4.71	0	36.1	LHB	184	56	6	26	.304
Road	5	1	2.55	0	49.1	RHB	149	37	2	15	.248
Day	1	2	4.50	0	18.0	Sc Pos	92	26	1	30	.283
Night	5	2	3.19	0	67.2	Clutch	13	4	0	0	.308

1991 Rankings (National League)

➡ 4th highest batting average allowed vs. left-handed batters (.304)

➡ 7th most GDPs induced per GDP situation (17.7%)

➡ Led the Reds in GDPs induced per GDP situation

PITCHING:

Despite a glittering minor league record (42-13 in 1988-90), the jury remains out on Chris Hammond. The lefthander was a .500 pitcher in 1991, going 7-7 in 18 starts. Hammond then missed the last several weeks of the season with arm problems which could be serious enough to affect his 1992 season.

Before being injured, Hammond did not impress volatile manager Lou Piniella, who likes to see more hard stuff. One of their more memorable blowups came late in the 1990 season on national TV; Piniella gave Hammond an animated chewing out during a visit to the mound.

Hammond relies heavily on his fine change-up, which he throws with an excellent arm motion that disguises the pitch well. But the lefthander might be guilty of throwing too many changes. Said an NL scout, "He won't challenge you with any of his pitches, and if you lay off his change, he is hittable. He has to move the ball around if he's not going to throw the hard stuff."

Hammond's fastball, curve and slider are all average. However, the Reds think his fastball would be better if used more. Hammond allowed nearly a hit per inning last year while striking out nearly as many as he walked. His margin for error was not great. Cincinnati must also be concerned about Hammond's durability. He broke down last season before logging even 100 innings. He also failed to complete any of his 18 starts, averaging barely five innings per outing.

HOLDING RUNNERS, FIELDING, HITTING:

Hammond has an average move to first and his quick delivery home is his best weapon against base stealers. He is a shaky fielder at times. However, Hammond proved last year to be an excellent hitting pitcher. He was on the leader board among NL pitchers with 12 hits, including three doubles, batting a robust .353.

OVERALL:

The Reds have yet to see the stuff which won Hammond so many games in the minors. Until the extent of his arm problems are ascertained, they can't count on Hammond for 1992.

CHRIS HAMMOND

Position: SP
Bats: L **Throws:** L
Ht: 6' 1" **Wt:** 190

Opening Day Age: 26
Born: 1/21/66 in Atlanta, GA
ML Seasons: 2

Overall Statistics

	W	L	ERA	G	GS	Sv	IP	H	R	BB	SO	HR
1991	7	7	4.06	20	18	0	99.2	92	51	48	50	4
Career	7	9	4.30	23	21	0	111.0	105	60	60	54	6

How Often He Throws Strikes

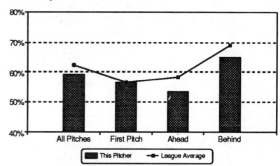

This Pitcher — League Average

1991 Situational Stats

	W	L	ERA	Sv	IP		AB	H	HR	RBI	AVG
Home	3	3	4.73	0	45.2	LHB	98	18	1	11	.184
Road	4	4	3.50	0	54.0	RHB	270	74	3	31	.274
Day	2	1	3.13	0	23.0	Sc Pos	84	25	0	36	.298
Night	5	6	4.34	0	76.2	Clutch	10	3	1	1	.300

1991 Rankings (National League)

➡ 10th most GDPs induced per GDP situation (16.7%)

HITTING:

After being a key to the Reds' 1990 pennant and then a World Series hero, Billy Hatcher receded to a more realistic plateau last season. Hatcher played a lot of center field because of Eric Davis' many absences, did some platoon time in left and ended up very close to the seasonal numbers he has usually compiled during his eight-year career.

However, like many Reds, Hatcher's performance was subpar in the first half when Cincinnati was trying to stay in the NL West race. He rebounded to have a decent year, but it was a matter of too little, too late.

Hatcher, as he demonstrated in the World Series, can find a groove where he sprays the ball to all fields and lays off breaking balls out of the strike zone. However, he largely remains a strictly pull, fastball hitter prone to chasing breaking pitches and trying to pull pitches away from him.

BASERUNNING:

Entering the 1991 season, Hatcher had averaged 35 steals per year in his previous five seasons. But last year he attempted 20 steals (11 successful) all year, a dramatic dropoff in what has been the strongest part of his game. Nagging injuries were one problem. His speed does not appear diminished, only his aggressiveness. He can be a dynamic baserunner when he's ready and willing.

FIELDING:

Hatcher has the range to play center, which he did extensively last year. However, his average throwing arm better suits him for left. For someone with his speed, Hatcher tends to play deeper than normal. This can result in some balls falling in front of him, especially in center.

OVERALL:

Hatcher is an uncomplaining, upbeat personality in the clubhouse and a guy whose skills, especially his running, are excellent commodities to have in reserve. However, it may be a stretch to play him every day, and he won't likely be a regular for Cincinnati unless there are injuries or trades.

BILLY HATCHER

Position: LF/CF
Bats: R **Throws:** R
Ht: 5'10" **Wt:** 190

Opening Day Age: 31
Born: 10/4/60 in
Williams, AZ
ML Seasons: 8

Overall Statistics

	G	AB	R	H	D	T	HR	RBI	SB	BB	SO	AVG
1991	138	442	45	116	25	3	4	41	11	26	55	.262
Career	886	3112	427	824	152	23	39	278	192	199	349	.265

Where He Hits the Ball

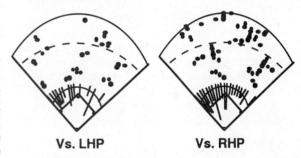

Vs. LHP   Vs. RHP

1991 Situational Stats

	AB	H	HR	RBI	AVG		AB	H	HR	RBI	AVG
Home	216	58	2	17	.269	LHP	130	36	1	11	.277
Road	226	58	2	24	.257	RHP	312	80	3	30	.256
Day	120	26	2	9	.217	Sc Pos	94	32	0	35	.340
Night	322	90	2	32	.280	Clutch	77	25	0	12	.325

1991 Rankings (National League)

→ 1st in highest batting average on a 3-2 count (.471)

→ 2nd lowest stolen base percentage (.550)

→ 4th in hit by pitch (7)

→ 7th highest batting average with runner in scoring position (.340)

→ Led the Reds in caught stealing (9), hit by pitch, batting average with runners in scoring position, batting average on a 3-2 count and bunts in play (12)

IN HIS PRIME

HITTING:

Poll any dozen major league general managers and ask them who they would choose to build a team around; it's a mortal lock that Barry Larkin's name will be mentioned. Though he again missed extensive time due to injuries (his 39-game absence was one of the biggest reasons the Reds didn't contend), Larkin continued to establish himself as one of the game's best players.

Larkin, who'd never homered more than 12 times in a season prior to last year, added a new dimension in 1991 by bashing home runs while still keeping his average above .300. As one NL pitching coach said, "A lot of power hitters learn how to hit for average. But there aren't many average hitters who learn how to add power while keeping their average up."

Larkin is so difficult to pitch to because of the way he uses all fields. He can hit the ball for power to right-center as easily as he can pull the ball out to left. He is an excellent fastball hitter who kills anything pitched up and away. The book on him is to try and keep the ball down with breaking balls and changes of speed.

BASERUNNING:

As a base stealer, Larkin reminds some NL veterans of Joe Morgan in that he doesn't steal bases for statistical purposes but is almost automatic when taking off in meaningful, late-inning situations. Larkin doesn't swipe as many sacks as Morgan used to, but his career success rate is an outstanding 82 percent.

FIELDING:

Defensively, Larkin has few peers. He has tremendous range and unequalled skill in throwing while still moving or off-balance. He had spells of erratic throwing in 1991, accounting for some of his 15 errors. However, many of his errors are made on balls most other shortstops just wave at.

OVERALL:

When the Reds get back in the race, Larkin will finally win deserved acclaim as one of the best all-around players in the game. He's an MVP waiting to happen.

BARRY LARKIN

Position: SS
Bats: R **Throws:** R
Ht: 6' 0" **Wt:** 190

Opening Day Age: 27
Born: 4/28/64 in Cincinnati, OH
ML Seasons: 6

Overall Statistics

	G	AB	R	H	D	T	HR	RBI	SB	BB	SO	AVG
1991	123	464	88	140	27	4	20	69	24	55	64	.302
Career	695	2589	402	762	118	24	58	290	133	210	233	.294

Where He Hits the Ball

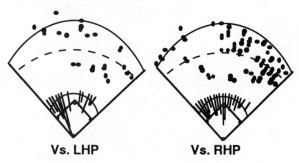

Vs. LHP   **Vs. RHP**

1991 Situational Stats

	AB	H	HR	RBI	AVG		AB	H	HR	RBI	AVG
Home	242	79	16	48	.326	LHP	135	44	8	22	.326
Road	222	61	4	21	.275	RHP	329	96	12	47	.292
Day	107	33	7	16	.308	Sc Pos	111	32	3	45	.288
Night	357	107	13	53	.300	Clutch	71	18	1	7	.254

1991 Rankings (National League)

- ➡ 2nd in on-base average vs. left-handed pitchers (.436)
- ➡ 3rd in slugging percentage vs. left-handed pitchers (.585) and steals of third (10)
- ➡ 4th most runs scored per time reached base (44.4%) and batting average at home (.326)
- ➡ 5th highest slugging percentage (.507)
- ➡ Led the Reds in triples (4), stolen bases (24), slugging percentage, on-base average (.378), stolen base percentage (80.0%), most pitches seen per plate appearance (3.94), runs scored per time reached base, batting average on an 0-2 count (.241), batting average with 2 strikes (.222), highest percentage of pitches taken (61.1%) and steals of third

HITTING:

If not for a change of pitchers on the final day of the season, Hal Morris might have won his first batting title. Morris had gone three-for-three against righthander Andy Benes to raise his average to .319. A fourth hit would have put Morris at .320 and ahead of Terry Pendleton. However, Benes was relieved by lefthander Rich Rodriguez, who retired Morris in his final at-bat to reduce the first baseman's average to .318.

It was nevertheless a superb season by Morris, especially considering he played much of the season with a shoulder injury and then, later in the year, with back problems. He has been compared to the Mets' Dave Magadan because of his ability to hit the ball to all fields. However, Morris has begun showing much more power than Magadan, hitting 14 homers and adding 33 doubles. The reason for the added power was Morris' improved ability to turn on more pitches and pull them for the long ball.

Morris is one of the league's best fastball hitters, which means teams will go deep into the count trying to get him to chase breaking balls and offspeed stuff. However, he fanned only 61 times in 478 at-bats.

BASERUNNING:

Though possessing average speed at best, Morris is a high percentage base stealer who judiciously picks his spots to run. Despite being pretty slow out of the batter's box, he grounded into only four double plays last year.

FIELDING:

Morris is only a fair first baseman with average range and throwing ability. He still has problems digging balls out of the dirt and committed nine errors last year.

OVERALL:

Manager Lou Piniella will still occasionally sit Morris against the Steve Averys of the world. But this is a guy who has stayed well above .300 ever since putting on a Reds uniform, and he is in the Cincinnati lineup to stay.

HAL MORRIS

Position: 1B
Bats: L **Throws:** L
Ht: 6' 4" **Wt:** 215

Opening Day Age: 27
Born: 4/9/65 in Fort Rucker, AL
ML Seasons: 4

Overall Statistics

	G	AB	R	H	D	T	HR	RBI	SB	BB	SO	AVG
1991	136	478	72	152	33	1	14	59	10	46	61	.318
Career	273	825	125	264	55	4	21	99	19	68	106	.320

Where He Hits the Ball

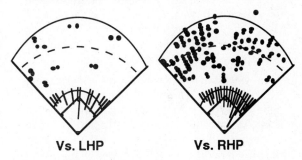

Vs. LHP   Vs. RHP

1991 Situational Stats

	AB	H	HR	RBI	AVG		AB	H	HR	RBI	AVG
Home	238	76	9	33	.319	LHP	103	26	1	12	.252
Road	240	76	5	26	.317	RHP	375	126	13	47	.336
Day	138	45	5	20	.326	Sc Pos	116	33	1	41	.284
Night	340	107	9	39	.315	Clutch	72	24	1	5	.333

1991 Rankings (National League)

- → 1st in batting average vs. right-handed pitchers (.336) and batting average after the 6th inning (.340)
- → 2nd in batting average (.318)
- → 4th in batting average on the road (.317)
- → 5th in on-base average vs. right-handed pitchers (.397)
- → Led the Reds in batting average, sacrifice flies (7), groundball/flyball ratio (1.6), most GDPs per GDP situation (4.0%), batting average in the clutch (.333), batting average with the bases loaded (.375) and batting average after the 6th inning

RANDY MYERS

Position: RP/SP
Bats: L **Throws:** L
Ht: 6' 1" **Wt:** 215

Opening Day Age: 29
Born: 9/19/62 in
Vancouver, WA
ML Seasons: 7

PITCHING:

Few players in baseball have seen their value change more quickly than Randy Myers. A year ago, Myers was the bullpen closer for the World Champion Cincinnati Reds. But during the course of the 1991 season he struggled as a closer before being supplanted by Rob Dibble, was moved into a middle-relief role which he resented, and was finally tried as a starter. Myers ended the season entrenched in manager Lou Piniella's doghouse and was likely trade bait over the winter.

How did Myers fall so far, so quickly? Well, the seeds of his decline were likely in place late in the triumphant 1990 season. Though Myers earned four postseason saves while not being scored upon, scouts were seeing a slight deterioration in his velocity. It was an ominous sign because Myers lives and dies with his heat. His slider is only average and he has never had the need to develop any offspeed pitches.

Once 1991 began, Myers began experiencing control problems. He walked 80 batters, the fifth-highest total in the National League, even though he pitched only 132 innings. Walks hurt Myers in the bullpen; then, when he was tried as a starter, they resulted in high pitch counts which negated any progress he could have made. Myers' inability to develop any quality pitch to go with his fastball also hurt him as a starter.

HOLDING RUNNERS, FIELDING, HITTING:

Myers has a solid pickoff move, though his delivery to the plate is somewhat slow. His delivery also leaves him in poor position to field. As a hitter, Myers did manage five hits last season. However, he struck out in 16 of his 33 plate appearances.

OVERALL:

No longer the Reds' closer, a likely clubhouse problem if used in any other bullpen role, and a bust as a starter, Myers likely wore out his welcome in Cincinnati. Look for him to be elsewhere in 1992. With better control, he could bounce back.

Overall Statistics

	W	L	ERA	G	GS	Sv	IP	H	R	BB	SO	HR
1991	6	13	3.55	58	12	6	132.0	116	61	80	108	8
Career	27	32	2.85	309	12	93	458.2	354	164	215	470	30

How Often He Throws Strikes

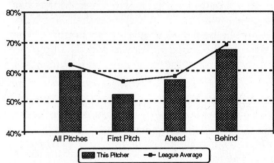

1991 Situational Stats

	W	L	ERA	Sv	IP		AB	H	HR	RBI	AVG
Home	3	5	3.75	5	72.0	LHB	122	35	3	18	.287
Road	3	8	3.30	1	60.0	RHB	358	81	5	40	.226
Day	2	2	2.40	1	30.0	Sc Pos	129	34	1	47	.264
Night	4	11	3.88	5	102.0	Clutch	169	47	2	20	.278

1991 Rankings (National League)

→ 2nd lowest winning percentage (.316)

→ 5th in walks allowed (80) and relief losses (7)

→ 6th in losses (13), lowest batting average allowed vs. right-handed batters (.226) and most baserunners allowed per 9 innings in relief (13.3)

→ 7th lowest percentage of inherited runners scored (21.1%)

→ Led the Reds in walks allowed, lowest batting average vs. right-handed batters and relief losses

HITTING:

As long as National League pitchers continue to try and throw fastballs by Paul O'Neill, he will continue to be one of the league's better power hitters. O'Neill led the Reds in 1991 with 28 home runs and 91 RBI, both career highs. With Eric Davis sidelined, O'Neill was Cincinnati's only consistent power threat.

Though obviously a quality player, O'Neill struggles against lefthanders, batting .201 vs. southpaws last year. All but three of his home runs came against right-handed pitchers while nearly half his strikeouts came at the hand of lefties in 194 fewer at-bats. Lefthanders offspeed stuff was death to O'Neill. Lefties mix speeds, keep the breaking stuff away and try not to get fastballs inside on him.

O'Neill also has a temper which can get him in trouble. National League umpires would likely vote O'Neill to their all-whiner team because of his hot-headed reactions to ball-strike calls. If he could curb his outbursts and get a better handle on offspeed pitches, O'Neill could become a genuine star.

BASERUNNING:

O'Neill is a fair runner who can be counted on to steal between 12-15 bases a year. However, he is not selective enough for someone with rather limited speed. He was 12-for-19 last year, and in his last two seasons he has stolen 25 bases and been caught 18 times, a very bad ratio.

FIELDING:

His range is only average but otherwise, O'Neill is one of the best right fielders in baseball. He has a strong, accurate arm made even better by his ability to charge the ball well and quickly get a throw off toward the infield.

OVERALL:

O'Neill is knocking on the door of stardom. He needs only to mature more and improve his production vs. left-handed pitching to become a 30-homer, 100-RBI anchor in the middle of the Reds' lineup.

PAUL O'NEILL

Position: RF
Bats: L **Throws:** L
Ht: 6' 4" **Wt:** 215

Opening Day Age: 29
Born: 2/25/63 in Columbus, OH
ML Seasons: 7

Overall Statistics

	G	AB	R	H	D	T	HR	RBI	SB	BB	SO	AVG
1991	152	532	71	136	36	0	28	91	12	73	107	.256
Career	651	2122	262	557	128	6	82	345	55	229	371	.262

Where He Hits the Ball

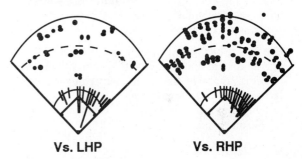

Vs. LHP   **Vs. RHP**

1991 Situational Stats

	AB	H	HR	RBI	AVG		AB	H	HR	RBI	AVG
Home	268	76	20	59	.284	LHP	169	34	3	15	.201
Road	264	60	8	32	.227	RHP	363	102	25	76	.281
Day	146	45	10	26	.308	Sc Pos	149	39	7	60	.262
Night	386	91	18	65	.236	Clutch	73	14	2	7	.192

1991 Rankings (National League)

→ 2nd in slugging percentage vs. right-handed pitchers (.562)

→ 3rd in doubles (36), lowest batting average on an 0-2 count (.048), lowest on-base average vs. left-handed pitchers (.254), lowest batting average on the road (.227) and lowest batting average after the 6th inning (.217)

→ 5th in intentional walks (14)

→ Led the Reds in home runs (28), doubles, RBIs (91), walks (73), intentional walks (14), strikeouts (107) and HR frequency (19 ABs per HR)

→ Led NL right fielders in fielding percentage (.994) and intentional walks

HITTING:

Joe Oliver wasn't healthy all season in 1991, and his shoulder problems were persistent enough for the Reds to end the season wondering if they might need to go find some catching. Oliver played only 94 games because of his shoulder injury. He did manage 11 homers and 41 RBI in only 269 at-bats.

However, Oliver batted just .216. He had problems in two areas. A pull hitter who can hit the ball a long way when he gets a fastball out over the plate and down, Oliver is very vulnerable to fastballs which crowd him inside. Also, many teams consistently retired him with any kind of breaking ball. If he learns to hit the breaking ball a bit better, Oliver would see more fastballs and his power potential suggests that he could be a consistent 15-20 home run hitter.

Oliver also has yet to prove he can be an everyday player due to his inability to hit right-handed pitching. Eight of his 11 homers came against lefthanders despite the fact that he received roughly the same number of at-bats against both righthanders and southpaws.

BASERUNNING:

The word "running" is used generously where Oliver is concerned. He is one of the slowest runners in the National League and no threat to either steal or take an extra base.

FIELDING:

Oliver's shoulder problems were evident in 1991. He made 11 errors and developed many bad habits behind the plate. The worst of these was a change in his release, which resulted in many of his throws tailing into runners. He is also prone to passed balls.

OVERALL:

Catching has become a worry for the Reds, and Lou Piniella was not pleased with Oliver's work last year. Oliver's shoulder is a problem, as are the many holes in his game. If scheduled offseason shoulder surgery returns him to full health, Oliver is capable of supplying some power; hopefully, he can iron out his defensive difficulties with a strong shoulder. But he'll need to play a lot better if he wants to remain the Reds' catcher.

JOE OLIVER

Position: C
Bats: R **Throws:** R
Ht: 6' 3" **Wt:** 210

Opening Day Age: 26
Born: 7/24/65 in Memphis, TN
ML Seasons: 3

Overall Statistics

	G	AB	R	H	D	T	HR	RBI	SB	BB	SO	AVG
1991	94	269	21	58	11	0	11	41	0	18	53	.216
Career	264	784	68	183	42	0	22	116	1	61	156	.233

Where He Hits the Ball

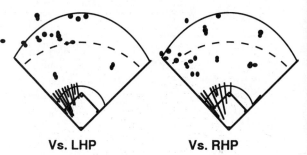

Vs. LHP   Vs. RHP

1991 Situational Stats

	AB	H	HR	RBI	AVG		AB	H	HR	RBI	AVG
Home	145	29	7	17	.200	LHP	131	30	8	27	.229
Road	124	29	4	24	.234	RHP	138	28	3	14	.203
Day	47	13	0	5	.277	Sc Pos	62	16	5	32	.258
Night	222	45	11	36	.203	Clutch	47	11	0	2	.234

1991 Rankings (National League)

→ 1st in lowest fielding percentage as a catcher (.980)

→ Led the Reds in GDPs (14)

PITCHING:

While the Reds' pitching staff crumbled all around him in 1991, veteran Ted Power was a steady, albeit unspectacular, source of relief. Power's 68 appearances ranked among the league leaders and led the Reds. He earned three of the 12 Reds' saves not earned by Rob Dibble. Until wearing down toward the end of the season, Power compiled a solid earned run average and hits-per-inning ratio.

As usual, Power was used almost exclusively in middle and long relief roles; he hasn't worked as a full-time closer since 1985, and his start for Pittsburgh in Game 6 of the 1990 playoffs is his only start in the last two seasons. Power's pitching repertoire has always lent itself more to relieving: though he is 37 years old, he relies on power pitching. His fastball still averages in the upper 80s and his style, especially in relief, is to come at hitters with heat.

When his fastball loses its sinking movement, Power can get in trouble because his slider and change-up are only average. That is evidenced by the .265 batting average against him. But Power proved in 1991 that his age has not caught up with him. He was a durable pitcher all season for Cincinnati, giving them 87 relief innings as well as reliability.

HOLDING RUNNERS, FIELDING, HITTING:

Power's slow delivery to the plate makes him vulnerable to base stealers. However, he is very diligent about holding runners close with repeated throws to first base. He has always been a good fielder, especially for someone his size. Power went hitless last year, striking out in three of his four plate appearances.

OVERALL:

Any pitcher Power's age is always going to have to fight to keep his job. However, with the Reds' staff likely to undergo significant upheaval, it's likely his experience and durability will be an asset which Cincinnati will find too valuable to relinquish.

TED POWER

Position: RP
Bats: R **Throws:** R
Ht: 6' 4" **Wt:** 220

Opening Day Age: 37
Born: 1/31/55 in Guthrie, OK
ML Seasons: 11

Overall Statistics

	W	L	ERA	G	GS	Sv	IP	H	R	BB	SO	HR
1991	5	3	3.62	68	0	3	87.0	87	37	31	51	6
Career	63	62	4.08	455	85	51	1015.0	1014	507	400	623	87

How Often He Throws Strikes

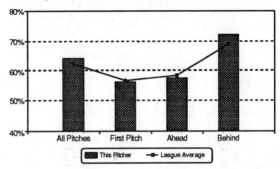

1991 Situational Stats

	W	L	ERA	Sv	IP		AB	H	HR	RBI	AVG
Home	5	0	3.04	2	50.1	LHB	171	50	4	20	.292
Road	0	3	4.42	1	36.2	RHB	157	37	2	16	.236
Day	1	1	3.54	1	20.1	Sc Pos	88	23	1	27	.261
Night	4	2	3.65	2	66.2	Clutch	104	27	1	9	.260

1991 Rankings (National League)

➡ 8th highest batting average allowed in relief (.265)

➡ Led the Reds in games pitched (68), holds (9) and relief innings (87)

HITTING:

In 1991, Jeff Reed was called upon for one of the busiest seasons of his largely part-time career. Reed responded with career highs in most offensive categories. His .267 average, most notably, was his best by 16 points. That said, Reed didn't exactly make Reds fans forget Johnny Bench. He drove in only 31 runs in 270 at-bats and managed only three homers; it was the third year in a row he's belted three dingers, and it equalled his career high. Virtually all of Reed's production predictably came versus right-handed pitching, against whom he played almost exclusively.

Reed is strictly a fastball hitter who does not try to pull but instead works on using the whole field. He is vulnerable to breaking stuff and anything thrown by lefthanders, who allowed him five hits in 26 ABs all year.

Cincinnati made no attempt to hide their efforts in scouting catchers over the course of the season's final weeks. Manager Lou Piniella talked often about how catcher Dan Wilson, the Reds 1990 number-one draft pick, has a chance to jump to the majors this season. All of these indicate that Reed didn't knock the Reds' eyes out with his 1991 performance.

BASERUNNING:

Like fellow Reds' catcher Joe Oliver, Reed is not a factor on the base paths. He's stolen a total of two bases in his eight year major league career. Even the element of surprise didn't help him in his one 1991 attempt.

FIELDING:

Reed has only an average arm and a slow release, which combines to make him vulnerable to base stealers. He does work his pitchers fairly well, using experienced pitch selection.

OVERALL:

Left-handed hitting catchers usually can find a job. Reed is no exception. But his job with the Reds could well be in jeopardy. He gives a work-man-like effort when called upon and if Cincinnati decides they want a change, Reed is likely to surface somewhere else.

JEFF REED

Position: C
Bats: L **Throws:** R
Ht: 6' 2" **Wt:** 190

Opening Day Age: 29
Born: 11/12/62 in Joliet, IL
ML Seasons: 8

Overall Statistics

	G	AB	R	H	D	T	HR	RBI	SB	BB	SO	AVG
1991	91	270	20	72	15	2	3	31	0	23	38	.267
Career	525	1400	101	328	63	6	13	117	2	139	199	.234

Where He Hits the Ball

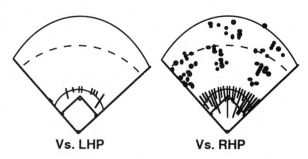

Vs. LHP   **Vs. RHP**

1991 Situational Stats

	AB	H	HR	RBI	AVG		AB	H	HR	RBI	AVG
Home	115	30	1	15	.261	LHP	26	5	0	5	.192
Road	155	42	2	16	.271	RHP	244	67	3	26	.275
Day	90	31	2	12	.344	Sc Pos	59	12	1	25	.203
Night	180	41	1	19	.228	Clutch	38	10	0	3	.263

1991 Rankings (National League)

➡ 6th lowest batting average on a 3-2 count (.087)

STAFF ACE

JOSE RIJO

Position: SP
Bats: R **Throws:** R
Ht: 6' 2" **Wt:** 210

Opening Day Age: 26
Born: 5/13/65 in San Cristobal, Dominican Republic
ML Seasons: 8

PITCHING:

If not for one misguided attempt to steal a base that resulted in an ankle injury and a month on the sidelines, Jose Rijo might well have won the National League Cy Young Award in 1991. No NL pitcher was better last year than Rijo, who proved his 1990 World Series MVP performance was no fluke.

Rijo was among league leaders in virtually every pitching category, including ERA (second best at 2.51), strikeouts and victories. He allowed 39 fewer hits than innings pitched, had a superb strikeout to walk ratio (3.1-to-1), and held opposing hitters to a .219 batting average (second lowest in the National League). The consummate pitching ace, Rijo lost successive starts only once all year.

Rijo features a fastball consistently clocked in the mid-90s with movement that rides in on left-handed batters. He also throws a slider, forkball and change-up. Rijo throws his change with what scouts and opposing batters believe is one of the best-disguised motions in the National League. The pitch becomes even more effective because Rijo is not afraid to use the change-up at any time in the count. He has had in the past a tendency to over-use his slider, but in the last two years he has largely shed that bad habit.

HOLDING RUNNERS, FIELDING, HITTING:

Rijo's pickoff move is not his strong point, though he has made some improvement. He has always had trouble holding runners close. However, Rijo can help himself in the field with his athleticism, and he has made himself into one of the best-hitting pitchers in the league. He had 14 hits last year with five RBI and nine sacrifices. After last season's misadventure, he is not likely to try many more stolen bases.

OVERALL:

It's easy to forget how young Rijo is (26) despite his 68 career victories and travels through three different organizations. He is a Cy Young Award waiting to happen, and one of these years he will avoid injury and win it.

Overall Statistics

	W	L	ERA	G	GS	Sv	IP	H	R	BB	SO	HR
1991	15	6	2.51	30	30	0	204.1	165	69	55	172	8
Career	68	58	3.39	223	151	3	1076.1	946	469	454	925	76

How Often He Throws Strikes

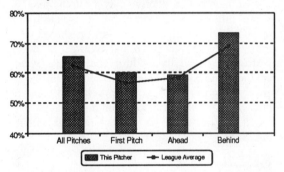

1991 Situational Stats

	W	L	ERA	Sv	IP		AB	H	HR	RBI	AVG
Home	9	0	2.99	0	99.1	LHB	436	110	5	45	.252
Road	6	6	2.06	0	105.0	RHB	319	55	3	16	.172
Day	4	2	1.70	0	53.0	Sc Pos	159	34	0	52	.214
Night	11	4	2.80	0	151.1	Clutch	36	8	0	2	.222

1991 Rankings (National League)

→ 1st in lowest slugging percentage allowed (.305), lowest on-base average allowed (.272), most run support per 9 innings (5.6) and ERA on the road (.2.06)

→ 2nd in ERA (2.51), winning percentage (.714), lowest batting average allowed (.219), highest stolen base percentage allowed (84.2%), least home runs per 9 innings (.35) and most strikeouts per 9 innings (7.6)

→ Led the Reds in ERA, wins (15), complete games (3), shutouts (1), strikeouts (172), balks (4), GDPs induced (15), winning percentage, strikeout/walk ratio (3.1) and lowest batting average allowed with runners in scoring position (.214)

HITTING:

The bottom line on Chris Sabo's 1991 season was excellent -- a .301 average with 26 homers, 88 RBI, 35 doubles and 91 runs scored. However, like a lot of other Reds, Sabo's season-ending numbers did not reflect how much he struggled during the early part of Cincinnati's season; most of his lusty hitting took place late in the year, when the Reds were already out of the race (.331 after the All-Star break). And those numbers did not reflect how Sabo was one of the reasons for the Reds' frequent clubhouse problems. His dugout skirmish with teammate Jose Rijo largely set the tone for Cincinnati's weak defense of its World Championship.

Nevertheless, once Sabo got locked in, he was one of the most productive players in the league. A pull hitter who has a very quick bat and looks to jerk fastballs, Sabo is the kind of hitter who many clubs try to pitch backwards. In other words, they will throw him change-ups when behind in the count. They will have their lefthanders try to crowd him or have their righthanders throw him breaking balls. When he gets a pitcher into a position where he knows a fastball is coming, Sabo is very dangerous.

BASERUNNING:

Sabo is an aggressive runner who will sometimes make a mistake and get thrown out trying for the extra base. However, he has deceptively good speed. He stole 19 bases in 25 attempts, and has averaged 26 steals a year in his career.

FIELDING:

With a strong, accurate arm and good hands, Sabo is an excellent third baseman. His range is above average and his instincts are among the best in the league.

OVERALL:

Sabo may not win a lot of popularity contests with his sometimes acerbic personality. But the numbers he's produced the last few years make up for a lot of other problems. He is one of the game's most well-rounded third basemen.

CHRIS SABO

Position: 3B
Bats: R **Throws:** R
Ht: 6' 0" **Wt:** 185

Opening Day Age: 30
Born: 1/19/62 in Detroit, MI
ML Seasons: 4

Overall Statistics

	G	AB	R	H	D	T	HR	RBI	SB	BB	SO	AVG
1991	153	582	91	175	35	3	26	88	19	44	79	.301
Career	520	1991	300	553	134	8	68	232	104	159	222	.278

Where He Hits the Ball

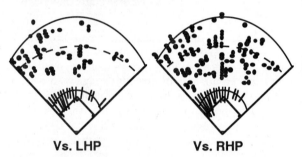

Vs. LHP   Vs. RHP

1991 Situational Stats

	AB	H	HR	RBI	AVG		AB	H	HR	RBI	AVG
Home	298	101	15	45	.339	LHP	193	69	9	29	.358
Road	284	74	11	43	.261	RHP	389	106	17	59	.272
Day	147	35	2	13	.238	Sc Pos	145	44	8	64	.303
Night	435	140	24	75	.322	Clutch	88	20	3	9	.227

1991 Rankings (National League)

→ 2nd in batting average vs. left-handed pitchers (.357), slugging percentage vs. left-handed pitchers (.596) and fielding percentage at third base (.966)

→ 3rd in hits (175) and batting average at home (.339)

→ 4th in total bases (294) and lowest ground-ball/flyball ratio (.75)

→ 5th in doubles (35)

→ Led the Reds in at-bats (582), runs (91), hits, singles (111), total bases, times on base (225), pitches seen (2,368), plate appearances (640), games (153) and batting average at home

PITCHING:

After getting relatively abbreviated auditions in each of the last two seasons, Scott Scudder will likely have the chance this year to be a permanent part of a major league starting rotation. Long considered one of the Reds' most desirable young pitchers, Scudder was the man Cleveland wanted most when they parted with Greg Swindell.

With a 6-9 record for the Reds last year, Scudder's biggest problem remains throwing strikes, especially with his breaking ball. He finished last season with more walks (56) than strikeouts (51). As one NL manager said, "When he's getting ahead of you consistently, he is tough to beat because he can use his good change and spot his fastball. But when he's behind, he has to come at you with the fastball, and it's hittable in those situations."

However, before his poor finish, Scudder was showing some progress. He made great strides in pitching to left-handed batters, who hit over 40 points lower against him last season than they did in 1990. He also dramatically cut down on gopher balls. In 1990, Scudder allowed 12 home runs in only 71.2 innings; last year, he was nailed for only six in 101.1. The key for him is always control. He has a repertoire of four major-league caliber pitches but must stay ahead in the count to make them effective.

HOLDING RUNNERS, FIELDING, HITTING:

Scudder has a poor pickoff move which makes him easy pickings for any base stealer. It is a part of his game which needs work for him to become a complete major league starter. However, he is a decent fielder with good instincts. Moving to the American League, he won't have to worry about his hitting until the Indians reach the World Series.

OVERALL:

Scudder was much coveted around baseball but just as highly regarded by the Reds, who thought he would become an established part of their rotation this season. Only the chance to get Swindell made them willing to part with Scudder.

SCOTT SCUDDER

Position: SP/RP
Bats: R **Throws:** R
Ht: 6' 2" **Wt:** 185

Opening Day Age: 24
Born: 2/14/68 in Paris, TX
ML Seasons: 3

Overall Statistics

	W	L	ERA	G	GS	Sv	IP	H	R	BB	SO	HR
1991	6	9	4.35	27	14	1	101.1	91	52	56	51	6
Career	15	23	4.54	71	41	1	273.1	256	147	147	159	32

How Often He Throws Strikes

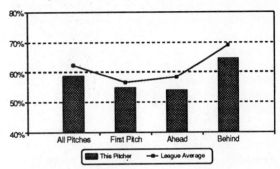

1991 Situational Stats

	W	L	ERA	Sv	IP		AB	H	HR	RBI	AVG
Home	3	6	5.34	0	55.2	LHB	215	54	3	23	.251
Road	3	3	3.15	1	45.2	RHB	155	37	3	18	.239
Day	1	1	6.33	0	21.1	Sc Pos	89	21	0	30	.236
Night	5	8	3.83	1	80.0	Clutch	39	13	1	6	.333

1991 Rankings (National League)

→ 7th in hit batsmen (6) and lowest winning percentage (.400)

→ Led the Reds in hit batsmen

CHRIS JONES

Position: LF
Bats: R **Throws:** R
Ht: 6' 2" **Wt:** 205

Opening Day Age: 26
Born: 12/16/65 in Utica, NY
ML Seasons: 1

Overall Statistics

	G	AB	R	H	D	T	HR	RBI	SB	BB	SO	AVG
1991	52	89	14	26	1	2	2	6	2	2	31	.292
Career	52	89	14	26	1	2	2	6	2	2	31	.292

HITTING, FIELDING, BASERUNNING:

On a club that could see several major changes, outfielder Chris Jones showed enough promise to warrant a long look this spring. Though known as a line drive hitter, Jones displayed excellent power, especially to the opposite field. Jones looks like he can hit major league fastballs, but he struggled when teams started mixing in sliders and offspeed stuff.

Jones' biggest problem was that pitchers quickly learned they didn't have to throw him strikes: he fanned 31 times while walking just twice in 89 at-bats, a ridiculously bad ratio. Jones will need to develop a lot more discipline if he expects to succeed at the major league level.

Though possessing good athletic tools, Jones also needs to refine his outfield skills. He seemed to have poor technique at times, especially with getting a good jump on the ball and getting into throwing position. He has better-than-average speed, especially in taking the extra base.

OVERALL:

The Reds have a lot of outfield "maybes." Maybe Eric Davis will be traded. Maybe Glenn Braggs won't rebound from his shoulder injury. Maybe Reggie Sanders won't be ready. In that kind of situation, a talented kid like Jones could end up sticking. Maybe he'll stop going after so many bad pitches.

CARMELO MARTINEZ

Position: 1B/LF
Bats: R **Throws:** R
Ht: 6' 2" **Wt:** 225

Opening Day Age: 31
Born: 7/28/60 in Dorado, Puerto Rico
ML Seasons: 9

Overall Statistics

	G	AB	R	H	D	T	HR	RBI	SB	BB	SO	AVG
1991	108	275	30	61	11	0	10	36	0	43	64	.222
Career	1003	2906	350	713	134	7	108	424	10	404	528	.245

HITTING, FIELDING, BASERUNNING:

The Reds were Carmelo Martinez's sixth career team and his third last year alone. That should tell you something. Martinez did pop 10 home runs in 275 at-bats, eight of those dingers coming against right-handed pitching. Frequently used as a platoon first sacker against lefties, Martinez hit only two homers in 131 at-bats while batting .221 against southpaws at his three stops last year. If Martinez can't hit lefties better, he's not going to have a job.

Martinez is strictly a fastball hitter who has trouble against any kind of breaking pitch or offspeed stuff. But his power is legitimate to all fields. He is a non-factor as a baserunner, and Martinez has gradually backslid as a fielder. His best position is first base, where he has decent hands. However, he made six errors in his limited play last year. He has become too much of a liability in the outfield to play there except in a pinch.

OVERALL:

Martinez is a free agent, and could conceivably return to the Reds as a bench player and pinch hitter with power. But his salary demands would have to be pretty modest. At this stage of his baseball life, Martinez has "Japanese League" written all over him.

TOP PROSPECT

LUIS QUINONES

Position: 2B/3B
Bats: B **Throws:** R
Ht: 5'11" **Wt:** 185

Opening Day Age: 29
Born: 4/28/62 in Ponce, Puerto Rico
ML Seasons: 7

REGGIE SANDERS

Position: CF
Bats: R **Throws:** R
Ht: 6' 1" **Wt:** 180

Opening Day Age: 24
Born: 12/1/67 in Florence, SC
ML Seasons: 1

Overall Statistics

	G	AB	R	H	D	T	HR	RBI	SB	BB	SO	AVG
1991	97	212	15	47	4	3	4	20	1	21	31	.222
Career	439	998	102	226	36	11	19	105	9	75	154	.226

Overall Statistics

	G	AB	R	H	D	T	HR	RBI	SB	BB	SO	AVG
1991	9	40	6	8	0	0	1	3	1	0	9	.200
Career	9	40	6	8	0	0	1	3	1	0	9	.200

HITTING, FIELDING, BASERUNNING:

Luis Quinones is a versatile player whom most managers would love to have on their bench. As a switch-hitter with some power, he is an excellen pinch hitting option. With all the Reds' injuries in 1991, Quinones ended up playing more than Cincinnati would have preferred.

Quinones is a dead fastball hitter; that's one reason he's been tough in the clutch, when pitchers tend to come in with the heater. He's one of those guys about whom a manager will threaten to fine his pitcher if he throws a fastball for a strike. Pitchers keep doing it, though, and Quinones knows how to take advantage. He has surprising power, with 18 homers in 697 at-bats over the last three seasons. Whether he's batting left-handed, where he was far more successful in 1991, or right-handed, Quinones should see a steady diet of breaking balls and offspeed pitches.

Quinones has below-average speed. Though an adequate fielder, he can play decently at second, short or third, but lacks range. Second base is probably his best position.

OVERALL:

Versatile players usually hang around because they are so tough to replace. So it is with Quinones, released by the Reds in the offseason; his ability to hit coming off the bench should be valuable to any contending team.

HITTING, FIELDING, BASERUNNING:

Cincinnati got only a brief look at Reggie Sanders last year, so the jury is out on whether he is ready for the big time. However, Sanders has big-time skills which create inevitable comparisons to a younger, healthier and happier Eric Davis.

Scouts certainly have taken notice. Said a top NL advance man, "He can be an impact player, one of those guys who can steal bases, hit for average and hit for power." In his nine-game trial last season, Sanders had trouble catching up with major league fastballs but he has hit in the .280 range in the minors. He's shown good patience along with a very quick bat.

Sanders has legitimate 40-stolen base kind of speed, though he didn't get a chance to run with the Reds. He seems likely to be a decent center fielder. He can outrun most balls in the outfield and has an above-average throwing arm.

OVERALL:

With Marge Schott seeking to shed Eric Davis' salary and personality, Sanders is going to get a chance to make the jump to the majors, even though he has only 86 games of experience at the AA level. He has Davis-type skills, but it's going to be some time before Sanders is ready to use them fully in the major leagues.

CINCINNATI REDS MINOR LEAGUE PROSPECTS

ORGANIZATION OVERVIEW:

Though they've won only one World Championship in the last 15 years, the Reds were a model organization for most of that time. Cincinnati believed passionately in player development, hiring the scouts and beating the bushes. The result was a steady flow of hot prospects, from Eric Davis through Barry Larkin and Rob Dibble. Unfortunately, that wonderful era is over. Under Marge Schott, the Reds have fired a lot of their best scouts, and others, feeling unappreciated, have left in disgust. Last summer Cincinnati let one of its top prospects, Reggie Jefferson, get away because of a foolish clerical error. There are some good players left in the Reds' system, but less than in most. It would be a surprising if they continue to produce top talent like they once did.

FREDDIE BENAVIDES

Position: SS
Bats: R **Throws:** R
Ht: 6' 2" **Wt:** 180
Opening Day Age: 25
Born: 4/7/66 in Laredo, TX

Recent Statistics

	G	AB	R	H	D	T	HR	RBI	SB	BB	SO	AVG
91 AAA Nashville	94	331	24	80	8	0	0	21	7	16	55	.242
91 NL Cincinnati	24	63	11	18	1	0	0	3	1	1	15	.286
91 MLE	94	321	20	70	7	0	0	17	5	14	56	.218

Benavides has both the range and the arm to play shortstop at the major league level. However, Barry Larkin is blocking his way, and his hitting skills are an even bigger problem. Benavides impressed people by hitting .286 while filling in for Larkin last summer, but that was most likely an illusion -- he'd never hit nearly that well in the minors, and his strikeout/walk ratio (15 Ks and one BB, that one intentional, in 63 ABs) was a joke. Benavides needs a lot of work.

GINO MINUTELLI

Position: P
Bats: L **Throws:** L
Ht: 6' 1" **Wt:** 178
Opening Day Age: 27
Born: 5/23/64 in Wilmington, DE

Recent Statistics

	W	L	ERA	G	GS	Sv	IP	H	R	BB	SO	HR
91 A Chston-wv	1	0	0.00	2	2	0	8.0	2	0	4	8	0
91 AAA Nashville	4	7	1.90	13	13	0	80.1	57	25	35	64	3
91 NL Cincinnati	0	2	6.04	16	3	0	25.1	30	17	18	21	5

The Reds could use some pitching help, and Minutelli, in their system since the mid-80s, has been around long enough to earn a shot. Minutelli had shoulder surgery in 1988, and his fastball isn't much. He got a brief chance last year, and the results -- five homers allowed in only 25.1 innings -- were not encouraging. Now nearly 28, he has to prove himself pretty quickly.

JOHN ROPER

Position: P
Bats: R **Throws:** R
Ht: 6' 0" **Wt:** 170
Opening Day Age: 20
Born: 11/21/71 in Moore County, NC

Recent Statistics

	W	L	ERA	G	GS	Sv	IP	H	R	BB	SO	HR
90 R Reds	7	2	0.97	13	13	0	74.0	41	10	31	76	1
91 A Chston-wv	14	9	2.31	27	27	0	186.2	133	59	67	189	5

Though he only pitched in A ball last year, the hard-throwing Roper has posted some awesome statistics in less than two full seasons. In 1990 he had a 0.97 ERA and allowed only 41 hits in 74 innings at Plant City. Last year at Charleston, he again fanned a man an inning and allowed only 133 hits in 187 innings while showing good control. Like Mo Sanford, he has a great curveball. The Reds love power pitchers, so watch this guy.

MO SANFORD

Position: P
Bats: R **Throws:** R
Ht: 6' 6" **Wt:** 220
Opening Day Age: 25
Born: 12/24/66 in Americus, GA

Recent Statistics

	W	L	ERA	G	GS	Sv	IP	H	R	BB	SO	HR
91 AA Chattanooga	7	4	2.74	16	16	0	95.1	69	37	55	124	7
91 AAA Nashville	3	0	1.60	5	5	0	33.2	19	7	22	38	0
91 NL Cincinnati	1	2	3.86	5	5	0	28.0	19	14	15	31	3

Considered a top power-pitching prospect by many, Sanford is a big, imposing righthander who has been blowing away hitters at every stop. But Sanford is not a pure fireballer; his best pitch is a wicked curve. Whether he makes it or not will largely depend on his ability to control the pitch. In the high minors and at Cincinnati last year, he had problems getting the ball over the plate.

DAN WILSON

Position: C
Bats: R **Throws:** R
Ht: 6' 3" **Wt:** 205
Opening Day Age: 23
Born: 3/25/69 in Arlington Heights, IL

Recent Statistics

	G	AB	R	H	D	T	HR	RBI	SB	BB	SO	AVG
90 A Chston-wv	32	113	16	28	9	1	2	17	0	13	18	.248
91 A Chston-wv	52	197	25	62	11	1	3	29	1	25	21	.315
91 AA Chattanooga	81	292	32	75	19	2	2	38	2	21	39	.257
91 MLE	81	281	24	64	17	1	1	29	1	14	40	.228

The Reds' top draft choice in 1990, Wilson is being rushed through the system because of the big club's desperate need for a catcher. His arm is excellent, and he's shown the ability to handle pitchers despite his lack of experience. But will he hit? Wilson batted only .257 in 81 games at AA last year, with no power. The Reds' report that Wilson is ready for the majors seems awfully optimistic, to say the least.

JEFF BAGWELL

FUTURE ALL-STAR

Position: 1B
Bats: R **Throws:** R
Ht: 6' 0" **Wt:** 195

Opening Day Age: 23
Born: 5/27/68 in Boston, MA
ML Seasons: 1

HITTING:

Jeff Bagwell added one last ingredient to a satisfying rookie season -- a strong finish. He did everything better the last month than the first, especially hit. In September, he applied the finishing touches to a successful rookie season, hitting at a .336 pace over his last 32 games. Another key statistic: he hit .333 (59-177) from the seventh inning on. He increased his RBI by 10 to 46 in the second half and the former Boston farmhand cut his strikeouts from 71 first-half whiffs to 45. The result for Bagwell was a richly deserved Rookie of the Year award.

This year, Bagwell is the hub of the Astro offense along with Craig Biggio, Ken Caminiti and Luis Gonzalez. His .294 batting average and club-high totals of 15 homers and 82 RBI mean a lot to the Astros. He is a perfect number-three man in the batting order, although an unorthodox hitter in some people's book because of his uppercut swing. His is not the classic swing. He had to adjust to a lot of high fastballs, but he adjusted well.

Bagwell has great bat speed and confidence, and he can drive the ball a good distance. He blasted a couple of tape-measure jobs -- one a 456-foot, upper deck shot in Pittsburgh -- and he could eventually hit 20 to 25 homers a season, even playing in the Astrodome.

BASERUNNING:

Bagwell is more alert than fast on the base paths. He stole seven bases in 11 tries and grounded into 12 double plays in 554 at-bats. He has average speed at best.

FIELDING:

Bagwell made the switch from third base to first base a week before the '91 season. He had a few early problems with his throws, but became a steady man with the glove. Bagwell committed 12 errors, but nine came in the first 70 games.

OVERALL:

With his strong arms and quick bat, Bagwell reminds some people of Steve Garvey (with a better batting eye) in his early years with the Dodgers. He is a confident hitter and is a cornerstone of the Astros' future hopes of building a contender.

Overall Statistics

	G	AB	R	H	D	T	HR	RBI	SB	BB	SO	AVG
1991	156	554	79	163	26	4	15	82	7	75	116	.294
Career	156	554	79	163	26	4	15	82	7	75	116	.294

Where He Hits the Ball

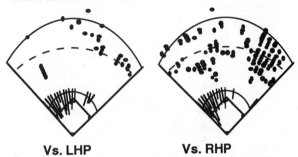

Vs. LHP   **Vs. RHP**

1991 Situational Stats

	AB	H	HR	RBI	AVG		AB	H	HR	RBI	AVG
Home	274	81	6	35	.296	LHP	206	66	7	37	.320
Road	280	82	9	47	.293	RHP	348	97	8	45	.279
Day	127	36	4	18	.283	Sc Pos	153	46	5	65	.301
Night	427	127	11	64	.297	Clutch	86	31	2	13	.360

1991 Rankings (National League)

→ 1st in hit by pitch (13) and batting average in the clutch (.361)

→ 2nd in batting average after the 6th innning (.333)

→ 3rd highest percentage of swings that missed (26.5%)

→ Led the Astros in home runs (15), total bases (242), RBIs (82), sacrifice flies (7), walks (75), hit by pitch, times on base (251), strikeouts (116), pitches seen (2,439), slugging percentage (.437), on-base average (.387), most pitches seen per plate appearance (3.75), batting average in the clutch and batting average on a 3-1 count (.571)

HITTING:

Craig Biggio batted around .300 all season, finishing with a team-high .295 average in '91. He became the first Astro catcher ever named a National League All-Star. Even so, the Astros may move Biggio to second base this year.

The switch, rumored for a year, happened briefly in the next-to-last series of the season at San Francisco. Biggio played the spot for three games and performed well enough in the very brief trial that the shift may become permanent in 1992. Biggio improved his catching techniques and his throwing last year, but he grew tired late in the season, and the Astros would like to preserve his legs at a less-demanding position. His hitting should prosper as a second baseman.

Biggio has become a good, consistent hitter who strokes the ball to all fields. He's not a home run man, but he has decent gap power. Biggio's RBI totals (46 in '91) are not impressive, but he got over half his at bats (318) in either the first or second spot in the lineup. Biggio has a quick bat, has good knowledge of the strike zone and has the ability to be a top ten hitter.

BASERUNNING:

Biggio's legs are a valuable commodity to the Astros. A move to second base would preserve his speed. He stole 19 bases last season and can double that total without the burden of catching. He was caught stealing only six times.

FIELDING:

His quick feet would serve Biggio well at second base and his arm is adequate there. As a catcher, he doesn't have the gun to bag baserunners (also a factor in the switch), but is a solid defensive catcher.

OVERALL:

If the Astros don't uncover another capable catcher, Biggio could remain behind the plate. But a shift to second base would prolong his career. Biggio says, "A lot of at-bats were given away from being tired." In '90, he balked at a move. This season it may prove the thing to do, especially since speed is one of Biggio's strongest assets.

CRAIG BIGGIO

Position: C
Bats: R **Throws:** R
Ht: 5'11" **Wt:** 180

Opening Day Age: 26
Born: 12/14/65 in Smithtown, NY
ML Seasons: 4

Overall Statistics

	G	AB	R	H	D	T	HR	RBI	SB	BB	SO	AVG
1991	149	546	79	161	23	4	4	46	19	53	71	.295
Career	483	1667	210	454	74	9	24	153	71	162	243	.272

Where He Hits the Ball

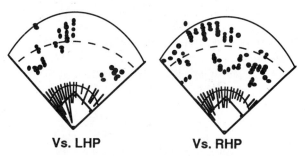

Vs. LHP   Vs. RHP

1991 Situational Stats

	AB	H	HR	RBI	AVG		AB	H	HR	RBI	AVG
Home	277	95	0	24	.343	LHP	186	51	1	11	.274
Road	269	66	4	22	.245	RHP	360	110	3	35	.306
Day	89	33	1	8	.371	Sc Pos	125	35	0	39	.280
Night	457	128	3	38	.280	Clutch	97	25	0	12	.258

1991 Rankings (National League)

→ 1st in least GDPs per GDP situation (1.8%) and batting average at home (.343)

→ 2nd in singles (130) and batting average on a 3-2 count (.382)

→ Led the Astros in batting average (.295), singles, least GDPs per GDP situation, batting average vs. right-handed pitchers (.306), batting average on a 3-2 count, batting average at home and steals of third (3)

→ Led NL catchers in batting average, runs (79), hits (161), singles, stolen bases (19), walks (53), times on base (216), pitches seen (2,080), on-base average (.358) and stolen base percentage (76.0%)

PITCHING:

Ryan Bowen is a two-pitch pitcher, but we're talking about two **real good** pitches. Bowen's curveball snaps, making batters talk to themselves, and his fastball crackles and pops. The former first-round draft choice (1986) spent a long apprenticeship in the minors polishing up those pitches, but finally earned a promotion to Houston last season. The Astros' youth movement is all about guys like Bowen -- talented and begging for an opportunity. When his shot came, the tightly-wound righthander responded with six wins in 10 decisions, but with an ERA (5.15) that needs to slim down.

Bowen made the jump from AAA Tucson in time to log 13 starts and gain valuable experience for a full run this season. He is a power pitcher with a good, live 90-MPH fastball and an exceptional curveball. His overhand curve has a very sharp break to it, and he has a problem keeping it in the strike zone. Bowen needs to curb his wildness (36 walks and eight wild pitches in 71.2 innings) along with his occasional bout of nervousness.

Bowen is working on a split-finger pitch as a change-up, and this will make him a more complete pitcher if perfected. He needs to challenge batters more with his fastball, his best pitch. When he gets his curveball over, Bowen can be tough.

HOLDING RUNNERS, FIELDING, HITTING:

Bowen is a good athlete with quick actions coming off the mound. His move to first base with a runner aboard could use a bit more polish. He's a good hitter with pop to the alleys despite limited experience.

OVERALL:

Bowen learns something each time he goes to the mound. When the Astros speak of the future, he is part of it. Bowen got his feet wet in '91; this year, he should be in the swim of things.

RYAN BOWEN

Position: SP
Bats: R **Throws:** R
Ht: 6' 0" **Wt:** 185

Opening Day Age: 24
Born: 2/10/68 in Hanford, CA
ML Seasons: 1

Overall Statistics

	W	L	ERA	G	GS	Sv	IP	H	R	BB	SO	HR
1991	6	4	5.15	14	13	0	71.2	73	43	36	49	4
Career	6	4	5.15	14	13	0	71.2	73	43	36	49	4

How Often He Throws Strikes

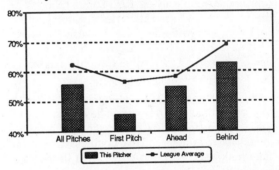

1991 Situational Stats

	W	L	ERA	Sv	IP		AB	H	HR	RBI	AVG
Home	3	2	3.16	0	42.2	LHB	160	46	2	25	.287
Road	3	2	8.07	0	29.0	RHB	112	27	2	9	.241
Day	3	1	2.95	0	21.1	Sc Pos	76	15	3	32	.197
Night	3	3	6.08	0	50.1	Clutch	9	3	0	0	.333

1991 Rankings (National League)

➡ Led the Astros in wild pitches (8)

GREAT RANGE

KEN CAMINITI

Position: 3B
Bats: B **Throws:** R
Ht: 6' 0" **Wt:** 200

Opening Day Age: 28
Born: 4/21/63 in
Hanford, CA
ML Seasons: 5

HITTING:

Until he masters switch-hitting, Ken Caminiti always will hear talk about how he should abandon batting from the left-hand side of the plate. Caminiti is a natural right-handed hitter but has switch-hit for nine years, since his college years at San Jose State. Caminiti put some of the critical discussion aside in '91 because he enjoyed his best all-around year. His batting average (.253) was two points shy of his best ever, and he achieved career highs in home runs (13) and RBI (80). Still, his righty numbers (.310, 9 HR, 44 RBI) are far better than when batting lefty (.213, 4 HR, 36 RBI).

In 1990, Caminiti struggled with a .242 average, four homers and only 51 RBI, so his rebound at the plate proved dramatic. He is gaining more confidence from the left side because he works hard at it. He's always analyzing his game, but that often works against him. Caminiti can worry himself into a slump.

Caminiti's also capable of getting red-hot, like the four-game binge last year when he knocked in 14 runs. He went 9-for-16 (.563) in the brief tear that included two homers and two doubles. His season stats rank right with the Astros' best third baseman in the last 25 years, Doug Rader.

BASERUNNING:

Caminiti is something of a plodder on the base paths, but he is a heady runner and makes up for his lack of speed by being alert in most situations. However, he stole only four bases in nine attempts.

FIELDING:

Caminiti is outstanding in the field despite his errors (23, up two from the year before). He makes all the plays at third base: the diving stop, the play in the hole, and coming in on the ball. You won't find a better arm at the position.

OVERALL:

Caminiti rebounded at the plate last season. There's no reason why he can't stay at the 80 RBI level, but it would surely help if he can improve his left-handed hitting. He's in his prime, and a team leader.

Overall Statistics

	G	AB	R	H	D	T	HR	RBI	SB	BB	SO	AVG
1991	152	574	65	145	30	3	13	80	4	46	85	.253
Career	559	1986	203	490	90	9	31	233	17	162	337	.247

Where He Hits the Ball

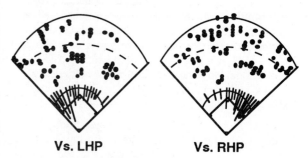

Vs. LHP   **Vs. RHP**

1991 Situational Stats

	AB	H	HR	RBI	AVG		AB	H	HR	RBI	AVG
Home	289	73	9	48	.253	LHP	232	72	9	44	.310
Road	285	72	4	32	.253	RHP	342	73	4	36	.213
Day	135	29	1	13	.215	Sc Pos	157	45	4	63	.287
Night	439	116	12	67	.264	Clutch	92	25	3	9	.272

1991 Rankings (National League)

→ 1st in lowest batting average vs. right-handed pitchers (.213), lowest cleanup slugging percentage (.341) and lowest slugging percentage vs. right-handed pitchers (.301)

→ 3rd lowest on-base average vs. right-handed pitchers (.289)

→ 4th in GDPs (18)

→ Led the Astros in doubles (30), intentional walks (7), GDPs, batting average with the bases loaded (.333) and slugging percentage vs. left-handed pitchers (.504)

→ Led NL third basemen in GDPs

HITTING:

The Astros keep measuring Casey Candaele for a bench role, but he keeps finding a way to squirm into the regular lineup. Candaele has value as a substitute with his versatility and ability to swing the bat. As a reserve, he makes his team stronger on the bench. But the formula always falls apart when the Astros discover that no one on the team can play second base better than Candaele does.

Last season, Mark McLemore got the job out of spring training, but he fizzled. Candaele wound up starting 119 games (96 at second base) and he batted .262 with a career-high 50 RBI. He had 461 at-bats, another career best. Once he made the lineup, Candaele found his stroke and put together a .273 finish (99-of-363) to raise his average from .224.

Candaele is a good little hitter. He hit better as a right-handed batter (.285 to .251), but his real asset is his hustle and drive. His spirit sparks a team and he's battled to put to rest all talk that he is not an everyday player, that the grind of the long season will wear him down. Candaele even had career highs of seven triples and four home runs. He's a clutch ballplayer and a fine contact hitter.

BASERUNNING:

An active runner, Candaele improved his stolen base/caught stealing ratio last year. He was successful in nine of 12 theft attempts. He's among the team's triple leaders each year, with 13 in two seasons.

FIELDING:

Candaele is aggressive in the field, charging balls and hustling to cover bases. His error total went up in '91 (from two to nine at second base), but Candaele played more innings. He plays the outfield well, too, though his arm is on the weak side.

OVERALL:

Once again Candaele's starting role is in jeopardy if the Astros switch Craig Biggio from catcher to second base. With the many experiments at that position, Candaele remains the safety valve.

CASEY CANDAELE

Position: 2B/LF
Bats: B **Throws:** R
Ht: 5' 9" **Wt:** 165

Opening Day Age: 31
Born: 1/12/61 in Lompoc, CA
ML Seasons: 5

Overall Statistics

	G	AB	R	H	D	T	HR	RBI	SB	BB	SO	AVG
1991	151	461	44	121	20	7	4	50	9	40	49	.262
Career	506	1423	156	367	63	19	8	106	27	125	151	.258

Where He Hits the Ball

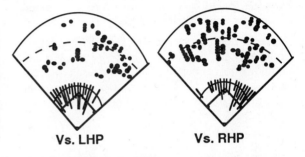

Vs. LHP   **Vs. RHP**

1991 Situational Stats

	AB	H	HR	RBI	AVG		AB	H	HR	RBI	AVG
Home	235	69	1	33	.294	LHP	158	45	1	13	.285
Road	226	52	3	17	.230	RHP	303	76	3	37	.251
Day	102	26	1	12	.255	Sc Pos	112	34	1	45	.304
Night	359	95	3	38	.265	Clutch	102	27	0	16	.265

1991 Rankings (National League)

→ 3rd least runs scored per time reached base (.273)

→ 8th highest batting average with 2 strikes (.251)

→ Led the Astros in intentional walks (7), batting average with 2 strikes and lowest percentage of swings that missed (13.0%)

→ Led NL second basemen in triples (7)

TOP PROSPECT

HITTING:

When the ball jumps off the bat of Andujar Cedeno, people stare in disbelief. Despite his slender frame, the young shortstop generates power like a muscular slugger. Cedeno has a quick bat and he is not afraid to swing it. He hit more homers (nine) in 67 games with Houston than in he did in 93 games at Tucson (seven) before his late-July promotion. "He can smoke the ball," says Astros manager Art Howe.

Cedeno is also a run producer despite his rookie status, driving across 36 runs. Of his 61 hits, 24 went for extra bases. He brings a lot of offense to the lineup at a position not used to that type of production. He has, says one National League manager, "strong wrists like (Hank) Aaron." He can get fooled by a pitch, then turn around and smash the same pitch out of the park.

Cedeno does, however, get fooled by a **lot** of pitches. Last year he struck out 74 times while walking only nine; he fanned in over 30 percent of his at-bats. He'll need to stop swinging at everything if he wants to be more than a .236 hitter.

BASERUNNING:

Cedeno runs well and moves with a fluid stride. His actions display a love for the game. He is just beginning to learn to study the pitchers and how to get a lead off the bag. He has good instincts.

FIELDING:

Fielding is Cedeno's raw spot. He must play the pop-up better, he doesn't charge certain balls and he needs to turn the double play more consistently. He made 18 errors at shortstop, six in the closing series at Atlanta in a pressure situation.

OVERALL:

The Astros feel confident hitching their wagon to Cedeno's star in 1992. His fielding should improve with maturity and playing on AstroTurf, but his bat will make the loudest noise -- if he can learn some strike zone judgement.

ANDUJAR CEDENO

Position: SS
Bats: R **Throws:** R
Ht: 6' 1" **Wt:** 168

Opening Day Age: 22
Born: 8/21/69 in La Romana, Dominican Republic
ML Seasons: 2

Overall Statistics

	G	AB	R	H	D	T	HR	RBI	SB	BB	SO	AVG
1991	67	251	27	61	13	2	9	36	4	9	74	.243
Career	74	259	27	61	13	2	9	36	4	9	79	.236

Where He Hits the Ball

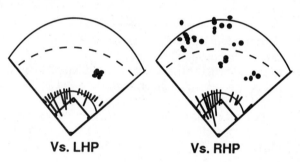

Vs. LHP   **Vs. RHP**

1991 Situational Stats

	AB	H	HR	RBI	AVG		AB	H	HR	RBI	AVG
Home	134	30	4	21	.224	LHP	80	17	0	10	.213
Road	117	31	5	15	.265	RHP	171	44	9	26	.257
Day	65	18	3	10	.277	Sc Pos	67	17	3	28	.254
Night	186	43	6	26	.231	Clutch	42	10	2	3	.238

1991 Rankings (National League)

→ 7th highest percentage of extra bases taken as a runner (68.8%)

→ 10th lowest batting average with an 0-2 count (.077)

PITCHING:

Last season, Jim Corsi carved out a niche for himself in the Houston Astros' bullpen despite losing all five of his decisions. Corsi did it the simple way: by throwing strikes. Nobody did that better among the team's retinue of relievers. He issued just 18 unintentional walks in 77.2 innings in a successful comeback effort from elbow surgery.

The former Oakland A's righthander found his spot as a middle reliever and finished up strongly, lending the Astros an experienced hand. His 3.71 ERA in 47 games lent stability to the pitching staff. Corsi was one of the few pitchers on the team to produce better numbers on the road than at home. He fashioned a 2.77 ERA in 23 road appearances for a team that finished 28-53 in road games.

Corsi throws a fastball, slider and a sinker that has good bite on it. The sinker rides in on right-handed hitters, and Corsi was much more effective against righties last year than he was versus lefties. He no longer throws as hard as in his A's days, but he hits 86 MPH as an average and is effective with good location of his pitches. Most importantly, Corsi doesn't walk himself into trouble. Of the 22 baserunners he inherited in '91, only four scored. His arm held up under the pitching load, too, as his 47 outings represented a career high.

HOLDING RUNNERS, FIELDING, HITTING:

Corsi has worked at improving his move with a runner at first base, but he tends to be a little slow to the plate. Though he committed only one error in the field last season, he is not quick off the mound, and would have to be considered a below-average fielder. He struck out in his lone at-bat.

OVERALL:

The Astros signed Corsi at the suggestion of Assistant GM Bob Watson and he turned out to be a good addition. Due to the Astros' youth movement, however, Corsi was placed on unconditional waivers in November of '91. He'll have to take his middle-relief abilities elsewhere.

JIM CORSI

Position: RP
Bats: R **Throws:** R
Ht: 6' 1" **Wt:** 210

Opening Day Age: 30
Born: 9/9/61 in Newton, MA
ML Seasons: 3

Overall Statistics

	W	L	ERA	G	GS	Sv	IP	H	R	BB	SO	HR
1991	0	5	3.71	47	0	0	77.2	76	37	23	53	6
Career	1	8	3.21	80	1	0	137.1	122	55	39	84	9

How Often He Throws Strikes

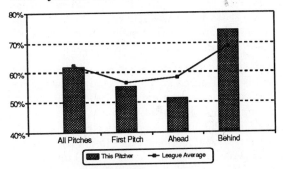

1991 Situational Stats

	W	L	ERA	Sv	IP		AB	H	HR	RBI	AVG
Home	0	3	4.66	0	38.2	LHB	153	44	5	18	.288
Road	0	2	2.77	0	39.0	RHB	141	32	1	16	.227
Day	0	0	2.53	0	21.1	Sc Pos	73	25	2	25	.342
Night	0	5	4.15	0	56.1	Clutch	57	21	3	14	.368

1991 Rankings (National League)

→ 7th in first batter efficiency (.167)

→ Led the Astros in most GDPs induced per GDP situation (14.7%) and first batter efficiency

PITCHING:

After seven seasons in Houston, Jim Deshaies appears to have reached the end of the line with the Astros. Deshaies has gone only 12-24 over the last two years, and budget-conscious Houston probably won't want to gamble that the free agent lefty can turn things around. With the Astros' youth drive in full gear, management promoted its most promising young arms and Deshaies was told to take the rest of the season off in early September.

Players are supposed to make a salary drive in their free agent year, but last season was the worst of Deshaies' career, both in terms of record (5-12) and ERA (4.98). His problems were evident from the beginning of most games in '91, as he was tagged for 32 first-inning runs in his 28 starts. In those games the first batter reached base 15 times, and all but five of them scored.

At 31, Deshaies is not the power pitcher of old and finds it necessary to make adjustments. He continued to rely on his high fastball last year, designing his pitching style for the spacious Astrodome. But Deshaies got a lot of fly balls at home that went for home runs (15 of them) on the road. Poor mechanics also plagued him in '91, especially with a change-up that kept drifting over the plate. The change makes all of his other pitches work, and when it doesn't, hitters can tee off on his 84 MPH fastball.

HOLDING, RUNNERS, FIELDING, HITTING:

Deshaies puts much effort into holding runners at first base, repeatedly throwing to the bag. However, his move to the plate is very slow. He handles balls back to the mound well, but his hitting is something of a washout.

OVERALL:

All indications were that Deshaies had pitched his last game for Houston. Despite the Astrodome advantage, his pitching during the last two years was so poor that his future must be considered in doubt. Given many teams' need for lefthanders, he'll undoubtedly be given a chance to revive his career.

JIM DESHAIES

Position: SP
Bats: L **Throws:** L
Ht: 6' 4" **Wt:** 220

Opening Day Age: 31
Born: 6/23/60 in
Massena, NY
ML Seasons: 8

Overall Statistics

	W	L	ERA	G	GS	Sv	IP	H	R	BB	SO	HR
1991	5	12	4.98	28	28	0	161.0	156	90	72	98	19
Career	61	60	3.72	183	180	0	1109.0	974	488	430	736	114

How Often He Throws Strikes

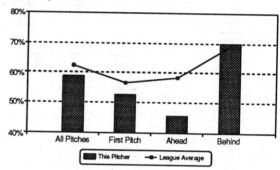

1991 Situational Stats

	W	L	ERA	Sv	IP		AB	H	HR	RBI	AVG
Home	2	3	3.72	0	65.1	LHB	104	29	4	19	.279
Road	3	9	5.83	0	95.2	RHB	498	127	15	59	.255
Day	0	3	7.11	0	19.0	Sc Pos	132	35	5	56	.265
Night	5	9	4.69	0	142.0	Clutch	52	13	0	3	.250

1991 Rankings (National League)

→ 1st in lowest winning percentage (.294) and lowest ERA on the road (5.83)

→ 2nd in balks (5)

→ 3rd in pickoff throws (295)

→ 7th in most home runs allowed (19) and runners caught stealing (14)

→ Led the Astros in losses (12), home runs allowed, balks, pickoff throws and runners caught stealing

HITTING:

Remove one line from Steve Finley's scouting report: "Can't hit left-handed pitching." Given the opportunity to play in all situations during his first year in Houston, the lefty-hitting Finley hung up a .250 mark against southpaws and batted .285 overall for the season. In his final year with Baltimore, the young outfielder hit .193 against lefties. But the Astros liked Finley's swing and approach at the plate and felt he would hit southpaws, given the opportunity. With the Orioles, Finley didn't play against tough lefties and got yanked for a pinch hitter when a southpaw entered the game.

Many predicted Finley would be no more than a fourth outfielder after joining Houston in the Glenn Davis trade. He turned those beliefs aside after struggling through April with a .203 batting average. From May 4 on, he compiled a .299 mark and showed talent in the leadoff spot. Finley went 31 for 82 (.378) leading off the game, with 11 of those hits going for extra bases. He's a good contact hitter with some pop in his bat, hitting eight homers, all on the road. Finley showed the ability to hold up over the long season.

BASERUNNING:

With his top-of-the-order speed, Finley served as a catalyst for the Houston offense. He runs very well, and can stretch an extra base out of his hits. Finley uses his speed as a weapon, stealing 34 bases to rank ninth in the league.

FIELDING:

Finley can do it all in the field. He can run a ball down, cut the ball off in the gaps, and he has a strong, accurate arm. He makes few mistakes in judgement and knows the game.

OVERALL:

Steady, all-around play in his first year in Houston made Finley an important part of the Astros' rebuilding process. He surprised some people with how well he played. Finley should become a fixture in the number-one or two spot in the lineup for quite awhile.

STEVE FINLEY

Position: CF/RF
Bats: L **Throws:** L
Ht: 6' 2" **Wt:** 180

Opening Day Age: 27
Born: 3/12/65 in Union City, TN
ML Seasons: 3

Overall Statistics

	G	AB	R	H	D	T	HR	RBI	SB	BB	SO	AVG
1991	159	596	84	170	28	10	8	54	34	42	65	.285
Career	382	1277	165	343	49	16	13	116	73	89	148	.269

Where He Hits the Ball

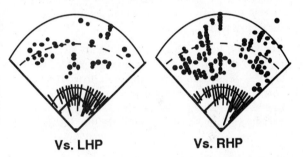

Vs. LHP   Vs. RHP

1991 Situational Stats

	AB	H	HR	RBI	AVG		AB	H	HR	RBI	AVG
Home	300	82	0	20	.273	LHP	184	46	1	16	.250
Road	296	88	8	34	.297	RHP	412	124	7	38	.301
Day	132	40	3	14	.303	Sc Pos	103	32	3	46	.311
Night	464	130	5	40	.280	Clutch	89	25	0	12	.281

1991 Rankings (National League)

→ 3rd in triples (10), games (159) and bunts in play (40)

→ 4th in at-bats (596)

→ 5th in singles (124) and caught stealing (18)

→ Led the Astros in at-bats, runs (84), hits (170), triples, total bases (242), sacrifice bunts (10), stolen bases (34), caught stealing, plate appearances (656), games, groundball/flyball ratio (1.6), runs scored per time reached base (39.3%), batting average with runners in scoring position (.311), batting average on the road (.297) and bunts in play (40)

HITTING:

Occasionally, a team force-feeds a player to the majors and he chokes. After making the leap from AA ball to Houston in 1991, Luis Gonzalez was one who enjoyed dining at the big league table. After a slow start during which he labored to hit .200, Gonzalez stepped up the pace. The lean outfielder batted .386 in a closing, 12-game rush to lift his average to .254 at the finish line.

Even more impressive was the way Gonzalez hit for power. Despite the handicap of playing in the Astrodome, the youngster had 52 extra-base hits; over 40 percent of his hits were extra-base blows. Gonzalez drove in 69 runs, but whiffed 101 times, a figure which should decrease once he learns to relax at the plate. He needs to improve his stroke versus southpaw pitching, against whom he hit only .172 with 13 RBI.

The young Astro has a short, quick stroke -- some refer to it as a classic swing -- and hitters with such swings usually are difficult to fool. This should prove the case with the former first baseman as he gains maturity. Gonzalez must learn patience and the strike zone better, but he shows every sign of being able to make adjustments.

BASERUNNING:

Gonzalez has decent speed (10 stolen bases in 17 attempts) and should improve that total as he learns the pitchers' moves. He is more of a careful baserunner than a daring one.

FIELDING:

In spring training, Gonzalez took the long hike from first base to left field. The Astros made the switch to get his bat in the lineup. He had the normal problems one expects, but Gonzalez limited his errors to five and was a much improved fielder by season's end. His arm is well below average.

OVERALL:

With his sweet batting stroke, Gonzalez has the ability to become an excellent power hitter and a big RBI threat. This year, he must display more consistency to take his game to the next level of development. He's a very exciting young slugger.

LUIS GONZALEZ

Position: LF
Bats: L **Throws:** R
Ht: 6' 2" **Wt:** 180

Opening Day Age: 24
Born: 9/3/67 in Tampa, FL
ML Seasons: 2

Overall Statistics

	G	AB	R	H	D	T	HR	RBI	SB	BB	SO	AVG
1991	137	473	51	120	28	9	13	69	10	40	101	.254
Career	149	494	52	124	30	9	13	69	10	42	106	.251

Where He Hits the Ball

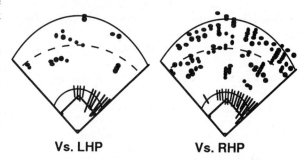

Vs. LHP   Vs. RHP

1991 Situational Stats

	AB	H	HR	RBI	AVG		AB	H	HR	RBI	AVG
Home	227	62	4	32	.273	LHP	122	21	1	13	.172
Road	246	58	9	37	.236	RHP	351	99	12	56	.282
Day	110	28	5	14	.255	Sc Pos	136	37	3	50	.272
Night	363	92	8	55	.253	Clutch	74	21	0	9	.284

1991 Rankings (National League)

- ➡ 1st in lowest batting average vs. left-handed pitchers (.172)
- ➡ 3rd in hit by pitch (8) and lowest slugging percentage vs. left-handed pitchers (.271)
- ➡ 4th in triples (9)
- ➡ 5th in lowest on-base average vs. left-handed pitchers (.257)
- ➡ Led the Astros in HR frequency (36.4 ABs per HR), batting average on an 0-2 count (.161) and slugging percentage vs. right-handed pitchers (.490)
- ➡ Led NL left fielders in triples (9)

STAFF ACE

PITCHING:

Don't call Pete Harnisch a hard luck pitcher. Although the numbers say otherwise, he doesn't buy it. "What can I do about it?," says the Houston righthander. "I don't worry about anything I can't control." Maybe so, but Harnisch's 12-9 record hardly indicates his excellent work last year. Manager Art Howe says, "With any kind of run support, Pete would have won 16 to 18 games for the season."

Harnisch, the former Baltimore Oriole, emerged last year as the ace of the Astros' pitching staff. His 12-9 record for a last-place team, 2.70 ERA (fifth in the National League) and opponents batting average (.212, tops in the N.L.) mark him as one of the league's premier hurlers despite his record.

Harnisch, who came to Houston in the Glenn Davis trade, is a bulldog competitor, one who pitches high in the strike zone and gets a lot of fly balls. Last year, Harnisch almost always had a smoking fastball and sharp slider. The big difference? Better control and the development of a good change-up. "He wasn't this kind of pitcher when I saw him in Baltimore," says one veteran scout. "He had trouble throwing strikes and he was inconsistent with his slider. He's still pretty much a thrower. His high fastball is his strikeout pitch."

HOLDING RUNNERS, FIELDING, HITTING:

Harnisch has a fairly quick move to first base, but his delivery to the plate isn't the fastest. He's only considered an average fielder, but he's sure-handed and made only one error in 216 innings pitched. Harnisch is an aggressive hitter by nature, but not too successful.

OVERALL:

The leader of a young Astros pitching staff who battles with the best of them, Harnisch is the type who will get the ball on Opening Day and take it from there. He used to think change-ups were for wimps, but as he makes the transition from thrower to pitcher, he could grow into a 20-game winner. With proper run support, that is.

PETE HARNISCH

Position: SP
Bats: R **Throws:** R
Ht: 6' 0" **Wt:** 207

Opening Day Age: 25
Born: 9/23/66 in Commack, NY
ML Seasons: 4

Overall Statistics

	W	L	ERA	G	GS	Sv	IP	H	R	BB	SO	HR
1991	12	9	2.70	33	33	0	216.2	169	71	83	172	14
Career	28	31	3.74	84	83	0	521.2	468	230	242	374	42

How Often He Throws Strikes

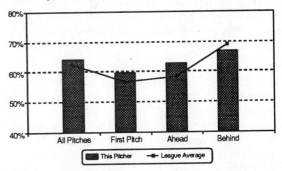

1991 Situational Stats

	W	L	ERA	Sv	IP		AB	H	HR	RBI	AVG
Home	7	4	2.41	0	119.1	LHB	457	107	10	35	.234
Road	5	5	3.05	0	97.1	RHB	339	62	4	28	.183
Day	2	2	4.40	0	43.0	Sc Pos	202	38	2	47	.188
Night	10	7	2.28	0	173.2	Clutch	83	11	0	3	.133

1991 Rankings (National League)

→ 1st in lowest batting average allowed (.212)

→ 2nd lowest batting average allowed with runners in scoring position (.188)

→ 3rd in highest stolen base percentage allowed (81.8%), least GDPs induced per 9 innings (.25), most strikeouts per 9 innings (7.1) and ERA at home (2.41)

→ Led the Astros in ERA (2.70), wins (12), games started (33), complete games (4), shutouts (2), innings (216.2), hits allowed (169), batters faced (900), strikeouts (172), pitches thrown (3,433), stolen bases allowed (27), strikeout/walk ratio (2.1) and winning percentage (.571)

PITCHING:

The 1991 season marked a milestone for Dwayne Henry. For the first time in his eight major league seasons, Henry spent the entire year in the bigs. Of course it helped that Henry finally pitched well enough to stick around. The possessor of a 5.43 lifetime ERA entering the season, Henry posted a 3.19 mark in a career-high 52 games, but it wasn't enough to save him from his release at season's end by the Astros.

Henry succeeded in '91 by finally learning to relax on the mound and allowing his natural ability work for him. After being released by Atlanta following the 1990 season (he'd previously pitched for the Rangers), Henry was invited to the Astros' spring camp as a non-roster player. He earned a spot with the bullpen-poor Astros and was effective all season. Opposing batters hit only .219 against the big, hard-throwing righthander.

Henry not only throws hard, but he does so consistently. He throws a fastball in the 92 MPH range and could be a dominating pitcher if he had more tricks in his bag. He has developed a decent slider, but everything he throws is hard. Henry needs to master a breaking ball or a change-up to be totally effective. Just enough of an offspeed pitch to mess up hitters' timing.

As a middle or late reliever, he needs to develop consistency with his fastball and slider. He had just two save opportunities in '91 and he nailed them down. Henry has always had control problems, and those continued last year with 39 walks in 67.2 innings. Also, half of the base runners he inherited (17 of 35) wound up scoring.

HOLDING RUNNERS, FIELDING, HITTING:

Henry doesn't work too hard at holding runners near the bag, but he covers balls hit around the mound very well. He had only one at-bat (a strikeout).

OVERALL:

Will Henry continue his success this year? Not with the Astros, but with Cincinnati, he might. He certainly has the arm, though better control would surely help. With his stuff, he has a shot at getting plenty of work in 1992.

DWAYNE HENRY

Position: RP
Bats: R **Throws:** R
Ht: 6' 3" **Wt:** 205

Opening Day Age: 30
Born: 2/16/62 in Elkton, MD
ML Seasons: 8

Overall Statistics

	W	L	ERA	G	GS	Sv	IP	H	R	BB	SO	HR
1991	3	2	3.19	52	0	2	67.2	51	25	39	51	7
Career	8	10	4.61	152	0	7	183.2	166	99	123	157	16

How Often He Throws Strikes

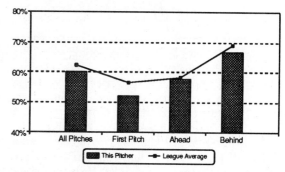

1991 Situational Stats

	W	L	ERA	Sv	IP		AB	H	HR	RBI	AVG
Home	3	1	3.26	2	38.2	LHB	133	30	4	23	.226
Road	0	1	3.10	0	29.0	RHB	100	21	3	16	.210
Day	0	0	1.86	1	9.2	Sc Pos	68	17	1	32	.250
Night	3	2	3.41	1	58.0	Clutch	84	21	1	18	.250

1991 Rankings (National League)

➡ 1st in highest percentage of inherited runners scored (48.6%)

➡ 9th lowest batting average allowed in relief (.219)

PITCHING:

Xavier Hernandez took one step backward in order to move several steps forward last season. It may have been just what Hernandez' pitching career needed going into 1992. Hernandez took his midseason demotion to AAA Tucson with a positive attitude and made the most of it.

Armed with a good sinker ball and forkball, the young righthander needed another pitch to gain an edge. He went to Tucson and worked on developing a breaking ball, and he returned with a slider that had some zip. Now, he has two pitches to throw against right-handed batters and two to throw against lefties, and he's become more effective. His late-season showing in '91 became one of the bright spots in the Astros' bullpen.

Hernandez' win at Cincinnati in mid-September broke a personal seven-game losing streak and he posted a 2-1 record with three saves in his final 12 appearances. This closing spurt took the sting out of a 2-7 season with a 4.71 ERA. Overall, he allowed only seven of 21 inherited base runners to score last season. "He's got a nice, loose arm, and I like the life on his fastball," said one scout who watched him work late in the year.

HOLDING RUNNERS, FIELDING, HITTING:

Hernandez is paying closer attention to runners, which is necessary, since his slow front leg kick gives them the chance to get a good jump. He went through 32 games without making an error, but got shut out at the plate, going 0-for-10 with seven strikeouts as a hitter.

OVERALL:

The Astros' closer job is wide open and Hernandez needs to hold his late-season form to challenge for the job this season. In three seasons, he's posted ERAs of 4.76, 4.62 and 4.71, so he's going to have to show that his September improvement wasn't just temporary. Most likely, he'll be used in a middle-innings role.

XAVIER HERNANDEZ

Position: RP/SP
Bats: L **Throws:** R
Ht: 6' 2" **Wt:** 185

Opening Day Age: 26
Born: 8/16/65 in Port Arthur, TX
ML Seasons: 3

Overall Statistics

	W	L	ERA	G	GS	Sv	IP	H	R	BB	SO	HR
1991	2	7	4.71	32	6	3	63.0	66	34	32	55	6
Career	5	8	4.68	73	7	3	148.0	151	83	64	86	16

How Often He Throws Strikes

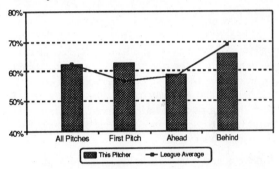

This Pitcher — League Average

1991 Situational Stats

	W	L	ERA	Sv	IP		AB	H	HR	RBI	AVG
Home	1	3	3.18	1	28.1	LHB	129	28	1	17	.217
Road	1	4	5.97	2	34.2	RHB	122	38	5	14	.311
Day	1	2	3.09	0	11.2	Sc Pos	76	20	3	27	.263
Night	1	5	5.08	3	51.1	Clutch	44	13	0	4	.295

1991 Rankings (National League)

➡ Led the Astros in lowest batting average allowed vs. left-handed batters (.217)

HOUSTON ASTROS

PITCHING:

With a strong first third of the season, Jimmy Jones revived his sagging pitching career last season. He made the Houston club as a non-roster invitee to spring training. Now he has to hang on to the job.

Originally signed by San Diego as a power pitcher, Jones drifted to the New York Yankees and became a free agent after two uneventful years. He landed with the Astros on a look-see basis and they gave him an opportunity. Jones is now a finesse guy, more of a thinking man's pitcher. He is not overpowering, but he throws a whole arsenal of pitches -- fastball, slow curve, harder curve, change-up -- and he changes speeds well.

An elbow problem removed Jones from the rotation late in the '91 season, but he should be part of Houston's plans for the future. He has proven he can pitch in the big leagues, especially when he has command of his pitches. Jones is a heady pitcher who knows how to set up hitters and make them hit his pitch. A native Texan, he displayed some consistency in winning four of his first five decisions as an Astro.

Jones pitched very well in the Astrodome, taking full advantage of the stadium's large dimensions. "He doesn't have the overpowering stuff like those two young guys (Darryl Kile and Ryan Bowen)," says one National League scout, "but he knows how to pitch. He's a good, solid pitcher when healthy."

HOLDING RUNNERS, FIELDING HITTING:

Jones has a decent pickoff move, but opponent baserunners were able steal 18 bases on him. His hitting stroke is no serious threat to opposing pitchers, but he will occasionally slap out a base hit.

OVERALL:

Jones' 1992 role depends on the progress of the team's young arms this spring. He can hold down the fourth or fifth starting roles or work as a long reliever. He'll turn 28 in April, and fits neatly into the club's youth movement.

JIMMY JONES

Position: SP
Bats: R **Throws:** R
Ht: 6' 2" **Wt:** 190

Opening Day Age: 27
Born: 4/20/64 in Dallas, TX
ML Seasons: 6

Overall Statistics

	W	L	ERA	G	GS	Sv	IP	H	R	BB	SO	HR
1991	6	8	4.39	26	22	0	135.1	143	73	51	88	9
Career	29	32	4.42	116	89	0	576.0	627	333	191	286	53

How Often He Throws Strikes

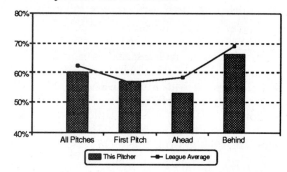

1991 Situational Stats

	W	L	ERA	Sv	IP		AB	H	HR	RBI	AVG
Home	4	3	3.08	0	96.1	LHB	348	105	6	40	.302
Road	2	5	7.62	0	39.0	RHB	182	38	3	19	.209
Day	2	1	2.12	0	29.2	Sc Pos	125	36	0	44	.288
Night	4	7	5.03	0	105.2	Clutch	31	5	0	2	.161

1991 Rankings (National League)

➡ 6th highest batting average allowed vs. left-handed batters (.302)

PITCHING:

Typical of the Houston Astros last season was Darryl Kile, a young pitcher just beginning to flex his muscles. Kile went through a learning process in '91, just like many of his teammates, and the tall righthander expects to be much-improved this year for the experience. With Houston's commitment to youth, Kile was among those Astro players thrown into the major league fire to see if they could hold their own. After a brief spell in the bullpen, he moved into the starting rotation and produced a 7-11 record with a 3.69 ERA.

Control difficulties and inexperience kept Kile from improving on those numbers. He walked 84 batters in 153.2 innings, but a lot of that had to do with trying to make the perfect pitch all the time. Kile struck out 100. He is a big (6-5) pitcher with a good, live arm and a lot of poise. The Astros had boasted of his vast potential for several years before his rookie debut, and Kile backed up those claims with his performance.

Kile and Ryan Bowen have the best curveballs on the staff. In fact, Kile has one of the best curveballs in the league right now, says one National Leaguer. He throws it 90 miles an hour and he's working on a change-up that is already very good. When he puts it all together, look out.

HOLDING RUNNERS, FIELDING, HITTING:

It's painful to watch Kile with a bat in his hands. He went 0-for-38, with 23 whiffs, as a rookie. In the field he made three errors, but he has a good, quick throw to the bag with a runner on base.

OVERALL:

At age 22 last season, Kile was the youngest starter in the Astros' rotation since 1977. He didn't pitch like it. With his exceptional pitches, he seems on the verge of bursting into the winner's circle in a big way. He has the ability to settle into the number-two spot in the rotation behind Pete Harnisch.

DARRYL KILE

Position: SP/RP
Bats: R **Throws:** R
Ht: 6' 5" **Wt:** 185

Opening Day Age: 23
Born: 12/2/68 in Garden Grove, CA
ML Seasons: 1

Overall Statistics

	W	L	ERA	G	GS	Sv	IP	H	R	BB	SO	HR
1991	7	11	3.69	37	22	0	153.2	144	81	84	100	16
Career	7	11	3.69	37	22	0	153.2	144	81	84	100	16

How Often He Throws Strikes

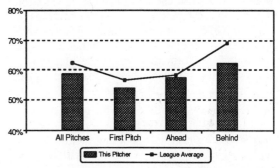

1991 Situational Stats

	W	L	ERA	Sv	IP		AB	H	HR	RBI	AVG
Home	4	5	3.36	0	77.2	LHB	343	90	7	36	.262
Road	3	6	4.03	0	76.0	RHB	242	54	9	34	.223
Day	1	5	5.08	0	33.2	Sc Pos	182	40	5	53	.220
Night	6	6	3.30	0	120.0	Clutch	31	7	1	6	.226

1991 Rankings (National League)

- → 2nd in walks allowed (84)
- → 3rd in balks (4)
- → 6th lowest winning percentage (.389)
- → 7th in hit batsmen (6)
- → 8th lowest batting average allowed with runners in scoring position (.220)
- → Led the Astros in walks allowed and hit batsmen

PITCHING:

After three years of agonizingly slow recovery from shoulder surgery, Rob Mallicoat returned to the major leagues in 1991, four seasons after shoulder problems derailed his career. The road was a tough haul, taking Mallicoat from the low minors in 1990 to Houston by the latter stages of 1991. He was able to renew his confidence and pitch his way into the team's plans as a long reliever.

Mallicoat missed all of 1988 and 1989 before starting all over in the instructional league. The lean lefthander began the 1991 season at AA Jackson, where he went 4-1 and averaged over a strikeout an inning. Promoted to AAA Tucson, Mallicoat was 4-4 and got a late call to Houston. Appearing in 24 games, he re-established his credentials, although his record (0-2, 3.86, one save) was nothing to brag about. Mallicoat displayed flashes of the form that had made him one of Houston's top prospects before his injury woes set him back after the 1987 season.

Mallicoat is again throwing with good velocity, averaging 86 to 88 MPH and occasionally topping 90. As his arm strength grew, he lost the feel for his curveball, creating problems with his control (13 walks in 23 innings). He relied on his slider again to combat this.

Mallicoat still needs to develop an offspeed pitch rather than be forced to come in with fastballs when behind in the count. But his breaking stuff is already major league. "He's got the best breaking ball of any lefthander in our organization," says Astro pitching coach Bob Cluck.

HOLDING RUNNERS, FIELDING, HITTING:

Mallicoat has a lefty's natural move to first base and he fields his position well -- one error in 24 games. He batted just once with the big club.

OVERALL:

Mallicoat beat the timetable for his return to the major leagues after his shoulder problems. This year, with Al Osuna, the Astros have two dependable lefties in the bullpen, something lacking during most of '91.

ROB MALLICOAT

Position: RP
Bats: L **Throws:** L
Ht: 6' 3" **Wt:** 180

Opening Day Age: 27
Born: 11/16/64 in St. Helen's, OR
ML Seasons: 2

Overall Statistics

	W	L	ERA	G	GS	Sv	IP	H	R	BB	SO	HR
1991	0	2	3.86	24	0	1	23.1	22	10	13	18	2
Career	0	2	4.50	28	1	1	30.0	30	15	19	22	2

How Often He Throws Strikes

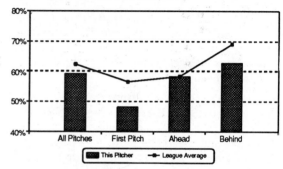

1991 Situational Stats

	W	L	ERA	Sv	IP		AB	H	HR	RBI	AVG
Home	0	1	8.59	0	7.1	LHB	38	10	1	9	.263
Road	0	1	1.69	1	16.0	RHB	47	12	1	7	.255
Day	0	0	1.80	1	10.0	Sc Pos	29	10	1	15	.345
Night	0	2	5.40	0	13.1	Clutch	35	11	1	10	.314

1991 Rankings (National League)

→ 8th in holds (11)
→ Led the Astros in holds

PITCHING:

The Astros didn't hesitate to turn the ball over to rookie lefthander Al Osuna last season. That was partly out of necessity, but also because of the team's growing dependence on him. Osuna set an Astros rookie record with 71 appearances, which tied for third on the club's single-season chart. Only one other lefty, Juan Agosto, has ever been more active for the Astros than Osuna (82 appearances in 1990 and 75 in 1988).

Osuna is part of a new generation; he advanced through the minors as a relief pitcher after signing out of the University of Southern California. In fact, he's never started a game in professional ball. Osuna often labored in the closer role for the Astors, converting just 12 of 21 save opportunities, but his work gave the Astros definite hope for the future. The rookie had to carry a heavy load in the bullpen as other closers failed, and he proved to be the most effective of those used as the late-inning stopper.

As a general rule relief pitchers throw two pitches, but Osuna's an exception. His best pitch is an excellent screwball, one which helped the southpaw hold righties to a .179 average. He also has an 88-MPH fastball and two different sliders -- a big one and a short one. Osuna's mostly a screwball/fastball pitcher, however. Controlling his pitches has been his big problem, and last year he averaged more than one walk every two innings.

HOLDING RUNNERS, FIELDING, HITTING:

Osuna usually works with men on base and has improved at holding runners. Considered an average fielder, he made only one error all season and went hitless in two plate appearances.

OVERALL:

Osuna rang up one-third of the Astros' saves in '91 and his role should grow this season. With a year under his belt, he figures to get better. Houston's search for a needed closer could begin and end with Osuna, but only if he develops better control of his varied stuff.

AL OSUNA

Position: RP
Bats: R **Throws:** L
Ht: 6' 3" **Wt:** 200

Opening Day Age: 26
Born: 8/10/65 in Inglewood, CA
ML Seasons: 2

Overall Statistics

	W	L	ERA	G	GS	Sv	IP	H	R	BB	SO	HR
1991	7	6	3.42	71	0	12	81.2	59	39	46	68	5
Career	9	6	3.58	83	0	12	93.0	69	45	52	74	6

How Often He Throws Strikes

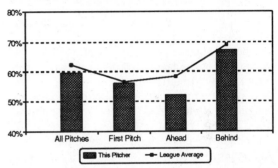

1991 Situational Stats

	W	L	ERA	Sv	IP		AB	H	HR	RBI	AVG
Home	4	3	4.35	5	41.1	LHB	109	26	3	21	.239
Road	3	3	2.45	7	40.1	RHB	184	33	2	17	.179
Day	1	0	0.40	3	22.1	Sc Pos	79	21	2	34	.266
Night	6	6	4.55	9	59.1	Clutch	199	41	4	32	.206

1991 Rankings (National League)

- → 1st in lowest save percentage (57.1%)
- → 2nd in blown saves (9)
- → 5th in relief wins (7) and lowest batting average allowed in relief (.201)
- → 6th in games pitches (71)
- → 8th in highest percentage of inherited runners scored (35.1%) and relief losses (6)
- → 9th in holds (10)
- → Led the Astros in games pitched, saves (12), save opportunities (21), blown saves, relief wins, relief losses and relief innings (81.2)

PITCHING:

In something of a career change, Mark Portugal went from starting pitcher in '91 to potential bullpen closer at season's end. Portugal had a good first half as a starter (8-5, 3.84), but then shifted to the bullpen after being banged around in August and early September. He agreed to make the switch when the club's young starting pitchers began flashing their skills. The results were mixed.

Whether permanent or not, the chunky righthander wanted to give it a shot and the Astros were anxious for a solution to one of their most pressing needs. Portugal ended the season 10-12 with a 4.49 ERA and only one save, so he obviously hasn't yet proven himself as a reliever.

Portugal is an aggressive pitcher and has the mentality for the closer's role. But he's also been the number-two starter behind Pete Harnisch; the development of the team's young arms will determine which direction he goes. He throws a fastball, curveball, slider and a dandy change-up. He gets great arm speed on the change and mystifies hitters. Portugal can throw it in the strike zone, right down the middle in the danger zone, and get away with it because of the deception of the pitch. Say one National Leaguer, "He has four pitches and all are above average. His change may be the best around."

HOLDING RUNNERS, FIELDING, HITTING:

Though he has had a tendency to put on weight, Portugal's a good athlete who prides himself on holding runners and pounces on any ball hit his way. His move to first is not exceptional, but he works fast and gets rid of the ball quickly. He is the best hitting pitcher on the Houston team.

OVERALL:

With neither Al Osuna, Curt Schilling nor anyone else having locked up Houston's closer role, the job could well fall to Portugal. He's always wanted to meet the late-inning challenge with the game on the line. It could come down to a decision between Osuna, Schilling and Portugal.

MARK PORTUGAL

Position: SP/RP
Bats: R **Throws:** R
Ht: 6' 0" **Wt:** 190

Opening Day Age: 29
Born: 10/30/62 in Los Angeles, CA
ML Seasons: 7

Overall Statistics

	W	L	ERA	G	GS	Sv	IP	H	R	BB	SO	HR
1991	10	12	4.49	32	27	1	168.1	163	91	59	120	19
Career	39	42	4.20	156	100	5	711.2	695	357	268	480	84

How Often He Throws Strikes

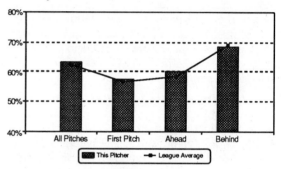

1991 Situational Stats

	W	L	ERA	Sv	IP		AB	H	HR	RBI	AVG
Home	4	5	3.06	1	79.1	LHB	366	89	10	45	.243
Road	6	7	5.76	0	89.0	RHB	271	74	9	34	.273
Day	5	4	5.11	1	49.1	Sc Pos	143	44	6	58	.308
Night	5	8	4.24	0	119.0	Clutch	58	20	2	9	.345

1991 Rankings (National League)

- ➡ 1st in highest ERA (4.49)
- ➡ 2nd in highest ERA on the road (5.76)
- ➡ 3rd most home runs allowed per 9 innings (1.0)
- ➡ 4th highest batting average allowed with runners in scoring position (.308)
- ➡ Led the Astros in losses (12), home runs allowed (19), GDPs induced (15), groundball/flyball ratio (1.3), lowest stolen base percentage allowed (63.2%), least pitches thrown per batter (3.55), most run support per 9 innings (4.5) and most GDPs induced per 9 innings (.80)

HITTING:

No player likes making the transition from starter to utility man, but Rafael Ramirez went through the process without a murmur of complaint. But while Ramirez won points for his attitude, he didn't win many raves for his play. The veteran batted only .236 coming off the bench last year, the second-lowest average of his career.

Ramirez remains a dependable hitter in clutch situations; it's just that those times are less frequent now. He still is capable of stringing together back-to-back game-winning pinch hits, as he did in early August games against Dodger reliever John Candelaria. But those moments were infrequent, and he hit only .231 (9-for-39) as a pinch swinger last year. Ramirez' overall average dropped 25 points from his 1990 level; with his noted impatience (.274 on-base average) and lack of power (11 extra-base hits in 233 at-bats), he has to hit over .260 to have any offensive value at all.

Ramirez remains adept at taking the pitch to center and right field, seldom pulling the ball. He's always been a good contact hitter, but last year he struck out almost as many times as in 1990 in about half as many at-bats -- another sign that his bat is slowing.

BASERUNNING:

Ramirez runs the bases well despite his years. He is alert at taking the extra base, but he's not much of a stolen base threat. He was only 3-for-6 last year.

FIELDING:

Ramirez' range has decreased and his arm is not a gun, yet he did an acceptable job in the field while playing short, second and third. He usually ranks among league leaders in errors, but committed only eight in mainly a utility role.

OVERALL:

If free agent Ramirez fails to remain with the Astros, he should land with another club as a bench player in 1992. His defensive skills are not overwhelming, however, and Ramirez will have to hit better than he did in 1991.

RAFAEL RAMIREZ

Position: SS/2B
Bats: R **Throws:** R
Ht: 5'11" **Wt:** 190

Opening Day Age: 33
Born: 2/18/59 in San Pedro de Macoris, Dominican Republic
ML Seasons: 12

Overall Statistics

	G	AB	R	H	D	T	HR	RBI	SB	BB	SO	AVG
1991	101	233	17	55	10	0	1	20	3	13	40	.236
Career	1466	5318	545	1388	218	31	52	471	112	257	597	.261

Where He Hits the Ball

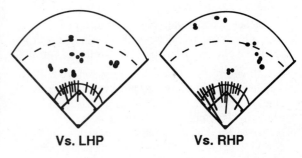

Vs. LHP   Vs. RHP

1991 Situational Stats

	AB	H	HR	RBI	AVG		AB	H	HR	RBI	AVG
Home	91	22	0	10	.242	LHP	110	27	1	14	.245
Road	142	33	1	10	.232	RHP	123	28	0	6	.228
Day	53	13	0	4	.245	Sc Pos	61	13	0	18	.213
Night	180	42	1	16	.233	Clutch	72	18	0	9	.250

1991 Rankings (National League)

→ 6th lowest batting average with 2 strikes (.129)
→ 8th lowest percentage of extra bases taken as a runner (29.4%)

PITCHING:

When Curt Schilling joined the Houston Astros last year, he quickly made known his all-consuming goal: to be the closer, the go-to guy in the bullpen. The former Baltimore set-up man has the disposition for the role, and he loves the challenge of being the late-inning man with the game on the line. He began the '91 season as the team's stopper, but things quickly went downhill. Schilling got cuffed around, the bad days far outweighing the good.

After pitching well early, Schilling blew several leads, his won-lost record dipped to 3-5 and his ERA rose to 4.86. He went to AAA Tucson to work out his problems and to get better command of his pitches. He fared better after his return, finishing the season with eight saves in 11 opportunities. Scouts from other clubs keep asking about Schilling's availability because of his arm strength. Some wonder whether he has closer's stuff, but almost everyone likes Schilling's arm.

Schilling throws a fastball that reaches 90 MPH, a slider and a split-fingered pitch that he uses as a change-up. The fastball is decidedly his best pitch. When Schilling throws strikes, he is impressive. But lack of command over his fastball got him behind in the count much too often. Mostly, it is a matter of mechanics; if he smooths things out, he can be effective.

HOLDING RUNNERS, FIELDING, HITTING:

Schilling did an excellent job holding baserunners last year, allowing only three successful steals in seven attempts. He moves well for his size in fielding balls, making only one error all season. He is an aggressive hitter, but seldom bats.

OVERALL:

A shot of success can boost Schilling's confidence and make him the Astros' number-one reliever. Going into spring training, the job was open. He has the talent to succeed as a reliever -- closer or not -- if he continues to mature.

CURT SCHILLING

Position: RP
Bats: R **Throws:** R
Ht: 6' 4" **Wt:** 215

Opening Day Age: 25
Born: 11/14/66 in Anchorage, AK
ML Seasons: 4

Overall Statistics

	W	L	ERA	G	GS	Sv	IP	H	R	BB	SO	HR
1991	3	5	3.81	56	0	8	75.2	79	35	39	71	2
Career	4	11	4.16	100	5	11	145.0	149	73	71	113	8

How Often He Throws Strikes

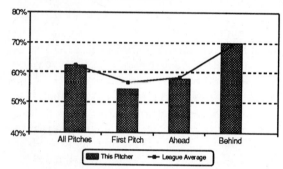

1991 Situational Stats

	W	L	ERA	Sv	IP		AB	H	HR	RBI	AVG
Home	3	3	3.64	3	47.0	LHB	149	38	1	14	.255
Road	0	2	4.08	5	28.2	RHB	142	41	1	24	.289
Day	0	1	4.15	1	17.1	Sc Pos	106	28	0	34	.264
Night	3	4	3.70	7	58.1	Clutch	138	39	1	20	.283

1991 Rankings (National League)

- ➡ 1st in worst first batter efficiency (.396)
- ➡ 2nd most baserunners allowed per 9 innings in relief (14.0)
- ➡ 5th most strikeouts per 9 innings in relief (8.45)
- ➡ 6th highest batting average allowed in relief (.271)
- ➡ Led the Astros in games finished (34) and most strikeouts per 9 innings in relief

HOUSTON ASTROS

HITTING:

Where have all the seasons gone, Gerald Young? Once a star player in the Houston Astros' firmament, Young has lost his place in that baseball galaxy. The bright shine of Young's half-season debut in 1987, when he batted .321, and the flashy spectacle of 65 stolen bases the next year have worn off in the struggles of the past three seasons.

The Astros don't really expect Young to hit .321 again, but they're finding it tough to retain belief in him. He can play the field with anyone, but hasn't been able to hold up his end at the plate. Young at least reversed the decline in his batting average last year (.257 in 1988, .233 in 1989 and .175 in 1990). But even with hard work, he only lifted his average to .218.

The Astros told Young he needed an attitude adjustment and the speedy center fielder tried to follow orders. They want him to hit the ball on the ground, use the bunt and take advantage of his speed. Maybe they've just given him **too** much advice, and compounded the problems. To his credit, Young makes decent contact, and he's learned to reach base frequently via the walk. Despite his lowly batting average, Young's .327 on-base average was ten points above the league average.

BASERUNNING:

Young's legs remain his biggest asset. He stole 16 bases in 21 attempts last year, and obviously could have stolen a lot more given increased playing time. His 76 percent success rate was the best of his career.

FIELDING:

Young can go get the ball in center field and has not allowed hitting woes to infringe on his defensive prowess. His arm is more than adequate for the job. He did not make an error in the field in '91.

OVERALL:

At 27, Young still has time to revive his career. His skills -- great speed, excellent defense, above-average ability to reach base -- might appeal to another club. But his chances for a regular job with the Astros seem pretty remote.

GERALD YOUNG

Position: CF
Bats: B **Throws:** R
Ht: 6' 2" **Wt:** 185

Opening Day Age: 27
Born: 10/22/64 in Tela, Honduras
ML Seasons: 5

Overall Statistics

	G	AB	R	H	D	T	HR	RBI	SB	BB	SO	AVG
1991	108	142	26	31	3	1	1	11	16	24	17	.218
Career	531	1679	235	418	54	16	3	105	147	210	193	.249

Where He Hits the Ball

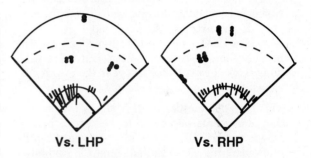

Vs. LHP   Vs. RHP

1991 Situational Stats

	AB	H	HR	RBI	AVG		AB	H	HR	RBI	AVG
Home	74	17	0	5	.230	LHP	78	19	1	4	.244
Road	68	14	1	6	.206	RHP	64	12	0	7	.188
Day	28	2	0	0	.071	Sc Pos	28	7	0	10	.250
Night	114	29	1	11	.254	Clutch	35	5	0	4	.143

1991 Rankings (National League)

→ Led the Astros in stolen base percentage (76.2%)

ERIC ANTHONY

Position: RF
Bats: L **Throws:** L
Ht: 6' 2" **Wt:** 195

Opening Day Age: 24
Born: 11/8/67 in San Diego, CA
ML Seasons: 3

Overall Statistics

	G	AB	R	H	D	T	HR	RBI	SB	BB	SO	AVG
1991	39	118	11	18	6	0	1	7	1	12	41	.153
Career	148	418	44	75	16	0	15	43	6	50	135	.179

HITTING, FIELDING, BASERUNNING:

Twice, the Houston Astros gave Eric Anthony the first shot as a starter in right field. Twice, he has gone down swinging. Anthony had a reasonable excuse in 1990 -- he was over-hyped, and when he didn't hit, he began to press. But when Anthony looked even worse last year, there were no excuses left.

This begs the question: will Anthony ever make the adjustments necessary to become a major league regular? Or, for that matter, even a fourth outfielder? It's show-and-tell time for Anthony. The Astros admittedly rushed him to the bigs in 1990. The second time around, though, he should have done better than a .153 batting average, better than 41 strikeouts in 118 at-bats, and better than one homer and 7 RBI. Anthony has tried to make adjustments, to make better contact, but he's got a large hole in his swing and the pitchers found it. He can hit fastballs into the upper deck. Breaking balls and offspeed pitches are another matter.

Anthony is an average baserunner, but has improved his play in the field with experience. He is still raw in a number of areas.

OVERALL:

At 24, it seems ludicrous to give up on Anthony, but he has little chance of making it with the Astros now. A change of scenery might do him a lot of good.

ANDY MOTA

Position: 2B
Bats: R **Throws:** R
Ht: 5'10" **Wt:** 180

Opening Day Age: 26
Born: 3/4/66 in Santo Domingo, Dominican Republic
ML Seasons: 1

Overall Statistics

	G	AB	R	H	D	T	HR	RBI	SB	BB	SO	AVG
1991	27	90	4	17	2	0	1	6	2	1	17	.189
Career	27	90	4	17	2	0	1	6	2	1	17	.189

HITTING, FIELDING, BASERUNNING:

As first impressions go, Andy Mota did not make the most of his promotion to Houston last season. Although he was the winner of back-to-back batting crowns in the minor leagues, Manny Mota's son struggled in his month with the Astros. He hit .189, with two doubles, one homer and six RBI.

Reputed to be a contact hitter, Mota struck out 17 times in 90 Astro at-bats. He showed no discipline whatsoever, drawing only one walk. Mota has hit everywhere he's played, but you sure couldn't prove that from the way he hit for the Astros.

Mota's play at second base did not assure the Astros he could handle a major league job defensively, either. He made three errors, had limited range in the field and did not display the skills required in playing around the bag. Perhaps too much was expected. Mota did display his advertised speed, though, stealing two bases without being caught.

OVERALL:

Mota must prove himself at the big league level. After watching Mota play second base the final month of '91, the Astros toyed with the idea of putting catcher Craig Biggio there. At 26, Mota is a bit old to be an up-and-coming prospect, but you've got to like his genes.

JAVIER ORTIZ

Position: LF
Bats: R **Throws:** R
Ht: 6' 4" **Wt:** 220

Opening Day Age: 29
Born: 1/22/63 in Boston, MA
ML Seasons: 2

ERIC YELDING

Position: SS
Bats: R **Throws:** R
Ht: 5'11" **Wt:** 165

Opening Day Age: 27
Born: 2/22/65 in Montrose, AL
ML Seasons: 3

Overall Statistics

	G	AB	R	H	D	T	HR	RBI	SB	BB	SO	AVG
1991	47	83	7	23	4	1	1	5	0	14	14	.277
Career	77	160	14	44	9	2	2	15	1	26	25	.275

Overall Statistics

	G	AB	R	H	D	T	HR	RBI	SB	BB	SO	AVG
1991	78	276	19	67	11	1	1	20	11	13	46	.243
Career	290	877	107	218	22	6	2	57	86	59	152	.249

HITTING, FIELDING, BASERUNNING:

In two seasons with Houston, Javier Ortiz has left no doubt that he can hit the ball as a reserve player and occasional starter. He's hit in the .275 range each year in a difficult role. Ortiz doesn't have much home run power, but he can drive the ball on occasion, and he has excellent plate discipline. Despite this, the Astros released Ortiz in their organizational house-cleaning.

After a 1990 call-up, Ortiz played well enough to push himself into the Astros' left field picture. But he tore ligaments in his left knee in a home plate collision and that shut him down after 30 games. This past year, Ortiz had not regained all of the limited speed he once had. When rookie Luis Gonzalez took hold of the left field spot, Ortiz was relegated to the bench. He went 5-for-21 (.239) as a pinch hitter.

Ortiz is only adequate in the field and doesn't have a great throwing arm. He stole some bases as a young minor leaguer, but Ortiz, 6-4 and 220, is no running threat.

OVERALL:

Ortiz, an aggressive hitter, has grown in the role of reserve, though he'd obviously like the chance to play more. He may not get the chance unless he can latch onto another club and immediately catch someone's eye.

HITTING, FIELDING, BASERUNNING:

Eric Yelding suffered setbacks in more than one area last season. He lost his starting job at shortstop, drew a demotion to the minors and suffered a fractured cheekbone and broken nose while playing at AAA Tucson.

The year was a definite downer for a young player who'd been considered one of the Astros' brighter young prospects. Handed a regular lineup spot as starting shortstop, Yelding batted .243 with only 13 extra-base hits. And Yelding, who'd been a terror on the base paths in 1990 with 64 steals, swiped only 11 bases in 20 attempts.

Both an infielder and an outfielder during his pro career, Yelding was moved back to shortstop as part of the Astros' master plan. He couldn't handle it, making 18 errors in 78 games at short. On a team rebuilding with young pitching and defense, this didn't cut it. Sent to Tucson to get himself together, Yelding got hit in the face by a pitch in another stroke of bad luck. While he was gone, Andujar Cedeno established himself as the Astros' shortstop, probably for years to come.

OVERALL:

Yelding faces heavy odds in any attempt to regain his old starting job at shortstop. His speed could push him into the outfield competition, where he logged playing time two years ago. That's probably his only hope for a regular berth.

ORGANIZATION OVERVIEW:

The Astros, as usual, are rebuilding. Throughout most of their history, this organization has had money problems, so it has tried to develop its own talent . . . the only route available. The results have been decidedly mixed. Last year, for instance, free agent losses enabled the Astros to wind up with seven of the top 50 picks in the draft; unfortunately, Houston wasn't able to sign several of them. That's all too typical. While Houston has talented people committed to youth in general manager Bill Wood and manager Art Howe, the franchise is for sale and the club's ownership is in flux. Who knows whether Wood and Howe will be around long enough to see their plans reach fruition?

GARY COOPER

Position: 3B
Bats: R **Throws:** R
Ht: 6' 1" **Wt:** 200

Opening Day Age: 27
Born: 8/13/64 in Lynwood, CA

Recent Statistics

	G	AB	R	H	D	THR	RBI	SB	BB	SO	AVG
91 AAA Tucson	120	406	86	124	25	6	14	75	7	66	108	.305
91 NL Houston	9	16	1	4	1	0	0	2	0	3	6	.250
91 MLE	120	379	53	97	21	4	6	47	4	41	120	.256

Does Gary Cooper have a great name? Yup. Is he a great prospect? Nope. At 27, Cooper finally reached AAA last year, showed some power and discipline, and batted .300 for the first time in his professional career. His glove skills are considered good. But Cooper's Pacific Coast League-inflated stats are not all that impressive. If the Astros let Ken Caminiti go and give their third base job to Cooper (his High Noon?), they're taking a big, big gamble.

JEFF JUDEN

Position: P
Bats: R **Throws:** R
Ht: 6' 7" **Wt:** 245

Opening Day Age: 21
Born: 1/19/71 in Salem, MA

Recent Statistics

	W	L	ERA	GG	GS	Sv	IP	H	R	BB	SO	HR
91 AA Jackson	6	3	3.10	16	16	0	95.2	84	43	44	75	4
91 AAA Tucson	3	2	3.18	10	10	0	56.2	56	28	25	51	2
91 NL Houston	0	2	6.00	4	3	0	18.0	19	14	7	11	3

Houston's top pick in 1989, Juden is huge and throws very hard; to the Astros, he's J.R. Richard and Nolan Ryan rolled into one. A former hockey player, Juden has an aggressive attitude, and his control, while not great, is improving. He has a chance to be an excellent pitcher, but it would probably help if the Astros don't hype him too much yet; he's had exactly 13 starts above the AA level.

KENNY LOFTON

Position: OF
Bats: L **Throws:** L
Ht: 5' 11" **Wt:** 175

Opening Day Age: 24
Born: 5/31/67 in East Chicago, IN

Recent Statistics

	G	AB	R	H	D	THR	RBI	SB	BB	SO	AVG
91 AAA Tucson	130	545	93	168	19	17	2	50	40	52	95	.308
91 NL Houston	20	74	9	15	1	0	0	0	2	5	19	.203
91 MLE	130	512	58	135	16	12	0	31	27	32	105	.264

Rated the top prospect in the Pacific Coast League by Baseball America, Lofton has the all-around athletic skills typical of such highly rated prospects: he can run, he can throw, he can play basketball. The key question is whether Lofton can hit a baseball, and the jury is still out on that one. Lofton hit very well in class A ball, but his AAA numbers were mediocre for the PCL, and he's shown almost no home run power. In Lofton's defense, he hasn't been playing baseball full-time all that long. He has a good chance, but this doesn't look like the 1992 Rookie of the Year.

DAVE ROHDE

Position: 2B
Bats: B **Throws:** R
Ht: 6' 2" **Wt:** 182

Opening Day Age: 27
Born: 5/8/64 in Los Altos, CA

Recent Statistics

	G	AB	R	H	D	THR	RBI	SB	BB	SO	AVG
91 AAA Tucson	73	253	36	94	10	4	1	40	15	52	34	.372
91 NL Houston	29	41	3	5	0	0	0	0	0	5	8	.122
91 MLE	73	233	22	74	8	3	0	25	10	32	39	.318

Curiously neglected, Rohde has spent two years at Tucson compiling stats that put Kenny Lofton's to shame, but all he's had to show for it has been a middling shot at a utility role. His glove seems decent enough, and the minor league stats surely indicate that he can hit. Rohde probably deserves a full shot at the Astros' second base job, but he may not get it this year. There's always expansion . . .

DONNELL WALL

Position: P
Bats: R **Throws:** R
Ht: 6' 1" **Wt:** 180

Opening Day Age: 24
Born: 7/11/67 in Potosi, MO

Recent Statistics

	W	L	ERA	GG	GS	Sv	IP	H	R	BB	SO	HR
90 A Asheville	6	8	5.18	28	22	1	132.0	149	87	47	111	18
91 A Burlington	7	5	2.03	16	16	0	106.2	73	30	21	102	4
91 A Osceola	6	3	2.09	12	12	0	77.1	55	22	11	62	3

An 18th-round draft choice out of Southwest Louisiana in 1989, Wall has been quietly compiling some very impressive stats at the class A level for the Astros. He throws strikes, he strikes people out, he doesn't give up many hits, and he wins. He's not as flashy as some of the other Astros' prospects, but he bears watching.

PITCHING:

In 1991, Tim Belcher was a much better pitcher than his 10-9 record would indicate. The Dodger offense simply shut down whenever he took the hill. Belcher had a 0.80 ERA in his ten wins and a 2.36 ERA in his 14 no-decisions. He did not record a win from June 23 until August 14, but in those eight starts in between, the team totalled only eleven runs in his support.

Belcher's best pitch is a 94-MPH four-seam fastball with good rising action, and the current waist-high strike zone is a real problem for him. He also throws a hard slider, a splitter and a curve that serves as his change when he can get it over. In fact, Belcher sometimes has control problems with all of his pitches. But he's tough to hit, especially for righthanders, who batted only .195 against him.

At times, Belcher can be his own worst enemy. Little things -- a walk, an error, a seemingly harmless scratch single -- bother him more than they should. He appears to lose some velocity and control from the stretch position; that and the lack of run support no doubt exacerbate the problem. Yet Belcher is the guy you want on the mound for a big game. Lifetime, he is 12-5, 1.90 ERA in September/October and 3-0 in postseason play.

HOLDING RUNNERS, FIELDING, HITTING:

When Belcher goes into a pitching funk, it affects him in every other phase of the game. He has no pickoff move to speak of, but normally fields his position well enough. Though he struck out over a third of the time, Belcher is a fine bunter and will send the occasional line drive into the outfield.

OVERALL:

Belcher has undeniably great stuff. Finally, at the age of 30, he is learning to keep his temper in check. With just a little luck, he could have won seven or eight more games last year. If he can stay healthy, Belcher is poised to become one of the most dominant pitchers in the league.

TIM BELCHER

Position: SP
Bats: R **Throws:** R
Ht: 6' 3" **Wt:** 223

Opening Day Age: 30
Born: 10/19/61 in Sparta, OH
ML Seasons: 5

Overall Statistics

	W	L	ERA	G	GS	Sv	IP	H	R	BB	SO	HR
1991	10	9	2.62	33	33	0	209.1	189	76	75	156	10
Career	50	38	2.99	138	119	5	806.0	680	309	261	633	57

How Often He Throws Strikes

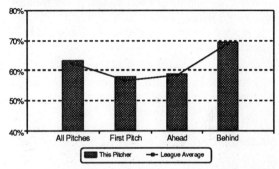

1991 Situational Stats

	W	L	ERA	Sv	IP		AB	H	HR	RBI	AVG
Home	7	4	2.67	0	121.1	LHB	445	122	4	33	.274
Road	3	5	2.56	0	88.0	RHB	344	67	6	33	.195
Day	2	3	3.28	0	57.2	Sc Pos	193	42	3	56	.218
Night	8	6	2.37	0	151.2	Clutch	97	26	0	6	.268

1991 Rankings (National League)

→ 2nd lowest batting average allowed vs. right-handed batters (.195)

→ 4th in lowest ERA (2.62) and least home runs allowed per 9 innings (.43)

→ 5th in lowest run support per 9 innings (3.4), ERA at home (2.67) and ERA on the road (2.56)

→ Led the Dodgers in ERA, games started (33), walks allowed (75), strikeouts (156), least home runs allowed per 9 innings, most strikeouts per 9 innings (6.7), ERA at home, lowest batting average allowed vs. right-handed batters and lowest batting average allowed with runners in scoring position (.218)

HITTING:

Brett Butler provided a core of consistency in what was an otherwise erratic Dodger attack last year. He hit .302 before his first All-Star appearance, .290 after. He hit .281 vs. lefties, .306 vs. righties. He hit .290 with the bases empty, .310 with runners on and .309 with runners in scoring position. All in all, Butler was everything the Dodgers expected when they signed him to a free agent contract before the season -- and then some.

In addition to his team-high 182 hits and .296 batting average, the consummate leadoff man drew 108 walks, raising his on-base average to .401, second in the N.L. Almost a third (59 of 182) of Butler's hits never left the infield, and 21 of them were bunts. Though his usual modus operandi is to slap the ball to the left side and then run like heck, Butler is capable of pulling the ball when the situation calls for it.

In fact, Butler is capable of doing a lot of things that don't show up in the box score. He saw a whopping average of 4.2 pitches per plate appearance, fouling off anything that wasn't to his liking. He is a master at expending the opposing pitcher's energy while protecting his own hurler.

BASERUNNING:

Though he stole a team-high 38 bases, Butler was thrown out an alarming 28 times. Even so, like he is at the plate, the little guy is a pest on the bases. He's a constant threat and will always take the extra base. In addition, he's a sliding clinic in action.

FIELDING:

Butler played an errorless 161 games in center field, establishing a new N.L. record. He played the role of field general, calling off Daniels and Strawberry on any ball he could reach. Though Butler has a weak arm, he always throws to the right base and hits the cutoff man.

OVERALL:

Butler was clearly the Dodgers' MVP on the field. He was among the N.L. leaders in many categories and solidified a potentially disastrous outfield. Though he'll be 35 this summer, he remains an outstanding player.

BRETT BUTLER

Position: CF
Bats: L **Throws:** L
Ht: 5'10" **Wt:** 160

Opening Day Age: 34
Born: 6/15/57 in Los Angeles, CA
ML Seasons: 11

Overall Statistics

	G	AB	R	H	D	T	HR	RBI	SB	BB	SO	AVG
1991	161	615	112	182	13	5	2	38	38	108	79	.296
Career	1521	5616	962	1606	202	88	41	400	396	762	606	.286

Where He Hits the Ball

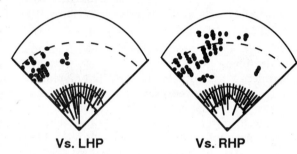

Vs. LHP   **Vs. RHP**

1991 Situational Stats

	AB	H	HR	RBI	AVG		AB	H	HR	RBI	AVG
Home	295	92	2	22	.312	LHP	256	72	0	14	.281
Road	320	90	0	16	.281	RHP	359	110	2	24	.306
Day	175	48	1	14	.274	Sc Pos	110	34	1	36	.309
Night	440	134	1	24	.305	Clutch	106	32	1	12	.302

1991 Rankings (National League)

➡ 1st in runs (112), singles (162), caught stealing (28), walks (108), times on base (291), pitches seen (3,064), plate appearances (730), games (161), lowest HR frequency (307.5 ABs per HR), leadoff on-base average (.401) and fielding percentage in center field (1.000)

➡ 2nd in at-bats (615), hits (182), on-base average (.401), groundball/flyball ratio (3.7), pitches seen per plate appearance (4.20) and bunts in play (51)

➡ Led the Dodgers in batting average (.296), at-bats, runs, hits, singles, stolen bases (38), caught stealing, walks, times on base, pitches seen, plate appearances, games and on-base average

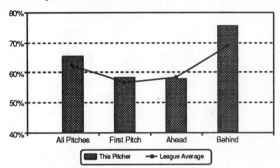

TOUGH ON LEFTIES

JOHN CANDELARIA

Position: RP
Bats: R **Throws:** L
Ht: 6' 6" **Wt:** 225

Opening Day Age: 38
Born: 11/6/53 in
Brooklyn, NY
ML Seasons: 17

PITCHING:

John Candelaria made the Dodger staff for one reason last year: his ability to get out left-handed hitters. They hit just .138 against him (righties hit .354). So time and again the gangly Candelaria would trudge in from the bullpen to record a single out, then flip the ball to pitching coach Ron Perranoski and trudge to the showers. He appeared in 59 games and pitched a total of 33.2 innings. No pitcher has ever worked so few innings in that many games.

Candelaria is tall with extremely long arms, making his release point seem to be halfway to first base. He cross-fires the fastball and cutter, then uses the slow curve as a change. Though he held the first (and often only) batter he faced to a paltry .179 average, opponents had good success at taking a shot at the first pitch fastball (.389 when hitting the first pitch).

Candelaria was quite effective in the first half of the season, posting a nifty 1.74 ERA up to the break. Then it all fell apart. His ERA after the All-Star game was 6.92 and opponents lit him up for a .364 average. Though he suffered with a sore knee all year, there was no discernible change in his motion or delivery; Candelaria simply lost his effectiveness as his aging body wore down over the long campaign.

HOLDING RUNNERS, FIELDING, HITTING:

Candelaria has a fair move and appears to get off the mound fairly well for his size. He handled only two chances all season, both successfully. He never made a plate appearance.

OVERALL:

The Dodgers believe in playing the percentages, yet they went most of the year with a 37 year old as the only southpaw coming out of their pen. The late season acquisition of Steve Wilson along with Candelaria's second half collapse may have signalled the end of his short career with the Dodgers. That might well mean retirement, but another contending club may be willing to give Candelaria a shot.

Overall Statistics

	W	L	ERA	G	GS	Sv	IP	H	R	BB	SO	HR
1991	1	1	3.74	59	0	2	33.2	31	16	11	38	3
Career	175	114	3.30	526	356	23	2481.1	2354	1010	570	1633	242

How Often He Throws Strikes

(bar chart: All Pitches, First Pitch, Ahead, Behind)
Legend: This Pitcher — League Average

1991 Situational Stats

	W	L	ERA	Sv	IP		AB	H	HR	RBI	AVG
Home	1	0	3.60	1	15.0	LHB	58	8	1	4	.138
Road	0	1	3.86	1	18.2	RHB	65	23	2	14	.354
Day	0	1	5.14	0	7.0	Sc Pos	44	10	1	15	.227
Night	1	0	3.38	2	26.2	Clutch	90	24	1	13	.267

1991 Rankings (National League)

- 1st in holds (19)
- 3rd lowest percentage of inherited runners scored (18.3%)
- Led the Dodgers in holds, blown saves (3), first batter efficiency (.179) and lowest percentage of inherited runners scored

HITTING:

Gary Carter followed up his surprisingly productive 1990 season for the Giants with an almost identical year for the Dodgers. Though he started slowly (.091 in April), Carter's average increased each month until September. For two different stretches, he stepped in as the full-time catcher when Mike Scioscia went down. He even filled in at first base a few times.

Carter's eyes light up when he spots a pitch he can pull: inside heat, hanging curve, anything offspeed. Otherwise, he's a selective hitter, though he doesn't walk a lot. Pitchers try to lure him into chasing something just off the outside corner, and he'll sometimes bite. Looking to pull, he moved on top of the plate more last year, and wound up getting hit by seven pitches, matching his career high despite his limited duty.

Carter offered glimpses of his old power last year, driving in 26 runs with 14 doubles and six homers. He proved that he needs to start in order to be productive. Carter went just 2-for-27 (.074) with one RBI as a pinch hitter.

BASERUNNING:

Carter is a 37-year-old catcher in the twilight of a probable Hall of Fame career. He's a smart, station-to-station baserunner who looks as though he's carrying an extra load on his back. Still, he stole two bases in four attempts.

FIELDING:

Carter was brought on board for his leadership qualities behind the plate. He was always on the same page as the staff and has an especially good rapport with the umpires. Except for blocking the plate, the team lost nothing when Carter was back there.

OVERALL:

The Dodgers signed Carter as an experienced insurance policy and it paid off handsomely. But with their aging roster, they didn't have a lot of interest in bringing the veteran back for 1992. Carter's is making a sentimental journey back to Montreal, where he began his major league career 18 seasons ago.

GARY CARTER

Position: C
Bats: R **Throws:** R
Ht: 6' 2" **Wt:** 214

Opening Day Age: 38
Born: 4/8/54 in Culver City, CA
ML Seasons: 18

Overall Statistics

	G	AB	R	H	D	T	HR	RBI	SB	BB	SO	AVG
1991	101	248	22	61	14	0	6	26	2	22	26	.246
Career	2201	7686	1001	2030	353	30	319	1196	39	815	960	.264

Where He Hits the Ball

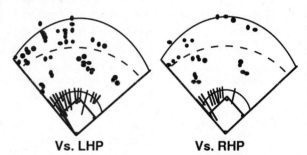

Vs. LHP   Vs. RHP

1991 Situational Stats

	AB	H	HR	RBI	AVG		AB	H	HR	RBI	AVG
Home	125	27	3	11	.216	LHP	151	38	3	14	.252
Road	123	34	3	15	.276	RHP	97	23	3	12	.237
Day	59	13	0	3	.220	Sc Pos	69	18	1	19	.261
Night	189	48	6	23	.254	Clutch	54	12	1	3	.222

1991 Rankings (National League)

- 2nd in batting average on a 3-1 count (.667)
- 4th in hit by pitch (7)
- Led the Dodgers in hit by pitch and batting average on a 3-1 count

PITCHING:

Though Tim Crews established a new career high with six saves, he had an uneven 1991. His ERA of 3.43 was his highest in five ML seasons and he blew three other save opportunities. Crews was actually a victim of his own success. His worst months (June, 5.40 ERA; September, 7.27) came in heavy usage right after his two best ones (May, 2.89; August, 1.23). When he's on, the team tends to call upon him often. Crews has a durable arm, but not one made of iron. Like any pitcher, when he gets tired, he gets hit.

Like many other Ron Perranoski projects, Crews lives on the outside corner. He likes to start with a slider away, hoping to either nick the corner or get the batter to flail at one that just misses. Batters do very well (.441) when they're able to hit that first pitch. He'll fire his mediocre fastball inside to back the hitter off a bit, then go right back to work on the outside edge.

Possessing great control, Crews walked only eight batters (unintentionally) in 76 innings. He can spot the ball just about where he wants it. All three of his pitches, fastball, slider and forkball, move down and away from right-handed hitters, who hit just .212 against him. However, those pitches end up where lefties like the ball, down and in, and they tend to feast on his offerings (.303).

HOLDING RUNNERS, FIELDING, HITTING:

Crews knows how to help himself on the mound. He has a pretty good move to first and fields his position well. He struck out and walked in his only two plate appearances in '91.

OVERALL:

Crews has established himself as the jack-of-all-trades in the Dodger bullpen. In the best of times, he's the first man up, ready to go three or four innings to keep the team in the game. It's a thank-less job, but one for which he is well-suited.

TIM CREWS

Position: RP
Bats: R **Throws:** R
Ht: 6' 0" **Wt:** 195

Opening Day Age: 31
Born: 4/3/61 in Tampa, FL
ML Seasons: 5

Overall Statistics

	W	L	ERA	G	GS	Sv	IP	H	R	BB	SO	HR
1991	2	3	3.43	60	0	6	76.0	75	30	19	53	7
Career	11	10	3.05	232	2	15	345.2	349	135	90	250	28

How Often He Throws Strikes

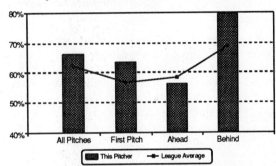

1991 Situational Stats

	W	L	ERA	Sv	IP		AB	H	HR	RBI	AVG
Home	2	1	2.95	4	36.2	LHB	142	43	3	19	.303
Road	0	2	3.89	2	39.1	RHB	151	32	4	17	.212
Day	1	0	2.05	3	22.0	Sc Pos	79	18	3	29	.228
Night	1	3	4.00	3	54.0	Clutch	93	24	3	13	.258

1991 Rankings (National League)

→ 5th highest batting average allowed vs. left-handed batters (.303)

→ Led the Dodgers in games pitched (60), relief innings (76) and least baserunners allowed per 9 innings in relief (11.1)

HITTING:

Kal Daniels' 1990 numbers (.296 BA, 27 HR, 94 RBI) seemed to prove that, despite years of nagging injuries, his hitting skills remained undiminished. Yet in '91 Daniels slumped to .249 with 17 HR and 73 RBI. One must now wonder whether his chronic knee problems have begun hampering his ability to drive the ball.

Daniels is a selective hitter with a thorough knowledge of the strike zone. He always walks a lot, but his strikeout totals have gone up every year as well. Daniels' whining about every called strike is hurting him at the plate; umpires are clearly losing their patience with him. He might need to become more aggressive. He hit .317 on the first pitch, but a dismal .139 with two strikes against him.

When things are going well for him, Daniels will hit the ball where it's pitched, occasionally showing tremendous power to left-center. Last year, he seemed uncertain at the plate, with many at-bats ending in feeble checked swings. Daniels' reputation as a clutch hitter could come into question should he have another year like this one (.237 in the late innings of close games).

BASERUNNING:

His hobbled gait makes it hard to believe that Daniels stole 27 bases for the Reds just four years ago. Now the pain and discomfort forces him to choose his spots. He was six for seven in steal attempts and can take the extra base when it's needed.

FIELDING:

Daniels is a fair outfielder at best. He gets a poor jump, especially on balls over his head, and will often give up on them too soon. Daniels is better on line drives in front of him and to the side, and is not afraid to leave his feet to make a catch. He has a below-average arm.

OVERALL:

Daniels' bad attitude is starting to catch up with him, even with his own teammates. His disappearing acts at crucial times are growing quite old. The club would like to move him, though his poor season might make that difficult.

KAL DANIELS

Position: LF
Bats: L **Throws:** R
Ht: 5'11" **Wt:** 205

Opening Day Age: 28
Born: 8/20/63 in Vienna, GA
ML Seasons: 6

Overall Statistics

	G	AB	R	H	D	T	HR	RBI	SB	BB	SO	AVG
1991	137	461	54	115	15	1	17	73	6	63	116	.249
Career	644	2126	370	615	114	8	98	335	87	343	439	.289

Where He Hits the Ball

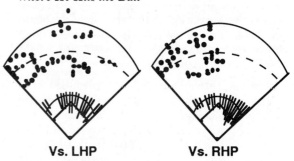

Vs. LHP   Vs. RHP

1991 Situational Stats

	AB	H	HR	RBI	AVG		AB	H	HR	RBI	AVG
Home	242	60	12	48	.248	LHP	206	52	6	36	.252
Road	219	55	5	25	.251	RHP	255	63	11	37	.247
Day	109	22	4	19	.202	Sc Pos	127	37	9	61	.291
Night	352	93	13	54	.264	Clutch	76	18	1	14	.237

1991 Rankings (National League)

→ 3rd lowest batting average (.250)

→ 5th least runs scored per time reached base (30.2%)

→ 7th in strikeouts (116)

→ 8th in highest groundball/flyball ratio (1.8) and lowest batting average at home (.248)

→ Led NL left fielders in strikeouts, groundball/flyball ratio and most pitches seen per plate appearances (3.83)

PITCHING:

Jim Gott entered the 1991 season throwing harder than he had in several years. He felt no more lingering effects, mental or physical, from his elbow surgery in early '89. So it was especially frustrating to be constantly pitching himself out of trouble in the first half. Gott had problems with his control, which pitching coach Ron Perranoski attributed to the righthander feeling "too strong" after favoring his tender arm over the previous two years.

After a particularly ineffective June (6.35 ERA), Gott finally found his groove. He became the workhorse of the bullpen, posting a fine 2.66 ERA in 47.1 innings of work after the All-Star break (3.45 ERA, 28.2 IP before). He ended up walking 3.8 batters per nine innings, not great but identical to his career ratio. Gott has the ability to bear down with men on base. First batters he faced compiled a .319 average, but that mark went down to .200 with men on base and sank to .167 with runners in scoring position.

Gott is a power pitcher. His fastball is registering in the low 90s again and he follows that up with a hard slider and an occasional curve. In Gott's splendid year for Pittsburgh in '88 (6 wins, 34 saves, 3.49 ERA), he struck out 76 batters in 77.1 innings of work. He fanned 73 in 76 IP in '91 with an ERA of 2.96; it certainly appears that Gott has regained his old form.

HOLDING RUNNERS, FIELDING, HITTING:

Gott's big leg kick makes him easy prey for base stealers. He moves well for a big man and gets off the mound in good shape. Gott swings a mean stick, but made just three plate appearances in 1991.

OVERALL:

The Dodgers signed Gott to a big two-year deal last winter. He pitched as well as anyone down the stretch (2.04 in September) and looks to be the main set-up man and co-closer with Roger Mc-Dowell next year.

JIM GOTT

Position: RP
Bats: R **Throws:** R
Ht: 6' 4" **Wt:** 220

Opening Day Age: 32
Born: 8/3/59 in Hollywood, CA
ML Seasons: 10

Overall Statistics

	W	L	ERA	G	GS	Sv	IP	H	R	BB	SO	HR
1991	4	3	2.96	55	0	2	76.0	63	28	32	73	5
Career	42	56	3.98	362	96	55	886.2	854	446	376	647	70

How Often He Throws Strikes

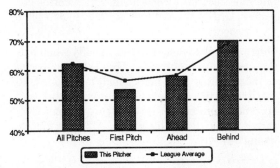

1991 Situational Stats

	W	L	ERA	Sv	IP		AB	H	HR	RBI	AVG
Home	1	0	2.68	1	37.0	LHB	141	27	2	9	.191
Road	3	3	3.23	1	39.0	RHB	141	36	3	15	.255
Day	2	0	2.35	0	15.1	Sc Pos	72	12	1	17	.167
Night	2	3	3.12	2	60.2	Clutch	68	15	0	10	.221

1991 Rankings (National League)

- ➡ 3rd most strikeouts per 9 innings in relief (8.6)
- ➡ 5th worst first batter efficiency (.319)
- ➡ 7th lowest batting average allowed vs. left-handed batters (.191)
- ➡ Led the Dodgers in blown saves (3), lowest batting average allowed vs. left-handed batters, relief ERA (2.96), relief innings (76), lowest batting average allowed in relief (.223) and most strikeouts per 9 innings in relief

HITTING:

Alfredo Griffin began the 1991 season as a question mark due to a career-threatening back injury. Last year Griffin missed considerable time with a toe injury, a fractured cheekbone and a sprained knee. Ironically, the stints on the bench may have kept the aging veteran fresh. When he was able to play, Griffin had a productive year for the Dodgers.

As a right-handed batter (.270 in '91), Griffin is an aggressive spray-hitter with some pop in his bat. Left-handed (.223), Griffin has one of the ugliest swings in the majors. At times, both feet appear to leave the ground. From either side, he likes to jump on the first-pitch fastball or, if that fails, the second-pitch fastball. Legendarily impatient, Griffin walked just 22 times in 385 plate appearances.

Griffin uses the whole field, especially when batting from the right side. The better-prepared teams play their right fielder shallow and close to the line. Griffin is never an automatic out and becomes more dangerous with runners on (.292) and especially late in the game (.313 from the 7th inning on).

BASERUNNING:

At 35, Griffin has a quick first step and runs quite well, though he's not much of a threat to steal any more. Although unsuccessful, his attempt to reach second after walking was one of the year's highlights.

FIELDING:

Griffin's principal value to the team is clearly as a stabilizing influence in an erratic infield. He positions himself well, has pretty good range and hits Murray's mitt from anywhere on the field. He'll make his share of errors, but wants the ball hit to him with the game on the line.

OVERALL:

Griffin is a real gamer. One fellow player nominated him as the team MVP after he came back just four weeks after cheekbone surgery. But with Jose Offerman waiting in the wings, it's very possible that free agent Griffin has played his last game as a Dodger.

ALFREDO GRIFFIN

Position: SS
Bats: B **Throws:** R
Ht: 5'11" **Wt:** 166

Opening Day Age: 35
Born: 3/6/57 in Santo Domingo, Dominican Republic
ML Seasons: 16

Overall Statistics

	G	AB	R	H	D	T	HR	RBI	SB	BB	SO	AVG
1991	109	350	27	85	6	2	0	27	5	22	49	.243
Career	1853	6535	723	1633	235	78	24	514	189	326	632	.250

Where He Hits the Ball

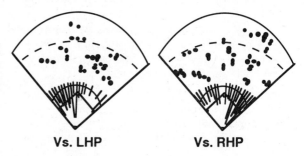

Vs. LHP   **Vs. RHP**

1991 Situational Stats

	AB	H	HR	RBI	AVG		AB	H	HR	RBI	AVG
Home	158	32	0	11	.203	LHP	148	40	0	9	.270
Road	192	53	0	16	.276	RHP	202	45	0	18	.223
Day	95	27	0	9	.284	Sc Pos	80	21	0	26	.262
Night	255	58	0	18	.227	Clutch	64	21	0	5	.328

1991 Rankings (National League)

→ 1st in lowest fielding percentage at shortstop (.960) and lowest batting average with the bases loaded (.083)

→ 3rd highest percentage of extra bases taken as a runner (75.0%)

→ 6th in lowest slugging percentage vs. left-handed pitchers (.290) and bunts in play (27)

→ Led the Dodgers in batting average in the clutch (.328) and steals of third (3)

PITCHING:

The Dodgers signed Kevin Gross largely due to his reputation as a workhorse. Gross had averaged over 200 innings per year over the previous six seasons and with a rotation full of question marks, that stability was quite attractive. Ironically, Gross went out and got hammered in his first three starts (13.50 ERA). He was given the starting assignment only seven more times the rest of the year and finished with only 115.2 IP.

Gross ended up as the club's self-declared "utility pitcher." As Orel Hershiser worked his way back from shoulder surgery, Gross had to be ready to back him up with three to five innings of work; he twice started on short notice when the former ace proved unable to answer the bell. Gross even filled in as the closer for a short time, picking up three saves in that role.

Gross throws a rising four-seam fastball and a hard slider, but the key to his success is getting his curve over. It breaks straight down and keeps the hitters off-balance. When opposing batters, especially lefties (.313 BA), sit on his fastball, Gross is in trouble. Opponents hit .391 on the first pitch and .339 when Gross got behind in the count. When he got ahead, they hit only .180.

HOLDING RUNNERS, FIELDING, HITTING:

Gross doesn't help himself much on the mound. Opposing runners love his high leg kick, and he's only a fair fielder at best. He can swing the bat, however, hitting .280 with three RBI in his limited plate appearances.

OVERALL:

Once he settled down, Gross pitched well. He had a 3.03 ERA and led the team with six wins after the All-Star break. He complained very little despite the way he was used, an admirable trait on a club that liked to hear itself whine. With Mike Morgan and Hershiser facing free agency and Bob Ojeda able to demand a trade, Gross will more than likely amass his usual 200 innings in '92.

KEVIN GROSS

Position: RP/SP
Bats: R **Throws:** R
Ht: 6' 5" **Wt:** 215

Opening Day Age: 30
Born: 6/8/61 in Downey, CA
ML Seasons: 9

Overall Statistics

	W	L	ERA	G	GS	Sv	IP	H	R	BB	SO	HR
1991	10	11	3.58	46	10	3	115.2	123	55	50	95	10
Career	90	101	3.99	311	231	4	1585.0	1570	767	633	1091	143

How Often He Throws Strikes

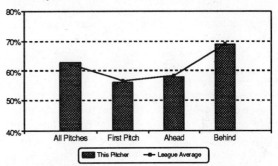

1991 Situational Stats

	W	L	ERA	Sv	IP		AB	H	HR	RBI	AVG
Home	7	3	2.79	1	61.1	LHB	233	73	6	32	.313
Road	3	8	4.47	2	54.1	RHB	214	50	4	16	.234
Day	3	4	4.08	0	35.1	Sc Pos	95	32	1	38	.337
Night	7	7	3.36	3	80.1	Clutch	109	32	2	12	.294

1991 Rankings (National League)

→ 2nd highest batting average allowed in relief (.285)

→ 3rd in highest batting average allowed vs. left-handed batters (.313) and most baserunners allowed per 9 innings in relief (13.8)

→ 8th in relief losses (6)

→ 9th in relief wins (6)

→ Led the Dodgers in blown saves (3), relief wins and relief losses

HITTING:

Lenny Harris is a good hitter: as the main Dodger third baseman for two seasons, he's batted .304 and .287, very respectable averages. But Harris has totalled only five homers in 860 at-bats in those two seasons, along with a total of only 67 RBI. That makes the Dodgers restless and yearn for the good old days of Ron Cey.

Harris is best when he raps the ball back through the middle or to the opposite field. He often gets himself out by pulling the ball, temporarily forgetting that he packs little power in his stocky body. Working him down and in will often work.

Harris has been labelled a platoon player from the beginning, but he held his own against all but the toughest lefties (.241). He jumps on the fastball from either side and generally makes contact. He knows how to protect the plate, striking out just 32 times in 429 ABs.

BASERUNNING:

Harris has very good speed, but he is not a good baserunner. He'll often blaze on toward the next bag only to find himself out by five steps. His base stealing improved last year (12 of 15), which may bode well for the future.

FIELDING:

Harris is the best second baseman on the team, but he rarely gets to play there. His great range is wasted at third, and his arm is only average. His natural exuberance will sometimes affect his decision-making on the field; twice last year he got caught trying to tag a runner coming into third and ended up getting no one.

OVERALL:

Vin Scully says that Harris is "guaranteed to make you smile, make you feel good." That is a valuable component on what is generally an uptight team. But it doesn't make up for the offense the Dodgers surrender by playing Harris. His skills -- both offensive and defensive -- are better suited for second, and that's where he may end up this year.

LENNY HARRIS

Position: 3B/2B/SS
Bats: L **Throws:** R
Ht: 5'10" **Wt:** 205

Opening Day Age: 27
Born: 10/28/64 in Miami, FL
ML Seasons: 4

Overall Statistics

	G	AB	R	H	D	T	HR	RBI	SB	BB	SO	AVG
1991	145	429	59	123	16	1	3	38	12	37	32	.287
Career	413	1238	163	349	43	6	8	101	45	91	100	.282

Where He Hits the Ball

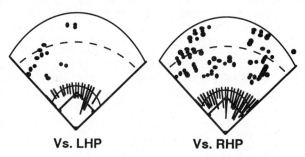

Vs. LHP   Vs. RHP

1991 Situational Stats

	AB	H	HR	RBI	AVG		AB	H	HR	RBI	AVG
Home	211	58	1	17	.275	LHP	87	21	1	9	.241
Road	218	65	2	21	.298	RHP	342	102	2	29	.298
Day	123	32	1	10	.260	Sc Pos	100	28	2	32	.280
Night	306	91	2	28	.297	Clutch	73	23	0	7	.315

1991 Rankings (National League)

➡ 2nd lowest fielding percentage at third base (.943)

➡ 5th in sacrifice bunts (12) and GDPs (17)

➡ Led the Dodgers in sacrifice bunts, GDPs, batting average with the bases loaded (.444) and batting average on an 0-2 count (.286)

➡ Led NL third basemen in sacrifice bunts, batting average on an 0-2 count, batting average with 2 strikes (.262), bunts in play (17) and highest percentage of swings put into play (52.4%)

PITCHING:

After a year of intense rehabilitative work, Orel Hershiser returned to the mound in late May of last season. He barely made it out of the first inning. Slowly but surely, however, Hershiser regained a semblance of his old form. Though he missed a few turns and lasted only an inning another time, Hershiser was 4-0, 3.22 ERA after the All-Star break (3-2, 3.80 before).

Hershiser clearly had problems loosening up his surgically-repaired shoulder. In Hershiser's first 30 pitches of each outing, opposing hitters pounded out a .317 average. They hit just .223 afterwards. Whether effective or not, Hershiser was on a strict 90-pitch count all year, facing only two batters after that mark. The Dodgers, understandably, preferred to err on the side of caution; hopefully, there won't be a need to do that this year.

Hershiser may have permanently lost some MPH on his fastball, but he never blew people away anyway. His cut fastball moves down and away, his sinker down and in, and he can hit the mitt all game long. Hershiser is especially tough once he's ahead in the count; opponents hit just .140 with two strikes on them.

HOLDING RUNNERS, FIELDING, HITTING:

For such a gangly guy, Hershiser fields his position very well. He has a pretty good move to first and gets rid of the ball quickly. He really knows how to handle the bat, hitting .258 last year. In bunt situations, Hershiser is just as likely to "butcher-boy" a chopper through the incoming infield as he is to lay one down.

OVERALL:

The Dodgers face an intriguing dilemma with the free agent Hershiser. Though not the old Hershiser, he went 2-0, 1.04 in September and the team posted a 16-5 mark in games that he started. Plus the fans adore him. Ultimately, it's hard to imagine Hershiser in another uniform. They'll probably agree to a deal loaded with incentive clauses.

OREL HERSHISER

Position: SP
Bats: R **Throws:** R
Ht: 6' 3" **Wt:** 192

Opening Day Age: 33
Born: 9/16/58 in Buffalo, NY
ML Seasons: 9

Overall Statistics

	W	L	ERA	G	GS	Sv	IP	H	R	BB	SO	HR
1991	7	2	3.46	21	21	0	112.0	112	43	32	73	3
Career	106	67	2.77	256	216	5	1594.1	1378	563	470	1100	79

How Often He Throws Strikes

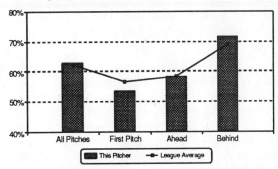

1991 Situational Stats

	W	L	ERA	Sv	IP		AB	H	HR	RBI	AVG
Home	3	2	3.27	0	63.1	LHB	208	59	2	20	.284
Road	4	0	3.70	0	48.2	RHB	225	53	1	20	.236
Day	2	0	5.16	0	22.2	Sc Pos	105	29	1	35	.276
Night	5	2	3.02	0	89.1	Clutch	7	1	0	0	.143

1991 Rankings (National League)

➡ 3rd in balks (4)
➡ Led the Dodgers in balks

LOS ANGELES DODGERS

PITCHING:

Jay Howell followed up an injury-plagued 1990 campaign with a year in which physical problems allowed him to pitch even less. Howell's left knee held up for the first half and he had 11 saves and a 2.67 ERA at the All-Star break. But it flared up on him in July and he pitched just 17.1 innings the rest of the year. Howell's unavailability down the stretch (when his problem was a strained elbow) had as much to do with the Dodgers failure as anything else.

Howell has always been a hard thrower, but the sharp downward break of his curveball makes it his strikeout pitch. He fanned 40 in 51 IP and showed exceptionally good control, issuing just eight unintentional walks. As has been the case in each of the last three years, Howell had better success against lefthanders (.175) than versus righties (.256).

Howell pitched well when he was available. He tallied 16 saves, the seventh straight season that he's reached that mark. He was very tough at home (6-2, 2.84), though the win total was inflated by the home team's uncanny ability to score in their last at-bat. His lack of success on the road (0-3, 3.72) was largely due to a stratospheric 8.22 ERA on turf.

HOLDING RUNNERS, FIELDING, HITTING:

Howell's big leg kick makes it relatively easy to steal against him, but since he's always pitching late in close games, he can get by. His knee slows down his fielding, too, though he's not really a terrible defensive player. Howell did not make a plate appearance last year and remains hitless in seven at-bats as a Dodger.

OVERALL:

Howell has been **the** bullpen leader the last four years, exhorting his fellow crew members into battle with Patton-like speeches. The arrival of Roger McDowell makes it unlikely that Howell, a free agent, will remain in LA. Howell has been a very effective closer when healthy, so somebody will no doubt take a chance on him.

JAY HOWELL

Position: RP
Bats: R **Throws:** R
Ht: 6' 3" **Wt:** 220

Opening Day Age: 36
Born: 11/26/55 in Miami, FL
ML Seasons: 12

Overall Statistics

	W	L	ERA	G	GS	Sv	IP	H	R	BB	SO	HR
1991	6	5	3.18	44	0	16	51.0	39	19	11	40	3
Career	50	46	3.41	433	21	149	696.0	649	281	241	571	42

How Often He Throws Strikes

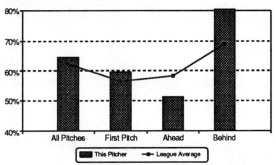

1991 Situational Stats

	W	L	ERA	Sv	IP		AB	H	HR	RBI	AVG
Home	6	2	2.84	8	31.2	LHB	97	17	1	11	.175
Road	0	3	3.72	8	19.1	RHB	86	22	2	8	.256
Day	0	0	4.15	5	13.0	Sc Pos	49	10	1	16	.204
Night	6	5	2.84	11	38.0	Clutch	137	25	2	14	.182

1991 Rankings (National League)

- 9th in least GDPs induced per GDP situation (3.1%) and relief wins (6)
- 10th in saves (16)
- Led the Dodgers in saves, games finished (35), save opportunities (18) and relief wins

STAFF ACE

RAMON MARTINEZ

Position: SP
Bats: L **Throws:** R
Ht: 6' 4" **Wt:** 173

Opening Day Age: 24
Born: 3/22/68 in Santo Domingo, Dominican Republic
ML Seasons: 4

PITCHING:

Only time will tell if Ramon Martinez' right arm has already begun paying the price for all those hard innings he has been asked to pitch. The 24 year old (though there are rumors that he is older) has averaged more than 220 innings pitched over the last three seasons. Martinez went into the All-Star break with a splendid 12-3, 2.54 mark only to go 5-10, 4.15 the rest of the way. And 11 of his 18 HR were allowed after August 1st.

There's a reason why Martinez is asked to finish games: the guy knows how to close it out. Opponents hit just .171 from the seventh inning on, and if the game was close, that average went down to .121. Furthermore, they hit .130 after he had thrown 120 pitches. Unfortunately, the Dodgers allow Martinez to continue from the 120-pitch point quite often.

The young Dominican throws in the low-to-mid-90s and has great motion when throwing the change-up. He has trouble getting his curveball over, especially in cold and/or damp weather. Martinez likes the conditions in Chavez Ravine; he is 21-6, 2.80 over the past two years there.

HOLDING RUNNERS, FIELDING, HITTING:

Martinez' lanky frame takes a while to unwind and runners take advantage. He gets off the mound fairly well, but will occasionally make a bad toss to a bag. He has finally decided to be a full-time left-handed hitter (after a few years of experimentation) and though he looks awkward, Martinez drove in nine runs last year.

OVERALL:

Martinez threw 133 pitches in a 10-3 win on September 1st, proving that Tommy Lasorda is not simply boasting when he says that he pays "no attention to pitch counts." Lasorda lost his last two aces to severe shoulder problems and one hopes that he will show more concern in protecting this one. Martinez has a chance to be one of the greats.

Overall Statistics

	W	L	ERA	G	GS	Sv	IP	H	R	BB	SO	HR
1991	17	13	3.27	33	33	0	220.1	190	89	69	150	18
Career	44	26	3.15	90	87	0	589.0	487	234	199	485	51

How Often He Throws Strikes

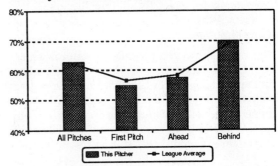

1991 Situational Stats

	W	L	ERA	Sv	IP		AB	H	HR	RBI	AVG
Home	9	4	2.91	0	105.0	LHB	453	102	7	39	.225
Road	8	9	3.59	0	115.1	RHB	375	88	11	40	.235
Day	6	5	2.74	0	72.1	Sc Pos	190	45	4	60	.237
Night	11	8	3.53	0	148.0	Clutch	66	8	1	2	.121

1991 Rankings (National League)

- → 2nd in shutouts (4) and least GDPs induced per 9 innings (.25)
- → 3rd in most pitches thrown per batter (3.84)
- → 4th in wins (17), hit batsmen (7) and lowest groundball/flyball ratio (.91)
- → 5th in complete games (6) and pitches thrown (3,516)
- → Led the Dodgers in wins (17), losses (13), games started (33), complete games, shutouts, home runs allowed (18), hit batsmen, pitches thrown and most run support per 9 innings (4.9)

PITCHING:

Roger McDowell joined the Dodgers' million dollar bullpen (four members earning over $1 million per year!) on the last day of July. He instantly became the club's late-inning guy, contributing 42.1 IP, seven saves and six wins (in nine decisions) in just over two months. McDowell needs a lot of work to be effective; he sure got it in LA, working seven of nine games during one stretch in August.

Even pitching coach Ron Perranoski was surprised to see how hard McDowell throws his fastball (low 90s at times), but it's his sinker that gets hitters out. It explodes down and in on righthanders, forcing them to hammer the ball into the ground. McDowell averaged 2.9 groundballs for every flyball once he joined the Dodgers. Why his ERA was so much higher at home (3.86) than on the road (0.95) is a mystery.

McDowell thrives on pressure situations, which is one of the main reasons the Dodgers picked him up. His September ERA was 1.50. Opposing batters hit .281 with the bases empty, .243 with runners on and .227 with men in scoring position. He appears to have the ability to bear down at crunch time, a crucial prerequisite for any closer.

HOLDING RUNNERS, FIELDING, HITTING:

With the double play such a big part of his game, McDowell must hold runners close. He pitches from a closed stance, but ends up in good fielding position. McDowell occasionally suffers from brain cramps on the mound, like when he threw home with two outs in a late-season game. Though McDowell handles the bat well in batting practice, he never made a plate appearance in a game for the Dodgers.

OVERALL:

With free agent Jay Howell's Dodger career probably over, McDowell looks like the new guy in town. His stand-up comedy approach to the game is a refreshing change from the current tight-lipped Dodgers. Should the front office ever make infield defense a priority, McDowell could be very tough.

ROGER McDOWELL

Position: RP
Bats: R **Throws:** R
Ht: 6' 1" **Wt:** 186

Opening Day Age: 31
Born: 12/21/60 in Cincinnati, OH
ML Seasons: 7

Overall Statistics

	W	L	ERA	G	GS	Sv	IP	H	R	BB	SO	HR
1991	9	9	2.93	71	0	10	101.1	100	40	48	50	4
Career	51	49	3.03	467	2	135	712.2	661	280	259	349	30

How Often He Throws Strikes

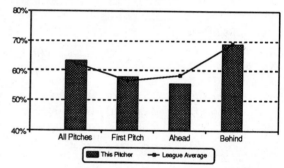

1991 Situational Stats

	W	L	ERA	Sv	IP		AB	H	HR	RBI	AVG
Home	5	5	3.48	4	51.2	LHB	196	53	2	26	.270
Road	4	4	2.36	6	49.2	RHB	185	47	2	21	.254
Day	0	2	3.71	2	26.2	Sc Pos	132	30	0	42	.227
Night	9	7	2.65	8	74.2	Clutch	258	70	3	29	.271

1991 Rankings (National League)

→ 1st in relief losses (9)

→ 2nd in worst first batter efficiency (.354) and least strikeouts per 9 innings in relief (4.4)

→ 3rd in relief wins (9) and relief innings (101.1)

→ 5th most baserunners allowed per 9 innings in relief (13.3)

→ 6th in games pitched (71)

→ 9th in holds (10), blown saves (5) and lowest batting average allowed with runners in scoring position (.227)

→ Led the Dodgers in relief wins (6 while with the Dodgers)

PITCHING:

By finishing 14-10 last year, Mike Morgan was finally able to shed the albatross of never having had a winning season in his 11-year major league career. Morgan established career highs in wins, innings pitched (236.1) and strikeouts (140). Always a fast starter, Morgan avoided the second half fade that had plagued him the two previous seasons. He was 4-0, 2.89 in the crucial month of September.

Morgan throws his two- and four-seam fastballs hard enough to keep batters honest, and he's got great control (2.3 walks per nine innings). He likes to work in and out, keeping the ball down so hitters will drive his heavy ball into the ground. Morgan gets incredible movement on his two-seamer. On his best days, it'll break a good eight inches away from left-handed batters. Many of Morgan's strikeouts come when hitters give up on a pitch that curls back over the inside corner.

Physically, Morgan is a horse. He's worked into the seventh inning in 44 of 66 starts over the last two years. He tends to hit the wall at 90 pitches, however; opponents hit .348 after that point last year. But Morgan allowed two earned runs or less in 21 of his 33 starts, so the team is almost always in the game with him on the mound.

HOLDING RUNNERS, FIELDING, HITTING:

Morgan likes to keep runners honest by mixing a variety of head bobs and step-offs with a fair move to first. His compact, efficient delivery leaves him in good fielding position and he plays his position well. At the plate, Morgan usually makes contact but rarely gets the ball to drop in safely.

OVERALL:

Morgan craves the respect and big money that better-than-average free agent pitchers command these days. He wants to be "a number-one or two starter," but never pitched like one until he hooked up with Ron Perranoski and Mike Scioscia. Though Morgan would be silly to leave the pitcher-friendly confines of Chavez Ravine, the free agent seems determined to do just that.

MIKE MORGAN

Position: SP
Bats: R **Throws:** R
Ht: 6' 2" **Wt:** 222

Opening Day Age: 32
Born: 10/8/59 in Tulare, CA
ML Seasons: 11

Overall Statistics

	W	L	ERA	G	GS	Sv	IP	H	R	BB	SO	HR
1991	14	10	2.78	34	33	1	236.1	197	85	61	140	12
Career	67	104	4.10	264	204	3	1385.1	1448	700	467	660	123

How Often He Throws Strikes

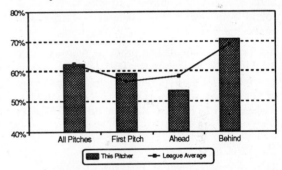

1991 Situational Stats

	W	L	ERA	Sv	IP		AB	H	HR	RBI	AVG
Home	6	5	3.32	1	119.1	LHB	495	113	9	41	.228
Road	8	5	2.23	0	117.0	RHB	376	84	3	29	.223
Day	5	4	1.98	1	72.2	Sc Pos	163	41	0	55	.252
Night	9	6	3.13	0	163.2	Clutch	90	23	1	8	.256

1991 Rankings (National League)

→ 2nd in GDPs induced (23), lowest slugging percentage allowed (.306), lowest ground-ball/flyball ratio (2.6) and ERA on the road (2.23)

→ 3rd in innings (236.1), lowest on-base average allowed (.278) and most GDPs induced per 9 innings (.88)

→ 5th least home runs allowed per 9 innings (.46) and lowest batting average allowed vs. right-handed batters (.223)

→ Led the Dodgers in games started (33), innings, hits allowed (197), batters faced (949), most stolen bases allowed (24), GDPs induced, winning percentage (.583) and strikeout/walk ratio (2.3)

HITTING:

Eddie Murray's 1991 season was gutted by a mysterious rib injury that no one wanted to discuss. After hitting .300 through the end of May, Murray went into a horrific slump that lasted two months. He hit .229 in June and .172 in July. Murray never asked to come out of the lineup, never blamed nor even mentioned the injury until the story was leaked in August. Who on the club knew about it is still uncertain.

Even at full strength, Murray had trouble from the right side, hitting just .217. Pitchers would bust him inside with fastballs, then try to fool him with off-speed stuff when they got ahead in the count. It worked, as Murray waved helplessly at a lot of balls, an unusual sight for him. His hit and walk totals both decreased substantially from past years.

Yet when it came time to produce, Murray came through. He delivered 96 RBI, only a couple below his lifetime average. And during the month of September, when the Dodgers were trying unsuccessfully to hold off Atlanta, he hit .351 with six homers and 23 RBI.

BASERUNNING:

Though slow, Murray is quite fun to watch on the base paths. Last year he stole 10 bases, matching his career high, in just 13 attempts. And though he won't challenge the league's best arms, Murray will take the extra base if it's there.

FIELDING:

It was not simply reputation that enabled Murray to win three Gold Gloves. He makes the throw to second as well as any right-handed first sacker, and seldom misplays grounders or bunts. Murray has problems with pop-ups hit behind him and will occasionally wander too far from the bag chasing a grounder in the hole.

OVERALL:

Murray's three years in LA have been very productive. The Dodgers have shown a reluctance to go with rookies, but Murray will be 36 next year. If he is willing to settle on a two-year deal, Murray might be able to cap off a magnificent career in his hometown.

EDDIE MURRAY

Position: 1B
Bats: B **Throws:** R
Ht: 6' 2" **Wt:** 222

Opening Day Age: 36
Born: 2/24/56 in Los Angeles, CA
ML Seasons: 15

Overall Statistics

	G	AB	R	H	D	T	HR	RBI	SB	BB	SO	AVG
1991	153	576	69	150	23	1	19	96	10	55	74	.260
Career	2288	8573	1279	2502	425	30	398	1469	86	1081	1150	.292

Where He Hits the Ball

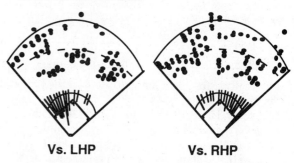

Vs. LHP   **Vs. RHP**

1991 Situational Stats

	AB	H	HR	RBI	AVG		AB	H	HR	RBI	AVG
Home	282	76	11	50	.270	LHP	254	55	6	40	.217
Road	294	74	8	46	.252	RHP	322	95	13	56	.295
Day	148	41	4	26	.277	Sc Pos	155	40	5	75	.258
Night	428	109	15	70	.255	Clutch	97	26	3	18	.268

1991 Rankings (National League)

➤ 3rd in lowest percentage of extra bases taken as a runner (20.5%) and intentional walks (17)

➤ 5th in GDPs (17)

➤ 7th lowest on-base average vs. left-handed pitchers (.269)

➤ Led the Dodgers in doubles (23), sacrifice flies (8), intentional walks, GDPs and steals of third (3)

➤ Led NL first basemen in GDPs and steals of third

HITTING:

Proclaimed the Dodgers' top prospect -- and their shortstop of the future -- Jose Offerman hasn't measured up in two pressure-filled trials with the big club. Offerman has batted only .181 over 171 at-bats, and has managed only three extra-base hits. People are beginning to get restless.

Though the Dodgers understandably want to maximize Offerman's blazing speed, there are serious doubts about his ability to hit left-handed. With the Dodgers, the switch-hitter has batted only .116 in 95 ABs while batting lefty. On the plus side, he has shown a particularly good eye hitting lefty, drawing 22 walks over that same span.

Right-handed, Offerman looks like a whole different hitter. While he has a loopy, lazy arc to his bat when batting left-handed, his swing from the right side is sure and compact. Offerman hit .300 as a righty in '91 and was very aggressive. He likes to drive fastballs, especially up in the strike zone, to left field and back through the box.

BASERUNNING:

Offerman has great speed, one of the few offensive attributes not enhanced by the thin air in AAA Albuquerque. He had stolen at least 57 bases every full year before '91 and will take an extra base on the slightest opportunity.

FIELDING:

Though Offerman's defense was shaky under pennant race pressure, he gets to balls, both on the ground and in the air, that others don't even dream of reaching. Like many young shortstops, however, he often tries to do too much. He'll exhibit his strong arm from an off-balance position, and the ball will often end up in the dirt or in the dugout.

OVERALL:

A controversial figure at age 23, Offerman has divided fans and baseball people over whether he can make it as a major league shortstop. Reportedly, Tommy Lasorda doesn't want to play him. But if the Dodgers don't give Offerman a chance to assert himself by playing him every day beginning in April, they could ruin his chances of ever succeeding in this impatient town.

JOSE OFFERMAN

Position: SS
Bats: B **Throws:** R
Ht: 6' 0" **Wt:** 160

Opening Day Age: 23
Born: 11/8/68 in San Pedro de Macoris, Dominican Republic
ML Seasons: 2

Overall Statistics

	G	AB	R	H	D	T	HR	RBI	SB	BB	SO	AVG
1991	52	113	10	22	2	0	0	3	3	25	32	.195
Career	81	171	17	31	2	0	1	10	4	29	46	.181

Where He Hits the Ball

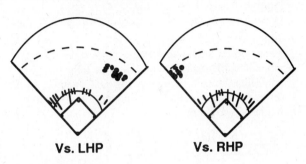

Vs. LHP   Vs. RHP

1991 Situational Stats

	AB	H	HR	RBI	AVG		AB	H	HR	RBI	AVG
Home	61	14	0	1	.230	LHP	50	15	0	2	.300
Road	52	8	0	2	.154	RHP	63	7	0	1	.111
Day	34	6	0	1	.176	Sc Pos	19	3	0	3	.158
Night	79	16	0	2	.203	Clutch	19	2	0	0	.105

1991 Rankings (National League)

➡ Did not rank near the top or bottom in any category

PITCHING:

After suffering through a year of long relief and occasional starting assignments with the Mets in 1990, Bob Ojeda came to the Dodgers with something to prove. He had a rough April (1-3, 5.32 ERA), but soon settled into a groove. As Ojeda has shown throughout his career, he was especially tough in the last month of the season (3-1, 2.33 in '91; 26-13 lifetime).

Ojeda lives on the outside edge of the plate. He'll drill his deceptively good fastball up and in, mostly to set up his change-up. Ojeda needs to get ahead in the count to be effective; both the patience of the opposing lineup and the umpire's interpretation of the strike zone have a lot to do with whether he'll be successful.

Ojeda has always been extremely tough for left-handed hitters. In '91, opponents hit .257 from either side, yet he remained effective. He has good control and an uncanny ability to bear down when trouble is brewing. Though he's not the complete game type, averaging just over six innings per start, Ojeda keeps his team in the game while he's in there.

HOLDING RUNNERS, FIELDING, HITTING:

Ojeda holds runners close with a variety of moves. He has a compact pitching motion, delivering the ball to the plate with a minimal leg kick and leaving himself in good fielding position. Ojeda pounded out his first homer in '91, his sixth year in the N.L., and his three RBI virtually doubled his career total.

OVERALL:

Ojeda did not like being passed over for what was supposed to be his final start of the season, and made noise about demanding a trade, as his contract enabled him to do. That was most likely a maneuver to gain a contract extension. Ojeda was born in LA and is perfectly suited for the home park. Also, the Dodgers have no other southpaws in the rotation. He should be back.

BOBBY OJEDA

Position: SP
Bats: L **Throws:** L
Ht: 6' 1" **Wt:** 195

Opening Day Age: 34
Born: 12/17/57 in Los Angeles, CA
ML Seasons: 12

Overall Statistics

	W	L	ERA	G	GS	Sv	IP	H	R	BB	SO	HR
1991	12	9	3.18	31	31	0	189.1	181	78	70	120	15
Career	107	88	3.60	311	253	1	1671.2	1605	746	568	1004	131

How Often He Throws Strikes

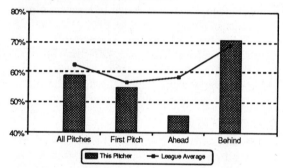

1991 Situational Stats

	W	L	ERA	Sv	IP		AB	H	HR	RBI	AVG
Home	6	4	3.01	0	98.2	LHB	136	35	1	11	.257
Road	6	5	3.38	0	90.2	RHB	569	146	14	61	.257
Day	2	3	4.85	0	29.2	Sc Pos	172	40	0	52	.233
Night	10	6	2.87	0	159.2	Clutch	38	12	0	2	.316

1991 Rankings (National League)

- ➡ 4th in highest on-base average allowed (.323) and lowest run support per 9 innings (3.4)
- ➡ 5th most runners caught stealing (15)
- ➡ 6th lowest strikeout/walk ratio (1.7)
- ➡ 7th highest groundball/flyball ratio (1.6)
- ➡ Led the Dodgers in pickoff throws (144), runners caught stealing and lowest stolen base percentage allowed (60.5%)

HITTING:

Will the real Juan Samuel please stand up (at the plate)? Dodger batting coach Ben Hines had Samuel switch to a lighter bat in late 1990, increasing his bat speed and allowing him to wait longer on the pitch. His torrid late-season surge in 1990 (.376-September/October) carried into '91, and Samuel went to the All-Star game hitting .313 with nine homers and 43 RBI. But his bat disappeared in the second-half (.224, three homers, 15 RBI).

What happened? In the first half of '91, Samuel was an aggressive opposite-field hitter who laid off bad pitches. He later relapsed into the wild swinger whom both the Phillies and Mets gave up on. Pitchers quickly caught on that they need not throw a strike to get Samuel out. Fastballs up, fastballs away, curve balls away, Samuel began swinging at (and missing) all of them. He struck out a team-high 133 times. Failure bred impatience and vice versa, a vicious cycle that he never spun out of.

BASERUNNING:

Samuel is a fine baserunner with excellent speed. He's always ready to take the extra base and seldom runs the team out of an inning. He stole a few less bases last year (23 in 31 attempts), but his position in the order and some hamstring problems were the probable causes for the decline.

FIELDING:

Samuel goes to his left fairly well, but has little range to his right. He has an accurate arm, but always needs an extra step to get something on it. In his eighth major league season, Samuel still refuses to use the backhand flip on double play grounders.

OVERALL:

In the winter of '90, the Dodgers offered Samuel arbitration solely to salvage the draft pick they would receive when he signed with another team. No one bit, and the team got a great half-season out of him. He's a free agent again, and though the Dodgers almost certainly won't enter the bidding, someone else will undoubtedly be willing to take a chance on him this time around.

JUAN SAMUEL

Position: 2B
Bats: R **Throws:** R
Ht: 5'11" **Wt:** 170

Opening Day Age: 31
Born: 12/9/60 in San Pedro de Macoris, Dominican Republic
ML Seasons: 9

Overall Statistics

	G	AB	R	H	D	T	HR	RBI	SB	BB	SO	AVG
1991	153	594	74	161	22	6	12	58	23	49	133	.271
Career	1234	4922	696	1277	235	81	128	551	341	332	1159	.259

Where He Hits the Ball

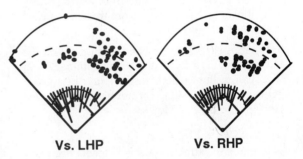

Vs. LHP   Vs. RHP

1991 Situational Stats

	AB	H	HR	RBI	AVG		AB	H	HR	RBI	AVG
Home	295	75	4	26	.254	LHP	250	63	7	27	.252
Road	299	86	8	32	.288	RHP	344	98	5	31	.285
Day	155	49	2	13	.316	Sc Pos	129	32	2	41	.248
Night	439	112	10	45	.255	Clutch	96	29	1	14	.302

1991 Rankings (National League)

→ 1st in lowest percentage of swings put into play (36.6%)

→ 2nd most errors at second base (17) and lowest fielding percentage at second base (.978)

→ 3rd in strikeouts (133)

→ 4th most pitches seen (2,553)

→ 5th in at-bats (594)

→ Led the Dodgers in triples (6), strikeouts, stolen base percentage (74.2%), slugging percentage vs. right-handed pitchers (.384) and batting average on the road (.288)

HITTING:

Mike Scioscia takes (and gives out) a physical beating behind the plate and last year it caught up with him. Silently suffering through a strained arch most of the year, Scioscia totalled his fewest number of at-bats since 1984. Yet his final totals (.264, 16 2B, 8 HR, 40 RBI) were amazingly consistent with the rest of his career. Only his performance against lefties suffered last year (.189; .297 vs RHP); southpaws hadn't given him that much trouble in the past.

Scioscia is a terrific situational hitter. He's got great bat control along with an uncanny ability to spot (or guess) who's covering the bag on the hit-and-run. Scioscia gets better as he works deeper in the count, hitting only .250 on the first pitch, but .290 after a first pitch strike. Wonderfully disciplined, he has walked more than he's struck out in each of his 12 seasons.

Scioscia is even better when the game is on the line, hitting .315 from the seventh inning on in '91. Throw him a high fastball late in a close game and you're asking for trouble. Just ask Doc Gooden.

BASERUNNING:

Though he is extremely slow, Scioscia has good instincts on the base paths. He'll take the extra base if it's there, but will often have to stay put to save running into an out. He stole four bases last year (in seven tries); one wonders if those catchers were conscious.

FIELDING:

No one blocks the plate better than Scioscia. Seldom do the pitchers shake him off, and he frames pitches for the ump very well. On foul pops, he knows Chavez Ravine's vast foul territories like the back of his face mask. His only weakness is his throwing arm, which is fair at best.

OVERALL:

Day-to-day, year-to-year, offensively and defensively, Scioscia is one of the steadiest performers in the game. He gives everything he's got every single inning. Both players and fans can learn a lot from observing his particular brand of work ethic.

MIKE SCIOSCIA

Position: C
Bats: L **Throws:** R
Ht: 6' 2" **Wt:** 229

Opening Day Age: 33
Born: 11/27/58 in Upper Darby, PA
ML Seasons: 12

Overall Statistics

	G	AB	R	H	D	T	HR	RBI	SB	BB	SO	AVG
1991	119	345	39	91	16	2	8	40	4	47	32	.264
Career	1324	4025	379	1054	192	9	65	422	26	535	276	.262

Where He Hits the Ball

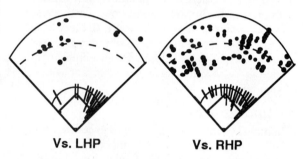

Vs. LHP   Vs. RHP

1991 Situational Stats

	AB	H	HR	RBI	AVG		AB	H	HR	RBI	AVG
Home	163	47	3	22	.288	LHP	106	20	3	13	.189
Road	182	44	5	18	.242	RHP	239	71	5	27	.297
Day	103	35	1	11	.340	Sc Pos	87	24	0	31	.276
Night	242	56	7	29	.231	Clutch	63	20	2	9	.317

1991 Rankings (National League)

→ 4th in lowest batting average vs. left-handed pitchers (.189), lowest percentage of swings that missed (10.1%) and highest percentage of swings put into play (54.1%)

→ 7th in lowest percentage of extra bases taken as a runner (27.3%) and lowest slugging percentage vs. left-handed pitchers (.292)

→ Led the Dodgers in lowest percentage of swings that missed and highest percentage of swings put into play

→ Led NL catchers in lowest percentage of swings that missed, highest percentage of swings put into play and highest percentage of pitches taken (60.8%)

LOS ANGELES DODGERS

HITTING:

Mike Sharperson is a fine hitter, especially against lefties. Proving that his .322 average vs. LHP in 1990 was no fluke, he increased it to .323 last year. Upon returning from an early-season injury, Sharperson found that he had lost his job as half of the third base platoon with Lenny Harris. But his productive bat eventually forced him back into the lineup against the many southpaws the Dodgers faced, and he hit .302 from June first onward.

Sharperson is the only true number-two hitter on the Dodger team. He can hit-and-run with the best of them and is patient enough to take a pitch or two. Once he gets ahead in the count, Sharperson will sit on the fastball and bang it back through the middle. He hit .349 after a 1-0 count.

Though he is no power threat (he did not homer until his 447th major league at-bat), Sharperson will occasionally turn on an inside fastball. Further adding to his value, he came off the bench to bat .273 as a pinch hitter.

BASERUNNING:

Sharperson was a perennial 15-20 steal man throughout his minor league career, and he swiped 15 bases for LA in 1990. He was just one for four in SB attempts last year; his leg problems and his place in the lineup were largely responsible for the drop. Sharperson still has better-than-average speed and good instincts on the base paths.

FIELDING:

As a third baseman, Sharperson is a bit of a matador with a fairly strong but erratic arm. His natural position is second base, but the club seldom uses him there. Instead, he is used as a valuable utility man, filling in at all four infield positions.

OVERALL:

Sharperson is a much more valuable player than his statistics might indicate. He is a fine offensive player, and his versatility gives the team several options. His bat skills are more in line with those of a second baseman, but he'll also probably see a lot of action at third.

MIKE SHARPERSON

Position: 3B
Bats: R **Throws:** R
Ht: 6' 3" **Wt:** 190

Opening Day Age: 30
Born: 10/4/61 in Orangeburg, SC
ML Seasons: 5

Overall Statistics

	G	AB	R	H	D	T	HR	RBI	SB	BB	SO	AVG
1991	105	216	24	60	11	2	2	20	1	25	24	.278
Career	349	789	87	218	35	5	5	75	18	87	102	.276

Where He Hits the Ball

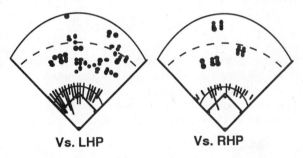

Vs. LHP   **Vs. RHP**

1991 Situational Stats

	AB	H	HR	RBI	AVG		AB	H	HR	RBI	AVG
Home	97	32	1	9	.330	LHP	158	51	2	15	.323
Road	119	28	1	11	.235	RHP	58	9	0	5	.155
Day	57	11	0	3	.193	Sc Pos	58	12	0	16	.207
Night	159	49	2	17	.308	Clutch	45	14	0	6	.311

1991 Rankings (National League)

- → 8th highest batting average vs. left-handed pitchers (.323)
- → Led the Dodgers in batting average vs. left-handed pitchers

HITTING:

From the All-Star game on, Darryl Strawberry was everything the Dodger fans paid for and more, hitting .290 with 20 HR and 69 RBI. Unfortunately, Strawberry had an unproductive first half (.229, 8 HR, 30 RBI) to go with it. He was tentative upon first arriving in LA, watching a lot of called third strikes whistle by before shaking his head and strolling out to the outfield.

Strawberry looks to turn on the inside pitch, especially down and in, and send it high and deep into the right field stands. Pitchers try to keep the ball away from him, and when he's going well, he'll drive it the other way. The Dodgers saw a lot of lefties in '91, and Strawberry actually hit southpaws better than he did righties.

Strawberry's ability to turn it up a notch was evidenced by his .302 average with men on base (.229 when empty). Curiously, 18 of his 28 HR came against just two teams, Houston and San Diego. However, his hot hitting in August, when he slugged 9 homers, and his .314 season batting average against the Braves were two important factors in helping the Dodgers stay in the race.

BASERUNNING:

Strawberry no longer seems interested in stealing bases. He takes a relatively small lead and was successful just over half the time he took off (10-for-18). He still has good speed, but maybe we are witnessing a transition to the next phase of his career: the station-to-station slugger.

FIELDING:

Strawberry is not a bad outfielder. He seldom gets a good jump, but his long stride chews up the turf quickly. His arm is surprisingly strong and accurate. His obvious physical gifts make everything look so easy. So why does he lose focus so often?

OVERALL:

No doubt a carryover from the world of New York tabloidism, Strawberry tends to display his leadership abilities in the newspapers. Should he ever learn to put it all together for an entire season, he could be the premier player in baseball. Until then, he'll inexplicably remain a disappointment to many people despite his 280 career homers before age 30 (Mike Schmidt had 235 at the same age.)

DARRYL STRAWBERRY

Position: RF
Bats: L **Throws:** L
Ht: 6' 6" **Wt:** 200

Opening Day Age: 30
Born: 3/12/62 in Los Angeles, CA
ML Seasons: 9

Overall Statistics

	G	AB	R	H	D	T	HR	RBI	SB	BB	SO	AVG
1991	139	505	86	134	22	4	28	99	10	75	125	.265
Career	1248	4408	748	1159	209	34	280	832	201	655	1085	.263

Where He Hits the Ball

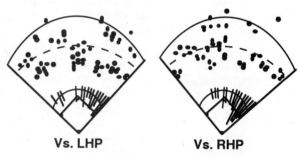

Vs. LHP   Vs. RHP

1991 Situational Stats

	AB	H	HR	RBI	AVG		AB	H	HR	RBI	AVG
Home	257	73	14	54	.284	LHP	228	63	11	43	.276
Road	248	61	14	45	.246	RHP	277	71	17	56	.256
Day	122	30	5	24	.246	Sc Pos	158	45	9	72	.285
Night	383	104	23	75	.272	Clutch	91	24	3	20	.264

1991 Rankings (National League)

→ 3rd in pitches seen per plate appearance (4.05)

→ 5th in strikeouts (125), HR frequency (18.0 ABs per HR) and lowest percentage of swings put into play (37.6%)

→ 7th in home runs (28)

→ 8th most runs scored per time reached base (40.6%)

→ Led the Dodgers in home runs, total bases (248), RBIs (99), slugging percentage (.491), HR frequency, most runs scored per time reached base and slugging percentage vs. left-handed pitchers (.478)

CHRIS GWYNN

Position: LF/RF
Bats: L **Throws:** L
Ht: 6' 0" **Wt:** 210

Opening Day Age: 27
Born: 10/13/64 in Los Angeles, CA
ML Seasons: 5

Overall Statistics

	G	AB	R	H	D	T	HR	RBI	SB	BB	SO	AVG
1991	94	139	18	35	5	1	5	22	1	10	23	.252
Career	256	391	48	100	12	3	10	53	2	21	69	.256

HITTING, FIELDING, BASERUNNING:

Chris Gwynn has made himself invaluable to the Dodgers as their top pinch hitter, delivering 13 hits (in 56 AB), two home runs and 13 RBI off the bench. Gwynn is very aggressive and confident with the game on the line. The confidence pays off, as he hit .300 with runners on (.215 with bases empty). Gwynn is more selective as a starter, but since he hit a paltry .098 with two strikes against him, he might be better served to just go up there hacking.

Gwynn has some power, with five homers in only 139 at-bats last year, and nearly a third of his hits went for extra bases. He has good instincts in every aspect of the game. Gwynn makes full use of what little speed he has, both on the bases and in the outfield. He gets a pretty good jump and his arm, though not in the same class as his brother's, is certainly adequate.

OVERALL:

Combine Gwynn's 1990-91 numbers and project them to 400 AB and you get .268, 14 HR, 63 RBI, pretty decent figures. Now 27, he should be playing every day, or at least be part of a platoon situation (he totalled only 28 at-bats vs. lefties in 1990-91). If the Dodgers end up getting a decent offer for Kal Daniels, it could be the former number-one draft pick's turn to shine.

DAVE HANSEN

Position: 3B
Bats: L **Throws:** R
Ht: 6' 0" **Wt:** 180

Opening Day Age: 23
Born: 11/24/68 in Long Beach, CA
ML Seasons: 2

Overall Statistics

	G	AB	R	H	D	T	HR	RBI	SB	BB	SO	AVG
1991	53	56	3	15	4	0	1	5	1	2	12	.268
Career	58	63	3	16	4	0	1	6	1	2	15	.254

HITTING, FIELDING, BASERUNNING:

Last year Dave Hansen came within one pinch hit (10-for-32, .313) of tying Pedro Guerrero's Dodger rookie record. Hansen was especially effective coming off the bench to lead off an inning (7-for-16, .438) and sparked several rallies late in the year.

Hansen is a line drive hitter with a little power who handles himself well at the plate. His minor league stats mark him as a patient hitter with excellent strike zone judgement. With the Dodgers last year he hit .313 (10-for-32) with two strikes against him, showing remarkable poise for a 22 year old.

Hansen has just average speed and will make the occasional rookie blunder on the base paths. The third sacker is as fearless in the field as he is at the plate. He attacks ground balls and exhibits an arm that is accurate and strong.

OVERALL:

Southpaw batting practice pitcher Tommy Lasorda made Hansen his pet project late in the year. He spent hours throwing his legendary curveball to the left-handed hitting third baseman. The kid hit .303 and .316 his last two years in the minors, and he clearly has some potential. It would not be a total surprise to see him in a third base platoon situation in '92.

STAN JAVIER

Position: LF/RF
Bats: B **Throws:** R
Ht: 6' 0" **Wt:** 185

Opening Day Age: 28
Born: 1/9/64 in San Francisco de Macoris, Dominican Republic
ML Seasons: 7

Overall Statistics

	G	AB	R	H	D	T	HR	RBI	SB	BB	SO	AVG
1991	121	176	21	36	5	3	1	11	7	16	36	.205
Career	628	1464	208	359	50	16	9	118	65	154	255	.245

HITTING, FIELDING, BASERUNNING:

After hitting .304 in his first season with the Dodgers, Stan Javier was rewarded last year with a spot on the bench. Javier's bat did not respond to the change, and his average tumbled all the way to .205.

The aggressive switch-hitter was 5-for-52 (.096) with 0 RBI as a pinch hitter. He hit .250 the rest of the time, but disappeared in the second half and ultimately had his smallest at-bat total since 1987. Javier has little home run power and only so-so plate discipline, so he has to hit for a good average in order to have much offensive value.

Fast and a good baserunner, Javier was 7-for-8 in stolen base attempts and is now 65-for-78 (83%) lifetime. He is also a very good center fielder, with great range and a fine arm. Javier's early season trial in the infield proved to be a failure. His many skills are just not well-served at the corners.

OVERALL:

Unless Kal Daniels is moved in the offseason, Javier is looking at another year of frustration. He must keep his chin up and learn how to better prepare himself for those late-inning at-bats. Javier should get the call in '93, when one of the expansion clubs will no doubt be building their outfield around him as their center fielder.

MITCH WEBSTER

Position: RF/LF/CF
Bats: B **Throws:** L
Ht: 6' 1" **Wt:** 185

Opening Day Age: 32
Born: 5/16/59 in Larned, KS
ML Seasons: 9

Overall Statistics

	G	AB	R	H	D	T	HR	RBI	SB	BB	SO	AVG
1991	107	203	23	42	8	5	2	19	2	21	61	.207
Career	906	2845	423	755	127	47	57	278	144	275	478	.265

HITTING, FIELDING, BASERUNNING:

It took him three teams and half a season, but Mitch Webster finally found his hitting stroke. The veteran outfielder hit .284 in LA after totalling .163 in Cleveland and Pittsburgh. Coming down the stretch, Webster proved to be a very valuable bench player for the Dodgers.

Though listed as a switch-hitter, Webster has become a platoon player. He hit just .172 from the left side (.240 right-handed). He is a line drive hitter with occasional power; over a third of his hits went for extra bases, including five triples in only 203 at-bats. But Webster's ever-increasing strikeout to walk ratio (61 to 21 last year) is becoming alarmingly high.

Webster averaged over 25 stolen bases per year from '86-90, but he was asked to steal just once in '91 with LA (he was thrown out). He still runs the bases well, though he's obviously lost a little speed. Webster is a good outfielder. He gets a good jump and makes the plays, but his arm is only fair.

OVERALL:

Webster fits in well with the Dodgers, understanding his role as a defensive replacement and pinch hitter. This is a welcome change on a team whose bench consists mostly of prospects who want to play every day. As a free agent, however, Webster will probably have to take a cut in pay to stay in LA.

ORGANIZATION OVERVIEW:

The Dodgers' once-vaunted player development record is now steeped in controversy. Last summer The Sporting News called the LA farm system the second-best in baseball. But many people quickly pointed out the obvious: if the Dodgers were so good at producing talent -- particularly hitting talent -- how come so few of their prospects ever made it in LA? The Dodgers do continue to develop fine pitchers. But their young hitters, aided by the friendly, high-altitude park at AAA Albuquerque (the Dukes' team batting average was .294 last year), tend to be very overrated. It doesn't help that, the older he gets, the more Tommy Lasorda seems to distrust young players. Lasorda, it was said, had to be forced to play the Dodgers' top prospect, Jose Offerman. It's not the best situation for Offerman or other young players who need patient handling.

CARLOS HERNANDEZ

Position: C
Bats: R **Throws:** R
Ht: 5' 11" **Wt:** 185

Opening Day Age: 24
Born: 5/24/67 in Bolivar, Venezuela

Recent Statistics

	G	AB	R	H	D	THR	RBI	SB	BB	SO	AVG
91 AAA Albuquerque	95	345	60	119	24	2	8	44	5	24	36	.345
91 NL Los Angeles	15	14	1	3	1	0	0	1	1	0	5	.214
91 MLE	95	319	39	93	17	0	5	28	3	16	38	.292

Hernandez, only the second Venezuelan to catch in the majors (Bo Diaz was first), seems the logical successor to Mike Scioscia, now 33. His defensive skills have improved greatly (he threw out 41% of opposing runners in AAA last year), and his hitting numbers keep getting better as well. If the Dodgers are serious about developing prospects, Hernandez will be Scioscia's backup this year.

ERIC KARROS

Position: 1B
Bats: R **Throws:** R
Ht: 6' 4" **Wt:** 210

Opening Day Age: 24
Born: 11/4/67 in Hackensack, NJ

Recent Statistics

	G	AB	R	H	D	THR	RBI	SB	BB	SO	AVG
91 AAA Albuquerque	132	488	88	154	33	8	22	101	3	58	80	.316
91 NL Los Angeles	14	14	0	1	1	0	0	1	0	1	6	.071
91 MLE	132	453	57	119	23	3	13	66	1	39	85	.263

The Dodgers face a dilemma with first sacker Karros. Eddie Murray is aging, and a free agent; one possibility would be to let him go and give the job to Karros. But Murray is still productive, and there's no guarantee that Karros can replace him any better than Greg Brock replaced Steve Garvey. Judging by recent history, the Dodgers will probably re-sign Murray.

PEDRO MARTINEZ

Position: P
Bats: R **Throws:** R
Ht: 6' 0" **Wt:** 154

Opening Day Age: 20
Born: 7/25/71 in Manoguayabo, DR

Recent Statistics

	W	L	ERA	GGS	Sv	IP	H	R	BB	SO	HR
90 R Great Falls	8	3	3.62	14 14	0	77.0	74	39	40	82	5
91 A Bakersfield	8	0	2.05	10 10	0	61.1	41	17	19	83	3
91 AA San Antonio	7	5	1.76	12 12	0	76.2	57	21	31	74	1
91 AAA Albuquerque	3	3	3.66	6 6	0	39.1	28	17	16	35	3

Ramon's younger brother (there's a third one, Jesus, in the low minors) had a fabulous year in '91, winning 18 games and fanning 192 at three levels. Pedro was rated the second-best prospect in the minors (behind the Giants' Royce Clayton) in The Sporting News rankings. Martinez has a major league fastball and slider, but he's very slender (154 pounds) and there's no guarantee that his arm will hold up under Lasorda-style usage. He's still a tremendous prospect at this point.

RAUL MONDESI

Position: OF
Bats: R **Throws:** R
Ht: 5' 11" **Wt:** 190

Opening Day Age: 21
Born: 3/12/71 in San Cristobal, DR

Recent Statistics

	G	AB	R	H	D	THR	RBI	SB	BB	SO	AVG
90 R Great Falls	44	175	35	53	10	4	8	31	30	11	30	.303
91 A Bakersfield	28	106	23	30	7	2	3	13	9	5	21	.283
91 AA San Antonio	53	213	32	58	10	5	5	26	7	8	47	.272
91 AAA Albuquerque	2	9	3	3	0	1	0	0	1	0	1	.333
91 MLE	55	210	24	49	7	2	3	18	4	5	52	.233

A young Dominican who's played only two seasons in the states, Mondesi clearly has major league defensive skills, with great range and an extraordinary arm. Mondesi is very fast, though he stole only 13 bases last year. His hitting is expected to improve, and it will need to. Almost everyone who's seen Mondesi play is very high on him.

JOHN WETTELAND

Position: P
Bats: R **Throws:** R
Ht: 6' 2" **Wt:** 195

Opening Day Age: 25
Born: 8/21/66 in San Mateo, CA

Recent Statistics

	W	L	ERA	GGS	Sv	IP	H	R	BB	SO	HR
91 AAA Albuquerque	4	3	2.79	41 4	20	61.1	48	22	26	55	5
91 NL Los Angeles	1	0	0.00	6 0	0	9.0	5	2	3	9	0

No kid at 25, Wetteland has already pitched in 59 games for the Dodgers. In 1989 and 1990, he mostly displayed a penchant for wild pitches and home run balls. In '91 he pitched very well at Albuquerque, however, and was very impressive in six outings with the Dodgers. Wetteland throws very hard, and his pitches have great movement; he finally seems ready, and a middle-relief role (at least) seems likely this year.

HITTING:

Bret Barberie was one of the last Expos cut in spring training in 1991. He went on to post very impressive numbers in less than a half season in AAA, batting .312 with both power and patience at Indianapolis. Eventually, Barberie was recalled to Montreal and became the club's most exciting hitter in September.

So far, Barberie has handled everything he's seen at the major league level. Along with hitting for average (.353), he showed that he possesses one of the best eyes on the team. Unlike the typical middle infielder, he drives the ball into the gap, and on occasion, out of the ballpark.

In the minors as well as in the majors Barberie was a streak hitter. He ended his season with the Expos by batting .469 in his last 49 at-bats with seven doubles, a triple, and seven walks. Though he wasn't around long enough for pitchers to develop a book on him, he hit both fastballs and breaking stuff, showing no apparent weaknesses in his offensive game.

BASERUNNING:

Barberie possesses better-than-average speed but needs some work on taking the extra base. He did not attempt a stolen base with Montreal but has potential, recording 10 steals in his limited time at Indianapolis.

FIELDING:

Defensive lapses cost Barberie a major league spot in the spring and troubled him during his initial stay with the Expos. He muffed routine grounders, rushed throws unnecessarily, and regularly appeared out of position. Most of his problems were at shortstop, where he fielded an atrocious .931. He has also played third, but second base is his best position. He moves well to both sides and has a strong, accurate arm.

OVERALL:

Barberie started the season as just a fair prospect in Montreal's deep minor league system but emerged by year-end as one of the league's most interesting young players. The Expos desperately need another productive bat in their lineup, but are overstocked with infielders. They may well make a deal to open up a position for Barberie.

BRET BARBERIE

Position: SS
Bats: B **Throws:** R
Ht: 5'11" **Wt:** 185

Opening Day Age: 24
Born: 8/16/67 in Long Beach, CA
ML Seasons: 1

Overall Statistics

	G	AB	R	H	D	T	HR	RBI	SB	BB	SO	AVG
1991	57	136	16	48	12	2	2	18	0	20	22	.353
Career	57	136	16	48	12	2	2	18	0	20	22	.353

Where He Hits the Ball

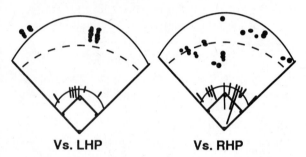

Vs. LHP   Vs. RHP

1991 Situational Stats

	AB	H	HR	RBI	AVG		AB	H	HR	RBI	AVG
Home	41	11	2	4	.268	LHP	37	10	1	5	.270
Road	95	37	0	14	.389	RHP	99	38	1	13	.384
Day	48	14	0	6	.292	Sc Pos	27	8	0	13	.296
Night	88	34	2	12	.386	Clutch	35	11	1	4	.314

1991 Rankings (National League)

→ 4th highest batting average on a 3-2 count (.370)

→ 6th lowest percentage of extra bases taken as a runner (26.7%)

→ Led the Expos in batting average on a 3-2 count

→ Led NL shortstops in batting average on a 3-2 count

PITCHING:

Following an impressive four start debut in 1990, Brian Barnes spent 1991 trying to duplicate those debut performances. In his first four starts of 1991, Barnes pitched fairly well twice and was shelled twice, running up an 8.38 ERA and an 0-2 record. That was a microcosm of Barnes' roller-coaster season.

Even in his quality starts, Barnes rarely pitched more than six innings and very often was hit hard the second time through the order. As a result he was the pitcher of record in less than half of his 27 starts. At the All-Star break, Barnes was just 0-3 in 11 starts with a 4.91 ERA, averaging less than six innings per start. Aside from a three-game streak in August of 21.1 innings without allowing an earned run, he continued his inconsistency in the second half.

Barnes limited opposing hitters to just a .233 average with a great change-up and an excellent curveball. However, he struggled all year to gain command of his less-than-overpowering fastball. Barnes constantly fell behind in the count; consequently, hitters were sitting on his change-up instead of being fooled by it. The result was one home run allowed every 10 innings and just over one walk every two innings -- the perfect mix for multi-run innings and trips to the mound by the manager.

HOLDING RUNNERS, FIELDING, HITTING:

Barnes is a terrible hitter. His .082 average in 49 at-bats was one of the worst among the league's pitchers. He did draw seven walks, however. Though he spent time in the Instructional League learning how to keep runners close, he remains vulnerable to the stolen base (20 in 28 attempts last season). He is a very average fielder.

OVERALL:

One should not be surprised to find a pitcher who relies primarily on offspeed pitches struggling his first season. Barnes showed that his stuff can get hitters out. If he gains command of his fastball, Barnes, who pitched his best games late in the season, can emerge as a quality starter.

BRIAN BARNES

Position: SP
Bats: L **Throws:** L
Ht: 5' 9" **Wt:** 170

Opening Day Age: 25
Born: 3/25/67 in Roanoke Rapids, NC
ML Seasons: 2

Overall Statistics

	W	L	ERA	G	GS	Sv	IP	H	R	BB	SO	HR
1991	5	8	4.22	28	27	0	160.0	135	82	84	117	16
Career	6	9	4.02	32	31	0	188.0	160	92	91	140	18

How Often He Throws Strikes

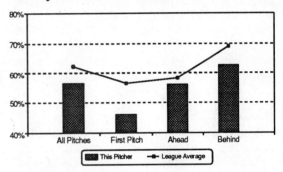

1991 Situational Stats

	W	L	ERA	Sv	IP		AB	H	HR	RBI	AVG
Home	1	5	4.24	0	68.0	LHB	104	25	3	13	.240
Road	4	3	4.21	0	92.0	RHB	476	110	13	57	.231
Day	2	2	4.89	0	35.0	Sc Pos	133	31	4	49	.233
Night	3	6	4.03	0	125.0	Clutch	29	7	0	3	.241

1991 Rankings (National League)

- ➡ 2nd in walks allowed (84)
- ➡ 7th in hit batsmen (6) and lowest batting average allowed vs. right-handed batters (.231)
- ➡ 10th highest ERA on the road (4.21)
- ➡ Led the Expos in walks allowed, hit batsmen, pickoff throws (203) and lowest batting average allowed vs. right-handed batters

HITTING:

Despite being plagued by a sore shoulder which ended his 1991 season prematurely, Ivan Calderon was the one consistent offensive force in the Expos' lineup, hitting .300 for the first time in his career. More importantly, he was the run producer the Expos had been looking for. Known as a clutch hitter with the White Sox, Calderon continued his impressive performance with men on base, batting .323 last year in such situations. He drove in 34 of 49 runners from third base with less than two out.

Aside from his consistency, Calderon, a Walt Hriniak student, is an excellent role model for Montreal's young hitters. Seldom retired by a pitcher's first offering, Calderon is patient enough to work a count and draw a walk. He is good at adjusting his approach depending on the pitcher, the ball-strike count, and the game situation. With two strikes, Calderon shortens his swing and tries to hit the ball where it is pitched. Early in the count, he will pull the ball for power.

BASERUNNING:

Calderon possesses good speed but has a tendency to overestimate it, sometimes turning his aggressiveness on the base paths into foolishness. His 16 caught stealings virtually negated the benefits of his 31 steals. Calderon gained some weight between 1990 and 1991, a condition which may partly explain baserunning miscalculations.

FIELDING:

Calderon was a very average defensive performer in 1991. He displayed average range and his sore shoulder limited the effectiveness of his throws. As he does on the base paths, Calderon gambles in left field, willing to give up the extra base in an attempt to make the spectacular catch. Late season surgery may force him to first base, where he did not look comfortable late last season.

OVERALL:

Despite suffering from some physical problems, Calderon had a solid 1991 season, and is expected to at least repeat his performance in '92. A move to first base would be against Calderon's wishes. Tough and athletic, he strongly prefers the outfield.

IVAN CALDERON

Position: LF
Bats: R **Throws:** R
Ht: 6' 1" **Wt:** 221

Opening Day Age: 30
Born: 3/19/62 in Fajardo, Puerto Rico
ML Seasons: 8

Overall Statistics

	G	AB	R	H	D	T	HR	RBI	SB	BB	SO	AVG
1991	134	470	69	141	22	3	19	75	31	53	64	.300
Career	794	2903	425	806	176	21	100	398	92	271	501	.278

Where He Hits the Ball

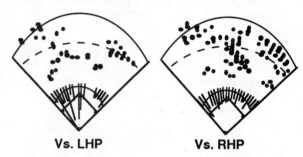

Vs. LHP   **Vs. RHP**

1991 Situational Stats

	AB	H	HR	RBI	AVG		AB	H	HR	RBI	AVG
Home	224	69	7	29	.308	LHP	161	57	11	31	.354
Road	246	72	12	46	.293	RHP	309	84	8	44	.272
Day	116	35	4	18	.302	Sc Pos	144	44	5	57	.306
Night	354	106	15	57	.299	Clutch	90	31	5	12	.344

1991 Rankings (National League)

→ 1st in slugging percentage vs. left-handed pitchers (.627)

→ 2nd in lowest batting average with the bases loaded (.111) and most errors in left field (7)

→ 3rd highest batting average vs. left-handed pitchers (.354)

→ Led the Expos in batting average (.300), home runs (19), total bases (226), RBIs (75), sacrifice flies (10), slugging percentage (.481), on-base average (.368), HR frequency (24.7 ABs per HR), batting average with runners in scoring position (.306) and batting average in the clutch (.344)

HITTING:

After enjoying a remarkably consistent rookie year, Delino Deshields' 1991 season never got untracked. DeShields went through a series of slumps affecting every aspect of his game. Eager to become what the Expos hoped for -- a number-three hitter -- DeShields flexed his muscles and upped his home run production from four to 10. But his new-found passion for the longball clearly had a downside. In the habit of overswinging rather than just making good contact, he struck out a league-leading 151 times -- a jump of more than 50% from 1990.

When he played within his talent, DeShields reaffirmed his judgement of the strike zone, walking 95 times -- fourth-best in the league. Despite all his problems and his .152 batting average after August 31st, DeShields still turned in a respectable .347 on-base percentage.

BASERUNNING:

When DeShields started the season with 12 consecutive stolen bases, it seemed that he had succeeded, with the help of coach Tommy Harper, in blending technique with his raw speed. But DeShields, carrying his batting slumps onto the base paths, was an unsure and error-prone baserunner the rest of the season. He still stole 56 bases, third-most in the N.L., but his 23 caught stealings were the league's second-highest total.

FIELDING:

In terms of raw ability, DeShields has what it takes to become a premier fielder. He can move gracefully to either side and is blessed with a very good arm. However, DeShields suffered through many lengthy defensive slumps last season. His 27 errors, many of them on routine plays, easily topped all major league second basemen.

OVERALL:

The subject of winter trade rumors, DeShields admitted that he tinkered with his stance too frequently last year. He promised to strengthen his body during the off season. He must also learn to pace himself and separate the different facets of his game. Nothing else can prevent him from developing into a star.

DELINO DeSHIELDS

Position: 2B
Bats: L **Throws:** R
Ht: 6' 1" **Wt:** 170

Opening Day Age: 23
Born: 1/15/69 in Seaford, DE
ML Seasons: 2

Overall Statistics

	G	AB	R	H	D	T	HR	RBI	SB	BB	SO	AVG
1991	151	563	83	134	15	4	10	51	56	95	151	.238
Career	280	1062	152	278	43	10	14	96	98	161	247	.262

Where He Hits the Ball

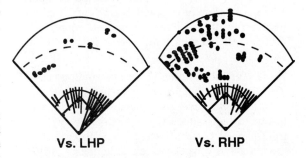

Vs. LHP   Vs. RHP

1991 Situational Stats

	AB	H	HR	RBI	AVG		AB	H	HR	RBI	AVG
Home	238	63	3	15	.265	LHP	189	41	3	14	.217
Road	325	71	7	36	.218	RHP	374	93	7	37	.249
Day	158	34	2	13	.215	Sc Pos	108	27	1	40	.250
Night	405	100	8	38	.247	Clutch	106	26	1	10	.245

1991 Rankings (National League)

→ 1st in strikeouts (151), lowest slugging percentage (.332), most pitches seen per plate appearance (4.24), lowest batting average on an 0-2 count (.040), lowest batting average on the road (.219) and lowest fielding percentage at second base (.962)

→ 2nd in lowest batting average (.238), caught stealing (23), pitches seen (2,853), highest percentage of pitches taken (63.3%)

→ 3rd in stolen bases (56)

→ Led the Expos in runs (83), caught stealing, walks (95), times on base (231), strikeouts, pitches seen, plate appearances (673), games (151), groundball/flyball ratio (2.1) and bunts in play (19)

PITCHING:

The Expos called up Jeff Fassero on June 4th, the day after they replaced Buck Rodgers with Tom Runnells. At Indianapolis, Fassero was an impressive 3-0 with a 1.47 ERA and four saves in 11 appearances, but no one expected him to spin the same magic at the major league level. In fact, a few days after his arrival, Runnells named Barry Jones his stopper.

That may have been a bad decision, because Fassero was awesome for the next two months. At one point, he pitched 12.2 consecutive shutout innings and retired 31 of 34 batters. In his first 32 innings of work he held the opposition to a .146 batting average. Meanwhile, Runnells still considered the ineffective Jones as his stopper. Fassero eventually returned to earth and was hit hard a few times, but he remained Montreal's premier reliever with eight saves in 11 opportunities.

Fassero's fastball doesn't have outstanding velocity (88 MPH), but it has great movement, and scouts praise his "good hard stuff." He also throws a hard slider which breaks away from right-handed batters. Fassero likes to challenge the hitter and usually gets ahead in the count. As a southpaw, he conversely held right-handed batters to just a .171 batting average in 129 at-bats, while left-handed hitters were able to manage .243. Fassero was stingy with extra-base hits, limiting the opposition to just a .266 slugging percentage.

HOLDING RUNNERS, FIELDING, HITTING:

Fassero is an alert fielder but his move to first is considered below average. However, he gave up just three stolen bases (in four attempts) last year. It's too soon to say, but Fassero looked comfortable at the plate. Though hitless in three at-bats, he did manage a walk and two sacrifice bunts.

OVERALL:

Fassero was a pleasant surprise in a dismal season for the Expos. He started off wonderfully, but performed in an average fashion when he was given more crucial relief assignments. But if he can't make it as a left-handed closer, he could be very valuable in middle relief.

JEFF FASSERO

Position: RP
Bats: L **Throws:** L
Ht: 6' 1" **Wt:** 180

Opening Day Age: 29
Born: 1/5/63 in Springfield, IL
ML Seasons: 1

Overall Statistics

	W	L	ERA	G	GS	Sv	IP	H	R	BB	SO	HR
1991	2	5	2.44	51	0	8	55.1	39	17	17	42	1
Career	2	5	2.44	51	0	8	55.1	39	17	17	42	1

How Often He Throws Strikes

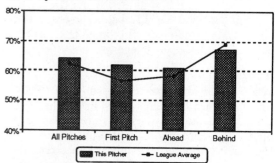

1991 Situational Stats

	W	L	ERA	Sv	IP		AB	H	HR	RBI	AVG
Home	2	2	2.17	3	29.0	LHB	70	17	0	11	.243
Road	0	3	2.73	5	26.1	RHB	129	22	1	9	.171
Day	0	4	2.61	2	20.2	Sc Pos	75	16	1	19	.213
Night	2	1	2.34	6	34.2	Clutch	118	25	0	14	.212

1991 Rankings (National League)

→ 2nd in least baserunners allowed per 9 innings in relief (9.3)

→ 4th lowest batting average allowed in relief (.196)

→ 6th in relief ERA (2.44)

→ Led the Expos in holds (7), relief ERA, lowest batting average allowed in relief, least baserunners allowed per 9 innings in relief and most strikeouts per 9 innings in relief (6.8)

HITTING:

In the baseball thesaurus, the phrases "barring injury" and "Mike Fitzgerald" go together. When spring training began last year, Fitzgerald was expected to be the Expos number-one catcher. A good part of his previous four years were spent recovering from a career-threatening injury to his right hand. Through it all, he'd shown the Expos that he was capable of producing some runs (142 RBI in 1,045 at-bats).

But when the season opened, Fitzgerald was in West Palm Beach rehabilitating from a fractured left hand. He joined the team in late May and was eased back into the lineup, but his bat went dead. On August 1, Fitzgerald was hitting a mighty .152 in 125 at-bats. Seeing limited duty, he caught fire the rest of the way. In his last 69 at-bats, Fitzgerald drove in 16 runs, hitting .304 with three homers.

Fitzgerald has a good eye and will take a walk as he waits patiently for a fastball. Unfortunately, he will also take a strikeout. He is a line drive hitter, but in certain situations, he'll try to crank one out of the park. Fitzgerald's late-season surge showed that he is still capable of delivering in clutch situations.

BASERUNNING:

The slow-footed Fitzgerald will surprise the opposition with the occasional delayed steal. He has stolen 12 bases in 15 attempts over the past two seasons. Otherwise, he's a one-base-at-a-time runner.

FIELDING:

Injuries have taken their toll on Fitzgerald's ability to throw runners out, but he remains a competent receiver. He moves well behind the plate and is good at receiving throws from the outfield. His handling of pitchers has been his forte. Buck Rodgers was convinced that Fitzgerald was one of the best in the league.

OVERALL:

A free agent, Fitzgerald questioned Tom Runnells' handling of the bullpen and worried that his game-calling abilities were underestimated. It took a while, but he showed he can still hit and, "barring injury," he should be able to help someone in 1992.

MIKE FITZGERALD

Position: C
Bats: R **Throws:** R
Ht: 5'11" **Wt:** 190

Opening Day Age: 31
Born: 7/13/60 in Long Beach, CA
ML Seasons: 9

Overall Statistics

	G	AB	R	H	D	T	HR	RBI	SB	BB	SO	AVG
1991	71	198	17	40	5	2	4	28	4	22	35	.202
Career	753	2127	201	505	93	9	42	276	29	270	398	.237

Where He Hits the Ball

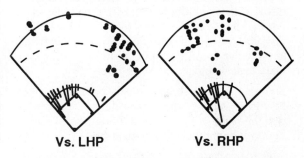

Vs. LHP   **Vs. RHP**

1991 Situational Stats

	AB	H	HR	RBI	AVG		AB	H	HR	RBI	AVG
Home	85	12	1	8	.141	LHP	86	20	3	19	.233
Road	113	28	3	20	.248	RHP	112	20	1	9	.179
Day	57	10	0	2	.175	Sc Pos	54	13	2	25	.241
Night	141	30	4	26	.213	Clutch	48	11	1	8	.229

1991 Rankings (National League)

- ➡ 2nd lowest percentage of runners caught stealing as a catcher (25.6%)
- ➡ 9th in lowest batting average with the bases loaded (.182) and lowest batting average with 2 strikes (.133)

HITTING:

A former offensive force, Andres Galarraga has slumped off to St. Louis. He'll need to play better than in 1991, when Expos' fans were left longing for those "disappointing" years (1989-1990) when Galarraga supplied a .256 average with 22 homers and 86 RBI. A knee problem which eventually required surgery kept Galarraga out of the lineup for a month, but the Expos hardly missed his production. He batted just .219 in 375 at-bats, providing just 33 RBI and nine home runs (one every 42 at-bats). Against southpaws, whom he once feasted upon, Galarraga batted an embarrassing .180 in 128 at-bats.

Every pitcher in the league, as well as 40 million baseball fans, knows that it is not necessary to throw strikes in order to retire Galarraga. Breaking ball in the dirt? No problem. Galarraga will give it a try. Fastball in his face? Why not? In fact, any pitcher found guilty of wasting a strike on Galarraga should pay a severe fine.

Swinging a sluggish bat -- many people thought he was 10 or 15 pounds overweight -- Galarraga was the worst in the league with runners in scoring position, hitting .174 in 98 at-bats.

BASERUNNING:

Galarraga slumped on the base paths as well. After stealing 10 bases in 11 attempts in 1990, he was 5-for-11 last season. Heavy and perhaps protecting his injured knee, Galarraga was less aggressive than usual.

FIELDING:

Despite all the distractions, Galarraga remains an exceptional first baseman. He has great range, scoops difficult throws out of the dirt, and smoothly initiates 3-6-3 double plays. Even so, scouts feel he doesn't have the quickness he had a few years ago.

OVERALL:

For Expo fans, the Big Cat had become the Big Scapegoat, and now he'll get a new start in St. Louis. Galarraga will be helped by the new, shortened dimensions in Busch Stadium. It would help even more if he got himself into better physical shape than he was during the 1991 season.

ANDRES GALARRAGA

Position: 1B
Bats: R **Throws:** R
Ht: 6' 3" **Wt:** 235

Opening Day Age: 30
Born: 6/18/61 in Caracas, Venezuela
ML Seasons: 7

Overall Statistics

	G	AB	R	H	D	T	HR	RBI	SB	BB	SO	AVG
1991	107	375	34	82	13	2	9	33	5	23	86	.219
Career	847	3082	394	830	168	14	106	433	54	224	790	.269

Where He Hits the Ball

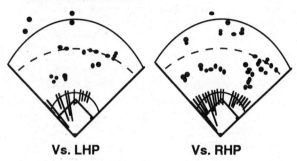

Vs. LHP   Vs. RHP

1991 Situational Stats

	AB	H	HR	RBI	AVG		AB	H	HR	RBI	AVG
Home	152	34	3	14	.224	LHP	128	23	6	17	.180
Road	223	48	6	19	.215	RHP	247	59	3	16	.239
Day	118	27	5	13	.229	Sc Pos	98	17	1	21	.173
Night	257	55	4	20	.214	Clutch	72	15	1	5	.208

1991 Rankings (National League)

→ 1st in lowest batting average with runners in scoring position (.174) and lowest on-base average vs. left-handed pitchers (.222)

→ 3rd lowest batting average vs. left-handed pitchers (.180)

→ 5th lowest batting average on a 3-1 count (.000)

→ 7th lowest batting average on 0-2 count (.071)

PITCHING:

For the second consecutive year, Mark Gardner gave the Expos three great months of pitching. Recovering from offseason surgery, Gardner missed the first month of the year, then started slowly. He did not get into a groove until mid-June. Then he began a sequence of 15 starts in which he won seven, lost six, (including a nine inning no-hitter), and posted a 2.39 ERA in 101.2 innings pitched. From that point on, as in 1990 when his season soured due to a tired arm, Gardner ceased to be effective. Over the last four weeks of the season, Gardner surrendered almost an earned run per inning, going 1-2 with a 8.20 ERA in 26.1 innings.

With his fastball and offspeed stuff just average, Gardner relies completely on his wicked curveball. He limited opposing hitters to a .230 batting average, tied for ninth best in the league. He was equally effective against both left-handed (.228) and right-handed (.233) hitters.

But Gardner is in trouble when his curve is not breaking sharply in and around the strike zone. Opposing hitters became more selective last year, walking more and striking out less. Trying to get ahead, Gardner had particular problems with the first batter of the inning, allowing him to reach base at a horrific .365 clip -- one of the worst figures among league starters.

HOLDING RUNNERS, FIELDING, HITTING:

Not blessed with a particularly good move, Gardner works hard at holding runners. Expo catchers were able to throw out 17 of 30 stolen base attempts against him -- one of the best ratios in the league. His fielding is adequate, considering that his delivery leaves him in poor position. Gardner is terrible at the plate.

OVERALL:

Gardner's tired arm in 1990 eventually required surgery. Last year's late season demise raises questions whether he can pitch effectively through an entire year. When his curve is on, he is one of the best pitchers in the league. To produce the numbers to prove it, the 30-year-old Gardner will have to show he can survive a full season.

MARK GARDNER

Position: SP
Bats: R **Throws:** R
Ht: 6' 1" **Wt:** 200

Opening Day Age: 30
Born: 3/1/62 in Los Angeles, CA
ML Seasons: 3

Overall Statistics

	W	L	ERA	G	GS	Sv	IP	H	R	BB	SO	HR
1991	9	11	3.85	27	27	0	168.1	139	78	75	107	17
Career	16	23	3.76	61	57	0	347.1	294	156	147	263	32

How Often He Throws Strikes

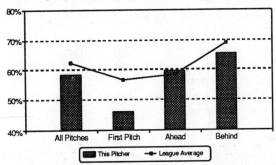

1991 Situational Stats

	W	L	ERA	Sv	IP		AB	H	HR	RBI	AVG
Home	4	4	2.51	0	64.2	LHB	381	87	10	41	.228
Road	5	7	4.69	0	103.2	RHB	223	52	7	27	.233
Day	2	7	4.69	0	63.1	Sc Pos	125	35	7	49	.280
Night	7	4	3.34	0	105.0	Clutch	51	11	1	2	.216

1991 Rankings (National League)

- → 1st in runners caught stealing (17)
- → 3rd in lowest strikeout/walk ratio (1.4), lowest stolen base percentage allowed (43.3%) and least run support per 9 innings (3.4)
- → 4th most pitches thrown per batter (3.83)
- → 7th in highest on-base average allowed (.318) and most home runs allowed per 9 innings (.91)
- → Led the Expos in losses (11), most home runs allowed (17), runners caught stealing, lowest stolen base percentage allowed, most strikeouts per 9 innings (5.7) and lowest batting average allowed vs. left-handed batters (.228)

GREAT SPEED

MARQUIS GRISSOM

Position: CF
Bats: R **Throws:** R
Ht: 5'11" **Wt:** 190

Opening Day Age: 24
Born: 4/17/67 in Atlanta, GA
ML Seasons: 3

HITTING:

Marquis Grissom began 1991 with a bang, momentarily dropping the word future from his "future star" tag only to return to the incomplete level of hitting which characterized his rookie season. Nonetheless, Grissom continued to display potential by raising his average ten points to .267 and belting 38 extra-base hits.

Up until early May, Grissom delivered both average and power in the number-two slot and, along with Ivan Calderon, carried the Expos' offense. From that point on, base stealing aside, Grissom virtually disappeared offensively until the last few weeks of the season. When Tom Runnells unwisely moved him to the leadoff spot for 30+ games, Grissom responded with a .235 average and nine walks in 149 at-bats.

Grissom worked deeper in the count in 1991 but often responded to breaking stuff outside the strike zone with weak fly balls. When putting the ball on the ground, Grissom is a constant source of pressure for opposing fielders. Considered by many scouts as the fastest right-handed hitter in the league in going from home to first, Grissom legged out 36 infield hits and reached base eight times on infield errors. Twenty-three percent of Grissom's career safeties have been infield hits, none of which are bunt hits.

BASERUNNING:

Speed is Grissom's best asset. Extremely comfortable in assessing pitchers and baserunning, he led the majors in steals with 76 and was fifth in the league in stolen base percentage (82%).

FIELDING:

Grissom perfected his defensive play in 1991. Combining speed, aggressiveness, sound judgement, and a strong throwing arm, Grissom should soon attract Gold Glove attention.

OVERALL:

In his first season as a regular, Grissom established himself as both an excellent baserunner and a fine defensive player at a crucial fielding position. Added maturity at the plate can easily perk Grissom's bat up to the .280, 15 homer range. He ended last season on a high note; now he has to take it from there.

Overall Statistics

	G	AB	R	H	D	T	HR	RBI	SB	BB	SO	AVG
1991	148	558	73	149	23	9	6	39	76	34	89	.267
Career	272	920	131	242	39	11	10	70	99	73	150	.263

Where He Hits the Ball

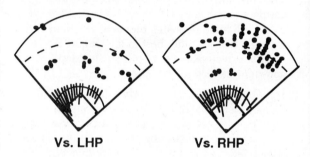

Vs. LHP   **Vs. RHP**

1991 Situational Stats

	AB	H	HR	RBI	AVG		AB	H	HR	RBI	AVG
Home	233	65	3	18	.279	LHP	211	60	3	18	.284
Road	325	84	3	21	.258	RHP	347	89	3	21	.256
Day	152	35	3	18	.230	Sc Pos	126	36	3	34	.286
Night	406	114	3	21	.281	Clutch	110	21	2	11	.191

1991 Rankings (National League)

→ 1st in stolen bases (76) and steals of third (18)

→ 2nd lowest leadoff on-base percentage (.278)

→ 4th in triples (9)

→ 5th highest stolen base percentage (81.7%)

→ Led the Expos in hits (149), singles (111), triples, stolen bases, stolen base percentage, runs scored per time reached base and steals of third

→ Led NL center fielders in stolen bases and steals of third

PITCHING:

After a meteoric rise through the minor leagues, Chris Haney learned his trade at the major league level and showed enough promise to be considered as one of the Expos' five starters in 1992.

Drafted 51st overall in the 1990 draft, Haney excelled immediately, posting a combined 1.66 ERA in 87 innings with three different minor league teams. Haney's difficulties with the Expos were typical for someone making his major league debut after just one year and 11 days of professional ball. He lacked stamina and was prone to wild streaks with 43 bases on balls and nine wild pitches in 84.2 innings. Haney's final numbers are a reflection of his inconsistency and mask the fact that he looked sharp in a number of his starts.

Lacking an overpowering fastball, Haney tended to approach hitters over- cautiously but displayed impressive composure in clutch situations, challenging the hitters instead of nibbling around the plate. Some scouts were impressed with both the quality of his curveball and his command of the fastball. Haney was very effective against left-handed hitters, limiting them to a .183 average in 60 at-bats.

HOLDING RUNNERS, FIELDING, HITTING:

Like many pitchers his age, Haney needs to fine tune his fielding. He possesses a good move to first and throws to the bag often. Last season he gave up only eight steals in 14 attempts. Haney has a relatively nice swing at the plate and makes contact. He produced just two singles and three sacrifices in 26 at-bats, but only struck out three times.

OVERALL:

Like Chris Nabholz and Brian Barnes before him, Haney received the latter part of his training at the major league level. As a rule, the Expos do not believe that Triple-A is an essential part of a starting pitcher's development, so Haney's mediocre statistics are less important than the promise he showed. Haney will almost certainly begin the season as part of the Expos' starting rotation.

CHRIS HANEY

Position: SP
Bats: L **Throws:** L
Ht: 6' 3" **Wt:** 185

Opening Day Age: 23
Born: 11/16/68 in Baltimore, MD
ML Seasons: 1

Overall Statistics

	W	L	ERA	G	GS	Sv	IP	H	R	BB	SO	HR
1991	3	7	4.04	16	16	0	84.2	94	49	43	51	6
Career	3	7	4.04	16	16	0	84.2	94	49	43	51	6

How Often He Throws Strikes

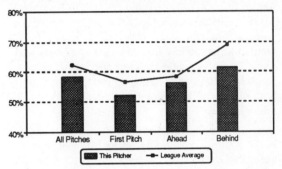

1991 Situational Stats

	W	L	ERA	Sv	IP		AB	H	HR	RBI	AVG
Home	3	2	2.42	0	44.2	LHB	60	11	0	6	.183
Road	0	5	5.85	0	40.0	RHB	276	83	6	35	.301
Day	0	0	1.69	0	10.2	Sc Pos	93	26	1	32	.280
Night	3	7	4.38	0	74.0	Clutch	7	1	0	0	.143

1991 Rankings (National League)

➞ 11th in wild pitches (9)
➞ Led the Expos in wild pitches

PITCHING:

Obtained from the White Sox with Ivan Calderon for Tim Raines, Barry Jones become the anchor of the worst bullpen in the major leagues. Jones didn't have a terrible year overall, but he did have a terrible time as a closer.

A great set-up man with the White Sox the previous two seasons in which he compiled a 14-6 record, Jones could not handle the stopper role. He blew eight of 21 save opportunities, and his other stats suffered after manager Tom Runnells named him his relief ace in early June.

According to some scouts, Jones gained a little weight and lost a little zip on both his fastball and his slider. He came to the Expos with the reputation of throwing inside but demonstrated a rather passive pitching style. He had trouble finding the plate all season long, especially against left-handed hitters. They hit .255 in 141 at-bats and drew 21 walks while striking out just 15 times. Jones had a tendency to miss the strike zone with high pitches and gave up one home run every 11 innings.

Interestingly, Jones continued to have problems in the National League. Heading into last season, his career stats were 16-8 with a 2.35 ERA in 104 A.L. appearances, compared to 6-9 with a 3.81 in 100 N.L. appearances.

HOLDING RUNNERS, FIELDING, HITTING:

Jones received just two at-bats in 77 games last season and succeeded in laying down a sacrifice bunt. Not very agile, Jones is a below-average defensive player who committed three errors, a significant amount for a relief pitcher. Jones possesses a decent move to first base.

OVERALL:

Jones was a major disappointment for Expos' management last season. He came with great set-up man credentials, but a set-up man needs a stopper and the Expos did not have one. So Jones took the job, even though he doesn't really have closer's stuff. The result: he will most probably pitch elsewhere in 1992.

BARRY JONES

Position: RP
Bats: R **Throws:** R
Ht: 6' 4" **Wt:** 225

Opening Day Age: 29
Born: 2/15/63 in Centerville, IN
ML Seasons: 6

Overall Statistics

	W	L	ERA	G	GS	Sv	IP	H	R	BB	SO	HR
1991	4	9	3.35	77	0	13	88.2	76	35	33	46	8
Career	26	26	3.16	281	0	22	356.0	316	145	156	213	27

How Often He Throws Strikes

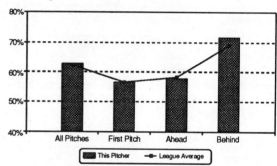

1991 Situational Stats

	W	L	ERA	Sv	IP		AB	H	HR	RBI	AVG
Home	1	2	2.70	6	40.0	LHB	141	36	2	15	.255
Road	3	7	3.88	7	48.2	RHB	168	40	6	29	.238
Day	0	1	2.59	7	24.1	Sc Pos	89	28	4	37	.315
Night	4	8	3.64	6	64.1	Clutch	185	53	5	34	.286

1991 Rankings (National League)

→ 1st in games pitched (77), most GDPs induced per GDP situation (20.0%) and relief losses (9)

→ 2nd lowest save percentage (61.9%)

→ 4th least strikeouts per 9 innings in relief (4.7)

→ 5th in blown saves (8)

→ 6th in games finished (46)

→ Led the Expos in games pitched, saves (13), games finished, save opportunites (21), blown saves, relief losses and relief innings (88.2)

HITTING:

Last year, Dave Martinez relived his 1990 experience complete with an extremely similar set of statistics. Though his home run total dropped from 11 to seven, he raised his average 16 points to a career-high .295.

Martinez began the season on the bench as the club's fourth outfielder, but injuries allowed him the opportunity to play semi-regularly. His numbers were excellent, forcing Montreal to consider whether Martinez deserves to play every day. His main weakness has always been his problems against lefties; though he's improved in recent years, Martinez batted only .237 against southpaws in '91. He certainly deserves to be in the lineup against righties with a .314 batting average while slugging .449 against them last year.

A fervent student when it comes to hitting, Martinez is intense during every at-bat. He takes many pitches, yet he does not draw a great number of walks. He often takes poor swings at breaking balls deep in the count. He has solidified his reputation as a clutch hitter. In 96 at-bats with runners in scoring position, Martinez hit .302.

BASERUNNING:

Though not a threat to lead the league in steals, Martinez is very dependable on the bases. He's averaged 18 steals per year since 1987; last year's performance (16-for-23) was typical for him.

FIELDING:

Martinez' solid glove work helps his claim to a starting position. He is excellent at all three outfield positions, displaying flashy range. Though his arm is considered below average in strength, it is accurate. He threw out two runners in the same inning last season and ended up the year with 10 assists in 112 games.

OVERALL:

After two solid seasons, Martinez presents the Expos with a dilemma. He clearly deserves platoon duty, at least, but can't squeeze into the Calderon-Grissom-Walker outfield unless someone slumps or is injured. If Ivan Calderon is moved to first base, Martinez may have another chance to prove that he is more than just an occasional platoon outfielder.

DAVE MARTINEZ

Position: RF/LF/CF
Bats: L **Throws:** L
Ht: 5'10" **Wt:** 175

Opening Day Age: 27
Born: 9/26/64 in Manhattan, NY
ML Seasons: 6

Overall Statistics

	G	AB	R	H	D	T	HR	RBI	SB	BB	SO	AVG
1991	124	396	47	117	18	5	7	42	16	20	54	.295
Career	701	2162	282	588	79	32	36	197	95	172	371	.272

Where He Hits the Ball

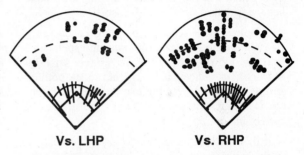

Vs. LHP   **Vs. RHP**

1991 Situational Stats

	AB	H	HR	RBI	AVG		AB	H	HR	RBI	AVG
Home	173	49	3	21	.283	LHP	93	22	0	8	.237
Road	223	68	4	21	.305	RHP	303	95	7	34	.314
Day	106	23	2	13	.217	Sc Pos	96	29	0	31	.302
Night	290	94	5	29	.324	Clutch	78	16	0	6	.205

1991 Rankings (National League)

→ 1st in batting average on an 0-2 count (.423)

→ 7th in batting average with 2 strikes (.253)

→ 9th in steals of third (5)

→ Led the Expos in least GDPs per GDP situation (4.9%), batting average on an 0-2 count, batting average with 2 strikes and lowest percentage of swings that missed (14.8%)

→ Led NL right fielders in batting average on an 0-2 count

PITCHING:

At an age (36) where most players are fading away, Dennis Martinez is experiencing career highlights. On July 28 against Los Angeles, he became only the 15th pitcher in baseball history to throw a perfect game. The rest of the season wasn't bad for him, either. He topped the league in ERA (2.39) and in shutouts (five). He tied Tom Glavine for the league lead in complete games (nine) and maintained the sixth best opposition batting average (.226).

Martinez, a recovered alcoholic, has triumphed off the field as well, producing moments that will not be forgotten. In his native Nicaragua, his perfect game touched off national celebrations. The nation's press heralded him as a national hero, a "great unifier" who "crosses party lines."

In Montreal, last season's pitching coach Larry Bearnarth stated that Martinez was indispensable, that he would not want to coach without Martinez' presence. He is a great model, both on and off the mound, for the team's youthful pitchers. Between starts, he works hard and takes great care of himself.

Martinez is a craftsman with overpowering stuff. Early in the game he will throw everything he has: a fastball, a sinking fastball, a hard curve, a slider and a change-up. Then he will adjust and throw what is most effective for the situation.

HOLDING RUNNERS, FIELDING, HITTING:

Both alert and agile, Martinez is an excellent fielder, and his defensive ability helped secure his perfect game. He has a decent move to first base, yet allowed 22 steals in 26 attempts. The weak-throwing Ron Hassey, his designated catcher, didn't help him in this area. Martinez hit .153 in 72 at-bats with four doubles and helped himself with 10 sacrifice hits.

OVERALL:

Martinez is the team's pitching coach by example, as well as its ace. He knows the limitations of both his pitches and his body. There is no reason not to expect another fine season.

DENNIS MARTINEZ

Position: SP
Bats: R **Throws:** R
Ht: 6' 1" **Wt:** 180

Opening Day Age: 36
Born: 5/14/55 in Granada, Nicaragua
ML Seasons: 16

STAFF ACE

Overall Statistics

	W	L	ERA	G	GS	Sv	IP	H	R	BB	SO	HR
1991	14	11	2.39	31	31	0	222.0	187	70	62	123	9
Career	177	145	3.71	491	410	5	2933.1	2878	1342	866	1546	274

How Often He Throws Strikes

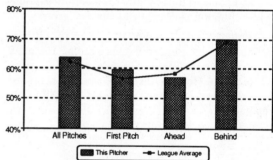

1991 Situational Stats

	W	L	ERA	Sv	IP		AB	H	HR	RBI	AVG
Home	7	4	2.16	0	96.0	LHB	489	114	4	34	.233
Road	7	7	2.57	0	126.0	RHB	340	73	5	28	.215
Day	3	2	2.34	0	42.1	Sc Pos	193	38	1	50	.197
Night	11	9	2.40	0	179.2	Clutch	127	26	1	6	.205

1991 Rankings (National League)

→ 1st in ERA (2.39), complete games (9), shutouts (5), highest stolen base percentage allowed (84.6%) and ERA at home (2.16)

→ 3rd in lowest slugging percentage allowed (.311) and least home runs allowed per 9 innings (.37)

→ Led the Expos in ERA, wins (14), losses (11), games started (31), complete games, shutouts, innings (222), hits allowed (187), batters faced (905), strikeouts (123), pitches thrown (3,353), most stolen bases allowed (22), GDPs induced (14), winning percentage (.560) and sacrifice bunts as a hitter (10)

PITCHING:

Following his impressive debut with the Expos in 1990, Chris Nabholz suffered through injuries in 1991 before re-establishing himself as one of the league's best young lefthanders. Tendinitis in his left shoulder twice forced Nabholz to spend time on the disabled list, and he missed 65 days in all. He did not regain his form until September, when he received National League Pitcher of the Month honors by winning each of his six starts and posting an ERA of 2.23.

Nabholz is equally effective against both right and left-handed hitters. He is more intelligent than he is overpowering, blending a good sinking fastball with an excellent curve and a good change-up. As part of his progress, he maintained a higher level of concentration and improved upon some of the weaknesses evident in his rookie year. Nabholz lowered his walks per nine innings from 4.1 to 3.3 and surrendered one less home run despite pitching 83.2 more innings. Nabholz permitted only five home runs in 153.2 innings last year, one of the best ratios in baseball.

Nabholz maintained his poise with runners on base but proved to be a little sloppy with batters leading off the inning. He allowed leadoff men an on-base percentage of .329 (one of the worst in the league) as opposed to a .307 mark overall.

HOLDING RUNNERS, FIELDING, HITTING:

Nabholz possesses a deceptively good move to first base. In 26 stolen base attempts against him, 11 runners were erased -- many of them surprised by his improved pickoff move. At 6-5, Nabholz isn't the most graceful fielder, but he gets the job done. Not much of a hitter (.115 batting average last year), Nabholz has difficulty bunting runners over and managed just three sacrifices all year.

OVERALL:

At 25, Nabholz enters 1992 as the top left-handed starter on the staff, ready to extend his previous flashes of brilliance over a lengthier period of time. A professional for just three years, the streaky Nabholz has both the smarts and the stuff to perform consistently at a high level.

CHRIS NABHOLZ

Position: SP
Bats: L **Throws:** L
Ht: 6' 5" **Wt:** 210

Opening Day Age: 25
Born: 1/5/67 in Harrisburg, PA
ML Seasons: 2

Overall Statistics

	W	L	ERA	G	GS	Sv	IP	H	R	BB	SO	HR
1991	8	7	3.63	24	24	0	153.2	134	66	57	99	5
Career	14	9	3.38	35	35	0	223.2	177	89	89	152	11

How Often He Throws Strikes

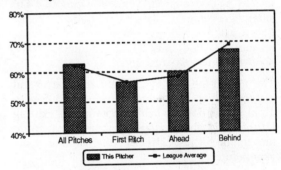

1991 Situational Stats

	W	L	ERA	Sv	IP		AB	H	HR	RBI	AVG
Home	3	5	3.36	0	75.0	LHB	95	22	2	8	.232
Road	5	2	3.89	0	78.2	RHB	471	112	3	43	.238
Day	1	2	5.21	0	38.0	Sc Pos	124	32	0	43	.258
Night	7	5	3.11	0	115.2	Clutch	30	6	0	2	.200

1991 Rankings (National League)

→ Did not rank near the top or bottom in any category

HITTING:

Six months after they signed then 16-year-old phenom Wilfredo Cordero, the Expos acquired Spike Owen with the hope that he would stabilize their shortstop position until Cordero was ready. That's exactly what Owen has done. Always steady, Owen has performed to expectations. But if Cordero has a good training camp in '92, the dependable will become expendable. In fact, last August Owen was rumored on his way to a contender until Cordero suffered a broken hand.

Having faded in the second half in both 1989 and 1990, Owen reversed a trend last season by finishing strongly, pushing his average to a four-year high of .254. In his last 69 games, Owen hit .294 in 214 at-bats and showed some power (.416 slugging average). Swinging at more fastballs, Owen was a much more aggressive hitter last season. He drew only 31 unintentional walks, about half his 1990 total of 58.

The switch-hitting Owen could make a useful platoon player. Last season, Owen hit .305 with 18 of his 22 doubles against southpaws. Batting left-handed, where offspeed pitches seem to tie him up, he hit just .210 last season and .214 the year before.

BASERUNNING:

On the base paths, Owen hustles to make the most of his ordinary speed, scampering from first to third or second to home on base hits. As a base stealer, Owen does not cut it. He was successful in only two of his eight attempts last year.

FIELDING:

Owen's range at shortstop is average at best, but he handles everything he gets to. Owen dropped to second in the league in fielding percentage last season (despite only eight errors) after finishing first the previous two years. His arm, though accurate, is only a little above average.

OVERALL:

Owen's Montreal future depends heavily on Cordero. If the youngster is ready, the cash-stricken Expos probably could not afford to keep Owen on the bench. He's a respected veteran, and other clubs would undoubtedly be interested in him. However, he may have to accept becoming a bench or platoon player.

SPIKE OWEN

Position: SS
Bats: B **Throws:** R
Ht: 5'10" **Wt:** 170

Opening Day Age: 30
Born: 4/19/61 in Cleburne, TX
ML Seasons: 9

Overall Statistics

	G	AB	R	H	D	T	HR	RBI	SB	BB	SO	AVG
1991	139	424	39	108	22	8	3	26	2	42	61	.255
Career	1155	3724	447	896	157	49	33	314	65	423	420	.241

Where He Hits the Ball

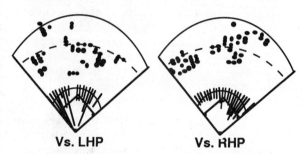

Vs. LHP   Vs. RHP

1991 Situational Stats

	AB	H	HR	RBI	AVG		AB	H	HR	RBI	AVG
Home	161	34	1	7	.211	LHP	200	61	1	12	.305
Road	263	74	2	19	.281	RHP	224	47	2	14	.210
Day	118	33	1	7	.280	Sc Pos	93	20	0	20	.215
Night	306	75	2	19	.245	Clutch	79	22	1	7	.278

1991 Rankings (National League)

- → 2nd highest fielding percentage at shortstop (.986)
- → 5th lowest batting average with runners in scoring position (.215)
- → 6th in triples (8)
- → 8th most GDPs per GDP situation (16.4%)
- → Led the Expos in intentional walks (11), batting average on a 3-1 count (.467) and highest percentage of swings put into play (51.2%)
- → Led NL shortstops in triples, intentional walks and batting average on the road (.281)

STRONG ARM

GIL REYES

Position: C
Bats: R **Throws:** R
Ht: 6' 2" **Wt:** 200

Opening Day Age: 28
Born: 12/10/63 in Santo
Domingo, Dominican
Republic
ML Seasons: 7

HITTING:

At 27, Gilberto Reyes was finally in a position to become a starting catcher last year. A former top prospect with the Dodgers, Reyes spent nine years in their farm system coping with alcohol addiction before the Expos gave him another chance in 1989. A year later, Reyes led the American Association in throwing out opposing base stealers (42.7%) and opened some eyes in the Expos organization.

Reyes did pretty well in the early going last season, sharing the catching duties with Ron Hassey. He had his average over the .300 mark in mid-June and even managed to put together a 10-game hitting streak. Yearning for the Gary Carter days when an Expo catcher could actually throw runners out, fans in Montreal wondered why Reyes didn't play more. They found out in the second half. Reyes struck out 33 times in his last 125 at-bats (26%) as his averaged plummeted to .217.

Reyes is a free swinger and, even on the rare occasions in which he makes contact, possesses a stroke devoid of any power. He had just nine extra-base hits, all doubles, in over 200 at-bats. Everything gets Reyes out. He's late on the fastball and confused by the breaking ball.

BASERUNNING:

For a catcher, Reyes has decent speed but lacks the judgement to be a good baserunner. He stole only two bases in six attempts last year.

FIELDING:

Reyes' vaunted arm is strong and accurate, and he threw out over 53% (39 of 77) of the runners attempting to steal on him. Reyes' other catching skills need work, however. He has trouble blocking pitches and blocking the plate. Only Benito Santiago committed more errors in the NL than Reyes' 11.

OVERALL:

Reyes will be given a chance at the catching job again this year. As the season progressed, his game calling improved. Members of the staff spoke well of his performance, and he was behind the plate for Mark Gardner's nine inning no-hitter. Even so, he won't get a full-time job unless he can improve his hitting.

Overall Statistics

	G	AB	R	H	D	T	HR	RBI	SB	BB	SO	AVG
1991	83	207	11	45	9	0	0	13	2	19	51	.217
Career	122	258	13	52	11	0	0	14	2	20	64	.202

Where He Hits the Ball

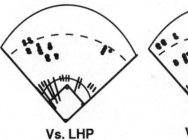
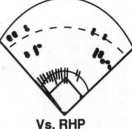

Vs. LHP   **Vs. RHP**

1991 Situational Stats

	AB	H	HR	RBI	AVG		AB	H	HR	RBI	AVG
Home	86	19	0	6	.221	LHP	97	18	0	4	.186
Road	121	26	0	7	.215	RHP	110	27	0	9	.245
Day	65	12	0	2	.185	Sc Pos	56	14	0	13	.250
Night	142	33	0	11	.232	Clutch	39	13	0	3	.333

1991 Rankings (National League)

→ Led NL catchers in highest percentage of runners caught stealing (53.1%)

MONTREAL EXPOS

PITCHING:

Succeeding the likes of Tim Burke, Barry Jones, Steve Frey, Scott Ruskin, Doug Piatt and Jeff Fassero, Mel Rojas is the Expos' current stopper of the month. Rojas spent over two months of the 1990 season refining his game in the minors after failing an early audition with the Expos. When he received his second chance last year, he showed promise in the closer's role.

Rojas, whose fastball can hit the mid-90s, also throws a forkball and a slider, but at this point he's more a thrower than a pitcher. In some early outings last season he looked absolutely terrible, appearing to have no idea how to pitch. Hampered by poor pitching mechanics, he has had difficulty establishing a consistent release point. Like many hard throwers with a relatively small stature, Rojas, 5-11, has a strained, overstretched motion.

After his early season bomb, Rojas was sent to the minors and was used primarily as a starter in order to smooth out his pitching form. He showed much more poise upon his return. In fact, the bouts of wildness that have plagued his entire professional career seemed to disappear as he struck out 34 batters and walked just 10 in 41 innings. Over the last month, he performed like a quality stopper -- 2-0 with five saves in 13 appearances and a 1.02 ERA.

HOLDING RUNNERS, FIELDING, HITTING:

Rojas has had problems with the other parts of his game. He is hitless in seven lifetime at-bats. He doesn't pay close attention to baserunners and does not have a good move to first. His pitching motion leaves him in a very awkward fielding position. Now that his pitching form has improved, these other deficiencies will be addressed.

OVERALL:

The Expos have been, and will probably continue to be, patient with Rojas since he is the team's hardest thrower. He may not yet be ready to become the club's terminator this year, but that's the role the Expos are grooming him for.

MEL ROJAS

Position: RP
Bats: R **Throws:** R
Ht: 5'11" **Wt:** 175

Opening Day Age: 25
Born: 12/10/66 in Haina, Dominican Republic
ML Seasons: 2

Overall Statistics

	W	L	ERA	G	GS	Sv	IP	H	R	BB	SO	HR
1991	3	3	3.75	37	0	6	48.0	42	21	13	37	4
Career	6	4	3.68	60	0	7	88.0	76	38	37	63	9

How Often He Throws Strikes

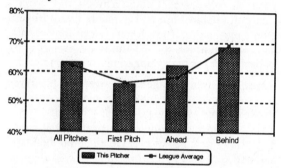

1991 Situational Stats

	W	L	ERA	Sv	IP		AB	H	HR	RBI	AVG
Home	1	2	3.12	2	17.1	LHB	89	22	2	15	.247
Road	2	1	4.11	4	30.2	RHB	95	20	2	7	.211
Day	1	0	2.00	1	9.0	Sc Pos	55	12	1	18	.218
Night	2	3	4.15	5	39.0	Clutch	78	13	1	7	.167

1991 Rankings (National League)

→ 7th least GDPs induced per GDP situation (3.0%)
→ Led the Expos in holds (7)

PITCHING:

Scott Ruskin has now been a professional pitcher for as long as he's been a professional outfielder. In 1990, Ruskin's 2.75 ERA as a reliever surprised everyone. However, in '91, only his third year on the mound, his numbers slipped and his development seemed to stall. Ruskin topped 60 appearances for the second straight season, but his ERA jumped up to 4.24. Ruskin received more closing opportunities amid last season's bullpen chaos, but failed to make an impression.

Ruskin's curveball is a quality out pitch, and the one that prompted his switch from the outfield to the mound. However, his other pitches -- a fastball and a change-up -- have been much easier to hit. Over the last two seasons, Ruskin has allowed almost a hit per inning and nearly one walk every two innings. Ruskin has had trouble throwing his curveball for strikes immediately upon entering a game.

The Expos would love to use the left-handed Ruskin as a situational late-inning reliever, but in each of the past two seasons, left-handed batters have given him more difficulty than righties have. Last season, lefties batted .275 against Ruskin, whereas righthanders hit .219.

HOLDING RUNNERS, FIELDING, HITTING:

Ruskin's athletic ability makes up for his lack of experience at the position. His fielding has improved greatly, as has his determination to hold runners close; one can anticipate further improvements in these areas. As a middle reliever, Ruskin does not receive many hitting opportunities. Too bad, because the former outfielder hit over .269 in parts of three minor league seasons.

OVERALL:

Ruskin has value to the Expos because he is a lefthander with a rubber arm. That value has been compromised, thus far, by his failure to handle left-handed batters. Considering that Ruskin is still relatively inexperienced, he might be able to correct this deficiency. Beginning 1992 however, he has lost his spot as the late-inning lefthander to Jeff Fassero and will begin the season as a middle reliever.

SCOTT
RUSKIN

Position: RP
Bats: R **Throws:** L
Ht: 6' 1" **Wt:** 185

Opening Day Age: 28
Born: 6/6/63 in
Jacksonville, FL
ML Seasons: 2

Overall Statistics

	W	L	ERA	G	GS	Sv	IP	H	R	BB	SO	HR
1991	4	4	4.24	64	0	6	63.2	57	31	30	46	4
Career	7	6	3.43	131	0	8	139.0	132	59	68	103	8

How Often He Throws Strikes

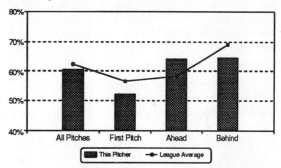

1991 Situational Stats

	W	L	ERA	Sv	IP		AB	H	HR	RBI	AVG
Home	3	2	1.93	2	28.0	LHB	91	25	0	10	.275
Road	1	2	6.06	4	35.2	RHB	146	32	4	17	.219
Day	0	1	4.82	1	18.2	Sc Pos	65	15	1	21	.231
Night	4	3	4.00	5	45.0	Clutch	114	29	1	12	.254

1991 Rankings (National League)

→ 2nd lowest percentage of inherited runners scored (16.7%)

→ 4th most GDPs per GDP situation (2.3%)

→ 5th highest relief ERA (4.24)

→ 9th in blown saves (5)

→ Led the Expos in holds (7), first batter efficiency (.186) and lowest percentage of inherited runners scored

PITCHING:

For the second straight season, the Expos used Bill Sampen as a middle reliever and emergency starter, and for the second straight season, his won-loss record was better than his performance. In 1990, Sampen was the beneficiary of generous offensive support and led the staff with 12 victories despite pitching just 90.1 innings. However, he did post a 2.99 ERA as a rookie, and his overall work showed promise for the future.

Sampen had another fine record last year (9-5), but that was about the only similarity to 1990. His ERA rose by over a run to 4.00, and his strikeout/walk ratio deteriorated from an excellent two-to-one mark in 1990 to almost one-to-one (52/46) in 1991. Sampen, who allowed only seven homers in 1990, allowed 13 in about the same number of innings in 1991. He allowed more homers per nine innings last year than anyone on the Expo staff (25 IP minimum).

Sampen possesses just one major league pitch -- an 88 MPH fastball. His slider is barely average and his change-up is non-existent. The Expos sent Sampen to AAA Indianapolis for over a month, but he returned with the same deficiencies. Though he's a righty, righthanders feasted on him, batting .291. Location was a year-long problem for him. One scout summed up Sampen's work succinctly: "Too many high pitches."

HOLDING RUNNERS, FIELDING, HITTING:

Sampen is an excellent athlete. He fields his position very well and looks good at the plate. He collected three hits in 13 at-bats (a .231 average) and laid down two sacrifice bunts. His big weakness is holding runners. His move to first is terrible and opposing baserunners exploited it by stealing 16 bases in 24 attempts.

OVERALL:

Despite his 21-12 record the last two years, Sampen is walking on thin ice. He regressed a lot last year and simply has to have better control in order to succeed. Sampen seems in no danger of losing his roster spot, but unless his breaking ball comes around, he may find himself being crowded out by other pitchers.

BILL SAMPEN

Position: RP/SP
Bats: R **Throws:** R
Ht: 6' 2" **Wt:** 190

Opening Day Age: 29
Born: 1/18/63 in Lincoln, IL
ML Seasons: 2

Overall Statistics

	W	L	ERA	G	GS	Sv	IP	H	R	BB	SO	HR
1991	9	5	4.00	43	8	0	92.1	96	49	46	52	13
Career	21	12	3.50	102	12	2	182.2	190	83	79	121	20

How Often He Throws Strikes

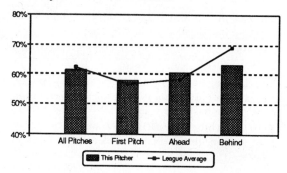

1991 Situational Stats

	W	L	ERA	Sv	IP		AB	H	HR	RBI	AVG
Home	4	2	3.31	0	35.1	LHB	180	46	7	25	.256
Road	5	3	4.42	0	57.0	RHB	172	50	6	25	.291
Day	5	2	3.18	0	39.2	Sc Pos	109	25	3	38	.229
Night	4	3	4.61	0	52.2	Clutch	66	22	1	9	.333

1991 Rankings (National League)

→ 9th in relief wins (6)
→ Led the Expos in relief wins

OVERLOOKED

LARRY WALKER

Position: RF/1B
Bats: L **Throws:** R
Ht: 6' 3" **Wt:** 210

Opening Day Age: 25
Born: 12/1/66 in Maple Ridge, BC
ML Seasons: 3

HITTING:

Though he raised his batting average by 49 points and increased his RBI total by 13, Larry Walker's final 1991 numbers don't tell the whole story behind his improvement. It was a season of adjustments which, in the end, showcased Walker as one of the league's most explosive young players.

At the All-Star break, Walker was hitting in the .230 range. Then he opened his stance, shortened his swing, and became a completely different hitter. In his last 71 games, Walker hit .338 in 263 at-bats with 43 RBI, 21 doubles, a triple and 10 homers -- all of which translated to a .540 slugging percentage. Walker more than held his own against southpaws, hitting .287 in 160 at-bats with some power.

In the second half, Walker showed more patience and stopped trying to pull every pitch. This development, combined with his shortened swing, enabled him to lower his strikeout frequency by about 20% without compromising any power. Still adept at crushing an opposing pitcher's mistake, Walker hit some of the longest home runs at Olympic Stadium last season.

BASERUNNING:

Walker, a fast, alert baserunner, was less aggressive and less successful in stealing bases last season. After swiping 21 bases in 28 attempts in 1990, he was 14-for-23 last year. There's no reason he can't do better.

FIELDING:

Walker can be quite spectacular in right field. He gets a great jump on the ball, covers a lot of ground, and throws with both accuracy and precision. Sure-handed, he committed just two errors there. Walker also started 39 games at first base, his first professional experience at that position. Completely out of his element at the outset, Walker showed great improvement as he went along and could probably become a better-than-average first baseman.

OVERALL:

Now 25 and entering his third season, Walker has made some adjustments and improved the consistency of his game. In 1992, the hot streaks should outnumber the slumps, and Walker will be counted on to produce bigger numbers.

Overall Statistics

	G	AB	R	H	D	T	HR	RBI	SB	BB	SO	AVG
1991	137	487	59	141	30	2	16	64	14	42	102	.290
Career	290	953	122	250	48	5	35	119	36	96	227	.262

Where He Hits the Ball

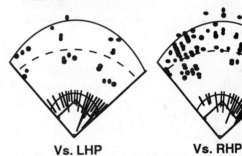

Vs. LHP   Vs. RHP

1991 Situational Stats

	AB	H	HR	RBI	AVG		AB	H	HR	RBI	AVG
Home	187	51	5	24	.273	LHP	160	46	4	25	.287
Road	300	90	11	40	.300	RHP	327	95	12	39	.291
Day	126	31	4	20	.246	Sc Pos	119	32	2	41	.269
Night	361	110	12	44	.305	Clutch	96	28	4	13	.292

1991 Rankings (National League)

→ 2nd in highest fielding percentage in right field (.991), highest percentage of swings that missed (28.2%) and lowest percentage of swings put into play (36.8%)

→ 7th lowest stolen base percentage (60.9%)

→ 8th in least runs scored per time reached base (31.4%) and lowest percentage of pitches taken (47.5%)

→ Led the Expos in doubles (30) and batting average on the road (.300)

→ Led NL right fielders in hit by pitch (5)

HITTING:

In 1991, Tim Wallach suffered through the most disappointing season of his career -- both as a hitter and as the captain of a team which virtually collapsed. Wallach established career lows in batting average (.225), doubles (22), extra-base hits (36) and slugging percentage (.334) and came close to his career lows in every other category. Given 492 at-bats in the cleanup spot, he drove in just 66 runs.

Throughout his career, Wallach's main deficiency has been his inability to adapt to the adjustments aimed at him by opposing pitchers. He will have a good year; the following year, the pitchers will adjust and Wallach will slump. Some hitters change their approach from game to game. The stubborn Wallach changes his from off season to off season.

Last season, Wallach struck out 100 times for the first time since 1984. He was impatient, falling behind in the count by swinging at pitches outside the strike zone. Wallach even had trouble getting around on the fastball, his favorite pitch.

BASERUNNING:

The slow-footed Wallach isn't fancy on the base paths but gets the job done. He is asked to form the latter part of a hit-and-run once in a while, which is not a wise idea. Wallach is only a 45 percent career basestealer, and was just two-for-six last year.

FIELDING:

Wallach has not lost his exceptional fielding ability. In fact, while still making all the plays that earned him a Gold Glove in 1990, Wallach lowered his error total from 21 to 14 in '91. Wallach is adept at both charging bunts and slow hoppers and diving to either his left or right. His arm is strong and accurate.

OVERALL:

Wallach went from being the team's MVP to the team's biggest disappointment. But a good season from Wallach in '92 is not out of the question. He's bounced back before. Judging from his 1991 numbers, he'll probably be asked to work out his problems from a less demanding position in the lineup than his customary fourth or fifth spot.

TIM WALLACH

Position: 3B
Bats: R **Throws:** R
Ht: 6' 3" **Wt:** 200

Opening Day Age: 34
Born: 9/14/57 in Huntington Park, CA
ML Seasons: 12

Overall Statistics

	G	AB	R	H	D	T	HR	RBI	SB	BB	SO	AVG
1991	151	577	60	130	22	1	13	73	2	50	100	.225
Career	1617	5992	684	1574	331	30	195	846	48	464	919	.263

Where He Hits the Ball

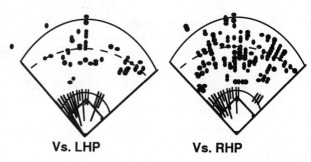

Vs. LHP   Vs. RHP

1991 Situational Stats

	AB	H	HR	RBI	AVG		AB	H	HR	RBI	AVG
Home	230	49	5	23	.213	LHP	185	41	5	21	.222
Road	347	81	8	50	.233	RHP	392	89	8	52	.227
Day	148	38	4	21	.257	Sc Pos	167	40	3	58	.240
Night	429	92	9	52	.214	Clutch	116	27	1	10	.233

1991 Rankings (National League)

→ 1st in lowest batting average (.225), lowest batting average at home (.213) and lowest batting average after the 6th inning (.205)

→ 2nd in lowest slugging percentage (.335), lowest on-base average (.292), lowest batting average vs. right-handed pitchers (.227), lowest cleanup slugging percentage (.343) and lowest slugging percentage vs. right-handed pitchers (.329)

→ 4th lowest on-base average vs. right-handed pitchers (.292)

→ Led the Expos in at-bats (577), hit by pitch (6), GDPs (12) and games (151)

→ Led NL third basemen in fielding percentage (.967) and hit by pitch

TOM FOLEY

Position: SS/1B
Bats: L **Throws:** R
Ht: 6' 1" **Wt:** 180

Opening Day Age: 32
Born: 9/9/59 in
Columbus, GA
ML Seasons: 9

Overall Statistics

	G	AB	R	H	D	T	HR	RBI	SB	BB	SO	AVG
1991	86	168	12	35	11	1	0	15	2	14	30	.208
Career	880	2252	208	558	111	18	26	219	28	198	318	.248

HITTING, FIELDING, BASERUNNING:

Thirty-two year old Tom Foley, once a valuable middle infielder, has seen his batting average fall for four straight seasons. Formerly an Expo regular, Foley has been unable to adjust to the role of utility player.

Since the arrival of Delino DeShields in 1990, Foley's statistics have been painfully similar: a .208 batting average in 168 at-bats last season and a .213 BA in 164 at-bats the year before. As a pinch hitter over the same period, Foley is just 4-for-24. Foley is patient at the plate and makes contact. He pulls the ball but has very little power and has not homered since 1989.

An excellent second baseman, Foley played just 15 innings at second last season. He is not nearly as good at shortstop or third base, where his arm is not quite strong enough. He is competent at first base, with one error in 31 games last year. Foley is a run-of-the-mill baserunner. He was two for two in stolen bases last season but was thrown out 21 times in 31 tries during the previous four seasons.

OVERALL:

The subject of trade rumors just a year ago, Foley no longer attracts the same kind of attention and thus will probably remain a utility player. Having seen his hitting skills diminish the last two seasons, Foley must maintain his defensive abilities.

STEVE FREY

Position: RP
Bats: R **Throws:** L
Ht: 5' 9" **Wt:** 170

Opening Day Age: 28
Born: 7/29/63 in
Southampton, PA
ML Seasons: 3

Overall Statistics

	W	L	ERA	G	GS	Sv	IP	H	R	BB	SO	HR
1991	0	1	4.99	31	0	1	39.2	43	31	23	21	3
Career	11	5	3.70	102	0	10	116.2	116	61	63	65	11

PITCHING, FIELDING, HITTING & HOLDING RUNNERS:

The surprise of the Expos bullpen in 1990 -- an 8-2 record, nine saves, and a 2.10 ERA -- Steve Frey took a couple of giant career-threatening backward steps in 1991. Frey was effective in 1990 despite walking as many batters as he struck out. Last season his control problems caught up with him and he struggled from the outset. He was sent to Indianapolis in June but displayed the same lack of control with 12 walks in 17 innings. When he was recalled, the pressure to throw strikes made him an easy target for opposing hitters.

For the season, opponents hit .281 against Frey, much higher than the .219 they managed in 1990 and the .256 they hit before his 1991 demotion. Frey no longer can hide the fact that he is a finesse pitcher who relies heavily on one pitch -- a curveball which breaks sharply out of the strike zone. Frey helps himself as a fielder and has a decent move to first. Opponents stole three bases in five attempts against him.

OVERALL:

At 28, it is unlikely that Frey will improve his other pitches. Last season, he was expected to handle the left-handed stopper role in the Expos' bullpen committee. Now he must compete against either Jeff Fassero or Scott Ruskin for a middle relief spot.

DOUG PIATT

Position: RP
Bats: L **Throws:** R
Ht: 6' 1" **Wt:** 185

Opening Day Age: 26
Born: 9/26/65 in Beaver, PA
ML Seasons: 1

Overall Statistics

	W	L	ERA	G	GS	Sv	IP	H	R	BB	SO	HR
1991	0	0	2.60	21	0	0	34.2	29	11	17	29	3
Career	0	0	2.60	21	0	0	34.2	29	11	17	29	3

PITCHING, FIELDING, HITTING & HOLDING RUNNERS:

After accumulating 251 strikeouts in 206.2 innings in three minor league seasons, Doug Piatt was given a couple of chances to make an impression with the Expos, a team in dire need of a hard-throwing reliever. For a brief period, like most of the members of the Expos' bullpen, Piatt earned the chance to become the team's stopper. Like the others, his performance suffered in the high-pressure role.

The Expos believe that Piatt has the temperament to become a good reliever. He pitches aggressively and is unafraid to claim the inside part of the strike zone. Piatt possesses a 91 MPH fastball but needs to gain both command of his change-up and better location with his slider. Opposing left-handed hitters slashed him to pieces, hitting .316 with three homers and 10 walks. But Piatt dominated righties, holding them to just a .159 average. His fielding is unexceptional and he needs to improve on his move to first base. He received just one at-bat.

OVERALL:

Piatt performed well in streaks last season. He pitched good ball following his recall in June but was optioned out a month later. He came back strong in September/October, striking out 21 batters in 20 innings while posting an ERA of 2.25. With those numbers, Piatt will be competing for a starring role in the Expos bullpen.

NELSON SANTOVENIA

Position: C
Bats: R **Throws:** R
Ht: 6' 3" **Wt:** 210

Opening Day Age: 30
Born: 7/27/61 in Pina del Rio, Cuba
ML Seasons: 5

Overall Statistics

	G	AB	R	H	D	T	HR	RBI	SB	BB	SO	AVG
1991	41	96	7	24	5	0	2	14	0	2	18	.250
Career	291	873	76	204	42	4	21	114	4	58	163	.234

HITTING, FIELDING, BASERUNNING:

If Nelson Santovenia could forget the 1991 season, he most certainly would. After a hellish 1990 season in which he batted just .190, spent some time in the minors, and underwent arthroscopic knee surgery, things figured to get better. In most ways they did not, though Santovenia swung a much better bat.

After initially refusing to play in Indianapolis, Santovenia spent most of his time there sharing the catching duties. He did get into 41 games with the Expos and was able to raise his 1990 average 60 points to .250. But Santovenia swings at almost everything, walking just twice in 96 at-bats last season. Otherwise, Santovenia has demonstrated a pretty good stroke and an uncanny ability to drive in runs (114 RBI in 873 career at-bats).

Behind the plate, Santovenia is a lot like Gilberto Reyes. He has an above-average arm (though not as strong as Reyes') but he is weak in blocking pitches, blocking the plate and calling a game. Santovenia is one of the slowest runners in baseball.

OVERALL:

The Expos have had their catching problems, which is one reason they're bringing Gary Carter back. Carter and Reyes both rate ahead of Santovenia; since all three are righty swingers, Santovenia's chances of making the roster are pretty slim. His only chance is that the Expos will value his hitting skills higher than Reyes' strong arm.

ORGANIZATION OVERVIEW:

The Expo farm system is frequently described as the best in baseball, and with good reason. Over the past few years, the Montreal system has pumped a steady stream of talent -- most of the Expo roster, in fact -- to the big club. Under the highly-regarded Dan Duquette, who succeeded Dave Dombrowski as the Montreal GM at the end of the 1991 season, the talent flow should continue. Still, the Expo franchise, so solid at the bottom, is shaky at the top, with a crumbling stadium, lack of fan support and rumblings about relocation to another city. Many talented players simply don't want to play in French-speaking Montreal. If the franchise is sold and/or moved to the U.S., the Expo future could look a whole lot brighter.

WILFREDO CORDERO

Position: SS   **Opening Day Age:** 20
Bats: R **Throws:** R   **Born:** 10/3/71 in
Ht: 6' 2" **Wt:** 185   Mayaguez, PR

Recent Statistics

	G	AB	R	H	D	T	H	R	RBI	SB	BB	SO	AVG
90 AA Jacksnville	131	444	63	104	18	4	7	40		9	56	122	.234
91 AAA Indianapols	98	360	48	94	16	4	11	52		8	26	89	.261
91 MLE	98	347	38	81	14	2	7	41		6	20	94	.233

Some people think the Expos' search for a superstar will end with shortstop Cordero. He's considered a fantastic fielder, and he's beginning to develop some power. However, Cordero has not yet hit for average, and there's some doubt as to whether he'll be ready to take over the Expo shortstop job this year, as some expect. He's still very young, and if he's in the majors in 1991, he's probably going to struggle. He has a lot to prove at the plate, though the Expos figure to be patient with him.

TODD HANEY

Position: 2B   **Opening Day Age:** 26
Bats: R **Throws:** R   **Born:** 7/30/65 in
Ht: 5' 9" **Wt:** 165   Galveston, TX

Recent Statistics

	G	AB	R	H	D	T	H	R	RBI	SB	BB	SO	AVG
90 AA Williamsprt	1	2	0	1	1	0	0	0		0	1	0	.500
90 AAA Calgary	108	419	81	142	15	6	1	36		16	37	38	.339
91 AAA Indianapols	132	510	68	159	32	3	2	39		11	47	49	.312
91 MLE	132	489	54	138	28	2	1	31		8	37	51	.282

The Expos are loaded with talented young infielders; Haney is another example. Haney hit very well in the Seattle system in '90, was traded to the Tigers last spring, then curiously released before Montreal picked him up. He is a scrappy second sacker in the Wally Backman/Chuck Knoblauch mold; he may need a trade to prove it, but he can almost certainly play in the majors.

MATT STAIRS

Position: 2B   **Opening Day Age:** 23
Bats: R **Throws:** R   **Born:** 2/27/69 in Saint
Ht: 5' 9" **Wt:** 175   John, N.B., Canada

Recent Statistics

	G	AB	R	H	D	T	H	R	RBI	SB	BB	SO	AVG
90 A Wst Plm Bch	55	184	30	62	9	3	3	30		15	40	19	.337
90 AA Jacksnville	79	280	26	71	17	0	3	34		5	22	42	.254
91 AA Harrisburg	129	505	87	168	30	10	13	78		23	66	47	.333
91 MLE	129	486	73	149	27	7	9	65		17	46	50	.307

Three reasons the Expos have considered trading DeShields are Bret Barberie, Todd Haney and Stairs. There's little doubt, after '91, that Stairs can hit; he has outstanding power for a small man, and fine speed as well. There are a few questions about his second base skills, but the consensus is that they'll find a spot for him. Stairs may play in AAA this year, but he shouldn't be in the minor leagues much longer. A bonus for the Expos: he's Canadian.

JOHN VANDERWAL

Position: OF   **Opening Day Age:** 25
Bats: L **Throws:** L   **Born:** 4/29/66 in Grand
Ht: 6' 1" **Wt:** 180   Rapids, MI

Recent Statistics

	G	AB	R	H	D	T	H	R	RBI	SB	BB	SO	AVG
91 AAA Indianapols	133	478	84	140	36	8	15	71		8	79	118	.293
91 NL Montreal	21	61	4	13	4	1	1	8		0	1	18	.213
91 MLE	133	459	67	121	32	5	10	57		6	62	125	.264

A third-round pick out of Western Michigan in 1987, VanderWal is a patient hitter with gap power and some home run potential. He's fast and considered a good defensive player, also. The one negative in his 1991 stats were his 118 strikeouts. He's well-seasoned by now and should make the Expo roster this year; he has a chance to get lots of playing time.

DAVID WAINHOUSE

Position: P   **Opening Day Age:** 24
Bats: L **Throws:** R   **Born:** 11/7/67 in
Ht: 6' 2" **Wt:** 190   Toronto, Ontario, Canada

Recent Statistics

	W	L	ERA	G	GS	Sv	IP	H	R	BB	SO	HR
91 AA Harrisburg	2	2	2.60	33	0	11	52.0	49	17	17	46	1
91 AAA Indianapols	2	0	4.08	14	0	1	28.2	28	14	15	13	1
91 NL Montreal	0	1	6.75	2	0	0	2.2	2	2	4	1	0

Another Canadian, Wainhouse was Montreal's first pick in 1988. A starter until '91, he made rapid progress when moved to the bullpen. Montreal needs a closer about as badly as they need a new stadium, and it would be no shock to find Wainhouse in the Expo relief corps this year. Chances are he'll break in as a middle reliever.

HITTING:

The Mets have now received two good years from Daryl Boston, proving that the White Sox made a mistake by letting him go. Given a chance to play, Boston has showed that he can hit for average, hit with power, and steal bases. He has displayed a positive attitude as a platooner and role player and has been a helpful influence in a generally unhappy clubhouse.

Boston ended up leading all Mets regulars with a .275 batting average in 1991. He picked up the pace considerably while playing on a regular basis after replacing the injured Vince Coleman in center field, hitting over .361 during one stretch of 15 games from June 23 to July 11.

Boston was a free swinger when he first reached the major leagues, but he has grown more disciplined every year. He has a good knowledge of opposing pitchers, and he knows how to use all fields. Boston is a tough out in clutch situations, and he is hard to double up.

BASERUNNING:

Boston has always had good speed. He stole 46 bases in 1984 and 46 more in 1986, splitting both seasons between Triple-A and the majors. Boston is a smart baserunner with a consistently high success rate in stealing bases. He can turn up the pace in key situations and is a clever, aggressive slider.

FIELDING:

Capable of playing all three outfield positions, Boston was the Mets' fourth outfielder and was frequently used as a defensive replacement in late innings. His speed helps him cover plenty of territory, and he has an exceptional throwing arm.

OVERALL:

Many observers felt that Boston deserved the regular right field job in 1991, after the departure of Darryl Strawberry. The Mets wanted a "big-name" hitter, however, and traded Bob Ojeda to get Hubie Brooks. Hindsight shows that Boston would have been a better choice, and would have allowed the Mets to keep a much-needed starting pitcher. Wherever the free agent plays in 1992, Boston will be an asset.

DARYL BOSTON

Position: CF/RF
Bats: L **Throws:** L
Ht: 6' 3" **Wt:** 205

Opening Day Age: 29
Born: 1/4/63 in Cincinnati, OH
ML Seasons: 8

Overall Statistics

	G	AB	R	H	D	T	HR	RBI	SB	BB	SO	AVG
1991	137	255	40	70	16	4	4	21	15	30	42	.275
Career	752	1972	284	493	100	19	54	189	85	167	332	.250

Where He Hits the Ball

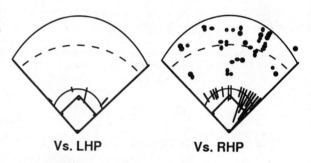

Vs. LHP   Vs. RHP

1991 Situational Stats

	AB	H	HR	RBI	AVG		AB	H	HR	RBI	AVG
Home	135	33	2	13	.244	LHP	31	6	1	1	.194
Road	120	37	2	8	.308	RHP	224	64	3	20	.286
Day	95	22	3	8	.232	Sc Pos	52	15	1	16	.288
Night	160	48	1	13	.300	Clutch	40	11	1	4	.275

1991 Rankings (National League)

→ Did not rank near the top or bottom in any category

HITTING:

When the Dodgers acquired Darryl Strawberry, their incumbent right fielder Hubie Brooks became expendable. The Mets, needing a veteran power hitter and a right fielder after the loss of Strawberry, were happy to take Brooks. They weren't so happy at the end of 1991, however. Hubie slumped in the second half of the season and underwent surgery for a herniated disk on September 12.

Prior to 1991, Brooks was among the most consistent hitters in the National League. From 1984 through 1990, Brooks average 16 home runs, 79 RBI, and compiled a .278 batting average. His home runs reached his normal level in 1991, but his average didn't: Brooks' .238 was a career low. Most painful for the Mets, his RBI output plummeted as he stopped hitting in clutch situations.

Brooks has traditionally been a free swinger. He cut down on his strikeouts in 1991, and worked more walks than he's had in any season since 1984. That may indicate that Brooks is finally developing some patience to go with his good eye and knowledge of the strike zone. The bad news is that his bat speed isn't what it used to be.

BASERUNNING:

Brooks was only 8-for-24 in steal attempts in 1989-1990, and finally quit trying so hard in 1991. By picking his spots more carefully, he nabbed three steals in four attempts. He isn't a threat at this stage of his career. He is aggressive, however, and will take an extra base when a fielder gets lackadaisical.

FIELDING:

A former shortstop and third baseman, Brooks has a good arm for right field, but he still looks awkward at times. The loss of speed has cut down his range and left him at a level that is just barely adequate in the field.

OVERALL:

The Mets were trying various personnel in right field during September 1991, including catcher Mackey Sasser and third baseman Howard Johnson. It's obvious that Brooks' future is not secure.

HUBIE BROOKS

Position: RF
Bats: R **Throws:** R
Ht: 6' 0" **Wt:** 205

Opening Day Age: 35
Born: 9/24/56 in Los Angeles, CA
ML Seasons: 12

Overall Statistics

	G	AB	R	H	D	T	HR	RBI	SB	BB	SO	AVG
1991	103	357	48	85	11	1	16	50	3	44	62	.238
Career	1454	5439	609	1480	263	31	139	750	60	362	922	.272

Where He Hits the Ball

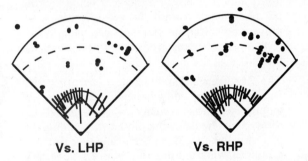

Vs. LHP   Vs. RHP

1991 Situational Stats

	AB	H	HR	RBI	AVG		AB	H	HR	RBI	AVG
Home	172	41	4	22	.238	LHP	121	30	5	17	.248
Road	185	44	12	28	.238	RHP	236	55	11	33	.233
Day	98	21	3	12	.214	Sc Pos	100	21	2	33	.210
Night	259	64	13	38	.247	Clutch	57	12	2	6	.211

1991 Rankings (National League)

➡ 2nd lowest fielding percentage in right field (.972)

➡ 3rd lowest batting average with runners in scoring position (.210)

PITCHING:

Tim Burke was the Expos' ace reliever for four years, averaging 21 saves per season from 1987 through 1990. In 1991 he became a set-up man and was traded to the Mets for Ron Darling on July 15. After a rough start in New York, Burke finally found his good stuff again and recorded a 1.10 ERA after August 21.

Burke is a classic sinker/slider pitcher with above-average velocity on his sinking fastball. He improved the sinker in late 1991 with a slightly different grip learned from pitching coach Mel Stottlemyre. Burke possesses a peculiar and distracting motion: in the middle of his delivery, he drops his right arm straight down and holds it motionless for a moment while moving his glove hand toward the plate. Because the move is so unlike any other pitcher, batters must re-think their timing whenever Burke takes the mound.

The Mets experimented successfully with Burke's stamina, letting him work up to three full innings and throw as many as 50 pitches. Burke showed that he can work all the way through an opposing lineup without tiring, and thus can help a bullpen when the middle relievers need rest. Most of the time, however, Burke appears in short set-up work, preceding John Franco.

HOLDING RUNNERS, FIELDING, HITTING:

Burke is a good fielder with a fine pickoff move. Opposition runners stole eight bases in nine attempts during 1991, but these steals occurred during his difficult period with Montreal when he had bigger pitching problems to worry about.

OVERALL:

Burke's long-standing inconsistency cost him the ace reliever's role in Montreal. The Expos' switch to a stopper-by-committee was a simple and resounding vote of "no confidence." After arriving in New York, however, Burke's mechanical adjustments made a huge difference, and he was extremely effective in the role of set-up man. He should keep that job and handle it well in 1992.

TIM BURKE

Position: RP
Bats: R **Throws:** R
Ht: 6' 3" **Wt:** 205

Opening Day Age: 33
Born: 2/19/59 in Omaha, NE
ML Seasons: 7

Overall Statistics

	W	L	ERA	G	GS	Sv	IP	H	R	BB	SO	HR
1991	6	7	3.36	72	0	6	101.2	96	46	26	59	8
Career	46	29	2.62	460	2	102	656.0	572	222	201	429	46

How Often He Throws Strikes

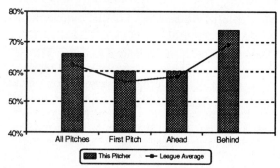

1991 Situational Stats

	W	L	ERA	Sv	IP		AB	H	HR	RBI	AVG
Home	2	2	2.16	4	50.0	LHB	192	57	2	26	.297
Road	4	5	4.53	2	51.2	RHB	193	39	6	15	.202
Day	1	4	5.52	1	31.0	Sc Pos	99	26	3	35	.263
Night	5	3	2.42	5	70.2	Clutch	208	48	3	23	.231

1991 Rankings (National League)

→ 1st in blown saves (10)

→ 2nd in relief innings (101.2)

→ 4th in games pitches (72)

→ 5th in relief losses (7)

→ 7th in highest batting average vs. left-handed batters (.297) and worst first batter efficiency (.308)

→ 9th in holds (10) and relief wins (6)

→ Led the Mets in holds (4 with the Mets)

GREAT SPEED

VINCE COLEMAN

Position: CF
Bats: B **Throws:** R
Ht: 6' 1" **Wt:** 185

Opening Day Age: 30
Born: 9/22/61 in
Jacksonville, FL
ML Seasons: 7

HITTING:

Vince Coleman was supposed to help New York fans forget Darryl Strawberry. Instead, he helped St. Louis fans forget Vince Coleman. After leading the National League in stolen bases every year from 1985 through 1990, Coleman pulled up lame with a hamstring injury and went on the disabled list twice in 1991.

Coleman is not a good hitter. He keeps his batting average in the respectable range by using his speed to beat out infield hits. He had only 13 extra base hits in 1991, a career low. Coleman simply tries to put the ball in play and get to first base, where his speed takes over.

One positive aspect of Coleman's offense in 1991 was that he posted a .347 on-base percentage, the second highest of his career. That didn't compare favorably with top leadoff hitters like Brett Butler (.401) and Lenny Dykstra (.391), but it showed progress. He really needs to draw more walks in the leadoff spot, which is the only place he can fit into a batting order. Stuck behind anyone else in another part of the lineup, he would eventually put footprints on their back.

BASERUNNING:

Coleman's baserunning ability pushes the limits of traditional scouting terminology; he runs well enough to be considered for the Hall of Fame on that aspect alone. At age 30, Coleman is already among the all-time stolen base leaders, presently tied with Maury Wills for 16th place. He doesn't steal 100 bases any more, but last year he swiped 37 in only 72 games.

FIELDING:

The Mets stretched Coleman's credentials to convert him from left field to center, a position he hadn't played in years. He has great range due to his speed, but he's still having adventures with Shea Stadium winds and he doesn't have a great arm.

OVERALL:

There were so many disappointments on the Mets roster in 1991 that Coleman's off year attracted relatively little attention. When the Mets regroup in 1992, Coleman will be back in the spotlight, especially with the speed-minded Jeff Torborg in the dugout.

Overall Statistics

	G	AB	R	H	D	T	HR	RBI	SB	BB	SO	AVG
1991	72	278	45	71	7	5	1	17	37	39	47	.255
Career	950	3813	611	1008	113	61	16	234	586	353	675	.264

Where He Hits the Ball

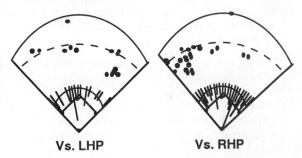

Vs. LHP   **Vs. RHP**

1991 Situational Stats

	AB	H	HR	RBI	AVG		AB	H	HR	RBI	AVG
Home	107	25	0	5	.234	LHP	105	26	1	4	.248
Road	171	46	1	12	.269	RHP	173	45	0	13	.260
Day	87	20	0	4	.230	Sc Pos	57	16	0	15	.281
Night	191	51	1	13	.267	Clutch	52	16	0	6	.308

1991 Rankings (National League)

→ 7th in stolen bases (37)

→ 8th in steals of third (6)

→ Led the Mets in triples (5), stolen bases, batting average in the clutch (.308) and bunts in play (17)

PITCHING:

Like the girl with a curl on her forehead, David Cone is two completely different pitchers. In seven bad outings in 1991, he gave up 39 earned runs in 33 innings. In his other 27 starts totaling 199.2 IP, he gave up only 46 earned runs, and he looked even better than his 2.07 ERA would indicate. Overall, Cone wound up with exactly 14 wins for the third year in a row, but there are people who think he should be winning more.

Cone is an enigmatic package of talent. Opposition hitters and managers often praise him for having the best stuff in the National League (fastball, slider, curve and splitter, all with great movement) but Cone also loses his concentration too easily and too frequently. The problem wasn't new in 1991. Back in 1990, Cone had an ERA over 6.00 in April and May, but then recovered supremely, to finish the season at 3.23.

Pitching coach Mel Stottlemyre and Cone agree that he is most effective when he doesn't try to be overpowering. Ironically, when Cone uses all his pitches, not intending to blow hitters away, he has his most dominant outings -- like the 19-strikeout performance with which he ended the 1991 season.

HOLDING RUNNERS, FIELDING, HITTING:

Cone doesn't let baserunners distract him. Though he makes a lot of throws to first, his attention is devoted to the batter. The opposition got away with 27 steals against him in 1991, often making it look easy. Cone is, however, a solid fielder. He is one of the better-hitting pitchers in the National League, often helping himself with a base hit or a sacrifice bunt.

OVERALL:

Despite the inconsistency, Cone must be regarded as one of the top starting pitchers in the game today. His long untouchable streaks every year prove that he still has all the skill that enabled him to compile a 20-3 record with a 2.22 ERA in 1988. By simply staying focused, Cone can avoid slumps and have another huge year in 1992.

DAVID CONE

Position: SP
Bats: L **Throws:** R
Ht: 6' 1" **Wt:** 190

Opening Day Age: 29
Born: 1/2/63 in Kansas City, MO
ML Seasons: 6

Overall Statistics

	W	L	ERA	G	GS	Sv	IP	H	R	BB	SO	HR
1991	14	14	3.29	34	34	0	232.2	204	95	73	241	13
Career	67	41	3.18	166	138	1	1017.1	858	398	349	966	77

How Often He Throws Strikes

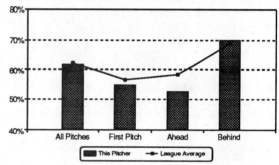

1991 Situational Stats

	W	L	ERA	Sv	IP		AB	H	HR	RBI	AVG
Home	6	7	3.91	0	115.0	LHB	545	135	7	47	.248
Road	8	7	2.68	0	117.2	RHB	323	69	6	31	.214
Day	4	5	4.21	0	57.2	Sc Pos	206	47	7	65	.228
Night	10	9	2.98	0	175.0	Clutch	84	19	1	5	.226

1991 Rankings (National League)

→ 1st in strikeouts (241), pitches thrown (3,743), pickoff throws (406) and most strikeouts per 9 innings (9.3)

→ 2nd in wild pitches (17), strikeout/walk ratio (3.3) and most pitches thrown per batter (3.88)

→ 3rd in losses (14)

→ 4th in stolen bases allowed (27) and least GDPs induced per 9 innings (.31)

→ Led the Mets in ERA (3.29), wins (14), complete games (5), shutouts (2), innings (232.2), walks allowed (73), strikeouts, wild pitches, pitches thrown, pickoff throws, strikeout/walk ratio and lowest batting average allowed with runners in scoring position (.228)

HITTING:

It took a strong second half by Kevin Elster to get his 1991 batting average up to .241. Early in the year, it looked like he would have trouble just matching his .219 career mark. Elster has a history of weak starts and good second half performances. He has decent power for a middle infielder, but his inability to hit for average, and his failure get on base consistently, have been long-standing sources of frustration in the Mets organization.

Elster is a hard swinger, not a contact hitter. He has produced steady, if unspectacular, offensive stats over the past four years. Consistency is normally a virtue, but Elster first reached the major leagues in 1986 at age 22. Most hitters show significant improvement in their mid-twenties, but Elster hasn't advanced noticeably. He still chases outside breaking pitches, and has trouble with right-handed pitchers in general.

BASERUNNING:

Elster is among the slower shortstops in the National League. He's stolen only 10 bases in his six-year career, and was 2-for-5 last year. He knows his limits, however, and doesn't make mistakes on the base paths.

FIELDING:

After shoulder surgery in September 1990, there were big questions concerning Elster's ability to make throws from deep in the hole. He performed this task adequately in 1991. Playing behind a pitching staff that generated a lot of fly balls, Elster set the major league record for consecutive errorless games by a shortstop in 1988-1989. He is a decent fielder, but the record was a fluke.

OVERALL:

Elster is a natural candidate to be platooned, after hitting nearly .300 against lefty pitchers and under .200 against righties in 1991. He kept his regular shortstop job in 1991 only because Howard Johnson proved inadequate at that position and because Garry Templeton couldn't hit a lick. After four seasons, it's fairly clear that Elster's defense is not spectacular enough to make up for his weak hitting. The Mets simply need to find another shortstop, which they might do.

KEVIN ELSTER

Position: SS
Bats: R **Throws:** R
Ht: 6' 2" **Wt:** 200

Opening Day Age: 27
Born: 8/3/64 in San Pedro, CA
ML Seasons: 6

Overall Statistics

	G	AB	R	H	D	T	HR	RBI	SB	BB	SO	AVG
1991	115	348	33	84	16	2	6	36	2	40	53	.241
Career	531	1566	166	351	75	6	34	174	10	142	240	.224

Where He Hits the Ball

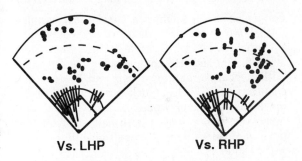

Vs. LHP   **Vs. RHP**

1991 Situational Stats

	AB	H	HR	RBI	AVG		AB	H	HR	RBI	AVG
Home	181	48	3	14	.265	LHP	159	47	1	14	.296
Road	167	36	3	22	.216	RHP	189	37	5	22	.196
Day	92	21	3	7	.228	Sc Pos	85	23	2	31	.271
Night	256	63	3	29	.246	Clutch	57	8	0	3	.140

1991 Rankings (National League)

➡ 1st in lowest batting average in the clutch (.140)

➡ Led the Mets in batting average vs. left-handed pitchers (.296) and on-base average vs. left-handed pitchers (.362)

PITCHING:

Sid Fernandez, one of the top starting pitchers in the National League from 1985 to 1990, didn't help the Mets much in 1991. Fernandez suffered a broken arm during spring training, and shortly after coming off the disabled list in July, he injured his knee and missed the remainder of the season. Sid's grand total of one victory accurately summarizes his frustrating 1991 season.

Fernandez is among the all-time leaders in lowest opponents' batting average allowed (.205). Although he hasn't been a big winner over the years (mainly due to lack of run support), he has been a terrific "big game" pitcher and is consistently tough on the opposition. When healthy, he is as good as any left-handed starter in the game today.

Fernandez' main pitch is a sneaky-fast, rising fastball which generates plenty of strikeouts and fly ball outs. Fielder assists are scarce when Sid is on the mound. He complements the fastball with a sharp-breaking curve and a straight change. Fernandez has much better control than his high walk total would indicate. When he misses the strike zone, it is usually half-intentional. Fernandez simply doesn't give in to dangerous hitters.

HOLDING RUNNERS, FIELDING, HITTING:

During the past two seasons, Fernandez has been working harder at holding runners, with fair results. The opposition recorded only three steals in his 44 innings during 1991. He is just adequate as a fielder, but he is a big asset with a bat in his hands.

OVERALL:

The two raps on Sid Fernandez are stamina and weight-watching. Both will be subjects of intense scrutiny from the first day of spring training until the end of the season in 1992. Fernandez gained weight while waiting for his wrist to heal during the first half of 1991, a fact that might be linked to the subsequent knee injury. If he can stay trim and work a full season without mishap, he can easily be a 20-game winner.

SID FERNANDEZ

Position: SP
Bats: L **Throws:** L
Ht: 6' 1" **Wt:** 230

Opening Day Age: 29
Born: 10/12/62 in Honolulu, HI
ML Seasons: 9

Overall Statistics

	W	L	ERA	G	GS	Sv	IP	H	R	BB	SO	HR
1991	1	3	2.86	8	8	0	44.0	36	18	9	31	4
Career	79	62	3.25	207	201	1	1256.1	930	496	500	1184	109

How Often He Throws Strikes

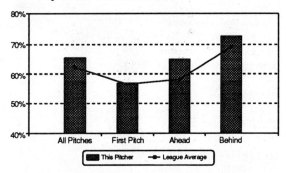

1991 Situational Stats

	W	L	ERA	Sv	IP		AB	H	HR	RBI	AVG
Home	1	1	1.42	0	19.0	LHB	35	13	1	3	.371
Road	0	2	3.96	0	25.0	RHB	127	23	3	13	.181
Day	0	0	-.--	0	0.0	Sc Pos	32	6	1	10	.188
Night	1	3	2.86	0	44.0	Clutch	4	1	0	0	.250

1991 Rankings (National League)

➜ Did not rank near the top or bottom in any category

STOPPER

JOHN FRANCO

Position: RP
Bats: L **Throws:** L
Ht: 5'10" **Wt:** 185

Opening Day Age: 31
Born: 9/17/60 in
Brooklyn, NY
ML Seasons: 8

PITCHING:

John Franco leads the National League in saves over the past six years, and already has a place among the all-time great relief pitchers. During 1991 Franco suffered some back pain that affected his performance, but he still finished the year with 30 saves, tying for third in the league.

Franco features a good fastball and slider, but his best pitch is a change-up. This offspeed wonder-pitch fades away from right-handed hitters; it moves so well that hitters and scouts have often called it a screwball. Thanks to the fade-away, Franco has been tough on lefty and righty hitters alike over the years. Surprisingly, it was the lefties who gave him the most trouble during 1991.

Franco is a true thinking man's pitcher. After eight years in the National League, he knows the hitters well. He is an expert at pitching to spots, moving the ball around, and changing speeds. Franco has an excellent understanding of the relationship between pitch location and fielder positioning, so he gets the most out of his defense.

HOLDING RUNNERS, FIELDING, HITTING:

Franco has a sharp pickoff move and pays close attention to runners. The opposition has stolen only 10 bases against him over the past two years. Fitting his ground ball style, Franco is a good fielder who covers plenty of ground and always knows what to do with the ball. He rarely comes to bat.

OVERALL:

Despite the 30 saves in 1991, Franco is coming off a weak season in which he yielded a .271 opponent's batting average. In 1992 he will need to reestablish himself as a dominant closer by giving up fewer hits and getting the opposition out more quickly. The prognosis is good. Franco has already shown that he can overcome his back pain with an exercise regimen, and he has previously come back strong after difficult periods (the second half of 1989). In 1992 he should continue advancing rapidly among the lifetime save leaders.

Overall Statistics

	W	L	ERA	G	GS	Sv	IP	H	R	BB	SO	HR
1991	5	9	2.93	52	0	30	55.1	61	27	18	45	2
Career	52	42	2.53	500	0	211	651.0	587	223	249	468	33

How Often He Throws Strikes

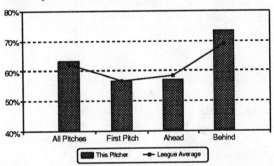

1991 Situational Stats

	W	L	ERA	Sv	IP		AB	H	HR	RBI	AVG
Home	1	4	3.00	18	27.0	LHB	53	18	0	6	.340
Road	4	5	2.86	12	28.1	RHB	172	43	2	24	.250
Day	1	2	2.45	9	18.1	Sc Pos	86	21	1	28	.244
Night	4	7	3.16	21	37.0	Clutch	202	55	2	27	.272

1991 Rankings (National League)

→ 1st in relief losses (9)

→ 3rd in saves (30) and save percentage (85.7%)

→ 4th in save opportunities (35)

→ 5th in games finished (48)

→ 7th highest batting average allowed in relief (.271)

→ Led the Mets in saves, games finished, save opportunites, save percentage, blown saves (5), relief losses and most strikeouts per 9 innings in relief (7.3)

PITCHING:

Dwight Gooden's path to the Hall of Fame took a detour in September 1991 when he underwent rotator cuff surgery. Before reaching age 27, Gooden had amassed 132 career victories. His astounding .714 winning percentage places him high atop the all-time list (even above Whitey Ford's .690 and Christy Mathewson's .665).

Gooden has two big pitches: a fastball with great velocity and movement, and a curve that breaks so sharply it was nicknamed "Lord Charles" when the regular term for a good curveball was just called "Uncle Charlie." Either one of the two main pitches can make Gooden a winner in any start; when both of them are working well, he is unhittable. Gooden has experimented with other pitches, but his main variants are changing locations and speeds on the heater and the hook.

Gooden's role gives definition to the term "franchise player." Although he has only one 20-win season in the record books, he has averaged over 16 wins per season during eight years in New York. He has been a workhorse who can give the bullpen a rest, but after throwing 149 pitches on April 13, Gooden never went beyond 128 in any outing during 1991.

HOLDING RUNNERS, FIELDING, HITTING:

Gooden's high leg kick has always given him trouble holding runners. He tried making adjustments a few years ago, but finally decided it was better to concentrate on the hitters and let the runners have their fun (which they do -- 33 steals in 1991). Gooden is a fine fielder, and like most of the Mets' pitchers, he is dangerous at the plate.

OVERALL:

The science of rotator cuff surgery has advanced considerably. The "R" operation no longer means that a pitcher's career is necessarily finished. Gooden has battled back from troubling injuries before. Nonetheless, there are serious questions about how well Gooden can perform in 1992. If he can't pitch effectively, the Mets will be devastated.

DWIGHT GOODEN

Position: SP
Bats: R **Throws:** R
Ht: 6' 3" **Wt:** 210

Opening Day Age: 27
Born: 11/16/64 in Tampa, FL
ML Seasons: 8

Overall Statistics

	W	L	ERA	G	GS	Sv	IP	H	R	BB	SO	HR
1991	13	7	3.60	27	27	0	190.0	185	80	56	150	12
Career	132	53	2.91	238	236	1	1713.2	1467	609	505	1541	87

How Often He Throws Strikes

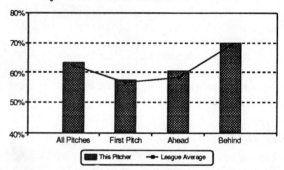

1991 Situational Stats

	W	L	ERA	Sv	IP		AB	H	HR	RBI	AVG
Home	9	3	3.55	0	106.1	LHB	412	104	4	35	.252
Road	4	4	3.66	0	83.2	RHB	309	81	8	38	.262
Day	4	3	3.70	0	58.1	Sc Pos	184	51	3	58	.277
Night	9	4	3.55	0	131.2	Clutch	62	13	1	4	.210

1991 Rankings (National League)

- ➤ 2nd in stolen bases allowed (33) and runners caught stealing (16)
- ➤ 4th in groundball/flyball ratio (2.1) and most strikeouts per 9 innings (7.1)
- ➤ 5th in run support per 9 innings (5.1)
- ➤ 6th in winning percentage (.650)
- ➤ Led the Mets in stolen bases allowed, runners caught stealing, winning percentage, groundball/flyball ratio, least pitches thrown per batter (3.59), most run support per 9 innings, most GDPs induced per 9 innings (.71) and ERA at home (3.56)

HITTING:

Todd Hundley first came up to the Mets in 1990 when catcher Mackey Sasser was injured. No one expected much offense, and Hundley batted .209. When Hundley returned in September 1991, the Mets hoped to see a good defensive catcher, and defense is all Hundley provided: he hit only .133 in 60 at-bats.

One positive sign is that Hundley showed more power in 1991. At AAA Tidewater, he produced 14 home runs while maintaining a respectable .273 average. He led his team in homers, RBI, and doubles. Those numbers offer reasonable hope that he can hit for power in the majors.

Hundley continues to look overmatched by major league pitching. He can be fooled by pitches out of the strike zone, and he can be punched out with a superior fastball. In order to become a productive major league hitter, he needs to improve further. He is still young enough to make big advances.

BASERUNNING:

Hundley fits the "new" mold of the major league catcher: smaller and quicker than the old stereotype of slow, lumbering backstops (note that his father, Randy, was a prototype of the new mold). Todd's total of 11 stolen bases in 1989-1990 will not likely be repeated in the majors, but his baserunning will undoubtedly surprise some lackadaisical fielders before the league gets used to him.

FIELDING:

Hundley's greatest strength is his ability to throw out runners. In the minor leagues, he has cut down almost half of those who tried to steal on him. At age 22, he still makes rookie mistakes, but he is progressing. In 1991 he showed quicker movement and better positioning around home plate. He is especially impressive pouncing on bunts.

OVERALL:

Hundley has a lot going for him: youth, bloodlines, a great arm, and developing power. He should improve steadily during the next few years, but is already capable of filling a major league role. Going into spring training 1992, Hundley was the frontrunner for the Mets number-one catching job.

TODD HUNDLEY

Position: C
Bats: B **Throws:** R
Ht: 5'11" **Wt:** 185

Opening Day Age: 22
Born: 5/27/69 in Martinsville, VA
ML Seasons: 2

Overall Statistics

	G	AB	R	H	D	T	HR	RBI	SB	BB	SO	AVG
1991	21	60	5	8	0	1	1	7	0	6	14	.133
Career	57	127	13	22	6	1	1	9	0	12	32	.173

Where He Hits the Ball

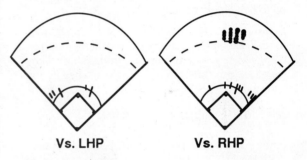

Vs. LHP   **Vs. RHP**

1991 Situational Stats

	AB	H	HR	RBI	AVG		AB	H	HR	RBI	AVG
Home	34	4	1	5	.118	LHP	19	2	0	3	.105
Road	26	4	0	2	.154	RHP	41	6	1	4	.146
Day	25	2	0	3	.080	Sc Pos	20	5	0	6	.250
Night	35	6	1	4	.171	Clutch	13	3	1	2	.231

1991 Rankings (National League)

➡ Did not rank near the top or bottom in any category

PITCHING:

Jeff Innis fits the mold of the classic submarine relief pitcher. With John Franco and Tim Burke ahead of him, Innis doesn't work in a closer role like Kent Tekulve or Dan Quisenberry, but he has the same type of stuff. He has been tougher on righty hitters, but is improving against lefties.

Innis has two main pitches, a sinking fastball and a slider. For a different look, he can also throw an occasional overhand curve that breaks straight down and a riding fastball that breaks in on right-handed hitters. Innis learned the knuckleball from Joe Niekro while in the minors, but he doesn't use it much. The key to success for Innis is keeping his sinker and slider down. Whenever he has trouble, anyone can see it coming: the pitches rise up to belt level and get belted.

A rubber-arm pitcher who can work every day, Innis is capable of pitching two or three innings, but the Mets prefer to keep his outings short. They never let him throw more than 40 pitches in any outing during 1991.

HOLDING RUNNERS, FIELDING, HITTING:

Innis has a reputation for not holding runners well, but in 1991 only six attempted steals were successful against him while five optimists were caught trying. He has worked at holding runners, with visible results. Innis is a competent fielder with a cool head. He almost never touches a bat.

OVERALL:

In another organization, Innis might have had a shot at a closer role some time during his career, but the Mets simply don't view him that way. At age 29 he is not likely to reach new heights, and it would take a rash of injuries for him to ascend to the top of the bullpen now. Nonetheless, he is a competent middle inning reliever, perfect for facing one or two tough right-handed hitters in a critical situation.

JEFF INNIS

Position: RP
Bats: R **Throws:** R
Ht: 6' 1" **Wt:** 180

Opening Day Age: 29
Born: 7/5/62 in Decatur, IL
ML Seasons: 5

Overall Statistics

	W	L	ERA	G	GS	Sv	IP	H	R	BB	SO	HR
1991	0	2	2.66	69	0	0	84.2	66	30	23	47	2
Career	2	8	2.72	145	1	1	195.1	171	70	47	117	13

How Often He Throws Strikes

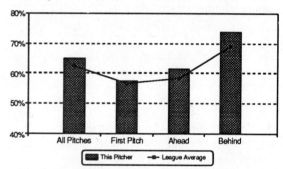

1991 Situational Stats

	W	L	ERA	Sv	IP		AB	H	HR	RBI	AVG
Home	0	2	2.59	0	48.2	LHB	124	31	1	15	.250
Road	0	0	2.75	0	36.0	RHB	178	35	1	21	.197
Day	0	0	1.61	0	28.0	Sc Pos	92	18	0	33	.196
Night	0	2	3.18	0	56.2	Clutch	80	19	0	9	.237

1991 Rankings (National League)

- 3rd least baserunners allowed per 9 innings in relief (9.5)
- 8th in highest percentage of inherited runners scored (35.1%), lowest batting average allowed in relief (.219) and least strikeouts per 9 innings in relief (5.0)
- 9th in games pitched (69)
- Led the Mets in games pitched, holds (4), lowest percentage of inherited runners scored, relief ERA (2.66), relief innings (84.2), lowest batting average allowed in relief and least baserunners allowed per 9 innings in relief

HITTING:

Fans in New York have the idea that Gregg Jefferies is a failed prospect, someone with promising minor league credentials who has never lived up to his potential. They imagine he has reached his prime without succeeding. The facts tell a different story. Jefferies is the same age as many "super-prospects" like Eric Karros and Tino Martinez. Jefferies' only problem is that he reached the major leagues while most players his age were toiling in the low minors.

Jefferies is simply a great natural hitter. Expectations are high because he has the sweet swing that scouts love from both sides of the plate. With his good eye, quick hands and ability to go with any pitch, Jefferies looks like a .300 hitter. His compact swing generates more power than the big cuts of many larger men. His only weakness is that he tries too hard, expanding the strike zone in pressure situations. He knows better, and it's frustrating.

BASERUNNING:

Jefferies' running game has developed faster than his hitting. His 26 stolen bases in 1991 came from careful reading of situations, not from raw speed. His 84% success rate in 1990-1991 shows how carefully he picks his spots. He is always aggressive and never misses an opportunity.

FIELDING:

During his short career, the Mets have moved Jefferies from shortstop to third base, then to second base, back to third, and back to second. He has held up admirably during this chaos, and he still has decent range and a good throwing arm. But he needs work on positioning at second base, and he is very weak on the double play.

OVERALL:

If Jefferies would just loosen up a little and learn how to laugh at himself, he might become a great hitter immediately. He takes every situation too seriously, on the field or off. You could blame this problem on media pressure, but it's a vicious circle that Jefferies himself will have to break.

GREGG JEFFERIES

Position: 2B/3B
Bats: B **Throws:** R
Ht: 5'10" **Wt:** 185

Opening Day Age: 24
Born: 8/1/67 in Burlingame, CA
ML Seasons: 5

Overall Statistics

	G	AB	R	H	D	T	HR	RBI	SB	BB	SO	AVG
1991	136	486	59	132	19	2	9	62	26	47	38	.272
Career	465	1713	246	472	96	9	42	205	63	140	134	.276

Where He Hits the Ball

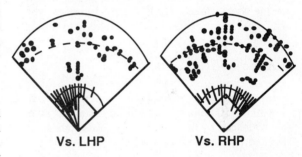

Vs. LHP   **Vs. RHP**

1991 Situational Stats

	AB	H	HR	RBI	AVG		AB	H	HR	RBI	AVG
Home	244	72	5	28	.295	LHP	174	51	1	18	.293
Road	242	60	4	34	.248	RHP	312	81	8	44	.260
Day	156	44	2	18	.282	Sc Pos	124	38	1	50	.306
Night	330	88	7	44	.267	Clutch	85	23	2	10	.271

1991 Rankings (National League)

- 2nd highest batting average on an 0-2 count (.333)
- 4th highest stolen base percentage (83.9%)
- 5th lowest percentage of swings that missed (10.4%)
- 7th highest percentage of swings put into play (52.8%)
- Led the Mets in batting average (.272), singles (102), stolen base percentage, batting average with the bases loaded (.400), batting average on an 0-2 count, batting average at home (.295) and highest percentage of swings put into play

FUTURE MVP?

HOWARD JOHNSON

Position: 3B/SS/RF
Bats: B **Throws:** R
Ht: 5'10" **Wt:** 195

Opening Day Age: 31
Born: 11/29/60 in Clearwater, FL
ML Seasons: 10

HITTING:

Howard Johnson had his best year ever in 1991. He led the National League in RBI and reached the "30/30" plateau for the third time, with 38 homers and 30 stolen bases. Five years ago, Johnson made a simple adjustment: he decided to look for the curveball and adjust to the fastball. He's been a terrific hitter ever since.

Johnson is a hard-swinging pull hitter from both sides of the plate. He strikes out frequently, but that's just a side-effect of his total offensive package. Johnson is dangerous in every situation. The only safe approach is to keep the ball away from him. In 1991 he made significant progress against left-handed pitchers, who had always given him trouble. Johnson is one of the best clutch hitters in the Mets' lineup. He is a crowd-pleaser who has won many games with dramatic, late-inning power hitting.

BASERUNNING:

Blessed with great speed, Johnson gets a good jump and runs aggressively. In his personal drive for the 30/30 club, he was a little too aggressive, as evidenced by the drop in his success rate from 81% in 1990 to 65% in 1991.

FIELDING:

Johnson was actually a member of the 30/30/30 club in 1991, because he made 31 errors to go with his other stats. The Mets started the 1991 season with Johnson installed "permanently" at shortstop, but the folly of that move became overwhelmingly obvious. As a third baseman, Johnson has poor range and a strong but erratic throwing arm. The Mets experimented with him in right field during September, and there's a strong chance he'll play there this year. His arm appears strong enough for the outfield; his range is a question mark.

OVERALL:

Johnson's progress as a hitter has coincided with his personal growth. Feeling more secure about his abilities during the past two years, he has become more of a team player. At the end of 1991, he was about the closest thing the Mets had to a team leader.

Overall Statistics

	G	AB	R	H	D	T	HR	RBI	SB	BB	SO	AVG
1991	156	564	108	146	34	4	38	117	30	78	120	.259
Career	1179	3959	624	1014	206	17	197	629	191	521	812	.256

Where He Hits the Ball

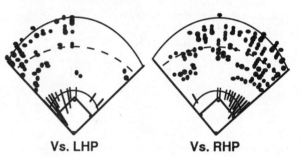

Vs. LHP **Vs. RHP**

1991 Situational Stats

	AB	H	HR	RBI	AVG		AB	H	HR	RBI	AVG
Home	280	75	21	64	.268	LHP	217	55	14	40	.253
Road	284	71	17	53	.250	RHP	347	91	24	77	.262
Day	185	45	13	42	.243	Sc Pos	152	42	6	74	.276
Night	379	101	25	75	.266	Clutch	97	24	6	19	.247

1991 Rankings (National League)

- 1st in home runs (38), RBIs (117), sacrifice flies (15), HR frequency (14.8 ABs per HR), lowest groundball/flyball ratio (.47), most runs scored per time reached base (48.0%), cleanup slugging percentage (.592) and lowest fielding percentage at third base (.926)
- 2nd in runs (108), slugging percentage (.535) and least GDPs per GDP situation (3.0%)
- 3rd in total bases (302)
- Led the Mets in home runs, at-bats (564), runs, hits (146), doubles (34), total bases, RBIs, sacrifice flies, caught stealing (16), intentional walks (12), times on base (225), strikeouts (120), pitches seen (2,488), games (156) and slugging percentage

DAVE MAGADAN

Position: 1B
Bats: L **Throws:** R
Ht: 6' 3" **Wt:** 200

Opening Day Age: 29
Born: 9/30/62 in Tampa, FL
ML Seasons: 6

HITTING:

Dave Magadan was one of the Mets' biggest disappointments in 1991, and they had many disappointments. In 1990, Magadan challenged for the NL batting crown. In 1991 he found himself challenged for playing time at first base by the weak-hitting Garry Templeton. What went wrong? Magadan had shoulder pain during the 1991 season, finally having surgery to remove torn cartilage from both shoulders on September 13. The physical problem was a big factor, but Magadan also had to deal with adjustments from the opposition pitchers, who showed him more respect after his .328 season in 1990.

Magadan is basically a singles hitter. He uses his patience and good knowledge of the strike zone, waiting for a pitch he can drive. In 1991 he was simply too patient. Magadan's 83 walks led the team, but the Mets would much prefer to see him swing more, get more hits, and (most importantly) drive in more runs.

BASERUNNING:

One reason the Mets don't want Magadan taking so many walks is that he is so slow on the bases. At age 29, he has only four career steals. The best you can say about his running game is that Magadan doesn't waste effort and doesn't make foolish mistakes.

FIELDING:

The perception in New York is that Magadan is not much of a fielder, but most of his critics are trying to compare him to predecessor Keith Hernandez, one of the all-time great gloves at first base. Magadan is actually a defensive asset. His range is only fair, but he has soft hands, positions himself well, and always knows what to do with the ball. In two years, he has made only seven errors.

OVERALL:

A career .305 hitter before 1991, Magadan is not going to stay down at the .258 level. The problem isn't batting average, however. As a slow runner with no home run power, Magadan must learn to swing more aggressively, especially with men on base.

Overall Statistics

	G	AB	R	H	D	T	HR	RBI	SB	BB	SO	AVG
1991	124	418	58	108	23	0	4	51	1	83	50	.258
Career	602	1767	242	519	101	10	18	226	4	291	204	.294

Where He Hits the Ball

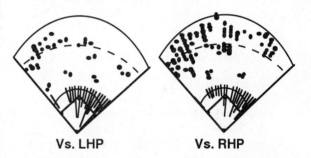

Vs. LHP   **Vs. RHP**

1991 Situational Stats

	AB	H	HR	RBI	AVG		AB	H	HR	RBI	AVG
Home	202	49	2	25	.243	LHP	151	37	0	12	.245
Road	216	59	2	26	.273	RHP	267	71	4	39	.266
Day	135	28	2	13	.207	Sc Pos	103	30	1	45	.291
Night	283	80	2	38	.283	Clutch	67	12	0	9	.179

1991 Rankings (National League)

➡ 1st in highest percentage of pitches taken (63.6%)

➡ 3rd in lowest percentage of swings that missed (9.0%)

➡ 4th in lowest slugging percentage (.342), least runs scored per time reached base (30.1%) and lowest slugging percentage vs. left-handed pitchers (.271)

➡ 5th in pitches seen per plate appearance (4.00)

➡ Led the Mets in walks (83), on-base average (.378), groundball/flyball ratio (1.3), most pitches seen per plate appearance, highest percentage of pitches taken and lowest percentage of swings that missed

HITTING:

After producing three consecutive seasons with 26 to 29 home runs and 95 to 99 RBI in 1986-1988, Kevin McReynolds gave people the idea that he would go on posting those numbers forever. Unfortunately, hitters decline with age, and McReynolds is a little past his peak at age 32. It is not surprising, and shouldn't be disappointing, that he is now performing somewhat below what his level was at age 28.

McReynolds is still one of the Mets' best hitters, always dangerous and especially tough in clutch situations. He got his fifth career grand slam in 1991, and hit .308 with men in scoring position. McReynolds modestly explains that he doesn't regard himself as a great clutch hitter; he simply expects to see good pitches in the strike zone when there are men on base. McReynolds is a pull hitter. He will jump on the first pitch if he likes what he sees.

BASERUNNING:

McReynolds has slowed down considerably since he stole 21 bases in 21 attempts in 1988. After achieving only six steals and getting caught six times in 1991, he is likely to be running less in the future. Although slower, McReynolds is still smart on the bases and won't miss opportunities.

FIELDING:

McReynolds' defensive abilities are almost too good for left field. He is a former center fielder, and the Mets considered using him, instead of Vince Coleman, to play center in 1991. In the end, they decided not to move McReynolds because he is doing so well where he is. He has excellent range and one of the best throwing arms in the league.

OVERALL:

Although a little past his prime, McReynolds is still one of the most valuable outfielders in the National League. He is a dangerous power hitter and a big defensive asset. With just a little luck, he could produce another 20-homer, 90 RBI season in 1992.

KEVIN McREYNOLDS

Position: LF/CF
Bats: R **Throws:** R
Ht: 6' 1" **Wt:** 215

Opening Day Age: 32
Born: 10/16/59 in Little Rock, AR
ML Seasons: 9

Overall Statistics

	G	AB	R	H	D	T	HR	RBI	SB	BB	SO	AVG
1991	143	522	65	135	32	1	16	74	6	49	46	.259
Career	1232	4519	615	1215	226	29	183	695	82	398	569	.269

Where He Hits the Ball

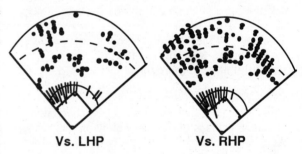

Vs. LHP   **Vs. RHP**

1991 Situational Stats

	AB	H	HR	RBI	AVG		AB	H	HR	RBI	AVG
Home	236	56	7	33	.237	LHP	189	49	6	21	.259
Road	286	79	9	41	.276	RHP	333	86	10	53	.258
Day	159	37	3	15	.233	Sc Pos	143	44	7	62	.308
Night	363	98	13	59	.270	Clutch	85	22	6	22	.259

1991 Rankings (National League)

➡ 2nd lowest groundball/flyball ratio (.68)

➡ 5th lowest batting average at home (.237)

➡ 8th highest percentage of swings put into play (52.7%)

➡ Led the Mets in batting average with runners in scoring position (.308), batting average on a 3-1 count (.539) and batting average on the road (.276)

➡ Led NL left fielders in fielding percentage (.992), doubles (32), lowest percentage of swings that missed (13.6%) and highest percentage of swings put into play

HITTING:

Mackey Sasser has always been a good hitter. His .272 average in 1991 was his lowest since joining the Mets, but he didn't have an off year. Sasser was a terror in key situations (.367 with men in scoring position). Despite totalling only 228 at-bats, he produced as many RBI as most of the catchers in the National League.

Mackey is a great contact hitter and a free swinger -- he rarely walks or strikes out. His ability to put the ball in play makes him a reliable pinch hitter, a role for which the Mets used him frequently in 1991. Sasser can hit to all fields. He isn't a classic home run hitter, but he has good line drive power. If Sasser wasn't such a slow runner, he would get a lot more extra-base hits.

BASERUNNING:

Sasser is so slow that he can make a third base coach look foolish for sending him home when an average runner would have scored easily. Sasser has yet to steal successfully in five major league seasons. He was caught in both his 1991 attempts; in 1990 he didn't try even once.

FIELDING:

Sasser, an adequate catcher at best, has yet to cure his nervous habit of pumping the ball when throwing back to the pitcher, a problem that creates steal opportunities. The Mets tried the former outfielder in right field late in 1991, and fans were amazed when, in his first appearance, he made a catch that ended up as the Mets "Play of the Year." Sasser has sure hands and the arm for right field, but his range is well below average. The Mets also tried Sasser at first base.

OVERALL:

At the end of 1991, it wasn't clear what position Sasser would play in 1992, or whether he even figured into the Mets' plans. One fact is certain: there will always be a major league job for a catcher who can hit .300 against righty pitchers and who can be relied upon to hit the ball hard in clutch situations.

MACKEY SASSER

Position: C/RF
Bats: L **Throws:** R
Ht: 6' 1" **Wt:** 210

Opening Day Age: 29
Born: 8/3/62 in Fort Gaines, GA
ML Seasons: 5

Overall Statistics

	G	AB	R	H	D	T	HR	RBI	SB	BB	SO	AVG
1991	96	228	18	62	14	2	5	35	0	9	19	.272
Career	342	830	77	238	52	5	13	117	0	37	64	.287

Where He Hits the Ball

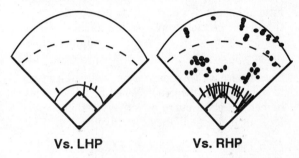

Vs. LHP   Vs. RHP

1991 Situational Stats

	AB	H	HR	RBI	AVG		AB	H	HR	RBI	AVG
Home	109	35	3	21	.321	LHP	29	5	0	2	.172
Road	119	27	2	14	.227	RHP	199	57	5	33	.286
Day	94	29	4	21	.309	Sc Pos	60	22	2	31	.367
Night	134	33	1	14	.246	Clutch	53	14	2	10	.264

1991 Rankings (National League)

→ Did not rank near the top or bottom in any category

PITCHING:

Rookie Pete Schourek joined the Mets' starting rotation in late August after Sid Fernandez and Dwight Gooden went out for the season. Schourek had been a middle reliever through most of 1991, after making his first major league appearance on April 9. He was only mediocre as a reliever, posting a 4.62 ERA and giving up more than a hit per inning in that role. Schourek did much better as a starter, the role he had in the minor leagues. He finished the season on a high note with a 2-0 record and a 2.79 ERA in his last three starts.

Schourek has a good fastball, but he isn't overpowering (88 MPH tops). He needs to move the fastball around and run it in against right-handed hitters. Schourek's curveball is especially effective when he can drop it on the outside corner against righties. He has a good straight change-up, and he can take velocity off the curve as well.

Because he isn't overpowering, Schourek needs to stay ahead in the count. When he falls behind, he can't use the curve effectively. When hitters look for the fastball, they can drive it.

HOLDING RUNNERS, FIELDING, HITTING:

Base stealers were 12 for 12 against Schourek in 1991. He gets respect for being a lefty, but if he doesn't improve, word is going to spread and even more people will run on him. Schourek is still learning the fine points of fielding around the mound, but as a former first baseman he handles himself well. He hit .555 in high school and is not an automatic out.

OVERALL:

For the first time in many years, the Mets may be looking for help in their starting pitcher department in 1992. Schourek is a viable candidate for a spot in the rotation. He was 16-5 as a minor league starter in 1990 and helped himself immensely with his strong finish in 1991.

PETE SCHOUREK

Position: RP/SP
Bats: L **Throws:** L
Ht: 6' 5" **Wt:** 195

Opening Day Age: 22
Born: 5/10/69 in Austin, TX
ML Seasons: 1

Overall Statistics

	W	L	ERA	G	GS	Sv	IP	H	R	BB	SO	HR
1991	5	4	4.27	35	8	2	86.1	82	49	43	67	7
Career	5	4	4.27	35	8	2	86.1	82	49	43	67	7

How Often He Throws Strikes

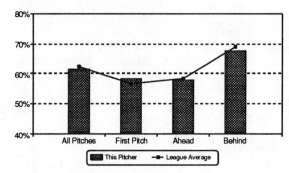

1991 Situational Stats

	W	L	ERA	Sv	IP		AB	H	HR	RBI	AVG
Home	4	1	3.31	0	49.0	LHB	110	29	2	18	.264
Road	1	3	5.54	2	37.1	RHB	221	53	5	34	.240
Day	3	1	5.23	0	31.0	Sc Pos	104	30	2	43	.288
Night	2	3	3.74	2	55.1	Clutch	42	6	1	5	.143

1991 Rankings (National League)

→ 1st in least GDPs induced per GDP situation (1.4%)

PITCHING:

A Rule Five draftee, Doug Simons had to spend the entire 1991 season on the Mets major league roster. If his minor league career had been uninterrupted, he probably would have been a starter at the Triple-A level. Working out of the Mets bullpen, he saw action mostly as a lefty-vs.-lefty situational reliever, a job he performed well. Overall, Simons pitched much better than his 5.19 ERA would indicate.

Simons has the full repertoire of a starting pitcher: a sinking fastball, a cut fastball, a straight change, a slurve, and a forkball. The slurve is a new pitch developed during 1991 with help from coach Mel Stottlemyre, adding velocity while taking away movement from his basic curveball. He can still throw a big overhand curve, but didn't use it as a short reliever during 1991. Working out of the pen, he stayed with the fastball and the slurve.

Simons was a workhorse in 1989 and 1990, pitching almost 200 innings each year. He said he found it difficult to stay sharp without getting as much use during 1991. The Mets finally gave Simons a starting assignment on September 30, but he gave up six earned runs in two innings, proving that he had indeed become stale.

HOLDING RUNNERS, FIELDING, HITTING:

Taking full advantage of the good view from the left side of the rubber, Simons holds baserunners well. His fielding skills are still maturing, but he is adequate. Simons won a collegiate batting title and will be a good-hitting major league pitcher, although he didn't bat much during 1991.

OVERALL:

Simons played Venezuelan winter ball in 1991-1992 under the watchful eye of Mets management, hoping to begin spring training with a credible shot at the starting rotation. At this stage of his career, he says he would prefer to work as a minor league starter rather than a major league reliever. Now that the Rule Five period is over, the Mets will probably take the same view if they have a choice.

DOUG SIMONS

Position: RP
Bats: L **Throws:** L
Ht: 6' 0" **Wt:** 170

Opening Day Age: 25
Born: 9/15/66 in Bakersfield, CA
ML Seasons: 1

Overall Statistics

	W	L	ERA	G	GS	Sv	IP	H	R	BB	SO	HR
1991	2	3	5.19	42	1	1	60.2	55	40	19	38	5
Career	2	3	5.19	42	1	1	60.2	55	40	19	38	5

How Often He Throws Strikes

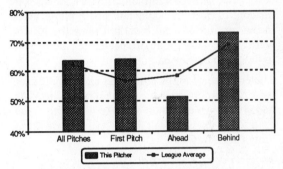

1991 Situational Stats

	W	L	ERA	Sv	IP		AB	H	HR	RBI	AVG
Home	1	1	4.91	0	36.2	LHB	87	17	0	9	.195
Road	1	2	5.63	1	24.0	RHB	137	38	5	25	.277
Day	1	0	4.39	1	26.2	Sc Pos	52	16	3	28	.308
Night	1	3	5.82	0	34.0	Clutch	59	13	1	6	.220

1991 Rankings (National League)

- → 3rd highest relief ERA (4.45)
- → 8th worst first batter efficiency (.306)

PITCHING:

After four years at the top of the pitching profession, Frank Viola fell on hard times in 1991. Before the season started, there was a scare about elbow chips in his left arm. Further diagnosis determined that Viola could avoid surgery, and he started the season well. At the All-Star break, Viola was 10-5 with a 2.80 ERA. But then he went to pieces: after the break he was 3-10, 5.53.

Viola's two great strengths have always been his sizzling fastball and his excellent control. The good fastball makes his curve and his outstanding change-up effective weapons because hitters can't be looking for them. During 1991, Viola lost just a little velocity and movement off the fastball, and it became a hittable pitch. He never lost his control (just 2.1 walks per nine innings, even in the horrible second half) but once the hitters were able to look for an offspeed pitch and adjust to the fastball, they had their fun.

The collapse of Viola coincided closely with the New York's demise in the pennant race. The Mets had always depended on Viola to win a big game or to stop a losing streak, but he failed to do those things after July.

HOLDING RUNNERS, FIELDING, HITTING:

One positive aspect of Viola's 1991 campaign is that he practically shut down the opposition running game, allowing only six steals and just a 27% success rate. Viola is a good fielder, but his years in the American League have left him a weak hitter.

OVERALL:

Before the 1991 season started, Viola was demanding the same money and length of contract as Dwight Gooden had just been given, and the New York fans and media were screaming that the Mets were foolish not to be granting his requests. Given Viola's weak 1991 campaign, that was probably a wise move; his contract demands this winter will probably determine whether he'll return to the Mets.

FRANK VIOLA

Position: SP
Bats: L **Throws:** L
Ht: 6' 4" **Wt:** 210

Opening Day Age: 31
Born: 4/19/60 in Hempstead, NY
ML Seasons: 10

Overall Statistics

	W	L	ERA	G	GS	Sv	IP	H	R	BB	SO	HR
1991	13	15	3.97	35	35	0	231.1	259	112	54	132	25
Career	150	125	3.72	342	341	0	2339.0	2336	1072	662	1601	258

How Often He Throws Strikes

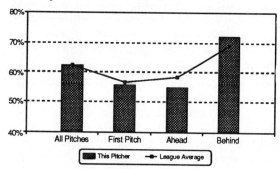

1991 Situational Stats

	W	L	ERA	Sv	IP		AB	H	HR	RBI	AVG
Home	8	8	4.26	0	122.2	LHB	193	45	5	22	.233
Road	5	7	3.64	0	108.2	RHB	712	214	20	77	.301
Day	6	5	3.09	0	96.0	Sc Pos	203	55	4	69	.271
Night	7	10	4.59	0	135.1	Clutch	92	29	3	9	.315

1991 Rankings (National League)

→ 1st in hits allowed (259), highest batting average allowed (.286), lowest stolen base percentage allowed (27.3%) and highest batting average allowed vs right-handed batters (.301)

→ 2nd in losses (15), home runs allowed (25), runners caught stealing (16) and highest slugging percentage allowed (.423)

→ 3rd in highest on-base average allowed (.325) and highest ERA at home (4.26)

→ Led the Mets in losses, games started (35), hits allowed, batters faced (980), home runs allowed, runners caught stealing, GDPs induced (16), lowest stolen base percentage allowed and sacrifice bunts as a hitter (10)

PITCHING:

Wally Whitehurst always wanted to be a Met starter. He got his chance when Sid Fernandez broke an arm during spring training in 1991. After Fernandez returned, Whitehurst stayed in the starting rotation as the Mets chose to remove Ron Darling. Unfortunately, Whitehurst ran out of gas almost immediately after Darling was traded away. After the All-Star break, he was 2-8 with a 5.56 ERA. He didn't get a start after September 6, as the Mets chose to look at younger talent.

Whitehurst is basically a curveball pitcher. He succeeds by throwing the curve for strikes and getting ahead in the count. He uses his fastball and slider to keep hitters off-balance so that they can't get their timing adjusted to the curve. Whitehurst also has a straight change-up, but he didn't have much success with it in 1991.

A very direct pitcher, Whitehurst likes to throw strikes and work efficiently. He doesn't try to strike people out, and he doesn't try to be too cute with trick pitches in precise locations. He simply wants the hitters to put the ball in play where the defense can handle it. In 1991, too many balls were hit where the fielders couldn't help.

HOLDING RUNNERS, FIELDING, HITTING:

Whitehurst is good at holding runners. Although there were plenty of men on base against him in 1991, he gave up only nine steals and held the opposition to a 53% stolen base success rate. Whitehurst is an adequate fielder and a good enough hitter that he is not an automatic out.

OVERALL:

The Mets had numerous pitching problems during 1991; Whitehurst's failure was only one of them. But he had a clear opportunity to emerge and solidify his place in the starting rotation, and he let his big chance get away. The best things going for Whitehurst in 1992 are a good track record as a middle reliever and the Mets' need for pitching help of all kinds.

WALLY WHITEHURST

Position: SP/RP
Bats: R **Throws:** R
Ht: 6' 3" **Wt:** 185

Opening Day Age: 28
Born: 4/11/64 in Shreveport, LA
ML Seasons: 3

Overall Statistics

	W	L	ERA	G	GS	Sv	IP	H	R	BB	SO	HR
1991	7	12	4.18	36	20	1	133.1	142	67	25	87	12
Career	8	13	3.93	83	21	3	213.0	222	101	39	142	19

How Often He Throws Strikes

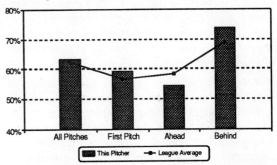

1991 Situational Stats

	W	L	ERA	Sv	IP		AB	H	HR	RBI	AVG
Home	3	7	4.43	0	61.0	LHB	270	80	7	30	.296
Road	4	5	3.98	1	72.1	RHB	248	62	5	30	.250
Day	1	5	5.23	1	43.0	Sc Pos	113	30	2	41	.265
Night	6	7	3.69	0	90.1	Clutch	43	14	1	4	.326

1991 Rankings (National League)

→ 3rd in balks (4)

→ 5th lowest winning percentage (.368)

→ 8th highest batting average allowed vs. left-handed batters (.296)

→ Let the Mets in balks and most GDPs induced per GDP situation (14.0%)

PITCHING:

After a dominating season at AA Jackson in 1990 (15-3 with a 1.65 ERA), Anthony Young got off to a slow start in 1991. First he tried to impress management by blowing away hitters during spring training; then, when he didn't make the big league roster on Opening Day, he continued his over-aggressive approach at AAA Tidewater with poor results. In late May, his coaches finally convinced him to go back to the style that made him successful in 1990. From that point, Young had a terrific season.

Like all sinker/slider pitchers, Young is most successful when he keeps the ball down in the strike zone. Young has a large repertoire, a source of temptation to try to do too much. He has a good slider, a curve, and a straight change. He can make the fastball stay up in the strike zone when he wants, and he can use a slow curve as a second change-of-pace pitch.

The Mets have been cautious about Young's stamina. In his eight major league starts, he never worked beyond the seventh inning, and never threw more than 93 pitches. Young has not been a long-distance pitcher in the minor leagues, either, producing only three complete games per year in 1990 and 1991.

HOLDING RUNNERS, FIELDING, HITTING:

Young pays close attention to baserunners, and the opposition is still studying his pickoff move. He yielded only three steals in ten games with the Mets in 1991, but he can expect to be tested more strenuously in 1992. In the field and at bat, Young is a true asset. In 1990 he hit .303 and, in the field, he tied for the most assists and double plays by a Texas League pitcher.

OVERALL:

Considering his solid background and strong performance as a late season call-up, Young is among the frontrunners for a starter's job in 1992. He has really learned how to pitch within himself, and has a chance to have a fine season in the Mets' rotation.

ANTHONY YOUNG

Position: SP
Bats: R **Throws:** R
Ht: 6' 2" **Wt:** 200

Opening Day Age: 26
Born: 1/19/66 in Houston, TX
ML Seasons: 1

Overall Statistics

	W	L	ERA	G	GS	Sv	IP	H	R	BB	SO	HR
1991	2	5	3.10	10	8	0	49.1	48	20	12	20	4
Career	2	5	3.10	10	8	0	49.1	48	20	12	20	4

How Often He Throws Strikes

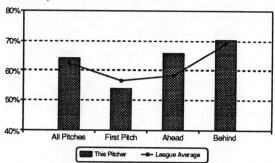

1991 Situational Stats

	W	L	ERA	Sv	IP		AB	H	HR	RBI	AVG
Home	1	3	3.77	0	28.2	LHB	112	33	3	11	.295
Road	1	2	2.18	0	20.2	RHB	75	15	1	8	.200
Day	1	3	2.79	0	29.0	Sc Pos	37	9	1	13	.243
Night	1	2	3.54	0	20.1	Clutch	5	3	1	1	.600

1991 Rankings (National League)

→ Did not rank near the top or bottom in any category

MARK CARREON

Position: LF/CF/RF
Bats: R **Throws:** L
Ht: 6' 0" **Wt:** 195

Opening Day Age: 28
Born: 7/9/63 in Chicago, IL
ML Seasons: 5

Overall Statistics

	G	AB	R	H	D	T	HR	RBI	SB	BB	SO	AVG
1991	106	254	18	66	6	0	4	21	2	12	26	.260
Career	272	596	73	162	26	0	21	65	5	42	74	.272

HITTING, FIELDING, BASERUNNING:

Mark Carreon is a good power hitter, noted for his performance in clutch situations. He first attracted attention in the major leagues by hitting four pinch hit home runs in 1989, and now holds the Mets' franchise record with eight pinch hit homers in his short career after belting three more in 1991. Carreon is a free swinger but is still a good contact hitter. By nature he is a pull hitter, but he knows how to use the opposite field when the situation requires. He hit the ball on the ground much more last year, and wound up grounding into a whopping 14 DPs in only 254 at-bats.

In the minor leagues, Carreon stole over 30 bases three times, but he hasn't been much of a threat to run in the majors. In 1991 he stole two bases in three attempts. Fielding is the aspect of his game that has held Carreon back from becoming an everyday player. He has trouble judging fly balls and simply isn't graceful. His arm is well below average.

OVERALL:

Carreon has twice won the job as the Mets' utility outfielder and top right-handed pinch hitter, but he hasn't been happy as a part-time player and has let his dissatisfaction be known. The Mets might accommodate his wishes and let him move on to greener pastures in 1992.

KEITH MILLER

Position: 2B/RF
Bats: R **Throws:** R
Ht: 5'11" **Wt:** 185

Opening Day Age: 28
Born: 6/12/63 in Midland, MI
ML Seasons: 5

Overall Statistics

	G	AB	R	H	D	T	HR	RBI	SB	BB	SO	AVG
1991	98	275	41	77	22	1	4	23	14	23	44	.280
Career	308	772	121	204	40	4	7	48	44	59	133	.264

HITTING, FIELDING, BASERUNNING:

Keith Miller is a thinking man's hitter. He does all the little things: goes with the pitch, bunts to get on base, hit-and-runs, hits behind the runner, whatever the manager wants. Miller had his best year ever in 1991, finishing with a .280 average for the first time since he was at Triple-A in 1988. What was most surprising was the power he displayed: 27 extra-base hits in only 275 at-bats, including 22 doubles. Miller, who had hit only three homers in four seasons, belted four in 1991, and his .411 slugging average was higher than that of Gregg Jefferies or Hubie Brooks.

Miller is a very good runner who could steal 30 to 40 bases per season if he played full time. Very versatile, he played all three outfield positions, second base, third base, and shortstop during 1991. His original position is second base, and he can play it very well. Miller has good range at all positions, and his arm is adequate for third base or right field.

OVERALL:

Miller was once slated to be the Mets' second baseman with Gregg Jefferies playing third and Kevin Elster at short. But when Howard Johnson learned how to hit a curveball, it changed that whole plan. If Johnson moves to outfield or first base, Miller could again become a viable regular.

CHARLIE O'BRIEN

Position: C
Bats: R **Throws:** R
Ht: 6' 2" **Wt:** 190

Opening Day Age: 30
Born: 5/1/61 in Tulsa, OK
ML Seasons: 6

Overall Statistics

	G	AB	R	H	D	T	HR	RBI	SB	BB	SO	AVG
1991	69	168	16	31	6	0	2	14	0	17	25	.185
Career	271	733	72	149	36	3	10	79	0	71	93	.203

HITTING, FIELDING, BASERUNNING:

How weak is Charlie O'Brien's hitting? It's so weak that when he hit safely in 13 of 22 games (a .267 streak), the Mets PR department made it a highlight in their media notes! Maybe the Mets were right; after 1990 and '91 seasons in which he batted .178 and then .185, "Charlie O'Brien hitting highlights" are judged by a different standard.

O'Brien does have a little power; he once hit 15 home runs in Double-A. Pitchers can't throw him fat pitches, but with a little effort they can get him out easily. In the rare cases when he gets on base, O'Brien is not a good runner.

The Mets' pitchers love throwing to O'Brien. He is a great game-caller who adapted to the National League without difficulty in the midst of the 1990 pennant race. He can do it all: handle pitchers, throw out runners, and cover the ground around home plate.

OVERALL:

O'Brien is probably better suited to the American League, where the presence of the DH in the lineup means that each team can afford to carry one weak hitter. With the Mets in 1991, there was serious talk that he should bat ninth. Nonetheless, his good defense may be enough to keep him in the majors for another year.

GARRY TEMPLETON

Position: SS/1B/3B
Bats: B **Throws:** R
Ht: 6' 0" **Wt:** 205

Opening Day Age: 36
Born: 3/24/56 in Lockey, TX
ML Seasons: 16

Overall Statistics

	G	AB	R	H	D	T	HR	RBI	SB	BB	SO	AVG
1991	112	276	25	61	10	2	3	26	3	10	38	.221
Career	2079	7721	893	2096	329	106	70	728	242	375	1092	.271

HITTING, FIELDING, BASERUNNING:

After acquiring him from San Diego early last season, the Mets discovered that Garry Templeton can still hit left-handed pitching (.344). In their excitement, they installed Templeton as a platoon first baseman late in the season, a decision that told more about the Mets than it did about Garry. A former star, Templeton is an aging hitter, crafty from experience but weakened by a loss of bat and foot speed. Templeton batted only .221, lowest of his 16-year career, in 1991. Combining the low average with his usual impatience (seven unintentional walks in 293 plate appearances), he posted a laughable on-base percentage of .246.

Acquired for defensive insurance purposes, Templeton compensates for his lack of range by positioning himself well at shortstop. He knows the league's hitters well, and he knows all the moves required of a middle infielder. Unfortunately, he is slowed down by chronic knee problems and simply can't move like he used to.

OVERALL:

At age 36, free agent Templeton may have trouble keeping a major league job in 1992. The former star, once traded even-up for Ozzie Smith, is near the end of his career. He has some value as a defensive backup and occasional pinch hitter, but his days as a regular are certainly behind him now.

NEW YORK METS MINOR LEAGUE PROSPECTS

ORGANIZATION OVERVIEW:

An organization that once produced a steady stream of great talent -- notably Dwight Gooden and Darryl Strawberry -- the Mets are now rebuilding their farm system. Drafting close to the end of every round each year has undoubtedly cost them some blue-chip prospects, and the Mets have also traded away some good young talent (such as Kevin Tapani and Rick Aguilera). The Met system was rated fifth-best in last year's Sporting News rankings, but that just seems like more New York hype. The better Met prospects are either a few years away or have holes in their game. And of course when they reach the Big Apple they'll be expected to be superstars from Day One.

TERRY BROSS

Position: P
Bats: R **Throws:** R
Ht: 6' 9" **Wt:** 230
Opening Day Age: 26
Born: 3/30/66 in El Paso, TX

Recent Statistics

	W	L	ERA	G	GS	Sv	IP	H	R	BB	SO	HR
91 AAA Tidewater	2	0	4.36	27	0	2	33.0	31	21	32	23	0
91 AA Williamsprt	2	0	2.49	20	0	5	25.1	13	12	11	28	1
91 NL New York	0	0	1.80	8	0	0	10.0	7	2	3	5	1

At 6-9 and 230 pounds, Bross looks like a power forward, and he's a fearsome sight coming in from the bullpen. Not surprisingly, he throws very hard, but his control has always been a big problem, and he doesn't have much besides the fastball. He looked good in a September trial, but the Mets still seem unsure about him. If Bross doesn't make their 40-man roster, anyone will be able to pick him up. He should be in somebody's bullpen this year.

JEROMY BURNITZ

Position: OF
Bats: L **Throws:** R
Ht: 6' 0" **Wt:** 190
Opening Day Age: 22
Born: 4/14/69 in Westminster, CA

Recent Statistics

	G	AB	R	H	D	THR	RBI	SB	BB	SO	AVG
90 A Pittsfield	51	173	37	52	6	5	6	22	12	45	39	.301
90 A St. Lucie	11	32	6	5	1	0	0	3	1	7	12	.156
91 AA Williamsprt	135	457	80	103	16	10	31	85	31	104	127	.225
91 MLE	135	445	67	91	14	7	25	71	22	74	137	.204

The Mets first pick in 1990, Burnitz led the minor leagues in homers last year while putting together a 30-30 season. He has speed, power, a good arm . . . and a lot to learn, judging from his .225 average in AA ball. Burnitz also drew 100 walks last year, meaning he could survive in the majors as a low-average power hitter. The Mets are expecting more; hopefully they're not expecting more than Burnitz can deliver.

JOSE MARTINEZ

Position: P
Bats: R **Throws:** R
Ht: 6' 2" **Wt:** 155
Opening Day Age: 21
Born: 4/1/71 in Guayubin, DR

Recent Statistics

	W	L	ERA	G	GS	Sv	IP	H	R	BB	SO	HR
90 R Mets	8	3	1.57	13	13	0	92.0	68	27	9	90	1
91 A Columbia	20	4	1.49	26	26	0	193.1	162	51	30	158	3

If you like to play a long shot, consider Martinez, the first minor leaguer to win 20 games since Gene Nelson in 1980. The 20-year-old Dominican had awesome stats at Class A Columbia, but his fastball is only low 80s; his best pitch is a change-up. The Mets will learn more about him as he moves up. For a pitching prospect, though, he sure has the right last name.

RICARDO OTERO

Position: OF
Bats: B **Throws:** L
Ht: 5' 7" **Wt:** 140
Opening Day Age: 19
Born: 4/15/72 in Vaga Baha, PR

Recent Statistics

	G	AB	R	H	D	THR	RBI	SB	BB	SO	AVG
91 R Kingsport	66	235	47	81	16	3	7	52	12	35	32	.345
91 A Pittsfield	6	24	4	7	0	0	0	2	4	2	1	.292

Another long shot, the Puerto Rican Otero was a 45th-round draft choice in 1990. But at age 19 he terrorized the Appalachian League, showing amazing power for such a small man. His lesser stats were impressive: more walks than strikeouts (very unusual for a young player, but especially a young Latin), and 12 steals in 16 attempts. Keep a close eye on this guy.

JULIO VALERA

Position: P
Bats: R **Throws:** R
Ht: 6' 2" **Wt:** 215
Opening Day Age: 23
Born: 10/13/68 in San Sebastian, PR

Recent Statistics

	W	L	ERA	G	GS	Sv	IP	H	R	BB	SO	HR
91 AAA Tidewater	10	10	3.83	26	26	0	176.1	152	79	70	117	12
91 NL New York	0	0	0.00	2	0	0	2.0	1	0	4	3	0

To many Met fans, Julio Valera will always be a symbol of the screwball Bud Harrelson era; Buddy chose to start Valera, fresh from the minors, in a must-win game against the Pirates late in 1990. A year ago Valera was considered one of the Mets' best pitching prospects, and he went on to have a big season -- big as in 252 pounds, unfortunately. Excess weight cost Valera a chance to pitch with the Mets last year, and he went on to have a so-so season at Tidewater. No, that wasn't Julio you saw floating over Fifth Avenue at the Macy's parade . . . but it might have been his pitching chances, unless he gets himself in shape. He still has the arm.

PITCHING:

Joe Boever inherited the right-handed set-up man's job last August 2nd when the Phillies traded Roger McDowell to the Dodgers. Boever was not very impressive in that role, suffering from control problems, but his durability in middle relief made him a very useful pitcher.

Boever is a two-pitch hurler, relying on a straight mid-80s fastball which he can throw to any part of the plate, and a palm ball. The palm ball is a combination change-up and curve: it comes in slower than his arm speed would suggest and then drops down sharply, often out of the strike zone. Hitters, particularly lefties, will take the pitch for a ball when they can pick up its rotation, and that was Boever's problem last year. He's in trouble when he has to rely on his fastball.

Phils officials think that Boever, a fly ball pitcher, will benefit from improvement by Wes Chamberlain and the return of ballhawk Lenny Dykstra. Boever also notes that he set a personal high in strikeouts per inning last year, evidence that his palm ball is still fooling hitters. Another key to his effectiveness is his use pattern. Boever is best when working on one or no days rest, and whenever possible, manager Jim Fregosi took advantage of this to good effect.

HOLDING RUNNERS, FIELDING, HITTING:

Boever's move is among the team's worst. He tends to tunnel in on the hitter, and his best pitch is a slow, downward-moving pitch; he prevents his catchers from catching base stealers. He fields his position well and made contact all three times that he batted, the only Phils pitcher to do so in 1990 and '91.

OVERALL:

Boever's rubber arm is a valued commodity, and improved outfield defense should help him this year. He'll need better control, but he can be a very tough pitcher in a middle relief role.

JOE BOEVER

Position: RP
Bats: R **Throws:** R
Ht: 6' 1" **Wt:** 212

Opening Day Age: 31
Born: 10/4/60 in St. Louis, MO
ML Seasons: 7

Overall Statistics

	W	L	ERA	G	GS	Sv	IP	H	R	BB	SO	HR
1991	3	5	3.84	68	0	0	98.1	90	45	54	89	10
Career	11	25	3.70	255	0	36	345.2	322	149	167	285	32

How Often He Throws Strikes

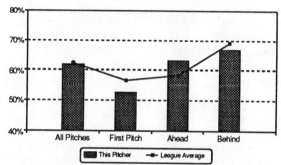

1991 Situational Stats

	W	L	ERA	Sv	IP		AB	H	HR	RBI	AVG
Home	2	1	3.17	0	54.0	LHB	171	44	4	25	.257
Road	1	4	4.67	0	44.1	RHB	197	46	6	26	.234
Day	0	2	7.08	0	20.1	Sc Pos	98	25	2	38	.255
Night	3	3	3.00	0	78.0	Clutch	158	36	4	11	.228

1991 Rankings (National League)

- ➡ 3rd highest percentage of inherited runners scored (42.9%)
- ➡ 5th in relief innings (98.1)
- ➡ 6th least GDPs induced per GDP situation (3.0%)
- ➡ 8th most baserunners allowed per 9 innings in relief (13.2)
- ➡ 9th most strikeouts per 9 innings in relief (8.1)
- ➡ Led the Phillies in relief innings

HITTING:

Wes Chamberlain was promoted to Philadelphia in midseason last year when Lenny Dysktra drove into a tree. Chamberlain proceeded to etch himself into the Phils scorecard for the next several seasons. He hit for power, finishing third in home runs to Dale Murphy and John Kruk, who each batted nearly 200 times more, and hit .240 overall despite batting only .168 for the last month of the season.

His late-season slump came as Chamberlain continued to tinker with his swing, earning him the nickname "Man of 1,000 Stances." Chamberlain takes one to three home run hacks per game reminiscent of the days of Dave Kingman. But he will mix in flat, line drive swings which take advantage of the alleys and his foot speed.

Pitchers no longer challenge Chamberlain, but try to move the ball in and out and not let him get set for any pitch. This approach led him to slump at the end of '91, but both he and the Phillies expect Chamberlain to adjust and continue to emerge as a solid offensive contributor.

BASERUNNING:

Chamberlain is swift and aggressive, but spent most of last year studying opposing catchers and outfielders. Expect him to steal 20 bases in 1992, with few caught-stealings, and add several doubles per year because of his fleet feet.

FIELDING:

Chamberlain is slow reading the ball off the bat, but moves and throws well and will spend time in winter ball working on getting a better jump. Scouts feel he'll improve in the field.

OVERALL:

The Phillies acquired Chamberlain because Pirate GM Larry Doughty didn't understand the waiver rule. Chamberlain, who murdered the Bucs last year, will make Doughty wish he spent more time on the rulebook -- 18 games a year for the next decade or so. Chamberlain is one of the proudest acquisitions of the Lee Thomas era in Philadelphia, and should occupy the third to fifth spots in the batting order for many years.

WES CHAMBERLAIN

Position: LF
Bats: R **Throws:** R
Ht: 6' 2" **Wt:** 215

Opening Day Age: 26
Born: 4/13/66 in Chicago, IL
ML Seasons: 2

Overall Statistics

	G	AB	R	H	D	T	HR	RBI	SB	BB	SO	AVG
1991	101	383	51	92	16	3	13	50	9	31	73	.240
Career	119	429	60	105	19	3	15	54	13	32	82	.245

Where He Hits the Ball

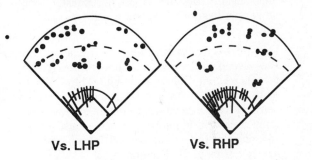

Vs. LHP   Vs. RHP

1991 Situational Stats

	AB	H	HR	RBI	AVG		AB	H	HR	RBI	AVG
Home	211	56	9	32	.265	LHP	140	38	7	26	.271
Road	172	36	4	18	.209	RHP	243	54	6	24	.222
Day	110	20	5	16	.182	Sc Pos	96	24	6	36	.250
Night	273	72	8	34	.264	Clutch	75	18	1	8	.240

1991 Rankings (National League)

→ Did not rank near the top or bottom in any category

PITCHING:

Bothered by bone spurs and an inconsistent delivery, Pat Combs went from a potential big winner to a struggling lefty last year. Combs was able to log only two victories before undergoing elbow surgery in June. He wound up missing the rest of the season.

The key to Combs' pitching has always been throwing his drop-off-the-table curveball for strikes. That's what he did in 1989, when he broke in by going 4-0 with a 2.09 ERA in six starts. But for the last two years, Combs has struggled to keep his arm in pace with his body on both his curve and change-up. Last year he was so out of sync that he walked 43 batters in only 64.1 innings. Combs has a decent, high-80s fastball, but he simply has to have good control in order to win.

Despite his frustrating season, manager Jim Fregosi and pitching coach Johnny Podres remain convinced that Combs can win. They plan to work intensely with him on smoothing out his delivery until it becomes a matter of repetition. They'd also like him to prepare more fully to take advantage of the weaknesses of opposing hitters the way Terry Mulholland does.

HOLDING RUNNERS, FIELDING, HITTING:

As his delivery fell apart, so did Combs' pickoff move and relatively quick delivery to the plate. Opponents stole 12 bases in 14 attempts, nearly one stolen base per start. Combs fields everything he can reach, but his mound struggles distracted his attention from his defense last year. He is a mediocre bunter, but does force pitchers to throw strikes to get him out.

OVERALL:

Combs will be 25 years old next season, and is only a couple of fairly minor adjustments away from becoming a consistent winner. Phillies GM Lee Thomas, who has collected 25 to 28-year-old prospects from other teams, is not likely to give up on him. Assuming he's healthy, Combs will get a full shot at one of the two available starting jobs this spring.

PAT COMBS

Position: SP
Bats: L **Throws:** L
Ht: 6' 4" **Wt:** 207

Opening Day Age: 25
Born: 10/29/66 in
Newport, RI
ML Seasons: 3

Overall Statistics

	W	L	ERA	G	GS	Sv	IP	H	R	BB	SO	HR
1991	2	6	4.90	14	13	0	64.1	64	41	43	41	7
Career	16	16	3.99	52	50	0	286.1	279	141	135	179	21

How Often He Throws Strikes

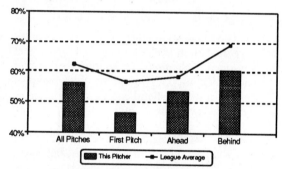

1991 Situational Stats

	W	L	ERA	Sv	IP		AB	H	HR	RBI	AVG
Home	1	2	6.03	0	31.1	LHB	43	9	1	3	.209
Road	1	4	3.82	0	33.0	RHB	209	55	6	27	.263
Day	0	1	6.52	0	9.2	Sc Pos	83	13	2	21	.157
Night	2	5	4.61	0	54.2	Clutch	16	1	0	0	.063

1991 Rankings (National League)

➡ Did not rank near the top or bottom in any category

PITCHING:

Danny Cox is a fiery competitor whom Lee Thomas and Jim Fregosi fondly recall from their days with the St. Louis Cardinals. After missing more than two full seasons with serious elbow problems, Cox made a heroic comeback with the Phillies last year, but he was no longer the pitcher that Thomas and Fregosi remembered. Cox has metamorphosed into a sinker-curveball-change-up pitcher, and last year he was a very inconsistent one.

Cox returned to the majors last April 27. Pitching seven strong innings, he emphasized staying ahead of hitters and changing speeds, as if he had become his old teammate John Tudor. After a brutal second start in which he was strafed for seven hits in one inning, Cox reeled off three good outings, only to be sidelined for a month with a strained groin muscle.

After returning, Cox made one more strong start. However, his sore elbow made his breaking pitches inconsistent, and he was taken out of the rotation in July. He could not regain his rotation spot with erratic, occasional starts during the rest of the season. Overall, Cox lasted barely five innings a start and allowed a homer every seven innings, nearly twice his previous career rate.

HOLDING RUNNERS, FIELDING, HITTING:

Cox has both a normal move and a "pickoff special" to keep runners close. His economical delivery gives catchers a good chance to throw out runners. A good athlete and enthusiastic competitor, Cox aggressively covers bases, takes throws at first, and tries to get lead runners on bunt plays. He is also a game hacker at the plate, and had a good enough eye to draw two walks last year.

OVERALL:

Cox can still pitch in the major leagues if he can change speeds consistently; that was his method during his good starts last year. But if his elbow problems don't allow him to do that, Cox will be lost in the shuffle of arms in spring training.

DANNY COX

Position: SP/RP
Bats: R **Throws:** R
Ht: 6' 4" **Wt:** 225

Opening Day Age: 32
Born: 9/21/59 in Northhampton, England
ML Seasons: 7

Overall Statistics

	W	L	ERA	G	GS	Sv	IP	H	R	BB	SO	HR
1991	4	6	4.57	23	17	0	102.1	98	57	39	46	14
Career	60	62	3.51	175	167	0	1088.0	1089	491	336	539	85

How Often He Throws Strikes

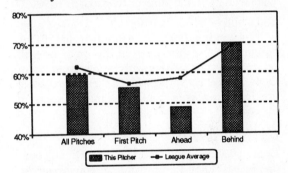

1991 Situational Stats

	W	L	ERA	Sv	IP		AB	H	HR	RBI	AVG
Home	2	4	4.41	0	49.0	LHB	189	52	7	32	.275
Road	2	2	4.72	0	53.1	RHB	191	46	7	21	.241
Day	2	2	4.67	0	27.0	Sc Pos	95	26	4	40	.274
Night	2	4	4.54	0	75.1	Clutch	21	5	0	3	.238

1991 Rankings (National League)

→ Did not rank near the top or bottom in any category

HITTING:

An injury-filled 1991 began for Darren Daulton when he was a passenger in Lenny Dykstra's car crash last May; that accident took the rap for Daulton's poor year with the glove and bat. The problem with blaming Daulton's injuries is that his 1991 batting attributes -- power, walks and a lousy batting average -- were the same ones he displayed throughout his career until 1990, a breakthrough season which earned him a three-year, $6.7 million contract.

Certainly the rib and back injuries curtailed Daulton's swing and slowed his bat speed. Moved down in the batting order, Daulton felt the need to hit for power instead of taking pitches, as he did when batting in the number-two spot in 1990.

Top Phillies' officials believe that Daulton's bat will rebound in 1992. But some fear that if they continue to use him deep in the order he will return to his pre-1990 poverty-line impression of Gene Tenace, complete with .200 batting average and lots of walks in front of the pitcher's spot in the order.

BASERUNNING:

Daulton's once-good speed is gone, but he none-theless has stolen 12 bases in 13 attempts over the last two years. Obviously a smart baserunner, he has tamed his approach to the bases in order to ward off recurring injuries.

FIELDING:

By any measure of defense, Daulton had the worst season of any Phillies catcher. Previously well-regarded by the team's pitchers as a fine pitch-caller, Daulton had trouble getting in sync with pitchers last year, and his bad back and ribs sapped his throws. Daulton allowed a gruesome 82 percent of baserunners to steal successfully.

OVERALL:

Severe back and rib injuries are as serious for catchers as arm injuries, and worse in one way: you can play through them, as Daulton attempted to do. Unfortunately, it is nearly impossible to play well with such injuries. While a winter of healing should help restore his health, manager Jim Fregosi has to find a way to harness Daulton's offensive skills and make them more useful to the team.

DARREN DAULTON

Position: C
Bats: L **Throws:** R
Ht: 6' 2" **Wt:** 200

Opening Day Age: 30
Born: 1/3/62 in Arkansas City, KS
ML Seasons: 8

Overall Statistics

	G	AB	R	H	D	T	HR	RBI	SB	BB	SO	AVG
1991	89	285	36	56	12	0	12	42	5	41	66	.196
Career	561	1629	183	361	73	4	48	200	21	253	338	.222

Where He Hits the Ball

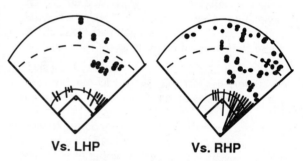

Vs. LHP   **Vs. RHP**

1991 Situational Stats

	AB	H	HR	RBI	AVG		AB	H	HR	RBI	AVG
Home	152	32	8	23	.211	LHP	96	14	2	9	.146
Road	133	24	4	19	.180	RHP	189	42	10	33	.222
Day	71	16	5	12	.225	Sc Pos	62	18	1	29	.290
Night	214	40	7	30	.187	Clutch	60	11	2	12	.183

1991 Rankings (National League)

→ 1st in lowest percentage of runners caught stealing as a catcher (17.6%)

→ 5th lowest batting average with 2 strikes (.127)

→ 7th in highest batting average with the bases loaded (.429) and lowest batting average with a 3-2 count (.093)

→ Led the Phillies in least GDPs per GDP situation (5.9%) and batting average with the bases loaded

→ Led NL catchers in batting average with the bases loaded

PITCHING:

While recording the first winning professional season of his career in 1991, Jose DeJesus demonstrated the kind of stuff that makes for long careers. At the same time, his unsightly walk totals call the effectiveness of such a career into question. DeJesus' improvement came as new pitching coach Johnny Podres helped him add a change-of-pace to the 90-MPH high fastballs which are his trademark.

The right-handed beanpole hits or misses the top of the strike zone with most pitches, which made another new pitch effective: a little drop-curve which hitters swung over because they were so used to his fastball. Confidence is the biggest remaining hurdle for the streaky 27 year old. After a slow start, DeJesus entered September at 10-4, 3.35, but lost his last five decisions in six starts, partly due to walking 26 batters in 34 innings.

DeJesus also struggled late in the year with his new change-up, and has made a consistent and smooth delivery a top project for spring training. For a flame-thrower, he is not much of a strikeout pitcher. His fastball is essentially level, and moves in or out rather than sinking or rising; this makes it relatively easy for opposing hitters to make contact, but very difficult to drive the ball anywhere.

HOLDING RUNNERS, FIELDING, HITTING:

DeJesus' slow delivery helps runners get a good jump, but his high fastballs are well suited to getting a catcher out of his crouch and throwing to second. Combined with his good move, he cut his opposition stolen base rate to 63 percent. His follow-through leaves him in poor position to field. While he swings gamely, DeJesus does not hit or bunt well, and runs poorly.

OVERALL:

DeJesus is a willing learner and hard worker. He needs to make his overhand motion consistent in order to keep his fastball at or near the top of the strike zone. But he has matured into a worthwhile third to fifth starter -- not bad for someone acquired for Steve Jeltz.

JOSE DeJESUS

Position: SP
Bats: R **Throws:** R
Ht: 6' 5" **Wt:** 213

Opening Day Age: 27
Born: 1/6/65 in Brooklyn, NY
ML Seasons: 4

Overall Statistics

	W	L	ERA	G	GS	Sv	IP	H	R	BB	SO	HR
1991	10	9	3.42	31	29	1	181.2	147	74	128	118	7
Career	17	18	3.77	58	53	1	322.1	257	151	214	209	18

How Often He Throws Strikes

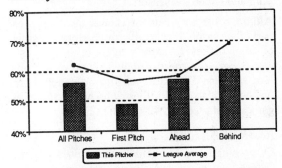

1991 Situational Stats

	W	L	ERA	Sv	IP		AB	H	HR	RBI	AVG
Home	4	5	3.39	0	77.0	LHB	376	87	1	41	.231
Road	6	4	3.44	1	104.2	RHB	279	60	6	23	.215
Day	2	1	3.62	0	37.1	Sc Pos	191	39	2	55	.204
Night	8	8	3.37	1	144.1	Clutch	57	16	1	7	.281

1991 Rankings (National League)

→ 1st in walks allowed (128), lowest strikeout/walk ratio (.9), highest on-base average allowed (.353), most pitches thrown per batter (3.91) and least home runs allowed per 9 innings (.35)

→ 5th in lowest batting average allowed (.224), lowest slugging percentage allowed (.318) and lowest batting average allowed with runners in scoring position (.204)

→ Led the Phillies in walks allowed, stolen bases allowed (19), runners caught stealing (11), GDPs induced (16), lowest batting average allowed, lowest slugging percentage allowed, least home runs per 9 innings, most GDPs induced per 9 innings (.79) and ERA on the road (3.44)

HITTING:

There have been two enduring raps against Lenny Dykstra: that he'll wear out or get hurt if he plays every day, and that he can't hit lefthanders. The first of these raps may have been strengthened in 1991, but the second was blasted away permanently.

For the second season in a row, Dykstra hit lefties, drew walks and stole bases. He appeared well on his way to a 120-run, 60 stolen base season when he drove his car into a tree May 5 on the way home from a party, injuring his ribs and back. While frenetic rehabilitation enabled Dykstra to return on July 15, a crash into an outfield wall in Cincinnati August 26 re-injured the Phils spark-plug and ended his season.

Although his car accident cannot be viewed as part of his baseball-related injury history, his style of play makes Dykstra's availability for 150 games per year questionable. This poses a problem because Dykstra's ability to reach base means a lot to the Phillies, who were 36-23 in games he started and 42-61 when he did not.

BASERUNNING:

Combining sheer homicidal aggressiveness with tremendous judgement, a great first step and good speed, a strong case can be made that Dykstra is the best baserunner in the National League. He stole bases more frequently last year, but was rarely caught.

FIELDING:

Dykstra's speed and anticipation make him a perennial entry among the league's best center fielders. He plays deep so that he can charge most balls, adding momentum to a weak arm.

OVERALL:

Dykstra has emerged as a star with the Phils as their best leadoff man since Richie Ashburn. The Phils hope he can match Ashburn's consistency and longevity, and jump-start enough offense to make them consistent winners in 1992.

LENNY DYKSTRA

Position: CF
Bats: L **Throws:** L
Ht: 5'10" **Wt:** 186

Opening Day Age: 29
Born: 2/10/63 in Santa Ana, CA
ML Seasons: 7

Overall Statistics

	G	AB	R	H	D	T	HR	RBI	SB	BB	SO	AVG
1991	63	246	48	73	13	5	3	12	24	37	20	.297
Career	846	2874	480	812	172	28	46	244	190	344	310	.283

Where He Hits the Ball

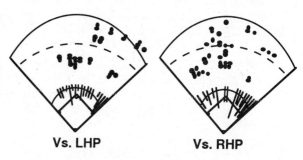

Vs. LHP	Vs. RHP

1991 Situational Stats

	AB	H	HR	RBI	AVG		AB	H	HR	RBI	AVG
Home	118	38	3	6	.322	LHP	94	29	2	6	.309
Road	128	35	0	6	.273	RHP	152	44	1	6	.289
Day	81	20	0	1	.247	Sc Pos	32	8	0	7	.250
Night	165	53	3	11	.321	Clutch	51	16	1	3	.314

1991 Rankings (National League)

- → 1st in stolen base percentage (85.7%) and lowest batting average on a 3-1 count (.000)
- → 3rd in leadoff on-base average (.387)
- → 4th in batting average with 2 strikes (.272)
- → 9th in steals of third (5)
- → Led the Phillies in stolen bases (24), stolen base percentage and steals of third
- → Led NL center fielders in stolen base percentage, batting average on a 3-2 count (.300) and batting average with 2 strikes

PITCHING:

Tommy Greene started the 1991 season as a 24-year-old washed-out former prospect. But after pitching a no-hitter May 23, and a three-hitter May 28, he was given a rotation slot that he never surrendered. Greene finished the year with 13 wins, the most in his seven-season professional career, and his 3.38 ERA was the best for any Phillies' starter.

Part of the former Brave's resurgence lay in trading Fulton County Stadium for Veterans Stadium. Greene throws a rising fastball 60 percent of the time, and it's easier to keep that pitch in the bigger Philadelphia park. As a result, Greene stopped trying to overthrow his fastball, and the pitch became more consistent. A smoother delivery also helped his slow-breaking curveball. Greene is still working on his change-up, and throws it sparingly.

Greene made the Phils in 1991 largely because he was out of options, and began the year in the bullpen. But after the no-hitter he really got it together and turned in an 8-4 second half. With his strong finish, Greene proved that he was adjusting to the league better than it was adjusting to him. He also showed no signs of fatigue despite working a career-high 207.2 innings.

HOLDING RUNNERS, FIELDING, HITTING:

The best hitter and athlete on the Phils' staff, Greene banged out 19 hits for a .268 average and helped himself win several games with his bat. His athleticism also shows in his good fielding, especially on turf. Greene has an involved delivery and a poor move to first base, making him fairly easy to steal on.

OVERALL:

When he arrived in Philadelphia as a throw-in to the Jeff Parrett-Jim Vatcher for Dale Murphy trade, Greene simply represented a 24 year old with a live arm -- another Phillies reclamation project. His fortunes changed so quickly that a visiting reporter last year asked: "Who else did the Phillies get in the Tommy Greene deal?"

TOMMY GREENE

Position: SP/RP
Bats: R **Throws:** R
Ht: 6' 5" **Wt:** 227

Opening Day Age: 25
Born: 4/6/67 in Lumberton, NC
ML Seasons: 3

Overall Statistics

	W	L	ERA	G	GS	Sv	IP	H	R	BB	SO	HR
1991	13	7	3.38	36	27	0	207.2	177	85	66	154	19
Career	17	12	3.75	55	40	0	285.1	249	128	98	192	32

How Often He Throws Strikes

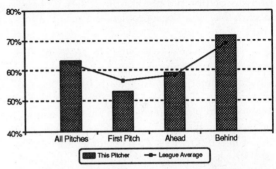

1991 Situational Stats

	W	L	ERA	Sv	IP		AB	H	HR	RBI	AVG
Home	6	4	3.31	0	108.2	LHB	453	116	12	52	.256
Road	7	3	3.45	0	99.0	RHB	315	61	7	30	.194
Day	5	3	3.58	0	65.1	Sc Pos	152	43	2	58	.283
Night	8	4	3.29	0	142.1	Clutch	59	13	1	4	.220

1991 Rankings (National League)

➜ 5th in lowest groundball/flyball ratio (.93) and least GDPs induced per 9 innings (.39)

➜ 6th in winning percentage (.650)

➜ 7th in home runs allowed (19) and most pitches thrown per batter (3.79)

➜ 8th in strikeouts (154), lowest on-base average allowed (.290) and highest batting average allowed with runners in scoring position (.283)

➜ Led the Phillies in ERA (3.38), home runs allowed, strikeouts, lowest on-base average allowed, most run support per 9 innings (4.4) and most strikeouts per 9 innings (6.7)

PITCHING:

When Mike Hartley came to the Phillies with Braulio Castillo for Roger McDowell last August 1, Philadelphia expectations were fairly modest. Dumping McDowell's hefty contract was a key to the deal, and so was acquiring the promising Castillo. Hartley represented little more than a good arm, something the pitching-poor Phils need to collect.

Hartley throws mostly curveballs and split-fingered fastballs, and has repeatedly said he needs to be a starter to succeed. After seeing him work, Phils coaches now agree, feeling that Hartley's lack of a hard fastball or other out pitch make him unsuited for bullpen work. The overstocked Dodger rotation did not afford Hartley a chance to start; that won't be a problem with the Phillies.

Still used as a reliever after arriving in Philadelphia, Hartley was very erratic. He saved the first game he pitched in, and pitched well until he came completely apart August 18, hitting the first two batters he faced, and then allowing a hit and two walks to blow a lead. After that appearance, he was used sparingly, and lack of work helped render him ineffective. That cemented the plan to use him as a starter. Hartley made a half dozen starts for the Dodgers in 1990 and was fairly effective.

HOLDING RUNNERS, FIELDING, HITTING:

Hartley is another Phils pitcher who is easy to steal on. Opponents say he telegraphs his move with awkward footwork, and last year he allowed 13 steals in 14 attempts. He fields bunts well, and frequently will try to get the lead runner going into second or third base. Hartley is a weak hitter.

OVERALL:

After begging to start for two years, Hartley will get his chance this spring. The Phillies will attempt to teach him the Johnny Podres change-up, and hope that pitch will help him become the fifth starter they need. If not, Hartley will go back to the bullpen, and try to be more consistent.

MIKE HARTLEY

Position: RP
Bats: R **Throws:** R
Ht: 6' 1" **Wt:** 197

Opening Day Age: 30
Born: 8/31/61 in Hawthorne, CA
ML Seasons: 3

Overall Statistics

	W	L	ERA	G	GS	Sv	IP	H	R	BB	SO	HR
1991	4	1	4.21	58	0	2	83.1	74	40	47	63	11
Career	10	5	3.52	95	6	3	168.2	134	73	77	143	18

How Often He Throws Strikes

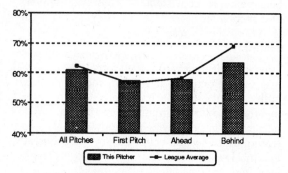

1991 Situational Stats

	W	L	ERA	Sv	IP		AB	H	HR	RBI	AVG
Home	3	0	4.19	0	43.0	LHB	159	38	5	18	.239
Road	1	1	4.24	2	40.1	RHB	153	36	6	26	.235
Day	1	0	4.95	0	20.0	Sc Pos	104	20	4	36	.192
Night	3	1	3.98	2	63.1	Clutch	75	15	0	11	.200

1991 Rankings (National League)

- ➡ 4th most baserunners allowed per 9 innings in relief (13.7)
- ➡ 6th highest percentage of inherited runners scored (39.5%)
- ➡ 7th in hit batsmen (6), wild pitches (10) and highest relief ERA (4.21)

HITTING:

Charlie Hayes' failing bat let Dave Hollins step in and claim the starting third base job for the Phillies in 1991. Hayes provided some pop with 53 RBI and 36 extra-base hits, including 12 homers, but his inability to reach base was too glaring a weakness for the Phillies to ignore. Of the 14 National League third basemen who started 40 or more games, Hayes finished dead last with a .257 on-base percentage.

Apart from occasional power, Hayes' major strength as a hitter is that he usually puts the ball into play. His bat picks up at Veterans Stadium, which is well-suited for a contact hitter with its spacious outfield and small foul territory. But by encouraging this style, his home park also aids in his undoing by falsely suggesting that putting the ball into play is, alone, enough to bring success.

Hayes has proven he can hit fastballs, but he's a sucker for breaking pitches, and is probably the Phillie least able to adjust his swing to offspeed pitches. He had a good first half in 1990, a good second half in 1991, but has to change his approach to have a good full season.

BASERUNNING:

Hayes is no threat as a base stealer (3-for-6 last year). His occasional lapses of concentration show up on the base paths just as much as they do in the batter's box.

FIELDING:

Though not many people know it, Hayes is one of the best defensive third basemen in the National League. He has a strong and accurate arm, and has successfully experimented with hop-throws when he has to get rid of the ball quickly. He remains one of the best in baseball going to his right, and moves surely to his left.

OVERALL:

Hayes' power and defensive skills are good enough to ensure his stay in the majors. But they will not guarantee that he'll continue to start at third base for the Phillies, who are exasperated by his lack of development. He's still only 26, and other teams might be interested in him.

CHARLIE HAYES

Position: 3B
Bats: R **Throws:** R
Ht: 6' 0" **Wt:** 210

Opening Day Age: 26
Born: 5/29/65 in Hattiesburg, MS
ML Seasons: 4

Overall Statistics

	G	AB	R	H	D	T	HR	RBI	SB	BB	SO	AVG
1991	142	460	34	106	23	1	12	53	3	16	75	.230
Career	388	1336	116	330	58	2	30	153	10	55	219	.247

Where He Hits the Ball

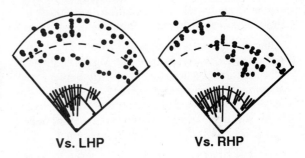

Vs. LHP   **Vs. RHP**

1991 Situational Stats

	AB	H	HR	RBI	AVG		AB	H	HR	RBI	AVG
Home	248	65	6	34	.262	LHP	190	49	4	22	.258
Road	212	41	6	19	.193	RHP	270	57	8	31	.211
Day	124	27	3	17	.218	Sc Pos	109	26	4	38	.239
Night	336	79	9	36	.235	Clutch	100	32	4	11	.320

1991 Rankings (National League)

→ 5th lowest percentage of pitches taken (45.4%)

→ 9th highest batting average with the bases loaded (.417)

→ Led the Phillies in batting average in the clutch (.320) and lowest percentage of swings that missed (19.8%)

HITTING:

Beset with continual injuries and pressured, when healthy, to offset the loss of Lenny Dykstra, Von Hayes made his 11th major league season his worst. Totally messed up, Hayes lost both the power and on-base ability which had long made him a solid offensive contributor.

Hayes' biggest problem last year may have been listening too carefully to critics who complained that he was too willing to draw a walk. A patient hitter who had averaged 86 walks a year since 1986, Hayes suddenly decided to go up there hacking. The result was an on-base percentage of .303, his worst ever. Complicating matters, Hayes suffered all season from nagging ankle, foot and wrist injuries that resulted in a loss of power. The inside fastballs which Hayes used to deposit in the seats became fly outs to right field.

Although Hayes was supposed to be out for the season after Randy Myers broke Von's wrist with a fastball in May, he returned in early September. Moving off the plate and working to pull the ball, Hayes briefly looked like his old self. But the pain in his throwing arm and wrist sidelined him once again. He ended the season with no home runs.

BASERUNNING:

Hayes continues to steal bases at a high rate of success (nine in 11 tries in 1991), takes bases aggressively, and breaks up double plays spiritedly. His one or two mistakes each year are over-publicized.

FIELDING:

Called upon to play 49 games in center field after Dykstra was injured, Hayes was competent, showing good range to each side and coming in aggressively on short fly balls. But the wrist and arm injuries have weakened his once-good throwing arm, and call his ability to play right and center field into question.

OVERALL:

Hayes' body fell prey to several nagging injuries in 1991, and he made things worse by trying to change his hitting style. With restored health and a return to his old patience, there's no reason that he can't be a valuable offensive performer -- even if the Phillies finally trade him.

VON HAYES

Position: CF/LF
Bats: L **Throws:** R
Ht: 6' 5" **Wt:** 188

Opening Day Age: 33
Born: 8/31/58 in Stockton, CA
ML Seasons: 11

Overall Statistics

	G	AB	R	H	D	T	HR	RBI	SB	BB	SO	AVG
1991	77	284	43	64	15	1	0	21	9	31	42	.225
Career	1401	4942	732	1333	265	35	139	667	242	675	750	.270

Where He Hits the Ball

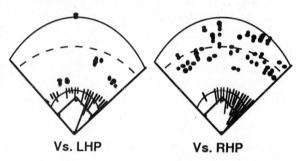

Vs. LHP   **Vs. RHP**

1991 Situational Stats

	AB	H	HR	RBI	AVG		AB	H	HR	RBI	AVG
Home	99	20	0	5	.202	LHP	90	24	0	8	.267
Road	185	44	0	16	.238	RHP	194	40	0	13	.206
Day	89	22	0	8	.247	Sc Pos	67	12	0	21	.179
Night	195	42	0	13	.215	Clutch	51	11	0	1	.216

1991 Rankings (National League)

→ Led the Phillies in hit by pitch (3) and batting average on a 3-1 count (.500)

HITTING:

Given little chance to win the Phillies' third base job in 1991 except by this book, Dave Hollins did just that -- at least when he was healthy. Though Hollins got into only 56 games, he made a big impression with a powerful bat that produced a hefty .510 slugging percentage.

For most of the first half of the season, Hollins was in AAA Scranton, mired in as bad a slump there as Charlie Hayes was in Philadelphia. Recalled to Philadelphia once he straightened himself out, Hollins hit consistently for both power and average while also showing a patient batting eye. The biggest problem Hollins faced was not National League pitching but an aching right shoulder which forced him out of the lineup repeatedly.

In the minor leagues, Hollins was known as a line drive hitter who hit a lot of doubles while homering in single digits. In two seasons with the Phillies, however, he has impressed with his home run hitting ability, bashing 11 dingers in only 265 at-bats. Hollins looks for fastballs early in the count and uses an uppercut swing to drive them into the seats. When the count runs longer, he becomes a more selective hitter who will accept a walk.

BASERUNNING:

A hard-nosed competitor, Hollins' baserunning savvy helps him stretch singles into doubles and doubles into triples. He has stolen as many as 20 bases in the minors, but swiped only one at the major league level in 1991.

FIELDING:

Hollins' third base arm was once rated the best in the Texas League, but he was hampered by his shoulder problems in 1991. An adequate glove man, he is not the equal of Charlie Hayes in quick reactions, but will probably improve with hard work.

OVERALL:

The Phils will give Hollins the third base job this spring if his shoulder has healed. If he continues to hit like he did last year, the team will find a spot for him, even if he cannot play third.

DAVE HOLLINS

Position: 3B
Bats: B **Throws:** R
Ht: 6' 1" **Wt:** 207

Opening Day Age: 25
Born: 5/25/66 in Buffalo, NY
ML Seasons: 2

Overall Statistics

	G	AB	R	H	D	T	HR	RBI	SB	BB	SO	AVG
1991	56	151	18	45	10	2	6	21	1	17	26	.298
Career	128	265	32	66	10	2	11	36	1	27	54	.249

Where He Hits the Ball

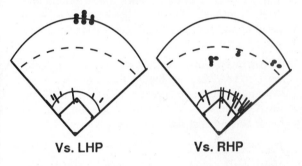

Vs. LHP   Vs. RHP

1991 Situational Stats

	AB	H	HR	RBI	AVG		AB	H	HR	RBI	AVG
Home	60	19	3	8	.317	LHP	45	20	3	10	.444
Road	91	26	3	13	.286	RHP	106	25	3	11	.236
Day	42	16	3	9	.381	Sc Pos	44	11	2	16	.250
Night	109	29	3	12	.266	Clutch	31	4	1	1	.129

1991 Rankings (National League)

→ Led the Phillies in hit by pitch (3)

HITTING:

A Phillie regular in 1989 and for much of 1990, Ricky Jordan became a part-time player in 1991. It might have been a demotion, but Jordan made the most of it, hitting with considerable power. Though he batted only 301 times, he drove in 49 runs, and 40 percent of his hits went for extra bases.

Jordan loves the high fastball, and most of his extra-base hits come on pitches upstairs. He's not a selective hitter, however, and pitchers are often successful "climbing the ladder" on the 6-3 Jordan, getting him to swing at pitches up around his Adam's apple. Jordan gets enough pitches in his wheelhouse to take advantage, but he's impatient and will seldom draw a walk -- he recorded only 14 (two of those intentional) last year. He loves to jump on the first pitch and was 25-for-62 (.403) when he put the first offering in play.

Jordan hit for power against both lefties and righties last year, but he batted for a much higher average against southpaws (.310). Curiously, he wasn't platooned all that much, logging most of his at-bats against righthanders.

BASERUNNING:

No threat to steal or take an extra base, Jordan beats out five or six hits per year because his foot speed is deceiving for a big man. He is unexceptional on the base paths otherwise.

FIELDING:

Hard work has made Jordan slightly above average at first base. He may be the best in the majors at coming off the bag for wayward throws and sweep-tagging the runner. However, his first step to ground balls is slow, and he may have the worst throwing arm in the major leagues.

OVERALL:

Expected to be a star after his .308, 69-game debut in 1988, Jordan has turned out to be something less than that. His lack of selectivity is probably his biggest weakness, but he can hit for both a decent average and good power. Used properly, particularly as a platoon player against lefties, he can be a pretty valuable hitter.

RICKY JORDAN

Position: 1B
Bats: R **Throws:** R
Ht: 6' 3" **Wt:** 209

Opening Day Age: 26
Born: 5/26/65 in Richmond, CA
ML Seasons: 4

Overall Statistics

	G	AB	R	H	D	T	HR	RBI	SB	BB	SO	AVG
1991	101	301	38	82	21	3	9	49	0	14	49	.272
Career	406	1421	174	393	79	7	37	211	7	57	189	.277

Where He Hits the Ball

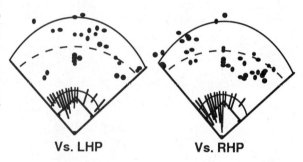

Vs. LHP   Vs. RHP

1991 Situational Stats

	AB	H	HR	RBI	AVG		AB	H	HR	RBI	AVG
Home	158	47	5	27	.297	LHP	126	39	4	19	.310
Road	143	35	4	22	.245	RHP	175	43	5	30	.246
Day	105	32	5	22	.305	Sc Pos	88	27	4	42	.307
Night	196	50	4	27	.255	Clutch	75	15	0	7	.200

1991 Rankings (National League)

➡ 10th most GDPs per GDP situation (15.5%)

➡ Led the Phillies in batting average with runners in scoring position (.307), batting average vs. left-handed pitchers (.310) and slugging percentage vs. left-handed pitchers (.500)

OVERLOOKED

JOHN KRUK

Position: 1B/LF/CF
Bats: L **Throws:** L
Ht: 5'10" **Wt:** 200

Opening Day Age: 31
Born: 2/9/61 in
Charleston, WV
ML Seasons: 6

HITTING:

John Kruk hit for power again in 1991, buttressing his oft-stated contention that his 20 homer, 91 RBI season in 1987 was not a fluke. Kruk had totalled only 24 homers from 1988 through 1990, but he had almost that many in 1991 alone (21). He also set career marks in doubles (27), runs scored (84) and RBI (92).

Usually an opposite field hitter who drove his home runs over the left-center field fence, Kruk made an adjustment late in 1990 which paid off last season. He added a shortened stroke to his repertoire, allowing him to pull high inside fastballs off right-handed pitchers. During the first half of the season, Kruk hit several home runs to right, and pitchers gave up trying to overpower him. In the second half he got more soft stuff, and was able to take it with power to the opposite field.

Kruk also improved last year against left-handed pitchers, who had held him to a .222 average and 15 RBI in 1990. He made some adjustments and wound up batting .297 with 35 RBI against southpaws in '91.

BASERUNNING:

Though an extremely aggressive baserunner, Kruk rarely hurls himself into an out. His declining speed led manager Jim Fregosi to cut down his stolen base attempts, but after Kruk's seven-for-seven performance in 1991, Fregosi may let him run a little more often.

FIELDING:

The best defensive first baseman, right fielder and left fielder on the team, Kruk has soft hands, a strong arm, and an uncanny knowledge of playing surfaces. He has overcome a slight problem scooping one-hop infield throws at first base; he might be a Gold Glove first baseman, committing just two errors all year at first base.

OVERALL:

Kruk's versatility is a wonderful weapon for a manager to have. He is skilled in three defensive positions. He can reach base, steal a base, take a walk or hit a home run. Quite simply, he can fit any role in the offense and many in the defense. He is simply invaluable to the Phillies.

Overall Statistics

	G	AB	R	H	D	T	HR	RBI	SB	BB	SO	AVG
1991	152	538	84	158	27	6	21	92	7	67	100	.294
Career	786	2441	348	711	112	25	69	376	45	378	442	.291

Where He Hits the Ball

Vs. LHP   **Vs. RHP**

1991 Situational Stats

	AB	H	HR	RBI	AVG		AB	H	HR	RBI	AVG
Home	276	79	8	48	.286	LHP	202	60	4	35	.297
Road	262	79	13	44	.302	RHP	336	98	17	57	.292
Day	134	35	6	16	.261	Sc Pos	131	36	5	65	.275
Night	404	123	15	76	.304	Clutch	103	29	1	12	.282

1991 Rankings (National League)

→ 4th in intentional walks (16)

→ 7th in sacrifice flies (9) and slugging percentage vs. right-handed pitchers (.512)

→ Led the Phillies in batting average (.294), home runs (21), runs (84), hits (158), triples (6), total bases (260), RBIs (92), sacrifice flies, walks (67), intentional walks, times on base (226), strikeouts (100), pitches seen (2,287), plate appearances (615), slugging percentage (.483) and on-base average (.368)

→ Led NL first basemen in fielding percentage (.997)

HITTING:

Mickey Morandini was demoted to AAA Scranton on Opening Day last year, but his prowess (and a Wally Backman slump) soon earned him a trip back to Philadelphia. Morandini showed he can play second base and hit singles and doubles against major league righthanders. He hit only .185 against lefthanders, however, and eventually wound up platooning with Randy Ready. Late in the year, as the Phils battled for third place, Ready was seeing the bulk of the action, even against some righties.

Morandini stands up fairly straight, well off the plate, and dives into pitches, making him very vulnerable to breaking balls from lefties. His style also makes it difficult for him to get around on an inside fastball. Morandini's good bat control does enable him to get wood on pitches from the middle of the plate out, whether high or low.

BASERUNNING:

Morandini has good speed, but his 13 stolen bases in 15 attempts were due more to a good first step and sound instincts than fast feet. Playing every day, Morandini could steal up to 25 bases with the same kind of efficiency. That same sound approach also enables him to take extra bases on poor-armed outfielders.

FIELDING:

Morandini, who was converted to second base from shortstop in 1990, out-gloved both Ready and Backman in 1991, establishing himself as the Phils best at the position. Morandini turns the double play well, and covers ground to his left more confidently than toward second. His good first step helps him play liners and soft flies. Phils coaches want him to work on balls hit up the middle, but they see his glove work as a strong point for his future.

OVERALL:

Morandini's strong performance against righties and in the field should keep him as a platoon partner for Randy Ready this season. If the 25 year old can solve his problems against lefties, he could emerge as a full-time starter and the team's new version of Tommy Herr.

MICKEY MORANDINI

Position: 2B
Bats: L **Throws:** R
Ht: 5'11" **Wt:** 167

Opening Day Age: 25
Born: 4/22/66 in Kittanning, PA
ML Seasons: 2

Overall Statistics

	G	AB	R	H	D	T	HR	RBI	SB	BB	SO	AVG
1991	98	325	38	81	11	4	1	20	13	29	45	.249
Career	123	404	47	100	15	4	2	23	16	35	64	.248

Where He Hits the Ball

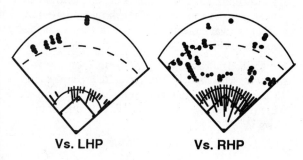

Vs. LHP   Vs. RHP

1991 Situational Stats

	AB	H	HR	RBI	AVG		AB	H	HR	RBI	AVG
Home	166	39	1	10	.235	LHP	65	12	0	3	.185
Road	159	42	0	10	.264	RHP	260	69	1	17	.265
Day	73	16	0	5	.219	Sc Pos	64	17	1	19	.266
Night	252	65	1	15	.258	Clutch	55	14	0	2	.255

1991 Rankings (National League)

➡ Led the Phillies in sacrifice bunts (6) and bunts in play (13)

PITCHING:

Terry Mulholland proved last year that his late 1990 surge was no fluke. His 232 innings, 16 wins and three shutouts demonstrated his arrival as the anchor of the Phillie staff. One other number highlights Mulholland's season: he hurled eight complete games in 34 starts, as many as the rest of the staff combined in their 128 starts.

The key to Mulholland's surge has been, simply, health. The season and a third since August 1990 has been the longest uninjured string of his major league career. For a pitcher who drives off his legs like Mulholland, staying healthy allows him to maintain a few critical MPH on his sinking fastball and slider. That extra velocity was enough to make the former Giant castoff the Phils top pitcher.

While he throws the slider and sinker 80 percent of the time, Mulholland also added a Johnny Podres-taught change-up last year. It confounded hitters, adding two strikeouts per 9 innings to his stats. The new pitch also helped the already control-minded Mulholland cut his walks to a career-low of just under two per nine innings.

The quiet, intense lefty prepares for each game more meticulously than almost any other pitcher, actually committing himself to a rough script of how to pitch each batter. This allows the defense to position itself with unusual confidence for each hitter, another reason for Mulholland's success.

HOLDING RUNNERS, FIELDING, HITTING:

Mulholland has an excellent move and he delivers the ball to the plate quickly. He allowed only six steals in 11 attempts last year. Mulholland has improved as a fielder, but his hard hands make him only adequate as a glove man. He can't hit, bunt or run.

OVERALL:

The last time the Phils unveiled an ace, Ken Howell promptly got injured. They are keenly aware that Mulholland is only a leg injury away from the ineffective pitcher who was available cheap in 1989. But with his strong preparation and devotion to fitness, Mulholland appears able to repeat or even improve on his strong 1991 performance.

TERRY MULHOLLAND

Position: SP
Bats: R **Throws:** L
Ht: 6' 3" **Wt:** 208

Opening Day Age: 29
Born: 3/9/63 in Uniontown, PA
ML Seasons: 5

Overall Statistics

	W	L	ERA	G	GS	Sv	IP	H	R	BB	SO	HR
1991	16	13	3.61	34	34	0	232.0	231	100	49	142	15
Career	32	38	3.89	116	94	0	628.2	641	297	169	328	44

How Often He Throws Strikes

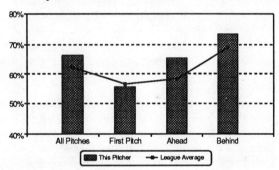

This Pitcher —— League Average

1991 Situational Stats

	W	L	ERA	Sv	IP		AB	H	HR	RBI	AVG
Home	11	2	2.96	0	130.2	LHB	157	40	6	20	.255
Road	5	11	4.44	0	101.1	RHB	730	191	9	69	.262
Day	5	5	3.18	0	73.2	Sc Pos	190	57	7	77	.300
Night	11	8	3.81	0	158.1	Clutch	113	26	3	11	.230

1991 Rankings (National League)

- ➝ 2nd most errors by a pitcher (5)
- ➝ 3rd in complete games (8) and shutouts (3)
- ➝ 5th in wins (16)
- ➝ Led the Phillies in wins, losses (13), games started (34), complete games, shutouts, innings (232), hits allowed (231), batters faced (956), pitches thrown (3,377), pickoff throws (144), GDPs induced (16), strikeout/walk ratio (2.9), groundball/flyball ratio (1.3), lowest stolen base percentage allowed (54.5%) and least pitches thrown per batter (3.53)

HITTING:

Dale Murphy essentially delivered the kind of cleanup-hitter season that he was expected to last year, coming close to the .250, 20-25 HR, 80-90 RBI standards set for him. But there's a rat loose in the kitchen. For the second consecutive season, Murphy showed that he can no longer hit right-handed pitching. Unfortunately, everyday players face righties about 65 percent of the time, and the Phillies feel they can't afford to have a weak stick in the lineup that often. Murphy is now scheduled to platoon with Von Hayes or some other left-handed hitter in 1992.

While struggling against righties, Murphy was still effective against southpaws in 1991. He waited for them to throw curveballs, particularly inside, and punished them whenever they arrived. However, Murphy can no longer handle high and outside heat. He is now a mistake hitter, and when pitchers don't make them, he doesn't hit them.

BASERUNNING:

After stealing nine bases in 11 tries in four months with the Braves in 1990, Murphy has attempted only two steals in 210 games with the Phillies. This is at the teams' behest: they fear his lack of speed will override even his usually sound instincts. Murphy is a hard-charging and spirited baserunner, but now takes a few less extra bases per year due to reduced aggressiveness.

FIELDING:

Once a Gold Glover, Murphy's arm remains strong, but his lateral range is limited to his right, and he plays fairly deep, allowing some soft hits to drop in front of him. He moves to the foul line well and has no fear of hitting the ground or a wall to catch balls.

OVERALL:

In 1991, pitchers began walking Wes Chamberlain and John Kruk to face Murphy with runners in scoring position. That forced the Phillies to confront Murphy's slowing bat speed and consider platooning him. Murphy will still play, and increased rest and platooning will keep him productive, but his playing time could be cut in half.

DALE MURPHY

Position: RF
Bats: R **Throws:** R
Ht: 6' 4" **Wt:** 221

Opening Day Age: 36
Born: 3/12/56 in Portland, OR
ML Seasons: 16

Overall Statistics

	G	AB	R	H	D	T	HR	RBI	SB	BB	SO	AVG
1991	153	544	66	137	33	1	18	81	1	48	93	.252
Career	2136	7856	1191	2095	348	39	396	1252	161	980	1720	.267

Where He Hits the Ball

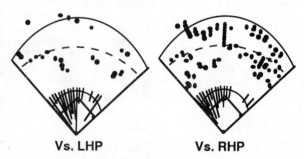

Vs. LHP   **Vs. RHP**

1991 Situational Stats

	AB	H	HR	RBI	AVG		AB	H	HR	RBI	AVG
Home	279	78	9	54	.280	LHP	192	57	5	25	.297
Road	265	59	9	27	.223	RHP	352	80	13	56	.227
Day	122	25	3	17	.205	Sc Pos	155	37	4	63	.239
Night	422	112	15	64	.265	Clutch	108	26	7	20	.241

1991 Rankings (National League)

- ➡ 2nd in GDPs (20), lowest on-base average vs. right-handed pitchers (.286) and lowest batting average on the road (.223)
- ➡ 3rd lowest batting average vs. right-handed pitchers (.227)
- ➡ 6th lowest batting average (.252)
- ➡ 8th lowest on-base average (.309) and least pitches seen per plate appearances (3.41)
- ➡ Led the Phillies in at-bats (544), doubles (33), GDPs, games (153), groundball/flyball ratio (1.5) and batting average on a 3-2 count (.323)
- ➡ Led NL right fielders in GDPs

HITTING:

Randy Ready was a threefold surprise for the Phillies in 1991. They expected him to hit for a little power, struggle at second base, and reach base at around the major league average. By season's end, however, Ready's defense and ability to get on base were so noticeable that they gladly forgave his power outage.

Ready is the consummate platoon player and pinch hitter, always prepared to swat left-handed pitchers. The key to his success lies in a very unusual stance which Ready began to use in 1990. He crouches over the plate, lifting his front knee up and bending his torso down, creating a strike zone reminiscent of Eddie Gaedel's. This channels pitches so that they are within a few inches of belt-height or they are called balls. The stance has made driving the ball deep very difficult for Ready, but has improved his ability to hit line drives and draw walks. These abilities became very useful to the Phillies after leadoff man Lenny Dykstra was lost for the season, as Ready was the only Dykstra replacement to enjoy any success from that slot.

BASERUNNING:

Ready is extremely aggressive on close plays, kicking his foot out high to jar the ball loose or at least punish anyone attempting to tag him. He is not a basestealer and is also very selective about taking extra bases, choosing mostly to pick on lazy players or poor arms.

FIELDING:

Ready's competent play at second base was the biggest surprise of the season. He turns the double play adequately. He has excellent first-step reactions on liners and ground balls but is a step slower than most second sackers going into the first base hole. He committed only three errors all year.

OVERALL:

Free agent Ready is tough on lefthanders, can play several positions and is a tough pinch hitter. The Phillies will try to keep this versatile contributor, who will land on his feet as a platooner somewhere in the major leagues if he does not return.

RANDY READY

Position: 2B
Bats: R **Throws:** R
Ht: 5'11" **Wt:** 182

Opening Day Age: 32
Born: 1/8/60 in San Mateo, CA
ML Seasons: 9

Overall Statistics

	G	AB	R	H	D	T	HR	RBI	SB	BB	SO	AVG
1991	76	205	32	51	10	1	1	20	2	47	25	.249
Career	636	1780	265	468	96	20	35	209	24	267	233	.263

Where He Hits the Ball

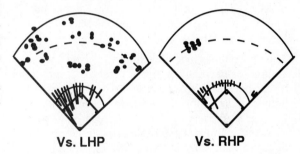

Vs. LHP   Vs. RHP

1991 Situational Stats

	AB	H	HR	RBI	AVG		AB	H	HR	RBI	AVG
Home	108	27	1	10	.250	LHP	147	39	1	18	.265
Road	97	24	0	10	.247	RHP	58	12	0	2	.207
Day	64	16	0	7	.250	Sc Pos	52	13	0	16	.250
Night	141	35	1	13	.248	Clutch	44	8	0	3	.182

1991 Rankings (National League)

- → 1st in batting average with 2 strikes (.286)
- → 6th highest on-base average vs. left-handed pitchers (.418)
- → Led the Phillies in batting average with 2 strikes and on-base average vs. left-handed pitchers

PITCHING:

After two so-so years in the Philadelphia bullpen, Wally Ritchie brought two new pitches with him into the 1991 season. It took a little while, but the difference soon became evident. The lefty posted a 2.27 ERA after the All-Star break and finished the year with a 2.50 mark, second-best on the club to Mitch Williams. As a result, Richie finally appears to have locked up a spot as a left-handed set-up man.

In 1989 and '90, Ritchie had to rely on his change-up as his out pitch. That wasn't enough, and Richie wound up walking a lot of batters in an attempt to paint the corners. But last year the slender hurler added a curve which handcuffed left-handed hitters and gave righty batters a new challenge. Even more importantly, Ritchie premiered a sinking fastball which he was able to throw for strikes.

The new pitches made Ritchie's old stand-by, the change-of-pace, even more effective, and he didn't have to nibble as much. After walking 17 batters in 26 innings in 1990, he issued the same number of free passes while working nearly twice an many innings in 1991. He also struck out 26, after whiffing only eight in '90. Ritchie's progress and newfound control made him Jim Fregosi's southpaw choice to bring into games with runners on base.

HOLDING RUNNERS, FIELDING, HITTING:

Ritchie's move is slow and perfunctory. Baserunners are able to read it, and both his sinker and curve are tough to catch and throw on stolen base attempts. He is a good fielder, however, finishing his motion balanced and able to move off the mound to either side. He rarely bats, and looks pretty ugly when he does.

OVERALL:

The Phillies are loaded with relievers who walk a lot of batters, and right now Ritchie's ability to throw strikes makes him the top set-up man on the team. If they don't sign Mitch Williams and adopt a bullpen-by-committee, Ritchie could even move into a major role.

WALLY RITCHIE

Position: RP
Bats: L Throws: L
Ht: 6' 2" Wt: 180

Opening Day Age: 26
Born: 7/12/65 in Glendale, CA
ML Seasons: 3

Overall Statistics

	W	L	ERA	G	GS	Sv	IP	H	R	BB	SO	HR
1991	1	2	2.50	39	0	0	50.1	44	17	17	26	4
Career	4	4	3.18	107	0	3	138.2	123	58	63	79	13

How Often He Throws Strikes

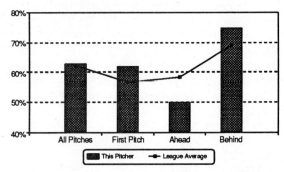

1991 Situational Stats

	W	L	ERA	Sv	IP		AB	H	HR	RBI	AVG
Home	1	2	2.03	0	31.0	LHB	62	10	1	7	.161
Road	0	0	3.26	0	19.1	RHB	126	34	3	13	.270
Day	0	0	2.65	0	17.0	Sc Pos	53	13	1	17	.245
Night	1	2	2.43	0	33.1	Clutch	75	18	2	9	.240

1991 Rankings (National League)

➡ Led the Phillies in holds (7)

PITCHING:

Bruce Ruffin has slumped every spring since 1988, so the Phillies decided to let him have his slump in Scranton last year. They didn't recall him until June, and the strategy campaign resulted in Ruffin's most effective season since his sensational rookie year of 1986. Even so, Ruffin managed only a 4-7 record.

Ruffin's three pitches have not changed. His best offering is a sinking fastball which hitters attempt to lay off so that they can fatten their batting average against his straight heater and slider. If he can throw his slider for strikes, Ruffin is effective, because then opponents have to swing at his sinker. But for about half his outings each year, the slider hangs, and Ruffin gets in big trouble.

Inconsistency in Ruffin's motion has been blamed for a lot of his difficulties, but it's becoming clear that slow seasonal starts are an even more serious problem for him. Ruffin's long-stated preference for starting rather than relieving was not borne out in 1991: his ERA and baserunners allowed per nine innings were virtually identical whether starting or relieving. Ruffin's first ten starts were noticeably better than his last five, however.

HOLDING RUNNERS, FIELDING, HITTING:

Ruffin has an efficient Tommy John-style delivery and pays close attention to runners, both of which make the lefthander tough to steal on. Ruffin's delivery leaves him in good position to field the ball. While he did not get a hit, he led the Phils with six sacrifice bunts and drew four walks, demonstrating that he worked hard to make an offensive contribution.

OVERALL:

Ruffin was dropped from the Phillies rotation in September because the team knows what he will do: pitch well for a dozen games and then slip back to mediocrity. He's done that for five straight seasons. Privately, club officials say that they'll know their staff is ready to contend when Ruffin isn't one of the teams' ten best pitchers. It might be best for all concerned for Ruffin to move on to another club.

BRUCE RUFFIN

Position: RP/SP
Bats: B **Throws:** L
Ht: 6' 2" **Wt:** 213

Opening Day Age: 28
Born: 10/4/63 in Lubbock, TX
ML Seasons: 6

Overall Statistics

	W	L	ERA	G	GS	Sv	IP	H	R	BB	SO	HR
1991	4	7	3.78	31	15	0	119.0	125	52	38	85	6
Career	42	58	4.16	198	134	3	889.0	980	477	359	479	60

How Often He Throws Strikes

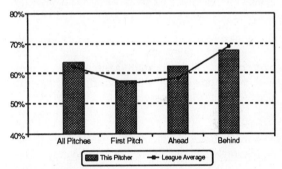

1991 Situational Stats

	W	L	ERA	Sv	IP		AB	H	HR	RBI	AVG
Home	3	3	3.21	0	75.2	LHB	111	28	1	12	.252
Road	1	4	4.78	0	43.1	RHB	348	97	5	35	.279
Day	0	1	6.67	0	27.0	Sc Pos	116	28	2	40	.241
Night	4	6	2.93	0	92.0	Clutch	55	18	0	3	.327

1991 Rankings (National League)

→ 4th highest batting average allowed vs. right-handed batters (.279)

→ Led the Phillies in most GDPs induced per GDP situation (11.1%) and most sacrifice bunts as a batter (6)

HITTING:

Dickie Thon has averaged 144 games per year in his three seasons as the Phils' shortstop, a mark exceeded only by Ozzie Smith among National Leaguers. But Thon's declining ability to pull fastballs and drive in runs imperils his ability to stay in that elite company.

At first glance, Thon's batting record appears creditable for a shortstop. He had remarkably similar stats in both 1990 and 1991: averages in the .250s, about 20 doubles per year, eight or nine homers and 45 RBI. But the Phils believe that with Thon's unwillingness to walk, he must hit .285 or above to justify an everyday spot in the lineup. Thon can't do that, and he didn't help his cause by hitting .220 with runners in scoring position last year.

Thon used to be a great fastball hitter, but his bat has slowed to the point where he can now be overpowered. He still can hit a pitcher's mistakes with more power than most shortstops; he just doesn't do it often enough, in the Phillies' eyes.

BASERUNNING:

Thon's first-step quickness has deteriorated, but he remains swift and steals bases efficiently. The only Phillie who can slide head-first or feet-first equally well, he beats a lot of close throws due to these practiced skills.

FIELDING:

Thon makes the plays he can reach, but that group shrinks slightly with every passing season. On longer throws, he often has to stop, set and stride before getting rid of the ball, a luxury many plays do not allow. He is adequate but no longer better than most other shortstops and the team fears a further decline.

OVERALL:

Thon is still one of the top 20 shortstops in the major leagues, but he is facing his 34th birthday. The Phils, understandably, don't want to subsidize the free agent's further decline with a hefty multi-year contract. He can probably play regularly in 1992 at his 1990-91 level, and his savvy could make him a valuable utility player afterwards.

DICKIE THON

Position: SS
Bats: R **Throws:** R
Ht: 5'11" **Wt:** 176

Opening Day Age: 33
Born: 6/20/58 in South Bend, IN
ML Seasons: 13

Overall Statistics

	G	AB	R	H	D	T	HR	RBI	SB	BB	SO	AVG
1991	146	539	44	136	18	4	9	44	11	25	84	.252
Career	1207	3929	443	1042	168	38	66	365	149	306	579	.265

Where He Hits the Ball

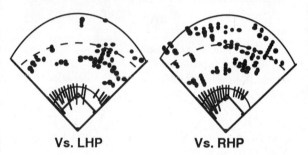

Vs. LHP   **Vs. RHP**

1991 Situational Stats

	AB	H	HR	RBI	AVG		AB	H	HR	RBI	AVG
Home	270	73	4	25	.270	LHP	205	53	2	14	.259
Road	269	63	5	19	.234	RHP	334	83	7	30	.249
Day	146	34	2	10	.233	Sc Pos	118	26	0	29	.220
Night	393	102	7	34	.260	Clutch	113	28	3	10	.248

1991 Rankings (National League)

→ 1st in lowest on-base average (.283) and least pitches seen per plate appearance (2.96)

→ 2nd least runs scored per time reached base (27.3%)

→ 3rd lowest percentage of pitches taken (44.0%)

→ 6th in lowest slugging percentage (.351) and lowest batting average with runners in scoring position (.220)

→ 7th lowest batting average (.252)

→ Led the Phillies in singles (105), caught stealing (5) and highest percentage of swings put into play (47.7%)

PITCHING:

Mitch Williams is hard to hit, hard to catch, and hard to figure. But what would you expect from a 30-save stopper whose nickname isn't the "Terminator," or some other confidence-giving appellation, but "Wild Thing"? For one thing, you would expect erratic performances, and the lefty hurler who once said "I pitch as if my hair is on fire" delivers, hurling marvelously for a game or a week and then spending an equal amount of time engrossed in a search for the strike zone. Williams actually allowed more walks (62) last year than he permitted hits (56).

Strictly a power pitcher, Williams has an excellent slider, but his best pitch is a 90-plus MPH fastball which moves like crazy. But while he throws impressive pitches, he also throws a lot of them. A 25-pitch inning in which he faces five batters and retires the side scoreless is Mitch's version of perfection. He's always on the edge, and as his 1987 and 1989 seasons showed, that can be a recipe for disaster as well as success.

FIELDING, HITTING, BASERUNNING:

Williams has a good move to first base and pitches confidently from the stretch, but his erratic control hinders his catchers' ability to catch and throw quickly. Last year, 12 of 14 runners successfully stole on him. Williams' delivery leaves him in an almost helpless fielding position, so it's no surprise that his lifetime fielding average is .852. Another one-of-a-kind Williams stat: he has more errors in his career (12) than he has putouts (10).

OVERALL:

Williams is one of a special breed of closers who rarely give up a hit, walk a lot of batters, throw huge numbers of pitches, and therefore are much more effective starting off an inning than coming in with men on base. In his good seasons, Williams strands the tying and go-ahead runs after he walks them aboard. In his poor seasons, they score. At 27, he figures to have plenty of both kinds of years left, but as a free agent, the Phils will have to shell out the big bucks to keep him.

MITCH WILLIAMS

Position: RP
Bats: L **Throws:** L
Ht: 6' 4" **Wt:** 205

Opening Day Age: 27
Born: 11/17/64 in Santa Ana, CA
ML Seasons: 6

Overall Statistics

	W	L	ERA	G	GS	Sv	IP	H	R	BB	SO	HR
1991	12	5	2.34	69	0	30	88.1	56	24	62	84	4
Career	35	36	3.33	436	3	114	511.0	367	213	384	486	35

How Often He Throws Strikes

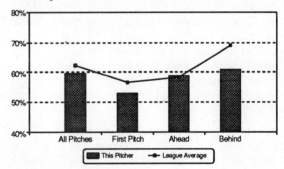

1991 Situational Stats

	W	L	ERA	Sv	IP		AB	H	HR	RBI	AVG
Home	9	2	2.11	17	47.0	LHB	68	13	0	6	.191
Road	3	3	2.61	13	41.1	RHB	240	43	4	21	.179
Day	3	4	2.03	10	31.0	Sc Pos	102	11	1	21	.108
Night	9	1	2.51	20	57.1	Clutch	245	44	4	25	.180

1991 Rankings (National League)

→ 1st in relief wins (12) and lowest batting average allowed in relief (.182)

→ 2nd in games finished (60), hit batsmen (8), save opportunities (39) and blown saves (9)

→ 3rd in saves (30), winning percentage (.706) and first batter efficiency (.145)

→ Led the Phillies in games pitches (69), saves, games finished, hit batsmen, save opportunities, winning percentage, save percentage (76.9%), blown saves, first batter efficiency, relief ERA (2.34), relief wins, lowest batting average allowed in relief, least baserunners per 9 innings in relief (12.8) and most strikeouts per 9 innings in relief (8.6)

DARRIN FLETCHER

Position: C
Bats: L **Throws:** R
Ht: 6' 1" **Wt:** 199

Opening Day Age: 25
Born: 10/3/66 in Elmhurst, IL
ML Seasons: 3

Overall Statistics

	G	AB	R	H	D	T	HR	RBI	SB	BB	SO	AVG
1991	46	136	5	31	8	0	1	12	0	5	15	.228
Career	62	167	9	38	9	0	2	15	0	7	21	.228

HITTING, FIELDING, BASERUNNING:

Acquired late in the 1990 season for pitcher Dennis Cook, ex-Dodger Darrin Fletcher capitalized on Darren Daulton's repeated rib injuries last season to confound critics who claimed that he could not handle pitchers and baserunners at the major league level. Unfortunately, Fletcher balanced his surge behind the plate with a downturn at bat.

Fletcher's AAA batting record indicates an ability to hit for average with gap power, but he hasn't duplicated that success at the major league level. The lefty batter did power enough inside pitches to put him on a 30-double pace over a full season. But major league hurlers soon learned that they didn't have to throw Fletcher strikes to get him out.

Defensively, Fletcher threw out runners more successfully than Daulton, and highlighted a season of defensive progress by catching Tommy Greene's no-hitter. His pitch selection has won the confidence of pitching coach Johnny Podres and the staff.

OVERALL:

As he turns 26 in 1992, Fletcher has all the attributes of a backup catcher: he is left-handed, throws well, and hasn't hit yet. If he can hit like the Mike LaValliere clone he was in the minors, Fletcher could be a solid major league catcher. One thing is for sure: catching behind "Injury, Thy name is Daulton," he will have plenty of opportunities to play.

JASON GRIMSLEY

Position: SP
Bats: R **Throws:** R
Ht: 6' 3" **Wt:** 182

Opening Day Age: 24
Born: 8/7/67 in Cleveland, TX
ML Seasons: 3

Overall Statistics

	W	L	ERA	G	GS	Sv	IP	H	R	BB	SO	HR
1991	1	7	4.87	12	12	0	61.0	54	34	41	42	4
Career	5	12	4.35	27	27	0	136.2	120	68	103	90	7

PITCHING, FIELDING, HITTING & HOLDING RUNNERS:

Jason Grimsley will be a starter for the Phillies as soon as he can throw strikes consistently. Unfortunately, neither the 24-year-old righthander nor team officials know what decade that will be.

Grimsley throws a sinking fastball and a straight curve, both of which dive down. Those pitches are tough to hit, but they're even tougher for Grimsley to control. Last year he threw 14 wild pitches, the third-highest total in the league, even though he worked only 61 innings. To complete the picture, Grimsley walked 41 batters, only one fewer than he struck out.

Manager Jim Fregosi and pitching coach Johnny Podres plan to stress a consistent release point for Grimsley, as they believe his wildness is a product of an inconsistent delivery. Grimsley also needs to speed up his delivery to the plate and improve his move to first base. His motion leaves him in poor position to field balls, but he covers first base alertly. Grimsley is no hitter, although he can bunt.

OVERALL:

With all of his faults, why do the Phils still see Grimsley as a major league starter? Because he is very hard to hit, possessing a major league fastball and curve. They believe they can smooth his motion and teach him a pickoff throw, polishing this rough gem into a pitcher. It'll take some work.

STEVE LAKE

Position: C
Bats: R **Throws:** R
Ht: 6' 1" **Wt:** 202

Opening Day Age: 35
Born: 3/14/57 in
Inglewood, CA
ML Seasons: 9

Overall Statistics

	G	AB	R	H	D	T	HR	RBI	SB	BB	SO	AVG
1991	58	158	12	36	4	1	1	11	0	2	26	.228
Career	412	952	75	227	33	5	12	93	1	38	132	.238

HITTING, FIELDING, BASERUNNING:

Now 35, Steve Lake is the very image of the number-two catcher. In nine seasons, he's never played more than 74 games or batted more than 179 times. His lifetime average is .238. Yet Lake sticks around, mostly because he can throw and handle pitchers.

In the lineup more last year because of Darren Daulton's injury, Lake saw his average drop to .228 after five straight seasons over .250. He was hitting about the same as always; the difference was that he was facing more righties, against whom he batted .188. Opposing teams continue to get Lake out with fastballs, challenging him inside and down.

Lake is far too slow to steal or take extra bases. His fiery demeanor expresses itself in his defense, where he is a great believer in challenging hitters and a constant goad to Phils' pitchers to throw strikes. His arm is one of the best around. While Lake only snared one-third of the 51 baserunners who attempted to steal on him in 1991, he has thrown out 118 of 229 during his career.

OVERALL:

Free agent Lake will be someone's backup catcher in '92 and '93, although his offense will slump if he winds up with a team whose number one is a right-handed hitter like himself. Used against lefties and to handle certain pitchers, he can be quite valuable.

STEVE SEARCY

Position: RP/SP
Bats: L **Throws:** L
Ht: 6' 1" **Wt:** 195

Opening Day Age: 27
Born: 6/4/64 in
Knoxville, TN
ML Seasons: 4

Overall Statistics

	W	L	ERA	G	GS	Sv	IP	H	R	BB	SO	HR
1991	3	3	6.59	34	5	0	71.0	81	56	44	53	10
Career	6	13	5.65	60	21	0	176.2	192	122	111	135	25

PITCHING, FIELDING, HITTING & HOLDING RUNNERS:

After watching him turn in an 8.41 ERA over the first half of last season, the Detroit Tigers decided to stop waiting for Steve Searcy to justify his "top prospect" status. When Detroit cut Searcy loose, Philadelphia GM Lee Thomas pounced on the 27-year-old lefthander, adding him to the Phils list of reclamation projects.

There's little question that Searcy has major league stuff. He has a good high 80s fastball that sinks with good movement, a slider which can be tough on left-handed hitters, and a change-up which he turns over a little bit. Controlling these pitches has always been a major problem for him -- he's walked 111 batters in only 176.2 major league innings -- and he's had problems with right-handed batters, who hit .302 against him last year. Tiger and Phil officials think he needs to pitch inside more; indeed, Searcy has never hit a batter in his major league career. Searcy has a good move to first, but it's compromised by a slow delivery to the plate. He can't hit, but he fields his position well.

OVERALL:

The Phils go into spring training hurting for pitching, and that gives Searcy a chance. Unless he takes back the inside half of home plate, however, long relief appears to be his best shot at making the team.

ORGANIZATION OVERVIEW:

Going back to the late '40s, the Phillies have a distinguished history in the field of player development. Hugh Alexander, possibly the greatest scout ever, is most closely associated with the Phils, and was in good part responsible for the 1980 World Champions. These facts make it even more sad to see the current state of the Phils' minor league system. Who was the last impact player they developed and kept -- Mike Schmidt, maybe? The Phils produce a representative number of players who make their major league roster, but it's hard to get excited about an organization whose "top prospect" a year ago was Mickey Morandini. The club's 1989 and 1990 first-round picks, both top-seven choices, have yet to make it past A ball. This is sad. What's Dallas Green's phone number?

ANDY ASHBY

Position: P | **Opening Day Age:** 24
Bats: R **Throws:** R | **Born:** 7/11/67 in Kansas
Ht: 6' 5" **Wt:** 180 | City, MO

Recent Statistics

	W	L	ERA	G	GS	Sv	IP	H	R	BB	SO	HR
91 AAA Scrantn-WB	11	11	3.46	26	26	0	161.1	144	78	60	113	12
91 NL Philadelphia	1	5	6.00	8	8	0	42.0	41	28	19	26	5

At 6-5, one would think Ashby would be able to dominate hitters, and he does -- at least when he can get the ball over the plate. Control is the big problem for this righty, who walked 19 in 42 innings (while going 1-5 with a 6.00 ERA) in his eight-start trial for the Phils. If he gets the ball over the plate he can win.

KIM BATISTE

Position: SS | **Opening Day Age:** 24
Bats: R **Throws:** R | **Born:** 3/15/68 in New
Ht: 6' 0" **Wt:** 178 | Orleans, LA

Recent Statistics

	G	AB	R	H	D	THR	RBI	SB	BB	SO	AVG
91 AAA Scranton-WB	122	462	54	135	25	6	1	41	18	11	72	.292
91 NL Philadelphia	10	27	2	6	0	0	0	1	0	1	8	.222
91 MLE	122	438	38	111	22	3	0	28	12	7	77	.253

Phillie shortstop Dickie Thon is aging and a free agent, and Batiste is the logical successor. Batiste's major league equivalents are not impressive, but he performed very well in the second half of last season. He's improved steadily over the last three years, both offensively and defensively, and should be the Phils' shortstop -- though probably not a star -- this year or next.

CLIFF BRANTLEY

Position: P | **Opening Day Age:** 23
Bats: R **Throws:** R | **Born:** 4/12/68 in Staten
Ht: 6' 2" **Wt:** 190 | Island, NY

Recent Statistics

	W	L	ERA	G	GS	Sv	IP	H	R	BB	SO	HR
91 AA Reading	4	3	1.94	11	11	0	69.2	50	17	25	51	3
91 AAA Scrantn-WB	2	4	3.80	8	8	0	47.1	44	26	25	28	2
91 NL Philadelphia	2	2	3.41	6	5	0	31.2	26	12	19	25	0

The Phils' second round draft pick in 1986, Brantley struggled throughout his professional career until 1991. He throws hard and generally keeps the ball low in the strike zone, yielding few home runs but having some trouble keeping the ball in the strike zone. Brantley made a good impression with the Phils last fall . . . but had trouble throwing strikes. Nonetheless, he has a chance this year.

BRAULIO CASTILLO

Position: OF | **Opening Day Age:** 23
Bats: R **Throws:** R | **Born:** 5/13/68 in Elias
Ht: 6' 0" **Wt:** 160 | Pina, DR

Recent Statistics

	G	AB	R	H	D	THR	RBI	SB	BB	SO	AVG
91 AA San Antonio	87	297	49	89	19	3	8	48	22	32	73	.300
91 AAA Scranton-WB	16	60	14	21	9	1	0	15	2	6	7	.350
91 NL Philadelphia	28	52	3	9	3	0	0	2	1	1	15	.173
91 MLE	103	338	44	91	23	1	5	44	15	23	86	.269

Castillo came to the Phils in the Roger McDowell deal, and got a golden opportunity in September when Lenny Dykstra went out for the year. He didn't do much, and the consensus is that Castillo, who's played only two seasons of professional ball, needs more seasoning. Castillo, who has had alcohol problems, appears to be taking his major league prospects seriously, learning and taking notes. He has a chance, but needs a lot of work.

TYLER GREEN

Position: P | **Opening Day Age:** 22
Bats: R **Throws:** R | **Born:** 2/18/70 in
Ht: 6' 5" **Wt:** 185 | Springfield, OH

Recent Statistics

	W	L	ERA	G	GS	Sv	IP	H	R	BB	SO	HR
91 A Batavia	1	0	1.20	3	3	0	15.0	7	2	6	19	0
91 A Clearwater	2	0	1.38	2	2	0	13.0	3	2	8	20	0

A College World Series star at Wichita State, Green signed late last year and got into only five games at Batavia and Clearwater. He blew hitters away, however, and the Phillies are so high on him that it shouldn't be long before he's in the Philadelphia rotation. Green's fastball is 90 MPH at best, and he relies on a variety of pitches. It would be a stretch to say that Green will make it to the majors in 1992 -- some shoulder problems late in the year are a worry -- but it's certainly possible.

PITCHING:

The main thing keeping Stan Belinda from becoming a first-rate closer is consistency. Belinda can be overpowering, as shown by his allowing only 50 hits and striking out 71 batters in 78.1 innings last season. He limited opponents to a .184 batting average. Despite those impressive numbers, he was only 7-5 with 16 saves and an ERA of 3.45. Belinda will be dominating in one appearance; in the next, he'll walk in the winning run or give up a game-winning home run.

A sidewinder, Belinda is a classic power reliever. He reaches back and tries to blow people away with a 91 MPH fastball. He is extremely difficult for right-handed hitters because of his delivery, but he needs to develop a consistent breaking pitch. He has experimented with a few different pitches, and the split-fingered fastball appears to be his best bet -- some of his most impressive outings came when his splitter was working.

Belinda's control is still spotty, and he walked over four batters per nine innings in 1991. He must get the first pitch over for a strike more often to be truly effective. He continually puts himself in a hole by falling behind in the count. On the other hand, he is durable and capable of pitching on back-to-back days if necessary.

HOLDING RUNNERS, FIELDING, HITTING:

Belinda needs to work on holding runners and fielding his position. As a hitter, he's forgettable. He is hitless in 12 career at-bats. However, he did draw a bases-loaded walk in 1991 for his first career RBI.

OVERALL:

With more experience and consistency, Belinda has a chance to be an outstanding closer. Once an amateur boxer, he brings that mentality to the mound. He enjoys the challenge of a pressure situation and rarely gets rattled. Belinda is still young and should grow into the closer's role on a club crying for a bullpen hammer. His NLCS performance against Atlanta -- a win and five scoreless innings -- should help his confidence.

STAN BELINDA

Position: RP
Bats: R **Throws:** R
Ht: 6' 3" **Wt:** 200

Opening Day Age: 25
Born: 8/6/66 in Huntingdon, PA
ML Seasons: 3

Overall Statistics

	W	L	ERA	G	GS	Sv	IP	H	R	BB	SO	HR
1991	7	5	3.45	60	0	16	78.1	50	30	35	71	10
Career	10	10	3.67	123	0	24	147.0	111	61	66	136	14

How Often He Throws Strikes

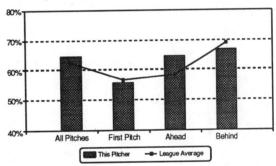

1991 Situational Stats

	W	L	ERA	Sv	IP		AB	H	HR	RBI	AVG
Home	2	1	1.94	13	41.2	LHB	123	25	4	12	.203
Road	5	4	5.15	3	36.2	RHB	149	25	6	26	.168
Day	2	1	4.50	4	20.0	Sc Pos	81	15	3	30	.185
Night	5	4	3.09	12	58.1	Clutch	159	30	5	23	.189

1991 Rankings (National League)

→ 2nd in first batter efficiency (.120) and lowest batting average allowed in relief (.184)

→ 5th in save percentage (80.0%) and relief wins (7)

→ 8th in least baserunners allowed per 9 innings in relief (10.2) and most strikeouts per 9 innings in relief (8.2)

→ Led the Pirates in save percentage, first batter efficiency, relief wins, relief innings (78.1), lowest batting average allowed in relief, least baserunners allowed per 9 innings in relief and most strikeouts per 9 innings in relief

HITTING:

Jay Bell is rapidly emerging into one of the top power-hitting shortstops in baseball. In 1991, only his second full major league season, Bell showed outstanding power. He hit 16 home runs, belted 56 extra-base hits and drove in 67 runs from the number-two spot in the Pirates' batting order.

Bell rests his bat on his right shoulder as the pitcher goes into his delivery. It may be a bit unorthodox, but it is Bell's way of keeping his bat back; he still generates good bat speed. He loves fastballs from the middle of the plate in and can turn on them. Breaking balls used to give him fits, but he is getting better in that area. He still strikes out a bit much, mainly on high-and-away fastballs or low-and-away breaking pitches.

Though a blossoming power hitter, Bell is excellent at doing the little things necessary as a number-two hitter. He is an outstanding bunter and has laid down 69 sacrifices over the past two seasons. He also does a good job of hitting behind runners. Bell concentrates more in clutch situations as shown by his 12-for-29 performance in last year's National League Championship Series. He is a much better hitter when there are men on base.

BASERUNNING:

Bell has good speed and uses intelligence on the base paths. He is aggressive but does not take foolish risks. He can steal a base and is good for about 10 a year.

FIELDING:

Bell is also becoming one of the game's steadiest defensive shortstops. Despite below-average range, he has a very strong arm and knows how to position himself. The glue of the Pirates' infield, he occasionally loses his concentration on routine plays, particularly potential double play grounders.

OVERALL:

Bell is on the verge of stardom. He is a rare power-hitting shortstop with sound fundamentals and above-average fielding ability. Only 26, he has many good years ahead of him.

JAY BELL

Position: SS
Bats: R **Throws:** R
Ht: 6' 1" **Wt:** 185

Opening Day Age: 26
Born: 12/11/65 in Eglin AFB, FL
ML Seasons: 6

Overall Statistics

	G	AB	R	H	D	T	HR	RBI	SB	BB	SO	AVG
1991	157	608	96	164	32	8	16	67	10	52	99	.270
Career	510	1812	262	460	89	20	30	184	31	167	342	.254

Where He Hits the Ball

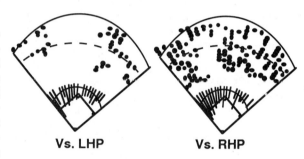

Vs. LHP   Vs. RHP

1991 Situational Stats

	AB	H	HR	RBI	AVG		AB	H	HR	RBI	AVG
Home	303	85	7	33	.281	LHP	194	56	6	28	.289
Road	305	79	9	34	.259	RHP	414	108	10	39	.261
Day	158	47	3	18	.297	Sc Pos	140	40	4	49	.286
Night	450	117	13	49	.260	Clutch	92	26	3	12	.283

1991 Rankings (National League)

- ➡ 1st in sacrifice bunts (30) and errors at shortstop (24)
- ➡ 3rd in at-bats (608) and plate appearances (697)
- ➡ 4th in bunts in play (34)
- ➡ 5th in games (157) and most runs scored per time reached base (43.6%)
- ➡ Led the Pirates in at-bats, singles (108), triples (8), sacrifice bunts, hit by pitch (4), strikeouts (99), pitches seen (2,519), plate appearances, games, most runs scored per time reached base, batting average on a 3-1 count (.563) and bunts in play

CLUTCH HITTER

BARRY BONDS

Position: LF
Bats: L **Throws:** L
Ht: 6' 1" **Wt:** 190

Opening Day Age: 27
Born: 7/24/64 in Riverside, CA
ML Seasons: 6

HITTING:

Barry Bonds proved in 1991 that his outstanding 1990 season was not an aberration. Though he did not quite match his incredible '90 numbers, he had a second straight MVP-caliber season.

Bonds does it all. He is a power hitter with an outstanding on-base percentage. His extremely quick swing has no wasted motion, and he is strong enough to take the ball out to all fields. His 4-for-27 performance in last year's National League Championship series notwithstanding, Bonds comes through in the clutch. When he is hot, there is little a pitcher can do: his quick wrists enable him to turn on any fastball and he can punish breaking balls.

Bonds is normally a patient hitter and has one of the sharpest eyes in the game. With this reputation established, he gets away with taking the closest of borderline pitches. At times, he will get frustrated from constantly being pitched around. In those periods, he will chase breaking balls in the dirt. Bonds has improved in clutch situations. In 1991, he hit .345 with men in scoring position and .338 in late-and-close situations.

BASERUNNING:

Bonds is fast and has become a much better percentage base stealer with experience. He continues to improve at reading pitchers and he is good for 40-50 steals a season at a success rate over 75%. He always looks to take the extra base.

FIELDING:

The best defensive left fielder in baseball, Bonds has outstanding range and is the master of racing to the line to reduce doubles into singles. He can also track down almost anything hit to the gap in left-center. His only drawback is his average arm, but he rarely misses a cut-off man or throws to the wrong base.

OVERALL:

Bonds has gone from potential to bona fide superstar in the past two seasons. He was a close runner-up in the '91 MVP balloting, and many people thought he deserved to win. When talking about the game's top players, he is at the top of the list.

Overall Statistics

	G	AB	R	H	D	T	HR	RBI	SB	BB	SO	AVG
1991	153	510	95	149	28	5	25	116	43	107	73	.292
Career	870	3111	563	837	184	31	142	453	212	484	521	.269

Where He Hits the Ball

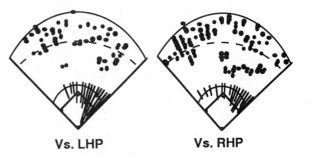

Vs. LHP   **Vs. RHP**

1991 Situational Stats

	AB	H	HR	RBI	AVG		AB	H	HR	RBI	AVG
Home	261	71	12	51	.272	LHP	201	57	7	39	.284
Road	249	78	13	65	.313	RHP	309	92	18	77	.298
Day	131	34	4	27	.260	Sc Pos	148	51	8	87	.345
Night	379	115	21	89	.303	Clutch	80	27	2	16	.338

1991 Rankings (National League)

→ 1st in on-base average (.410) and on-base average vs. right-handed pitchers (.425)

→ 2nd in RBIs (116), sacrifice flies (13), walks (107), intentional walks (25) and fielding percentage in left field (.991)

→ 3rd in times on base (260)

→ Led the Pirates in home runs (25), RBIs, sacrifice flies, stolen bases (43), caught stealing (13), walks, intentional walks, hit by pitch (4), slugging percentage (.514), on-base average (.410), HR frequency (20.4 ABs per HR), batting average with runners in scoring position (.345), batting average in the clutch (.338) and steals of third (9)

HITTING:

Bobby Bonilla sacrificed a little power for average last season. However, he was still one of the top RBI men in the game. The big switch-hitter decided to cut down on his swing and not try to pull every pitch. The results were that he walked more and improved his batting average to a career-high .302 while his home runs declined; after three consecutive seasons of 24 or more homers, his total slipped to 18 in '91. However, Bonilla posted career-highs in on-base percentage (.391) and walks (90). He also retained gap power; his 44 doubles led the league last season.

Bonilla believes in finding his pitch, preferably a fastball, and hitting it hard. He is strong enough to take any pitch out of the park, but he is also patient enough to work the count in his favor. Bonilla is a better overall hitter from the left side of the plate, but generates more power as a righty -- he is not an easy out from either side. Bonilla is a big run producer, notching 100 RBIs in three of the past four seasons. He hit .308 with men in scoring position last season.

BASERUNNING:

Bonilla moves well for a big man, though a constant battle with his weight (240 pounds) may soon reduce his speed. He rarely steals but is agile enough to take the extra base when he has a chance.

FIELDING:

Because of injuries to third baseman Jeff King and John Wehner, Bonilla spent much time shuttling between right field and third in 1991. After leading the league in errors as a third baseman in 1988 and 1989, Bonilla again committed 13, one more than Chris Sabo made in 750 more innings. He has a strong arm but has some trouble judging fly balls in the outfield. Still, he is less of an overall liability in right.

OVERALL:

Bonilla was eligible for free agency at the end of last season. Strapped by a low budget, it was doubtful that the Pirates could afford to keep him. Wherever he goes, he will make a sudden impact in the middle of a lineup.

BOBBY BONILLA

Position: RF/3B
Bats: B **Throws:** R
Ht: 6' 3" **Wt:** 240

Opening Day Age: 29
Born: 2/23/63 in New York, NY
ML Seasons: 6

Overall Statistics

	G	AB	R	H	D	T	HR	RBI	SB	BB	SO	AVG
1991	157	577	102	174	44	6	18	100	2	90	67	.302
Career	918	3294	510	931	201	37	116	526	28	397	497	.283

Where He Hits the Ball

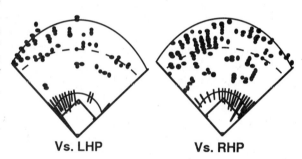

Vs. LHP   Vs. RHP

1991 Situational Stats

	AB	H	HR	RBI	AVG		AB	H	HR	RBI	AVG
Home	285	88	9	51	.309	LHP	232	66	14	47	.284
Road	292	86	9	49	.295	RHP	345	108	4	53	.313
Day	153	52	8	31	.340	Sc Pos	159	49	6	75	.308
Night	424	122	10	69	.288	Clutch	83	22	3	14	.265

1991 Rankings (National League)

- → 1st in doubles (44)
- → 2nd in times on base (266) and on-base average vs. right-handed pitchers (.418)
- → 3rd in sacrifice flies (11)
- → 4th in runs (102), hits (174), on-base average (.391) and batting average vs. right-handed pitchers (.313)
- → 5th in walks (90), plate appearances (680), games (157) and batting average on an 0-2 count (.304)
- → Led the Pirates in batting average (.302), runs, hits, doubles, total bases (284), times on base, games, batting average vs. right-handed pitchers and batting average at home (.309)

HITTING:

The adjustments Steve Buechele has made as a hitter are finally paying off. The payoff has just been a little later arriving than expected. During spring training of 1990, while still with the Texas Rangers, Buechele concentrated on staying back on pitches, feeling he was lunging too often. However, a broken wrist he suffered in April effectively wiped out that season.

The new-look Buechele showed his stuff in 1991, even after being traded to the Pirates on Aug. 30. He posted career highs in the triple crown categories with a combined .262 average, 22 home runs and 85 RBI. Buechele is a fastball hitter, but his new approach helps him make better contact on breaking pitches. Righthanders still have success by throwing breaking balls away -- Buechele's weakness has always been an inability to hit righties. He showed noticeable improvement in 1991, hitting .251 against them with good power.

Buechele strikes out a lot, 97 times last season. However, he shows decent patience, is a good bunter and a good hitter when behind in the count. He hit well with runners in scoring position, batting .302 with eight homers.

BASERUNNING:

Buechele is not a base stealer, getting thrown out in all five 1991 tries. He has average speed and is aggressive on the bases. However, he will occasionally run himself into an out.

FIELDING:

Defense has always been Buechele's strong point; he has quick reflexes and a strong arm. Before being traded to Pittsburgh, he set an American League single-season record for fielding percentage with just three errors and a .991 mark. He is a little unsure on artificial turf, though, committing four errors in 31 games with the Pirates. He also has experience at second base and can play shortstop in a pinch.

OVERALL:

Buechele found himself in the right place at the right time. He went on the open market as a free agent following a career year in 1991. With so many teams searching for a quality third baseman, he figured to be an attractive player.

STEVE BUECHELE

Position: 3B/2B
Bats: R **Throws:** R
Ht: 6' 2" **Wt:** 200

Opening Day Age: 30
Born: 9/26/61 in Lancaster, CA
ML Seasons: 7

Overall Statistics

	G	AB	R	H	D	T	HR	RBI	SB	BB	SO	AVG
1991	152	530	74	139	22	3	22	85	0	49	97	.262
Career	911	2813	353	679	120	14	98	357	14	254	548	.241

Where He Hits the Ball

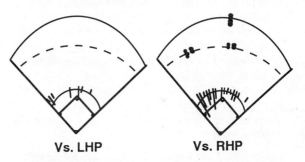

Vs. LHP   Vs. RHP

1991 Situational Stats

	AB	H	HR	RBI	AVG		AB	H	HR	RBI	AVG
Home	251	69	9	32	.275	LHP	131	39	9	26	.298
Road	279	70	13	53	.251	RHP	399	100	13	59	.251
Day	85	19	4	15	.224	Sc Pos	149	45	8	66	.302
Night	445	120	18	70	.270	Clutch	108	27	3	21	.250

1991 Rankings (National League)

➡ Did not rank near the top or bottom in any category

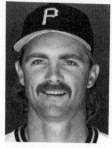

WORKHORSE

DOUG DRABEK

Position: SP
Bats: R **Throws:** R
Ht: 6' 1" **Wt:** 185

Opening Day Age: 29
Born: 7/25/62 in
Victoria, TX
ML Seasons: 6

PITCHING:

After winning the Cy Young Award in 1990, the only direction Doug Drabek could head in 1991 was down. That's exactly the way he went, but the fall looked worse than it really was. After going 22-6 with a 2.76 ERA in '90, Drabek's record dropped to 15-14 last season. However, luck was not on his side -- he lost six games by one run despite receiving the eighth-highest run support in the league. Drabek's bad luck continued in the playoffs, when he was 1-1 despite allowing only one run in 15 innings. He lost a memorable 1-0 heartbreaker to Steve Avery in Game Six of the NLCS.

After winning a record $3.35 million settlement in arbitration following the 1990 season, Drabek admittedly put pressure on himself at the start of the year. He tried to overpower people and make every pitch perfect. Drabek is at his best when he mixes his pitches and changes speeds. His fastball is good, though not overpowering, while his slider and curveball are outstanding. He also mixes in an adequate change-up. When he consistently gets both breaking pitches over, he can shut anyone down.

Drabek isn't one to pile up strikeouts, but he gets ground ball after ground ball when he is on his game. He is the Pirates' workhorse, logging 234.2 innings in 1991, fourth-most in the NL. He is also a good big-game pitcher, winning the National League East clincher each of the past two seasons. His playoff performance did nothing to undermine that reputation.

HOLDING RUNNERS, FIELDING, HITTING:

With hard work, Drabek has become more adept at holding runners, but still allowed 29 runners out of 44 to steal safely. He does not beat himself in the field. A good athlete, he is quick off the mound in fielding bunts and covering first base. He is also not an automatic out at the plate and has occasional extra-base power.

OVERALL:

With a little bit of luck, Drabek could have been a 20-game winner again in 1991. He is a master craftsman who fully understands the art of pitching. As long as he doesn't try to become a strike-out king, he is always a threat to win 20.

Overall Statistics

	W	L	ERA	G	GS	Sv	IP	H	R	BB	SO	HR
1991	15	14	3.07	35	35	0	234.2	245	92	62	142	16
Career	84	59	3.19	192	183	0	1237.2	1135	486	333	719	108

How Often He Throws Strikes

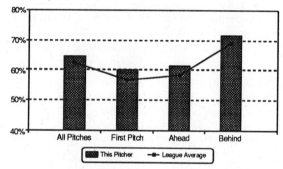

1991 Situational Stats

	W	L	ERA	Sv	IP		AB	H	HR	RBI	AVG
Home	9	8	2.40	0	131.0	LHB	530	152	8	49	.287
Road	6	6	3.91	0	103.2	RHB	364	93	8	30	.255
Day	5	4	3.35	0	78.0	Sc Pos	210	51	3	61	.243
Night	10	10	2.93	0	156.2	Clutch	72	23	2	8	.319

1991 Rankings (National League)

→ 2nd in hits allowed (245), ERA at home (2.40) and errors by a pitcher (5)

→ 3rd in losses (14) and most stolen bases allowed (29)

→ 4th in innings (234.2) and highest batting average allowed (.274)

→ 5th in games started (35), batters faced (977), runners caught stealing (15) and highest on-base average allowed (.321)

→ Led the Pirates in losses, games started, innings, hits allowed, batters faced, walks allowed (62), strikeouts (142), pitches thrown (3,507), stolen bases allowed, runners caught stealing and ERA at home

HITTING:

On the brink of living up to being the top choice in the 1986 draft, Jeff King's future is again questionable. King finally started to shed the "wasted draft pick" label in the second half of 1990, his first full major-league season. He hit 14 homers, including 11 in the second half of the season.

However, King's status is again cloudy after playing in only 33 games in 1991 because of a lower back strain. He went on the disabled list for good on June 13. The Pirates felt rest would cure the problem, but King faced back surgery in late October. The injury came at the worst possible time in King's career. Based on his second-half performance of '90, he is a player capable of producing 20 homers and 80 RBIs.

King is basically a straight-away hitter with power from gap-to-gap. He rarely pulls the ball. One knock on him is that he worries so much about power that he sacrifices batting average and on-base percentage. More than anything, King needs to relax and stop trying to live up to being the number-one pick. He strives so much for perfection that he is often too hard on himself in times of failure.

BASERUNNING:

King has average speed but good instincts. He is not a stolen base threat but looks to take an extra base when outfielders are napping. He stole three bases in his 33 games last season.

FIELDING:

King is a solid defensive third baseman who has shown signs of greater improvement. He has good first-step quickness and goes toward the line extremely well. Shoulder problems limit his arm strength but he compensates with accuracy.

OVERALL:

King has an unsettled future. If he overcomes his back problem, he has a chance to be a good run-producer. If not, his injuries can take the blame for his wash-out as the nation's top amateur choice.

JEFF KING

Position: 3B
Bats: R **Throws:** R
Ht: 6' 1" **Wt:** 185

Opening Day Age: 27
Born: 12/26/64 in Marion, IN
ML Seasons: 3

Overall Statistics

	G	AB	R	H	D	T	HR	RBI	SB	BB	SO	AVG
1991	33	109	16	26	1	1	4	18	3	14	15	.239
Career	235	695	93	159	31	5	23	90	10	55	99	.229

Where He Hits the Ball

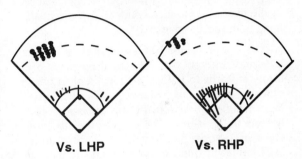

Vs. LHP   Vs. RHP

1991 Situational Stats

	AB	H	HR	RBI	AVG		AB	H	HR	RBI	AVG
Home	63	14	3	10	.222	LHP	31	10	1	4	.323
Road	46	12	1	8	.261	RHP	78	16	3	14	.205
Day	30	8	0	4	.267	Sc Pos	28	8	1	13	.286
Night	79	18	4	14	.228	Clutch	16	4	1	3	.250

1991 Rankings (National League)

→ Did not rank near the top or bottom in any category

PITCHING:

Bob Kipper spent three years quietly establishing himself as one of the top left-handed set-up relievers in the National League. In 1991, everything fell apart. His ERA soared to 4.65 and opponents hit .276 against him last season. He also surrendered seven home runs in 60 innings, prompting some Pirate fans to tag him with the disparaging nickname "Round-Tripper" Kipper. The longball has always been a problem for him.

After being converted from a starter in 1988, Kipper adjusted well to the bullpen. When pitching well, he mixes a good fastball with above-average breaking pitches and a decent change-up. He usually has pretty good control of each; however, too many fastballs went right down the heart of the plate and too many sliders and curveballs hung in the strike zone in 1991.

Kipper's top attribute has been his ability to get left-handed hitters out. He will drop down and throw sidearm to lefties, getting them to chase breaking pitches low and away. However, lefties tagged him last season, hitting .321 with four homers in 78 at-bats. The tougher the situation, the worse Kipper performed. The opposition hit .317 both with runners on base and runners in scoring position. Kipper does have durability and poise. Those were about the only parts of his game that did not leave him in 1991.

HOLDING RUNNERS, FIELDING, HITTING:

As a lefty, Kipper uses his natural advantage in holding baserunners. He pays close attention to runners and they do not get a big jump. He is also an adequate fielder. He isn't a factor when he gets a rare at-bat, as evidenced by a .137 career average.

OVERALL:

Kipper was able to file for free agency after last season. Since everyone seems to need lefties, he figured to draw some interest. After seven seasons, Kipper is still only 27 and young enough to bounce back. However, his poor 1991 probably cost him some money.

BOB KIPPER

Position: RP
Bats: R **Throws:** L
Ht: 6' 2" **Wt:** 185

Opening Day Age: 27
Born: 7/8/64 in Aurora, IL
ML Seasons: 7

Overall Statistics

	W	L	ERA	G	GS	Sv	IP	H	R	BB	SO	HR
1991	2	2	4.65	52	0	4	60.0	66	34	22	38	7
Career	24	34	4.33	246	45	11	523.1	487	278	203	347	73

How Often He Throws Strikes

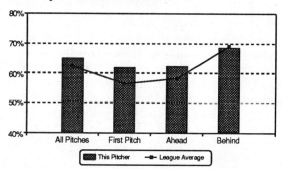

1991 Situational Stats

	W	L	ERA	Sv	IP		AB	H	HR	RBI	AVG
Home	1	1	6.75	1	30.2	LHB	78	25	4	15	.321
Road	1	1	2.45	3	29.1	RHB	161	41	3	17	.255
Day	0	0	5.24	1	22.1	Sc Pos	63	20	3	25	.317
Night	2	2	4.30	3	37.2	Clutch	78	21	3	14	.269

1991 Rankings (National League)

→ 2nd highest relief ERA (4.65)

→ 4th highest batting average allowed in relief (.276)

→ 7th most baserunners allowed per 9 innings in relief (13.2)

→ Led the Pirates in lowest percentage of inherited runners scored (27.3%)

PITCHING:

Bill Landrum is baseball's version of the disappearing man. In the first half of a season, he is a dominating closer. In the second half, he seldom gets a save opportunity. Such has been the case in each of the past two seasons, though Landrum has led the Pirates in saves for three straight years. Before the All-Star break in 1990-91, he converted 27 of 30 save opportunities. Post All-Star, he has cashed in on just three of eight.

Shoulder problems hampered Landrum's effectiveness and availability in both seasons. Though not serious enough to require surgery, he has often been unavailable to pitch on consecutive days. As the season progresses, Landrum loses the pop off his 90+ MPH fastball. Without his best pitch, he becomes very hittable.

There is a chance that Landrum may become a starter. He has put a lot of work into developing his breaking and offspeed pitches in the past year. In any role, the Pirates have themselves a bargain -- they signed Landrum as a six-year minor-league free agent before the 1988 season. After having posted two saves in parts of three seasons with Cincinnati and the Cubs, he has shut the door on 56 wins in the past three seasons. In a shaky bullpen, he has been as reliable as anyone when healthy.

HOLDING RUNNERS, FIELDING, HITTING:

In 1989, when he saved 26 games, Landrum rarely had to worry about holding runners. Last season, however, Landrum allowed nine of 10 to steal safely. He has a below-average move and runners take liberties. He is an adequate fielder but no threat with the bat.

OVERALL:

Injuries have taken their toll on Landrum in the past two seasons. When healthy, he is still effective. However, he hasn't been able to handle the load of a full-time closer. At this point, a lot of baseball people feel he would better in a middle relief or set-up role -- and a shot as a starter is another possibility.

BILL LANDRUM

Position: RP
Bats: R **Throws:** R
Ht: 6' 2" **Wt:** 205

Opening Day Age: 33
Born: 8/17/58 in Columbia, SC
ML Seasons: 6

Overall Statistics

	W	L	ERA	G	GS	Sv	IP	H	R	BB	SO	HR
1991	4	4	3.18	61	0	17	76.1	76	32	19	45	4
Career	17	12	3.13	232	2	58	319.2	315	126	109	197	14

How Often He Throws Strikes

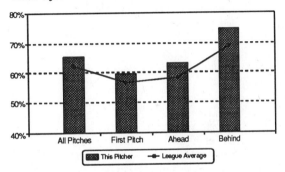

1991 Situational Stats

	W	L	ERA	Sv	IP		AB	H	HR	RBI	AVG
Home	1	1	1.80	9	35.0	LHB	139	38	2	18	.273
Road	3	3	4.35	8	41.1	RHB	162	38	2	18	.235
Day	0	2	1.65	2	16.1	Sc Pos	82	23	0	32	.280
Night	4	2	3.60	15	60.0	Clutch	175	43	3	19	.246

1991 Rankings (National League)

→ 5th in first batter efficiency (.155)

→ 6th in save percentage (77.3%)

→ 7th in saves (17) and games finished (43)

→ Led the Pirates in games pitched (61), saves, games finished, save opportunities (22), blown saves (5) and relief ERA (3.18)

HITTING:

Mike LaValliere is a good contact hitter at the bottom of the Pirate batting order. LaValliere has minimal power and the next leg hit he gets will be his first. However, he is a good major league hitter because he keeps the ball in play and rarely strikes out.

Though he tied a career high with three home runs last season, LaValliere has no illusions about his power. He just tries to lay his bat on the ball and find a hole somewhere with his compact swing. He has become particularly adept at dumping outside pitches the other way into short left field. Pitchers must be careful not to lay many fat pitches over the heart of the plate.

LaValliere can surprise by turning on an occasional fastball. Normally a dependable clutch hitter, LaValliere batted just .108 in late-and-close situations last season. However, he is a .429 career hitter with the bases loaded and a tough out in any situation.

BASERUNNING:

LaValliere lost 20 pounds before the 1991 season and it may have paid off. He stole two bases, his first since 1988, and legged out two triples to double his career total. Actually, LaValliere is among the slowest players in the game. He takes it one base at a time.

FIELDING:

Four knee operations have quietly eroded LaValliere's defensive skills. He threw out only 30 percent of would-be base stealers in 1991. Though no longer the Gold Glove winner of 1987, LaValliere is still a plus behind the plate. He takes charge, calls a good game and has the total confidence of his pitching staff.

OVERALL:

LaValliere, though no great star, is a fine major league catcher. Over the past two seasons, he has combined with platoon-mate Don Slaught to form one of the better catching corps in the game. Good catchers are hard to find and LaValliere was a free agent at the end of last season. The Pirates knew that they had to find a way to keep him.

MIKE LaVALLIERE

Position: C
Bats: L **Throws:** R
Ht: 5'10" **Wt:** 210

Opening Day Age: 31
Born: 8/18/60 in Charlotte, NC
ML Seasons: 8

Overall Statistics

	G	AB	R	H	D	T	HR	RBI	SB	BB	SO	AVG
1991	108	336	25	97	11	2	3	41	2	33	27	.289
Career	641	1841	144	499	84	4	14	214	5	244	179	.271

Where He Hits the Ball

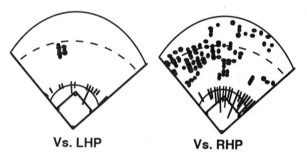

Vs. LHP   Vs. RHP

1991 Situational Stats

	AB	H	HR	RBI	AVG		AB	H	HR	RBI	AVG
Home	163	54	1	22	.331	LHP	54	12	0	14	.222
Road	173	43	2	19	.249	RHP	282	85	3	27	.301
Day	100	34	1	16	.340	Sc Pos	95	25	1	39	.263
Night	236	63	2	25	.267	Clutch	37	4	0	3	.108

1991 Rankings (National League)

→ 1st in lowest percentage of extra bases taken as a runner (12.0%)

→ 6th most GDPs per GDP situation (17.2%)

→ 8th in batting average with the bases loaded (.417)

→ Led the Pirates in batting average with the bases loaded

→ Led NL catchers in highest fielding percentage (.998)

HITTING:

From an offensive standpoint, what you see is what you get with Jose Lind. After four full years as a major league regular, Lind's level of production is a .260-.265 average with a decent number of doubles, few homers or walks and a fair RBI count from the number-eight spot.

Lind, who holds the bat with his hands slightly apart, has not shown improvement as a hitter. He insists on hitting everything to the opposite field, even thigh-high fastballs over the middle of the plate. The opposite-field approach makes him a decent contact hitter but robs him of any power he might generate. He is strong enough to pull the ball if he so desires.

Lind is an adequate bunter and decent on the hit-and-run. However, he grounded into 19 double plays with his propensity for making ground ball contact. Once a patient hitter, Lind became overanxious at times in 1991. For an eighth-place hitter, though, he is a decent run producer. He drove in a career-high 54 runs in 1991 and hit .280 with runners in scoring position.

BASERUNNING:

Though his athletic ability is well known in Pittsburgh, Lind does not take full advantage of his good speed. After stealing 15 bases in each of his first two full seasons, he has combined for that many in the past two years. He is an adequate baserunner but does not take as many extra bases as he should.

FIELDING:

Lind is peerless as a defensive second baseman. He gets to almost any ball hit between first and second and has an outstanding arm. His leaping ability rivals that of an NBA player. Lind is also a master at turning the double play with his soft hands and quick feet. He always plays under control and makes the routine plays.

OVERALL:

Though Lind could be more productive with the bat, his dazzling glove work fits into any lineup. He makes up for his offensive weaknesses by taking away countless hits over the course of a season.

JOSE LIND

Position: 2B
Bats: R **Throws:** R
Ht: 5'11" **Wt:** 175

Opening Day Age: 27
Born: 5/1/64 in Toabaja, Puerto Rico
ML Seasons: 5

Overall Statistics

	G	AB	R	H	D	T	HR	RBI	SB	BB	SO	AVG
1991	150	502	53	133	16	6	3	54	7	30	56	.265
Career	644	2348	254	607	97	22	8	210	47	154	259	.259

Where He Hits the Ball

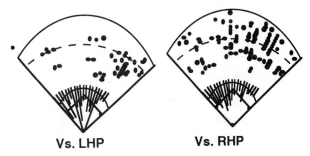

Vs. LHP   Vs. RHP

1991 Situational Stats

	AB	H	HR	RBI	AVG		AB	H	HR	RBI	AVG
Home	262	64	2	30	.244	LHP	167	45	2	15	.269
Road	240	69	1	24	.287	RHP	335	88	1	39	.263
Day	119	36	0	13	.303	Sc Pos	118	33	1	47	.280
Night	383	97	3	41	.253	Clutch	80	20	0	4	.250

1991 Rankings (National League)

- ➡ 2nd highest fielding percentage at second base (.989)
- ➡ 3rd in GDPs (19), lowest slugging percentage (.339) and least pitches seen per plate appearance (3.26)
- ➡ 4th lowest HR frequency (167 ABs per HR)
- ➡ Led the Pirates in singles (108), GDPs, groundball/flyball ratio (1.7), lowest percentage of swings that missed (14.2%) and highest percentage of swings put into play (48.9%)
- ➡ Led NL second basemen in GDPs

PITCHING:

In 1991, the question "Whatever happened to Roger Mason, one-time hot prospect with the Tigers and Giants in the mid-1980s?" was answered. He finally made it big in the major leagues, pitching for a division champion with the Pirates after pitching just 1.1 inning in the majors since 1987. Needing any bullpen help they could get, the Pirates called up Mason from their Class AAA Buffalo farm club in early August. They got more from the journeyman than they could have ever hoped.

After compiling a solid 9-5 record as a starter and reliever with Buffalo, Mason was superb out of the Pirates' bullpen. He went 3-2 with three saves. He also showed Houdini-like ability in allowing just one of 21 inherited baserunners to score and by limiting hitters to a .200 average with runners in scoring position and just .197 in clutch situations.

Mason has found his niche as a short reliever. He relies on using just two pitches, a 90 MPH tailing fastball and a good split-fingered pitch. Though Mason is strong enough to keep his velocity during a nine-inning stint, the lack of an effective third pitch has always hampered him. He throws a slider, which acts more as a cut fastball. Mason also found the good control he lacked the first time around, walking only six in 29.2 innings in 1991, though the splitter often dives into the dirt.

HOLDING RUNNERS, FIELDING, HITTING:

Tall and gangly, Mason is awkward in the field and doesn't have a good move to first. However, he pays close attention to runners and the game situation. He has only an .075 lifetime batting average but is a decent bunter.

OVERALL:

Slowed by elbow problems earlier in his career, Mason never developed as a starter. However, he had a magical final two months out of the bullpen for the Pirates in 1991. The magic continued in the playoffs, when Mason worked 4.1 scoreless innings and came through with a crucial save in Game Five. He has a remote shot to win the closer's job in 1992.

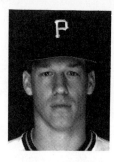

ROGER MASON

Position: RP
Bats: R **Throws:** R
Ht: 6' 6" **Wt:** 215

Opening Day Age: 33
Born: 9/18/58 in Bellaire, MI
ML Seasons: 6

Overall Statistics

	W	L	ERA	G	GS	Sv	IP	H	R	BB	SO	HR
1991	3	2	3.03	24	0	3	29.2	21	11	6	21	2
Career	9	11	4.06	52	23	4	168.2	160	88	69	126	13

How Often He Throws Strikes

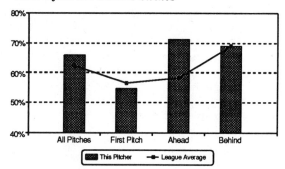

1991 Situational Stats

	W	L	ERA	Sv	IP		AB	H	HR	RBI	AVG
Home	2	1	3.24	2	16.2	LHB	52	11	1	6	.212
Road	1	1	2.77	1	13.0	RHB	53	10	1	4	.189
Day	1	0	6.35	2	5.2	Sc Pos	30	6	0	7	.200
Night	2	2	2.25	1	24.0	Clutch	61	12	1	7	.197

1991 Rankings (National League)

→ Did not rank near the top or bottom in any category

HITTING:

Lloyd McClendon is a valuable player coming off the Bucco bench against left-handed pitching. The hard-hitting McClendon terrorizes lefties; he hit .350 against them last season with six home runs. Conversely, righthanders give him fits and have prevented him from being more than a role player. He compiled only a .130 average against righties in 46 at-bats in 1991.

For his career, McClendon has been far more effective against left-handed pitching. He likes pitches up and in and makes lefties pay when they get one in his zone. He usually pulls lefthanders and can take them out of the park. However, he struggles with just about anything on the outside part of the plate. Righties continually make him chase pitches out of the strike zone.

Though he's been considered a free swinger, McClendon has good strike zone judgement, and he will take an occasional walk. He is a dangerous hitter off the bench and has at least one pinch hit homer in each of his five major league seasons. He can turn a game around in a hurry.

BASERUNNING:

The stocky McClendon navigates the bases decently. He can steal a base if the pitcher isn't paying attention (two for three last year). He picks his spots to take an extra base, and is usually successful.

FIELDING:

McClendon plays a lot of positions but does not distinguish himself at any. Originally a catcher, he rarely puts on the gear any more. He is now primarily a first baseman-outfielder. He handles first base decently and his work in left field and right field is passable; he is willing to play third base if needed. McClendon is not in the majors because of his glove.

OVERALL:

At age 32, McClendon finally spent a full season in the majors last year. He is a good bench player who provides some power. He handles the pressure of pinch hitting well and is effective as an occasional starter against lefties.

LLOYD McCLENDON

Position: 1B/RF
Bats: R **Throws:** R
Ht: 5'11" **Wt:** 210

Opening Day Age: 33
Born: 1/11/59 in Gary, IN
ML Seasons: 5

Overall Statistics

	G	AB	R	H	D	T	HR	RBI	SB	BB	SO	AVG
1991	85	163	24	47	7	0	7	24	2	18	23	.288
Career	347	741	94	184	31	1	26	103	14	88	113	.248

Where He Hits the Ball

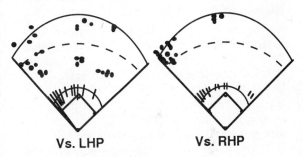

Vs. LHP   Vs. RHP

1991 Situational Stats

	AB	H	HR	RBI	AVG		AB	H	HR	RBI	AVG
Home	66	15	2	7	.227	LHP	117	41	6	19	.350
Road	97	32	5	17	.330	RHP	46	6	1	5	.130
Day	49	12	2	6	.245	Sc Pos	60	15	2	18	.250
Night	114	35	5	18	.307	Clutch	38	10	0	5	.263

1991 Rankings (National League)

→ 4th in batting average vs. left-handed pitchers (.350) and on-base average vs. left-handed pitchers (.429)

→ 6th in batting average on a 3-2 count (.353)

→ 7th in slugging percentage vs. left-handed pitchers (.547)

→ Led the Pirates in batting average/on-base average/slugging percentage vs. left-handed pitchers and batting average on a 3-2 count

→ Led the NL first basemen in batting average/on-base average/slugging percentage vs. left-handed pitchers and batting average on a 3-2 count

HITTING:

Orlando Merced turned two former Pirate weaknesses into strengths last season. With the free agent defections of Wally Backman and Sid Bream following the 1990 season, the Pirates needed both a leadoff man and a first baseman against right-handed pitching. Merced, after being the last player cut in spring training, returned to fill both voids.

The switch-hitting rookie came back to the majors just one week into the season. Though rarely used at the top of the order in the minor leagues, Merced fit right into the Bucs' leadoff spot, showing outstanding patience for a young hitter. He will take pitches to work the count in his favor but hits well when behind in the count, too.

Merced fit snugly into the role of platoon first baseman as well. He's a much better hitter from the left side of the plate, batting .285 against righties last season compared to .208 against lefties. Unlike many young hitters, Merced is not baffled by breaking balls. He has some power but is mainly a line drive hitter to all fields. He handles pressure situations extremely well, hitting .326 with runners in scoring position and .353 as a pinch hitter last year.

BASERUNNING:

Merced has good speed and goes from first to third and second to home very well. However, he has yet to translate his speed into base stealing prowess. He stole only eight bases last year but should improve on that with experience.

FIELDING:

Merced has played every position but pitcher and shortstop in his professional career. He has no problems at first base, where he is steady. He may eventually move to the outfield, however. Merced spent time in the Florida Instructional League learning to catch after the 1990 season and is adequate enough for emergency use.

OVERALL:

Merced will not have to worry about being the last cut this spring. He has established himself as a solid player with an outside chance at stardom; a hard worker, he must first learn to hit lefties to be an everyday player.

ORLANDO MERCED

Position: 1B
Bats: B **Throws:** R
Ht: 5'11" **Wt:** 175

Opening Day Age: 25
Born: 11/2/66 in San Juan, Puerto Rico
ML Seasons: 2

Overall Statistics

	G	AB	R	H	D	T	HR	RBI	SB	BB	SO	AVG
1991	120	411	83	113	17	2	10	50	8	64	81	.275
Career	145	435	86	118	18	2	10	50	8	65	90	.271

Where He Hits the Ball

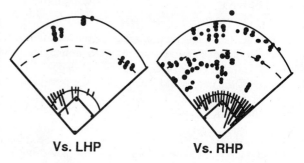

Vs. LHP   Vs. RHP

1991 Situational Stats

	AB	H	HR	RBI	AVG		AB	H	HR	RBI	AVG
Home	192	49	5	22	.255	LHP	53	11	0	6	.208
Road	219	64	5	28	.292	RHP	358	102	10	44	.285
Day	116	36	4	25	.310	Sc Pos	95	31	6	46	.326
Night	295	77	6	25	.261	Clutch	62	13	3	12	.210

1991 Rankings (National League)

→ 2nd lowest fielding percentage at first base (.988)

→ 3rd highest percentage of pitches taken (63.1%)

→ 7th highest on-base average vs. right-handed pitchers (.388)

→ Led the Pirates in highest percentage of pitches taken

PITCHING:

In 1990, the Pittsburgh Pirates wished Vicente Palacios could have pitched in the playoffs, but he was ineligible. In 1991, he was eligible, but the Pirates elected not to even place him on their postseason roster. Palacios looked headed for a prominent role with the Pirates going into 1991. He pitched 15 scoreless relief innings in September/October, 1990 after his recall from Class AAA Buffalo -- many of those innings were in crucial situations.

However, following an inconsistent 1991, Palacios' status is now in doubt. He has already undergone two rotator cuff operations in his career, then missed a month last season with shoulder problems. There is question as to how long his shoulder can hold up.

Palacios throws hard and has an above-average fastball and nasty slider. He complements the hard stuff with an offspeed pitch he calls the "taco" pitch. He grips it like a knuckleball and it breaks sharply down like a forkball. However, the pitch moves with better velocity than a knuckler. His stuff is good but often he cannot control it well enough. He has to throw strikes on a more consistent basis.

Palacios has the ability to both start and relieve. He has been successful in both roles, throwing a shutout early in the 1991 season and saving three games during the pennant race in 1990.

HOLDING RUNNERS, FIELDING, HITTING:

Palacios has shown dramatic improvement at holding runners in recent seasons. His delivery to the plate is much quicker and he pays more attention to runners on first. He is nothing special as a fielder. As a hitter, he is 2-for-35 for an .057 lifetime batting average.

OVERALL:

This figures to be the make-or-break year for Palacios, whose future is clouded by his history of shoulder problems. At age 28, he may be a little too young to give up on. However, he is getting too old for the prospect label. He must make his move in 1992.

VINCE PALACIOS

Position: RP/SP
Bats: R **Throws:** R
Ht: 6' 3" **Wt:** 195

Opening Day Age: 28
Born: 7/19/63 in Mataloma, Mexico
ML Seasons: 4

Overall Statistics

	W	L	ERA	G	GS	Sv	IP	H	R	BB	SO	HR
1991	6	3	3.75	36	7	3	81.2	69	34	38	64	12
Career	9	6	3.95	56	14	6	150.1	128	66	64	100	16

How Often He Throws Strikes

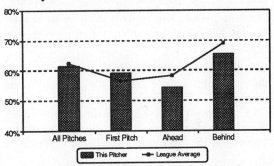

1991 Situational Stats

	W	L	ERA	Sv	IP		AB	H	HR	RBI	AVG
Home	4	1	2.05	0	48.1	LHB	137	32	2	13	.234
Road	2	2	6.21	3	33.1	RHB	166	37	10	24	.223
Day	0	1	8.10	1	10.0	Sc Pos	73	16	1	20	.219
Night	6	2	3.14	2	71.2	Clutch	70	19	2	9	.271

1991 Rankings (National League)

→ 8th least GDPs induced per GDP situation (3.1%)

PITCHING:

Bob Patterson is not dazzling, but he is quietly effective. He does not have overpowering stuff and relies on good location to get hitters out. He has a decent fastball and a good curveball. With only average velocity, Patterson needs to keep the ball low in the strike zone. When he gets pitches up, hitters turn on them.

The two strengths Patterson brings to the party are outstanding control and the ability to neutralize left-handed hitters. He walked only 15 batters in 65.2 innings last season, an important facet of his game -- his fastball isn't good enough to bail him out when behind in the count. Patterson also held lefties to a .181 batting average and five extra-base hits in 83 at-bats last season. His breaking pitches dart down and away from left-handed hitters, causing them to flail away harmlessly.

Patterson has good stamina and can give his club three or four innings out of the bullpen when necessary. He has also started in the past and can fill a spot role when needed. He did not pitch well in pressure situations last year, though, as opponents hit .333 with runners in scoring position.

FIELDING, HOLDING RUNNERS, HITTING:

Patterson is truly the game's top glove man -- he began marketing "Dr. Glove," a foam designed to help soften the leather in baseball gloves. Happily, he's a good endorsement for his product; he's a good fielder and is excellent at holding runners. Last season, opponents were one of six in steal attempts with Patterson pitching. He is only an .087 career hitter.

OVERALL:

Patterson, who will turn 33 early in the 1992 season, will never be a star. However, he has become a decent role reliever whose value lies in getting left-handed hitters out. With his ability to spot start, he is a good guy to have on a pitching staff.

BOB PATTERSON

Position: RP
Bats: R **Throws:** L
Ht: 6' 2" **Wt:** 192

Opening Day Age: 32
Born: 5/16/59 in Jacksonville, FL
ML Seasons: 6

Overall Statistics

	W	L	ERA	G	GS	Sv	IP	H	R	BB	SO	HR
1991	4	3	4.11	54	1	2	65.2	67	32	15	57	7
Career	19	18	4.53	150	21	8	270.1	289	143	74	195	26

How Often He Throws Strikes

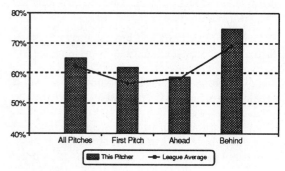

1991 Situational Stats

	W	L	ERA	Sv	IP		AB	H	HR	RBI	AVG
Home	2	2	4.94	0	27.1	LHB	83	15	1	8	.181
Road	2	1	3.52	2	38.1	RHB	168	52	6	28	.310
Day	1	2	5.59	2	19.1	Sc Pos	63	21	3	30	.333
Night	3	1	3.50	0	46.1	Clutch	77	20	4	12	.260

1991 Rankings (National League)

- 5th in holds (13)
- 8th highest relief ERA (4.19)
- 9th highest batting average allowed in relief (.264)
- Led the Pirates in holds

HITTING:

Gary Redus has always heard more about what he doesn't do on the field than what he does. He has heard career-long criticism for trying to hit too many homers, swinging at too many bad pitches and not hitting the ball on the ground enough. Redus has cut out many of his negatives through the years, but the tags still follow him.

Redus has become a solid platoon player on back-to-back National League East championship clubs. He still hits the ball in the air a lot, though not as frequently as in his younger days. He still chases high fastballs and low breaking balls away. Redus is not exactly Wade Boggs, but he's willing to take pitches and draw walks.

Though he hits for a low average -- his .246 mark in 1991 was three points below his lifetime figure -- Redus is a productive player. He has some pop in his bat and can start rallies. He may not have lived up to the big expectations placed on him in his younger days, but he has become a reliable part-time player who makes solid contributions.

BASERUNNING:

Though 35, Redus shows no signs of slowing down. He is outstanding at reading pitchers and his stolen base success rate is always above average. He accelerates from first to third as fast as anyone in the league. Redus stays in very good shape and his legs prove it.

FIELDING:

Redus' best position is designated hitter. The problem is that he plays in the National League. He has seen extensive action at first base the past three years without showing improvement. Hard grounders can handcuff him and throws in the dirt also cause him problems. His speed affords him good range in the outfield, but he gets late jumps and has trouble going back on balls. His arm is also below average.

OVERALL:

Allowed to play within his limitations in Pittsburgh, Redus is a solid platoon/bench player. He rarely does the spectacular but provides steady production. He also provides an elder statesman-type influence in the clubhouse.

GARY REDUS

Position: 1B
Bats: R **Throws:** R
Ht: 6' 1" **Wt:** 195

Opening Day Age: 35
Born: 11/1/56 in Tanner, AL
ML Seasons: 10

Overall Statistics

	G	AB	R	H	D	T	HR	RBI	SB	BB	SO	AVG
1991	98	252	45	62	12	2	7	24	17	28	39	.246
Career	988	3082	535	768	163	44	81	307	307	437	622	.249

Where He Hits the Ball

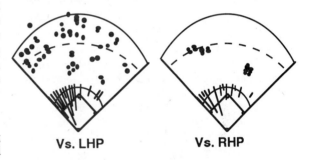

Vs. LHP   Vs. RHP

1991 Situational Stats

	AB	H	HR	RBI	AVG		AB	H	HR	RBI	AVG
Home	125	35	3	11	.280	LHP	173	43	5	15	.249
Road	127	27	4	13	.213	RHP	79	19	2	9	.241
Day	52	6	1	3	.115	Sc Pos	49	7	1	18	.143
Night	200	56	6	21	.280	Clutch	51	14	1	6	.275

1991 Rankings (National League)

- ➡ 2nd highest stolen base percentage (85.0%)
- ➡ 5th highest percentage of extra bases taken as a runner (70.6%)
- ➡ Led the Pirates in stolen base percentage
- ➡ Led NL first basemen in stolen bases (17) and stolen base percentage

HITTING:

If you take away the second half of the 1990 season and the first half of 1991, Don Slaught would be considered one of the top hitters in the game. Slaught hit .382 before the All-Star break in 1990 and .206 after. In 1991, he batted .218 in the first half and .373 after. The Pirates would obviously like more consistency, but they're happy with Slaught's overall results: a .300 average in 1990 and a .295 mark in 1991.

Slaught has little power but hits line drives to all fields. Standing close to the plate, he is basically a fastball hitter, though good hard stuff inside gives him trouble. Slaught will jump on fastballs on the outside part of the plate, going the opposite way. Pitchers can get him to chase breaking balls away. However, he drives change-ups.

Slaught is an outstanding bunter and a threat on the suicide squeeze. Overall, he handles the bat quite well and is good on hit-and-run plays. Though a right-handed hitter, he hits righties as well as lefties -- he compiled a .340 average against righthanders last season while hitting .262 against lefties.

BASERUNNING:

With 14 stolen bases in 10 seasons, Slaught is not exactly Craig Biggio. However, he moves decently on the base paths and can take an extra base.

FIELDING:

The knock on Slaught is that he is weak defensively. Though not a Gold Glove winner, he is adequate behind the plate and calls a decent game. Spending time on his footwork in recent years has paid off in Slaught's throwing. He gunned down 39 percent of runners trying to steal in 1991. He is not a good receiver, though, and tends to lunge at the ball instead of getting behind it. Durability is also a problem for him, with seven disabled list stints in 10 seasons.

OVERALL:

In-season consistency is obviously not a phrase associated with Slaught. However, he has played well on the whole as part of a catching platoon with Mike LaValliere. He has given the Pirates the top catching platoon tandem in the league.

DON SLAUGHT

Position: C
Bats: R **Throws:** R
Ht: 6' 1" **Wt:** 190

Opening Day Age: 33
Born: 9/11/58 in Long Beach, CA
ML Seasons: 10

Overall Statistics

	G	AB	R	H	D	T	HR	RBI	SB	BB	SO	AVG
1991	77	220	19	65	17	1	1	29	1	21	32	.295
Career	917	2816	294	771	176	23	55	314	14	202	415	.274

Where He Hits the Ball

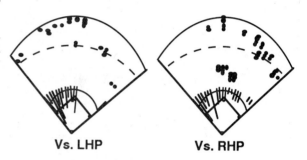

Vs. LHP   Vs. RHP

1991 Situational Stats

	AB	H	HR	RBI	AVG		AB	H	HR	RBI	AVG
Home	118	38	0	15	.322	LHP	126	33	0	11	.262
Road	102	27	1	14	.265	RHP	94	32	1	18	.340
Day	50	14	0	5	.280	Sc Pos	67	19	0	27	.284
Night	170	51	1	24	.300	Clutch	39	11	1	8	.282

1991 Rankings (National League)

→ 2nd lowest percentage of extra bases taken as a runner (13.4%)

PITCHING:

Long considered a pitcher with outstanding potential, John Smiley delivered in 1991. His record was 20-8, tying Atlanta's Tom Glavine and Minnesota's Scott Erickson for the major league lead in victories. The most wins Smiley had compiled in any of his previous four seasons was 13.

Maturity played a major role in Smiley's emergence last year. Long noted for his temper and for fighting himself on the mound, Smiley became more composed and relaxed last season. He was rarely rattled in tight situations, though he did not get past the second inning in two National League Championship Series losses.

Smiley is a power pitcher who can turn to finesse in the right situations. His fastball routinely surpasses 90 MPH and shatters many bats while his slider has real bite. He also mixes in a nasty change-up which he disguises very well (and which is considered his best pitch by many scouts). Smiley's overhand curve is still erratic and he plans to put extensive work into developing it in spring training. For a young left-handed power pitcher, Smiley has outstanding control. He walked only 44 in 207.2 innings last season. However, his stamina is questionable after completing only two of 32 starts last year.

HOLDING BASERUNNERS, FIELDING AND HITTING:

Smiley put in long hours last spring working on holding runners and shortening his leg kick. The work helped as opponents were only 18 of 31 in steal attempts against him. He has also begun paying attention to his fielding and no longer makes mistakes like failing to back up bases. Smiley is an adequate bunter but a .110 lifetime hitter.

OVERALL:

Expecting 20 wins a season from Smiley may be a little too much. However, he came into his own in '91 and should consistently win 15-18 games for many years to come. A key to this season will be how well he shakes off last year's nightmarish postseason.

JOHN SMILEY

Position: SP
Bats: L **Throws:** L
Ht: 6' 4" **Wt:** 200

Opening Day Age: 27
Born: 3/17/65 in Phoenixville, PA
ML Seasons: 6

Overall Statistics

	W	L	ERA	G	GS	Sv	IP	H	R	BB	SO	HR
1991	20	8	3.08	33	32	0	207.2	194	78	44	129	17
Career	60	42	3.57	196	117	4	854.0	787	375	229	534	78

How Often He Throws Strikes

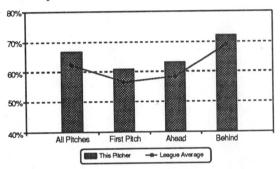

1991 Situational Stats

	W	L	ERA	Sv	IP		AB	H	HR	RBI	AVG
Home	10	5	2.98	0	99.2	LHB	153	30	3	12	.196
Road	10	3	3.17	0	108.0	RHB	621	164	14	59	.264
Day	8	1	2.67	0	67.1	Sc Pos	153	40	2	46	.261
Night	12	7	3.27	0	140.1	Clutch	60	14	0	3	.233

1991 Rankings (National League)

- → 1st in wins (20) and winning percentage (.714)
- → 5th highest strikeout/walk ratio (2.9)
- → 7th in least baserunners per 9 innings (10.4) and highest batting average allowed vs. right-handed batters (.264)
- → Led the Pirates in wins, home runs allowed (17), winning percentage, lowest batting average allowed (.251), lowest stolen base percentage allowed (58.1%), least baserunners allowed per 9 innings (10.4) and most strikeouts per 9 innings (5.6)

PINPOINT CONTROL

ZANE SMITH

Position: SP
Bats: L **Throws:** L
Ht: 6' 2" **Wt:** 200

Opening Day Age: 31
Born: 12/28/60 in
Madison, WI
ML Seasons: 8

PITCHING:

When Zane Smith gets that sinking feeling, it's a good thing. Smith relies on a fastball with excellent sinking motion. When his sinker is right, he can be as tough as any left-handed pitcher in the league. He will watch a parade of batters step to the plate and beat the pitch into the ground -- last season, he induced 27 double play grounders.

Smith's troubles come when the sinker isn't sharp. His fastball is average and he is very hittable when it comes in above the knee. Smith also throws a curveball, a slider and a change-up. The curveball breaks sharply away from lefties while the slider ties up righties. His change is adequate.

Control is Smith's strong point. In 1990 he walked only 2.1 batters per nine innings, which is excellent; in '91, he reduced that figure by one whole walk, to a minuscule 1.1, the top mark in the National League. At one point, he went 282 consecutive innings without issuing a walk to a leadoff batter. It's possible that Smith is becoming a little **too** obsessed with not walking batters. Last year he yielded one more hit per nine innings than in 1990, and his ERA rose from 2.55 to 3.20.

Smith has good stamina, pitching 228 innings last season and completing six games. He prefers to pitch with a slightly tired arm because it gives the sinker better movement. After performing well in pressure situations in 1990, Smith had a few problems in 1991. Hitters batted .301 off him with runners in scoring position.

FIELDING, HOLDING RUNNERS, HITTING:

Smith is a good fielder who does not make mistakes, though for a lefty, he does not hold runners exceptionally well. He allowed 26 of 34 steal attempts to be successful in 1991. He is not an automatic out as a hitter, is a good bunter and rarely clogs the bases.

OVERALL:

Smith, 67-78 lifetime, has finally found consistent success in Pittsburgh. Since being acquired from Montreal in August of 1990, he is 22-12. He's only 31 and has several productive years ahead of him.

Overall Statistics

	W	L	ERA	G	GS	Sv	IP	H	R	BB	SO	HR
1991	16	10	3.20	35	35	0	228.0	234	95	29	120	15
Career	67	78	3.58	258	194	3	1344.1	1335	636	464	772	77

How Often He Throws Strikes

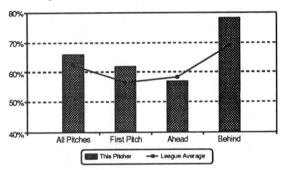

1991 Situational Stats

	W	L	ERA	Sv	IP		AB	H	HR	RBI	AVG
Home	11	3	2.78	0	129.1	LHB	146	39	1	12	.267
Road	5	7	3.74	0	98.2	RHB	727	195	14	76	.268
Day	4	4	4.53	0	51.2	Sc Pos	183	55	4	72	.301
Night	12	6	2.81	0	176.1	Clutch	76	20	1	8	.263

1991 Rankings (National League)

→ 1st in GDPs induced (27), strikeout/walk ratio (4.2), groundball/flyball ratio (2.7) and most GDPs induced per 9 innings (1.1)

→ 3rd in shutouts (3) and sacrifice bunts as a hitter (13)

→ 4th in hits allowed (234) and most run support per 9 innings (5.1)

→ 5th in wins (16), games started (35), complete games (6) and highest batting average allowed (.268)

→ Led the Pirates in games started, complete games, shutouts, pickoff throws (151), GDPs induced, lowest on-base average allowed (.292), groundball/flyball ratio and least pitches thrown per batter (3.46)

PITCHING:

Randy Tomlin is almost a split personality. Off the field, he is polite, reserved and barely speaks above a whisper. On the field, he is a fierce competitor who does not give in to hitters. The little lefthander has a below-average (84 MPH) fastball. However, he baffles hitters by changing speeds and throwing with an unorthodox motion.

Tomlin's main pitch is his "Vulcan-grip" change-up. He jams the ball between his middle and ring fingers, reminiscent of the Vulcan sign in "Star Trek." Hitters, accustomed to swinging at 90 MPH pitches, can only flail at his painfully-slow offerings. When he is throwing the change for strikes, it makes for a frustrating day for the opponent. Tomlin throws his pitches from a cross-fire motion, presenting the illusion that he is throwing from somewhere between first and second base. It particularly poses a problem for left-handed batters, who hit just .172 against him last season.

Tomlin can go the distance as shown by his four complete games and two shutouts in 27 starts last season, his first full year in the majors. He also has good control, which he needs as a finesse pitcher. Tomlin did become more hittable in tough situations last year. He allowed a .282 average with runners in scoring position and .314 in late-and-close situations.

FIELDING, HOLDING RUNNERS, HITTING:

Tomlin is a good fielder and exceptionally good at spearing shots through the box. He is extremely tough to run against because of his delivery. Possessor of an excellent move, he picked off eight runners last season. After going 1-for-25 as a rookie, he improved as a hitter last season with a .192 average.

OVERALL:

Tomlin is establishing himself as a crafty little lefty in the mode of Harvey Haddix and Bobby Shantz. He pitched better than his 8-7 record, and at only 25 years of age has a chance to be a solid major league starter for a long time.

RANDY TOMLIN

Position: SP
Bats: L Throws: L
Ht: 5'11" Wt: 179

Opening Day Age: 25
Born: 6/14/66 in Bainbridge, MD
ML Seasons: 2

Overall Statistics

	W	L	ERA	G	GS	Sv	IP	H	R	BB	SO	HR
1991	8	7	2.98	31	27	0	175.0	170	75	54	104	9
Career	12	11	2.85	43	39	0	252.2	232	99	66	146	14

How Often He Throws Strikes

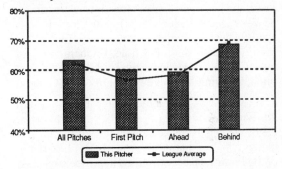

1991 Situational Stats

	W	L	ERA	Sv	IP		AB	H	HR	RBI	AVG
Home	5	4	2.83	0	92.1	LHB	134	23	1	10	.172
Road	3	3	3.16	0	82.2	RHB	535	147	8	53	.275
Day	1	2	2.98	0	45.1	Sc Pos	156	44	1	49	.282
Night	7	5	2.98	0	129.2	Clutch	51	16	2	5	.314

1991 Rankings (National League)

- → 2nd lowest batting average allowed vs. left-handed batters (.172)
- → 3rd in sacrifice bunts as a hitter (13)
- → 5th highest batting average allowed vs. right-handed batters (.275)
- → Led the Pirates in ERA (2.98), hit batsmen (6), balks (3), lowest slugging percentage allowed (.354), least home runs allowed per 9 innings (.46), ERA on the road (3.16) and lowest batting average allowed vs. left-handed batters

HITTING:

Andy Van Slyke may not be the hitter he was in 1988 (.288-25-100). But happily, he is not the hitter he was in 1989 (.237-9-53) either. Instead, Van Slyke has leveled off at a very productive, if unspectacular, level over the past two seasons. He has become a decent average hitter with some power and the ability to produce runs.

Van Slyke is tough on righthanders, feasting on their fastballs. However, his struggles against lefties returned in 1991. After having solved lefties in 1990, Van Slyke hit just .195 against them in 1991. Southpaws can make him look very bad on breaking pitches away.

Van Slyke has cut his strikeouts down in recent years and has a good eye at the plate. Sometimes, however, his patience works against him. He has spells where he never swings at the first pitch, putting himself in an 0-1 hole. Pitchers will just put a fastball right down the middle on the first pitch, knowing Van Slyke probably won't swing.

The veteran has helped the Pirates to two straight NL East titles with big September performances. He drove in 21 runs in September during '90 and batted .347 for that month in '91. But like many of the Pirates, he has struggled in postseason play, batting .184 (9-for-49) in 1990-91.

BASERUNNING:

Van Slyke is fast and aggressive on the bases and is annually among the base stealing percentage leaders. However, he is now a little more cautious after suffering a series of nagging injuries over the years. He stole a career-low 10 bases last year.

FIELDING:

Van Slyke is a true Gold Glove center fielder. His once-tremendous range has dropped a notch, but he remains a ball hawk with a strong arm. He is fearless, crashing into fences and skidding head first across artificial turf. Opponents do not run on him.

OVERALL:

It is unlikely Van Slyke will ever duplicate his great 1988 season, and the Pirates don't really expect him to. They are happy with him at his current level: a dangerous hitter who leads by example with his all-out play in center field.

ANDY VAN SLYKE

Position: CF
Bats: L **Throws:** R
Ht: 6' 2" **Wt:** 195

Opening Day Age: 31
Born: 12/21/60 in Utica, NY
ML Seasons: 9

Overall Statistics

	G	AB	R	H	D	T	HR	RBI	SB	BB	SO	AVG
1991	138	491	87	130	24	7	17	83	10	71	85	.265
Career	1236	4123	617	1109	206	70	130	599	208	500	796	.269

Where He Hits the Ball

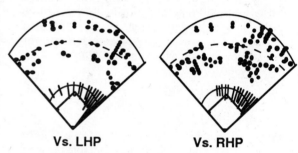

Vs. LHP   Vs. RHP

1991 Situational Stats

	AB	H	HR	RBI	AVG		AB	H	HR	RBI	AVG
Home	265	60	9	46	.226	LHP	185	36	4	23	.195
Road	226	70	8	37	.310	RHP	306	94	13	60	.307
Day	148	43	7	28	.291	Sc Pos	132	37	1	55	.280
Night	343	87	10	55	.254	Clutch	71	19	2	11	.268

1991 Rankings (National League)

→ 2nd highest fielding percentage in center field (.997)

→ 3rd in sacrifice flies (11) and lowest batting average at home (.226)

→ 5th in least GDPs per GDP situation (4.0%), lowest batting average with the bases loaded (.143) and lowest batting average after the 6th inning (.221)

→ 6th in most runs scored per time reached base (42.4%) and lowest batting average vs. left-handed pitchers (.195)

→ Led the Pirates in hit by pitch, most pitches seen per plate appearance (3.94) and least GDPs per GDP situation

PITCHING:

Bob Walk just keeps rolling along in his steady if unspectacular way. Though plagued by groin and hamstring problems, Walk posted a solid 9-2 record for the Pirates last season as a starter. In the National League Championship Series, he was outstanding out of the bullpen. In three vital long relief appearances against Atlanta, Walk posted a 1.93 ERA in 9.1 innings and earned a save with a three inning stint in Game One.

Walk relies on experience and guile. He has lost something off his fastball as he has aged, but he still gets people out by effectively changing speeds. Walk's curveball has a big break and he must throw it for strikes to be successful. He tries to establish his curve on the first pitch to almost every hitter. He also throws a slider and change-up, mainly for show.

Injuries have plagued Walk throughout the last three seasons and reduced him to almost a part-time starter. He is a pitcher who maxes out at six or seven innings, failing to complete any of his 20 starts last season. Walk has good control; however, his curveball occasionally gets away from him, explaining his 11 wild pitches in 1991.

Walk has come full circle in his career. When he broke in with the Philadelphia Phillies in 1980, he was a free spirit and tagged with the nickname "Whirlybird." Today, he is a respected member of the Pirates' staff because of his competitiveness.

FIELDING, HOLDING RUNNERS, HITTING:

As he is in every other aspect of the game, Walk is not a pretty fielder but gets the job done. He has a slow delivery to the plate but makes up for it with a quick move to first. Walk is a battler at the plate and hit his first career home run last season off the Chicago Cubs' Danny Jackson.

OVERALL:

A free agent, the 35-year-old Walk planned on returning to Pittsburgh. Though injury-prone, Walk is versatile and gives a good effort every time he takes the mound.

BOB WALK

Position: SP/RP
Bats: R **Throws:** R
Ht: 6' 4" **Wt:** 217

Opening Day Age: 35
Born: 11/26/56 in Van Nuys, CA
ML Seasons: 12

Overall Statistics

	W	L	ERA	G	GS	Sv	IP	H	R	BB	SO	HR
1991	9	2	3.60	25	20	0	115.0	104	53	35	67	10
Career	82	61	3.88	282	208	3	1344.0	1325	654	493	708	110

How Often He Throws Strikes

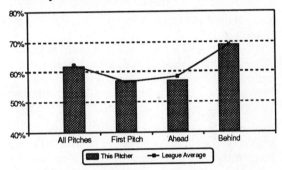

1991 Situational Stats

	W	L	ERA	Sv	IP		AB	H	HR	RBI	AVG
Home	4	2	3.48	0	62.0	LHB	244	63	5	24	.258
Road	5	0	3.74	0	53.0	RHB	189	41	5	24	.217
Day	3	1	3.41	0	31.2	Sc Pos	101	28	3	38	.277
Night	6	1	3.67	0	83.1	Clutch	17	5	0	1	.294

1991 Rankings (National League)

➡ 5th in wild pitches (11)
➡ Led the Pirates in wild pitches

NEAL HEATON

Position: RP
Bats: L **Throws:** L
Ht: 6' 1" **Wt:** 205

Opening Day Age: 32
Born: 3/3/60 in Jamaica, NY
ML Seasons: 10

Overall Statistics

	W	L	ERA	G	GS	Sv	IP	H	R	BB	SO	HR
1991	3	3	4.33	42	1	0	68.2	72	37	21	34	6
Career	76	95	4.35	332	202	10	1438.0	1512	764	490	653	152

PITCHING, FIELDING, HITTING & HOLDING RUNNERS:

Few players suffered a bigger fall than Neal Heaton in 1991. After being selected to the All-Star Game in 1990, Heaton did not even make the Pirates' postseason roster last year. A sore shoulder bumped Heaton out of the starting rotation in 1990; he has never regained his stature with the Pirates and spent 1991 as the staff's 11th pitcher.

Heaton still has some value with his ability to start and relieve. He is probably better off in the bullpen because he does not have a large repertoire. His main pitch is a 92 MPH fastball. He also throws a hard slider and an offspeed pitch called the "screw-knuckle-change."

Heaton's defense is below average. He has a slow wind up and a high leg kick. That combination leaves him in poor fielding position and allows runners to get big jumps. Heaton loves to hit and is far from being an automatic out. He also has good speed, and will occasionally look to steal a base. He is good enough to see action as a pinch runner.

OVERALL:

Though Heaton worked in 42 games last year, most of them were unimportant assignments, and it's obvious he does not have a role in Pittsburgh. His best bet would be a trade, though his $1 million salary makes dealing him difficult.

GARY VARSHO

Position: RF
Bats: L **Throws:** R
Ht: 5'11" **Wt:** 190

Opening Day Age: 30
Born: 6/20/61 in Marshfield, WI
ML Seasons: 4

Overall Statistics

	G	AB	R	H	D	T	HR	RBI	SB	BB	SO	AVG
1991	99	187	23	51	11	2	4	23	9	19	34	.273
Career	252	395	49	99	22	4	4	35	19	25	59	.251

HITTING, FIELDING, BASERUNNING:

Last season Gary Varsho proved that he was more than just a decent pinch hitter. In parts of three seasons with the Chicago Cubs (1988-90), pinch swinging was about all Varsho was ever asked to do. Traded to the Pirates last year, he was given more playing time and quickly proved to be a decent all-around player. Varsho's .273 average as a bench player and part-time outfielder gave the Pirates a boost on their way to the NL East title.

A contact hitter, Varsho has a little pop in his bat, too, knocking 17 extra-base hits in 187 at-bats. Primarily, he is a line drive hitter who sprays the ball around. Earlier in his career, Varsho constantly experimented with his swing. However, he has become a disciple of the Charlie Lau school in recent seasons, with a balanced stance and good weight shift.

Varsho has above-average speed and is very aggressive. He constantly looks for an opening that will allow him to take an extra base. Varsho is shaky in the outfield and has problems judging fly balls. He does have a strong arm, though, and plays an adequate first base.

OVERALL:

Varsho has found a home in Pittsburgh. Pirates' manager Jim Leyland finds at-bats for his subs, and Varsho has flourished in this new situation.

JOHN WEHNER

Position: 3B
Bats: R **Throws:** R
Ht: 6' 3" **Wt:** 204

Opening Day Age: 24
Born: 6/29/67 in Pittsburgh, PA
ML Seasons: 1

Overall Statistics

	G	AB	R	H	D	T	HR	RBI	SB	BB	SO	AVG
1991	37	106	15	36	7	0	0	7	3	7	17	.340
Career	37	106	15	36	7	0	0	7	3	7	17	.340

HITTING, FIELDING, BASERUNNING:

Like his fellow Pirate third baseman Jeff King, John Wehner spent the 1991 winter recovering from back problems. After a phenomenal major league debut, Wehner underwent surgery in September to remove a ruptured disk. Before the back problem, Wehner stunned everyone by hitting .340 in 37 games.

Wehner's batting stance is unique, to say the least. He keeps his hands far from his body and rocks back into hitting position as the pitcher delivers. It is Wehner's way of generating bat speed. The fear is that he will be unable to turn on hard inside fastballs. So far Wehner has exhibited little home run power. However, with a 6-foot-3, 204-pound frame, he should hit some long balls with experience.

Despite his size, Wehner runs well and was a base stealer in the minors. Not noted for his defense in the minors, he played well at third base for the Pirates, showing quick feet, a strong arm and the ability to make the spectacular play. His performance has caused the Pirates to rethink their plan of converting him into a first baseman.

OVERALL:

The Pirates are optimistic Wehner will be ready for the start of spring training. Steve Buechele is a free agent and Jeff King is on the mend from his own back problems. Wehner figures to be a key figure in the third base picture.

CURT WILKERSON

Position: 2B/3B/SS
Bats: B **Throws:** R
Ht: 5' 9" **Wt:** 173

Opening Day Age: 30
Born: 4/26/61 in Petersburg, VA
ML Seasons: 9

Overall Statistics

	G	AB	R	H	D	T	HR	RBI	SB	BB	SO	AVG
1991	85	191	20	36	9	1	2	18	2	15	40	.188
Career	849	2128	244	522	68	22	6	150	61	119	350	.245

HITTING, FIELDING, BASERUNNING:

Curtis Wilkerson is a player in regression. Since hitting a career-high .293 with the Texas Rangers in 1988, Wilkerson's batting average has slipped in each of the last three seasons. In 1991, after signing with the Pirates as a free agent, he batted only .188. A game-winning grand slam off St. Louis' Lee Smith accounted for one of his few highlights.

A switch-hitter, Wilkerson hits for better average from the right side. Like most switch-hitters, he likes the ball up batting right-handed and down when hitting left-handed. Wilkerson struggles with breaking stuff. If a pitcher establishes his offspeed pitch, Wilkerson is in trouble. Once he falls behind in the count, he is an almost automatic out.

Wilkerson has good speed but rarely tries to steal. As a baserunner, he is alert and aggressive. He can play three infield positions, but his best is second base, and he can go to his left well. His range is barely adequate at shortstop and his reflexes are not good at third base.

OVERALL:

Wilkerson's major league career may be in jeopardy. He is a free agent, but with clubs looking to save money by giving jobs to lesser-paid players, Wilkerson could struggle to find a job.

ORGANIZATION OVERVIEW:

A last-place franchise with an aging roster, little money and few fans only seven years ago, the Pirates have made a remarkable comeback. Under Syd Thrift, the Bucs traded for young talent like Bonilla, Van Slyke, Drabek and Bell. Thrift also rebuilt Pittsburgh's farm system, which has produced players like Bonds, Lind, Smiley and Belinda (some of whom pre-dated the Thrift era). Thrift is long gone, and under Larry Doughty the Pirates have won two division titles. Now, there are problems. A careless mistake cost Pittsburgh Wes Chamberlain; top pick Jeff King has had a disappointing career; Doughty took a risk by trading top prospects Kurt Miller and Hector Fajardo for Steve Buechele; and a lot of the Bucs may depart because they want more bucks. The farm system has few blue chippers, and Pittsburgh may soon be back to square one.

STEPHEN COOKE

Position: P **Opening Day Age:** 22
Bats: R **Throws:** L **Born:** 1/14/70 in Kanai,
Ht: 6' 6" **Wt:** 200 HI

Recent Statistics

	W	L	ERA	G	GS	Sv	IP	H	R	BB	SO	HR
90 A Welland	2	3	3.52	11	11	0	46.0	36	21	17	43	2
91 A Augusta	5	4	2.82	11	11	0	60.2	50	28	35	52	0
91 A Salem	1	0	4.85	2	2	0	13.0	14	8	2	5	0
91 AA Carolina	3	3	2.26	9	9	0	55.2	39	21	19	46	2

A former LSU basketball recruit, Cooke is tall and thin -- some say too thin. He throws hard and keeps the ball down in the strike zone; he's allowed only four homers in 175.1 professional innings. His control needs work, but it's not horrible. Cooke appears to be a very fine prospect, only a year or two away from the majors.

CARLOS GARCIA

Position: SS **Opening Day Age:** 24
Bats: R **Throws:** R **Born:** 10/15/67 in
Ht: 6' 2" **Wt:** 160 Tachira, Venezuela

Recent Statistics

	G	AB	R	H	D	THR	RBI	SB	BB	SO	AVG
91 AAA Buffalo	127	463	62	123	21	6	7	60	30	33	78	.266
91 NL Pittsburgh	12	24	2	6	0	2	0	1	0	1	8	.250
91 MLE	127	448	51	108	19	4	5	49	21	27	82	.241

A shortstop with speed and great defensive ability, Garcia has Jay Bell standing in his way with the Pirates. That's just as well for now, because Garcia's bat skills still need some polishing. His glove appears so good, however, that he won't have to hit very much to earn a major league job. With a little improvement, Garcia could soon be somebody's regular shortstop.

PAUL MILLER

Position: P **Opening Day Age:** 26
Bats: R **Throws:** R **Born:** 4/27/65 in
Ht: 6' 5" **Wt:** 215 Burlington, WI

Recent Statistics

	W	L	ERA	G	GS	Sv	IP	H	R	BB	SO	HR
91 AA Carolina	7	2	2.42	15	15	0	89.1	69	29	35	69	4
91 AAA Buffalo	5	2	1.48	10	10	0	67.0	41	17	29	30	2
91 NL Pittsburgh	0	0	5.40	1	1	0	5.0	4	3	3	2	0

A lowly 53rd-round draft pick in 1987, Miller was lightly regarded until '90, when he posted ERAs below 2.50 at both Class A and AA. Miller continued to impress in 1991, even making a start for the Pirates. He's not a radar-gun popper, and he struck out only one more than he walked for Buffalo. But he allowed few hits, and he seems to know how to pitch. He has an outside chance to make the big club this year.

TIM WAKEFIELD

Position: P **Opening Day Age:** 25
Bats: R **Throws:** R **Born:** 8/2/66 in
Ht: 6' 2" **Wt:** 200 Melbourne, FL

Recent Statistics

	W	L	ERA	G	GS	Sv	IP	H	R	BB	SO	HR
90 A Salem	10	14	4.73	28	28	0	190.1	187	109	85	127	24
91 AAA Buffalo	0	1	11.57	1	1	0	4.2	6	1	4	3	0
91 AA Carolina	15	8	2.90	26	25	0	183.0	155	68	51	120	13

An eighth-round pick from Florida Tech in 1988, Wakefield is one of the few knuckleballers left in professional baseball. He's already had an interesting career: he was drafted as a first baseman, but a .189 season prompted the Pirates to shift him to the mound. Knuckleballers often take a long, long time to develop, and Wakefield is well ahead of schedule. If his knuckler is as good as it's looked so far, he could have a very productive (and lengthy) career.

KEVIN YOUNG

Position: 3B **Opening Day Age:** 22
Bats: R **Throws:** R **Born:** 6/16/69 in Kansas
Ht: 6' 3" **Wt:** 210 City, KS

Recent Statistics

	G	AB	R	H	D	THR	RBI	SB	BB	SO	AVG
90 A Welland	72	238	46	58	16	2	5	30	10	31	39	.244
91 A Salem	56	201	38	63	11	4	6	28	3	20	34	.313
91 AA Carolina	75	263	36	90	19	6	3	33	9	15	38	.342
91 AAA Buffalo	4	9	1	2	1	0	0	2	1	0	0	.222
91 MLE	79	265	33	85	18	5	2	32	6	11	41	.321

Young, who has had less than two seasons of professional ball, made big strides last year, finishing with a promotion to AAA. Young is fast and has power potential, though he hasn't hit many home runs yet. His defense has been hampered by some arm problems, but he seems okay now. Young will probably be at Buffalo this year; he should not be there very long.

PITCHING:

To quote the best source for information of this sort -- this book, in 1990 -- "To explain the success of Juan Agosto as a relief pitcher is to delve into the great unknown." And that was when Agosto was good. His most recent campaigns produced ERAs of 4.29 and 4.81, and it appears that the mystery is over. Agosto throws a screwball, curve and a sinker but has no fastball, relying on control and guile. In 1990 and 1991 his hits allowed, walks, and hit batsmen took a dizzying upward leap. He allowed 14.5 baserunners per nine innings in 1991, worst among N.L. relievers.

Agosto's sinker is still sinking, as witnessed by his nearly three-to-one ratio of ground balls to fly balls, but his control has slipped. Agosto's greatest strength was his ability to battle back from behind in the count; in 1991 he seemed unable to do so.

After appearing in 13 of the Cards first 20 games, Agosto was predicting 90 appearances for himself. By the All-Star break, however, he had a 5.75 ERA and had lost the confidence of Joe Torre. His appearances fell from 49 in the first half to just 23 in the second. Consequently, he pitched on at least three days rest 13 times in the second half, after only five such rest periods in the first. His second half ERA was 3.41. Used judiciously, Agosto can still pitch.

HOLDING RUNNERS, FIELDING, HITTING:

Being a lefty helps Agosto control the running game, with only 12 attempts against him and just seven successful. He committed two errors, but is a competent fielder. You should change the oil in your car more often than Agosto bats.

OVERALL:

The presence of Frank DiPino, or any other capable lefty, will benefit Agosto, who clearly shows the strain of having over 300 appearances in four years. He is not simply overworked, however; he has been aided greatly by his home parks. His control is slipping, and he is 34. Left-handed relievers have nine lives, but Agosto is likely on his eighth.

JUAN AGOSTO

Position: RP
Bats: L **Throws:** L
Ht: 6' 2" **Wt:** 190

Opening Day Age: 34
Born: 2/23/58 in Rio Piedras, Puerto Rico
ML Seasons: 11

Overall Statistics

	W	L	ERA	G	GS	Sv	IP	H	R	BB	SO	HR
1991	5	3	4.81	72	0	2	86.0	92	52	39	34	4
Career	38	29	3.80	498	1	29	570.2	565	273	236	279	27

How Often He Throws Strikes

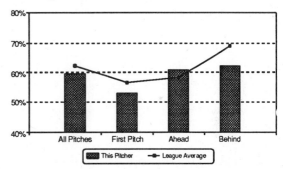

1991 Situational Stats

	W	L	ERA	Sv	IP		AB	H	HR	RBI	AVG
Home	3	2	4.21	2	47.0	LHB	96	26	0	14	.271
Road	2	1	5.54	0	39.0	RHB	220	66	4	42	.300
Day	0	2	4.05	0	20.0	Sc Pos	96	37	1	49	.385
Night	5	1	5.05	2	66.0	Clutch	99	24	1	10	.242

1991 Rankings (National League)

- ➡ 1st in highest relief ERA (4.81), highest batting average allowed in relief (.291), most baserunners allowed per 9 innings in relief (14.5) and least strikeouts per 9 innings in relief (3.6)
- ➡ 2nd in hit batsmen (8) and highest percentage of inherited runners scored (46.1%)
- ➡ 4th in games pitched (72) and worst first batter efficiency (.322)
- ➡ Led the Cardinals in games pitched, hit batsmen, most GDPs induced per GDP situation and relief innings (86)

PITCHING:

The Cardinals have finally decided that Cris Carpenter is a short man, and in 1991 let him set up Lee Smith. Carpenter appeared in a career-high 59 games but only twice threw more than two innings and never more than three. Consequently, he could air out his 90 MPH heater and go after hitters. He limited opponents to a .220 average, best on the Cardinals, and his 10 wins in relief earned him the nickname "the buzzard" among his teammates.

Carpenter's record in relief was deserved, though he was lavishly supported with six runs per nine innings pitched. He won six straight in 20 appearances between April 21 and June 10 (only Mitch Williams won more games in relief in '91). He strained a ligament in his index finger and missed the last month of the season or his totals might have been more impressive.

Only eight of 37 inherited runners scored off Carpenter, and in his first inning of work he held opponents to a .202 average. He allowed just 10 baserunners per nine innings, and that includes nine intentional walks.

So how did Carpenter get collared with a 4.23 ERA? His major weakness was his tendency to groove the first pitch and to try to throw the ball past hitters when he fell behind in the count. He should learn from those mistakes.

HOLDING RUNNERS, FIELDING, HITTING:

Carpenter is a wonderful athlete and didn't commit an error last year. He has a strong throw to first and keeps runners close, allowing only three steals in seven attempts. In just three at-bats, he managed one hit with an RBI.

OVERALL:

The Cardinals used a number one pick on Carpenter in 1987 and obviously expected more than a middle reliever. However, good set-up men are growing in stature and Carpenter, who was tied for sixth in the league with 12 holds, has the potential to be one of the best. Look for a lower ERA and more strikeouts in 1992.

CRIS CARPENTER

Position: RP
Bats: R **Throws:** R
Ht: 6' 1" **Wt:** 185

Opening Day Age: 27
Born: 4/5/65 in St.Augustine, FL
ML Seasons: 4

Overall Statistics

	W	L	ERA	G	GS	Sv	IP	H	R	BB	SO	HR
1991	10	4	4.23	59	0	0	66.0	53	31	20	47	6
Career	16	11	3.99	107	13	0	189.2	184	92	57	112	15

How Often He Throws Strikes

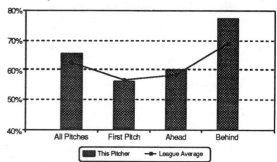

1991 Situational Stats

	W	L	ERA	Sv	IP		AB	H	HR	RBI	AVG
Home	5	1	3.37	0	34.2	LHB	123	28	0	13	.228
Road	5	3	5.17	0	31.1	RHB	118	25	6	17	.212
Day	2	0	0.00	0	13.1	Sc Pos	72	15	1	21	.208
Night	8	4	5.30	0	52.2	Clutch	106	23	4	13	.217

1991 Rankings (National League)

- ➡ 2nd in relief wins (10)
- ➡ 5th least baserunners allowed per 9 innings in relief (10.0)
- ➡ 6th in holds (12) and highest relief ERA (4.23)
- ➡ 8th lowest percentage of inherited runners scored (21.6%)
- ➡ Led the Cardinals in lowest batting average allowed vs. left-handed batters (.228), lowest percentage of inherited runners scored, relief wins and lowest batting average allowed in relief (.220)

PITCHING:

Rheal Cormier (RAY-al KORE-mee-ay) was promoted to St. Louis in 1991 despite a 4.23 ERA and a 7-9 record in AAA Louisville. While those numbers aren't impressive, Cormier's control is. He issued 31 walks in 127.2 innings in the minors in 1991, and 97 walks in 442.2 career minor league innings. He also struck out 307 hitters in the minors, working his way to the majors in less than three minor league seasons. He throws a lot of sinkers which he mixes with his fastball, and he throws everything for strikes.

Cormier won his first major league start August 15, defeating the Mets 4-1, and joined the rotation for the rest of the season. His control was better than advertised as he walked just eight in 67.2 innings; his strikeouts were down, but he still fanned 38. Cormier tossed two complete games, but he tires late in games. Through 60 pitches he held opposition hitters to a .220 average, but after that they beat him up at a .374 pace.

Right-handed hitters seem to be able to pick up Cormier's sinker pretty well, smacking every extra-base hit (and seven of the eight walks) he allowed. Cormier absolutely dominated lefties. Whether he can do better against righthanders remains to be seen, but he needs to be relieved earlier or develop some stamina to be successful.

HOLDING RUNNERS, FIELDING, HITTING:

Cormier did an excellent job holding runners, and only one of four baserunners attempting to steal on him was successful. His fielding was also fine at a perfect 1.000. At Louisville Cormier batted .118, but he hit a very fine .238 after being called up to St. Louis.

OVERALL:

Cormier is a competitor who doesn't want to come out of a close game. Working into the late innings may inflate his numbers now, but it should help his stamina and toughness in the long run. His control is phenomenal, his potential is enormous, and he's pitching in a great pitchers' park. The Cards have a rough gem to work with who shows promise of being a double-figure winner in their rotation.

RHEAL CORMIER

Position: SP
Bats: L **Throws:** L
Ht: 5'10" **Wt:** 185

Opening Day Age: 24
Born: 4/23/67 in
Moneton, Canada
ML Seasons: 1

Overall Statistics

	W	L	ERA	G	GS	Sv	IP	H	R	BB	SO	HR
1991	4	5	4.12	11	10	0	67.2	74	35	8	38	5
Career	4	5	4.12	11	10	0	67.2	74	35	8	38	5

How Often He Throws Strikes

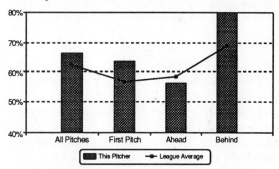

This Pitcher / League Average

1991 Situational Stats

	W	L	ERA	Sv	IP		AB	H	HR	RBI	AVG
Home	4	2	4.08	0	39.2	LHB	48	7	0	2	.146
Road	0	3	4.18	0	28.0	RHB	219	67	5	25	.306
Day	3	0	3.32	0	21.2	Sc Pos	58	17	1	21	.293
Night	1	5	4.50	0	46.0	Clutch	14	6	1	3	.429

1991 Rankings (National League)

➡ Did not rank near the top or bottom in any category

PITCHING:

In 1991, Jose DeLeon came within a whisker of being the worst supported pitcher in baseball for the second straight year. (He lost the honor to Kirk McCaskill by .01 run.) Mostly due to lack of support, and despite some changes in his pitching philosophy that helped him to a career-low 2.71 ERA, he struggled to a 5-9 record. At least DeLeon didn't lead the league in losses for the third time in his career.

DeLeon has been a terrific strikeout pitcher in the past, but in 1991 it appeared his velocity had decreased -- a scout measured his fastball at only 85 MPH in one outing. DeLeon relies more now on his slider and split-fingered fastball, getting fewer strikeouts but inducing more ground balls. He also throws a curve, but mainly for variety. DeLeon's control has never been good, but it was better last year than in 1990.

No pitcher can win without support. His teammate's offense was actually worse than it seems. Of the 57 runs scored for DeLeon, 20 came in two games, leaving him with less than 2.3 runs per nine innings in his other 26 starts! In five August starts, DeLeon pitched 29 innings and allowed 7 earned runs. His ERA was 2.17, but his record was 0-1.

DeLeon, who hadn't had any arm problems until this season, was sidelined for three weeks from August 28 to September 23 by a strained muscle in his right shoulder.

HOLDING RUNNERS, FIELDING, HITTING:

DeLeon has an average pickoff move, but he gave increased attention to baserunners in 1991, and only 12 of 24 runners were successful. He is an average fielder, but made no errors in 1991. DeLeon swings hard and strikes out often. He can deliver the sacrifice when called upon to move a runner.

OVERALL:

DeLeon is the best losing pitcher in baseball. Everything he did on the mound in 1991 should have helped his team win. A trade may be beneficial for DeLeon, but the Cardinals would be crazy to let him go. The wins have to come if he keeps pitching as well as he did in 1991. Don't they?

JOSE DeLEON

Position: SP
Bats: R **Throws:** R
Ht: 6' 3" **Wt:** 215

Opening Day Age: 31
Born: 12/20/60 in Rancho Viejo, La Vega, Dominican Republic
ML Seasons: 9

Overall Statistics

	W	L	ERA	G	GS	Sv	IP	H	R	BB	SO	HR
1991	5	9	2.71	28	28	0	162.2	144	57	61	118	15
Career	73	105	3.68	261	243	4	1579.2	1286	711	697	1343	122

How Often He Throws Strikes

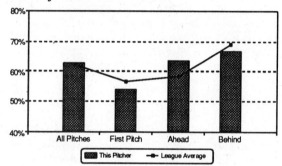

1991 Situational Stats

	W	L	ERA	Sv	IP		AB	H	HR	RBI	AVG
Home	3	4	2.42	0	89.1	LHB	326	82	9	25	.252
Road	2	5	3.07	0	73.1	RHB	277	62	6	21	.224
Day	2	3	2.51	0	46.2	Sc Pos	124	21	2	31	.169
Night	3	6	2.79	0	116.0	Clutch	37	12	1	5	.324

1991 Rankings (National League)

- ➡ 1st in lowest groundball/flyball ratio (.84) and lowest run support per 9 innings (3.2)
- ➡ 4th in ERA at home (2.42)
- ➡ 6th in ERA (2.71)
- ➡ 7th in hit batsmen (6), lowest stolen base percentage allowed (50.0%) and least GDPs induced per 9 innings (.44)
- ➡ Led the Cardinals in ERA, runners caught stealing (12), most strikeouts per 9 innings (6.5) and ERA at home

HITTING:

Left fielder Bernard Gilkey looked good as gold in spring training as he led the Cardinals with 33 hits and had a .407 average. Gilkey is a prototypical Cardinal in that his blazing speed is his greatest weapon. He also has a fine eye, consistently walking more than he strikes out. He was chosen the American Association's Best Baserunner and Most Exciting Player in 1990, and was a AAA All-Star.

His '91 season was not that exciting. Gilkey had steadily improved as a minor league hitter, which caused unrealistic expectations. He has never topped .300 and has little power, though he legs his share of doubles. After a .260 April, which thrilled the Cardinals, he faded badly.

Before he could break his slump, Gilkey had to go on the disabled list with a broken thumb. After his return he seemed to have trouble with good fastballs -- the thumb injury might have hampered his ability to grip the bat -- and eventually he was sent to the minors. In Louisville, Gilkey's hitting woes continued, plus he pulled a quadriceps muscle; except for brief action, his season was over.

BASERUNNING:

It was disappointing to the Cardinals that Gilkey managed only 22 steal attempts, 14 successfully. He had some trouble early, and just as he was getting comfortable, suffered his injury. He will be a 30-steal man in the future, and more if he can play every day.

FIELDING:

Gilkey's great speed and good arm were evident in the spacious St. Louis outfield. He had six outfield assists and just one error in only half a season. He is a fine outfielder with excellent range.

OVERALL:

Though he batted only .216, Gilkey's season wasn't a total disaster. He drew 39 walks in 81 games and only struck out 33 times. With his speed and ability to make contact, it would be a major surprise if he failed to get his on-base percentage to a respectable level. Gilkey's thumb injury obviously hampered him, so the Cardinals aren't too discouraged by his poor rookie season.

BERNARD GILKEY

Position: LF
Bats: R **Throws:** R
Ht: 6' 0" **Wt:** 170

Opening Day Age: 25
Born: 9/24/66 in St. Louis, MO
ML Seasons: 2

Overall Statistics

	G	AB	R	H	D	T	HR	RBI	SB	BB	SO	AVG
1991	81	268	28	58	7	2	5	20	14	39	33	.216
Career	99	332	39	77	12	4	6	23	20	47	38	.232

Where He Hits the Ball

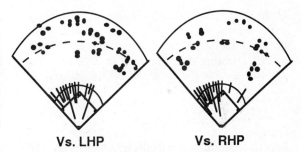

Vs. LHP   Vs. RHP

1991 Situational Stats

	AB	H	HR	RBI	AVG		AB	H	HR	RBI	AVG
Home	149	32	2	10	.215	LHP	137	26	2	9	.190
Road	119	26	3	10	.218	RHP	131	32	3	11	.244
Day	89	20	3	7	.225	Sc Pos	62	13	0	15	.210
Night	179	38	2	13	.212	Clutch	39	10	1	5	.256

1991 Rankings (National League)

→ 1st in lowest batting average with 2 strikes (.102)

→ 2nd in most GDPs per GDP situation (22.9%) and lowest slugging percentage vs. left-handed pitchers (.270)

→ 3rd lowest leadoff on-base average (.299)

→ 4th in lowest batting average with the bases loaded (.125) and lowest batting average on a 3-2 count (.036)

→ 5th lowest batting average vs. left-handed pitchers (.190)

→ 9th lowest stolen base percentage (63.6%)

→ Led the Cardinals in batting average on a 3-1 count (.500)

HITTING:

Pedro Guerrero's salary drive took a detour on July 7 when he broke his leg in a collision with his own catcher. He missed six weeks, and never got untracked afterwards. Guerrero has been one of the best all-around hitters in baseball for years, and though his first-half numbers indicate that he can still hit -- .284 with 53 RBI before the All-Star break -- there are signs that his skills are eroding.

Guerrero's slugging percentage has been in more-or-less steady decline for five or six years, but in 1991 even his solid first half produced just a .361 slugging mark. His on-base average, usually in the .350 to .400 range, was only .326. He had curious problems with left-handed pitching, going homerless in 160 at-bats for the season.

Guerrero still strikes out very seldom and hits the ball hard; more good seasons are not out of the question. He had a few of his patented hot streaks in 1991, earning N.L. Player of the Week honors just before he broke his leg. In 30 July at-bats, he slugged .700 and hit .367.

BASERUNNING:

Guerrero's immobility is well documented. Knee injuries, age, and artificial turf have erased the image of the player who stole 45 bases between 1982 and 1983. Still, he surprised some batteries in 1991, stealing four bases, but did not challenge outfielders' arms and had only 12 doubles.

FIELDING:

Guerrero led National League first basemen in errors with 16 and had a fielding average of .984. He plays deep and near the line to prevent extra-base hits, leaving Jose Oquendo responsible for anything hit in the hole. Shoulder troubles have affected his throwing.

OVERALL:

The next time Guerrero puts on a St. Louis uniform, it will probably be for an Old Timers game, as his days with the Cardinals seem to be over. Guerrero's poor 1991 season will undoubtedly cost him free agent money, but a lot of scouts still think he can be a productive hitter. It'll almost certainly have to be as a DH for an American League team.

PEDRO GUERRERO

Position: 1B
Bats: R **Throws:** R
Ht: 6' 0" **Wt:** 197

Opening Day Age: 35
Born: 6/29/56 in San Pedro de Macoris, Dominican Republic
ML Seasons: 14

Overall Statistics

	G	AB	R	H	D	T	HR	RBI	SB	BB	SO	AVG
1991	115	427	41	116	12	1	8	70	4	37	46	.272
Career	1493	5246	720	1586	261	28	214	882	95	598	837	.302

Where He Hits the Ball

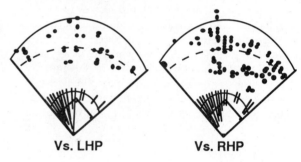

Vs. LHP   Vs. RHP

1991 Situational Stats

	AB	H	HR	RBI	AVG		AB	H	HR	RBI	AVG
Home	216	61	4	42	.282	LHP	160	41	0	15	.256
Road	211	55	4	28	.261	RHP	267	75	8	55	.281
Day	115	32	3	19	.278	Sc Pos	143	50	3	64	.350
Night	312	84	5	51	.269	Clutch	71	18	1	13	.254

1991 Rankings (National League)

→ 1st in lowest fielding percentage at first base (.984)

→ 2nd highest batting average with runners in scoring position (.350)

→ 3rd lowest cleanup slugging percentage (.363)

→ 6th highest batting average on an 0-2 count (.290)

→ Led the Cardinals in sacrifice flies (7), batting average with runners in scoring position and batting average on an 0-2 count

→ Led NL first basemen in errors (16)

PITCHING:

Ken Hill is a tall, lanky, hard-throwing righthander who in the past has relied mainly on a fastball and hard curve. Those pitches were still effective in 1991, but Hill's development of a new forkball made a big difference. He went 11-10, his first winning season in the majors, and only Pete Harnisch allowed fewer hits per inning among National League starters.

Walks have always been a problem for Hill, but he made some progress in 1991. He still has trouble throwing strikes when behind in the count. However, Hill ranked fourth among N.L. leaders in opponent's batting average with a .224 mark, so he was able to absorb the walks.

Hill had a breakthrough year in Louisville in 1990 where he developed the forkball, allowing just 47 hits in 67.1 innings. He is a power pitcher, not afraid to throw inside, and he records steady, if unspectacular, strikeout totals. In August Hill went on the 15-day disabled list with a strained right elbow, which helps explain his poor pitching in July and early August. The rest did him good -- he had a 23-inning scoreless streak and went 3-1 in his final seven outings.

HOLDING RUNNERS, FIELDING, HITTING:

Hill throws over to first often, but base stealers were successful in 19 of 30 attempts. He fields his position well, and committed only one error. He tied for the team lead with seven sacrifice hits and equalled Bob Tewksbury's four walks by Cards' pitchers. He didn't hit for much average, but did manage to collect three RBI on five hits and score two runs.

OVERALL:

Hill, who pitched very well for the Cardinals in 1991, was traded to the Expos after the season for Andres Galarraga. Hill still had control problems last year, and if he has to rely on very low hit totals to be effective, he could be in for a long season. But if the forkball remains a potent weapon, Hill could make it a long season for N.L. batters.

KEN HILL

Position: SP
Bats: R **Throws:** R
Ht: 6' 2" **Wt:** 175

Opening Day Age: 26
Born: 12/14/65 in Lynn, MA
ML Seasons: 4

Overall Statistics

	W	L	ERA	G	GS	Sv	IP	H	R	BB	SO	HR
1991	11	10	3.57	30	30	0	181.1	147	76	67	121	15
Career	23	32	4.03	84	78	0	470.2	428	226	205	297	31

How Often He Throws Strikes

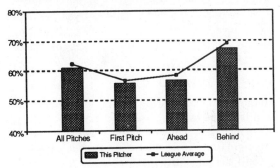

1991 Situational Stats

	W	L	ERA	Sv	IP		AB	H	HR	RBI	AVG
Home	6	4	3.18	0	87.2	LHB	367	87	8	36	.237
Road	5	6	3.94	0	93.2	RHB	289	60	7	33	.208
Day	6	2	2.14	0	67.1	Sc Pos	130	33	5	50	.254
Night	5	8	4.42	0	114.0	Clutch	63	14	2	6	.222

1991 Rankings (National League)

- ➡ 4th lowest batting average allowed (.224)
- ➡ 6th lowest run support per 9 innings (3.5)
- ➡ 7th in hit batsmen (6)
- ➡ 8th lowest strikeout/walk ratio (1.8)
- ➡ Led the Cardinals in walks allowed (67), strikeouts (121), wild pitches (7), pitches thrown (2,756), stolen bases allowed (19), lowest batting average allowed, lowest slugging percentage allowed (.346) and sacrfice bunts as a batter (7)

HITTING:

Rex(citable) Hudler had a disappointing season in 1991. Of course, by Hudler's standards, winning the World Series is all that counts and the statistics don't matter. There is no player in the National League who gives more of himself than Rex Hudler. Hudler wants to be a regular, but suffers from A) not hitting well enough to be a regular outfielder, and B) not fielding well enough to be a regular infielder.

Hudler's .227 average last year was a sharp decline from the .282 mark he posted in 1990. He slipped against lefties, who he usually handles well, and dropped over 200 points in his rare shots at righthanders. Hudler's power also suffered, going from seven home runs to just one. Trying to be more patient, he lost ground last year, seldom swinging at the first pitch but consistently getting behind in the count. With two strikes, he batted only .136.

BASERUNNING:

Hudler is the most daring runner on the team. He will try to advance a base on every opportunity, no matter how remote. Hudler was caught stealing eight times in 16 attempts at second, but was 4-for-4 stealing third base.

FIELDING:

Hudler makes some amazing plays. Once he had to run full speed and dive for a ball already going past him, but still robbed Herm Winningham of extra bases. The Cardinals won 1-0. In another game he dove head first and crashed his head into the wall but made the catch. He had to leave the game after that one, but even the opposition Met players came out to give him an ovation. Hudler has a below-average outfield arm, but his range and aggressiveness make up for it.

OVERALL:

Hudler provides leadership by example, on and off the field, and fills more than just a utility role for the Cardinals. Young players such as Lankford, Gilkey, Pena, and Zeile benefit by having Hudler around. He pushes everyone around him to work a little harder. However, if he opens 1992 hitting .175, his enthusiasm may not be able to save him.

REX HUDLER

Position: LF/CF
Bats: R **Throws:** R
Ht: 6' 0" **Wt:** 180

Opening Day Age: 31
Born: 9/2/60 in Tempe, AZ
ML Seasons: 7

Overall Statistics

	G	AB	R	H	D	T	HR	RBI	SB	BB	SO	AVG
1991	101	207	21	47	10	2	1	15	12	10	29	.227
Career	406	857	118	215	43	7	18	65	75	40	132	.251

Where He Hits the Ball

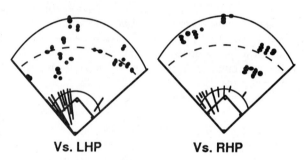

Vs. LHP	Vs. RHP

1991 Situational Stats

	AB	H	HR	RBI	AVG		AB	H	HR	RBI	AVG
Home	105	25	1	9	.238	LHP	155	39	1	10	.252
Road	102	22	0	6	.216	RHP	52	8	0	5	.154
Day	60	13	1	8	.217	Sc Pos	47	14	0	14	.298
Night	147	34	0	7	.231	Clutch	39	8	0	1	.205

1991 Rankings (National League)

➡ 5th lowest stolen base percentage (60.0%)

➡ 10th lowest on-base average vs. left-handed pitchers (.282)

➡ Led the Cardinals in steals of third (4)

HITTING:

The 1990 trade that brought switch-hitting Felix Jose from Oakland for batting champion Willie McGee worked like a charm for St. Louis, as Jose earned All-Star status immediately. Jose had shown signs of improvement in the 25 games he played after he came to St. Louis in 1990. He consolidated those gains in 1991.

Jose burst out of the box in April, hitting .354 with a .595 slugging average. He couldn't sustain that pace, but only hit below .282 during one month, July, when he batted .266. On September 1 Jose had his first two-homer game, and hit three more before the season ended. That was no fluke; he has upper-deck power, and the potential to hit 20 or more homers.

Never known for his patience, Jose showed some improvement last year with 50 walks. An excellent fastball hitter, he still can't resist the urge to jump on the first pitch, and it's hard to knock the results; last year he batted .373 when he put the first offering in play. He was an excellent clutch hitter in '91, batting .343 with runners in scoring position.

BASERUNNING:

Jose has good speed on the base paths, although he's a little rough as a base stealer. He stole 20 bases and is a constant threat to run, but he was caught 12 times. He'll challenge outfielders' arms, but he often runs himself into foolish outs.

FIELDING:

Jose has good right field skills with decent range and a terrific arm. His 14 outfield assists tied for the league lead for right fielders, and he cut down runners at second, third, and home. As with his running, however, Jose's defensive work is erratic at times.

OVERALL:

Despite Jose's excellent numbers last year, scouts are surprisingly split about his future. Some see him as a definite star who will run, throw and hit with power. Others see an immature player whose stats, however good, will hide a lot of clubhouse problems. Jose is not yet 27, however, and if he needs to develop some maturity, there's still plenty of time.

FELIX JOSE

Position: RF
Bats: B **Throws:** R
Ht: 6' 1" **Wt:** 190

Opening Day Age: 26
Born: 5/8/65 in Santo Domingo, Dominican Republic
ML Seasons: 4

Overall Statistics

	G	AB	R	H	D	T	HR	RBI	SB	BB	SO	AVG
1991	154	568	69	173	40	6	8	77	20	50	113	.305
Career	308	1057	128	299	59	7	19	135	33	78	208	.283

Where He Hits the Ball

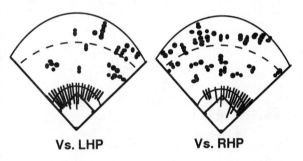

Vs. LHP   Vs. RHP

1991 Situational Stats

	AB	H	HR	RBI	AVG		AB	H	HR	RBI	AVG
Home	280	83	3	39	.296	LHP	262	78	2	30	.298
Road	288	90	5	38	.313	RHP	306	95	6	47	.310
Day	164	51	5	33	.311	Sc Pos	143	49	3	68	.343
Night	404	122	3	44	.302	Clutch	91	32	3	8	.352

1991 Rankings (National League)

- ➡ 2nd in doubles (40)
- ➡ 3rd in batting average with the bases loaded (.500)
- ➡ 5th in batting average (.305), hits (173) and batting average in the clutch (.352)
- ➡ Led the Cardinals in batting average, at-bats (568), hits, doubles, total bases (249), slugging percentage (.438), batting average in the clutch , batting average on a 3-2 count (.350), batting average on the road (.313), batting average after the 6th inning (.314) and batting average with 2 strikes (.243)

RAY LANKFORD

Position: CF
Bats: L **Throws:** L
Ht: 5'11" **Wt:** 180

Opening Day Age: 24
Born: 6/5/67 in Modesto, CA
ML Seasons: 2

HITTING:

Ray Lankford was handed the Cardinals' center field job last year when they traded Willie McGee and let Vince Coleman go as a free agent. Lankford had proven his mettle in a 39-game trial in 1990, hitting .286 with speed, power, and a .353 on-base percentage. Although Lankford couldn't match those numbers in 1991, he improved steadily throughout the season.

Early in the season, Lankford tried hard to make contact but was making a lot of soft outs. Later he began to swing with more authority. He was moved to the leadoff spot late in the year, and though his numbers didn't really look like a leadoff hitter's, they were very good. In September he hit .277 with six homers, slugged .509, and stole 11 bases in 12 attempts. Lankford showed he could handle the fastball, and improved against breaking stuff as the year wore on. His trouble in drawing walks (only 41) is still a problem.

BASERUNNING:

Lankford's baserunning is excellent already and should get better. He stole 44 bases, his high as a professional, and led the league with 15 triples. Lankford was caught stealing 20 times, and was often caught leaning at first and retired in rundowns. Despite getting on base only 184 times, he still scored 83 runs, a rate that trailed only Ron Gant and Howard Johnson, sluggers who drove themselves in over 30 times each.

FIELDING:

Lankford is often spectacular in center field. He covers the gaps in left center and right center and can go deep to rob hitters of extra-base hits. Lankford's six errors equalled Ron Gant's for most by an N.L. center fielder. Lankford may overestimate his below average arm, as he had only seven assists and seemed surprised when runners challenged him.

OVERALL:

Lankford has a bright future. He didn't win the Rookie of the Year Award honors, but he may turn out to be the most exciting of the '91 crop with his speed and range of skills. If he can regain the batting eye he displayed as a minor leaguer, he can become a major league star.

Overall Statistics

	G	AB	R	H	D	T	HR	RBI	SB	BB	SO	AVG
1991	151	566	83	142	23	15	9	69	44	41	114	.251
Career	190	692	95	178	33	16	12	81	52	54	141	.257

Where He Hits the Ball

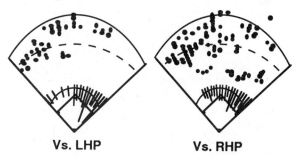

Vs. LHP   **Vs. RHP**

1991 Situational Stats

	AB	H	HR	RBI	AVG			AB	H	HR	RBI	AVG
Home	283	67	4	33	.237		LHP	220	52	0	26	.236
Road	283	75	5	36	.265		RHP	346	90	9	43	.260
Day	146	38	4	19	.260		Sc Pos	133	38	1	54	.286
Night	420	104	5	50	.248		Clutch	91	23	1	14	.253

1991 Rankings (National League)

- ➡ 1st in triples (15) and errors in center field (6)
- ➡ 3rd in most runs scored per time reached base (45.1%) and lowest batting average with the bases loaded (.125)
- ➡ 4th in lowest batting average (.251), stolen bases (44), caught stealing (20), least GDPs per GDP situation (3.7%) and lowest batting average at home (.237)
- ➡ 5th lowest on-base average (.301)
- ➡ Led the Cardinals in triples, stolen bases, caught stealing, strikeouts (114) and most runs scored per time reached base

PITCHING:

Rookie righthander Omar Olivares gave no indication in spring training, or early in the 1991 season, that he would become one of the mainstays of the Cardinal starting rotation. Olivares earned his only major league save on April 20 vs Philadelphia, then was optioned to Louisville on the 24th with a 5.14 ERA.

At Louisville Olivares was used as a starter before being recalled to stay on May 24. He didn't pitch well at first, but gradually lowered his ERA, never had a losing month, and went 9-6 during the second half with a 3.07 ERA. Olivares carried shutouts through eight innings in three of his last five starts. He was very consistent, pitching into the sixth inning in 21 of his last 22 starts.

Olivares tries to get hitters to hit ground balls, and since he doesn't try to overpower anyone, he has great stamina and can last late into games. His fastball is above-average at 89 MPH, and he also throws a slider with a sweeping break, while using a split-fingered fastball as his offspeed pitch. His pitches often miss low, and walks can be a problem for him. His .316 on-base percentage allowed was one of the worst in the league.

HOLDING RUNNERS, FIELDING, HITTING:

Olivares keeps runners close, but does not yet have a polished move to first. He committed two errors, but helps make up for any fielding deficiencies with his hitting. Olivares had three doubles among his 12 hits, and six RBI. Olivares is a candidate to lead N.L. pitchers in home runs some day. He showed some power to center and coaxed a couple of walks while striking out 16 times.

OVERALL:

Olivares came over to the Cards from the Padre system, where he tantalized overanxious minor league hitters into hitting a ton of ground balls. Though just 24, he is a highly regarded pitcher, and his second half performance bodes well for 1992. If he can keep the walks under control, he should be fine.

OMAR OLIVARES

Position: SP
Bats: R **Throws:** R
Ht: 6' 1" **Wt:** 185

Opening Day Age: 24
Born: 7/6/67 in Mayaguez, Puerto Rico
ML Seasons: 2

Overall Statistics

	W	L	ERA	G	GS	Sv	IP	H	R	BB	SO	HR
1991	11	7	3.71	28	24	1	167.1	148	72	61	91	13
Career	12	8	3.53	37	30	1	216.2	193	89	78	111	15

How Often He Throws Strikes

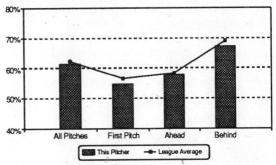

1991 Situational Stats

	W	L	ERA	Sv	IP		AB	H	HR	RBI	AVG
Home	7	5	3.33	1	97.1	LHB	345	81	5	32	.235
Road	4	2	4.24	0	70.0	RHB	264	67	8	32	.254
Day	2	2	4.74	0	38.0	Sc Pos	123	33	1	43	.268
Night	9	5	3.41	1	129.1	Clutch	56	13	1	1	.232

1991 Rankings (National League)

→ 5th in lowest strikeout/walk ratio (1.5) and lowest stolen base percentage allowed (47.6%)

→ 7th least strikeouts per 9 innings (4.9)

→ Led the Cardinals in pickoff throws (129), winning percentage (.611), groundball/fly-ball ratio (1.6) and lowest stolen base percentage allowed

GREAT RANGE

JOSE OQUENDO

Position: 2B/SS
Bats: B **Throws:** R
Ht: 5'10" **Wt:** 160

Opening Day Age: 28
Born: 7/4/63 in Rio Piedras, Puerto Rico
ML Seasons: 8

HITTING:

Jose Oquendo fell from his career high average of .291 in 1989 to .252 in 1990. He was expected to rebound in 1991, to at least above .250. But Oquendo didn't rebound and hit a soft .240. Oquendo has no power, and opposition fielders know they can play shallow and steal hits.

Oquendo got off to a slow start, hitting .200 in April and a dismal .146 in May. He found a groove in mid-July, and by mid-August had raised his average to .275, but then went into another swoon. Oquendo got only six hits in September, and his poor finish threatens his status as a regular.

A patient hitter, Oquendo has had more walks than strikeouts every season since 1987. Despite the poor hitting, he had a very fine .357 on-base percentage last year, drawing 67 walks. Careful not to chase pitches out of the strike zone, he's a good breaking ball hitter, but in the last couple of years pitchers have had increasing success over-powering him with fastballs.

BASERUNNING:

Oquendo has poor baserunning instincts, is not fast, and is hesitant to run. He has stolen only one base in each of the last two seasons. If a speedy runner is needed, Geronimo Pena will pinch run.

FIELDING:

Jose Oquendo is an outstanding defensive second baseman. He has it all: terrific range, a very strong arm, and a solid glove. He can go up the middle and still cover the territory to his left to protect Pedro Guerrero. He is not the best in the league on the pivot, but is still a Gold Glove candidate.

OVERALL:

The Cardinal offense is really not strong enough to support Oquendo, and Geronimo Pena, who has some sock, is pushing him at second base. Oquendo will have to do better in 1992 or he will become Ozzie Smith's caddie. He is still a valuable player, and is only 28. He was a fine hitter in 1989, and could be again.

Overall Statistics

	G	AB	R	H	D	T	HR	RBI	SB	BB	SO	AVG
1991	127	366	37	88	11	4	1	26	1	67	48	.240
Career	987	2745	285	717	91	18	12	221	33	375	328	.261

Where He Hits the Ball

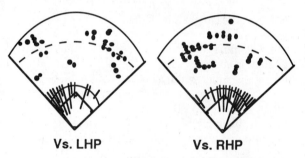

Vs. LHP   **Vs. RHP**

1991 Situational Stats

	AB	H	HR	RBI	AVG		AB	H	HR	RBI	AVG
Home	184	48	0	14	.261	LHP	150	36	1	15	.240
Road	182	40	1	12	.220	RHP	216	52	0	11	.241
Day	92	23	1	11	.250	Sc Pos	80	20	0	25	.250
Night	274	65	0	15	.237	Clutch	64	19	1	6	.297

1991 Rankings (National League)

- → 3rd highest fielding percentage at second base (.988)
- → 6th in intentional walks (13)
- → 7th lowest percentage of swings that missed (11.7%)
- → Led the Cardinals in intentional walks

HITTING:

Manager Joe Torre made a controversial decision when he decided to move veteran backup catcher Tom Pagnozzi into the starting lineup last year. Torre felt Todd Zeile would hit better as a third baseman and Pagnozzi would improve the Cardinal defense behind the plate. The plan worked and paid dividends.

Pagnozzi's .264 batting average was the highest for a Cardinal regular catcher since Ted Simmons hit .303 in 1980, and he had no significant platoon differential. Pagnozzi had never hit a triple before 1991; last year he had five. He isn't a power hitter, but equalled his career high of two home runs and hit 24 doubles. Pagnozzi makes contact, striking out only 63 times. He looked good against both fastballers and breaking-ballers, and his only real negative was his low total of 36 walks.

Pagnozzi drove in a career-high 57 runs and had the highest Cardinal RBI game of the season, driving home six runs on May 26 at New York. Although he caught a lot of games, he finished the season strongly. He hit .348 in 26 games after September 1 with an on-base percentage of .416.

BASERUNNING:

Pagnozzi tied Tim McCarver's modern day single-season record of nine stolen bases by a Cardinal catcher. Torre somewhat obsessively tried to help Pagnozzi achieve the record by having him run at will, but Pag was caught in each of his final three attempts, including the last in his only appearance as a pinch runner. If not for the weak finish, Pagnozzi wouldn't have had such a poor stealing record (9-for-22).

FIELDING:

Pagnozzi won a Gold Glove for his excellent defensive work in 1991. He committed only seven errors while throwing out 70 of 156 basestealers (45%). The pitchers have confidence in Pagnozzi's pitch selection and in his ability to prevent wild pitches.

OVERALL:

Pagnozzi, at 29, may be ready to come into his own. His defense is of All-Star caliber, and he hasn't yet received the fan recognition he deserves. However, N.L. opponents are becoming aware of the receiver's talents.

TOM PAGNOZZI

Position: C
Bats: R **Throws:** R
Ht: 6' 1" **Wt:** 190

Opening Day Age: 29
Born: 7/30/62 in Tucson, AZ
ML Seasons: 5

Overall Statistics

	G	AB	R	H	D	T	HR	RBI	SB	BB	SO	AVG
1991	140	459	38	121	24	5	2	57	9	36	63	.264
Career	369	1002	86	258	51	5	6	107	11	71	164	.257

Where He Hits the Ball

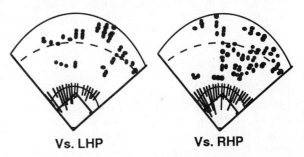

Vs. LHP   Vs. RHP

1991 Situational Stats

	AB	H	HR	RBI	AVG		AB	H	HR	RBI	AVG
Home	221	50	2	23	.226	LHP	201	51	2	25	.254
Road	238	71	0	34	.298	RHP	258	70	0	32	.271
Day	118	36	2	25	.305	Sc Pos	134	35	1	53	.261
Night	341	85	0	32	.249	Clutch	84	16	0	3	.190

1991 Rankings (National League)

→ 1st in lowest stolen base percentage (40.9%) and least runs scored per time reached base (23.6%)

→ 2nd in highest percentage of runners caught stealing as a catcher (44.9%), lowest HR frequency (230 ABs per HR) and lowest batting average at home (.226)

→ 6th least pitches seen per plate appearance (3.37)

→ 7th lowest slugging percentage (.351)

→ Led NL catchers in triples (5), caught stealing (13), intentional walks (6), groundball/flyball ratio (1.6), batting average on an 0-2 count (.219) and batting average on the road (.298)

HITTING:

Geronimo Pena is a second baseman looking for a place to play. It looked as if he was being groomed for third base, but Todd Zeile has taken that spot. At shortstop, Ozzie Smith has found the fountain of youth. Pena is a better hitter than Jose Oquendo, and has some power, but hasn't shown quite enough to replace Oquendo at second base.

The switch-hitting Pena has struggled from the left side, hitting just .185 in 1991. He had a lot of problems in particular with righties' breaking stuff. He fared a lot better as a right-handed batter, hitting for average and power. Pena batted .301 with a .527 slugging percentage against southpaw pitching.

Joe Torre got Pena into games as often as was possible last year. The youngster started two games in left field, 39 games at second, and was used 11 times as a pinch hitter. Clearly, Torre liked Pena's hitting potential.

BASERUNNING:

Pena is an excellent baserunner, stealing 15 bases in 20 attempts; he was a great minor league basestealer, leading the minors with 80 steals in 1987. He didn't ground into a double play during the season. Torre utilized Pena's speed, using him 31 times as a pinch runner and he scored 12 runs.

FIELDING:

In 1990 at Louisville, the Cardinals tried to move Pena to third base, but the experiment was given up in July as Pena couldn't adjust from second to third base. Pena has the skills to be a fine second baseman, with above average range and quickness.

OVERALL:

The Cardinals have a lot of guys who can't hit lefthanders, which makes Pena a valuable commodity. He is only 25 and has the power, the speed, and the tools of a major leaguer. Torre wants Pena to play in the winter leagues to get more experience in left field, perhaps considering some platoon work for him. The Cardinals will find some use for Pena, but if he wants to be a regular, he has to hit righties better.

GERONIMO PENA

Position: 2B
Bats: B **Throws:** R
Ht: 6' 1" **Wt:** 170

Opening Day Age: 25
Born: 3/29/67 in Distrito Nacional, Dominican Republic
ML Seasons: 2

Overall Statistics

	G	AB	R	H	D	T	HR	RBI	SB	BB	SO	AVG
1991	104	185	38	45	8	3	5	17	15	18	45	.243
Career	122	230	43	56	10	3	5	19	16	22	59	.243

Where He Hits the Ball

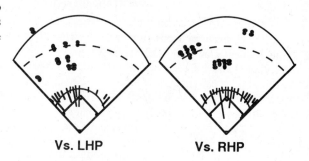

Vs. LHP   Vs. RHP

1991 Situational Stats

	AB	H	HR	RBI	AVG		AB	H	HR	RBI	AVG
Home	91	20	1	4	.220	LHP	93	28	4	13	.301
Road	94	25	4	13	.266	RHP	92	17	1	4	.185
Day	60	16	3	5	.267	Sc Pos	51	11	0	12	.216
Night	125	29	2	12	.232	Clutch	41	7	1	3	.171

1991 Rankings (National League)

➡ Led the Cardinals in hit by pitch (5)

PITCHING:

Veteran righthander Bryn Smith bounced back quickly from his only major league trip to the disabled list in 1990 to lead the club with 31 starts in 1991. Smith does not throw hard but is a smart pitcher who moves the ball around, throws strikes, and uses a sinker and offspeed palmball to keep his strikeouts at a respectable level. In 1991 his consistency bore the fruit of his 100th victory. "This is like 300 for me," said Smith. "I know I'll never win 200." Smith has won more than 12 games only once in his career, and notched an even dozen last season. He was the second-best supported pitcher in the league in '91, with 5.5 runs per game, and he should have won 15 or more. The same could be said for his entire career.

Opposing managers load their lineups with left-handers against Smith, but he was much improved against them in 1991 after a poor 1990. Smith allowed only 10.9 baserunners per nine innings, but it should be noted that his strikeout-to-walk ratio, while good at two-to-one, is a slip from his established rate of around 2.5-to-one.

HOLDING RUNNERS, FIELDING, HITTING:

Smith has never held runners very well but improved slightly from 1990. Still, 19 of 27 (70%) baserunners were successful despite the craft of Tom Pagnozzi. Smith fielded 1.000 and is a thorough professional defensively. He's also among the best hitting pitchers in the league. He had an eight-game hitting streak and batted .246 for the season, leading the pitching staff with eight RBI. As a Cardinal, Smith has hit .250 over two seasons.

OVERALL:

Smith should be able to post ten or more wins, even at age 36. He is not going to help a team as the number-one or two starter, however. The Cardinals are still rebuilding, and though Smith's innings and consistency are valuable to them, he may have greater value in a trade for some younger players.

BRYN SMITH

Position: SP
Bats: R **Throws:** R
Ht: 6' 2" **Wt:** 205

Opening Day Age: 36
Born: 8/11/55 in Marietta, GA
ML Seasons: 11

Overall Statistics

	W	L	ERA	G	GS	Sv	IP	H	R	BB	SO	HR
1991	12	9	3.85	31	31	0	198.2	188	95	45	94	16
Career	102	88	3.43	341	249	6	1740.1	1658	768	416	1010	135

How Often He Throws Strikes

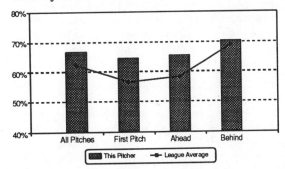

1991 Situational Stats

	W	L	ERA	Sv	IP		AB	H	HR	RBI	AVG
Home	5	4	3.52	0	107.1	LHB	441	120	7	50	.272
Road	7	5	4.24	0	91.1	RHB	308	68	9	34	.221
Day	2	2	4.01	0	49.1	Sc Pos	164	41	5	63	.250
Night	10	7	3.80	0	149.1	Clutch	25	7	0	2	.280

1991 Rankings (National League)

- ➡ 2nd in least pitches thrown per batter (3.26) and most run support per 9 innings (5.5)
- ➡ 3rd least strikeouts per 9 innings (4.3)
- ➡ 4th in hit batsmen (7)
- ➡ 7th highest ERA (3.85)
- ➡ Led the Cardinals in wins (12), games started (31), complete games (3), innings (198.2), batters faced (818), home runs allowed (16), stolen bases allowed (19), strikeout/walk ratio (2.1), lowest on-base average allowed (.297), most run support per 9 innings and lowest batting average allowed with runners in scoring position (.250)

LEE SMITH

STOPPER

Position: RP
Bats: R **Throws:** R
Ht: 6' 6" **Wt:** 250

Opening Day Age: 34
Born: 12/4/57 in
Jamestown, LA
ML Seasons: 12

PITCHING:

Lee Smith had a career year in 1991, bettering all of his stellar seasons with the Cubs, Red Sox, and Cardinals. Smith added a new pitch, an 83-MPH split-fingered fastball, to his 93-MPH heater and hard slider, and befuddled National League hitters. He recorded a career- and major league-high 47 saves, breaking the National League record for saves in a season. His 300th save came in his 703rd game, the second-fastest to 300 behind Bruce Sutter who needed 661 games. Big Lee moved ahead of Rich Gossage into third place on the all-time save list. Only Jeff Reardon has more saves among active pitchers.

Las year Smith appeared in 67 games, becoming the second player in major league history (the other was Ron Perranoski) to appear in 50 or more games for 10 straight seasons. He has blown only 11 of 85 save opportunities in two seasons with the Cardinals.

In 73 innings, Smith walked only 13, and five were intentional. He struck out 67 batters, an excellent average of 8.3 per nine innings, but it should be noted that it was the first time since 1984 that he failed to fan a batter per inning. His 2.34 ERA was third among N.L. relievers.

HOLDING RUNNERS, FIELDING, HITTING:

Smith is huge at 6-6 and is listed at 250 pounds more as a courtesy than anything else. For a big guy he fields his position adequately. Though he throws heat, he delivers his pitches slowly, and runners stole 10 bases in 12 attempts. Big Lee does not bat.

OVERALL:

The Cardinals make noise about using Todd Worrell more if he returns in 1992, easing the strain on the aging, knee-weary Smith. At age 34 the extra pounds are taking a toll on his body. Smith's arm is fine, but he was tired by season's end and troubled by a groin strain. His weight and supposed imminent collapse have been the subjects of winter discussion since 1985, and he's still the best. He should be again in 1992. Without Smith, the Cardinals can't even dream of contention.

Overall Statistics

	W	L	ERA	G	GS	Sv	IP	H	R	BB	SO	HR
1991	6	3	2.34	67	0	47	73.0	70	19	13	67	5
Career	61	65	2.84	717	6	312	992.1	857	347	376	990	59

How Often He Throws Strikes

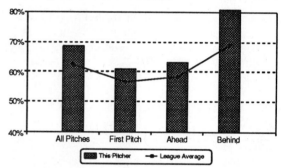

This Pitcher ■ League Average

1991 Situational Stats

	W	L	ERA	Sv	IP		AB	H	HR	RBI	AVG
Home	6	1	1.38	26	45.2	LHB	165	42	3	19	.255
Road	0	2	3.95	21	27.1	RHB	116	28	2	12	.241
Day	2	1	3.00	14	21.0	Sc Pos	87	23	2	27	.264
Night	4	2	2.08	33	52.0	Clutch	230	58	5	29	.252

1991 Rankings (National League)

→ 1st in saves (47), games finished (61), save opportunites (53) and save percentage (88.7%)

→ 3rd lowest relief ERA (2.34)

→ 6th most strikeouts per 9 innings in relief (8.3)

→ 7th in blown saves (6)

→ Led the Cardinals in saves, games finished, save opportunities, save percentage, blown saves, first batter efficiency (.270), relief ERA and most strikeouts per 9 innings in relief

HITTING:

Ozzie Smith entered the 1991 season under the cloud of his 1990 performance, his poorest since his first year in St. Louis (1982). Would the Cardinals exercise their option for 1992? Smith was looking for four more years and a raise on his $2 million contract, while the Cardinals held a buyout option in the event of further deterioration.

Smith responded with the second-highest average of his career and an All-Star season. He corrected the most troubling aspect of 1990 by raising his average 73 points against right-handed pitchers. Smith continues to exhibit the batting eye that has made him fourth among active players in walk/strikeout ratio, behind only Wade Boggs, Willie Randolph, and Mike Scioscia; he has never fanned even 50 times in a season. From either side, he likes the ball upstairs.

BASERUNNING:

There is no lack of evidence that Smith still has plenty of speed and baserunning smarts. He scored 96 runs, including his 1,000th career run. He reached the 20+ stolen base mark for the 14th straight season and was second on the team with 35 stolen bases, giving him 499 career steals. Smith still takes extra bases and challenges defenses. His 22 infield singles and six bunt hits led the Cards.

FIELDING:

Smith made just eight errors last year, surpassing Larry Bowa's National League record of nine for shortstops in 150+ games, set back in 1972. The Gold Glove winner still has excellent range, especially on pop-ups, and plays the hitters well. Smith's 79 double plays were second in the league, and he was a big help to Todd Zeile, who was trying to learn the ropes at third base. He may not be the old Wizard, but there still aren't many like him.

OVERALL:

Smith will definitely be back in 1992, and with the way the Cardinals have been cutting contracts over the last few years, they should have the money to give him that four-year deal. Smith is now off the map of normal career progression, and, like Carlton Fisk or Nolan Ryan, could be a productive player for many more years.

OZZIE SMITH

Position: SS
Bats: B **Throws:** R
Ht: 5'10" **Wt:** 160

Opening Day Age: 37
Born: 12/26/54 in Mobile, AL
ML Seasons: 14

Overall Statistics

	G	AB	R	H	D	T	HR	RBI	SB	BB	SO	AVG
1991	150	550	96	157	30	3	3	50	35	83	36	.285
Career	2076	7569	1006	1955	327	55	22	650	499	890	490	.258

Where He Hits the Ball

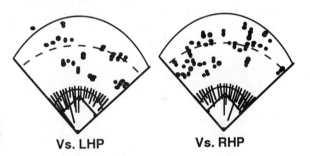

Vs. LHP   Vs. RHP

1991 Situational Stats

	AB	H	HR	RBI	AVG		AB	H	HR	RBI	AVG
Home	291	94	2	28	.323	LHP	248	65	3	25	.262
Road	259	63	1	22	.243	RHP	302	92	0	25	.305
Day	150	43	0	12	.287	Sc Pos	138	38	1	43	.275
Night	400	114	3	38	.285	Clutch	76	18	0	13	.237

1991 Rankings (National League)

→ 2nd in lowest percentage of swings that missed (8.8%) and highest percentage of swings put into play (55.4%)

→ 3rd lowest HR frequency (183 ABs per HR)

→ 5th in groundball/flyball ratio (2.0) and batting average at home (.323)

→ Led the Cardinals in runs (96), singles (121), walks (83), times on base (241), plate appearances (641), on-base average (.380), groundball/flyball ratio, stolen base percentage (79.5%), batting average at home and bunts in play (15)

→ Led NL shortstops in fielding percentage (.988)

PITCHING:

In 1991, Scott Terry was rebounding from offseason arthroscopic surgery to repair torn cartilage in his right shoulder, and the Cardinals weren't sure what to expect from him. Terry came through with his best season since his 9-6, 2.92 ERA year of 1988. He appeared in a career-high 65 games, all in relief. It was the first season since 1987 that Terry pitched exclusively out of the bullpen.

Terry led the club's right-handed relievers with 80.1 innings pitched and led the staff with 15 holds. Whitey Herzog sent him to the bullpen after he gave up 14 homers in less than 150 innings in 1989. It helped Terry; he gave up only one homer in 1991, and used his 89-MPH fastball to fan 52 while issuing just 18 unintentional walks. He throws both a cut fastball and a sinker, keeping the ball down, and last year induced twice as many ground balls as fly balls. Terry also throws a slider and a so-so change, but he's primarily a fastballer. Terry seems to have mastered the mechanical changes that helped him finish strong in 1990.

Despite the good pitching, Terry was weakest when he needed to be toughest: when facing his first batter. He allowed a .298 average to first hitters, walking eight. He had only one rough stretch, in July, though an injury shut him down in September.

HOLDING RUNNERS, FIELDING, HITTING:

Terry is an excellent fielder who spent over three seasons as an outfielder before becoming a pitcher. He made no errors, wild pitches, or balks. Ten runners attempted to steal, and seven were successful. Terry had only seven at-bats, but managed a run and a RBI.

OVERALL:

Terry didn't appear in any games after September 13th. He developed an inflammation in his right shoulder which was not determined to be serious. However, he was held out the rest of the season as a precaution. Terry proved valuable to the Cards during the season and will be expected to pitch in the same middle relief role in '92.

SCOTT TERRY

Position: RP
Bats: R **Throws:** R
Ht: 5'11" **Wt:** 195

Opening Day Age: 32
Born: 11/21/59 in Hobbs, NM
ML Seasons: 6

Overall Statistics

	W	L	ERA	G	GS	Sv	IP	H	R	BB	SO	HR
1991	4	4	2.80	65	0	1	80.1	76	31	32	52	1
Career	24	28	3.73	236	40	8	499.1	491	234	176	262	35

How Often He Throws Strikes

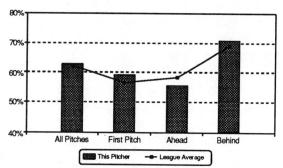

1991 Situational Stats

	W	L	ERA	Sv	IP		AB	H	HR	RBI	AVG
Home	4	1	1.19	0	45.1	LHB	171	41	1	18	.240
Road	0	3	4.89	1	35.0	RHB	134	35	0	13	.261
Day	1	1	2.00	0	18.0	Sc Pos	91	18	1	30	.198
Night	3	3	3.03	1	62.1	Clutch	132	35	1	17	.265

1991 Rankings (National League)

→ 2nd in holds (15)
→ 9th worst first batter efficiency (.298)
→ Led the Cardinals in holds

PITCHING:

Bob Tewksbury didn't become a rotation starter until age 30; he was derailed along the way by five trips to the disabled list. He made 20 starts in 1990, showcasing his amazing control by walking only 11 hitters -- two intentional -- in 131 innings as a starter. In 1991 he made 30 starts for the Cards, and pitching coach Joe Coleman urged Tewksbury to pitch inside and use his breaking ball to set up his fastball.

A smart veteran, Tewksbury was able to quickly assimilate Coleman's approach to pitching. With his 84 MPH fastball, he still only struck out 75 batters, but the heater was more effective than ever before. Tewksbury works quickly, throwing the not-very-fastball just off the black. He also throws a slider, curve and change-up, none of which are exceptional pitches. He gets clobbered often, but also fools many hitters.

Tewksbury allowed opponents a .281 average -- only Frank Viola was worse in the N.L. -- and gave up the league's third-most hits per inning. So, though he walked just 38, he allowed a dangerous 11.7 baserunners per nine. His ERA of 3.25 kept his team close enough for the Cards to go 18-12 in his 30 starts.

HOLDING RUNNERS, FIELDING, HITTING:

Runners don't take big leads off Tewksbury, though he rarely throws over. His control is so good that Tom Pagnozzi always receives the pitch in an excellent position to throw. Only 20 runners attempted to steal on him, and 10 were caught. Tewksbury will attempt the play at second on a sacrifice, and is a good fielder, though he made two errors. He's a swinger at the plate, hitting .155 and scoring five runs.

OVERALL:

Tewksbury, Omar Olivares, Bryn Smith, and Rheal Cormier will fill out the Cardinal rotation behind DeLeon. Tewksbury walks a fine line with his "let 'em hit it" philosophy, but his great control makes it work. He should continue as a rotation starter in 1991.

BOB TEWKSBURY

Position: SP
Bats: R **Throws:** R
Ht: 6' 4" **Wt:** 200

Opening Day Age: 31
Born: 11/30/60 in Concord, NH
ML Seasons: 6

Overall Statistics

	W	L	ERA	G	GS	Sv	IP	H	R	BB	SO	HR
1991	11	12	3.25	30	30	0	191.0	206	86	38	75	13
Career	32	34	3.67	104	84	1	551.1	611	269	116	214	37

How Often He Throws Strikes

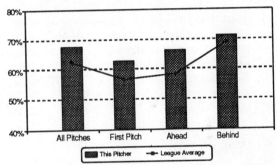

This Pitcher — League Average

1991 Situational Stats

	W	L	ERA	Sv	IP		AB	H	HR	RBI	AVG
Home	6	3	3.24	0	94.1	LHB	406	113	4	38	.278
Road	5	9	3.26	0	96.2	RHB	327	93	9	41	.284
Day	4	6	2.95	0	64.0	Sc Pos	169	48	4	64	.284
Night	7	6	3.40	0	127.0	Clutch	43	10	1	3	.233

1991 Rankings (National League)

→ 1st in least pitches thrown per batter (3.11) and least strikeouts per 9 innings (3.5)

→ 2nd highest batting average allowed (.281) and most GDPs induced per 9 innings (.90)

→ 4th in GDPs induced (19) and highest slugging percentage allowed (.413)

→ 6th lowest stolen base percentage allowed (50.0%)

→ Led the Cardinals in losses (12), complete games (3), hits allowed (206), GDPs induced, least pitches thrown per batter, least home runs allowed per 9 innings (.61), most GDPs induced per 9 innings, ERA on the road (3.26) and most sacrifice bunts as a batter (7)

HITTING:

Milt Thompson returned to doing what he does best in 1991: coming off the bench as a super sub. After signing a big contract before the 1990 season, Thompson flopped as a regular. With the arrival of Bernard Gilkey, Ray Lankford, and Felix Jose, Thompson was used mostly against righthanders. He responded with his best offensive season, even if you consider his .216 batting average in 74 at-bats against lefties.

Thompson hit well over .400 in April and May, but when Gilkey was injured he was forced to play against all kinds of pitchers and his average steadily dropped. In September, playing almost every day, Thompson hit just .243 with 18 strikeouts.

Still very fast, Thompson has always been an extreme ground ball hitter who attempts to take advantage of his speed. He hit almost three times as many balls on the ground as in the air last year, but corrected his tendency to pull everything to second base. Thompson loves the low fastball, and thrives when he can lay off the high heat. A smart hitter, he uses the whole field.

BASERUNNING:

Thompson has always been a good baserunner. He slapped 16 doubles and legged out five triples among his 100 hits. He is a threat to steal, and usually successful stealing a base at critical times. His 16-for-25 mark in 1991 is below his career success rate; he can do better.

FIELDING:

Thompson helps the Cardinals by being able to play all three outfield positions. He's probably best in left field; though he gets a good jump, he lacks the range of a classic center fielder, and his arm is a little weak for right. But he does a respectable job at each spot.

OVERALL:

Thompson has a great attitude and is an unselfish player. Returned to his comfort zone in 1991, he was a valuable player for the Cardinals. The greatest obstacle in his path is Bernard Gilkey, and their roles might be reversed if Gilkey doesn't learn to hit lefties.

MILT THOMPSON

Position: LF
Bats: L **Throws:** R
Ht: 5'11" **Wt:** 170

Opening Day Age: 33
Born: 1/5/59 in
Washington, DC
ML Seasons: 8

Overall Statistics

	G	AB	R	H	D	T	HR	RBI	SB	BB	SO	AVG
1991	115	326	55	100	16	5	6	34	16	32	53	.307
Career	871	2774	367	777	115	34	33	241	173	235	459	.280

Where He Hits the Ball

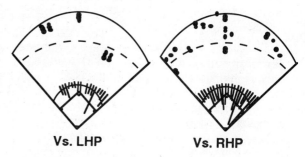

Vs. LHP	Vs. RHP

1991 Situational Stats

	AB	H	HR	RBI	AVG		AB	H	HR	RBI	AVG
Home	159	45	4	21	.283	LHP	74	16	1	6	.216
Road	167	55	2	13	.329	RHP	252	84	5	28	.333
Day	94	28	1	11	.298	Sc Pos	86	19	0	26	.221
Night	232	72	5	23	.310	Clutch	71	20	1	11	.282

1991 Rankings (National League)

- → 7th lowest batting average with runners in scoring position (.221)
- → Led NL left fielders in least GDPs per GDP situation (5.8%)

HITTING:

The Cardinals showed some nerve last year, moving young catcher Todd Zeile to a new position, third base. The experiment worked mainly because Zeile, who had a few problems learning his new position, labored hard to improve and didn't let the position switch affect his hitting. On the contrary, Zeile's offensive skills continued to grow.

Zeile provided the Cardinals with solid hitting, raising his average to .280. His home run total dropped from 15 in his rookie season to 11, but he led the team and belted 50 extra-base hits. The biggest improvement was in raising his RBI total from 57 to 81. As a rookie Zeile had looked overmatched against good fastballers, and hit only .163 with runners in scoring position. There were no such problems last year, when he improved his scoring position average to .304.

Though still very young, Zeile is already a very selective hitter, with 62 walks last season. Zeile in fact may be a little too selective, sometimes missing chances to pull the trigger, but the Cards won't mess with success.

BASERUNNING:

Zeile is an aggressive runner on the base paths and legged out three triples to go with his 36 doubles. He had 28 steal attempts last year after only six in 1990, and his 17 steals adds a new dimension to his offensive game.

FIELDING:

Nobody expected Zeile to win a Gold Glove last season, least of all Zeile, who resisted the move. His 25 errors led the league and his range is just average, but he made many errors late in the season and fatigue could have been a factor. When he learns that he doesn't have to hurry his throws his fielding will be much improved.

OVERALL:

Zeile is poised to become a star. He is a selective hitter with power, and the fences at Busch Stadium are being moved in for 1992. His defensive game is already decent despite extremely limited experience at third. If the Cardinals' new team jells in the next few years, he could be the cleanup hitter for a championship team.

TODD ZEILE

Position: 3B
Bats: R **Throws:** R
Ht: 6' 1" **Wt:** 190

Opening Day Age: 26
Born: 9/9/65 in Van Nuys, CA
ML Seasons: 3

Overall Statistics

	G	AB	R	H	D	T	HR	RBI	SB	BB	SO	AVG
1991	155	565	76	158	36	3	11	81	17	62	94	.280
Career	327	1142	145	300	64	7	27	146	19	138	185	.263

Where He Hits the Ball

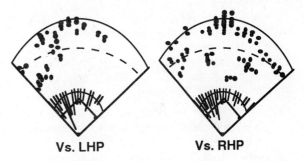

Vs. LHP   Vs. RHP

1991 Situational Stats

	AB	H	HR	RBI	AVG		AB	H	HR	RBI	AVG
Home	279	83	7	50	.297	LHP	237	72	5	33	.304
Road	286	75	4	31	.262	RHP	328	86	6	48	.262
Day	155	50	4	24	.323	Sc Pos	158	48	1	64	.304
Night	410	108	7	57	.263	Clutch	104	30	1	8	.288

1991 Rankings (National League)

- → 1st in batting average with the bases loaded (.600) and most errors at third base (25)
- → 3rd in doubles (36)
- → 4th in most pitches seen per plate appearance (4.00) and highest percentage of pitches taken (62.2%)
- → 5th in pitches seen (2,552)
- → Led the Cardinals in home runs (11), RBIs (81), hit by pitch (5), GDPs (15), pitches seen, games (155), HR frequency (51.4 ABs per HR), most pitches seen per plate appearance and highest percentage of pitches taken

WILLIE FRASER

Position: RP
Bats: R **Throws:** R
Ht: 6' 1" **Wt:** 206

Opening Day Age: 27
Born: 5/26/64 in New York, NY
ML Seasons: 6

Overall Statistics

	W	L	ERA	G	GS	Sv	IP	H	R	BB	SO	HR
1991	3	5	5.35	48	1	0	75.2	77	48	32	37	13
Career	34	39	4.39	208	57	5	619.0	595	328	223	309	82

PITCHING, FIELDING, HITTING & HOLDING RUNNERS:

Willie Fraser was forced from California's rotation after two years as a starter in 1987 and 1988 due to his tendency to give up the gopher ball. Working out of the bullpen in 1989 and 1990, he reined in the long ball and helped the Angels, posting ERAs of 3.24 and 3.08.

Fraser went to the Blue Jays in the Devon White/Junior Felix trade, but his old problem with home runs returned. Those problems worsened after the Cardinals claimed him on waivers on June 26th, and even pitching inside to hitters (six hit batters in 75.2 innings) didn't help him. Fraser throws a fastball in the mid-80s, a slider, and a forkball which he uses as a change-up, but he has no strikeout pitch and gives up a lot of extra-base hits when he falls behind in the count. Fraser is a good fielder, but his usual fine control of the running game was lost in 1991 and he allowed 11 steals in 16 attempts.

OVERALL:

When Scott Terry and Cris Carpenter were hurt in September, Fraser allowed only 14 baserunners in 16 innings and had 12 strikeouts. However, he still wound up with a 4.93 ERA with the Cards for the season. Fraser had two good years before 1991, so he'll probably get another shot in 1992, though maybe not in St. Louis.

RICH GEDMAN

Position: C
Bats: L **Throws:** R
Ht: 6' 0" **Wt:** 212

Opening Day Age: 32
Born: 9/26/59 in Worcester, MA
ML Seasons: 12

Overall Statistics

	G	AB	R	H	D	T	HR	RBI	SB	BB	SO	AVG
1991	46	94	7	10	1	0	3	8	0	4	15	.106
Career	992	3054	326	772	172	12	87	374	3	225	487	.253

HITTING, FIELDING, BASERUNNING:

Signed before the 1991 season, Rich Gedman was an adequate backup for regular catcher Tom Pagnozzi, who played the position so well that he was rarely replaced. Gedman was the "Sunday" starter behind the plate, starting 27 games.

Gedman hit only .106, but to paraphrase manager Joe Torre, "So what? If you play as little as Gedman, the average doesn't mean anything. Are you going to play him more if he hits .400?" Well, maybe. Gedman's average was a big drop from 1990, when he hit .202 in about the same playing time. However, three of Gedman's 10 hits were home runs and two of the homers produced game-winning RBI. He was 0-for-6 as a pinch hitter.

Gedman really wasn't effective defensively, committing five errors and three passed balls. He also tossed out only 10 of 40 base stealers. But he communicates well with his pitchers and has 12 years of major league experience. The Cards' ERA with Gedman behind the plate (3.33) was almost half a run better than with Pagnozzi.

OVERALL:

Torre said he wanted Gedman to come back, and the Cards signed him for 1992. On the horizon, the Cardinals have an excellent defensive catcher in Ray Stephens at Louisville (AAA). A spring training battle should develop. Stephens has been at Louisville since 1986 and will be pushing Gedman for the backup catcher role.

BOB McCLURE

Position: RP
Bats: R **Throws:** L
Ht: 5'11" **Wt:** 188

Opening Day Age: 38
Born: 4/29/53 in
Oakland, CA
ML Seasons: 17

Overall Statistics

	W	L	ERA	G	GS	Sv	IP	H	R	BB	SO	HR
1991	1	1	4.96	45	0	0	32.2	37	19	13	20	4
Career	65	54	3.82	613	73	52	1098.1	1060	525	467	671	96

PITCHING, FIELDING, HITTING & HOLDING RUNNERS:

Veteran Bob McClure was signed to a free agent contract by the Cardinals last June 24, when they were desperate for a left-handed reliever. McClure had been released by the Angels on June 17, and pitching coach Joe Coleman and manager Joe Torre, who had been an Angels' broadcaster, thought he could help. McClure is traditionally tough on lefties, and 1991 was no exception. However righties blasted him, as they hit .354 with power.

The Cardinals definitely got the best of McClure's season. After a 9.31 ERA with California, he posted a 3.13 mark in St. Louis and a 1.74 gem of a half after the All-Star break. He gave up just one home run and allowed only seven of 31 inherited runners to score, an excellent mark. Defensively, McClure fit right in with the Cards' pitching staff, playing errorless ball. The veteran of six teams knows how to keep runners close; only two runners attempted to steal, and both were thrown out.

OVERALL:

McClure is 39 years old and near the end of his playing career. His curve still breaks, but it has never been that effective against righties, and he is losing his heat. It would be surprising if the Cardinals can find a spot for him, but his good second half may find him work somewhere.

GERALD PERRY

Position: 1B
Bats: L **Throws:** R
Ht: 6' 0" **Wt:** 190

Opening Day Age: 31
Born: 10/30/60 in
Savannah, GA
ML Seasons: 9

Overall Statistics

	G	AB	R	H	D	T	HR	RBI	SB	BB	SO	AVG
1991	109	242	29	58	8	4	6	36	15	22	34	.240
Career	885	2747	333	727	126	11	51	339	137	274	304	.265

HITTING, FIELDING, BASERUNNING:

Gerald Perry became an unexpectedly valuable player for the Cardinals last season. Signed as a free agent after playing with Kansas City in 1990, Perry's role was to pinch hit and fill in occasionally in the outfield and first base. He did a good job in his often-difficult bench role. As a pinch hitter, Perry had a team-best 13 RBI and batted .268 (11-for-41). Though Perry hit only .240 overall, he hit .319 (23-for-72), with runners in scoring position. Perry liked the wide-open spaces of Busch Stadium and hit a career-high four triples in only 242 at-bats.

When Pedro Guerrero went out with a broken leg in July, Perry came in to play first base. There wasn't a big difference in their defensive play, as Perry committed five errors. Perry has good, if untamed, speed, with 137 lifetime stolen bases. He's probably lost a step or so, but last year he swiped 15 bases in 23 attempts.

OVERALL:

Perry is a valuable left-handed bat off the bench, and has probably found a new career as a pinch hitter. He doesn't have the offensive skills to be a regular at the positions he can play defensively, first and left, but he can bring a lot to a club in a part-time role.

ORGANIZATION OVERVIEW:

When the Cardinals dropped to last place in the National League East in 1990, a lot of people thought they'd be in for a long rebuilding process. Guess again; the Redbirds finished second in 1991, and have a youthful roster which should contend for the next several years. In Joe Torre, St. Louis has a manager who's completely unafraid to put a young player into his lineup. Cardinal farm director Ted Simmons, who, like Torre, was a major league regular before he turned 21, has been accused by some of moving players up the system too quickly. If that's the case, it doesn't look it's done them much harm so far. The St. Louis system seems to be in very good hands.

JOHN ERICKS

Position: P
Bats: R **Throws:** R
Ht: 6' 7" **Wt:** 220
Opening Day Age: 24
Born: 6/16/67 in Oak Lawn, IL

Recent Statistics

	W	L	ERA	GGS	Sv	IP	H	R	BB	SO	HR
90 A St. Pete	2	1	1.57	4 4	0	23.0	16	5	6	25	0
90 AA Arkansas	1	2	9.39	4 4	0	15.1	17	19	19	19	2
91 AA Arkansas	5	14	4.77	25 25	0	139.2	138	94	84	103	6

The Cardinals top pick in 1988, Ericks has proven beyond doubt that he can throw very, very hard. What he hasn't proven is that he can throw strikes. In 386.1 minor league innings, he has fanned 399 men, but walked 237. Things were no better for Ericks last year in AA ball; if anything, they were worse. Ericks has a fastballer's chance, however, and that's a real chance. The Cards may want to try him as a reliever, but they probably don't want to give up on him a starter yet.

MARK GRATER

Position: P
Bats: R **Throws:** R
Ht: 5' 10" **Wt:** 205
Opening Day Age: 28
Born: 1/19/64 in Rochester, PA

Recent Statistics

	W	L	ERA	GGS	Sv	IP	H	R	BB	SO	HR
91 AAA Louisville	3	5	2.02	58 0	12	80.1	68	20	33	53	1
91 NL St. Louis	0	0	0.00	3 0	0	3.0	5	0	2	0	0

A 23rd round draft pick in 1986, Grater has taken his time moving up the Cardinal system, but not for lack of good pitching. A career reliever, he's never had an ERA higher than 3.18, and he's recorded as many as 32 saves in a season. Short and stocky, he keeps the ball low and has allowed exactly one -- that's one -- home run in each of the last four seasons. At 28, he's as ready as he'll ever be, and he has a real chance to make the Cardinal staff -- and do well this year.

DONOVAN OSBORNE

Position: P
Bats: B **Throws:** L
Ht: 6' 2" **Wt:** 195
Opening Day Age: 22
Born: 6/21/69 in Roseville, CA

Recent Statistics

	W	L	ERA	GGS	Sv	IP	H	R	BB	SO	HR
90 A Hamilton	0	2	3.60	4 4	0	20.0	21	8	5	14	0
90 A Savannah	2	2	2.61	6 6	0	41.1	40	20	7	28	2
91 AA Arkansas	8	12	3.63	26 26	0	166.0	177	82	43	130	6

Donovan Osborne may have the least intimidating name for a pitcher since Orel Hershiser, but he's made an impression in a short career of less than two professional seasons. The Cardinals' first pick out of Nevada-Las Vegas in 1990, Osborne already has a good repertoire (fastball, slider, change), has posted excellent walk/strikeout ratios, and has been tough to take out of the yard (eight homers allowed in 227.1 professional innings). Thus far he's done everything except win (10-16 record). That should change this year.

STAN ROYER

Position: 3B
Bats: R **Throws:** R
Ht: 6' 3" **Wt:** 195
Opening Day Age: 24
Born: 8/31/67 in Olney, IL

Recent Statistics

	G	AB	R	H	D	THR	RBI	SB	BB	SO	AVG
91 AAA Louisville	138	523	48	133	29	6 14	74	1	43	126	.254
91 NL St. Louis	9	21	1	6	1	0 0	1	0	1	2	.286
91 MLE	138	508	39	118	27	5 11	60	0	36	125	.232

Royer, who came over from Oakland in the Willie McGee trade, is a big third sacker who has some power (49 extra-base hits last year). His swing appears to have some holes, though -- a lot of strikeouts, not many walks -- and he's never hit much for average. His defensive skills are decent, but he's been error-prone. Royer's best hope seems to be to wait for expansion; he's not much of a threat to Todd Zeile's job.

DMITRI YOUNG

Position: SS
Bats: B **Throws:** R
Ht: 6' 2" **Wt:** 215
Opening Day Age: 18
Born: 10/11/73 in Vicksburg, MS

Recent Statistics

	G	AB	R	H	D	THR	RBI	SB	BB	SO	AVG
91 R Johnson Cty	37	129	22	33	10	0 2	22	2	21	28	.256

Superstars usually develop early, and that's why you have to keep an eye on Young; when he was 12 years old, he was in high school leading his team with a .564 average. (Now that's a prospect.) The Cardinals first pick last year (fourth overall), Young showed a great batting eye and outstanding power at age 17. Baseball America rated him the number-two prospect in the Appalachian League. Hmm, they say Ted Simmons likes to move those youngsters along. You wouldn't think . . .?

LARRY ANDERSEN

Position: RP
Bats: R **Throws:** R
Ht: 6' 3" **Wt:** 205

Opening Day Age: 38
Born: 5/6/53 in Portland, OR
ML Seasons: 14

PITCHING:

Always regarded as a solid middle reliever and legendary free spirit, Larry Andersen earned a new reputation for toughness in 1991. After signing the first multi-year contract of his career via "new-look" free agency, Andersen was soon bothered by a painful herniated disc in his neck. Rather than succumb to the disabled list, Andersen instead tried to keep pitching. He ended up being disabled twice but still managed a career-high 13 saves in only 38 appearances for San Diego.

Ideally, Andersen should be used in set-up roles rather than as a closer. Before his neck became too painful, he allowed only one run in his first 13 outings. He also permitted only six of 23 inherited runners to score.

At his age (39), Andersen cannot be allowed to pitch several days in succession -- he has to be careful about a lot of things. He missed a week last season after slipping in his hot tub and pulling a muscle in his chest, a notable Southern California injury.

Andersen still throws one of baseball's best sliders and uses it on almost 90 percent of his pitches. He also maintained his usual excellent strikeout-to-walk ratio. Andersen did not allow a home run last season and in the last two seasons has given up only two homers in 142 innings.

HOLDING RUNNERS, FIELDING, HITTING:

Andersen is vulnerable to stolen bases because of his high leg kick. However, he uses a variety of tactics to confuse runners, such as holding the ball longer and using an assortment of pickoff moves. Andersen is a good fielder who is rarely caught out of position. He is, however, one of the worst hitters on earth, with four hits in his entire career and none in the last two years.

OVERALL:

Andersen is one of those rare pitchers who has improved with age. For another year at least, he should be an important part of the Padres' bullpen, especially if Craig Lefferts or someone else asserts himself as the team's closer.

Overall Statistics

	W	L	ERA	G	GS	Sv	IP	H	R	BB	SO	HR
1991	3	4	2.30	38	0	13	47.0	39	13	13	40	0
Career	35	34	3.11	572	1	47	866.2	819	346	267	629	50

How Often He Throws Strikes

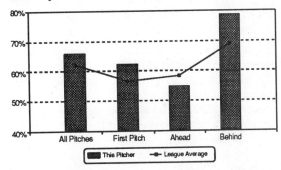

1991 Situational Stats

	W	L	ERA	Sv	IP		AB	H	HR	RBI	AVG
Home	3	0	2.19	8	24.2	LHB	89	25	0	10	.281
Road	0	4	2.42	5	22.1	RHB	79	14	0	6	.177
Day	0	0	1.23	3	7.1	Sc Pos	49	11	0	15	.224
Night	3	4	2.50	10	39.2	Clutch	126	28	0	12	.222

1991 Rankings (National League)

→ Did not rank near the top or bottom in any category

CY YOUNG STUFF

ANDY BENES

Position: SP
Bats: R **Throws:** R
Ht: 6' 6" **Wt:** 238

Opening Day Age: 24
Born: 8/20/67 in
Evansville, IN
ML Seasons: 3

PITCHING:

There had been growing debate before 1991 about whether Andy Benes would be better suited to pitching out of the bullpen. Since being rushed to the majors in 1989, Benes had barely been a .500 pitcher and the questions mounted last season when he got off to a 4-10 start through mid-July.

But then Benes finally put it all together. He went back to throwing his overpowering fastball instead of overusing his slider and change. Over the season's final two months, there was no better starting pitcher in the National League. In his final 15 starts, Benes went 11-1 with a 1.77 ERA -- that included a 10-game winning streak, the longest in the National League in two years. He ended up setting career highs in innings, wins and strikeouts (167).

Benes has developed a fastball that has some movement in contrast to the flat fastball which he originally brought to the majors. Surprisingly, the heater does not have great velocity, topping out around 90 MPH but mostly averaging around 85 or 86. It moves, however, and that's the difference. Benes' slider has become effective and he has begun to develop a feel for changing speeds. He is still vulnerable to the home run ball, having allowed a staff-high 23 last year.

HOLDING RUNNERS, FIELDING, HITTING:

Despite Benes' big, slow delivery, basestealers were only successful on 10 of 21 attempts. For the second straight year, he had trouble with balks, being called for four. For a big man, he is a capable fielder. Benes also has some power as a batter, hitting the second home run of his career last season. Unfortunately, it was one of only two hits he managed in 62 at-bats.

OVERALL:

Benes' big finish should end any speculation of conversion to a reliever. He is only 24 years old, and just four years removed from being the first player taken in the 1988 amateur draft. This may be the season he emerges as one of the league's dominant pitchers for a full season.

Overall Statistics

	W	L	ERA	G	GS	Sv	IP	H	R	BB	SO	HR
1991	15	11	3.03	33	33	0	223.0	194	76	59	167	23
Career	31	25	3.32	75	74	0	482.0	422	191	159	373	48

How Often He Throws Strikes

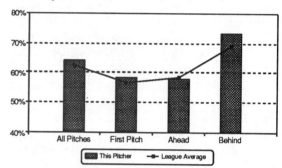

1991 Situational Stats

	W	L	ERA	Sv	IP		AB	H	HR	RBI	AVG
Home	6	5	3.73	0	111.0	LHB	466	107	13	38	.230
Road	9	6	2.33	0	112.0	RHB	370	87	10	32	.235
Day	7	2	2.76	0	71.2	Sc Pos	153	30	3	43	.196
Night	8	9	3.15	0	151.1	Clutch	88	21	1	6	.239

1991 Rankings (National League)

→ 2nd least run support per 9 innings (3.3)

→ 3rd in balks (4), lowest groundball/flyball ratio (.91), ERA on the road (2.33) and lowest batting average allowed with runners in scoring position (.196)

→ 4th lowest stolen base percentage allowed (47.6%)

→ 5th in home runs allowed (23) and lowest on-base average allowed (.285)

→ Led the Padres in ERA (3.03), wins (15), games started (33), complete games (4), innings (223), home runs allowed, walks allowed (59), hit batsmen (4), strikeouts (167), balks, pitches thrown (3,448), runners caught stealing (11) and strikeout/walk ratio (2.8)

PITCHING:

A 22 year old who wasn't recalled until last August, Ricky Bones had a glittering major league debut -- he pitched seven shutout innings while allowing just two hits in a victory over the World Champion Cincinnati Reds. Things had to go downhill from there and did. Bones had a three-game winning streak in early September, aided by the Padres scoring 26 runs in the three games. But in between, he struggled and ended up 4-6 with a high 4.83 earned run average.

On a club whose pitching staff is in flux, Bones remains a promising part of their future. He was signed out of Puerto Rico at age 17 and has made steady progress through the San Diego farm system. What is unsettling about him is that, despite posting winning records at each step through the minors, Bones allowed more hits than innings pitched in every season above A-ball. The same was true last year in his 11-start trial with the Padres.

The reason Bones allows so many hits is that he does not have one overwhelming pitch. He throws a rising fastball, curve, slider and split-fingered pitch, none of which are outstanding, so he needs to pitch from ahead in the count. When he stays ahead of hitters, his variety of pitches works well. But when he falls behind and must come in with a fastball, he is very vulnerable. If Bones improves his control, his well-rounded repertoire can be effective.

HOLDING RUNNERS, FIELDING, HITTING:

Bones has an average move to first but still needs to improve his delivery to the plate. Teams were willing to wait for hits against Bones rather than trying to steal bases (0-for-1 in stolen base attempts). He has solid athletic instincts in the field. Bones also shows some potential as a bunter, with four successful sacrifices.

OVERALL:

The Padres' rotation is wide open behind Bruce Hurst and Andy Benes; Bones will have a clear shot at winning a spot in the rotation. His youth and flashes of success last season will likely give him an even shot at winning a job.

RICKY BONES

Position: SP
Bats: R **Throws:** R
Ht: 5'10" **Wt:** 175

Opening Day Age: 23
Born: 4/7/69 in Salinas, PR
ML Seasons: 1

Overall Statistics

	W	L	ERA	G	GS	Sv	IP	H	R	BB	SO	HR
1991	4	6	4.83	11	11	0	54.0	57	33	18	31	3
Career	4	6	4.83	11	11	0	54.0	57	33	18	31	3

How Often He Throws Strikes

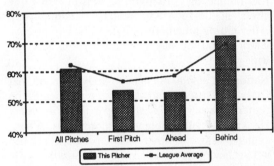

1991 Situational Stats

	W	L	ERA	Sv	IP		AB	H	HR	RBI	AVG
Home	3	3	5.40	0	33.1	LHB	116	31	2	19	.267
Road	1	3	3.92	0	20.2	RHB	96	26	1	11	.271
Day	1	3	3.74	0	21.2	Sc Pos	44	16	2	26	.364
Night	3	3	5.57	0	32.1	Clutch	2	0	0	0	.000

1991 Rankings (National League)

➡ Did not rank near the top or bottom in any category

HITTING:

In what was an unsettled San Diego outfield in the beginning of 1991, the left field spot was Jerald Clark's to win or lose. After looking for a while like he would nail down the job, Clark faded badly over the season's second half and may have lost his last chance.

Things started out so nicely. Clark won the Opening Day starting job and came out of the gate playing well, knocking in 13 runs in his first 20 games. But on April 30, he injured his Achilles tendon after slipping on a wet field in New York and ended up on the disabled list. He stayed there until May 20, and when he returned he began to slump. Clark had one more hot streak left, hitting four homers and driving in 13 runs in a 15-game stretch in mid-June. After that, the bottom fell out. After hitting nine homers in his first 216 at-bats, Clark would hit only one homer in his last 153 trips.

National League pitchers quickly learned that Clark was strictly a lowball hitter who could be retired with any kind of stuff up in the strike zone. He was also vulnerable to breaking balls. A hard swinger who is at times undisciplined, Clark has not yet made enough adjustments to survive in the majors on an every-day basis.

BASERUNNING:

Clark has below average speed and is no threat to steal bases. Because of his big swing, he is also slow to get out of the batter's box, as evidenced by his 10 GDPs last season in limited play.

FIELDING:

At best, Clark is less than adequate in the outfield. He has poor range and a below-average arm in both strength and accuracy. Clark is able to play first base reasonably well, but won't get much chance with durable Fred McGriff ahead of him.

OVERALL:

At 28, Clark has passed the age of being a prospect. He may never be more than an extra man because of his defensive deficiencies and inconsistency. However, his power (16 homers in 526 lifetime at-bats) will likely land him a job somewhere.

JERALD CLARK

Position: LF/1B/RF
Bats: R **Throws:** R
Ht: 6' 4" **Wt:** 202

Opening Day Age: 28
Born: 8/10/63 in
Crockett, TX
ML Seasons: 4

Overall Statistics

	G	AB	R	H	D	T	HR	RBI	SB	BB	SO	AVG
1991	118	369	26	84	16	0	10	47	2	31	90	.228
Career	193	526	43	122	23	1	16	68	2	39	127	.232

Where He Hits the Ball

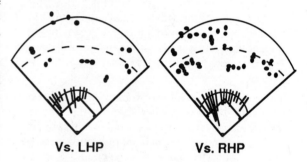

Vs. LHP   **Vs. RHP**

1991 Situational Stats

	AB	H	HR	RBI	AVG		AB	H	HR	RBI	AVG
Home	195	41	8	29	.210	LHP	126	22	4	13	.175
Road	174	43	2	18	.247	RHP	243	62	6	34	.255
Day	105	23	3	13	.219	Sc Pos	88	21	3	36	.239
Night	264	61	7	34	.231	Clutch	71	16	2	12	.225

1991 Rankings (National League)

➡ 2nd in lowest batting average vs. lefthanded pitchers (.175) and lowest on-base average vs. left-handed pitchers (.239)

➡ 4th lowest batting average with 2 strikes (.122)

➡ 6th in hit by pitch (6)

➡ 8th lowest slugging percentage vs. left-handed pitchers (.294)

➡ Led the Padres in hit by pitch

HITTING:

Considering the price they paid, the San Diego Padres had to feel let down by Tony Fernandez at season's end. After an excellent start, Fernandez struggled during the second half, while Roberto Alomar, the infielder the Padres sacrificed for Fernandez, was the best player on Toronto's division championship team. Fernandez' average dropped nearly 40 points after mid-June; his .272 mark was the second-lowest of his career in any full season. He had a career-low 38 runs batted in and managed only 36 extra-base hits.

In his defense, Fernandez labored over the second half with a bad right thumb which required postseason surgery. However, it was also evident that National League pitchers began to adjust their approach to Fernandez, and the switch-hitter was not able to respond. He hit breaking balls better right-handed but was easily buried by hard stuff. Batting left-handed, he hit fastballs better but was vulnerable to being pitched away.

There was a time when Fernandez delivered some power (41 doubles in 1988 and 17 triples in 1990). However, though he had 27 doubles in 1991, he has totalled only eight home runs in the last two years. Fernandez remains effective as a hit-and-run man, especially from the left side.

BASERUNNING:

Fernandez is still an above-average base stealer, going 23-for-32 last year on the base paths. He has good speed, but also grounds into a few double plays.

FIELDING:

Fernandez arrived in the NL with a reputation as another Ozzie Smith with the glove. However, he was often eaten alive by the natural grass field in San Diego and ended up with 20 errors. His range remains excellent.

OVERALL:

On the whole, Fernandez was an average player for the Padres in his first year in the National League (although as shortstops go, he out-produced most). To make the big trade with Toronto successful, however, he needs to be a lot better in '92. Fernandez had the right to demand a trade after the season, and there was talk that San Diego might accommodate him.

TONY FERNANDEZ

Position: SS
Bats: B **Throws:** R
Ht: 6' 2" **Wt:** 175

Opening Day Age: 29
Born: 6/30/62 in San Pedro de Macoris, Dominican Republic
ML Seasons: 9

Overall Statistics

	G	AB	R	H	D	T	HR	RBI	SB	BB	SO	AVG
1991	145	558	81	152	27	5	4	38	23	55	74	.272
Career	1173	4510	591	1294	219	66	44	442	161	340	418	.287

Where He Hits the Ball

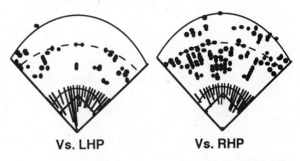

Vs. LHP   Vs. RHP

1991 Situational Stats

	AB	H	HR	RBI	AVG		AB	H	HR	RBI	AVG
Home	271	79	1	17	.292	LHP	184	48	2	13	.261
Road	287	73	3	21	.254	RHP	374	104	2	25	.278
Day	144	37	3	16	.257	Sc Pos	117	36	1	33	.308
Night	414	115	1	22	.278	Clutch	87	24	0	6	.276

1991 Rankings (National League)

→ 5th lowest HR frequency (140 ABs per HR)

→ 7th lowest slugging percentage vs. right-handed pitchers (.369)

→ 8th in highest percentage of extra bases taken as a runner (68.3%) and lowest slugging percentage (.360)

→ Led the Padres in doubles (27), stolen base percentage (71.9%), most runs scored per time reached base (39.1%) and bunts in play (18)

→ Led NL shortstops in caught stealing (9), batting average vs. right-handed pitchers (.278) and on-base average vs. right-handed pitchers (.344)

CLUTCH HITTER

TONY GWYNN

Position: RF
Bats: L **Throws:** L
Ht: 5'11" **Wt:** 210

Opening Day Age: 31
Born: 5/9/60 in Los
Angeles, CA
ML Seasons: 10

HITTING:

It is a measure of Tony Gwynn's greatness that a year in which he had the third-best batting average in the National League would be considered a disappointment. However, his final standing in the batting race is also an indication of the way he was hitting before a knee problem slowed him down. The injury hampered him for much of the second half before requiring surgery in September. Gwynn missed the final four weeks, and this ruined his chance for a fifth career batting title.

Gwynn was hitting .378 on June 22 and was on a pace for a 100-RBI season. However, after the All-Star break, he had the most prolonged slump of his career, hitting only .247 the entire second half with just 14 RBI. The slump was largely due to the knee problem, which resulted in an operation to clean out loose particles and smooth out cartilage.

Nothing has changed with Gwynn. He remains the toughest batter to strike out in the majors (just 19 times in 530 at-bats) and a tough man in clutch situations (.377 with men in scoring position). Gwynn continues to drive outside pitches to left. However, in the last two years, he has tried pulling the ball more.

BASERUNNING:

His knee injury and weight problems have just about ended Gwynn's status as one of the most dependable base stealers in baseball. He managed only eight steals in 16 attempts in 1991. However, Gwynn is still one of the more intelligent runners in the game.

FIELDING:

The knee and extra weight have affected Gwynn's outfield range to the point where he sometimes doesn't reach balls he used to routinely run down. Gwynn remains an excellent outfielder, however, with one of the better right-field arms in the N.L.

OVERALL:

Relieved of the clubhouse problems he suffered in 1990, Gwynn last season found new unwelcome distractions with his knee injury. He's now over 30 with a body that many have recently been predicting would break down. This could be a crossroads season for a player considered a potential Hall of Famer.

Overall Statistics

	G	AB	R	H	D	T	HR	RBI	SB	BB	SO	AVG
1991	134	530	69	168	27	11	4	62	8	34	19	.317
Career	1335	5181	765	1699	248	72	53	550	246	460	275	.328

Where He Hits the Ball

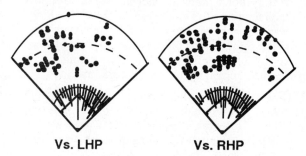

Vs. LHP   **Vs. RHP**

1991 Situational Stats

	AB	H	HR	RBI	AVG		AB	H	HR	RBI	AVG
Home	244	75	1	21	.307	LHP	211	62	2	19	.294
Road	286	93	3	41	.325	RHP	319	106	2	43	.332
Day	150	44	0	15	.293	Sc Pos	130	49	1	55	.377
Night	380	124	4	47	.326	Clutch	89	31	1	9	.348

1991 Rankings (National League)

→ 1st in batting average with runners in scoring position (.377), lowest percentage of swings that missed (6.9%) and highest percentage of swings put into play (61.0%)

→ 2nd in triples (11) and batting average on the road (.325)

→ 3rd in batting average (.317), groundball/flyball ratio (3.1) and batting average with 2 strikes (.282)

→ 4th in singles (126)

→ Led the Padres in batting average, hits (168), singles, doubles (27), triples, groundball/flyball ratio, batting average with runners in scoring position and batting average in the clutch (.348)

PITCHING:

For two years, Greg Harris had been one of the best middle and long relievers in baseball. But one of the first moves suggested by Padres GM Joe McIlvaine when he arrived was to make Harris into a starter. After missing over two months with a tender elbow, Harris came back to prove that his home should remain in the rotation. In his second start back from the disabled list, he took a no-hitter into the eighth inning of an eventual win over New York. And during a 12-start span beginning in August, Harris went 7-2 with a 1.88 earned run average that included the N.L.'s first back-to-back 1-0 shutouts since 1988.

In a total of 17 starts after the elbow problems, Harris proved he was healthy. He ended the year with a 2.23 ERA which would have led the league had he pitched the necessary innings to qualify. The only down side in an otherwise long list of positive numbers were the 16 home runs Harris allowed in 133 innings.

Harris has always had an outstanding fastball and one of the best curveballs in baseball. However, he will also hang his share of curves, which largely accounts for that high home run total. As a result, he has worked with pitching coach Mike Roarke on developing an offspeed weapon to show hitters in addition to the heater and curve.

HOLDING RUNNERS, FIELDING, HITTING:

Harris has worked hard to develop a better pickoff move. He does a solid job of holding runners, though he is like many Padres' pitchers in that he sometimes depends too much on Benito Santiago's arm. Harris is an average fielder and occasionally can help himself with the bat, especially as a bunter.

OVERALL:

Harris has always wanted the chance to start, and now he finally has his wish. If he stays healthy, there's no reason why he cannot be a solid winner and give the Padres' a super 1-2-3 punch of himself, Benes and Bruce Hurst.

GREG W. HARRIS

Position: SP
Bats: R **Throws:** R
Ht: 6' 2" **Wt:** 187

Opening Day Age: 28
Born: 12/1/63 in Greensboro, NC
ML Seasons: 4

Overall Statistics

	W	L	ERA	G	GS	Sv	IP	H	R	BB	SO	HR
1991	9	5	2.23	20	20	0	133.0	116	42	27	95	16
Career	27	22	2.34	152	29	15	403.1	327	123	131	313	30

How Often He Throws Strikes

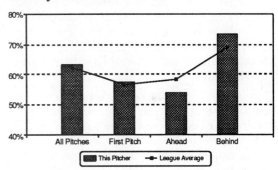

1991 Situational Stats

	W	L	ERA	Sv	IP		AB	H	HR	RBI	AVG
Home	5	2	1.85	0	73.0	LHB	309	78	12	27	.252
Road	4	3	2.70	0	60.0	RHB	189	38	4	13	.201
Day	4	0	1.64	0	38.1	Sc Pos	96	15	2	21	.156
Night	5	5	2.47	0	94.2	Clutch	81	12	0	1	.148

1991 Rankings (National League)

→ Led the Padres in shutouts (2)

HITTING:

Ever since his selection as a number-one draft pick in 1986, Thomas Howard has been considered one of the Padres' best prospects. Howard had batted over .300 at almost every stop on his road to San Diego, including a .328 mark at AAA Las Vegas in 1990. But after finally getting some extended playing time last season following his recall from the minors, Howard got mixed reviews. On the positive side, he showed excellent athletic skills and had some flashes of offensive promise. However, Howard managed only a .249 average in 281 at-bats and had just 22 RBI.

A switch-hitter, Howard batted .286 from the right side, but received only 28 right-handed at-bats. Ninety percent of his at-bats came hitting lefty, as he was often used in a platoon with Darrin Jackson; as a lefthander, he hit only .245. Howard can hit a fastball, and N.L. pitchers quickly learned that he could be retired with breaking balls, either curves or sliders.

Howard has good speed and is a threat on occasion to bunt for a hit. He also had one pinch hit home run, but that was an aberration. Howard has never shown much consistent power at any level of the minors, and that was also true with the Padres last year, as he managed only four home runs.

BASERUNNING:

Howard has been a double-figure base stealer throughout his professional career. He stole 10 bases last year but was also caught seven times, indicating a need for better judgement.

FIELDING:

Howard has excellent potential as a center fielder, with above-average range and a strong and accurate arm. His defense is likely his biggest strength as a player.

OVERALL:

For years, San Diego has been looking for an everyday center fielder. However, barring any major move or trade, it is likely Howard and others will get a chance to share time. Howard will earn time with his defense and his speed, not with his bat.

THOMAS HOWARD

Position: CF/LF/RF
Bats: B **Throws:** R
Ht: 6' 2" **Wt:** 198

Opening Day Age: 27
Born: 12/11/64 in Middletown, OH
ML Seasons: 2

Overall Statistics

	G	AB	R	H	D	T	HR	RBI	SB	BB	SO	AVG
1991	106	281	30	70	12	3	4	22	10	24	57	.249
Career	126	325	34	82	14	3	4	22	10	24	68	.252

Where He Hits the Ball

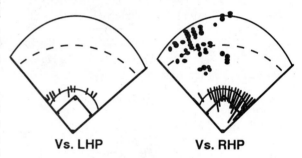

Vs. LHP   Vs. RHP

1991 Situational Stats

	AB	H	HR	RBI	AVG		AB	H	HR	RBI	AVG
Home	140	36	4	14	.257	LHP	28	8	1	2	.286
Road	141	34	0	8	.241	RHP	253	62	3	20	.245
Day	77	22	2	6	.286	Sc Pos	70	20	2	19	.286
Night	204	48	2	16	.235	Clutch	61	12	1	7	.197

1991 Rankings (National League)

➡ Did not rank near the top or bottom in any category

HITTING:

With their third base spot a wasteland inhabited by a succession of failures including Jim Presley, Scott Coolbaugh, Garry Templeton and Paul Faries, the Padres obtained Jack Howell last July 30 in a trade that sent outfield bust Shawn Abner to the California Angels. The opportunity was there, but Howell didn't seize it any more than the others: he hit only .206 in 58 games with the Padres, with six homers and 16 RBI.

Howell, a left-handed hitter, ended up platooning at third since he is basically helpless against left-handed pitching (.103 overall last year). National League scouts quickly spotted the several holes in Howell's swing. He was jammed with inside stuff repeatedly. Though he would sometimes go to the opposite field with outside pitches, most teams pitched away from Howell's power zone.

Howell's power has become sporadic at best. After hitting 59 homers in 1987-89 with California, he's totalled only 16 in the last two. As a result, Howell hardly made the Padres feel that their third-base dilemma is behind them.

BASERUNNING:

Howell didn't attempt a steal for San Diego, and has only 13 steals in 27 attempts in his career. At least he is aggressive on the base paths in breaking up double plays and taking the extra base.

FIELDING:

Howell made only two errors in 54 third base games for San Diego. He showed good range but his arm is average. Howell has good reflexes, but no longer makes the play on slow rollers the way he once did. Some scouts considered him to be a good 10 pounds overweight last year.

OVERALL:

Howell is 30 years old, and no longer a promising youngster; he's established himself as a low-average hitter with declining power. Barring an off season move for a third baseman, however, the Padres will likely give him a chance to win their third base job against righties. It's not so much an endorsement of Howell as it is an indication of the lack of alternatives.

JACK HOWELL

Position: 3B/2B
Bats: L **Throws:** R
Ht: 6' 0" **Wt:** 190

Opening Day Age: 30
Born: 8/18/61 in Tucson, AZ
ML Seasons: 7

Overall Statistics

	G	AB	R	H	D	T	HR	RBI	SB	BB	SO	AVG
1991	90	241	35	50	5	1	8	23	1	29	44	.207
Career	737	2268	294	535	111	15	84	274	13	265	539	.236

Where He Hits the Ball

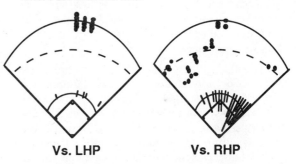

Vs. LHP   Vs. RHP

1991 Situational Stats

	AB	H	HR	RBI	AVG		AB	H	HR	RBI	AVG
Home	117	24	3	12	.205	LHP	29	3	0	0	.103
Road	124	26	5	11	.210	RHP	212	47	8	23	.222
Day	73	14	2	7	.192	Sc Pos	48	14	1	13	.292
Night	168	36	6	16	.214	Clutch	39	13	2	5	.333

1991 Rankings (National League)

→ Did not rank near the top or bottom in any category

PITCHING:

Bruce Hurst was on his way to a 20-win season and possible Cy Young Award consideration when he suffered a string of no-decisions and then elbow problems which sidelined him for the season's final three weeks. The elbow injury was not considered serious, but Hurst is creeping toward the age when any physical problem is cause for concern.

However, the Padres had little to worry about with Hurst for most of last season. After surprisingly giving him a hefty contract extension, Hurst got off to a superb start. He won his first four decisions and later won five straight starts beginning in mid-July and extending into August. But after his record moved to 14-5 with a win over Houston on August 7, Hurst would be victorious only once more before the sore elbow sidelined him for good on September 17.

Even with the elbow woes, Hurst was a horse. He went six or more innings in his first 29 starts and pitched at least eight innings in 13 starts. As always, he was a master at mixing his pitches. Hurst uses a forkball, slider and offspeed curve while spotting his deceptive fastball with excellent control. Despite having only average velocity, Hurst is a solid strikeout pitcher because of his ability to change speeds and put the ball where he wants.

HOLDING RUNNERS, FIELDING, HITTING:

Hurst is a true professional who helps himself in many ways. He has one of the best pickoff moves in baseball, last year leading the Padres with seven. He is also an excellent fielder. Hurst has also made himself a useful hitter. He had nine hits and six RBI and was among league leaders with 12 sacrifices last year.

OVERALL:

Assuming his elbow problems are not chronic, Hurst supplies the young Padres staff with a dependable ace around which to grow. He is a savvy pro who is great in the clubhouse and, should San Diego contend, a proven big-game pitcher.

BRUCE HURST

Position: SP
Bats: L **Throws:** L
Ht: 6' 3" **Wt:** 219

Opening Day Age: 34
Born: 3/24/58 in St. George, UT
ML Seasons: 12

Overall Statistics

	W	L	ERA	G	GS	Sv	IP	H	R	BB	SO	HR
1991	15	8	3.29	31	31	0	221.2	201	89	59	141	17
Career	129	101	3.84	334	314	0	2149.1	2172	1005	667	1525	227

How Often He Throws Strikes

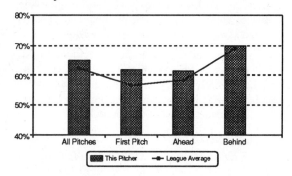

This Pitcher / League Average

1991 Situational Stats

	W	L	ERA	Sv	IP		AB	H	HR	RBI	AVG
Home	7	5	3.34	0	126.2	LHB	136	24	1	10	.176
Road	8	3	3.22	0	95.0	RHB	699	177	16	65	.253
Day	2	0	3.24	0	33.1	Sc Pos	169	44	4	58	.260
Night	13	8	3.30	0	188.1	Clutch	90	19	0	4	.211

1991 Rankings (National League)

- ➡ 3rd least pitches thrown per batter (3.37)
- ➡ 4th lowest batting average allowed vs left-handed batters (.176)
- ➡ 5th in winning percentage (.652) and sacrifice bunts as a batter (12)
- ➡ 7th in wins (15)
- ➡ Led the Padres in wins, complete games (4), hits allowed (201), batters faced (909), walks allowed (59), pickoff throws (163), GDPs induced (14), winning percentage, lowest slugging average allowed (.340) and sacrifice bunts as a batter

HITTING:

Nearing the point where the Padres were getting ready to give up on him, Darrin Jackson turned around his career in 1991 and became one of San Diego's most pleasant surprises. Jackson, who entered the season with 13 career homers, proceeded to blast 21 last year. He averaged one home run for every 17.1 at-bats, a very impressive rate, while playing in a career-high 122 games.

Always a dead high fastball hitter who tried to pull everything, Jackson last season learned how to better adjust to breaking balls. He still sat on heat, and he was still retired most easily by breaking stuff, but he was able to fight off breaking pitches better, work deeper counts and get pitchers into more situations in which they had to throw him the fastball. Then Jackson took advantage.

Never a very patient hitter, Jackson drew only 27 walks, which still surpassed his career total of 23. He also batted only .269 with men in scoring position, one reason why he drove in only 49 runs despite the high home run total.

BASERUNNING:

Despite a reputation for better-than-average speed, Jackson is not much of a threat. He stole only five bases in eight attempts last season. He's a hustling baserunner, however, and will take the extra base if he has the opportunity.

FIELDING:

Jackson has very good range but an average arm, which is not helped by poor footwork that often leaves him in the wrong position to throw. Baserunners usually can run on Jackson for an extra base.

OVERALL:

With the Padres in need of extra offense, especially from their outfield, Jackson has dramatically increased his worth with his burst of home run power. He finished the season strongly, further raising hopes. However, Jackson now must prove he wasn't just a one-year fluke to further assert himself as a key man in the Padres' future.

DARRIN JACKSON

Position: CF/LF
Bats: R **Throws:** R
Ht: 6' 0" **Wt:** 186

Opening Day Age: 28
Born: 8/22/63 in Los Angeles, CA
ML Seasons: 6

Overall Statistics

	G	AB	R	H	D	T	HR	RBI	SB	BB	SO	AVG
1991	122	359	51	94	12	1	21	49	5	27	66	.262
Career	362	846	109	215	34	4	34	98	13	50	155	.254

Where He Hits the Ball

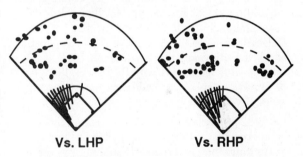

Vs. LHP   **Vs. RHP**

1991 Situational Stats

	AB	H	HR	RBI	AVG		AB	H	HR	RBI	AVG
Home	174	45	12	24	.259	LHP	163	43	11	26	.264
Road	185	49	9	25	.265	RHP	196	51	10	23	.260
Day	113	28	9	18	.248	Sc Pos	78	21	4	30	.269
Night	246	66	12	31	.268	Clutch	65	11	3	7	.169

1991 Rankings (National League)

→ 7th lowest batting average in the clutch (.169)
→ Led the Padres in least GDPs per GDP situation (8.8%)

PITCHING:

Despite earning 23 saves for the second year in a row with the Padres, Craig Lefferts won't cherish 1991 as a season to remember. Lefferts blew seven save opportunities, ranking among league leaders in that negative category. For the first time in his career he allowed more hits than innings pitched. His 3.91 ERA was nearly a run higher than his career ERA entering last season, and was the highest he's ever turned in. Opposing hitters batted .285 against him. Lefferts was nicked for five home runs and had a poor 1-6 record.

After allowing seven of his first 16 inherited runners to score, Lefferts was replaced as closer by Larry Andersen. His inconsistency was reflected in his decreased number of appearances -- 54, the fewest of his career. All this would be more ominous were it not for the fact that Lefferts finished the season well. Over his last 13 appearances, he allowed only two earned runs in 18 innings while going 1-1 with five saves, the type of numbers San Diego had been accustomed to seeing from the lefthander.

Lefferts' problems stemmed from a streak where he continually got the ball up in the strike zone, something that is especially damaging for a pitcher who relies heavily on his screwball and sinker. Never one to overpower batters, Lefferts becomes vulnerable when he's pitching from behind in the count. Even in his best years, Lefferts has never been the 30-save kind of closer.

HOLDING RUNNERS, FIELDING, HITTING:

Lefferts has a good left-handed move to first and is capable of holding runners close. He is also a solid fielder. Like all late-inning relievers, his hitting is rarely a factor. He went hitless in his six at-bats last season, striking out four times.

OVERALL:

In the final year of a three-year contract, Lefferts' role this season could undergo some change. San Diego is in the market for an established closer and if one is obtained, Lefferts will slide into more of a set-up role. That might be better for him, even if it's less glamourous.

CRAIG LEFFERTS

Position: RP
Bats: L **Throws:** L
Ht: 6' 1" **Wt:** 209

Opening Day Age: 34
Born: 9/29/57 in Munich, West Germany
ML Seasons: 9

Overall Statistics

	W	L	ERA	G	GS	Sv	IP	H	R	BB	SO	HR
1991	1	6	3.91	54	0	23	69.0	74	35	14	48	5
Career	40	50	3.03	582	5	100	831.1	742	318	241	530	77

How Often He Throws Strikes

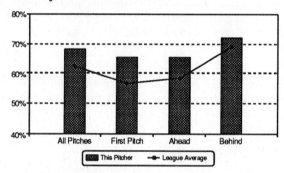

1991 Situational Stats

	W	L	ERA	Sv	IP		AB	H	HR	RBI	AVG
Home	0	5	3.46	10	41.2	LHB	64	18	1	17	.281
Road	1	1	4.61	13	27.1	RHB	196	56	4	25	.286
Day	0	3	3.86	7	18.2	Sc Pos	70	20	0	32	.286
Night	1	3	3.93	16	50.1	Clutch	186	50	4	33	.269

1991 Rankings (National League)

- 3rd in worst first batter efficiency (.333) and highest batting average allowed in relief (.285)
- 5th in save opportunities (30)
- 6th in saves (23) and blown saves (7)
- Led the Padres in saves, games finished (40), save opportunities, save percentage (76.7%), blown saves, relief losses and most strikeouts per 9 innings in relief (6.3)

PITCHING:

There was no more pleasant a surprise for San Diego last year than Mike Maddux, who was out of a job last spring after being released by the Dodgers. Maddux attended a booster club luncheon in Las Vegas for the Padres' Triple-A club where he sought out GM Joe McIlvaine and persuaded McIlvaine to give him an invitation to spring training. Maddux ended up earning a spot on San Diego's Opening Day roster and went on to be one of the Padres' most valuable pitchers.

Maddux shared the club lead in appearances with a career-high 64 while also achieving personal bests with his 7-2 record, 2.46 ERA and five saves. He allowed 20 fewer hits than innings pitched, opposing batters hit only .221 against him and, despite all the extra work, he got better as the year progressed. Maddux allowed only two runs in his last 23.2 innings, a stretch that covered 13 outings and included two wins and three saves.

The biggest factors in Maddux's turnaround were control and maturity. Coming up through the Philadelphia farm system, Maddux always had good stuff, including an excellent curve and an above-average slider and fastball. However, he often labored with his control, and in tough situations he would invariably get burned. But last year, he harnessed much of his ability and blossomed in the middle and long relief role.

HOLDING RUNNERS, FIELDING, HITTING:

Maddux has only an average pickoff move, but was tough on to base stealers in '91 (only 5 of 12 were successful). He is a good fielder with excellent defensive instincts. Maddux has never been a threatening hitter, last year managing one hit in 13 at-bats.

OVERALL:

It's rare when someone can salvage a career virtually overnight but that's what Maddux did in 1991. He'll have to prove he can do it again, but with his arm there's no reason why he can't succeed. Maddux established himself as an effective middle reliever last year and his role will likely grow with San Diego.

MIKE MADDUX

Position: RP
Bats: L **Throws:** R
Ht: 6' 2" **Wt:** 180

Opening Day Age: 30
Born: 8/27/61 in Dayton, OH
ML Seasons: 6

Overall Statistics

	W	L	ERA	G	GS	Sv	IP	H	R	BB	SO	HR
1991	7	2	2.46	64	1	5	98.2	78	30	27	57	4
Career	17	16	4.05	139	36	6	346.2	350	176	118	212	22

How Often He Throws Strikes

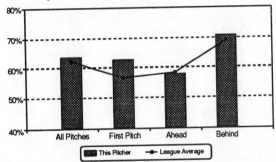

1991 Situational Stats

	W	L	ERA	Sv	IP		AB	H	HR	RBI	AVG
Home	5	1	1.75	1	51.1	LHB	171	42	0	12	.246
Road	2	1	3.23	4	47.1	RHB	182	36	4	14	.198
Day	2	0	2.33	1	27.0	Sc Pos	92	17	0	20	.185
Night	5	2	2.51	4	71.2	Clutch	102	23	0	13	.225

1991 Rankings (National League)

→ 5th lowest percentage of inherited runners scored (19.1%)

→ 7th in relief innings (98.2) and least baserunners allowed per 9 innings in relief (10.1)

→ 9th in relief ERA (2.62) and relief wins (6)

→ Led the Padres in games pitched (64), holds (9), first batter efficiency (.293), lowest percentage of inherited runners scored, relief ERA, relief wins, relief innings, lowest batting average allowed in relief (.227) and least baserunners allowed per 9 innings in relief

FUTURE MVP?

FRED McGRIFF

Position: 1B
Bats: L **Throws:** L
Ht: 6' 3" **Wt:** 215

Opening Day Age: 28
Born: 10/31/63 in Tampa, FL
ML Seasons: 6

HITTING:

In effect, San Diego traded Joe Carter for Fred McGriff in a swap that left winners on both sides. Carter helped lead the Blue Jays to a division title, while changing leagues had little effect on McGriff. He achieved a career high in RBI (106) while hitting over 30 homers for the fourth straight season. And those numbers become even more impressive when you look more closely at McGriff's season.

With Tony Gwynn damaged goods for half a season and without a lot of other protection in the lineup, McGriff was pitched around repeatedly -- he was intentionally walked an N.L.-high 26 times. But McGriff still came through, hitting 14 of his 31 home runs against left-handed pitching after entering the season with only 19 career homers against lefthanders.

National League teams had some success crowding McGriff from the belt up, keeping him from getting his arms extended and pulling the ball with his awesome power. He is a dangerous low-ball hitter, and teams tried to get him to chase fastballs up and out of the strike zone. They also attempted to make McGriff fish for outside breaking balls, though he has excellent power to left-center. The strategy worked sometimes, as evidenced by McGriff's 135 strikeouts.

BASERUNNING:

McGriff will steal the occasional base (four steals in five tries last year). He is sometimes guilty of coasting a little, costing himself some chances at extra bases.

FIELDING:

The one blemish in his otherwise solid season was McGriff's work around first base. He made a career-high 14 errors, many of them due to non-chalance. However, he has excellent range and good hands around the bag.

OVERALL:

All the numbers indicate McGriff's talent. But there are detractors who say he disappears in pennant races and is not a clutch, big-game performer. The only way we'll know if he's progressed in that area is for San Diego to build a contender around him.

Overall Statistics

	G	AB	R	H	D	T	HR	RBI	SB	BB	SO	AVG
1991	153	528	84	147	19	1	31	106	4	105	135	.278
Career	731	2472	432	687	118	9	156	411	25	457	630	.278

Where He Hits the Ball

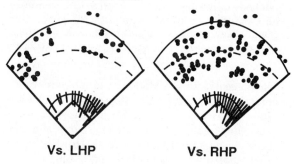

Vs. LHP   **Vs. RHP**

1991 Situational Stats

	AB	H	HR	RBI	AVG		AB	H	HR	RBI	AVG
Home	239	67	18	53	.280	LHP	213	58	14	48	.272
Road	289	80	13	53	.277	RHP	315	89	17	58	.283
Day	135	36	8	27	.267	Sc Pos	144	39	8	73	.271
Night	393	111	23	79	.282	Clutch	72	16	2	7	.222

1991 Rankings (National League)

➡ 1st in intentional walks (26)

➡ 2nd in strikeouts (135), HR frequency (17.0 ABs per HR) and most errors at first base (14)

➡ 3rd in walks (105), on-base average (.396) and on-base average vs. right-handed pitchers (.406)

➡ 4th in home runs (31) and RBIs (106)

➡ 5th in times on base (254) and highest percentage of swings that missed (25.9%)

➡ Led the Padres in home runs, runs (84), total bases (261), RBIs, sacrifice flies (7), walks, intentional walks, times on base, strikeouts, pitches seen (2,492), plate appearances (642), games (153), slugging percentage (.494) and on-base average

JOSE MELENDEZ

Position: RP/SP
Bats: R **Throws:** R
Ht: 6' 2" **Wt:** 175

Opening Day Age: 26
Born: 9/2/65 in
Naguabo, Puerto Rico
ML Seasons: 2

PITCHING:

A waiver pickup out of the Seattle organization, Jose Melendez could end up being a steal for San Diego after displaying some excellent potential. After starting the 1991 season at AAA Las Vegas where he went 7-0 with excellent control, Melendez was recalled on May 31 and ended up being used in a variety of roles.

Melendez started the first six games upon his recall, going 3-3. He then went to the bullpen and posted a 3-2 record with three saves in 22 relief appearances. The Padres put Melendez back into the rotation during the season's final two weeks, and he went 2-0 in three starts. In Melendez, the Padres uncovered another versatile pitcher similar to Mike Maddux who could prove valuable by being plugged into assorted roles. Also like Maddux, however, Melendez is not a kid. He was originally part of the Pittsburgh organization where he pitched from 1984 through 1988 before being picked by Seattle in the minor-league draft.

Melendez is what scouts like to call a "long-armer," a pitcher with an easy flowing motion. He possesses a good sinking fastball (87 MPH), an above average curve and decent change, with which he mixes a split-fingered pitch. He demonstrated good control and proved difficult to hit, limiting opposing hitters to a .221 average. He was, however, susceptible to home runs, allowing 11 in 93.2 innings.

HOLDING RUNNERS, FIELDING, HITTING:

Melendez has a better-than-average pickoff move, especially for someone with so little major league experience. He is also a good fielder. He had two hits in 20 at-bats but also struck out 14 times, indicating he is not likely to become a factor as a batter.

OVERALL:

After eight seasons of professional ball, Melendez is still only 26 years old. With the Padres, his future is likely to be in the bullpen as a middle and long man. To put his renewed value in perspective, he was supposedly the stumbling block in a big November Padres-Reds deal. The Padres wouldn't include him as part of the trade.

Overall Statistics

	W	L	ERA	G	GS	Sv	IP	H	R	BB	SO	HR
1991	8	5	3.27	31	9	3	93.2	77	35	24	60	11
Career	8	5	3.73	34	9	3	99.0	85	43	27	67	13

How Often He Throws Strikes

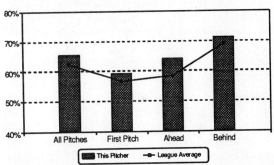

1991 Situational Stats

	W	L	ERA	Sv	IP		AB	H	HR	RBI	AVG
Home	5	3	3.30	1	46.1	LHB	176	40	6	17	.227
Road	3	2	3.23	2	47.1	RHB	172	37	5	15	.215
Day	1	2	3.72	3	29.0	Sc Pos	52	12	0	19	.231
Night	7	3	3.06	0	64.2	Clutch	77	18	2	9	.234

1991 Rankings (National League)

→ Led the Padres in errors by a pitcher (2)

PITCHING:

People have been burying Dennis Rasmussen for years only to have the tall lefthander fool them in the end. But now the end might be getting close for Rasmussen, who labored through a rugged 1991 season and has not had a solid season since 1988 (16-10, 3.43). It had appeared that Rasmussen was finished with the team prior to last season until the Padres signed him for one year shortly before spring training.

Rasmussen then developed a sore shoulder during spring training and did not make his first start until May 25. He came out of the gate pitching well, going 3-1 with a 0.71 ERA in his first five starts. Then the bottom fell out. Rasmussen suffered through a nine-game losing streak, a stretch in which the Padres didn't help matters by scoring an average of only 1.6 runs per nine innings for him. Rasmussen briefly rebounded by going 3-1 in his next six starts before going winless in the season's final three weeks.

Rasmussen continues to rely on a big-breaking curve ball. He has never been one to challenge hitters despite having a decent fastball. He did become tougher on left-handed hitters last year, but righthanders pounded him at a .280 clip. His days could be numbered, with the influx of younger Padre pitchers.

HOLDING RUNNERS, FIELDING, HITTING:

Rasmussen makes an effort to try to hold baserunners, but he does not have a great move to first. He'll pick off a napping runner on occasion, but his slow delivery makes him vulnerable to stolen bases. He is also not the most agile of fielders. Rasmussen can help with his bat; he led Padre pitchers last year with a .136 average and is a .193 lifetime hitter.

OVERALL:

Soon to be 33, Rasmussen has made a career of having good years exactly when it looks like his days are numbered. However, he likely won't get another chance with San Diego, and his value has appreciably diminished around baseball as well.

DENNIS RASMUSSEN

Position: SP
Bats: L **Throws:** L
Ht: 6' 7" **Wt:** 233

Opening Day Age: 32
Born: 4/18/59 in Los Angeles, CA
ML Seasons: 9

Overall Statistics

	W	L	ERA	G	GS	Sv	IP	H	R	BB	SO	HR
1991	6	13	3.74	24	24	0	146.2	155	74	49	75	12
Career	86	73	4.09	234	224	0	1379.0	1339	699	492	805	166

How Often He Throws Strikes

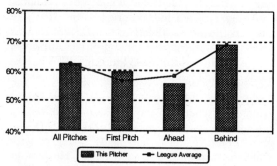

1991 Situational Stats

	W	L	ERA	Sv	IP		AB	H	HR	RBI	AVG
Home	4	5	3.88	0	60.1	LHB	104	24	2	10	.231
Road	2	8	3.65	0	86.1	RHB	468	131	10	53	.280
Day	3	3	3.59	0	42.2	Sc Pos	120	31	3	50	.258
Night	3	10	3.81	0	104.0	Clutch	36	10	0	2	.278

1991 Rankings (National League)

→ 2nd lowest winning percentage (.316)

→ 3rd highest batting average allowed vs. right-handed batters (.280)

→ 6th in losses (13)

→ Led the Padres in losses and most stolen bases allowed (21)

BIP
ROBERTS

Position: 2B/LF/CF
Bats: B **Throws:** R
Ht: 5' 7" **Wt:** 160

Opening Day Age: 28
Born: 10/27/63 in
Berkeley, CA
ML Seasons: 5

HITTING:

Injuries killed the 1991 season for Bip Roberts, and somewhere along the way he went from the team's catalyst to likely off season trade bait. Alternating between second base and the outfield, Roberts first was sidelined with back spasms and then with bruises after an outfield collision. He then injured his knee in mid-August and required surgery to repair torn cartilage, returning to play 19 games in September.

All the down time resulted in down numbers. Roberts batted a respectable .281, but that was a drop of 28 points from 1990. A switch-hitter, he was far more effective batting left-handed for the second straight year. However, for a player of his skills, Roberts struck out too much (71 times) while earning too few walks (37). The lack of discipline had been a problem early in Roberts' career and resurfaced in 1991.

N.L. teams still try to get Roberts out with breaking balls, since he has always been a good fastball hitter. He'll chase balls out of the strike zone, especially batting left-handed.

BASERUNNING:

Roberts is not a flat-out burner and must rely on good jumps instead of pure speed to steal bases. The injuries were an obvious problem in 1991 and both his total (26) and success rate (70%) were not nearly as good as in 1990 (42 and 79%).

FIELDING:

It's still a matter of debate as to what Roberts' best position might be. He's probably best at second base, but has never had the chance to play there for a full season. As an outfielder, he can play both left and center, showing decent range but a poor arm.

OVERALL:

For some reason, by late last season Roberts seemed to be another of the growing legion of players to end up on the wrong side of manager Greg Riddoch. If he isn't traded, Roberts is San Diego's only bona fide leadoff hitter. However, if the Padres do offer Roberts around, a lot of clubs will be interested.

Overall Statistics

	G	AB	R	H	D	T	HR	RBI	SB	BB	SO	AVG
1991	117	424	66	119	13	3	3	32	26	37	71	.281
Career	489	1559	286	454	69	16	16	113	107	156	212	.291

Where He Hits the Ball

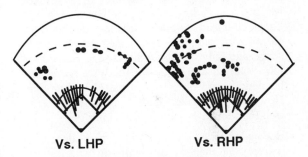

Vs. LHP   Vs. RHP

1991 Situational Stats

	AB	H	HR	RBI	AVG		AB	H	HR	RBI	AVG
Home	223	64	3	17	.287	LHP	119	30	0	8	.252
Road	201	55	0	15	.274	RHP	305	89	3	24	.292
Day	116	36	3	10	.310	Sc Pos	79	25	1	28	.316
Night	308	83	0	22	.269	Clutch	68	19	1	7	.279

1991 Rankings (National League)

→ 3rd highest batting average on a 3-1 count (.625)

→ 9th lowest slugging percentage vs. left-handed pitchers (.294)

→ Led the Padres in stolen bases (26), caught stealing (11), batting average on a 3-1 count and batting average on a 3-2 count (.286)

→ Led NL second basemen in batting average on a 3-1 count

PITCHING:

There are few commodities more sought after in baseball than the reliable left-handed reliever. For evidence, just look at the long list of retreads (the Dan Schatzeder, Ray Searage ilk) who annually trot from team to team solely because they can throw both left-handed and frequently. The Padres have to feel very good about the development of Rich Rodriguez, who in 1991 established himself as a dependable southpaw out of the pen.

Rodriguez was originally the property of the Mets, but was buried in the minors. Ironically, it was then-Mets VP Joe McIlvaine who okayed the minor 1988 deal that sent Rodriguez to San Diego in exchange for the immortal Brad Pounders. Now Rodriguez has become an asset for McIlvaine's Padres. Rodriguez shared the San Diego club lead in appearances last year with 64. He allowed only 10 of 49 inherited runners to score, and only 66 hits in 80 innings. He did the job usually asked of him, namely to retire left-handed hitters who batted only .221 against him. However, Rodriguez needs to improve his control. He walked 44 batters in 80 innings.

Rodriguez hides the ball well with a deceptive delivery that makes it especially difficult for lefties to see the ball. He relies heavily on a slider while showing an occasional curveball. Against right-handed hitters, Rodriguez will also turn over his fastball, giving it a screwball-like look that breaks in on righties.

HOLDING RUNNERS, FIELDING, HITTING:

Rodriguez has only a fair move to first. He does a decent job of holding on runners and is an average fielder. He is hitless in eight lifetime at-bats.

OVERALL:

Good left-handed middle relievers are worth their weight in gold. After years of watching lefthanders like Pat Clements, Derek Lilliquist and Eric Nolte, the Padres are very happy to have Rodriguez around.

RICH RODRIGUEZ

Position: RP
Bats: R **Throws:** L
Ht: 5'11" **Wt:** 200

Opening Day Age: 29
Born: 3/1/63 in Downey, CA
ML Seasons: 2

Overall Statistics

	W	L	ERA	G	GS	Sv	IP	H	R	BB	SO	HR
1991	3	1	3.26	64	1	0	80.0	66	31	44	40	8
Career	4	2	3.10	96	1	1	127.2	118	48	60	62	10

How Often He Throws Strikes

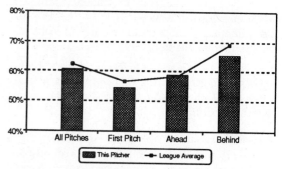

1991 Situational Stats

	W	L	ERA	Sv	IP		AB	H	HR	RBI	AVG
Home	1	1	4.58	0	37.1	LHB	95	21	3	12	.221
Road	2	0	2.11	0	42.2	RHB	187	45	5	22	.241
Day	2	1	3.47	0	23.1	Sc Pos	91	19	1	27	.209
Night	1	0	3.18	0	56.2	Clutch	82	16	4	14	.195

1991 Rankings (National League)

→ 4th most GDPs induced per GDP situation (19.1%)

→ 5th least strikeouts per 9 innings in relief (4.7)

→ 6th lowest percentage of inherited runners scored (20.4%)

→ Led the Padres in games pitched (64) and most GDPs induced per GDP situation

HITTING:

Another fast finish, something of a trademark, helped Benito Santiago to one of his best overall seasons in 1991. Santiago hit 17 homers, one less than his personal best, and he added a career-high 87 RBI. Nevertheless, there was talk by season's end that the Padres wouldn't mind trading him in their ongoing purge of anyone who is in the doghouse of manager Greg Riddoch. At one point last season, Riddoch benched Santiago for not running out an infield pop, and the two often quarreled about pitch selection.

Despite frequent sessions with batting coach Merv Rettenmund, Santiago also did not appreciably change his undisciplined batting style. He struck out 114 times with only 23 walks. Teams were successful in getting Santiago to swing at high fastballs and breaking balls in the dirt.

As he's done before, Santiago saved some of his best production for late in the season when the Padres were basically out of the race. He drove in 36 runs in San Diego's final 40 games.

BASERUNNING:

Hardly the typical catcher on the base paths, Santiago nevertheless sometimes gives himself too much credit as a base stealer. He stole eight bases last year but was caught 10 times. With his wild swing, he is also very slow getting out of the batter's box. He grounded into a league-high 21 double plays.

FIELDING:

No catcher has a better arm than Santiago. But teams are less hesitant about running on him than they once were. Santiago threw out only 38 percent (57 of 150) of opposing base stealers. Amazingly, he threw out 25 of 59 from his knees. However, Santiago is guilty of too many errors trying for pickoffs, and Padres pitchers continue to have trouble with his pitch selection.

OVERALL:

This amazingly talented catcher could be headed elsewhere. In new surroundings, Santiago might well go to the next step and become a true superstar. For some reason, he seems stalled in development in San Diego, even if it's at a very lofty plateau compared to most catchers.

BENITO SANTIAGO

Position: C
Bats: R **Throws:** R
Ht: 6' 1" **Wt:** 182

Opening Day Age: 27
Born: 3/9/65 in Ponce, Puerto Rico
ML Seasons: 6

Overall Statistics

	G	AB	R	H	D	T	HR	RBI	SB	BB	SO	AVG
1991	152	580	60	155	22	3	17	87	8	23	114	.267
Career	683	2486	275	661	103	15	75	333	60	118	464	.266

Where He Hits the Ball

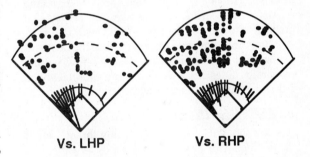

Vs. LHP   **Vs. RHP**

1991 Situational Stats

	AB	H	HR	RBI	AVG		AB	H	HR	RBI	AVG
Home	287	70	6	34	.244	LHP	204	58	8	35	.284
Road	293	85	11	53	.290	RHP	376	97	9	52	.258
Day	139	45	6	25	.324	Sc Pos	171	47	6	72	.275
Night	441	110	11	62	.249	Clutch	106	35	4	20	.330

1991 Rankings (National League)

→ 1st in GDPs (21) and lowest on-base average vs. right-handed pitchers (.284)

→ 2nd lowest fielding percentage as a catcher (.985)

→ Led the Padres in at-bats (580), sacrifice flies (7), GDPs, batting average with the bases loaded (.375) and steals of third (5)

→ Led NL catchers in errors (14), home runs (17), at-bats, total bases (234), RBIs (87), sacrifice flies, strikeouts (114), GDPs, plate appearances (614), games (152) and slugging percentage (.403)

HITTING:

Desperate for infield help and some added pop, the Padres dealt veteran Garry Templeton to New York last year for veteran Tim Teufel. Teufel supplied some power, hitting 11 homers in 97 games for San Diego while alternating between second and third base. Teufel accounted for 24 of his 42 Padre RBI on home runs.

Though the Padres played him every day, Teufel demonstrated once again that he is a platoon player. He hit 88 points higher against left-handed pitching with 54 of his 77 strikeouts coming against righthanders.

Teufel is a fastball hitter who has a good knowledge of the strike zone and will take pitches for walks. However, he is vulnerable to breaking balls in the strike zone as well as changes of speed. Most clubs try never to throw him a fastball in the strike zone but instead use the heater as a waste pitch against him. Teufel's low batting average hides his value as a run-producer who draws a huge number of walks.

BASERUNNING:

Never thought of as a basestealing threat, Teufel unveiled an all-new skill in 1991 by stealing nine bases in 12 attempts. One reason was that he usually hit in the sixth or seventh spot of the order and was thus more free to run than when batting second, the lineup position he often occupied for the Mets.

FIELDING:

Teufel displayed equal ability at both second base and third. At second, he lacks range and is only fair at making the double play pivot. His lack of range is not as serious at third, but he has only an average third base arm. Teufel can also play first, though he has below-average skills there.

OVERALL:

Teufel is one of those guys who is quite valuable as a part-timer on a good club. As an everyday player, he does not appreciably make a team better. His '92 role on the Padres is uncertain, but he could end up an everyday player at either second or third.

TIM TEUFEL

Position: 2B/3B
Bats: R **Throws:** R
Ht: 6' 0" **Wt:** 175

Opening Day Age: 33
Born: 7/7/58 in Greenwich, CT
ML Seasons: 9

Overall Statistics

	G	AB	R	H	D	T	HR	RBI	SB	BB	SO	AVG
1991	117	341	41	74	16	0	12	44	9	51	77	.217
Career	876	2666	366	684	164	10	73	323	19	329	447	.257

Where He Hits the Ball

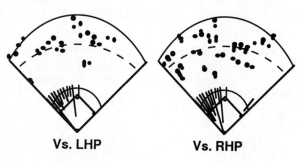

Vs. LHP   Vs. RHP

1991 Situational Stats

	AB	H	HR	RBI	AVG		AB	H	HR	RBI	AVG
Home	162	37	6	24	.228	LHP	133	36	7	27	.271
Road	179	37	6	20	.207	RHP	208	38	5	17	.183
Day	93	20	2	12	.215	Sc Pos	94	20	6	35	.213
Night	248	54	10	32	.218	Clutch	72	17	3	10	.236

1991 Rankings (National League)

- 4th lowest batting average with runners in scoring position (.213)
- 6th highest percentage of pitches taken (61.8%)
- Led the Padres in slugging percentage vs. left-handed pitchers (.544) and on-base average vs. left-handed pitchers (.397)

PITCHING:

After four straight years of pitching 200 or more innings, the wheels came off in 1991 for 36-year-old Ed Whitson. He developed elbow tendinitis within the season's first two months, then tried a brief comeback in late June. Whitson had to return to the disabled list and eventually underwent arthroscopic surgery on July 15 to remove a bone spur.

The season was a washout for Whitson, who in 1990 had the best year of his career and was one of the best starting pitchers in the National League. He ended up with a 4-6 record and 5.03 ERA, numbers which are meaningless because of his physical problems. The good news is that he checked out all right physically at the end of the season. San Diego indicated that they would renew Whitson's option for 1992 and their reports suggested he should return to 100 percent.

If that's the case, then National League hitters will again see one of the most intelligent pitchers in baseball. Whitson is a master at keeping hitters off-balance by using an excellent change-up, throwing his fastball at several different speeds and then spotting his slider and curve. With a repertoire that does not include any one overpowering pitch, Whitson must have control. When last healthy in 1990, he averaged less than two walks per nine innings.

HOLDING RUNNERS, FIELDING, HITTING:

Whitson does a decent job of holding runners. He is an average fielder, but at times does not have swift reactions to balls hit in front of the mound. Whitson has made himself into a decent hitter, though he managed only three hits in 24 at-bats last season.

OVERALL:

There is no bigger key to the Padres becoming contenders than Whitson. If his elbow is 100 percent and he returns to something close to his 1990 form, then the Padres will have added one of the most dependable starting pitchers in the league to their staff; a healthy Whitson gives them a very competitive starting rotation. Without him, they will be looking to fill some big holes in their staff.

ED WHITSON

Position: SP
Bats: R **Throws:** R
Ht: 6' 3" **Wt:** 202

Opening Day Age: 36
Born: 5/19/55 in Johnson City, TN
ML Seasons: 15

Overall Statistics

	W	L	ERA	G	GS	Sv	IP	H	R	BB	SO	HR
1991	4	6	5.03	13	12	0	78.2	93	47	17	40	13
Career	126	123	3.79	452	333	8	2240.2	2240	1045	698	1266	211

How Often He Throws Strikes

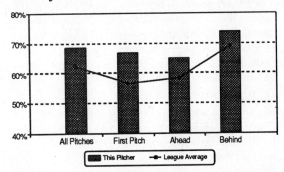

1991 Situational Stats

	W	L	ERA	Sv	IP		AB	H	HR	RBI	AVG
Home	0	3	5.18	0	33.0	LHB	180	51	5	15	.283
Road	4	3	4.93	0	45.2	RHB	131	42	8	28	.321
Day	2	3	6.61	0	31.1	Sc Pos	54	20	3	25	.370
Night	2	3	3.99	0	47.1	Clutch	16	3	0	1	.188

1991 Rankings (National League)

→ 6th most GDPs induced per GDP situation (18.2%)

SCOTT COOLBAUGH

Position: 3B
Bats: R **Throws:** R
Ht: 5'11" **Wt:** 195

Opening Day Age: 25
Born: 6/13/66 in
Binghampton, NY
ML Seasons: 3

Overall Statistics

	G	AB	R	H	D	T	HR	RBI	SB	BB	SO	AVG
1991	60	180	12	39	8	1	2	15	0	19	45	.217
Career	152	411	40	89	15	1	6	35	1	38	104	.217

HITTING, FIELDING, BASERUNNING:

The Padres acquired Scott Coolbaugh from Texas before the 1991 season, hoping he might be the answer to their third base problem. Coolbaugh had been considered one of Texas' better prospects for several years, but didn't do much in an extended 1990 trial.

He didn't do much in San Diego, either. After playing fairly regularly for two months, Coolbaugh ended up spending most of the season in the minors. The reasons for the demotion weren't hard to find. He batted only .217 with precious little run production (two homers and 15 RBI). Coolbaugh seemed overmatched by National League hard stuff, striking out 45 times in only 180 at bats. He was buried inside by fastballs on his hands.

Coolbaugh is no basestealing threat, having been caught on all three of his 1991 attempts. He was also erratic in the field, making seven errors in his limited playing time. He has decent range but has an erratic throwing arm, and he lacks quickness on slow rollers.

OVERALL:

Unless San Diego obtains an established third baseman, Coolbaugh will likely get a chance in spring training to show improvement. However, he hasn't shown the power he had once hinted at, and he's quickly gone from prospect to suspect.

JOHN COSTELLO

Position: RP
Bats: R **Throws:** R
Ht: 6' 1" **Wt:** 180

Opening Day Age: 31
Born: 12/24/60 in New York, NY
ML Seasons: 4

Overall Statistics

	W	L	ERA	G	GS	Sv	IP	H	R	BB	SO	HR
1991	1	0	3.09	27	0	0	35.0	37	15	17	24	2
Career	11	6	2.97	119	0	4	157.2	141	62	64	104	13

PITCHING, FIELDING, HITTING & HOLDING RUNNERS:

Ex-Cardinal and Expo John Costello bounced three times between the Padres and AAA Las Vegas last year, which is normal for him; Costello has pitched in both the majors and minors in each of the last four seasons. With the Padres, he had some success as a middle and long reliever. He allowed only four of 13 inherited runners to score and allowed runs in just seven of his 27 outings. Overall, Costello's 3.09 ERA was the second-lowest of his major league career.

Costello is not an overpowering pitcher. He relies on moving the ball around, throwing an average fastball which he turns over some to left-handed hitters. Lefties hit 60 points less against him than righthanders. That's a key for him; if Costello can handle major league lefties, he'll be able to stick around. He'll have to improve his .303 opponents average versus righties, however.

Costello is a good fielder but has only an average move to first and is slow coming to the plate, making him vulnerable to base stealers.

OVERALL:

Costello isn't going to move into anyone's starting rotation or be a closer. But he can be a decent ninth or tenth man on a staff and prove helpful in long relief situations -- especially if he can continue to handle left-handed hitters.

JOSE MOTA

Position: 2B
Bats: B **Throws:** R
Ht: 5' 9" **Wt:** 155

Opening Day Age: 27
Born: 3/16/65 in Santo Domingo, Dominican Republic
ML Seasons: 1

Overall Statistics

	G	AB	R	H	D	T	HR	RBI	SB	BB	SO	AVG
1991	17	36	4	8	0	0	0	2	0	2	7	.222
Career	17	36	4	8	0	0	0	2	0	2	7	.222

HITTING, FIELDING, BASERUNNING:

Jose Mota was one of six Padres to get a start at second base in 1991. Mota didn't see much action, however, playing in only 17 games and getting just 36 at-bats. He didn't make much of an impression, batting .222 with no extra-base hits and no steals. Mota has hit over .300 in the minors, however, so some ability is present.

The son of ex-National League outfielder and pinch hitter Manny Mota, Jose's minor league record indicates little power but good strike zone discipline along with the ability to hit for a decent average. Mota is also a fair defensive player, though he lacks great range at second. He has some speed, nabbing 15 stolen bases at AAA Las Vegas last year, but he was also caught 10 times. Mota's been around; he was originally drafted by the Pirates, and has also been the property of the Dodger and Indian organizations.

OVERALL:

Considering how wide open the Padres' second base situation is, Mota will likely get a shot like every other San Diego infielder. However, he is hardly a fresh-faced prospect who can be expected to improve. He'll be 27 on Opening Day and isn't likely to suddenly show much power or be a productive major league run producer overnight. He has a chance to stick as a reserve.

ADAM PETERSON

Position: SP
Bats: R **Throws:** R
Ht: 6' 3" **Wt:** 190

Opening Day Age: 26
Born: 12/11/65 in Long Beach, CA
ML Seasons: 5

Overall Statistics

	W	L	ERA	G	GS	Sv	IP	H	R	BB	SO	HR
1991	3	4	4.45	13	11	0	54.2	50	33	28	37	10
Career	5	11	5.46	39	27	0	155.0	167	103	65	75	24

PITCHING, FIELDING, HITTING & HOLDING RUNNERS:

With Ed Whitson injured and the Padres looking for at least a fifth starter, San Diego gave righthander Adam Peterson a trial last year. Peterson, who came over from the White Sox in a spring trade, made 11 starts for the Padres, ending up with a 3-4 record and 4.45 ERA, hardly overpowering results. However, he did pitch a six-inning, two-hit shutout in one start.

Though he had some good years in the White Sox system -- going 40-21 in 1987- 89 -- Peterson has no overpowering pitch. He must mix his average fastball and slider to be effective. He can be tough on right-handed hitters who batted .196 compared to an average of .278 by lefties. Peterson also is usually around the plate; that's the reason why he has always been vulnerable to home runs, allowing 10 in only 54.2 innings in 1991.

Peterson is a competent fielder and has a fairly quick delivery home, which helps against base stealers. He didn't get a hit last year (0-for-13).

OVERALL:

Despite Peterson's good minor league record, he's 5-11 lifetime with a 5.46 ERA in the big time. It's uncertain whether or not he will stick with the Padres this year. His best chance is as a long reliever.

ORGANIZATION OVERVIEW:

The Padre team which won the 1984 National League pennant had some very good young talent (Tony Gwynn, Alan Wiggins, Kevin McReynolds, Eric Show, Dave Dravecky) and was expected to win more titles. That never happened. Although San Diego continued to produce talented players like the Alomar brothers, Benito Santiago, Carlos Baerga, Andy Benes and Greg Harris, the Padres have been only marginal contenders at best. The Padres often seemed to expect too much from their young players, trading many of them away while they were still short of their prime years. Things should be better now that Joe McIlvaine and Greg Riddoch are in charge, but there's some rebuilding to do; the Padre system has few top prospects.

JAY GAINER

Position: 1B
Bats: L **Throws:** L
Ht: 6' 0" **Wt:** 188

Opening Day Age: 25
Born: 10/8/66 in
Panama City, FL

Recent Statistics

	G	AB	R	H	D	THR	RBI	SB	BB	SO	AVG
90 A Spokane	74	281	41	100	21	0 10	54	4	31	49	.356
91 A High Desert	127	499	83	131	17	0 32	120	4	52	105	.263

What power numbers! Gainer led the minor leagues with 32 homers, and the California League with 120 RBI. Before getting too carried away, look at Gainer's average (.263), his strikeout total (105), his age (25), and the park at High Desert, which is the friendliest in the California League. However, Gainer has had only two seasons of professional experience; in the other, he led the Northwest League with a .356 average. Gainer wasn't even chosen one of the top ten prospects in the California League, but keep an eye on him. If he's any good, he'll move up fast.

MATTHEW MIESKE

Position: OF
Bats: R **Throws:** R
Ht: 6' 0" **Wt:** 185

Opening Day Age: 24
Born: 2/13/68 in
Midland, MI

Recent Statistics

	G	AB	R	H	D	THR	RBI	SB	BB	SO	AVG
90 A Spokane	76	291	59	99	20	0 12	63	25	45	43	.340
91 A High Desert	133	492	108	168	36	6 15	119	39	94	82	.341

Jay Gainer's sidekick, Mieske has helped his partner terrorize two leagues in two seasons. Like Gainer, he was a 1990 draftee who had an impressive debut at Spokane, hitting .340 and leading the Northwest League in homers and RBI. Mieske's the better prospect, though; he's younger, plays better defense, has more speed and a better batting eye. If you're going to keep one eye on Gainer this year, keep both of them on Mieske.

FRANK SEMINARA

Position: P
Bats: R **Throws:** R
Ht: 6' 2" **Wt:** 195

Opening Day Age: 24
Born: 5/16/67 in
Brooklyn, NY

Recent Statistics

	W	L	ERA	G	GS	Sv	IP	H	R	BB	SO	HR
90 A Pr William	16	8	1.90	25	25	0	170.1	136	51	52	132	5
91 AA Wichita	15	10	3.38	27	27	0	176.0	173	86	68	107	10

A Brooklyn boy, Seminara attended Columbia and was in the Yankee system until this year, when the Padres acquired him. He's been largely ignored, but it's hard to see why: Seminara has a 2.90 minor league ERA, with decent strikeout totals. He led the Carolina League in ERA in 1990, and had a fine year in a hitters park at Wichita this season. His record the last two years is 31-18. He's a finesse pitcher, not the kind that excites people, but it looks like he can pitch.

DAVE STATON

Position: 1B
Bats: R **Throws:** R
Ht: 6' 5" **Wt:** 215

Opening Day Age: 23
Born: 4/12/68 in
Seattle, WA

Recent Statistics

	G	AB	R	H	D	THR	RBI	SB	BB	SO	AVG
90 A Riverside	92	335	56	97	16	1 20	64	4	52	78	.290
90 AA Wichita	45	164	26	50	11	0 6	31	0	22	37	.305
91 AAA Las Vegas	107	375	61	100	19	1 22	74	1	44	89	.267
91 MLE	107	350	36	75	13	0 13	44	0	26	96	.214

Big and strong, Staton definitely has power, averaging a homer every 17 at-bats in his minor league career. Thus far his game is very incomplete, however: he's big and lumbering, a poor defensive player, and he struck out about once every four at-bats with Las Vegas. Staton does draw some walks, and he has a .301 lifetime minor league average. Don't start worrying, Fred McGriff; Staton will probably get another year in AAA.

DAN WALTERS

Position: C
Bats: R **Throws:** R
Ht: 6' 2" **Wt:** 190

Opening Day Age: 25
Born: 8/15/66 in
Brunswick, ME

Recent Statistics

	G	AB	R	H	D	THR	RBI	SB	BB	SO	AVG
90 AA Wichita	58	199	25	59	12	0 7	40	0	21	21	.296
90 AAA Las Vegas	53	184	19	47	9	0 3	26	0	13	24	.255
91 AAA Las Vegas	96	293	39	93	22	0 4	44	0	22	35	.317
91 MLE	96	269	23	69	15	0 2	26	0	13	37	.257

Walters, a catcher who used to be in the Houston system, has had an unpredictable career, and his .317 season at Las Vegas last year was by far the best of his seven minor league seasons. His major league equivalents are not very good, however, and Walters has little power or speed. He looks like a potential backup catcher; don't expect a starring role.

HITTING:

For a while in the early part of the 1991 season, it appeared as if Dave Anderson might finally get a chance to earn a permanent starting job. The Giants started the season without Jose Uribe, who was injured, and they quickly gave up on Mike Benjamin. That left the shortstop job to Anderson, more or less by default. Never a great defensive player, he didn't hit well enough to last as a regular.

Anderson is primarily a low-ball, all-fields hitter who tends to chop down at the ball -- that hurts him some at Candlestick Park, where the high grass slows down a lot of ground balls that might get through an artificial-turf infield. He batted only .197 at Candlestick last year while finishing at .313 on the road.

Anderson's a smart hitter who knows the strike zone and will take pitchers deep into counts. He also hits the curve and the offspeed pitch well; pitchers do him a favor by throwing him such pitches because he isn't quick-wristed enough to handle good heat on a consistent basis.

BASERUNNING:

Anderson is slowing down a bit, and long-standing back problems have deprived him of much of the above-average speed he once had. But he still runs the bases with a high degree of intelligence, and can be depended upon to make good decisions.

FIELDING:

Anderson got most of his playing time at shortstop last year, but can play all four infield positions. That makes him an ideal utility man, and it is in this role that the Giants would prefer to use him. He really doesn't have the arm strength to be an above-average shortstop.

OVERALL:

Anderson has proven to be a useful player for the Giants since they signed him two years ago. He never has complained about his utility man status, and contributed somewhat when he was handed the starting shortstop job for a month-long period. Anderson has definite value and probably will again be the Giants' primary utility man.

DAVE ANDERSON

Position: SS/1B
Bats: R **Throws:** R
Ht: 6' 2" **Wt:** 184

Opening Day Age: 31
Born: 8/1/60 in Louisville, KY
ML Seasons: 9

Overall Statistics

	G	AB	R	H	D	T	HR	RBI	SB	BB	SO	AVG
1991	100	226	24	56	5	2	2	13	2	12	35	.248
Career	822	1942	234	466	69	12	16	135	49	202	320	.240

Where He Hits the Ball

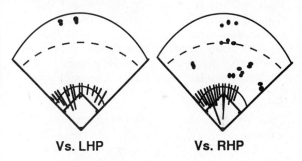

Vs. LHP   **Vs. RHP**

1991 Situational Stats

	AB	H	HR	RBI	AVG		AB	H	HR	RBI	AVG
Home	127	25	1	9	.197	LHP	81	12	1	3	.148
Road	99	31	1	4	.313	RHP	145	44	1	10	.303
Day	91	20	0	5	.220	Sc Pos	52	9	0	8	.173
Night	135	36	2	8	.267	Clutch	62	17	0	4	.274

1991 Rankings (National League)

➡ Did not rank near the top or bottom in any category

HITTING:

Kevin Bass has not found home very hospitable since signing a lucrative three-year free agent deal with the San Francisco Giants before the 1990 season. In fact, rumors concerning a possible buyout and/or waiving of the no-trade clause in Bass' contract were spreading late in the 1991 campaign.

For the third straight year, Bass, a native of nearby Redwood City, was plagued by injuries. He spent a month on the disabled list in July because of a bad knee. When he did play he never seemed relaxed at the plate. He played as if he had to prove in each game that he had earned that big contract.

Bass still has the quick-wristed, elegant swing that he brought with him from Houston. The problem is that he has lost some bat speed, and the elegance comes from the upward arc -- he uppercuts everything, and a very high percent of the pitches he saw last season were breaking balls.

BASERUNNING:

Bass is a decent baserunner, but no longer takes many chances. This decline could be the result of his injuries. Bass is no longer much of a base stealing threat, although he might be if he played for a team that ran more.

FIELDING:

Bass' defensive long suit is his arm strength and accuracy; from that standpoint, he has filled a right field need for the Giants when healthy. He also goes back on a ball just about as well as anyone. Overall, he is a superior defensive outfielder.

OVERALL:

Due mainly to the no-trade clause in his contract, Bass is likely to be with the Giants on Opening Day. But he has fallen out of favor, mostly because he has been unable to stay healthy. Bass must have a solid season in 1992 to remain a viable major league entity.

KEVIN BASS

Position: RF/LF
Bats: B **Throws:** R
Ht: 6' 0" **Wt:** 190

Opening Day Age: 32
Born: 5/12/59 in Redwood City, CA
ML Seasons: 10

Overall Statistics

	G	AB	R	H	D	T	HR	RBI	SB	BB	SO	AVG
1991	124	361	43	84	10	4	10	40	7	36	56	.233
Career	1132	3710	469	1000	180	34	95	468	120	256	496	.270

Where He Hits the Ball

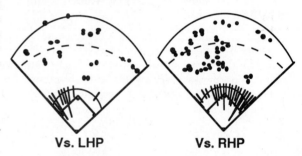

Vs. LHP   **Vs. RHP**

1991 Situational Stats

	AB	H	HR	RBI	AVG		AB	H	HR	RBI	AVG
Home	167	35	5	17	.210	LHP	113	27	6	15	.239
Road	194	49	5	23	.253	RHP	248	57	4	25	.230
Day	133	25	2	12	.188	Sc Pos	96	19	3	33	.198
Night	228	59	8	28	.259	Clutch	68	16	2	13	.235

1991 Rankings (National League)

- 2nd lowest batting average with runners in scoring position (.198)
- 5th most GDPs per GDP situation (18.2%)
- 10th lowest percentage of extra bases taken as a runner (31.6%)
- Led the Giants in GDPs (12)
- Led NL right fielders in batting average on a 3-1 count (.500)

PITCHING:

Rod Beck was one of the more pleasant surprises on the San Francisco Giants' pitching staff in 1991, especially after his second promotion during the All-Star break. Beck was used primarily in long relief, but showed his no-nonsense approach by retiring 24 of the 31 men he faced in first-batter situations. Beck wasn't known as a control pitcher in the minors, but he walked only 13 in 52.1 innings with the big club.

Beck is a swarthy, burly guy who pitches a lot like he looks. Although he has been used both in relief and as a starter in the Giants' organization, he seems best suited for relief. He has a riding fastball and likes to pitch inside, but he also can sink the fastball. He changes speeds very seldom, and his slider and curve are little more than wrinkles, although he seemed able to throw them for strikes even when behind in the count. He tries to keep his job as uncomplicated as he can, and that style seems to work well for him.

HOLDING RUNNERS, FIELDING, HITTING:

Beck has an ordinary move to first, and usually doesn't pay much attention to runners. With his fairly compact motion, he gives his catcher something of a head start. Beck is not a good fielder, largely because his mobility is very limited. He sometimes takes silly chances when fielding bunts and nubbers. As a hitter, he had only two at-bats, but singled off the Braves' John Smoltz in his first major league plate appearance.

OVERALL:

Beck has a get-after-them approach that appealed to Giants' manager Roger Craig, and his velocity is such that he can challenge most hitters and get away with it. Moreover, he's around the plate almost all the time. Beck intends to lose 20 pounds during the off season, and that could help him assume a prominent role with San Francisco in 1992.

ROD BECK

Position: RP
Bats: R **Throws:** R
Ht: 6' 1" **Wt:** 215

Opening Day Age: 23
Born: 8/3/68 in Burbank, CA
ML Seasons: 1

Overall Statistics

	W	L	ERA	G	GS	Sv	IP	H	R	BB	SO	HR
1991	1	1	3.78	31	0	1	52.1	53	22	13	38	4
Career	1	1	3.78	31	0	1	52.1	53	22	13	38	4

How Often He Throws Strikes

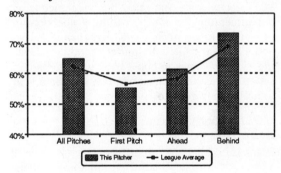

1991 Situational Stats

	W	L	ERA	Sv	IP		AB	H	HR	RBI	AVG
Home	0	1	3.86	1	25.2	LHB	89	26	4	10	.292
Road	1	0	3.71	0	26.2	RHB	105	27	0	16	.257
Day	0	0	3.65	0	12.1	Sc Pos	59	19	0	22	.322
Night	1	1	3.83	1	40.0	Clutch	32	8	1	3	.250

1991 Rankings (National League)

→ Did not rank near the top or bottom in any category

PITCHING:

Known for his consistency while in the American League, Bud Black had several stretches last year that almost justified the four-year, $10 million free agent contract he signed before the season. At other times, like when he was allowing one of his 25 homers (tied for second-most in the league), his pitches looked like dirigibles.

Adjusting to the lower National League strike zone might have been a problem for Black. He tends give up a lot of fly balls and likes to tempt batters to try to hit under the ball. That got him into trouble, especially in midsummer air on the road. Black's road ERA was a horrid 5.28.

Black also had trouble with his offspeed pitches. His velocity was as expected, but he seemed to be experimenting too much, willingly abandoning one of his many pitches -- slider, change, curve and a half-forkball, half-splitter -- and then lacking the confidence to come back with it. Batters sat on the fastball against him late in counts, and too often they got one.

HOLDING RUNNERS, FIELDING, HITTING:

Black is excellent at holding runners, which isn't a forte of the Giants' staff. He catalogued runners quickly, even though he was in an unfamiliar league, and often crossed them up with a variety of techniques. Defensively, he is better than adequate, although at times he can be too aggressive in going after a lead runner. Considering he had been in the American League, Black proved quite adroit with the bat. He had three doubles with six RBI and batted .183 for the season.

OVERALL:

Black's season wasn't as bad as his 12-16 record might indicate. That record reflects his inconsistency more than it does his overall effectiveness. He was a positive influence on the Giants' younger pitchers, and he seldom followed one bad outing with another. Ideally, he should be the Giants' number-three or four starter -- a guy who can win 15 or 16 games with a good club.

BUD BLACK

Position: SP
Bats: L **Throws:** L
Ht: 6' 2" **Wt:** 185

Opening Day Age: 34
Born: 6/30/57 in San Mateo, CA
ML Seasons: 11

Overall Statistics

	W	L	ERA	G	GS	Sv	IP	H	R	BB	SO	HR
1991	12	16	3.99	34	34	0	214.1	201	104	71	104	25
Career	95	98	3.74	333	232	11	1681.0	1598	777	499	850	164

How Often He Throws Strikes

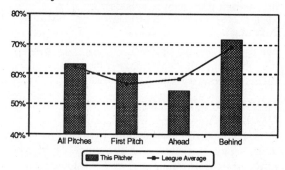

1991 Situational Stats

	W	L	ERA	Sv	IP		AB	H	HR	RBI	AVG
Home	8	7	2.81	0	112.0	LHB	175	48	6	27	.274
Road	4	9	5.28	0	102.1	RHB	625	153	19	65	.245
Day	5	1	3.00	0	60.0	Sc Pos	153	40	5	62	.261
Night	7	15	4.37	0	154.1	Clutch	64	14	0	7	.219

1991 Rankings (National League)

→ 1st in losses (16) and balks (6)

→ 2nd in most home runs allowed (25) and most home runs allowed per 9 innings (1.1)

→ 3rd in shutouts (3), GDPs induced (20) and highest ERA on the road (5.28)

→ Led the Giants in losses, games started (34), complete games (3), shutouts, innings (214.1), batters faced (893), home runs allowed, wild pitches (6), balks, pitches thrown (3,184), GDPs induced, most GDPs induced per 9 innings (.84) and lowest batting average allowed vs. right-handed batters (.245)

PITCHING:

Jeff Brantley has made a career of alternately delighting and infuriating San Francisco Giants fans. Brantley's 1991 season contained mostly pleasing numbers, but he was unable to shake his maddening proclivity for creating his own messes to escape from.

Brantley began the season as a co-closer with Dave Righetti, but eventually lost that role. One reason was his tendency to ride the ball high and out of the strike zone. Batters began laying off Brantley's chest-level offerings, and he wound up allowing 135 baserunners in only 95 innings. But only 27 (20 percent) of those runners scored.

Brantley delights manager Roger Craig because of his ability to make the big pitch in crucial situations; he allowed only a .161 batting average with runners in scoring positoin. When he isn't trying to challenge hitters, everything he throws -- split-fingered fastball, sinker, slider, curve -- comes in heavy and hard to pull. Brantley is good at pitching from behind, using his breaking stuff to set up his fastball. He won't let anybody commandeer the inside corner against him.

Still, there was that tendency to pitch himself into trouble. In one game against Cincinnati when the Giants were on the verge of getting back into the race, Brantley walked the first three batters he faced, retired the next two and then walked home the winning run in the bottom of the ninth inning.

HOLDING RUNNERS, FIELDING, HITTING:

Brantley is tireless in pursuing the finer aspects of his game, and it shows. He is persistent and quick to first base, and challenges baserunners the same way he does hitters. He covers a lot of ground defensively and seldom makes a mental mistake. As a hitter, he can get a bunt down when necessary.

OVERALL:

It's impossible not to admire Brantley for his bulldog attitude and his unwillingness to back down from hitters, and his overall numbers didn't represent a large drop from his 1990 All-Star season. Still, it's hard to envision him as a consistent closer simply because he gets himself into too many predicaments.

JEFF BRANTLEY

Position: RP
Bats: R **Throws:** R
Ht: 5'11" **Wt:** 190

Opening Day Age: 28
Born: 9/5/63 in Florence, AL
ML Seasons: 4

Overall Statistics

	W	L	ERA	G	GS	Sv	IP	H	R	BB	SO	HR
1991	5	2	2.45	67	0	15	95.1	78	27	52	81	8
Career	17	7	2.94	190	2	35	300.0	278	108	128	222	23

How Often He Throws Strikes

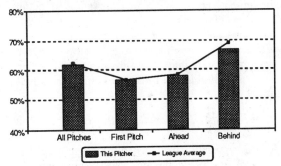

1991 Situational Stats

	W	L	ERA	Sv	IP		AB	H	HR	RBI	AVG
Home	2	0	2.14	7	42.0	LHB	185	38	3	16	.205
Road	3	2	2.70	8	53.1	RHB	161	40	5	20	.248
Day	3	0	2.57	5	35.0	Sc Pos	118	19	1	28	.161
Night	2	2	2.39	10	60.1	Clutch	235	55	5	19	.234

1991 Rankings (National League)

→ 1st in lowest batting average allowed with runners in scoring position (.161)
→ 6th in holds (12) and relief innings (95.1)
→ 7th in relief ERA (2.45)
→ 9th in games finished (39)
→ Led the Giants in games pitched (67), wild pitches (6), most stolen bases allowed (17), holds, lowest batting average allowed with runners in scoring position, relief ERA, relief innings and most strikeouts per 9 innings in relief (7.6)

PITCHING:

John Burkett was without much question the San Francisco Giants' best pitcher in 1990 and for the first four months of 1991. Last August 11, the day the Giants reached .500 for the first and only time since April, Burkett was 9-5 with a 3.27 ERA.

It was about that time that Burkett, whose durability never had been in question, began to complain of a tired arm. His ERA promptly ballooned, eventually increasing almost a full point. Manager Roger Craig skipped Burkett's turn several times late in the year, and the rest seemed to help.

Burkett's arm fatigue made it unnecessary for other teams to respect his fastball, which normally has good velocity and very good downward movement. His curve, however, showed better bite, especially against left-handed hitters, and one possible benefit of his experience last year was that he had no choice but to develop the curve as another "out" pitch. He gets into trouble when he tries to nibble too much and isn't confrontational.

HOLDING RUNNERS, FIELDING, HITTING:

It's quite possible that Burkett throws to first base as much as any pitcher in baseball. He has been known to throw as many as 25 times over to first in a game. It helped him hold opposition baserunners to only 17 steals in 33 attempts (52%) despite an average move. He isn't a particularly good fielder, either, but he has reached the point where he doesn't hurt himself much in sacrifice situations. Burkett is a brutal hitter, with 26 strikeouts in 55 at-bats, but he isn't a bad bunter, getting down nine sacrifice bunts.

OVERALL:

Burkett isn't the type of pitcher who can be a team's ace. Ideally, he should be a number three or four, and apparently the workload he had to absorb as the top man took its toll on his arm. On the positive side, his arm fatigue apparently was nothing clinical, and there's no reason to think he won't again be a factor for the Giants in 1992.

JOHN BURKETT

Position: SP
Bats: R **Throws:** R
Ht: 6' 2" **Wt:** 210

Opening Day Age: 27
Born: 11/28/64 in New Brighton, PA
ML Seasons: 3

Overall Statistics

	W	L	ERA	G	GS	Sv	IP	H	R	BB	SO	HR
1991	12	11	4.18	36	34	0	206.2	223	103	60	131	19
Career	26	18	4.00	72	66	1	416.2	431	199	124	254	39

How Often He Throws Strikes

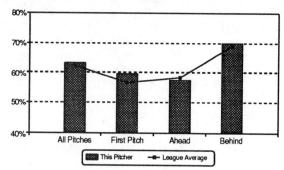

This Pitcher   League Average

1991 Situational Stats

	W	L	ERA	Sv	IP		AB	H	HR	RBI	AVG
Home	6	6	3.54	0	109.1	LHB	467	137	14	62	.293
Road	6	5	4.90	0	97.1	RHB	337	86	5	39	.255
Day	4	6	3.28	0	82.1	Sc Pos	197	63	2	76	.320
Night	8	5	4.78	0	124.1	Clutch	54	12	3	8	.222

1991 Rankings (National League)

→ 1st in hit batsmen (10)

→ 2nd in pickoff throws (344), runners caught stealing (16), highest on-base average allowed (.332) and highest batting average allowed with runners in scoring position (.320)

→ 3rd highest batting average allowed (.277)

→ 4th highest ERA (4.18)

→ 5th highest ERA on the road (4.90)

→ Led the Giants in games started (34), complete games (3), hits allowed (223), hit batsmen (10), pickoff throws, most stolen bases allowed (17), most runners caught stealing, strikeout/walk ratio (2.2) and least pitches thrown per batter (3.45)

CLUTCH HITTER

WILL CLARK

Position: 1B
Bats: L **Throws:** L
Ht: 6' 1" **Wt:** 190

Opening Day Age: 28
Born: 3/13/64 in New Orleans, LA
ML Seasons: 6

HITTING:

Will Clark vowed after the 1990 season, much of which he played on a nerve-damaged foot, that the San Francisco Giants would see his best offensive year yet in 1991. As it turned out, Clark exceeded his major league high only in RBIs. But his other totals all were excellent, and are more impressive considering the fact that among his teammates, only Matt Williams was a season-long source of support.

The main thing that Clark regained when the nerve damage in his foot healed was his ability to hit line drives to left field. Without the ability to plant in 1990, he began looping the bat. In 1991, though, he returned to line-drive normalcy. Pitchers had started working him to the low-outside corner, usually with breaking balls, but he quickly filled that hole in his swing. He also adjusted his stance slightly, closing it even more than it was previously, a la Stan Musial, to give increased outside-plate coverage.

BASERUNNING:

Clark's speed is now slightly below average. He doesn't take as many chances as he did in his earlier years, but that's probably just as well because his baserunning had at times fallen into the almost-reckless category. He no longer is a threat to steal, but the Giants will occasionally start him on a hit-and-run.

FIELDING:

Clark was a first-time Gold Glove winner in '91, and deserved it. He is very mobile around the bag, and handles low throws beautifully. His only weakness is his throwing arm, which he injured when he was a rookie. But he remains daring, even when throwing.

OVERALL:

Given Clark's durability, conditioning, and age (28), it wouldn't be a stretch to think that he could have ten more productive seasons. It's reasonable, given his current level of play, to think he'll end up with 400 home runs and more than 2,500 hits. This is a hitter on track for the Hall of Fame, and he's at his peak. It's still a bit early to call him the Stan Musial of his generation, but Clark is getting closer.

Overall Statistics

	G	AB	R	H	D	T	HR	RBI	SB	BB	SO	AVG
1991	148	565	84	170	32	7	29	116	4	51	91	.301
Career	884	3265	536	985	182	34	146	563	38	370	594	.302

Where He Hits the Ball

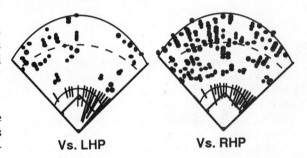

Vs. LHP   Vs. RHP

1991 Situational Stats

	AB	H	HR	RBI	AVG		AB	H	HR	RBI	AVG
Home	283	80	17	47	.283	LHP	197	47	9	40	.239
Road	282	90	12	69	.319	RHP	368	123	20	76	.334
Day	198	68	13	42	.343	Sc Pos	152	51	10	84	.336
Night	367	102	16	74	.278	Clutch	89	27	3	23	.303

1991 Rankings (National League)

→ 1st in total bases (303), slugging percentage (.536) and slugging percentage vs. right-handed pitchers(.581)

→ 2nd in RBIs (116), batting average vs. right-handed pitchers (.334) and fielding percentage at first base (.997)

→ 3rd in batting average on the road (.319)

→ Led the Giants in runs (84), hits (170), doubles (32), triples (7), total bases, RBIs, intentional walks (12), times on base (223), slugging percentage, on-base average (.359), most runs scored per time reached base (37.7%), least GDPs per GDP situation (4.1%) and batting average with the bases loaded (.333)

PITCHING:

Kelly Downs, less than a year removed from career-threatening rotator-cuff surgery, began the 1991 season in a familiar place: the disabled list. Used as a spot starter and long reliever after he was activated, Downs pitched so poorly that the Giants were on the verge of giving up on him.

Finally in July, manager Roger Craig made him a set-up man, and Downs shocked everybody for about a month. He took two full points off his ERA. Using smoother mechanics dictated by his surgery, he discovered he could throw with velocity without having to throw as hard, and he gave the staff a much-needed intimidator. Downs' upturn ended when he gave up a crucial grand-slam home run to Cincinnati's Barry Larkin in early August. But overall he was one of the team's few reasonably useful pitchers during the Giants' collapse late in the season.

Downs' velocity remains above average, and he can hop the ball when he comes straight over the top. He has an improving change-up. Downs will mix in a slider and curveball from time to time, but he was at his best when he went with non-breaking stuff, changing speeds and grips to get movement and variety.

HOLDING RUNNERS, FIELDING, HITTING:

Downs is persistent in runners-on situations, but is a trifle awkward from the stretch and doesn't get rid of the ball quickly enough. He is a better fielder than he was before his injury because he now finishes in a balanced position, but he sometimes makes bad decisions. He is a poor hitter and an average bunter.

OVERALL:

Very talented, Downs has had ongoing problems with injuries and, when healthy, the Giants never seemed to find a role to fit him. He may have finally found that role as a set-up man. The Giants have plenty of relievers, and his future might not be with them, but it's still possible to envision Downs becoming a very good set-up man or even a closer -- if his arm holds up.

KELLY DOWNS

Position: RP/SP
Bats: R **Throws:** R
Ht: 6' 4" **Wt:** 205

Opening Day Age: 31
Born: 10/25/60 in Ogden, UT
ML Seasons: 6

Overall Statistics

	W	L	ERA	G	GS	Sv	IP	H	R	BB	SO	HR
1991	10	4	4.19	45	11	0	111.2	99	59	53	62	12
Career	46	36	3.65	158	103	1	699.2	640	311	243	461	51

How Often He Throws Strikes

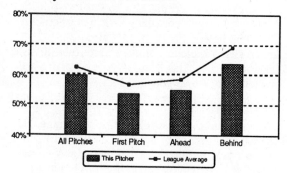

1991 Situational Stats

	W	L	ERA	Sv	IP		AB	H	HR	RBI	AVG
Home	5	2	3.90	0	55.1	LHB	220	58	6	31	.264
Road	5	2	4.47	0	56.1	RHB	195	41	6	26	.210
Day	4	0	4.54	0	37.2	Sc Pos	120	23	4	42	.192
Night	6	4	4.01	0	74.0	Clutch	46	10	1	4	.217

1991 Rankings (National League)

➡ 5th in relief wins (7)
➡ Led the Giants in relief wins and lowest batting average allowed in relief (.223)

HITTING:

An afterthought pickup from Milwaukee at the start of the '91 season, Mike Felder somewhat surprisingly had the best season of a checkered career. Felder gradually worked his way into the Giants' outfield rotation, mostly in left field when Kevin Mitchell was injured. For a time he was among the National League batting leaders.

Felder showed consistency from either side of the plate -- he was exclusively a right-handed hitter before turning professional. He also showed a willingness to be pesky and patient instead of overswinging, as had been his wont with the Brewers. He hits almost exclusively to the opposite field now instead of trying to pull the ball. Although he was easily jammed, he has developed a good inside-out swing to compensate.

Even with all that, though, Felder couldn't keep his job as a regular after Mitchell returned and Darren Lewis arrived, starting only nine games after July 21. One problem was that he started chasing the inside pitches that he has never been able to handle. Additionally, losing his leadoff spot gave him fewer opportunities to bunt his way on, something he does extremely well.

BASERUNNING:

Felder led the Giants in stolen bases even though he didn't play much during the final two months. He has excellent speed and the intelligence to put that speed to good use on the bases, although he did incur manager Roger Craig's wrath with over-aggressiveness at times.

FIELDING:

Felder is mobile and quick to find the ball in any direction. He can play all three outfield positions, but is best suited for left field because his arm strength is average at best. His arm is accurate, though, and he covers a lot of ground.

OVERALL:

Felder's problem with the Giants is that they don't think of him as a long-term solution in the outfield, where they have a lot of good prospects. They like him, but will have trouble finding him playing time. Felder might be ideal for one of the expansion teams in 1993.

MIKE FELDER

Position: LF/CF/RF
Bats: B **Throws:** R
Ht: 5' 8" **Wt:** 160

Opening Day Age: 29
Born: 11/18/62 in Vallejo, CA
ML Seasons: 7

Overall Statistics

	G	AB	R	H	D	T	HR	RBI	SB	BB	SO	AVG
1991	132	348	51	92	10	6	0	18	21	30	31	.264
Career	587	1481	233	372	37	22	9	117	129	121	142	.251

Where He Hits the Ball

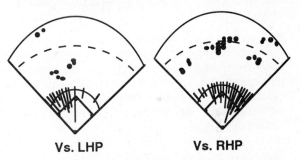

Vs. LHP   Vs. RHP

1991 Situational Stats

	AB	H	HR	RBI	AVG		AB	H	HR	RBI	AVG
Home	168	48	0	10	.286	LHP	107	29	0	4	.271
Road	180	44	0	8	.244	RHP	241	63	0	14	.261
Day	127	30	0	9	.236	Sc Pos	61	17	0	17	.279
Night	221	62	0	9	.281	Clutch	64	13	0	6	.203

1991 Rankings (National League)

- 5th in bunts in play (28) and lowest batting average on a 3-1 count (.000)
- 8th highest stolen base percentage (77.8%)
- Led the Giants in stolen bases (21), stolen base percentage and bunts in play
- Led NL left fielders in sacrifice bunts (4), stolen base percentage and bunts in play

HITTING:

The only reason Terry Kennedy wasn't completely forgotten last year was because he did the Giants' post-game radio show. San Francisco's on- and off-field treatment of Kennedy made it fairly obvious that they do not consider him part of their plans.

Kennedy sat and watched early in the season as rookie Steve Decker played his way out of the job given him by pre-camp decree. Kennedy got more at-bats during the middle of the campaign, but again was relegated to the bench after the All-Star break when Kirt Manwaring established himself as the number-one man. The result was that Kennedy posted the lowest totals of his career in almost every category, including games played.

Not surprisingly, inactivity took its toll. When Kennedy did play, he ceased being a contact hitter because he felt he had to produce big numbers to regain a starting spot. Kennedy hit under the ball constantly, and saw almost nothing but breaking pitches, usually high in the strike zone. A fairly patient hitter in his first two years with San Francisco, he reverted to his previous form, drawing only seven unintentional walks for the season.

BASERUNNING:

Roger Craig probably could run the bases more rapidly than Kennedy, who nonetheless gives full effort and will take somebody on in a collision situation. One highlight: Kennedy got his first triple since 1987. Of course, the two outfielders fell down chasing the ball, but . . .

FIELDING:

Kennedy had good rapport with the older members of the Giants' pitching staff. But most of those pitchers are gone now, and Manwaring knows the younger guys better. Physically, Kennedy has never been a great defensive catcher, and at 35 he won't get any quicker.

OVERALL:

To the Giants, Kennedy's main value now would be as a seldom-used backup, a guidance counselor and left-handed pinch hitter -- if they want him at all. He's a free agent, and if he wants a chance at a bigger role, he'll have to try another team.

TERRY KENNEDY

Position: C
Bats: L **Throws:** R
Ht: 6' 4" **Wt:** 220

Opening Day Age: 35
Born: 6/4/56 in Euclid, OH
ML Seasons: 14

Overall Statistics

	G	AB	R	H	D	T	HR	RBI	SB	BB	SO	AVG
1991	69	171	12	40	7	1	3	13	0	11	31	.234
Career	1491	4979	474	1313	244	12	113	628	6	365	855	.264

Where He Hits the Ball

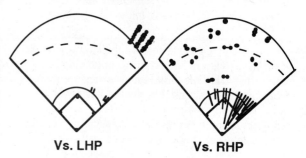

Vs. LHP   Vs. RHP

1991 Situational Stats

	AB	H	HR	RBI	AVG		AB	H	HR	RBI	AVG
Home	75	18	2	11	.240	LHP	10	3	1	3	.300
Road	96	22	1	2	.229	RHP	161	37	2	10	.230
Day	56	12	0	4	.214	Sc Pos	39	9	1	10	.231
Night	115	28	3	9	.243	Clutch	28	5	1	3	.179

1991 Rankings (National League)

➡ 3rd highest percentage of runners caught stealing as a catcher (44.3%)

KIRT MANWARING

Position: C
Bats: R **Throws:** R
Ht: 5'11" **Wt:** 190

Opening Day Age: 26
Born: 7/15/65 in Elmira, NY
ML Seasons: 5

HITTING:

Because of a broken finger, Kirt Manwaring's 1991 season didn't really begin until mid-July. But once the San Francisco Giants committed to him as their number-one catcher, they got an unexpected bonus. Never before considered any kind of offensive threat, Manwaring was one of their steadier bats as they climbed back to the .500 mark in mid-August.

Manwaring's average was a respectable .258 before a 6-for-47 September dropped him down to .222, the level the Giants had come to expect. At the plate, Manwaring doesn't have the bat speed to handle a good fastball, especially in on his hands. He will hit the breaking ball, but he doesn't get too many.

Manwaring usually makes contact, and is an excellent bunter, one of the best on the team. But overall, he's one of the weakest offensive players in baseball. Manwaring had only nine walks and nine extra-base hits (all doubles) last year, meaning that almost his entire offensive value was reflected in his batting average. At season's end, his batting average was .225.

BASERUNNING:

Manwaring has fair speed, but the Giants don't want him to run. He isn't very aggressive and is strictly a station-to-station guy most of the time, although he's smart and doesn't take foolhardy chances.

FIELDING:

The Giants have long said Manwaring has the agility, arm strength and acumen to be an outstanding catcher. That's true, but the difference in his improvement last year was his assertiveness. Not a commanding person by nature, he had seemed intimidated by the Giants' numerous veteran pitchers. Manwaring became much more assertive when he got a chance to work with the younger staff the Giants have been unveiling.

OVERALL:

The Giants' young pitchers flourished with Manwaring behind the plate. He's a more mature receiver than Steve Decker, and will enter spring training with the Giants' catching job his to win or lose in 1992. Whether he'll hit enough to hold it is a big question.

Overall Statistics

	G	AB	R	H	D	T	HR	RBI	SB	BB	SO	AVG
1991	67	178	16	40	9	0	0	19	1	9	22	.225
Career	206	514	42	114	20	3	1	53	3	22	75	.222

Where He Hits the Ball

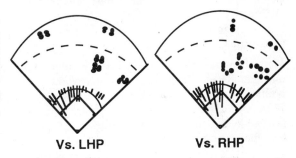

Vs. LHP   Vs. RHP

1991 Situational Stats

	AB	H	HR	RBI	AVG		AB	H	HR	RBI	AVG
Home	90	24	0	11	.267	LHP	65	20	0	9	.308
Road	88	16	0	8	.182	RHP	113	20	0	10	.177
Day	68	13	0	8	.191	Sc Pos	42	11	0	19	.262
Night	110	27	0	11	.245	Clutch	26	6	0	3	.231

1991 Rankings (National League)

➝ Did not rank near the top or bottom in any category

PITCHING:

When the San Francisco Giants promoted Paul McClellan from the minors last July, it was only because several pitchers with lesser minor league numbers had already failed to give the Giants much help. The organization was out of patience with McClellan, a mercurial type who was strictly a fastball pitcher with little predilection to allow himself to be taught.

But this seemed to be a new Paul McClellan. He brought to the majors a split-fingered fastball, a forkball and a slider to go with his fastball, and he was throwing his fastball to spots instead of trying to blow it past people. More importantly, his temperament seemed very much under control. McClellan struggled in the final month after pitching extremely well in his first few outings, but he seemed to be at the start of a personal transformation.

McClellan never will be a corner-painter, but manager Roger Craig liked his aggression. His problem was that he gave up 12 home runs in only 71 innings. Hitters knew he would come with the fastball late in counts or after falling behind, and they teed off on him.

HOLDING RUNNERS, FIELDING, HITTING:

McClellan is below major league standards at holding runners. He needs help with his footwork from the stretch; he often tangles himself to such an extent that runners can go at will. He's a very aggressive and eager fielder, but sometimes lets his initiative cloud his judgement. He is a good athlete, and he might become a decent hitter.

OVERALL:

McClellan proved last year that he has good enough stuff to survive at the major league level, and his self-control has made a quantum leap. The next challenge will be to improve his other pitches to the point where hitters can't sit on the fastball if he falls behind in the count. The Giants appear interested in him again, and he could be a member of their starting rotation in 1992.

PAUL McCLELLAN

Position: SP
Bats: R **Throws:** R
Ht: 6' 2" **Wt:** 180

Opening Day Age: 26
Born: 2/8/66 in San Mateo, CA
ML Seasons: 2

Overall Statistics

	W	L	ERA	G	GS	Sv	IP	H	R	BB	SO	HR
1991	3	6	4.56	13	12	0	71.0	68	41	25	44	12
Career	3	7	5.26	17	13	0	78.2	82	51	31	46	15

How Often He Throws Strikes

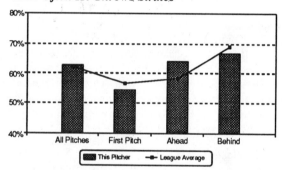

This Pitcher — League Average

1991 Situational Stats

	W	L	ERA	Sv	IP		AB	H	HR	RBI	AVG
Home	2	2	4.33	0	35.1	LHB	143	39	7	20	.273
Road	1	4	4.79	0	35.2	RHB	127	29	5	15	.228
Day	1	3	4.11	0	35.0	Sc Pos	64	17	4	25	.266
Night	2	3	5.00	0	36.0	Clutch	11	2	0	1	.182

1991 Rankings (National League)

→ Did not rank near the top or bottom in any category

HITTING:

Willie McGee won the National League batting title by proxy in 1990 after being traded by the St. Louis Cardinals to Oakland in September. In 1991, back in the NL, McGee almost won the batting title in person as a late charge left him just short of the top.

As expected, McGee's chop-hitting style was not well-suited for Candlestick Park, and he batted only .270 at home. But he more than made up for that on the road, particularly road turf, and he was a paragon of consistency all season. He lifted his average over .300 in the second game of the season, and it did not drop below that level all year. McGee also was the Giants' best clutch hitter, registering a .343 mark with runners in scoring position.

McGee is a flick hitter who is difficult to fool with offspeed or breaking stuff because he takes almost no stride. His open stance helps him get his hands extended against inside pitches; he'll usually inside-out those pitches, going to the opposite field well over half the time. McGee remains one of the most pronounced ground ball hitters in baseball, and with only 34 walks last year, one of the more impatient ones.

BASERUNNING:

At age 33, McGee still hasn't slowed much, but takes fewer chances and is less inclined to seek out contact. He had only 17 steals last season, and probably will steal even less than that as he ages.

FIELDING:

McGee met the Giants' expectations in center field, though he suffered from occasional lapses in concentration. He goes out on balls well and adjusted quickly to Candlestick's tricky winds, but his throwing is acceptable at best.

OVERALL:

No longer the MVP-caliber player of his youth, McGee has his limitations, but consistent .300 hitters aren't easy to come by. Moreover, the Giants generally liked his demeanor and professionalism both on the field and in the clubhouse. McGee should be a key performer for San Francisco again in 1992.

WILLIE
McGEE

Position: CF/RF
Bats: B **Throws:** R
Ht: 6' 1" **Wt:** 195

Opening Day Age: 33
Born: 11/2/58 in San Francisco, CA
ML Seasons: 10

Overall Statistics

	G	AB	R	H	D	T	HR	RBI	SB	BB	SO	AVG
1991	131	497	67	155	30	3	4	43	17	34	74	.312
Career	1324	5195	717	1548	237	81	56	603	294	286	790	.298

Where He Hits the Ball

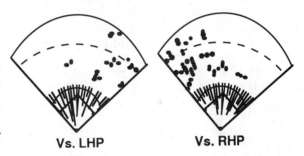

Vs. LHP   Vs. RHP

1991 Situational Stats

	AB	H	HR	RBI	AVG		AB	H	HR	RBI	AVG
Home	222	60	2	20	.270	LHP	154	52	2	20	.338
Road	275	95	2	23	.345	RHP	343	103	2	23	.300
Day	187	65	1	21	.348	Sc Pos	105	36	0	35	.343
Night	310	90	3	22	.290	Clutch	85	28	1	8	.329

1991 Rankings (National League)

→ 1st in groundball/flyball ratio (4.0) and batting average on the road (.345)

→ 4th highest batting average (.312)

→ 5th highest batting average with runners in scoring position (.343)

→ Led the Giants in batting average, singles (118), caught stealing (9), groundball/flyball ratio, batting average with runners in scoring position, batting average in the clutch (.329), batting average vs. left-handed pitchers (.338), batting average on an 0-2 count (.250), batting average on the road, batting average with 2 strikes (.249) and steals of third (3)

HITTING:

Perhaps it was simply that playing hurt all the time finally caught up with Kevin Mitchell. The 1989 National League Most Valuable Player ran out of gas at almost the exact same time that the San Francisco Giants did in 1991 -- and the result was catastrophic for both. Mitchell had only five home runs and 15 RBI after August 11, the one and only day all season that the Giants were at .500. Bothered by a strained groin muscle, he started only five of the Giants' final 25 games.

Mitchell is so heavily muscled that his flexibility is easily compromised. He has had wrist problems for some time, and knee surgery cost him 20 games early in the season. Mitchell, as is his wont, gamely tried to play through those and other injuries, but it was apparent toward the end of the season that his strength was severely affected. Mitchell especially had trouble with inside pitches, which used to be absolute no-nos against him. Even so, he homered once every 13.7 at-bats last year, an outstanding rate.

BASERUNNING:

Mitchell is a fierce, attacking baserunner when he is healthy. He wasn't in 1991, and seemed to lose some of his zeal for collisions and chance-taking. Mitchell's speed would now have to be classified as below average. He stole only two bases in five attempts last year.

FIELDING:

Mitchell, once better than average, is now a weak left fielder. He is fearless when confronted by walls, but is very slow in all directions. And although his arm is accurate, it is not very strong. However, proposed switch back to the infield would probably be a mistake.

OVERALL:

An independent spirit, Mitchell occasionally has incurred the wrath of management because he isn't a lock-step marcher. He tends to be distant from many of his teammates, too. It would be a major surprise if he were to be traded, but it no longer would be a shock -- especially considering he still has market value and could fetch some much-needed pitching.

KEVIN MITCHELL

Position: LF
Bats: R **Throws:** R
Ht: 5'11" **Wt:** 210

Opening Day Age: 30
Born: 1/13/62 in San Diego, CA
ML Seasons: 7

Overall Statistics

	G	AB	R	H	D	T	HR	RBI	SB	BB	SO	AVG
1991	113	371	52	95	13	1	27	69	2	43	57	.256
Career	801	2749	421	756	138	20	162	481	26	317	496	.275

Where He Hits the Ball

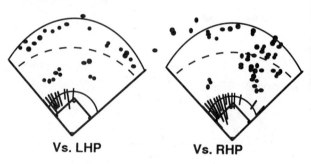

Vs. LHP   Vs. RHP

1991 Situational Stats

	AB	H	HR	RBI	AVG		AB	H	HR	RBI	AVG
Home	190	46	9	30	.242	LHP	114	31	7	22	.272
Road	181	49	18	39	.271	RHP	257	64	20	47	.249
Day	149	38	9	26	.255	Sc Pos	99	24	6	39	.242
Night	222	57	18	43	.257	Clutch	61	9	2	7	.148

1991 Rankings (National League)

→ 2nd in lowest batting average in the clutch (.148) and lowest fielding percentage in left field (.970)

→ 3rd in cleanup slugging (.524)

→ 8th in highest batting average on a 3-1 count (.545) and lowest batting average on a 3-2 count (.098)

→ 9th in home runs (27)

→ Led the Giants in batting average on a 3-1 count

→ Led NL left fielders in home runs

PITCHING:

For the first four months of 1991, Francisco Oliveras was perhaps the most consistent pitcher the San Francisco Giants had. Picked up from Minnesota in an afterthought trade the year before, Oliveras, 29, was thought to be a long shot to make the club.

Oliveras doesn't throw particularly hard and doesn't have any signature pitch to depend on in a crucial situation. Perhaps, in fact, that was his big advantage: Nobody knew what to expect from him. He would throw his curve, which has little movement but lots of rotation, even on a 3-and-0 count. He throws his slider harder than most pitchers, so it functions as a cut fastball that moves just enough to prevent people from sitting on his fastball.

Oliveras doesn't have much in the way of an offspeed pitch; even his curve is thrown fairly hard. His fastball isn't that fast, so all of his pitches are thrown at similar speeds; he was hit hard during the final two months of the season as hitters finally stopped waiting on offspeed pitches that never came. Moreover, he started short-arming the ball and seemed to be having major problems with his mechanics.

HOLDING RUNNERS, FIELDING, HITTING:

Oliveras uncoils slowly and isn't deceptive in his runner-holding techniques, but he had some success against basestealers by throwing to first more often than most pitchers. He moves fairly well off the mound and has good instincts on comebackers, but hesitates and doesn't always make good decisions. He isn't much of a hitter or bunter.

OVERALL:

Oliveras was on the verge of establishing a long-term future for himself with the Giants after four months in 1991. But his ERA suddenly ballooned from 2.41 to 3.86. Oliveras, at a relatively advanced age for a fringe major leaguer, probably will be evaluated more on the basis of his last two months than on his first four. He still figures in the Giants' plans, but that could change quickly if their younger pitchers emerge next spring.

FRANCISCO OLIVERAS

Position: RP
Bats: R **Throws:** R
Ht: 5'10" **Wt:** 180

Opening Day Age: 29
Born: 1/31/63 in Santurce, Puerto Rico
ML Seasons: 3

Overall Statistics

	W	L	ERA	G	GS	Sv	IP	H	R	BB	SO	HR
1991	6	6	3.86	55	1	3	79.1	69	36	22	48	12
Career	11	12	3.74	100	11	5	190.1	180	86	58	113	25

How Often He Throws Strikes

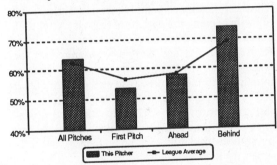

1991 Situational Stats

	W	L	ERA	Sv	IP		AB	H	HR	RBI	AVG
Home	5	2	3.51	3	33.1	LHB	151	41	5	21	.272
Road	1	4	4.11	0	46.0	RHB	134	28	7	17	.209
Day	2	3	3.48	2	31.0	Sc Pos	64	16	2	25	.250
Night	4	3	4.10	1	48.1	Clutch	90	25	4	13	.278

1991 Rankings (National League)

→ 6th in first batter efficiency (.167)

→ 7th least strikeouts per 9 innings in relief (5.0)

→ 9th in holds (10), lowest percentage of inherited runners scored (22.6%) and relief wins (6)

→ Led the Giants in least baserunners per 9 innings in relief (10.4)

PITCHING:

Unlike most of the players who contributed to the San Francisco Giants' demise in 1991, Dave Righetti was more of a victim. The Giants played so horribly early in the season that Righetti, who was signed as a free agent after 11 seasons with the New York Yankees, almost never had a chance to perform as a closer.

Manager Roger Craig wound up bringing Righetti into non-closing situations just to get him some work, and as a result Righetti seemed to lose his situational sharpness. When he was called upon to close games, he seemed to be experimenting with so many pitches that his fastball went by the wayside.

The turning point came in July, when Righetti and his wife became the parents of triplets. After that, baseball seemed to become fun for him again. Righetti relaxed and started throwing with the loose-limbed rhythm that was one of his characteristics with the Yankees. He still used his other pitches (curve, slider, sinker, change-up), but the fastball -- thrown at 93 MPH with good downward movement -- again was his out pitch. At one point, he retired the first man he faced 18 straight times, striking out seven.

HOLDING RUNNERS, FIELDING, HITTING:

Righetti isn't particularly deceptive or quick to first base, nor does he give top priority to holding runners; that didn't hurt him much in 1991, as NL runners were still learning his move. He comes off the mound a bit off-balance, and that sometimes adversely affects his fielding, but he's quick in coverage and backup situations. He doesn't bat enough to worry about his hitting.

OVERALL:

After the triplets were born, Righetti did some of the best work of his career, and looked like he could be as successful in the National League as he was in the American. He gets a lot of fly balls, and in a league with larger parks and more artificial turf, he should be ideal. Moreover, he is only 33 and throws as hard as ever.

DAVE RIGHETTI

Position: RP
Bats: L **Throws:** L
Ht: 6' 4" **Wt:** 212

Opening Day Age: 33
Born: 11/28/58 in San Jose, CA
ML Seasons: 12

Overall Statistics

	W	L	ERA	G	GS	Sv	IP	H	R	BB	SO	HR
1991	2	7	3.39	61	0	24	71.2	64	29	28	51	4
Career	76	68	3.13	583	76	248	1207.2	1063	477	501	991	69

How Often He Throws Strikes

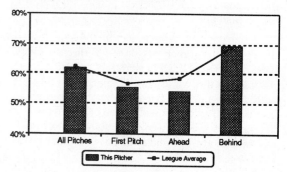

1991 Situational Stats

	W	L	ERA	Sv	IP		AB	H	HR	RBI	AVG
Home	1	4	4.14	14	37.0	LHB	72	12	0	9	.167
Road	1	3	2.60	10	34.2	RHB	195	52	4	23	.267
Day	2	4	4.44	8	26.1	Sc Pos	81	24	1	29	.296
Night	0	3	2.78	16	45.1	Clutch	187	45	4	26	.241

1991 Rankings (National League)

→ 1st in first batter efficiency (.071) and lowest percentage of inherited runners scored (15.6%)
→ 4th in games finished (49) and save percentage (82.8%)
→ 5th in saves (24) and relief losses (7)
→ 6th in save opportunities (29)
→ Led the Giants in saves, games finished, save opportunities, save percentage, blown saves (5), first batter efficiency, lowest percentage of inherited runners scored and relief losses

PITCHING:

Ever the survivor, Don Robinson spent almost the entire 1991 season on a lifeboat. The Giants never were in serious contention, and during the season purged themselves of older pitchers such as Rick Reuschel and Mike LaCoss. Robinson was bumped from the starting rotation by a succession of young prospects, and didn't pitch particularly well early in the season either as a spot starter or as a reliever.

But he came on toward the end of the season as manager Roger Craig continued to give him opportunities, and he probably saved himself by pitching a near complete-game victory after taking the mound on 10 minutes notice.

Robinson is well suited for Candlestick Park because he gives up a lot of fly balls that are swallowed by the wind. His home ERA was 2.77 last season, while on the road it was 6.03. Robinson doesn't get cute and he doesn't use an extensive repertoire. He changes speeds and locations constantly, but doesn't really throw an out-and-out breaking pitch. He doesn't make pitching more complicated than it is.

HOLDING RUNNERS, FIELDING, HITTING:

Robinson is as tricky holding runners on first as he is simple when dealing with batters. He has a slide step and a few other techniques that he varies to hold runners, and is surprisingly quick when he wheels to first. He also fields his position fairly well, although he no longer moves off the mound easily because he has been injured so often. Robinson is still one of the best-hitting pitchers, rivalling many position players.

OVERALL:

Robinson is only 34, but seems much older. Roger Craig considers him valuable because he never complains and keeps his team in the game regardless of the role into which he is thrust. He also has a down-home personality that makes him approachable for young pitchers. Though Robinson is a free agent, he's likely to be back next season, barring more injury problems and assuming he keeps his vow to lose some weight.

DON ROBINSON

Position: RP/SP
Bats: R **Throws:** R
Ht: 6' 4" **Wt:** 240

Opening Day Age: 34
Born: 6/8/57 in Ashland, KY
ML Seasons: 14

Overall Statistics

	W	L	ERA	G	GS	Sv	IP	H	R	BB	SO	HR
1991	5	9	4.38	34	16	1	121.1	123	64	50	78	12
Career	107	102	3.75	513	218	57	1897.2	1826	871	636	1225	168

How Often He Throws Strikes

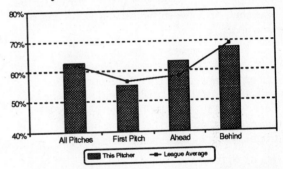

1991 Situational Stats

	W	L	ERA	Sv	IP		AB	H	HR	RBI	AVG
Home	3	2	2.77	0	61.2	LHB	251	70	5	36	.279
Road	2	7	6.03	1	59.2	RHB	214	53	7	26	.248
Day	2	2	3.51	1	51.1	Sc Pos	115	42	3	52	.365
Night	3	7	5.01	0	70.0	Clutch	36	11	1	3	.306

1991 Rankings (National League)

→ Did not rank near the top or bottom in any category

HITTING:

Robby Thompson was the guinea pig in perhaps the most disastrous of the San Francisco Giants' ill-fated experiments in 1991. Once that experiment was over, though, Thompson had one of the best -- and healthiest -- seasons of his six-year major league career.

After leadoff man Brett Butler defected to Los Angeles via free agency, Giants manager Roger Craig immediately announced that Thompson would be San Francisco's number one hitter. It seemed a moonstruck choice; Thompson was a career .257 hitter who walked seldom, struck out a lot and didn't have the requisite speed. He was batting .222 when Craig ended the experiment. Thompson's numbers steadily improved as he was shuttled between the second, sixth and seventh spots.

One positive aspect of the leadoff experiment, though, was that Thompson became more conscious of the need to lay off the outside breaking ball, and his walk-to-strikeout ratio improved noticeably (34 to 96 in 1990, 63 to 95 in 1991). He has excellent power to both gaps, but he has some trouble reaching the outside fastball.

BASERUNNING:

Thompson gets a decent jump, but his speed is only adequate and he never has completely mastered pitchers' moves. It's not unusual for him to be fooled into retreating to the bag when the pitcher delivers to the plate. But he does a good job taking the extra base on the base paths.

FIELDING:

Thompson is steady, reliable and intelligent at second base, and he remains among the best in the National League when it comes to turning the double play. He does have limitations, though, especially when it comes to range.

OVERALL:

Relatively free from the back problems that have bothered him for years, Thompson responded with another strong year for the Giants. Next to Will Clark, he probably has been the team's steadiest player in the Roger Craig era. Now that the leadoff experiment is mercifully over, Thompson should be able to benefit from the lessons it taught him. But, his back will remain a question mark.

ROBBY THOMPSON

Position: 2B
Bats: R **Throws:** R
Ht: 5'11" **Wt:** 170

Opening Day Age: 29
Born: 5/10/62 in West Palm Beach, FL
ML Seasons: 6

Overall Statistics

	G	AB	R	H	D	T	HR	RBI	SB	BB	SO	AVG
1991	144	492	74	129	24	5	19	48	14	63	95	.262
Career	855	2983	433	768	149	33	71	293	82	270	638	.257

Where He Hits the Ball

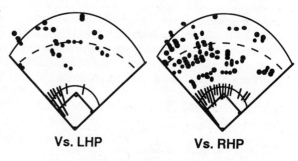

Vs. LHP   **Vs. RHP**

1991 Situational Stats

	AB	H	HR	RBI	AVG		AB	H	HR	RBI	AVG
Home	241	71	11	26	.295	LHP	135	38	7	16	.281
Road	251	58	8	22	.231	RHP	357	91	12	32	.255
Day	172	49	7	20	.285	Sc Pos	96	22	2	28	.229
Night	320	80	12	28	.250	Clutch	82	23	1	8	.280

1991 Rankings (National League)

- ➡ 6th in hit by pitch (6) and lowest batting average on the road (.231)
- ➡ 7th lowest batting average vs. right-handed pitchers (.255)
- ➡ Led the Giants in sacrifice bunts (11), walks (63), hit by pitch, pitches seen (2,210), most pitches seen plate appearances (3.86), highest slugging percentage vs. left-handed pitchers (.511), batting average after the 6th inning (.295), batting average after the 6th inning (.313) and highest percentage of pitches taken (54.3%)
- ➡ Led NL second basemen in sacrifice bunts, hit by pitch, least GDPs per GDP situation (5.5%) and batting average after the 6th inning

HITTING:

The San Francisco Giants have never had more than modest offensive expectations of Jose Uribe, but he usually was steady. That was not the case in 1991. Uribe was torrid for one short period and worse than torpid for the rest of the season.

Uribe started the season on the disabled list with a heel problem, and later spent another stint on the DL with a leg laceration. Mike Benjamin and Dave Anderson came and went at shortstop; Uribe, meanwhile, was struggling to keep his average above .150. Then he went on a binge, getting five hits in one game and raising his average above .250 before tailing off at the end.

Uribe is strictly a slap hitter from either side of the plate, but is much more efficient batting righty. He has trouble handling any sort of breaking ball while batting left-handed, and is almost helpless against a good slider on the hands. Right-handed, he's more selective and will pull the ball occasionally. He also makes much better contact from the right side and might wind up abandoning switch-hitting entirely, as he did for a short time in 1989.

BASERUNNING:

Uribe is reasonably quick, but isn't fast and is not much of a challenger of catchers or outfielders. He tends to play it safe on the bases and doesn't have the stature or the inclination to be a takeout guy.

FIELDING:

Uribe remains a better-than-average major league shortstop, but his declining range is beginning to cause problems for him. He especially has problems going to his right. On the plus side, he has excellent hands, a strong arm and a good working relationship with second baseman Robby Thompson.

OVERALL:

The Giants all but abandoned Uribe during his two stints on the disabled list. His late streak might have given him one last chance, but at 32 he's beginning to wear thin on the Giants. They are likely to give rookie Royce Clayton a long, hard look during the spring.

JOSE URIBE

Position: SS
Bats: B **Throws:** R
Ht: 5'10" **Wt:** 165

Opening Day Age: 32
Born: 1/21/60 in San Cristobal, Dominican Republic
ML Seasons: 8

Overall Statistics

	G	AB	R	H	D	T	HR	RBI	SB	BB	SO	AVG
1991	90	231	23	51	8	4	1	12	3	20	33	.221
Career	927	2849	279	686	89	33	17	203	71	234	395	.241

Where He Hits the Ball

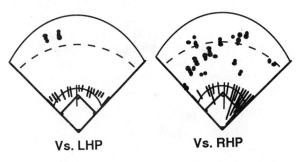

Vs. LHP   Vs. RHP

1991 Situational Stats

	AB	H	HR	RBI	AVG		AB	H	HR	RBI	AVG
Home	115	27	0	7	.235	LHP	60	15	0	3	.250
Road	116	24	1	5	.207	RHP	171	36	1	9	.211
Day	97	26	0	3	.268	Sc Pos	52	13	0	10	.250
Night	134	25	1	9	.187	Clutch	29	6	0	0	.207

1991 Rankings (National League)

→ 2nd lowest batting average on a 3-2 count (.000)

HITTING:

Matt Williams looks more like an accountant than a baseball player. Sometimes his swing makes him look like an accountant, too, especially when he's guessing wrong. But Williams can hit the ball as far as anybody in the game; with 101 career home runs at age 26, he may wish he were an accountant to better tally his homers (and his pennies) before his career is through.

Williams has a tendency to try and crush every ball he sees, and as a result he was in the .200 range early last season. But he steadied himself and enjoyed four solid months after that. His home run total was the highest ever by a San Francisco Giants third baseman.

Williams is getting better at going with the outside breaking ball, a good thing since that's usually all he gets. He's a surprisingly good low-ball hitter for a righty swinger. However, Williams has struck out four times as much as he's walked during his career, and did not improve in that area in 1991. Poor discipline is a big reason that he's prone to long slumps.

BASERUNNING:

Williams is quicker than he looks and gets a decent jump, but he doesn't have immediate acceleration and isn't a good base stealer. His concentration has been known to wander on the bases, but he usually makes good decisions.

FIELDING:

Williams, who won his first Gold Glove last season, has such great reactions that he sometimes looks as though he ought to be wearing pads and a mask. On the minus side, his range isn't that much above average, and he'll force off-balance, ill-advised throws once in a while. Still, he's so good defensively that the Giants play him even when he is in the most epochal of slumps.

OVERALL:

It is easy to forget that Williams is only 26 and still is learning the game, because his feats are so prodigious. His slumps tend to get protracted, due to impatience both at the plate and with himself. Still, this is a long-time All-Star, and he and Will Clark are the only absolute untouchables on the Giant roster.

MATT D. WILLIAMS

Position: 3B
Bats: R **Throws:** R
Ht: 6' 2" **Wt:** 205

Opening Day Age: 26
Born: 11/28/65 in Bishop, CA
ML Seasons: 5

Overall Statistics

	G	AB	R	H	D	T	HR	RBI	SB	BB	SO	AVG
1991	157	589	72	158	24	5	34	98	5	33	128	.268
Career	536	1899	235	466	84	11	101	310	17	104	447	.245

Where He Hits the Ball

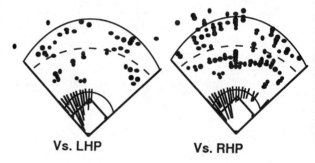

Vs. LHP   Vs. RHP

1991 Situational Stats

	AB	H	HR	RBI	AVG		AB	H	HR	RBI	AVG
Home	289	83	17	46	.287	LHP	165	46	7	25	.279
Road	300	75	17	52	.250	RHP	424	112	27	73	.264
Day	232	69	17	44	.297	Sc Pos	148	36	4	55	.243
Night	357	89	17	54	.249	Clutch	92	20	4	13	.217

1991 Rankings (National League)

- 1st in lowest percentage of pitches taken (41.9%) and highest percentage of swings that missed (31.3%)
- 2nd in home runs (34)
- 3rd in HR frequency (17.3 ABs per HR) and lowest percentage of swings put into play (37.4%)
- 4th in total bases (294) and strikeouts (128)
- 5th in games (157) and lowest on-base average vs. right-handed pitchers (.308)
- Led the Giants in home runs, at-bats (589), sacrifice flies (7), hit by pitch (6), strikeouts, plate appearances (635), games and HR frequency

TOUGH ON LEFTIES

PITCHING:

Trevor Wilson established himself as a viable major league pitcher for the San Francisco Giants in 1991, although his bosses (again) often seemed at a loss when it came to handling him.

Manager Roger Craig went into the season with the idea that Wilson, used primarily as a starter in 1990, would be the ideal left-handed set-up man for the Giant bullpen. In fairness to Craig, that decision largely was based on necessity, but it seemed to have a detrimental effect on Wilson. Trying too hard to throw strikes, he reverted to his old habits of depending too much on his fastball and on letting his emotions control him. Finally, more out of exasperation than anything else, Craig put him back into the starting rotation. As a starter, Wilson turned his season around, finishing with a staff-high 13 wins.

Wilson is still primarily a fastball pitcher, and is particularly tough on left-handed hitters because his fastball tends to rise up and in on them. The rest of Wilson's arsenal isn't that far above average, but it is getting better. He showed more confidence in his curveball after returning to the starting rotation. He's still working on his slider and change.

HOLDING RUNNERS, FIELDING, HITTING:

Wilson has a deceptive little jump-move to first base, and he gets rid of the ball quickly. He had six pickoffs, and nobody stole a base against him after July 30. He is a reasonably good fielder, although sometimes he'll unwisely try to make the spectacular play. Wilson, a hopeless hacker in the past, hit and bunted well all season, and even hit a home run.

OVERALL:

Wilson is still learning to channel his competitive fire, and he is up in the strike zone too often for Craig's liking. But he was the Giants' only reliable starter during the final two months of 1991. Look for him to be in the starting rotation from the beginning of the season, whether Craig likes it that way or not.

TREVOR WILSON

Position: SP/RP
Bats: L Throws: L
Ht: 6' 0" Wt: 175

Opening Day Age: 25
Born: 6/7/66 in Torrance, CA
ML Seasons: 4

Overall Statistics

	W	L	ERA	G	GS	Sv	IP	H	R	BB	SO	HR
1991	13	11	3.56	44	29	0	202.0	173	87	77	139	13
Career	23	23	3.81	89	54	0	373.2	313	173	158	242	27

How Often He Throws Strikes

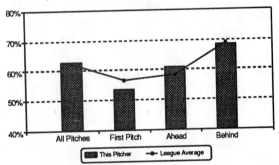

1991 Situational Stats

	W	L	ERA	Sv	IP		AB	H	HR	RBI	AVG
Home	8	4	2.71	0	119.2	LHB	160	27	1	13	.169
Road	5	7	4.81	0	82.1	RHB	580	146	12	62	.252
Day	9	1	2.88	0	90.2	Sc Pos	177	47	4	63	.266
Night	4	10	4.12	0	111.1	Clutch	67	14	1	4	.209

1991 Rankings (National League)

→ 1st in lowest batting average allowed vs. left-handed batters (.169)

→ 2nd in lowest stolen base percentage allowed (40.0%)

→ 5th in pickoff throws (240), groundball/fly-ball ratio (2.0) and most GDPs induced per 9 innings (.80)

→ Led the Giants in ERA (3.56), wins (13), walks allowed (77), strikeouts (139), winning percentage (.542), lowest batting average allowed (.234), lowest slugging percentage allowed (.343) and lowest on-base average allowed (.308)

MIKE BENJAMIN

Position: SS
Bats: R **Throws:** R
Ht: 6' 3" **Wt:** 195

Opening Day Age: 26
Born: 11/22/65 in Euclid, OH
ML Seasons: 3

Overall Statistics

	G	AB	R	H	D	T	HR	RBI	SB	BB	SO	AVG
1991	54	106	12	13	3	0	2	8	3	7	26	.123
Career	90	168	25	26	6	1	4	11	4	10	37	.155

HITTING, FIELDING, BASERUNNING:

With Jose Uribe starting the 1991 season on the disabled list, Mike Benjamin became the San Francisco Giants' Opening Day shortstop by default. He proceeded to default on the opportunity.

Benjamin played only six games and went one-for-21 before it became obvious that he simply couldn't handle major league pitching. Although he eventually appeared in 54 big-league games between trips to AAA Phoenix, Benjamin's squalid .123 average said it all about his lost season. He has some power, but he has far too sweeping a swing for somebody his size. He doesn't know the strike zone very well and was utterly befuddled by offspeed pitches.

Benjamin's defense was somewhat better, and he showed a capability for making the throw from deep in the hole. But he also has a tendency to throw before setting his feet, and he hasn't shown he can make the double play with any consistency. He has pretty good speed, but didn't get much of a chance to display it last year.

OVERALL:

Until last year, Benjamin was considered a legitimate long-range candidate for the shortstop job. Last year might have ended that candidacy. He has some ability, but will have to radically streamline his batting style to get another shot at the majors, at least with the Giants.

STEVE DECKER

Position: C
Bats: R **Throws:** R
Ht: 6' 3" **Wt:** 205

Opening Day Age: 26
Born: 10/25/65 in Rock Island, IL
ML Seasons: 2

Overall Statistics

	G	AB	R	H	D	T	HR	RBI	SB	BB	SO	AVG
1991	79	233	11	48	7	1	5	24	0	16	44	.206
Career	94	287	16	64	9	1	8	32	0	17	54	.223

HITTING, FIELDING, BASERUNNING:

San Francisco Giants manager Roger Craig wanted to build confidence in Steve Decker last year, so he said before the start of spring training that the catching job belonged to the 25-year-old rookie, who had batted .296 in a 15-game September trial in 1990.

Decker, indeed, seemed to have the dominating presence that Craig sought behind the plate. But the major league curveball proved insurmountable to him during the first two months of the season, and he let his poor offense affect his catching to the point where he became almost a statue behind the plate. Veteran pitchers complained openly about Decker's inability to work with them, and he began to stiff-arm the ball. Exasperated, the Giants sent Decker to Phoenix, but had to recall him after only one game because Kirt Manwaring broke a finger. He responded to some degree to the demotion, but never won his job back.

OVERALL:

The Giants were disappointed by Decker last season, especially when he waited three days to report to Phoenix after being sent down. But management also realizes that they rushed him into a situation that he was ill-prepared to handle. Kirt Manwaring probably will retain the catching job at the start of this season, but Decker remains prominent in the Giants' plans at the position.

TOMMY HERR

Position: 2B
Bats: B **Throws:** R
Ht: 6' 0" **Wt:** 196

Opening Day Age: 36
Born: 4/4/56 in
Lancaster, PA
ML Seasons: 13

Overall Statistics

	G	AB	R	H	D	T	HR	RBI	SB	BB	SO	AVG
1991	102	215	23	45	8	1	1	21	9	45	28	.209
Career	1514	5349	676	1450	254	41	28	574	188	627	584	.271

HITTING, FIELDING, BASERUNNING:

Tommy Herr's career clearly was at a crossroads after he was released by the New York Mets last August 4, less than one year removed from a presentable .261 season. The Giants signed him as infield insurance at a time when they thought they had a chance to creep back into the National League West race. But that hope soon faded, and Herr got only 60 at-bats in a month and a half with the Giants.

Though he had only two extra-base hits, Herr batted a respectable .250 for the Giants, and had a fine on-base average of .384. He had almost as many walks (13) as hits (15). But Herr's bat and foot speed reflected his age, although he did play a good second base during his rare opportunities there. His other start was at third base -- the first time in his major league career that he had played that position.

OVERALL:

Herr did not have much of a chance to make an impression with the Giants, who were looking for middle-infield help at a time when they were plagued by injuries. Herr still believes he can play regularly in the major leagues, and while that may be a lot to hope for at age 36, he can help a team in a bench role.

DARREN LEWIS

Position: CF
Bats: R **Throws:** R
Ht: 6' 0" **Wt:** 175

Opening Day Age: 24
Born: 8/28/67 in
Berkeley, CA
ML Seasons: 2

Overall Statistics

	G	AB	R	H	D	T	HR	RBI	SB	BB	SO	AVG
1991	72	222	41	55	5	3	1	15	13	36	30	.248
Career	97	257	45	63	5	3	1	16	15	43	34	.245

HITTING, FIELDING, BASERUNNING:

The Giants didn't want to rush Darren Lewis to the majors, but they didn't have much choice when Willie McGee went on the disabled list July 12. Lewis, who had been acquired from Oakland in an off season trade, gave them an instant burst of energy.

Inserted into the leadoff spot, Lewis started off well, prompting top praise from Roger Craig, and was still hitting .298 in mid-August when everything fell apart. Lewis has no power, yet he suddenly seemed obsessed with trying to pull and uppercut everything. Pitchers discovered that he opened his shoulder too early and thus was helpless against outside breaking balls. The more he pressed, the worse his situation got, and Craig finally had to bench him -- effectively for the rest of the season -- when his slump reached 1- for-43.

Lewis runs extremely well and with a great deal of eagerness, stealing 13 bases in 20 tries. Defensively, he was outstanding a times, terrible at others. Most of his mistakes were related to over-aggression, though, and can be corrected. His arm is strong.

OVERALL:

Lewis wasn't ready for the long-term demands of the majors last year, but he's only 24. Presently, he's the most likely candidate in the organization to be the Giants' center fielder of the future -- provided the team is willing to live with his total lack of power.

ORGANIZATION OVERVIEW:

Though the Giants were in the World Series only three years ago, they need help: pitching help, catching help, shortstop help, outfield help. With an impressive group of prospects, however, they seem close to getting it. Shortstop Royce Clayton was rated the top prospect in the minors last year by The Sporting News, and though that's probably a stretch, there are plenty of very talented players in the system in both the low and high minors. There's so much talent, in fact, that we had to leave the very highly regarded Johnny Ard, Rich Huisman and John Patterson, among others, off this list. The only question is whether manager Roger Craig and GM Al Rosen, who are both in their sixties and would like to get a world championship for San Francisco, will have enough patience with youth. The hunch is that they will.

ROYCE CLAYTON

Position: SS
Bats: R **Throws:** R
Ht: 6' 0" **Wt:** 175
Opening Day Age: 22
Born: 1/2/70 in Burbank, CA

Recent Statistics

	G	AB	R	H	D	THR	RBI	SB	BB	SO	AVG
91 AA Shreveport	126	485	84	136	22	8	5	68	36	61	102	.280
91 NL San Francisco	9	26	0	3	1	0	0	2	0	1	6	.115
91 MLE	126	465	66	116	19	4	3	53	23	40	109	.249

The shortstop position is the weakest one in the Giant lineup, and the only debate is about when Clayton will take the job, this year or next. Clayton is an excellent fielder with an outstanding arm, and his '91 season was his best with the bat. He has a good eye, extra-base power, and can steal 30 or more bases. If the Giants give Clayton the job and he falls short, they won't give up on him; they'll just give him the year at AAA he hasn't yet had.

JUAN GUERRERO

Position: 3B
Bats: R **Throws:** R
Ht: 5' 11" **Wt:** 160
Opening Day Age: 25
Born: 2/1/67 in San Pedro De Macoris, DR

Recent Statistics

	G	AB	R	H	D	THR	RBI	SB	BB	SO	AVG
90 AA Shreveport	118	390	55	94	21	1	16	47	4	26	74	.241
91 AA Shreveport	128	479	78	160	40	2	19	94	14	46	88	.334
91 MLE	128	456	61	137	35	1	14	73	9	30	94	.300

While teammates Clayton, Hosey and Patterson were getting all the ink, Guerrero was putting together the best offensive numbers of any Giants' AA player. Though he only weighs 160, the young Dominican has outstanding power, and 1991 was his breakthrough year. Defense may be a question -- Guerrero's already played second, third and the outfield -- but this young man can hit.

STEVE HOSEY

Position: OF
Bats: R **Throws:** R
Ht: 6' 3" **Wt:** 218
Opening Day Age: 23
Born: 4/2/69 in Oakland, CA

Recent Statistics

	G	AB	R	H	D	THR	RBI	SB	BB	SO	AVG
90 A San Jose	139	479	85	111	13	6	16	78	16	71	139	.232
91 AA Shreveport	126	409	79	120	21	5	17	74	24	56	87	.293
91 MLE	126	392	62	103	18	3	13	58	15	37	93	.263

The Giants first draft choice out of Fresno State in 1989, Hosey had a poor year at San Jose in 1990 (.232), but rebounded to have a great season at AA Shreveport last year. Hosey has excellent power, and though he's a big man, possesses good speed also. His outfield skills are also very good, with a fine throwing arm. Hosey has an outside chance to make the Giants roster this year, but chances are that he'll play in AAA.

SALOMON TORRES

Position: P
Bats: R **Throws:** R
Ht: 5' 11" **Wt:** 150
Opening Day Age: 20
Born: 3/11/72 in San Pedro De Macoris, DR

Recent Statistics

	W	L	ERA	G	GS	Sv	IP	H	R	BB	SO	HR
91 A Clinton	16	5	1.41	28	28	0	210.2	148	48	47	214	4

A Dominican from that popular place, San Pedro de Macoris, Torres terrorized the Midwest League at age 19 last year. He's already a well-rounded pitcher, with fastball, curve, slider, change and control. It should be pointed out that the Clinton park helps pitchers look good, but **this** good? In two years of pro ball, Torres has a 27- 6 record with a 1.14 ERA in 300.2 innings as a starter.

TED WOOD

Position: OF
Bats: L **Throws:** L
Ht: 6' 2" **Wt:** 170
Opening Day Age: 25
Born: 1/4/67 in Mansfield, OH

Recent Statistics

	G	AB	R	H	D	THR	RBI	SB	BB	SO	AVG
91 AAA Phoenix	137	512	90	159	38	6	11	109	12	86	96	.311
91 NL San Francisco	10	25	0	3	0	0	0	1	0	2	11	.120
91 MLE	137	476	57	123	30	3	7	69	7	55	100	.258

Tall and thin, ex-Olympian Wood has rapidly improved in three seasons of professional ball: .258 and then .265 at Shreveport, then .311 at Phoenix last year. Wood has good speed, a strong arm and good range; he doesn't look like a big home run hitter, but he has plenty of gap power, with 55 extra-base hits last year. And he has a great batting eye. The Sporting News rated Wood the number-seven prospect in the minors last year. That's way too high, but Wood has a lot of major league skills.

About STATS, Inc.

It all starts with the **system**. The STATS scoring method, which includes pitch-by-pitch information and the direction, distance, and velocity of each ball hit into play, yields an immense amount of information. Sure, we have all the statistics you're used to seeing, but where other statistical sources stop, STATS is just getting started.

Then, there's the **network**. Our information is timely because our game reporters send their information by computer as soon as the game is over. Statistics are checked, rechecked, updated, and are available daily.

Analysis comes next. STATS constantly searches for new ways to use this wealth of information to open windows into the workings of baseball. Accurate numbers, intelligent computer programming, and a large dose of imagination all help coax the most valuable information from its elusive cover.

Finally, distribution!

For 12 years now STATS has served Major League teams including the White Sox, Athletics and Yankees. The boxscores that STATS provides to the *Associated Press* and *USA Today* have revolutionized what baseball fans expect from a boxscore. *Sports Illustrated* and *The Sporting News* regularly feature STATS, Inc. while *ESPN's* nightly baseball coverage is supported by a full-time STATS statistician. We provide statistics for *Earl Weaver Baseball*, *Rotisserie Baseball*, the syndicated newspaper game *Dugout Derby*, and many other baseball games and fantasy leagues all over the country.

For the baseball fan, STATS publishes monthly and year-end reports on each Major League team. We offer a host of year-end statistical breakdowns on paper or disk that cover hitting, pitching, catching, baserunning, throwing, and more. STATS even produces custom reports on request.

Computer users with modems can access the STATS computer for information with **STATS On-Line**. If you own a computer with a modem, there is no other source with the scope of baseball information that STATS can offer.

STATS and Bill James enjoy an on-going affiliation that has produced several baseball products including the *STATS 1992 Major League Handbook*, the *STATS 1992 Minor League Handbook* and *Bill James Fantasy Baseball*, designed by Bill James himself. This is the ultimate fantasy baseball game, allowing you to manage your own team and compete with other team owners around the country. STATS also produces a similarly-designed head-to-head fantasy football game, *STATS Fantasy Football*.

Always looking for innovative approaches, STATS has other exciting future projects underway for sports fans nationwide. It is the purpose of STATS, Inc. to make the best possible sports information available to all interests: fans, players, teams, or media. For more information write to:

STATS, Inc.
7366 North Lincoln Ave.
Lincolnwood, IL 60646-1708

. . . or call us at 1-708-676-3322. We can send you a STATS brochure, a free Bill James Fantasy Baseball information kit, and/or information on STATS On-Line.

To maintain our information, STATS hires people around the country to cover games using the STATS scoring method. If you are interested in applying for a game reporter's position, please write or call STATS.

For the story behind the numbers, check out another STATS' publication: *The STATS 1992 Baseball Scoreboard*. The first edition of this book in 1990 took the nation's baseball fans by storm. This all new edition, available in many bookstores or directly from STATS, is back with the same great writing, great graphics and stats you won't find anywhere else.

Index

A

B

Brantley, Cliff	572
Brantley, Jeff	651
Bream, Sid	382
Brett, George	180
Briley, Greg	299
Brogna, Rico	176
Brooks, Hubie	525
Bross, Terry	547
Brown, Kevin	326
Brown, Kevin D.	222
Browne, Jerry	132
Browning, Tom	429
Brunansky, Tom	56
Buechele, Steve	577
Buhner, Jay	300
Burke, Tim	526
Burkett, John	652
Burks, Ellis	57
Burnitz, Jeromy	547
Bush, Randy	228
Butler, Brett	476

C

Cadaret, Greg	251
Calderon, Ivan	502
Caminiti, Ken	454
Campbell, Kevin	298
Candaele, Casey	455
Candelaria, John	477
Candiotti, Tom	352
Canseco, Jose	277
Carpenter, Cris	600
Carreon, Mark	545
Carter, Gary	478
Carter, Jeff	127
Carter, Joe	353
Castillo, Braulio	572
Castillo, Frank	405
Cedeno, Andujar	456
Cerutti, John	155
Chamberlain, Wes	549
Charlton, Norm	430
Chitren, Steve	278
Clancy, Jim	383
Clark, Jack	58
Clark, Jerald	626
Clark, Will	653

Clayton, Royce	670
Clemens, Roger	59
Cochrane, Dave	321
Cole, Alex	133
Coleman, Vince	527
Combs, Pat	550
Cone, David	528
Conine, Jeff	200
Cooke, Stephen	598
Coolbaugh, Scott	644
Cooper, Gary	474
Cooper, Scott	77
Cora, Joey	103
Cordero, Wilfredo	523
Cormier, Rheal	601
Corsi, Jim	457
Costello, John	644
Cotto, Henry	301
Cox, Danny	551
Crews, Tim	479
Crim, Chuck	204
Cron, Chris	101
Curtis, Chad	101
Cuyler, Milt	156

D

Daniels, Kal	480
Darling, Ron	279
Darwin, Danny	75
Dascenzo, Doug	406
Daugherty, Jack	327
Daulton, Darren	552
Davis, Alvin	302
Davis, Chili	229
Davis, Eric	431
Davis, Glenn	30
Davis, Mark	181
Davis, Storm	182
Dawson, Andre	407
Dayley, Ken	371
Decker, Steve	668
Deer, Rob	157
DeJesus, Jose	553
DeLeon, Jose	602
Delgado, Carlos	373
Delucia, Rich	303
Dempsey, Rick	222

Deshaies, Jim	458	Finley, Steve	459
DeShields, Delino	503	Fisk, Carlton	105
DeSilva, John	176	Fitzgerald, Mike	505
Devereaux, Mike	31	Flanagan, Mike	33
Diaz, Mario	346	Fleming, Dave	323
Dibble, Rob	432	Fletcher, Darrin	570
Dickson, Lance	426	Fletcher, Scott	106
Disarcina, Gary	101	Foley, Tom	521
Doran, Billy	433	Fossas, Tony	60
Downing, Brian	328	Franco, John	531
Downs, Kelly	654	Franco, Julio	329
Drabek, Doug	578	Fraser, Willie	620
Dressendorfer, Kirk	298	Freeman, Marvin	400
Ducey, Rob	373	Frey, Steve	521
Duncan, Mariano	434	Frohwirth, Todd	34
Dunston, Shawon	408	Fryman, Travis	159
Dykstra, Lenny	554		

E

Eckersley, Dennis	280
Egloff, Bruce	152
Eichhorn, Mark	82
Eiland, Dave	272
Eisenreich, Jim	183
Eldred, Cal	224
Elster, Kevin	529
Ericks, John	622
Erickson, Scott	230
Espinoza, Alvaro	252
Evans, Dwight	32

F

Fajardo, Hector	348
Fariss, Monty	348
Farr, Steve	253
Fassero, Jeff	504
Felder, Mike	655
Felix, Junior	83
Fermin, Felix	134
Fernandez, Alex	104
Fernandez, Sid	530
Fernandez, Tony	627
Fetters, Mike	99
Fielder, Cecil	158
Finley, Chuck	84

G

Gaetti, Gary	85
Gagne, Greg	231
Gainer, Jay	646
Gakeler, Dan	160
Galarraga, Andres	506
Gallagher, Dave	86
Gallego, Mike	281
Gant, Ron	384
Gantner, Jim	205
Garces, Rich	249
Garcia, Carlos	598
Gardiner, Mike	61
Gardner, Mark	507
Gedman, Rich	620
George, Chris	224
Geren, Bob	272
Gibson, Kirk	184
Gibson, Paul	161
Gilkey, Bernard	603
Gladden, Dan	232
Glavine, Tom	385
Gleaton, Jerry Don	162
Gohr, Greg	176
Gomez, Leo	35
Gonzalez, Juan	330
Gonzalez, Luis	460
Gooden, Dwight	532
Gordon, Tom	185
Gossage, Goose	331

Gott, Jim	481		Hatcher, Billy	437
Grace, Mark	409		Hayes, Charlie	557
Grahe, Joe	87		Hayes, Von	558
Grater, Mark	622		Heath, Mike	400
Gray, Jeff	62		Heaton, Neal	596
Grebeck, Craig	107		Henderson, Dave	282
Green, Tyler	572		Henderson, Rickey	283
Greene, Tommy	555		Henke, Tom	356
Greenwell, Mike	63		Henneman, Mike	164
Griffey Jr, Ken	304		Henry, Doug	207
Griffin, Alfredo	482		Henry, Dwayne	462
Grimsley, Jason	570		Hernandez, Carlos	499
Grissom, Marquis	508		Hernandez, Roberto	125
Gross, Kevin	483		Hernandez, Xavier	463
Gross, Kip	435		Herr, Tommy	669
Gruber, Kelly	354		Hershiser, Orel	485
Gubicza, Mark	186		Hesketh, Joe	65
Guerrero, Juan	670		Hibbard, Greg	109
Guerrero, Pedro	604		Higuera, Teddy	208
Guetterman, Lee	254		Hill, Glenallen	135
Guillen, Ozzie	108		Hill, Ken	605
Gullickson, Bill	163		Hillegas, Shawn	136
Guthrie, Mark	247		Hoiles, Chris	36
Gutierrez, Ricky	53		Hollins, Dave	559
Guzman, Jose	332		Holman, Brian	306
Guzman, Juan	355		Honeycutt, Rick	284
Gwynn, Chris	497		Horn, Sam	37
Gwynn, Tony	628		Hosey, Steve	670
			Hough, Charlie	110
			Houston, Tyler	402
H			Howard, Dave	187
			Howard, Thomas	630
			Howe, Steve	257
Habyan, John	255		Howell, Jack	631
Hall, Mel	256		Howell, Jay	486
Hamelin, Bob	200		Hoy, Pete	77
Hamilton, Darryl	206		Hrbek, Kent	234
Hammond, Chris	436		Hudler, Rex	606
Haney, Chris	509		Huff, Mike	125
Haney, Todd	523		Hundley, Todd	533
Hansen, Dave	497		Hunter, Brian	386
Hanson, Erik	305		Hurst, Bruce	632
Hare, Shawn	176		Huson, Jeff	333
Harnisch, Pete	461			
Harper, Brian	233			
Harris, Greg	64			
Harris, Greg W.	629		**I**	
Harris, Lenny	484			
Hartley, Mike	556		Incaviglia, Pete	165
Harvey, Bryan	88		Innis, Jeff	534

J

Jackson, Bo	111
Jackson, Danny	410
Jackson, Darrin	633
Jackson, Mike	307
Jacoby, Brook	285
Jaha, John	224
James, Chris	137
Javier, Stan	498
Jeffcoat, Mike	334
Jefferies, Gregg	535
Jefferson, Reggie	150
Johnson, Howard	536
Johnson, Jeff	258
Johnson, Lance	112
Johnson, Randy	308
Jones, Barry	510
Jones, Calvin	309
Jones, Chipper	402
Jones, Chris	448
Jones, Doug	138
Jones, Jimmy	464
Jones, Tracy	322
Jordan, Ricky	560
Jose, Felix	607
Joyner, Wally	89
Juden, Jeff	474
Justice, Dave	387

K

Kamieniecki, Scott	259
Karkovice, Ron	113
Karros, Eric	499
Kelly, Mike	402
Kelly, Pat	260
Kelly, Roberto	261
Kennedy, Terry	656
Key, Jimmy	357
Kiecker, Dana	75
Kile, Darryl	465
King, Eric	139
King, Jeff	579
Kipper, Bob	580
Klesko, Ryan	402
Klink, Joe	286
Knoblauch, Chuck	235

Koslofski, Kevin	200
Krueger, Bill	310
Kruk, John	561

L

Lake, Steve	571
Lancaster, Les	411
Landrum, Bill	581
Landrum, Ced	424
Langston, Mark	90
Lankford, Ray	608
Larkin, Barry	438
Larkin, Gene	236
LaValliere, Mike	582
Leach, Terry	237
Leary, Tim	262
Lee, Manuel	358
Lee, Mark	209
Lefferts, Craig	634
Leibrandt, Charlie	388
Leiter, Mark	166
Leius, Scott	238
Lemke, Mark	389
Lennon, Patrick	323
Lewis, Darren	669
Lewis, Mark	140
Lind, Jose	583
Livingstone, Scott	175
Lofton, Kenny	474
Lopez, Javy	402
Lyons, Steve	76

M

Maas, Kevin	263
MacDonald, Bob	359
Macfarlane, Mike	188
Machado, Julio	210
Mack, Shane	239
Maddux, Greg	412
Maddux, Mike	635
Magadan, Dave	537
Magnante, Mike	198
Mahomes, Pat	249
Maldonado, Candy	360
Mallicoat, Rob	466

Manuel, Barry	348	Mitchell, Keith	401
Manwaring, Kirt	657	Mitchell, Kevin	660
Martel, Ed	274	Molitor, Paul	211
Martinez, Carlos	141	Mondesi, Raul	499
Martinez, Carmelo	448	Montgomery, Jeff	191
Martinez, Chito	38	Moore, Mike	288
Martinez, Dave	511	Morandini, Mickey	562
Martinez, Dennis	512	Morgan, Mike	489
Martinez, Edgar	311	Morris, Hal	439
Martinez, Jose	547	Morris, Jack	240
Martinez, Pedro	499	Morton, Kevin	66
Martinez, Ramon	487	Moseby, Lloyd	167
Martinez, Tino	312	Mota, Andy	472
Mason, Roger	584	Mota, Jose	645
Mathews, Terry	335	Mulholland, Terry	563
Mattingly, Don	264	Mulliniks, Rance	361
Maurer, Rob	348	Munoz, Pedro	247
Mayne, Brent	189	Murphy, Dale	564
McCaskill, Kirk	91	Murphy, Rob	313
McClellan, Paul	658	Murray, Eddie	490
McClendon, Lloyd	585	Mussina, Mike	43
McClure, Bob	621	Mutis, Jeff	152
McDonald, Ben	39	Myers, Greg	362
McDowell, Jack	114	Myers, Randy	440
McDowell, Roger	488		
McElroy, Chuck	413		
McGee, Willie	659	**N**	
McGriff, Fred	636		
McGwire, Mark	287	Nabholz, Chris	513
McIntosh, Tim	224	Naehring, Tim	76
McNeely, Jeff	77	Nagy, Charles	142
McRae, Brian	190	Navarro, Jaime	212
McReynolds, Kevin	538	Neagle, Denny	248
Melendez, Jose	637	Nelson, Gene	289
Melvin, Bob	40	Newfield, Marc	323
Merced, Orlando	586	Newman, Al	241
Mercedes, Luis	53	Newson, Warren	126
Mercker, Kent	390	Nichols, Rod	143
Merullo, Matt	126	Nilsson, Dave	224
Mesa, Jose	51	Nixon, Otis	391
Meulens, Hensley	265	Nokes, Matt	266
Mieske, Matthew	646	Nunez, Edwin	223
Milacki, Bob	41		
Miller, Keith	545		
Miller, Kurt	348	**O**	
Miller, Paul	598		
Milligan, Randy	42	O'Brien, Charlie	546
Mills, Alan	274	O'Brien, Pete	314
Minutelli, Gino	450	O'Neill, Paul	441

Offerman, Jose	491	Phillips, Tony	168
Ojeda, Bobby	492	Piatt, Doug	522
Olerud, John	363	Plantier, Phil	68
Olin, Steve	144	Plesac, Dan	213
Olivares, Omar	609	Plunk, Eric	273
Oliver, Joe	442	Polonia, Luis	93
Oliveras, Francisco	661	Poole, Jim	46
Olson, Greg	392	Portugal, Mark	468
Olson, Gregg	44	Power, Ted	443
Oquendo, Jose	610	Puckett, Kirby	243
Orosco, Jesse	145	Pulliam, Harvey	200
Orsulak, Joe	45		
Ortiz, Javier	473		
Ortiz, Junior	248	**Q**	
Ortor., John	100		
Osborne, Donovan	622	Quantrill, Paul	77
Osuna, Al	467	Quinones, Luis	449
Otero, Ricardo	547	Quintana, Carlos	69
Otto, Dave	146	Quirk, Jamie	296
Owen, Spike	514		

P

Pagliarulo, Mike	242	**R**	
Pagnozzi, Tom	611		
Palacios, Vince	587	Radinsky, Scott	119
Pall, Donn	115	Raines, Tim	120
Palmeiro, Rafael	336	Ramirez, Manuel	152
Palmer, Dean	337	Ramirez, Rafael	469
Parker, Dave	371	Ramos, John	274
Parrish, Lance	92	Randolph, Willie	214
Pasqua, Dan	116	Rasmussen, Dennis	638
Patterson, Bob	588	Ready, Randy	565
Patterson, Ken	117	Reardon, Jeff	70
Paulino, Elvin	426	Redus, Gary	589
Pecota, Bill	192	Reed, Jeff	444
Pena, Alejandro	393	Reed, Jody	71
Pena, Geronimo	612	Reimer, Kevin	338
Pena, Tony	67	Reyes, Gil	515
Pendleton, Terry	394	Reynolds, Harold	315
Perez, Melido	118	Rhodes, Arthur	52
Perez, Pascual	267	Righetti, Dave	662
Perez, Yorkis	426	Rijo, Jose	445
Perry, Gerald	621	Riles, Ernest	297
Peters, Don	298	Ripken, Billy	47
Peterson, Adam	645	Ripken, Cal	48
Petralli, Geno	347	Ritchie, Wally	566
Pettis, Gary	347	Ritz, Kevin	175
		Rivera, Luis	72
		Roberts, Bip	639
		Robinson, Don	663

Robinson, Jeff	94		Seminara, Frank	646
Rodriguez, Frank	77		Sharperson, Mike	495
Rodriguez, Ivan	339		Shaw, Jeff	151
Rodriguez, Rich	640		Sheffield, Gary	215
Rogers, Kenny	340		Shumpert, Terry	195
Rohde, Dave	474		Sierra, Ruben	343
Rojas, Mel	516		Silvestri, Dave	274
Roper, John	450		Simons, Doug	541
Rose, Bobby	100		Skinner, Joel	147
Rowland, Rich	176		Slaught, Don	590
Royer, Stan	622		Slocumb, Heathcliff	417
Ruffin, Bruce	567		Slusarski, Joe	290
Ruffin, Johnny	127		Smiley, John	591
Ruskin, Scott	517		Smith, Bryn	613
Russell, Jeff	341		Smith, Dave	418
Ryan, Nolan	342		Smith, Dwight	425
			Smith, Lee	614
			Smith, Lonnie	395
S			Smith, Ozzie	615
			Smith, Willie	274
Saberhagen, Bret	193		Smith, Zane	592
Sabo, Chris	446		Smoltz, John	396
Salazar, Luis	414		Sojo, Luis	96
Salkeld, Roger	323		Sorrento, Paul	249
Salmon, Tim	101		Sosa, Sammy	121
Sampen, Bill	518		Spehr, Tim	199
Samuel, Juan	493		Spiers, Bill	216
Sanchez, Rey	426		Sprague, Ed	372
Sandberg, Ryne	415		Stairs, Matt	523
Sanders, Deion	401		Stanley, Mike	344
Sanders, Reggie	449		Stanton, Mike	397
Sanderson, Scott	268		Staton, Dave	646
Sanford, Mo	450		Steinbach, Terry	291
Santiago, Benito	641		Stevens, Lee	97
Santovenia, Nelson	522		Stewart, Dave	292
Sasser, Mackey	539		Stieb, Dave	364
Sax, Steve	269		Stillwell, Kurt	196
Scanlan, Bob	416		Stottlemyre, Todd	365
Schaefer, Jeff	322		Strawberry, Darryl	496
Schilling, Curt	470		Stubbs, Franklin	217
Schofield, Dick	95		Surhoff, B.J.	218
Schooler, Mike	316		Sutcliffe, Rick	419
Schourek, Pete	540		Sveum, Dale	223
Scioscia, Mike	494		Swan, Russ	317
Scudder, Scott	447		Swindell, Greg	148
Seanez, Rudy	152		Swift, Bill	318
Searcy, Steve	571			
Segui, David	49			
Seitzer, Kevin	194			

T

Tabler, Pat	372
Tanana, Frank	169
Tapani, Kevin	244
Tartabull, Danny	197
Taubensee, Eddie	152
Taylor, Wade	270
Telford, Anthony	53
Templeton, Garry	546
Terrell, Walt	170
Terry, Scott	616
Tettleton, Mickey	171
Teufel, Tim	642
Tewksbury, Bob	617
Thigpen, Bobby	122
Thomas, Frank	123
Thome, Jim	151
Thompson, Milt	618
Thompson, Robby	664
Thon, Dickie	568
Thurman, Gary	199
Timlin, Mike	366
Tomlin, Randy	593
Torres, Salomon	670
Trammell, Alan	172
Treadway, Jeff	398

U

Uribe, Jose	665

V

Valera, Julio	547
Valle, Dave	319
Van Poppel, Todd	298
Van Slyke, Andy	594
VanderWal, John	523
Varsho, Gary	596
Vaughn, Greg	219
Vaughn, Mo	73
Velarde, Randy	273
Ventura, Robin	124
Villanueva, Hector	420
Viola, Frank	542

Vizcaino, Jose	425
Vizquel, Omar	320

W

Wainhouse, David	523
Wakefield, Tim	598
Walk, Bob	595
Walker, Chico	421
Walker, Larry	519
Wall, Donnell	474
Wallach, Tim	520
Walters, Dan	646
Walton, Jerome	422
Ward, Duane	367
Ward, Turner	373
Webster, Lenny	249
Webster, Mitch	498
Wegman, Bill	220
Wehner, John	597
Weiss, Walt	293
Welch, Bob	294
Wells, David	368
Wendell, Turk	426
West, David	245
Wetteland, John	499
Whitaker, Lou	173
White, Devon	369
Whitehurst, Wally	543
Whiten, Mark	149
Whitson, Ed	643
Wickman, Robert	127
Wilkerson, Curt	597
Wilkins, Rick	423
Williams, Bernie	271
Williams, Jeff	53
Williams, Matt D.	666
Williams, Mitch	569
Williamson, Mark	50
Willis, Carl	246
Wilson, Dan	450
Wilson, Mookie	370
Wilson, Trevor	667
Wilson, Willie	295
Winfield, Dave	98
Witt, Bobby	345
Wohlers, Mark	399

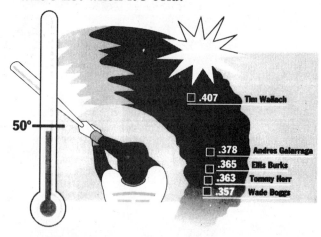
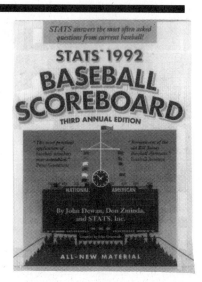